© **PEÑÍN EDICIONES**

**Production team:**
Editor-in-chief and tasting director: José Peñín
Co-ordinator: Carlos González
Data processing: Erika Laymuns
Texts: José Peñín, Carlos González, Maite Corsín
Managing editor: Ángeles Cosano
Tasting team: Carlos González and Maite Corsín
Tasting support team: Paloma López-Piña and Javier Luengo
Cover design, layout and desktop publishing: Grupo Peñín Art Department
Javier Herrán, Marta Gómez y Mati Durán
Advertising: Ana Alós
Photography: Massimiliano Polles

PUBLISHER BY: GRUPO PEÑÍN
Arga, 11
28002 Madrid - Spain
Tel.: 00 34 91 411 94 64 Fax: 00 34 91 515 94 99
comunicacion@grupopenin.com
www.grupopenin.com

ISBN: 978-84-95203-58-8
Legal Deposite: M-40335-2009
Printer: GRÁFICAS DEVA

DISTRIBUTOR: GRUPO COMERCIAL ANAYA
Juan Ignacio Luca de Tena, 15
Tel: 00 34 91 393 88 00
28027 Madrid

The main novelty in this year's edition is of an editorial nature. In the 20th anniversary of the first edition of our Guide, the moment has come to renovate it with a more manageable format as well as a more alluring and modern –if we considered the classicism of the average wine guide– cover page. Yet again our leadership within the wine-publishing sector in Spain permits us to undertake such change, and we are sure it will be for the better.

In consideration to the increasing number of wines tasted and in order to put a necessary limit to the size of our Guide, we have destined less room in it for those wineries that did not send their wines for our evaluation. Thus, they will be excluded henceforth both from the region and the final index, save a mere mention of the winery's name at the end of each wine-region's chapter, although we will still include those we deem indispensable given their reputation, even if we have to do it against their will; in such cases we will acquire their wines in specialized shops with the sole goal in mind to be of service to the consumer, who should be kept informed about the real quality of those particular wines.

## LATEST FROM SPANISH WINES IN THE 2010 EDITION

There is a genuine interest to make quality wines and to determine where that minimum of quality should lie. In that sense, and for the first time, we are glad to announce we have not rated a single wine within the "not recommendable" category –i.e., those that score 60 points or below–, just the logic culmination of a slow and steady qualitative progress over the last few years. On the other hand, the leading pack gets bigger by the day in a fertile effort to achieve excellence.

White still renderings and cavas have been the stars of this edition, the former thanks to the way they have let out the fact that Spain is not only red wine territory and that there are also some splendid, racy white wines (Rías Baixas with albariño and Rueda with verdejo have both had a memorable 2008 vintage); the latter, our formidable sparkling renderings, have improved exquisitely from the moment the classic cava stereotype from Catalonia was abandoned along with some traditional practices to 'induce' age, like adding old wines to the dosage, in favour of more progressive methods like proper management of the lees and the use of the carbonic from the second fermentation in the bottle to achieve a better, more balanced ageing model. Likewise, it is amazing the way the viura from Rioja has achieved such character and complexity in some new barrel-fermented renderings, along with the most classic, oak-aged examples, which have managed some sort of improvement, too. The 2008 vintage will be remembered as an exemplary one thanks to the excellence of some winemakers, for it was surely a difficult one to handle and not at all homogenous in terms of quality, the sort of situation when typically terroir, talent and perseverance come to the fore. Some other vintages still in the market like the cooler 2007 has given us the chance to rediscover the most prominent varietal features in almost every region. As for the warmer 2005 vintage, it has now reached a formidable level of maturity, while the 2006 renderings from the northernmost regions are showing well too, although they lack the richness and character of the 2005's.

Curiously enough, the middle and the southern parts of Spain have had a cooler 2008 vintage, even when not as rich in terms of expression as that of 2004, which is just now started to show all its so far only presumed potential, given it had higher levels of acidity and a solid set of tannins that required a long process of harmonization in the bottle to achieve the sheer elegance it is now displaying.

José Peñín

**José Peñín** is the most knowledgeable, influential and international Spanish wine critic. A career spanning three decades makes him the most prolific and authoritative wine journalist in Spanish language. Besides other important recognitions, in 2007 he was given the Special Prize of the International Jury at the **World Gourmand Cookbook Awards**.

The **Peñín Guide to Spanish Wine** has a professional team specialized in the sensory evaluation of wines from all the different Spanish wine regions. They deal with an impressive database –including over a hundred thousand tasting notes from previous editions of the Guide–, which provides them with not only the availability of a significant historical record, but also the opportunity to trace each wine's scoring progress through the years, thus minimizing the possibility of a wine getting the wrong score due to a 'bad bottle'. Wines that scored 91 points or more undergo a re-tasting that allows the team to compare products of similar quality on a single-event evaluation basis. The team comprises José Peñín as tasting director; **Carlos González**, an agricultural engineer and PhD in Oenology, Marketing and Viticulture with also a vast professional experience in wine business; and **Maite Corsín,** a wine journalist with a great expertise in wine marketing and a record-breaking nine-year spell tasting for the Guide alongside José Peñín.

## TASTING SUPPORT TEAM

The tasting support team is composed of **Carlos del Hoyo**, our international consultant in Grupo Peñín and a great expert in the identification –in wine-tasting terms– of the best price/quality ratio, and our two in-house senior wine editors, **Paloma López-Piña and Javier Luengo**.

# SUMMARY

## -CONTENTS

# SUMMARY

## ACKNOWLEDGMENTS

We thank those **Consejos Reguladores** (regulatory boards) that have so readily cooperated with the Guide providing their buildings and professional staff to make our tasting possible, a task which in some cases was not carried out in the end due to organizational faults on our part. We have to thank also –and very especially– **José Matás** from **Enoteca Casa Bernal**, in El Palmar (Murcia); **Juan Luis Pérez de Eulate** from **La Vinoteca**, a splendid wine shop in Palma de Mallorca; **Casa del Vino La Baranda** from El Sauzal and particularly **José Alfonso González Lorente**, as well as the **Casa del Vino of Gran Canaria**; the restaurant **Vizzeria**, in Falset (Tarragona); **Viniteca Mayol**, in Torroja del Priorat (Tarragona) and **Vinatería Pámpano** in Almendralejo (Badajoz).

## WINE-PRODUCING REGIONS

In Spain there are currently 73 DOs, including the sole six "Vino de Pago" designations that there are so far: Dominio de Valdepusa, Finca Élez, Dehesa del Carrizal, Pago Guijoso, Señorío de Arínzano and Pago de Otazu.

In a way, the "pago" designation seems to complicate the wine map even further, but it is being driven –albeit in a less revolutionary fashion– by highly influential Consejos Reguladores such as Rioja, in line with the concept proposed by the Wine Law (Ley del Vino) of 2003, which defines "pago" as a rural location with its own unique and differentiated characteristics, and at least a five-year market record under the same name.

Equally in the DO Ca. Priorat, the Catalonian wineries of Álvaro Palacios, Celler Pasanau, Mas Martinet and Clos Mogador asked a few years back their Consejo Regulador, which has full powers to determine qualification standards, trazability, production, etc., to promote the creation of a new category under the "vi de finca qualificada" (qualified single plot) label, now fully implemented. In the meantime, the Consejo Regulador has also approved a brand new category, "vi de vila" (town's wine, in Catalonian language) within the DO, which will be given its seal of approval in the second semester of 2009. Producers of some 12 municipalities (Gratallops, Poboleda, Porrera, etc.) of the area will be able to label their wines as "vi de vila", a sort of subcategory within the DO. In the same context, the Consejo Regulador has designed a new wine map of the different sub-zones associated to each town or subcategory. To start with, it is forbidden to buy grapes from other areas or towns, so these "vi de vila" will be made exclusively from estate grown grapes.

As for the Guide, all the DOs are listed in alphabetical order, whilst the rest of the labels under the "Vino de la Tierra" label, as well as the VCPRD wines and "Vinos de Mesa", are also listed in strictly alphabetical order. The latter has also been listed by autonomous community: Andalucía, Aragón, Baleares, Castilla-La Mancha, Castilla-León, Cataluña, Extremadura, La Rioja, Navarra and Valencia. Finally, the section "Sparkling Wines–Traditional Method" comprises the sparkling wines made in the same way as cava, by the method of secondary fermentation in the bottle, but within regions of production outside the DO Cava or any other designation of origin.

The following sections are found in each chapter:
-A map of the DO and the largest areas of vineyard concentration.

-An overview of the region with a brief commentary on its current situation and foreseeable future.

-The general characteristics of each region's wines.

-A rating (excellent, very good, good, average and mediocre) of the harvest according to our wine-tasting team and the evaluation of the final products as they are ready to hit the market, a much more realistic approach to quality than the official one, based on an evaluation of the wines in their post-fermentative state and so with some notes directly derived from vinification, fermentative or else.

-A list of wineries and tasting notes.

## WINERIES

These are listed in alphabetical order within the wine-producing region to which they belong. For each winery, the name, address and telephone number are given, as well as the most relevant details. This information is supplied by the producers up to 30 June 2006. All the basic information relating to general details (address, telephone numbers and brands on the market) has been updated practically 100% in this edition, although it is possible that other details (number of casks, production, percentage destined for exports, etc.) correspond to the information collated in the previous edition, due to not having received the requested information for the 2007 Guide by the deadline indicated.

If the same company produces wines grouped in different DO wine-producing regions, the information available for that company will appear in all the entries and, in the wineries index section, they will be entered for each area or wine-producing region in which they operate. The most frequent case will relate to companies that simultaneously produce cava and wines from other Catalonian DO regions.

# WINES

The wines and their corresponding tasting notes make up the bulk of the text. They are always displayed after the information about the winery that produces them, according to the following specifications:
Each wine appears with its brand name, ageing and vintage (if supplied by the producer). Also, the type of wine, the DO to which it belongs, the approximate retail price supplied by the winery and the percentages for domestic and foreign sales are specified.

- As a new feature, in this 2007 edition, and given the overriding objective not to increase the number of pages any more than is necessary, in order to ensure it remains handy to use, only wines whose score is equal to or higher than 80 will appear with tasting notes. For the rest, only the score will be given.

# INDEXES

As well as the usual alphabetical indexes listed by wine brands and wineries, there is an index of the best wines from each DO region to easily distinguish the most prominent wines from each area at a glance. Furthermore, a list of Designations of Origin and "Vinos de la Tierra" is included, ordered by autonomous region, as well as another list of wine-producing groups with all the associated wineries.
The objective of this book is to quickly and efficiently inform readers about the characteristics of wines that can be found on the market during the last quarter of 2006 and throughout 2007. The opinions that are expressed are the sole responsibility of José Peñín and his team, and should only be appraised in relation to the faith that the reader has in his evaluation.

These classifications should, furthermore, be interpreted with a 6% maximum margin of error.

Except for wines with a marked character, the tasting has been simplified by highlighting the most significant aspects and those most easily detected by a consumer. Detailed and technical descriptions have been avoided, which we believe to be decidedly confusing for the average consumer. However, there is a list of terms that might appear quite technical to the less experienced consumer.

## WHEN THE WINES ARE TASTED

The majority of the tasting takes place from the end of January to 30 June. As such, any samples received after that time will not appear in the Guide. For each area, a tasting period is established, so that the increased number of wine tastings required can be carried out systematically in a relatively short space of time.

## HOW THE SAMPLES WERE RECEIVED

We have not set out in search of wines that missed the deadline, unless we thought they might achieve a high score, due to their quality, from previous experience. Increasingly, wineries appreciate the prestige that the Peñín Guide is gaining year after year and so there is a rise in the number of samples received. Almost all the best Spanish wines have been submitted by the wineries. The absentees, however, are due to the misgivings on the part of the producers that their wines will end up at the bottom of the heap. It could also be because the winery has sold all of its production, either because of high demand or a poor harvest. Sometimes, an obvious omission may be detected due to an unintentional error attributable to Peñín Ediciones. Should the winery be responsible, we would resort to purchasing the wine on the market, again always provided the brand had a relatively well-established reputation.

## SCORING SYSTEM

As this guide is being used more and more at an international level, we have chosen the American scoring system, in which 0 equals 50. This classification represents the different qualities of the wines in general terms, noting concepts detailed within each range of 10 points, except in the range from 90 to 100, which has been divided into two parts in order to add more accuracy and credibility to the highest scores. In view of this, the reader must refer to this page to find the general description related to the particular classification and then look at the specific description of the wine according to the following scale:

### 95-100 Exceptional
This wine excels among those of a similar type, vintage and region. It is extremely impressive in every sense: full of complex elements, both on the nose and the palate, produced by a combination of soil, variety, method of production and ageing. It is elegant and out of the ordinary, far exceeding commercial standards and, in some cases, unknown to the general public.

### 90-94 Excellent
Wines with the same attributes as above, but with less outstanding or individual characteristics.

### 80-89 Very good
A wine that stands out due to the elements acquired during the wine making and/or ageing process or the inherent qualities of the grape variety. A wine with specific characteristics, but without highlighting any particular attributes of the soil.

### 70-79 Good
Although not as distinctive, the wine fully reflects the characteristics of its type and wineproducing region. There are no defects, but no virtues either.

### 60-69 Average
An acceptable wine in which slight defects can be detected, but not losing too much in the overall effect.

### 50-59 Not recommended
A harmless but unenjoyable wine. It may be oxidised or have defects due to ageing or late racking; it may be an old wines past its best or a young wine with unfavourable yeasty aromas.

## THE NUMBER OF WINES TASTED

It is difficult to give an accurate figure, because the majority of debatable wines, from 60 points onwards, were reviewed on numerous occasions. In addition to the wines tasted and commented on, approximately 1,000 repeat tastings need to be taken into account.

## HOW THE WINES ARE CLASSIFIED AND RATED

José Peñín, like the majority of specialist writers, is opposed to numerical ratings. However, pure and simple descriptions of wine-tastings, without any indication of score, do not explain sufficiently, to the less proficient consumer, the differences between the brands, when faced with the dilemma of which wine to choose between two or more with similar descriptions. It is clear that the negative and positive descriptions have their respective limits without the need for ratings; and it could be considered sufficient to establish categories of good, very good and excellent. But the author does not want to use these terms by way of classification, when there is a need to differentiate a good wine with 70 points from another with 75 points.

## HOW THE WINE-TASTINGS ARE CARRIED OUT

Unlike comparative and blind tastings, José Peñín and his team carry out the tastings with the identity of the wine revealed because, sometimes, between two wines from the same brand and vintage, there can be some differences based on their respective development in bottle depending on the condition of the stopper. This fact, which should not be considered as a defect, can, in turn, affect the rating, to a certain degree. Their experience, which allows them to overcome the influence of the label and, therefore, their knowledge of the winery's history, makes it possible to provide a fair assessment, as there are rarely large differences in quality that are not related to natural factors affecting the harvest.

It is clear that, unless tastings of the same wines are to be carried out by various wine-tasting groups or commissions in various sittings, the results obtained in a single blind tasting for an annual publication will never be fair, unless the identity of the wines are revealed to the members and they know about the general line of work of the winery. Here is the method for carrying out the wine-tastings. A general impression is obtained not only from the results of the various tastings carried out in different places, situations and times, but also the line, style and quality classification of the winery is taken into account. It is rare for two bottles of the same brand, type and method of ageing (Crianza, Reserva or Gran Reserva) to obtain scores of more than three points difference (in the Guide, for example, 75 and 78), even though they are produced from different harvests. Instead, it is more likely that they are awarded higher scores, due to the significant changes in production methods and raw materials sourced by the winery.

The author's general knowledge about the style (generally consistent) of each winery, throughout the last four years,

reduces the errors of blind tasting, where, at times, the defects originating inside a particular bottle (not scored) can be confused with deficiencies in the production and ageing (scored) of the wine. With new wineries (or brands that are appearing in the guide for the first time and contrast with the usual style of the company under review), the wine-tasting team can carry out small survey amongst colleagues and compare opinions with other collaborators.

On the other hand, we are aware that in Spain, due to a relatively consistent climate in most parts of the regions, and, of course, to the astuteness for blending wines that was a long-standing practice in most wineries, the variations in vintage are fewer than the changes in style. The latter practice is normally stated and also detected in the wine tasting.

## TASTINGS OF PREMATURELY-BOTTLED WINES

In previous editions relatively lower scores have appeared for high quality wines bottled in a period of less than three months. It is clear that after six months this wine is worthy of a higher classification in view of its improvement, both on the nose and the palate, but with no means for adjustment, it has to wait until the following year's edition. Even allowing for, and disregarding, the negative factors implied by tasting a wine in the period stated (underdeveloped fruit, unbalanced oak and wine, rather harsh tannins), it is risky to score a wine higher than the senses perceive. Therefore, the wine-tasting team advises wineries that are uncertain as to whether the wine has fully developed, in terms of taste and smell, to abstain from submitting samples under these circumstances, as both the winery and the team could run the risk of discrediting the brand due to incorrect scoring. In these cases it would be more appropriate to submit a sample from the previous harvest with fully established characteristics, even if it has sold out at the winery, as there is still the possibility that there will be some available on the market which is a prerequisite for publication in the Guide.

## HOW TO INTERPRET THE TASTING NOTES

In each description of a wine, two types of concept are presented:

## OBJECTIVE

These are the "measurable" descriptions, which are not conditioned by any personal idiosyncrasies of the taster, and which can easily be compared by any enthusiast.

Colour: the intensity and clarity; for example, if the wine is intense, open, pale, cloudy, limpid, etc.

Aroma: intensity, defects, excess aroma of one element contained in the wine (e.g. wood and type of grape variety, fruity or not, ageing, etc.)

Taste: intensity and structure; whether it is meaty, with body, rounded, the essential flavours (acidity, bitterness – tannins – sweet, acidic, saline) and all those described for the aroma.

## SUBJECTIVE

These are the "non measurable" descriptions, of a personal nature, referenced by comparison with other products known to José Peñín and his team through experience, and whose purpose is to help to guide the reader. Examples: colour – "golden, cherry, old gold, mahogany, straw-coloured, etc.."; nose and palate – "dark-roasted flavour, jam, cherry, attic, etc."

For another wine taster, for example, dark-roasted flavour could be equivalent to a toasty hint and "attic" summarised as dust or old wood.

## HOW TO INTERPRET THE INFORMATION ON THE WINERIES

We would like to draw your attention to the use of oak in many Spanish wines that appear on the market that do not indicate the ageing, such as oak, casks, crianza, etc. It is increasingly more common for many wines to reach the market after three or four months in cask, with the aim of making them more refined and finished. In this sense, we are merely informing the reader that the wine has been aged in cask, without specifying the number of months. If the characteristic "oak" appears on the label, we will include it in the identification of the wine.

The abbreviations used:

| | |
|---|---|
| B | BLANCO (WHITE) |
| BC | BLANCO CRIANZA |
| BFB | BLANCO FERMENTADO EN BARRICA (WHITE BARREL FERMENTED) |

| | |
|---|---|
| RD | ROSADO (ROSÉ) |
| T | TINTO (RED) |
| TC | TINTO CRIANZA |
| TR | TINTO RESERVA |
| TGR | TINTO GRAN RESERVA |
| FI | FINO |
| MZ | MANZANILLA |
| OL | OLOROSO |
| OLV | OLOROSO VIEJO |
| AM | AMONTILLADO |
| PX | PEDRO XIMÉNEZ |
| PC | PALO CORTADO |
| CR | CREAM |
| PCR | PALE CREAM |
| GE | GENEROSO |
| ESP | ESPUMOSO (SPARKLING WINE) |
| BR | BRUT |
| BN | BRUT NATURE |
| SC | SECO (DRY) |
| SS | SEMISECO (SEMI-DRY) |
| S/C | SIN COSECHA (NON VINTAGE) |

## WINES NOT TASTED

There are two groups of wines not tasted:

a) Wines belonging to wineries that have only submitted some of their brands. b) Wines belonging to wineries that have not submitted any samples.

In the case of a), the absence can be due either to the wine having sold out in thewinery (an absurd reason given that the wine could still be available on the market), orto the producer's belief that, as they were lower quality brands, they would by awardeda lower score. In this latter case, we deduce that this refers to inferior wines to otherstasted and classified from these producers. As the brands already received allow us togain an understanding of the style of the winery, we will not insist on the missing labelsbeing submitted. In the case of b) we definitely know that, apart from rare exceptions, the wines wouldnot achieve a score of more than 79. However, we have made every effort to update the basic details (address, telephone number and brands sold) and, of course, we will continue toask them to submit samples for tastings for future editions.

# VARIETIES

## THE MAIN SPANISH WHITE VARIETIES

**~ Airén.** It is the main white grape in La Mancha producing the largest single variety volume of wine in the world. When grown on a large scale without proper care it provides very uninteresting wines. However, with good care, it offers white wines of a pale colour and a fruity nose that are smooth and pleasant on the palate, although lacking remarkable features.

**~ Albarín.** Grown mainly in Asturias, in Cangas de Narcea. Its characteristic flavour falls somewhere between sweet and herbaceous, with the latter feature more pronounced when yields are high. In recent years it has been increasingly grown in the VT León region to an overwhelming quality. Given its short ripening cycle, even when grown in high and relatively sunny regions –as it is the case of that part of León–, it easily achieves an alcohol content of 14%, retaining a fresh acidity with hints of herbs and white fruits.

**~ Albariño.** Mainly produced on the Atlantic coast of Galicia, it is a high quality grape typical of humid and not too sunny regions, and therefore thought to have its origins in central Europe. Its wines are fruity and floral, with a characteristically fat, fleshy, lingering taste.

**~ Albillo.** A considerably neutral variety, low in acidity and with a tendency to oxidise, it produces smooth wines with high glycerine content but no remarkable features. Once the main table wine grape throughout Castile, its early-ripening cycle and high sugar levels afforded its reputation in historic wines such as those of San Martín de Valdeiglesias, known as 'blancos pardillos', slightly coloured –oxidized– whites. Albillo is the dominant variety in San Martín de Valdeiglesias, a sub-region in the DO Vinos de Madrid, and is also grown in higher areas of La Palma –in the Canary Islands– and in Ribera del Duero.

**~ Cayetana blanca.** Grown in Extremadura, mainly in Tierra de Barros, it adapts easily to clay soils and hot climates, yielding light wines with some singular herbal – not herbaceous– notes. It has a pleasant freshness, which is easily lost after the first year in the bottle.

**~ Dona Blanca.** Grown mainly in the DO Monterrei, in the province of Orense. Also known as moza fresca and valenciana in Bierzo, some experts identify it as the merseguera from the Mediterranean coast of Valencia. It is characterized by some fine herbal nuances and good acidity, and it performs well when blended with *godello*.

**~ Forastera Gomera.** Found predominantly in La Gomera along with listán (in both the white and red versions) and the indigenous negramoll, it was one of the grape varieties considered "of interest" when the former vinos de la tierra (VT) designation became DO. Particularly interesting are its colour intensity (lemony yellow), aroma (ripe white fruit) and acidity, all of them characteristics that can be found in the best young wines.

**~ Garnacha blanca.** Considered the Mediterranean white grape par excellence, it is grown mainly in Catalonia (Empordà, Priorat, and above all Terra Alta), and characterised by pleasant herb, hay and scrubland nuances, some warm, alcoholic notes on the palate and its capacity to age wonderfully in the rancio style when aged in wood and winemakers resort to lee-stirring practices.

**~ Godello.** Another high quality Galician white grape cultivated in Valdeorras and Monterrei –in the province of Ourense– as well as in the Bierzo region, in León. Its high glycerol level and acidity provides pleasant bittersweet notes along with high alcohol content.

**~ Hondarrabi Zuri.** This variety is used to produce txakoli in the Basque provinces of Vizcaya and Guipúzcoa. Perfectly adapted to a cool and humid climate, it yields fresh and fruity wines with lovely green grass and apple notes and a refreshing acidity.

**~ Jaén.** Grown mainly in Andalusia, jaén is an old grape variety, already mentioned by Alonso de Herrera in 1513. Another ampelographer of the XVIII century, García de la Leña, mentions two types of jaén: jaén blanco and jaén doradillo. About the latter he recalls: "The grape has a somewhat golden colour, after which it is named: its skin is a little harder than that of the blanco and ripens later". Herbaceousness is the main feature of the wines made from jaén, along with some mineral nuances, although there has been little research on its performance with selected yeasts.

~ **Lado.** This variety, as subtle as it is scarce, is found in DO Ribeiro. The white wines in that region are made by blending different grape varieties, a way to add complexity and nuances to the renderings. Lado is added to provide lightness, aromatic intensity and acidity.

~ **Listán blanca.** Cultivated in the Canary Islands, it provides wines with a singular character that falls between ripe grape and mountain herbs notes. It is balsamic and even more so if grown in vineyards on dry and difficult terrains (Valle de Güímar), whereas in more humid regions such as Tacoronte-Acentejo, Valle de la Orotava and –to a lesser extent– Ycoden-Daute-Isora, this variety shows herbal notes and some sweetness.

~ **Loureiro.** Another Galician variety used to add complexity and round wines off. It is a highly aromatic grape, although it is used in blends in only tiny proportions. There is also a red loureiro, which is very scarce. The white one is best known for an aroma reminiscent of bay leaf (loureiro in Galician language).

~ **Macabeo (o viura).** It is the main variety for quality white Rioja wines and also cavas. Its slow oxidation pattern makes it ideal for barrel ageing. The wine is pale and light, with hints of green fruits when yields are high. Recent research has proved macabeo cultivated in poor soils and under low-yield growing patterns –just the opposite to current practices in Penedès and La Rioja– yields grapes of higher quality.

~ **Malvar.** The main white grape variety in the region of Madrid, it has a smooth texture, a good fruity character and some sweetness that combines brilliantly with airén, as well as being an ideal grape to make wines with sobremadre (with the skins), the most popular winemaking practice within the region.

~ **Malvasía.** It gave name to the most famous sweet wine of the Middle Ages and, although it reigned throughout the Mediterranean region, it is now relegated to Italy, Portugal (it is the main grape variety in Madeira) and Spain. Considered nobler than moscatel, it produces very aromatic whites with a highly original taste that falls somewhere between musky and bitter. In the Mediterranean basin there are many clones and types of this age-old grape variety. The best-known examples in Spain are the malvasías from the Canary Islands and the town of Sitges in Catalonia, and it is also produced in smaller quantities in Navarra and La Rioja. Aromatic and historic as it gets (its Greek provenance links it to the oldest winemaking in the Western world), known in Catalonia as subirat parent, its huge character is promoting its renaissance in the Mediterranean coast as well as in the inland regions.

~ **Merseguera.** A variety cultivated in Valencia, basically in the Alto Turia and on a lesser scale in Utiel-Requena. It provides whites with a grassy character, dry mountain herbs and a light almondy background; it has a little more body than cayetana blanca and airén. So far there is no evidence of any improvement in its quality with the application of new winemaking methods.

~ **Moscatel.** Generally used in the production o sweet mistela wines, it yields aromatic, neat wines that are very fragrant and fresh when young. It is grown in Levante, Cádiz, Málaga and the Ebro valley, the latter an area where they grow mainly the type known as moscatel de grano menudo, used in the production of high quality sweet wines.

~ **Palomino.** This is the grape variety par excellence in the region of Jerez. Its fast evolution makes it ideal for the production of 'vinos generosos' (fortified wines). It has little body and a fresh pungent flavour with bitter almond nuances. Palomino is also grown in the provinces of Galicia, León and Valladolid.

~ **Pardina.** Is the most characteristic white grape in Extremadura, particularly abundant in the regions of Tierra de Barros and Ribera Baja. New winemaking methods are helping to reveal a lovely character of mountain herbs and white ripe fruit, and it also shows a lovely character on the palate.

~ **Parellada.** IGrown in the higher regions of Catalonia. It is a delicate grape and therefore very difficult to grow. Its low-alcoholic wines are pale, with delicate aromas and a light body. It is also a complementary variety in cava production.

~ **Pedro Ximénez.** Mainly grown in the provinces of Córdoba and Málaga. The wines from Montilla-Moriles are made from this grape and its fast evolution makes it suitable for the production of dry and sweet fortified wines, as well as ¬blended with moscatel, for the sweet wines of Málaga. When made into dry wines, it shows a pleasant, easy palate with a slight sweetness.

~ **Picapoll.** A grape native to the Catalonian region of Pla de Bages, and it is also grown in the Languedoc in France. According to some theories its name comes from the spots I has on the skin and according to others from its sharp acidity. Although it is traditionally used blended with other varieties (mainly macabeo and parellada), new wave producers such as Abadal have used it in single-varietal wines given its intense, fruity aromas of flowers and herbs.

~ **Torrontés.** It is used blended –along with godello, albariño, treixadura and loureiro– in modern Ribeiro wines, and gives musts of a somewhat neutral taste –partly to high-yielding production patterns–, and therefore less intense and more acidic than its white counterparts. Outside Spain, it is the most popular grape for white wine production in Argentina.

~ **Treixadura.** The main grape variety from Ribeiro, it is similar to albariño but not as refined and with less glycerol content. Its taste is reminiscent of ripe apples and it blends beautifully with the albariño. Floral and fruity in character, it is a good quality grape; however, it does have a limited production.

~ **Verdejo.** This is perhaps the Spanish white variety most integrated with the ecosystem of the plateau and, therefore,

best adapted to the continental climate of Castile. When selected yeasts are not used, its wines are characterized by flavours that are both pleasantly herbal and fruity, with some structure on the palate, leading to a typically bitter finish, but with a background of sweetness that provides a lot of character. It grows well when planted in alluvial soils and areas with strong day-night temperature contrast.

~ **Vijariego.** It is one of the oldest indigenous Spanish grape varieties, grown exclusively in the Canary Islands and Andalusia (mainly in the provinces of Granada and Almería). It has a fruity character with some pleasant herbal and balsamic nuances. A very interesting white grape, even when barrel-fermented.

~ **Xarel.lo.** A very harmonious, balanced grape variety, but with more body than the other characteristic Catalonian grapes, parellada and macabeo. It shows a splendid character when is grown under low-yield production patterns and manages to ripen properly.

~ **Zalema.** The name stems from the Arabic "salem", meaning peace. This variety, exclusive to the DO Condado de Huelva, is full, fruity and fresh on the nose, characterised by fruit notes bordering on exotic. On the

## GEOGRAPHICAL DISTRIBUTION OF THE MAIN WHITE GRAPES

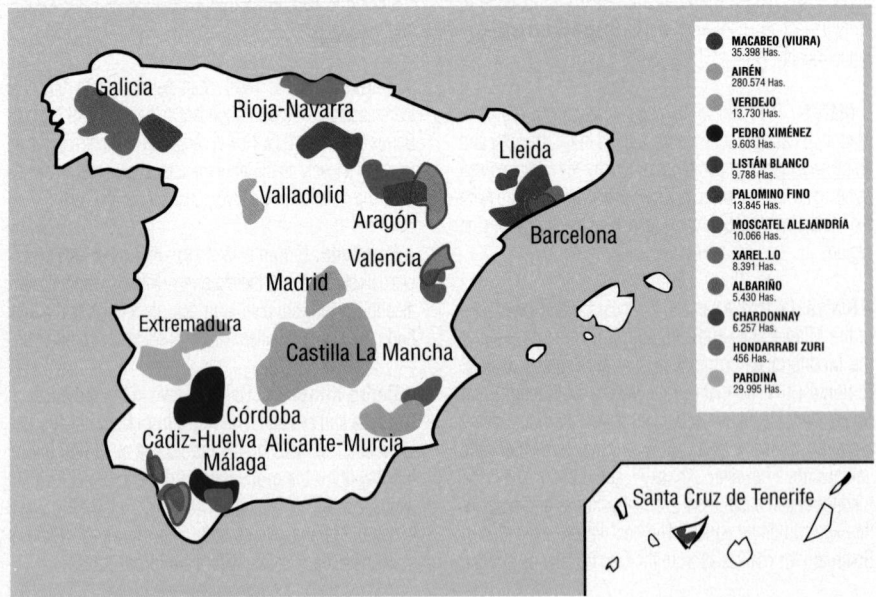

MACABEO (VIURA)
35.398 Has.

AIRÉN
280.574 Has.

VERDEJO
13.730 Has.

PEDRO XIMÉNEZ
9.603 Has.

LISTÁN BLANCO
9.788 Has.

PALOMINO FINO
13.845 Has.

MOSCATEL ALEJANDRÍA
10.066 Has.

XAREL.LO
8.391 Has.

ALBARIÑO
5.430 Has.

CHARDONNAY
6.257 Has.

HONDARRABI ZURI
456 Has.

PARDINA
29.995 Has.

Galicia · Rioja-Navarra · Lleida · Valladolid · Aragón · Barcelona · Valencia · Madrid · Extremadura · Castilla La Mancha · Córdoba · Cádiz-Huelva · Alicante-Murcia · Málaga · Santa Cruz de Tenerife

palate, in addition to freshness, its more prominent feature is a smooth, ripe aftertaste with hints of flowers and apple peel.

## THE MAIN SPANISH RED VARIETIES

~ **Bobal.** A typical grape of the high areas of Levante, and particularly abundant in Utiel-Requena. Very intense in terms of colour, with brilliant reflections thanks to its high acidity, it has generally low alcohol content, though. It has also a fresh, not too intense nose, and makes good rosé wines. When the grape comes from old vines, a more pronounced wild-berry character appears. An improved knowledge on low-yield viticulture is giving rise to meatier and more tannic reds with excellent ageing potential.

~ **Brancellao.** A variety characterised by small to medium-size bunches and light-coloured flesh, it provides structure. It is grown in Ribeira Sacra along with merenzao, although to a much lesser extent than mencía.

~ **Caíño.** Found in both white and red versions, the former authorised in Rías Baixas, the latter one of the main varieties in Ribeiro.

~ **Callet.** Native to Mallorca, for years it has been considered a second-rate grape, producing musts with very little colour due to high-yield production patterns. However, young wine growers from around the town of Felanitx have given it a new lease of life over the last few years thanks to selective work on old vines and low yields, producing wines with good colour and high alcohol content. It is usually blended with cabernet sauvignon, manto negro or tempranillo to improve the wines ageing potential and add complexity. The skin needs to fully ripen to avoid its typical herbaceous notes.

~ **Cariñena.** Perhaps the Spanish variety more capable to stand overripeness. With old vines and in warm dry soils it can be obtained a good fruit expression of great freshness and dry and lively tannins, although only above 14 % alcohol content. It generally shows hints of wild red berries that are fresher than those related to monastrell and garnacha. It is usually blended with garnacha, which has a somewhat weaker tannic structure. It is grown mainly in Tarragona (Priorat and Montsant).

~ **Garnacha.** For many decades this has been the main Spanish grape variety in terms of production. In recent times its wines have improved in colour, character and depth, thanks to a considerable average reduction in yield. As it tends, like monastrell, to oxidize easily, to keep a good colour is crucial, but it does have an enormous fruit expression with a certain touch of sweetness, maybe not as pronounced as monastrell. It is grown mainly in the warm regions of La Rioja, Navarra, Aragón and Catalonia, i.e., along the Ebro River Valley. In Toledo and to the west of Madrid there is a clone of garnacha with slightly less colour and tannins.

~ **Garnacha tintorera.** The main characteristic of this grape is that its pulp is coloured, which makes it a very sought after grape to give colour to bulk wines. Traditionally known as the alicante bouschet hybrid, some authors say it is grape variety on its own right native from Alicante, Toledo and Ciudad Real. Some recent single-varietal renderings in the DO Almansa have proved its great aromatic and fruity character, as well as its capability to provide body and structure on the palate.

~ **Graciano.** This is a classic Rioja grape, which, as it was grown in less accessible areas of La Rioja, was used only in small proportions and mainly to improve both the acidity and the fruit expression of tempranillo. As soon as it was discovered that planted in warmer areas the grape grew richer in fruit and colour expression, single-varietal wines began to emerge. It has a great aromatic character with hints of blueberries and is fresher and more vigorous than the tempranillo grown in warmer regions. Most of the graciano is planted in La Rioja and in the hottest parts of Valencia and Extremadura.

~ **Hondarribi Beltza.** The red txakoli variety has its origins –and it is cultivated exclusively– within the geographical boundaries of the Basque Country. It is characterised by a high acidity and strong fruit and wild herbs aromas. As well as being made into varietal wines, it is also part of rosé blends along with its white counterpart, hondarribi zuri. Some French experts maintain that it is very similar to cabernet franc as it is also grown in the French region of Irulegui.

~ **Juan García.** Native to the region of Fermoselle, in the province of Zamora (Castilla-León), where it is the main variety. It can provide interesting young wines of moderate alcoholic content. However, its thin skin makes it a fragile variety in areas of high humidity or when it comes to lengthy ageing periods.

**~ Listán Negra.** This grape is grown in the Canary Islands and yields brilliant red wines with a marked balsamic nose, hints of eucalyptus and some fresh, juicy red fruit notes. Its average low tannic level makes it more suitable for the production of young wines.

**~ Manto negro.** Native to the Balearic Islands, it is especially abundant in the DO Binissalem, in Mallorca, although is also found in Pla i Llevant. It yields typical ripe fruit aromas along with hints of caramel. On the palate it is quite balanced, although it is normally blended with another local grape –callet– or some other international varieties.

**~ Marselan.** A fairly new variety (just under a decade old), it is a hybrid or crossbreed of cabernet sauvignon and garnacha and it first went on the market in 2002. Its aromatic and sensory profile is characterised by a stimulating opposition between a high concentration of fruity and spicy notes and the subtlety of its tannins, which makes it one of the grapes with the greatest potential in the Mediterranean area. Its tendency to ripen very quickly makes it prone to over-maturation.

**~ Mencía.** The cultivation of this grape is limited to the northeast of the Iberian Peninsula, and it is abundant in the border of the provinces of León and Zamora with the region of Galicia. Quite similar to cabernet franc, it yields fruity wines, rich in colour and acidity when grown in cooler regions with sufficient water. Recently, deeper, more concentrated reds are being made thanks to more careful winemaking and lower yields.

**~ Monastrell.** Of Spanish provenance and known in France as mourvèdre, the monastrell is characterised by its suitability to regions with little rainfall and high temperatures. It is almost entirely grown in the limestone soils of the provinces of Alicante and Murcia. It has a lot of fruit expression, though of a candied-fruit kind, as well as sweet and soft tannins. It is prone to oxidation, and therefore excellent for sweet and rancio wines. It needs to reach 13.5º of potential alcohol and the wine should not age for more than 10 months for the fruit to achieve full expression. Except in the areas already mentioned, where monastrell is vinified on its own, in cooler regions like Catalonia it is usually blended with other varieties.

**~ Moristel.** It is grown within the geographical boundaries of Somontano, like parraleta, although from a sensory point of view it is slightly sweeter, with certain rusticity, some candied-fruit notes and cherry preserve.

## GEOGRAPHICAL DISTRIBUTION OF THE MAIN RED GRAPES

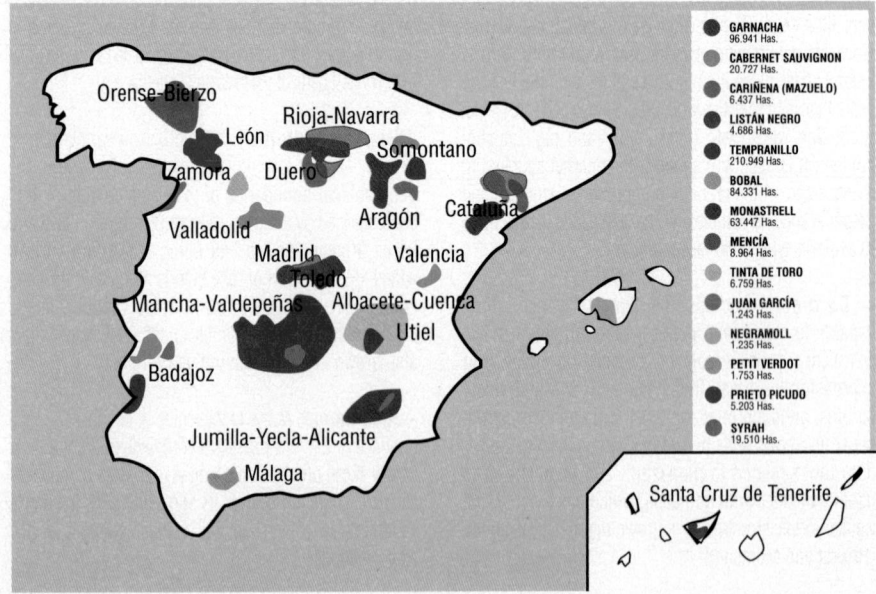

~ **Negramoll.** A grape cultivated in the Canary Islands, particularly in the island of La Palma. It has less character than listán, but more structure and tannins. When harvested late, it sometimes shows a juicy blackcurrant character.

~ **Parraleta.** A grape variety indigenous to Somontano region and not found anywhere else, its main characteristic is a lovely rusticity; it also shows some balsamic (herbal) character derived from its typical notes of wild berries —mainly strawberries and raspberries— as well as spices.

~ **Prieto picudo.** Grown in the area comprised between the towns of Benavente (Zamora) and Astorga (León), and from there to the border of the province of Palencia. Its main characteristic is to grow even in extreme climatic conditions. Its wines have usually a dark cherry colour and shows intense red fruit notes similar to those made of mencía, but with some added, pleasant herbal hints and more tannins, given it has a thicker skin. It is also similar to graciano.

~ **Rufete**. Grown exclusively in the Sierra de Salamanca and therefore the flagship of the wine region of Arribes del Duero, it generally provides wines light in both colour and body. Its tendency to oxidization asks for careful winemaking, but the best examples keep some singular characteristics: herbs, spices, and blackthorn berry notes both on the palate and on the nose.

~ **Sumoll.** Its indigenous character is still a matter of dispute between different Catalonian regions, although Conca de Barberà acts as the most vehement defender. Easy to grow and therefore a very popular choice at the end of the 19th Century to produce "vinos de pasto" (bulk wines) in a region, Catalonia, that was leading back then Spanish red wine production.

~ **Tempranillo.** The most widely grown grape variety in Spain as a result of two factors: its adaptability to extreme continental climate and its tannic structure, which allows for longer wood-ageing periods. Its general characteristics can be summed up in a fruity aroma and a flavour that is less "virile" than those of cabernet sauvignon or syrah, as well as smoother tannins. It prefers continental climates with a sharp temperature contrast and lots of sunshine hours, therefore it is grown in almost all continental zones of Spain and hardly found in coastal regions or humid areas under Atlantic rainfall patterns.

~ **Tinta de Toro.** An old clone of tempranillo, which manages in a hot region like Toro to achieve the same acidity levels as in Ribera del Duero, only with a higher alcohol content. The best red wines come from rocky and sandy areas, and shows more similarities with the Portuguese tinta roriz for its fine herbal background than with the tempranillo from Ribera del Duero. It has the same fruit potential as garnacha, with just a touch drier character. Its palate is generally one of ripe black fruit with abundant dry tannins capable to balance out sweetness beautifully.

~ **Trepat.** An early variety in terms of bud-break and late in terms of harvesting, it is vigorous, with large berries, plenty of seeds, thick skin and compact bunches. It yields rosé wines very light in colour and body, with moderate alcoholic content and a well-balanced acidity. It is grown mainly in DO Costers del Segre and DO Conca de Barberá, its native soil and where it has traditionally been made into single-varietal rosé wines through a light maceration process.

## THE MAIN FOREIGN VARIETIES CULTIVATED IN SPAIN

~ **Cabernet Franc (red).** Like cabernet sauvignon it comes from the Bordeaux region, although it gives more supple and fruitier wines. It is thought to be related to mencía —a grape abundantly grown in regions like Galicia and Castile—, and it is mainly grown in Catalonia.

~ **Cabernet Sauvignon (red).** Originally from France and typical the Bordeaux region, its wines are ideal for ageing, very intense in colour, with strong tannins and a penetrating aroma of violets and berries. In Spain it has acclimatised perfectly to areas such as Penedès, Navarra and Ribera del Duero, and it is difficult to find a red wine producing area in which this champion variety has not been planted in recent years.

~ **Chardonnay (white).** Originally from Burgundy (France), it has become the most valuable white grape in the world. The wines, characterised by a slight smoky nose and —given its high dry extract, glycerine levels and low oxidation tendency— achieve good results when aged in wood. Perfectly adapted to different Spanish regions (Penedès, Costers del Segre, Navarra, Somontano, etc.), it is being authorised in numerous DOs.

~ **Gewürztraminer (white).** One of the varieties of the "traminer" species, of a spicy flavour and originally from the Alsace region (France) and Germany, it is grown in Spain on a limited scale in Somontano and Penedès, but the wines produced are not obviously as famous as the ones produced in the above mentioned European regions. In Spain its musky character is more prominent than the spicy one.

~ **Marsanne (white).** Part of the great varietal trio – along with viognier and roussane– from the Rhône valley and originally from the region of Montélimar, it is characterised by mineral and exotic fruit (melon) notes and a lovely, unctuous palate. It is hard to find in single-varietal form, since it requires the aromatic contribution of more intense varieties from that region like viognier.

~ **Merlot (red).** Again of French origin, this grape variety has a dark blue colour and a very thick skin. Although it ripens earlier than cabernet sauvignon, it grows well in hot-climate regions. It is widely grown in Spain in Somontano and Catalonia, and to a lesser extent in Alicante and Murcia.

~ **Petit Verdot (red).** Again originally from Bordeaux, it is hardly found in that region and is relatively new to Spain, where it is associated more to the whims of some producers (Marqués de Griñón, Abadía Retuerta) than to an specific geographical area, although the best results are achieved in continental regions with lots of annual sunshine hours (Jumilla, Alicante, Toledo and Ronda). The existing Spanish examples yield aromatic notes of fresh, ripe berries, have good intensity both on the palate and the nose –thanks to their late ripening pattern– and achieve high alcohol levels.

~ **Pinot Noir (red).** The classic grape variety from Burgundy and Champagne, its fruit has a small size and a dark violet skin that provides a lot of colour. However, its wines lose colour faster, turning orangey. In warm climates it loses its complexity and elegance. It is mainly grown in Catalonia.

~ **Riesling (white).** The most famous white wines from Alsace, the Moselle an the Rhine regions, are produced from this grape. The berry is small, yellowish in colour and low yielding. In Spain, where is mainly grown in Catalonia, produces fresh, fruity and floral dry wines, which are not as great and complex as those from the European regions mentioned above.

~ **Roussane (white).** Like marsanne, it comes from the Rhône river valley wine region. It is present in the best wines from the most significant appellations such as Hermitage, Saint Joseph, Côtes du Rhône, Châteauneuf du Pape and Corbières. Despite its tendency to oxidise it can provide subtle wines that age magnificently in the bottle. Its aromas are reminiscent of apricot, with floral (narcissus), citric and sometimes honey notes. It has a somewhat unctuous character making it very attractive on the palate. At present we can find some examples of it in Catalonia.

~ **Sauvignon blanc (white).** A quality white grape with small berries and a lovely golden colour when properly ripe. It is mainly grown in Bordeaux (Graves) and the Loire region, although it has acclimatised to other countries such as Argentina, Chile, Uruguay, California and above all New Zealand. In Spain it is mainly grown in the DO Rueda and to a lesser extent in Catalonia. It has a taste of tropical fruits and a slight floral nuance.

~ **Syrah (red).** This is the grape of the Rhône valley and Australia par excellence and, ideally suited to warm regions it is becoming very fashionable in Spain. The grapes are ovoid and small with a very pleasant flavour. Its wine has a characteristic aroma of violets and very ripe black fruit. At present it has become a very popular grape in Jumilla (the first place in Spain where it was grown), where it is blended with monastrell, as well as other parts of Spain that enjoy a Mediterranean–continental climate.

~ **Viognier (white).** The jewel of the Rhone valley is growing fast in popularity all over the world and has acclimatised well in Spain thanks to the similarity of the Mediterranean climate with its region of origin. Considered a noble grape, it ages with grace, has a floral and fruity character with hints of herbs and lots of depth, and in the best renderings it shows also great complexity. Mainly grown in Catalonia, Teruel, and Toledo.

## THE INFLUENCE OF THE DIFFERENT VARIETES ON THE COLOUR OF WINES

### RED WINES
**Tempranillo.** When young it has a garnet red cherry colour, with an intense velvet rim that gives a sense of immaturity.
**Garnacha.** Violet rim and a slightly orangey cherry tone at the core. .
**Cabernet Sauvignon.** Pronounced red colour, with a swift change from solid ripe cherry in the centre to purple at the rim.
**Garnacha Tintorera** (called alicante in Galicia and León) has high pigmentation levels both in the skin and in the must, the reason why it is grown in regions with little sunlight –such as Galicia– to compensate for the lack of colour typical of cooler climates. However the finest quality is found in Almansa, where more of it is grown.

### ROSÉ WINES
**Cariñena.** Pomegranate notes at the rim.
**Cabernet Sauvignon.** Raspberry notes.
**Garnacha.** Purple with a shade of mauve.

### WHITE WINES
**Xarel-lo.** It yields wines that are usually straw-coloured with yellow reflections, very similar to albariño.
**Parellada.** It usually yields pale wines, given that is generally grown in higher regions and hardly manage to complete its ripening cycle. When blended with xarel-lo, wines tend to have higher alcohol levels and a moderate acidity, which makes a good blend for cava production.
**Chardonnay.** It yields a more yellow hue thanks to the colour of its skin..

# TERROIR

This is the magical term used by the French to express the intimate association between a soil of homogeneous characteristics, a variable microclimate and the grape varieties adapted to them, therefore a key element to produce a wine with its own personality and able to stand out from the rest.

## The origin

Terroir is in France the cornerstone of both their vine-growing philosophy and their appellation system. It is used not only to define regions of a certain entity and size, but also to delimit small areas of just a few hectares, as it is the case of the cru in Bordeaux and the even smaller clos in Burgundy.

## The concept in Spain

Although the system of designations of origin is similar to that of the French appellations, the geographical demarcations were created in Spain on a much larger scale, either due to the influence of a group of growers, historical or even political reasons, and only occasionally in attention to soil and climate. The designation Vinos de Pago has not been a serious option until recently and only as the result of an increased interest in the singularity of vineyards, and it is being used mainly for commercial purposes to identify a higher status in the vineyard hierarchy. However, it is important to make a distinction between the French cru, which identifies a soil of very defined and similar characteristics transferred to the bottle, from the Spanish pago, which refers to an undivided estate with different types of soils where wines are blended together before being bottled.

## The concept in the New World

The New World has made of the grape variety the real star of their system, and branded the concept of terroir as unrealistically poetic or even as a mere marketing strategy. The New World has also promoted high-yields policies to a point where the grape variety completely loses its character, and therefore the soil and climate (terroir) expression is lost likewise. But there is a point of contradiction in the respect most Australian, Californian and even Chilean growers show for their old vineyards and use this concept —deeper and more abundant roots absorb mineral minerals from the soil much better— as a way to produce wines of greater complexity. At present, some exceptional single estate wines are also being produced in these countries.

## How to manage *terroir*?

Perhaps the most important practical philosophy associated with terroir is the respect for all the natural elements (climate, soil, etc.) which, by definition, cannot be manipulated. On the other hand, to achieve the greatest possible expression from the land demands quality practices: to limit yields, and to use the best available training and watering methods to appropriately manage the vigour of the vines.

## Are some terroirs better than others?

There is no democracy when it comes to wines and terroirs. Therefore there are terroirs that, given the nature of their soil and climate, produce finer wines than others and even wines with a greater complexity and the ability to age much better, for no apparent reason.

## What are the main types of soil that produce quality wines?

Neither age, geological composition or texture of the soil are determinant quality factors. We can find that excellent wines can come from all sorts of soils (clay, slate, alluvial, limestone, etc.). The only common factors seem to be that these soils are very poor and almost in every case unable to grow any other plant but vines, and that they have an excellent natural drainage, which may even be improved by man if necessary, in a way that water supply to the plant is strictly controlled; in other words, the soil has the necessary mechanisms to balance shortage or surplus of water, depending on rainfall and latitude.

## Is an ideal soil enough?

A typical soil cross-section found in many parts of Spain is that of a vineyard with a top layer of stones (gravel, pebbles, slate), which helps to increase temperature and therefore ensures a better ripening cycle, followed by a second layer of sand that drains the water, and below that a third layer of clay to retain the humidity in the subsoil, but this optimal soil pattern must also have environmental and climatic factors in harmony with it. For example, a red wine from Priorat with the same soil pattern at a higher altitude would be entirely different. And the same would happen if we had the same poor slate soil but without the fresh breezes coming off the Sierra del Montsant. In addition, we must remember that the better a given variety is adapted to the soil and climate, the more character it will be able to extract from the soil.

# THE BEST TERROIRS IN SPAIN

The terroirs listed below (more or less in order of importance) are the predominant ones in Spain:

~ **Slate soils.** Priorat, some areas of Cebreros (Ávila), Arribes del Duero, Ribeira Sacra, La Axarquía (Málaga), highest areas in Valle de Güímar (Tenerife), some areas in Calatayud and the northeast part of Empordà.

~ **Stony soils.** The best estates of Toro, certain estates in Tarragona (Falset, Conca de Barberà and Terra Alta), some areas in Ribera de Navarra, areas close to the Duero river in Rueda and some areas in Rioja Baja.

~ **Predominantly limestone soils with some clay.** Rioja Alavesa and surrounding regions, Sonsierra, Rioja Alta, in Ribera del Duero the area closer to Valladolid, Calatayud, Jumilla, Yecla, Jerez, Montilla-Moriles, Terra Alta, Alicante, Cigales, Costers del Segre and Somontano.

~ **Sandy (siliceous) and granite soils.** Rías Baixas, Valdeorras, Ribeiro, Ribeira Sacra, Fermoselle, the area north of Méntrida and the western area of Vinos de Madrid.

~ **Volcanic soils.** Lanzarote, Hierro, Valle de Güímar, Gran Canaria, Monte de Lentiscal, La Palma, Ycoden-Daute-Isora and Abona.

# THE INFLUENCE OF THE SOIL ON THE AROMA OF WINES

The type of soil subtly modifies the aroma of wine.

~ **Granite and sandy soils.** They produce neat wines with pure, well-defined aromas that perfectly identify the grape variety, although they may at times show a high alcohol content due to the excessive drainage of the soil, which promotes concentration, as it is the case of the wines from Galicia or the red Garnachas from San Martín de Valdeiglesias, made from grapes grown on soils with low moisture retention.

~ **Gravel or stony vineyards** (as found in some parts of Rueda and Toro). They yield wines with earthy aromas and flinty notes, which merge well with ripe grape nuances achieved thanks to the stones being warmed up by sunlight.

~ **Slate soils and mineral-rich soils.** In Priorat, Arribes del Duero, Cebreros and La Axarquía the wines always have slight hints of mineral, roasted coffee and overall toasty aromas, the same notes found in the Portuguese wines from the Upper Duero valley, the birthplace of Port.

~ **Volcanic soils.** These soils are found in Lanzarote, Hierro, La Palma, and certain areas of Tenerife. Their wines have slightly burnt and iodised nuances.

~ **Clay soils** (the majority within Spain). By retaining water, they provide higher yields and necessarily lower quality grapes. The wines have therefore less expression and, especially in white wines, there can appear some herbaceous notes if the vineyard is located on flat and humid areas. Clay is needed deep down in the subsoil to retain the moisture and to ensure an adequate feeding of the vine through the roots.

~ **Ferruginous soils.** They are difficult soils to produce quality wines. In general, ferruginous clay soils give the grapes a high level of iron, which should be eliminated, and a somewhat rustic and slightly burnt note.

~ **Limestone-rich soils** (found in Burgundy –Côtes de Nuits–, Champagne, Jumilla, Jerez or Rioja Alavesa). These soils add a note of elegance to the wines, which are overall better, richer and more complex.

# CLIMATES AND MICROCLIMATES

The climate plays a decisive role in vine growing. Factors such as temperature, rainfall or the amount of sunshine will determine winemaking and the differences in style. Spain, which occupies a territory where both the Atlantic and the Mediterranean climate merge, is therefore subject to a great variety of climatic conditions within a limited area.

## THE COMPLEXITY OF SPANISH OROGRAPHY.

High plateaus, river valleys, terraces, plots and ravines outline the real backbone of the peninsular geographic profile, mountain ranges that, curiously enough, run from northeast to southwest, and make up large catchment areas open to the west where 80% of the humid currents from the southwest come and manage to make up for mild temperatures; rains which appear precisely when the grape has not formed in the plant, but are nevertheless necessary to feed the roots, which is what really matters. The low rainfall in the mainland (due to a permanent and dominant high pressure zone over the Azore Islands during the growing period of the vine) considerably reduces humidity in comparison with a large part of Italy and the rest of Europe. This accounts for poor organic levels in the soil but a richer mineral content, which greatly favours vine growing.

Descriptions of all the climatic patterns found in Spain are listed below.

# ATLANTIC CLIMATE

Produced by the influence of the Atlantic Ocean, it is characterised by mild temperatures and a high degree of humidity, with rains happening all year round. There is a large mass of water situated to the west and its influence depends on maritime currents and water temperature differential.

## WINE PRODUCING REGIONS:

~ **Northern Tenerife**. The moisture does not come from the storms which usually occur a little more to the north, but from humid trade winds blowing from the northeast, which, when colliding with the warm air mass from the mountainous relief of Tenerife, create an accumulation of clouds known locally as 'panza de burro' (donkey's paunch) that keeps stable the level of humidity along the coastline from Tacoronte-Acentejo to the Valle de Orotava and, to a certain degree, up in the Ycoden–Daute–Isora area.

Wines with high acidity, low alcohol content and a touch of malic acid.

~ **Galicia**. A region entirely influenced by the Atlantic, not only because of the level of humidity and the sea breezes, but also the frequency of the storms coming in from west to east and bringing great quantities of rain. In areas further inland with less rainfall, microclimates may form and the grape will ripen more easily, such as the O'Rosal and Condado de Tea areas.

Grapes —and wines— that sometimes struggle to mature, high in malic acid, with a moderate alcohol content and also high acidity.

~ **Txakoli**. Like Galicia, it has a 100% Atlantic climate influence with also a high rainfall. This calls for the use of suitable, well-adapted varieties with little room for alternative grapes with better acidity levels, except those that do well in very cool and wet climates such as riesling. The vines must face south, which creates problems as the vineyards are found mainly on the northern slopes.

Fresh, acidic whites, with hints of green apples and floral notes. Very dry reds, slightly herbaceous and with aroma of red berries.

# ATLANTIC-CONTINENTAL CLIMATE

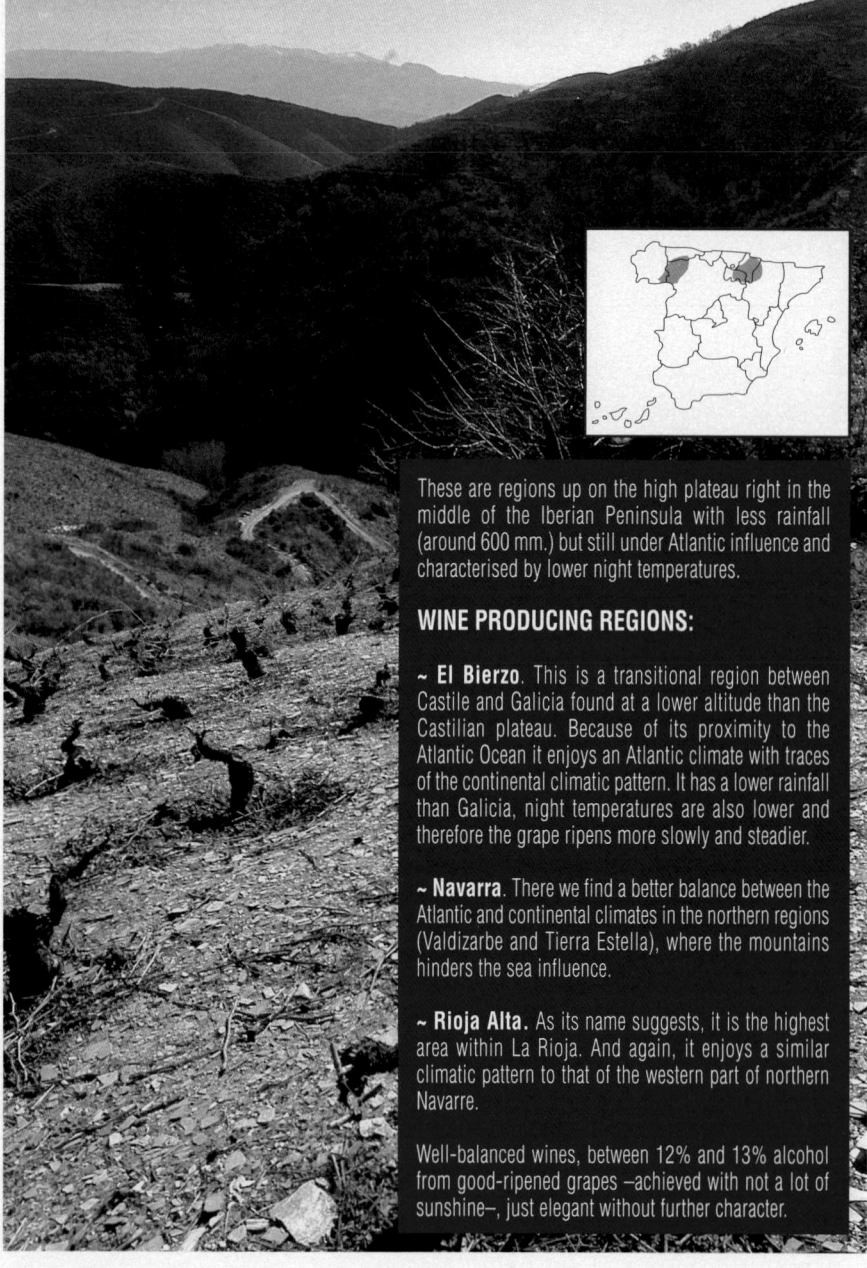

These are regions up on the high plateau right in the middle of the Iberian Peninsula with less rainfall (around 600 mm.) but still under Atlantic influence and characterised by lower night temperatures.

## WINE PRODUCING REGIONS:

**~ El Bierzo**. This is a transitional region between Castile and Galicia found at a lower altitude than the Castilian plateau. Because of its proximity to the Atlantic Ocean it enjoys an Atlantic climate with traces of the continental climatic pattern. It has a lower rainfall than Galicia, night temperatures are also lower and therefore the grape ripens more slowly and steadier.

**~ Navarra**. There we find a better balance between the Atlantic and continental climates in the northern regions (Valdizarbe and Tierra Estella), where the mountains hinders the sea influence.

**~ Rioja Alta.** As its name suggests, it is the highest area within La Rioja. And again, it enjoys a similar climatic pattern to that of the western part of northern Navarre.

Well-balanced wines, between 12% and 13% alcohol from good-ripened grapes –achieved with not a lot of sunshine–, just elegant without further character.

# CONTINENTAL–ATLANTIC CLIMATE

Mainly characterised by a huge contrast between day and night temperatures. The sunlight during the day provides good ripening, slowed down by cool night temperatures that ultimately help to preserve good acidity levels. The Atlantic influence comes from the rains that arrive from the ocean during spring and autumn.

## WINE PRODUCING REGIONS

~ **Castilla–León**. Includes the DO Ribera del Duero, located in the Duero river valley and partly influenced by altitude; Rueda –to the southwest, at a lower altitude, enjoying a milder climate–, Toro and Cigales.

Wines with good colour and alcohol content and with a great acid structure.

# ATLANTIC-MEDITERRANEAN CLIMATE

This might seem a strange combination, but the area is very close to both seas and is therefore influenced by both climates, perhaps a little more Mediterranean and just moderated by the Atlantic.

## WINE PRODUCING REGIONS:

~ **Jerez**. When the cool western wind blows, the climate is sufficiently Atlantic to form heavy condensation at night. But in summer, when the drier easterly wind blows, the climate becomes clearly Mediterranean.

~ **Huelva**. The Atlantic influence is not as obvious since, in spite of its western location, the southern exposure give it a more Mediterranean influence.

Wines with moderate alcohol and acidity, although in the case of generoso (fortified) wines, particularly common in this area, this is irrelevant as there is alcohol addition.

# CONTINENTAL–MEDITERRANEAN CLIMATE

The rainfall is similar to a Continental–Atlantic climatic pattern; the vineyards are located at a lower altitude and therefore are closer to the sea, in spite of its situation on a plateau.

## WINE PRODUCING REGIONS

Castilla-La Mancha, Montilla-Moriles and Ribera del Guadiana; Campo de Borja, Cariñena and Calatayud in Aragón; Costers del Segre, southern part of Navarra, Rioja Baja and Rioja Alavesa.

Wines with higher alcohol content and lower acidity.

# MEDITERRANEAN CLIMATE

It is characterised by low rainfall and altitude.

WINE PRODUCING REGIONS:

Valencia, Clariano, Alto Turia, Alicante, Murcia with two of its three winegrowing regions (Yecla and Jumilla); practically all the wine regions in Catalonia but especially the coastal one. The vines are capable of enduring longer ageing periods, a circumstance that yields wines with higher alcohol levels, even though these are vines with a long vegetative cycle more suited to warmer climates.

Full-bodied wines, slightly warm nose, notes of dry earth and very ripe, jammy black fruit.

# VITICULTURAL MICROCLIMATES

These are climates that occur in very small areas, such as a single town, vineyard or even just a vine. In this section we will concentrate on those microclimates that affect small plots and are more common in Spanish vineyards.

## MOUNTAIN MICROCLIMATES

It affects vineyards surrounded by forest, located on uneven slopes and which have different expositions (north, south, east, or west). The grapes ripen unevenly as the sun does not shine homogenously on the vineyard. There are even microclimates within the microclimate. However, the common factor is that they are 'enclosed' areas.

**Where to find them?** In San Martin de Valdeiglesias (Madrid), La Axarquía (Málaga), Alto Turia (Valencia), Sierra de Francia (Salamanca), Cebreros (Ávila) or the extraordinarily qualitative Catalonian Priorat.

## VALLEY MICROCLIMATES

These are usually found north of the 40° latitude line. Normally, we have a river running through a valley acting as a hinge between the two slopes, which are partially or completely protected by mountains. The vines grown on the slopes will have shorter growing cycles than those on the plain, but they will also have different alcohol levels depending on the exposition and the incline.

**Two sides of the valley.** The southern bank of a river means more sunlight, as the sun rays fall almost perpendicularly, while on the northern slope the rays are oblique which means a longer ripening period and consequently more acidic wines and greater ageing potential. This is what happens in Ribera del Duero with vineyards like Vega Sicilia and Viña Mayor, located on the north-facing slopes and able to produce grapes with same sugar levels as those on the opposite side (Pesquera, Dehesa de los Canónigos, Hacienda Monasterio).

When the orientation of the valley is north–south and the slopes go east to west, ripening is also different. An east or southwest orientation in a northern latitude such as Côte de Nuits in Burgundy means they can take advantage of the sun from daybreak. But the same situation in Spain does not have any special advantages. The worst orientation is west, as high temperatures during the day are capped with an excess of sunlight in the afternoon, the hottest time of the day.

**The altitude factor.** Ripening improves with an increase in altitude, as vines get away from the humidity and cooler climate of the lower areas. Only when we go 100 metres above the valley do cold night temperatures make ripening difficult. Equally, the vineyard on a plain will be more productive and therefore grapes would be of inferior quality.

**Where to find them?** In extreme growing-conditions areas such as Ribera del Duero, Lerma river valley (a more exposed area with a harsher climate which produces lighter wines), Rioja Alavesa (when we add the foehn effect, rainfall gets lower on the opposite side of the mountain range there and the wines have deeper colour and a higher alcohol content) and Rioja Alta (vineyards with less sunlight and higher rainfall levels, which slow down ripening patterns giving wines with less colour and more acidity).

## FLUVIAL MICROCLIMATE

It is given in areas close to a river, which benefit from valley climate. However, there is an element of risk in being at such low altitude and near a mass of water, for ground temperature is lower than in areas higher up, more evaporation takes place generating mists and a greater risk of frost and vine diseases. The only positive side of it happens in stony, alluvial areas, when heat accumulated in the stones helps ripening.

**Where to find it?** Some Rueda vineyards near the Duero as well as the vineyards of Vega Sicilia and Abadia Retuerta, also located along that river.

## MARITIME MICROCLIMATE

Determined by the positive influence that the sea has on very hot, sunny areas to slow down the growing cycle. It is very common in southern areas where they grow varieties that require a lot of sunshine and benefit from the alternating temperatures regime provided by the sea breezes.

**Its influence on ageing.** The influence of the sea also brings about a slower and less oxidative wood-ageing period, as it happens in El Puerto de Santa María

and Sanlúcar de Barrameda. It used to be compulsory for the wines from Málaga (at its very port) and Oporto (in Vila Nova de Gaia, near the coast).

**Where to find it?** In the area of La Marina in Alicante and La Axarquía in Málaga, where the moscatel grape needs a certain amount of humidity but also lots of sunshine. In Jerez, the best vineyards are found on the highest hills open to westerly sea breezes. In the north of Tenerife, the trade winds from the northeast moderate the alcohol content of the grape and keep acidity levels high.

# THE INFLUENCE OF THE CLIMATE ON THE COLOUR OF WINES

The climate can have a definitive influence on the colour of wines as proved by the following examples.

**Pedro Ximénez wines.** The grapes are dehydrated after the harvest. They are placed on esparto grass mats and sunned until they turn to raisins and take on a brownish, ochre colour. The resulting wine is dark. This is due to a process similar to caramelization, as the sun burns the grapes and concentrates the sugar by reducing the volume of water. Also, oxidation takes place during ageing under the solera system, darkening the wine even further. Depending on the length of the ageing period the colour will be lighter or darker

**Sunning in glass bonbonnes.** This is only done in Rueda and Catalonia. As a way to accelerate ageing, the wine is put in glass containers and left in the open; day-night temperature differences provide a similar effect to that of more common summer-winter annual ageing. The sun causes the white whine to turn a yellow-reddish colour after just a few months.

**The colour of red wines.** It is clear that the pigmentation of grapes is produced by the sun. But a very dark grape is not necessarily ready to be made into wine. Although very unlikely in sunny climates, its sugar level may not be sufficient. However, it is also quite common for the colour and the sugars to be right and the skin still unripe. This often happens in warm regions where, as well as testing sugar and acid levels with a refractometer, the skins and pips are checked for ripeness since, occasionally, sugars form and pigmentation takes place before the skin has fully ripened. Therefore, paradoxically, there are reds from very sunny regions with herbaceous notes although the colour is deep and the alcohol content is above 12.5%.

* A cabernet sauvignon wine from Lérida is exposed to more sunlight than a cabernet sauvignon from Bordeaux. The wines from the French region have a lively violet rim, while the ones from Lérida tend to have light ochre tones, although they still keep a good balance thanks to modern winemaking methods.

* Monastrell wines from Catalonia, Provence, Jumilla or Alicante also differ. In the latter two areas, sunlight hours and the high alcohol content gives them a bluish-coppery hue, while those to the north show a redder, more lively colour.

# THE INFLUENCE OF THE CLIMATE ON THE AROMA OF WINES

In cold and humid regions (such as txakoli in the Basque Country, Galicia, and the north of Portugal), high rainfall makes it difficult for the grape to fully ripen, and therefore wines are low in alcohol and high in acidity. Given their high malic acid content, white wines from those areas show a slight note of cider or apple, even when malolactic fermentation is induced to help reduce acidity.

However, the same variety can show a whole new character under different climates. The Mediterranean varieties, which are the most common in Spain, tend to lose a lot of their aromatic expression in higher, more humid regions.

This is what happens to garnacha grown in Rioja Alta, as opposed to that of Rioja Baja. The wine of the former will have less colour intensity, but it will be more elegant and suitable for ageing thanks to a greater acidity that, on the other hand, may mask its aromatic expression.

A similar thing happens to parellada, a fine, classy white grape which needs the cool temperatures of the higher regions of Penedès, in Catalonia, to show at its best, while it loses some of its finesse in warmer climates.

As to the tempranillo, while it will typically, with a slow and balanced ripening cycle, display red mulberry notes, it will show a blackberry jam, slightly "cooked" character with a faster and deeper maturation, brought usually about by higher temperatures.

# CUALIFICATION OF 2008 VINTAGE BY DO ACCORDING TO PEÑÍN GUIDE

| Denominación de Origen | Rating | Denominación de Origen | Rating |
|---|---|---|---|
| ABONA | VERY GOOD | MONDÉJAR | AVERAGE |
| ALELLA | VERY GOOD | MONTERREI | EXCELLENT |
| ALICANTE | EXCELLENT | MONTILLA-MORILES | VERY GOOD |
| ALMANSA | VERY GOOD | MONTSANT | EXCELLENT |
| ARABAKO TXAKOLINA | VERY GOOD | NAVARRA | GOOD |
| ARLANZA | GOOD | PENEDÈS | VERY GOOD |
| ARRIBES | VERY GOOD | PLA DE BAGES | VERY GOOD |
| BIERZO | AVERAGE | PLA I LLEVANT | VERY GOOD |
| BINISSALEM MALLORCA | GOOD | PRIORAT | VERY GOOD |
| BIZKAIKO TXAKOLINA | VERY GOOD | RÍAS BAIXAS | EXCELLENT |
| BULLAS | VERY GOOD | RIBEIRA SACRA | VERY GOOD |
| CALATAYUD | VERY GOOD | RIBEIRO | VERY GOOD |
| CAMPO DE BORJA | VERY GOOD | RIBERA DEL DUERO | VERY GOOD |
| CARIÑENA | GOOD | RIBERA DEL GUADIANA | VERY GOOD |
| CATALUNYA | GOOD | RIBERA DEL JÚCAR | VERY GOOD |
| CAVA | VERY GOOD | RIOJA | VERY GOOD |
| CIGALES | GOOD | RUEDA | EXCELLENT |
| CONCA DE BARBERÀ | VERY GOOD | SOMONTANO | VERY GOOD |
| CONDADO DE HUELVA | VERY GOOD | TACORONTE-ACENTEJO | GOOD |
| COSTERS DEL SEGRE | VERY GOOD | TARRAGONA | VERY GOOD |
| EL HIERRO | GOOD | TERRA ALTA | GOOD |
| EMPORDÀ-COSTA BRAVA | GOOD | TIERRA DE LEÓN | GOOD |
| GETARIAKO TXAKOLINA | VERY GOOD | TIERRA DEL VINO DE ZAMORA | VERY GOOD |
| GRAN CANARIA | AVERAGE | TORO | EXCELLENT |
| JEREZ-XÉRÈS-SHERRY MANZANILLA DE SANLÚCAR DE BARRAMEDA | EXCELLENT | UCLÉS | AVERAGE |
| JUMILLA | GOOD | UTIEL-REQUENA | GOOD |
| LA GOMERA | N/A | VALDEORRAS | VERY GOOD |
| LA MANCHA | VERY GOOD | VALDEPEÑAS | EXCELLENT |
| LA PALMA | VERY GOOD | VALENCIA | VERY GOOD |
| LANZAROTE | GOOD | VALLE DE GÜIMAR | VERY GOOD |
| MÁLAGA-SIERRAS DE MÁLAGA | VERY GOOD | VALLE DE LA OROTAVA | GOOD |
| MANCHUELA | VERY GOOD | VINOS DE MADRID | VERY GOOD |
| MÉNTRIDA | VERY GOOD | YCODEN-DAUTE-ISORA | GOOD |
|  |  | YECLA | GOOD |

# WINERIES AND THE TASTING OF THE WINES BY DESIGNATION OF ORIGIN

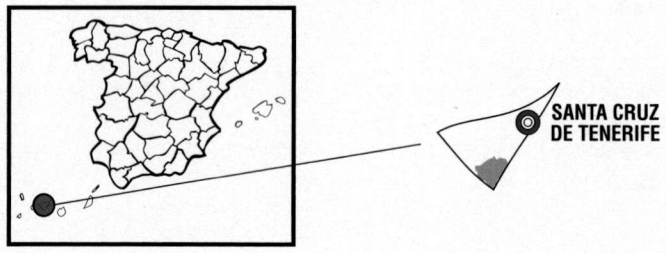

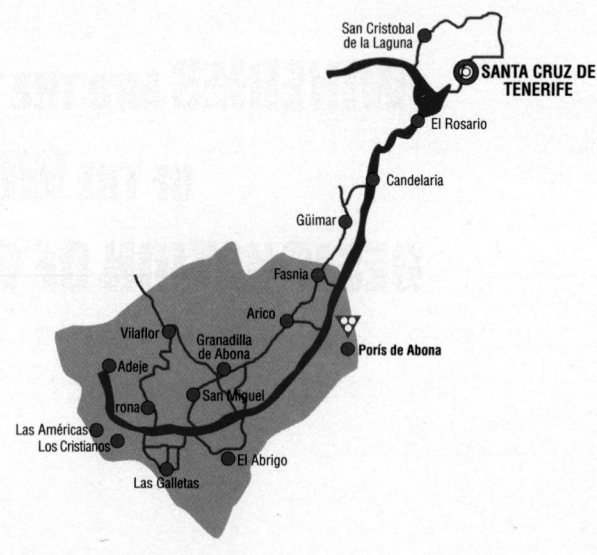

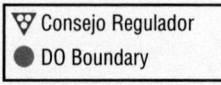

▽ Consejo Regulador
● DO Boundary

## NEWS

In Abona, the region with the highest vineyard altitude in Spain, wineries are trying to exploit that advantage through more suitable vineyard practices. A good example of that will is the huge amount of wines of very different profiles the wineries are now producing. The coop Cumbres de Abona makes up to 13 different wines, some of them from grapes grown at 1750 metres of altitude, a height at which Frontos, another local winery, seem to be rejoicing too. The local producers should go on researching in order to recuperate the local grape varieties (gual, marmajuelo, verdello or vijariego) with the added difficulty to adapt them to the pergola training system, the most common in the region, keeping enough canopy to avoid an excess of sunlight. Another difficulty for the islanders of Tenerife is the diversity of ecotypes present in the north and the south side of the island, which do not provide the opportunity of a homogenous vintage. Abona is still white wine territory, although there is a new wave of very expressive and original reds made from baboso negro reaching good ratings like Tierra de Frontos Clásico, Flor de Chasna or Magmático, the latter adding listán negra, tempranillo and syrah to the blend. Listán blanca is the main grape to make whites, although those from malvasía like Tierras de Aponte and Testamento are still the top wines in terms of balance and complexity.

## LOCATION

In the southern area of the island of Tenerife, with vineyards which occupy the slopes of the Teide down to the coast. It covers the municipal districts of Adeje, Arona, Vilaflor, San Miguel de Abona, Granadilla de Abona, Arico and Fasnia.

## CLIMATE

Mediterranean on the coastal belt, and gradually cools down inland as a result of the trade winds. Rainfall varies between 350 mm per year on the coast and 550 mm inland. In the highest region, Vilaflor, the vineyards do not benefit from these winds as they face slightly west. Nevertheless, the more than 200 Ha of this small plateau produce wines with an acidity of 8 g/l due to the altitude, but with an alcohol content of 13%, as this area of the island has the longest hours of sunshine.

## SOIL.

Distinction can be made between the sandy and calcareous soil inland and the more clayey, well drained soil of the higher regions, seeing as they are volcanic. The so-called 'Jable' soil is very typical, and is simply a very fine whitish volcanic sand, used by the local winegrower to cover the vineyards in order to retain humidity in the ground and to prevent weeds from growing. The vineyards are located at altitudes which range between 300 and 1,750 m (the better quality grapes are grown in the higher regions), which determines different grape harvesting dates in a period spanning the beginning of August up to October.

## GRAPE VARIETIES:

**White:** *Bastardo Blanco, Bermejuela, Forastera Blanca, Güal, Listán Blanca* (majority with 1,869 Ha), *Malvasía, Moscatel, Pedro Ximénez, Sabro, Torrontés, Verdello, Vijariego.* The white varieties make up the majority of the vineyards.

**Red:** *Bastardo Negro, Cabernet Sauvignon, Castellana Negra, Listán Negro, Listán Prieto, Malvasía Rosada, Moscatel Negro, Negramoll, Pinot Noir, Rubí Cabernet, Syrah, Tempranillo, Tintilla, Vijariego Negro.*

| | |
|---|---|
| Hectares of Vineyard | 1,150 |
| Nº Viticulturists | 1,229 |
| Nº of Bodegas | 19 |
| 2008 Harvest | Very Good |
| 2008 Production | 605,996 l. |
| Marketing | 100% domestic |

# DO ABONA

**CONSEJO REGULADOR.**
Martín Rodríguez, 9
38588 Porís de Abona - Arico (Tenerife)
☎: 922 164 241 - Fax: 922 164 135.
@ crdoabona@terra.es

## GENERAL CHARACTERISTICS OF THE WINES:

| | |
|---|---|
| **WHITES** | They have a pale yellow colour with a fruity and sometimes floral nose and are dry, pleasant and well-balanced on the palate. |
| **ROSÉS** | They are characterised by their pink colour and are light and pleasant to drink, although less fragrant than those from Tacoronte. |
| **REDS** | Although less representative than the white wines, they have a deep cherry-red, with a red berries and bramble nose and a somewhat light structure. |

## 2008 VINTAGE RATING:

# VERY GOOD

## BODEGA FRONTOS

Lomo Grande, 1 Los Blanquitos
38600 Granadilla de Abona (Santa Cruz de Tenerife)
☎: 922 777 253 - Fax: 922 777 246
bodega@tierradefrontos.com
www.tierradefrontos.com

TIERRA DE FRONTOS BLANCO CLÁSICO 2008 B
gual, verdell, marmajuelo, albillo

**86** Colour: pale. Nose: ripe fruit, white flowers, citrus fruit.
Palate: flavourful, fruity, fresh.

TIERRA DE FRONTOS ECOLÓGICO 2008 B
listán blanco 100%

**86** Colour: pale. Nose: powerful, ripe fruit, fresh fruit, floral.
Palate: flavourful, fruity, fresh.

TIERRA DE FRONTOS SEMISECO ECOLÓGICO 2008 B
listán blanco 100%

**83**

TIERRA DE FRONTOS MALVASÍA DULCE 2008 B
malvasia 100%

**80**

TIERRA DE FRONTOS BLANCO SELECCIÓN 2007 B
verdello 50%, malvasia 50%

**85** Colour: bright straw. Nose: powerful, dry nuts, honeyed
notes, spicy. Palate: flavourful, powerful, fleshy, warm.

TIERRA DE FRONTOS 2008 RD
tintilla 100%

**74**

TIERRA DE FRONTOS TINTO CLÁSICO 2008 T
baboso negro 100%

**90** Colour: cherry, garnet rim. Nose: powerful, ripe fruit,
raspberry, warm, balsamic herbs. Palate: flavourful, powerful,
spicy, ripe fruit.

## BODEGA MENCEY CHASNA

Marta, 3 Chimiche
38594 Granadilla de Abona (Tenerife)
☎: 922 777 285 - Fax: 922 777 259
ventas@menceychasna.com

LOS TABLEROS 2008 B BARRICA
listán blanco

**88** Colour: straw. Nose: expressive, complex, ripe fruit,
sweet spices, citrus fruit, floral. Palate: flavourful, fruity, fresh,
creamy.

MENCEY DE CHASNA 2008 B
listán blanco 100%

**85** Colour: pale. Nose: fresh fruit, ripe fruit, floral. Palate:
fruity, fresh, light-bodied.

LOS TABLEROS 2007 T BARRICA
listán negro, syrah, tempranillo, ruby cabernet

**87** Colour: cherry, garnet rim. Nose: powerful, varietal, ripe
fruit, sweet spices, toasty. Palate: flavourful, powerful, fleshy.

MENCEY DE CHASNA 2007 T
listán negro 60%, tempranillo 40%, syrah %, ruby cabernet %

**67**

## COOPERATIVA CUMBRES DE ABONA

Camino del Viso, s/n
38589 Arico (Santa Cruz de Tenerife)
☎: 922 768 604 - Fax: 922 768 234
cumbresabona@wanadoo.es
www.cumbresabona.com

TESTAMENTO MALVASÍA DRY 2008 B

**87** Colour: pale. Nose: powerful, varietal, ripe fruit, citrus
fruit, floral. Palate: flavourful, fruity, fresh, fleshy.

TESTAMENTO MALVASÍA 2008 B BARRICA

**87** Colour: bright straw. Nose: fresh fruit, fruit expression,
varietal, grassy, citrus fruit. Palate: flavourful, fruity, fresh, fleshy.

FLOR DE CHASNA SEMISECO 2008 B

**85** Colour: pale. Nose: grassy, expressive, ripe fruit, fresh
fruit. Palate: flavourful, fruity, fresh, sweetness.

FLOR DE CHASNA AFRUTADO 2008 B

**84**

CUMBRES DE ABONA 2008 B

**82**

FLOR DE CHASNA 2008 B

**81**

CUMBRES DE ABONA 2008 RD

**74**

# DO ABONA

FLOR DE CHASNA 2008 T BARRICA

**89** Colour: bright cherry. Nose: ripe fruit, sweet spices, creamy oak, expressive. Palate: flavourful, fruity, toasty, round tannins.

MAGMATICO 2008 T
listán negro, tempranillo, syrah

**88** Colour: cherry, purple rim. Nose: expressive, fresh fruit, red berry notes, floral. Palate: flavourful, fruity, good acidity, round tannins.

FLOR DE CHASNA 2008 T

**86** Colour: cherry, purple rim. Nose: expressive, fresh fruit, red berry notes, floral. Palate: flavourful, fruity, good acidity, round tannins.

CUMBRES DE ABONA 2008 T

**83**

FLOR DE CHASNA 2007 T

**89** Colour: cherry, garnet rim. Nose: medium intensity, candied fruit, fruit liqueur notes, dark chocolate. Palate: flavourful, fleshy, sweet, spicy.

TESTAMENTO MALVASÍA DULCE 2008 B DULCE

**82**

TESTAMENTO MALVASÍA ESENCIA 2006 B DULCE

**88** Colour: bright golden. Nose: powerful, candied fruit, fruit liqueur notes, sweet spices, pattiserie. Palate: flavourful, powerful, fleshy, sweet.

ALMAVERDE
ALMAZUL
VIÑA PERAZA
ALMAORO

## PEDRO HERNÁNDEZ TEJERA

Ctra. Archifira, s/n
38570 Fasnia (Tenerife)
☎: 616 920 832

VIÑA ARESE AFRUTADO 2008 B

**86** Colour: pale. Nose: fresh fruit, white flowers, earthy notes. Palate: flavourful, fruity, fresh.

VIÑA ARESE 2008 T

**82**

VIÑA ARESE 2007 T BARRICA

**80**

## S.A.T. REVERÓN E HIJOS

Los Quemados, s/n
38620 Vilaflor (Tenerife)
☎: 607 867 206

PAGOS REVERÓN 2008 B

**82**

PAGO REVERÓN 2008 T

**83**

PAGOS REVERÓN 2007 T BARRICA

**85** Colour: cherry, garnet rim. Nose: powerful, ripe fruit, sweet spices, toasty. Palate: flavourful, powerful, fine bitter notes, round tannins.

## SOCIEDAD COOP. SAN MIGUEL

Carretera General del Sur, 5
38620 San Miguel de Abona (Tenerife)
☎: 922 700 300 - Fax: 922 700 301
bodega@casanmiguel.com
www.casmi.net

VIÑA TAMAIDE 2008 B

**87** Colour: pale. Nose: powerful, fresh fruit, ripe fruit, floral. Palate: flavourful, fruity, fresh.

CHASNERO 2008 B

**83**

VIÑA TAMAIDE AFRUTADO 2008 B

**78**

MARQUES DE FUENTE B

**88** Colour: bright straw. Nose: expressive, complex, pattiserie, sweet spices, ripe fruit. Palate: flavourful, fleshy, complex, spicy.

VIÑA TAMAIDE 2008 T

**84**

CHASNERO 2008 T

**82**

MARQUES DE FUENTE 2007 T

**80**

## TIERRAS DE APONTE

La Capellanía, 34 Taucho
38677 Adeje (Santa Cruz de Tenerife)
☎: 609 248 017 - Fax: 637 322 019
comercial@tierrasdeaponte.com
www.tierrasdeaponte.com

TIERRAS DE APONTE MALVASÍA DULCE 2006 B
malvasia 100%

**89** Colour: bright golden. Nose: spicy, dark chocolate, candied fruit, honeyed n otes. Palate: fleshy, complex, sweet, good acidity, long.

TIERRAS DE APONTE TRADICIONAL 2008 T

**83**

TIERRAS DE APONTE VENDIMIA SELECCIONADA 2008 T
Vigiriego 60%, rubí cabernet 40%

**83**

SOME OTHER WINERIES WITHIN THE DO:

**BODEGAS DE VILAFLOR**
**HIMACOPASA**
**JOSÉ JEREMIAS AMARAL DELGADO**
**LA ORTIGOSA S.L.**
**MARISOL DÍAZ QUINTERO**
**RAFAEL YUSEF DELGADO**
**SOCIEDAD COOPERATIVA LAS ERAS DE ARICO**
**TOMÁS FRÍAS GONZÁLEZ**
**VIÑA VIEJA S.A.T.**
**VIÑAFLOR TENERIFE S.L.**

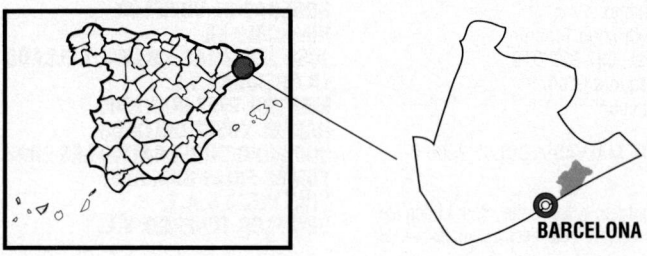

BARCELONA

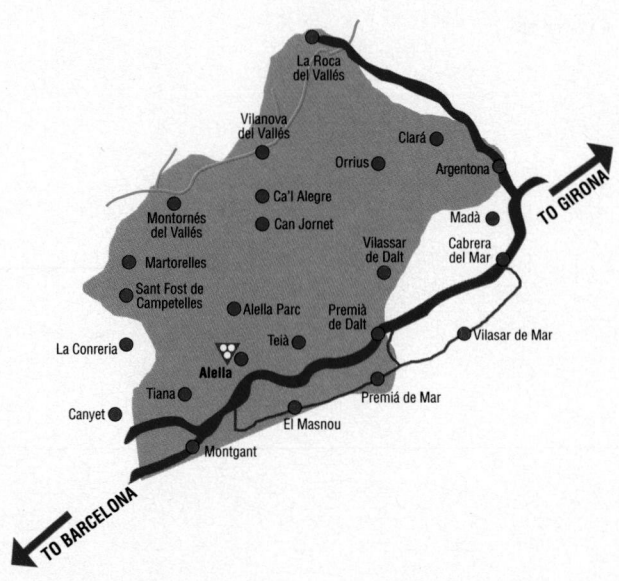

La Roca
del Vallés

Vilanova
del Vallés

Clará

Orrius

Argentona

TO GIRONA

Ca'l Alegre

Montornés
del Vallés

Can Jornet

Madà

Vilassar
de Dalt

Cabrera
del Mar

Martorelles

Sant Fost de
Campetelles

Alella Parc

Premià
de Dalt

Vilasar de Mar

La Conreria

Teià

Alella

Tiana

Premià de Mar

Canyet

El Masnou

Montgant

TO BARCELONA

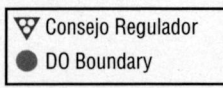
Consejo Regulador

● DO Boundary

## NEWS

This small region close to the city of Barcelona has been, in terms of quality, a matter of two wineries, Alta Alella and Alella Vinícola.  But this year a house from Rioja, Castillo de Sajazarra, has joined the ranks of the DO with In Vita, a white wine made from sauvignon blanc and the local pansa blanca planted between the sea and the Montseny. The best wines from the region are certainly white and rosé renderings (Roura, Alta Alella Parvus), although more and more single-variety reds from syrah or garnacha can be found nowadays. In the mostly dry vintage of 2008 –with just some heavy rains in September that delayed the harvest– wines appear lighter in colour but altogether balanced, with a rich fruit expression and good acidity. The pansa blanca (local name for xarel.lo) is harmoniously blended with sauvignon blanc or garnacha blanca, and the elegant and warm viogner shows exceedingly well in the new bottling by one of the pioneer hoses in the region, Marqués de Alella.

## LOCATION

It extends over the regions of El Maresme and el Vallès in Barcelona. It covers the municipal districts of Alella, Argentona, Cabrils, El Masnou, La Roca del Vallès, Martorelles, Montornès del Vallès, Montgat, Orrius, Premià de Dalt, Premià de Mar, Santa Mª de Martorelles, Sant Fost de Campsentelles, Teià, Tiana, Vallromanes, Vilanova del Vallès and Vilasar de Salt. The main feature of this region is the urban environment which surrounds this small stretch of vineyards; in fact, one of the smallest DO's in Spain.

## CLIMATE

A typically Mediterranean microclimate with mild winters and hot dry summers. The coastal hills play an important role, as they protect the vines from cold winds and condense the humidity from the sea.

## SOIL

Distinction can be made between the clayey soils of the interior slope of the coastal mountain range and the soil situated along the coastline. The latter, known as Sauló, is the most typical. Almost white in colour, it is renowned for it high permeability and great capacity to retain sunlight, which makes for a better ripening of the grapes.

## GRAPE VARIETIES:

**White:** *Pansa Blanca* (similar to the *Xarel·lo* from other regions in Catalonia), *Garnatxa Blanca, Pansa Rosada, Picapoll, Malvasía, Macabeo, Parellada, Chardonnay, Sauvignon Blanc* and *Chenin Blanc*.
**Red (minority):** *Garnatxa Negra, Ull de Llebre* (*Tempranillo*), *Merlot, Pinot Noir, Syrah* and *Cabernet Sauvignon*.

| Hectares of Vineyard | 314,7 |
|---|---|
| Nº Viticulturists | 92 |
| Nº of Bodegas | 7 |
| 2008 Harvest | Very Good |
| 2007 Production | 635,768 l. |
| Marketing | 96.3% domestic 3.7% export |

# DO ALELLA

## CONSEJO REGULADOR
Masía Can Magarola, s/n. 08328 Alella (Barcelona).
☎: 935 559 153 - Fax: 935 405 249
@ doalella@doalella.org
www.doalella.org

## GENERAL CHARACTERISTICS OF THE WINES:

| | |
|---|---|
| **WHITES** | These are the most characteristic of the region. One can distinguish between the traditional Alella, light, fruity and quite supple (although not sweet), and the other dry wines with a pale straw colour which are fresh, fruity, well-balanced, slightly supple with a persistent nose. There are also examples of white wines fermented in barrels. |
| **ROSÉS** | These are not the most abundant, although very good rosé wines are produced which are very flavourful on the palate. |
| **REDS** | The most interesting examples in the region are those that include foreign varieties in the blend, especially *Merlot* and *Cabernet Sauvignon*, which stand out for their unique fruity character. |

## 2008 VINTAGE RATING:

# VERY GOOD

## ALELLA VINÍCOLA

Angel Guimerà, 62
08328 Alella (Barcelona)
☎: 935 403 842 - Fax: 935 401 648
comercial@alellavinicola.com
www.alellavinicola.com

IVORI 2008 B
pansa blanca 60%, chardonnay 20%, sauvignon blanc 10%, moscatel 10%

**88** Colour: coppery red. Nose: grapey, honeyed notes, dry nuts. Palate: full, flavourful, good acidity, good structure, fine bitter notes.

MARFIL CLÀSSIC 2008 B
pansa blanca 100%

**82**

MARFIL BLANCO SECO 2008 B
pansa blanca 100%

**82**

MARFIL MUY DULCE 2003 B
pansa blanca 100%

**92** Colour: light mahogany. Nose: dry nuts, dried fruit, honeyed notes, expressive. Palate: full, rich, powerful, sweet, great length.

MARFIL GENEROSO SEMI 1976 B
pansa blanca 100%

**90** Colour: amber. Nose: smoky, dry nuts, honeyed notes, fruit preserve. Palate: rich, powerful, good acidity, great length.

MARFIL 2006 TC
garnacha 40%, cabernet sauvignon 40%, syrah 15%, merlot 5%

**85** Colour: deep cherry, brick rim edge. Nose: fruit preserve, sweet spices, balanced. Palate: warm, flavourful, good acidity, round tannins.

MARFIL VIOLETA 2003 T
garnacha 100%

**90** Colour: dark-red cherry, brick rim edge. Nose: dried fruit, dry nuts, expressive, sweet spices. Palate: full, good acidity, flavourful, slightly dry, soft tannins.

MARFIL GENEROSO SEC 1976 BLANCO DULCE
pansa blanca 100%

**88** Colour: amber. Nose: honeyed notes, dried fruit, dry nuts, powerfull. Palate: light-bodied, fresh, fine bitter notes, great length.

VALLMORA

## ALTA ALELLA

Can Genis, s/n
08391 Tiana (Barcelona)
☎: 934 693 720 - Fax: 934 691 343
altaalella@altaalella.cat
www.altaalella.cat

DADES ALTA ALELLA BLANC DOLÇ 2008 B
chardonnay, viognier, pansa blanca

**90** Colour: pale. Nose: candied fruit, ripe fruit, citrus fruit, honeyed notes. Palate: flavourful, fruity, fleshy, fresh.

ALTA ALELLA LANIUS 2008 B
chardonnay, viognier, pansa blanca, sauvignon blanc

**89** Colour: pale. Nose: complex, lees reduction notes, characterful, dried flowers. Palate: full, fruity, fresh.

EXEO 2008 B
chardonnay, viognier

**85** Aroma ripe fruit, tropical fruit, warm. Palate: rich, fresh, fruity, flavourful.

ALTA ALELLA PARVUS CHARDONNAY 2008 B
chardonnay

**84**

ALTA ALELLA PARVUS 2008 RD
cabernet sauvignon

**87** Colour: light cherry. Nose: fresh fruit, violet drops, expressive, red berry notes. Palate: flavourful, rich, good finish, fruity.

ALTA ALELLA ORBUS 2007 TC
syrah

**90** Colour: cherry, purple rim. Nose: floral, expressive, mineral, fruit preserve. Palate: rich, fruity, fruity aftestaste, spicy, warm.

ALTA ALELLA PARVUS SYRAH 2007 T
syrah

**88** Colour: deep cherry, garnet rim. Nose: macerated fruit, balsamic herbs, elegant, floral. Palate: full, fruity, good acidity, grainy tannins, good structure.

ALTA ALELLA DOLÇ MATARÓ 2008 TINTO DULCE
mataro

**87** Colour: cherry, garnet rim. Nose: powerful, overripe fruit, candied fruit. Palate: flavourful, fleshy, sweet.

## BODEGAS CASTILLO DE SAJAZARRA

Del Río, s/n
26212 Sajazarra (La Rioja)
☎: 941 320 066 - Fax: 941 320 251
bodega@castillo-de-sajazarra.com
www.castillo-de-sajazarra.com

IN VITA 2008 B
pansa blanca, sauvignon blanc

**90** Colour: bright straw. Nose: fresh fruit, white flowers, citrus fruit, grassy. Palate: flavourful, fruity, fresh, sweetness.

## JUAN ANTONIO PÉREZ ROURA

Felipe II, 143
08027 (Barcelona)
☎: 933 527 456 - Fax: 933 524 339
roura@roura.es
www.roura.es

ROURA SAUVIGNON BLANC 2008 B
sauvignon blanc 100%

**83**

ROURA MERLOT ROSAT 2008 RD
merlot 100%

**85** Colour: rose, purple rim. Nose: fresh fruit, herbaceous, wild herbs, dry stone. Palate: light-bodied, fresh, fruity, mineral.

ROURA CRIANZA TRES CEPS 2006 TC
cabernet sauvignon 50%, merlot 30%, syrah 20%

**86** Colour: deep cherry, garnet rim. Nose: ripe fruit, toasty, spicy, new oak, balanced. Palate: light-bodied, fruity, easy to drink, round tannins.

## PARXET

Mas Parxet s/n
08391 Tiana (Barcelona)
☎: 933 950 811 - Fax: 933 955 500
info@parxet.es
www.parxet.es

MARQUÉS DE ALELLA PANSA BLANCA 2008 B
pansa blanca 100%

**88** Colour: bright straw. Nose: fresh fruit, grassy, floral, fine lees. Palate: flavourful, good acidity, fruity.

MARQUÉS DE ALELLA PANSA BLANCA XAREL.LO 2008 B

**87** Colour: bright straw. Nose: fresh fruit, floral, elegant, dry stone. Palate: flavourful, full, fruity, great length.

MARQUÉS DE ALELLA VIOGNIER 2008 B
viognier

**87** Colour: straw. Nose: fresh fruit, fragrant herbs, fruit expression. Palate: fleshy, fruity, good acidity.

MARQUÉS DE ALELLA ALLIER 2007 BFB
chardonnay 100%

**89** Colour: bright golden. Nose: fruit liqueur notes, spicy, characterful, fragrant herbs. Palate: rich, full, powerful, good structure, good acidity, spicy.

SOME OTHER WINERIES WITHIN THE DO:

**CELLER ALTRABANDA S.C.P.**
**CELLER J. MESTRE**

## NEWS

Alicante has everything to become a flagship for quality wines and wine tours. Its vineyards, associated to the Costa Blanca (White Coast) region, are a big sale in Alicante, the region's capital city. Also the most valued region in sensory terms within the autonomous region of Valencia, it has reached an even higher standard this year with a fresher, more expressive vintage compared to the previous one. A great vintage without the shadow of a doubt: low rainfall and grapes harvested with just optimal maturity and acidity levels. As a result, our tasting shows rosé wines of note, with great structure and fruity notes and a rich acidity, as well as white wines featuring moscatel with plenty of white fruit (apricot) and floral notes that afford complexity. Pretty much in line with this sort of excellence, red wines made from monastrell show up to the fresh standard expected from that variety, as shown in the previous vintage. All in all, red, rosé and white wines from Alicante, along with the sweet aged fondillón wines make up a broad and interesting all-year-round choice.

## LOCATION

In the province of Alicante (covering 51 municipal districts), and a small part of the province of Murcia. The vineyards extend over areas close to the coast (in the surroundings of the capital city of Alicante, and especially in the area of La Marina, a traditional producer of Moscatel), as well as in the interior of the province.

## CLIMATE

Distinction must be made between the vineyards situated closer to the coastline, where the climate is clearly Mediterranean and somewhat more humid, and those inland, which receive continental influences and have a lower level of rainfall.

## SOIL

In general, the majority of the soils in the region are of a dun limestone type, with little clay and hardly any organic matter.

## GRAPE VARIETIES:

**White:** *Merseguera, Moscatel de Alejandría, Macabeo, Planta Fina, Verdil, Airén, Chardonnay* and *Sauvignon Blanc.*
**Red:** *Monastrell, Garnacha* Tinta (*Alicante* or *Giró*), *Garnacha Tintorera, Bobal, Tempranillo, Cabernet Sauvignon, Merlot, Pinot Noir* and *Syrah.*

| | |
|---|---|
| Hectares of Vineyard | 9,456 |
| Nº Viticulturists | 2,454 |
| Nº of Bodegas | 51 |
| 2008 Harvest | Excellent |
| 2007 Production | 15,359,827 |
| Marketing | 75.5% domestic 24.5% export |

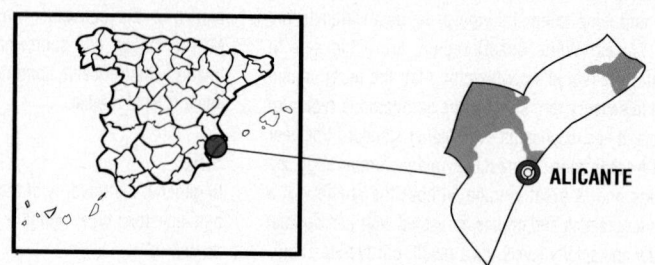

Banyeres
Alcoy
Ben
Beneixama
Beni
Campo
de Mirra
Carrascar de
la Font Roja
Villena
Biar
Onil
Ibi
Torreman
Vinalopó River
Castalla
Jijona
Sax
Tibi
Salinas
Elda
E
Monóvar
San Vicent
del Raspeig
Mub
El Pinós
Novelda
Monforte
del Cid
Aspa
ALICANTE
La Romana
Algueña
Torrellano
El Altet
Hondón de
los Frailes
Crevillent
Elche
TO MURCIA
Santa Pola

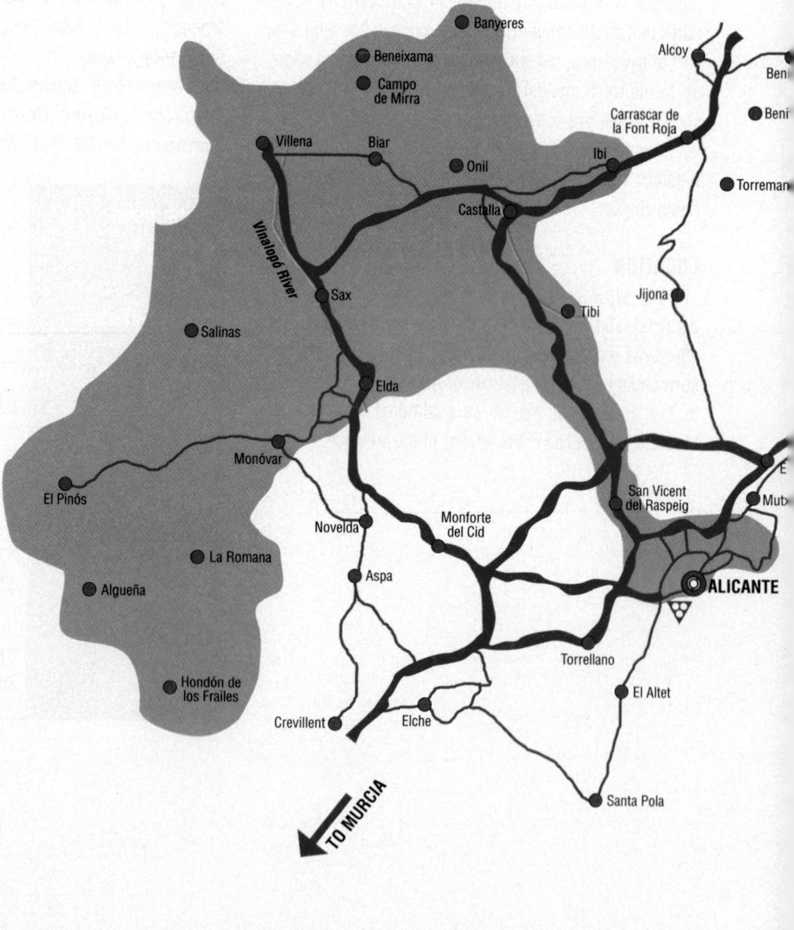

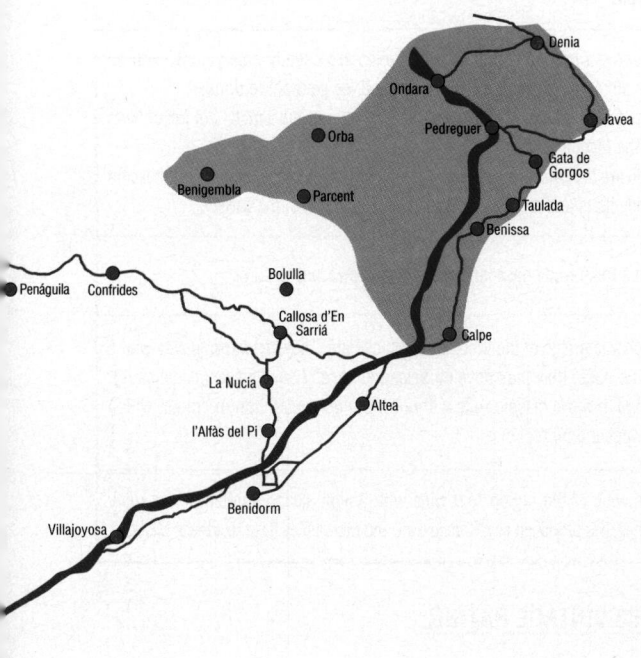

Denia
Ondara
Orba
Pedreguer
Javea
Gata de Gorgos
Benigembla
Parcent
Taulada
Benissa
Penáguila
Confrides
Bolulla
Callosa d'En Sarriá
Calpe
La Nucia
Altea
l'Alfàs del Pi
Villajoyosa
Benidorm
llo

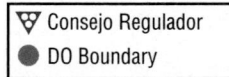

▽ Consejo Regulador
● DO Boundary

# DO ALICANTE

**CONSEJO REGULADOR.**
Orense, 3, Entlo. Dcha. 03003 Alicante.
☎: 965 984 478 - Fax: 965 229 295
@ crdo.alicante@crdo
www. alicante.org

## GENERAL CHARACTERISTICS OF THE WINES:

| | |
|---|---|
| **WHITES** | The young white wines produced from local varieties are usually pale yellow, with an honest, fruity nose, although maybe not too intense, and are pleasant to drink.<br>There are also some Chardonnays which reflect the character of the variety, but full of hints of ripe fruit due to the Mediterranean climate.<br>More significant still are the sweet Muscatels of the region of Marina, which are reminiscent of honey, with grapey hints and a musky character characteristic of the variety. |
| **ROSÉS** | These are pink with a fresh fruity nose: and are easy and pleasant to drink. |
| **REDS** | The red wines are characteristic of the Mediterranean climate. They are warm, meaty with a fine structure; on the nose: they may develop balsamic noses (fallen leaves, eucalyptus). There is also a range of more classic reds without too much extraction of colour, which unfortunately may appear a bit rusty. |
| **FONDILLÓN** | This is the historic wine of the region (old wine with a high alcohol content and a rusty character). Sometimes, it is produced as a Rancio wine and other times it is mixed with Mistelas. |

## 2008 VINTAGE RATING:

# EXCELLENT

## AGRO-CASTELLÓ

Rda. P. Leandro Calvo, 2
46700 Gandía (Valencia)
☎: 962 871 241 - Fax: 962 878 818
cesardeborja@yahoo.com

FINCA COLLADO 2007 BFB
chardonnay, moscatel

**83**

FINCA COLLADO 2005 T
merlot, cabernet sauvignon

**87** Colour: bright cherry. Nose: ripe fruit, sweet spices, varietal, toasty. Palate: flavourful, fruity, toasty, round tannins.

## AGROXALO

La Virgen, 43
03727 Jalón (Alicante)
☎: 606 945 691 - Fax: 965 730 658
info@agroxalo.com
www.agroxalo.com

CASTA MARINA 2008 B
moscatel

**87** Colour: bright straw. Nose: fresh, fresh fruit, white flowers, expressive. Palate: flavourful, fruity, good acidity, balanced.

PANSULA B

**87** Colour: bright straw. Nose: fresh, fresh fruit, white flowers, expressive. Palate: flavourful, fruity, good acidity, sweet.

TROS DEL PINAR 2007 T

**80**

MEDITERRANEO ESP

**78**

## BODEGA COOPERATIVA DE ALGUEÑA COOP. V.

Ctra. Rodriguillo, km. 29.500
03668 Algueña (Alicante)
☎: 965 476 113 - Fax: 965 476 229
bodcoopalguenya@terra.es

TORREVIÑAS 2008 B

**84**

TORREVIÑAS LÁGRIMA RD

**87** Colour: rose, purple rim. Nose: powerful, ripe fruit, red berry notes, floral, expressive. Palate: fleshy, powerful, fruity, fresh.

FONDONET 2008 T

**86** Colour: bright cherry. Nose: creamy oak, expressive, overripe fruit, fruit preserve, powerfull. Palate: flavourful, fruity, great length, sweet.

CASA JIMÉNEZ 2005 TC

**85** Colour: cherry, garnet rim. Nose: ripe fruit, spicy, creamy oak, toasty. Palate: powerful, flavourful, toasty, round tannins.

TORREVIÑAS DOBLE PASTA T
monastrell

**85** Colour: black cherry. Nose: expressive, fruit preserve, powerfull. Palate: flavourful, fruity, good acidity, round tannins.

FONDILLÓN 1980

**87** Colour: iodine, amber rim. Nose: powerful, complex, elegant, dry nuts, toasty. Palate: rich, fine bitter notes, fine solera notes, long, spicy.

## BODEGA COOPERATIVA SANT VICENTE FERRER

Avda. Las Palmas, 32
03725 Teulada (Alicante)
☎: 965 740 051 - Fax: 965 740 489
bodega@coop-santvicent.com
www.coop-santvicent.com

VIÑA TEULADA 2008 B JOVEN
moscatel 100%

**86** Colour: bright straw. Nose: fresh, fresh fruit, white flowers, expressive. Palate: flavourful, fruity, good acidity, balanced.

TEULADA
TEGULATA
PITÁGORA

## BODEGA FRANCISCO GÓMEZ

Pj. Finca La Serrata - Ctra. Villena Pinoso, km. 8,5
03400 Villena (Alicante)

☎: 965 979 195 - Fax: 965 979 196
santiago.gomez@grupoinvercon.net

FRUTO NOBLE SAUVIGNON BLANC 2007 B

**84**

BOCA NEGRA MONASTRELL 2006 TC
monastrell

**90** Colour: bright cherry. Nose: ripe fruit, sweet spices, creamy oak, expressive, balsamic herbs, undergrowth. Palate: flavourful, fruity, toasty, round tannins, fresh.

**MORATILLAS 2006 TC**

**88** Colour: cherry, garnet rim. Nose: ripe fruit, spicy, creamy oak, toasty, complex, caramel. Palate: powerful, flavourful, toasty, round tannins, fresh.

**SERRATA 2005 TC**

**89** Colour: cherry, garnet rim. Nose: ripe fruit, spicy, creamy oak, toasty, complex. Palate: powerful, flavourful, toasty, round tannins, easy to drink.

**FRUTO NOBLE 2005 T**

**87** Colour: bright cherry. Nose: sweet spices, creamy oak, expressive, ripe fruit, aged wood nuances. Palate: flavourful, fruity, toasty, round tannins, easy to drink.

## BODEGA J. BELDA

Avda. Conde Salvaterra, 54
46635 Fontanars dels Alforins (Valencia)
☎: 962 222 245 - Fax: 962 222 245
info@danielbelda.com
www.danielbelda.com

**MIGJORN 2006 T**

**86** Colour: black cherry. Nose: spicy, toasty, complex, overripe fruit, fruit liqueur notes. Palate: powerful, flavourful, toasty, round tannins.

## BODEGA JOAQUÍN GÁLVEZ

Avda. de la Paz, 24
03400 Villena (Alicante)
☎: 630 44 5 0
donpela1996@gmail.com

**LEVA DANIEL'S 2006 T**
tempranillo 40%, syrah 60%, merlot %

**90** Colour: dark-red cherry, purple rim. Nose: complex, floral, creamy oak. Palate: fleshy, fruity, fresh, round tannins, elegant.

## BODEGA NUESTRA SEÑORA DE LAS VIRTUDES COOP. V.

Ctra. de Yecla, 9
03400 Villena (Alicante)
☎: 965 802 187 - Fax: 965 813 387
coopvillena@coopvillena.com
www.coopvillena.com

**VINALOPÓ 2008 B**
macabeo, sauvignon blanc

**87** Colour: bright straw. Nose: fresh, fresh fruit, expressive, wild herbs. Palate: flavourful, fruity, good acidity, balanced.

**VINALOPÓ 2008 RD**
monastrell

**87** Colour: rose, purple rim. Nose: powerful, ripe fruit, red berry notes, floral, expressive. Palate: fleshy, powerful, fruity.

**VINALOPÓ 2008 T**
monastrell, merlot

**86** Colour: cherry, purple rim. Nose: expressive, fresh fruit, red berry notes, floral. Palate: flavourful, fruity, good acidity, round tannins.

**VINALOPÓ SELECCIÓN 2007 T**
monastrell, syrah

**84**

**VINALOPÓ PETIT VERDOT 2007 T**
petit verdot

**83**

**VINALOPÓ 2005 TC**
monastrell, cabernet sauvignon

**86** Colour: cherry, garnet rim. Nose: ripe fruit, spicy, creamy oak, toasty, complex. Palate: powerful, flavourful, toasty, round tannins.

**VINALOPÓ 2002 TR**
monastrell, cabernet sauvignon

**84**

**TESORO DE VILLENA RESERVA ESPECIAL FONDILLÓN 1972 SOLERA**
monastrell

**75**

## BODEGA SANTA CATALINA DEL MAÑAN

Ctra. Monóvar-Pinoso, km. 10,5
03649 Mañan Monóvar (Alicante)
☎: 966 960 096 - Fax: 966 960 096
bodegamanan@terra.es

**BLANCO CHARDONNAY MAÑA 2008 B**
chardonnay 100%

**85** Colour: bright straw. Nose: fresh, white flowers, expressive, spicy, sun-drenched nuances. Palate: flavourful, fruity, good acidity, balanced.

**ROSADO SYRAH MAÑA 2008 RD**
syrah 100%

**85** Colour: rose, purple rim. Nose: powerful, ripe fruit, floral, expressive, candied fruit. Palate: fleshy, powerful, fruity, fresh.

**TORRENT DEL MAÑA 2008 T**
monastrell 85%, merlot 15%

**84**

**TINTO MERLOT MAÑA 2007 T**
merlot 100%

**86** Colour: bright cherry. Nose: ripe fruit, sweet spices, creamy oak, expressive. Palate: flavourful, fruity, toasty, round tannins.

**MAÑA RUSTIC 2002 T**
cabernet sauvignon 100%

**87** Colour: cherry, garnet rim. Nose: ripe fruit, spicy, creamy oak, toasty, complex. Palate: powerful, flavourful, toasty, round tannins.

TERRA DEL MAÑA

## BODEGA XALO

Ctra. Xaló Alcali s/n
03727 Xaló (Alicante)
☎: 966 480 034 - Fax: 966 480 808
info@bodegasxalo.com
www.bodegasxalo.com

**BAHIA DE DÉNIA MOSCATEL DE LA MARINA ALTA 2008 B JOVEN**

**90** Colour: bright straw. Nose: fresh, white flowers, expressive, candied fruit, pattiserie. Palate: flavourful, fruity, good acidity, balanced.

VALL DE XALO B

**85** Colour: bright straw. Nose: fresh, white flowers, expressive. Palate: fruity, good acidity, balanced.

VALL DE XALO B JOVEN

**84**

VALL DE XALO RD JOVEN

**88** Colour: rose, purple rim. Nose: powerful, ripe fruit, red berry notes, floral, expressive. Palate: fleshy, powerful, fruity, fresh.

VALL DE XALO T JOVEN

**85** Colour: bright cherry. Nose: ripe fruit, sweet spices, expressive, fruit preserve. Palate: flavourful, fruity, toasty, round tannins, sweetness.

VALL DE XALO T JOVEN

**78**

CASTELL D'AINSA

## BODEGAS BERNABÉ NAVARRO

Ctra. Villena-Cañada, km. 3 Finca Casa Balaguer
03400 Villena (Alicante)
☎: 966 770 353 - Fax: 966 770 353
info@bodegasbernabenavarro.com
www.bodegasbernabenavarro.com

**BERYNA 2007 T**
monastrell 60%, otras 40%

**92** Colour: cherry, garnet rim. Nose: spicy, creamy oak, toasty, complex, fruit preserve, warm. Palate: powerful, flavourful, toasty, round tannins.

**CASA BALAGUER 2006 T**
monastrell 50%, otras 50%

**94** Colour: bright cherry. Nose: ripe fruit, sweet spices, creamy oak, expressive, mineral. Palate: flavourful, fruity, toasty, round tannins.

**BERYNA SELECCIÓN 2005 T**
monastrell 50%, tempranillo 40%, cabernet sauvignon 10%

**94** Colour: cherry, garnet rim. Nose: ripe fruit, spicy, creamy oak, toasty, complex, mineral. Palate: powerful, flavourful, toasty, round tannins, balanced, good acidity.

**DULCE CHRISTINA**

## BODEGAS BOCOPA

Paraje Les Pedreres, Autovía A-31, KM. 200 - 201
03610 Petrer (Alicante)
☎: 966 950 489 - Fax: 966 950 406
direccion@bocopa.com
www.bocopa.com

**MARINA ESPUMANTE 2008 B**
moscatel 100%

**84**

**SOL DE ALICANTE MOSCATEL B**
moscatel 100%

**88** Colour: golden. Nose: powerful, floral, honeyed notes, candied fruit, fragrant herbs. Palate: flavourful, sweet, fresh, fruity, good acidity, long.

**MARINA ALTA 2008 B**
moscatel 100%

**86** Colour: bright straw. Nose: fresh, fresh fruit, expressive, jasmine. Palate: flavourful, fruity, good acidity, balanced.

**TERRETA ROSÉ 2008 RD**
monastrell 100%

**88** Colour: rose, purple rim. Nose: powerful, ripe fruit, red berry notes, floral, expressive. Palate: fleshy, powerful, fruity, fresh.

**ALCANTA 2008 T**
monastrell 100%

**86** Colour: cherry, purple rim. Nose: expressive, fresh fruit, red berry notes, floral. Palate: flavourful, fruity, good acidity, round tannins.

**LAUDUM MONASTRELL ESPECIAL 2006 T**
monastrell 100%

**89** Colour: cherry, garnet rim. Nose: ripe fruit, spicy, creamy oak, toasty, complex, varietal, cedar wood. Palate: powerful, flavourful, toasty, round tannins, good structure.

**LAUDUM GARNACHA SYRAH 2006 T**
garnacha 50%, syrah 50%

**86** Colour: cherry, garnet rim. Nose: ripe fruit, spicy, creamy oak, toasty, complex. Palate: powerful, flavourful, toasty, grainy tannins, spirituous.

**LAUDUM CABERNET SAUVIGNON 2006 T**
cabernet sauvignon 100%

**86** Colour: cherry, garnet rim. Nose: ripe fruit, spicy, creamy oak, toasty, complex, fruit liqueur notes, aromatic coffee. Palate: powerful, flavourful, toasty, round tannins.

**LAUDUM PETIT VERDOT 2006 T**
petit verdot 100%

**85** Colour: cherry, garnet rim. Nose: ripe fruit, spicy, creamy oak, toasty, complex, cedar wood. Palate: powerful, flavourful, toasty, round tannins.

**ALCANTA 2004 TC**
monastrell 50%, tempranillo 50%

**86** Colour: bright cherry. Nose: ripe fruit, sweet spices, expressive. Palate: flavourful, fruity, toasty, round tannins.

**LAUDUM 2004 TC**
monastrell 70%, cabernet sauvignon 15%, merlot 15%

**85** Colour: cherry, garnet rim. Nose: ripe fruit, spicy, creamy oak, toasty, complex, wet leather. Palate: powerful, flavourful, toasty, round tannins.

**SOL DE ALICANTE DULCENEGRA T**
monastrell 100%

**87** Colour: cherry, garnet rim. Nose: spicy, complex, overripe fruit, dried fruit. Palate: powerful, flavourful, toasty, round tannins.

## BODEGAS FAELO

Poeta Miguel Hernández, 60
03201 Elche (Alicante)
☎: 655 856 898
info@vinosladama.com
www.vinosladama.com

**LA PALMA BLANCA 2008 B**
moscatel 100%

**89** Colour: golden. Nose: powerful, floral, honeyed notes, candied fruit. Palate: flavourful, sweet, fresh, fruity, good acidity, long.

**L'ALBA DE FAELO 2008 RD**
syrah 100%

**84**

**LA DAMA 2005 TC**
cabernet sauvignon 40%, petit verdot 40%, monastrell 20%

**88** Colour: bright cherry. Nose: ripe fruit, sweet spices, creamy oak, expressive. Palate: flavourful, fruity, toasty, round tannins, spirituous.

## BODEGAS GUTIÉRREZ DE LA VEGA

Les Quintanes, 1
03792 Parcent (Alicante)
☎: 966 405 266 - Fax: 966 405 257

info@castadiva.es
www.castadiva.es

**CASTA DIVA ESENCIAL 2008 B**
moscatel 100%

**93** Colour: bright straw. Nose: fresh, fresh fruit, white flowers, expressive, varietal. Palate: flavourful, fruity, good acidity, balanced, sweet.

**CASTA DIVA FURTIVA LÁGRIMA 2008 B**
moscatel 100%

**92** Colour: bright yellow. Nose: powerful, ripe fruit, sweet spices, fragrant herbs, faded flowers. Palate: rich, smoky aftertaste, flavourful, fresh, good acidity.

**CASTA DIVA COSECHA MIEL 2008 B**
moscatel 100%

**91** Colour: golden. Nose: powerful, floral, honeyed notes, candied fruit, fragrant herbs, citrus fruit. Palate: flavourful, sweet, fresh, fruity, good acidity, long, fine bitter notes.

**CASTA DIVA COSECHA DORADA 2008 B**
moscatel 100%

**84**

**CASTA DIVA LA DIVA 2007 BC**
moscatel 100%

**88** Colour: golden. Nose: powerful, honeyed notes, candied fruit, fragrant herbs, toasty. Palate: flavourful, sweet, fresh, fruity, good acidity, long.

**CASTA DIVA RESERVA REAL 2002 B RESERVA**
moscatel 100%

**92** Colour: golden. Nose: powerful, honeyed notes, candied fruit, fragrant herbs, faded flowers. Palate: flavourful, sweet, fresh, fruity, good acidity, long.

**CASTA DIVA RECONDITA ARMONIA 2007 T**
monastrell 100%

**90** Colour: bright cherry. Nose: sweet spices, expressive, candied fruit. Palate: flavourful, fruity, toasty, round tannins.

**ROJO Y NEGRO 2006 T**
giró 100%

**86** Colour: cherry, garnet rim. Nose: spicy, toasty, complex, fruit preserve. Palate: powerful, flavourful, toasty, round tannins.

**CASTA DIVA PRÍNCIPE DE SALINAS 2006 TC**
monastrell 100%

**80**

## CASTA DIVA FONDILLÓN 1999
monastrell 100%

**92** Colour: dark-red cherry, garnet rim. Nose: powerful, characterful, fruit liqueur notes, dried fruit. Palate: flavourful, sweetness, pruney, spicy.

## CASTA DIVA FONDILLÓN 1987 1987
monastrell 100%

**93** Colour: pale ruby, brick rim edge. Nose: fruit liqueur notes, overripe fruit, fruit liqueur notes, roasted almonds, aromatic coffee, acetaldehyde. Palate: flavourful, good structure, spirituous, sweetness.

## CASTA DIVA FONDILLÓN SOLERA 1978
monastrell 100%

**92** Colour: light mahogany. Nose: characterful, fruit liqueur notes, fruit liqueur notes, acetaldehyde, tar. Palate: balanced, spirituous, sweetness, spicy.

## CASTA DIVA ALEJANDRÍA

## BODEGAS MURVIEDRO

Ampliación Polígono El Romeral, s/n
46340 Requena (Valencia)
☎: 962 329 003 - Fax: 962 329 002
murviedro@murviedro.es
www.murviedro.es

## CUEVA DEL PERDÓN 2006 T
monastrell 60%, syrah 40%

**87** Colour: cherry, garnet rim. Nose: expressive, ripe fruit, sweet spices, dark chocolate. Palate: flavourful, long, fine tannins.

## DULCE DE MURVIEDRO 2008 MOSCATEL
moscatel 100%

**85** Colour: bright yellow. Nose: varietal, candied fruit, grapey, honeyed notes. Palate: sweet, unctuous, good acidity.

## BODEGAS PARCENT

Avda. Denia, 15 (Ctra. Parcent Alcalali)
03792 Parcent (Alicante)
☎: 636 536 693 - Fax: 966 405 467
armando@bodegasparcent.com
www.bodegasparcent.com

## DOLÇ D'ART 2008 B
moscatel 100%

**86** Colour: bright straw. Nose: fresh, fresh fruit, white flowers, expressive. Palate: flavourful, fruity, good acidity, balanced.

## AURO 2008 B
moscatel 50%, chardonnay 50%

**84**

## GRÀ D'OR BLANCO SECO 2008 B
moscatel 100%

**83**

## ROSAT 2008 RD
merlot 50%, giró 50%

**78**

## COMTAT DE PARCENT 2006 TC
cabernet sauvignon 40%, merlot 40%, giró 20%

**83**

## FRUIT D'AUTOR 2008 VINO DE LICOR

**82**

## BODEGAS SANBERT

Ctra. Pinoso - Fortuna SN Partida de Rodriguillo
03658 Pinoso (Alicante)
☎: 965 978 603 - Fax: 965 978 274
bodegasanbert@yahoo.es
www.sanbert.com

ALFAQUI 2008 B
moscatel 70%, merseguera 30%

## 83

CAMPS DE GLORIA 2006 B
moscatel 100%

**90** Colour: bright straw. Nose: fresh, white flowers, expressive, candied fruit, fruit liqueur notes. Palate: flavourful, fruity, good acidity, balanced, sweet.

ALFAQUI 2008 RD
monastrell 100%

## 82

RODRIGUILLO MONASTRELL 2008 T
monastrell 100%

**86** Colour: bright cherry. Nose: ripe fruit, sweet spices, creamy oak, expressive. Palate: flavourful, fruity, toasty, round tannins.

ALFAQUI 2008 T
monastrell 100%

## 81

DOCTUS 2006 TC
monastrell 100%

## 81

RODRIGUILLO 2006 TC
monastrell 100%

**88** Colour: cherry, garnet rim. Nose: ripe fruit, spicy, creamy oak, toasty, complex. Palate: powerful, flavourful, toasty, round tannins.

## BODEGAS SIERRA SALINAS

Paraje del Puerto s/n
03400 Villena (Alicante)
☎: 968 791 271 - Fax: 968 791 900
office@sierrasalinas.com
www.sierrasalinas.com

MO SALINAS 2007 T
monastrell

**88** Colour: bright cherry. Nose: ripe fruit, sweet spices, creamy oak, expressive. Palate: flavourful, fruity, round tannins.

MIRA SALINAS 2007 T

**91** Colour: very deep cherry, purple rim. Nose: dry stone, elegant, spicy, fruit preserve. Palate: round, powerful, round tannins, toasty.

SALINAS 1237 2006 T
garnacha tinta, cabernet sauvignon, monastrell

**94** Colour: black cherry. Nose: dark chocolate, powerfull, complex, fruit preserve, mineral, sweet spices, creamy oak. Palate: flavourful, powerful, concentrated, round tannins.

MIRA SALINAS 2006 T
monastrell, cabernet sauvignon, garnacha tinta

**93** Colour: bright cherry. Nose: sweet spices, creamy oak, expressive, mineral, fruit preserve. Palate: flavourful, fruity, toasty, round tannins.

PUERTO SALINAS 2006 T
monastrell, cabernet sauvignon, garnacha tinta

**90** Colour: bright cherry. Nose: ripe fruit, sweet spices, creamy oak, expressive. Palate: flavourful, fruity, toasty, slightly dry, soft tannins.

## BODEGAS TERRA NATURA

Pintor Juan Gris, 26
03400 Villena (Alicante)
☎: 965 801 486 - Fax: 965 800 978
export@bodegasterranatura.com
www.aymnavarro.com

MIGUEL NAVARRO SELECCIÓN 2008 B
moscatel

**90** Colour: bright straw. Nose: fresh, fresh fruit, white flowers, expressive, varietal. Palate: flavourful, fruity, good acidity, balanced.

TERRA NATURA TEMPRANILLO 2008 RD
tempranillo 100%

**87** Colour: rose, purple rim. Nose: powerful, ripe fruit, red berry notes, floral, expressive. Palate: fleshy, powerful, fruity, fresh.

TERRA NATURA MONASTRELL TEMPRANILLO 2008 T
monastrell 80%, tempranillo 20%

**87** Colour: bright cherry. Nose: sweet spices, creamy oak, expressive, balsamic herbs, violets. Palate: flavourful, fruity, toasty, round tannins.

MIGUEL NAVARRO SELECCIÓN MONASTRELL TEMPRANILLO 2007 T
monastrell 80%, tempranillo 20%

**90** Colour: cherry, garnet rim. Nose: ripe fruit, spicy, creamy oak, toasty, complex, macerated fruit. Palate: powerful, flavourful, toasty, round tannins, spirituous.

MIGUEL NAVARRO SELECCIÓN SYRAH MERLOT 2007 T
syrah 50%, merlot 50%

**90** Colour: bright cherry. Nose: ripe fruit, sweet spices, creamy oak, expressive. Palate: flavourful, fruity, toasty, round tannins.

MIGUEL NAVARRO SELECCIÓN 2005 TC
monastrell 70%, syrah 30%

**89** Colour: bright cherry. Nose: sweet spices, creamy oak, expressive, fruit liqueur notes. Palate: flavourful, toasty, round tannins, warm.

ALEBUS
GRAN FONDILLÓN 1970

## BODEGAS Y VIÑEDOS EL SEQUÉ

Paraje El Sequé, 59
03650 Pinoso (Alicante)
☎: 945 600 119 - Fax: 945 600 850
elseque@artadi.com

EL SEQUÉ 2007 T ROBLE
monastrell 80%, syrah 10%, cabernet sauvignon 10%

**94** Colour: bright cherry. Nose: sweet spices, creamy oak, expressive, mineral, fresh fruit. Palate: flavourful, fruity, toasty, round tannins.

EL SEQUÉ 2006 T ROBLE
monastrell, garnacha, syrah

**91** Colour: bright cherry. Nose: ripe fruit, sweet spices, creamy oak, red berry notes, mineral. Palate: flavourful, fruity, toasty, round tannins.

LADERAS DE EL SEQUÉ

## E. MENDOZA S.L.U.

Partida El Romeral, s/n
Apartado 351
03580 Alfás del Pi (Alicante)
☎: 965 888 639 - Fax: 965 889 232
bodegas-mendoza@bodegasmendoza.com
www.bodegasmendoza.com

ENRIQUE MENDOZA MOSCATEL DE LA MARINA 2008 B

**91** Colour: bright straw. Nose: fresh, fresh fruit, white flowers, expressive, balsamic herbs, varietal, citrus fruit. Palate: flavourful, fruity, good acidity, balanced, sweet.

ENRIQUE MENDOZA SHIRAZ 2005 TC
syrah

**91** Colour: bright cherry. Nose: ripe fruit, sweet spices, creamy oak, expressive. Palate: flavourful, fruity, toasty, round tannins.

ESTRECHO MONASTRELL 2005 T
monastrell

**91** Colour: cherry, purple rim. Nose: expressive, red berry notes, ripe fruit, lactic notes. Palate: flavourful, good acidity, slightly dry, soft tannins, powerful.

ENRIQUE MENDOZA MERLOT 2005 TC
merlot

**88** Colour: cherry, garnet rim. Nose: spicy, creamy oak, toasty, complex, fruit preserve. Palate: powerful, flavourful, toasty, grainy tannins.

ENRIQUE MENDOZA SANTA ROSA 2004 TR

**93** Colour: cherry, garnet rim. Nose: spicy, creamy oak, toasty, complex, fruit liqueur notes, powerfull, characterful. Palate: powerful, flavourful, toasty, round tannins.

ENRIQUE MENDOZA CABERNET SAUVIGNON - SHIRAZ 2004 TR
cabernet sauvignon, syrah

**89** Colour: cherry, garnet rim. Nose: ripe fruit, spicy, creamy oak, toasty, complex. Palate: powerful, flavourful, toasty, round tannins.

DOLÇ DE MENDOZA

## FRANCISCO YAGO PUCHE S.L.

Finca El Mojón. Paraje La Boquera
30510 Villena (Alicante)
☎: 968 790 765 - Fax: 968 790 765
boyago@boyago.es

CASA EL MOJÓN 2006 T JOVEN
monastrell 40%, tempranillo 40%, garnacha 20%

**86** Colour: bright cherry. Nose: ripe fruit, sweet spices, creamy oak, expressive, fruit liqueur notes. Palate: flavourful, fruity, toasty, round tannins, spirituous.

FRANCISCO YAGO MONASTRELL SYRAH 2002 TR
monastrell 50%, syrah 50%

**85** Colour: cherry, garnet rim. Nose: ripe fruit, spicy, creamy oak, toasty, complex, fruit liqueur notes. Palate: powerful, flavourful, toasty, round tannins.

CASA EL MOJÓN 2002 TC
monastrell 40%, tempranillo 40%, garnacha 20%

**82**

BOYAGO

## LA BODEGA DE PINOSO

Pº de la Constitución, 82
03650 Pinoso (Alicante)
☎: 965 477 040 - Fax: 966 970 149
info@labodegadepinoso.com
www.labodegadepinoso.com

LA TORRE DEL RELOJ MACABEO 2008 B
macabeo 85%, airén 15%

**87** Colour: bright straw. Nose: fresh, fresh fruit, expressive, varietal. Palate: flavourful, fruity, good acidity, balanced.

VERMADOR ECOLÓGICO 2008 B
macabeo 85%, airén 15%

**85** Colour: bright straw. Nose: white flowers, expressive, warm, macerated fruit. Palate: flavourful, fruity, good acidity, balanced.

LA TORRE DEL RELOJ 2008 RD
monastrell 85%, tempranillo 10%, syrah 5%

**84**

VERMADOR ECOLÓGICO 2008 RD
monastrell 100%

**82**

VERGEL 2007 T
monastrell 6%, merlot 10%, alicante bouchet 84%

**89** Colour: very deep cherry. Nose: ripe fruit, spicy, mineral, earthy notes. Palate: flavourful, powerful, fleshy.

PONTOS 2007 T
monastrell 100%

**88** Colour: cherry, garnet rim. Nose: ripe fruit, spicy, creamy oak, toasty, complex. Palate: powerful, flavourful, toasty, round tannins, sweet.

LA TORRE DEL RELOJ MONASTRELL 2007 T
monastrell 85%, merlot 10%, tempranillo 5%

**87** Colour: cherry, purple rim. Nose: expressive, fresh fruit, red berry notes, floral. Palate: flavourful, fruity, good acidity, round tannins.

VERMADOR ECOLÓGICO MONASTRELL 2007 T BARRICA
monastrell 85%                              HHHHH3,3€

**86** Colour: cherry, purple rim. Nose: expressive, fruit preserve. Palate: flavourful, fruity, good acidity, round tannins.

**PONTOS CEPA 50 2006 T**
monastrell 100%

**88** Colour: cherry, garnet rim. Nose: ripe fruit, spicy, toasty, complex, aged wood nuances. Palate: powerful, flavourful, toasty, round tannins.

**PONTOS 1932 ALTA EXPRESIÓN 2006 T**
monastrell 100%

**88** Colour: cherry, garnet rim. Nose: ripe fruit, spicy, creamy oak, toasty, complex, fruit liqueur notes. Palate: powerful, flavourful, toasty, round tannins, sweetness.

**PONTOS 2005 TC**
monastrell, merlot, cabernet sauvignon

**87** Colour: cherry, garnet rim. Nose: spicy, creamy oak, toasty, complex, fruit liqueur notes. Palate: powerful, flavourful, toasty, round tannins.

**VERMADOR ECOLÓGICO MONASTRELL 2008 BARRICA**

**86** Colour: deep cherry, garnet rim. Nose: ripe fruit, varietal, expressive. Palate: flavourful, fruity, good acidity, slightly green tannins.

## PRIMITIVO QUILES

Mayor, 4
03640 Monóvar (Alicante)
☎: 965 470 099 - Fax: 966 960 235
info@primitivoquiles.com
www.primitivoquiles.com

**PRIMITIVO QUILES MONASTRELL-MERLOT 2007 T ROBLE**
monastrell 60%, merlot 40%

**85** Colour: bright cherry. Nose: sweet spices, creamy oak, expressive, fruit preserve, overripe fruit. Palate: flavourful, fruity, toasty, round tannins.

**PRIMITIVO QUILES MONASTRELL 2005 TC**
monastrell

**85** Colour: pale ruby, brick rim edge. Nose: elegant, spicy, wet leather, aged wood nuances, fruit liqueur notes, fruit liqueur notes. Palate: spicy, fine tannins, elegant, long.

**RASPAY 2003 T**

**83**

**GRAN IMPERIAL GE RESERVA ESPECIAL**
moscatel

**90** Colour: dark mahogany. Nose: complex, fruit liqueur notes, dried fruit, pattiserie, toasty. Palate: sweet, rich, unctuous, powerful.

**PRIMITIVO QUILES FONDILLÓN 1948 GE GRAN RESERVA**
monastrell

**87** Colour: iodine, amber rim. Nose: roasted almonds, fruit liqueur notes, fruit liqueur notes, dried fruit, acetaldehyde. Palate: sweetness, warm, good acidity.

**PRIMITIVO QUILES MOSCATEL EXTRA VINO DE LICOR**
moscatel

**86** Colour: dark mahogany. Nose: fruit liqueur notes, candied fruit, aromatic coffee, caramel. Palate: spirituous, sweetness, spicy.

**EL ABUELO FONDILLÓN**

## PRODUCTOS AGRÍCOLAS JUAN PORSELLANES

Avda. País Valencia, 4
Benissa (Alicante)

☎: 965 730 200
info@porsellanes.com

## AGULLO 2007 T
tempranillo 80%, cabernet sauvignon 20%

**88** Colour: dark-red cherry, orangey edge. Nose: powerful, characterful, fruit liqueur notes, ripe fruit, fruit liqueur notes, creamy oak. Palate: flavourful, long, great length, slightly dry, soft tannins.

## ENTREPINS 2007 T
merlot 82%, cabernet sauvignon 18%

**85** Colour: black cherry, orangey edge. Nose: characterful, fruit preserve, grassy. Palate: flavourful, spirituous, long, soft tannins.

## MAS DE CARAITA 2007 T
tempranillo, syrah, garnacha
**83**

## LA SORT MOSCATEL ECOLÓGICO MOSCATEL
moscatel
**83**

MOSCATEL PORSELLANES

## SALVADOR POVEDA

CV 830 - Ctra. Salinas, km. 3
03640 Monovar (Alicante)
☎: 966 960 180 - Fax: 965 473 389
salvadorpoveda@salvadorpoveda.com
www.salvadorpoveda.com

## TOSCAR MONASTRELL 2007 T

**87** Colour: bright cherry. Nose: varietal, medium intensity, macerated fruit, fruit expression. Palate: flavourful, fruity, fresh.

## TOSCAR CABERNET SAUVIGNON 2005 TC

**89** Colour: cherry, garnet rim. Nose: fruit preserve, overripe fruit, warm, roasted coffee. Palate: sweetness, fleshy, concentrated, powerful.

## TOSCAR MERLOT 2005 TC

**87** Colour: cherry, garnet rim. Nose: powerful, characterful, ripe fruit, toasty, dark chocolate. Palate: powerful, fleshy, concentrated, sweetness.

POVEDA TEMPRANILLO 2005 TC

**87** Colour: very deep cherry. Nose: powerful, warm, slightly evolved, roasted coffee, sweet spices. Palate: fleshy, sweetness, powerful.

## BORRASCA 2004 T

**86** Colour: cherry, garnet rim. Nose: medium intensity, fruit liqueur notes, fruit liqueur notes, spicy. Palate: powerful, spirituous, sweetness.

## TOSCAR SYRAH T

**85** Colour: deep cherry. Nose: powerful, characterful, ripe fruit, floral. Palate: flavourful, fruity, fine bitter notes, good acidity.

## FONDILLÓN 1987 1987 GE GRAN RESERVA

**90** Colour: iodine, amber rim. Nose: powerful, characterful, fruit liqueur notes, candied fruit, aged wood nuances, varnish.

VIÑA VERMETA

## VINS DEL COMTAT

Turballos, 1-3
03820 Alicante (Alicante)
☎: 965 593 194 - Fax: 965 593 590
info@vinsdelcomtat.com
www.vinsdelcomtat.com

## CRISTAL.LI B

**90** Colour: bright straw. Nose: fresh, fresh fruit, white flowers, expressive, varietal. Palate: flavourful, fruity, good acidity, balanced.

## VERDEVAL B

**85** Colour: bright straw. Nose: fresh, fresh fruit, white flowers, expressive. Palate: flavourful, fruity, good acidity, balanced.

## SERRELLA 2006 T

**89** Colour: cherry, garnet rim. Nose: ripe fruit, spicy, creamy oak, toasty, expressive. Palate: powerful, flavourful, toasty, round tannins.

## MAIGMÓ T

**85** Colour: cherry, garnet rim. Nose: spicy, toasty, complex, powerfull, dried fruit, overripe fruit, tar. Palate: powerful, flavourful, toasty, balanced.

# DO ALICANTE

SOME OTHER WINERIES WITHIN THE DO:

**BODEGA COOPERATIVA CAMPO DE SAN BLAS**
**BODEGA Y VIÑEDOS DEL ARZOBISPO**
**BODEGAS ESTEVAN**
**BODEGAS FONDARIUM**
**BODEGAS Y VIÑEDOS DE MURCIA S.L.**
**BROTONS S.L.**
**COMERCIAL GRUPO FREIXENET S.A.**
**COMPAÑIA DE VINOS DE TELMO RODRÍGUEZ**
**EL CARCHE**
**VIÑA PRADO**

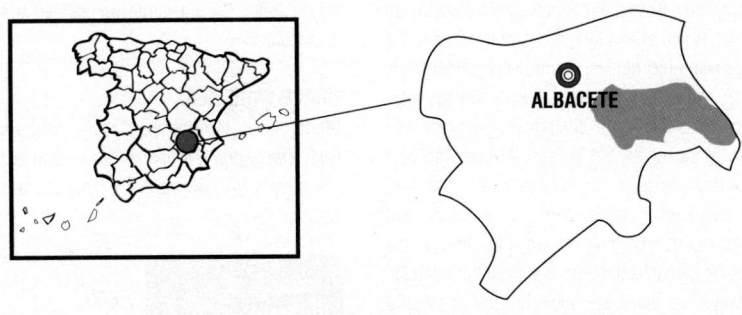

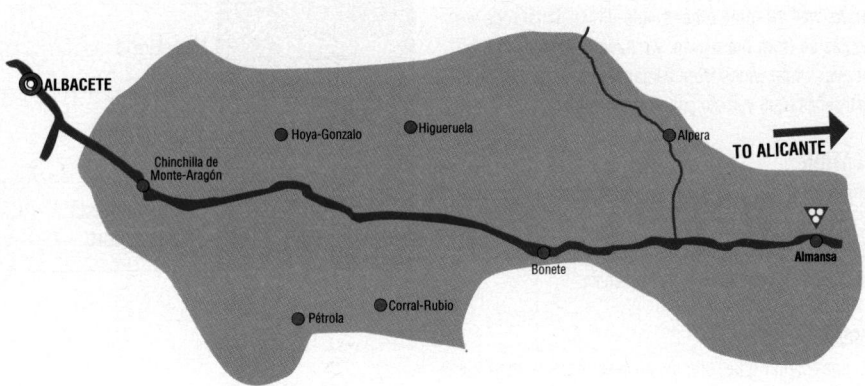

ALBACETE

Hoya-Gonzalo

Higueruela

Alpera

TO ALICANTE

Chinchilla de
Monte-Aragón

Bonete

Almansa

Pétrola

Corral-Rubio

▽ Consejo Regulador
● DO Boundary

# DO ALMANSA

## NEWS

Almansa has got the hang of its more planted grape variety, garnacha tintorera. From bulk grape used to add colour to blends and after a long adaptation period to the new vine-growing techniques, the grape is yielding now much better wines, performing brilliantly vintage after vintage regardless of climatic differences. There are very few wineries in the region, but Bodegas Almanseñas, with their label Adara, comes up top. Behind this success there are four well-known winemakers of national and international repute who have managed to show all the potential of the garnacha tintorera in a most harmonious, balanced way. The wines are powerful, full of mineral character and singularity given that is planted at 800 meters, which accounts for higher acidity to counterbalance the high level of tannins and richness typical of this grape variety. We are talking about a winery with great weight in international markets, along with Atalaya and the rest of producers from the region, that have managed to sell abroad over two million bottles every year. As well as some other single-dimensional reds we have tasted from the region, we have had access to the first ever white wines from Almansa, made by Bodegas Almanseñas from verdejo and sauvignon blanc.

## LOCATION

In the eastern region of the province of Albacete. It covers the municipal areas of Almansa, Alpera, Bonete, Corral Rubio, Higueruela, Hoya Gonzalo, Pétrola and the municipal district of El Villar de Chinchilla.

## CLIMATE

Of a continental type, somewhat less extreme than the climate of La Mancha, although the summers are very hot, with temperatures which easily reach 40 °C. Rainfall, on the other hand, is scant, an average of about 350 mm a year. The majority of the vineyards are situated on the plains, although there are a few situated on the slopes.

## SOIL

The soil is limy, poor in organic matter and with some clayey areas. The vineyards are situated at an altitude of about 700 m.

## GRAPE VARIETIES:

**White:** *Airén, Verdejo* and *Sauvignon Blanc.*
**Red:** *Garnacha Tintorera* (most popular), *Cencibel* (*Tempranillo*), *Monastrell* (second most popular), *Syrah.*

| | |
|---|---|
| Hectares of Vineyard | 7,600 |
| Nº Viticulturists | 750 |
| Nº of Bodegas | 13 |
| 2008 Harvest | Very Good |
| 2007 Production | 19,000,000 l. |
| Marketing | 22.7% domestic 77.3% export |

**CONSEJO REGULADOR.**
Méndez Núñez, 5. Aptdo. 158
02640 Almansa (Albacete).
☎: 967 340 258 - Fax: 967 310 842
@ crdo@tvalmansa.es

## GENERAL CHARACTERISTICS OF THE WINES:

| | |
|---|---|
| **WHITES** | These are produced mainly from the *Airén* variety. They are pale yellow, light, fruity and pleasant, in line with the wines from La Mancha. |
| **ROSÉS** | These are pink or salmon pink; fresh and fruity with an honest nose and are usually full - bodied and easy drinking. |
| **REDS** | The *Garnacha Tintorera* has over the past few years recovered the prominence of the DO, producing strong, fruity, fresh and meaty wines, especially since it is now bottled more selectively instead of being sold in bulk. Up to then, the most characteristic reds were the young wines of *Cencibel*, with an intense cherry colour and a fruity character. All of them stand out for a certain acidity on the palate due to the altitude of the vineyards. |

## 2008 VINTAGE RATING:

# VERY GOOD

## BODEGA DEHESA EL CARRASCAL

Pasaje de Lodares Portal 3 - 2 D
02001 Albacete (Albacete)
☎: 967 240 458 - Fax: 967 210 989
dehesacarrascal@terra.es
www.vinoselcarrascal.com

TUDON'S 2006 T
petit verdot 100%

**87** Colour: cherry, garnet rim. Nose: balanced, warm, spicy, fruit preserve. Palate: flavourful, fruity, great length, round tannins.

TUDON'S 2005 TC
syrah 100%

**84**

## BODEGAS ALMANSEÑAS

Ctra. de Alpera, km. 96,6 Finca Venta la Vega
02640 Almansa (Albacete)
☎: 967 098 116 - Fax: 963 840 526
adaras@ventalavega.com
www.ventalavega.com

ADARAS 2008 B
sauvignon blanc, verdejo

**90** Colour: bright straw. Nose: fresh, varietal, ripe fruit, floral, sweet spices. Palate: flavourful, fruity, fresh, spicy.

DULCE DE ADARAS 2008 B
100% sauvignon blanc

**83**

LA HUELLA DE ADARAS 2008 B
45% verdejo, 40% sauvignon blanc, 15% monastrell

**83**

CALIZO DE ADARAS 2008 T
50% garnacha tinta, 30% monastrell, 10% petit verdot 10%syrah

**85** Colour: cherry, purple rim. Nose: fresh fruit, red berry notes, floral. Palate: flavourful, fruity, good acidity, round tannins.

LA HUELLA DE ADARAS 2007 T JOVEN
garnacha tinta, monastrell, syrah

**91** Colour: deep cherry. Nose: powerful, expressive, varietal, fresh, fruit expression. Palate: powerful, flavourful, fruity, fresh.

ADARAS 2006 T

**91** Colour: bright cherry. Nose: ripe fruit, sweet spices, creamy oak, expressive, mineral, dark chocolate. Palate: flavourful, fruity, toasty, round tannins.

LA HUELLA DE ADARAS 2006 T
garnacha 60%, monastrell 30%, syrah 10%

**84**

ADARAS 2005 T
garnacha tintorera

**90** Colour: very deep cherry. Nose: powerful, varietal, characterful, mineral, sweet spices. Palate: flavourful, powerful, concentrated, spicy, round tannins.

LA VEGA DE ADARAS 2005 T
garnacha 70%, monastrell 30%

**88** Colour: cherry, garnet rim. Nose: spicy, creamy oak, toasty, complex, fruit preserve. Palate: powerful, flavourful, toasty, round tannins, warm.

## BODEGAS ATALAYA

Ctra. Almansa - Ayora, km. 1
02640 Almansa (Albacete)
☎: 968 435 022 - Fax: 968 716 051
info@orowine.com

ATALAYA 2008 T
monastrell, garnacha, otras

**90** Colour: cherry, garnet rim. Nose: expressive, ripe fruit, red berry notes, floral. Palate: flavourful, powerful, fleshy, ripe fruit, round tannins.

ATALAYA 2007 T
monastrell, garnacha, otras

**88** Colour: cherry, garnet rim. Nose: powerful, fruit preserve, warm, toasty. Palate: powerful, flavourful, concentrated, spicy, round tannins, roasted-coffee aftertaste.

## BODEGAS EL TANINO

Sol, s/n
02696 Hoya Gonzalo (Albacete)
☎: 967 589 126 - Fax: 967 589 127
info@bodegaseltanino.com
www.bodegaseltanino.com

1752 2006 T BARRICA
garnacha tintorera

**88** Colour: black cherry. Nose: powerful, characterful, ripe fruit, fruit liqueur notes, sweet spices. Palate: powerful, flavourful, fleshy, complex, concentrated.

## BODEGAS PIQUERAS

Pol. Ind. El Mugrón, Zapateros, 11
02640 Almansa (Albacete)
☎: 967 341 482 - Fax: 967 345 480
bodpiqueras@almansa.org
www.bodegaspiqueras.es

CASTILLO DE ALMANSA 2004 TR
monastrell, tempranillo, syrah, garnacha tintorera

**86** Colour: dark-red cherry, orangey edge. Nose: fruit preserve, fine reductive notes, tobacco, cocoa bean, aromatic coffee. Palate: good acidity, classic aged character, spicy, round tannins.

TERRA GRANDE
VALCANTO

## COOPERATIVA AGRARIA SANTA QUITERIA. BODEGA TINTORALBA

Baltasar González Sáez, 34
02694 Higueruela (Albacete)
☎: 967 287 012 - Fax: 967 287 031
direccion@tintoralba.com
www.tintoralba.com

HIGUERUELA 2008 T
garnacha tintorera 100%

**89** Colour: cherry, purple rim. Nose: expressive, fresh fruit, red berry notes, floral. Palate: flavourful, fruity, good acidity, round tannins.

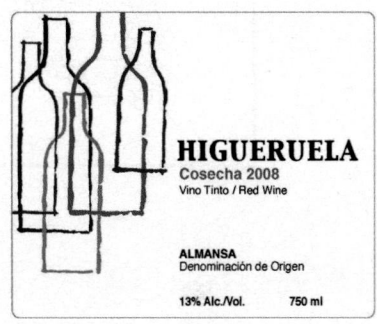

HIGUERUELA
Cosecha 2008
Vino Tinto / Red Wine

ALMANSA
Denominación de Origen

13% Alc./Vol.          750 ml

DULCE TINTORALBA 2008 T
garnacha tintorera 100%

**82**

## HACIENDA EL ESPINO

Ctra. de Ayora, km. 98
02640 Almansa (Albacete)
☎: 967 318 003 - Fax: 967 344 561
haciendaelespino@almansa.com
www.haciendaelespino.com

1707 SYRAH 2007 T
syrah 100%

**84**

1707 VARIEDADES 2005 T
garnacha, pinot noir, cabernet sauvignon, merlot, syrah

**82**

SOME OTHER WINERIES WITHIN THE DO:

**SANTA ROSA S.L.**

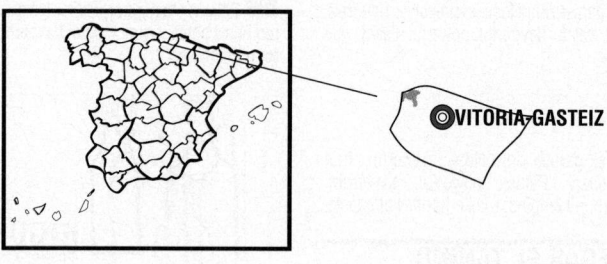

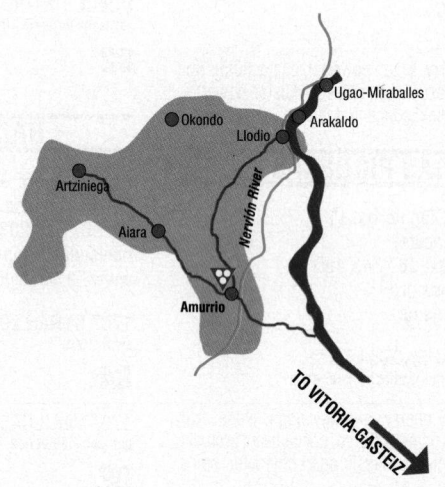

▽ Consejo Regulador
● DO Boundary

## NEWS

From just one and a half hectare in 1986, a group of vine growers in Ayala valley –to the northwest of the province of Álava and closer to the Atlantic– have managed to reach the current 70 hectares, which are now part of the DO Arabako Txakolina. Thanks to the steady effort of the producers in foreign markets, the six wineries that are part of the DO keep selling abundantly abroad and have known a great success in USA. In the next few years the Consejo Regulador will increase the vineyard surface to compensate for the production decreases of vintages like 2008, where abundant spring rains did away with a whole 24% of the harvest. Less wine but of better quality, apparently and according to our tasting, although of just two wines, in which we notice the carbonic trait typical of txakolis from Getaria and Bilbao, as well as some varietal nuances, with an overall riper fruit character on the nose and on the palate, given that this inner region usually gets more sunshine hours.

## LOCATION

It covers the region of Aiara (Ayala), situated in the north west of the province of Alava on the banks of the Nervion river basin. Specifically, it is made up of the municipalities of Amurrio, Artziniega, Aiara (Ayala), Laudio (Llodio) and Okondo.

## CLIMATE

Similar to that of the DO Bizkaiko Txakolina, determined by the influence of the Bay of Biscay, although somewhat less humid and slightly drier and fresher. In fact, the greatest risk in the region stems from frost in the spring. However, it should not be forgotten that part of its vineyards borders on the innermost plantations of the DO Bizkaiko Txakolina.

## SOIL

A great variety of formations are found, ranging from clayey to fundamentally stony, precisely those which to date are producing the best results and where fairly stable grape ripening is achieved.

## GRAPE VARIETIES:

**Main:** *Hondarrabi Zuri* (80%).
**Authorized:** *Petit Manseng, Petit Corbu* and *Gross Manseng*.

| | |
|---|---|
| **Hectares of Vineyard** | 70 |
| **N° Viticulturists** | 37 |
| **N° of Bodegas** | 6 |
| **2008 Harvest** | Very Good |
| **2007 Production** | 196,101 l. |
| **Marketing** | 80% domestic 20% export |

**CONSEJO REGULADOR.**
Plaza Dionisio Aldama (Galería Comercial). Apto. 36
01470 Amurrio (Álava).
☎: 945 892 308 - Fax: 945 891 211
@dotxakolialava@mundofree.com
www.arabakotxakolina.com

## GENERAL CHARACTERISTICS OF THE WINES:

| | |
|---|---|
| **WHITES** | Produced mainly from the autochthonous variety *Hondarrabi Zuri*, the Txakoli from Álava is very similar to those from the other two provinces of the Basque Country, especially those from Bizkaia. They are pale steely or greenish, with hints of fresh herbs and a fruity character slightly more aged than their neighbours. On the palate, they are slightly more round and full-bodied thanks to a slightly higher alcohol content and, although fresh, they are less acidic on the palate. |

## 2008 VINTAGE RATING:

## VERY GOOD

## BELDUI TXAKOLINA

Beldui Baserria-Gardea
01400 Laudio (Álava)
☎: 946 728 148
info@beldui.com
www.beldui.com

BELDUI TXAKOLINA 2008 B
hondarrabi zuri

**81**

## OKONDO TXAKOLINA

Barrio Jandiola, 16 (Caserío Aretxabala)
48001 Okondo (Alava)
☎: 945 898 516 - Fax: 944 238 650
admon@senoriodeastobiza.com
www.seniriodeastobiza.com

SEÑORÍO DE ASTOBIZA 2008 B
hondarrabi zuri 55%, gros manseng 30%, petit corbu 15%

**86** Colour: pale. Nose: fresh fruit, grassy. Palate: rich, fruity, good acidity, correct.

SOME OTHER WINERIES WITHIN THE DO:

**CASA DEL TXAKOLI**

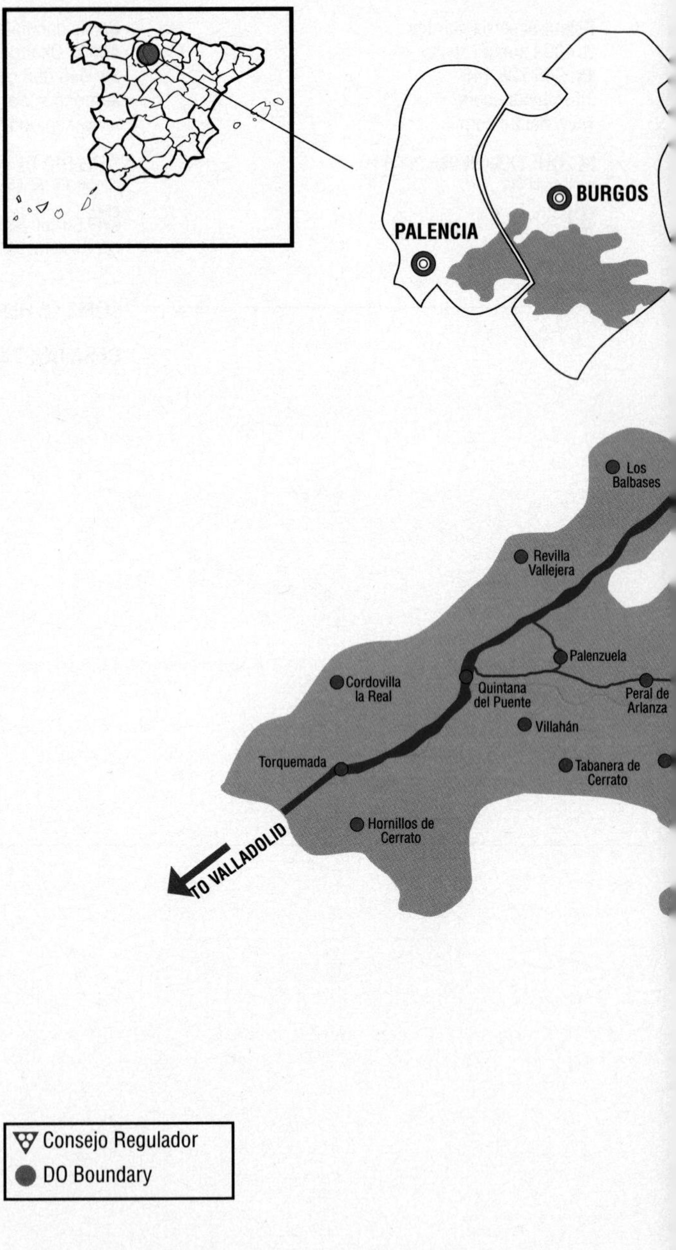

BURGOS

PALENCIA

Los Balbases

Revilla Vallejera

Palenzuela

Cordovilla la Real

Quintana del Puente

Peral de Arlanza

Villahán

Torquemada

Tabanera de Cerrato

Hornillos de Cerrato

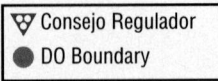
TO VALLADOLID

▽ Consejo Regulador
● DO Boundary

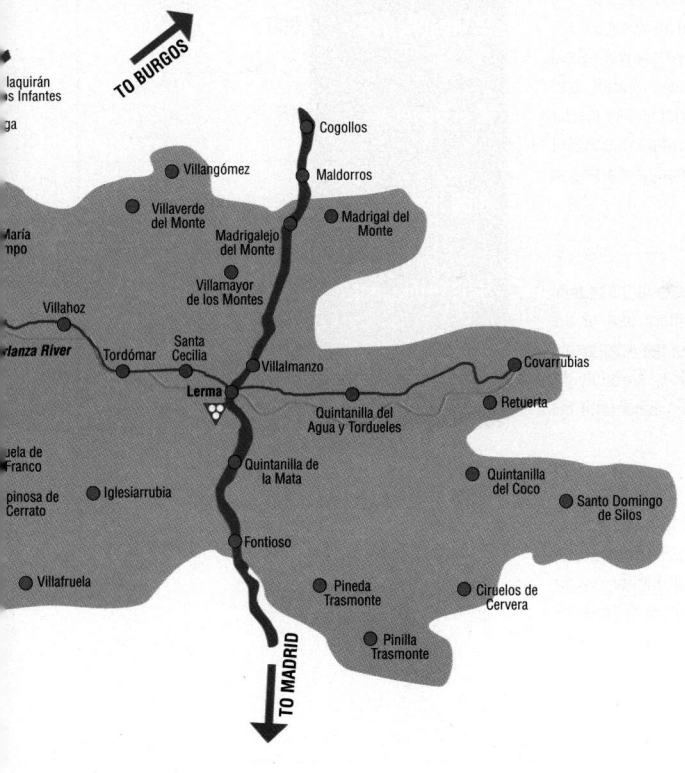

laquirán
s Infantes

ga

TO BURGOS

Cogollos

Villangómez

Maldorros

María
npo

Villaverde
del Monte

Madrigalejo
del Monte

Madrigal del
Monte

Villamayor
de los Montes

Villahoz

*lanza River*

Santa
Cecilia

Tordómar

Villalmanzo

Covarrubias

Lerma

Retuerta

Quintanilla del
Agua y Tordueles

uela de
Franco

Quintanilla de
la Mata

pinosa de
Cerrato

Iglesiarrubia

Quintanilla
del Coco

Santo Domingo
de Silos

Fontioso

Villafruela

Pineda
Trasmonte

Ciruelos de
Cervera

TO MADRID

Pinilla
Trasmonte

# DO ARLANZA

## NEWS
Wines from Arlanza have come of age after the début as DO. The first relevant feature is consistency, a homogeneous style between wines and vintages, something quite complicated to achieve considering that is the coolest region in Castilla y León. The wines from the 2008 vintage are not many, maybe dwindled by a late and irregular harvest, with also lower ratings compared to last year's. All in all they are powerful renderings, surely more apt for long oak ageing able to soft down a tempranillo, high in colour and tannins, planted in rocky and gravel soils at high altitude and in a cool region. There are some new wines, with the best coming from Bodegas Buezo, and some good examples from older wineries such as Bodegas Arlanza. Nevertheless, the best ratings go to the complex, powerful wines of the 2004 vintage, which are keeping amazingly well. Save those from Buezo, pretty interesting overall and pioneering the use of foreign grape varieties like merlot and pinot noir, the rest show pretty humble in concept and ratings. All in all, good value for money, starting at around 3€.

## LOCATION
With the medieval city of Lerma at the core of the region, Arlanza occupies the central and southern part of the province of Burgos, on the river valleys of the Arlanza and its subsidiaries, all the way westwards through 13 municipal districts of the province of Palencia until the Pisuerga River is reached.

## CLIMATE
The climate of this wine region is said to be one of the harshest within Castilla y León, with lower temperatures towards the western areas and rainfall higher on the eastern parts, in the highlands of the province of Soria.

## SOIL
Soil in the region is not particularly deep, with soft rocks underneath and good humidity levels. The landscape is one of rolling hills where vines are planted on varied soils, from limestone to calcareous, with abundant granite on certain areas.

## GRAPE VARIETIES:
**Red:** *Tempranillo, Garnacha* and *Mencía.*
**White:** *Albillo* and *Viura*

| | |
|---|---|
| Hectares of Vineyard | 450 |
| Nº Viticulturists | 300 |
| Nº of Bodegas | 15 |
| 2008 Harvest | Very Good |
| 2007 Production | 670,000 l. |
| Marketing | 94.5% domestic 5.5% export |

**CONSEJO REGULADOR.**
Ronda de la Cárcel, 4. 09340 Lerma (Burgos).
☎: 947 171 046 - Fax: 947 171 046
@ info@arlanza.org
www.arlanza.org

**GENERAL CHARACTERISTICS OF THE WINES:**

| | |
|---|---|
| **REDS** | Mostly made from *Tempranillo* grapes, they keep certain similarities with those from Ribera de Duero -both regions enjoy an extreme Atlantic climate-, although they have a stronger roasted character, fresher fruit and softer tannins. As we travel westwards and the altitude gets lower, wines get more powerful and increase their alcohol content, but probably the greatest potential still to be achieved is related to acidity levels. |

<u>**2008 VINTAGE RATING:**</u>

**GOOD**

## BODEGAS ARLANZA S.C.P.

Ctra. Madrid-Irún km 203, 800
09390 Villalmanzo (Burgos)
☎: 947 172 070 - Fax: 947 170 259
comercial@bodegasarlanza.com
www.bodegasarlanza.com

**DOMINIO DE MANCILES 2007 B**
viura 50%, albillo 50%

**87** Colour: bright straw. Nose: fresh fruit, wild herbs, citrus fruit. Palate: flavourful, fruity, balanced, good acidity, good finish.

**DOMINIO DE MANCILES 2008 RD**
tempranillo 60%, garnacha 40%

**84**

**DOMINIO DE MANCILES 2007 T ROBLE**
tempranillo 80%, cabernet sauvignon 15%, mencía 5%

**86** Colour: bright cherry, garnet rim. Nose: sweet spices, fruit expression, dark chocolate. Palate: flavourful, fruity, round tannins.

**DOMINIO DE MANCILES 2007 T**
tempranillo 80%, cabernet sauvignon 15%, mencía 5%

**84**

**DOMINIO DE MANCILES 2004 TC**
tempranillo 80%, cabernet sauvignon 15%, mencía 5%

**85** Colour: black cherry. Nose: characterful, ripe fruit, spicy, dark chocolate. Palate: flavourful, fine bitter notes, slightly dry, soft tannins.

**DOMINIO DE MANCILES 2003 TR**
tempranillo 100%

**84**

**VALDEMANSILLA 2002 TC**
tempranillo 80%, cabernet sauvignon 15%, mencía 5%

**86** Colour: cherry, garnet rim. Nose: ripe fruit, medium intensity, spicy, fine reductive notes. Palate: balanced, fruity, good acidity.

## BODEGAS SIERRA

Ctra. Madrid-Irún km 203,700
09390 Villalmanzo (Burgos)
☎: 947 170 083 - Fax: 947 170 083
info@bodegassierra.com
www.bodegassierra.com

**CASTILLO DE URA 2004 TC**

**82**

**ITINERE ESP**
tempranillo blanco

**85** Colour: bright golden. Nose: lees reduction notes, pattiserie, dry nuts. Palate: fruity, easy to drink, sweetness.

CASCAJUELO
PRADO LERMA
SUEÑOS DEL DUQUE

## BODEGAS VIÑA VALDABLE

Gómes Salazar, 18
09346 Covarrubias (Burgos)
☎: 947 406 533 - Fax: 947 406 596
info@valdable.com

**VIÑA VALDABLE 2008 T**
tempranillo 100%

**88** Colour: deep cherry, purple rim. Nose: fresh fruit, varietal, expressive, sweet spices. Palate: flavourful, fruity, powerful, sweetness.

**VIÑA VALDABLE 2005 TC**
tempranillo 100%

**83**

**VIÑA LETICIA 2004 TR**
tempranillo 100%

**85** Colour: deep cherry, garnet rim. Nose: fruit preserve, balanced, sweet spices. Palate: light-bodied, fruity, good acidity, roasted-coffee aftertaste.

## BODEGAS Y VIÑEDOS GARMENDIA

Finca Santa Rosalia, s/n Revilla Vallegera
34260 Vizmalo (Burgos)
☎: 947 166 171 - Fax: 947 166 147
maria@bodegasgarmendia.com
www.bodegasgarmendia.com

**GARMENDIA 2008 RD**
garnacha 60%, tempranillo 40%

**85** Colour: raspberry rose. Nose: fresh fruit, red berry notes, floral. Palate: rich, fruity, spicy, fresh.

**GARMENDIA 2008 T**
tempranillo 100%

**86** Colour: cherry, purple rim. Nose: fresh fruit, varietal, expressive, red berry notes. Palate: fruity, fresh, easy to drink, light-bodied.

## BUEZO VS. VG

Paraje Valdeazadón
09342 Mahamud (Burgos)
☎: 947 616 899 - Fax: 947 616 885
rfranco@buezo.com
www.buezo.com

**BUEZO TEMPRANILLO 2004 TC**
tempranillo 100%

**89** Colour: dark-red cherry. Nose: powerfull, creamy oak, cocoa bean, earthy notes, fruit liqueur notes. Palate: flavourful, fresh, good acidity, roasted-coffee aftertaste, round tannins.

**BUEZO NATTAN 2004 TC**

**90** Colour: bright cherry. Nose: ripe fruit, sweet spices, creamy oak, expressive, mineral. Palate: flavourful, fruity, toasty, round tannins.

**BUEZO PETIT VERDOT 2004 TC**
petit verdot 50%, tempranillo 50%

**89** Colour: cherry, garnet rim. Nose: ripe fruit, floral, elegant, sweet spices. Palate: powerful, good acidity, roasted-coffee aftertaste.

**BUEZO VARIETALES 2004 TC**
tempranillo 50%, merlot 25%, cabernet sauvignon 25%

**88** Colour: black cherry. Nose: fruit preserve, floral, elegant, aromatic coffee. Palate: fresh, short, round tannins, roasted-coffee aftertaste.

## LA COLEGIADA

Ctra. Madrid-Irún, km. 203
Vía de Servicio Villalmanzo
09340 Lerma (Burgos)
☎: 947 177 030 - Fax: 947 177 004
info@tintolerma.com
www.tintolerma.com

**TINTO LERMA 2006 TC**

**87** Colour: deep cherry. Nose: ripe fruit, spicy, dark chocolate, creamy oak. Palate: good structure, round, fine tannins.

## PAGOS DE NEGREDO VIÑEDOS

Avda. Casado del Alisal, 26
34001 Palencia (Palencia)
☎: 979 700 450 - Fax: 979 702 171
administracion@pagosdenegredo.com
www.pagosdenegredo.com

**PAGOS DE NEGREDO MAGNUM 2005 TC**
tempranillo

**87** Colour: black cherry. Nose: creamy oak, toasty, ripe fruit. Palate: powerful, fruity, toasty, flavourful.

# DO ARLANZA

PAGOS DE NEGREDO 2005 TC
tempranillo 100%

## 84

## VITIVINICOLA LADRERO S.L.

Avda. de la Paz, 4
34230 Torquemada (Palencia)
☎: 979 800 545 - Fax: 979 800 545
bodega@ladrero.e.telefonica.net
www.bodegasladrero.es

SEÑORÍO DE VALDESNEROS 2008 RD
tempranillo 100%

## 80

SEÑORÍO DE VALDESNEROS 2005 TC
tempranillo 100%

## 82

SOME OTHER WINERIES WITHIN THE DO:

**ARLESE NEGOCIOS**
**BODEGAS MONTE AMÁN S.L.**
**COVARRUBIAS SALUD S.L.**
**PALACIO DE LERMA**

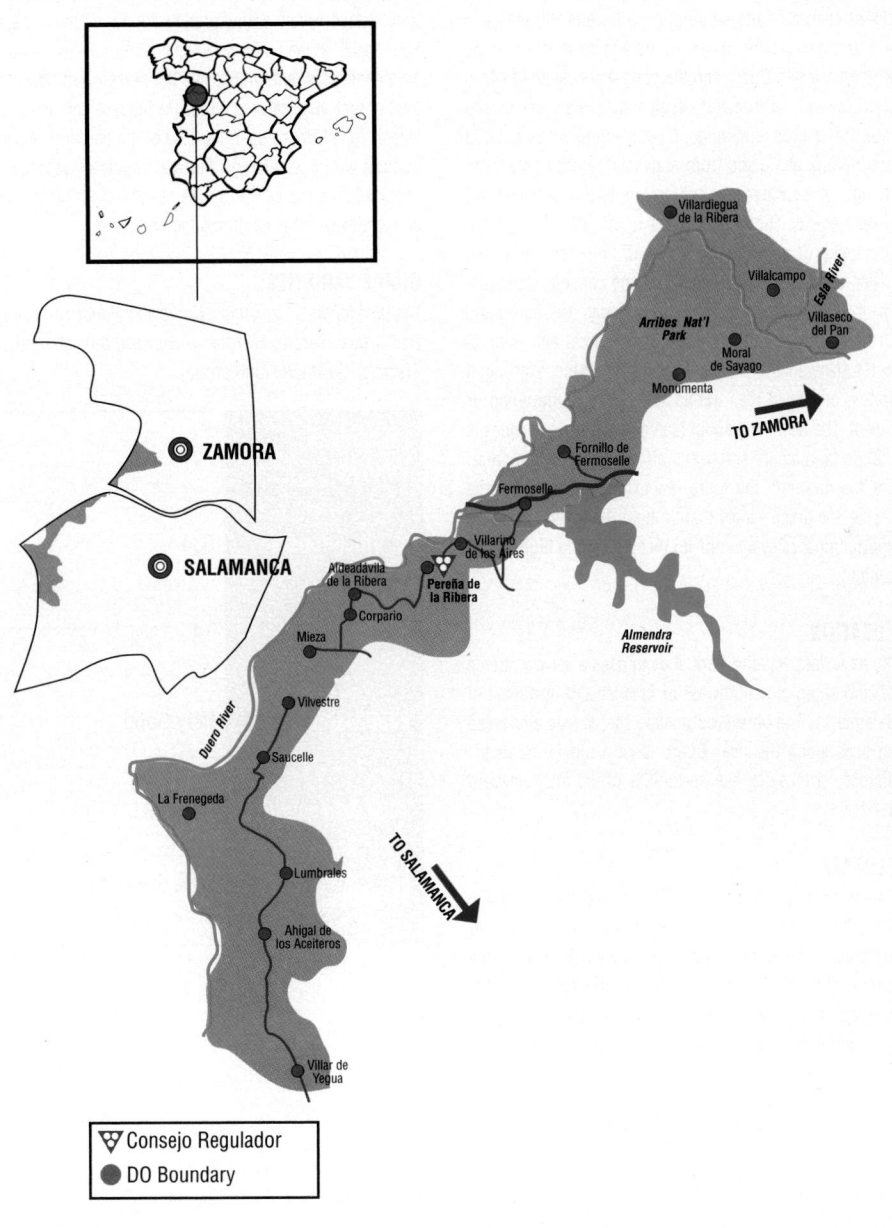

Villardiegua de la Ribera
Villalcampo
Esla River
Villaseco del Pan
Arribes Nat'l Park
Moral de Sayago
Monumenta

ZAMORA

Fornillo de Fermoselle
Fermoselle

SALAMANCA

Villarino de los Aires
Aldeadávila de la Ribera
Pereña de la Ribera
Corpario
Mieza

Almendra Reservoir

TO ZAMORA

Duero River

Vilvestre

Saucelle

La Frenegeda

TO SALAMANCA

Lumbrales

Ahigal de los Aceiteros

Villar de Yegua

▽ Consejo Regulador
● DO Boundary

## NEWS

This geographically diverse DO is coming up with wines full of character and singularity. Different altitudes and vineyard expositions, its wines are similar to those of the Portuguese Alto Douro and the powerfully coloured wines from Zamora. To assess the region adequately, we have to look at the aged renderings, for the young wines of 2008 are literally two made from malvasía; we can give faith, though, of their aromatic expression, unctuous palate and greater acidity. The flagship grape of the DO is juan garcía, previously used to make rosé and light reds and now giving shape to brilliant, powerful and concentrated reds, the likes of those from Terrazgo Bodegas de Crianza and Ocellum Durii, with even some rose petal and mineral notes. Nowadays, the best examples come from aged wines, blends of juan garcía and rufete, tempranillo or bruñal. The best thing about juan garcía for based wines is that its tannins are softer and afford an easier structure. For the moment, there are few examples of the scarce bruñal, the grape variety that brought Ribera de Pelazas to international relevance for its meatiness and high tannin content.

## LOCATION

In Las Arribes National Park, it comprises a narrow stretch of land along the southwest of Zamora and northeast of Salamanca. The vineyards occupy the valleys and steep terraces along the river Duero. Just a single municipal district, Fermoselle, has up to 90% of the total vineyard surface.

## CLIMATE

This wine region has a strong Mediterranean influence, given the prominent decrease in altitude that the territory features from the flat lands of the Sáyago area along the Duero valley until the river reaches Fermoselle, still in the province of Zamora. Rainfall is low all through the year, even during the averagely hot summer.

## SOIL

The region has shallow sandy soils with abundant quartz and stones, even some granite found in the area of Fermoselle. In the territory which is part of the province of Salamanca it is quite noticeable the presence of slate, the kind of rock also featured on the Portuguese part along the Duero, called Douro the other side of the border. The slate subsoil works a splendid thermal regulator capable of accumulating the heat from the sunshine during the day and to slowly release it during the night time.

## GRAPE VARIETIES:

**White:** *Malvasía, Verdejo, Albillo* and *Puesta en cruz.*
**Red:** *Juan García, Rufete, Tempranillo* (preferential); *Mencía, Garnacha* (authorized).

| | |
|---|---|
| Hectares of Vineyard | 750 |
| Nº Viticulturists | 634 |
| Nº of Bodegas | 14 |
| 2008 Harvest | Very Good |
| 2007 Production | 421,200 l. |
| Marketing | 90% domestic 10% export |

**CONSEJO REGULADOR.**
La Almofea, 95.
37175 Pereña de la Ribera (Salamanca)
☎: 923 573 413 - Fax: 923 573 209
@ info@doarribes.com
www.vinoarribesduero.com

## GENERAL CHARACTERISTICS OF THE WINES:

| WHITES | Very rare and made from *Malvasía*, they get all the benefits from sunshine and altitude as well as the mineral notes derived from the slate subsoil. |
|---|---|
| REDS | Wines made with *Juan García* or *Rufete* are lighter both in colour and body and oxidize easily, although they can show an eminently fruity character when the grapes get the appropriate sunshine hours or the blend with other grape varieties is also adequate. Nevertheless, proper vineyard management is achieving a smaller grape size and thus stronger colour for the final wines made from these two varieties. Also quite noticeable are the strong mineral nuances provided by the slate subsoil that renders these wines very similar to those from the Douro, the name that the river Duero gets once it has got over the Portuguese border. |

### 2008 VINTAGE RATING:

## VERY GOOD

# DO ARRIBES

## BODEGAS RIBERA DE PELAZAS

Camino de la Ermita
37175 Pereña de la Ribera (Salamanca)
☎: 902 108 031
bodega@bodegasriberadepelazas.com
www.bodegasriberadepelazas.com

**ABADENGO MALVASÍA 2008 B**
malvasia 100%

**87** Colour: bright straw. Nose: ripe fruit, scrubland. Palate: unctuous, fruity, fine bitter notes, mineral.

**ABADENGO JUAN GARCÍA 2007 T ROBLE**
juan garcía

**88** Colour: light cherry, garnet rim. Nose: medium intensity, earthy notes, spicy, expressive. Palate: balanced, fresh, good acidity.

**GRAN ABADENGO 2005 TR**
juan garcía 100%

**90** Colour: cherry, garnet rim. Nose: warm, balanced, floral, macerated fruit. Palate: balanced, flavourful, ripe fruit, great length, soft tannins, round tannins.

**ABADENGO 2005 TC**
juan garcía 100%

**87** Colour: cherry, garnet rim. Nose: medium intensity, varietal, fruit expression, undergrowth. Palate: flavourful, easy to drink, balanced.

**BRUÑAL 2004 TC**
bruñal 100%

**89** Colour: dark-red cherry, orangey edge. Nose: ripe fruit, creamy oak, aromatic coffee, sweet spices. Palate: round tannins, fruity, flavourful, good structure.

## HACIENDA MARQUÉS DE LA CONCORDIA

Ctra. El Ciego, s/n

26350 Cenicero (La Rioja)
☎: 914 365 900 - Fax: 914 365 932
iruiz@haciendas-espana.com
www.haciendas-espana.com

**HACIENDA ZORITA 2006 TC**
tempranillo 100%

**88** Colour: very deep cherry, garnet rim. Nose: fruit liqueur notes, sweet spices, new oak. Palate: powerful, full, fruity, good acidity, round tannins, great length.

**DURIUS MAGISTER 2005 T**
tempranillo 60%, merlot 13%, malbec 13%, cabernet sauvignon 13%

**90** Colour: cherry, garnet rim. Nose: spicy, aromatic coffee, dark chocolate, fruit liqueur notes. Palate: flavourful, warm, spicy, round tannins.

## LA SETERA

Calzada 7
49232 Fornillos de Fermoselle (Zamora)
☎: 980 612 925 - Fax: 980 612 925
lasetera@lasetera.com
www.lasetera.com

**LA SETERA MALVASIA 2008 B**
malvasia 100%

**86** Colour: straw. Nose: fresh fruit, fruit expression, fresh. Palate: fruity, fresh, fine bitter notes.

**LA SETERA SELECCIÓN ESPECIAL 2007 T**
touriga nacional 100%

**92** Colour: very deep cherry. Nose: balanced, fruit expression, ripe fruit, mineral, complex. Palate: flavourful, fresh fruit tannins.

**LA SETERA 2007 T**
juan garcía 100%

**86** Colour: cherry, garnet rim. Nose: fresh, medium intensity, red berry notes. Palate: fruity, flavourful, good structure, fleshy, round tannins.

**LA SETERA 2006 TC**
juan garcía 100%

**89** Colour: deep cherry. Nose: expressive, elegant, ripe fruit, pattiserie, sweet spices, cocoa bean. Palate: flavourful, round tannins, spirituous.

## OCELLUM DURII

Saun Juan 56 - 58
49220 Fermoselle (Zamora)

☎: 983 390 606 - Fax: 983 394 224
ocellumdurii@hotmail.com

CONDADO DE FERMOSEL 2007 T ROBLE

**84**

CONDADO DE FERMOSEL"TRANSITIUM DURII"
2006 T

**91** Colour: bright cherry, garnet rim. Nose: fruit expression, expressive, powerfull. Palate: flavourful, concentrated, fleshy, balsamic, round tannins.

CONDADO DE FERMOSEL"TRANSITIUM DURII"
2005 T
juan garcía 70%, tempranillo 30%

**91** Colour: bright cherry, garnet rim. Nose: ripe fruit, dark chocolate, spicy. Palate: flavourful, powerful, fruity, balsamic, great length.

## TERRAZGO BODEGAS DE CRIANZA S.L.

Portugal, 7
49232 Fornillos de Fermoselle (Zamora)
☎: 657 689 542
terrazgobc@yahoo.es
www.terrazgo.com

TERRAZGO 2006 T

**92** Colour: bright cherry. Nose: sweet spices, creamy oak, expressive, mineral, ripe fruit, red berry notes, scrubland. Palate: flavourful, fruity, toasty, round tannins. Personality.

SOME OTHER WINERIES WITHIN THE DO:

**BODEGA COOP. VIRGEN DE LA BANDERA
BODEGAS ARRIBES DE DUERO
BODEGAS LAS GAVIAS
COOPERATIVA SAN BARTOLOMÉ**

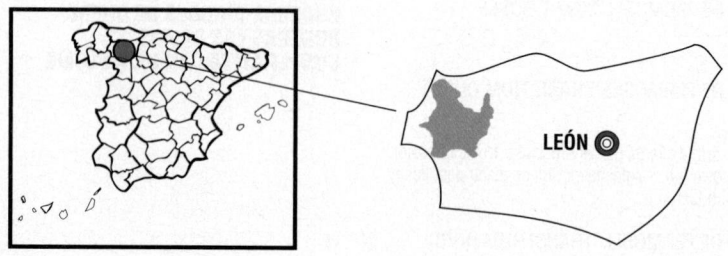

LEÓN ◉

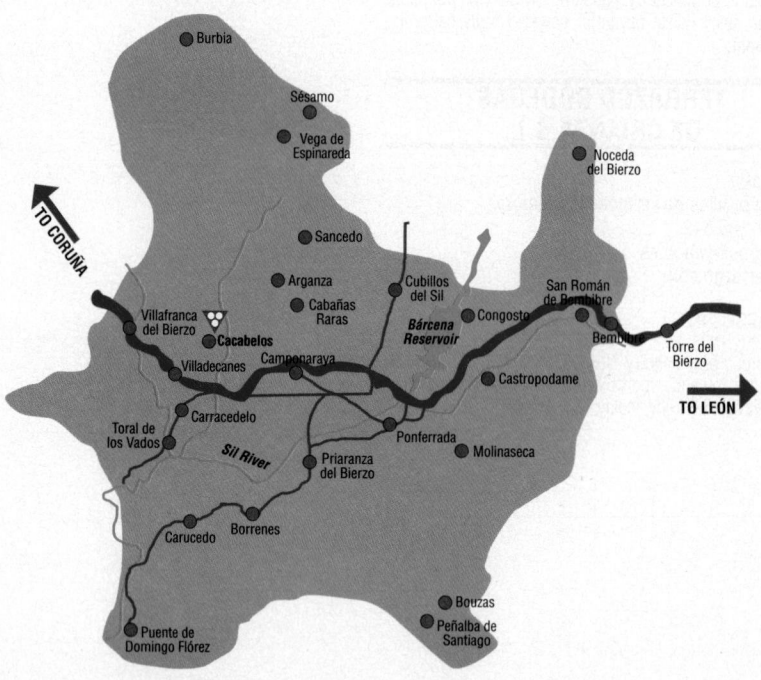

Burbia

Sésamo

Vega de Espinareda

Noceda del Bierzo

TO CORUÑA

Sancedo

Arganza

Cubillos del Sil

Cabañas Raras

San Román de Bembibre

Villafranca del Bierzo

Congosto

Bárcena Reservoir

Cacabelos

Bembibre

Villadecanes

Camponaraya

Torre del Bierzo

TO LEÓN

Carracedelo

Castropodame

Toral de los Vados

Ponferrada

Sil River

Molinaseca

Priaranza del Bierzo

Carucedo

Borrenes

Bouzas

Peñalba de Santiago

Puente de Domingo Flórez

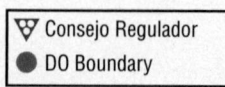

▽ Consejo Regulador
● DO Boundary

## NEWS

To enjoy Bierzo we have to separate the chaff from the grain, particularly between the latest vintages, or else to go for consolidated wines made by winemakers of repute. From the tasting of the 2008 wines we can tell the grapes mature fully, accounting for the concentrated fruit notes typical of modern Bierzo but to a certain extent foreign to mencía. It would have been enough to allow a proper maturation of the skin and leave it there, but there was an excess of confidence, the bunches were left in the vine, sugar levels went up and the acidity dwindled fast, so wines are sweeter –although alcohol levels are not particularly high– and lack freshness. Godello and rosé wines are nevertheless a good alternative.

Of the amazing 2007, the excellent expression of a well-ripe mencía remains intact, save some examples, which seem to have lost their fruit completely. The ratings are 2 to 3 points lower for the same wines one year after. The 2006 vintage shows a much better shape and wines of real stature, although with a rich, alcoholic edge –over 14,5%– and some splendid reserva and grand reserva renderings with an even better backbone. The expression of the mencía is still a little subdued, but the fruit notes are managing little by little to come on top of the oak ones. There are hardly no new wineries in the region, and the best ones –Raúl Pérez, Descendientes de J. Palacios, Dominio de Tares– keep coming up with singular wines based on microclimate, soil and varietal expression.

## LOCATION

In the north west of the province of León. It covers 23 municipal areas and occupies several valleys in mountainous terrain and a flat plain at a lower altitude than the plateau of León, with higher temperatures accompanied by more rainfall. It may be considered an area of transition between Galicia, León and Asturias.

## CLIMATE

Quite mild and benign, with a certain degree of humidity due to Galician influence, although somewhat dry like Castilla. Thanks to the low altitude, late frost is avoided quite successfully and the grapes are usually harvested one month before the rest of Castilla. The average rainfall per year is 721 mm.

## SOIL

In the mountain regions, it is made up of a mixture of fine elements, quartzite and slate. In general, the soil of the DO is humid, dun and slightly acidic. The greater quality indices are associated with the slightly sloped terraces close to the rivers, the half - terraced or steep slopes situated at an altitude of between 450 and 1,000 m.

## GRAPE VARIETIES:

**Red:** *Mencía* or *Negra* (65%), *Garnacha Tintorera* (5.5%), *Merlot, Cabernet Sauvignon, Tempranillo.*
**White:** *Doña Blanca* (10%), *Palomino* (15%), *Malvasía* (3%), *Godello* (1.5%).

| | |
|---|---|
| Hectares of Vineyard | 3,969 |
| Nº Viticulturists | 4,137 |
| Nº of Bodegas | 55 |
| 2008 Harvest | Very Good |
| 2007 Production | 9,620,100 l. |
| Marketing | 88.02% domestic 11.98% export |

# DO BIERZO

**CONSEJO REGULADOR.**
Los Morales, 1. Apdo. Correos 41.
24540 Cacabelos (León)
☎: 987 549 408 - Fax: 987 547 077
@ info@crdobierzo.es
@ comunicacion@crdobierzo.es
www.crdobierzo.es

## GENERAL CHARACTERISTICS OF THE WINES:

| | |
|---|---|
| **WHITES** | These are pale yellow, light, fresh and fruity, although not too defined. The ones with most character are those that contain the *Godello* variety. |
| **ROSÉS** | The colour can range from onion skin to pink tones; on the nose, strawberry and raspberry noses dominate, typical of the *Mencía* variety, which must make up at least 50% of the blend. In general, they are light and supple. |
| **REDS** | These are the most characteristic wines of the denomination. Those that most stand out are the young wines of normal vinification or produced using the carbonic maceration procedure. Sometimes there is a risk of a slightly low acidity due to the fast ripening of the *Mencía* in such a mild climate. They have an intense cherry colour with a brilliant violet edge and are fruity with a very robust nose (strawberries, blackberries) typical of the variety; on the palate they are dry, light and fruity with a great varietal character. Barrel - aged red wines are also produced. |

## 2008 VINTAGE RATING:

# AVERAGE

## AGRIBERGIDUM

Antigua Carretera N-VI, km. 403,5
24547 Pieros, Cacabelos (León)
☎: 987 546 279 - Fax: 987 548 026
vinos@agribergidum.es
www.agribergidum.es

CASTRO BERGIDUM GODELLO 2008 B

**84**

ENCOMIENDA TEMPLARIA GODELLO 2008 B

**82**

CASTRO BERGIDUM 2008 RD

**87** Colour: rose, purple rim. Nose: rose petals, raspberry. Palate: fruity, flavourful, fruity aftestaste, sweetness.

CASTRO BERGIDUM MENCÍA 2008 T
mencía

**88** Colour: very deep cherry, garnet rim. Nose: ripe fruit, varietal, expressive, earthy notes. Palate: full, good acidity, powerful, fruity.

ENCOMIENDA TEMPLARIA 2006 TC

**86** Colour: dark-red cherry. Nose: powerful, pattiserie, toasty, fruit preserve. Palate: fleshy, spirituous, slightly evolved, spicy, ripe fruit.

ENCOMIENDA TEMPLARIA 2002 TR

**88** Colour: dark-red cherry. Nose: elegant, medium intensity, fruit expression, fine reductive notes, aromatic coffee, creamy oak. Palate: elegant, round, smoky aftertaste, creamy.

## ARTURO GARCIA, VIÑEDOS Y BODEGAS

La Escuela, 3
24516 Perandones (León)
☎: 987 553 000 - Fax: 987 553 004
info@bodegarturo.com
www.bodegarturo.com

HACIENDA SAEL GODELLO 2008 B
godello 100%

**82**

HACIENDA SAEL MENCÍA 2008 T
mencía 100%

**88** Colour: cherry, purple rim. Nose: expressive, fresh fruit, red berry notes, floral, varietal, characterful. Palate: flavourful, fruity, good acidity, round tannins, powerful, good structure.

SOLAR DE SAEL 2006 T BARRICA
mencía 100%

**85** Colour: bright cherry. Nose: ripe fruit, sweet spices, creamy oak, expressive, candied fruit. Palate: flavourful, fruity, round tannins, spicy, sweetness.

SOLAR DE SAEL 2005 TC

**87** Colour: cherry, garnet rim. Nose: ripe fruit, spicy, creamy oak, toasty, short. Palate: powerful, flavourful, toasty, round tannins, balsamic, spicy.

SOLAR DE SAEL 2004 TR
mencía 100%

**81**

SOLAR DE SAEL 2003 TGR
mencía 100%

**84**

## BERNARDO ÁLVAREZ

San Pedro, 75
24430 Villadecanes (León)
☎: 987 562 129 - Fax: 987 562 129
migarron@bodegasbernardoalvarez.e.telefonica.net

CAMPO REDONDO GODELLO 2008 B
godello 100%

**82**

VIÑA MIGARRÓN 2008 RD
mencía 100%

**84**

VIÑA MIGARRÓN 2008 T
mencía 100%

**85** Colour: dark-red cherry. Nose: macerated fruit, varietal, powerfull. Palate: sweetness, powerful, flavourful, fruity.

CAMPO REDONDO 2006 T ROBLE
mencía 100%

**91** Colour: deep cherry. Nose: varietal, powerfull, complex, undergrowth, mineral, cocoa bean, cedar wood, fruit expression. Palate: elegant, round, fruity, flavourful.

VIÑA MIGARRÓN 2004 TC
mencía 100%

**83**

## BODEGA ANTONIO JOSÉ SILVA BROCO

Ctra. General, 4
24516 Parandones (León)
☎: 987 553 043

**LAGAR DE CAXÁN 2008 T**
mencía 100%

**86** Colour: deep cherry, garnet rim. Nose: ripe fruit, earthy notes, expressive. Palate: flavourful, varietal, powerful, unctuous.

**LAGAR DE CAXÁN 2007 T**
mencía 100%

**86** Colour: dark-red cherry. Nose: fresh, powerfull, fruit preserve. Palate: fruity, flavourful, spirituous.

## BODEGA CABILDO DE SALAS

Constantilla, 8
24414 Sala de los Barrios (León)
☎: 606 326 335
bodega@cabildodesalas.com
www.cabildodesalas.com

**CABILDO DE SALAS MENCÍA CENTENARIA 2007 T**
mencía 100%

**86** Colour: very deep cherry. Nose: creamy oak, aged wood nuances, ripe fruit. Palate: fleshy, spirituous, sweetness, powerful, flavourful.

**CABILDO DE SALAS 2007 T ROBLE**
mencía 100%

**85** Colour: very deep cherry. Nose: ripe fruit, fruit liqueur notes, sweet spices, roasted coffee. Palate: powerful, fleshy, fruity, creamy, ripe fruit.

## BODEGA DEL ABAD

Ctra. N-VI, km 396
24549 Carracedelo (León)
☎: 987 562 417 - Fax: 987 562 428
vinos@bodegadelabad.com
www.bodegadelabad.com

**ABAD DOM BUENO GODELLO 2008 B**
godello 100%

**83**

**GOTIN DEL RISC LÍAS 2007 B**
godello 100%

**91** Colour: bright straw. Nose: powerful, neat, ripe fruit, fresh, scrubland, grassy. Palate: flavourful, rich, fruity, fresh, fleshy.

**CARRACEDO 2006 T**
mencía 100%

**90** Colour: deep cherry. Nose: ripe fruit, sweet spices, creamy oak, expressive, aromatic coffee. Palate: flavourful, fruity, toasty, round tannins, powerful, spirituous, roasted-coffee aftertaste.

**GOTIN DEL RISC ESSENCIA 2006 T ROBLE**
mencía 100%

**90** Colour: deep cherry. Nose: cocoa bean, roasted coffee, fruit expression, ripe fruit, varietal. Palate: powerful, flavourful, fruity, ripe fruit, creamy.

**ABAD DOM BUENO 2006 T ROBLE**
mencía 100%

**87** Colour: very deep cherry. Nose: red berry notes, fruit liqueur notes, varietal, characterful, spicy, creamy oak. Palate: powerful, flavourful, spirituous, sweetness, toasty.

**GOTIN DE GOTIN T**
mencía 100%

**86** Colour: dark-red cherry, garnet rim. Nose: fruit liqueur notes, sweet spices, creamy oak, warm. Palate: full, rich, fruity, grainy tannins.

## BODEGA LA CAVA DEL BIERZO

Las Flores s/n
24530 Villafranca del Bierzo (León)
☎: 987 562 156 - Fax: 987 562 156

**VAL TODIL 2008 T MACERACIÓN CARBÓNICA**
mencía

**88** Colour: deep cherry. Nose: powerful, varietal, ripe fruit, toasty. Palate: powerful, flavourful, fruity, fleshy.

**VAL TODIL 2008 T**
mencía

**86** Colour: dark-red cherry. Nose: ripe fruit, varietal, powerfull, toasty, balsamic herbs. Palate: fresh, fruity, flavourful.

## BODEGA LUZDIVINA AMIGO

Ctra. Villafranca, 10
24516 Parandones (León)
☎: 987 544 826 - Fax: 987 544 826
info@bodegaluz.com
www.bodegaluz.com

VIÑADEMOYA 2007 T
mencía 100%

## 84

BALOIRO 2006 TC
mencía 100%

**92** Colour: deep cherry. Nose: powerful, varietal, complex, fruit liqueur notes, ripe fruit, creamy oak, aromatic coffee.

VIÑADEMOYA LEIROS 2006 T
mencía 100%

**88** Colour: very deep cherry. Nose: ripe fruit, sweet spices, creamy oak, expressive. Palate: flavourful, fruity, round tannins, roasted-coffee aftertaste, warm.

### BODEGA MARTÍNEZ YEBRA

San Pedro, 96
24530 Villadecanes (León)
☎: 987 562 082 - Fax: 987 562 082
info@bodegamartinezyebra.es
www.bodegamartinezyebra.es

CANES 2008 T

**86** Colour: dark-red cherry. Nose: powerful, varietal, maceration notes, ripe fruit. Palate: round tannins, powerful, flavourful, fruity, fleshy.

VIÑADECANES TRES RACIMOS 2005 T
mencía 100%

**86** Colour: deep cherry. Nose: creamy oak, cocoa bean, ripe fruit. Palate: spirituous, powerful, flavourful, toasty.

VIÑADECANES 2004 T
mencía 100%

**88** Colour: cherry, garnet rim. Nose: ripe fruit, aromatic coffee, creamy oak. Palate: powerful, fleshy, spirituous.

### BODEGA Y VIÑEDOS LUNA BEBERIDE

Ctra. Madrid-Coruña, km. 402
24540 Cacabelos (León)
☎: 987 549 002 - Fax: 987 549 214
info@lunabeberide.es
www.lunabeberide.es

LB LUNA BEBERIDE B

## 83

MENCÍA LUNA BEBERIDE T
mencía

**90** Colour: dark-red cherry, garnet rim. Nose: fresh fruit, elegant, expressive. Palate: unctuous, fruity, good structure, good finish, good acidity.

### BODEGAS ADRIÁ S.L.

Antigua Ctra. Madrid - Coruña, km. 408
24500 Villafranca del Bierzo (León)
☎: 987 540 907 - Fax: 987 540 347
info@bodegasadria.com
www.bodegasdria.com

VEGA MONTÁN GODELLO 2008 B
godello 100%

## 78

VEGA MONTÁN 2008 B
dona blanca 90%, godello 10%

## 76

VEGA MONTÁN 2008 RD
mencía 100%

## 79

VEGA MONTÁN 2008 T
mencía 100%

**87** Colour: deep cherry, garnet rim. Nose: ripe fruit, floral. Palate: rich, fresh, spicy.

VEGA MONTÁN 2007 T ROBLE
mencía 100%

**86** Colour: dark-red cherry, garnet rim. Nose: ripe fruit, aged wood nuances, sweet spices, new oak, balanced. Palate: fruity, good acidity, roasted-coffee aftertaste.

VEGA MONTÁN "ECLIPSE" 2005 T
mencía 100%

**90** Colour: deep cherry. Nose: ripe fruit, sweet spices, expressive, cocoa bean, undergrowth. Palate: flavourful, fruity, toasty, powerful, slightly dry, soft tannins.

### BODEGAS EL LINZE

Duque de Liria, 9
28015 (Madrid)
☎: 636 161 479
info@ellinze.com
www.ellinze.com

MARTA CIBELINA 2007 T
mencía 100%

**88** Colour: cherry, garnet rim. Nose: powerful, balsamic herbs, scrubland, toasty, fresh fruit. Palate: flavourful, varietal, mineral, slightly acidic.

## BODEGAS OTERO SANTÍN

Ortega y Gasset, 10
24400 Ponferrada (León)
☎: 987 410 101 - Fax: 987 418 544

OTERO SANTÍN B JOVEN

**87** Nose: ripe fruit, tropical fruit, expressive, mineral. Palate: light-bodied, fruity, good acidity.

OTERO SANTÍN RD JOVEN

**85** Colour: rose, purple rim. Nose: fresh fruit, violet drops, neat. Palate: light-bodied, fruity, fine bitter notes, correct.

VALDECAMPO
COMPLUDO

## BODEGAS PEIQUE

El Bierzo s/n
24530 Valtuille de Abajo (León)
☎: 987 562 044 - Fax: 987 562 044
bodega@bodegaspeique.com
www.bodegaspeique.com

PEIQUE TINTO MENCÍA 2008 T
mencía 100%

**87** Colour: very deep cherry, purple rim. Nose: varietal, ripe fruit, expressive, floral. Palate: rich, fruity, good acidity, grainy tannins, powerful.

PEIQUE VIÑEDOS VIEJOS 2006 T ROBLE
mencía 100%

**92** Colour: deep cherry. Nose: aromatic coffee, creamy oak, mineral, fresh fruit, violet drops. Palate: powerful, flavourful, varietal, fruity, spirituous, toasty, fruity aftestaste.

PEIQUE SELECCIÓN FAMILIAR 2005 T
mencía 100%

**92** Colour: cherry, garnet rim. Nose: ripe fruit, spicy, creamy oak, toasty, complex. Palate: powerful, flavourful, toasty, round tannins, ripe fruit, roasted-coffee aftertaste.

## BODEGAS VALD'URIA

Travieso, 10
24550 Villamartín de la Abadía (León)

☎: 987 547 027 - Fax: 987 547 027
mitiba21@hotmail.com

VAL D'URIA 2007 T
mencia 100%

**88** Colour: very deep cherry. Nose: varietal, aged wood nuances, caramel. Palate: spirituous, good structure, fruity, sweetness.

## BODEGAS Y VIÑEDO MENGOBA

San Francisco, E
24416 Santo Tomás de las Ollas (León)
☎: 649 940 800
gregory@mengoba.com
www.mengoba.com

MENGOBA SOBRE LÍAS 2008 B
godello , dona blanca

**91** Colour: straw. Nose: scrubland, undergrowth, fruit expression, characterful, varietal, creamy oak, smoky. Palate: complex, fruity, good acidity, fine bitter notes.

MENGOBA MENCÍA DE ESPANILLO 2008 T

**90** Colour: very deep cherry. Nose: expressive, fresh fruit, red berry notes, floral, balsamic herbs. Palate: flavourful, fruity, good acidity, round tannins, toasty, roasted-coffee aftertaste, varietal.

## BODEGAS Y VIÑEDOS CANTALOBOS

Avda. de Galicia, 5
24540 Cacabelos (León)
☎: 987 548 079
vinos@cantalobos.es
www.cantalobos.es

CANTALOBOS S.C. T

**83**

CANTALOBOS 2003 TC

**87** Colour: dark-red cherry. Nose: ripe fruit, fruit liqueur notes, powerfull, creamy oak, sweet spices. Palate: flavourful, ripe fruit, creamy, sweet tannins.

## BODEGAS Y VIÑEDOS CASTRO VENTOSA

Finca El Barredo, s/n
24530 Valtuille de Abajo (León)
☎: 987 562 148 - Fax: 987 562 191

castroventosa@telefonica.net
www.castroventosa.com

## CASTRO VENTOSA 2008 T
mencía

**89** Colour: very deep cherry, garnet rim. Nose: ripe fruit, varietal, expressive, mineral. Palate: fruity, complex, balanced.

## EL CASTRO DE VALTUILLE JOVEN 2007 T

**89** Colour: cherry, garnet rim. Nose: elegant, ripe fruit, spicy, scrubland. Palate: flavourful, fleshy, spicy, round tannins.

## CASTRO VENTOSA"VINTAGE" 2006 T
mencía

**90** Colour: bright cherry. Nose: ripe fruit, sweet spices, creamy oak, expressive. Palate: flavourful, fruity, toasty, round tannins.

## VALTUILLE CEPAS CENTENARIAS 2005 T ROBLE

**93** Colour: dark-red cherry. Nose: varietal, powerfull, complex, scrubland, creamy oak, cocoa bean, fruit expression. Palate: powerful, flavourful, fruity, mineral, toasty.

## EL CASTRO DE VALTUILLE 2005 T

**90** Colour: deep cherry. Nose: sweet spices, creamy oak, expressive, fruit liqueur notes. Palate: flavourful, fruity, toasty, round tannins, spicy, creamy.

## CASTRO VENTOSA"VINTAGE" 2005 T

**89** Colour: dark-red cherry. Nose: spicy, creamy oak, ripe fruit. Palate: powerful, fleshy, sweetness, spirituous.

## BODEGAS Y VIÑEDOS GANCEDO

Parcela 467, Pol. 6 c/Vistalegre
24548 Quilós (León)
☎: 987 134 980 - Fax: 987 563 278
info@bodegasgancedo.com
www.bodegasgancedo.com

## VAL DE PAXARIÑAS "CAPRICHO" 2008 B
godello 80%, dona blanca 20%

**87** Colour: straw. Nose: earthy notes, fresh fruit, closed, characterful, varietal. Palate: sweetness, rich, fruity, flavourful.

## HERENCIA DEL CAPRICHO 2007 BFB
godello 80%, dona blanca 20%

**93** Colour: golden. Nose: smoky, creamy oak, fragrant herbs, undergrowth, mineral. Palate: powerful, flavourful, rich, complex, creamy, mineral, smoky aftertaste.

## XESTAL 2006 T
mencía

**91** Colour: bright cherry. Nose: ripe fruit, sweet spices, creamy oak, expressive. Palate: flavourful, fruity, toasty, round tannins, fruity aftestaste.

UCEDO

## BODEGAS Y VIÑEDOS HIJOS DE LISARDO GARCÍA

Ctra. Parandones - Horta, 32
24516 Parandones - Toral de los Vados (León)
☎: 987 544 009 - Fax: 987 544 034
comercial@vinosmiranda.com
www.vinosmiranda.com

VIÑA MIRANDA B

**84**

VIÑA MIRANDA 2007 T

**81**

SEÑORÍO DE PARANDONES T

**86** Colour: light cherry. Nose: fresh, powerfull, varietal, ripe fruit. Palate: fresh, fruity, flavourful.

## BODEGAS Y VIÑEDOS PAIXAR

Ribadeo, 56
24500 Villafranca del Bierzo (León)
☎: 987 549 002 - Fax: 987 549 214

PAIXAR MENCÍA 2006 T

**91** Colour: deep cherry. Nose: powerful, warm, expressive, fruit expression, ripe fruit, undergrowth, creamy oak, dark chocolate. Palate: spirituous, powerful, flavourful, roasted-coffee aftertaste, spicy.

## CASAR DE BURBIA

Traversía la Constitución s/n
24549 Carracedelo (León)
☎: 987 562 910 - Fax: 987 562 850
info@casardeburbia.com
www.casardeburbia.com

TEBAIDA 2007 T

**92** Colour: bright cherry. Nose: ripe fruit, sweet spices, creamy oak, expressive, toasty. Palate: flavourful, fruity, toasty, round tannins.

CASAR DE BURBIA 2007 T

**90** Colour: cherry, garnet rim. Nose: ripe fruit, spicy, creamy oak, roasted coffee. Palate: powerful, flavourful, toasty, round tannins.

LIARAN 2007 T

**90** Colour: cherry, purple rim. Nose: expressive, red berry notes, dark chocolate, toasty. Palate: flavourful, fruity, good acidity, round tannins.

HOMBROS 2006 T

**93** Colour: bright cherry. Nose: sweet spices, creamy oak, red berry notes, lactic notes. Palate: flavourful, fruity, toasty, round tannins.

## CEPAS DEL BIERZO

Ctra. de Sanabria, 111
24400 Ponferrada (León)
☎: 987 412 333 - Fax: 987 412 912
coocebier@coocebier.e.telefonica.net

DON OSMUNDO 2006 T ROBLE

**83**

ESCARIL
FANEIRO

## COBERTIZO DE VIÑARAMIRO

San Pelayo, 2
24530 Valtuille de Abajo (León)
☎: 987 562 157 - Fax: 987 562 157

COBERTIZO 2008 T
mencía

**86** Colour: deep cherry, garnet rim. Nose: ripe fruit, varietal, expressive. Palate: flavourful, fruity, concentrated.

COBERTIZO 2005 T
mencía

**88** Colour: deep cherry. Nose: aromatic coffee, cedar wood, creamy oak, fruit liqueur notes, ripe fruit. Palate: spirituous, warm, powerful, flavourful, fruity.

## COOPERATIVA COMARCAL VINÍCOLA DEL BIERZO

Ctra. Columbrianos a Ocero s/n
24412 Cabañas Raras (León)
☎: 987 421 755 - Fax: 987 421 755
vinicolabierzo@hotmail.com

CABAÑAS ORO 2008 B
dona blanca 50%, palomino 50%

**77**

CABAÑAS ORO S.C. TC
mencía 100%

**84**

CABAÑAS ORO S.C. T ROBLE

**82**

CABAÑAS ORO 2008 T
mencía 100%

**73**

CABAÑAS ORO 2000 TR
mencía 100%

**85** Colour: pale ruby, brick rim edge. Nose: spicy, fine reductive notes, fruit liqueur notes, cedar wood. Palate: spicy, fine tannins, long, round.

## DESCENDIENTES DE J. PALACIOS

Avda. Calvo Sotelo, 6
24500 Villafranca del Bierzo (León)
☎: 987 540 821 - Fax: 987 540 851
info@djpalacios.com

PÉTALOS DEL BIERZO 2007 T

**93** Colour: bright cherry. Nose: sweet spices, creamy oak, expressive, fresh fruit, red berry notes. Palate: fruity, toasty, round tannins, powerful, varietal.

VILLA DE CORULLÓN 2006 T

**95** Colour: bright cherry. Nose: ripe fruit, creamy oak, expressive, fragrant herbs. Palate: flavourful, fruity, toasty, round tannins, powerful, varietal, complex.

LAS LAMAS 2006 T

**94** Colour: cherry, garnet rim. Nose: expressive, elegant, fragrant herbs, balsamic herbs, floral, ripe fruit, red berry notes. Palate: flavourful, fruity, fleshy, spicy, round tannins.

## ESTEFANIA

Ctra. Dehesas - Posada, s/n
24390 Ponferrada (León)
☎: 987 420 015 - Fax: 987 420 015
info@tilenus.com
www.tilenus.com

## TILENUS 2008 T
mencía 100%

**80**

## TILENUS ENVEJECIDO EN ROBLE 2006 T ROBLE
mencía 100%

**88** Colour: garnet rim. Nose: creamy oak, cocoa bean, fruit expression, varietal. Palate: flavourful, fruity, toasty, roasted-coffee aftertaste.

## TILENUS 2005 TC
mencía 100%

**90** Colour: dark-red cherry. Nose: creamy oak, smoky, fruit liqueur notes, fruit expression. Palate: powerful, flavourful, fruity, spirituous, sweetness, round tannins.

## TILENUS 2004 TC
mencía

**89** Colour: bright cherry, bright ochre rim. Nose: fruit preserve, elegant, balanced, sweet spices, cocoa bean. Palate: light-bodied, fruity, round tannins, balanced.

## TILENUS PAGOS DE POSADA 2003 TR
mencía 100%

**89** Colour: dark-red cherry. Nose: spicy, creamy oak, fruit preserve, fruit liqueur notes. Palate: powerful, flavourful, sweetness, spirituous.

## TILENUS PIEROS 2002 T
mencía 100%

**91** Colour: deep cherry. Nose: complex, elegant, fine reductive notes, tobacco, fruit expression, cocoa bean. Palate: round, good acidity, elegant, fruity, flavourful, soft tannins.

## LA SERRANA S.L.

Los Pinares, 69
24530 Villadecanes (León)
☎: 699 447 611 - Fax: 987 463 167

bodegalaserrana@yahoo.es

## LEGUS 2007 T JOVEN
mencía 100%

**87** Colour: deep cherry. Nose: fresh, powerfull, varietal. Palate: fruity, flavourful, fleshy.

## UTTARIS 2007 T JOVEN
mencía 100%

**84**

## UTTARIS 2004 TC

**88** Colour: dark-red cherry. Nose: varietal, powerfull, macerated fruit, aromatic coffee, creamy oak. Palate: balsamic, flavourful, fruity.

## LEGUS TC

**84**

MONCLOA DE SAN LÁZARO

## LOSADA, VINOS DE FINCA

Ctra. Villafranca LE-713, km. 12
24540 Cacabelos (León)
☎: 988 337 900 - Fax: 988 337 901
losada@losadavinosdefinca.com
www.losadavinosdefinca.com

## LOSADA 2007 T
mencía

**89** Colour: deep cherry. Nose: toasty, spicy, new oak, macerated fruit. Palate: flavourful, powerful, complex, spirituous, roasted-coffee aftertaste, toasty.

## ALTOS DE LOSADA 2006 T
mencía

**92** Colour: very deep cherry. Nose: toasty, sweet spices, undergrowth, mineral, fresh fruit, fruit expression, powerfull, varietal, complex. Palate: spirituous, powerful, flavourful, sweetness.

## MARTÍN CÓDAX S.A.U.

Burgans, 91
36663 Vilariño-Cambados (Pontevedra)
☎: 986 526 040 - Fax: 986 526 901
comercial@martincodax.com
www.martincodax.com

## CUATRO PASOS 2008 RD
mencía 100%

**87** Colour: rose, purple rim. Nose: ripe fruit, varietal. Palate: fruity, flavourful, powerful, round.

**CUATRO PASOS 2007 T ROBLE**
mencía 100%

**88** Colour: very deep cherry. Nose: ripe fruit, sweet spices, creamy oak, expressive, damp earth, mineral. Palate: flavourful, toasty, round tannins, good structure, powerful.

**MARTÍN SARMIENTO 2005 T**
mencía 100%

**90** Colour: very deep cherry. Nose: powerful, warm, fruit preserve, fruit liqueur notes, roasted coffee. Palate: flavourful, powerful, spirituous, spicy, toasty.

## MENCIAS DE DOS S.L.

Bernal Díaz del Castillo, 1- 2
47400 Medina del Campo (Valladolid)
☎: 983 103 223 - Fax: 983 816 561
alejandra@sitiosdebodega.com
www.sitiosdebodega.com

**AMBOS MENCÍA 2008 T**
mencía 100%

**88** Colour: very deep cherry, garnet rim. Nose: ripe fruit, balanced, creamy oak, sweet spices. Palate: flavourful, fruity, good acidity, fine bitter notes.

**DE 2 2008 T**
mencía 100%

**88** Colour: very deep cherry, garnet rim. Nose: ripe fruit, powerfull, varietal, earthy notes, roasted coffee. Palate: full, flavourful, fruity, creamy.

**AMBOS MENCÍA 2005 T ROBLE**
mencía 100%

**89** Colour: very deep cherry. Nose: aromatic coffee, sweet spices, fruit liqueur notes, fruit liqueur notes. Palate: powerful, flavourful, sweetness, roasted-coffee aftertaste, toasty.

## PÉREZ CARAMÉS S.A.

Peña Picón, s/n
24500 Villafranca del Bierzo (León)
☎: 987 540 197 - Fax: 987 540 314
info@perezcarames.com
www.perezcarames.com

**CASAR DE VALDAIGA 2007 T**
mencía

**78**

## PRADA A TOPE

La Iglesia, s/n
24546 Canedo (León)
☎: 902 400 101 - Fax: 987 567 000
info@pradaatope.es
www.pradaatope.es

**PALACIO DE CANEDO 2008 B**
godello 100%

**84**

**PALACIO DE CANEDO 2008 RD**
mencía 75%, godello 25%

**84**

**PALACIO DE CANEDO 2008 T MACERACIÓN CARBÓNICA**
mencía 100%

**86** Colour: very deep cherry, garnet rim. Nose: ripe fruit, floral, expressive. Palate: flavourful, fruity, easy to drink.

**PALACIO DE CANEDO MENCÍA 2007 T**
mencía 100%

**87** Colour: deep cherry. Nose: toasty, dark chocolate, ripe fruit. Palate: powerful, flavourful, good structure, sweetness, varietal, toasty, fruity.

**PRADA A TOPE 2006 T BARRICA**
mencía 100%

**90** Colour: deep cherry. Nose: fruit expression, fresh fruit, aromatic coffee, creamy oak. Palate: powerful, full, flavourful, complex, toasty, fruity aftestaste.

**PALACIO DE CANEDO 2004 TC**
mencía 100%

**89** Colour: cherry, garnet rim. Nose: fresh, varietal, complex. Palate: powerful, flavourful, fruity, complex, creamy, fruity aftestaste.

**PRADA A TOPE 2002 TR**
mencía 100%

**87** Colour: pale ruby, brick rim edge. Nose: spicy, fine reductive notes, aged wood nuances, fruit liqueur notes, cigar. Palate: spicy, fine tannins, elegant.

## RAUL PÉREZ BODEGAS Y VIÑEDOS

Bulevar Rey Juan Carlos 1º Rey de España, 11 B
24400 Ponferrada (León)
raulperez@raulperezbodegas.es
www.raulperezbodegas.es

## ULTREIA "DE VALTUILLE" 2007 T
mencía 100%

**95** Colour: dark-red cherry, garnet rim. Nose: faded flowers, fresh fruit, damp earth, aromatic coffee, cedar wood, creamy oak. Palate: powerful, flavourful, fruity, fresh, complex, smoky aftertaste, toasty, soft tannins.

## RIBAS DEL CUA

Finca Robledo, Aptdo. de Correo 83
24540 Cacabelos (León)
☎: 987 971 018 - Fax: 987 971 016
bodega@ribasdelcua.com
www.ribasdelcua.com

RIBAS DEL CÚA PRIVILEGIO 2006 T

**89** Colour: cherry, garnet rim. Nose: ripe fruit, spicy, creamy oak, toasty, complex, medium intensity, dry stone. Palate: powerful, flavourful, toasty, round tannins, spirituous, complex.

## SOTO DEL VICARIO

Ctra. Cacabelos San Clemente, Pol. 908 Parcela 155
24547 San Clemente (León)
☎: 670 983 534 - Fax: 926 666 029
sandra.luque@pagodelvicario.com
www.sotodelvicario.com

SOTO DEL VICARIO GO DE GODELLO 2008 B
godello 100%

**91** Colour: bright yellow. Nose: ripe fruit, sweet spices, fragrant herbs. Palate: flavourful, rich, good acidity, unctuous.

SOTO DEL VICARIO MEN SELECCIÓN 2007 T
mencía 100%

**90** Colour: dark-red cherry, garnet rim. Nose: ripe fruit, elegant, floral, sweet spices, creamy oak, cocoa bean. Palate: fruity, long, spicy, round tannins.

SOTO DEL VICARIO MEN DE MENCÍA 2006 T
mencía 100%

**91** Colour: bright cherry, garnet rim. Nose: ripe fruit, aromatic coffee, cocoa bean, mineral. Palate: good structure, creamy, round tannins, elegant.

## TENOIRA GAYOSO, S.A.T.

Doctor Aren, 8
24500 Villafranca del Bierzo (León)
☎: 699 950 747 - Fax: 987 540 307
info@tenoiragayoso.com
www.tenoiragayoso.com

TENOIRA 2008 T
mencía 100%

**85** Colour: very deep cherry, garnet rim. Nose: fresh fruit, floral, varietal. Palate: fruity, good acidity, powerful.

## VALSANZO

Manuel Azaña, 9
Edificio Ambassador, Local 15
47014 (Valladolid)
☎: 983 150 150 - Fax: 983 150 151
valsanzo@valsanzo.com
www.valsanzo.com

TERRAS CÚA 2005 TC
mencía 100%

**88** Colour: cherry, garnet rim. Nose: fruit liqueur notes, macerated fruit, cocoa bean, creamy oak. Palate: spirituous, powerful, flavourful, spirituous, sweetness.

## VINOLE WINES, S.L.

Ignacio Serrano 167
47008 (Valladolid)
☎: 610 540 250 - Fax: 983 246 385
info@vinolewines.com
www.vinolewines.com

LA BUENA SUERTE 2006 T
mencía

**89** Colour: cherry, garnet rim. Nose: ripe fruit, spicy, creamy oak, toasty, complex, macerated fruit, sweet spices. Palate: powerful, flavourful, toasty, round tannins, spirituous.

## VINOS DE ARGANZA

Río Ancares, 2
24560 Toral de los Vados (León)

# DO BIERZO

☎: 987 544 831 - Fax: 987 563 532
admon@vinosdearganza.com
www.vinosdearganza.com

**FLAVIUM 2008 T**
mencía

**86** Colour: very deep cherry, garnet rim. Nose: fresh fruit, floral, varietal. Palate: unctuous, fruity, grainy tannins, flavourful.

**SÉCULO 2008 T**
mencía

**85** Colour: dark-red cherry, garnet rim. Nose: ripe fruit, varietal, balanced. Palate: full, fruity, varietal, correct, fine bitter notes.

**ENSUEÑO 2008 T**
mencía

**79**

**FLAVIUM 2006 TC**
mencía

**90** Colour: garnet rim. Nose: varietal, fresh, expressive, mineral, cocoa bean, spicy. Palate: powerful, flavourful, fruity, fresh, mineral, fruity aftestaste, toasty.

**SÉCULO 2006 TC**
mencía

**85** Colour: dark-red cherry. Nose: creamy oak, sweet spices, fruit expression, ripe fruit. Palate: powerful, flavourful, toasty, slightly dry, soft tannins.

**FLAVIUM 2004 TR**
mencía

**85** Colour: dark-red cherry. Nose: roasted coffee, ripe fruit. Palate: powerful, flavourful, fleshy, ripe fruit, roasted-coffee aftertaste.

**SÉCULO 2003 TR**
mencía

**86** Colour: dark-red cherry. Nose: medium intensity, complex, varietal, aromatic coffee, creamy oak. Palate: round, balanced, flavourful, soft tannins.

## VINOS DEL BIERZO S. COOP.

Avda. Constitución, 106
24540 Cacabelos (León)
☎: 987 546 150 - Fax: 987 549 236
info@vinosdelbierzo.com
www.vinosdelbierzo.com

**VINICIO GODELLO 2008 B**
godello 100%

**83**

**VIÑA ORO 2008 B**
dona blanca 100%

**79**

**VIÑA ORO 2008 RD**
mencía 100%

**78**

**VINICIO S.C. T**
mencía 100%

**78**

**VIÑA ORO 2007 T**
mencía 100%

**86** Colour: deep cherry. Nose: varietal, complex, fresh, ripe fruit, creamy oak. Palate: fruity, fresh, green.

**CARRALERO 2007 T**
mencía 100%

**79**

**GUERRA SELECCIÓN 2007 T**
mencía 100%

**75**

**GUERRA 2006 T**
mencía 100%

**82**

**GUERRA 2003 TC**
mencía 100%

**85** Colour: dark-red cherry. Nose: medium intensity, short, closed, ripe fruit. Palate: correct, flavourful, fruity, soft tannins.

**VINICIO 2001 TR**
mencía 100%

**88** Colour: pale ruby, brick rim edge. Nose: elegant, spicy, fine reductive notes, aged wood nuances, fruit liqueur notes. Palate: spicy, fine tannins, elegant, long.

**SEÑORÍO DEL BIERZO 2001 TR**
mencía 100%

**86** Colour: pale ruby, brick rim edge. Nose: complex, old leather, fine reductive notes, ripe fruit, fruit expression, cocoa bean. Palate: slightly acidic, round, soft tannins.

## VINOS VALTUILLE S.L.

La Fragua, s/n
24530 Valtuille de Abajo (León)
☎: 679 491 428 - Fax: 987 549 425
pagodevaldoneje@yahoo.es

PAGO DE VALDONEJE 2008 T

**87** Colour: very deep cherry. Nose: macerated fruit, maceration notes, ripe fruit. Palate: fleshy, good structure, powerful, flavourful, fruity aftestaste, fruity, sweetness.

PAGO DE VALDONEJE "VIÑAS VIEJAS" 2006 T

**90** Colour: deep cherry. Nose: ripe fruit, sweet spices, creamy oak, expressive. Palate: flavourful, toasty, round tannins, creamy, ripe fruit, mineral, roasted-coffee aftertaste.

## VIÑA ALBARES

Camino Real s/n
24310 Albares de la Ribera (León)
☎: 987 233 768 - Fax: 987 220 034
info@vinaalbares.com
www.vinaalbares.com

TIERRAS DE ALBARES 2007 T JOVEN
mencía 100%

**72**

## VIÑAS DEL BIERZO

Ctra. Ponferrada a Cacabelos s/n
24410 Camponaraya (León)
☎: 987 463 009 - Fax: 987 450 323
vdelbierzo@granbierzo.com
www.granbierzo.com

MARQUÉS DE CORNATEL 2008 B
godello 100%

**83**

NARAYA 2008 B
dona blanca 80%, malvasia 20%

**77**

VALMAGAZ 2008 B
godello 70%, malvasia 30%

**77**

VIÑABIER 2008 B
dona blanca 60%, godello 40%

**65**

MARQUÉS DE CORNATEL 2008 RD
mencía 100%

**86** Colour: rose. Nose: violet drops, raspberry, fresh fruit. Palate: fresh, fruity, flavourful, varietal.

VALMAGAZ 2008 RD

**80**

VIÑABIER 2008 RD
mencía 100%

**80**

NARAYA 2008 RD

**78**

MARQUÉS DE CORNATEL 2008 T ROBLE
mencía 100%

**86** Colour: deep cherry, garnet rim. Nose: ripe fruit, toasty, aged wood nuances, aromatic coffee, balanced. Palate: light-bodied, good acidity, toasty, fruity.

VALMAGAZ MENCÍA 2008 T
mencía 100%

**84**

NARAYA 2008 T
mencía 100%

**83**

VIÑABIER 2008 T
mencía 100%

**80**

GRAN BIERZO 2004 TC
mencía 100%

**82**

GRAN BIERZO 2003 TR
mencía 100%

**87** Colour: bright cherry. Nose: medium intensity, neat, closed, ripe fruit, aromatic coffee, creamy oak. Palate: round, good acidity, fruity, flavourful, soft tannins.

FUNDACION 1963 2000 TR
mencía 100%

**84**

## VIÑEDOS Y BODEGAS DOMINIO DE TARES

Los Barredos, 4 Polígono Bierzo Alto
24318 San Román de Bembibre (León)
☎: 987 514 550 - Fax: 987 514 570
info@dominiodetares.com
www.dominiodetares.com

DOMINIO DE TARES GODELLO 2008 B
godello 100%

**90** Colour: bright yellow. Nose: powerful, ripe fruit, sweet spices, creamy oak, fragrant herbs. Palate: rich, smoky aftertaste, flavourful, fresh, good acidity.

ARREBATO RD CRIANZA
mencía

**89** Colour: rose, purple rim. Nose: fresh fruit, varietal, expressive. Palate: light-bodied, fruity, good acidity, good structure.

DOMINIO DE TARES BALTOS 2007 T
mencía 100%

**89** Colour: black cherry, garnet rim. Nose: ripe fruit, creamy oak, sweet spices, balanced, floral. Palate: flavourful, round, roasted-coffee aftertaste.

TARES P. 3 2005 T ROBLE
mencía 100%

**92** Colour: very deep cherry. Nose: powerful, complex, damp earth, roasted coffee, cocoa bean, fruit expression. Palate: powerful, spirituous, fleshy, creamy, ripe fruit, round tannins.

DOMINIO DE TARES CEPAS VIEJAS 2005 TC
mencía 100%

**91** Colour: very deep cherry. Nose: powerful, expressive, ripe fruit, roasted coffee, dark chocolate. Palate: powerful, flavourful, spirituous, slightly dry, soft tannins.

BEMBIBRE 2005 T
mencía 100%

**88** Colour: cherry, garnet rim. Nose: ripe fruit, spicy, creamy oak, toasty. Palate: powerful, flavourful, round tannins, good finish, spicy.

## VIÑEDOS Y BODEGAS PITTACUM

De la Iglesia, 11
24546 Arganza, El Bierzo (León)
☎: 987 548 054 - Fax: 987 548 028
pittacum@pittacum.com
www.pittacum.com

3 OBISPOS 2008 RD CRIANZA
mencía 100%

**82**

PITTACUM AUREA 2006 TC
mencía 100%

**92** Colour: deep cherry. Nose: mineral, damp earth, macerated fruit, creamy oak, cocoa bean. Palate: powerful, full, spirituous, flavourful, creamy, ripe fruit.

PITTACUM 2006 T
mencía 100%

**92** Colour: cherry, garnet rim. Nose: ripe fruit, spicy, creamy oak, toasty, complex, cocoa bean. Palate: powerful, flavourful, toasty, round tannins, roasted-coffee aftertaste.

SOME OTHER WINERIES WITHIN THE DO:

**BODEGA DIONISIO NIETO BLANCO
BODEGA ISABEL FERNANDA GUERRERO
BODEGAS Y VIÑEDOS BERGIDENSES
BROCO MARTÍNEZ
SEÑORÍO DE PEÑALBA S.A.
VIÑEDOS Y BODEGAS COMENDADOR S.L.
VITICULTORES BERCIANOS S.L.**

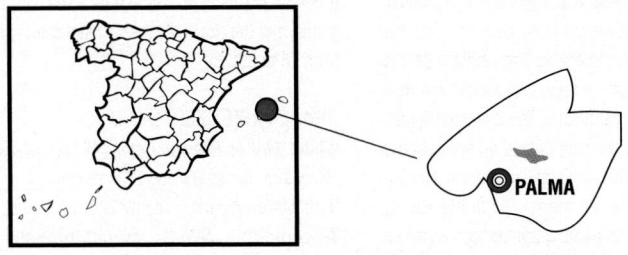

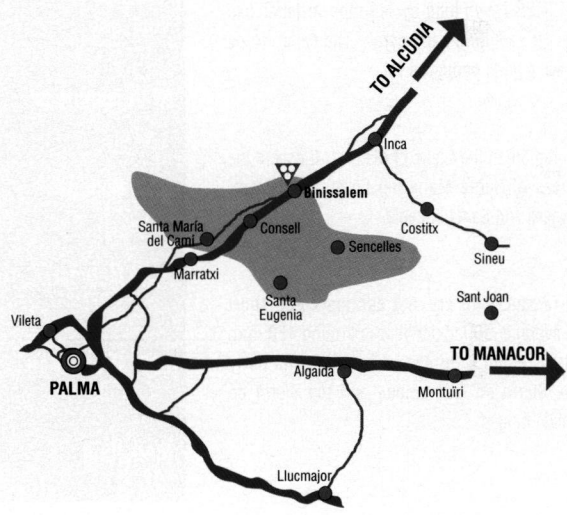

☒ Consejo Regulador
● DO Boundary

## NEWS

The young wines from the 2008 vintage, deemed a splendid one, are not necessarily the winners in a positive 2008 vintage where the best is yet to come in the shape of barrel aged crianza wines. In the young renderings the difficulties are evident mostly in reds, being white and rosé wines the most singular examples. The prensal blanca, also called moll locally, is showing beautifully when barrel fermented or in blends with chardonnay or moscatel giving shape to wines to floral, lovely wines. The bottle-ageing reds, mainly from the manto negro grape variety, are more concentrated in colour and structure, with soft tannins and some lovely, earthy, creamy and floral notes. The wineries Macià Batle and Biniagual are the leading manto negro defendants, blended with long-cycle grape varieties like merlot, cabernet sauvignon and syrah. The callet grape variety is showing quite poorly, as yet.

## LOCATION

In the central region on the island of Majorca. It covers the municipal areas of Santa María del Camí, Binissalem, Sencelles, Consell and Santa Eugenia.

## CLIMATE

Mild Mediterranean, with dry, hot summers and short winters. The average rainfall per year is around 450 mm. The production region is protected from the northerly winds by the Sierra de Tramuntana and the Sierra de Alfabia mountain ranges.

## SOIL

The soil is of a brownish - grey or dun limey type, with limestone crusts on occasions. The slopes are quite gentle, and the vineyards are situated at an altitude ranging from 75 to 200 m.

## GRAPE VARIETIES:

**White:** *Moll* or *Prensal Blanc* (46 Ha), *Macabeo, Parellada, Moscatel* and *Chardonnay.*

**Red:** *Manto Negro* (majority 229 Ha), *Callet, Tempranillo, Syrah, Monastrell* and *Cabernet Sauvignon* (second red variety 56 Ha) and *Merlot.*

| | |
|---|---|
| Hectares of Vineyard | 607,12 |
| Nº Viticulturists | 145 |
| Nº of Bodegas | 16 |
| 2008 Harvest | Very Good |
| 2007 Production | 1,340,422 l. |
| Marketing | 91.5% domestic 8.5% export |

**CONSEJO REGULADOR.**
Concepció, 7. 07350 Binissalem (Mallorca).
☎: 971 886 577 - Fax: 971 886 522
@ info@binissalemdo.com
www.binissalemdo.com

## GENERAL CHARACTERISTICS OF THE WINES:

| | |
|---|---|
| **WHITES** | These are straw yellow in colour. They are characterised by their wild, fruity traits, with hints of mountain herbs and a very Mediterranean character; the best, in which the personality of the local *Prensal* grapes stands out, provide a great complexity of nuances and excellent balance on the palate. |
| **ROSÉS** | These are pink and are characterised by their hints of aged wood, typical of the vineyards that receive a lot of sunshine. |
| **REDS** | These are the most characteristic of the region and represent almost three quarters of the production of the denomination. There are young and, especially, aged wines. Their character is determined by the peculiarities of the *Manto Negro* autochthonous variety, which provides an essence of ripe fruits and hints of caramel; on the palate, the wines are well - balanced and persistent. |

## 2008 VINTAGE RATING:

# GOOD

## BINIGRAU

Fiol, 33
07143 Biniali (Illes Balears)
☎: 971 512 023 - Fax: 971 886 495
info@binigrau.es
www.binigrau.es

E-ROSAT DE BINIGRAU 2008 RD
manto negro 50%, merlot 50%

**84**

E-NEGRE DE BINIGRAU

## BODEGA BINIAGUAL

Llogueret de Biniagual, Ap. de Correo, 5
07350 Binissalem (Mallorca)
☎: 971 886 040 - Fax: 971 886 108
info@bodegabiniagual.com
www.biniagual.com

FINCA BINIAGUAL - VERÁN 2006 T

**89** Colour: cherry, garnet rim. Nose: ripe fruit, spicy, creamy oak, complex, earthy notes. Palate: powerful, flavourful, toasty, round tannins.

GRAN VERÁN 2005 T

**90** Colour: cherry, garnet rim. Nose: ripe fruit, spicy, creamy oak, toasty, complex, balsamic herbs. Palate: flavourful, toasty, classic aged character, fine tannins.

VERÁN 2008

**89** Colour: salmon. Nose: fresh fruit, earthy notes, pattiserie. Palate: elegant, rich, flavourful, fruity.

## CELLER TIANNA NEGRE

Finca Es Pinaret, Camí d'es Mitjans
Polígono 7 - Parcela 67
07350 Binissalem (Mallorca) (Balears)
☎: 971 226 200 - Fax: 971 226 201
celler@tunel.com
www.tiannanegre.com

RANDEMAR 2008 B
prensal, moscatel

**88** Colour: bright straw. Nose: fresh, fresh fruit, expressive, tropical fruit. Palate: flavourful, fruity, good acidity, balanced.

SES NINES DOLÇ B
prensal, moscatel

**84**

SES NINES 2008 T
manto negro, callet, cabernet sauvignon

**87** Colour: cherry, purple rim. Nose: floral, sweet spices, ripe fruit. Palate: fruity, flavourful, spicy, great length.

RANDEMAR 2008 T
manto negro, cabernet sauvignon, callet

**85** Colour: cherry, purple rim. Nose: white flowers, red berry notes, lactic notes. Palate: flavourful, spicy, fine bitter notes, great length.

SES NINES 2007 T
manto negro, syrah, callet

**89** Colour: cherry, garnet rim. Nose: ripe fruit, red berry notes, creamy oak. Palate: flavourful, good structure, toasty, soft tannins.

## JAUME DE PUNTIRÓ

Pza. Nova, 23
07320 Santa María del Cami (Mallorca (Baleares))
☎: 971 620 023 - Fax: 971 620 023
pere@vinsjaumedepuntiro.com
www.vinsjaumedepuntiro.com

DAURAT 2008 BFB
prensal 100%

**86** Colour: bright yellow. Nose: powerfull, ripe fruit, sweet spices, creamy oak. Palate: rich, smoky aftertaste, flavourful, fresh, good acidity.

JAUME DE PUNTIRÓ BLANC 2008 B
prensal 100%

**84**

JAUME DE PUNTIRÓ ROSAT 2008 RD
manto negro 100%

**80**

JAUME DE PUNTIRÓ CARMESÍ 2006 T
manto negro 80%, callet 20%

**87** Colour: dark-red cherry. Nose: fruit liqueur notes, floral. Palate: flavourful, powerful, round tannins.

JAUME DE PUNTIRÓ PORPRAT 2006 T

**87** Colour: cherry, garnet rim. Nose: ripe fruit, cocoa bean, creamy oak, wild herbs. Palate: powerful, good structure, toasty, round tannins.

### JAUME DE PUNTIRÓ CAFÓ 2005 T

**86** Colour: pale ruby, brick rim edge. Nose: fruit liqueur notes, spicy, balsamic herbs. Palate: powerful, full, great length, toasty, round tannins.

### JAUME DE PUNTIRÓ MOSCATEL 2007 B DULCE
moscatel 100%

**85** Colour: yellow, pale. Nose: medium intensity, white flowers, fruit preserve. Palate: sweet, flavourful, long.

### J.P. 2005 TC
manto negro, cabernet sauvignon

**86** Colour: cherry, garnet rim. Nose: fresh, ripe fruit, dry nuts, aromatic coffee. Palate: flavourful, spirituous, good structure.

### BUC 2005 TC
manto negro, cabernet sauvignon

**85** Colour: cherry, garnet rim. Nose: sweet spices. Palate: flavourful, powerful, fleshy, spicy, easy to drink.

## JOSÉ L. FERRER (FRANJA ROJA)

Conquistador, 103
07350 Binissalem (Balears)
☎: 971 511 050 - Fax: 971 870 084
info@vinosferrer.com
www.vinosferrer.com

### VERITAS 2008 BFB
prensal

**81**

### JOSÉ L. FERRER BLANC DE BLANCS 2008 B
prensal

**80**

### JOSÉ L. FERRER 2008 RD

**79**

### JOSÉ L. FERRER 2006 TC

**85** Colour: cherry, garnet rim. Nose: ripe fruit, spicy, creamy oak, complex. Palate: powerful, flavourful, toasty, round tannins.

### JOSÉ L. FERRER SELECCIÓN 100 2003 TR

**85** Colour: pale ruby, brick rim edge. Nose: toasty, aromatic coffee, fruit liqueur notes. Palate: flavourful, powerful, slightly dry, soft tannins.

### BRUT VERITAS 2007 BN

**81**

### BRUT VERITAS 2006 BN

**79**

### VERITAS DOLÇ 2008 MOSCATEL
moscatel grano menudo

**87** Colour: bright yellow. Nose: grapey, honeyed notes, fruit preserve. Palate: flavourful, sweet, fine bitter notes, balanced.

### AUTÉNTICO

# DO BINISSALEM MALLORCA

## MACIÀ BATLE

Camí Coanegra, s/n
07320 Santa María del Camí (Balears)
☎: 971 140 014 - Fax: 971 140 086
correo@maciabatle.com
www.maciabatle.com

MACIÀ BATLE BLANC DE BLANCS 2008 B
prensal, chardonnay

**87** Colour: bright straw. Nose: fresh, fresh fruit, expressive, tropical fruit. Palate: flavourful, fruity, good acidity, balanced.

MACIÀ BATLE BLANC DE BLANCS ÚNIC 2007 BFB
prensal 70%, chardonnay 30%

**90** Colour: bright golden. Nose: characterful, smoky, sweet spices, fruit expression. Palate: flavourful, full, smoky aftertaste, great length.

MACIÀ BATLE 2008 RD
manto negro, callet

**80**

P. DE MARÌA 2007 T

**93** Colour: cherry, garnet rim. Nose: ripe fruit, wild herbs, sweet spices, creamy oak. Palate: good structure, elegant, round tannins.

MACIÀ BATLE 2006 TC

**86** Colour: bright cherry. Nose: overripe fruit, wild herbs, sweet spices. Palate: fruity, balanced, round tannins.

MACIÀ BATLE RESERVA PRIVADA 2005 TR

**90** Colour: cherry, garnet rim. Nose: ripe fruit, spicy, creamy oak, toasty, complex. Palate: powerful, flavourful, toasty, round tannins.

## VINS NADAL

Ramón Llull, 2
07350 Binissalem (Balears)
☎: 971 511 058 - Fax: 971 870 150
albaflor@vinsnadal.com
www.vinsnadal.com

ALBAFLOR 2008 B
prensal 78%, moscatel 22%

**79**

ALBAFLOR 2008 RD
manto negro 46%, merlot 40%, cabernet sauvignon 14%

**87** Colour: rose, bright. Nose: red berry notes, raspberry, floral. Palate: flavourful, fruity, full.

ALBAFLOR 2006 TC
manto negro 50%, cabernet sauvignon 37%, merlot 13%

**84**

ALBAFLOR 2005 TR
manto negro 50%, merlot 30%, cabernet sauvignon 20%

**83**

## VINYA TAUJANA

Balanguera 40
07142 Santa Eugenia (Mallorca)
☎: 971 144 494 - Fax: 971 144 494
vinyataujana@gmail.com

VINYA TAUJANA BLANC DE BLANC 2008 B
moll 100%

**80**

TORRENT FALS 2006 TC
manto negro 64%, syrah 19%, cabernet sauvignon 12%

**81**

## VINYES I VINS CA SA PADRINA

Camí dels Horts. s/n
07140 Sencelles (Balears)
☎: 686 933 991 - Fax: 971 612 400
cellercasapadrina@gmail.com

MANTONEGRO GONZÁLEZ SUÑER 2007 T ROBLE

**84**

SOME OTHER WINERIES WITHIN THE DO:

**ANTONIO NADAL
CA'N RAMIS
RAMANYÀ**

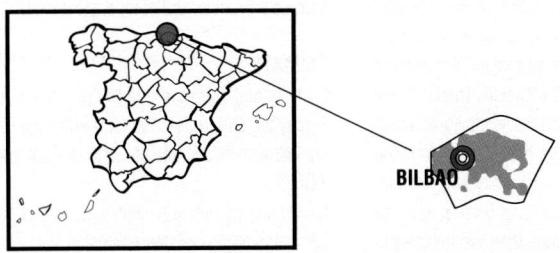

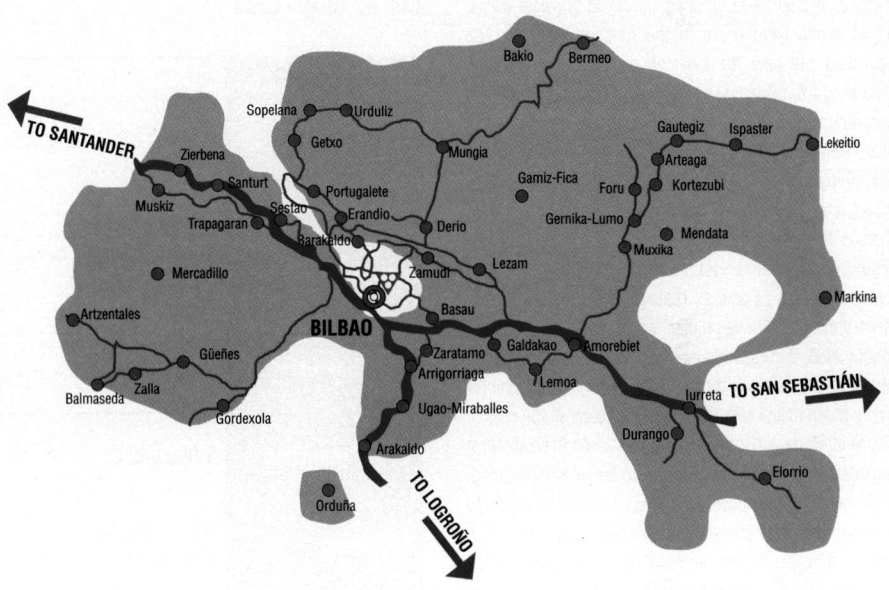

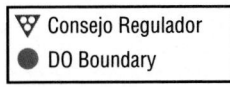

Consejo Regulador
DO Boundary

# DO BIZKAIKO TXAKOLINA

## NEWS

The wine region between the towns of Bakio and Balmaseda is showing a increasingly fighting, forward character in the promotion of its wines as well as in its regulations, which seem to focus on making wines more popular to consumers, lowering their acidity levels. To the wines made from local varieties and the 'exotic' ones made from the French folle blanche, we have got to add new varieties like sauvignon blanc, chardonnay and riesling, although we should not forget the local grapes, for vine growers are not allowed to plant more than two hectares of the foreign ones. All in all, the txakoli from Biscay seem to become less of a txakoli and more of an accomplished, global wine thanks to new –in the region– winemaking methods like barrel-fermenting, sparkling or sweet wines, all of which have room in the new regulations. The sparkling will bear the label of 'espumoso de Bizkaia' (sparkling from Biscay) to single it out from the traditional sparkling wines. On the other hand, late harvest wines will also become special wines, controlled and certified by the DO, although they can not use the 'txakoli' back label. Red wines hardly represent 5% of the total production, and there is an important effort to improve clone selection with the hondarribi beltza ¬(some recent studies relate it to cabernet franc) as well as research with the pinot noir. Regardless of all those studies, we have valued a vintage, that of 2008, that reminds us of the freshness of the 2007, showing wines of a limpid, fresh and herbal character pretty much in line with the typical character of the region. The leading pack (Doniene, Uriondo, Iñaki Aretxabaleta) includes those that have resorted to lee or wood ageing, and therefore the more complex examples manage to overtake the more classic Itsas Mendi renderings, of an easier character. In the red wine realm we have noticed some faults in terms of maturation, both in terms of soil and variety choice.

## LOCATION

In the province of Vizcaya. The production region covers both coastal areas and other areas inland.

## CLIMATE

Quite humid and mild due to the influence of the Bay of Biscay which tempers the temperatures. Fairly abundant rainfall, with an average of 1,000 to 1,300 mm per year.

## SOIL

Mainly clayey, although slightly acidic on occasions, with a fairly high organic matter content.

## GRAPE VARIETIES:

**White:** *Hondarrabi Zuri, Folle Blanche.*
**Red:** *Hondarrabi Beltza.*

| Hectares of Vineyard | 276 |
|---|---|
| Nº Viticulturists | 291 |
| Nº of Bodegas | 56 |
| 2008 Harvest | Very Good |
| 2007 Production | 1,069,982 l. |
| Marketing | 96% domestic 4% export |

**CONSEJO REGULADOR.**
Bº Garaioltza, 23. 48196 Lezama (Vizcaya).
☎: 944 555 063 - Fax: 944 556 245
@ prvegetal@lorra-cg.net
www.bizkaikotxakolina.org

## GENERAL CHARACTERISTICS OF THE WINES:

| | |
|---|---|
| **WHITES** | These are the most characteristic of the denomination. They are characterised by their dull, straw yellow with, on occasions, green glimmer; their nose combines floral and fruity notes, although they have a more herbaceous character than those of Getaria due to the *Folle Blanche* variety, together with the *Hondarrabi* Zuri variety. on the palate they are light, easy drinking and have a freshness that gives them their high acidity. |
| **ROSÉS** | In the region, this type of wine is known as 'Ojo de Gallo', rooster's eye. They represent a very small proportion of the production; they are fresh and light, although on the palate they tend to be quite acidic. |
| **REDS** | As with the rosé wines they are also a minority product; in fact, they are only produced in regions with a certain tradition. In general, they are excessively acidic. |

## 2008 VINTAGE RATING:

## VERY GOOD

## BASALBEITIKO TXAKOLINA

Barrio Goitioltza, 37 Caserío Basalbeiti
48196 Lezama (Bizkaia)
☎: 944 556 146

BASALBEITIKO 2008 B

**80**

## BIKANDI TXAKOLINA

Artabila, 5
48200 Durango ()
☎: 946 816 519

BIKANDI TXACOLINA 2008 B

**84**

## BODEGA BERROJA

Ctra. de Zugastieta al balcón de Bizkaia.
Ajuria Barrio Berroja
48392 Muxika (Bizkaia)
☎: 944 106 254 - Fax: 946 309 390
txakoli@bodegaberroja.com
www.bodegaberroja.com

AGUIRREBEKO 2008 B

**85** Colour: straw. Nose: citrus fruit, dried herbs, balsamic herbs. Palate: fruity, fresh, good structure, flavourful.

BERROIA 2008 B

**83**

BERROJA 2006 B

**86** Colour: golden. Nose: sun-drenched nuances, macerated fruit, dried herbs, petrol notes, waxy notes. Palate: good acidity, elegant, fine bitter notes, unctuous, balsamic, spicy.

## BODEGA ELIZALDE

Barrio Mendraka, 1
48230 Elorrio (Bizkaia)
☎: 946 820 000 - Fax: 946 820 000
kerixa@gmail.com

MENDRAKA 2008 B
hondarrabi zuri 95%, otras 5%

**87** Colour: yellow, greenish rim. Nose: citrus fruit, fruit expression, scrubland, spicy. Palate: elegant, fruity, fresh, carbonic notes, good acidity.

## BODEGA JON ANDER REKALDE

San Roke Bekoa, 11 (Artxanda)
48150 Sondika ()
☎: 944 458 631

ARTXANDA 2008 B

**86** Colour: bright straw. Nose: floral, grapey, saline. Palate: fresh, fruity, carbonic notes, full.

## BODEGA URIARTE

Barrio Acillcona-Cº Eguskiza
48113 Fika (Bizkaia)
☎: 946 153 140 - Fax: 946 153 535
info@txakoli-uriarte.com
www.txakoli-uriarte.com

URIARTE 2008 B
hondarrabi zuri 75%, folle blanch 5%, riesling 5%, chardonnay 5%

**84**

URIARTE ESPECIAL 2007 B
hondarrabi zuri 100%

**86** Colour: bright yellow. Nose: candied fruit, spicy, balsamic herbs. Palate: fresh, fruity, full.

IKUS GARRI

## BODEGAS GURRUTXAGA S.L.

Baurdo Auzoa, s/n
48289 Mendexa (Bizkaia)
☎: 946 844 937

GURRUTXAGA 2008 B

**86** Colour: straw, greenish rim. Nose: fruit expression, floral, fresh fruit, saline. Palate: fruity, fresh, good acidity.

GURRUTXAGA 2008 RD

**84**

## DONIENE GORRONDONA TXAKOLINA

Gibelorratzagako San Pelaio, 1
48130 Bakio (Bizkaia)

☎: 946 194 795 - Fax: 946 195 831
gorrondona@donienegorrondona.com
www.donienegorrondona.com

**DONIENE 2008 BFB**
hondarrabi zuri

**91** Colour: yellow. Nose: grapey, candied fruit, dry nuts, scrubland, creamy oak. Palate: flavourful, rich, carbonic notes.

**DONIENE 2008 B**
hondarrabi zuri

**88** Colour: bright straw. Nose: expressive, citrus fruit, fresh fruit, scrubland. Palate: flavourful, fruity, good acidity, long.

**GORRONDONA 2008 B**
hz, hb, munemahatsa

**87** Colour: bright straw. Nose: citrus fruit, candied fruit, dried herbs, saline. Palate: flavourful, carbonic notes, fresh, balsamic.

**GORRONDONA 2008 T**
hondarrabi beltza

**82**

**DONIENE 2006 ESP**
hondarrabi zuri, muemahatsa

**82**

## ERDIKOETXE LANDETXEA

Goitioltza, 38
48196 Lezama (Bizkaia)
☎: 944 573 285 - Fax: 944 573 285
erdikoetxelandetxea@hotmail.com
www.nekatur.net

**ERDIKOETXE 2008 B**

**82**

**ERDIKOETXE 2008 T**

**77**

## GARKALDE TXAKOLINA

Barrio Goitioltza, 8 - Caserio Garkalde
48196 Lezama (Bizkaia)
☎: 944 556 412

**GARKALDE TXACOLINA 2008 B**

**84**

## GARRATZ TXAKOLINA

Iñigo López de Haro, 2 - 4º H
48300 Gernika (Bizkaia)
☎: 946 255 021

**GARRATZ 2008 B**

**84**

## IÑAKI ARETXABALETA

Barrio Garaioltza, 92 Bis
48196 Lezama (Bizkaia)
☎: 944 556 508

**MAGALARTE IÑAKI ARETXABALETA 2008 B**

**86** Colour: bright straw. Nose: grapey, macerated fruit, balsamic herbs. Palate: balsamic, good acidity, fine bitter notes, fine bead.

**MAGALARTE IÑAKI ARETXABALETA 2007 BFB**

**88** Colour: bright yellow. Nose: balsamic herbs, macerated fruit, rancio notes, cedar wood, spicy. Palate: fleshy, full, good acidity, round.

## ITSASMENDI

Barrio Arane, 3
48300 Gernika (Bizkaia)
☎: 946 270 316 - Fax: 946 251 032
info@bodegasitsasmendi.com
www.bodegasitsasmendi.com

**ITSASMENDI Nº 7 2007 B**
hondarrabi zuri, riesling

**87** Colour: bright straw, golden. Nose: characterful, balsamic herbs, macerated fruit, petrol notes, saline. Palate: slightly tart, fine bitter notes, fruity, fresh.

**ITSAS MENDI UREZTI 2006 VINO DULCE NATURAL BARRICA**

**90** Colour: golden. Nose: complex, dry nuts, sun-drenched nuances, spicy, petrol notes, balsamic herbs. Palate: powerful, flavourful, complex, elegant, fine bitter notes.

**ITSAS MENDI 2008 B**

**88** Colour: straw. Nose: floral, dried herbs, macerated fruit, grapey, pattiserie. Palate: fruity, flavourful, carbonic notes.

**GORKA IZAGUIRRE 2008 B**

**87** Colour: bright straw. Nose: macerated fruit, grapey, balsamic herbs, spicy. Palate: flavourful, full, balsamic.

**UIXAR 2008 B**

**87** Colour: bright yellow, greenish rim. Nose: grapey, macerated fruit, dried herbs, fragrant herbs, sweet spices, balsamic herbs. Palate: fruity, flavourful, rich, good acidity.

**EGIA ENEA 2008 B**

**86** Colour: bright straw. Nose: macerated fruit, dried herbs, floral. Palate: fruity, fresh, full, flavourful.

**MARKO 2008 B**

**86** Colour: bright straw. Nose: complex, fresh, macerated fruit, dried herbs. Palate: full, fruity, fresh, long.

**TORREKO TXAKOLINA 2008 B**

**86** Colour: straw, greenish rim. Nose: candied fruit, grapey, scrubland, spicy. Palate: round, good acidity, balsamic, full.

**E-GALA 2008 B**

**86** Colour: bright straw, greenish rim. Nose: white flowers, expressive, macerated fruit, balanced, powerfull. Palate: flavourful, fruity, good acidity, balanced.

**NEKESOLO 2008 B**

**85** Colour: bright straw. Nose: expressive, candied fruit, elegant, macerated fruit, dried flowers. Palate: flavourful, fruity, good acidity, balanced.

**MUNETABERRI 2008 B**

**85** Colour: bright straw. Nose: fresh, fresh fruit, expressive, candied fruit, dried flowers. Palate: flavourful, fruity, good acidity.

**ETXANO 2008 B**

**84**

AMUNATEGI
LARRONDO
ARRIORTU

## ITURRIALDE S.L.

Barrio Legina, s/n
48195 Larrabetzu (Bizkaia)
☎: 946 742 706 - Fax: 946 741 221
txakoli@gorkaizagirre.com
www.gorkaizagirre.com

## JOSÉ ETXEBARRÍA URRUTIA

Txonebarri-C. Igartua, s/n
48110 Gatika (Bizkaia)
☎: 946 742 010

TXAKOLI ETXEBARRÍA 2008 B

**80**

## LA ANTIGUA TXAKOLINA

Burgos Kalea, 20 Bajo
48460 Orduña ()
☎: 945 384 097

TXACOLI ANTIGUAKO-AMA 2008 B

**86** Colour: yellow. Nose: candied fruit, macerated fruit, sweet spices. Palate: fresh, fruity, flavourful, carbonic notes.

## MAGALARTE ZAMUDIO

Arteaga Auzoa, 107
48170 Zamudio (Bizkaia)
☎: 944 521 431 - Fax: 944 521 431
magalarte@hotmail.com

MAGALARTE JABI ARETXABALETA 2008 B

**83**

ARTEBAKARRA 2008 B

**81**

## MERRUTXU

Caserío Merrutxu, Arboliz 15
48311 Ibarrangelu (Bizkaia)
☎: 946 276 435
info@merrutxu.com
www.merrutxu.com

MERRUTXU 2008 B
hondarrabi zuri, folle blanch

**85** Nose: citrus fruit, balsamic herbs, dried herbs, floral. Palate: elegant, fresh, fruity, flavourful, full.

## OXINBALTZA

Barrio Maguna 27 Caserío Oxinbaltza
48392 Muxika (Bizkaia)
☎: 639 317 611
oxinbaltza@oxinbaltza.com
www.oxinbaltza.com

OXINBALTZA 2008 B
hondarrabi zuri, petit courbu

**87** Colour: straw. Nose: citrus fruit, fruit expression,

balsamic herbs, dried flowers, sweet spices. Palate: fruity, fresh, flavourful.

## TXAKOLI LARRABE

Barrio Garaioltza, 103 - Caserío Usategi
48196 Lezama (Bizkaia)
☎: 944 564 91

TXACOLI LARRABE 2008 B

**83**

## TXAKOLI TXABARRI

Juan Antonio del Yelmo, 1 4C
48860 Zalla (Bizkaia)
☎: 946 390 947 - Fax: 946 390 947
itxasa@yahoo.es

TXABARRI 2008 B
hondarrabi zuri 80%, riesling 10%, sauvignon blanc 10%

**85** Colour: bright yellow, greenish rim. Nose: balsamic herbs, macerated fruit, grapey, wild herbs. Palate: full, flavourful, good acidity, long.

TXABARRI 2008 RD

**79**

TXABARRI 2008 T
hondarrabi baltza 100%

**83**

## URIONDO

Barrio Urriondo, 2
48480 Zaratamo (VBizkaia)
☎: 946 711 870
uriondo.txakoli@gmail.com

URIONDO CUVÉE 2008 BFB
ondarrabi, mune matja

**90** Colour: bright yellow. Nose: powerfull, ripe fruit, sweet spices, creamy oak, fragrant herbs. Palate: rich, smoky aftertaste, flavourful, fresh, good acidity.

URIONDO 2008 B
ondarrabi, mune matja

**87** Colour: pale. Nose: fresh fruit, floral, grassy. Palate: flavourful, fruity, fresh.

# DO BIZKAIKO TXAKOLINA

## VIRGEN DE LOREA

Barrio de Lorea
48860 Otxaran-Zalla (Bizkaia)
☎: 946 390 296 - Fax: 946 670 521
espancor@cnb.informail.es

SEÑORÍO DE OTXARAN 2008 B

**88** Colour: bright yellow. Nose: ripe fruit, grapey, balsamic herbs, dried herbs, spicy. Palate: round, elegant, fruity, flavourful.

ARETXAGA 2008 B

**80**

SOME OTHER WINERIES WITHIN THE DO:

**AGIRRE LLONA**
**AXPE (JOSE A. BILBAO)**
**AYARZA**
**GURE AHALEGINAK**
**JUAN ANTONIO OLEAGA ARRIAGA**
**LA ANTIGUA TXAKOLINA**
**OTXANDURI UPATEGIA**
**RUFINO ISASI**
**SASIA BASERRIA**
**TXAKOLI AITABITXI**
**TXAKOLI ARITXOLA**
**TXAKOLI LLARENA**

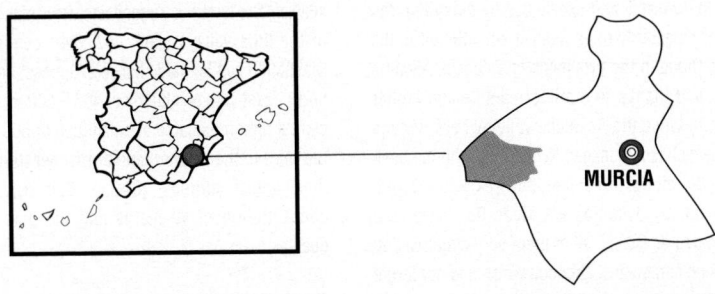

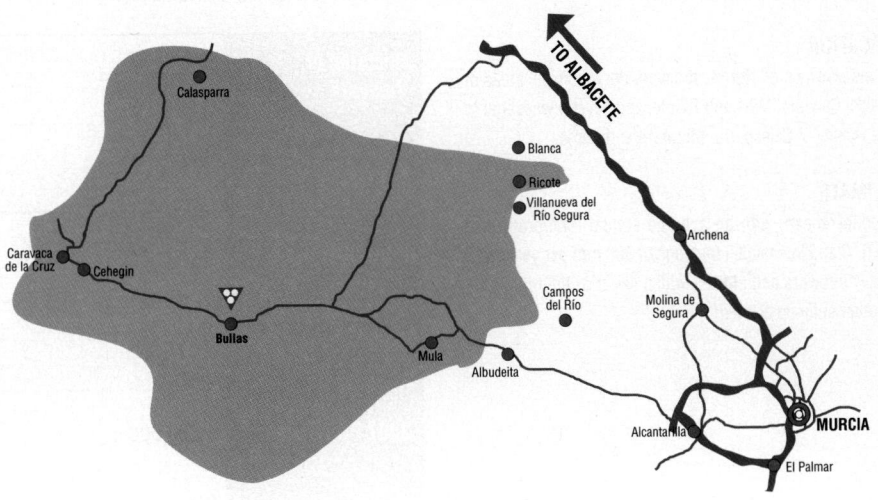

- △▽ Consejo Regulador
- ● DO Boundary

## NEWS

The smallest of the DOs within Murcia region continues its steady rise to notoriety and excellence by defending the character and singularity of its monastrell, different to the other clones found in the provinces of Valencia, Alicante and Murcia, and thanks to a milder climate and higher altitude, for instance the Aceniche valley where Bodega Monastrell –which has managed to come up with the best, highly aromatic monastrell wines this year– is located. Some other notable wineries are Madroño, Partal and Molino y Lagares de Bullas, all of them very dynamic and forward-looking companies, although we should not forget to mention Nuestra Señora del Rosario, an old coop which pioneered old vine philosophy as well as export policies to a great extent: 90% of the wine from Bullas we find in foreign markets comes from them.

## LOCATION

In the province of Murcia. It covers the municipal areas of Bullas, Cehegín, Mula and Ricote, and several vineyards in the vicinity of Calasparra, Moratalla and Lorca.

## CLIMATE

Mediterranean, with an average annual temperature of 15.6 °C and low rainfall (average of 300 mm per year). The heavy showers and storms which occur in the region are another defining element.

## SOIL

Brownish - grey limey soil, with limestone crusts, and alluvial. The terrain is rugged and determined by the layout of the little valleys, each with their own microclimate. Distinction can be made between 3 areas: one to the north north - east with an altitude of 400 – 500 m; another in the central region, situated at an altitude of 500 – 600 m; and the third in the western and north - western region, with the highest altitude (500 – 810 m), the highest concentration of vineyards and the best potential for quality.

## GRAPE VARIETIES:

**White:** *Macabeo* (main) and *Airén*.
**Red:** *Monastrell* (main), *Tempranillo, Cabernet Sauvignon, Syrah, Merlot* and *Garnacha*.

| | |
|---|---|
| Hectares of Vineyard | 2,258 |
| Nº Viticulturists | 609 |
| Nº of Bodegas | 14 |
| 2008 Harvest | Very Good |
| 2007 Production | 1,800,000 l. |
| Marketing | 75% domestic 25% export |

**CONSEJO REGULADOR.**

Avda. de Murcia, 4. 30180 Bullas (Murcia).

☎: 968 652 601 - Fax: 968 652 601

@ consejoregulador@vinosdebullas.es

## GENERAL CHARACTERISTICS OF THE WINES:

| WHITES | Produced with *Macabeo* and *Airén*, they are pale yellow and have pleasant fruity notes. |
|---|---|
| ROSÉS | The varietal character of those produced with *Monastrell* stands out. They are light, pleasant and easy drinking. Those produced from Garnacha are full - bodied on the palate. |
| REDS | Those produced from *Monastrell* and *Tempranillo* stand out for their Mediterranean character, sun - drenched fruit and fruity character, although they are less rounded than those of Jumilla and Alicante. On the other hand, their inclusion in the blend of the new varieties recently approved by the Council should afford greater structure and longevity to the red wines. |

## 2008 VINTAGE RATING:

# VERY GOOD

## BODEGA BALCONA

Democracia, 7
30180 Bullas (Murcia)
☎: 968 652 891
bodegabalcona@larural.es
www.partal-vinos.com

**PARTAL SELECCIÓN 37 BARRICAS 2004 T**
monastrell 65%, tempranillo 35%, cabernet sauvignon %

**87** Colour: bright cherry. Nose: ripe fruit, expressive, spicy, aromatic coffee. Palate: flavourful, toasty, round tannins, balanced, fine bitter notes.

**PARTAL VINO DE AUTOR 2002 T**
monastrell 60%, syrah 40%, tempranillo %, cabernet sauvignon %

**88** Colour: bright cherry. Nose: ripe fruit, sweet spices, creamy oak, expressive, earthy notes. Palate: flavourful, fruity, toasty, round tannins.

## BODEGA MONASTRELL

Pareje El Aceniche
30430 Cemejin (Murcia)
☎: 968 653 708 - Fax: 968 653 708
ageh@telefonica.net
www.bodegamonastrell.com

**CHAVEO 2006 T**
monastrell 100%

**87** Colour: cherry, garnet rim. Nose: toasty, complex, fruit preserve, fruit liqueur notes, spicy. Palate: powerful, flavourful, toasty, round tannins, roasted-coffee aftertaste.

**VALCHE 2005 TC**
monastrell 100%

**93** Colour: bright cherry. Nose: sweet spices, creamy oak, expressive, mineral, fruit preserve. Palate: flavourful, toasty, round tannins, powerful.

**CHAVEO DULCE T**
monastrell 100%

**82**

ALMUDI

## BODEGAS CONTRERAS

Los Ríos, 2
30812 Avilés, Lorca (Murcia)
☎: 968 492 836 - Fax: 968 492 836

info@bodegas-contreras.com
www.bodegas-contreras.com

**UVIO 2007 TC**
monastrell, syrah, cabernet sauvignon

**86** Colour: bright cherry. Nose: sweet spices, expressive, fruit preserve, roasted coffee. Palate: flavourful, toasty, round tannins, balsamic.

**SORTIUS MONASTRELL 2007 T**
monastrell

**85** Colour: bright cherry. Nose: sweet spices, creamy oak, fruit preserve, fruit liqueur notes. Palate: flavourful, toasty, pruney, grainy tannins.

**SORTIUS SYRAH 2007 T ROBLE**
syrah

**88** Colour: bright cherry. Nose: ripe fruit, sweet spices, creamy oak, varietal. Palate: flavourful, fruity, toasty, round tannins.

## BODEGAS DEL ROSARIO

Avenida de la Libertad s/n
30180 Bullas (Murcia)
☎: 968 652 075 - Fax: 968 653 765
info@bodegasdelrosario.com
www.bodegasdelrosario.com

**LAS REÑAS MACABEO 2008 B**
macabeo 100%

**88** Colour: bright straw. Nose: ripe fruit, neat, expressive, white flowers. Palate: fresh, ripe fruit, good acidity, unctuous.

**LAS REÑAS MONASTRELL 2008 RD**
monastrell 100%

**85** Colour: light cherry. Nose: ripe fruit, dried flowers, medium intensity. Palate: flavourful, fruity, good acidity.

**LAS REÑAS MONASTRELL 2008 T**
monastrell 80%, tempranillo 20%

**87** Colour: cherry, purple rim. Nose: ripe fruit, lactic notes, dried flowers, varietal, fresh. Palate: fruity, good finish, flavourful, easy to drink.

**3000 AÑOS 2006 T**
monastrell 50%, syrah 50%

**93** Colour: very deep cherry. Nose: powerful, ripe fruit, fruit expression, sweet spices, creamy oak, dark chocolate. Palate: flavourful, powerful, fleshy, complex, long, round tannins.

**LAS REÑAS MONASTRELL - SHIRAZ 2006 TC**
monastrell 80%, syrah 20%

**86** Colour: cherry, garnet rim. Nose: ripe fruit, expressive, spicy, warm. Palate: powerful, fruity, flavourful, round tannins, toasty.

**LAS REÑAS 2006 T BARRICA**
monastrell 80%, tempranillo 20%

**84**

## BODEGAS MADROÑAL

Partal, 6
30180 Bullas (Murcia)
☎: 968 655 183 - Fax: 968 654 479
madro-1@hotmail.com

## SISCAR 2008 T
monastrell

**89** Colour: bright cherry. Nose: ripe fruit, sweet spices, creamy oak, expressive. Palate: flavourful, fruity, toasty, harsh oak tannins.

## SISCAR 2007 T
monastrell 100%

**85** Colour: bright cherry. Nose: sweet spices, fruit preserve, overripe fruit. Palate: flavourful, toasty, round tannins, balsamic.

## MADROÑAL 2005 TC
monastrell 80%, syrah 20%

**86** Colour: cherry, garnet rim. Nose: spicy, creamy oak, toasty, complex, fruit preserve. Palate: powerful, flavourful, toasty, round tannins.

## MADROÑAL DE LA FAMILIA 2004 TC
monastrell 80%, syrah 20%

**86** Colour: very deep cherry. Nose: characterful, complex, fruit expression, ripe fruit, aromatic coffee, dark chocolate. Palate: flavourful, harsh oak tannins, ripe fruit.

## BODEGAS MERCADER-QUESADA

Herrera, 22
30180 Bullas (Murcia)
☎: 968 654 205 - Fax: 968 654 205
pilarquesadagil@yahoo.es
www.mundoenologico.com

## MERCADER QUESADA VENDIMIA T
monastrell

**88** Colour: cherry, purple rim. Nose: expressive, fresh fruit, red berry notes, floral. Palate: flavourful, fruity, good acidity, round tannins.

## MERCADER QUESADA SELECCIÓN MONASTRELL ECOLÓGICO T

**86** Colour: cherry, garnet rim. Nose: spicy, toasty, complex. Palate: powerful, flavourful, toasty, round tannins.

## CARRASCALEJO

Finca El Carrascalejo, s/n
30180 Bullas (Murcia)
☎: 968 652 003 - Fax: 968 652 003
carrascalejo@carrascalejo.com
www.carrascalejo.com

## CARRASCALEJO RD

**80**

## CARRASCALEJO T

**86** Colour: cherry, purple rim. Nose: expressive, fresh fruit, red berry notes, floral. Palate: flavourful, fruity, good acidity, round tannins.

## CARRASCALEJO TC

**86** Colour: bright cherry. Nose: sweet spices, expressive, fruit preserve, mineral. Palate: flavourful, toasty, round tannins, fine bitter notes.

## COOPERATIVA VINÍCOLA AGRARIA SAN ISIDRO

Pl. Ind. Marimingo,
Altiplano, s/n
30180 Bullas (Murcia)
☎: 968 654 991 - Fax: 968 652 160
bodegasanisidro@terra.es

## CEPAS DEL ZORRO MACABEO 2008 B
macabeo 100%

**84**

## CEPAS DEL ZORRO 2008 RD
monastrell 80%, garnacha 20%

**85** Colour: rose, purple rim. Nose: ripe fruit, red berry notes, floral, expressive. Palate: fleshy, powerful, fruity, fresh.

## CEPAS DEL ZORRO 2008 T
monastrell 75%, tempranillo 20%, syrah 5%

**83**

## CEPAS DEL ZORRO BARRICA 2007 T
monastrell 70%, tempranillo 20%, syrah 10%

**87** Colour: bright cherry. Nose: ripe fruit, cocoa bean, dark chocolate. Palate: flavourful, fruity, toasty, round tannins.

## CEPAS DEL ZORRO 2005 TC
monastrell 70%, tempranillo 20%, syrah 10%

**84**

## FERNANDO CARREÑO PEÑALVER

Andalucía, 40
30430 Cehegín (Murcia)
☎: 968 740 004 - Fax: 968 740 004
carrenobodegas@terra.es

## MARMALLEJO 2005 TC

**85** Colour: cherry, garnet rim. Nose: ripe fruit, spicy, creamy oak, toasty. Palate: powerful, flavourful, toasty, round tannins.

## MOLINO Y LAGARES DE BULLAS

Paraje Venta del Pino, ctra. Portugalés, km. 12
30180 Bullas (Murcia)
☎: 638 046 694 - Fax: 968 654 494
lavia@bodegaslavia.com
www.bodegaslavia.com

**LAVIA+ 2006 T**
monastrell 100%

**90** Colour: cherry, garnet rim. Nose: toasty, complex, elegant, aromatic coffee, fruit liqueur notes. Palate: flavourful, toasty, round tannins, balanced.

**LAVIA MONASTRELL SYRAH 2006 TC**
monastrell 70%, syrah 30%

**88** Colour: bright cherry. Nose: sweet spices, expressive, fruit preserve, fragrant herbs. Palate: flavourful, fruity, round tannins, balsamic, spicy.

**LAVIA+ 2005 T**
monastrell 100%

**92** Colour: bright cherry. Nose: ripe fruit, sweet spices, expressive, fragrant herbs. Palate: flavourful, fruity, toasty, round tannins.

## SOME OTHER WINERIES WITHIN THE DO:

**A. GARCÍA NOGUEROL**
**BODEGAS LOS CEPEROS**

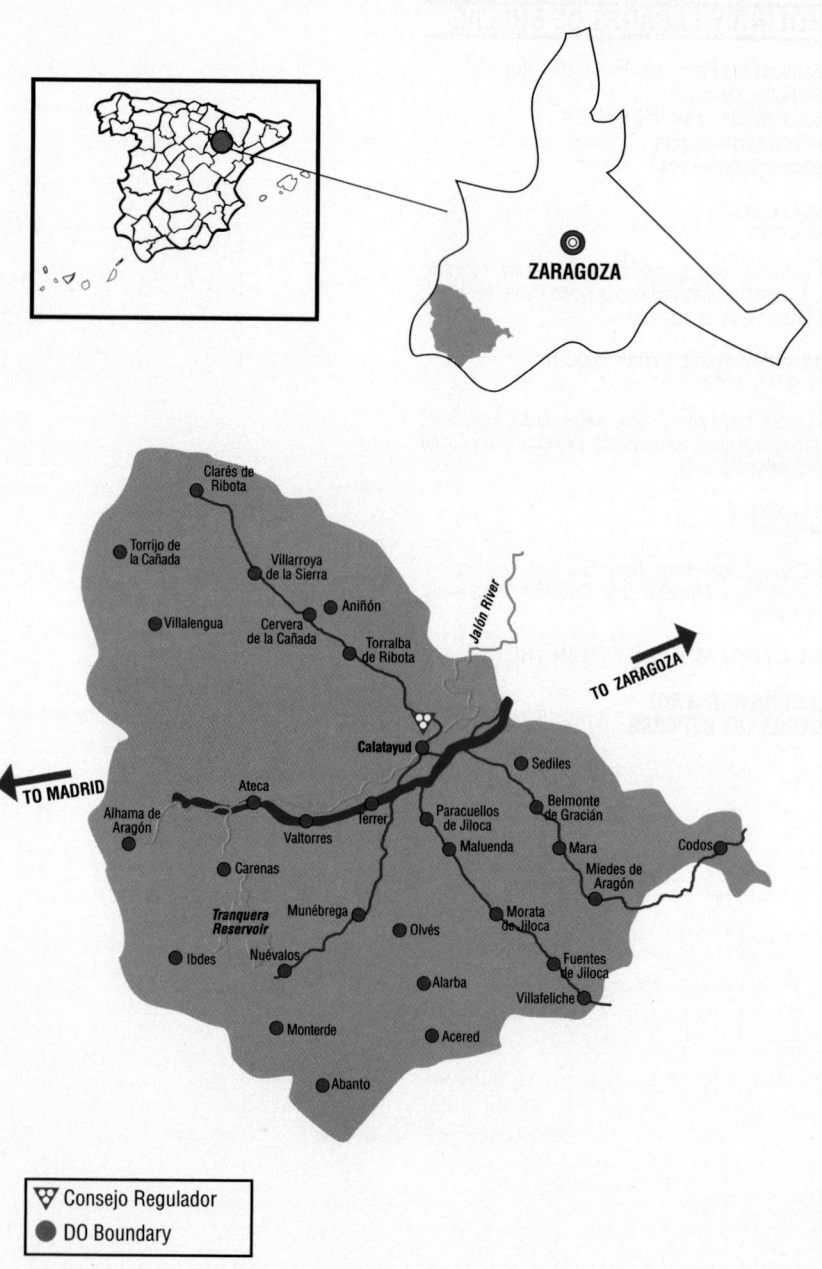

ZARAGOZA

Clarés de Ribota

Torrijo de la Cañada

Villarroya de la Sierra

Aniñón

Villalengua

Cervera de la Cañada

Torralba de Ribota

Jalón River

TO ZARAGOZA

Calatayud

Sediles

TO MADRID

Ateca

Belmonte de Gracián

Alhama de Aragón

Valtorres

Terrer

Paracuellos de Jiloca

Maluenda

Mara

Codos

Carenas

Miedes de Aragón

Tranquera Reservoir

Munébrega

Olvés

Morata de Jiloca

Ibdes

Nuévalos

Alarba

Fuentes de Jiloca

Villafeliche

Monterde

Acered

Abanto

▽ Consejo Regulador

● DO Boundary

## NEWS

As it happened in Cariñena, the total production figure in Calatayud was lower, although here the problem seem to be more acute since we are talking about the biggest region in terms of vineyard surface within the autonomous region of Aragón; while the average harvest means around 18 million kilograms, 2008 came to just 8, a 60% lower. The reason behind it is the uprooting proposed and financed by the EU that will mean Calatayud will comprise soon no more than 2.500 hectares, when the total figure just a few years ago was 40.000. This circumstance seems to be particularly poignant in the case of high vineyards with slate soils so suitable for quality vine growing. But to the local coops, which control 90 of those elevated vineyards –the highest within Aragón– low yields and grape prices have turned vine growing into a bad business. Nevertheless, the quality of the wines of this exporting region (85% of its production goes to USA, UK and other foreign markets) remains as high as that of last year's. Red wines are fresh and fruity, typical of a cool vintage, and we even find some complexity when harvesting was delayed in high vineyards until mid November. But probably 2007 was even greater. The garnachas from that vintage show round and supple, with riper nuances and more complexity when aged in quality oak, while the whites go unnoticed and it will be interesting to start thinking about other grape varieties beyond macabeo which could benefit from the highly qualitative slate soils. The rosé wines show quite nicely too, although with no further surprises, as it is the case with those reds with an average price of some 4€. The top wines are high in alcohol, generally made from old vine garnacha grapes, have lots of expression and prices accordingly high, and come from consolidated wineries such as Virgen de la Sierra, Bodegas y Viñedos del Jalón, Ateca, San Alejandro and San Gregorio.

## LOCATION

It is situated in the western region of the province of Zaragoza, along the foothills of the Sistema Ibérico, outlined by the network of rivers woven by the different tributaries of the Ebro: Jalón, Jiloca, Manubles, Mesa, Piedra and Ribota, and covers 46 municipal areas of the Ebro Valley.

## CLIMATE

Semi - arid and dry, although somewhat cooler than Cariñena and Borja, with cold winters, an average annual temperature which ranges between 12 and 14 °C, and a period of frost of between 5 and 7 months which greatly affects the production. The average rainfall ranges between 300 – 550 mm per year, with great day/night temperature contrasts during the ripening season.

## SOIL

In general, the soil has a high limestone content. It is formed by rugged stony materials from the nearby mountain ranges and is on many occasions accompanied by reddish clay. The region is the most rugged in Aragón, and the vineyards are situated at an altitude of between 550 and 880 m.

## GRAPE VARIETIES:

**White:** Preferred: *Macabeo* (25%) and *Malvasía*.
Authorized: *Moscatel de Alejandría, Garnacha Blanca* and *Chardonnay*.
**Red:** Preferred: *Garnacha Tinta* (61.9%), *Tempranillo* (10%) and *Mazuela*.
**Authorized:** *Monastrell, Cabernet Sauvignon, Merlot* and *Syrah*.

| | |
|---|---|
| Hectares of Vineyard | 5,350 |
| Nº Viticulturists | 2,702 |
| Nº of Bodegas | 15 |
| 2008 Harvest | N/A |
| 2007 Production | 5,918,384 l. |
| Marketing | 15% domestic 85% export |

# DO CALATAYUD

**CONSEJO REGULADOR.**
Pol. Industrial La Charluca, 39. Apdo. Correos 40
50300 Calatayud (Zaragoza)
☎: 976 884 260 - Fax: 976 885 912
@ administracion@docalatayud.com
www.docalatayud.com

## GENERAL CHARACTERISTICS OF THE WINES:

| WHITES | These are pale yellow and are characterised by their fresh, fruity style. There is some experience with fermentation in barrels. |
|---|---|
| ROSÉS | These constitute the most characteristic product of the region and are excellent value for money. Produced mainly from *Garnacha*, they stand out for their fine varietal expression, their brilliant raspberry colour, their freshness, their strong nose and their full-bodiedness, typical of the variety. |
| REDS | The *Garnacha* grapes give these wines a lively dark colour. The finest examples have quite a strong nose, with notes of ripe black fruit; on the palate they are full-bodied and sometimes somewhat warm. |

## 2008 VINTAGE RATING:

# VERY GOOD

## AGUSTÍN CUBERO

La Charluca, s/n
50300 Calatayud (Zaragoza)
☎: 976 882 332 - Fax: 976 887 512
calatayud@bodegascubero.com
www.bodegascubero.com

CASTILLO DEL MAGO 2008 T
garnacha, tempranillo

**86** Colour: cherry, purple rim. Nose: powerful, ripe fruit, toasty, dark chocolate. Taste flavourful, fruity, round tannins.

UNUS 2007 T
syrah

**90** Colour: cherry, garnet rim. Nose: fruit preserve, dark chocolate, toasty. Taste flavourful, powerful, ripe fruit, spicy.

STYLO 2007 T

**89** Colour: cherry, garnet rim. Nose: powerful, ripe fruit, dark chocolate, sweet spices, earthy notes. Palate: flavourful, fruity, fleshy, round tannins.

## BODEGA CASTILLO DE MALUENDA

Avda. José Antonio, 61
50340 Maluenda (Zaragoza)
☎: 976 893 017 - Fax: 976 546 969
info@castillodemaluenda.com
www.castillodemaluenda.com

CASTILLO DE MALUENDA 2008 RD
garnacha 100%

**79**

VIÑA ALARBA VOLCÁN 2008 T
tempranillo 100%

**90** Colour: cherry, garnet rim. Nose: expressive, mineral, ripe fruit, spicy. Palate: flavourful, fleshy, fruity, round tannins.

CASTILLO DE MALUENDA 2008 T
tempranillo 60%, syrah 40%

**88** Colour: cherry, purple rim. Nose: powerful, balsamic herbs, scrubland, ripe fruit. Palate: flavourful, fruity, good acidity, round tannins.

CASTILLO DE MALUENDA VIÑAS VIEJAS 2008 T
garnacha 100%

**88** Colour: deep cherry. Nose: ripe fruit, red berry notes, fragrant herbs, dried flowers. Palate: flavourful, fruity, balsamic, round tannins.

CASTILLO DE MALUENDA GARNACHA SYRAH 2008 T
garnacha 60%, syrah 40%

**88** Colour: cherry, garnet rim. Nose: powerful, ripe fruit, fruit expression, floral. Palate: flavourful, ripe fruit, round tannins.

ALTO LAS PIZARRAS 2006 T
garnacha 100%

**92** Colour: cherry, garnet rim. Nose: expressive, elegant, ripe fruit, spicy, aromatic coffee. Palate: flavourful, ripe fruit, spicy, fine tannins.

CLARAVAL 2006 T
garnacha 50%, syrah 20%, cabernet sauvignon 20%, tempranillo 10%

**87** Colour: cherry, garnet rim. Nose: powerful, ripe fruit, warm, spicy. Palate: flavourful, spicy, ripe fruit.

LAS PIZARRAS 2005 T
garnacha 100%

**89** Colour: bright cherry. Nose: ripe fruit, sweet spices, creamy oak, mineral. Palate: flavourful, fruity, toasty, round tannins.

CASTILLO DE MALUENDA 2005 TC
tempranillo 60%, garnacha 30%, cabernet sauvignon 10%

**88** Colour: bright cherry. Nose: ripe fruit, sweet spices, lactic notes. Palate: flavourful, fruity, toasty, round tannins.

VIÑA ALARBA PAGO SAN MIGUEL 2005 T
garnacha 85%, syrah 15%

**87** Colour: cherry, garnet rim. Nose: fruit liqueur notes, ripe fruit, warm, toasty. Palate: flavourful, spicy, round tannins.

## BODEGA COOPERATIVA VIRGEN DE LA SIERRA

Avda. de la Cooperativa, 21-23
50310 Villarroya de la Sierra (Zaragoza)
☎: 976 899 015 - Fax: 976 899 132
oficina@bodegavirgendelasierra.com

ALBADA 2008 B
macabeo

**88** Colour: bright straw. Nose: floral, ripe fruit, wild herbs. Palate: flavourful, fruity, fresh, fleshy.

CRUZ DE PIEDRA 2008 B
macabeo

**84**

CRUZ DE PIEDRA 2008 RD
garnacha

**85** Colour: brilliant rose. Nose: fresh fruit, red berry notes, wild herbs. Palate: flavourful, fruity, fresh.

CRUZ DE PIEDRA 2008 T
garnacha

**86** Colour: cherry, purple rim. Nose: grassy, varietal, fresh fruit. Palate: flavourful, fruity, round tannins.

CRUZ DE PIEDRA CAPRICHO 2007 T
garnacha

**93** Colour: bright cherry. Nose: ripe fruit, sweet spices, creamy oak, expressive, cocoa bean, lactic notes. Palate: flavourful, fruity, toasty, round tannins.

ALBADA 2007 T
garnacha

**88** Colour: cherry, garnet rim. Nose: medium intensity, mineral, ripe fruit, warm. Palate: flavourful, powerful, spicy.

CRUZ DE PIEDRA CAPRICHO 2006 T
garnacha

**88** Colour: cherry, garnet rim. Nose: ripe fruit, fruit liqueur notes, warm, aromatic coffee. Palate: flavourful, powerful, spicy, round tannins.

ALBADA CALATAYUD SUPERIOR 2005 TR
garnacha 94%, merlot 6%

**91** Colour: cherry, garnet rim. Nose: powerful, ripe fruit, fruit preserve, creamy oak. Palate: flavourful, concentrated, spicy, round tannins.

ALBADA 2002 TR
tempranillo 45%, garnacha 25%, syrah 15%, cabernet sauvignon 15%

**88** Colour: cherry, garnet rim. Nose: ripe fruit, spicy, creamy oak, toasty. Palate: powerful, flavourful, toasty, round tannins.

## BODEGA SAN GREGORIO

Ctra. Villalengua s/n
50312 Cervera de la Cañada (Zaragoza)
☎: 976 899 206 - Fax: 976 896 240
tresojos@bodegasangregorio.com
www.bodegasangregorio.com

ARMANTES 2008 B
macabeo

**81**

ARMANTES 2008 RD
garnacha 50%, tempranillo 50%

**83**

ARMANTES SELECCIÓN ESPECIAL 2008 T
garnacha 60%, tempranillo 22%, syrah 6%, cabernet sauvignon 6%, merlot 6%

**89** Colour: cherry, purple rim. Nose: fresh fruit, red berry notes, floral, grassy, spicy. Palate: flavourful, fruity, good acidity, round tannins.

ARMANTES 2008 T
garnacha 50%, tempranillo 50%

**88** Colour: cherry, purple rim. Nose: fresh fruit, red berry notes, floral. Palate: flavourful, fruity, good acidity, round tannins.

TRES OJOS TEMPRANILLO 2008 T
tempranillo

**88** Colour: cherry, purple rim. Nose: fresh fruit, red berry notes, floral. Taste flavourful, fruity, good acidity, round tannins.

TRES OJOS GARNACHA 2008 T
garnacha

**86** Colour: cherry, purple rim. Nose: fresh fruit, red berry notes, varietal, grassy. Palete: flavourful, fruity, good acidity, round tannins.

MANGA DEL BRUJO 2007 T
garnacha 65%, syrah 15%, tempranillo 15%, monastrell 5%, mazuelo 5%

**90** Colour: cherry, purple rim. Nose: powerful, expressive, complex, sweet spices, aromatic coffee. Palate: flavourful, fruity, spicy, round tannins.

ARMANTES SELECCIÓN ESPECIAL 2007 T
garnacha, tempranillo, syrah, cabernet sauvignon, merlot

**89** Colour: dark-red cherry. Nose: ripe fruit, powerfull, new oak, mineral. Palate: powerful, flavourful, ripe fruit, creamy, round tannins.

TRES OJOS SHIRAZ MERLOT 2007 T
syrah 60%, merlot 40%

**87** Colour: cherry, purple rim. Nose: red berry notes, ripe fruit, scrubland. Palate: flavourful, fruity, good acidity, round tannins.

## ARMANTES GARNACHA VIEJA 2006 TC

**88** Colour: cherry, garnet rim. Nose: ripe fruit, spicy, mineral. Taste flavourful, fruity, spicy, round tannins.

## ARMANTES SELECCIÓN 20 BARRICAS 2004 TR

**86** Colour: cherry, garnet rim. Nose: ripe fruit, fruit preserve, sweet spices, dark chocolate. Taste flavourful, fleshy, spicy, round tannins.

## BODEGAS ATECA

Ctra. Nacional II,s/n
50200 Ateca (Zaragoza)
☎: 629 261 379 - Fax: 968 716 051
info@orowine.com

### GARNACHA DE FUEGO 2008 T
garnacha 100%

**89** Colour: cherry, garnet rim. Nose: ripe fruit, floral, spicy, mineral. Palate: flavourful, powerful, good structure, spicy, ripe fruit, round tannins.

### ATTECA 2007 T
garnacha 100%

**89** Colour: cherry, garnet rim. Nose: expressive, elegant, mineral, ripe fruit, fresh fruit. Palate: flavourful, fruity, fresh, good acidity.

### ATTECA ARMAS 2006 T
garnacha 100%

**89** Colour: cherry, garnet rim. Nose: powerful, ripe fruit, warm, roasted coffee, dark chocolate. Palate: flavourful, powerful, fleshy, spicy.

## BODEGAS GUERRERO SEBASTIAN

Ctra. Daroca, 6
50347 Acered (Zaragoza)
☎: 976 896 704 - Fax: 976 896 704
info@bodegasguerrerosebastian.com
www.bodegasguerrerosebastian.com

### AZERÉ 2008 B
macabeo 100%

**82**

### AZERÉ GARNACHA + DE 50 2006 T
garnacha 100%

**90** Colour: cherry, garnet rim. Nose: expressive, mineral, ripe fruit, floral, new oak. Palate: flavourful, powerful, ripe fruit, spicy, round tannins.

### AZERÉ 2006 TC
garnacha 100%

**88** Colour: cherry, garnet rim. Nose: powerful, ripe fruit, floral, mineral, sweet spices. Palate: flavourful, spicy, ripe fruit, easy to drink.

## BODEGAS LANGA

Ctra. Nacional II, km. 241,700
50300 Calatayud (Zaragoza)
☎: 976 881 818 - Fax: 976 884 463
info@bodegas-langa.com
www.bodegas-langa.com

### LANGA 2008 RD
cabernet sauvignon 50%, syrah 50%

**80**

### LAJAS 2007 T
garnacha 90%, otras 10%

**91** Colour: cherry, purple rim. Nose: powerful, ripe fruit, mineral, sweet spices. Palate: flavourful, powerful, fleshy, round tannins.

### LANGA GARNACHA CENTENARIA 2007 T
garnacha 100%

**88** Colour: cherry, garnet rim. Nose: new oak, toasty, dark chocolate, ripe fruit. Palate: powerful, ripe fruit, round tannins.

### LANGA MERLOT 2007 T
merlot 100%

**85** Colour: cherry, garnet rim. Nose: powerful, ripe fruit, dark chocolate, aged wood nuances. Palate: powerful, fleshy, sweetness, round tannins.

### REYES DE ARAGÓN MERLOT SYRAH 2006 T
merlot 50%, syrah 50%

**88** Colour: cherry, garnet rim. Nose: powerful, ripe fruit, scrubland, toasty. Palate: powerful, flavourful, fleshy.

### REYES DE ARAGÓN 2006 TC
cabernet sauvignon 50%, garnacha 50%

**88** Colour: cherry, garnet rim. Nose: powerful, ripe fruit, spicy. Palate: flavourful, powerful, spicy, round tannins.

### REAL DE ARAGÓN CENTENARIA 2006 T
garnacha 100%

**88** Colour: cherry, garnet rim. Nose: powerful, ripe fruit, sweet spices, creamy oak. Palate: flavourful, powerful, spicy, round tannins.

## LANGA CABERNET SYRAH 2006 T
cabernet sauvignon 50%, syrah 50%

**87** Colour: cherry, garnet rim. Nose: powerful, ripe fruit, toasty. Palate: flavourful, powerful, fleshy, ripe fruit.

## REYES DE ARAGÓN 2004 TR
merlot 50%, garnacha 50%

**88** Colour: cherry, garnet rim. Nose: toasty, dark chocolate, fruit preserve. Palate: flavourful, sweetness, spicy.

## BODEGAS LUGUS

El Charquillo s/n
50300 Calatayud (Zaragoza)
☎: 976 884 748 - Fax: 976 466 831
lugus@bodegaslugus.com
www.bodegaslugus.com

### LUG 2005 TC
garnacha 100%

**88** Colour: cherry, garnet rim. Nose: powerful, ripe fruit, fruit preserve, spicy, new oak, dark chocolate. Palate: flavourful, powerful, ripe fruit, round tannins.

## BODEGAS SAN ALEJANDRO

Ctra. Calatayud - Cariñena, km. 16
50330 Miedes de Aragón (Zaragoza)
☎: 976 892 205 - Fax: 976 890 540
bodegas@san-alejandro.com
www.san-alejandro.com

### BALTASAR GRACIÁN VENDIMIA SELECCIONADA 2008 B
macabeo 100%

**85** Colour: straw. Nose: floral, fresh fruit, ripe fruit, tropical fruit. Palate: flavourful, fruity, fresh, fleshy.

### BALTASAR GRACIÁN BLANCO DE HIELO 2008 B
macabeo 100%

**78**

### BALTASAR GRACIÁN VENDIMIA SELECCIONADA 2008 RD
garnacha 100%

**87** Colour: raspberry rose. Nose: elegant, candied fruit, dried flowers, fragrant herbs, red berry notes. Palate: light-bodied, flavourful, good acidity, long, spicy.

### BALTASAR GRACIÁN VENDIMIA SELECCIONADA 2008 T
garnacha 100%

**87** Colour: cherry, purple rim. Nose: powerful, fresh fruit, floral, mineral, grassy. Palate: flavourful, balsamic, round tannins.

### BALTASAR GRACIÁN GARNACHA VIÑAS VIEJAS 2007 T
garnacha 100%

**91** Colour: bright cherry. Nose: ripe fruit, creamy oak, lactic notes, cocoa bean, mineral. Palate: flavourful, fruity, toasty, round tannins.

### BALTASAR GRACIÁN TEMPRANILLO VIÑAS VIEJAS 2007 T ROBLE
tempranillo 100%

**90** Colour: bright cherry. Nose: ripe fruit, sweet spices, creamy oak, scrubland. Palate: flavourful, fruity, toasty, round tannins.

### BALTASAR GRACIÁN EXPRESIÓN 2007 T ROBLE
garnacha 53%, tempranillo 19%, syrah 28%

**88** Colour: cherry, garnet rim. Nose: powerful, ripe fruit, sweet spices, dark chocolate. Palate: flavourful, fruity, fresh.

### BALTASAR GRACIÁN CALATAYUD SUPERIOR 2005 T
garnacha 100%

**94** Colour: cherry, garnet rim. Nose: ripe fruit, spicy, creamy oak, toasty, complex, mineral, fragrant herbs. Palate: powerful, flavourful, toasty, round tannins.

### BALTASAR GRACIÁN 2004 TR
garnacha 70%, tempranillo 20%, cabernet sauvignon 10%

**90** Colour: cherry, garnet rim. Nose: ripe fruit, spicy, creamy oak, toasty, fragrant herbs. Palate: powerful, flavourful, toasty, round tannins.

### BALTASAR GRACIÁN 2004 TC
garnacha 60%, tempranillo 30%, syrah 10%

**89** Colour: bright cherry, garnet rim. Nose: ripe fruit, sweet spices, creamy oak, expressive, mineral. Palate: flavourful, fruity, toasty, round tannins.

LAS ROCAS

## LOBBAN WINE

Creueta, 24
08784 St. Jaume Sesoliveres (Barcelona)
☎: 667 551 695
pamelageddes@terra.es
www.lapamelita.com

EL GORDITO 2005 T
garnacha 45%, syrah 45%, tempranillo 10%

**87** Colour: cherry, garnet rim. Nose: powerful, ripe fruit, aromatic coffee, warm. Palate: flavourful, powerful, spicy.

## SOME OTHER WINERIES WITHIN THE DO:

**BODEGAS Y VINOS ÁNGEL LUIS PABLO URIOL**
**GALGO WINES**
**NIÑO JESÚS S.A.T.**
**SOCIEDAD COOP. VIRGEN DE LA PEANA**

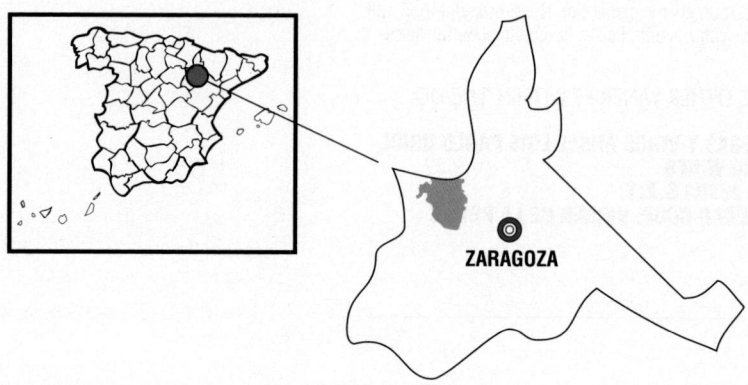

ZARAGOZA

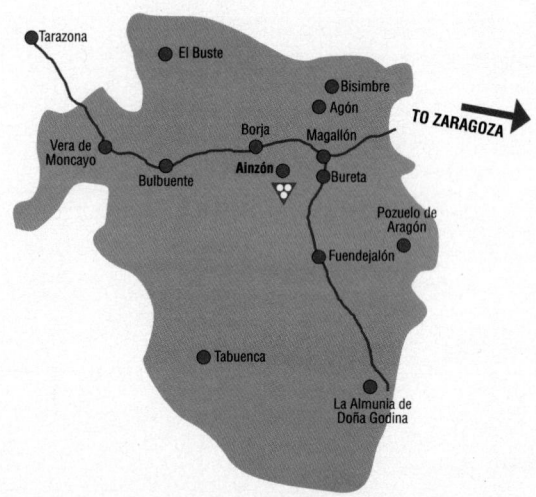

Tarazona

El Buste

Bisimbre

Agón

TO ZARAGOZA

Vera de Moncayo

Borja

Magallón

Ainzón

Bulbuente

Bureta

Pozuelo de Aragón

Fuendejalón

Tabuenca

La Almunia de Doña Godina

▽ Consejo Regulador
● DO Boundary

## NEWS

The production decrease of around 30% in Campo de Borja for the 2008 vintage has not affected the overall quality. This Spanish DO, part of the autonomous region of Aragón, located in the town of Ainzón and pretty much controlled by cooperatives, still keeps high production figures of nearly thirty million kilograms. The vines –surely the oldest in the region– affected by this decrease were those on the slopes of mount Montcayo. In the wines tasted this year we can appreciate the effect of day-night temperature contrast, which provides a slower ripening pattern and richer fruit notes. White wines have improved a lot and the rosé renderings show lovely red fruit notes and a fine floral character. Old garnacha vines are in wonderful shape and show all their quality potential and elegance in the wines from Bodegas Alto Moncayo, Borsao (also participated by Alto Moncayo) and Bodegas Aragonesas. A new winery, Pagos de Moncayo, is working intensely on terroir expression. The DO, named as the "Empire of Garnacha", is bottling lovely, rich, creamy and almost liquereux garnacha wines of an intensely aromatic character. These varietal wines come mostly from the so-called "garnachas de monte" or mountain garnachas, usually old vines planted at high altitude. The lower-rated, medium range wines, are blends destined for a less knowledgeable type of consumer. Sales figures for the DO are up, helped by good marketing strategies promoted mainly in international markets by some of the most dynamic and forward-looking wineries.

## LOCATION

The DO Campo de Borja is made up of 16 municipal areas, situated in the north west of the province of Zaragoza and 60 km from the capital city, in an area of transition between the mountains of the Sistema Ibérico (at the foot of the Moncayo) and the Ebro Valley: Agón, Ainzón, Alberite, Albeta, Ambel, Bisimbre, Borja, Bulbuente, Burueta, El Buste, Fuendejalón, Magallón, Malejan, Pozuelo de Aragón, Tabuenca and Vera del Moncayo.

## CLIMATE

A rather extreme continental climate, with cold winters and dry, hot summers. One of its main characteristics is the influence of the 'Cierzo', a cold and dry north - westerly wind. Rainfall is rather scarce, with an average of between 350 and 450 mm per year.

## SOIL

The most abundant are brownish - grey limey soils, terrace soils and clayey ferrous soils. The vineyards are situated at an altitude of between 350 and 700 m on small slightly rolling hillsides, on terraces of the Huecha river and the Llanos de Plasencia, making up the Somontano del Moncayo.

## GRAPE VARIETIES:

**White:** *Macabeo, Moscatel, Chardonnay.*
**Red:** *Garnacha* (majority with 75%), *Tempranillo, Mazuela, Cabernet Sauvignon, Merlot, Syrah.*

| | |
|---|---|
| Hectares of Vineyard | 7,432 |
| Nº Viticulturists | 1,267 |
| Nº of Bodegas | 17 |
| 2008 Harvest | Good |
| 2007 Production | 16,600,000 l. |
| Marketing | 58.8% domestic 41.2 export |

**CONSEJO REGULADOR.**
Subida de San Andrés, 6
50570 Ainzón (Zaragoza).
☎: 976 852 122 - Fax: 976 868 806
@ vinos@campodeborja.com
www.campodeborja.com

## GENERAL CHARACTERISTICS OF THE WINES:

| | |
|---|---|
| **WHITES** | Mainly produced from *Macabeo*, they are light, fresh and pleasant. There is also experience with white wines fermented in barrels. |
| **ROSÉS** | With notably fine quality, they are produced mainly from *Garnacha*; they are somewhat fresher than those of Cariñena and stand out for the full-bodied character that the variety provides. |
| **REDS** | Also based on the *Garnacha*, they are the most important type of wine in the region. In their youth, dark cherry coloured, they have a fine intense nose and offer notes of ripe black fruit; they are flavourful, fruity and meaty. The Crianza reds are somewhat lighter and more round; the Reservas and Gran Reservas produced in the traditional manner, however, may have animal nuances and hints of reduced fruit with the rusty character of the *Garnacha*. |

## 2008 VINTAGE RATING:

# VERY GOOD

## BODEGAS ALTO MONCAYO

Residencia Paraíso, 1 Esc. B 1 E
50008 (Zaragoza)
☎: 976 867 807 - Fax: 976 868 147
info@bodegasaltomoncayo.com

AQUILÓN 2006 T
garnacha 100%

**95** Colour: cherry, garnet rim. Nose: closed, ripe fruit, fruit preserve, sweet spices, creamy oak. Palate: flavourful, powerful, fleshy, concentrated, spicy, round tannins.

ALTO MONCAYO 2006 T
garnacha 100%

**94** Colour: cherry, garnet rim. Nose: powerfull, expressive, characterful, ripe fruit, fruit preserve, sweet spices, creamy oak. Palate: flavourful, powerful, fleshy, complex, round tannins.

ALTO MONCAYO VERATÓN 2006 T
garnacha 100%

**91** Colour: cherry, garnet rim. Nose: powerfull, warm, ripe fruit, mineral, sweet spices. Palate: flavourful, ripe fruit, balanced, fine bitter notes.

## BODEGAS ARAGONESAS

Ctra. Magallón, s/n
50529 Fuendejalón (Zaragoza)
☎: 976 862 153 - Fax: 976 862 363
luis@bodegasaragonesas.com
www.bodegasaragonesas.com

COTO DE HAYAS 2008 B
chardonnay

**86** Colour: yellow, pale. Nose: neat, fresh fruit, tropical fruit. Palate: fresh, fruity, easy to drink.

COTO DE HAYAS 2007 BFB

**86** Colour: bright yellow. Nose: powerfull, ripe fruit, sweet spices, fragrant herbs. Palate: rich, smoky aftertaste, flavourful, fresh, good acidity.

COTO DE HAYAS 2008 RD
garnacha, cabernet sauvignon

**85** Colour: rose, bright. Nose: expressive, red berry notes, rose petals. Palate: flavourful, slightly acidic, good finish.

COTO DE HAYAS GARNACHA CENTENARIA 2008 T
garnacha

**91** Colour: bright cherry. Nose: ripe fruit, sweet spices, creamy oak, expressive. Palate: flavourful, fruity, toasty, round tannins.

COTO DE HAYAS SOLO 09 SYRAH 2008 T
syrah

**88** Colour: cherry, purple rim. Nose: powerfull, characterful, ripe fruit, floral, warm. Palate: powerful, spicy, pruney, round tannins.

COTO DE HAYAS 2008 T
garnacha, syrah

**87** Colour: cherry, purple rim. Nose: expressive, red berry notes, floral. Palate: flavourful, fruity, good acidity, round tannins.

COTO DE HAYAS TEMPRANILLO CABERNET 2008 T ROBLE
tempranillo, cabernet sauvignon

**87** Colour: cherry, garnet rim. Nose: medium intensity, ripe fruit, scrubland, floral. Palate: flavourful, powerful, spicy.

FAGUS DE COTO DE HAYAS 2007 T
garnacha

**91** Colour: black cherry. Nose: ripe fruit, fruit expression, toasty, earthy notes, dark chocolate, fruit liqueur notes. Palate: powerful, flavourful, fleshy, fine bitter notes, roasted-coffee aftertaste.

COTO DE HAYAS GARNACHA CENTENARIA 2007 T
garnacha

**89** Colour: bright cherry. Nose: powerfull, fruit expression, fresh fruit, balsamic herbs, sweet spices. Palate: fresh, fruity, flavourful, good acidity, harsh oak tannins.

DON RAMÓN 2007 T BARRICA
garnacha 75%, tempranillo 25%

**87** Colour: cherry, garnet rim. Nose: expressive, red berry notes, floral, sweet spices. Palate: flavourful, long, fruity aftestaste, great length, harsh oak tannins.

FAGUS DE COTO DE HAYAS 2006 T
garnacha 100%

**91** Colour: very deep cherry. Nose: expressive, complex, ripe fruit, dry stone, cocoa bean, cedar wood, fruit liqueur notes, aged wood nuances, creamy oak. Palate: flavourful, fleshy, round tannins, fine bitter notes, spirituous.

COTO DE HAYAS 2006 TC

**89** Colour: bright cherry. Nose: ripe fruit, sweet spices, roasted coffee. Palate: flavourful, fruity, toasty, round tannins.

CASTILLO DE FUENDEJALON 2006 TC

**86** Colour: pale ruby, brick rim edge. Nose: overripe fruit, fruit liqueur notes, sweet spices. Palate: flavourful, sweetness, toasty, grainy tannins.

COTO DE HAYAS 2005 TR

**89** Colour: dark-red cherry, garnet rim. Nose: powerfull, ripe fruit, warm, spicy, roasted coffee. Palate: flavourful, powerful, spicy, long.

COTO DE HAYAS 2005 TC
garnacha 60%, tempranillo 40%

**88** Colour: cherry, garnet rim. Nose: neat, powerfull, ripe fruit, fruit liqueur notes. Palate: good structure, powerful, fleshy, slightly dry, soft tannins.

DON RAMÓN 2005 TC
garnacha 75%, tempranillo 25%

**87** Colour: cherry, garnet rim. Nose: fruit liqueur notes, sweet spices. Palate: flavourful, great length, slightly dry, soft tannins.

MOSÉN CLETO 2005 TC
garnacha 75%, tempranillo 25%

**85** Colour: cherry, garnet rim. Nose: ripe fruit, fruit liqueur notes. Palate: flavourful, toasty, good finish.

COTO DE HAYAS 2004 TR
garnacha

**90** Colour: cherry, garnet rim. Nose: spicy, toasty, ripe fruit. Palate: flavourful, spicy, round tannins.

OXIA 2004 TC
garnacha

**88** Colour: deep cherry. Nose: aged wood nuances, new oak, cedar wood, short, fresh fruit. Palate: lacks expression, toasty.

COTO DE HAYAS MOSCATEL 2008
VINO DULCE NATURAL
moscatel

**86** Colour: bright straw. Nose: medium intensity, fresh, candied fruit. Palate: flavourful, fruity, sweetness.

COTO DE HAYAS MISTELA VINO DULCE NATURAL
garnacha

**88** Colour: cherry, garnet rim. Nose: fruit liqueur notes, candied fruit, sweet spices. Palate: spirituous, sweet, powerful, great length.

ARAGUS

CRUCILLÓN

## BODEGAS BORDEJÉ

Ctra. Borja - Rueda, km. 3
50570 Ainzón (Zaragoza)
☎: 976 868 080 - Fax: 976 868 989
pedidos@bodegasbordeje.com
www.bodegasbordeje.com

ABUELO NICOLÁS 2007 T
merlot 100%

**82**

PAGO DE ROMEROSO 2006 T
tempranillo 100%

**88** Colour: black cherry. Nose: powerfull, complex, ripe fruit, warm, dark chocolate. Palate: flavourful, powerful, round tannins.

LELES DE BORDEJE 2006 T
garnacha 100%

**88** Colour: bright cherry. Nose: ripe fruit, sweet spices, roasted coffee, smoky. Palate: flavourful, fruity, toasty, round tannins.

PAGO DE HUECHASECA 2005 T
tempranillo 45%, merlot 40%, cabernet sauvignon 15%

**89** Colour: very deep cherry. Nose: ripe fruit, dark chocolate, aged wood nuances, mineral. Palate: flavourful, spicy, ripe fruit.

DON PABLO 2003 TR
tempranillo 50%, garnacha 50%

**83**

BORDEJÉ 2000 TR
tempranillo 50%, garnacha 50%

**82**

## BODEGAS BORSAO S.A.

Ctra. Nac. 122, km. 63
50540 Borja (Zaragoza)
☎: 976 867 116 - Fax: 976 867 752
i.alberto@bodegasborsao.com
www.bodegasborsao.com

BORSAO SELECCIÓN 2008 RD
garnacha

**85** Colour: light cherry. Nose: neat, fresh fruit, wild herbs. Palate: fresh, fruity, easy to drink.

**BORSAO SELECCIÓN 2008 T JOVEN**
garnacha 70%, syrah 20%, tempranillo 10%

**87** Colour: very deep cherry. Nose: neat, red berry notes, floral. Palate: flavourful, easy to drink, long.

**BORSAO TRES PICOS GARNACHA 2007 T**
garnacha

**91** Colour: cherry, garnet rim. Nose: powerfull, expressive, ripe fruit, mineral. Palate: flavourful, fruity, spicy, round tannins.

**BORSAO BOLE 2007 T**
garnacha, syrah

**89** Colour: dark-red cherry. Nose: expressive, faded flowers, sweet spices, ripe fruit. Palate: flavourful, full, great length, round tannins.

**BORSAO SELECCIÓN 2006 TC**
garnacha, tempranillo, merlot

**88** Colour: very deep cherry. Nose: characterful, fruit liqueur notes, creamy oak. Palate: flavourful, toasty, round tannins.

**BORSAO SELECCIÓN 2005 TR**
garnacha, tempranillo, cabernet sauvignon

**90** Colour: cherry, garnet rim. Nose: ripe fruit, spicy, creamy oak, toasty, complex. Palate: powerful, flavourful, toasty, round tannins.

## CRIANZAS Y VIÑEDOS SANTO CRISTO

Ctra. Tabuenca, s/n
50570 Ainzón (Zaragoza)
☎: 976 869 696 - Fax: 976 868 097
info@bodegas-santo-cristo.com
www.bodegas-santo-cristo.com

**VIÑA COLLADO 2008 B**
macabeo 100%

**85** Colour: bright straw. Nose: fresh, fresh fruit, white flowers, expressive. Palate: flavourful, fruity, good acidity, balanced.

**MOSCATEL AINZÓN 90 DÍAS 2007 B BARRICA**
moscatel 100%

**91** Colour: golden. Nose: powerfull, floral, honeyed notes, candied fruit, fragrant herbs. Palate: flavourful, sweet, fresh, fruity, good acidity, long.

**VIÑA COLLADO 2008 RD**
garnacha 100%

**88** Colour: rose, purple rim. Nose: powerfull, ripe fruit, red berry notes, floral, expressive. Palate: fleshy, powerful, fruity, fresh.

**VIÑA COLLADO 2008 T**
garnacha 60%, tempranillo 40%

**89** Colour: cherry, purple rim. Nose: neat, ripe fruit, dried flowers. Palate: spicy, long, flavourful, round tannins.

**TERRAZAS DEL MONCAYO 2007 T ROBLE**
garnacha 100%

**90** Colour: very deep cherry. Nose: powerfull, fruit liqueur notes, sweet spices, creamy oak. Palate: flavourful, sweetness, spicy, round tannins.

**CAYUS SELECCIÓN 2007 T**
garnacha 100%

**83**

**SANTO CRISTO 60 ANIVERSARIO 2006 T**
garnacha 100%

**89** Colour: cherry, garnet rim. Nose: ripe fruit, dried flowers. Palate: full, flavourful, spicy, fine bitter notes, slightly dry, soft tannins.

**PEÑAZUELA SELECCIÓN 2006 T ROBLE**
garnacha 100%

**88** Colour: cherry, purple rim. Nose: neat, fruit liqueur notes, faded flowers. Palate: good structure, varietal, fleshy, great length.

**VIÑA AINZÓN 2005 TR**

**87** Colour: cherry, garnet rim. Nose: expressive, ripe fruit, fruit liqueur notes, creamy oak. Palate: flavourful, good structure, fine bitter notes.

**VIÑA AINZÓN 2005 TC**
garnacha 60%, tempranillo 30%, cabernet sauvignon 10%

**86** Colour: cherry, garnet rim. Nose: characterful, ripe fruit, fruit liqueur notes, sweet spices. Palate: flavourful, full, spicy, great length.

**VIÑA AINZÓN PREMIUM 2005 TR**
garnacha 100%

**83**

**VIÑA AINZÓN 2003 TR**
garnacha 70%, tempranillo 30%

**85** Colour: pale ruby, brick rim edge. Nose: characterful, fruit preserve. Palate: flavourful, full, balanced, round tannins.

MOSCATEL AINZÓN 2008 VINO DE LICOR
moscatel 100%

**85** Colour: bright straw. Nose: candied fruit, honeyed notes, fragrant herbs. Palate: flavourful, powerful, sweetness.

## PAGOS DEL MONCAYO

Ctra. Z-372, km. 1,6
50580 Vera de Moncayo (Zaragoza)
☎: 976 900 256 - Fax: 976 900 257
info@pagosdelmoncayo.com
www.pagosdelmoncayo.com

PAGOS DEL MONCAYO 2008 T
garnacha 65%, syrah 35%

**88** Colour: cherry, garnet rim. Nose: elegant, scrubland, balsamic herbs, ripe fruit. Palate: flavourful, fruity, spicy.

PAGOS DEL MONCAYO SYRAH 2008 T
syrah 100%

**88** Colour: cherry, purple rim. Nose: powerfull, ripe fruit, floral, scrubland, balsamic herbs. Palate: flavourful, fruity, good structure, spicy.

PAGOS DEL MONCAYO 2007 T
garnacha 100%

**90** Colour: cherry, purple rim. Nose: medium intensity, ripe fruit, scrubland, creamy oak, mineral. Palate: flavourful, fleshy, ripe fruit, great length.

## RUBERTE HERMANOS

Tenor Fleta, s/n
50520 Magallón (Zaragoza)
☎: 976 858 106 - Fax: 976 858 475
info@bodegasruberte.com
www.bodegasruberte.com

RUBERTE 2008 B
macabeo

**83**

RUBERTE 2008 RD

**86** Colour: rose, purple rim. Nose: medium intensity, red berry notes, ripe fruit. Palate: flavourful, fruity, fresh.

F DE ALIANA 2008 TC
garnacha

**90** Colour: cherry, purple rim. Nose: expressive, red berry notes, violets, lactic notes, sweet spices. Palate: flavourful, balanced, great length.

RUBERTE 2008 T JOVEN
garnacha

**86** Colour: cherry, purple rim. Nose: fruit preserve, dried flowers. Palate: powerful, flavourful, round tannins.

RUBERTE TRESOR T
garnacha

**88** Colour: cherry, garnet rim. Nose: powerfull, fruit liqueur notes, overripe fruit, toasty. Palate: fleshy, concentrated, slightly dry, soft tannins.

RUBERTE VINO DE LICOR T

**87** Colour: cherry, garnet rim. Nose: medium intensity, candied fruit, raspberry. Palate: flavourful, fleshy, warm, fine bitter notes.

MUZA ALCORAZ
ALIANA
MORAVIÑA
CAMINO AL MONCAYO

SOME OTHER WINERIES WITHIN THE DO:

**BODEGAS AGRO-FRAGO**
**DELFÍN PARDOS BONA**
**MARECA**
**ROMÁN S.C.**
**VINOS CERRO CORPENT S.L.**

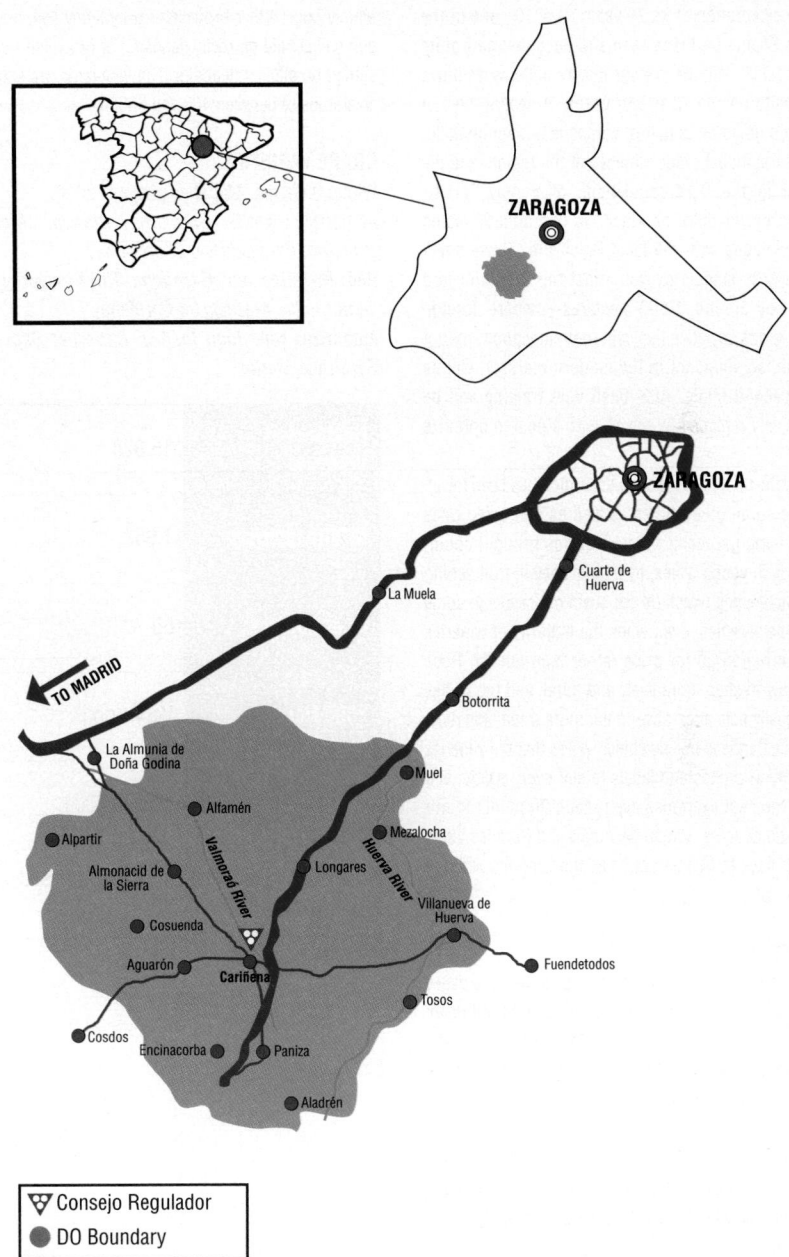

☒ Consejo Regulador
● DO Boundary

## NEWS

With the celebration of its 75 years as a DO –one of the oldest in Spain– Cariñena seems to have lost part of its vigour in 2008, with the average quality of its wines down a few points compared to last year's. A second sort of celebration going on is that of garnacha and tempranillo, the most traditional grape varieties in the region, and the inclusion in the DO's regulations of a new variety, crespiello or vidadillo, of which we had already tasted various vintages with the label Pulchrum. These small turns towards singularity will affect the DO's vineyard surface –of around 1.600 hectares–, where foreign (French) grape varieties like cabernet sauvignon, merlot and syrah, so abundant in the modern markets, will be playing second fiddle. Also bush vine training will be progressively replaced by guyot, with a goal to optimize costs.

This year, the total production in the region has been lower. There are some green notes as well as confected ones even in young garnacha wines, features brought about, particularly in young wines, by a deficiency in fruit setting and late harvesting which do not seem noticeable in some other grape varieties, even when the majority of wineries within the region go for price rather than quality. Rosé wines show fresher, more lively and floral, and the whites are an equally safe alternative to the more traditional reds. In any case Cariñena means choice, given that the wineries have plenty of brands and labels to suit every palate, and some of the best examples even reach 90 points in our rating. Pago de Aylés, Virgen del Águila and Grandes Vinos y Viñedos have to be mentioned as the wineries with the best potential.

## LOCATION

In the province of Zaragoza, and occupies the Ebro valley covering 14 municipal areas: Aguarón, Aladrén, Alfamén, Almonacid de la Sierra, Alpartir, Cariñena, Cosuenda, Encinacorba, Longares, Mezalocha, Muel, Paniza, Tosos and Villanueva de Huerva.

## CLIMATE

A continental climate, with cold winters, hot summers and low rainfall. The viticulture is also influenced by the effect of the 'Cierzo'.

## SOIL

Mainly poor; either brownish - grey limey soil, or reddish dun soil settled on rocky deposits, or brownish - grey soil settled on alluvial deposits. The vineyards are situated at an altitude of between 400 and 800 m.

## GRAPE VARIETIES:

**White:** Preferred: *Macabeo* (majority 20%).
Authorized white: *Garnacha Blanca, Moscatel Romano, Parellada* and *Chardonnay*.
**Red:** Preferred red: *Garnacha Tinta* (majority 55%), *Tempranillo, Mazuela* (or *Cariñena*).
**Authorized red:** *Juan Ibáñez, Cabernet Sauvignon, Syrah* and *Merlot*.

| | |
|---|---|
| Hectares of Vineyard | 15,925 |
| Nº Viticulturists | 1,952 |
| Nº of Bodegas | 55 |
| 2008 Harvest | Very Good |
| 2007 Production | 50,388,200 l. |
| Marketing | 47.72% domestic 52.28% export |

**CONSEJO REGULADOR.**
Camino de la Platera, 7. 50400 Cariñena (Zaragoza)
☎: 976 793 031 - Fax: 976 621 107
@ consejoregulador@docarinena.com
@ promocion@docarinena.com
www.docarinena.com

## GENERAL CHARACTERISTICS OF THE WINES:

| WHITES | These are not the most important of the region. They are characterised by their straw yellow colour, notes of ripe fruit and fruity character. |
|---|---|
| ROSÉS | Most are the result of new technology: they are pink, with fine fruit intensity and flavourful on the palate, thanks to the intervention of the *Garnacha*. |
| REDS | These are the wines par excellence of the region, quite robust with a warm character. The young wines have a dark cherry colour with hints of violet and noses of ripe fruit reminiscent of blackberries and plums; thanks to the *Garnacha*, they are also very flavourful on the palate. The Crianza wines maintain these characteristics, although they are more supple due to being aged in barrels; these may display balsamic notes and dark-roasted flavours; on the palate they are supple and warm. These long-aged wines, if only produced from *Garnacha*, may have rough notes due to the fact that this grape variety does not age very well. |

## 2008 VINTAGE RATING:

# GOOD

## BIOENOS S.L.

Mayor, 88
50400 Cariñena (Zaragoza)
☎: 976 620 045 - Fax: 976 622 082
bioenos@bioenos.com
www.bioenos.com

PULCHRUM CRESPIELLO 2006 T
vidadielo 100%

**87** Colour: black cherry. Nose: powerful, fruit preserve, overripe fruit, new oak. Palate: powerful, fleshy, pruney, balsamic.

PULCHRUM CRESPIELLO 2004 T
vidadillo

**88** Colour: cherry, garnet rim. Nose: powerful, ripe fruit, balsamic herbs, sweet spices. Palate: flavourful, powerful, fleshy.

## BODEGA ESTEBAN MARTIN

Camino Virgen de Lagunas s/n
50461 Alfamén (Zaragoza)
☎: 976 625 016 - Fax: 976 625 029
villarllorente@hotmail.com

ESTEBAN MARTÍN 2008 B

**87** Colour: pale. Nose: ripe fruit, tropical fruit, honeyed notes. Palate: fruity, fresh, flavourful, light-bodied.

ESTEBAN MARTÍN CHARDONNAY
SELECCIÓN 2008 B

**80**

ESTEBAN MARTÍN 2005 TC

**88** Colour: cherry, garnet rim. Nose: medium intensity, ripe fruit, sweet spices. Palate: flavourful, fresh, spicy.

ESTEBAN MARTÍN 2004 TR

**83**

## BODEGAS AÑADAS

Ctra. Aguarón, Km 47,100
50400 Cariñena (Zaragoza)
☎: 976 793 016 - Fax: 976 620 448
bodega@carewines.com
www.carewines.com

CARE CHARDONNAY 2008 B
chardonnay 100%

**86** Colour: pale. Nose: fruit preserve, floral, grassy. Palate: fruity, fresh, rich.

CARE 2008 RD
cabernet sauvignon 50%, tempranillo 50%

**87** Colour: rose, purple rim. Nose: medium intensity, candied fruit, red berry notes. Palate: sweetness, rich, fruity, fresh.

CARE 2007 T ROBLE
syrah 50%, tempranillo 50%

**89** Colour: cherry, purple rim. Nose: powerful, ripe fruit, red berry notes, lactic notes, sweet spices, creamy oak. Palate: flavourful, powerful, fleshy, round tannins.

CARE XCLNT 2006 T
cabernet sauvignon 45%, syrah 45%, garnacha 10%

**90** Colour: cherry, garnet rim. Nose: powerful, ripe fruit, warm, toasty, dark chocolate, damp undergrowth. Palate: flavourful, powerful, fleshy, fine bitter notes, round tannins.

CARE 2006 TC
merlot 50%, tempranillo 50%

**88** Colour: cherry, garnet rim. Nose: toasty, dark chocolate, fruit preserve. Palate: spicy, ripe fruit, round tannins.

CARE FINCA BANCALES 2005 T BARRICA
garnacha 85%, cabernet sauvignon 15%

**88** Colour: cherry, garnet rim. Nose: powerful, ripe fruit, overripe fruit, sweet spices. Palate: flavourful, powerful, fleshy, round tannins.

## BODEGAS DEL SEÑORÍO S.A.

Afueras, s/n
50108 Almonacid de la Sierra (Zaragoza)
☎: 976 627 225 - Fax: 976 627 225

info@bodegasdelsenorio.com
www.bodegasdelsenorio.com

SENDA LASARDA 2008 B

**86** Colour: pale. Nose: medium intensity, fresh fruit, tropical fruit, floral. Palate: fruity, fresh, light-bodied.

DOBLE EXCELENT 2004 TC

**83**

SEÑORÍO DE LA OBRA 2004 TR

**81**

SEÑORÍO DE LA OBRA 2002 TGR

**81**

## BODEGAS IGNACIO MARÍN

San Valero, 1
50400 Cariñena (Zaragoza)
☎: 976 621 129 - Fax: 976 621 031
comercial@ignaciomarin.com
www.ignaciomarin.com

DUQUE DE MEDINA 2008 B

**84**

DUQUE DE MEDINA 2008 T

**87** Colour: cherry, purple rim. Nose: fresh fruit, red berry notes, floral. Palate: flavourful, fruity, good acidity, round tannins.

MARÍN GARNACHA 2005 T

**88** Colour: cherry, garnet rim. Nose: medium intensity, ripe fruit, candied fruit, sweet spices. Palate: flavourful, powerful, spicy.

MARÍN MERLOT 2005 T

**79**

CAMPO MARÍN 2003 TR

**80**

BARÓN DE LAJOYOSA 2001 TGR

**79**

GRAN STATUS T

**87** Colour: cherry, purple rim. Nose: medium intensity, ripe fruit, red berry notes, sweet spices. Palate: flavourful, fruity, fresh.

BARÓN DE LAJOYOSA MOSCATEL VINO DE LICOR

**87** Colour: bright straw. Nose: candied fruit, fruit liqueur notes, honeyed notes. Palate: sweet, flavourful, warm, good acidity.

## BODEGAS LALAGUNA GARCÍA

Ctra. Comarcal A-1304
de Longares a Alfamés, km. 1,28

50460 Longares (Zaragoza)
☎: 657 804 783 - Fax: 976 369 980
bodegaslalaguna@bodegaslalaguna.com
www.bodegaslalaguna.com

**LALAGUNA 2008 B**
macabeo 100%

**87** Colour: bright straw. Nose: fresh, fresh fruit, white flowers. Palate: flavourful, fruity, good acidity, balanced.

**LALAGUNA 2008 RD**
garnacha 100%

**80**

**LALAGUNA 2008 T**
garnacha 100%

**78**

**LALAGUNA 2006 TC**
garnacha 70%, mazuelo 20%, tempranillo 10%

**81**

**FINCA GUISANA 2002 T**
garnacha 70%, tempranillo 30%

**84**

## BODEGAS LOMABLANCA

Ctra. de Valencia, km. 459
50460 Longarés (Zaragoza)
☎: 976 145 100 - Fax: 976 142 621
info@bodegaslomablanca.com
www.bodegaslomablanca.com

**GABARDA CHARDONNAY 2008 B**
chardonnay 100%

**87** Colour: pale. Nose: powerful, ripe fruit, tropical fruit, floral. Palate: flavourful, fruity, fresh.

**GABARDA 2008 T MACERACIÓN CARBÓNICA**
tempranillo 100%

**88** Colour: cherry, purple rim. Nose: expressive, fresh fruit, red berry notes, floral. Palate: flavourful, fruity, good acidity, round tannins.

**GABARDA II 2007 T**
garnacha, tempranillo, syrah

**85** Colour: cherry, purple rim. Nose: ripe fruit, red berry notes, spicy. Palate: flavourful, fruity, fresh.

**GABARDA III 2005 T**
merlot, cabernet sauvignon, tempranillo

**86** Colour: cherry, garnet rim. Nose: sweet spices, toasty, dark chocolate, ripe fruit. Palate: powerful, flavourful, spicy, round tannins.

**GABARDA PV 2004 T**

**88** Colour: cherry, garnet rim. Nose: powerful, warm, ripe fruit, grassy, scrubland, toasty. Palate: flavourful, powerful, fleshy, spicy, round tannins.

**GABARDA IV 2004 TC**
garnacha, cabernet sauvignon, syrah

**87** Colour: cherry, garnet rim. Nose: powerful, fruit preserve, overripe fruit, sweet spices. Palate: powerful, flavourful, pruney.

## BODEGAS PRINURII

Ctra. N 330 (Zaragoza-Valencia), km. 449,150
50400 Cariñena (Zaragoza)
☎: 976 621 039 - Fax: 976 620 714
ivan@bodegasprinur.com
www.bodegasprinur.com

**PRINUR CHARDONNAY 2008 B**

**87** Colour: bright straw. Nose: ripe fruit, fresh fruit, grassy. Palate: flavourful, light-bodied, fruity.

**PRINUR VIÑAS VIEJAS 2005 T**

**92** Colour: cherry, garnet rim. Nose: powerful, varietal, red berry notes, ripe fruit, creamy oak, sweet spices. Palate: flavourful, fleshy, fruity, spicy, round tannins.

**PRINUR RED PASSION 2008 RD**

**89** Colour: raspberry rose. Nose: elegant, floral, ripe fruit. Palate: flavourful, fruity, rich, fine bitter notes.

PRINUR MACABEO 2008 B

**82**

PRINUR BLUE JEANS 2008 T

**87** Colour: deep cherry. Nose: medium intensity, ripe fruit, spicy, scrubland. Palate: flavourful, powerful, fleshy, good acidity.

PRINUR SELECCIÓN CALAR 2005 T

**90** Colour: cherry, garnet rim. Nose: powerful, ripe fruit, red berry notes, toasty, new oak. Palate: flavourful, powerful, fleshy, ripe fruit, round tannins.

## BODEGAS SAN VALERO

Ctra. Nacional 330, km. 450
50400 Cariñena (Zaragoza)
☎: 976 620 400 - Fax: 976 620 398
bsv@sanvalero.com
www.sanvalero.com

CARINVS MUSCAT 2008 B
moscatel 100%

**83**

MONTE DUCAY 2008 B
macabeo 100%

**83**

CARINVS CHARDONNAY 2008 B
chardonnay 100%

**78**

CARINVS 2008 RD
syrah 60%, cabernet sauvignon 40%

**87** Colour: rose, purple rim. Nose: powerful, ripe fruit, violet drops, faded flowers. Palate: rich, fruity, flavourful.

MONTE DUCAY 2008 RD
garnacha 90%, cabernet sauvignon 10%

**82**

CARINVS 2007 T ROBLE
tempranillo 20%, garnacha 20%, cabernet sauvignon 20%, merlot 20%

**87** Colour: cherry, purple rim. Nose: powerful, ripe fruit, lactic notes, creamy oak. Palate: flavourful, powerful, fleshy.

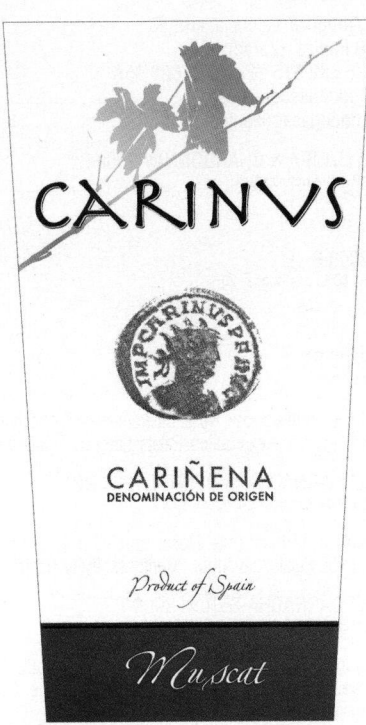

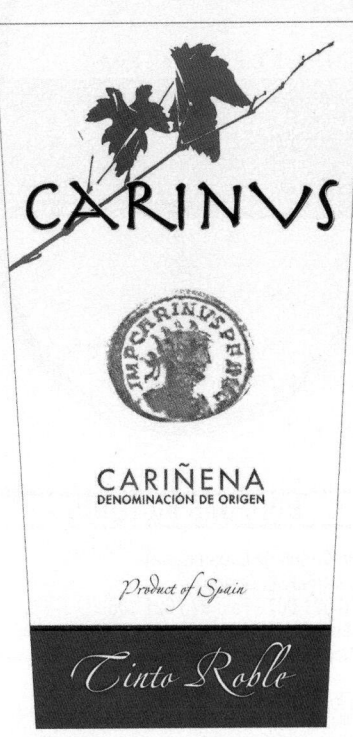

**MONTE DUCAY 2008 T**
garnacha, tempranillo, cabernet sauvignon

**84**

**MONTE DUCAY 2002 TGR**
tempranillo 60%, cabernet sauvignon 30%, garnacha 10%

**86** Colour: cherry, garnet rim. Nose: spicy, dark chocolate, aromatic coffee, ripe fruit. Palate: flavourful, classic aged character, ripe fruit, round tannins.

**MARQUÉS DE TOSOS 2004 TR**
tempranillo, garnacha

**87** Colour: pale ruby, brick rim edge. Nose: spicy, aromatic coffee, pattiserie, fruit liqueur notes. Palate: flavourful, light-bodied, spicy.

## BODEGAS VICTORIA

Camino Virgen de Lagunas, s/n
50400 Cariñena (Zaragoza)
☎: 976 621 007 - Fax: 976 621 106
info@bodegasvictoria.com
www.bodegasvictoria.com

**FINCA PARDINA 2007 T**
tempranillo 70%, cabernet sauvignon 20%, syrah 10%

**89** Colour: bright cherry. Nose: sweet spices, creamy oak, expressive, floral, macerated fruit. Palate: flavourful, fruity, toasty, round tannins.

**DOMINIO DE LONGAZ PARCELA 79 2007 T**
tempranillo 50%, syrah 50%

**89** Colour: bright cherry. Nose: ripe fruit, sweet spices, creamy oak, expressive, floral, undergrowth. Palate: flavourful, fruity, toasty, powerful tannins, fleshy.

**DOMINIO DE LONGAZ PREMIUM 2006 T**
syrah 40%, cabernet sauvignon 30%, merlot 30%

**91** Colour: bright cherry. Nose: ripe fruit, sweet spices, creamy oak, expressive, white flowers, earthy notes. Palate: flavourful, fruity, toasty, soft tannins.

**LONGUS 2006 T**
cabernet sauvignon 40%, syrah 30%, merlot 30%

**91** Colour: cherry, garnet rim. Nose: ripe fruit, spicy, creamy oak, toasty, complex. Palate: powerful, flavourful, toasty, round tannins.

## BODEGAS VIRGEN DEL AGUILA

Ctra. Zaragoza-Valencia, km. 53
50480 Paniza (Zaragoza)
☎: 976 622 515 - Fax: 976 622 958
info@bodegasaguila.com
www.bodegasaguila.com

**JABALÍ VIURA & CHARDONNAY 2008 B**
viura 80%, chardonnay 20%

**83**

**VAL 2008 B**
macabeo 80%, chardonnay 20%

**80**

**VAL 2008 RD**
garnacha 100%

**87** Colour: brilliant rose. Nose: medium intensity, fresh fruit, red berry notes, fruit expression. Palate: flavourful, fruity, fresh.

**JABALÍ GARNACHA-CABERNET 2008 RD**
garnacha 90%, cabernet sauvignon 10%

**86** Colour: brilliant rose. Nose: candied fruit, red berry notes, floral. Palate: flavourful, sweetness, fruity, fresh.

**JABALÍ GARNACHA-SYRAH 2008 T**
garnacha 60%, syrah 40%

**90** Colour: cherry, purple rim. Nose: red berry notes, ripe fruit, sweet spices, creamy oak, cocoa bean. Palate: fruity, fresh, flavourful.

**VAL 2008 T**
tempranillo 50%, garnacha 30%, syrah 20%

**85** Colour: cherry, purple rim. Nose: red berry notes, violet drops, lactic notes. Palate: flavourful, fruity, fresh.

**SEÑORÍO DEL ÁGUILA 2004 TC**
tempranillo, garnacha, cabernet sauvignon

**83**

**SEÑORÍO DEL ÁGUILA 2002 TR**
tempranillo, garnacha, cabernet sauvignon

**83**

**JABALÍ TEMPRANILLO - CABERNET 2008**
tempranillo 60%, cabernet sauvignon 40%

**91** Colour: cherry, purple rim. Nose: ripe fruit, red berry notes, sweet spices, lactic notes. Palate: flavourful, fruity, rich, round tannins.

## BODEGAS Y VIÑEDOS MONFIL S.L.

Avda. del Ejército 40,
50400 Cariñena (Zaragoza)
☎: 976 793 070 - Fax: 976 620 054
ana@monfil.com
www.monfil.com

**MONFIL MACABEO 2008 B**
macabeo

**84**

**MONFIL SHIRAZ 2007 T**
syrah

**78**

**MONFIL GARNACHA 2007**
garnacha

**81**

## CAMPOS DE LUZ

Avda. Diagonal, 590, 5 - 1
08021 Barcelona (Barcelona)
☎: 660 445 464
montse@vinergia.com
www.vinergia.es

**CAMPOS DE LUZ 2008 B**
chardonnay, viura, moscatel

**83**

**CAMPOS DE LUZ 2008 T**
garnacha 100%

**85** Colour: cherry, purple rim. Nose: powerful, grassy, floral. Palate: powerful, flavourful, fine bitter notes.

**CAMPOS DE LUZ 2006 TC**
garnacha 100%

**85** Colour: cherry, garnet rim. Nose: medium intensity, ripe fruit, sweet spices. Palate: flavourful, ripe fruit, round tannins.

## COVINCA SOC. COOP.

Camino de la Estación, s/n
50460 Longares (Zaragoza)
☎: 976 142 653 - Fax: 976 142 402
gerencia@covinca.es
www.axialvinos.com

**TORRELONGARES 2008 B**
macabeo 100%

**86** Colour: bright straw. Nose: fresh, fresh fruit, white flowers. Palate: flavourful, fruity, good acidity, balanced.

**TORRELONGARES 2008 RD**

**81**

**TORRELONGARES VARIETALES SYRAH 2008 T**
syrah 100%

**87** Colour: cherry, purple rim. Nose: powerful, ripe fruit, red berry notes, wild herbs. Palate: powerful, fleshy, fruity, good structure, good acidity.

**TORRELONGARES SELECCIÓN 50 2007 T**
garnacha 100%

**83**

**TERRAI 2006 T**
garnacha 100%

**91** Colour: cherry, garnet rim. Nose: mineral, dark chocolate, aged wood nuances, ripe fruit. Palate: flavourful, good structure, balanced, fine bitter notes, round tannins.

TORRELONGARES GARNACHA 2008
garnacha 100%

**88** Colour: cherry, garnet rim. Nose: powerful, ripe fruit, new oak, toasty, dark chocolate. Palate: flavourful, powerful, spicy, round tannins.

## GRANDES VINOS Y VIÑEDOS S.A.

Ctra. Valencia Km 45,700
50400 Cariñena (Zaragoza)
☎: 976 621 261 - Fax: 976 621 253
info@grandesvinos.com
www.grandesvinos.com

ANAYÓN CHARDONNAY 2008 BFB
chardonnay

**90** Colour: bright yellow. Nose: ripe fruit, creamy oak, sweet spices, fragrant herbs. Palate: rich, flavourful, fresh, good acidity.

MONASTERIO DE LAS VIÑAS 2008 B
macabeo

**84**

CORONA DE ARAGÓN 2008 B
macabeo, chardonnay

**83**

ANAYÓN CHARDONNAY 2007 BFB
chardonnay

**87** Colour: bright golden. Nose: fruit preserve, candied fruit, sweet spices. Palate: flavourful, fleshy, fruity, ripe fruit, fine bitter notes, long, smoky aftertaste.

CORONA DE ARAGÓN MOSCATEL B
moscatel

**88** Colour: bright straw. Nose: expressive, varietal, candied fruit, honeyed notes. Palate: flavourful, good structure, ripe fruit.

MONASTERIO DE LAS VIÑAS 2008 RD
garnacha

**87** Colour: brilliant rose. Nose: elegant, floral, red berry notes, scrubland. Palate: flavourful, fruity, fresh.

CORONA DE ARAGÓN 2008 RD
garnacha, syrah

**83**

CORONA DE ARAGÓN 2008 T
garnacha

**86** Colour: cherry, garnet rim. Nose: powerful, ripe fruit, floral. Palate: flavourful, powerful, fruity.

MONASTERIO DE LAS VIÑAS 2008 T
cariñena

**83**

ANAYÓN GARNACHA 2007 T
garnacha

**89** Colour: cherry, garnet rim. Nose: roasted coffee, creamy oak, spicy, ripe fruit. Palate: fleshy, powerful, harsh oak tannins.

CORONA DE ARAGÓN DISPARATES SYRAH 2007 T
syrah

**88** Colour: cherry, purple rim. Nose: powerful, ripe fruit, sweet spices, creamy oak. Palate: fleshy, powerful, ripe fruit, round tannins.

CORONA DE ARAGÓN DISPARATES CARIÑENA 2007 T
cariñena

**84**

CORONA DE ARAGÓN DISPARATES TEMPRANILLO 2007 T
tempranillo

**84**

CORONA DE ARAGÓN 2006 TC
cabernet sauvignon, garnacha, cariñena

**88** Colour: cherry, garnet rim. Nose: aged wood nuances, spicy, ripe fruit, fruit liqueur notes. Palate: flavourful, powerful, spicy, round tannins.

Crianza · 2006

ANAYÓN 2006 T
cabernet sauvignon

**91** Colour: cherry, purple rim. Nose: creamy oak, aged wood nuances, ripe fruit. Palate: powerful, flavourful, fleshy, slightly dry, soft tannins.

MONASTERIO DE LAS VIÑAS 2006 TC
cariñena

**85** Colour: cherry, garnet rim. Nose: roasted coffee, dark chocolate, fruit preserve. Palate: spicy, round tannins, fine bitter notes.

CORONA DE ARAGÓN 2005 TR
cabernet sauvignon, garnacha, cariñena

**87** Colour: deep cherry, orangey edge. Nose: powerful, spicy, aromatic coffee, pattiserie. Palate: flavourful, good structure, easy to drink, spicy.

MONASTERIO DE LAS VIÑAS 2005 TR
cariñena

**85** Colour: cherry, garnet rim. Nose: candied fruit, overripe fruit, spicy, aged wood nuances, caramel. Palate: flavourful, light-bodied, classic aged character, easy to drink.

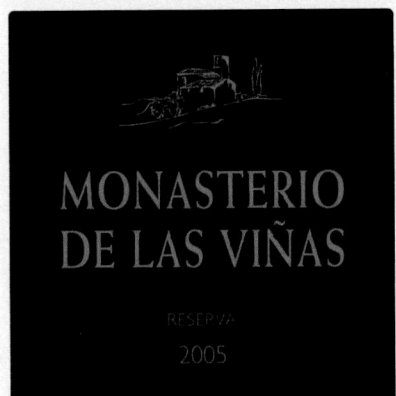

MONASTERIO DE LAS VIÑAS 2003 TGR
cabernet sauvignon, cariñena

**86** Colour: cherry, garnet rim. Nose: powerful, warm, candied fruit, dark chocolate, spicy. Palate: flavourful, classic aged character, spicy.

CORONA DE ARAGÓN 2003 TGR
cabernet sauvignon, cariñena, garnacha

**85** Colour: cherry, garnet rim. Nose: powerful, ripe fruit, roasted coffee, dark chocolate. Palate: flavourful, powerful, fleshy, round tannins.

## HACIENDA MOLLEDA

Ctra. Belchite, km 29,3
50154 Tosos (Zaragoza)
☎: 976 620 702 - Fax: 976 620 102

hm@haciendamolleda.com
www.haciendamolleda.com

HACIENDA MOLLEDA 2007 T ROBLE
garnacha 100%

**74**

HACIENDA MOLLEDA GARNACHA 2006 T ROBLE
garnacha 100%

**89** Colour: cherry, garnet rim. Nose: mineral, dry stone, ripe fruit, sweet spices. Palate: flavourful, powerful, spicy, round tannins.

HACIENDA MOLLEDA 2006 T
tempranillo, garnacha

**70**

HACIENDA MOLLEDA 2004 T ROBLE
tempranillo, garnacha, cabernet sauvignon, syrah, cariñena

**82**

HACIENDA MOLLEDA 2003 T ROBLE
tempranillo, garnacha

**81**

HACIENDA MOLLEDA 2002 TC
tempranillo 100%

**81**

HACIENDA MOLLEDA 2001 TC
tempranillo 100%

**87** Colour: cherry, garnet rim. Nose: aged wood nuances, pattiserie, candied fruit. Palate: flavourful, light-bodied, easy to drink, spicy.

## HEREDAD ANSÓN

Camino Eras Altas s/n
50450 Muel (Zaragoza)
☎: 976 141 133 - Fax: 976 141 133
info@bodegasheredadanson.com
www.bodegasheredadanson.com

HEREDAD DE ANSÓN 2008 B
macabeo

**83**

HEREDAD DE ANSÓN 2008 RD
garnacha

**79**

HEREDAD DE ANSÓN 2008 T
merlot 50%, syrah 50%

**88** Colour: cherry, purple rim. Nose: powerful, ripe fruit, red berry notes. Palate: flavourful, powerful, ripe fruit.

LIASÓN 2008 T
garnacha

**78**

LEGUM 2007 T
garnacha

**88** Colour: cherry, garnet rim. Nose: creamy oak, new oak, toasty, cocoa bean, ripe fruit. Palate: powerful, fleshy, spicy, harsh oak tannins.

HEREDAD DE ANSÓN VENDIMIA SELECCIONADA 2007 T
garnacha 85%, syrah 15%

**85** Colour: deep cherry, orangey edge. Nose: powerful, candied fruit, fruit liqueur notes, dark chocolate, aromatic coffee. Palate: spicy, classic aged character, ripe fruit.

## JORDAN DE ASSO

Cariñena, 55
50408 Aguarón (Zaragoza)
☎: 976 620 291 - Fax: 976 230 270
info@jordandeasso.com
www.jordandeasso.com

JORDAN DE ASSO 2005 T
tempranillo 40%, syrah 30%, cabernet sauvignon 30%

**88** Colour: cherry, garnet rim. Nose: fruit preserve, creamy oak, dark chocolate. Palate: flavourful, powerful, spicy.

JORDAN DE ASSO 2005 TR

**88** Colour: cherry, garnet rim. Nose: powerful, ripe fruit, sweet spices, toasty. Palate: flavourful, powerful, ripe fruit, round tannins.

## LONG WINES

Avda. del Monte, 46
28120 Algete (Madrid)
☎: 916 221 305 - Fax: 916 220 029
william@william-long.com
www.longwines.com

PLEYADES SHIRAZ 2008 T

**86** Colour: cherry, purple rim. Nose: powerful, varietal, ripe fruit, scrubland. Palate: powerful, fleshy, fruity.

PLEYADES SHIRAZ 2007 T
syrah

**84**

PLEYADES 2005 TR
cariñena, garnacha, syrah

**91** Colour: cherry, garnet rim. Nose: balanced, ripe fruit, lactic notes, creamy oak, new oak, sweet spices. Palate: flavourful, powerful, fleshy, round tannins, mineral.

## MANUEL MONEVA E HIJOS S.L.

Avda. Zaragoza, 10
50108 Almonacid de la Sierra (Zaragoza)
☎: 976 627 020 - Fax: 976 627 334
monevahijos@terra.es

VIÑA VADINA 2008 RD

**83**

VIÑA VADINA GARNACHA 2008 T

**82**

VIÑA VADINA SELECCIÓN ESPECIAL 2007 T

**86** Colour: bright cherry. Nose: ripe fruit, sweet spices, creamy oak. Palate: flavourful, fruity, toasty, round tannins.

## PAGO DE AYLÉS

Finca Ayles. Carretera A-1101 km. 24
50152 Mezalocha (Zaragoza)
☎: 976 140 473 - Fax: 976 140 268
info@bodegasayles.com
www.bodegasayles.com

AYLES TEMPRANILLO 2008 RD

**81**

AYLÉS 4 VARIETALES 2008 T

**88** Colour: cherry, purple rim. Nose: powerful, ripe fruit, fruit expression. Palate: powerful, flavourful, fleshy.

AYLÉS "TRES DE 3000" 2007 T

**93** Colour: cherry, garnet rim. Nose: powerful, ripe fruit, fruit liqueur notes, earthy notes, creamy oak, dark chocolate, new oak. Palate: powerful, fleshy, fine bitter notes, powerful tannins.

AYLÉS "TRES DE 3000" 2006 T

**90** Colour: cherry, garnet rim. Nose: powerful, ripe fruit, sweet spices, new oak, toasty. Palate: flavourful, powerful, spicy, round tannins.

## AYLÉS MERLOT-TEMPRANILLO 2006 T

**87** Colour: cherry, garnet rim. Nose: medium intensity, ripe fruit, spicy, cocoa bean. Palate: flavourful, spicy, round tannins.

## AYLÉS 2005 TC

**88** Colour: cherry, garnet rim. Nose: candied fruit, ripe fruit, spicy, aromatic coffee. Palate: flavourful, powerful, fleshy, spicy.

## AYLÉS 2004 TC

**88** Colour: cherry, garnet rim. Nose: powerful, overripe fruit, dark chocolate, cocoa bean. Palate: flavourful, sweetness, spicy.

## QUINTA MAZUELA

Ctra. La Almunia, s/n
50400 Cariñena (Zaragoza)
☎: 976 620 138 - Fax: 976 620 138
quintamazuela@telefonica.net

## QUINTA MAZUELA 2007 T ROBLE
merlot 50%, cabernet sauvignon 40%, syrah 10%

**86** Colour: dark-red cherry. Nose: overripe fruit, powerfull, balsamic herbs, scrubland. Palate: powerful, fleshy, sweetness, round tannins.

## QUINTA MAZUELA 2005 T ROBLE
tempranillo 60%, merlot 40

**84**

## SOLAR DE URBEZO

San Valero, 14
50400 Cariñena (Zaragoza)
☎: 976 621 968 - Fax: 976 620 549
info@solardeurbezo.es
www.solardeurbezo.es

## URBEZO CHARDONNAY 2008 B
chardonnay 100%

**83**

## ALTIUS 2008 RD
merlot

**89** Colour: rose, purple rim. Nose: fresh fruit, spicy, characterful, dried flowers. Palate: carbonic notes, fruity, powerful, good acidity.

## URBEZO MERLOT 2008 RD
merlot 100%

**84**

## ALTIUS GARNACHA VIÑAS VIEJAS 2008 T
garnacha 100%

**88** Colour: cherry, garnet rim. Nose: medium intensity, ripe fruit, red berry notes, fragrant herbs. Palate: flavourful, ripe fruit, light-bodied.

## ALTIUS SYRAH 2008 T
syrah 100%

**88** Colour: light cherry. Nose: varietal, red berry notes, fresh fruit, expressive. Palate: spicy, easy to drink, round tannins, fruity.

## URBEZO GARNACHA VIÑAS VIEJAS 2008 T

**84**

## VIÑA URBEZO 2008 T
garnacha 30%, tempranillo 40%, syrah 30%

**82**

## DANCE DEL MAR 2007 T
tempranillo, merlot

**88** Colour: deep cherry. Nose: varietal, expressive, ripe fruit, fragrant herbs, sweet spices. Palate: flavourful, fruity, good structure, fine bitter notes.

## ALTIUS 2006 TC
tempranillo 40%, cabernet sauvignon 30%, merlot 20%, syrah 10%

**86** Colour: cherry, garnet rim. Nose: medium intensity, warm, ripe fruit. Palate: ripe fruit, round tannins.

## URBEZO 2005 TC
tempranillo 40%, cabernet sauvignon 30%, merlot 20%, syrah 10%

**87** Colour: cherry, garnet rim. Nose: floral, fresh fruit, spicy. Palate: flavourful, fruity, fresh, fine tannins.

## URBEZO 2003 TR
cariñena, syrah, cabernet sauvignon, merlot

**88** Colour: pale ruby, brick rim edge. Nose: spicy, fine reductive notes, wet leather, aged wood nuances, fruit liqueur notes. Palate: spicy, fine tannins, long.

## URBEZO 2002 TGR
garnacha 50%, cabernet sauvignon 50%

**85** Colour: pale ruby, brick rim edge. Nose: fruit preserve, spicy, toasty, cedar wood. Palate: harsh oak tannins, aged character, warm, good acidity.

## TIERRA DE CUBAS

Ctra. A-220, km. 24
50400 Cariñena (Zaragoza)

# DO CARIÑENA

☎: 976 621 300 - Fax: 976 622 153
proveedores@tierradecubas.es

TIERRA DE CUBAS 2007 T ROBLE

**90** Colour: cherry, garnet rim. Nose: powerful, warm, ripe fruit, creamy oak, dark chocolate, aromatic coffee. Palate: flavourful, powerful, spicy, round tannins.

## VINNICO EXPORT

De la Muela, 16
03730 Jávea (Alicante)
☎: 965 791 967 - Fax: 966 461 471
info@vinnico.com
www.vinnico.com

FLOR DEL MONTGÓ OLD VINES GARNACHA 2008 T
garnacha 100%

**83**

CASTILLO DE SABIKA 2008 T
garnacha 100%

**82**

## VIÑAZAGROS

Juan Carlos I, 9
50461 Alfamen (Zaragoza)
☎: 976 626 002 - Fax: 976 626 002
vinazagros@vinazagros.com
www.vinazagros.com

VIÑA ZAGROS MMIV 2004 T
tempranillo, cabernet sauvignon, garnacha

**86** Colour: bright cherry, garnet rim. Nose: expressive, medium intensity, fruit liqueur notes, toasty, fruit preserve. Palate: spirituous, spicy, classic aged character.

## VIÑEDOS Y BODEGAS PABLO

Avda. Zaragoza, 16
50108 Almonacid de la Sierra (Zaragoza)
☎: 976 627 037 - Fax: 976 627 102
granviu@granviu.com
www.granviu.com

MENGUANTE GARNACHA BLANCA 2008 B
garnacha blanca

**88** Colour: bright straw. Nose: varietal, elegant, ripe fruit, tropical fruit. Palate: flavourful, fruity, fresh, fleshy.

MENGUANTE TEMPRANILLO 2007 T ROBLE
tempranillo

**88** Colour: cherry, garnet rim. Nose: expressive, ripe fruit, creamy oak, new oak. Palate: flavourful, powerful, spicy, round tannins.

MENGUANTE GARNACHA 2007 T
garnacha

**83**

MENGUANTE SELECCIÓN GARNACHA 2006 T
garnacha

**87** Colour: cherry, garnet rim. Nose: medium intensity, ripe fruit, spicy. Palate: flavourful, fine bitter notes, spicy.

GRAN VÍU GARNACHA DEL TERRENO 2004 T
garnacha

**91** Colour: cherry, garnet rim. Nose: elegant, earthy notes, ripe fruit, sweet spices, toasty. Palate: flavourful, fleshy, spicy, round tannins.

GRAN VÍU FINCA SANTIAGA 2004 T
garnacha, tempranillo, vidadillo, cabernet sauvignon

**90** Colour: cherry, garnet rim. Nose: mineral, powerfull, ripe fruit, spicy, toasty. Palate: flavourful, powerful, fleshy, spicy, round tannins.

GRAN VÍU SELECCIÓN 2002 T
garnacha, tempranillo, cabernet sauvignon, syrah

**89** Colour: cherry, garnet rim. Nose: warm, varietal, pattiserie, toasty. Palate: flavourful, powerful, fleshy, spicy.

## WINNER WINES

Avda. del Mediterráneo, 38
28007 Madrid (Madrid)
☎: 915 019 042 - Fax: 915 017 794
winnerwines@ibernoble.com
www.ibernoble.com

NAIF 2004 TR

**82**

SOME OTHER WINERIES WITHIN THE DO:

**BODEGAS CONDALES DEL NORTE
CAMINO DEL BOSQUE S.C.L.
CAÑALABA S.L.
GENARO TEJERO
JOSE ANTONIO VALERO TORRES
SUCESORES DE MANUEL PIQUER
TOSOS ECOLÓGICA**

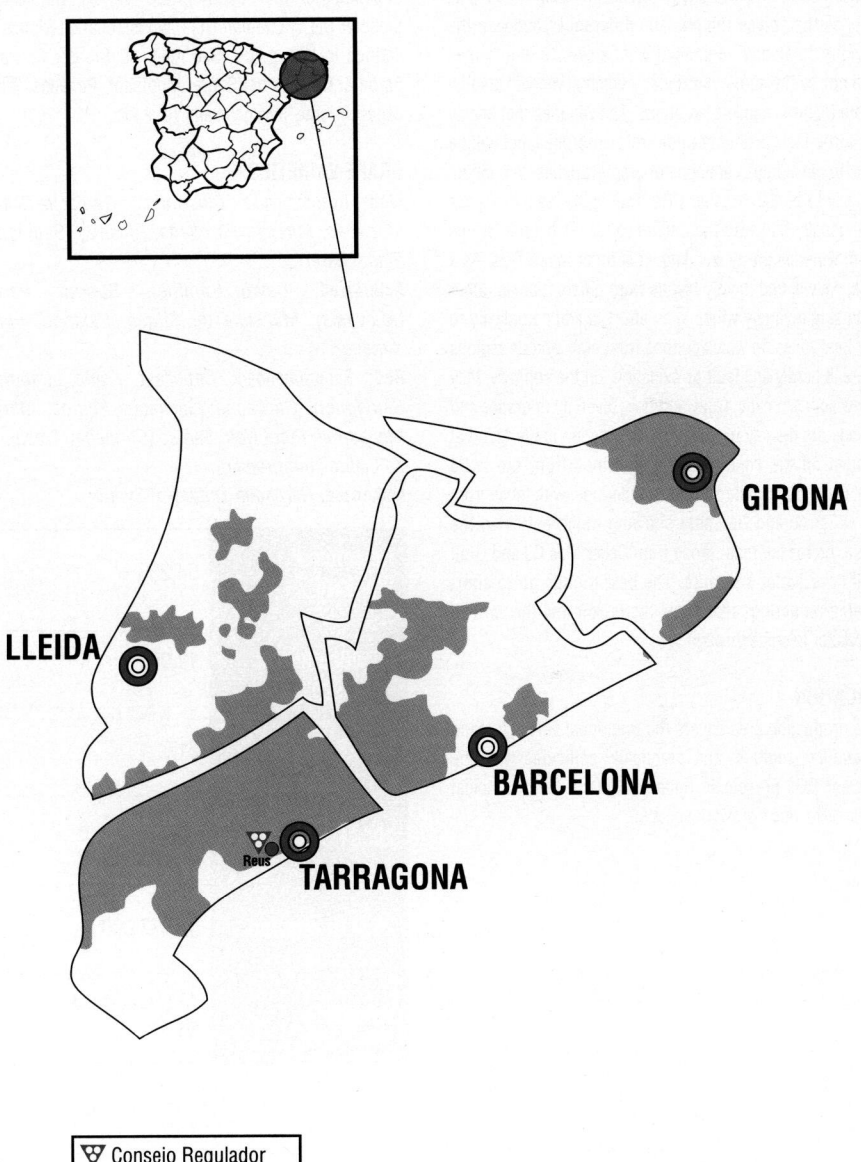

GIRONA

LLEIDA

BARCELONA

Reus

TARRAGONA

▽ Consejo Regulador
● DO Boundary

## NEWS

It is logical to find diversity of styles and ratings in a DO as vast as this; given the climatic differences between the various Catalonian regions, it will be easy to think wines will not be the same, particularly when some will also be more mature –aged– than others. The wineries that decide to bottle their products under this umbrella label will be able to use a huge catalogue of grape varieties, something usually forbidden in other DOs. That is the reason why we will usually find with the Catalunya back label new wines from wineries pretty well known in other major DOs. As a rule, we will find mostly blends from different areas rather than single-variety wines in an effort to add complexity to the final wines. In wines coming from high altitude regions there is hardly any fault or oxidation, on the contrary, they show very aromatic, fruity and fine. Diversity of grapes and blends are the key to it all. Also interesting is the fact that almost all the wines are young wines from the 2008 vintage, mostly white and rosé renderings, with those from Ca N'Estruc and De Casta showing much better on the nose. As for the reds, those from Celler Mas Gil and Grau Vell have better structure. The best ratings go to short ageing renderings that allow the terroir and the varietal character to shine through.

## LOCATION

The production area covers the traditional vine - growing Catalonian regions, and practically coincides with the current DOs present in Catalonia plus a few municipal areas with vine - growing vocation.

## CLIMATE AND SOIL

Depending on the location of the vineyard, the same as those of the Catalonian DO's, whose characteristics are defined in this guide. See Alella, Empordà, Conca de Barberà, Costers del Segre, Montsant, Penedès, Pla de Bages, Priorat, Tarragona and Terra Alta.

## GRAPE VARIETIES:

**White:** Recommended: *Chardonnay, Garnacha Blanca, Macabeo, Muscat, Parellada, Riesling, Sauvignon Blanc, Xarel·lo.*

**Authorized:** *Gewürztraminer, Subirat Parent (Malvasía), Malvasía de Sitges, Picapoll, Pedro Ximénez.*

**Red:** Recommended: *Cabernet Franc, Cabernet Sauvignon, Garnacha, Garnacha Peluda, Merlot, Monastrell, Pinot Noir, Samsó (Cariñena), Trepat, Ull de Llebre (Tempranillo).*

**Authorized:** *Garnacha Tintorera, Syrah.*

| | |
|---|---|
| Hectares of Vineyard | 54,233 |
| Nº Viticulturists | 12,007 |
| Nº of Bodegas | 217 |
| 2008 Harvest | Very Good |
| 2007 Production | 35,977,000 l. |
| Marketing | 43.5% domestic 56.5% export |

**CONSEJO REGULADOR.**
Passeig Sunyer, 4 - 6. 43204 Reus (Tarragona)
☎: 977 328 103 - Fax: 977 321 357
@ info@do-catalunya.com
www.do-catalunya.com

## GENERAL CHARACTERISTICS OF THE WINES:

| | |
|---|---|
| **WHITES** | In general, the autochtonous varieties from Catalonia predominate, *Macabeo, Xarel·lo* and *Parellada.* They are straw yellow and have a fresh and fruity nose; on the palate they are light and easy drinking. One can also find some *Chardonnay*, which are somewhat fruitier, typical of the variety, although not excessively, as they come from high-yield vineyards. |
| **ROSÉS** | These are quite modern; most are pink or raspberry pink in colour and the nose is fresh and fruity with hints of red berries; on the palate they are light and correct. |
| **REDS** | These may be produced from autochtonous grapes, especially *Ull de Llebre* (*Tempranillo*) and *Garnacha.* Cherry-coloured, they tend to be fruity on the nose with notes of wild berries; on the palate they are fruity, without too much body, although easy drinking. There are also examples of foreign varieties, especially, which can have balsamic and, on occasions, vegetative notes and which have a greater structure on the palate. |

## 2008 VINTAGE RATING:

# GOOD

## ALBET I NOYA

Can Vendrell de la Codina, s/n
08739 Sant Pau D'Ordal (Barcelona)
☎: 938 994 812 - Fax: 938 994 930
albetinoya@albetinoya.cat
www.albetinoya.cat

ALBET I NOYA PETIT ALBET NEGRE 2008 T
tempranillo, garnacha

**87** Colour: cherry, purple rim. Nose: expressive, fresh fruit, red berry notes, floral. Palate: flavourful, fruity, good acidity, round tannins.

CAN VENDRELL DE LA CODINA

## BODEGA CASTELL D'ENCUS

Ctra. Tremp a Sta. Engracia, km. 5
25630 Talarn (Lleida)
☎: 934 876 666
rbobet@encus.org
www.encus.org

ETICA 2008 B
riesling, albariño

**90** Colour: pale. Nose: fresh fruit, grapey, wild herbs. Palate: balanced, round, long, good acidity.

## BODEGAS MIGUEL TORRES

Miguel Torres i Carbó, 6
08203 Vilafranca del Penedés (Barcelona)
☎: 938 177 400 - Fax: 938 177 444
mailadmin@torres.es
www.torres.es

VIÑA SOL 2008 B

**87** Colour: bright straw. Nose: fresh, white flowers, expressive, fresh fruit. Palate: flavourful, fruity, good acidity, balanced.

VIÑA ESMERALDA 2008 B

**86** Colour: pale. Nose: fresh fruit, citrus fruit, white flowers, varietal. Palate: flavourful, fruity, fresh, sweetness.

NEROLA XAREL.LO 2006 B
xarel.lo, garnacha blanca

**87** Colour: bright straw. Nose: ripe fruit, fresh fruit, grassy. Palate: flavourful, fruity, fresh, fleshy.

DECASTA 2008 RD

**89** Colour: rose, purple rim. Nose: ripe fruit, red berry notes, floral, expressive, lactic notes. Palate: fleshy, powerful, fruity, fresh.

SANGRE DE TORO 2007 T
garnacha, mazuelo

**88** Colour: cherry, garnet rim. Nose: toasty, creamy oak, ripe fruit. Palate: flavourful, powerful, fleshy, spicy, ripe fruit.

GRAN SANGRE DE TORO 2005 TR
garnacha 60%, mazuelo 25%, syrah 15%

**86** Colour: cherry, garnet rim. Nose: powerfull, ripe fruit, toasty, spicy. Palate: flavourful, fleshy, spicy.

NEROLA SYRAH MONASTRELL 2005 T
syrah, monastrell

**86** Colour: bright cherry. Nose: ripe fruit, sweet spices, creamy oak, expressive. Palate: flavourful, fruity, toasty, round tannins.

SAN VALENTÍN
CORONAS

## BODEGAS PUIGGROS

Ctra. de Manresa, km. 13
08711 Odena (Barcelona)
☎: 932 105 638
bodegaspuiggros@telefonica.net
www.bodegaspuiggros.com

SENTITS BLANCS 2008 B
garnacha blanca 100%

**90** Colour: bright yellow. Nose: powerfull, ripe fruit, sweet spices, creamy oak, tropical fruit. Palate: rich, smoky aftertaste:, flavourful, fresh, good acidity.

## BODEGAS ROQUETA

Ctra. de Vic, 81
08241 Manresa (Barcelona)
☎: 938 743 511 - Fax: 938 737 204
info@roqueta.com
www.abadal.net

RAMÓN ROQUETA CHARDONNAY 2008 B
chardonnay 80%, macabeo 20%

**84**

**SYNERA 2008 B**
macabeo 80%, moscatel 20%

**82**

**RAMÓN ROQUETA CABERNET SAUVIGNON 2006 T**
cabernet sauvignon 100%

**84**

**RAMÓN ROQUETA CABERNET SAUVIGNON 2008 RD**
cabernet sauvignon

**84**

**SYNERA 2008 RD**
garnacha 50%, tempranillo 50%

**83**

**RAMÓN ROQUETA CABERNET SAUVIGNON 2008 T**
cabernet sauvignon 100%

**85** Colour: cherry, purple rim. Nose: powerfull, ripe fruit, grassy. Palate: powerful, spicy, round tannins.

**RAMÓN ROQUETA TEMPRANILLO 2008 T**
tempranillo 100%

**84**

**SYNERA 2007 T BARRICA**
merlot 70%, tempranillo 30%

**88** Colour: cherry, purple rim. Nose: powerfull, ripe fruit, earthy notes, sweet spices, dark chocolate, toasty. Palate: flavourful, powerful, fleshy.

**SYNERA 2004 TC**
merlot 70%, tempranillo 30%

**81**

## CA N'ESTRUC

Ctra. C-1414, km. 1, 05
08292 Esparreguera (Barcelona)
☎: 937 777 017 - Fax: 937 771 108
canestruc@vilaviniteca.es

**IDOIA BLANC 2008 BFB**

**92** Colour: bright yellow. Nose: fresh, expressive, grassy, smoky. Palate: complex, fresh, fruity, flavourful, rich, varietal.

**CA N'ESTRUC BLANC 2008 B**

**88** Colour: straw. Nose: fresh fruit, balsamic herbs, grassy. Palate: fruity, fresh, flavourful.

**CA N'ESTRUC 2008 RD**
merlot, cabernet sauvignon

**87** Colour: rose, purple rim. Nose: varietal, powerfull, fresh, raspberry. Palate: powerful, flavourful, fine bitter notes.

**IDOIA 2008 T**

**90** Colour: deep cherry. Nose: complex, mineral, ripe fruit, spicy, creamy oak, aroma:tic coffee. Palate: powerful, flavourful, fleshy, toasty, smoky aftertaste, mineral.

**CA N'ESTRUC 2008 T**

**87** Colour: deep cherry. Nose: expressive, varietal, powerfull, earthy notes, characterful. Palate: good structure, fruity, fresh, powerful, flavourful.

## CASTELL D'ENCÚS

Ctra. Tremp a Sta. Engracia, km. 5

25630 Talarn (Lleida)
☎: 934 876 666
rbobet@encus.org
www.encus.org

ETICA 2008 B
Riesling, albariño

**90** Colour: pale. Nose: fresh fruit, grapey, wild herbs. Palate: balanced, round, long, good acidity.

## CAVAS DEL AMPURDÁN

Pza. del Carme, 1
17491 Perelada (Girona)
☎: 972 538 011 - Fax: 972 538 277
perelada@castilloperelada.com
www.blancpescador.com

MASIA PERELADA 2008 B
macabeo 70%, garnacha blanca 30%

**85** Colour: pale. Nose: grassy, white flowers, citrus fruit, fresh fruit. Palate: fruity, fresh, light-bodied.

BLANC PESCADOR SEGUNDA GENERACIÓN 2008 B
garnacha blanca 60%, sauvignon blanc 40%

**85** Colour: bright straw. Nose: fresh, fresh fruit, white flowers, expressive. Palate: flavourful, fruity, good acidity, balanced.

MASIA PERELADA 2008 RD
garnacha 65%, tempranillo 35%

**85** Colour: rose, purple rim. Nose: red berry notes, ripe fruit, violet drops. Palate: flavourful, fruity, fleshy.

## CAVES CONDE DE CARALT S.A.

Ctra. Sant Sadurní-Sant Pere de Riudebitlles, km. 5
08775 Torrelavit (Barcelona)
☎: 938 917 070 - Fax: 938 996 006
seguraviudas@seguraviudas.es
www.freixenet.es

CONDE DE CARALT BLANC DE BLANCS 2008 B
xarel.lo 40%, parellada 30%, macabeo 30%

**84**

CONDE DE CARALT 2008 RD
tempranillo 40%, garnacha 40%, cariñena 20%

**82**

CONDE DE CARALT 2005 TR
tempranillo 85%, cabernet sauvignon 15%

**83**

## CELLER CERCAVINS

Pol. 8 Parcela 17
25340 Verdú (Lleida)
☎: 973 348 114 - Fax: 973 348 114
info@cellercercavins.com
www.cellercercavins.com

EGOM 2006 T

**88** Colour: dark-red cherry. Nose: fruit liqueur notes, fruit liqueur notes, balsamic herbs. Palate: powerful, flavourful, round tannins, balsamic.

## CELLER MAS GIL

Afores, s/n
17251 Calonge (Girona)
☎: 972 661 486 - Fax: 972 661 462
info@closdagon.com
www.closdagon.com

CLOS D'AGON 2008 B
roussanne 42%, viognier 36%, marsanne 22%

**92** Colour: bright straw. Nose: white flowers, ripe fruit, fruit expression, citrus fruit, grassy. Palate: flavourful, fruity, rich, ripe fruit.

CLOS VALMAÑA 2008 B
viognier 48%, roussanne 28%, marsanne 24%

**87** Colour: bright straw. Nose: faded flowers, ripe fruit, citrus fruit, tropical fruit. Palate: flavourful, fleshy, pruney.

CLOS D'AGON 2007 T
cabernet franc 32%, syrah 26%, cabernet sauvignon 22%, merlot 13%, petit verdot 7%

**94** Colour: cherry, purple rim. Nose: powerfull, characterful, earthy notes, mineral, ripe fruit, new oak, toasty. Palate: flavourful, powerful, fleshy, spicy, ripe fruit, slightly dry, soft tannins.

CLOS VALMAÑA 2007 TC
syrah 36%, merlot 28%, cabernet sauvignon 18%, cabernet franc 14%, petit verdot 4%

**93** Colour: cherry, garnet rim. Nose: spicy, creamy oak, toasty, earthy notes, powerfull, ripe fruit. Palate: powerful, flavourful, toasty, round tannins.

## CELLER PASCONA

Camí dels Fontals, s/n
43730 Falset (Tarragona)

☎: 609 291 770 - Fax: 977 117 098
info@pascona.com
www.pascona.com

PASCONA BLANC 2008 B
macabeo 100%

**82**

## CLOS MONTBLANC

Ctra. Montblanc-Barbera, s/n
43422 Barberá de la Conca (Tarragona)
☎: 977 887 030 - Fax: 977 887 032
info@closmontblanc.com
www.closmontblanc.com

PROYECTO CU4TRO 2008 B

**87** Colour: bright straw. Nose: powerfull, fresh fruit, ripe fruit, citrus fruit. Palate: flavourful, fruity, fresh, fleshy.

FINCA CARBONELL 2008 B

**83**

FINCA CARBONELL 2007 T

**84**

PROYECTO CU4TRO 2005 T

**81**

ALENYA

## FERMÍ BOHIGAS

Finca Can Maciá s/n
08711 Ódena (Barcelona)
☎: 938 048 100 - Fax: 938 032 366
tecnic@bohigas.es
www.bohigas.es

MAS MACIÀ XAREL.LO 2008 B
xarel.lo 100%

**88** Colour: bright straw. Nose: ripe fruit, citrus fruit, tropical fruit. Palate: flavourful, fleshy, fruity, fresh.

BOHIGAS BLANC DE TRES LUXE 2008 B
garnacha 50%, xarel.lo 40%, sauvignon blanc 10%

**87** Colour: bright straw. Nose: grassy, white flowers, ripe fruit, citrus fruit. Palate: flavourful, fruity, fresh, fleshy.

BOHIGAS BLANC DE BLANCS 2008 B
xarel.lo 85%, parellada 15%

**84**

BOHIGAS CHARDONNAY 2007 BFB
chardonnay 100%

**87** Colour: bright straw. Nose: powerfull, candied fruit, citrus fruit, sweet spices, pattiserie. Palate: flavourful, fleshy, fine bitter notes.

BOHIGAS CABERNET SAUVIGNON 2005 TC
cabernet sauvignon 100%

**84**

MAS MACIÀ CABERNET SAUVIGNON 2004 TC
cabernet sauvignon 100%

**82**

## GRAU VELL

Can Grau Vell, s/n
08784 Hostalets de Pierola (Barcelona)
☎: 676 586 933 - Fax: 932 684 965
info@grauvell.cat

ALCOR 2006 T

**92** Colour: very deep cherry. Nose: aroma:tic coffee, fresh fruit, fruit expression. Palate: powerful, flavourful, complex, spirituous, creamy, mineral.

ALCOR 2005 T

**93** Colour: deep cherry. Nose: ripe fruit, fruit expression, fruit liqueur notes, sweet spices, roasted coffee. Palate: complex, powerful, flavourful, spirituous, good structure.

## JAUME GRAU - VINS GRAU

Ctra. C-37 de Igualada a Manresa, km. 75,5
08255 Maians (Barcelona)
☎: 938 356 002 - Fax: 938 356 812
info@vinsgrau.com
www.vinsgrau.com

CLOS DEL RECÓ 2008 B
macabeo 40%, xarel.lo 40%, perguada 20%

**78**

CLOS DEL RECÓ 2008 RD
merlot , tempranillo

**78**

CLOS ESTRADA 2008 T
tempranillo 100%

**86** Colour: bright cherry, garnet rim. Nose: short, ripe fruit. Palate: flavourful, fruity, balanced, fruity aftestaste.

## JAUME SERRA

Ctra. de Vilanova, km. 2,5
08800 Vilanova i la Geltru (Barcelona)
☎: 938 936 404 - Fax: 938 142 262
jaumeserra@jgc.es
www.vinosdefamilia.com

VIÑA DEL MAR 2008 B
**84**

VIÑA DEL MAR SEMIDULCE 2008 B
xarel.lo, macabeo
**79**

VIÑA DEL MAR 2008 RD
**83**

VIÑA DEL MAR 2008 T
**80**

## JEAN LEÓN

Pago Jean León
08775 Torrelavit (Barcelona)

☎: 938 995 512 - Fax: 938 995 517
jeanleon@jeanleon.com
www.jeanleon.com

TERRASOLA TEMPRANILLO 2008 TC
tempranillo
**85** Colour: cherry, garnet rim. Nose: toasty, sweet spices, aroma:tic coffee, ripe fruit. Palate: flavourful, powerful, ripe fruit.

TERRASOLA SYRAH GARNACHA 2006 TC
**86** Colour: cherry, garnet rim. Nose: ripe fruit, spicy, creamy oak, toasty. Palate: powerful, flavourful, toasty, round tannins.

## LA XARMADA

Hisenda Casa Llivi, s/n
08796 Pacs del Penedés (Barcelona)
☎: 938 171 237 - Fax: 938 171 546
laxarmada@laxarmada.com
www.laxarmada.com

LA XARMADA 2008 B
chenin blanc 50%, chardonnay 50%
**87** Colour: pale. Nose: expressive, fresh fruit, grassy. Palate: flavourful, fruity, fresh, good acidity.

LA XARMADA MERLOT 2008 RD
**76**

LA XARMADA TURDUS SELECCIÓ 2008 T
syrah 60%, merlot 30%, cabernet sauvignon 10%
**85** Colour: black cherry. Nose: powerfull, fruit preserve, fruit liqueur notes, fragrant herbs. Palate: fleshy, sweetness, fine bitter notes.

LA XARMADA 2008 T
tempranillo 70%, syrah 30%
**83**

LA XARMADA MERLOT 2008 T
merlot 100%
**82**

LA XARMADA MERLOT 2007 T
merlot 100%
**86** Colour: dark-red cherry. Nose: powerfull, fruit preserve, fruit liqueur notes, toasty, dark chocolate. Palate: powerful, sweetness, spirituous.

LA XARMADA TURDUS SELECCIÓ 2007 T
syrah 60%, merlot 30%, cabernet sauvignon 10%
**84**

## MASET DEL LLEÓ

Avda. Barcelona, 31 Pol.g Sant Pere Molanta
08734 Olerdola (Barcelona)
☎: 902 200 250 - Fax: 938 921 333
info@maset.com
www.maset.com

MASET DEL LLEÓ SYRAH 2005 TR
syrah
**89** Colour: cherry, garnet rim. Nose: ripe fruit, spicy, creamy oak, toasty, new oak. Palate: powerful, flavourful, toasty, round tannins.

## MASIA BACH

Ctra. Martorell - Capellada, km. 20,5
08635 Sant Esteve de Sesrovires (Barcelona)
☎: 937 714 052 - Fax: 937 713 309

info@bach.es
www.bach.es

**VIÑA EXTRÍSIMO 2008 RD**
tempranillo, cabernet sauvignon, garnacha

**84**

## OLIVEDA S.A.

La Roca, 3
17750 Capmany (Girona)
☎: 972 549 012 - Fax: 972 549 106
comercial@grupoliveda.com
www.grupoliveda.com

**MASIA OLIVEDA CHARDONNAY 2008 B**
chardonnay

**88** Colour: bright straw. Nose: fresh fruit, citrus fruit, floral. Palate: flavourful, fruity, fresh, varietal.

**MASIA OLIVEDA MERLOT 2007 TC**
merlot

**87** Colour: cherry, garnet rim. Nose: powerfull, fruit liqueur notes, ripe fruit, spicy. Palate: powerful, spirituous, concentrated, spicy.

**MASIA OLIVEDA CABERNET SAUVIGNON 2007 T**
cabernet sauvignon

**85** Colour: cherry, garnet rim. Nose: medium intensity, ripe fruit, fruit liqueur notes, toasty. Palate: powerful, ripe fruit, spicy.

**DON JOSÉ 2006 TC**
tempranillo, samso, cabernet sauvignon

**77**

**MASIA OLIVEDA 2005 TC**
tempranillo, garnacha, syrah

**85** Colour: cherry, garnet rim. Nose: spicy, dark chocolate, ripe fruit, toasty. Palate: powerful, spicy, round tannins.

## PORTAL DEL MONTSANT

DaH, 74
43775 Marça (Tarragona)
☎: 977 178 486 - Fax: 934 173 591
portal@portaldelmontsant.com
www.portaldelmontsant.com

**SANTES 2008 B**
macabeo 100%

**89** Colour: bright straw. Nose: fresh, fresh fruit, white flowers, expressive, citrus fruit. Palate: flavourful, fruity, good acidity, balanced.

**SANTES 2007 T**
tempranillo 100%

**87** Colour: black cherry. Nose: creamy oak, toasty, dark chocolate, ripe fruit. Palate: fleshy, powerful, flavourful, powerful tannins.

## ROCAMAR

Major, 80
08755 Castellbisbal (Barcelona)
☎: 937 711 205
info@rocamar.net

**MASIA RIBOT 2008 B**
xarel.lo

**81**

**MASIA RIBOT MERLOT 2007 T**

**77**

**MASIA RIBOT TEMPRANILLO 2007 T**

**75**

**MASIA RIBOT CABERNET SAUVIGNON 2006 T**

**83**

PALANGRE

## UNIÓ CORPORACIÓ ALIMENTARIA - CELLERS UNIÓ

Joan Oliver, 16-24
43206 Reus (Tarragona)
☎: 977 330 055 - Fax: 977 330 070
reus@cellersunio.com
www.cellersunio.com

**MASIA PUBILL 2008 B**
garnacha blanca 60%, macabeo 25%, chardonnay 15%

**77**

**MASIA PUBILL 2008 RD**
garnacha 60%, merlot 40%

**78**

**MASIA PUBILL NEGRE 2008 T**
garnacha 60%, ull de llebre 40%

**84**

**MASIA PUBILL 2006 TC**
garnacha 50%, ull de llebre 35%, cabernet sauvignon 15%

# DO CATALUNYA

## 82

**MASIA PUBILL 2005 TR**
ull de llebre 40%, garnacha 40%, cabernet sauvignon 20%

## 83

**MASIA PUBILL 2002 TGR**
cariñena 50%, garnacha 30%, cabernet sauvignon 20%

## 83

---

# VINOS ROSTEI

Cami Mas Rostei, s/n
17255 Begur (Girona)
☎: 629 568 302
vinosrostei@telefonica.net
www.vinosrostei.com

**ROSTEI 2005 TC**
cabernet sauvignon 60%, merlot 40%

## 82

**ROSTEI 2003 TR**
cabernet sauvignon 60%, merlot 40%

## 83

SOME OTHER WINERIES WITHIN THE DO:

**BODEGAS PINORD
CELLER COOPERATIU DE SALELLES
CELLER J. MESTRE
CELLERS TRIADA
CLOS VITIS
CUVÉE SANTAMARÍA
HOSPITAL DE SANT JOAN BAPTISTA
DE SITGES
JAUME GRAU - VINS GRAU
JUAN ANTONIO PÉREZ ROURA
LEONARDO CANO PEÑA (VINS I CAVES
ARTESANALS VALLBONA D'ANOIA)
SOL DE BRUGÀS
U MÉS U FAN TRES
VALLFORMOSA
VINS PRAVI S.L.**

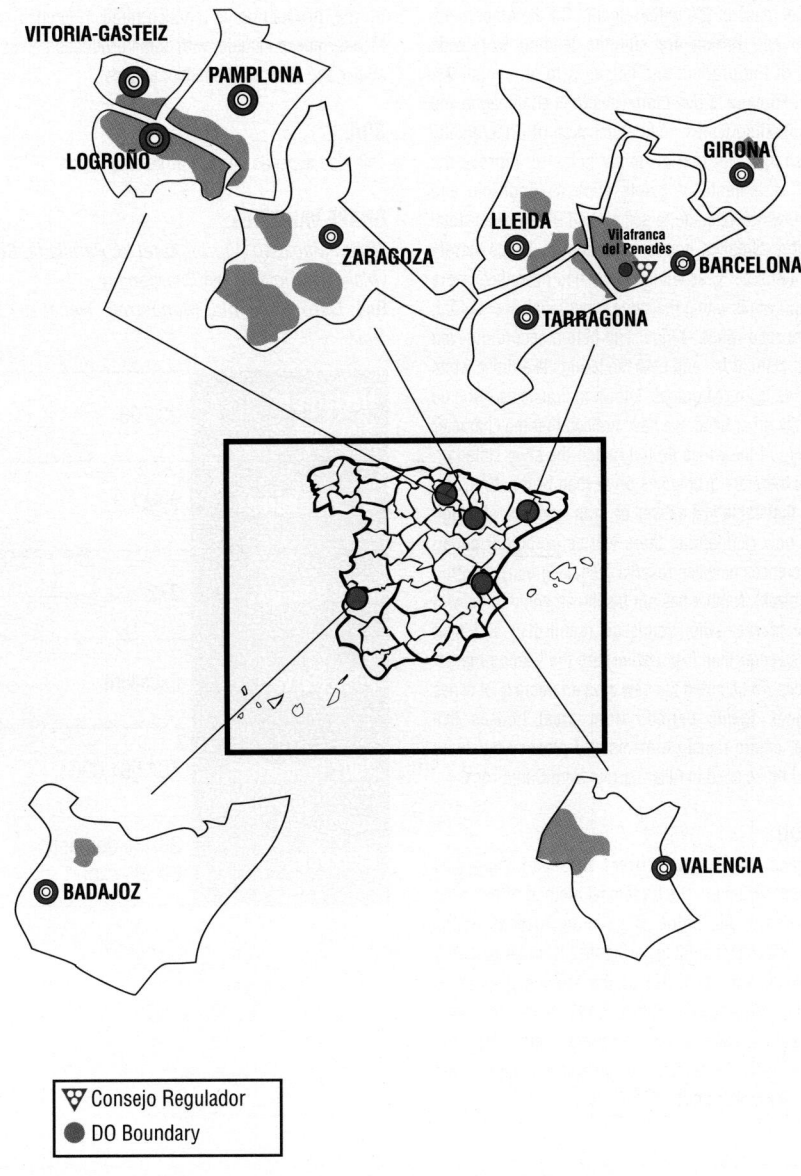

Consejo Regulador
DO Boundary

## NEWS

Step by step, consumers are more prone to drink cava, the sparkling Catalonian star wine, although it has known an overall decrease of 9% within Spain. On the other hand, Germans and British are still the leading worldwide drinkers of the product and helped it to an overall 9% increase. Foreigners buy more cava than champagne and Italian sparkling wines, mainly because of price/quality relationship, a fact that evidently helps to improve the financial statements of giants such as Codorníu and Freixenet, which manage to sell abroad 90% of their total production. Smaller houses manage to bottle hardly 600.000 units per year. All in all, we find nowadays more brands and wines within the same winery than ever before; also more rosé wines –bigger and better, according even to French standards– and new renderings like those white cavas made from red grapes, known in France as blanc de noir. On the other hand, we have noticed that the character and quality of the wines do not match the style stated on the label: there are brut wines dryer than brut nature, and reservas that could just as well be gran reservas, although with the new regulations there will be no colour-coded label differences between reserva (usually green) and gran reserva (black). Neither has our tasting anything to do with what the market tells: semiseco (semi-dry) and brut (slightly sweeter than brut nature) are the leading market preferences. To be noted the new cava aristocracy of wines with longer ageing periods from great houses like Gramona, where research meets and pleases our taste buds, and those aged in Allier barrels from Sumarroca.

## LOCATION

The defined Cava region covers the sparkling wines produced according to the traditional method of a second fermentation in the bottle of 63 municipalities in the province of Barcelona, 52 in Tarragona, 12 in Lleida and 5 in Girona, as well as those of the municipal areas of Laguardia, Moreda de Álava and Oyón in Álava, Almendralejo in Badajoz, Mendavia and Viana in Navarra, Requena in Valencia, Ainzón and Cariñena in Zaragoza, and a further 18 municipalities of La Rioja.

## CLIMATE

That of each producing region stated in the previous epigraph. Nevertheless, the region in which the largest part of the production is concentrated (Penedès) has a Mediterranean climate, with some production areas being cooler and situated at a higher altitude.

## SOIL

This also depends on each producing region.

## GRAPE VARIETIES:

**White:** *Macabeo* (*Viura*), *Xarel.lo, Parellada, Subirat* (*Malvasía Riojana*) and *Chardonnay*.
**Red:** *Garnacha Tinta, Monastrell, Trepat* and *Pinot Noir*.

| | |
|---|---|
| Hectares of Vineyard | 33,706 |
| Nº Viticulturists | 7,547 |
| Nº of Bodegas | 272 |
| 2008 Harvest | Excellent |
| 2007 Production | 164,691,000 l. |
| Marketing | 39.1% domestic 60.9% export |

**CONSEJO REGULADOR**
Avinguda Tarragona, 24
08720 Vilafranca del Penedés (Barcelona)
☎: 938 903 104 - Fax: 938 901 567
@ consejo@cava.es
www.crcava.es

## GENERAL CHARACTERISTICS OF THE WINES:

| | |
|---|---|
| **YOUNG CAVAS** | Their youth is due to a shorter ageing period in the bottle (the minimum stipulated by the Consejo is nine months). They are somewhat lighter, fresher and easier to drink; they have notes of fruit and vegetables. |
| **WITH LONGER AGEING PERIODS** | (For the Gran Reserva, the wines have to be aged for a minimum of 30 months in the bottle). They have more complex notes due to the longer time that the yeasts remain in the bottles. There is a distinction between the more traditional styles, normally with noses of dried fruit and bitter almonds, sometimes also due to the inclusion of old wine in the expedition liqueur, although this custom is gradually dying out. The more modern styles combine slightly fruity and floral notes, even herbs, with hints of toast and nuts; they are also characterised by their refinement and elegance, typical of champagne. |
| **CHARDONNAY BASED** | These are characterised by their greater body on the palate and a light oily mouthfeel; on the nose they may sometimes develop noses of tropical fruit. |

## 2008 VINTAGE RATING:

# VERY GOOD

## AGRÍCOLA DE BARBERÀ

Comercio, 40
43422 Barberà de la Conca (Tarragona)
☎: 977 887 035 - Fax: 977 887 035
cobarbera@doconcadebarbera.com

CASTELL DE LA COMANDA 2004 BR
GRAN RESERVA
macabeo 50%, parellada 50%

**85** Colour: bright golden. Nose: dry nuts, fragrant herbs, complex, lees reduction notes. Palate: powerful, flavourful, good acidity, fine bead, fine bitter notes.

CASTELL DE LA COMANDA 2004 BN
GRAN RESERVA
macabeo 50%, parellada 50%

**86** Colour: bright golden. Nose: dry nuts, fragrant herbs, complex. Palate: powerful, flavourful, good acidity, fine bead, fine bitter notes.

CASTELL DE LA COMANDA 2003 BN
GRAN RESERVA
macabeo 50%, parellada 50%

**87** Colour: bright golden. Nose: fine lees, dry nuts, fragrant herbs, complex. Palate: powerful, flavourful, good acidity, fine bead, fine bitter notes.

## AGUSTÍ TORELLÓ MATA

La Serra, s/n
08770 Sant Sadurní d'Anoia (Barcelona)
☎: 938 911 173 - Fax: 938 912 616
info@agustitorellomata.com
www.agustitorellomata.com

AGUSTÍ TORELLÓ MATA ROSAT 2007 BR RESERVA
trepat 100%

**88** Colour: rose, purple rim. Nose: powerfull, ripe fruit, red berry notes, floral, expressive. Palate: fleshy, powerful, fruity, fresh.

AGUSTÍ TORELLÓ MATA 2006 BR RESERVA
macabeo 38%, parellada 35%, xarel.lo 27%

**89** Colour: bright straw. Nose: medium intensity, fresh fruit, dried herbs, fine lees, floral. Palate: fresh, fruity, flavourful, good acidity.

AGUSTÍ TORELLÓ MATA BARRICA 2006 BN
RESERVA
macabeo 100%

**90** Colour: bright golden. Nose: fine lees, dry nuts, fragrant herbs, complex, sweet spices. Palate: powerful, flavourful, good acidity, fine bead, fine bitter notes.

BAYANUS 375ML 2006 BN RESERVA
macabeo 41%, xarel.lo 28%, parellada 31%

**90** Colour: bright straw. Nose: dried herbs, fine lees, floral, fruit preserve. Palate: fresh, fruity, flavourful, good acidity.

AGUSTÍ TORELLÓ MATA 2005 BN GRAN RESERVA
macabeo 35%, xarel.lo 34%, parellada 31%

**89** Colour: bright golden. Nose: fine lees, dry nuts, fragrant herbs, complex. Palate: powerful, flavourful, good acidity, fine bead, fine bitter notes.

AGUSTÍ TORELLÓ MATA MAGNUM 2004 BN GRAN
RESERVA
macabeo 39%, parellada 33%, xarel.lo 28%

**90** Colour: bright straw. Nose: fresh fruit, dried herbs, fine lees, floral, lactic notes. Palate: fresh, fruity, flavourful, good acidity.

KRIPTA 2004 BN GRAN RESERVA
macabeo 45%, parellada 35%, xarel.lo 20%

**88** Colour: bright yellow. Nose: expressive, fine lees, fresh fruit, balanced. Palate: flavourful, fruity, fresh, fine bitter notes.

## ALBET I NOYA

Can Vendrell de la Codina, s/n
08739 Sant Pau D'Ordal (Barcelona)
☎: 938 994 812 - Fax: 938 994 930
albetinoya@albetinoya.cat
www.albetinoya.cat

ALBET I NOYA DOLÇ DE POSTRES RESERVA

**87** Colour: bright straw. Nose: candied fruit, fruit expression. Palate: flavourful, sweet, fresh.

ALBET I NOYA BRUT ROSAT PINOT NOIR BR

**89** Colour: onion pink. Nose: elegant, candied fruit, fragrant herbs, red berry notes, rose petals. Palate: light-bodied, flavourful, good acidity, long, spicy.

ALBET I NOYA BRUT 21 BARRICA BR BARRICA

**89** Colour: bright straw. Nose: medium intensity, fresh fruit, dried herbs, fine lees, floral, sweet spices, creamy oak. Palate: fresh, fruity, flavourful, good acidity.

ALBET I NOYA PETIT ALBET BR

**89** Colour: bright straw. Nose: fresh fruit, dried herbs, fine lees, floral. Palate: fresh, fruity, flavourful, good acidity.

ALBET I NOYA BR

**88** Colour: bright straw. Nose: fresh fruit, dried herbs, fine lees, floral. Palate: fresh, fruity, flavourful, good acidity.

ALBET I NOYA BRUT 21 BR

**87** Colour: bright straw. Nose: fresh fruit, dried herbs, fine lees, floral, fruit preserve. Palate: fresh, fruity, flavourful, good acidity.

ALBET I NOYA BN RESERVA

**89** Colour: bright straw. Nose: fresh fruit, dried herbs, fine lees, floral, sweet spices. Palate: fresh, fruity, flavourful, good acidity.

## ALELLA VINÍCOLA

Angel Guimerà, 62
08328 Alella (Barcelona)
☎: 935 403 842 - Fax: 935 401 648
comercial@alellavinicola.com
www.alellavinicola.com

MARFIL ROSAT 2006 BR
garnacha 50%, trepat 50%

**84**

MARFIL 2007 BN
macabeo, parellada, pansa blanca, chardonnay

**84**

IVORI 2006 BN FERMENTADO EN BARRICA
chardonnay 50%, pansa blanca 50%

**89** Colour: bright golden. Nose: fine lees, dry nuts, fragrant herbs, complex. Palate: powerful, flavourful, good acidity, fine bead, fine bitter notes.

## ALSINA & SARDÀ

Barrio Les Tarumbes, s/n
08733 Pla del Penedés (Barcelona)
☎: 938 988 132 - Fax: 938 988 671
alsina@alsinasarda.com
www.alsinasarda.com

PINOT NOIR ROSAT DE ALSINA & SARDA RD
pinot noir

**86** Colour: rose. Nose: powerfull, ripe fruit, red berry notes, floral, expressive. Palate: fleshy, powerful, fruity, fresh.

ALSINA & SARDÁ 2005 BR GRAN RESERVA
macabeo, xarel.lo, parellada

**86** Colour: bright golden. Nose: dry nuts, fragrant herbs, complex. Palate: powerful, flavourful, good acidity, fine bead, fine bitter notes.

ALSINA & SARDÁ 2005 BN RESERVA
macabeo, xarel.lo, parellada

**86** Colour: bright straw. Nose: medium intensity, fresh fruit, dried herbs, floral. Palate: fresh, fruity, flavourful, good acidity.

ALSINA & SARDÁ 2004 BN GRAN RESERVA

**87** Colour: bright golden. Nose: fine lees, dry nuts, fragrant herbs, complex, candied fruit. Palate: powerful, flavourful, good acidity, fine bead, fine bitter notes.

ALSINA & SARDÁ SELLO 2004 BN GRAN RESERVA
macabeo, xarel.lo, parellada

**87** Colour: bright golden. Nose: fine lees, fragrant herbs, complex, candied fruit. Palate: powerful, flavourful, good acidity, fine bead, fine bitter notes.

ALSINA & SARDÁ 2006 BRUT ROSADO
trepat

**87** Colour: rose, purple rim. Nose: powerfull, ripe fruit, red berry notes, floral. Palate: fleshy, powerful, fruity, fresh.

## AMETLLER CIVILL

Viladomat 140 bis 3º 4º
08015 (Barcelona)
☎: 933 208 439 - Fax: 933 208 437
ametller@ametller.com
www.ametller.com

MANUEL DE CABANYES 2005 BN
parellada, macabeo, xarel.lo

**86** Colour: bright golden. Nose: fine lees, dry nuts, complex, waxy notes. Palate: powerful, flavourful, good acidity, fine bead, fine bitter notes.

MANUEL DE CABANYES 2004 BN RESERVA
parellada, xarel.lo, macabeo

**86** Colour: bright golden. Nose: fine lees, fragrant herbs, complex, candied fruit. Palate: powerful, flavourful, good acidity, fine bead, fine bitter notes.

## AVINYÓ CAVAS

Masia Can Fontanals
08793 Avinyonet del Penedés (Barcelona)

# DO CAVA

☎: 938 970 055 - Fax: 938 970 691
avinyo@avinyo.com
www.avinyo.com

**AVINYÓ ROSAT RD**
pinot noir 100%

## 82

**AVINYÓ BR RESERVA**
macabeo 60%, xarel.lo 25%, parellada 15%

**85** Colour: bright straw. Nose: medium intensity, fresh fruit, floral. Palate: fresh, fruity, flavourful, good acidity.

**AVINYÓ SELECCIÓ LA TICOTA BN GRAN RESERVA**
xarel.lo 65%, macabeo 35%

**88** Colour: bright straw. Nose: medium intensity, fresh fruit, dried herbs, fine lees, floral. Palate: fresh, fruity, flavourful, good acidity, round.

**AVINYÓ BN RESERVA**
macabeo 55%, xarel.lo 35%, parellada 10%

**87** Colour: bright straw. Nose: medium intensity, fresh fruit, dried herbs, fine lees, floral. Palate: fresh, fruity, flavourful, good acidity.

## BODEGAS BORDEJÉ

Ctra. Borja - Rueda, km. 3
50570 Ainzón (Zaragoza)
☎: 976 868 080 - Fax: 976 868 989
pedidos@bodegasbordeje.com
www.bodegasbordeje.com

**BORDEJÉ ROSADO DE GARNACHA 2007 BN**
garnacha 100%

**86** Colour: rose, purple rim. Nose: powerfull, ripe fruit, red berry notes, floral, expressive. Palate: fleshy, powerful, fruity, fresh.

**BORDEJÉ CHARDONNAY 2007 BN**
chardonnay 100%

## 83

**BORDEJÉ 2005 BN**
macabeo 100%

## 77

## BODEGAS CAPITÀ VIDAL

Ctra. Villafranca-Igualada, km. 30
08733 Pla del Penedés (Barcelona)
☎: 938 988 630 - Fax: 938 988 625
capitavidal@capitavidal.com

www.capitavidal.com

**FUCHS DE VIDAL 2003 BN**

## 83

**FUCHS DE VIDAL CUVÈE ESPECIAL BN RESERVA**
macabeo 40%, xarel.lo 35%, parellada 25%

**85** Colour: bright straw. Nose: dried herbs, floral, fruit preserve. Palate: fresh, fruity, flavourful, good acidity.

**FUCHS DE VIDAL UNIC BN**
chardonnay 50%, pinot noir 35%, macabeo 15%, xarel.lo %, parellada %

## 83

**GRAN FUCHS DE VIDAL BN**
macabeo, xarel.lo, parellada

## 82

**PALAU SOLÁ**

## BODEGAS CASTELL D'OR

Mare Rafols, 3 1 D
08720 Vilafranca del Penedès (Barcelona)
☎: 938 905 385 - Fax: 938 905 446
castelldor@castelldor.com
www.castelldor.com

**COSSETANIA BR RESERVA**

**88** Colour: bright straw. Nose: fresh fruit, dried herbs, fine lees, floral. Palate: fresh, flavourful, good acidity, sweetness.

**FRANCOLI BR RESERVA**

**87** Colour: bright straw. Nose: dried herbs, fine lees, floral, ripe fruit. Palate: fresh, fruity, flavourful, good acidity.

**CASTELL COMANDA BR**

**87** Colour: bright straw. Nose: medium intensity, fresh fruit, floral. Palate: fresh, fruity, flavourful, good acidity, balanced.

**FLAMA D'OR ROSÉ BR**

**85** Colour: coppery red. Nose: powerfull, ripe fruit, floral, macerated fruit. Palate: fleshy, powerful, fruity, fresh.

**FRANCOLI ROSAT BR RESERVA**

## 84

**CASTELL COMANDA BN**

**88** Colour: bright straw. Nose: medium intensity, dried herbs, fine lees, floral, sweet spices. Palate: fresh, fruity, flavourful, good acidity.

## FLAMA D'OR BRUT IMPERIAL BN

**87** Colour: bright golden. Nose: fine lees, dry nuts, fragrant herbs, complex, white flowers. Palate: powerful, flavourful, good acidity, fine bead, fine bitter notes.

## FRANCOLI BN

**87** Colour: bright straw. Nose: medium intensity, fresh fruit, fine lees, floral. Palate: fresh, fruity, flavourful, good acidity.

## FLAMA D'OR BN

**86** Colour: bright straw. Nose: medium intensity, fresh fruit, dried herbs, floral. Palate: fresh, fruity, flavourful, good acidity.

## BODEGAS ESCUDERO

Ctra. de Arnedo, s/n
26587 Gravalos (La Rioja)
☎: 941 398 008 - Fax: 941 398 070
info@bodegasescudero.com
www.bodegasescudero.com

### DIORO BACO BR
100% chardonnay

**84**

### DIORO BACO BR
100% pinot noir

**83**

### DIORO BACO EXTRA BRUT
100% chardonnay

**86** Colour: bright straw. Nose: fresh fruit, dried herbs, fine lees, floral. Palate: fresh, fruity, flavourful, good acidity.

## BENITO ESCUDERO ABAD

## BODEGAS FAUSTINO

Ctra. de Logroño, s/n
01320 Oyón (Alava)
☎: 945 622 500 - Fax: 945 622 106
info@bodegasfaustino.es
www.bodegasfaustino.es

### CAVA FAUSTINO ROSADO RD RESERVA

**85** Colour: coppery red. Nose: powerfull, ripe fruit, red berry notes, floral, expressive. Palate: fleshy, powerful, fruity, fresh.

### CAVA FAUSTINO BR RESERVA

**85** Colour: bright straw. Nose: medium intensity, fresh fruit, dried herbs, fine lees. Palate: fresh, fruity, flavourful, good acidity.

## BODEGAS GRAMONA

Industria, 34-36
08770 Sant Sadurní D'Anoia (Barcelona)
☎: 938 910 113 - Fax: 938 183 284
comunicacion@gramona.com
www.gramona.com

### GRAMONA GRAN CUVÉE DE POSTRE RESERVA
xarel.lo 33%, macabeo 33%, parellada 33%

**88** Colour: bright yellow. Nose: powerfull, characterful, dry nuts. Palate: balanced, fine bitter notes, sweet, flavourful.

### GRAMONA IMPERIAL 2004 BR GRAN RESERVA
xarel.lo 50%, macabeo 40%, chardonnay 10%

**92** Colour: bright straw. Nose: fresh fruit, dried herbs, fine lees, floral, expressive, elegant. Palate: fresh, flavourful, good acidity, full.

### GRAMONA CELLER BATLLE 2000 BR GRAN RESERVA
xarel.lo 70%, macabeo 30%

**92** Colour: bright golden. Nose: fine lees, dry nuts, complex, elegant. Palate: powerful, flavourful, good acidity, fine bead, fine bitter notes.

### GRAMONA CELLER BATLLE 1998 BR GRAN RESERVA
xarel.lo 70%, macabeo 30%

**96** Colour: bright golden. Nose: candied fruit, expressive, characterful, complex, lees reduction notes, dry nuts. Palate: flavourful, fleshy, complex, fine bitter notes, fine bead.

### GRAMONA ALLEGRO BR RESERVA
chardonnay 33%, macabeo 33%, xarel.lo 33%

**89** Colour: bright straw. Nose: medium intensity, fresh fruit, dried herbs, fine lees, floral. Palate: fresh, fruity, flavourful, good acidity.

### GRAMONA ARGENT 2005 BRUT RESERVA
chardonnay 100%

**92** Colour: bright yellow. Nose: elegant, fresh, ripe fruit, varietal, fine lees. Palate: good acidity, fine bead, fruity, creamy.

### GRAMONA III LUSTROS 2002 BN GRAN RESERVA
xarel.lo 70%, macabeo 30%

**91** Colour: bright golden. Nose: fine lees, dry nuts, fragrant herbs, complex. Palate: powerful, flavourful, good acidity, fine bead, fine bitter notes.

### GRAMONA ROSÉ BRUT ROSADO GRAN RESERVA
pinot noir 100%

**87** Colour: rose. Nose: elegant, ripe fruit, red berry notes. Palate: good acidity, fine bead, ripe fruit.

### GRAMONA LA SUITE SC RESERVA
xarel.lo 33%, macabeo 33%, parellada 33%

**88** Colour: bright yellow. Nose: powerfull, characterful, roasted almonds, candied fruit. Palate: balanced, good acidity, fine bitter notes.

## BODEGAS HISPANO SUIZAS

Travesía de la Industria, 5
46370 Campos Arcis (Requena) (Valencia)
☎: 661 894 200 - Fax: 963 523 975
ceo@bodegashispanosuizas.com
www.bodegashispanosuizas.com

### TANTUM ERGO CHARDONNAY PINOT NOIR 2007 BN
chardonnay, pinot noir

**88** Colour: bright straw. Nose: medium intensity, fresh fruit, dried herbs, fine lees, floral. Palate: fresh, fruity, flavourful, good acidity.

### TANTUM ERGO PINOT NOIR ROSÉ 2007 BN
pinot noir 100%

**80**

## BODEGAS J. TRIAS

Comerç, 6
08720 Vilafranca del Penedés (Barcelona)
☎: 938 902 627 - Fax: 938 901 724
bodegas@jtrias.com
www.jtrias.com

### TRIAS BATLLE ROSADO 2007 BR
trepat

**84**

### TRIAS 2006 BR RESERVA
xarel.lo, macabeo, parellada

**86** Colour: bright straw. Nose: medium intensity, fresh fruit, dried herbs, fine lees, floral. Palate: fresh, fruity, flavourful, good acidity.

### TRIAS 2006 BN RESERVA
macabeo, xarel.lo, parellada

**86** Colour: bright straw. Nose: medium intensity, fresh fruit, dried herbs, fine lees, floral. Palate: fresh, fruity, flavourful, good acidity.

### TRIAS BATLLE 2004 BN GRAN RESERVA
xarel.lo, macabeo, parellada, chardonnay

**88** Colour: bright straw. Nose: medium intensity, fresh fruit, dried herbs, fine lees, floral, pattiserie, smoky. Palate: fresh, fruity, flavourful, good acidity.

## BODEGAS LANGA

Ctra. Nacional II, km. 241,700
50300 Calatayud (Zaragoza)
☎: 976 881 818 - Fax: 976 884 463
info@bodegas-langa.com
www.bodegas-langa.com

### REYES DE ARAGÓN BR RESERVA
macabeo 75%, chardonnay 25%

**82**

### REYES DE ARAGÓN BN RESERVA
chardonnay 75%, macabeo 25%

**85** Colour: bright straw. Nose: medium intensity, fresh fruit, dried herbs, fine lees, floral. Palate: fresh, fruity, flavourful, good acidity.

**REYES DE ARAGÓN BN GRAN RESERVA**
chardonnay 75%, macabeo 25%

**82**

**REYES DE ARAGÓN SELECCIÓN FAMILIAR BN**
chardonnay 75%, macabeo 25%

**82**

## BODEGAS OLARRA

Avda. de Mendavia, 30
26009 Logroño (La Rioja)
☎: 941 235 299 - Fax: 941 253 703
bodegasolarra@bodegasolarra.es
www.bodegasolarra.es

**AÑARES BR**
viura 100%

**84**

**AÑARES BN**
viura 100%

**86** Colour: bright straw. Nose: medium intensity, fresh fruit, dried herbs, fine lees, floral. Palate: fresh, fruity, flavourful, good acidity.

## BODEGAS ONDARRE

Ctra. de Aras, s/n
31230 Viana (Navarra)
☎: 948 645 300 - Fax: 948 646 002
bodegasondarre@bodegasondarre.es
www.bodegasondarre.es

**ONDARRE MILLENNIUM BR**
viura 100%

**86** Colour: bright straw. Nose: medium intensity, fresh fruit, dried herbs, fine lees, floral, complex. Palate: fresh, fruity, flavourful, good acidity, sweetness.

**ONDARRE BR RESERVA**
viura 100%

**82**

## BODEGAS ROMALE

Pol. Ind. Parc. 6 Manz. D
06200 Almendralejo (Badajoz)
☎: 924 667 255 - Fax: 924 665 877
romale@romale.com
www.romale.com

**PRIVILEGIO DE ROMALE 2006 BN RESERVA**
macabeo 60%, parellada 40%

**81**

**VIÑA ROMALE**

## BODEGAS TORROJA

Nogueral, 3
46357 Azagador (Valencia)
☎: 962 304 232 - Fax: 962 303 833
herve@bodegastorroja.com
www.bodegastorroja.com

**SYBARUS BN**
macabeo 80%, chardonnay 20%

**82**

## BODEGAS TROBAT

Castelló, 10
17780 Garriguella (Gerona)
☎: 972 530 092 - Fax: 972 552 530
toni.madern@bmark.es
www.bodegastrobat.com

**CELLER TROBAT 2005 BN**

**88** Colour: bright golden. Nose: fine lees, dry nuts, complex. Palate: powerful, flavourful, good acidity, fine bead, fine bitter notes, creamy.

**CELLER TROBAT BN**

**89** Colour: bright golden. Nose: fine lees, dry nuts, fragrant herbs, complex. Palate: powerful, flavourful, good acidity, fine bead, fine bitter notes.

**GRAN AMAT**

## BODEGUES SUMARROCA S.L.

Barrio El Rebato, s/n
08739 Subirats (Barcelona)
☎: 938 911 092 - Fax: 938 911 778
sumarroca@sumarroca.es
www.sumarroca.es

**CAVA SUMARROCA PINOT NOIR 2006 RD**
pinot noir 100%

**89** Colour: onion pink. Nose: elegant, candied fruit, dried flowers, fragrant herbs, red berry notes. Palate: light-bodied, flavourful, good acidity, long, spicy.

## SUMARROCA 2006 BR RESERVA
parellada, macabeo, xarel.lo, chardonnay

**89** Colour: bright straw. Nose: fresh fruit, dried herbs, fine lees, floral. Palate: fresh, fruity, flavourful, good acidity.

## SUMARROCA NÚRIA CLAVEROL 2005 BR RESERVA
xarel.lo, chardonnay, parellada

**94** Colour: bright straw. Nose: dried herbs, fine lees, floral, ripe fruit, elegant. Palate: fresh, fruity, flavourful, good acidity.

## CAVA SUMARROCA GRAN BRUT ALLIER 2005 BR GRAN RESERVA
chardonnay, xarel.lo, macabeo

**93** Colour: bright golden. Nose: dry nuts, fragrant herbs, complex, fine lees. Palate: powerful, flavourful, good acidity, fine bead, fine bitter notes, creamy.

## SUMARROCA GRAN BRUT 2003 BR
chardonnay, xarel.lo, macabeo

**92** Colour: bright straw. Nose: dried herbs, fine lees, floral, ripe fruit. Palate: fresh, fruity, flavourful, good acidity, creamy.

## SUMARROCA 2005 BN GRAN RESERVA
parellada, macabeo, xarel.lo, chardonnay

**91** Colour: bright straw. Nose: fresh fruit, dried herbs, fine lees, floral, elegant. Palate: fresh, fruity, flavourful, good acidity.

## CAVA SUMARROCA CUVÉE 2004 BN GRAN RESERVA
parellada, chardonnay

**90** Colour: bright straw. Nose: dried herbs, fine lees, floral, expressive, candied fruit. Palate: fresh, fruity, flavourful, good acidity.

## BOLET VINOS Y CAVAS

Finca Mas Lluet
08732 Castellvi de la Marca (Barcelona)
☎: 938 918 153 - Fax: 938 918 437
cavasbolet@cavasbolet.com
www.cavasbolet.com

## BOLET 2007 BR
pinot noir

**86** Colour: coppery red. Nose: powerfull, ripe fruit, red berry notes, floral, smoky. Palate: fleshy, powerful, fruity, fresh.

## BOLET 2006 BR RESERVA

**84**

## BOLET ECO 2006 BN RESERVA
xarel.lo, macabeo, parellada

**88** Colour: bright straw. Nose: medium intensity, fresh fruit, dried herbs, fine lees, floral. Palate: fresh, fruity, flavourful, good acidity.

## BOLET 2003 BN GRAN RESERVA
xarel.lo, macabeo, parellada

**87** Colour: bright golden. Nose: fine lees, dry nuts, fragrant herbs, complex. Palate: powerful, flavourful, good acidity, fine bead, fine bitter notes.

## BOLET SELECCIÓN FAMILIAR 2001 BN
xarel.lo, macabeo, parellada

**84**

## CA N'ESTELLA

Masia Can Estella
08635 Sant Esteve Sesrovires (Barcelona)
☎: 934 16 1 3 - Fax: 934 161 620
e.mallol@fincacanestella.com

## RABETLLAT I VIDAL BRUT CA N'ESTELLA BR

**86** Colour: bright straw. Nose: medium intensity, fresh fruit, dried herbs, fine lees, floral. Palate: fresh, fruity, flavourful, good acidity.

## RABETLLAT I VIDAL BN

**87** Colour: bright straw. Nose: medium intensity, fresh fruit, fine lees, floral, scrubland. Palate: fresh, fruity, flavourful, good acidity.

## RABETLLAT I VIDAL RESERVA DE LA FINCA BN

**86** Colour: bright straw. Nose: medium intensity, dried herbs, fine lees, faded flowers. Palate: fresh, fruity, flavourful, good acidity.

## RABETLLAT I VIDAL BRUT ROSADO

**85** Colour: rose. Nose: macerated fruit, red berry notes, smoky, spicy. Palate: fleshy, fruity, fresh, flavourful.

## CAN DESCREGUT

Masia Can Descregut s/n
08735 Vilobi del Penedès (Barcelona)
☎: 938 978 273 - Fax: 938 170 786
candescregut@hotmail.com
www.montdarac.com

MONT D'ARAC ROSAT RD
trepat

**86** Colour: rose, purple rim. Nose: powerfull, ripe fruit, red berry notes, floral, expressive. Palate: fleshy, powerful, fruity, fresh.

MONT D'ARAC BN
macabeo, xarel.lo, parellada

**88** Colour: bright straw. Nose: medium intensity, dried herbs, floral, tropical fruit. Palate: fresh, fruity, flavourful, good acidity.

## CAN FEIXES (HUGUET)

Finca Can Feixes s/n
08718 Cabrera D'Anoia (Barcelona)
☎: 937 718 227 - Fax: 937 718 031
canfeixes@canfeixes.com
www.canfeixes.com

HUGUET 2005 BR GRAN RESERVA
parellada 50%, macabeo 25%, pinot noir 25%

**88** Colour: bright straw. Nose: medium intensity, fresh fruit, fine lees, floral, candied fruit. Palate: fresh, fruity, flavourful, good acidity, easy to drink.

HUGUET 2005 BN GRAN RESERVA
parellada 50%, macabeo 25%, pinot noir 25%

**87** Colour: bright straw. Nose: medium intensity, dried herbs, fine lees, floral, candied fruit. Palate: fresh, fruity, flavourful, good acidity.

## CAN RÀFOLS DELS CAUS

Can Rafols del Caus s/n
08739 Avinyonet del Penedés (Barcelona)
☎: 938 97 0 0 - Fax: 938 970 370
canrafolsdelscaus@canrafolsdelscaus.com
www.canrafolsdelscaus.com

GRAN CAUS 2004 BN
xarel.lo 50%, macabeo 30%, chardonnay 20%

**87** Colour: bright golden. Nose: dry nuts, complex, ripe fruit. Palate: powerful, flavourful, good acidity, fine bead, fine bitter notes.

GRAN CAUS BN

**85** Colour: onion pink. Nose: elegant, candied fruit, dried flowers, fragrant herbs, red berry notes, spicy. Palate: light-bodied, flavourful, good acidity, long, spicy.

## CANALS & MUNNÉ

Ctra. Sant Sadurní a Vilafranca, km. 0, 5
08770 Sant Sadurní d'Anoia (Barcelona)

☎: 938 910 318 - Fax: 938 911 945
info@canalsimunne.com
www.canalsimunne.com

CANALS & MUNNÉ ROSÉ 2006 RD RESERVA
merlot, pinot noir

**83**

CANALS & MUNNÉ INSUPERABLE 2007 BR
macabeo, xarel.lo, parellada

**90** Colour: bright straw. Nose: medium intensity, fresh fruit, dried herbs, fine lees, floral. Palate: fresh, fruity, flavourful, good acidity, balanced.

CANALS & MUNNÉ RESERVA DE L'AVI
2004 BR GRAN RESERVA
macabeo, xarel.lo, parellada, chardonnay

**88** Colour: bright golden. Nose: fine lees, dry nuts, fragrant herbs, complex. Palate: powerful, flavourful, good acidity, fine bead, fine bitter notes.

CANALS & MUNNÉ MAGNUM 2005 BN
macabeo, xarel.lo, parellada, chardonnay

**88** Colour: bright yellow. Nose: fine lees, dry nuts, fragrant herbs, complex. Palate: powerful, flavourful, good acidity, fine bead, fine bitter notes.

CANALS & MUNNÉ 2005 BN
macabeo, xarel.lo, parellada, chardonnay

**86** Colour: bright straw. Nose: medium intensity, fresh fruit, dried herbs, floral. Palate: fresh, fruity, flavourful, good acidity.

CANALS & MUNNÉ GRAN DUC XXI 2004 BN GRAN RESERVA
macabeo, xarel.lo, chardonnay, pinot noir

**89** Colour: bright golden. Nose: fine lees, dry nuts, fragrant herbs, complex. Palate: powerful, flavourful, good acidity, fine bead, fine bitter notes.

CANALS & MUNNÉ EL SERRALET DEL GUINEU
2004 BN GRAN RESERVA
chardonnay, pinot noir

**88** Colour: bright golden. Nose: dry nuts, fragrant herbs, complex. Palate: powerful, flavourful, good acidity, fine bead, fine bitter notes.

CANALS & MUNNÉ (37,5 CL.) 2004 BN
macabeo, xarel.lo, parellada, chardonnay

**85** Colour: bright straw. Nose: medium intensity, dried herbs, floral, candied fruit. Palate: fresh, fruity, flavourful, good acidity.

## CANALS CANALS

Avda. Mare de Deu Montserrat, 9
08769 Castellví de Rosanes (Barcelona)
☎: 937 755 446 - Fax: 937 741 719
cava@canalscanals.com
www.canalscanals.com

MARTA DELUXE 2004 BN GRAN RESERVA
xarel.lo, macabeo, parellada

**88** Colour: bright golden. Nose: fine lees, dry nuts, fragrant herbs, complex. Palate: powerful, flavourful, good acidity, fine bead, fine bitter notes.

CANALS CANALS GRAN RESERVA NUMERADA 2004 BN GRAN RESERVA
xarel.lo, macabeo, parellada

**87** Colour: bright straw. Nose: medium intensity, fresh fruit, dried herbs, fine lees, floral. Palate: fresh, fruity, flavourful, good acidity.

RAMÓN CANALS 2004 BN GRAN RESERVA
xarel.lo, macabeo, parellada

**85** Colour: bright golden. Nose: fine lees, dry nuts, fragrant herbs, complex. Palate: powerful, flavourful, good acidity, fine bead, fine bitter notes.

## CANALS NADAL

Ponent, 2
08733 El Pla del Penedés (Barcelona)
☎: 938 988 081 - Fax: 938 989 050
cava@canalsnadal.com
www.canalsnadal.com

CANALS NADAL 2006 RD RESERVA
trepat 100%

**88** Colour: onion pink. Nose: elegant, candied fruit, dried flowers, fragrant herbs, red berry notes. Palate: light-bodied, flavourful, good acidity, long, spicy.

CANALS NADAL 2006 BR RESERVA
macabeo 40%, xarel.lo 45%, parellada 15%

**90** Colour: bright golden. Nose: fine lees, dry nuts, fragrant herbs, complex. Palate: powerful, flavourful, good acidity, fine bead, fine bitter notes.

CANALS NADAL VINTAGE 20 ANIVERSARI 2005 BR
chardonnay 40%, macabeo 30%, xarel.lo 20%, parellada 10%

**89** Colour: bright straw. Nose: medium intensity, fresh fruit, dried herbs, fine lees, floral, spicy. Palate: fresh, fruity, flavourful, good acidity.

ANTONI CANALS NADAL BRUT CUPADA SELECCIÓ 2006 BN
macabeo 50%, xarel.lo 40%, parellada 10%

**90** Colour: bright golden. Nose: fine lees, dry nuts, fragrant herbs, complex, candied fruit. Palate: powerful, flavourful, good acidity, fine bead, fine bitter notes.

CANALS NADAL 2006 BN
macabeo 45%, xarel.lo 40%, parellada 15%

**87** Colour: bright straw. Nose: medium intensity, fresh fruit, dried herbs, floral. Palate: fresh, fruity, flavourful, good acidity.

CANALS NADAL 2005 BN GRAN RESERVA
macabeo 50%, xarel.lo 40%, parellada 10%

**88** Colour: bright golden. Nose: fine lees, fragrant herbs, complex, citrus fruit. Palate: powerful, flavourful, good acidity, fine bead, fine bitter notes.

## CANALS Y NUBIOLA S.A.

Pza. Santiago Rusinyol, s/n
08770 Sant Sadurní D'Anoia (Barcelona)
☎: 938 917 025 - Fax: 938 910 126
canalsnubiola@canalsnubiola.es
www.canalsnubiola.es

CANALS & NUBIOLA 2006 BR
xarel.lo 40%, macabeo 30%, parellada 30%

**85** Colour: bright straw. Nose: medium intensity, floral, pattiserie. Palate: fresh, fruity, flavourful, good acidity.

CANALS & NUBIOLA 2006 BN
macabeo 33%, xarel.lo 33%, parellada 33%

**78**

CANALS & NUBIOLA SEMISEC 2007 SS
xarel.lo 50%, macabeo 40%, parellada 10%

**86** Colour: bright straw. Nose: medium intensity, fresh fruit, fine lees, rancio notes. Palate: fresh, fruity, flavourful, good acidity, full.

## CASTELL D'AGE

Carretera, 6-8
08782 La Beguda Baixa (Barcelona)
☎: 937 725 181 - Fax: 937 727 061
info@castelldage.com
www.castelldage.com

CASTELL D'AGE ROSADO BR

**87** Colour: rose, purple rim. Nose: powerfull, ripe fruit, red berry notes, floral, expressive. Palate: fleshy, powerful, fruity, fresh.

### CASTELL D'AGE ECOLÒGIC BN RESERVA

**87** Colour: bright straw. Nose: medium intensity, fresh fruit, dried herbs, fine lees, floral. Palate: fresh, fruity, flavourful, good acidity.

### CASTELL D'AGE CHARDONNAY ECOLÓGICO BN

**87** Colour: bright straw. Nose: fresh fruit, dried herbs, fine lees, floral. Palate: fresh, fruity, flavourful, good acidity.

### CASTELL D'AGE BN GRAN RESERVA

**87** Colour: bright golden. Nose: fine lees, dry nuts, complex. Palate: powerful, flavourful, good acidity, fine bead, fine bitter notes.

### CASTELL D'AGE POCULUM BONI GENI BN RESERVA

**84**

### ANNE MARIE COMTESSE BN RESERVA

**83**

---

### POCULUM BONI GENI

## CASTELL SANT ANTONI

Passeig del Parc, 13
08770 Sant Sadurní d'Anoia (Barcelona)
☎: 938 183 099 - Fax: 938 183 099
cava@castellsantantoni.com
www.castellsantantoni.com

### CASTELL SANT ANTONI "GRAN BRUT" BR GRAN RESERVA

**92** Colour: bright golden. Nose: fine lees, dry nuts, fragrant herbs, complex. Palate: powerful, flavourful, good acidity, fine bead, fine bitter notes.

### CASTELL SANT ANTONI GRAN BRUT MAGNUM BR RESERVA

**91** Colour: bright straw. Nose: ripe fruit, fine lees, elegant, balanced, expressive. Palate: fruity, flavourful, good acidity, fine bitter notes, fine bead.

### CASTELL SANT ANTONI 37,5 CL. BR

**90** Colour: bright straw. Nose: candied fruit, neat, fresh, floral. Palate: balanced, elegant, fine bead, good acidity, fine bitter notes.

### CASTELL SANT ANTONI POSTRE BR

**85** Colour: straw. Nose: medium intensity, ripe fruit, balanced. Palate: correct, sweet, easy to drink.

### CASTELL SANT ANTONI 2003 BN GRAN RESERVA

**91** Colour: bright golden. Nose: fine lees, dry nuts, complex, ripe fruit, elegant. Palate: powerful, flavourful, good acidity, fine bead, fine bitter notes.

### CASTELL SANT ANTONI MAGNUM 2001 BN GRAN RESERVA

**92** Colour: bright straw. Nose: elegant, expressive, balanced, fine lees, candied fruit. Palate: flavourful, good structure, ripe fruit, fine bead.

### CASTELL SANT ANTONI TORRE DE L'HOMENATGE 1999 BN GRAN RESERVA

**92** Colour: bright golden. Nose: powerfull, candied fruit, faded flowers, dry nuts, pattiserie. Palate: flavourful, fleshy, sweetness, aged character, fine bead.

### CASTELL SANT ANTONI CUVÉE MILLENNIUM BN GRAN RESERVA

**89** Colour: bright straw. Nose: balanced, medium intensity, spicy, fresh, ripe fruit. Palate: good acidity, correct, balanced.

### CASTELL SANT ANTONI GRAN BARRICA BN GRAN RESERVA

**89** Colour: bright yellow. Nose: medium intensity, elegant, ripe fruit, spicy. Palate: flavourful, powerful, concentrated, good acidity.

### CASTELL SANT ANTONI 37,5 CL. BN

**89** Colour: bright straw. Nose: medium intensity, fruit expression, floral. Palate: balanced, fresh, good acidity, fine bitter notes.

### CASTELL SANT ANTONI GRAN ROSAT BN RESERVA ESPECIAL
pinot noir

**88** Colour: rose. Nose: spicy, fresh fruit, medium intensity, raspberry. Palate: good acidity, fine bead, balanced, fine bitter notes.

### CASTELL SANT ANTONI CUVÉE MILLENNIUM BN

**85** Colour: brilliant rose. Nose: fruit expression, medium intensity. Palate: easy to drink, good acidity, correct.

## CASTELLBLANCH

Avda. Casetes Mir, s/n
08770 Sant Sadurní D'Anoia (Barcelona)
☎: 938 917 025 - Fax: 938 910 126
castellblanch@castellblanch.es
www.castellblanch.es

CASTELLBLANCH ROSADO 2007 RD
trepat 70%, garnacha 30%

**82**

CASTELLBLANCH BRUT ZERO 2006 BR RESERVA
parellada 50%, macabeo 31%, xarel.lo 10%, chardonnay 9%

**87** Colour: bright straw. Nose: fresh fruit, dried herbs, fine lees, floral. Palate: fresh, fruity, flavourful, good acidity.

CASTELLBLANCH GRAN CUVEÉ 2006 BR RESERVA
xarel.lo 60%, macabeo 30%, parellada 10%

**86** Colour: bright straw. Nose: fresh fruit, dried herbs, fine lees, floral. Palate: fresh, fruity, flavourful, good acidity.

CASTELLBLANCH EXTRA 2006 BR RESERVA
macabeo 33%, xarel.lo 33%, parellada 33%

**84**

CASTELLBLANCH GRAN CUVEÉ 2006 BN RESERVA
parellada 40%, xarel.lo 30%, macabeo 30%

**87** Colour: bright straw. Nose: fresh fruit, dried herbs, floral. Palate: fresh, fruity, flavourful, good acidity.

CASTELLBLANCH DOS LUSTROS 2005 BN RESERVA
parellada 40%, macabeo 28%, xarel.lo 20%, chardonnay 12%

**84**

## CASTELLROIG - FINCA SABATÉ I COCA

Ctra. Sant Sadurní d'Anoia a Vilafranca del Penedés, km. 1
08739 Subirats (Barcelona)
☎: 938 911 927 - Fax: 938 914 055
info@castellroig.com
www.castellroig.com

CASTELLROIG 2006 BN RESERVA
xarel.lo, macabeo, parellada

**89** Colour: bright golden. Nose: fine lees, dry nuts, complex, dried herbs. Palate: powerful, flavourful, good acidity, fine bead, fine bitter notes.

SABATE I COCA RESERVA FAMILIAR 2005 BN
xarel.lo

**91** Colour: bright golden. Nose: fine lees, dry nuts, fragrant herbs, complex. Palate: powerful, flavourful, good acidity, fine bead, fine bitter notes, round.

CASTELLROIG 2004 BN GRAN RESERVA
xarel.lo, macabeo

**88** Colour: bright golden. Nose: fine lees, dry nuts, fragrant herbs, complex, candied fruit. Palate: powerful, flavourful, good acidity, fine bead, fine bitter notes.

CASTELLROIG MAGNUM 2003 BN GRAN RESERVA
xarel.lo, macabeo

**90** Colour: bright golden. Nose: fine lees, dry nuts, complex, spicy. Palate: powerful, flavourful, good acidity, fine bead, fine bitter notes, round.

## CAVA BERDIÉ

Les Conilleres
08732 Castellví de la Marca (Barcelona)
☎: 938 919 735 - Fax: 938 919 735
info@berdieromagosa.com
www.cavaberdie.com

BERDIÉ 2007 BR
macabeo, xarel.lo, parellada

**87** Colour: bright straw. Nose: fresh fruit, dried herbs, floral. Palate: fresh, fruity, flavourful, good acidity, balanced.

BERDIÉ BRUT ROSÉ 2007 BR
monastrell, garnacha

**86** Colour: rose, purple rim. Nose: powerfull, ripe fruit, red berry notes, floral, expressive. Palate: fleshy, powerful, fruity, fresh.

BERDIÉ 2007 BN
macabeo, xarel.lo, parellada

**87** Colour: bright straw. Nose: fresh fruit, dried herbs, fine lees, floral. Palate: fresh, fruity, flavourful, good acidity.

BERDIÉ 2006 BN RESERVA
macabeo, xarel.lo, parellada

**88** Colour: bright straw. Nose: dried herbs, fine lees, fresh fruit. Palate: fresh, fruity, flavourful, good acidity.

BERDIÉ 2005 BN GRAN RESERVA
macabeo, xarel.lo, parellada

**88** Colour: bright straw. Nose: medium intensity, fresh fruit, dried herbs, fine lees, floral. Palate: fresh, fruity, flavourful, good acidity.

## CAVA CRISTINA COLOMER BERNAT

Diputació, 58
08770 Sant Sadurní D'Anoia (Barcelona)
☎: 938 910 804 - Fax: 938 913 034
ccolomer@cavescolomer.com
www.cavescolomer.com

COLOMER HOMENATGE A GAUDI PINOT NOIR
ROSÉ 2006 RD
pinot noir

## 84

COLOMER COSTA 2007 BN
xarel.lo, macabeo, parellada

**90** Colour: bright straw. Nose: fresh fruit, dried herbs, fine lees, floral. Palate: fresh, fruity, flavourful, good acidity.

COLOMER PRESTIGE 2005 BN
xarel.lo, macabeo, parellada, chardonnay, pinot noir

**90** Colour: bright golden. Nose: dry nuts, fragrant herbs, complex. Palate: powerful, flavourful, good acidity, fine bead, fine bitter notes.

COLOMER RESERVA "ER" 2004 BN RESERVA
xarel.lo, macabeo, parellada, chardonnay, pinot noir

**88** Colour: bright golden. Nose: dry nuts, fragrant herbs, complex. Palate: powerful, flavourful, good acidity, fine bead, fine bitter notes.

## CAVA GUILERA

Masia Artigas, s/n
08734 Lavern-Subirats (Barcelona)
☎: 938 993 085 - Fax: 938 993 491
info@cavaguilera.com
www.cavaguilera.comartesansdelavid.com

GUILERA BR RESERVA

## 83

GUILERA BN

## 84

GUILERA EXTRA BRUT RESERVA

**87** Colour: bright golden. Nose: fine lees, dry nuts, fragrant herbs, complex, candied fruit. Palate: powerful, flavourful, good acidity, fine bead, fine bitter notes.

GUILERA EXTRA BRUT GRAN RESERVA

**86** Colour: bright golden. Nose: fine lees, dry nuts, fragrant herbs, complex. Palate: powerful, flavourful, good acidity, fine bead, fine bitter notes.

GUILERA SS RESERVA

## 80

## CAVA JOSEP M. FERRET GUASCH

Barri L'alzinar, 68
08739 Font-Rubí (Barcelona)
☎: 938 979 037 - Fax: 938 979 414
ferretguasch@ferretguasch.com
www.ferretguasch.com

JOSEP M. FERRET GUASCH 2005 RD GRAN RESERVA

**85** Colour: brilliant rose. Nose: powerfull, ripe fruit, red berry notes, floral, expressive. Palate: fleshy, powerful, fruity, fresh.

JOSEP M. FERRET GUASCH 2005 BR RESERVA

**89** Colour: bright straw. Nose: medium intensity, fresh fruit, dried herbs, fine lees, floral. Palate: fresh, fruity, flavourful, good acidity, balanced.

VALLDEFERRET 2001 BR GRAN RESERVA

**88** Colour: bright golden. Nose: dry nuts, fragrant herbs, complex, lees reduction notes. Palate: powerful, flavourful, good acidity, fine bead, fine bitter notes.

JOSEP M. FERRET GUASCH 2005 BN RESERVA

**89** Colour: bright straw. Nose: fresh fruit, dried herbs, fine lees, floral, neat. Palate: fresh, fruity, flavourful, good acidity.

FERRET GUASCH COUPAGE SARA 2004 BN GRAN RESERVA

**89** Colour: bright golden. Nose: fine lees, dry nuts, fragrant herbs, complex. Palate: powerful, flavourful, good acidity, fine bead, fine bitter notes.

JOSEP M. FERRET GUASCH 2003 BN GRAN RESERVA

**88** Colour: bright golden. Nose: fine lees, dry nuts, fragrant herbs, complex. Palate: powerful, flavourful, good acidity, fine bead, fine bitter notes.

## CAVA MARIA CASANOVAS

Montserrat, 117
08770 Sant Sadurní d'Anoia (Barcelona)
☎: 938 910 812 - Fax: 938 911 572
mariacasanovas@brutnature.com
www.mariacasanovas.com

## MARÍA CASANOVAS 2006 BN GRAN RESERVA
chardonnay 42%, pinot noir 38%, tradicionales 20%

**90** Colour: bright golden. Nose: dry nuts, fragrant herbs, complex. Palate: powerful, flavourful, good acidity, fine bead, fine bitter notes.

## MARÍA CASANOVAS BN RESERVA
pinot noir

**86** Colour: rose, purple rim. Nose: powerfull, ripe fruit, red berry notes, floral. Palate: fleshy, powerful, fruity, fresh.

ROIG OLLÉ

## CAVA RECAREDO

Tamarit, 10
08770 Sant Sadurní D'Anoia (Barcelona)
☎: 938 910 214 - Fax: 938 911 697
cava@recaredo.es
www.recaredo.com

## RECAREDO 2005 BN GRAN RESERVA
xarel.lo 64%, macabeo 28%, parellada 8%

**90** Colour: bright golden. Nose: fine lees, dry nuts, complex, balsamic herbs. Palate: powerful, flavourful, good acidity, fine bead, fine bitter notes.

## RECAREDO 2004 BN GRAN RESERVA
xarel.lo 55%, macabeo 30%, chardonnay 15%

**90** Colour: bright golden. Nose: fine lees, dry nuts, fragrant herbs, complex, smoky. Palate: powerful, flavourful, good acidity, fine bead, fine bitter notes.

## RECAREDO BRUT DE BRUTS 2002 BN GRAN RESERVA
macabeo 72%, xarel.lo 28%

**89** Colour: bright golden. Nose: fine lees, dry nuts, fragrant herbs, complex. Palate: powerful, flavourful, good acidity, fine bead, fine bitter notes.

## TURO D'EN MOTA 1999 BN RESERVA
xarel.lo

**90** Colour: bright golden. Nose: scrubland, fruit preserve, spicy. Palate: good structure, flavourful, powerful.

## CAVA ROSELL GALLART

Montserrat, 56
08770 Sant Sadurní d'Anoia (Barcelona)
☎: 938 912 073 - Fax: 938 183 539
rosell-gallart@terra.es

## TERESA MATA I GARRIGA 2007 BN
macabeo, xarel.lo, parellada, chardonnay

**87** Colour: bright golden. Nose: dry nuts, fragrant herbs, complex, candied fruit. Palate: powerful, flavourful, good acidity, fine bead, fine bitter notes.

## ROSELL GALLART 2006 BN
macabeo, xarel.lo, parellada, chardonnay

**84**

## ROSELL GALLART MAGNUM 2001 BN GRAN RESERVA
macabeo, xarel.lo, parellada, chardonnay

**88** Colour: bright golden. Nose: dry nuts, complex. Palate: powerful, flavourful, good acidity, fine bitter notes.

## CAVA VIDAL I FERRÉ

Nou, 2
43815 Les Pobles (Tarragona)
☎: 977 638 554 - Fax: 977 638 554
vidaliferre@terra.es

## VIDAL I FERRÉ BR RESERVA

**87** Colour: bright straw. Nose: medium intensity, fresh fruit, dried herbs, fine lees, floral, characterful. Palate: fresh, fruity, flavourful, good acidity.

## VIDAL I FERRÉ BN GRAN RESERVA

**90** Colour: bright straw. Nose: medium intensity, fresh fruit, dried herbs, fine lees, floral, complex. Palate: fresh, fruity, flavourful, good acidity.

## VIDAL I FERRÉ BN RESERVA

**85** Colour: bright straw. Nose: medium intensity, fresh fruit, fine lees, floral, scrubland. Palate: fresh, fruity, flavourful, good acidity.

## VIDAL I FERRÉ SS

**88** Colour: bright golden. Nose: fine lees, dry nuts, fragrant herbs, complex, spicy. Palate: powerful, flavourful, good acidity, fine bead, fine bitter notes.

## CAVA VIVES AMBRÓS

Mayor, 39
43812 Montferri (Tarragona)
☎: 639 521 652 - Fax: 977 606 579
covives@tinet.org
www.vivesambros.com

**VIVES AMBRÒS 2006 BR**
xarel.lo 40%, macabeo 35%, parellada 25%

**86** Colour: bright straw. Nose: medium intensity, fresh fruit, dried herbs, floral, pattiserie. Palate: fresh, fruity, flavourful, good acidity.

**VIVES AMBRÒS 2005 BN**
xarel.lo 40%, macabeo 35%, chardonnay 25%

**86** Colour: bright straw. Nose: medium intensity, fresh fruit, fine lees, floral, citrus fruit, balsamic herbs, fine reductive notes. Palate: fresh, fruity, flavourful, good acidity.

**VIVES AMBRÒS SALVATGE 2004 BN**
xarel.lo 60%, macabeo 40%

**87** Colour: bright golden. Nose: fine lees, dry nuts, fragrant herbs, complex. Palate: powerful, flavourful, good acidity, fine bead, fine bitter notes.

## CAVA XAMÓS

Gran Vía 806, Bajos 84
08013 (Barcelona)
☎: 932 462 287
xamos@xamos.net
www.xamos.net

**XAMÓS ELEGANT RESERVA**

**87** Colour: bright straw. Nose: expressive, fresh, citrus fruit, pattiserie. Palate: fruity, fresh, flavourful, balanced.

**DOGMA BN**

**85** Colour: bright straw. Nose: powerfull, fresh, fresh fruit, scrubland. Palate: fruity, fresh, flavourful.

## CAVAS CONDE DE VALICOURT

Sant Antoni, 33-39
08770 Sant Sadurní D'Anoia (Barcelona)
☎: 938 910 036 - Fax: 938 910 696
cavas@condedevalicourt.com
www.condedevalicourt.com

**CONDE DE VALICOURT COUPAGE DE ALICIA 2007 BR RESERVA**
parellada 40%, macabeo 30%, xarel.lo 30%

**88** Colour: bright golden. Nose: fine lees, dry nuts, fragrant herbs, complex. Palate: powerful, flavourful, good acidity, fine bead, fine bitter notes, creamy.

**CONDE DE VALICOURT PAS DE SUCRE 2005 BN GRAN RESERVA**
parellada 40%, macabeo 30%, xarel.lo 30%

**89** Colour: bright straw. Nose: medium intensity, fresh fruit, dried herbs, fine lees, floral. Palate: fresh, fruity, flavourful, good acidity.

**CONDE DE VALICOURT MAJESTUOSO 2005 BN GRAN RESERVA**
macabeo 40%, xarel.lo 40%, parellada 20%

**88** Colour: bright golden. Nose: dry nuts, fragrant herbs, complex. Palate: powerful, flavourful, good acidity, fine bead, fine bitter notes.

## CAVAS DEL CASTILLO DE PERELADA

Avenida Barcelona, 78
08720 Vilafranca del Penedés (Barcelona)
☎: 938 180 676 - Fax: 938 180 926
dvilamitjana@castilloperalada.com
www.castilloperelada.com

**CASTILLO PERELADA CUVÉE 2007 RD**

**87** Colour: rose, purple rim. Nose: powerfull, ripe fruit, red berry notes, floral, expressive. Palate: fleshy, powerful, fruity, fresh.

**CASTILLO PERELADA RD**
trepat 60%, monastrell 20%, pinot noir 20%

**87** Colour: rose, purple rim. Nose: powerfull, ripe fruit, red berry notes, floral, expressive. Palate: fleshy, powerful, fruity, fresh.

**TORRE GALATEA BR**
pinot noir 50%, trepat 25%, monastrell 25%

**88** Colour: rose, purple rim. Nose: powerfull, ripe fruit, red berry notes, floral, expressive. Palate: fleshy, powerful, fruity, fresh.

**CASTILLO PERELADA BR RESERVA**
macabeo 40%, xarel.lo 30%, parellada 30%

**87** Colour: bright golden. Nose: fine lees, dry nuts, fragrant herbs, complex. Palate: powerful, flavourful, good acidity, fine bead, fine bitter notes.

**GRAN CLAUSTRO DE CASTILLO PERELADA 2007 BN**
chardonnay 48%, xarel.lo 27%, parellada 25%

**89** Colour: bright golden. Nose: fine lees, dry nuts, fragrant herbs, complex, white flowers. Palate: powerful, flavourful, good acidity, fine bead, fine bitter notes.

**CASTILLO PERELADA CUVÉE ESPECIAL 2007 BN**
macabeo 30%, parellada 30%, xarel.lo 25%, chardonnay 15%

**91** Colour: bright yellow. Nose: fine lees, dry nuts, fragrant herbs, complex. Palate: powerful, flavourful, good acidity, fine bead, fine bitter notes.

CASTILLO PERELADA 2006 BN
parellada 50%, xarel.lo 25%, macabeo 25%

**87** Colour: bright yellow. Nose: fine lees, fragrant herbs, complex, floral, fruit expression. Palate: powerful, flavourful, good acidity, fine bead, fine bitter notes.

GRAN CLAUSTRO CUVÉE ESPECIAL DE CASTILLO PERELADA 2005 BN GRAN RESERVA
chardonnay 38%, xarel.lo 32%, parellada 30%

**87** Colour: bright straw. Nose: medium intensity, fresh fruit, dried herbs, fine lees, floral, complex. Palate: fresh, fruity, flavourful, good acidity.

CASTILLO PERELADA BN
chardonnay

**88** Colour: bright yellow. Nose: fine lees, dry nuts, fragrant herbs, complex. Palate: powerful, flavourful, good acidity, fine bead, fine bitter notes.

## CAVAS EL MAS FERRER

S. Sebastia, 25 C'al Avi
08739 Subirats (Barcelona)
☎: 938 988 292 - Fax: 938 988 545
info@elmasferrer.com
www.elmasferrer.com

EL MAS FERRER 2007 BR
parellada 36%, macabeo 34%, xarel.lo 30%

**87** Colour: bright straw. Nose: medium intensity, fresh fruit, dried herbs, floral. Palate: fresh, fruity, flavourful, good acidity.

EL MAS FERRER 2006 BR RESERVA
macabeo 32,5%, xarel.lo 35%, parellada 32,5%

**86** Colour: bright straw. Nose: medium intensity, fresh fruit, dried herbs, fine lees, floral. Palate: fresh, fruity, flavourful, good acidity.

MAS FERRER 2005 BN GRAN RESERVA
xarel.lo 37%, parellada 33%, macabeo 30%

**89** Colour: bright straw. Nose: medium intensity, fresh fruit, dried herbs, fine lees, floral. Palate: fresh, fruity, flavourful, good acidity.

EL MAS FERRER 2005 BN
xarel.lo 37,5%, parellada 32,5%, macabeo 30%

**86** Colour: bright straw. Nose: medium intensity, fresh fruit, dried herbs, floral. Palate: fresh, fruity, flavourful, good acidity.

EL MAS FERRER SEGLE XXI 2004 EXTRA BRUT GRAN RESERVA
xarel.lo 40%, macabeo 30%, parellada 30%

**88** Colour: bright straw. Nose: medium intensity, dried herbs, fine lees, floral, candied fruit, spicy. Palate: fresh, fruity, flavourful, good acidity.

## CAVAS FERRET

Avda. de Catalunya, 36
08736 Guardiola de FontRubí (Barcelona)
☎: 938 979 148 - Fax: 938 979 285
ferret@cavasferret.com
www.cavasferret.com

CELIA DE FERRET 2003 RD GRAN RESERVA
pinot noir 80%, garnacha 20%, monastrell %

**88** Colour: onion pink. Nose: elegant, candied fruit, dried flowers, fragrant herbs, red berry notes. Palate: light-bodied, flavourful, good acidity, long, spicy.

FERRET BR RESERVA
macabeo 40%, parellada 40%, xarel.lo 20%

**88** Colour: bright straw. Nose: fresh fruit, dried herbs, fine lees, floral. Palate: fresh, fruity, flavourful, good acidity.

FERRET 2004 BN GRAN RESERVA
macabeo 40%, parellada 35%, xarel.lo 25%

**90** Colour: bright golden. Nose: fine lees, fragrant herbs, complex. Palate: powerful, flavourful, good acidity, fine bead, fine bitter notes.

ALTRE NOS FERRET 2003 BN GRAN RESERVA
xarel.lo 50%, chardonnay %, xarel.lo 35%, parellada 15%

**90** Colour: bright golden. Nose: dry nuts, fragrant herbs, complex, lees reduction notes. Palate: powerful, flavourful, good acidity, fine bead, fine bitter notes.

### EZEQUIEL FERRET 2001 BN GRAN RESERVA
xarel.lo 50%, parellada 50%, macabeo %

**87** Colour: bright straw. Nose: dried herbs, fine lees, floral, candied fruit. Palate: fresh, fruity, flavourful, good acidity.

### FERRET BN RESERVA
macabeo 40%, parellada 40%, xarel.lo 20%

**88** Colour: bright straw. Nose: medium intensity, fresh fruit, dried herbs, fine lees, floral. Palate: fresh, fruity, flavourful, good acidity.

## CAVAS HILL

Bonavista, 2
08734 Moja (Alt Penedès) (Barcelona)
☎: 938 900 588 - Fax: 938 170 246
cavashill@cavashill.com
www.cavashill.com

### CAVAS HILL ORO BR
macabeo 45%, xarel.lo 35%, parellada 20%

**82**

### CAVA ROSADO HILL BR
garnacha 60%, monastrell 40%

**80**

### HILLIUM 2005 BN GRAN RESERVA
xarel.lo, macabeo, parellada, chardonnay

**89** Colour: bright straw. Nose: ripe fruit, fruit expression, dried flowers. Palate: flavourful, fruity, fresh, fine bitter notes.

### CAVAS HILL BRUT BRUTÍSIMO 2005 BN GRAN RESERVA
xarel.lo 40%, chardonnay 30%, macabeo 15%, parellada 15%

**85** Colour: bright straw. Nose: medium intensity, fresh fruit, dried herbs, fine lees, floral. Palate: fresh, fruity, flavourful, good acidity.

### CAVAS HILL BRUT DE BRUT BN RESERVA
xarel.lo 40%, macabeo 25%, parellada 25%, chardonnay 10%

**84**

## CAVAS LAVERNOYA

Finca La Porchada
08729 Sant Marsal (Barcelona)
☎: 938 912 202 - Fax: 938 911 159

lavernoya@lavernoya.com
www.lavernoya.com

### LÁCRIMA BACCUS PRIMERÍSIMO GRAN CUVÉE BR GRAN RESERVA

**88** Colour: bright straw. Nose: powerfull, fresh, elegant, fine lees. Palate: flavourful, fine bead, fine bitter notes, great length.

### LAVERNOYA GRAN CUVÉE BR

**88** Colour: golden, bright yellow. Nose: powerfull, roasted almonds, fine reductive notes, lees reduction notes, expressive. Palate: fresh, flavourful, fine bead, fine bitter notes.

### LÁCRIMA BACCUS HERETAT BR

**87** Colour: bright yellow, golden. Nose: dry nuts, powerfull, fresh fruit. Palate: fresh, fruity, flavourful.

### LÁCRIMA BACCUS SUMMUM BN GRAN RESERVA

**89** Colour: bright straw. Nose: expressive, pattiserie, faded flowers, lees reduction notes. Palate: flavourful, fresh, good finish, elegant, fine bitter notes.

### LAVERNOYA BN RESERVA

**88** Colour: bright straw. Nose: powerfull, elegant, floral, ripe fruit. Palate: flavourful, good acidity, fruity.

### HERETAT DE LACRIMA BACCUS BN GRAN RESERVA

**86** Colour: yellow, bright golden. Nose: fresh, fine lees, dry nuts. Palate: fine bead, fresh, fine bitter notes.

## CAVAS MESTRES

Plaça Ajuntament, 8
08770 Sant Sadurní D'Anoia (Barcelona)
☎: 938 910 043 - Fax: 938 911 611
cava@mestres.es
www.mestres.es

### MESTRES 1312 2006 BR RESERVA
parellada 40%, xarel.lo 30%, macabeo 30%

**88** Colour: bright straw. Nose: medium intensity, dried herbs, fine lees, floral. Palate: fresh, fruity, flavourful, good acidity.

### MESTRES MAS VÍA 1997 BR GRAN RESERVA
xarel.lo 60%, macabeo 20%, parellada 20%

**89** Colour: bright golden. Nose: fine lees, dry nuts, fragrant herbs, complex. Palate: powerful, flavourful, good acidity, fine bead, fine bitter notes, rich.

**ELS CUPATGES DE MESTRES 80 ANIVERSARIO BR RESERVA**

**91** Colour: bright straw. Nose: fresh, neat, balanced, white flowers. Palate: flavourful, fleshy, complex, good structure, fruity.

**MESTRES COQUET 2005 BN RESERVA**
macabeo 35%, xarel.lo 35%, parellada 30%

**89** Colour: bright straw. Nose: fine lees, sweet spices, pattiserie, ripe fruit. Palate: flavourful, powerful, good structure, fruity, spicy.

**ELENA DE MESTRES ROSADO 2005 BN RESERVA ESPECIAL**
trepat 65%, monastrell 35%

**86** Colour: rose. Nose: medium intensity, ripe fruit, floral. Palate: flavourful, fruity, fresh.

**MESTRES VISOL 2004 BN GRAN RESERVA**
xarel.lo 40%, macabeo 35%, parellada 25%

**90** Colour: bright golden. Nose: fine lees, dry nuts, fragrant herbs, complex. Palate: powerful, flavourful, good acidity, fine bead, fine bitter notes.

**CLOS NOSTRE SENYOR 2001 BN GRAN RESERVA**
xarel.lo 60%, macabeo 20%, parellada 20%

**88** Colour: bright golden. Nose: dry nuts, complex, spicy, faded flowers. Palate: powerful, flavourful, good acidity, fine bead, fine bitter notes, unctuous.

## CAVAS PUIG MUNTS

Revall, 38
08760 Martorell (Barcelona)
☎: 937 755 216 - Fax: 937 740 213
puigmunts@puigmunts.com
www.puigmnts.com

**PUIG MUNTS GRAN RESERVA ESPECIAL 2004 BR GRAN RESERVA**
macabeo, xarel.lo, parellada

**85** Colour: bright straw. Nose: dried herbs, floral, fruit preserve. Palate: fresh, fruity, flavourful, good acidity.

**PUIG MUNTS 2005 BN**
macabeo, xarel.lo, parellada

**87** Colour: bright golden. Nose: fine lees, dry nuts, fragrant herbs, complex. Palate: powerful, flavourful, good acidity, fine bead, fine bitter notes.

**PUIG MUNTS 2004 BN GRAN RESERVA**
macabeo, xarel.lo, parellada

**88** Colour: bright golden. Nose: dry nuts, fragrant herbs, complex, lees reduction notes. Palate: powerful, flavourful, good acidity, fine bead, fine bitter notes.

**PUIG MUNTS GRAN RESERVA ESPECIAL 2004 BN GRAN RESERVA**
macabeo, xarel.lo, parellada

**85** Colour: bright golden. Nose: dry nuts, fragrant herbs, complex, toasty. Palate: powerful, flavourful, good acidity, fine bitter notes, slightly evolved.

## CAVAS SANSTRAVÉ

De la Conca, 10
43412 Solivella (Tarragona)
☎: 977 892 165 - Fax: 977 892 073
bodega@sanstrave.com
www.sanstrave.com

**SANSTRAVÉ 2004 BN GRAN RESERVA**
macabeo, parellada, chardonnay

**87** Colour: bright golden. Nose: dry nuts, complex, spicy. Palate: powerful, flavourful, good acidity, fine bead, fine bitter notes.

## CAVAS SIGNAT

Escultor Llimona, s/n
08328 Alella (Barcelona)
☎: 935 403 400 - Fax: 935 401 471
signat@signat.es
www.signat.es

**SIGNAT MAGNUM 2006 RESERVA**
macabeo 35%, parellada 34%, xarel.lo 28%, chardonnay 3%

**90** Colour: bright straw. Nose: medium intensity, balanced, fresh fruit, tropical fruit. Palate: balanced, fine bitter notes, good structure, fresh.

**SIGNAT 5 ESTRELLAS 2006 BR RESERVA**
macabeo 35%, parellada 34%, xarel.lo 28%, chardonnay 3%

**88** Colour: straw. Nose: spicy, ripe fruit, dried flowers. Palate: balanced, fine bitter notes, fine bead, good acidity.

**SIGNAT RESERVA IMPERIAL 2005 BR RESERVA**
macabeo 35%, parellada 35%, xarel.lo 26%, chardonnay 4%

**92** Colour: bright straw. Nose: candied fruit, elegant, white flowers, fine lees, dry nuts, grassy. Palate: good structure, fruity, sweetness, good acidity.

**SIGNAT 2006 BN**
macabeo 35%, parellada 35%, xarel.lo 25%, chardonnay 5%

**88** Colour: straw. Nose: expressive, fresh, fresh fruit. Palate: good structure, balanced, fine bitter notes, fine bead, spicy.

## CAVES CONDE DE CARALT S.A.

Ctra. Sant Sadurní-Sant Pere de Riudebitlles, km. 5
08775 Torrelavit (Barcelona)
☎: 938 917 070 - Fax: 938 996 006
seguraviudas@seguraviudas.es
www.freixenet.es

CONDE DE CARALT BLANC DE BLANCS BR
macabeo 60%, xarel.lo 20%, parellada 10%

**89** Colour: bright straw. Nose: medium intensity, fresh fruit, dried herbs, fine lees, floral. Palate: fresh, fruity, flavourful, good acidity.

CONDE DE CARALT BR
macabeo 50%, xarel.lo 20%, parellada 30%

**87** Colour: bright straw. Nose: medium intensity, fresh fruit, dried herbs, fine lees, floral. Palate: fresh, fruity, flavourful, good acidity.

CONDE DE CARALT CHARDONNAY 2004 BN
chardonnay 85%, macabeo 15%

**83**

## CAVES M. BOSCH

Ctra. San Martí Sarroca s/n
08737 Torroella de Foix (Barcelona)
☎: 938 405 488 - Fax: 938 403 026
info@grupombosch.com
www.cavesmbosch.com

M. BOSCH RESERVA FAMILIAR BN RESERVA
macabeo, xarel.lo, parellada

**87** Colour: bright straw. Nose: medium intensity, fresh fruit, dried herbs, fine lees, floral. Palate: fresh, fruity, flavourful, good acidity.

## CELLER CARLES ANDREU

Sant Sebastià, 19
43423 Pira (Tarragona)
☎: 977 887 404 - Fax: 977 887 427
info@cavandreu.com
www.cavandreu.com

CAVA RESERVA BRUT NATURE CARLES ANDREU 2006
parellada, macabeo, chardonnay

**90** Colour: bright golden. Nose: fine lees, dry nuts, fragrant herbs, complex, white flowers. Palate: powerful, flavourful, good acidity, fine bead, fine bitter notes.

CAVA RESERVA BARRICA BRUT NATURE CARLES ANDREU 2006
parellada %, macabeo %, chardonnay %

**90** Colour: bright straw. Nose: medium intensity, fresh fruit, dried herbs, fine lees, floral. Palate: fresh, fruity, flavourful, good acidity. Personality.

CAVA BRUT NATURE CARLES ANDREU 2006
parellada, macabeo

**89** Colour: bright straw. Nose: medium intensity, fresh fruit, dried herbs, fine lees, floral, complex. Palate: fresh, fruity, flavourful, good acidity.

CAVA ROSADO RESERVA BARRICA BRUT CARLES ANDREU 2006
trepat 100%

**89** Colour: onion pink. Nose: elegant, candied fruit, dried flowers, red berry notes, dry nuts. Palate: light-bodied, flavourful, good acidity, long, spicy. Personality.

CAVA BRUT CARLES ANDREU 2006
parellada, macabeo

**88** Colour: bright straw. Nose: medium intensity, fresh fruit, dried herbs, fine lees, floral, spicy. Palate: fresh, fruity, flavourful, good acidity.

CAVA ROSADO BRUT CARLES ANDREU 2006
trepat 100%

**88** Colour: rose, purple rim. Nose: powerfull, ripe fruit, red berry notes, floral, expressive, smoky. Palate: fleshy, powerful, fruity, fresh.

## CELLER COOPERATIU D'ARTÉS SCCL - CAVES ARTIUM

Ctra. Rocafort, 44
08271 Artés (Barcelona)
☎: 938 305 325 - Fax: 938 306 289
artium@cavesartium.com
www.cavesartium.com

LLUÍS GUITART 2006 BR
macabeo 40%, xarel.lo 40%, parellada 20%

**84**

ARTIUM 2004 BR
macabeo 40%, xarel.lo 30%, parellada 30%

**85** Colour: bright straw. Nose: medium intensity, fresh fruit, dried herbs, floral. Palate: fresh, fruity, flavourful, good acidity.

ARTIUM ROSAT 2004 BR RESERVA
trepat 100%

**83**

ARTIUM 2004 BN RESERVA
macabeo 40%, xarel.lo 40%, parellada 20%

**87** Colour: bright golden. Nose: dry nuts, fragrant herbs, complex, spicy. Palate: powerful, flavourful, good acidity, fine bead, fine bitter notes.

ARTIUM 1908 BN GRAN RESERVA
macabeo, xarel.lo, parellada

**88** Colour: bright golden. Nose: dry nuts, fragrant herbs, complex. Palate: powerful, flavourful, good acidity, fine bead, fine bitter notes.

LLUIS GUITART 2006 SS
macabeo 40%, xarel.lo 40%, parellada 20%

**86** Colour: bright straw. Nose: medium intensity, fresh fruit, dried herbs, fine lees, floral, spicy. Palate: fresh, fruity, flavourful, good acidity, creamy.

ARTIUM ROSAT 2004 SS RESERVA
trepat 100%

**87** Colour: onion pink. Nose: elegant, candied fruit, dried flowers, fragrant herbs, red berry notes. Palate: light-bodied, flavourful, good acidity, long, spicy.

## CELLER JORDI LLUCH

Barrio Les Casetes, s/n
08777 Sant Quinti de Mediona (Barcelona)
☎: 938 988 138 - Fax: 938 988 138
vinyaescude@vinyaescude.com
www.vinyaescude.com

VINYA ESCUDÉ 2007 BN
macabeo, xarel.lo, parellada

**86** Colour: bright straw. Nose: medium intensity, fresh fruit, dried herbs, fine lees, floral. Palate: fresh, fruity, flavourful, good acidity.

VINYA ESCUDÉ 523 2006 EXTRA BRUT RESERVA
macabeo, xarel.lo, parellada

**86** Colour: bright straw. Nose: medium intensity, dried herbs, fine lees, floral, candied fruit. Palate: fresh, fruity, flavourful, good acidity.

## CELLER MARIOL

Joan Miro, s/n
43786 Batea (Tarragona)
☎: 934 367 628 - Fax: 934 500 281

celler@cellermariol.es
www.cellermariol.es

CELLER MARIOL ARTESANAL ROSADO 36 MESES BR
parellada, monastrell

**85** Colour: rose. Nose: candied fruit, spicy, roasted almonds. Palate: flavourful, sweetness, fine bitter notes.

CELLER MARIOL BN GRAN RESERVA
macabeo, xarel.lo, parellada

**88** Colour: bright golden. Nose: dry nuts, fragrant herbs, complex, lees reduction notes. Palate: powerful, flavourful, good acidity, fine bead, fine bitter notes.

CELLER MARIOL ARTESANAL 18 MESES BN
macabeo, xarel.lo, parellada

**88** Colour: bright straw. Nose: medium intensity, fresh fruit, dried herbs, fine lees, floral. Palate: fresh, fruity, flavourful, good acidity.

CELLER MARIOL CAVA ARTESANAL 48 MESES BN RESERVA
macabeo, xarel.lo, parellada

**87** Colour: bright golden. Nose: fine lees, dry nuts, fragrant herbs, complex. Palate: powerful, flavourful, good acidity, fine bead, fine bitter notes.

## CELLER VELL S.A.

Partida Mas Solanes, s/n
08770 Sant Sadurní D'Anoia (Barcelona)
☎: 938 910 290 - Fax: 938 183 246
info@cellervell.com
www.cellervell.com

CELLER VELL CUVÈE LES SOLANES BN RESERVA

**87** Colour: bright golden. Nose: dry nuts, fragrant herbs, complex, spicy. Palate: powerful, flavourful, good acidity, fine bead, fine bitter notes, unctuous.

ESTRUCH NATURE CLASSIC BN

**84**

CELLER VELL 2006 EXTRA BRUT
garnacha, pinot noir

**85** Colour: rose, purple rim. Nose: powerfull, ripe fruit, red berry notes, floral, expressive. Palate: fleshy, powerful, fruity, fresh.

## CELLERS CAROL VALLÈS

Can Parellada s/n - Corral del Mestre

08739 Subirats (Barcelona)
☎: 938 989 078 - Fax: 938 988 413
info@cellerscarol.com
www.cellerscarol.com

### GUILLEM CAROL PINOT NOIR ROSAT 2005 RD RESERVA
pinot noir 100%

**83**

### GUILLEM CAROL MILLENIUM 1999 BR GRAN RESERVA
parellada 35%, xarel.lo 30%, macabeo 20%, chardonnay 15%

**88** Colour: bright golden. Nose: dry nuts, fragrant herbs, complex, pattiserie. Palate: powerful, flavourful, good acidity, fine bead, fine bitter notes.

### PARELLADA I FAURA 2006 BN RESERVA
parellada 40%, macabeo 30%, xarel.lo 30%

**90** Colour: bright golden. Nose: dry nuts, fragrant herbs, complex. Palate: powerful, flavourful, good acidity, fine bead, fine bitter notes.

### PARELLADA I FAURA MILLENIUM 2005 BN RESERVA
macabeo 40%, xarel.lo 30%, parellada 30%

**88** Colour: bright straw. Nose: dried herbs, fine lees, floral. Palate: fresh, fruity, flavourful, good acidity.

### GUILLEM CAROL 2004 BN GRAN RESERVA
parellada 40%, xarel.lo 40%, chardonnay 20%

**88** Colour: bright golden. Nose: dry nuts, fragrant herbs, complex. Palate: powerful, flavourful, fine bead.

### GUILLEM CAROL CHARDONNAY PINOT NOIR 2004 BN RESERVA
chardonnay 60%, pinot noir 40%

**88** Colour: bright straw. Nose: medium intensity, fresh fruit, fine lees, floral. Palate: fresh, fruity, flavourful, good acidity.

## CELLERS PLANAS ALBAREDA

Crta. Guardiola, km. 3
08735 Vilobí del Penedès (Barcelona)
☎: 938 922 143 - Fax: 938 922 143
planasalbareda@yahoo.es

### PLANAS ALBAREDA ROSAT 2006 BR
trepat

**87** Colour: rose. Nose: elegant, candied fruit, dried flowers, fragrant herbs, red berry notes. Palate: flavourful, good acidity, long, spicy, fruity.

### PLANAS ALBAREDA BR
macabeo, xarel.lo, parellada

**86** Colour: bright straw. Nose: fresh fruit, dried herbs, fine lees, floral. Palate: fresh, fruity, flavourful, good acidity.

### PLANAS ALBAREDA RESERVA DE L'AVI BN RESERVA
macabeo, xarel.lo, parellada

**88** Colour: bright straw. Nose: fresh fruit, dried herbs, floral. Palate: fresh, fruity, flavourful, good acidity.

### PLANAS ALBAREDA BN RESERVA
macabeo, xarel.lo, parellada

**86** Colour: bright straw. Nose: medium intensity, fresh fruit, floral, grassy. Palate: fresh, fruity, flavourful, good acidity.

### PLANAS ALBAREDA BN
macabeo, xarel.lo, parellada

**83**

## CODORNÍU

Avda. Jaume Codorníu, s/n
08770 Sant Sadurní D'Anoia (Barcelona)
☎: 938 183 232 - Fax: 938 910 822
s.martin@codorniu.es
www.codorniu.com

### CODORNÍU PINOT NOIR RD
pinot noir 100%

**90** Colour: onion pink. Nose: elegant, candied fruit, dried flowers, fragrant herbs, red berry notes. Palate: light-bodied, flavourful, good acidity, long, spicy.

### NON PLUS ULTRA CODORNÍU REINA Mª CRISTINA 2006 BR RESERVA
chardonnay 50%, macabeo 20%, parellada 20%, xarel.lo 10%

**90** Colour: bright straw. Nose: medium intensity, fresh fruit, dried herbs, fine lees, fine reductive notes. Palate: fresh, fruity, flavourful, good acidity.

### JAUME CODORNÍU BR
chardonnay 50%, macabeo 30%, parellada 20%

**91** Colour: bright straw. Nose: medium intensity, dried herbs, fine lees, floral, pattiserie, spicy. Palate: fresh, fruity, flavourful, good acidity, full.

### ANNA DE CODORNÍU BR RESERVA
chardonnay 70%, parellada 15%, xarel.lo 10%, macabeo 5%

**89** Colour: bright straw. Nose: medium intensity, fresh fruit, fine lees, floral, fine reductive notes. Palate: fresh, fruity, flavourful, good acidity, long.

### PLANAS ALBAREDA BR

**ANNA DE CODORNÍU ROSÉ BR RESERVA**
pinot noir 70%, monastrell 20%, chardonnay 10%

**89** Colour: rose, purple rim. Nose: red berry notes, floral, expressive, elegant. Palate: fleshy, powerful, fruity, fresh.

**GRAN PLUS ULTRA BN RESERVA**
chardonnay 60%, parellada 40%

**91** Colour: bright straw. Nose: medium intensity, fresh fruit, dried herbs, fine lees, floral, spicy, fine reductive notes. Palate: fresh, fruity, flavourful, good acidity, full.

## COOPERATIVA DE VITICULTORS DE MONTBLANC S.C.C.L.

Muralla de Santa Tecla, 54 - 56
43400 Montblanc (Tarragona)
☎: 977 860 016 - Fax: 977 860 929
info@cavapontvell.com
www.cavapontvell.com

**PONT VELL 2006 BR**
macabeo 60%, parellada 40%

**86** Colour: bright straw. Nose: medium intensity, fresh fruit, dried herbs, floral. Palate: fresh, fruity, flavourful, good acidity.

**PONT VELL MIL.LENIUM 2006 BN RESERVA**
macabeo 60%, parellada 40%

**88** Colour: bright golden. Nose: dry nuts, fragrant herbs, complex. Palate: powerful, flavourful, good acidity, fine bead, fine bitter notes.

**PONT VELL 2006 BN**
macabeo 60%, parellada 40%

**84**

## COVIDES VIÑEDOS Y BODEGAS

Rambla Nostra Senyora, 45
08720 Vilafranca del Penedès (Barcelona)
☎: 938 172 552 - Fax: 938 171 798
covides@covides.com
www.covides.com

**DUC DE FOIX CUVÉE PARA POSTRES**
macabeo, xarel.lo, parellada

**87** Colour: bright straw. Nose: medium intensity, fresh fruit, dried herbs, fine lees, floral. Palate: fresh, fruity, flavourful, good acidity.

**DUC DE FOIX ROSADO BR**
trepat

**85** Colour: onion pink. Nose: elegant, candied fruit, dried flowers, fragrant herbs, red berry notes. Palate: light-bodied, flavourful, good acidity, long, spicy.

**DUC DE FOIX BN**
macabeo, xarel.lo, parellada

**86** Colour: bright straw. Nose: medium intensity, fresh fruit, dried herbs, fine lees, floral. Palate: fresh, fruity, flavourful, good acidity.

## COVIÑAS COOP. V.

Avda. Rafael Duyos s/n
46340 Requena (Valencia)
☎: 962 300 680 - Fax: 962 302 651
covinas@covinas.com
www.covinas.com

**MARQUES DE PLATA BR**
macabeo 75%, parellada 12,5%, xarel.lo 12,5%

**84**

**MARQUES DE PLATA BN**
macabeo, xarel.lo, parellada

**87** Colour: bright straw. Nose: medium intensity, dried herbs, fine lees, floral, candied fruit. Palate: fresh, fruity, flavourful, good acidity, balanced.

## DOMINIO DE LA VEGA

Ctra. Madrid - Valencia, km. 270,6
46390 San Antonio. Requena (Valencia)
☎: 962 320 570 - Fax: 962 320 330
info@dominiodelavega.com
www.dominiodelavega.com

**DOMINIO DE LA VEGA ESPECIAL BR RESERVA**

**91** Colour: bright straw. Nose: medium intensity, fresh fruit, dried herbs, fine lees, floral. Palate: fresh, fruity, flavourful, good acidity.

**DOMINIO DE LA VEGA PINOT NOIR BR**

**88** Colour: onion pink. Nose: elegant, candied fruit, dried flowers, fragrant herbs, red berry notes. Palate: light-bodied, flavourful, good acidity, long, spicy.

**DOMINIO DE LA VEGA BR**

**87** Colour: bright straw. Nose: fresh fruit, dried herbs, floral, toasty. Palate: fresh, fruity, flavourful, good acidity, balanced.

### ARTEMAYOR CAVA BN

**90** Colour: bright yellow. Nose: sweet spices, roasted almonds, lactic notes, ripe fruit. Palate: flavourful, powerful, fleshy, fruity, fresh.

### DOMINIO DE LA VEGA BN

**88** Colour: bright straw. Nose: fresh fruit, fine lees, floral, neat. Palate: fresh, fruity, flavourful, good acidity.

### DOMINIO DE LA VEGA ESPECIAL BN RESERVA

**88** Colour: bright straw. Nose: fresh fruit, dried herbs, fine lees, floral. Palate: fresh, fruity, flavourful, good acidity.

## DURAN

Font, 2
08769 Castellví de Rosanes (Barcelona)
☎: 937 755 446 - Fax: 937 741 719
cava@cavaduran.com
www.cavaduran.com

### DURAN 5V 2005 BR GRAN RESERVA
chardonnay, pinot noir, xarel.lo, macabeo, parellada

**85** Colour: bright straw. Nose: medium intensity, fresh fruit, dried herbs, fine lees, floral, balsamic herbs. Palate: fresh, fruity, flavourful, good acidity.

### DURAN 2004 BR GRAN RESERVA
xarel.lo, macabeo, parellada, chardonnay

**84**

### DURAN 2004 BN GRAN RESERVA
xarel.lo, macabeo, parellada, chardonnay, pinot noir

**86** Colour: bright golden. Nose: fine lees, dry nuts, fragrant herbs, complex. Palate: powerful, flavourful, good acidity, fine bead, fine bitter notes.

## ELVIWINES S.L.

Granollers, 27 G
08173 Sant Cugat (Barcelona)
☎: 935 343 026 - Fax: 935 441 374
info@elviwines.com
www.elviwines.com

### ADAR CAVA 2006 BR
macabeo, xarel.lo, parellada

**88** Colour: bright straw. Nose: medium intensity, fresh fruit, fine lees, floral, scrubland. Palate: fresh, fruity, flavourful, good acidity.

## FERMÍ BOHIGAS

Finca Can Maciá s/n
08711 Ódena (Barcelona)
☎: 938 048 100 - Fax: 938 032 366
tecnic@bohigas.es
www.bohigas.es

### MAS MACIÀ BR

**83**

### ROSSINYOL DE MORAGAS BN
macabeo, xarel.lo, parellada

**85** Colour: bright straw. Nose: medium intensity, ripe fruit, honeyed notes, dried flowers. Palate: fruity, flavourful, good acidity.

### BOHIGAS BN GRAN RESERVA

**83**

## FINCA TORREMILANOS BODEGAS PEÑALBA LÓPEZ

Finca Torremilanos
09400 Aranda de Duero (Burgos)
☎: 947 512 852 - Fax: 947 572 856
torremilanos@torremilanos.com
www.torremilanos.com

### PEÑALBA-LÓPEZ 2006 BN
viura, chardonnay

**87** Colour: yellow, straw. Nose: citrus fruit, fresh fruit, fine lees. Palate: good acidity, correct, great length, fruity aftestaste.

## FRANCISCO DOMÍNGUEZ CRUCES - EL XAMFRÀ

Lavernó, 23-27
08770 Sant Sadurní D'Anoia (Barcelona)
☎: 938 910 182 - Fax: 938 910 176
info@elxamfra.com
www.elxamfra.com

### EL XAMFRÀ BRUT DE CASA BR GRAN RESERVA

**89** Colour: bright golden. Nose: fine lees, dry nuts, complex. Palate: powerful, flavourful, good acidity, fine bead, fine bitter notes, balanced.

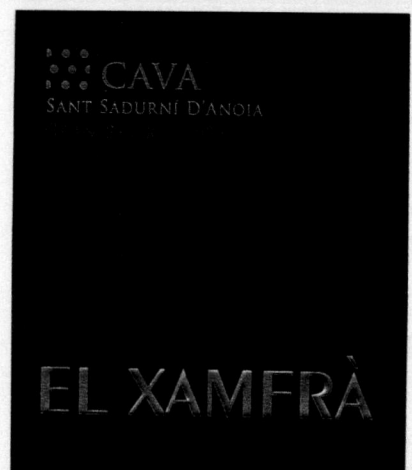

**EL XAMFRÀ BN RESERVA**

**85** Colour: bright straw. Nose: medium intensity, fruit expression, balanced. Palate: fruity, flavourful, good acidity, correct, balanced.

**EL XAMFRÀ BRUT ROSADO**
**84**

## FREIXA RIGAU

Santa Llucía, 15
17750 Capmany (Girona)
☎: 972 549 012 - Fax: 972 549 106
comercial@grupoliveda.com
www.grupoliveda.com

**FAMILIA OLIVEDA 2007 BR**

**87** Colour: bright straw. Nose: medium intensity, fresh fruit, dried herbs, floral. Palate: fresh, fruity, flavourful, good acidity.

**GRAN RIGAU BRUT DE BRUTS 2004 BR**

**86** Colour: bright straw. Nose: medium intensity, fresh fruit, dried herbs, floral. Palate: fresh, fruity, flavourful, good acidity.

**FAMILIA OLIVEDA 2006 BN RESERVA**

**87** Colour: bright straw. Nose: medium intensity, fresh fruit, floral, grassy. Palate: fresh, fruity, flavourful, good acidity.

**FREIXA RIGAU NATURE MIL.LÈSSIMA RESERVA FAMILIAR 2004 BN**

**88** Colour: bright yellow. Nose: fine lees, dry nuts, fragrant herbs, complex. Palate: powerful, flavourful, good acidity, fine bead, fine bitter notes.

**GRAN RIGAU CHARDONNAY 2004 BN**

**86** Colour: bright straw. Nose: fresh fruit, fine lees, floral, varietal. Palate: fresh, fruity, flavourful, good acidity.

**GRAN RIGAU ROSADO 2004 BN RESERVA**
pinot noir

**85** Colour: rose, purple rim. Nose: powerfull, ripe fruit, red berry notes, expressive. Palate: fleshy, powerful, fruity, fresh.

## FREIXENET

Joan Sala, 2
08770 Sant Sadurní D'Anoia (Barcelona)
☎: 938 917 000 - Fax: 938 183 095
freixenet@freixenet.es
www.freixenet.es

**MERITUM 2004 BR**
xarel.lo, macabeo, parellada

**90** Colour: bright golden. Nose: fine lees, dry nuts, fragrant herbs, complex. Palate: powerful, flavourful, good acidity, fine bead, fine bitter notes.

**CUVÉE D.S. 2004 BR RESERVA**

**88** Colour: bright golden. Nose: medium intensity, ripe fruit, expressive, dried herbs. Palate: ripe fruit, fruity, fresh.

**RESERVA REAL BR RESERVA**

**92** Colour: bright straw. Nose: fresh fruit, dried herbs, fine lees, floral. Palate: fresh, fruity, flavourful, good acidity.

**BRUT BARROCO BR RESERVA**

**90** Colour: bright straw. Nose: medium intensity, fresh fruit, dried herbs, fine lees, floral. Palate: fresh, fruity, flavourful, good acidity.

**TREPAT BR**
trepat 100%

**89** Colour: raspberry rose, coppery red. Nose: elegant, candied fruit, dried flowers, fragrant herbs. Palate: light-bodied, flavourful, good acidity, long, spicy.

**CORDÓN NEGRO BR**

**88** Colour: bright straw. Nose: medium intensity, fresh fruit, dried herbs, fine lees, floral. Palate: fresh, fruity, flavourful, good acidity.

FREIXENET CARTA NEVADA BR

## 82

FREIXENET VINTAGE 2005 BN

**88** Colour: bright straw. Nose: fresh fruit, dried herbs, fine lees, floral. Palate: fresh, fruity, flavourful, good acidity.

FREIXENET PRIMER CUVÉE BN

**90** Colour: bright straw. Nose: medium intensity, fresh fruit, dried herbs, fine lees, floral. Palate: fresh, fruity, flavourful, good acidity.

## GASTON COTY S.A.

Avernó, 30
08770 Sant Sadurní D'Anoia (Barcelona)
☎: 938 183 602 - Fax: 938 913 461
lorigan@lorigancava.com
www.lorigancava.com

L'O DE L'ORIGAN RD ESPUMOSO

**88** Colour: raspberry rose. Nose: fine lees, faded flowers, smoky. Palate: fine bead, fine bitter notes, reductive nuances.

L'O DE L'ORIGAN MAGNUM BN

**92** Colour: golden, bright yellow. Nose: powerfull, fine lees, candied fruit, floral. Palate: flavourful, powerful, fleshy, fine bead, good acidity, elegant, balanced.

L'O DE L'ORIGAN BN

**89** Colour: bright golden. Nose: neat, expressive, fruit preserve, fine lees. Palate: fruity, fresh, full.

L'O DE L' ORIGAN ROSADO BN

**88** Colour: salmon, bright. Nose: characterful, expressive, red berry notes, candied fruit. Palate: good structure, flavourful, great length, fine bead, fine bitter notes.

## GIRÓ DEL GORNER

Masia Giró del Gorner, s/n
08797 Puigdálber (Barcelona)
☎: 938 988 032
gorner@girodelgorner.com
www.girodelgorner.com

GORNER 2007 BR RESERVA
macabeo 50%, parellada 30%, xarel.lo 20%

**88** Colour: bright straw. Nose: fresh fruit, dried herbs, fine lees, floral. Palate: fresh, fruity, flavourful, good acidity.

GORNER 2006 BN RESERVA
macabeo 50%, parellada 30%, xarel.lo 20%

**88** Colour: bright straw. Nose: fresh fruit, dried herbs, fine lees, floral. Palate: fresh, fruity, flavourful, good acidity.

GORNER VINTAGE 2005 BN GRAN RESERVA
macabeo 50%, parellada 30%, xarel.lo 20%

**89** Colour: bright golden. Nose: dry nuts, fragrant herbs, complex. Palate: powerful, flavourful, good acidity, fine bead, fine bitter notes.

## GIRÓ RIBOT

Finca El Pont, s/n
08972 Santa Fe del Penedés (Barcelona)
☎: 938 974 050 - Fax: 938 974 311
comercial@giroribot.es
www.giroribot.es

GIRÓ RIBOT AVANTGARDE BR RESERVA
xarel.lo 50%, chardonnay 25%, macabeo 15%, parellada 10%

**87** Colour: bright straw. Nose: medium intensity, fresh fruit, dried herbs, fine lees, floral. Palate: fresh, fruity, flavourful, good acidity.

PAUL CHENEAU BLANC DE BLANCS BR RESERVA
macabeo 47%, xarel.lo 33%, parellada 20%

**87** Colour: bright straw. Nose: medium intensity, fresh fruit, dried herbs, fine lees, floral, scrubland. Palate: fresh, fruity, flavourful, good acidity.

GIRÓ RIBOT AB ORIGINE BR RESERVA
macabeo 50%, xarel.lo 30%, parellada 20%

**86** Colour: bright straw. Nose: medium intensity, fine lees, floral, candied fruit. Palate: fresh, fruity, flavourful, good acidity.

GIRÓ RIBOT AB ORIGINE BR
trepat 85%, pinot noir 15%

## 82

GIRÓ RIBOT MARE 2004 BN GRAN RESERVA
xarel.lo 50%, macabeo 30%, parellada 20%

**88** Colour: bright straw. Nose: medium intensity, fresh fruit, dried herbs, floral, balsamic herbs. Palate: fresh, fruity, flavourful, good acidity, long.

GIRÓ RIBOT AB ORIGINE 2003 BN GRAN RESERVA
macabeo 50%, xarel.lo 30%, parellada 20%

**88** Colour: bright straw. Nose: medium intensity, fresh fruit, dried herbs, fine lees, floral. Palate: fresh, fruity, flavourful, good acidity, complex.

## GIRÓ RIBOT TENDENCIAS EXTRA BRUT
macabeo 50%, xarel.lo 30%, macabeo 20%

**85** Colour: bright straw. Nose: medium intensity, fresh fruit, floral. Palate: fresh, fruity, flavourful, good acidity, unctuous.

## GRAN DUCAY BODEGAS

Ctra. N-330, km. 450
50400 Cariñena (Zaragoza)
☎: 976 620 400 - Fax: 976 620 398
bsv@sanvalero.com
www.sanvalero.com

GRAN DUCAY ROSÉ 2007 RD
garnacha 100%

**85** Colour: rose, purple rim. Nose: powerfull, ripe fruit, red berry notes, floral, expressive. Palate: fleshy, powerful, fruity, fresh.

GRAN DUCAY 2007 BN
macabeo 50%, xarel.lo 30%, parellada 20%

**85** Colour: bright straw. Nose: medium intensity, fresh fruit, dried herbs, fine lees. Palate: fresh, fruity, flavourful, good acidity.

## GRIMAU DE PUJADES

Castell de Les Pujades s/n
08732 La Munia (Barcelona)
☎: 938 918 031 - Fax: 938 918 426
grimau@grimau.com
www.grimau.com

GRIMAU BR
macabeo, xarel.lo, parellada

**84**

GRIMAU RESERVA FAMILIAR BN
macabeo, parellada, chardonnay, xarel.lo

**88** Colour: bright golden. Nose: fine lees, dry nuts, fragrant herbs, complex. Palate: powerful, flavourful, good acidity, fine bead, fine bitter notes.

GRIMAU MAGNUM BN
macabeo, xarel.lo, parellada

**87** Colour: bright golden. Nose: fine lees, dry nuts, fragrant herbs, complex. Palate: powerful, flavourful, good acidity, fine bead, fine bitter notes.

GRIMAU BN
macabeo, xarel.lo, parellada

**86** Colour: bright straw. Nose: medium intensity, fresh fruit, dried herbs, floral. Palate: fresh, fruity, flavourful, good acidity.

TRENCADÍS DE GRIMAU BN
macabeo, parellada, chardonnay, xarel.lo

**86** Colour: bright yellow. Nose: faded flowers, ripe fruit, medium intensity. Palate: fine bitter notes, good acidity.

## HACIENDA MARQUÉS DE LA CONCORDIA

Ctra. El Ciego, s/n
26350 Cenicero (La Rioja)
☎: 914 365 900 - Fax: 914 365 932
iruiz@haciendas-espana.com
www.haciendas-espana.com

MM PREMIUM CUVÉE MILLESIME 2005 BR GRAN RESERVA

**90** Colour: bright straw. Nose: fresh fruit, dried herbs, fine lees, floral. Palate: fresh, fruity, flavourful, good acidity, sweetness.

MM BRUT VINTAGE BR
macabeo 30%, parellada 30%, chardonnay 25%, xarel.lo 15%

**90** Colour: bright straw. Nose: fresh fruit, dried herbs, fine lees, floral. Palate: fresh, fruity, flavourful, good acidity.

## HERETAT MAS TINELL

Ctra. de Vilafranca a St. Martí Sarroca, km. 0,5
08720 Vilafranca del Penedés (Barcelona)
☎: 938 170 586 - Fax: 938 170 500
oscar.re@mastinell.com
www.mastinell.com

HERETAT MAS TINELL 2006 RD RESERVA
trepat 100%

**89** Colour: onion pink. Nose: elegant, candied fruit, dried flowers, fragrant herbs, red berry notes. Palate: light-bodied, flavourful, good acidity, long, spicy.

HERETAT MAS TINELL BRUT REAL 2006 BR RESERVA
macabeo 30%, xarel.lo 28%, parellada 36%, chardonnay 6%

**88** Colour: bright straw. Nose: fresh fruit, dried herbs, fine lees, floral. Palate: fresh, fruity, flavourful, good acidity.

HERETAT MAS TINELL NATURE REAL 2007 BN GRAN RESERVA
xarel.lo 35%, parellada 33%, macabeo 25%, chardonnay 7%

**87** Colour: bright golden. Nose: dry nuts, fragrant herbs, complex. Palate: powerful, flavourful, good acidity, fine bitter notes.

### HERETAT MAS TINELL CARPÈ DIEM RESERVA ESPECIAL 2004 BN RESERVA
chardonnay 40%, parellada 40%, xarel.lo 20%

**90** Colour: bright straw. Nose: fresh fruit, dried herbs, fine lees, floral, elegant. Palate: fresh, fruity, flavourful, good acidity.

### TERRA DE MARCA BN RESERVA

**84**

### CRISTINA MAS TINELL 2004 EXTRA BRUT GRAN RESERVA
parellada 50%, xarel.lo 22%, chardonnay 20%, reserva 8%

**90** Colour: bright golden. Nose: fine lees, dry nuts, fragrant herbs, complex. Palate: powerful, flavourful, good acidity, fine bead, fine bitter notes.

## J. M. SOGAS MASCARÓ

Amalia Soler, 35
08720 Vilafranca del Penedés (Barcelona)
☎: 650 370 691

### SOGAS MASCARÓ BR

**85** Colour: bright golden. Nose: fine lees, fragrant herbs, complex. Palate: powerful, flavourful, good acidity, fine bead, fine bitter notes.

### SOGAS MASCARÓ BN

**87** Colour: bright straw. Nose: medium intensity, fresh fruit, dried herbs, fine lees, floral. Palate: fresh, fruity, flavourful, good acidity.

## JANÉ VENTURA

Ctra. Calafell, 2
43700 El Vendrell (Tarragona)
☎: 977 660 118 - Fax: 977 661 239
janeventura@janeventura.com
www.janeventura.com

### JANÉ VENTURA ROSÉ BR RESERVA
garnacha 100%

**88** Colour: rose, purple rim. Nose: powerfull, ripe fruit, red berry notes, floral, expressive. Palate: fleshy, powerful, fruity, fresh.

### JANÉ VENTURA VINTAGE BN GRAN RESERVA
xarel.lo 45%, macabeo 30%, parellada 25%

**90** Colour: bright straw. Nose: medium intensity, fresh fruit, dried herbs, fine lees, floral, elegant. Palate: fresh, fruity, flavourful, good acidity.

### JANÉ VENTURA BN RESERVA
macabeo 30%, xarel.lo 30%, parellada 40%

**89** Colour: bright straw. Nose: medium intensity, fresh fruit, dried herbs, fine lees, floral. Palate: fresh, fruity, flavourful, good acidity.

## JAUME GIRÓ I GIRÓ

Montaner i Oller, 1-1
08770 Sant Sadurní d'Anoia (Barcelona)
☎: 938 910 165 - Fax: 938 911 271
cavagiro@cavagiro.com
www.cavagiro.com

### JAUME GIRÓ I GIRÓ RD

**82**

### JAUME GIRÓ I GIRÓ 2006 BR RESERVA
parellada 40%, macabeo 35%, xarel.lo 20%, chardonnay 5%

**87** Colour: bright straw. Nose: dried herbs, fine lees, floral, candied fruit. Palate: fresh, fruity, flavourful, good acidity.

### JAUME GIRÓ I GIRÓ BOMBONETTA 2004 BR
xarel.lo 45%, parellada 35%, chardonnay 20%

**88** Colour: bright straw. Nose: fresh fruit, dried herbs, fine lees, floral. Palate: fresh, fruity, flavourful, good acidity.

### GRANDALLA 2004 BR
xarel.lo 45%, parellada 35%, chardonnay 20%

**87** Colour: bright straw. Nose: medium intensity, fresh fruit, dried herbs, fine lees, floral. Palate: fresh, fruity, flavourful, good acidity.

### JAUME GIRÓ I GIRÓ HOMENATGE DE CAL REI 2002 BR
parellada 55%, macabeo 45%

**87** Colour: bright straw. Nose: fresh fruit, dried herbs, fine lees, floral. Palate: fresh, fruity, flavourful, good acidity.

### JAUME GIRÓ I GIRÓ 2006 BN RESERVA
parellada 40%, macabeo 35%, xarel.lo 20%, chardonnay 5%

**86** Colour: bright golden. Nose: fine lees, dry nuts, fragrant herbs, complex, elegant, dried flowers. Palate: powerful, flavourful, good acidity, fine bead, fine bitter notes.

### JAUME GIRÓ I GIRÓ SELECTE 2005 BN RESERVA
xarel.lo 45%, parellada 35%, chardonnay 20%

**88** Colour: bright straw. Nose: medium intensity, fresh fruit, dried herbs, fine lees, floral. Palate: fresh, fruity, flavourful, good acidity.

JAUME GIRÓ I GIRÓ 2002 BN GRAN RESERVA
macabeo 55%, parellada 45%

**87** Colour: bright golden. Nose: fine lees, dry nuts, fragrant herbs, complex. Palate: powerful, flavourful, good acidity, fine bead, fine bitter notes.

JAUME GIRÓ I GIRÓ BN

**87** Colour: bright straw. Nose: medium intensity, fresh fruit, dried herbs, fine lees, floral. Palate: fresh, fruity, flavourful, good acidity.

SALDONI

## JAUME LLOPART ALEMANY

Font Rubí, 9
08736 Font-Rubí (Barcelona)
☎: 938 979 133 - Fax: 938 979 133
info@jaumellopartalemany.com
www.jaumellopartalemany.com
JAUME LLOPART RESERVA FAMILIAR BR
macabeo, xarel.lo, parellada

**86** Colour: bright straw. Nose: medium intensity, fresh fruit, dried herbs, floral. Palate: fresh, fruity, flavourful, good acidity.

JAUME LLOPART ALEMANY 2005 BN GRAN
RESERVA
macabeo, xarel.lo, parellada

**88** Colour: bright golden. Nose: fine lees, dry nuts, fragrant herbs, complex. Palate: powerful, flavourful, good acidity, fine bead, fine bitter notes.

JAUME LLOPART ALEMANY RESERVA FAMILIAR
BN RESERVA
macabeo, xarel.lo, parellada

**86** Colour: bright straw. Nose: dried herbs, fine lees, floral, candied fruit. Palate: fresh, fruity, flavourful, good acidity.

JAUME LLOPART ALEMANY RESERVA
FAMILIAR BN
pinot noir, tempranillo

**85** Colour: rose. Nose: powerfull, ripe fruit, red berry notes, floral, expressive. Palate: fleshy, powerful, fruity, fresh.

## JAUME SERRA

Ctra. de Vilanova, km. 2,5
08800 Vilanova i la Geltru (Barcelona)

☎: 938 936 404 - Fax: 938 142 262
jaumeserra@jgc.es
www.vinosdefamilia.com

CRISTALINO BR
macabeo 50%, parellada 35%, xarel.lo 15%

**88** Colour: bright straw. Nose: medium intensity, fresh fruit, dried herbs, fine lees, floral, pattiserie. Palate: fresh, fruity, flavourful, good acidity, round.

CRISTALINO ROSADO BR
trepat 60%, pinot noir 40%

**84**

JAUME SERRA BR RESERVA
macabeo 45%, parellada 25%, xarel.lo 15%, chardonnay 15%

**83**

JAUME SERRA BR RESERVA
trepat 60%, pinot noir 40%

**82**

JAUME SERRA VINTAGE 2005 BN
macabeo 30%, chardonnay 30%, parellada 25%, xarel.lo 15%

**84**

JAUME SERRA CHARDONNAY 2004 BN
chardonnay 100%

**82**

## JOAN RAVENTÓS ROSELL

Heretat Vall-Ventós, s/n Carretera Sant Sadurní a
Masquefa, km. 6, 5
08783 Masquefa (Barcelona)
☎: 937 725 251 - Fax: 937 727 191
correu@raventosrosell.com
www.raventosrosell.com

JOAN RAVENTÓS ROSELL BN

**88** Colour: bright golden. Nose: dry nuts, fragrant herbs, complex, lees reduction notes, toasty. Palate: powerful, flavourful, good acidity, fine bead, fine bitter notes.

GRADIVA
JOAN RAVENTÓS ROSELL
HERETAT VALL-VENTÓS

## JOAN SARDÀ

Ctra. Vilafranca- St. Jaume dels Domenys, km. 8,1
08732 Castellvi de la Marca (Barcelona)

☎: 937 720 900 - Fax: 937 721 495
joansarda@joansarda.com
www.joansarda.com

## JOAN SARDÀ BR RESERVA

**86** Colour: bright straw. Nose: dried herbs, fine lees, floral, ripe fruit. Palate: fresh, fruity, flavourful, good acidity, sweetness.

## JOAN SARDÁ ROSÉ BR RESERVA

**85** Colour: rose. Nose: powerfull, ripe fruit, red berry notes, floral, expressive. Palate: fleshy, powerful, fruity, fresh.

## JOAN SARDÀ BN RESERVA

**88** Colour: bright straw. Nose: medium intensity, fresh fruit, dried herbs, fine lees, floral. Palate: fresh, fruity, flavourful, good acidity.

## JOAN SARDÀ MILLENIUM BN RESERVA

**87** Colour: bright straw. Nose: fresh fruit, dried herbs, fine lees, floral. Palate: fresh, fruity, flavourful, good acidity.

## JOSEP FERRET I MATEU

Avda. Penedés, 27
08730 Sta. Margarida i Monjos (Barcelona)
☎: 938 980 105 - Fax: 938 980 584
ferretmateu@ferretmateu.com
www.ferretmateu.com

FERRET I MATEU RD
trepat

**88** Colour: rose, purple rim. Nose: powerfull, ripe fruit, red berry notes, floral, expressive. Palate: fleshy, powerful, fruity, fresh.

MARIA MATEU CHARDONNAY BN
**84**

FERRET I MATEU BN
macabeo, xarel.lo, parellada
**84**

## JUAN ANTONIO PÉREZ ROURA

Felipe II, 143
08027 (Barcelona)
☎: 933 527 456 - Fax: 933 524 339
roura@roura.es
www.roura.es

ROURA BR
xarel.lo 70%, chardonnay 30%

**85** Colour: bright straw. Nose: fresh fruit, dried herbs, floral. Palate: fresh, fruity, flavourful, good acidity.

ROURA BRUT NATURE 5 * BN RESERVA
chardonnay 50%, xarel.lo 50%

**87** Colour: bright golden. Nose: dry nuts, fragrant herbs, complex. Palate: powerful, flavourful, good acidity, fine bead, fine bitter notes.

ROURA BN
xarel.lo 50%, chardonnay 50%

**85** Colour: bright straw. Nose: fresh fruit, dried herbs, fine lees, floral. Palate: flavourful, good acidity.

ROURA ROSAT BN
pinot noir 100%
**84**

## JUVÉ Y CAMPS

Sant Venat, 1
08770 Sant Sadurní D'Anoia (Barcelona)
☎: 938 911 000 - Fax: 938 912 100
comunicacio@juveycamps.com
www.juveycamps.com

JUVÉ & CAMPS ROSÉ PINOT NOIR RD
pinot noir 100%

**86** Colour: rose, purple rim. Nose: powerfull, ripe fruit, red berry notes, floral, expressive, fine lees. Palate: fleshy, powerful, fruity, fresh.

JUVÉ & CAMPS MILESIMÉ CHARDONNAY 2007 BR GRAN RESERVA
chardonnay 100%

**91** Colour: bright golden. Nose: fine lees, dry nuts, fragrant herbs, complex, candied fruit, smoky. Palate: powerful, flavourful, good acidity, fine bead, fine bitter notes.

GRAN JUVÉ & CAMPS 2005 BR GRAN RESERVA
macabeo 30%, parellada 30%, chardonnay 25%, xarel.lo 15%

**90** Colour: bright golden. Nose: fine lees, dry nuts, fragrant herbs, complex, spicy. Palate: powerful, flavourful, good acidity, fine bead, fine bitter notes.

JUVÉ & CAMPS CINTA PÚRPURA BR RESERVA
macabeo 40%, parellada 40%, xarel.lo 20%

**89** Colour: bright golden. Nose: fine lees, dry nuts. Palate: powerful, flavourful, good acidity, fine bead, fine bitter notes.

JUVÉ & CAMPS RESERVA DE LA FAMILIA 2006 BN RESERVA
parellada 34%, macabeo 33%, xarel.lo 33%

**90** Colour: bright golden. Nose: fine lees, dry nuts, fragrant herbs, complex. Palate: powerful, flavourful, good acidity, fine bead, fine bitter notes, elegant.

JUVÉ & CAMPS RESERVA DE LA FAMILIA MAGNUM 2006 BN RESERVA
parellada 34%, macabeo 33%, xarel.lo 33%

**90** Colour: bright golden. Nose: fine lees, dry nuts, complex, elegant. Palate: good acidity, fine bead, fine bitter notes.

## LA XARMADA

Hisenda Casa Llivi, s/n
08796 Pacs del Penedés (Barcelona)
☎: 938 171 237 - Fax: 938 171 546
laxarmada@laxarmada.com
www.laxarmada.com

JOSEP A. DE SANGENIS BN
chardonnay 50%, macabeo 25%, xarel.lo 25%

**86** Colour: bright straw. Nose: dried herbs, fine lees, floral, fruit liqueur notes. Palate: fresh, fruity, flavourful, good acidity.

HERETAT DE SANGENÍS BN
chardonnay 50%, macabeo 20%, xarel.lo 20%, parellada 10%

**78**

HERETAT DE SANGENÍS ROSADO BN
trepat 100%

**77**

## LAR DE BARROS - INVIOSA

Aptdo. de Correos 291
Ctra. Ex-300, p.k. 55,9 P.I. Dehesa del Pedregal, Naves 4-5-6
06200 Almendralejo (Badajoz)
☎: 924 671 235 - Fax: 924 687 231
info@lardebarros.com
www.lardebarros.com

MARQUÉS DE LARES BR
macabeo 100%

**83**

BONAVAL BR
macabeo 100%

**80**

LAR DE PLATA BR
macabeo 100%

**78**
EXTREM DE BONAVAL BN RESERVA
macabeo 100%

**87** Colour: bright straw. Nose: medium intensity, fresh fruit, dried herbs, fine lees, floral. Palate: fresh, fruity, flavourful, good acidity.

BONAVAL ROSADO BN
garnacha 100%

**86** Colour: rose, purple rim. Nose: powerfull, ripe fruit, red berry notes, floral, expressive. Palate: fleshy, powerful, fruity, fresh.

BONAVAL BN GRAN RESERVA
macabeo 100%

**84**

BONAVAL NUEVO MILENIO BN
macabeo 100%

**79**
LAR DE PLATA BN
macabeo 100%

**71**

BONAVAL SC
macabeo 100%

**83**

LAR DE PLATA SC
macabeo 100%

**83**

MARQUÉS DE LARES SS
macabeo 100%

**86** Colour: bright straw. Nose: medium intensity, fresh fruit, dried herbs, floral. Palate: fresh, fruity, flavourful, good acidity, balanced.

## LLOPART

Ctra. de Sant Sadurni - Ordal, km. 4
08739 Subirats (Barcelona)
☎: 938 993 125 - Fax: 938 993 038
llopart@llopart.es
www.llopart.es

LLOPART IMPERIAL 2005 BR GRAN RESERVA
xarel.lo 45%, macabeo 40%, parellada 10%, chardonnay 5%

**87** Colour: bright straw. Nose: fresh fruit, dried herbs, fine lees, floral. Palate: fresh, fruity, flavourful, good acidity.

### LLOPART EX-VITE 2003 BR GRAN RESERVA
xarel.lo 60%, macabeo 40%

**88** Colour: bright straw. Nose: dried herbs, fine lees, floral, candied fruit. Palate: fresh, fruity, flavourful, good acidity.

### LLOPART ROSÉ BR RESERVA
monastrell 60%, garnacha 20%, pinot noir 20%

**87** Colour: rose. Nose: powerfull, ripe fruit, red berry notes, floral, expressive. Palate: fleshy, powerful, fruity, fresh.

### LLOPART INTEGRAL 2006 BN RESERVA
parellada 45%, chardonnay 30%, macabeo 25%

**86** Colour: bright straw. Nose: fine lees, floral, ripe fruit, grassy. Palate: fresh, fruity, flavourful, good acidity.

### LLOPART 2006 BN RESERVA
macabeo 35%, xarel.lo 30%, parellada 25%, chardonnay 10%

**86** Colour: bright straw. Nose: fresh fruit, dried herbs, floral. Palate: fresh, fruity, flavourful, good acidity.

### LLOPART MICROCOSMOS ROSÉ 2005 BN GRAN RESERVA
pinot noir 85%, monastrell 15%

**86** Colour: onion pink. Nose: elegant, candied fruit, dried flowers, fragrant herbs, red berry notes. Palate: light-bodied, flavourful, good acidity, long, spicy.

### LLOPART LEOPARDI 2003 BN GRAN RESERVA
macabeo 40%, xarel.lo 30%, parellada 15%, chardonnay 15%

**91** Colour: bright straw. Nose: fresh fruit, dried herbs, fine lees, floral, balanced. Palate: fresh, fruity, flavourful, good acidity.

### LLOPART NÉCTAR TERRENAL SEMIDULCE RESERVA
xarel.lo 70%, parellada 30%

**85** Colour: bright straw. Nose: medium intensity, dried herbs, floral, candied fruit. Palate: fresh, fruity, flavourful, good acidity, sweet.

## LOXAREL

Masia Can Mayol, s/n
08735 Vilobí del Penedés (Barcelona)
☎: 938 978 001 - Fax: 938 978 111
loxarel@loxarel.com
www.loxarel.com

### 999 DE LOXAREL BR
pinot noir, trepat

**85** Colour: rose, purple rim. Nose: powerfull, ripe fruit, red berry notes, floral, expressive. Palate: fleshy, powerful, fruity, fresh.

### LOXAREL VINTAGE 2006 BN RESERVA
xarel.lo, chardonnay, parellada

**88** Colour: bright straw. Nose: medium intensity, fresh fruit, dried herbs, fine lees, floral. Palate: fresh, fruity, flavourful, good acidity.

### LOXAREL VINTAGE 2005 BN RESERVA
xarel.lo, chardonnay

**82**

### LOXAREL 2004 BN GRAN RESERVA
xarel.lo, chardonnay

**87** Colour: bright golden. Nose: fine lees, dry nuts, fragrant herbs, complex, toasty. Palate: powerful, flavourful, good acidity, fine bead, fine bitter notes.

### MM DE LOXAREL BN GRAN RESERVA
pinot noir, chardonnay

**88** Colour: bright golden. Nose: fine lees, dry nuts, fragrant herbs, complex. Palate: powerful, flavourful, good acidity, fine bead, fine bitter notes, sweetness, creamy.

### LOXAREL RESERVA FAMILIA BN GRAN RESERVA
xarel.lo, chardonnay, parellada

**87** Colour: bright golden. Nose: fine lees, dry nuts, fragrant herbs, complex. Palate: powerful, flavourful, good acidity, fine bead, fine bitter notes.

### REFUGI DE LOXAREL BN RESERVA
xarel.lo, chardonnay

**85** Colour: yellow. Nose: candied fruit, toasty, medium intensity. Palate: sweetness, fine bitter notes, balanced.

## MARCELINO DÍAZ

Mecánica s/n
06200 Almendralejo (Badajoz)

☎: 924 677 548 - Fax: 924 660 977
bodega@madiaz.com
www.madiaz.com

**PUERTA PALMA BR**
macabeo

**82**

**PUERTA PALMA BN RESERVA**
macabeo, parellada

**83**

## MARQUÉS DE MONISTROL

Monistrol d'Anoia, s/n
08770 Sant Sadurní d'Anoia (Barcelona)
info@haciendas-espana.com
www.haciendas-espana.com

**MARQUÉS DE MONISTROL PREMIUM 2005 BR**

**87** Colour: onion pink. Nose: elegant, candied fruit, dried flowers, fragrant herbs, red berry notes. Palate: light-bodied, flavourful, good acidity, long, spicy..

**MARQUÉS DE MONISTROL PREMIUM CUVÉE BR**

**85** Colour: onion pink. Nose: candied fruit, dried flowers, fragrant herbs, red berry notes, medium intensity. Palate: light-bodied, flavourful, long, spicy..

**MARQUÉS DE MONISTROL PREMIUM CUVÉE 2005 BN GRAN RESERVA**

**88** Colour: bright straw. Nose: medium intensity, fresh fruit, dried herbs, fine lees, floral. Palate: fresh, fruity, flavourful, good acidity, full.

**MARQUÉS DE MONISTROL BN**

**87** Colour: bright straw. Nose: medium intensity, fresh fruit, dried herbs, fine lees, floral, elegant. Palate: fresh, fruity, flavourful, good acidity.

**CLOS MONISTROL EXTRA BRUT**

**86** Colour: bright golden. Nose: dry nuts, fragrant herbs, complex, spicy. Palate: powerful, flavourful, good acidity, fine bead, fine bitter notes.

## MARRUGAT

Doctor Pasteur, 6
08720 Vilafranca del Penedés (Barcelona)
☎: 938 903 066 - Fax: 938 170 979
pinord@pinord.es
www.pinord.com

**MARRUGAT ROSADO 2007 BR**
trepat 100%

**87** Colour: onion pink. Nose: candied fruit, dried flowers, fragrant herbs, red berry notes. Palate: light-bodied, flavourful, good acidity, long, spicy.

**MARRUGAT COSECHA SELECCIONADA 2007 BR**
xarel.lo 40%, macabeo 30%, parellada 30%

**87** Colour: bright straw. Nose: medium intensity, dried herbs, fine lees, floral, candied fruit. Palate: fresh, fruity, flavourful, good acidity.

**DIBON 2007 BR RESERVA**
xarel.lo 40%, macabeo 30%, parellada 30%

**85** Colour: bright straw. Nose: medium intensity, fresh fruit, dried herbs, fine lees, floral. Palate: fruity, flavourful, good acidity, sweetness.

**MARRUGAT + NATURA ECOLÓGICO 2007 BR**
xarel.lo 50%, parellada 50%

**84**

**MARRUGAT GRAN BRUT 2005 BR RESERVA**
xarel.lo 60%, macabeo 20%, parellada 20%

**86** Colour: bright straw. Nose: medium intensity, fresh fruit, dried herbs, fine lees, floral. Palate: fresh, fruity, flavourful, good acidity.

**MARRUGAT CHARDONNAY BRUT FAMILIAR 2005 BR RESERVA**
chardonnay 95%, parellada 5%

**85** Colour: bright straw. Nose: medium intensity, fresh fruit, fine lees, floral, balsamic herbs. Palate: fresh, fruity, flavourful, good acidity.

**MARRUGAT 2005 BN GRAN RESERVA**
xarel.lo 60%, macabeo 20%, parellada 20%

**85** Colour: bright straw. Nose: medium intensity, fresh fruit, dried herbs, fine lees, floral, smoky. Palate: fresh, fruity, flavourful, good acidity.

**MARRUGAT SUSPIRUM 2004 BN**
xarel.lo 60%, macabeo 15%, parellada 15%, chardonnay 10%

**85** Colour: bright straw. Nose: medium intensity, dried herbs, candied fruit. Palate: fresh, fruity, flavourful, good acidity.

**MARRUGAT COSECHA SELECCIONADA 2007 SS**
xarel.lo 40%, macabeo 30%, parellada 30%

**84**

**DIBON 2007 SS**
xarel.lo 40%, macabeo 30%, parellada 30%

**84**

## MARTÍ SERDÀ

Ctra. D'Igualada a Vilafranca, km. 31.300
08792 Santa Fe del Penedés (Barcelona)
☎: 938 974 411 - Fax: 938 974 405
info@martiserda.com
www.martiserda.com

MARTÍ SERDÀ BR
macabeo 35%, parellada 35%, xarel.lo 30%

**87** Colour: bright straw. Nose: medium intensity, fresh fruit, dried herbs, fine lees, floral. Palate: fresh, fruity, flavourful, good acidity.

MARTÍ SERDÀ CHARDONNAY BR
chardonnay 100%

**85** Colour: bright straw. Nose: medium intensity, fresh fruit, dried herbs, floral. Palate: fresh, fruity, flavourful, good acidity.

MARTÍ SERDÀ BR
garnacha 35%, pinot noir 35%, trepat 30%

**84**

MARTÍ SERDÀ CUVÉE REAL BN
macabeo 50%, xarel.lo 25%, vino reserva 25%

**87** Colour: bright straw. Nose: medium intensity, fresh fruit, dried herbs, fine lees, floral. Palate: fresh, fruity, flavourful, good acidity.

MARTÍ SERDÀ BN RESERVA
macabeo, xarel.lo, chardonnay

**86** Colour: bright straw. Nose: fresh fruit, dried herbs, fine lees, floral. Palate: fresh, fruity, flavourful, good acidity.

MARTÍ SERDÀ BN RESERVA
xarel.lo, macabeo, cabernet franc

**83**

## MAS BERTRAN VITICULTORS S.L.

Avda. Josep Anselm Clavé, 25
08731 St. Martí Sarroca (Barcelona)
☎: 938 990 859 - Fax: 938 990 859
info@masbertranviticultors.com
www.masbertranviticultors.com

BALMA 2006 BN RESERVA
xarel.lo 45%, macabeo 30%, parellada 25%

**89** Colour: bright straw. Nose: medium intensity, fresh fruit, dried herbs, fine lees, floral. Palate: fresh, fruity, flavourful, good acidity.

BALMA 2005 BN RESERVA
xarel.lo 42%, parellada 30%, macabeo 28%

**88** Colour: bright golden. Nose: fine lees, dry nuts, fragrant herbs, complex, spicy. Palate: powerful, flavourful, good acidity, fine bead, fine bitter notes.

## MAS CODINA

Barri El Gorner, s/n Mas Codina
08797 Puigdalber (Barcelona)
☎: 938 988 166 - Fax: 938 988 166
cavesmascodina@hotmail.com

MAS CODINA 2006 BR
macabeo 46%, xarel.lo 27%, parellada 14%, chardonnay 13%

**87** Colour: bright straw. Nose: medium intensity, fresh fruit, dried herbs, fine lees, floral. Palate: fresh, fruity, flavourful, good acidity.

MAS CODINA 2006 BN RESERVA
macabeo 46%, xarel.lo 27%, parellada 14%, chardonnay 13%

**88** Colour: bright straw. Nose: fresh fruit, dried herbs, fine lees, floral. Palate: fresh, fruity, flavourful, good acidity.

MAS CODINA 2005 BN RESERVA ESPECIAL
macabeo 44%, chardonnay 30%, xarel.lo 26%

**88** Colour: bright straw. Nose: medium intensity, fresh fruit, dried herbs, fine lees, floral. Palate: fresh, fruity, flavourful, good acidity.

## MASCARÓ

Casal, 9
08720 Vilafranca del Penedés (Barcelona)
☎: 938 901 628 - Fax: 938 901 359
mascaro@mascaro.es
www.mascaro.es

MASCARÓ "MONARCH" BR GRAN RESERVA

**88** Colour: bright golden. Nose: fine lees, dry nuts, fragrant herbs, complex. Palate: powerful, flavourful, good acidity, fine bead, fine bitter notes.

MASCARÓ ROSADO "RUBOR AURORAE" BR

**88** Colour: coppery red. Nose: elegant, candied fruit, dried flowers, fragrant herbs, red berry notes. Palate: light-bodied, flavourful, good acidity, long, spicy.

MASCARÓ NIGRUM BR

**87** Colour: bright golden. Nose: fine lees, dry nuts, fragrant herbs, complex, candied fruit. Palate: powerful, flavourful, good acidity, fine bead, fine bitter notes, sweetness.

MASCARÓ BN

**85** Colour: bright straw. Nose: medium intensity, dried herbs, fine lees, floral, candied fruit. Palate: fresh, fruity, flavourful, good acidity.

CUVÉE ANTONIO MASCARÓ EXTRA BRUT GRAN RESERVA

**86** Colour: bright golden. Nose: dry nuts, fragrant herbs, complex, toasty. Palate: powerful, flavourful, good acidity, fine bead, fine bitter notes.

## MASET DEL LLEÓ

Av. Barcelona, 31 Pol.g Sant Pere Molanta
08734 Olerdola (Barcelona)
☎: 902 200 250 - Fax: 938 921 333
info@maset.com
www.maset.com

MASET DEL LLEÓ ROSÉ RD

**85** Colour: onion pink. Nose: elegant, candied fruit, dried flowers. Palate: light-bodied, flavourful, good acidity, long, spicy.

MASET DEL LLEÓ (NU) BR RESERVA

**88** Colour: bright straw. Nose: medium intensity, fresh fruit, dried herbs, fine lees, floral, pattiserie. Palate: fresh, fruity, flavourful, good acidity.

MASET DEL LLEÓ BN

**87** Colour: bright straw. Nose: medium intensity, fresh fruit, dried herbs, fine lees, floral, balsamic herbs. Palate: fresh, fruity, flavourful, good acidity.

MASET DEL LLEÓ COUVÉE L'AVI PAU BN RESERVA

**86** Colour: bright golden. Nose: fine lees, dry nuts, fragrant herbs, complex, macerated fruit. Palate: powerful, flavourful, good acidity, fine bead, fine bitter notes.

MASET DEL LLEÓ BN RESERVA

**86** Colour: bright straw. Nose: medium intensity, fine lees, floral, citrus fruit, scrubland. Palate: fresh, fruity, flavourful, good acidity, rich.

## MASIA PUIGMOLTÓ

Barrio de Sant Marçal, 67
08732 Castellet i La Gornal (Barcelona)
☎: 938 186 119 - Fax: 938 918 169
avalles@emendis.es

www.emendis.es
EMENDIS 2007 RD
trepat 100%

**84**

EMENDIS 2007 BR
xarel.lo 50%, macabeo 25%, parellada 25%

**86** Colour: bright straw. Nose: medium intensity, dried herbs, floral, ripe fruit. Palate: fresh, fruity, flavourful, good acidity.

EMENDIS 2007 BN RESERVA
xarel.lo 50%, macabeo 25%, parellada 25%

**91** Colour: bright straw. Nose: powerfull, elegant, complex, ripe fruit, grassy. Palate: good acidity, fine bead, flavourful, fruity, light-bodied.

EMENDIS IMUM BN RESERVA

**86** Colour: bright straw. Nose: medium intensity, fresh fruit, dried herbs, fine lees, floral. Palate: fresh, fruity, flavourful, good acidity.

## MATA I COLOMA

Ctra. St. Boi-La Llaguna, km. 10
08770 Sant Sadurní (Barcelona)
☎: 938 183 968 - Fax: 938 183 968
info@matacoloma.com
www.matacoloma.com

PERE MATA RESERVA FAMILIA 2006 BN
macabeo, xarel.lo, parellada

**88** Colour: bright straw. Nose: medium intensity, fresh fruit, dried herbs, fine lees, floral. Palate: fresh, fruity, flavourful, good acidity.

PERE MATA 2006 BN
macabeo, xarel.lo, parellada

**86** Colour: bright golden. Nose: fine lees, fragrant herbs, complex. Palate: powerful, flavourful, good acidity, fine bead, fine bitter notes.

PERE MATA L'ENSAMBLATGE 2005 BN
macabeo, xarel.lo, parellada

**86** Colour: bright straw. Nose: medium intensity, fresh fruit, dried herbs, fine lees, floral. Palate: fresh, fruity, flavourful, good acidity.

## MONT MARÇAL

Finca Manlleu
08732 Castellví de la Marca (Barcelona)

☎: 938 918 281 - Fax: 938 919 045
mrivas@mont-marcal.com
www.mont-marcal.com

## MONT MARÇAL BR RESERVA
xarel.lo 40%, macabeo 30%, parellada 20%, chardonnay 10%

**85** Colour: bright straw. Nose: medium intensity, fresh fruit, dried herbs, fine lees, floral. Palate: fresh, fruity, flavourful, good acidity.

## MONT MARÇAL EXTREMARIUM BR
xarel.lo 50%, macabeo 20%, parellada 15%, chardonnay 15%

**85** Colour: bright straw. Nose: ripe fruit, lees reduction notes, characterful. Palate: fruity, fine bitter notes, good acidity, good finish.

## MONT MARÇAL BR RESERVA

**85** Colour: rose, purple rim. Nose: powerfull, ripe fruit, red berry notes, floral, expressive. Palate: fleshy, powerful, fruity, fresh.

## MONT-FERRANT

Corsega, 73, 1
08029 (Barcelona)
☎: 934 191 000 - Fax: 934 193 170
montferrant@montferrant.com
www.montferrant.com

## MONT-FERRANT ROSÉ BR

**89** Colour: rose, purple rim. Nose: powerfull, ripe fruit, red berry notes, floral, expressive. Palate: fleshy, powerful, fruity, fresh.

## MONT FERRANT MEDALLA D'OR BR RESERVA

**88** Colour: bright golden. Nose: fine lees, dry nuts, fragrant herbs, complex. Palate: powerful, flavourful, good acidity, fine bead, fine bitter notes.

## MONT FERRANT GRAN CUVÉE BR

**87** Colour: bright straw. Nose: medium intensity, floral, ripe fruit. Palate: fresh, fruity, flavourful, good acidity.

## MONT-FERRANT BR RESERVA

**86** Colour: bright straw. Nose: medium intensity, dried herbs, floral. Palate: fresh, fruity, flavourful, good acidity, balanced.

## MONT-FERRANT BLANES NATURE BRUT EXTRA

**88** Colour: bright straw. Nose: fresh fruit, dried herbs, fine lees, floral. Palate: fresh, fruity, flavourful, good acidity.

## LUIS JUSTO VILLANUEVA BN

**90** Colour: bright straw. Nose: medium intensity, fresh fruit, fine lees, floral, grassy. Palate: fresh, fruity, flavourful, good acidity.

## MONT-FERRANT VINTAGE BN

**88** Colour: bright golden. Nose: dry nuts, fragrant herbs, complex, toasty. Palate: powerful, flavourful, good acidity, fine bead, fine bitter notes.

## BERTA BOUZY EXTRA BRUT

**90** Colour: bright straw. Nose: fresh fruit, fine lees, floral. Palate: fresh, fruity, flavourful, good acidity, creamy.

## AGUSTÍ VILARET EXTRA BRUT

**89** Colour: bright golden. Nose: dry nuts, fragrant herbs, complex. Palate: powerful, flavourful, good acidity, fine bead, fine bitter notes.

## MUNGUST

San Josep, 10-11-12
08784 Sant Jaume Sesrovires (Barcelona)
☎: 937 860 148 - Fax: 937 763 016
cavesmungust@ya.com

## PERE MUNNÉ DURÁN ETIQUETA NEGRA 2005 BN
xarel.lo 50%, macabeo 40%, parellada 10%

**86** Colour: bright golden. Nose: fine lees, dry nuts, fragrant herbs, complex. Palate: powerful, flavourful, good acidity, fine bead, fine bitter notes.

## MUNGUST 2004 BN RESERVA
xarel.lo 50%, macabeo 40%, parellada 10%

**86** Colour: bright golden. Nose: fine lees, dry nuts, fragrant herbs, complex, citrus fruit. Palate: powerful, flavourful, good acidity, fine bead, fine bitter notes.

## NADAL

Finca Nadal de la Boadella, s/n
08733 El Pla del Penedès (Barcelona)
☎: 938 988 011 - Fax: 938 988 443
nadal@nadal.com
www.nadal.com

## NADAL ROSAT 2006 BR RESERVA
pinot noir 100%

**87** Colour: onion pink. Nose: elegant, candied fruit, dried flowers, fragrant herbs, red berry notes. Palate: light-bodied, flavourful, good acidity, long, spicy.

**NADAL ESPECIAL 2005 BN GRAN RESERVA**
parellada 52%, macabeo 43%, xarel.lo 5%

**88** Colour: bright golden. Nose: dry nuts, fragrant herbs, complex, powerfull. Palate: powerful, flavourful, good acidity, fine bead, fine bitter notes.

**NADAL SALVATGE 2003 BN GRAN RESERVA**
macabeo 78%, xarel.lo 17%, parellada 5%

**88** Colour: bright golden. Nose: fine lees, dry nuts, fragrant herbs, complex. Palate: powerful, flavourful, good acidity, fine bead, fine bitter notes.

## OLIVELLA I BONET

Casetes Puigmoltó, 26
43720 L'Arboç (Tarragona)
☎: 977 670 433 - Fax: 977 670 433
olivellaibonet@hotmail.com

**MONT CARANAC CHARDONNAY 2007 BR**
chardonnay

**87** Colour: bright straw. Nose: fresh fruit, fine lees, floral, grassy. Palate: fresh, fruity, flavourful, good acidity.

**MONT CARANAC 2007 BN**
xarel.lo, macabeo, parellada

**83**

**OLIVELLA I BONET BN**
xarel.lo, macabeo, parellada

**84**

## ORIOL ROSSELL

Propietat Can Cassanyes s/n
08732 St. Marçal (Barcelona)
☎: 977 671 061 - Fax: 977 671 050
oriolrossell@oriolrossell.com
www.oriolrossell.com

**ORIOL ROSSELL 2006 RD**
trepat

**87** Colour: rose. Nose: elegant, candied fruit, dried flowers, fragrant herbs, red berry notes. Palate: light-bodied, flavourful, good acidity, long, spicy.

**ORIOL ROSSELL 2006 BN RESERVA**
macabeo, xarel.lo, parellada

**87** Colour: bright straw. Nose: medium intensity, fresh fruit, dried herbs, fine lees, floral. Palate: fresh, fruity, flavourful, good acidity.

**ORIOL ROSSELL RESERVA DE LA PROPIETAT 2004 BN GRAN RESERVA**
macabeo, xarel.lo, parellada

**88** Colour: bright golden. Nose: dry nuts, fragrant herbs, complex, lees reduction notes. Palate: powerful, flavourful, good acidity, fine bead, fine bitter notes.

**ORIOL ROSSELL 2004 BN GRAN RESERVA**
macabeo, xarel.lo, parellada

**87** Colour: bright golden. Nose: fine lees, dry nuts, complex. Palate: powerful, flavourful, good acidity, fine bead, fine bitter notes.

## PAGO DE THARSYS

Ctra. Nacional III, Km 274
46340 Requena (Valencia)
☎: 962 303 354 - Fax: 962 329 000
pagodetharsys@pagodetharsys.com
www.pagodetharsys.com

**PAGO DE THARSYS BRUT ROSADO 2006 BR RESERVA**
garnacha 100%

**88** Colour: rose, purple rim. Nose: powerfull, ripe fruit, red berry notes, floral, expressive. Palate: fleshy, powerful, fruity, fresh.

**PAGO DE THARSYS MILLESIME 2005 BR RESERVA**
macabeo 70%, parellada 20%, chardonnay 10%

**88** Colour: bright golden. Nose: fine lees, dry nuts, fragrant herbs, complex. Palate: powerful, flavourful, good acidity, fine bead, fine bitter notes.

**CARLOTA SURIA 2007 BN**
macabeo 70%, parellada 30%

**88** Colour: bright straw. Nose: fresh fruit, dried herbs, fine lees, floral. Palate: fresh, fruity, flavourful, good acidity.

**PAGO DE THARSYS 2006 BN**
macabeo 80%, chardonnay 20%

**88** Colour: bright straw. Nose: fresh fruit, dried herbs, fine lees, floral, ripe fruit. Palate: fresh, fruity, flavourful, good acidity.

**PAGO DE THARSYS 2005 BN GRAN RESERVA**
macabeo 80%, parellada 20%

**87** Colour: bright golden. Nose: fine lees, dry nuts, fragrant herbs, complex. Palate: powerful, flavourful, good acidity, fine bead, fine bitter notes, sweetness.

## PARATÓ

Can Respall de Renardes
08733 (Barcelona)

☎: 938 988 182 - Fax: 938 988 510
info@parato.es
www.parato.es

**PARATÓ PINOT NOIR 2008 RD**
pinot noir

**85** Colour: light cherry. Aroma powerfull, ripe fruit, red berry notes, raspberry. Palate: fleshy, powerful, fruity.

**PARATÓ PINOT NOIR 2007 RD**
pinot noir 100%

**82**

**PARATÓ BR**
macabeo, xarel.lo, parellada

**88** Colour: bright straw. Nose: fresh fruit, fine lees, floral, fruit expression. Palate: fresh, fruity, flavourful, good acidity, balanced.

**RENARDES CUV'EE ESPECIAL 2008 BN**
macabeo, xarel.lo, parellada

**85** Colour: bright straw. Nose: fresh fruit, floral, grassy. Palate: fresh, fruity, flavourful, good acidity.

**PARATÓ 2007 BN**
macabeo, xarel.lo, parellada

**85** Colour: bright straw. Nose: medium intensity, fresh fruit, dried herbs, floral. Palate: fresh, fruity, good acidity.

ELIAS I TERNS

## PARÉS BALTÀ

Masía Can Baltá, s/n
08796 Pacs del Penedés (Barcelona)
☎: 938 901 399 - Fax: 938 901 143
paresbalta@paresbalta.com
www.paresbalta.com

**PARÉS BALTÀ ROSE RD**

**87** Colour: coppery red. Nose: elegant, candied fruit, dried flowers, fragrant herbs, red berry notes. Palate: light-bodied, flavourful, good acidity, long, spicy.

**BLANCA CUSINÉ 2006 BR**
pinot noir, chardonnay

**91** Colour: bright straw. Nose: fresh fruit, dried herbs, fine lees, floral, expressive. Palate: fresh, fruity, flavourful, good acidity.

**PARÉS BALTÀ SELECTIO BR**
xarel.lo, chardonnay, macabeo, parellada

**89** Colour: bright straw. Nose: medium intensity, fresh fruit, dried herbs, fine lees, floral. Palate: fresh, fruity, flavourful, good acidity.

**PARÉS BALTÀ BR RESERVA**
parellada, macabeo, xarel.lo

**87** Colour: bright straw. Nose: medium intensity, fresh fruit, fine lees, floral, balsamic herbs. Palate: fresh, fruity, flavourful, good acidity.

**PARES BALTA BN**
xarel.lo, parellada, macabeo

**85** Colour: bright straw. Nose: medium intensity, fresh fruit, dried herbs, fine lees, floral. Palate: fresh, fruity, flavourful, good acidity.

## PARXET

Mas Parxet s/n
08391 Tiana (Barcelona)
☎: 933 950 811 - Fax: 933 955 500
info@parxet.es
www.parxet.es

**PARXET CUVÉE DESSERT RD**
pinot noir

**85** Colour: onion pink. Nose: elegant, candied fruit, dried flowers, fragrant herbs, red berry notes. Palate: good acidity, long, spicy, sweet.

**PARXET TITIANA PINOT NOIR BR**
pinot noir

**88** Colour: onion pink. Nose: elegant, candied fruit, dried flowers, fragrant herbs, red berry notes. Palate: light-bodied, flavourful, good acidity, long, spicy.

**PARXET BR**
pansa blanca, macabeo, parellada

**88** Colour: bright straw. Nose: fresh fruit, dried herbs, fine lees, floral, fresh. Palate: fresh, fruity, flavourful, good acidity.

**PARXET TITIANA CHARDONNAY BR**
chardonnay

**88** Colour: bright straw. Nose: fresh fruit, dried herbs, fine lees, floral, expressive, toasty. Palate: fresh, fruity, flavourful, good acidity.

**PARXET BR RESERVA**
pansa blanca, macabeo, parellada

**87** Colour: bright golden. Nose: fine lees, dry nuts, fragrant herbs, complex. Palate: powerful, flavourful, good acidity, fine bead, fine bitter notes.

# DO CAVA

**PARXET ANIVERSARIO PA-88 BN**
chardonnay, pinot noir

**90** Colour: bright straw. Nose: fresh fruit, dried herbs, fine lees, floral, elegant. Palate: fresh, fruity, flavourful, good acidity.

**PARXET BN**
pansa blanca, macabeo, parellada

**88** Colour: bright straw. Nose: medium intensity, fresh fruit, dried herbs, fine lees, floral. Palate: fresh, fruity, flavourful, good acidity.

**PARXET MARÍA CABANE 2005 EXTRA BRUT GRAN RESERVA**
pansa blanca, macabeo, parellada

**90** Colour: bright golden. Nose: fine lees, dry nuts, fragrant herbs, complex. Palate: powerful, flavourful, good acidity, fine bead, fine bitter notes.

## PERE VENTURA

Ctra. de Vilafranca, km. 0,4
08770 Sant Sadurní D'Anoia (Barcelona)
☎: 938 183 371 - Fax: 938 912 679
info@pereventura.com
www.pereventura.com

**PERE VENTURA ROSÉ RD**
trepat 100%

**86** Colour: rose. Nose: elegant, candied fruit, dried flowers, fragrant herbs, red berry notes. Palate: light-bodied, flavourful, good acidity, long, spicy.

**PERE VENTURA BR RESERVA**
xarel.lo 35%, macabeo 35%, parellada 30%

**87** Colour: bright yellow. Nose: faded flowers, candied fruit, fruit expression. Palate: good acidity, fine bead, balanced.

**PERE VENTURA TRESOR BN**
xarel.lo 40%, macabeo 40%, parellada 20%

**87** Colour: bright straw. Nose: fresh fruit, dried herbs, fine lees. Palate: fresh, fruity, flavourful, good acidity.

**PERE VENTURA CUPATGE D'HONOR BN RESERVA**
xarel.lo 70%, chardonnay 30%

**85** Colour: bright straw. Nose: medium intensity, dried herbs, floral, candied fruit. Palate: fresh, fruity, flavourful, good acidity.

## RAVENTÓS I BLANC

Plaça del Roure
08770 Sant Sadurní D'Anoia (Barcelona)

☎: 938 183 262 - Fax: 938 912 500
raventos@raventos.com
www.raventos.com

**L'HEREU DE RAVENTÓS I BLANC 2006 BR RESERVA**

**90** Colour: bright straw. Nose: medium intensity, fresh fruit, dried herbs, fine lees, floral. Palate: fresh, fruity, flavourful, good acidity.

**L'HEREU DE NIT 2006 BR**

**90** Colour: onion pink. Nose: elegant, candied fruit, dried flowers, fragrant herbs, red berry notes. Palate: light-bodied, flavourful, good acidity, long, spicy.

**ELISABET RAVENTÓS 2003 BR**

**87** Colour: bright yellow. Nose: medium intensity, candied fruit, fruit preserve. Palate: sweetness, flavourful, fruity.

**RAVENTÓS I BLANC GRAN RESERVA DE LA FINCA 2004 BN GRAN RESERVA**

**89** Colour: bright straw. Nose: ripe fruit, fruit expression, floral. Palate: flavourful, powerful, fresh, fine bead.

**RAVENTÓS I BLANC MAGNUM GRAN RESERVA DE LA FINCA 2003 BN GRAN RESERVA**

**92** Colour: bright yellow. Nose: fine lees, dry nuts, fragrant herbs, complex. Palate: powerful, flavourful, good acidity, fine bead, fine bitter notes.

**MANUEL RAVENTÓS 2001 BN GRAN RESERVA**

**90** Colour: bright golden. Nose: fine lees, dry nuts, fragrant herbs, complex. Palate: powerful, flavourful, good acidity, fine bead, fine bitter notes.

## REXACH BAQUES

Santa María, 12
08736 Guardiola de Font-Rubí (Barcelona)
☎: 938 979 170 - Fax: 938 979 335
info@rexachbaques.com
www.rexachbaques.com

**REXACH BAQUES BN GRAN RESERVA**

**88** Colour: bright straw. Nose: powerfull, candied fruit, citrus fruit, faded flowers, dry nuts. Palate: flavourful, spicy, fine bitter notes, fine bead.

## RIMARTS

Avda. Cal Mir, 44
08770 Sant Sadurní D'Anoia (Barcelona)

☎: 938 912 775 - Fax: 938 912 775
rimarts@rimarts.net
www.rimarts.net

## RIMARTS 2007 BR RESERVA
xarel.lo, macabeo, parellada

**87** Colour: bright straw. Nose: medium intensity, fresh fruit, dried herbs, fine lees, floral. Palate: fresh, fruity, flavourful, good acidity, balanced.

## RIMARTS CHARDONNAY 2006 BN RESERVA
chardonnay

**88** Colour: bright straw. Nose: dried herbs, fine lees, floral, neat, varietal, ripe fruit. Palate: fresh, fruity, flavourful, good acidity.

## RIMARTS 2006 BN RESERVA
xarel.lo, macabeo, parellada

**87** Colour: bright straw. Nose: dried herbs, fine lees, floral, ripe fruit. Palate: fresh, fruity, flavourful, good acidity.

## RIMARTS 2005 BN GRAN RESERVA
xarel.lo, macabeo, parellada, chardonnay

**88** Colour: bright golden. Nose: fine lees, dry nuts, fragrant herbs, complex. Palate: powerful, flavourful, good acidity, fine bead, fine bitter notes.

## UVAE 2003 BN RESERVA
xarel.lo, chardonnay

**84**

# ROGER GOULART

Corsega, 73 1
08029 (Barcelona)
☎: 934 191 000 - Fax: 934 193 170
rogergoulart@rogergoulart.com
www.rogergoulart.com

## ROGER GOULART BR RESERVA

**88** Colour: bright straw. Nose: medium intensity, fresh fruit, dried herbs, fine lees, floral, spicy. Palate: fresh, fruity, flavourful, good acidity.

## ROGER GOULART BR

**87** Colour: rose, purple rim. Nose: powerfull, ripe fruit, red berry notes, floral, expressive. Palate: fleshy, powerful, fruity, fresh.

## ROGER GOULART BRUT EXTRA GRAN RESERVA

**88** Colour: bright straw. Nose: medium intensity, fresh fruit, fine lees, floral, balsamic herbs. Palate: fresh, fruity, flavourful, good acidity.

## ROGER GOULART BN

**88** Colour: bright golden. Nose: fine lees, dry nuts, fragrant herbs. Palate: powerful, flavourful, good acidity, fine bead, fine bitter notes.

## ROGER GOULART GRAN CUVÉE 2004 EXTRA BRUT

**89** Colour: bright straw. Nose: medium intensity, fresh fruit, dried herbs, fine lees, floral. Palate: fresh, fruity, flavourful, good acidity.

## ROGER GOULART SS

**87** Colour: bright straw. Nose: medium intensity, fresh fruit, fine lees, floral, scrubland. Palate: fresh, fruity, flavourful, good acidity.

# ROSELL & FORMOSA

Rambla de la Generalitat, 14
08770 Sant Sadurní D'Anoia (Barcelona)
☎: 938 911 013 - Fax: 938 911 967
rformosa@roselliformosa.com
www.roselliformosa.com

## ROSELL I FORMOSA ROSAT BR
garnacha 50%, monastrell 50%

**85** Colour: rose, purple rim. Nose: powerfull, ripe fruit, red berry notes, expressive. Palate: fleshy, powerful, fruity, fresh.

## ROSELL I FORMOSA BR
macabeo 40%, xarel.lo 35%, parellada 25%

**84**

## ROSELL I FORMOSA 2004 BN GRAN RESERVA
macabeo 45%, xarel.lo 30%, parellada 25%

**86** Colour: bright straw. Nose: medium intensity, dried herbs, floral, lees reduction notes, candied fruit. Palate: fresh, fruity, flavourful, good acidity.

## DAURAT "BRUT DE BRUTS" BN
macabeo 45%, xarel.lo 30%, parellada 25%

**83**

# ROVELLATS

Pau Claris, 136
08009 (Barcelona)
☎: 934 880 575 - Fax: 934 880 819
rovellats@cavasrovellats.com
www.cavasrovellats.com

## ROVELLATS ROSÉ 2006 RD RESERVA
garnacha 80%, monastrell 20%

# DO CAVA

**85** Colour: rose, purple rim. Nose: powerfull, ripe fruit, red berry notes, expressive. Palate: fleshy, powerful, fruity, fresh.

ROVELLATS PREMIER BRUT 2007 BR
parellada 85%, macabeo 9%, xarel.lo 6%

**87** Colour: bright straw. Nose: fresh fruit, dried herbs, fine lees, floral, fruit expression. Palate: fresh, fruity, flavourful, good acidity.

ROVELLATS IMPERIAL 2006 BR RESERVA
macabeo 60%, parellada 25%, xarel.lo 15%

**88** Colour: bright straw. Nose: medium intensity, fresh fruit, dried herbs, fine lees, floral. Palate: fresh, fruity, flavourful, good acidity.

ROVELLATS 2004 BN GRAN RESERVA
xarel.lo 55%, macabeo 29%, parellada 16%

**88** Colour: bright golden. Nose: dry nuts, fragrant herbs, complex. Palate: powerful, flavourful, good acidity, fine bitter notes.

## SEGURA VIUDAS

Crta. Sant Sadurní a St. Pere de Riudebitlles, km. 5
08775 Torrelavit (Barcelona)
☎: 938 917 070 - Fax: 938 996 006
seguraviudas@seguraviudas.es
www.seguraviudas.com

SEGURA VIUDAS BRUT VINTAGE 2005 BR
macabeo 67%, parellada 33%

**88** Colour: bright straw. Nose: medium intensity, fresh fruit, dried herbs, fine lees, floral. Palate: fresh, fruity, flavourful, good acidity.

LAVIT BRUT BR
trepat 80%, monastrell 10%, garnacha 10%

**91** Colour: onion pink. Nose: elegant, candied fruit, dried flowers, fragrant herbs, red berry notes. Palate: light-bodied, flavourful, good acidity, long, spicy.

SEGURA VIUDAS RESERVA HEREDAD BR RESERVA
macabeo 67%, parellada 33%

**87** Colour: bright straw. Nose: medium intensity, fresh fruit, dried herbs, fine lees, floral. Palate: fresh, fruity, good acidity.

SEGURA VIUDAS BR RESERVA
macabeo 50%, parellada 35%, xarel.lo 15%

**83**

LAVIT 2006 BN
macabeo 60%, parellada 40%

**89** Colour: bright straw. Nose: medium intensity, fresh fruit, dried herbs, fine lees, floral. Palate: fresh, fruity, flavourful, good acidity.

TORRE GALIMANY 2005 BN
xarel.lo

**88** Colour: bright golden. Nose: fine lees, dry nuts, fragrant herbs, complex. Palate: powerful, flavourful, good acidity, fine bead, fine bitter notes.

ARIA BN
macabeo 60%, xarel.lo 20%, parellada 20%

**87** Colour: bright straw. Nose: medium intensity, fresh fruit, dried herbs, fine lees, floral. Palate: fresh, fruity, flavourful, good acidity.

## TORELLÓ

Can Martí de Baix
08790 Sant Sadurni D'Anoia (Barcelona)
☎: 938 910 793 - Fax: 938 910 877
torello@torello.es
www.torello.es

TORELLÓ DOLÇ 2006 RESERVA
macabeo, xarel.lo, parellada

**86** Colour: golden. Nose: smoky, pattiserie, spicy, dried herbs. Palate: full, creamy.

TORELLÓ ROSÉ 2006 BR RESERVA
monastrell, garnacha

**88** Colour: onion pink. Nose: elegant, candied fruit, dried flowers, fragrant herbs, red berry notes. Palate: light-bodied, flavourful, good acidity, long, spicy.

TORELLÓ 2006 BR RESERVA
macabeo, xarel.lo, parellada

**86** Colour: bright straw. Nose: medium intensity, fresh fruit, fine lees, floral, pattiserie, spicy. Palate: fresh, fruity, flavourful, good acidity.

TORELLO 225 2005 BN GRAN RESERVA
macabeo, xarel.lo, parellada

**87** Colour: bright golden. Nose: fine lees, dry nuts, fragrant herbs, complex, macerated fruit. Palate: powerful, flavourful, good acidity, fine bead, fine bitter notes.

TORELLÓ 2005 BN GRAN RESERVA
macabeo, xarel.lo, parellada

**86** Colour: bright straw. Nose: medium intensity, fresh fruit, dried herbs, fine lees, floral, pattiserie. Palate: fresh, fruity, flavourful, good acidity.

## TORRE ORIA

Carretera Pontón - Utiel, km. 3
46390 El Derramador (Valencia)
☎: 962 320 289 - Fax: 962 320 311
santiago.sancho@natra.es
www.torreoria.com

MARQUES DE REQUENA RD

**83**

MARQUES DE REQUENA BR

**86** Colour: bright straw. Nose: fresh fruit, dried herbs, fine lees, floral. Palate: fresh, fruity, flavourful, good acidity.

TORRE ORIA BR RESERVA

**85** Colour: bright straw. Nose: medium intensity, fresh fruit, dried herbs, fine lees, floral. Palate: fresh, fruity, flavourful, good acidity.

TORRE ORIA CENTENARIO BN

**88** Colour: yellow, bright straw. Nose: neat, fruit expression, grassy, fine lees. Palate: fruity, balanced, great length.

MARQUES DE REQUENA BN

**88** Colour: bright yellow. Nose: neat, expressive, fruit expression, grassy. Palate: flavourful, good acidity, balsamic.

TORRE ORIA SS

**84**

## TORRENS MOLINER

Ctra Sant Sadurni - Piera BV-2242 Km 10
08784 La Fortesa (Alt Penedès)
☎: 938 911 033 - Fax: 938 911 761
tormol@torrensmoliner.com
www.torrensmoliner.com

TORRENS & MOLINER GRAN SELECCIÓ BN GRAN RESERVA

**86** Colour: bright golden. Nose: fine lees, dry nuts, fragrant herbs, complex. Palate: powerful, flavourful, good acidity, fine bead, fine bitter notes.

TORRENS & MOLINER RESERVA PARTICULAR BN RESERVA

**86** Colour: bright golden. Nose: fine lees, dry nuts, fragrant herbs, complex. Palate: powerful, flavourful, good acidity, fine bead, fine bitter notes.

## U MES U FAN TRES

Masia Navinés B Els Pujols
08736 Guardiola de Font-Rubí (Barcelona)
☎: 938 974 069 - Fax: 938 974 724
umesu@umesufan3.com
www.umesufan3.com

1 + 1 = 3 2006 BR
macabeo, xarel.lo, parellada

**86** Colour: bright straw. Nose: medium intensity, fresh fruit, dried herbs, fine lees, floral. Palate: fresh, fruity, flavourful, good acidity, sweetness.

1 + 1 = 3 PINOT NOIR 2006 BN
pinot noir

**86** Colour: rose, purple rim. Nose: powerfull, ripe fruit, red berry notes, floral, expressive. Palate: fleshy, powerful, fruity, fresh.

1 + 1 = 3 2005 BN
macabeo, xarel.lo, parellada

**88** Colour: bright straw. Nose: fresh fruit, fine lees, floral, grassy. Palate: fresh, fruity, flavourful, good acidity.

1 + 1 = 3 2005 BN FERMENTADO EN BARRICA
xarel.lo, chardonnay

**85** Colour: bright straw. Nose: medium intensity, dried herbs, fine lees, floral, sweet spices, ripe fruit. Palate: fresh, fruity, flavourful, good acidity.

1 + 1 = 3 ESPECIAL 2003 BN GRAN RESERVA
chardonnay, pinot noir

**89** Colour: bright golden. Nose: fine lees, dry nuts, fragrant herbs, complex. Palate: powerful, flavourful, good acidity, fine bead, fine bitter notes.

1 + 1 = 3 RESERVA FAMILIAR BN

**88** Colour: bright straw. Nose: dried herbs, fine lees, floral, ripe fruit. Palate: fresh, fruity, flavourful, good acidity.

## UNIÓN VINÍCOLA DEL ESTE

Pl El Romeral c/ Construcción 74
46340 Requena (Valencia)
☎: 962 323 343 - Fax: 962 349 413
cava@uveste.es

NASOL DE RECHENNA 2007 BR
macabeo 100%

**89** Colour: pale. Nose: expressive, fresh, fresh fruit, floral. Palate: fruity, fresh.

VEGA MEDIEN 2007 BR
macabeo 80%, chardonnay 20%

**87** Colour: bright straw. Aroma medium intensity, fresh fruit, dried herbs, fine lees, floral. Palate: fresh, fruity, flavourful, good acidity.

VEGA MEDIEN 2007 DULCE
macabeo 80%, chardonnay 20%

**84**

VEGA MEDIEN 2007 SS
macabeo 100%

**84**

## VALLDOSERA

Pol. Ind. Clot de Moja, Calle Merlot, 11
08734 Moja (Barcelona)
☎: 938 904 353 - Fax: 938 904 334
info@2msiqualitywines.com
www.fincavalldosera.com

MS 4.7 BN

**89** Colour: bright straw. Nose: ripe fruit, spicy, complex. Palate: flavourful, powerful, fleshy, good structure, fine bitter notes.

VALLDOSERA BN

**86** Colour: bright straw. Nose: powerfull, ripe fruit, spicy. Palate: flavourful, powerful, fleshy, good structure, good acidity.

SUBIRAT PARENT BN

**85** Colour: bright yellow. Nose: powerfull, ripe fruit, candied fruit, dried flowers. Palate: flavourful, sweetness, fruity, fresh.

BLANC PLATÍ BN

**82**

## VALLFORMOSA

La Sala, 45
08735 Vilobi del Penedés (Barcelona)
☎: 938 978 286 - Fax: 938 978 355
vallformosa@vallformosa.es
www.vallformosa.com

GALA DE VALLFORMOSA 2005 BR GRAN RESERVA
macabeo, xarel.lo, parellada, chardonnay

**86** Colour: bright straw. Nose: medium intensity, ripe fruit, fine lees. Palate: fresh, fruity, fine bitter notes.

CARLA DE VALLFORMOSA BR RESERVA
xarel.lo, macabeo, parellada

**85** Colour: yellow, greenish rim. Nose: fresh fruit, citrus fruit, fine lees. Palate: fresh, light-bodied, correct.

ERIC DE VALLFORMOSA BN RESERVA
parellada, chardonnay

**88** Colour: bright golden. Nose: tropical fruit, candied fruit, fine lees, smoky. Palate: balanced, smoky aftertaste.

CHANTAL DE VALLFORMOSA BRUT ROSADO
garnacha, monastrell

**85** Colour: rose. Nose: citrus fruit, medium intensity, ripe fruit. Palate: easy to drink, fruity, long.

ORIOL DE VALLFORMOSA

## VÍA DE LA PLATA

Zugasti, 9
06200 Almendralejo (Badajoz)
☎: 924 661 155 - Fax: 924 661 155
cava@bodegasviadelaplata.com
www.bodegasviadelaplata.com

VÍA DE LA PLATA 2007 BN
chardonnay 100%

**85** Colour: bright golden. Nose: dry nuts, complex, white flowers. Palate: powerful, flavourful, good acidity, fine bead, fine bitter notes.

## VICENTE GANDÍA PLA

Ctra. Cheste a Godelleta s/n
46370 Chiva (Valencia)
☎: 962 524 242 - Fax: 962 524 243
info@vicentegandia.com
www.vicentegandia.com

**HOYA DE CADENAS 2008 BN**
macabeo 100%

**89** Colour: bright yellow, pale. Nose: neat, fresh fruit, citrus fruit, wild herbs. Palate: good structure, complex, flavourful, long.

## VILARNAU

Carretera d'Espiells, km. 1,4
Finca "Can Petit"
08770 Sant Sadurní d'Anoia (Barcelona)
☎: 938 912 361 - Fax: 938 912 361
castelldevilarnau@castelldevilarnau.es
www.gonzalezbyass.com

**VILARNAU BRUT ROSÉ RD**

**88** Colour: rose. Nose: elegant, candied fruit, dried flowers, fragrant herbs, red berry notes. Palate: light-bodied, flavourful, good acidity, long, spicy.

**ALBERT DE VILARNAU BR FERMENTADO EN BARRICA**

**91** Colour: bright straw. Nose: medium intensity, fresh fruit, dried herbs, fine lees, sweet spices, pattiserie. Palate: fresh, fruity, flavourful, good acidity.

**VILARNAU VINTAGE BR GRAN RESERVA**

**90** Colour: bright straw. Nose: fresh fruit, dried herbs, fine lees, floral, elegant. Palate: fresh, fruity, flavourful, good acidity.

**VILARNAU BR**

**86** Colour: bright straw. Nose: medium intensity, fresh fruit, dried herbs, fine lees, floral. Palate: fresh, fruity, flavourful, good acidity.

**ALBERT DE VILARNAU CHARDONNAY BN RESERVA**

**91** Colour: bright straw. Nose: medium intensity, fresh fruit, dried herbs, fine lees, floral, varietal. Palate: fresh, fruity, flavourful, good acidity.

**VILARNAU BN**

**87** Colour: bright straw. Nose: fresh fruit, fine lees, grassy. Palate: fresh, fruity, flavourful, good acidity.

## VINÍCOLA I SECCIÓ DE CRÉDIT SANT ISIDRE DE NULLES

Estació, s/n
43887 Nulles (Tarragona)
☎: 977 614 965 - Fax: 977 602 622

casinulles@casinulles.com
www.vinicoladenulles.com

**ADERNATS DOLÇ 2006**
macabeo 82%, parellada 10%, xarel.lo 8%

**89** Colour: bright straw. Nose: medium intensity, fresh fruit, dried herbs, fine lees, floral. Palate: fresh, fruity, flavourful, good acidity, creamy.

**ADERNATS 2006 BR**
macabeo 82%, parellada 10%, xarel.lo 8%

**90** Colour: bright golden. Nose: fine lees, dry nuts, fragrant herbs, complex. Palate: powerful, flavourful, good acidity, fine bead, fine bitter notes.

**ADERNATS ROSAT 2006 BR**
trepat 100%

**89** Colour: onion pink. Nose: elegant, candied fruit, dried flowers, fragrant herbs, red berry notes, rose petals. Palate: light-bodied, flavourful, good acidity, long, spicy.

**ADERNATS 2005 BR GRAN RESERVA**
chardonnay 50%, macabeo 30%, parellada 20%

**88** Colour: bright straw. Nose: medium intensity, fresh fruit, dried herbs, fine lees, floral. Palate: fresh, fruity, flavourful, good acidity.

**ADERNATS 2006 BN**
macabeo 82%, parellada 10%, xarel.lo 8%

**90** Colour: bright straw. Nose: medium intensity, fresh fruit, dried herbs, fine lees, floral, spicy, pattiserie. Palate: fresh, fruity, flavourful, good acidity.

**ADERNATS 2005 BN GRAN RESERVA**
chardonnay 50%, macabeo 30%, xarel.lo 20%

**90** Colour: bright straw. Nose: medium intensity, fresh fruit, dried herbs, fine lees, floral, fine reductive notes. Palate: fresh, fruity, flavourful, good acidity.

## VINÍCOLA DE SARRAL I SELECCIÓ DE CREDIT

Avda. de la Conca, 33
43424 Sarral (Tarragona)
☎: 977 890 031 - Fax: 977 890 136
cavaportell@covisal.es
www.cava-portell.com

**PORTELL 2007 RD**
trepat 100%

**84**

PORTELL 2007 BR
macabeo 70%, parellada 30%

**87** Colour: bright straw. Nose: medium intensity, fresh fruit, floral, fruit expression. Palate: fresh, fruity, flavourful, good acidity.

PORTELL 2006 BN
macabeo 80%, parellada 20%

**83**

PORTELL VINTAGE 2005 BN
macabeo 65%, parellada 35%

**86** Colour: bright yellow. Nose: fine lees, dry nuts, fragrant herbs, complex. Palate: powerful, flavourful, good acidity, fine bead, fine bitter notes.

## VINS EL CEP

Can Llopart de Les Alzines
08770 Sant Sadurní D'Anoia (Barcelona)
☎: 938 912 353 - Fax: 938 183 956
info@elcep.com
www.elcep.com

MARQUÉS DE GELIDA PINOT NOIR 2006 BR RESERVA
pinot noir 100%

**86** Colour: onion pink, rose. Nose: elegant, candied fruit, dried flowers, fragrant herbs, red berry notes. Palate: light-bodied, flavourful, good acidity, long, spicy.

L'ALZINAR 2006 BR RESERVA
xarel.lo 40%, macabeo 30%, parellada 20%, chardonnay 10%

**85** Colour: bright straw. Nose: medium intensity, fresh fruit, dried herbs, fine lees, floral. Palate: fresh, fruity, flavourful, good acidity.

MARQUÉS DE GELIDA ECOLÒGIC 2006 BR
xarel.lo 35%, macabeo 30%, parellada 25%, chardonnay 10%

**85** Colour: bright straw. Nose: medium intensity, fresh fruit, dried herbs, fine lees, floral, wild herbs. Palate: fresh, fruity, flavourful, good acidity.

MARQUÉS DE GELIDA BRUT EXCLUSIVE 2005 BR
macabeo 35%, xarel.lo 35%, parellada 15%, chardonnay 15%

**83**

L'ALZINAR 2005 BN RESERVA
xarel.lo 40%, macabeo 30%, parellada 30%

**86** Colour: bright straw. Nose: medium intensity, fresh fruit, dried herbs, fine lees. Palate: fresh, fruity, flavourful, good acidity.

MARQUÉS DE GELIDA GRAN SELECCIÓ 2003 BN GRAN RESERVA
macabeo 30%, xarel.lo 35%, parellada 20%, chardonnay 15%

**89** Colour: bright golden. Nose: dry nuts, fragrant herbs, complex, toasty. Palate: powerful, flavourful, good acidity, fine bead, fine bitter notes.

L'ALZINAR 2003 BN GRAN RESERVA
xarel.lo 40%, macabeo 25%, chardonnay 20%, parellada 15%

**88** Colour: bright golden. Nose: fine lees, dry nuts, fragrant herbs, complex. Palate: powerful, flavourful, good acidity, fine bead, fine bitter notes.

MARQUÉS DE GELIDA 2003 BN GRAN RESERVA
macabeo 25%, xarel.lo 35%, parellada 25%, chardonnay 15%

**87** Colour: bright straw. Nose: medium intensity, fresh fruit, dried herbs, fine lees, floral. Palate: fresh, fruity, flavourful, good acidity.

MARQUÉS DE GELIDA HOMENATGE 2003 BN GRAN RESERVA
macabeo 35%, xarel.lo 25%, parellada 25%, chardonnay 15%

**85** Colour: bright golden. Nose: dry nuts, complex. Palate: powerful, flavourful, good acidity, fine bead, fine bitter notes.

## VINS I CAVES CUSCÓ BERGA

Esplugues, 7
08793 Avinyonet del Penedès (Barcelona)
☎: 938 970 164 - Fax: 938 970 164
cuscoberga@cuscoberga.com
www.cuscoberga.com

CUSCÓ BERGA 2006 BR
parellada 40%, macabeo 30%, xarel.lo 30%

**86** Colour: bright straw. Nose: medium intensity, fresh fruit, dried herbs, fine lees, floral. Palate: fresh, fruity, flavourful, good acidity.

CUSCÓ BERGA 2005 BR GRAN RESERVA
parellada 40%, macabeo 30%, xarel.lo 30%

**87** Colour: bright golden. Nose: fine lees, dry nuts, fragrant herbs, complex. Palate: powerful, flavourful, good acidity, fine bead, fine bitter notes.

CUSCÓ BERGA 2006 BN
parellada 40%, macabeo 30%, xarel.lo 30%

**86** Colour: bright straw. Nose: medium intensity, dried herbs, fine lees, candied fruit, floral. Palate: fresh, fruity, flavourful, good acidity.

## VINS I CAVES TUTUSAUS

Plaça de la Creu, 1
08795 Olesa de Bonesvalls (Barcelona)
☎: 938 984 181 - Fax: 938 984 181
info@cavestutusaus.com
www.cavestutusaus.com

VALL DOLINA 2006 BN
xarel.lo 57%, macabeo 25%, parellada 11%, chardonnay 7%

**89** Colour: bright golden. Nose: fine lees, dry nuts, fragrant herbs, complex, fine reductive notes. Palate: powerful, flavourful, good acidity, fine bead, fine bitter notes.

CAVA TUTUSAUS 2005 BN
xarel.lo 54%, macabeo 27%, parellada 12%, chardonnay 7%

**88** Colour: bright straw. Nose: medium intensity, fresh fruit, dried herbs, fine lees, floral, fine reductive notes. Palate: fresh, fruity, flavourful, good acidity.

## VIÑA TORREBLANCA

Finca Masia Torreblanca, s/n
08734 Miquel D'Olérdola (Barcelona)
☎: 938 915 066 - Fax: 938 900 102
info@vinatorreblanca.com
www.vinatorreblanca.com

TORREBLANCA BR

**86** Colour: bright straw. Nose: medium intensity, dried herbs, floral, ripe fruit. Palate: fresh, fruity, flavourful, good acidity.

TORREBLANCA BR

**85** Colour: rose. Nose: powerfull, ripe fruit, red berry notes, floral, expressive. Palate: fleshy, powerful, fruity, fresh.

TORREBLANCA BN

**86** Colour: bright straw. Nose: medium intensity, fresh fruit, dried herbs, floral. Palate: fresh, fruity, flavourful, good acidity.

TORREBLANCA EXTRA BRUT RESERVA

**86** Colour: bright straw. Nose: medium intensity, dried herbs, floral, ripe fruit. Palate: fresh, fruity, flavourful, good acidity.

## VIÑEDOS Y BODEGAS VEGALFARO

Ctra. Pontón - Utiel, km. 3
46340 Requena (Valencia)

☎: 962 320 680 - Fax: 962 321 126
rodolfo@vegalfaro.com
www.vegalfaro.com

VEGALFARO 2006 BN
chardonnay, macabeo

**85** Colour: yellow, pale. Nose: wild herbs, fruit expression. Palate: fresh, fruity, easy to drink.

## WINNER WINES

Avda. del Mediterráneo, 38
28007 Madrid (Madrid)
☎: 915 019 042 - Fax: 915 017 794
winnerwines@ibernoble.com
www.ibernoble.com

JUVENALS BR RESERVA
macabeo, xarel.lo, parellada

**84**

SOME OTHER WINERIES WITHIN THE DO:

**ALTA ALELLA**
**ANTONI VILAMAJÓ SAUMELL**
**ARVIC ARETEY**
**BLANCHER ESPUMOSOS DE CAVA**
**BODEGA Y VIÑEDOS DEL ARZOBISPO**
**BODEGAS ESCUDERO**
**BODEGAS LUIS ALEGRE**
**BONET CABESTANY**
**CAN QUETU**
**CAN RAMON VITICULTORS DEL MONTGRÓS**
**CANALS Y DOMINGO**
**CASTELL DEL MIRALL**
**CATASÚS I CASANOVAS**
**CAVA ALMIRALL**
**CAVA FONPINET**
**CAVA GIBERT**
**CAVA LINCON (SALVADOR MATA OLIVA)**
**CAVA MIQUEL PONS**
**CAVA ROMAGOSA TORNÉ**
**CAVAS BERTHA**
**CAVES JOAN BUNDÓ**
**CAVES MONASTELL**
**CAVES NAVERÁN**
**CAVES OLIVÉ BATLLORI**
**CAYTUSA**
**CELLER CAN PUJOL**
**CELLER COOPERATIU DE VILAFRANCA S.C.C.L.**
**CELLER J. MESTRE**

CELLERS DE CAN SURIOL DEL CASTELL
CELLERS DE L'ARBOÇ
CELLERS GRAU DORÍA
CELLERS TRIADA
CELLERS VIVES GAU S.L.
CHOZAS CARRASCAL
EUDALD MASSANA NOYA
EXPLOTACIÓN VITIVINÍCOLA DEL PENEDÉS
MONTSARRA
FÉLIX TORNÉ CALDÚ
HERETAT MAS JORNET
JOAN BLANCH
JOAN PUJOL VILALLONGA
JOSÉ MARÍA ROSELL MIR
JOSEP FONT VERDIELL
JOSEP MASACHS
LAMARCA WINES
LEONARDO CANO PEÑA (VINS I CAVES
ARTESANALS VALLBONA D'ANOIA)
LUDEN S.A.
M. RIGOL ORDI
MARTÍN SOLER
MAS OLIVÉ
MAS ROMANI
MASIA BACH
MASIA PAPIOL
MASÍA SAGUÉ
MASOLIVÉ S.A.
MONTAU DE SADURNÍ
MONTESQUIUS
PAGÉS ENTRENA
PERE RIUS
RAVENTÓS GUASCH
REXACH BAQUES
ROBERT J. MUR
ROS MASANA, FÉLIX
ROSA MARÍA TORRES S.L.
SIMÓ DE PALAU
SOER-JOVÉL
SOLA RAVENTÓS
VALLORT VINYATERS
VINÍCOLA DEL NORDEST

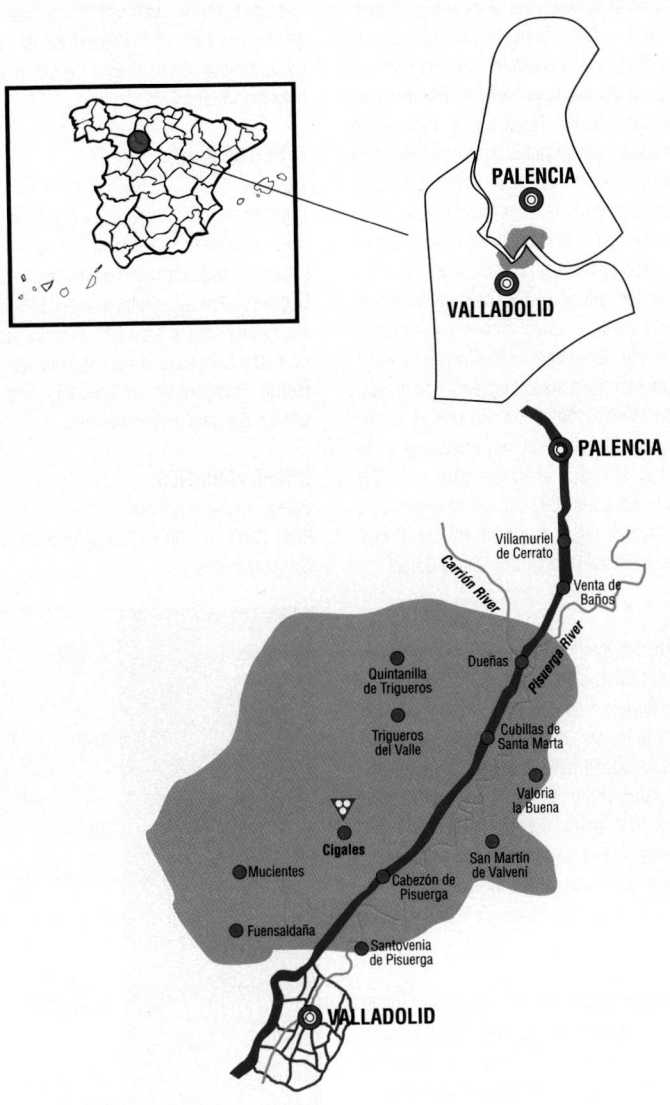

PALENCIA

VALLADOLID

PALENCIA

Villamuriel
de Cerrato

Carrión River

Venta de
Baños

Quintanilla
de Trigueros

Dueñas

Pisuerga River

Trigueros
del Valle

Cubillas de
Santa Marta

Valoria
la Buena

Cigales

Mucientes

San Martín
de Valvení

Cabezón de
Pisuerga

Fuensaldaña

Santovenia
de Pisuerga

VALLADOLID

☒ Consejo Regulador

● DO Boundary

# DO CIGALES

## NEWS

Cigales gets a definitive confirmation as a red wine region. Its traditional claret and rosé wines, although they still account for 40% of the wines tasted for our guide and are the biggest sellers of the DO, have been overshadowed by red wines from tempranillo. Rosé wines show more mature and with some overripe notes, even when the 2008 vintage was slightly cooler than average, while the reds get higher ratings compared to the last edition of our guide, thanks probably to grape selection. On the other hand we find that wines made by the local coops, which show no regard whatsoever for selection, show pretty unbalanced. The other vintages we have tasted show a concentrated, even slightly hot character and on the verge of over-ripening. They are red wines made from very ripe grapes, with high extract, abundant tannins and colour. In the oldest vintages it is noticeable that they are losing in the bottle their former aromatic character very fast. The reserva wines from 2003 and 2004 show slightly reductive off-odours and animal notes. The best are the always reliable and exquisite César Príncipe and Ovidio García.

## LOCATION

The region stretches to the north of the Duero depression and on both sides of the Pisuerga, bordered by the Cérvalos and the Torozos hills. The vineyards are situated at an altitude of 750 m; the DO extends from part of the municipal area of Valladolid (the wine estate known as 'El Berrocal') to the municipality of Dueñas in Palencia, also including Cabezón de Pisuerga, Cigales, Corcos del Valle, Cubillas de Santa Marte, Fuensaldaña, Mucientes, Quintanilla de Trigueros, San Martín de Valvení, Santovenia de Pisuerga, Trigueros del Valle and Valoria la Buena.

## CLIMATE

The climate is continental with Atlantic influences, and is marked by great contrasts in temperature, both yearly and day/night. The summers are extremely dry; the winters are harsh and prolonged, with frequent frost and fog; rainfall is irregular.

## SOIL

The soil is sandy and limy with clay loam which is settled on clay and marl. It has an extremely variable limestone content which, depending on the different regions, ranges between 1% and 35%.

## TYPES OF WINE
### Rosés:
**Cigales Nuevo.** Produced with at least 60% of the *Tinta del País* variety and at least 20% of white varieties. The vintage must be displayed on the label.
**Cigales.** Produced with at least 60% of the *Tinta del País* variety and at least 20% of white varieties. Marketed from 31st December of the following year.
**Reds.** Produced with at least 85% of the Tinta del País and the *Garnacha Tinta* varieties.

## GRAPE VARIETIES:
**White:** *Verdejo, Albillo.*
**Red:** *Tinta del País* (*Tempranillo*), *Garnacha Tinta, Garnacha Gris.*

| | |
|---|---|
| Hectares of Vineyard | 2,500 |
| Nº Viticulturists | 562 |
| Nº of Bodegas | 35 |
| 2008 Harvest | N/A |
| 2007 Production | 5,050,000 l. |
| Marketing | 75% domestic 25% export |

**CONSEJO REGULADOR.**
Corro Vaca, 5. 47270 Cigales (Valladolid)
☎: 983 580 074 - Fax: 983 586 590
@ consejo@do-cigales.es
www.do-cigales.es

## GENERAL CHARACTERISTICS OF THE WINES:

| ROSÉS | There is a distinction between the more traditional rosé wines, with the classic onion skin colour, fresh, fruity, with medium-intensity, roasted and light and supple on the palate; and the more modern rosé wines: raspberry-coloured with more powerful noses and greater fruitiness on the palate. There are also Crianza rosé wines aged for a minimum of six months in barrel and one year in the bottle. |
|---|---|
| REDS | Young and Crianza wines are produced. The first are typical fresh, fruity red wines that are pleasant and easy drinking. Those that are aged in barrels are quite correct and well-balanced. The best stand out for having obtained more colour and greater concentration, thanks to the use of finer wood and a greater fruity expression and to the Terroir. |

## 2008 VINTAGE RATING:

## GOOD

## BODEGA CÉSAR PRÍNCIPE

Ctra. Fuensaldaña - Mucientes, km. 1
47194 Fuensaldaña (Valladolid)
☎: 629 779 282 - Fax: 983 523 260
cesarprincipe@wanadoo.es

CÉSAR PRÍNCIPE 2006 T BARRICA
tempranillo 100%

**93** Colour: cherry, garnet rim. Nose: powerfull, characterful, complex, mineral, ripe fruit, sweet spices, dark chocolate. Palate: flavourful, fleshy, sweetness, round tannins.

## BODEGA COOPERATIVA DE CIGALES

Las Bodegas s/n
47270 Cigales (Valladolid)
☎: 983 580 135 - Fax: 983 580 682
bcc@bodegacooperativacigales.com
www.bodegacooperativacigales.com

COMPROMISO 2008 RD

**87** Colour: onion pink. Nose: elegant, candied fruit, dried flowers, fragrant herbs, red berry notes. Palate: light-bodied, flavourful, good acidity, long, spicy.

TORONDOS 2008 RD

**81**

TORONDOS RD ROBLE

**78**

TORONDOS 2008 T

**81**

TORONDOS 2006 TC

**85** Colour: cherry, garnet rim. Nose: ripe fruit, sweet spices, dark chocolate. Palate: flavourful, fleshy, spicy, round tannins.

TORONDOS 2004 TR

**88** Colour: cherry, garnet rim. Nose: powerfull, ripe fruit, toasty, aromatic coffee, wet leather. Palate: fine bitter notes, warm, long, round tannins.

VILLULLAS
VIÑATORONDOS

## BODEGA HIRIART

Los Gatos, s/n

47270 Cigales (Valladolid)
☎: 983 580 094 - Fax: 983 100 701
ines@bodegahiriart.es
www.bodegahiriart.es

ROSADO HIRIART 2008 RD
tempranillo 70%, garnacha 20%, verdejo 10%

**86** Colour: coppery red. Nose: expressive, red berry notes, floral. Palate: flavourful, fresh, ripe fruit.

## BODEGA OVIDIO GARCÍA

Pº Zorrilla, 9
47007 Valladolid
☎: 983 474 085 - Fax: 983 474 085
info@ovidiogarcia.com
www.ovidiogarcia.com

OVIDIO GARCÍA ESENCIA 2007 TC

**91** Colour: bright cherry. Nose: ripe fruit, sweet spices, creamy oak, complex. Palate: flavourful, fruity, toasty, round tannins.

OVIDIO GARCÍA ESENCIA 2006 TC

**91** Colour: cherry, garnet rim. Nose: ripe fruit, fruit preserve, toasty, sweet spices, cocoa bean. Palate: flavourful, fleshy, fine bitter notes, round tannins.

OVIDIO GARCÍA ESENCIA 2005 TC

**91** Colour: cherry, garnet rim. Nose: mineral, lactic notes, ripe fruit, red berry notes. Palate: flavourful, fleshy, fruity, round tannins.

## BODEGA VALDELOSFRAILES

Ctra. Cubillas s/n
47160 Cubillas de Santa Marta (Valladolid)

☎: 902 430 170 - Fax: 902 430 189
valdelosfrailes@matarromera.es
www.valdelosfrailes.es

VALDELOSFRAILES 2008 RD
tempranillo 80%, verdejo 20%

**83**

VALDELOSFRAILES 2008 T
tempranillo 100%

**87** Colour: cherry, purple rim. Nose: ripe fruit, sweet spices, medium intensity. Palate: flavourful, fleshy, ripe fruit.

SELECCIÓN PERSONAL CARLOS MORO
VALDELOSFRAILES 2005 T
tempranillo 100%

**91** Colour: cherry, garnet rim. Nose: ripe fruit, spicy, complex, powerfull, new oak, toasty. Palate: powerful, flavourful, toasty, concentrated, round tannins.

VALDELOSFRAILES PRESTIGIO 2005 T
tempranillo 100%

**90** Colour: bright cherry. Nose: ripe fruit, sweet spices, creamy oak, scrubland. Palate: flavourful, fruity, toasty, round tannins.

VALDELOSFRAILES VENDIMIA SELECCIONADA
2005 T
tempranillo 100%

**90** Colour: cherry, garnet rim. Nose: spicy, creamy oak, toasty, powerfull, ripe fruit. Palate: powerful, flavourful, toasty, round tannins.

VALDELOSFRAILES PAGO DE LAS COSTANAS 2003 T
tempranillo 100%

**90** Colour: cherry, garnet rim. Nose: ripe fruit, spicy, creamy oak, toasty, complex, wet leather. Palate: powerful, flavourful, toasty, round tannins.

## BODEGAS LEZCANO-LACALLE

Carretera Valoria, s/n

47282 Trigueros del Valle (Valladolid)
☎: 629 280 515 - Fax: 983 586 697
oficina@bodegaslezcano.es
www.bodegaslezcano.es

DOCETAÑIDOS 2008 RD
tempranillo 80%, albillo 20%, verdejo %, sauvignon blanc %

**84**

MAUDES 2005 TC
tempranillo 80%, merlot 15%, cabernet sauvignon 5%

**87** Colour: bright cherry. Nose: ripe fruit, sweet spices, creamy oak, warm. Palate: flavourful, toasty, round tannins.

LEZCANO-LACALLE DÚ 2003 T
tempranillo 80%, merlot 15%, cabernet sauvignon 5%

**88** Colour: cherry, garnet rim. Nose: powerfull, fruit preserve, fine reductive notes, toasty. Palate: fleshy, powerful.

LEZCANO-LACALLE 2003 T
tempranillo 80%, merlot 15%, cabernet sauvignon 5%

**87** Colour: cherry, garnet rim. Nose: fruit liqueur notes, fruit liqueur notes, toasty, sweet spices, aromatic coffee. Palate: flavourful, powerful, spicy, round tannins.

## BODEGAS REMIGIO DE SALAS JALÓN

Carril de Vinateras s/n. Dueñas
34210 Dueñas (Palencia)
☎: 979 780 056
amada@remigiodesalasjalon.com;
www.remigiodesalasjalon.com

LAS LUCERAS 2006 T

**88** Colour: cherry, garnet rim. Nose: candied fruit, ripe fruit, sweet spices, cocoa bean. Palate: flavourful, spicy, ripe fruit.

## BODEGAS RODRIGUEZ SANZ S.L.

Santa María, 6
47270 Cigales (Valladolid)
☎: 983 580 006 - Fax: 983 580 006
rodriguezsanz@telefonica.net

ROSAN 2008 RD

**86** Colour: light cherry. Nose: elegant, fresh fruit, red berry notes, floral. Palate: flavourful, fruity, fresh.

## BODEGAS SANTA RUFINA

Pago Fuente La Teja Polígono 3, Parcela 102

47290 Cubillas de Santa Marta (Valladolid)
☎: 983 585 202 - Fax: 983 585 202
info@bodegassantarufina.com
www.bodegassantarufina.com

UBALINDA VENDIMIA SELECCIONADA 2008 RD
tempranillo

**83**

VIÑA RUFINA 2006 TC
tempranillo 100%

**82**

## BODEGAS Y VIÑEDOS ALFREDO SANTAMARÍA

Poniente 14
47290 Cubillas de Santa Marta (Valladolid)
☎: 983 585 006 - Fax: 983 440 770
info@bodega-santamaria.com
www.bodega-santamaria.com

VALVINOSO 2008 RD
tempranillo 80%, albillo 10%, verdejo 10%

**82**

TRASCASAS 2006 TR
tempranillo 100%

**92** Colour: cherry, garnet rim. Nose: powerfull, expressive, lactic notes, ripe fruit, red berry notes, sweet spices, creamy oak. Palate: fleshy, flavourful, fruity, rich.

PAGO EL CORDONERO
ALFREDO SANTAMARÍA

## BODEGAS Y VIÑEDOS PILCAR

Ctra. Valoria, km. 3.6
47200 (Valladolid)
☎: 983 502 263 - Fax: 983 502 253
info@pilcar.com
www.pilcar.com

VIÑA CONCEJO 2006 T

**89** Colour: cherry, garnet rim. Nose: powerfull, mineral, new oak, toasty, sweet spices. Palate: fleshy, powerful, flavourful, round tannins.

CARREDUEÑAS

## BODEGAS Y VIÑEDOS SINFORIANO VAQUERO

Ctra. Villalba, km. 1,100
47194 Mucientes (Valladolid)
☎: 983 663 008 - Fax: 983 660 465
sinfo@sinforianobodegas.com
www.sinforianobodegas.com

SINFO 2008 T ROBLE

**88** Colour: cherry, garnet rim. Nose: powerfull, sweet spices, dark chocolate, toasty, ripe fruit. Palate: flavourful, fleshy, spicy, round tannins.

SINFORIANO 2007 TC

**89** Colour: cherry, garnet rim. Nose: powerfull, new oak, cedar wood, toasty, ripe fruit. Palate: fleshy, powerful, harsh oak tannins.

SINFO 2007 T ROBLE
tempranillo 100%

**87** Colour: cherry, garnet rim. Nose: aromatic coffee, toasty, ripe fruit, warm. Palate: ripe fruit, spicy, good acidity, round tannins.

SINFORIANO 2006 TC
tempranillo 100%

**89** Colour: cherry, garnet rim. Nose: powerfull, warm, fruit liqueur notes, toasty, sweet spices. Palate: flavourful, fleshy, spicy, round tannins.

SINFORIANO 2006 TR

**88** Colour: dark-red cherry. Nose: powerfull, characterful, ripe fruit, sweet spices, toasty. Palate: flavourful, fleshy, spicy, ripe fruit.

SINFORIANO 2005 TR
tempranillo 100%

**88** Colour: black cherry. Nose: powerfull, fruit preserve, fruit liqueur notes, toasty, dark chocolate. Palate: powerful, warm.

## BODEGAS Y VIÑEDOS VALERIANO

Camino de las Bodegas, s/n
47290 Cubillas de Santa Marta (Valladolid)
☎: 983 585 085 - Fax: 983 585 186
bodegasvaleriano@wanadoo.es
www.bodegasvaleriano.com

VIÑA SESMERO 2008 RD
tinta del país 60%, albillo 30%, garnacha 10%

## 82

EL BERROJO 2008 RD
tinta del país 60%, verdejo 30%, garnacha 10%

## 77

VALERIANO JOVEN 2008 T
tinta del país 100%

## 76

VALERIANO 2006 TC
tinta del país 100%

**85** Colour: cherry, garnet rim. Nose: powerfull, ripe fruit, fruit liqueur notes, toasty, new oak. Palate: powerful, flavourful, fleshy, fine bitter notes.

## COMPAÑIA DE VINOS MIGUEL MARTÍN

Ctra. Burgos - Portugal, km. 101
47290 Cubillas de Santa María (Valladolid)
☎: 983 250 319 - Fax: 983 250 329
exportacion@ciadevinos.com
www.ciadevinos.com

CASA CASTILLA 2008 RD

**85** Colour: rose, purple rim. Nose: fresh fruit, red berry notes, fruit expression. Palate: unctuous, fruity, flavourful, good acidity, easy to drink.

VIÑA GOY 2008 RD

## 84

## FINCA MUSEUM

Ctra. Cigales - Corcos, km. 3
47270 Cigales (Valladolid)
☎: 983 581 029 - Fax: 983 581 030
info@bodegasmuseum.com
www.bodegasmuseum.com

MUSEUM 2004 TC
tempranillo 100%

**86** Colour: cherry, garnet rim. Nose: powerfull, wet leather, toasty. Palate: sweetness, spirituous, toasty.

MUSEUM REAL 2004 TR
tempranillo 100%

**86** Colour: cherry, garnet rim. Nose: aromatic coffee, spicy, wet leather. Palate: flavourful, sweetness, spicy, long.

## FRUTOS VILLAR (CIGALES)

Camino Los Barreros, s/n
47270 Cigales (Valladolid)
☎: 983 586 868 - Fax: 983 580 180
bodegasfrutosvillar@bodegasfrutosvillar.com
www.bodegasfrutosvillar.com

CONDE ANSUREZ 2008 RD
tempranillo, otras

**86** Colour: rose. Nose: medium intensity, ripe fruit, floral. Palate: flavourful, powerful, fleshy.

CALDERONA 2008 RD
tempranillo, otras

**85** Colour: rose. Nose: candied fruit, ripe fruit, red berry notes, scrubland. Palate: flavourful, fruity, sweetness.

CALDERONA 2008 T
tempranillo

**86** Colour: cherry, purple rim. Nose: powerfull, varietal, ripe fruit, red berry notes. Palate: flavourful, fruity, grainy tannins.

CONDE ANSUREZ 2006 TC
tempranillo

**88** Colour: cherry, garnet rim. Nose: toasty, sweet spices, new oak, ripe fruit. Palate: flavourful, fleshy, powerful, toasty.

CALDERONA 2005 TR
tempranillo

**91** Colour: cherry, garnet rim. Nose: spicy, creamy oak, toasty, complex, lactic notes, ripe fruit. Palate: powerful, flavourful, toasty, round tannins.

CALDERONA 2005 TC
tempranillo

**88** Colour: cherry, garnet rim. Nose: medium intensity, ripe fruit, red berry notes, sweet spices. Palate: flavourful, fruity, spicy.

## GONZÁLEZ LARA S.A.

Ctra. Fuensaldaña s/n
47194 Mucientes (Valladolid)
☎: 983 587 881 - Fax: 983 587 881
gonzalezlara@bodegasgonzalezlara.com
www.bodegasgonzalezlara.com

FUENTE DEL CONDE 2008 RD

**84**

DEOGRACIAS 2006 RD FERMENTADO EN BARRICA

**83**

FUENTE DEL CONDE 2006 TC

**88** Colour: cherry, garnet rim. Nose: ripe fruit, lactic notes, new oak, sweet spices. Palate: flavourful, fleshy, round tannins.

## HIJOS DE CRESCENCIA MERINO S.L.

Mayor, 15
47280 Corcos del Valle (Valladolid)
☎: 983 580 118 - Fax: 983 580 118
eugenio@bodegashcmerino.com
www.bodegashcmerino.com

VIÑA CATAJARROS 2008 RD

**84**

## HIJOS DE FÉLIX SALAS

Corrales, s/n
47280 Corcos del Valle (Valladolid)
☎: 983 580 378 - Fax: 983 580 262
hijosfelixsalas@hotmail.com

FÉLIX SALAS 2008 RD

**84**

VIÑA PICOTA 2008 RD

**75**

PRELADO DE ARMEDILLA 2004 TC

**88** Colour: cherry, garnet rim. Nose: powerfull, characterful, fruit liqueur notes, ripe fruit, spicy, toasty. Palate: flavourful, fleshy, powerful, fine bitter notes.

FÉLIX SALAS 2004 TC

**87** Colour: cherry, garnet rim. Nose: fruit liqueur notes, spicy, lactic notes, red berry notes, new oak. Palate: flavourful, fleshy, ripe fruit, round tannins.

## HIJOS DE MARCOS GÓMEZ S.L.

Cuarto San Pedro s/n
47194 Mucientes (Valladolid)

☎: 983 587 764 - Fax: 983 587 764
salvueros@wanadoo.es

SALVUEROS 2008 RD

**84**

## HIJOS DE RUFINO IGLESIAS S.L.

La Canoniga, 25
47194 Mucientes (Valladolid)
☎: 983 587 778 - Fax: 983 587 778
bodega@hijosderufinoiglesias.com

CARRATRAVIESA 2008 RD
tempranillo 80%, garnacha %, albillo %, verdejo %

**86** Colour: rose. Nose: ripe fruit, red berry notes, floral. Palate: flavourful, fleshy, fruity, fresh.

RUFINO IGLESIAS
MILLATOS

## LA LEGUA

Ctra. Cigales km 1
47194 Fuensaldaña (Valladolid)
☎: 983 583 244 - Fax: 983 583 172
lalegua@lalegua.com
www.lalegua.com

LA LEGUA 2008 T
tempranillo 100%

**83**

LA LEGUA 2007 T ROBLE
tempranillo 100%

**86** Colour: cherry, garnet rim. Nose: spicy, dark chocolate, toasty, ripe fruit. Palate: flavourful, fleshy, spirituous, round tannins.

LA LEGUA 2006 TC
tempranillo 100%

**86** Colour: cherry, garnet rim. Nose: powerfull, varietal, ripe fruit, cocoa bean, sweet spices. Palate: flavourful, fleshy, round tannins.

LA LEGUA CAPRICHO 2005 T
tempranillo 100%

**87** Colour: dark-red cherry. Nose: powerfull, roasted coffee, dark chocolate, ripe fruit. Palate: powerful, warm, fine bitter notes, spicy, round tannins.

## PINEDO MENESES S.L.

Picón del Rollo, s/n
47280 Corcos del Valle (Valladolid)
☎: 983 586 877 - Fax: 983 586 877

LUBOL 2008 RD
# 84

PINEDO MENESES

## TRASLANZAS

Barrio de las Bodegas, s/n
47194 Mucientes (Valladolid)
☎: 639 641 123 - Fax: 946 020 263
traslanzas@traslanzas.com
www.traslanzas.com

TRASLANZAS 2005 T
tempranillo 100%

**90** Colour: black cherry. Nose: powerfull, warm, ripe fruit, scrubland, spicy. Palate: flavourful, fleshy, ripe fruit, round tannins.

### SOME OTHER WINERIES WITHIN THE DO:

**AVELINO VEGAS**
**AMALIO DEL POZO**
**ANDRÉS HERRERO VALLEJO**
**BODEGAS LAGAR DE SEM**
**BODEGAS SAN ANTON C.B.**
**COMPAÑIA DE VINOS DE TELMO RODRÍGUEZ**
**FARRÁN DIEZ BODEGAS Y VIÑEDOS S.L.**
**HERMÓGENES C.B.**
**MONT-FERRANT**
**M. LUISA CENTENO VÁSQUEZ**
**SOLAR DE LAGUNA**

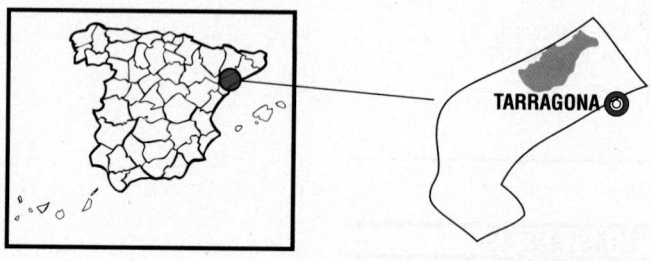

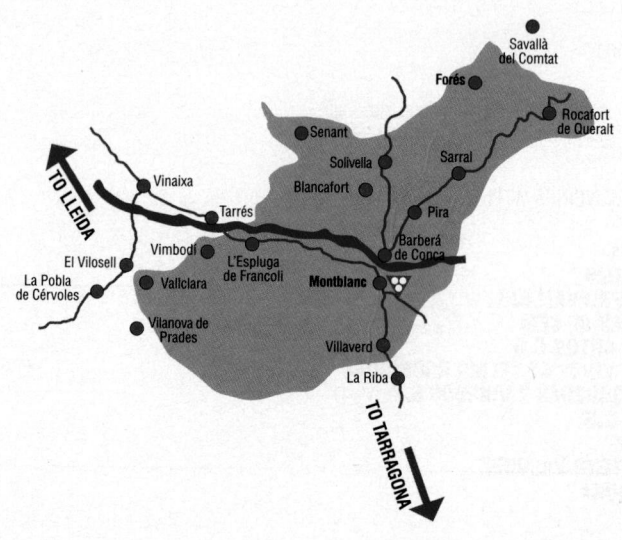

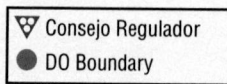

☼ Consejo Regulador
● DO Boundary

## NEWS

The headline: "Far too many cooperatives in Conca de Barberá". There are still eight of them almost exclusively dedicated to making base wine for cava, but only three of them have a bottling line. That is probably one of the reasons why, in a complicated vintage like 2008, with lots of rainfall and some mildiu happening at fruit setting – particularly evident in tempranillo and merlot–, there were no reasons to be optimistic. In our tasting for this year's edition the best results are achieved by white and rosé wines, with Montblanc and Mas Foraster leading the pack. Step by step, the local trepat is achieving all its presumed potential in rosé renderings of a light colour but an exceeding aromatic character. As for the rest, there is a bit of everything depending on the altitude of the vineyard, and the proximity of it to the mountains or to the sea. Vilanova de Prades, the latest area to become a subzone – still under way–, will be the highest within the DO at 800 meters and slate soils (llicorella) typical of Priorat. Wines from the 2007 vintage are full of colour, tannins and fruit expression, with some good renderings from French varietals and even a red wine from trepat that has a wonderful balsamic character. The rest of the crianza renderings manage beautifully to soften down the tannins and offer a much more complex aromatic expression than the average wines from the region.

## LOCATION

In the north of the province of Tarragona with a production area covering 14 municipalities, to which two new ones have recently been added: Savallà del Comtat and Vilanova de Prades.

## CLIMATE

Mediterranean and continental influences, as the vineyards occupy a river valley surrounded by mountain ranges without direct contact with the sea.

## SOIL

The soil is mainly brownish-grey and limy. The vines are cultivated on slopes protected by woodland. An important aspect is the altitude which gives the wines a fresh, light character.

## GRAPE VARIETIES:

**White:** *Macabeo, Parellada* (majority 3,300 Ha) *Chardonnay, Sauvignon Blanc.*
**Red:** *Trepat, Ull de Llebre (Tempranillo), Garnatxa, Cabernet Sauvignon, Merlot, Syrah, Pinot Noir.*

| Hectares of Vineyard | 5,600 |
|---|---|
| Nº Viticulturists | 1,300 |
| Nº of Bodegas | 22 |
| 2008 Harvest | Very Good |
| 2007 Production | 478,781 l. |
| Marketing | 62% domestic 38% export |

# DO CONCA DE BARBERÁ

**CONSEJO REGULADOR.**
Sant Josep, 18
43400 Montblanc (Tarragona)
☎: 977 861 232 - Fax: 977 862 424
@ cr@doconcadebarbera.com
www.doconcadebarbera.com

## GENERAL CHARACTERISTICS OF THE WINES:

| | |
|---|---|
| **WHITES** | Pale and brilliant, they are fruity, pleasant to drink and very light, although not excessively roasted. |
| **ROSÉS** | Raspberry-pink coloured, quite modern in their production style, with red fruit noses, slightly fresh, flavourful and well-balanced. |
| **REDS** | These are quite light and easy drinking, for the moment, with characteristics more adapted to producing young wines than for Crianza wines, except in the case of the most experienced producers who produce powerful, meaty and concentrated red wines. |

## 2008 VINTAGE RATING:

## VERY GOOD

# DO CONCA DE BARBERÁ

## ABADÍA DE POBLET

Passeig de l'Abat Conill, 6
43448 Poblet (Tarragona)
☎: 977 870 358 - Fax: 977 870 191
v.sanchez@codorniu.es

LES MASIES DE POBLET 2006 T
pinot noir

**84**

ABADÍA DE POBLET 2005 T
pinot noir

**88** Colour: bright cherry, bright ochre rim. Nose: fruit preserve, expressive, spicy. Palate: flavourful, full, fruity, good acidity, harsh oak tannins.

## BODEGAS CASTELL D'OR

Mare Rafols, 3 1 D
08720 Vilafranca del Penedès (Barcelona)
☎: 938 905 385 - Fax: 938 905 446
castelldor@castelldor.com
www.castelldor.com

CASTELL DE LA COMANDA 2008 B
parellada 20%, macabeo 80%

**78**

CASTELL DE LA COMANDA 2008 RD
trepat 100%

**82**

FRANCOLI 2008 T
trepat 50%, tempranillo 50%

**87** Colour: cherry, garnet rim. Nose: fruit liqueur notes, fruit preserve, aromatic coffee. Palate: powerful, fruity, slightly dry, soft tannins.

FRANCOLI 2003 TC
cabernet sauvignon 60%, tempranillo 40%

**85** Colour: deep cherry. Nose: raspberry, macerated fruit, balsamic herbs, spicy. Palate: fleshy, flavourful, round tannins.

FRANCOLI 2001 TR
cabernet sauvignon 60%, tempranillo 40%

**87** Colour: dark-red cherry. Nose: macerated fruit, caramel, sweet spices. Palate: fleshy, flavourful, spirituous.

## BODEGAS MIGUEL TORRES

Miguel Torres i Carbó, 6
08203 Vilafranca del Penedés (Barcelona)
☎: 938 177 400 - Fax: 938 177 444
mailadmin@torres.es
www.torres.es

MILMANDA 2007 B

**87** Colour: golden. Nose: elegant, macerated fruit, sun-drenched nuances, dried flowers. Palate: flavourful, full, fruity, balsamic, great length.

GRANS MURALLES 2005 T
monastrell ,samsó ,garnacha

**94** Colour: black cherry, purple rim. Nose: smoky, sweet spices, fruit liqueur notes, mineral, scrubland. Palate: flavourful, spirituous, good structure, good acidity.

## CARLANIA CELLER

Hort d'en Cirera, 23
43422 Barberá de la Conca (Tarragona)
☎: 977 887 375
info@carlania.com
www.carlania.com

CARLANIA 2008 B
macabeo ,trepat

**78**

CARLANIA 2008 RD
trepat

**76**

CARLANIA 2008 T ROBLE
ull de llebre ,trepat ,merlot

**85** Colour: dark-red cherry. Nose: fruit preserve, earthy notes, smoky. Palate: fleshy, powerful, balsamic, smoky aftertaste.

## CAVAS SANSTRAVÉ

De la Conca, 10
43412 Solivella (Tarragona)
☎: 977 892 165 - Fax: 977 892 073
bodega@sanstrave.com
www.sanstrave.com

SANSTRAVÉ FINCA GASSET 2007 BFB
chardonnay 100%

**88** Colour: golden. Nose: macerated fruit, scrubland, dry stone. Palate: flavourful, full, balsamic, good finish.

**SANSTRAVÉ PARTIDA DELS JUEUS 2006 TR**
merlot 80%, garnacha 20%

**87** Colour: pale ruby, brick rim edge. Nose: sweet spices, creamy oak, balsamic herbs, ripe fruit. Palate: fleshy, flavourful, classic aged character.

**SANSTRAVÉ FINCA GASSET SYRAH 2004 TR**
syrah 100%

**85** Colour: dark-red cherry, garnet rim. Nose: fruit preserve, honeyed notes, aromatic coffee. Palate: powerful, sweetness.

**SANSTRAVÉ FINCA GASSET 2002 TGR**
cabernet sauvignon 60%, tempranillo 40%

**84**

## CELLER CAL JOAN

Església, 4
43425 Montbrió de la Marca (Tarragona)
☎: 977 898 150
ccaljoan@gmail.com

**TROS D'ENYOR 2008 RD**
merlot 50%, ull de llebre 50%

**83**

**TROS D'ENYOR 2007 T**
merlot 60%, ull de llebre 40%

**84**

## CELLER CARLES ANDREU

Sant Sebastià, 19
43423 Pira (Tarragona)
☎: 977 887 404 - Fax: 977 887 427
info@cavandreu.com
www.cavandreu.com

**VINO TINTO TREPAT CARLES ANDREU 2007 T**
trepat 100%

**91** Colour: cherry, garnet rim. Nose: ripe fruit, balsamic herbs, complex, varietal. Palate: fleshy, fruity, full, balsamic, great length.

## CELLER JORDI LLORENS

Prim, 5-7
43411 Blancafort (Tarragona)
☎: 629 204 672
cellerjll@gmail.com

**CELLER JORDI LLORENS MACABEU PARELLADA 2008 B**
macabeo ,parellada

**78**

**ATIQETE CABERNET 2007 T BARRICA**
cabernet sauvignon

**89** Colour: ruby red. Nose: warm, expressive, balsamic herbs, undergrowth, macerated fruit. Palate: powerful, flavourful, balsamic, great length.

## CELLER MAS FORASTER

Camino Ermita de Sant Josep, s/n
43400 Montblanc (Tarragona)
☎: 977 860 229 - Fax: 977 875 037
info@josepforaster.com
www.josepforaster.com

**JOSEP FORASTER BLANC SELECCIÓ 2008 B**
garnacha blanca 40%, macabeo 30%, chardonnay 30%

**84**

**JOSEP FORASTER COLLITA 2008 T**
tempranillo 90%, cabernet sauvignon 10%

**88** Colour: black cherry, purple rim. Nose: fruit expression, macerated fruit, balsamic herbs, mineral. Palate: fleshy, fruity, fresh fruit tannins.

**JOSEP FORASTER 2006 TC**
cabernet sauvignon 40%, syrah 30%, tempranillo 30%

**90** Colour: dark-red cherry. Nose: fruit liqueur notes, fruit preserve, caramel, dry stone. Palate: powerful, flavourful, complex.

**JOSEP FORASTER SELECCIÓ 2005 TC**
cabernet sauvignon 90%, tempranillo 10%

**87** Colour: black cherry. Nose: fruit liqueur notes, fruit liqueur notes, roasted coffee, sweet spices, aromatic coffee. Palate: powerful, good structure, concentrated, slightly dry, soft tannins.

## CELLER MOLI DELS CAPELLANS

Avenir, 24 3 - 5
43800 Valls (Tarragona)
☎: 651 034 221
info@molidelscapellans.com
www.molidelscapellans.com

**MOLÍ DELS CAPELLANS 2008 B**
parellada ,muscat

**87** Colour: golden. Nose: fresh fruit, citrus fruit, dried herbs. Palate: flavourful, full, fruity.

**MOLÍ DELS CAPELLANS 2007 BFB**
Chardonnay

**85** Colour: golden. Nose: ripe fruit, sun-drenched nuances, spicy. Palate: flavourful, full, rich.

**MOLÍ DELS CAPELLANS SELECCIÓ 2007 T**
syrah ,tempranillo

**86** Colour: dark-red cherry. Nose: fruit liqueur notes, earthy notes, balsamic herbs. Palate: powerful, good structure, concentrated.

## CELLERS ROSET S.L.

Finca de Sant Feliu - Crta. Tàrrega, s/n
43410 La Guardia del Prats (Tarragona)
☎: 937 369 690 - Fax: 937 361 303
info@brescat.com
www.brescat.com

**BRESCAT 2006 TC**

**87** Colour: cherry, garnet rim. Nose: ripe fruit, spicy, creamy oak. Palate: fleshy, full, flavourful, smoky aftertaste.

**ROGENT T**
cabernet sauvignon

**89** Colour: pale ruby, brick rim edge. Nose: creamy oak, aged wood nuances, balsamic herbs. Palate: fleshy, flavourful, round tannins.

## CLOS MONTBLANC

Carretera Montblanc-Barbera, s/n
43422 Barberá de la Conca (Tarragona)
☎: 977 887 030 - Fax: 977 887 032
info@closmontblanc.com
www.closmontblanc.com

**CLOS MONTBLANC XIPELLA BLANC 2008 B**

**87** Colour: straw. Nose: citrus fruit, white flowers. Palate: light-bodied, fruity, flavourful.

**CASTILLO DE MONTBLANC MACABEO/ CHARDONNAY 2008 B**

**85** Colour: bright straw. Nose: fresh fruit, balsamic herbs, dried flowers. Palate: flavourful, fruity, fresh, balsamic.

**CLOS MONTBLANC CHARDONNAY 2008 BFB**

**85** Colour: bright golden. Nose: candied fruit, dry nuts, balsamic herbs, creamy oak. Palate: fruity, good structure, full, smoky aftertaste.

**CLOS MONTBLANC SAUVIGNON BLANC PREMIUM 2008 B**

**84**

**CLOS MONTBLANC ROSAT PREMIUM 2008 RD**

**88** Colour: light cherry. Nose: warm, powerfull, macerated fruit, red berry notes, balsamic herbs, floral. Palate: fleshy, full, flavourful, great length.

**CASTILLO DE MONTBLANC 2008 RD**

**87** Colour: rose. Nose: fruit liqueur notes, macerated fruit, spicy, floral. Palate: powerful, flavourful, fruity, great length.

**CASTILLO DE MONTBLANC TEMPRANILLO 2007 T**

**90** Colour: cherry, garnet rim. Nose: fruit liqueur notes, roasted coffee, undergrowth, balsamic herbs. Palate: complex, good structure, fresh, full.

**CLOS MONTBLANC SYRAH PREMIUM 2006 T**

**90** Colour: ruby red. Nose: macerated fruit, toasty, varietal, floral. Palate: fleshy, full, flavourful, round tannins.

**CLOS MONTBLANC PINOT NOIR PREMIUM 2005 TC**

**89** Colour: ruby red, garnet rim. Nose: fruit expression, macerated fruit, scrubland, floral, cedar wood. Palate: fleshy, flavourful, good acidity.

**CLOS MONTBLANC MERLOT PREMIUM 2005 TC**

**89** Colour: dark-red cherry, garnet rim. Nose: complex, expressive, creamy oak, spicy, balsamic herbs. Palate: fleshy, flavourful, balsamic, easy to drink.

**CLOS MONTBLANC XIPELLA PREMIUM 2005 T**

**88** Colour: pale ruby, brick rim edge. Nose: cedar wood, creamy oak, fine reductive notes. Palate: fleshy, rich, full.

**CLOS MONTBLANC MASÍA LES COMES 2004 TR**

**89** Colour: dark-red cherry, ruby red. Nose: characterful, mineral, cedar wood, fruit preserve. Palate: fleshy, concentrated, balsamic.

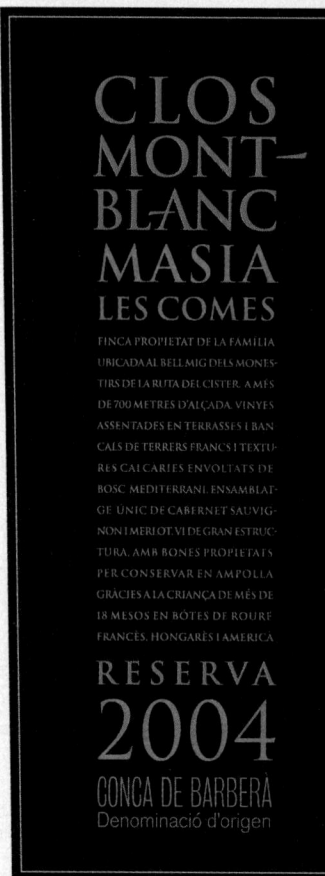

CLOS
MONT-
BLANC
MASIA
LES COMES

FINCA PROPIETAT DE LA FAMÍLIA
UBICADA AL BELL MIG DELS MONES-
TIRS DE LA RUTA DEL CISTER. A MÉS
DE 700 METRES D'ALÇADA. VINYES
ASSENTADES EN TERRASSES I BAN
CALS DE TERRERS FRANCS I TEXTU-
RES CALCÀRIES ENVOLTATS DE
BOSC MEDITERRANI. ENSAMBLAT-
GE ÚNIC DE CABERNET SAUVIG-
NON I MERLOT. VI DE GRAN ESTRUC-
TURA. AMB BONES PROPIETATS
PER CONSERVAR EN AMPOLLA
GRÀCIES A LA CRIANÇA DE MÉS DE
18 MESOS EN BÓTES DE ROURE
FRANCÈS, HONGARÈS I AMERICA

RESERVA
2004
CONCA DE BARBERÀ
Denominació d'origen

## GATZARA VINS

Josep M. Tossas, 47 1 - 2
43400 Montblanc (Tarragona)
☎: 977 861 175 - Fax: 977 861 175
info@gatzaravins.com

GATZARA 2008 T
merlot 52%, ull de liebre 30%, trepat 18%

**88** Colour: dark-red cherry. Nose: fruit preserve, sweet spices, balsamic herbs. Palate: powerful, rich, flavourful, powerful tannins.

GATZARA 2007 TC
merlot 55%, cabernet sauvignon 45%

**88** Colour: black cherry. Nose: fruit liqueur notes, fruit preserve, dark chocolate, balsamic herbs. Palate: powerful, fruity, concentrated, great length.

## MAS DEL TOSSAL

Comerç s/n
43422 Barberà de la Conca (Tarragona)
☎: 618 546 050
pepburguera@yahoo.es

ESPURNA 2007 T
cabernet franc ,syrah

**90** Colour: black cherry, purple rim. Nose: fruit liqueur notes, fruit liqueur notes, dry stone. Palate: powerful, flavourful, spirituous, powerful tannins.

## RENDE MASDEU S.L.

Avda. Catalunya, 44
43440 L'Espluga de Francolí  (Tarragona)
☎: 977 871 361 - Fax: 977 871 361
rendemasdeu@terra.es
www.rendemasdeu.com

RENDÉ MASDEU SYRAH 2008 RD
syrah 100%

**88** Colour: rose, purple rim. Nose: raspberry, red berry notes, violet drops. Palate: fleshy, rich, flavourful, balsamic.

RENDÉ MASDEU MERLOT 2006 TC
merlot 100%

**89** Colour: dark-red cherry. Nose: fruit liqueur notes, fruit liqueur notes, roasted almonds. Palate: powerful, rich, concentrated, good acidity.

RENDÉ MASDEU CABERNET 2006 TC
cabernet sauvignon 90%, syrah 10%

**88** Colour: black cherry. Nose: characterful, fruit preserve, balsamic herbs, floral. Palate: fleshy, powerful, concentrated, good acidity.

ARNAU

## ROSA MARÍA TORRES S.L.

Avda. Anguera, 2
43424 Sarral (Tarragona)
☎: 977 890 013 - Fax: 977 890 173
info@rosamariatorres.com
www.rosamariatorres.com

VIOGNIER 2007 BFB

**83**

RD ROURE 2006 T

**87** Colour: dark-red cherry. Nose: raspberry, macerated fruit, balsamic herbs, aromatic coffee. Palate: powerful, flavourful, concentrated, balsamic.

---

VINYA PLANS

## VINICOLA DE SARRAL I SELECCIÓ DE CREDIT

Avda. de la Conca, 33
43424 Sarral (Tarragona)
☎: 977 890 031 - Fax: 977 890 136
cavaportell@covisal.es
www.cava-portell.com

PORTELL BLANC DE BLANCS 2008 B
macabeo 80%, parellada 20%

**85** Colour: bright straw. Nose: fresh fruit, citrus fruit, dried herbs, balsamic herbs. Palate: flavourful, fruity, fresh.

AMBARÍ 2008 B
macabeo ,parellada

**82**

PORTELL TREPAT 2008 RD
trepat 100%

**88** Colour: rose, purple rim. Nose: powerfull, ripe fruit, red berry notes, floral, expressive. Palate: fleshy, powerful, fruity, fresh.

PORTELL MERLOT 2007 T
merlot 100%

**88** Colour: very deep cherry. Nose: fruit expression, macerated fruit, balsamic herbs, toasty. Palate: fleshy, fruity, full.

PORTELL SELECCIÓ 2 ANY 2006 T
tempranillo 70%, cabernet sauvignon 15%, merlot 15%

**88** Colour: cherry, garnet rim. Nose: macerated fruit, raspberry, dry nuts, balsamic herbs, smoky. Palate: powerful, flavourful, complex, balsamic.

PORTELL 2004 TR
merlot 50%, cabernet sauvignon 40%, tempranillo 10%

**89** Colour: dark-red cherry. Nose: cedar wood, dark chocolate, undergrowth, fruit liqueur notes. Palate: complex, spirituous, fine tannins, balsamic.

PORTELL 2008 BLANCO DE AGUJA
parellada 20%, macabeo 80%

**82**

PORTELL TREPAT 2008 ROSADO DE AGUJA
trepat 100%

**78**

## VIVER DE CELLERISTES GUSPI

Avda. Arnau de Ponç, 10
43423 Pira (Tarragona)
☎: 636 816 724
josep.guspi@hotmail.com
www.viverdecelleristes.concadebarbera.cat

GUSPI PINETELL 2007 T
merlot

**87** Colour: cherry, purple rim. Nose: varietal, ripe fruit, fruit expression, mineral. Palate: fruity, flavourful, powerful, fruity aftestaste, round tannins.

GUSPI EMBIGATS DE LA MARÍA 2007 T
tempranillo

**87** Colour: dark-red cherry. Nose: ripe fruit, varietal, powerfull, earthy notes. Palate: fruity, flavourful, fleshy, round tannins.

SOME OTHER WINERIES WITHIN THE DO:

**AGRÍCOLA DE BARBERÀ
BODEGAS BELLOD, S.A.
CAL CELDONI
CELLER ESCODA - SANAHUJA
COOP. AGRÍCOLA DE ROCAFORT DEL QUERALT
COOPERATIVA AGRÍCOLA DE PIRA
COOPERATIVA AGRÍCOLA I CAIXA AGRÍCOLA
DE BLANCAFORT S.C.C.L.
VI I VINYES DE CABESTANY**

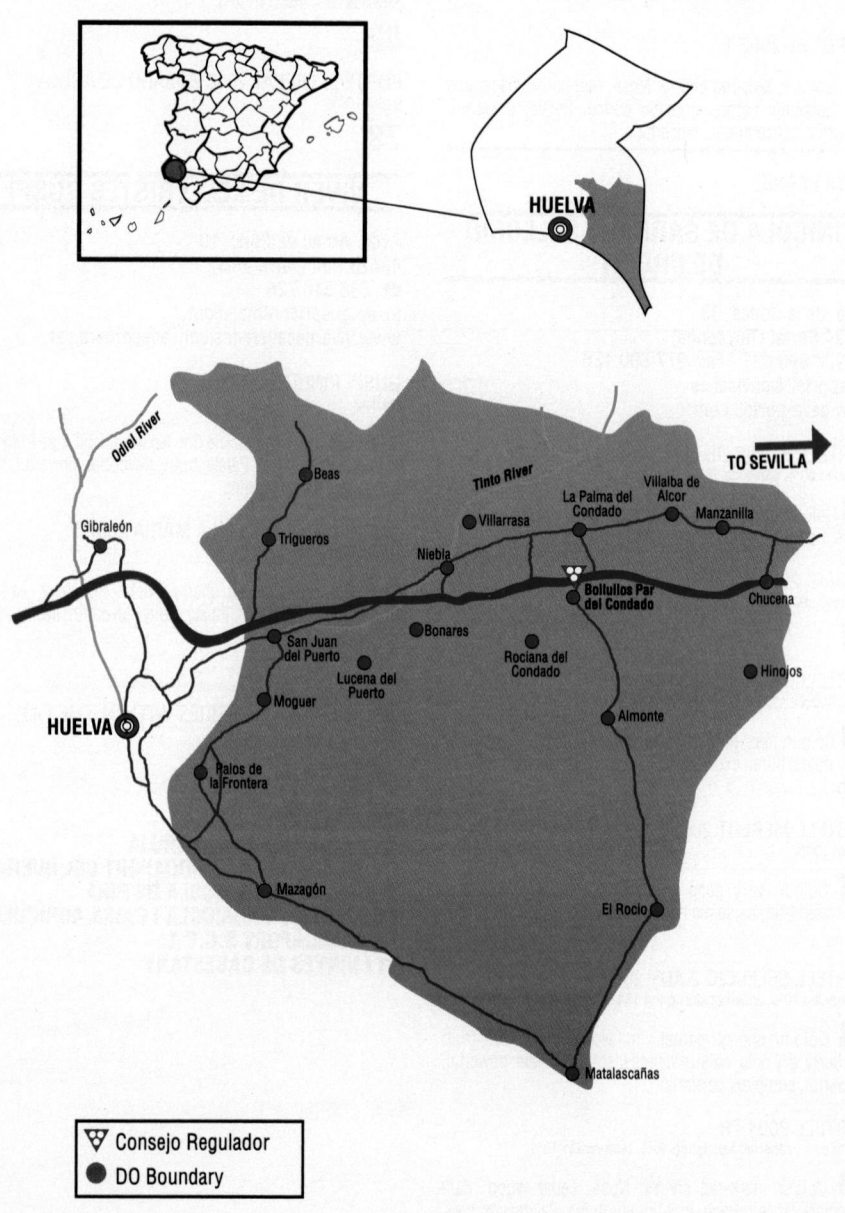

Consejo Regulador
DO Boundary

## NEWS

The so-called "Discovery Wines" have incorporated new grape varieties such as colombard, sauvignon blanc and chardonnay and there is also some will to promote red wine making as well. For the moment, the Consejo Regulador has permitted the use of syrah, tempranillo, merlot, cabernet sauvignon and cabernet franc. In any case, production figures for 2008 were a third lower than in 2007 in an attempt to get healthier grapes. With less bunches per vine, what they got was a longer ripening cycle that eventually provided meatier, bigger wines compared to those of 2007, and an overall fresher vintage. This is particularly evident in white wines made from zalema, which show abundant notes of tropical fruit rather than the floral ones typical of the variety. Nevertheless, the biggest surprise came from Aldea Blanca, a creamy, elegant white made from colombard.

Also singular are the so-called 'orange wines' (vinos de naranja), abundant in elegant, toasty ageing notes as well as those of macerated orange peel. And finally, there are some generosos that are as good as those from Jerez reaching easily ratings between 80 and 85 points.

## LOCATION

In the south east of Huelva. It occupies the plain of Bajo Guadalquivir. The production area covers the municipal areas of Almonte, Beas, Bollullos Par del Condado, Bonares, Chucena, Gibraleón, Hinojos, La Palma del Condado, Lucena del Puerto, Manzanilla, Moguer, Niebla, Palos de la Frontera, Rociana del Condado, San Juan del Puerto, Villalba del Alcor, Villarrasa and Trigueros.

## CLIMATE

Mediterranean in nature, with certain Atlantic influences. The winters and springs are fairly mild, with long hot summers. The average annual temperature is 18 °C, and the average rainfall per year is around 550 mm, with a relative humidity of between 60% and 80%.

## SOIL

In general, flat and slightly rolling terrain, with fairly neutral soils of medium fertility. The soil is mainly reddish, brownish-grey with alluvium areas in the proximity of the Guadalquivir.

## GRAPE VARIETIES:

**White:** *Zalema* (majority with 86% of vineyards), *Palomino, Listán de Huelva, Garrido Fino, Moscatel de Alejandría* and *Pedro Ximénez.*

| | |
|---|---|
| Hectares of Vineyard | 4,470 |
| Nº Viticulturists | 2,354 |
| Nº of Bodegas | 36 |
| 2008 Harvest | Excellent |
| 2007 Production | 7,767,745 l. |
| Marketing | 95% domestic 5% export |

# DO CONDADO DE HUELVA

**CONSEJO REGULADOR**
Avda. 28 de Febrero, s/n
21710 Bollullos Par del Condado (Huelva)
☎: 959 410 322 - Fax: 959 413 859.
@ cr@condadodehuelva.es
www.condadodehuelva.es

## GENERAL CHARACTERISTICS OF THE WINES:

| | |
|---|---|
| **YOUNG WHITES** | Produced from the autochtonous *Zalema* variety, they are characterised by their slightly vegetative notes with hints of scrubland; they are pleasant and easy drinking. |
| **CONDADO PÁLIDO** | These are quite similar to the other Finos of Andalusia (Jerezanos and Montillanos). *Palomino* grapes are used in their production, the same as those used for Jerez, although they have somewhat less biological character. |
| **CONDADO VIEJO** | These are the most traditional wines of the region, although now only produced in a few cellars, and come from the oldest Soleras. |

## 2008 VINTAGE RATING:

# VERY GOOD

## AGROALIMENTARIA VIRGEN DEL ROCÍO

Avda. de Cabezudos, s/n
21730 Almonte (Huelva)
☎: 959 406 146 - Fax: 959 407 052
administracion@raigal.com
www.raigal.com

RAIGAL B

**80**

TEJARES CONDADO PÁLIDO FI

**78**

TEJARES CONDADO DULCE GE

**77**

## BODEGAS CONTRERAS RUIZ S.L.

Almonte, 5
21720 Rociana del Condado (Huelva)
☎: 959 416 426 - Fax: 959 416 744
contreras@bodegascontreras.com

VIÑA CONTRERAS 2008 B
zalema 100%

**87** Colour: bright straw. Nose: fresh, fresh fruit, white flowers, varietal. Palate: flavourful, fruity, good acidity, balanced.

VIÑA BARREDERO 2008 B
zalema 100%

**85** Colour: bright straw. Nose: fresh, fresh fruit, white flowers. Palate: flavourful, fruity, balanced, fine bitter notes.

LAS BOTAS

## BODEGAS DEL DIEZMO NUEVO

Sor Ángela de la Cruz, 56
21800 Moguer (Huelva)
☎: 959 370 004 - Fax: 959 370 004
info@bodegadiezmonuevo.com

MELQUÍADES SÁENZ B

**87** Colour: bright straw. Nose: floral, wild herbs, ripe fruit, citrus fruit. Palate: sweet, balanced, good acidity.

VIÑA EL PATRIARCA B

**77**

PATRIARCA MELQUIADES SAENZ CONDADO PÁLIDO OL

**86** Colour: light mahogany. Nose: powerfull, characterful, candied fruit, overripe fruit. Palate: sweet, spirituous, correct.

## BODEGAS DOÑANA

Labradores, 2
21710 Bollulos del Condado (Huelva)
☎: 959 411 513
bodegasdonana@terra.es

ALDEA BLANCA BFB
colombard

**88** Colour: bright yellow. Nose: powerfull, ripe fruit, sweet spices, creamy oak, fragrant herbs. Palate: rich, smoky aftertaste, flavourful, fresh, good acidity.

VIÑA DOÑANA B
zalema

**83**

VIÑA DOÑANA 2006 TC
syrah

**83**

VIÑA DOÑANA 2005 TC
syrah

**83**

RETOÑO T ROBLE

**82**

## BODEGAS IGLESIAS

Teniente Merchante, 2
21710 Bollullos del Condado (Huelva)
☎: 959 410 439 - Fax: 959 410 463
bodegasiglesias@bodegasiglesias.com
www.bodegasiglesias.com

UZT TARDÍA 2008 B
zalema

**83**

% UZ CIEN X CIEN UVA ZALEMA 2008 B JOVEN
zalema 100%

**82**

RICA HEMBRA SOLERA 1980 GE
zalema 80%, pedro ximénez 20%

**85** Colour: dark mahogany. Nose: powerfull, tar, varnish, sun-drenched nuances. Palate: powerful, sweet, unctuous.

LETRADO SOLERA 1992 GE SOLERA
zalema 100%

**84**

PAR VINO NARANJA VINO DE LICOR
zalema 80%, pedro ximénez 20%

**88** Colour: iodine, amber rim. Nose: powerfull, expressive, candied fruit, citrus fruit. Palate: sweet, flavourful, pruney.

EXQUISITA

## BODEGAS OLIVEROS

Rábida, 12
21710 Bollullos Par del Condado (Huelva)
☎: 959 410 057 - Fax: 959 410 057
oliveros@bodegasoliveros.com
www.bodegasoliveros.com

JUAN JAIME SEMIDULCE 2008 B
zalema 100%

**80**

OLIVEROS VINO NARANJA 2003
pedro ximénez 70%, zalema 30%

**80**

OLIVEROS OLOROSO 2002
palomino 70%, garrido 30%

**73**

OLIVEROS FINO 2004 CONDADO PÁLIDO
palomino 100%

**82**

OLIVEROS PEDRO XIMÉNEZ 2006 PX
pedro ximénez 100%

**90** Colour: dark mahogany. Nose: complex, fruit liqueur notes, dried fruit, pattiserie, toasty. Palate: sweet, rich, unctuous, powerful.

## BODEGAS PRIVILEGIO DEL CONDADO S.L.

San José, 2
21710 Bollullos del Condado (Huelva)

☎: 959 410 261 - Fax: 959 410 171
comercial@vinicoladelcondado.com
www.vinicoladelcondado.com

MIORO 2008 B
zalema

**84**

MIORO GRAN SELECCIÓN 2007 B
zalema, moscatel

**85** Colour: yellow, bright straw. Nose: expressive, fresh fruit, grassy, honeyed notes. Palate: flavourful, fruity, good finish.

MIORO 1955 2005 B

**88** Colour: bright yellow. Nose: powerfull, ripe fruit, sweet spices, creamy oak, fragrant herbs. Palate: rich, smoky aftertaste, flavourful, fresh, good acidity.

DON CONDADO SEMI-DULCE B

**75**

VDM VINO DULCE DE NARANJA

**86** Colour: old gold, amber rim. Nose: candied fruit, fruit liqueur notes, citrus fruit. Palate: flavourful, powerful, sweet.

MISTERIO VINO DULCE GE

**84**

VDM VINO DULCE MOSCATEL GE

**80**

MISTERIO CREAM GE

**77**

## BODEGAS RAPOSO (JOSÉ ANTONIO RAPOSO)

Miguel Hernández, 31
21710 Bollullos Par del Condado (Huelva)
☎: 959 410 565 - Fax: 959 413 821
bodegas-raposo@terra.es

M.F. LA NUEZ CONDADO PÁLIDO

**87** Colour: yellow, golden. Nose: characterful, dry nuts, wild herbs, flor yeasts. Palate: flavourful, fine bitter notes.

AVELLANERO OLOROSO CONDADO VIEJO CRIANZA

**85** Colour: light mahogany. Nose: expressive, candied fruit, dry nuts. Palate: spirituous, flavourful, fine solera notes.

**AVELLANERO CREAM GE**

**87** Colour: light mahogany. Nose: warm, dried fruit, aromatic coffee, pattiserie. Palate: spirituous, flavourful, pruney.

**RAPOSO MOSCATEL PASAS GE**

**85** Colour: dark mahogany. Nose: powerfull, varietal, overripe fruit, sun-drenched nuances. Palate: sweet, powerful, varietal.

ROSA MORENA
VIÑA COLOMBINA
VIÑA LA NUEZ
SOLERA MORENA CLARA
LA CACHIFA
SELECTO M.C.A
LA FLAMENCA

## BODEGAS SAUCI

Doctor Fleming, 1
21710 Bollullos del Condado (Huelva)
☎: 959 410 524 - Fax: 959 410 331
bodegassauci@terra.es
www.bodegassauci.es

**SAUCI B JOVEN**
zalema 100%
**80**

**ESPINAPURA CONDADO PÁLIDO**
palomino 100%

**87** Colour: yellow, bright golden. Nose: balanced, medium intensity, flor yeasts, saline. Palate: flavourful, easy to drink.

**SAUCI CREAM SOLERA 1890 CR**
palomino 75%, pedro ximénez 25%

**86** Colour: iodine, amber rim. Nose: fruit preserve, candied fruit, powerfull. Palate: flavourful, sweet, spicy.

**RIODIEL SOLERA 1980 GE**
palomino 100%
**80**

**SAUCI VINO DULCE VINO DE LICOR**
pedro ximénez 80%, palomino 20%

**86** Colour: iodine, amber rim. Nose: powerfull, spicy, aged wood nuances, roasted almonds, candied fruit. Palate: powerful, sweet, spicy.

S' NARANJA

## DÍAZ

P.I. El Lirio c/Toneleros, 6
21710 Bollullos del Condado (Huelva)
☎: 959 410 340 - Fax: 959 408 095
diaz@bodegasdiaz.com
www.bodegasdiaz.com

**VADO DEL QUEMA 2008 B**
zalema 100%

**80**

**1955 CONDADO PÁLIDO CONDADO PÁLIDO**
palomino 100%

**82**

**ONUBIS GE**
moscatel 100%

**86** Colour: dark mahogany. Nose: characterful, grapey, candied fruit, creamy oak. Palate: sweet, unctuous, spirituous.

**1955 GE**
zalema 50%, listán 50%

**86** Colour: iodine, amber rim. Nose: fruit liqueur notes, fruit liqueur notes, dry nuts. Palate: sweetness, fine bitter notes, long.

**NARANJA DE ORO VINO NARANJA**
zalema 100%

**84**

## MARQUÉS DE VILLALUA

Ctra. A-472, km. 25,2
21860 Villalba del Alcor (Huelva)
☎: 959 420 905 - Fax: 959 421 141
bodega@marquesdevillalua.com
www.marquesdevillalua.com

**MARQUÉS DE VILLALÚA 2008 B**

**86** Colour: pale. Nose: ripe fruit, citrus fruit, floral. Taste flavourful, ripe fruit.

SANTA AGUEDA
ERMITA DE SANTA AGUEDA
AGUADULCE DE VILLALÚA

## VINÍCOLA VALVERDEJO S.L.

Ctra. Gibraleón - Trigueros km 2
21500 Gibraleón (Huelva)

# DO CONDADO DE HUELVA

☎: 959 240 215 - Fax: 959 240 900
mateobarba@vinicolavalverdejo.com
www.vinicolavalverdejo.com

TORREUMBRÍA 2008 B
palomino

**81**

TORREUMBRIA 2006 T
tempranillo, cabernet sauvignon, merlot

**84**

TORRECANALES OL

**86** Colour: light mahogany. Nose: candied fruit, roasted
almonds, sweet spices. Palate: sweet, pruney, spirituous.

MATEO BARBA
PANTURRANO

SOME OTHER WINERIES WITHIN THE DO:

**BODEGAS ANDRADE S.L.
COOP. NUESTRA SEÑORA DE GUÍA
NUESTRA SEÑORA DEL SOCORRO
VINÍCOLA MANZANILLERA**

## NEWS

Costers del Segre is one of those regions from where you could expect huge qualitative differences between its wineries –there are 25 of them– given their singular microclimates. Believe it or not, it is one of the biggest wine regions in Spain in terms of surface, for it comprises the whole of the province of Lleida and six different subzones, a diversity that definitely does not help to sell its wines. In Artesa, to the northwest of the capital city, Lleida, we will encounter wines of a fresher character from early ripening grapes well suited to extreme climatic patterns; to the southeast, in the subzones of Vall de Ríu Corb and Les Garrigues, wines are richer and more alcoholic, given that vines get there more sunlight hours. In Raimat, a subzone cut to measure to its namesake winery, wines are more mediterranean in style. The reason for all the latest vintages to be so homogenous in quality is probably the ability of the wineries to have come to work exclusively with selected soils, climates and grape varieties. As in the previous editions of our guide, the top ratings go to white wines based on macabeo and blended with chardonnay, and Cérvoles, Auzells, Missenyora and Castell del Remei are the leading houses. But there also room for other grapes like –marselan, cabernet franc, albariño, pinot noir, moscatel– and blends. The production decrease of almost 35% compared to last year has hardly been noticed in terms of quality, for the grapes were overall quite healthy.

## LOCATION

In the southern regions of Lleida, and a few municipal areas of Tarragona. It covers the sub-regions of: Artesa de Segre, Garrigues, Pallars Jussà, Raimat, Segrià and Valls del Riu Corb.

## CLIMATE

Rather dry continental climate in all the sub-regions, with minimum temperatures often dropping below zero in winter, summers with maximum temperatures in excess of 35° on occasions, and fairly low rainfall figures: 385 mm/year in Lleida and 450 mm/year in the remaining regions.

## SOIL

The soil is mainly calcareous and granitic in nature. Most of the vineyards are situated on soils with a poor organic matter content, brownish-grey limestone, with a high percentage of limestone and very little clay.

## GRAPE VARIETIES:

**White:** Preferred, *Macabeo, Xarel·lo, Parellada, Chardonnay, Garnacha Blanca.*
Authorized white: *Albariño, Riesling, Sauvignon Blanc.*
**Red:** Preferred, *Garnacha Negra, Ull de Llebre (Tempranillo), Cabernet Sauvignon, Merlot, Monastrell, Trepat, Samsó, Pinot Noir.*
Authorized red: *Syrah.*

| Hectares of Vineyard | 4,719 |
|---|---|
| Nº Viticulturists | 656 |
| Nº of Bodegas | 31 |
| 2008 Harvest | N/A |
| 2007 Production | 118,685 l. |
| Marketing | 60% domestic 40% export |

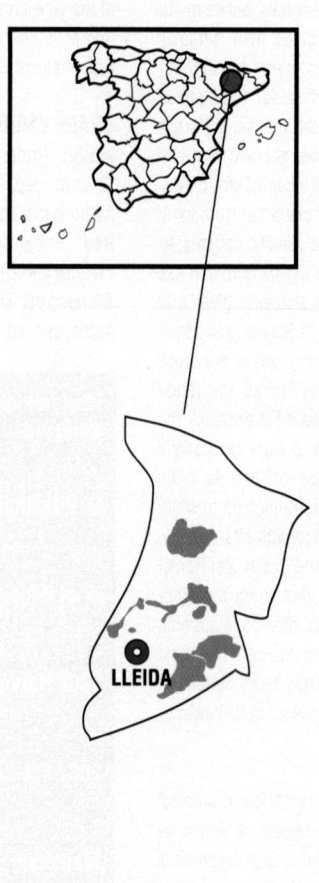

▽ Consejo Regulador
● DO Boundary

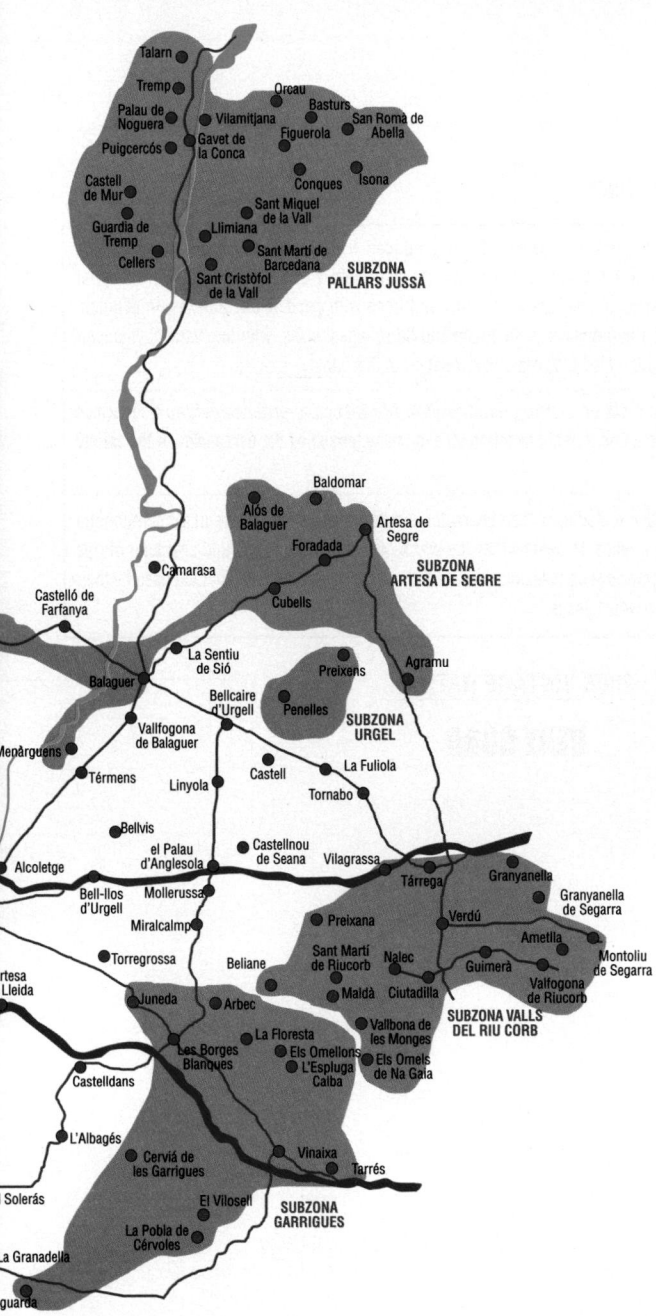

Talarn
Tremp
Orcau
Palau de Noguera
Vilamitjana
Basturs
San Romà de Abella
Gavet de la Conca
Figuerola
Puigcercós
Castell de Mur
Conques
Isona
Sant Miquel de la Vall
Guàrdia de Tremp
Llimiana
Sant Martí de Barcedana
Cellers
Sant Cristòfol de la Vall
**SUBZONA PALLARS JUSSÀ**

Baldomar
Alòs de Balaguer
Artesa de Segre
Foradada
Camarasa
**SUBZONA ARTESA DE SEGRE**
Castelló de Farfanya
Cubells
La Sentiu de Sió
Preixens
Agramu
Balaguer
Bellcaire d'Urgell
Penelles
**SUBZONA URGEL**
Menàrguens
Vallfogona de Balaguer
Térmens
Linyola
Castell
La Fuliola
Tornabo
Bellvis
el Palau d'Anglesola
Castellnou de Seana
Vilagrassa
Alcoletge
Tàrrega
Granyanella
Bell-llos d'Urgell
Mollerussa
Granyanella de Segarra
Miralcamp
Preixana
Verdú
Ametlla
Torregrossa
Beliane
Sant Martí de Riucorb
Nalec
Guimerà
Montoliu de Segarra
Artesa de Lleida
Maldà
Ciutadilla
Valfogona de Riucorb
Juneda
Arbec
**SUBZONA VALLS DEL RIU CORB**
La Floresta
Vallbona de les Monges
Les Borges Blanques
Els Omellons
Els Omels de Na Gaia
Castelldans
L'Espluga Calba
L'Albagés
Vinaixa
Cerviá de les Garrigues
Tarrés
El Solerás
El Vilosell
**SUBZONA GARRIGUES**
La Pobla de Cérvoles
La Granadella
aguarda

# DO COSTERS DEL SEGRE

**CONSEJO REGULADOR**
Complex de la Capallera, 97. 25192 Lleida
☎: 973 264 583 - Fax: 973 266 078
@secretari@costersdelsegre.es
www.costersdelsegre.es

## GENERAL CHARACTERISTICS OF THE WINES:

| | |
|---|---|
| **WHITES** | There is a distinction between those produced from traditional grapes (*Macabeo, Parellada* and *Xarel·lo*), which follow the parameters of the white wines from other Catalonian regions. They are light, fruity and fresh with good acidity indexes. In addition, there are the Chardonnays, both young and barrel-aged wines, with fine varietal character and following the Mediterranean interpretation of this variety. |
| **ROSÉS** | Produced from *Ull de Llebre* (*Tempranillo*), *Merlot* or *Cabernet Sauvignon*, the wines are pink, with a fine fruit character, fresh and characterised by the personality of the variety used. |
| **REDS** | The wines have a Mediterranean character, single varietal or a mixture of autochthonous and foreign varieties. In general they are warm, with a powerful nose and character of ripe fruit. Some may develop balsamic aromas and, on the palate, they are characterised by their warmth and flavourfulness. |

## 2008 VINTAGE RATING:

# VERY GOOD

## BODEGAS COSTERS DEL SIÓ

Ctra. de Agramunt, Km. 4,2
25600 Balaguer (Lérida)
☎: 973 424 062 - Fax: 973 424 112
bodegas@costersio.com
www.costersio.com

**VIÑA DEL SIÓS 2008 B**
sauvignon blanc 71%, chardonnay 25%, pinot noir 4%

**85** Colour: yellow, coppery red. Nose: grapey, macerated fruit, faded flowers. Palate: rich, fresh, flavourful.

**VIÑA DEL SIÓS 2008 RD**
garnacha tinta 50%, syrah 50%

**87** Colour: rose, purple rim. Nose: powerfull, ripe fruit, red berry notes, floral. Palate: fleshy, powerful, fruity, fresh.

**SIÓS SELECCIÓN 2007 T**
syrah 50%, garnacha 40%, others 10%

**89** Colour: dark-red cherry. Nose: fruit preserve, mineral, spicy, cocoa bean. Palate: fleshy, powerful, slightly dry, soft tannins.

**VIÑA DEL SIÓS 2007 T**
tempranillo 70%, merlot 30%

**87** Colour: dark-red cherry. Nose: ripe fruit, spicy, aromatic coffee, balsamic herbs. Palate: fleshy, powerful, flavourful, spirituous.

**ALTO SIÓS 2006 T**
syrah 70%, tempranillo 30%

**90** Colour: dark-red cherry. Nose: macerated fruit, red berry notes, balsamic herbs, damp earth. Palate: warm, good acidity, flavourful, balsamic.

AROCHO
FLOR DEL SIÓ

## CASTELL D'ENCÚS

Ctra. Tremp a Sta. Engracia, km. 5
25630 Talarn (Lleida)
☎: 934 876 666
rbobet@encus.org
www.encus.org

**EKAM 2008 B**

**90** Colour: bright straw. Nose: grassy, white flowers, ripe fruit. Palate: flavourful, fruity, fresh, rich.

## CASTELL DEL REMEI

Finca Castell del Remei s/n

25333 Castell del Remei (Lleida)
☎: 973 580 200 - Fax: 973 718 312
info@castelldelremei.com
www.castelldelremei.com

**CASTELL DEL REMEI ODA BLANC 2008 BFB**
chardonnay, macabeo

**91** Colour: bright yellow. Nose: ripe fruit, sweet spices, fragrant herbs. Palate: rich, smoky aftertaste, flavourful, fresh, good acidity.

**CASTELL DEL REMEI BLANC PLANELL 2008 B**
sauvignon blanc, macabeo

**88** Colour: bright straw. Nose: fresh, fresh fruit, expressive, scrubland. Palate: flavourful, fruity, good acidity, balanced, full.

**CASTELL DEL REMEI GOTIM BRU 2007 T**
cabernet sauvignon, tempranillo, merlot, garnacha

**86** Colour: deep cherry. Nose: balsamic herbs, fruit preserve. Palate: fleshy, concentrated, round tannins.

**CASTELL DEL REMEI 1780 2005 T**
cabernet sauvignon, tempranillo, garnacha

**89** Colour: cherry, garnet rim. Nose: characterful, fruit preserve, aged wood nuances, creamy oak, undergrowth. Palate: powerful, flavourful, spirituous.

**CASTELL DEL REMEI ODA 2006 T**
merlot, cabernet sauvignon, tempranillo

**90** Colour: dark-red cherry, bright ochre rim. Nose: fruit liqueur notes, ripe fruit, balsamic herbs, dried herbs, sweet spices. Palate: fleshy, concentrated, full.

## CELLER ANALEC

Crta. s/n. 25341, Nalec (Lleida)
☎: 973 303 190 / 618 139 317
info@analec.net
www.analec.net

ANALEC B ESPUMOSO
**83**

ANALEC RD ESPUMOSO
**84**

ANALEC 2007 T
**86** Colour: bright cherry. Nose: fruit preserve, balsamic herbs, sweet spices. Palate: spirituous, fruity, full.

## CELLER CASA PATAU

Costa del Senyor, s/n
25139 Menarguens (Lleida)
☎: 973 180 367
patau2@eresmas.com
www.casapatau.com

CASA PATAU 2005 TR
cabernet sauvignon 75%, merlot 15%, ull de llebre 10%

**87** Colour: dark-red cherry, garnet rim. Nose: fruit preserve, fruit expression, creamy oak, aromatic coffee. Palate: fleshy, powerful, spirituous.

## CELLER CERCAVINS

Pol. 8 Parcela 17
25340 Verdú (Lleida)
☎: 973 348 114 - Fax: 973 348 114
info@cellercercavins.com
www.cellercercavins.com

GUILLA 2008 BFB

**89** Colour: bright yellow. Nose: powerfull, sweet spices, creamy oak, fragrant herbs, candied fruit. Palate: rich, smoky aftertaste, flavourful, fresh, good acidity.

GUILLAMINA 2008 BFB

**85** Colour: bright yellow. Nose: ripe fruit, sweet spices, creamy oak, fragrant herbs. Palate: rich, smoky aftertaste, flavourful, fresh, good acidity.

BRU DE VERDÚ 2007 T

**87** Colour: bright cherry. Nose: ripe fruit, sweet spices, creamy oak, expressive, scrubland. Palate: flavourful, fruity, toasty, round tannins.

BRU DE VERDÚ 14 2006 T
**84**

## CELLER TORRES DE SANUI, S.L.

Camí Torres de Sanui - La Cerdera s/n
25193 Lleida
☎: 973 050 202 - Fax: 973 050 202
celler@desanui.com

DE SANUI BLANC 2008 B BARRICA
chardonnay 40%, riesling 30%, macabeo 20%, moscatel 10%

**87** Colour: yellow. Nose: scrubland, balsamic herbs, sweet spices. Palate: fruity, fresh, elegant.

DE SANUI BLANC BARRICA 2007 B

**88** Colour: bright yellow. Nose: fragrant herbs, ripe fruit, sweet spices, cocoa bean, creamy oak. Palate: flavourful, powerful, sweetness, rich, fruity.

DE SANUI NEGRE JOVE 2008 T
syrah 35%, garnacha 35%, tempranillo 30%
**80**

DE SANUI NEGRE JOVE 2007 T
syrah, garnacha, ull de llebre
**83**

DE SANUI NEGRE 2006 TC
garncha 35%, syrah 40%, merlot 25%

**86** Colour: dark-red cherry. Nose: fruit liqueur notes, aromatic coffee. Palate: powerful, spirituous, round tannins.

DE SANUI NEGRE 2005 TC
garnacha, syrah, merlot

**85** Colour: dark-red cherry. Nose: dark chocolate, sweet spices, ripe fruit, characterful. Palate: flavourful, powerful, fleshy, toasty.

## CELLER VILA CORONA

Camí els Nerets, s/n
25654 Vilamitjana (Lleida)
☎: 973 652 638 - Fax: 973 652 638
vila-corona@avired.com
www.vilacorona.cat

**VILA CORONA RIESLING 2008 B**
riesling 100%

**87** Colour: bright yellow. Nose: ripe fruit, creamy oak, fragrant herbs, scrubland, characterful. Palate: rich, smoky aftertaste, flavourful, fresh, good acidity.

**LLABUSTES ULL DE LLEBRE 2007 T**
ull de llebre 100%

**85** Colour: deep cherry. Nose: fruit expression, fruit preserve, wild herbs. Palate: fleshy, fruity, full.

**LLABUSTES CABERNET SAUVIGNON 2006 TC**
cabernet sauvignon 100%

**89** Colour: cherry, garnet rim. Nose: ripe fruit, spicy, creamy oak, toasty, complex, balsamic herbs. Palate: powerful, flavourful, toasty, round tannins.

**LLABUSTES MERLOT 2006 T**
merlot 100%

**88** Colour: cherry, garnet rim. Nose: ripe fruit, dry nuts, undergrowth, earthy notes. Palate: fleshy, full, round tannins.

## CÉRVOLES CELLER

Avda. Les Garrigues, 26
25471 La Pobla de Cèrvoles (Lleida)
☎: 973 580 200 - Fax: 973 718 312
info@castelldelremei.com
www.cervoles.com

**CÉRVOLES DOLÇ T**
garnacha, cabernet sauvignon

**85** Colour: cherry, garnet rim. Nose: powerfull, fruit preserve, overripe fruit. Palate: powerful, fleshy, sweet, good acidity.

**CÉRVOLES 2007 T**

**87** Colour: cherry, garnet rim. Nose: medium intensity, ripe fruit, dark chocolate, sweet spices. Palate: flavourful, powerful, fleshy, fruity.

**CÉRVOLES 2006 T**
tempranillo 38%, cabernet sauvignon 32%, garnacha 18%, merlot 12%

**90** Colour: black cherry. Nose: mineral, dry stone, fruit preserve, scrubland. Palate: powerful, full, good structure, round tannins, good acidity.

**CÉRVOLES 2008 BFB**
chardonnay 60%, macabeo 40%

**92** Colour: bright yellow. Nose: powerfull, ripe fruit, sweet spices, fragrant herbs. Palate: rich, smoky aftertaste, flavourful, fresh, good acidity.

2008
BLANC FERMENTAT EN ROURE ALLIER
COSTERS DEL SEGRE | LA POBLA DE CÉRVOLES
LLEIDA | ESPAÑA

Cérvoles

**CÉRVOLES ESTRATS 2005 T**
cabernet sauvignon 45%, tempranillo 28%, garnacha 27%

**93** Colour: dark-red cherry, bright ochre rim. Nose: fruit expression, macerated fruit, earthy notes, undergrowth, mineral, complex. Palate: fleshy, spirituous, flavourful, balsamic, soft tannins.

## COOPERATIVA D'ARTESA DE SEGRE

Ctra. Artesa - Montblanc, km. 1
25730 Artesa de Segre (Lleida)
☎: 973 400 098 - Fax: 973 400 646
celler@coopartesa.com
www.coopartesa.com

**SYMER 365 2008 T**
syrah, merlot                                    8,2€

**84**

**DEL IRIS G**
**VALLS DEL MONTSEC**

## L'OLIVERA

La Plana s/n
25268 Vallbona de les Monges (Lleida)

# DO COSTERS DEL SEGRE

☎: 973 330 276 - Fax: 973 330 276
olivera@olivera.org
www.olivera.org

**MISSENYORA 2008 BFB**
macabeo 100%

**92** Colour: bright straw. Nose: fresh, fresh fruit, white flowers, expressive, scrubland. Palate: flavourful, fruity, good acidity, balanced.

**BLANC DE MARGES 2008 BFB**
parellada 66%, viognier 33%, moscatel %, chardonnay %, sauvignon blanc %

**90** Colour: bright yellow. Nose: ripe fruit, sweet spices, creamy oak, grassy. Palate: rich, smoky aftertaste, flavourful, fresh, good acidity.

**EIXADERS 2008 BFB**
chardonnay 100%

**89** Colour: bright straw. Nose: fresh, fresh fruit, expressive, balsamic herbs. Palate: flavourful, fruity, good acidity, balanced.

**BLANC DE SERÈ 2008 B**
macabeo 60%, parellada 30%, chardonnay 10%

**88** Colour: bright straw. Nose: fresh, fresh fruit, white flowers, expressive. Palate: flavourful, fruity, good acidity, balanced.

**AGALIU 2008 BFB**
macabeo 100%

**87** Colour: straw. Nose: balsamic herbs, grapey, white flowers. Palate: full, flavourful.

**RASIM VIMADUR 2007 B**
garnacha blanca, cartoixa, malvasia          21€

**88** Colour: bright golden. Nose: citrus fruit, honeyed notes, dry nuts, scrubland, waxy notes. Palate: sweet, fruity, flavourful, good acidity, creamy.

**BLANC DE ROURE 2007 B**
parellada 30%, macabeo 60%, chardonnay 10%     HHHH7,2€

**87** Colour: bright yellow. Nose: macerated fruit, balsamic herbs, fine lees. Palate: fresh, flavourful.

**RASIM VIMADUR 2006 T BARRICA**
garnacha, syrah, merlot          HHH17€

**90** Colour: black cherry, garnet rim. Nose: fruit liqueur notes, mineral, aromatic coffee, dark chocolate. Palate: powerful, good structure, round tannins, pruney, roasted-coffee aftertaste.

## MAS BLANCH I JOVÉ

Paratge Llinars, Pol. 9, Parc. 129

25471 La Pobla de Cérvoles (Lleida)
☎: 973 050 018 - Fax: 973 391 151
jove.sara@gmail.com
www.masblanchijove.com

**SAÓ BLANC 2007 BFB**
macabeo 100%

**89** Colour: bright straw. Nose: fresh, fresh fruit, expressive, smoky, balsamic herbs. Palate: flavourful, fruity, good acidity, balanced, rich.

**SAÓ EXPRESSIU 2006 T**
garnacha 55%, cabernet sauvignon 25%, tempranillo 20%

**90** Colour: deep cherry. Nose: fruit expression, macerated fruit, violet drops, balsamic herbs. Palate: fleshy, flavourful, full, round tannins.

**SAÓ ABRIVAT 2006 T**
tempranillo 40%, garnacha 35%, cabernet sauvignon 15%, merlot 10%

**89** Colour: bright cherry. Nose: ripe fruit, dry nuts, dried herbs, spicy. Palate: fleshy, flavourful, round tannins.

## MONESTIR DEL TALLAT

Ctra. Reus-El Morell, Km. 7,8
43760 El Morell (Tarragona)
☎: 977 840 655 - Fax: 977 842 146
vermut@vermutyzaguirre.com
www.vermutyzaguirre.com

**MONESTIR DEL TALLAT MERLOT 2006 T**
**82**

**MONESTIR DEL TALLAT CABERNET SAUVIGNON 2004 TR**
**82**

ERMITA DELS DIUMENGES

## RAIMAT

Ctra. Lleida s/n
25111 Raimat (Lleida)
☎: 973 724 000 - Fax: 973 724 061
v.sanchez@codorniu.es
www.raimat.es

**RAIMAT ABADÍA BLANC DE BLANC 2008 B**
chardonnay, albariño

**89** Colour: bright straw. Nose: fresh, fresh fruit, white flowers, expressive. Palate: flavourful, fruity, good acidity, balanced, good structure.

**RAIMAT VIÑA 24 ALBARIÑO 2008 B**
albariño

**88** Colour: bright straw. Nose: citrus fruit, grassy, elegant, ripe fruit. Palate: round, flavourful, fruity, fresh.

**RAIMAT VIÑA 27 2008 B**
chardonnay

**88** Colour: pale. Nose: mineral, ripe fruit, elegant, tropical fruit. Palate: full, rich, flavourful, fruity aftestaste, round.

**RAIMAT VIÑA 32 CABERNET 2006 TC**
cabernet sauvignon

**88** Colour: deep cherry, orangey edge. Nose: fruit preserve, green pepper, creamy oak, spicy, dark chocolate. Palate: unctuous, balanced, good acidity, round tannins, fruity, fleshy.

**RAIMAT VIÑA 54 SHIRAZ 2006 TC**
syrah

**87** Colour: dark-red cherry, orangey edge. Nose: fruit preserve, creamy oak, sweet spices, smoky. Palate: fruity, fleshy, flavourful, varietal, slightly dry, soft tannins.

**RAIMAT VIÑA 19 MERLOT 2006 TC**
merlot

**86** Colour: cherry, garnet rim. Nose: ripe fruit, spicy, creamy oak. Palate: unctuous, fruity, good acidity, soft tannins.

**RAIMAT ABADÍA 2006 CRIANZA**
cabernet sauvignon, merlot, tempranillo

**87** Colour: cherry, garnet rim. Nose: fruit preserve, red berry notes, sweet spices. Palate: flavourful, fruity, grainy tannins, warm.

**RAIMAT GRAN BRUT BR**
chardonnay, pinot noir

**91** Colour: bright golden. Nose: elegant, expressive, dry nuts, candied fruit. Palate: flavourful, fruity, fresh, fleshy.

**RAIMAT CHARDONNAY BR**
chardonnay, pinot noir

**88** Colour: bright straw. Nose: medium intensity, fresh fruit, fine lees, floral, grassy. Palate: fresh, fruity, flavourful, good acidity.

**RAIMAT BN**
chardonnay, pinot noir

**90** Colour: bright golden. Nose: fine lees, dry nuts, complex, sweet spices, faded flowers. Palate: powerful, flavourful, good acidity, fine bead, fine bitter notes.

## TOMÀS CUSINÉ

Plaça Sant Sebastià, 13
25457 El Vilosell (Lleida)

☎: 973 176 029 - Fax: 973 175 945
info@tomascusine.com
www.tomascusine.com

**AUZELLS 2008 B**
macabeo, sauvignon blanc, parellada, chardonnay, moscatel, others

**93** Colour: bright straw. Nose: varietal, expressive, complex, grapey. Palate: fresh, fruity, rich, powerful, flavourful, sweetness.

**VILOSELL 2007 T**
tempranillo 62%, merlot 13%, cabernet sauvignon 14%, syrah 5%, garnacha 3%, cariñena 3%

**91** Colour: deep cherry. Nose: fresh fruit, violet drops, creamy oak, undergrowth. Palate: creamy, toasty, mineral, fruity, fresh, powerful.

**GEOL 2006 T**
merlot 45%, cabernet sauvignon 40%, cabernet franc 5%, marselan 5%

**92** Colour: very deep cherry. Nose: ripe fruit, sweet spices, creamy oak, expressive, roasted coffee. Palate: fruity, round tannins, powerful, spirituous, toasty.

## VALL DE BALDOMAR

Ctra. de Alós de Balaguer, s/n
25737 Baldomar (Lleida)
☎: 973 402 205 - Fax: 932 104 040
baldomar@smc.es

**CRISTIARI 2008 B**

**89** Colour: bright yellow. Nose: powerfull, ripe fruit, sweet spices, fragrant herbs, fine lees. Palate: rich, flavourful, fresh, good acidity, balsamic.

**CRISTIARI 2008 RD**

**81**

**CRISTIARI D'ALÒS MERLOT 2008 T ROBLE**

**87** Colour: bright cherry. Nose: ripe fruit, sweet spices, creamy oak, expressive, balsamic herbs. Palate: flavourful, fruity, toasty, round tannins.

**BALDOMÀ SELECCIÓ 2008 T**

**85** Colour: bright cherry. Nose: ripe fruit, sweet spices. Palate: fruity, round tannins, fleshy.

## VINYA ELS VILARS

Camí de Puiggrós, s/n
25140 Arbeca (Lleida)
☎: 973 149 144 - Fax: 973 160 719

vinyavilars@terra.es
www.vinyaelsvilars.com

**VILARS 2006 T**
merlot 50%, syrah 50%

**87** Colour: dark-red cherry. Nose: fruit preserve, earthy notes, aromatic coffee, expressive. Palate: concentrated, powerful, harsh oak tannins.

**LEIX 2006 T**
syrah 100%

**86** Colour: deep cherry, purple rim. Nose: aromatic coffee, spicy, fruit preserve, earthy notes. Palate: fleshy, powerful, round tannins.

## VINYA L'HEREU DE SERÓ

Molí s/n
25739 Seró (Artesa de Segre) (Lleida)
☎: 639 311 175 - Fax: 973 400 472
vinyalhereu@vinyalhereu.com
www.vinyalhereu.com

**PETIT GREALÓ 2006 T**
syrah 40%, merlot 30%, cabernet sauvignon 30%

**87** Colour: dark-red cherry. Nose: cocoa bean, sweet spices, fruit preserve, mineral. Palate: powerful, good structure, powerful tannins.

**FLOR DE GREALÓ 2005 T**
merlot 40%, syrah 30%, cabernet sauvignon 30%

**87** Colour: black cherry, garnet rim. Nose: roasted coffee, undergrowth, fruit preserve. Palate: fleshy, spirituous, powerful, round tannins.

<u>SOME OTHER WINERIES WITHIN THE DO:</u>

**CAR VINÍCOLAS REUNIDAS S.A.**
**CASA PARDET**
**CELLER COMALATS**
**CELLER TEIXIDÓ**

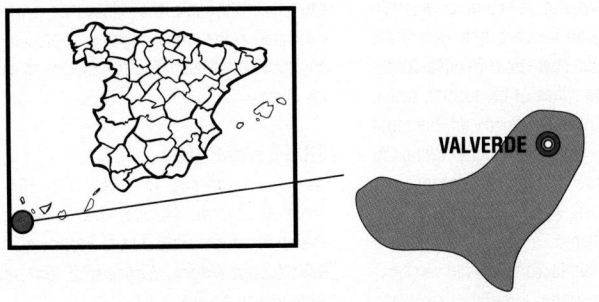

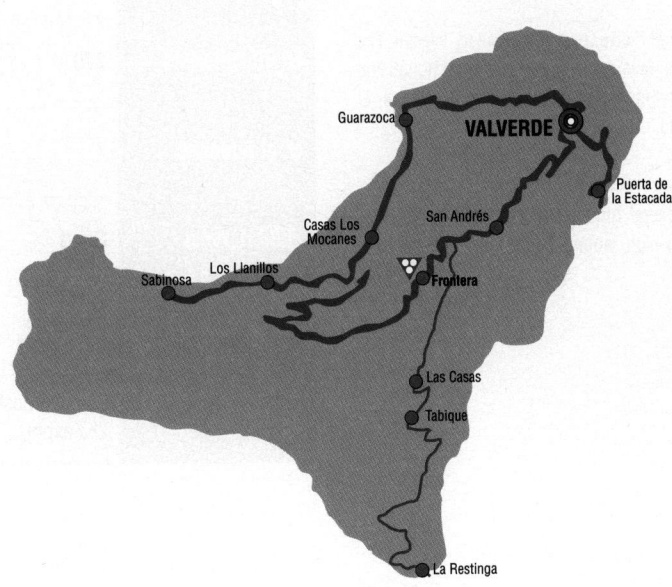

☒ Consejo Regulador
● DO Boundary

## NEWS

The wines from El Hierro ara more and more abundant, thanks to the promotional skills of its two main wineries: the cooperatives of Frontera an Tanajara, both part of the Viñátigo group, which has also interests in Ycoden-Daute-Isora. Of the two coops, the wines of the former, which controls 95% of the vineyard of El Hierro– are the most representative, although we have given higher ratings to those from Tanajara, that show overall more elegance and terroir expression, particularly with single-variety wines from vijariego and baboso negro. Finally, the indigenous verijadiego or vijariego (in both its white and red versions) is shining as the local star grape, a variety that yields complex wines with a lovely structure. On the other hand, the blends are far more discreet.

## LOCATION

On the island of El Hierro, part of the Canary Islands. The production area covers the whole island, although the main growing regions are Valle del Golfo, Sabinosa, El Pinar and Echedo.

## CLIMATE

Fairly mild in general, although higher levels of humidity are recorded in high mountainous regions. Rainfall is relatively low.

## SOIL

Volcanic in origin, with a good water retention and storage capacity. Although the vineyards were traditionally cultivated in the higher regions, at present most of them are found at low altitudes, resulting in an early ripening of the grapes.

## GRAPE VARIETIES:

**White:** *Verijadiego* (majority with 50% of all white varieties), *Listán Blanca, Bremajuelo, Uval (Gual), Pedro Ximénez, Baboso* and *Moscatel*.
**Red:** *Listán Negro, Negramoll, Baboso Negro* and *Verijadiego Negro*.

| | |
|---|---|
| Hectares of Vineyard | 207 |
| Nº Viticulturists | 270 |
| Nº of Bodegas | 7 |
| 2008 Harvest | Good |
| 2007 Production | 215,000 l. |
| Marketing | 98% domestic 2% export |

**CONSEJO REGULADOR**
Oficina de Agricultura
El Matorral, s/n. 38911 Frontera (Sta. Cruz de Tenerife)
☎: 922 556 064 / 922 559 744 - Fax: 922 559 691
@doelhierro@hotmail.com
www.elhierro.tv

## GENERAL CHARACTERISTICS OF THE WINES:

| | |
|---|---|
| **WHITES** | These are the most characteristic wines of the island. They are produced mainly from the *Vijariego* and *Listán Blanco* varieties. They are straw yellow, quite fresh and fruity and, on occasions, they have notes of tropical fruit. |
| **ROSÉS** | These are characterised by their orangey raspberry colour and are quite fresh and fruity. |
| **REDS** | These are characterised by their good quality. Likewise, they are quite full-bodied and fruity. |

## 2008 VINTAGE RATING:

## GOOD

## BODEGAS VIÑÁTIGO

Cabo Verde, s/n
38440 La Guancha (Tenerife)
☎: 922 828 768 - Fax: 922 829 936
vinatigo@vinatigo.com
www.vinatigo.com

TANAJARA VIJARIEGO NEGRO 2007 T
vijariego 100%

**88** Colour: cherry, garnet rim. Nose: elegant, ripe fruit, spicy, cocoa bean, mineral. Palate: balanced, flavourful, spicy, fine tannins.

TANAJARA BABOSO NEGRO 2007 T
baboso negro 100%

**85** Colour: pale ruby, brick rim edge. Nose: spicy, smoky, toasty, fruit liqueur notes. Palate: flavourful, fleshy, fine bitter notes, warm.

## SDAD. COOPERATIVA DEL CAMPO FRONTERA VINÍCOLA INSULAR

El Matorral, 55
38911 Frontera (Tenerife)
☎: 922 556 016 - Fax: 922 556 042
coopfrontera@cooperativafrontera.com
www.cooperativafrontera.com

VIÑA FRONTERA 2008 B
Vigiriego 60%, listán blanco 40%

**86** Colour: pale. Nose: floral, fresh fruit. Palate: flavourful, fruity, fresh.

VIÑA FRONTERA AFRUTADO 2008 B
Vigiriego 60%, listán blanco 30%, gual, baboso and bremajuelo 10%

**82**

VIÑA FRONTERA VERIJADIEGO 2007 T
Vigiriego 100%

**83**

VIÑA FRONTERA 2007 T
listán negro 85%, negramoll 15%

**81**

VIÑA FRONTERA 2005 T

**84**

GRAN SALMOR 2005 BLANCO DULCE RESERVA
bremajuelo 60%, Vigiriego 30%, gual 10%

**88** Colour: light mahogany. Nose: powerfull, candied fruit, fruit liqueur notes, honeyed notes, toasty. Palate: flavourful, fleshy, sweet, spicy.

## SOME OTHER WINERIES WITHIN THE DO:

**BODEGAS TANAJARA S.L.**
**EL TESORO**
**UWE URBACH**

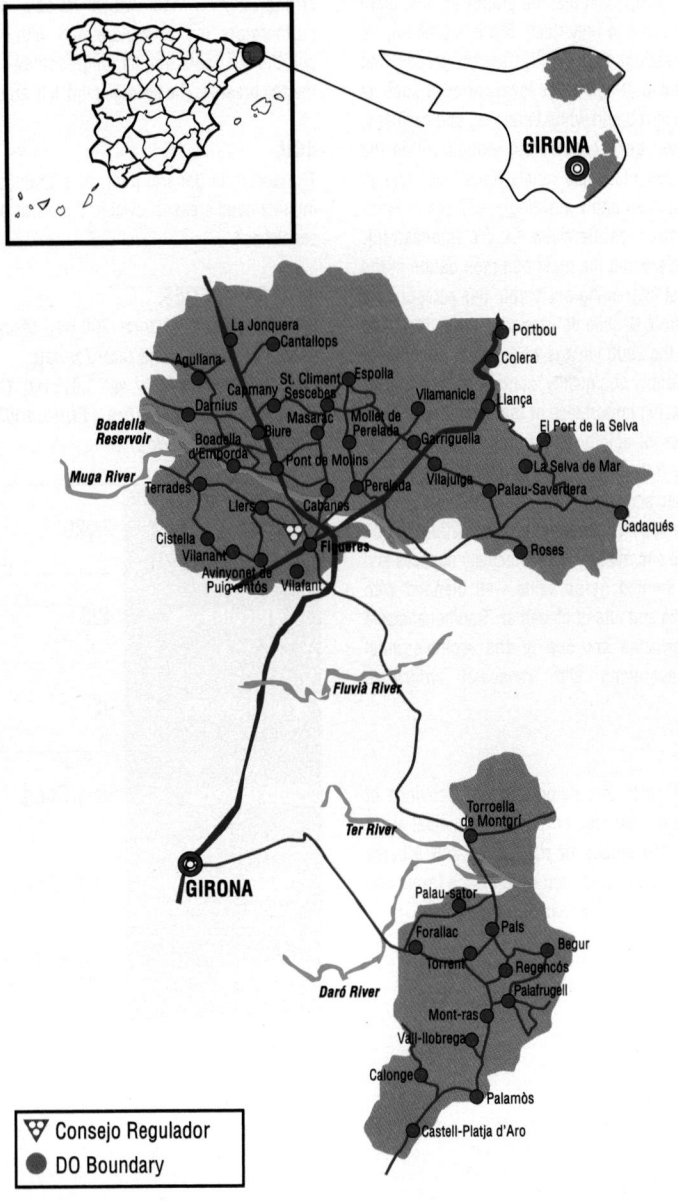

GIRONA

Portbou
Colera
Llança
La Jonquera
Cantallops
Agullana
St. Climent
Sescebes
Espolla
Vilamanicle
Canmany
Darnius
Masarac
Mollet de
Perelada
El Port de la Selva
Boadella
Reservoir
Biure
Garriguella
Boadella
d'Emporda
Muga River
Pont de Molins
Vilajuïga
La Selva de Mar
Palau-Saverdera
Terrades
Perelada
Cadaqués
Llers
Cabanes
Cistella
Figueres
Roses
Vilanant
Avinyonet de
Puigventós
Vilafant

Fluvià River

Ter River

Torroella
de Montgrí

GIRONA

Palau-sator
Forallac
Pals
Begur
Torrent
Regencós
Palafrugell
Daró River
Mont-ras
Vall-llobrega
Calonge
Palamòs
Castell-Platja d'Aro

▽ Consejo Regulador
● DO Boundary

## NEWS

Empordà has every feature needed to become a truly singular wine region, given that the grapes planted there need lots of sunshine to fully ripen. But it is probably its huge varietal catalogue of mostly foreign grapes that hinders the coming of age of the local varieties such as garnacha (both in red and white versions) and cariñena, which have never been considered enough within the region. When made into single-variety wines, even foreign grapes like syrah can show amazingly well (as in Finca Garbet) or Castillo de Perelada Ex Ex (monastrell), although blends are still the most common option in the region. The most interesting one within this category are the renderings from Castillo de Perelada, Masía Serra and Oliver Contí. In the 2008 vintage white wines show at its best, both in quantity and quality, something that tells us about the increasing importance of that category, but the rains left a trace of acidity and a lack of balance that overshadow the fruit expression. The same happened to rosé wines: closed and lacking fruit. Good also the reserva wines from previous vintages, even from 2002, which show meaty, rich and mineral, with chocolaty nuances and notes of ripe, sunned grape skins well blended with creamy oak notes and lots of character. Traditional sweet wines from garnacha are one of the region's most treasured wines along with moscatel unfortified renderings.

## LOCATION

In the far north west of Catalonia, in the province of Girona. The production area covers 40 municipal areas and is situated the slopes of the Rodes and Alberes mountain ranges forming an arch which leads from Cape Creus to what is known as the Garrotxa d'Empordà.

## CLIMATE

The climatology is conditioned by the 'Tramontana', a strong north wind which affects the vineyards. Furthermore, the winters are mild, with hardly any frost, and the summers hot, although somewhat tempered by the sea breezes. The average rainfall is around 600 mm.

## SOIL

The soil is in general poor, of a granitic nature in the mountainous areas, alluvial in the plains and slaty on the coastal belt.

## GRAPE VARIETIES:

**White:** *Garnacha Blanca* (200 Ha), *Macabeo* (100 Ha), *Moscatel*, *Xarel·lo* and *Chardonnay*.
**Red:** *Cariñena* (majority with 1,815 Ha), *Garnacha Tinta* (150 Ha), *Ull de Llebre* (*Tempranillo*), *Cabernet Sauvignon* and *Merlot*.

| | |
|---|---|
| Hectares of Vineyard | 2,020 |
| Nº Viticulturists | 423 |
| Nº of Bodegas | 45 |
| 2008 Harvest | Very Good |
| 2007 Production | 5,219,254 l. |
| Marketing | 93.5% domestic 6.5% export |

**CONSEJO REGULADOR**
Avda. Marignane, 2. Apto. Correos 186
17600 Figueres (Gerona)
☎: 972 507 513 - Fax: 972 510 058
@ doempcb@teleline.es

## GENERAL CHARACTERISTICS OF THE WINES:

| | |
|---|---|
| **WHITES** | Those produced from autochthonous varieties are fresh and flavourful on the palate and persistent; their nose is reminiscent of hay and apples. Single variety wines from Chardonnay are also produced. |
| **ROSÉS** | These are pink-raspberry coloured with a fruity nose and are relatively intense, fresh and light. |
| **REDS** | Novell red wines are produced (they are marketed immediately after the harvest to be consumed within the year) with a deep cherry-red colour, easy drinking with good acidity levels and a red berry nose. The Crianza wines are aromatic with notes of spices; on the palate they are flavourful and pleasant to drink. |
| **LICOROSOS** | Traditional wines of the region produced from *Garnacha*. Red amber in colour, the nose has notes of Mistela and Rancio; on the palate they stand out for their sweetness and stickiness. |

## 2008 VINTAGE RATING:

## GOOD

## AV BODEGUERS

Sant Baldiri s/n
17781 Vilamaniscle (Girona)
☎: 676 231 199
info@avbodeguers.com
www.avbodeguers.com

NEREUS 2008 T BARRICA
merlot, syrah, garnacha blanca

**76**

## BODEGAS GELAMA

Estació, 6
17493 Vilajuiga ()
☎: 972 530 031 - Fax: 972 530 031
roger_rius@yahoo.es

GELAMA 2008 RD
garnacha 100%

**80**

GELAMA SAMSÓ 2008 T
cariñena 100%

**78**

## BODEGAS TROBAT

Castelló, 10
17780 Garriguella (Gerona)
☎: 972 530 092 - Fax: 972 552 530
toni.madern@bmark.es
www.bodegastrobat.com

NOBLE CHARDONNAY BLANC DE BLANCS 2008 B
chardonnay 100%

**86** Colour: straw. Nose: fresh, varietal, characterful. Palate: good structure, fruity, rich, flavourful.

AMAT MERLOT 2008 RD
merlot 100%

**84**

AMAT "ULL DE LLEBRE" 2008 T
tempranillo 100%

**83**

AMAT TEMPRANILLO 2006 T
tempranillo 100%

**82**

NOBLE CABERNET SAUVIGNON 2005 T
cabernet sauvignon 80%, garnacha 20%

**82**

TROBAT

## CASTELL DE BIART S.A.

Carretera de Vilarnadal - Perelada, km. 1,8
17763 Masarac (Girona)
☎: 972 510 008 - Fax: 972 510 008
info@castelldebiart.es
www.castelldebiart.es

CASTELL DE BIART SAUVIGNON BLANC 2007 B
sauvignon blanc 100%

**75**

CASTELL DE BIART 2003 T

**85** Colour: cherry, garnet rim. Nose: powerfull, ripe fruit, aged wood nuances, fruit liqueur notes. Palate: fleshy, spicy, round tannins.

CASTELL DE BIART GARNATXA DE L'EMPORDÀ T

**88** Colour: pale ruby, brick rim edge. Nose: toasty, rancio notes, aged wood nuances, spicy, cigar. Palate: fleshy, flavourful, full, good structure.

DOLÇ DE BIART GARNATXA DE L'EMPORDÀ MISTELA

**89** Colour: dark-red cherry. Nose: fruit preserve, sweet spices, balsamic herbs, undergrowth. Palate: powerful, full, concentrated, good acidity.

PLA DE BIART
GENI DE BIART

## CASTILLO DE CAPMANY

Plaza del Fort, 5
17750 Capmany (Girona)
☎: 972 549 043 - Fax: 972 549 043
jlmoll@terra.es
www.castillodecapmany.com

CASTILLO OLIVARES 2005 T

**85** Colour: cherry, garnet rim. Nose: powerfull, ripe fruit, toasty, sweet spices, dark chocolate. Palate: flavourful, powerful, fleshy, fine bitter notes.

MOLL DE ALBA 2003 TR

**85** Colour: cherry, garnet rim. Nose: fine reductive notes, fruit preserve, spicy. Palate: flavourful, fruity, fine bitter notes, round tannins.

## CASTILLO DE PERELADA

Plaça del Carmen, 1
17491 Perelada (Girona)
☎: 972 538 011 - Fax: 972 538 277
perelada@castilloperelada.com
www.castilloperelada.com

**CASTILLO PERELADA CHARDONNAY 2008 B**
chardonnay 100%

**90** Colour: pale. Nose: fruit expression, fresh fruit, varietal, elegant, complex, fragrant herbs, smoky. Palate: fruity, powerful, flavourful, complex, creamy.

**CASTILLO PERELADA GARNATXA 2008 B**
garnacha blanca 100%

**89** Colour: straw. Nose: varietal, medium intensity, complex, fresh fruit. Palate: light-bodied, fruity, fresh, flavourful.

**CASTILLO DE PERELADA SAUVIGNON BLANC 2008 B**
sauvignon blanc 100%

**86** Colour: straw. Nose: powerfull, varietal, fresh, fruit expression. Palate: fruity, light-bodied, flavourful.

**CASTILLO PERELADA FINCA LA GARRIGA 2008 B**

**86** Colour: straw. Nose: closed, varietal, medium intensity. Palate: fruity, fresh, flavourful.

**CASTILLO PERELADA BLANC DE BLANCS 2008 B**
macabeo 50%, garnacha blanca 25%, chardonnay 20%,
sauvignon blanc 5%

**84**

**CASTILLO PERELADA CABERNET SAUVIGNON 2008 RD**
cabernet sauvignon 100%

**87** Colour: rose, purple rim. Nose: ripe fruit, varietal, fresh. Palate: powerful, flavourful, fruity, fresh.

**CASTILLO PERELADA 2008 RD**
garnacha 40%, cariñena 30%, tempranillo 20%, syrah 10%

**85** Colour: rose. Nose: fresh fruit, violet drops. Palate: light-bodied, flavourful, fruity, fresh.

**CASTILLO PERELADA FINCA MALAVEÏNA 2007 T**
merlot 40%, cabernet sauvignon 25%, syrah 20%, garnacha 15%

**87** Colour: deep cherry. Nose: medium intensity, woody, aged wood nuances, roasted coffee, candied fruit. Palate: fruity, flavourful, toasty.

**CASTILLO PERELADA LA GARRIGA 2007 T**
samsó 100%

**79**

**CASTILLO PERELADA CABERNET SAUVIGNON 2006 T**
cabernet sauvignon 100%

**88** Colour: cherry, garnet rim. Nose: ripe fruit, sweet spices, balanced. Palate: fruity, fleshy, round tannins.

**CASTILLO DE PERELADA 3 FINCAS 2006 TC**
garnacha 30%, cariñena 35%, cabernet sauvignon 25%, merlot 10%

**88** Colour: deep cherry. Nose: ripe fruit, dry stone, creamy oak, toasty. Palate: fleshy, powerful, flavourful, fruity.

**CASTILLO PERELADA FINCA ESPOLLA 2006 T**
monastrell 60%, syrah 40%

**87** Colour: bright cherry, garnet rim. Nose: balanced, warm, fruit liqueur notes. Palate: powerful, balanced, round tannins.

**CASTILLO DE PERELADA EX EX 7 2005 T**
monastrell 100%

**93** Colour: cherry, garnet rim. Nose: powerfull, expressive, aromatic coffee, dark chocolate, creamy oak, ripe fruit. Palate: flavourful, fleshy, fine bitter notes, round tannins.

**FINCA GARBET 2005 TR**
syrah 100%

**91** Colour: deep cherry. Nose: powerfull, complex, fruit expression, aromatic coffee, creamy oak. Palate: complex, full, powerful, flavourful, roasted-coffee aftertaste.

**CASTILLO DE PERELADA 5 FINCAS 2005 TR**
merlot 40%, garnacha 20%, cabernet sauvignon 15%, syrah 15%, tempranillo 5%, cabernet franc %

**91** Colour: deep cherry. Nose: fruit expression, ripe fruit, mineral, spicy, toasty. Palate: powerful, flavourful, spirituous, creamy, roasted-coffee aftertaste.

GRAN CLAUSTRO DE CASTILLO PERELADA 2004 T
cabernet sauvignon 50%, merlot 20%, garnacha 15%, samsó 15%

**90** Colour: cherry, garnet rim. Nose: ripe fruit, spicy, toasty. Palate: powerful, flavourful, toasty, round tannins.

CASTILLO PERELADA GARNATXA DE L'EMPORDÀ
garnacha roja 80%, garnacha blanca 20%

**92** Colour: mahogany, iodine, amber rim. Nose: fruit preserve, dry nuts, aged wood nuances, spicy, toasty, cigar, mineral. Palate: elegant, fine bitter notes, unctuous, good acidity, creamy, long.

## CELLER ARCHÉ PAGÈS

Sant Climent, 31
17750 Capmany (Girona)
☎: 972 549 229 - Fax: 972 549 229
bonfill@capmany.com
www.cellerarchepages.com

SÀTIRS 2008 B
macabeo 100%

**87** Colour: straw. Nose: fresh fruit, medium intensity, varietal. Palate: powerful, flavourful, fruity.

SÀTIRS 2008 RD
cabernet sauvignon, garnacha, merlot

**81**

SÀTIRS 2008 T

**70**

CARTESIUS 2005 T
garnacha 50%, cabernet sauvignon 30%, merlot 20%

**90** Colour: cherry, garnet rim. Nose: powerfull, ripe fruit, sweet spices, creamy oak. Palate: flavourful, powerful, fleshy, round tannins.

BONFILL 2005 T
garnacha 70%, cabernet sauvignon 30%

**90** Colour: cherry, garnet rim. Nose: spicy, creamy oak, toasty, complex, earthy notes, ripe fruit. Palate: powerful, flavourful, toasty, round tannins.

SÀTIRS 2004 T
garnacha 40%, cabernet sauvignon 30%, merlot 30%

**84**

CARTESIUS 2004
garnacha 50%, merlot 30%, cabernet sauvignon 20%

**88** Colour: cherry, garnet rim. Nose: ripe fruit, medium intensity, caramel, cocoa bean. Palate: fruity, balanced, fruity aftestaste, spicy.

## CELLER CAN SAIS

Raval de Dalt, 10
17253 Vall-llobrega (Girona)
☎: 972 318 033
correu@cellercansais.com
www.cellercansais.com

CAN SAIS MESTRAL 2008 B
macabeo 65%, garnacha blanca 35%, malvasia 5%

**80**

CAN SAIS ENCANTERI 2003 B
malvasia 100%

**85** Colour: light mahogany. Nose: rancio notes, cigar, roasted almonds, varnish. Palate: flavourful, spirituous, round, spicy, fine solera notes.

CAN SAIS GREGAL 2008 RD
garnacha 50%, merlot 50%

**82**

CAN SAIS TEMPTACIÓ 2008 T
ull de llebre 100%

**78**

CAN SAIS MIGJORN 2007 T
samsó 100%

**74**

CAN SAIS SELECCIÓ 2005 T
ull de llebre 55%, samsó 25%, merlot 15%, garnacha 5%

**82**

CAN SAIS SUM 2004 T
samsó 50%, ull de llebre 25%, merlot 25%

## 83

**CAN SAIS PRIVILEGI 2007 TINTO DULCE**
garnacha 100%

**87** Colour: deep cherry. Nose: grapey, fruit preserve, red berry notes, smoky, floral. Palate: sweet, rich, flavourful, round tannins.

## CELLER COOPERATIU D'ESPOLLA

Carretera Roses, s/n
17753 Espolla (Girona)
☎: 972 563 049 - Fax: 972 563 178
ccespolla@telefonica.es

**MUSCAT D'EMPORDÀ ESPOLLA 2008 B**
moscatel 100%

**87** Colour: golden. Nose: powerfull, floral, honeyed notes, candied fruit, fragrant herbs. Palate: flavourful, sweet, fresh, fruity, good acidity, long.

**CASTELL DE PANISSARS 2007 BFB**
moscatel 100%

## 83

**CASTELL DE PANISSARS 2008 RD**
merlot 100%

## 80

**CASTELL DE PANISSARS 2006 TC**
samsó 40%, garnacha 30%, ull de llebre 30%

## 83

**CLOS DE LES DÒMINES 2005 TR**
merlot 45%, cabernet sauvignon 35%, samsó 20%

**88** Colour: deep cherry, orangey edge. Nose: powerfull, ripe fruit, toasty, dark chocolate, aged wood nuances. Palate: flavourful, powerful, fleshy, spicy.

**GARNATXA D'EMPORDÀ ESPOLLA DULCE NATURAL GRAN RESERVA**
garnacha blanca 65%, garnacha roja 35%

**87** Colour: light mahogany, iodine. Nose: dry nuts, aged wood nuances, spicy, roasted almonds. Palate: powerful, flavourful, spirituous, round, good acidity.

## CELLER GENERI

Plaça Teresa Palleja, 3
17707 Agullana (Girona)
☎: 972 535 505 - Fax: 972 535 505
generiagallana@gmail.com

**PRAT D'EGNA NEGRE 2004 T ROBLE**
merlot, cabernet sauvignon

## 84

**PRAT D'EGNA NEGRE 2005**

## 84

## CELLER MARIA PAGÈS

Pujada, 6
17750 Capmany (Girona)
☎: 972 549 160 - Fax: 972 549 160
cellermpages@terra.es
www.cellermariapages.com

**SERRASAGUÉ VINYA DE HORT 2008 B**
garnacha blanca 65%, chardonnay 20%, moscatel 15%

## 76

**SERRASAGUÉ 2008 RD**
cabernet franc 66%, cabernet sauvignon 33%

**86** Colour: rose, purple rim. Nose: red berry notes, fresh fruit, violet drops, varietal, powerfull, expressive. Palate: sweetness, powerful, flavourful, ripe fruit.

**SERRASAGUÉ 2005 TC**
cabernet sauvignon 50%, garnacha 35%, cabernet franc 15%

**86** Colour: dark-red cherry, orangey edge. Nose: macerated fruit, medium intensity, creamy oak, cocoa bean. Palate: fruity, flavourful, round tannins, spicy.

**SERRASAGUÉ 2004 TC**
cabernet sauvignon 50%, garnacha 35%, cabernet franc 15%

**87** Colour: very deep cherry, garnet rim. Nose: ripe fruit, expressive, spicy, dark chocolate. Palate: ripe fruit, toasty, balanced, powerful.

**GARNATXA D'EMPORDÀ MARÍA PAGÈS 2007 RESERVA**
garnacha blanca 50%, garnacha 50%

**88** Colour: mahogany. Nose: fruit liqueur notes, dry nuts, aged wood nuances, caramel. Palate: unctuous, good acidity, full, flavourful, fine solera notes.

**GARNATXA D'EMPORDÀ MARÍA PAGÈS VINO DULCE NATURAL RESERVA**
garnacha blanca, garnacha

**85** Colour: light mahogany, amber. Nose: rancio notes, toasty, tobacco, fine reductive notes, fruit liqueur notes, fruit liqueur notes. Palate: creamy, flavourful, rich, sweetness.

## CELLER MARTÍ FABRA

Barrio Vic, 26
17751 Sant Climent Sescebes (Girona)
☎: 972 563 011 - Fax: 972 563 867
info@cellermartifabra.com

**VERD ALBERA 2008 B**
garnacha blanca 60%, moscatel 30%, garnacha rosada 5%, chardonnay 5%

**88** Colour: straw. Nose: complex, elegant, fresh, fragrant herbs, medium intensity. Palate: fresh, fruity, flavourful.

**MASÍA CARRERAS 2007 BFB**
cariñena blanca 40%, cariñena rosada 30%, garnacha blanca 10%, garnacha rosada 10%, picapoll 10%

**90** Colour: bright yellow. Nose: smoky, scrubland, fruit expression, fresh fruit, complex, varietal. Palate: elegant, round, powerful, flavourful, complex, good acidity, smoky aftertaste.

**FLOR D'ALBERA 2007 BFB**
moscatel 100%

**88** Colour: bright yellow. Nose: varietal, powerfull, complex, fruit expression, smoky. Palate: powerful, flavourful, slightly acidic.

**MASÍA PAIRAL CAN CARRERAS MOSCAT 2006 B**
moscatel 100%

**88** Colour: golden. Nose: powerfull, honeyed notes, candied fruit, spicy, dried flowers. Palate: flavourful, sweet, fresh, fruity, good acidity, long.

**LLADONER 2008 RD**
garnacha 100%

**80**

**MARTÍ FABRA SELECCIÓ VINYES VELLES 2006 T ROBLE**
garnacha 70%, cariñena 10%, tempranillo 10%, syrah 5%, cabernet sauvignon 5%

**86** Colour: dark-red cherry. Nose: toasty, honeyed notes, macerated fruit. Palate: sweetness, fleshy, powerful, flavourful.

**MASÍA CARRERAS NEGRE 2006 T**
garnacha 50%, cariñena 35%, tempranillo 5%, syrah 5%, cabernet sauvignon 5%

**86** Colour: deep cherry. Nose: smoky, woody, ripe fruit. Palate: spirituous, flavourful, oaky.

**MASÍA PAIRAL CAN CARRERAS GARNATXA DE L'EMPORDÀ**
garnacha blanca, garnacha rosada, garnacha

**84**

## CELLER MARTÍN FAIXÓ

Ctra. de Roses a Cadaqués
17488 Cadaqués (Girona)
☎: 972 159 401
info@cellermartinfaixo.com
www.cellermartinfaixo.com

**PERAFITA PICAPOLL 2008 B**
picapoll 100%

**78**

**PERAFITA ROSAT 2008 RD**
cabernet sauvignon 67%, garnacha 33%

**87** Colour: salmon. Nose: ripe fruit, varietal, fresh. Palate: powerful, flavourful, fruity, fresh, good acidity.

**PERAFITA 2006 TC**
merlot 55%, garnacha 35%, cabernet sauvignon 10%

**85** Colour: bright cherry, garnet rim. Nose: ripe fruit, sweet spices, tar. Palate: harsh oak tannins, powerful.

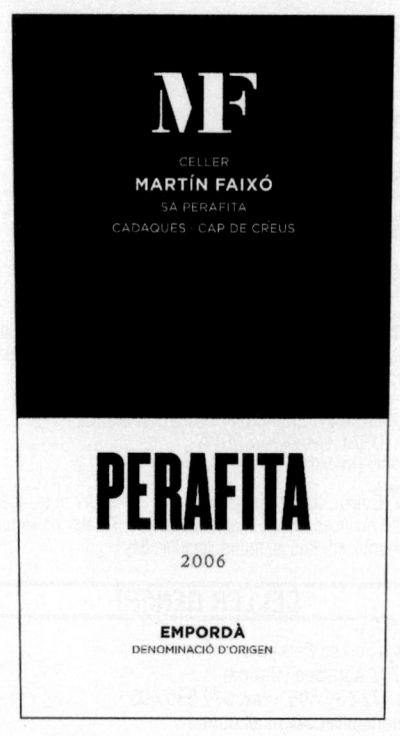

CADAC 2005 TR

**85** Colour: deep cherry. Nose: sweet spices, woody, ripe fruit. Palate: good structure, powerful, sweetness.

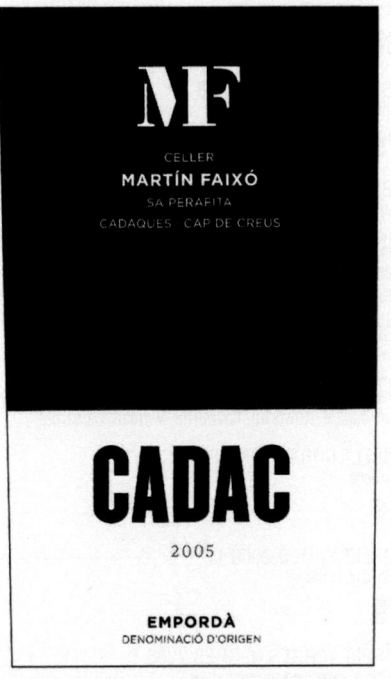

## CELLERS SANTAMARIA

Plaça Mayor, 6
17750 Capmany (Girona)
☎: 972 549 033 - Fax: 972 549 022
info@granrecosind.com
www.granrecosind.com

GRAN RECOSIND 2005 TR
merlot 100%

**86** Colour: cherry, garnet rim. Nose: powerfull, ripe fruit, dark chocolate, cocoa bean, creamy oak. Palate: flavourful, fleshy, spicy, round tannins.

GRAN RECOSIND 2002 TR
cabernet sauvignon 100%

**89** Colour: pale ruby, brick rim edge. Nose: candied fruit, spicy, cedar wood, caramel. Palate: elegant, classic aged character, round tannins, flavourful.

## COOPERATIVA AGRÍCOLA DE GARRIGUELLA

Ctra. de Roses, s/n
17780 Garriguella (Girona)
☎: 972 530 002 - Fax: 972 531 747
info@cooperativagarriguella.com
www.cooperativagarriguella.com

DINARELLS 2008 B
macabeo 60%, garnacha blanca 35%, moscatel 5%

**83**

PUNTILS 2008 B
garnacha blanca 65%, moscatel 35%

**83**

DINARELLS 2008 RD
samsó 40%, garnacha 40%, cabernet sauvignon 20%

**87** Colour: brilliant rose. Nose: rose petals, medium intensity, neat, expressive. Palate: fruity, light-bodied, powerful, flavourful, fresh.

PUNTILS 2008 RD
garnacha 50%, merlot 30%, samsó 20%

**84**

GARRIGUELLA NOVELL 2008 T
merlot 60%, garnacha 40%

**88** Colour: deep cherry, dark-red cherry. Nose: ripe fruit, fruit expression, raspberry. Palate: fruity, flavourful, powerful, fresh.

DINARELLS 2008 T
garnacha 40%, samsó 30%, cabernet sauvignon 30%

**85** Colour: dark-red cherry. Nose: fruit liqueur notes, varietal, red berry notes. Palate: green, balsamic, fruity aftestaste.

GARRIGUELLA 2006 TC
merlot, cabernet sauvignon, samsó, garnacha

**86** Colour: very deep cherry, garnet rim. Nose: dark chocolate, ripe fruit, creamy oak. Palate: powerful, rich, round tannins.

PUNTILS 2006 T
garnacha 40%, merlot 40%, samsó 20%

**85** Colour: dark-red cherry, garnet rim. Nose: ripe fruit, creamy oak, sweet spices. Palate: spirituous, full, fruity, warm.

GARRIGUELLA GARNATXA D'EMPORDÁ NEGRA

**85** Colour: cherry, garnet rim. Nose: fruit liqueur notes, dry nuts, roasted almonds, cocoa bean. Palate: unctuous, good acidity, creamy, fruity aftestaste.

## GARRIGUELLA GARNATXA D'EMPORDÁ ROJA 2003 VINO DULCE NATURAL
garnacha 100%

**87** Colour: coppery red, iodine. Nose: rancio notes, aged wood nuances, fruit liqueur notes, mineral, balsamic herbs. Palate: powerful, full, flavourful, good acidity.

## EMPORDALIA

Ctra. Roses, s/n
17494 Pau (Girona)
☎: 972 530 140 - Fax: 972 530 528
info@empordalia.com
www.empordalia.com

### SINOLS 2008 B
garnacha blanca 50%

**83**

### SINOLS 2008 RD
garnacha 40%, cariñena 30%, syrah 30%, merlot %, tempranillo %

**80**

### SINOLS NEGRE 2008 T
garnacha 50%, cariñena 50%

**82**

### SINOLS 2006 TC
garnacha 35%, cariñena 25%, cabernet sauvignon 25%, merlot 15%

**86** Colour: dark-red cherry, orangey edge. Nose: ripe fruit, creamy oak, sweet spices. Palate: round tannins, ripe fruit, easy to drink, spicy, fleshy.

### SINOLS MOSCATELL DE L'EMPORDÀ 2008 B DULCE
moscatel 100%

**85** Colour: straw. Nose: candied fruit, honeyed notes, fruit liqueur notes, balsamic herbs. Palate: unctuous, elegant, good acidity.

### SINOLS GARNATXA DE L'EMPORDA VINO DULCE NATURAL
garnacha roja 100%

**88** Colour: light cherry, coppery red. Nose: fruit liqueur notes, fruit liqueur notes, spicy, mineral. Palate: flavourful, full, fresh.

## ESPELT VITICULTORS

Mas Espelt
17493 Vilajuiga (Girona)
☎: 972 531 727 - Fax: 972 531 741
info@espeltviticultors.com
www.espeltviticultors.com

### ESPELT CHARDONNAY 2008 B
chardonnay 100%

**83**

### ESPELT VAILET 2008 B
garnacha blanca, macabeo

**80**

### ESPELT MARENY 2008 B
sauvignon blanc, moscatel

**79**

### ESPELT QUINZE ROURES 2007 BFB
garnacha blanca, garnacha gris

**88** Colour: bright yellow. Nose: complex, expressive, fine lees, smoky, creamy oak. Palate: elegant, powerful, flavourful, complex, balsamic, smoky aftertaste.

### ESPELT LLEDONER 2008 RD
garnacha

**87** Colour: rose. Nose: varietal, powerfull, expressive, fresh fruit. Palate: powerful, flavourful, varietal, balsamic.

### ESPELT CORALÍ 2008 RD
garnacha

**81**

### ESPELT SAULÓ 2008 T
garnacha, cariñena

**79**

### ESPELT TERRES NEGRES 2006 T
cariñena, cabernet sauvignon

**88** Colour: deep cherry, garnet rim. Nose: medium intensity, ripe fruit, scrubland. Palate: powerful, toasty, round tannins.

### ESPELT VIDIVÍ 2006 T
garnacha, merlot

**86** Colour: cherry, garnet rim. Nose: fruit preserve, spicy. Palate: flavourful, fruity aftestaste, soft tannins.

### ESPELT COMABRUNA 2006 T
syrah, cariñena, marselan

**81**

### ESPELT KASUMI 2005 T
cariñena 100%

**88** Colour: cherry, garnet rim. Nose: creamy oak, roasted almonds, fruit preserve, earthy notes. Palate: fleshy, sweetness, full, round.

### ESPELT GARNATXA JOVE T
garnacha

**85** Colour: light cherry. Nose: fruit liqueur notes, fruit liqueur notes, red berry notes, spicy. Palate: sweet, rich, unctuous.

ESPELT AIRAM VINO DE LICOR
garnacha, garnacha rosada

**86** Colour: coppery red, bright ochre rim. Nose: fruit liqueur notes, dry nuts, spicy, new oak. Palate: unctuous, fresh, flavourful.

QUINZE ROURES

## JOAN SARDÀ

Ctra. Vilafranca- St. Jaume dels Domenys, km. 8,1
08732 Castellvi de la Marca (Barcelona)
☎: 937 720 900 - Fax: 937 721 495
joansarda@joansarda.com
www.joansarda.com

CAP DE CREUS NACRE 2008
lledoner roig, lledoner blanco

**76**

CAP DE CREUS CORALL 2008
lladoner, samsó

**70**

FEIXES DEL PORT

## LAVINYETA

Ctra. de Mollet de Peralada a Masarac, s/n
17752 Mollet de Peralada (Girona)
☎: 647 748 809 - Fax: 972 505 323
lavinyeta@yahoo.es
www.lavinyeta.es

HEUS BLANC 2008 B

**78**

HEUS ROSAT 2008 RD
syrah 27%, merlot 26%, samsó 25%, garnacha tinta 22%

**83**

HEUS 2008 T
garnacha, syrah, merlot, cabernet franc

**80**

LLAVORS 2007 T
cabernet sauvignon, MERLOT, cariñena, garnacha

**83**

PUNTIAPART 2006 T
cariñena, cabernet sauvignon, merlot

**90** Colour: dark-red cherry. Nose: macerated fruit, varietal, powerfull, creamy oak, caramel. Palate: powerful, flavourful, sweetness, spicy, toasty.

SOLS DULCE

## LORDINA

Ctra. de Roses, km. 9,5
17493 Vilajuiga (Girona)
☎: 629 578 001 - Fax: 934 340 480
lordina7@gmail.com
www.lordina.net

LORDINA GRANIT 2006 T
syrah, garnacha, cariñena

**88** Colour: bright cherry, garnet rim. Nose: powerfull, macerated fruit, warm, earthy notes. Palate: fruity, good structure, elegant.

LORDINA 2006 T
syrah, garnacha

**84**

## MAS ESTELA

Mas Estela
17489 Selva de Mar (Girona)
☎: 972 126 176 - Fax: 972 388 011
masestela@hotmail.com
www.masestela.com

VINYA SELVA DE MAR 2006 T
garnacha 50%, syrah 30%, cariñena 20%

**89** Colour: cherry, garnet rim. Nose: fruit preserve, expressive, dark chocolate, aged wood nuances, medium intensity. Palate: round tannins, fruity, flavourful, concentrated.

QUINDALS 2006 T
garnacha 90%, sumoll 5%, cariñena 5%

**84**

ESTELA DOLÇ SOLERA
garnacha 100%

**90** Colour: pale ruby, brick rim edge. Nose: smoky, spicy, mineral, fruit liqueur notes, complex. Palate: powerful, flavourful, unctuous, round, creamy, toasty.

MAS ESTELA MOSCATELL 2005 BLANCO DULCE
moscatel 100%

**88** Colour: bright golden. Nose: spicy, pattiserie, citrus fruit, honeyed notes, balsamic herbs. Palate: fruity, full, flavourful, good acidity, fine bitter notes.

VI DE LLUNA

## MAS LLUNES

Ctra. de Roses, s/n
17780 Garriguela (Girona)
☎: 972 552 684 - Fax: 972 530 112
masllunes@masllunes.es
www.masllunes.es

MARAGDA 2008 B
garnacha blanca 80%, macabeo 10%, roussane 10%

**77**

NIVIA 2007 BFB
garnacha blanca 65%, samsó 35%

**83**

MARAGDA 2008 RD
garnacha 60%, merlot 40%

**83**

CERCIUM 2007 T
garnacha 30%, samsó 25%, syrah 20%, cabernet sauvignon 15%, merlot 10%

**82**

RHODES 2006 T
samsó 55%, syrah 30%, merlot 15%

**89** Colour: very deep cherry, garnet rim. Nose: ripe fruit, cocoa bean, spicy, new oak. Palate: flavourful, balanced, good acidity, round tannins.

EMPÓRION 2005 TC
cabernet sauvignon 70%, merlot 15%, syrah 15%

**86** Colour: dark-red cherry. Nose: ripe fruit, creamy oak, aged wood nuances, mineral. Palate: fruity, round tannins, fruity aftestaste.

## MAS OLLER

Ctra. GI-652, km. 0,23
17123 Torrent (Girona)
☎: 972 300 001
mas_oller@yahoo.es

MAS OLLER 2008 B
picapoll 70%, malvasia 30%

**92** Colour: bright yellow. Nose: rose petals, fresh fruit, complex, characterful, varietal, powerfull. Palate: spirituous, good structure, fruity, powerful, flavourful.

MAS OLLER 2008 T
syrah, garnacha, cabernet sauvignon

**93** Colour: dark-red cherry. Nose: ripe fruit, fresh fruit, expressive, powerfull. Palate: fruity, flavourful, full, round tannins, mineral, toasty.

AQUAREL.LO

## MAS POLIT

Raval de la Font, 1
17781 Vilamaniscle (Girona)
☎: 636 482 472
celler@maspolit.com
www.maspolit.com

MAS POLIT NEGRE 2007 T
garnacha 45%, cabernet sauvignon 35%, syrah 20%

**77**

MAS POLIT CLOS D'ILLA 2007
syrah 70%, cabernet sauvignon 30%

**85** Colour: dark-red cherry. Nose: varietal, powerfull, characterful, macerated fruit. Palate: sweetness, fruity, flavourful, toasty.

## MASIA SERRA

Dels Solés, 20
17750 Cantallops (Girona)
☎: 972 531 765 - Fax: 972 531 766
masiaserra@masiaserra.com

CTÒNIA 2008 BFB

**92** Colour: straw. Nose: elegant, complex, ripe fruit, mineral, scrubland. Palate: powerful, flavourful, rich, fresh, smoky aftertaste.

IO MASIA SERRA 2004 T

**90** Colour: deep cherry. Nose: toasty, spicy, aged wood nuances, ripe fruit, undergrowth. Palate: fleshy, powerful, flavourful, smoky aftertaste.

GNEIS 2003 T

**92** Colour: very deep cherry. Nose: caramel, creamy oak, ripe fruit. Palate: fleshy, complex, sweetness, spirituous, good structure, powerful, toasty, roasted-coffee aftertaste.

## OLIVEDA S.A.

La Roca, 3
17750 Capmany (Girona)
☎: 972 549 012 - Fax: 972 549 106
comercial@grupoliveda.com
www.grupoliveda.com

RIGAU ROS CHARDONNAY 2008 BFB
chardonnay

**88** Colour: bright straw. Nose: expressive, fresh fruit, smoky. Palate: rich, powerful, flavourful, creamy, smoky aftertaste.

RIGAU ROS BLANCO DE FLOR 2008 B
chardonnay, xarel.lo, macabeo

**85** Colour: straw. Nose: fresh fruit, medium intensity, neat. Palate: round, powerful, flavourful, fruity.

FUROT 2008 B JOVEN
sauvignon blanc 100%

**79**

RIGAU ROS 2008 RD
merlot, garnacha, samsó

**83**

FINCA FUROT 2005 TC
samsó

**87** Colour: cherry, garnet rim. Nose: roasted almonds, red berry notes, ripe fruit, aged wood nuances. Palate: easy to drink, fruity, soft tannins.

FINCA FUROT 2003 TR
cabernet sauvignon, garnacha, merlot

**88** Colour: pale ruby, brick rim edge. Nose: powerfull, ripe fruit, toasty, spicy. Palate: flavourful, powerful, fleshy, round tannins.

RIGAU ROS 2003 TGR
cabernet sauvignon, samso

**86** Colour: pale ruby, brick rim edge. Nose: sweet spices, cocoa bean, fruit preserve. Palate: flavourful, classic aged character, aged character, soft tannins.

RIGAU ROS CABERNET SAUVIGNON 2002 TR
cabernet sauvignon, s

**86** Colour: pale ruby, brick rim edge. Nose: fruit preserve, sweet spices, cocoa bean, fine reductive notes. Palate: fruity, flavourful, soft tannins, aged character.

## OLIVER CONTI

Puignau, s/n
17750 Capmany (Girona)
☎: 972 193 161 - Fax: 972 193 040
dolors@oliverconti.com
www.oliverconti.com

OLIVER CONTI TREYU 2008 B
gewürztraminer 52%, macabeo 38%, sauvignon blanc 10%

**88** Colour: straw. Nose: grapey, fruit expression, varietal, powerfull. Palate: complex, fresh, fruity.

OLIVER CONTI 2007 B BARRICA
gewürztraminer 50%, sauvignon blanc 50%

**87** Colour: bright yellow. Nose: macerated fruit, varietal, expressive, mineral, smoky, creamy oak. Palate: elegant, fresh, fruity, flavourful, balsamic, smoky aftertaste.

OLIVER CONTI CARLOTA 2007 T
cabernet franc 75%, cabernet sauvignon 25%

**91** Colour: deep cherry. Nose: fruit preserve, tobacco, balsamic herbs, sweet spices, toasty. Palate: fleshy, full, powerful, grainy tannins.

OLIVER CONTI ARA 2007 T
cabernet sauvignon 52%, cabernet franc 22%, garnacha 12%, merlot 10%, petit verdot 4%

**91** Colour: deep cherry. Nose: spicy, aromatic coffee, fruit expression, mineral. Palate: creamy, spicy, balsamic, elegant, round.

OLIVER CONTI TURÓ NEGRE 2007 T
merlot 42%, cabernet sauvignon 40%, cabernet franc 18%

**88** Colour: dark-red cherry. Nose: sweet spices, creamy oak, ripe fruit, medium intensity. Palate: flavourful, powerful, roasted-coffee aftertaste, ripe fruit.

OLIVER CONTI 2005 TR
cabernet sauvignon 45%, merlot 40%, petit verdot 10%, marcelan 5%

**91** Colour: dark-red cherry. Nose: sweet spices, aromatic coffee, ripe fruit, complex, varietal. Palate: complex, fruity, powerful, flavourful, roasted-coffee aftertaste, mineral.

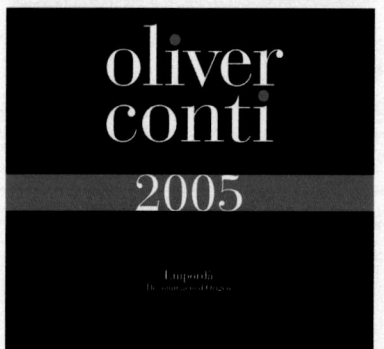

## PERE GUARDIOLA S.L.

Ctra. GI-602, km. 2,9
17750 Capmany (Gerona)
☎: 972 549 096 - Fax: 972 549 097
vins@pereguardiola.com
www.pereguardiola.com

FLORESTA 2008 B
chardonnay, macabeo

**83**

JONCARIA CHARDONNAY 2008 B

**80**

JONCARIA MOSCAT 2005 BFB
moscatel 100%

**89** Colour: bright yellow. Nose: powerfull, elegant, fine reductive notes, faded flowers. Palate: complex, flavourful, full, rich, varietal.

FLORESTA 2008 RD
garnacha, merlot, syrah

**83**

FLORESTA 2008 T
syrah, mazuelo, cabernet sauvignon, garnacha

**86** Colour: deep cherry. Nose: varietal, fresh, expressive, complex. Palate: fresh, fruity, powerful, varietal, balsamic.

FLORESTA 2005 TC

**87** Colour: cherry, garnet rim. Nose: powerfull, ripe fruit, toasty, aged wood nuances. Palate: flavourful, powerful, fleshy, spicy.

CLOS FLORESTA 2004 TR

**88** Colour: bright cherry. Nose: ripe fruit, sweet spices, creamy oak. Palate: flavourful, fruity, toasty, round tannins.

JONCARIA MERLOT 2003 TR

**85** Colour: pale ruby, brick rim edge. Nose: fruit preserve, cedar wood, fine reductive notes. Palate: aged character, full, flavourful.

TORRE DE CAPMANY GARNATXA D'EMPORDÀ
VINO DE LICOR

**85** Colour: coppery red. Nose: spicy, toasty, fruit liqueur notes, dry nuts. Palate: powerful, full, flavourful, sweetness.

TORRE DE CAPMANY GARNATXA D'EMPORDÀ
VINO DULCE NATURAL GRAN RESERVA

**88** Colour: light mahogany. Nose: dry nuts, toasty, aged wood nuances, undergrowth. Palate: flavourful, rich, spirituous, fresh.

## ROIG PARALS

Garriguella, 8
17752 Mollet de Peralada (Girona)
☎: 972 634 320 - Fax: 972 306 209
lworld@hotmail.com
www.roigparals.com

## SAMSÓ VINYES VELLES 2005 T
samsó 85%, merlot 15%

**86** Colour: cherry, garnet rim. Nose: powerfull, warm, ripe fruit, aged wood nuances, toasty. Palate: flavourful, spicy, round tannins.

## PLA DEL MOLÍ 2005 T
cabernet sauvignon 70%, merlot 30%

**85** Colour: cherry, garnet rim. Nose: powerfull, ripe fruit, toasty, warm. Palate: powerful, spicy, ripe fruit, toasty, round tannins.

## TERRA REMOTA

Els Tallats
17751 Sant Climent Sescebes (Girona)
☎: 972 193 727
terraremota@hotmail.com
www.terraremota.com

### TERRA REMOTA CAMINANTE 2007 B
garnacha blanca 40%, chardonnay 30%, chenin blanc 30%

**90** Colour: bright yellow. Nose: powerfull, ripe fruit, sweet spices, creamy oak, fragrant herbs. Palate: rich, smoky aftertaste, flavourful, fresh, good acidity.

### TERRA REMOTA CAMINITO 2007 RD
cabernet sauvignon 50%, syrah 50%

**87** Colour: raspberry rose. Nose: medium intensity, fine reductive notes, fruit preserve. Palate: sweetness, correct, spicy, ripe fruit.

### TERRA REMOTA CAMINITO 2008 T

**88** Colour: raspberry rose. Nose: fresh fruit, violet drops, red berry notes. Palate: fresh, fruity, flavourful, sweetness.

### TERRA REMOTA CLOS ADRIEN 2006 T
syrah 90%, tempranillo 10%

**90** Colour: cherry, garnet rim. Nose: powerfull, expressive, ripe fruit, fruit preserve, sweet spices. Palate: flavourful, fleshy, sweetness, fruity, long.

### TERRA REMOTA CAMINO 2006 T
syrah 40%, garnacha 30%, cabernet sauvignon 30%

**87** Colour: cherry, garnet rim. Nose: fruit preserve, fruit liqueur notes, sweet spices. Palate: ripe fruit, flavourful, powerful.

## VINICOLA DEL NORDEST

Empolla, 9
17752 Mollet de Peralada (Girona)
☎: 972 563 150 - Fax: 972 545 134
vinicola@vinicoladelnordest.com
www.vinicoladelnordest.com

### ANUBIS NEGRE DE LES COSTES 2003 TR

**84**

### ANUBIS GARNATXA DE L'EMPORDÀ 1996 DULCE NATURAL GRAN RESERVA

**89** Colour: light mahogany, iodine. Nose: fruit liqueur notes, dry nuts, toasty, dark chocolate, aged wood nuances, cigar. Palate: rich, flavourful, complex, creamy, toasty.

COVEST
VINYA FARRIOL
GARRIGAL

## VINYA IVO

Apdo. 100 S'Alqueria
17488 Cadaques (Girona)
contact@vinya-ivo.com
www./vinyaivo.wordpress.com

### S'ALQUERIA 2006 T
samso, garnacha, macabeo, petit verdot

**91** Colour: black cherry. Nose: powerfull, characterful, ripe fruit, dark chocolate, toasty, aromatic coffee. Palate: flavourful, powerful, fleshy, spicy, round tannins.

## VINYES D'OLIVARDOTS

Paratge Olivadots s/n
17750 Capmany (Gerona)
☎: 650 395 627
vdo@olivardots.com
www.olivardots.com

### GRESA EXPRESSIÓ 2006 T
garnacha 30%, syrah 30%, cariñena 20%, cabernet sauvignon 20%

**91** Colour: bright cherry, garnet rim. Nose: balanced, expressive, elegant, ripe fruit, cocoa bean, mineral. Palate: complex, good structure, creamy.

GRESA EXPRESSIÓ 2007 T
garnacha 30%, cariñena 30%, syrah 20%, cabernet sauvignon 20%

**90** Colour: dark-red cherry. Nose: ripe fruit, creamy oak, sweet spices. Palate: round tannins, flavourful, fruity, rich, spicy.

## VINYES DELS ASPRES

Requesens, 7
17708 Cantallops (Alt Empordà Catalunya)
☎: 972 463 146 - Fax: 972 420 662
vinyesdelsaspres@vinyesdelsaspres.cat
www.vinyesdelsaspres.cat

BLANC DELS ASPRES 2007 BC
garnacha blanca 100%

**81**

VI DE PANSES DELS ASPRES 2004 B
garnacha roja 100%

**89** Colour: old gold. Nose: roasted almonds, spicy, rancio notes, aged wood nuances, dry nuts, candied fruit. Palate: rich, fresh, full, flavourful.

ORIOL 2008 T
cariñena 35%, cabernet sauvignon 28%, garnacha 21%, tempranillo 16%

**87** Colour: dark-red cherry. Nose: macerated fruit, toasty. Palate: fleshy, powerful, flavourful, fruity.

S'ALOU 2005 TC
garnacha 47%, cabernet sauvignon 27%, syrah 13%, cariñena 13%

**89** Colour: cherry, garnet rim. Nose: ripe fruit, spicy, creamy oak, cocoa bean. Palate: fleshy, complex, fruity, balanced.

NEGRE DELS ASPRES 2005 TC
cariñena 46%, cabernet sauvignon 34%, garnacha 20%

**84**

BAC DE LES GINESTERES VINO DULCE NATURAL 2000 DULCE
garnacha roja 100%

**86** Colour: light mahogany, iodine, amber rim. Nose: roasted almonds, toasty, cedar wood, aged wood nuances. Palate: powerful, flavourful, good acidity, toasty, fine solera notes.

## SOME OTHER WINERIES WITHIN THE DO:

**BODEGAS MAS VIDA S.L.**
**CELLER MAS PATIRÀS**

# DO GETARIAKO TXAKOLINA

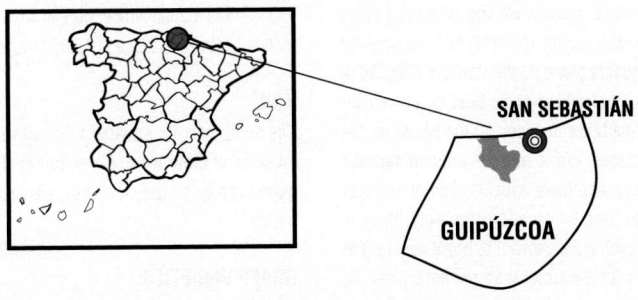

☖ Consejo Regulador
● DO Boundary

*Peñín Guide to Spanish Wine* **263**

# DO GETARIAKO TXAKOLINA

## NEWS
The wineries from Getaria are getting a more professional approach in every sense, for now we find at last that every single bottle from the region that reaches the shelves bears the seal of quality given by the Consejo Regulador. They also maintain that lively carbonic bead typical of their nature and some fine bitter nuances on the palate for the 2007 and 2008 vintages. Some wineries are bottling their wines almost in May, and there appear notes of fine lees and macerated ripe fruit, which add complexity; there is also room for improvement in respect to bottle ageing. The 2008 vintage was a little warmer than previous ones, so the txakolis show more expression and certain richness, with slightly sweeter and very harmonious notes on the palate. The people from Txomin Etxaniz seem to be in an experimental mood with their late harvest renderings of hondarribi zuri, which show enormous acidity and a fine 'German' nose leaning towards honeyed nuances. This same house has come up with two different bottlings of the same wine, one of them bearing an entirely English label. The attempt to make reds within the region has become a solitary, sad one.

## LOCATION
On the coastal belt of the province of Guipuzcoa, covering the vineyards situated in the municipal areas of Aia, Getaria and Zarauz, at a distance of about 25 km from San Sebastián.

## CLIMATE
Fairly mild, thanks to the influence of the Bay of Biscay. The average annual temperature is 13°C, and the rainfall is plentiful with an average of 1,600 mm per year.

## SOIL
The vineyards are situated in small valleys and gradual hillsides at altitudes of up to 200 m. They are found on humid brownish-grey limy soil, which are rich in organic matter.

## GRAPE VARIETIES:
**White:** *Hondarrabi Zuri* (majority with 90% of all vineyards).
**Red:** *Hondarrabi Beltza.*

| Hectares of Vineyard | 402 |
|---|---|
| Nº Viticulturists | 100 |
| Nº of Bodegas | 23 |
| 2008 Harvest | Good |
| 2007 Production | 1,580,000 l. |
| Marketing | 95% domestic 5% export |

## CONSEJO REGULADOR

Parque Aldamar, 4 bajo. 20808 Getaria (Gipuzkoa)
☎: 943 140 383 - Fax: 943 896 030
@info@getariakotxakolina.com
www.getariakotxakolina.com

## GENERAL CHARACTERISTICS OF THE WINES:

| WHITES | Produced from the autochtonous variety Hondarrabi Zuri; nevertheless, they may include a small percentage of red grapes (*Hondarrabi Beltza*) in the blend. The Txakoli from Getaria is characterised by its pale steely colour; the clean and frank nose of the wine, with pleasant herby notes and, in the best case, with floral traits; on the palate it is very fresh due to its high acidity, and light; it may also seem a bit carbonic. |
| --- | --- |

## 2008 VINTAGE RATING:

## VERY GOOD

# DO GETARIAKO TXAKOLINA

## AGERRE

Agerre Baserria - Bº Askizu
20808 Getaria (Guipúzcoa)
☎: 943 140 446 - Fax: 943 140 446
txakaguerre@terra.es

AGERRE 2008 B
hondarrabi zuri

**85** Colour: pale, greenish rim. Nose: fresh, fresh fruit, expressive, citrus fruit, scrubland. Palate: flavourful, fruity, good acidity, carbonic notes.

SAN MARTIN 2007 B
hondarrabi zuri

**86** Colour: bright straw, greenish rim. Nose: candied fruit, macerated fruit, balsamic herbs, spicy. Palate: fresh, full, fruity, dry, fine bead.

## AIZPURUA

San Prudentzio Auzoa, 36
20808 Getaria (Guipúzcoa)
☎: 943 580 922
bodegaaizpurua@txakoli.com

AIZPURUA. B 2008 B

**85** Colour: straw, greenish rim. Nose: balsamic herbs, macerated fruit, scrubland. Palate: fine bitter notes, fresh, fruity, flavourful.

AIALLE

## AMEZTOI

Barrio Eitzaga, 10
20808 Getaria (Guipúzcoa)
☎: 943 140 918 - Fax: 940 250 320
ameztoi@txakoliameztoi.com
www.txakoliameztoi.com

AMEZTOI 2008 B

**87** Colour: bright straw, greenish rim. Nose: citrus fruit, candied fruit, spicy, dried herbs. Palate: fresh, fruity, flavourful, good structure.

RUBENTIS

## BASA LORE

Santa Bárbara Auzoa - Buzón 1
20800 Zarautz (Guipúzcoa)
☎: 943 132 231 - Fax: 943 834 747
basa-lore@mixmail.com

BASA LORE 2008 B

**85** Colour: bright straw. Nose: candied fruit, grapey, pattiserie, spicy, white flowers. Palate: fruity, full, dry.

IGARTZETA

## BODEGA REZABAL

Itsas Begi Etxea, 628
20800 Zarautz (Guipúzcoa)
☎: 943 580 599 - Fax: 943 580 775
rezabal_txakolina@yahoo.es

REZABAL 2008 B
hondarrabi zuri

**86** Colour: pale, greenish rim. Nose: candied fruit, wild herbs, mineral, floral. Palate: fresh, fruity, balsamic, fine bitter notes.

ARRI

## BODEGAS SANTARBA

Santa Bárbara, 7 buzon Nº 8
20800 Zarautz (Guipúzcoa)
☎: 943 140 452 - Fax: 943 140 452

SANTARBA 2008 B

**84**

## ETXETXO

Etxetxo Baserria
20808 Getaria (Guipúzcoa)
☎: 943 140 085 - Fax: 943 140 146
etxetxo@euskalnet.net

ETXETXO 2008 B

**84**

## GAÑETA

Agerre Goikoa Baserria
20808 Getaria (Guipúzcoa)
☎: 943 140 174 - Fax: 943 140 174

GAÑETA 2008 B

**87** Colour: straw. Nose: macerated fruit, balsamic herbs, spicy, white flowers. Palate: flavourful, fruity, rich, fine bitter notes, good acidity.

## TALAI-BERRI

Talai Mendi Auzoa 728
20800 Zarautz (Gipuzkoa)
☎: 943 132 750 - Fax: 943 132 750
info@talaiberri.com
www.talaiberri.com

TALAI BERRI 2008 B
hondarrabi zuri 90%, hondarrabi beltza 10%

**87** Colour: pale, greenish rim. Nose: complex, expressive, scrubland, grapey, macerated fruit, floral. Palate: good structure, full, flavourful, fresh, balsamic.

FINCA JAKUE 2008 B
hondarrabi zuri 100%

**86** Colour: bright straw. Nose: candied fruit, maceration notes, spicy. Palate: full, fruity, flavourful, long.

TALAI-BERRI 2008 T
hondarrabi beltza 100%

**77**

## TXAKOLI GAINTZA S.L.

Caserío Gaintza
20808 Getaria (Guipúzcoa)
☎: 943 140 032 - Fax: 943 896 038
info@txakoligaintza.com

AITAKO CEPAS CENTENARIAS 2007 B

**85** Colour: bright straw. Nose: grapey, citrus fruit, scrubland. Palate: fresh, fruity, flavourful, balsamic.

GAINTZA

## TXAKOLI ULACIA

Cristóbal Balenciaga, 9
20808 Getaria (Guipúzcoa)
☎: 943 140 893

ULACIA 2008 B

**86** Colour: straw. Nose: macerated fruit, faded flowers, fragrant herbs. Palate: fruity, rich, flavourful.

## TXAKOLI ZUDUGARAI

Ctra. Zarautz - Aia. B. Laurgain
20809 Aia (Guipúzcoa)
☎: 943 134 625 - Fax: 943 835 952
txakolizudugarai@euskalnet.net
www.txakolizudugarai.com

ZUDUGARAI 2008 B
hondarrabi zuri 90%, hondarrabi batza 10%          5,25€

**81**

AMATS

## TXOMIN ETXANIZ

Txomin Etxaniz
20808 Getaria (Guipúzcoa)
☎: 943 140 702 - Fax: 943 140 464
txakoli@txominetxaniz.com
www.txominetxaniz.com

TXOMIN ETXANIZ WHITE WINE 2008 B

**85** Colour: straw. Nose: citrus fruit, tropical fruit, balsamic herbs, spicy. Palate: fruity, fresh, fine bitter notes.

Txomin Etxaniz
GETARIA
WHITE WINE

Getariako Txakolina
DENOMINACIÓN DE ORIGEN

TXOMIN ETXANIZ 2008 B

**85** Colour: bright straw. Nose: macerated fruit, sun-drenched nuances, dried herbs, faded flowers. Palate: fruity, full, flavourful, fine bitter notes.

TXOMIN ETXANIZ - UYDI VENDIMIA TARDÍA 2006 B

**86** Colour: golden, greenish rim. Nose: balsamic herbs, candied fruit, honeyed notes, wild herbs, elegant. Palate: sweet, fresh, flavourful.

TXOMIN ETXANIZ BEREZIA 2008

**88** Colour: straw. Nose: balsamic herbs, grapey, macerated fruit, faded flowers, spicy. Palate: elegant, fine bitter notes, fresh, fruity, full.

TXOMIN ETXANIZ - BIRBIRRA DEG. 2009 ESP

**80**

TXOMIN ETXANIZ - BIRBIRRA 2006 ESP

**78**

## URKI TXAKOLINA

Urki Txakolina
20808 Getaria (Guipúzcoa)
☎: 943 140 049 - Fax: 943 140 049
info@urkitxakolina.com
www.urkitxakolina.com

URKI 2008 B
hondarrabi zuri 100%

**83**

SOME OTHER WINERIES WITHIN THE DO:

**AKARREGI TXIKI**
**ARREGI**
**EIZAGUIRRE**

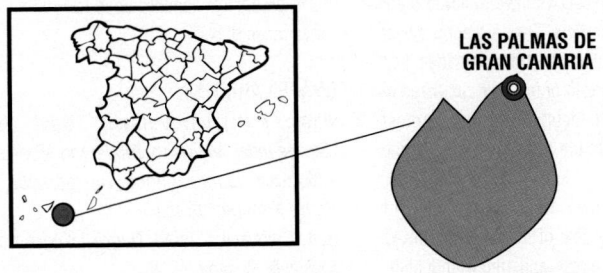

LAS PALMAS DE
GRAN CANARIA

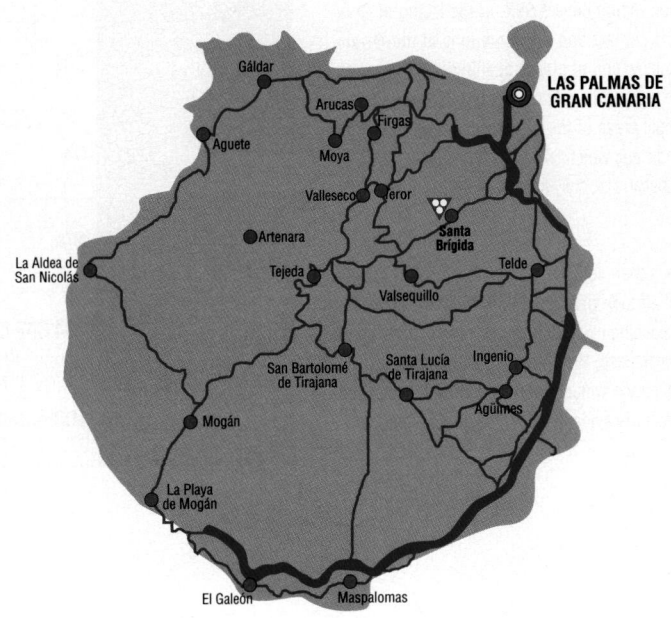

LAS PALMAS DE
GRAN CANARIA

▽ Consejo Regulador
● DO Boundary

## NEWS

Very few wines tasted, just around ten –less than ever before–, although, to be honest, we have to agree there were some interesting renderings. They are semi-sweet whites made by young producers from two wineries, Los Berrazales and Bentayga, a breath of fresh air compared to the average mediocrity and difficulties that are the most common feature coming from the rest of wineries. Of the former we should point out its wondrous semi-dry moscatel from grapes grown on a sunny plot of subtropical climate near the sea; of the latter, its brand Agala, a semi-sweet, night-harvest rendering from a high-altitude plot at 1300 meters. Overall, some really good prospects.

## LOCATION

The production region covers 99% of the island of Gran Canaria, as the climate and the conditions of the terrain allow for the cultivation of grapes at altitudes close to sea level up to the highest mountain tops. The DO incorporates all the municipal areas of the island, except for the Tafira Protected Landscape which falls under an independent DO, Monte de Lentiscal, also fully covered in this Guide.

## CLIMATE

As with the other islands of the archipelago, the differences in altitude give rise to several microclimates which create specific characteristics for the cultivation of the vine. Nevertheless, the climate is conditioned by the influence of the trade winds which blow from the east and whose effect is more evident in the higher-lying areas.

## SOIL

The vineyards are found both in coastal areas and on higher grounds at altitudes of up to 1500 m, resulting in a varied range of soils.

## GRAPE VARIETIES:

**White:** Preferred: *Malvasía, Güal, Marmajuelo* (*Bermejuela*), *Vijariego, Albillo* and *Moscatel*.
Authorized: *Listán Blanco, Burrablanca, Torrontés, Pedro Ximénez, Brebal*.
**Red:** Preferred: *Listán Negro, Negramoll, Tintilla, Malvasía Rosada*.
**Authorized:** *Moscatel Negra*.

| | |
|---|---|
| Hectares of Vineyard | 237 |
| Nº Viticulturists | 337 |
| Nº of Bodegas | 63 |
| 2008 Harvest | N/A |
| 2007 Production | 234,697 l. |
| Marketing | 100% domestic |

**CONSEJO REGULADOR**
Calvo Sotelo, nº 26
35300 Sta Brígida (Gran Canaria)
☎: 928 640 462.

## GENERAL CHARACTERISTICS OF THE WINES:

| | |
|---|---|
| **WHITES** | Yellow straw, the nose tends to be of herbs with fruity notes. Sweet wines from *Moscatel* are also produced with the characteristic musky nuance of the variety, with honey and herb notes. |
| **ROSÉS** | These have an onion skin colour; they are fruity, but with a character still to be defined. |
| **REDS** | With a deep cherry-red colour, they offer some fruity notes and characteristic balsamic hints, without too much body on the palate. |

### 2008 VINTAGE RATING:

# AVERAGE

## BODEGAS BENTAYGA

El Alberconcillo, s/n
35360 Tejeda (Palmas de Gran Canaria)
☎: 928 426 047 - Fax: 928 418 795
info@bodegasbentayga.com
www.bodegasbentayga.com

AGALA DULCELENA DULCE 2008 B

**84**

AGALA 2008 B

**75**

AGALA VENDIMIA NOCTURNA 2008 B SEMIDULCE

**87** Colour: bright straw. Nose: powerfull, ripe fruit, citrus fruit, grassy. Palate: flavourful, sweetness, balanced, good acidity.

## BODEGAS DE LA FAMILIA FLICK

Avda. de Escaleritas, 112
35011 Las Palmas de Gran Canaria (Gran Canaria)
☎: 928 289 055 - Fax: 928 206 512
jflick@grupoflick.com

VIÑA MONTEALTO 2008 T

**73**

## BODEGAS ENRIQUE ALFONSO ORTEGA

La Cantera, 9
35217 Valsequillo
☎: 928 570 595
grupolacantera@terra.es

VIÑA CANTERA 2008 B

**86** Color: bright straw. Nose: powerfull, white flowers, jasmine, fresh fruit. Palate: flavourful, sweet, fruity.

VIÑA CANTERA 2008 T

**81**

## LA HIGUERA MAYOR

Ctra. de Teide a Santa Brígida, El Palmital GC 80,
Pto. km., 7,5. Telde (Las Palmas de Gran Canaria)
☎: 630 285 454
lahigueramayor@telefonica.net
www.lahigueramayor.com

LA HIGUERA MAYOR 2007 T
castellana , negramoll , tintilla

**72**

## LOS BERRAZALES

Finca La Laja
35480 Valle de Agaete (Las Palmas)
☎: 928 898 154 - Fax: 928 898 154
lugojorge3@hotmail.com

LOS BERRAZALES 2008 B

**89** Colour: pale. Nose: expressive, fresh fruit, citrus fruit, white flowers, grassy. Palate: flavourful, sweet, fruity, fleshy.

LOS BERRAZALES 2008 T

**70**

## MOGARÉN

Las Moranas, 2 Las Vegas
35216 Valsequillo (Gran Canaria)
☎: 600 553 268
bodegasmogaren@yahoo.es
www.bodega-mogaren.com

GRAN MOGARÉN 2008 T BARRICA

**82**

SOME OTHER WINERIES WITHIN THE DO:

**ANSITE**
**BODEGAS AGUAYRO**
**BODEGAS LAS TIRAJANAS**
**DIEGO ÇAMBRELENG ROCA**
**EL BATÁN**
**EL EUCALIPTO**
**EL RINCÓN**
**EL SOLAPÓN**
**FRANCISCO PEÑATE RIVERO**
**FRONTÓN DE ORO S.A.T.**
**HEREDEROS CARMEN RODRÍGUEZ MILLÁN**
**HOYA CHIQUITA**
**LA MONTAÑA**
**LA ORILLA**
**LAUREANO ROCA DE ARMAS**
**MANUEL QUINTANA NARANJO**
**MARCIAL RIVERO MIRANDA**
**MONDALÓN PICACHOS S.L.**
**RAMOSAT**
**SANTIAGO ROBAINA LEÓN**

**SARAMEMA S.L.**
**SEÑORIO DE AGÜIMES**
**TABLERO DE LA DATA**
**VINO EL CASERÍO**
**VINOS DE JUAN INGLÉS**
**VIÑA ANGOA**
**VIÑA CENTRO**
**VIÑA TABAIBA S.L.**

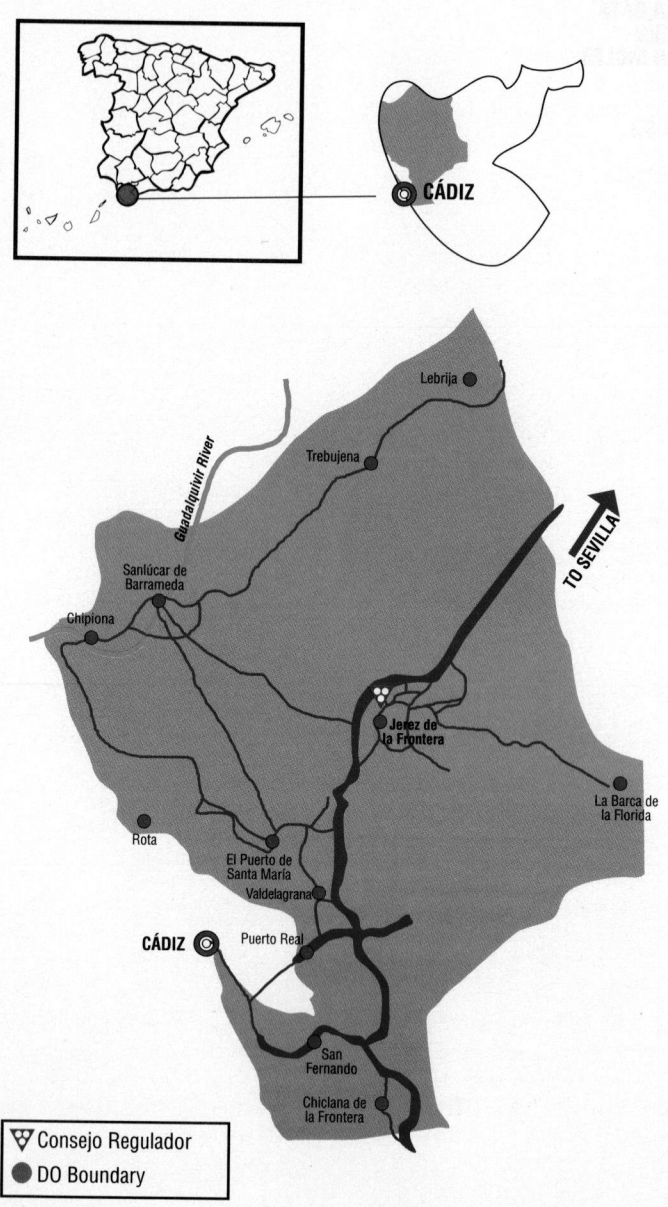

CÁDIZ

Lebrija

Guadalquivir River

Trebujena

TO SEVILLA

Sanlúcar de
Barrameda

Chipiona

Jerez de
la Frontera

La Barca de
la Florida

Rota

El Puerto de
Santa María

Valdelagrana

CÁDIZ

Puerto Real

San
Fernando

Chiclana de
la Frontera

▽ Consejo Regulador
● DO Boundary

## NEWS

Jerez still remains the wine region with the highest percentage of wines over 90 points. With a huge promotional campaign masterminded by the Consejo Regulador, the whole range of sherry wines –fino, manzanilla, oloroso, palo cortado, cream, pale cream and pedro ximénez– have reinforced not only their image but also their food-pairing capabilities. There are ten different sherry categories, although statistics seem to focus only on fino and the sweet cream concept said to be made-to-measure for the international markets. A sheer novelty is the fact that the region will include in the new regulations the sweet moscatel wines from the towns of Chipiona and Chiclana; wines that, contrary to the nature of those from Málaga and some other peninsular moscateles do not undergo fermentation. The new regulations will also put an end to the disputes between fino and manzanilla regarding nature, naming and geography: they will be called manzanillas those that end their ageing in the area of Sanlúcar de Barrameda, even when they come originally from other zones and wineries within the Marco de Jerez or sherry region.

In the region's overall rating, this year the manzanillas have managed to steal the limelight, having increased their ratings an average of four points, favoured by their quality and the more pronounced, pungent and longer nature of the so called "biological ageing". Carbon filtering previous to bottling has become more rare, so the average colour is brighter. The star wines are those from Equipo Navazos, a team that has managed to find the rarest and oldest sherry stocks to bottle –all numbered– very complex wines. Also to be followed are the VOS and VORS from Barbadillo, as well as their younger renderings.

## LOCATION

In the province of Cádiz. The production area covers the municipal districts of Jerez de la Frontera, El Puerto de Santa María, Chipiona, Trebujena, Rota, Puerto Real, Chiclana de la Frontera and some estates in Lebrija.

## CLIMATE

Warm with Atlantic influences. The west winds play an important role, as they provide humidity and help to temper the conditions. The average annual temperature is 17.5°C, with an average rainfall of 600 mm per year.

## SOIL

The so-called 'Albariza' soil is a key factor regarding quality. This type of soil is practically white and is rich in calcium carbonate, clay and silica. It is excellent for retaining humidity and storing winter rainfall for the dry summer months. Moreover, this soil determines the so-called 'Jerez superior'. It is found in Jerez de la Frontera, Puerto de Santa María, Sanlúcar de Barrameda and certain areas of Trebujena. The remaining soil, known as 'Zona', is muddy and sandy.

## GRAPE VARIETIES:

**White:** *Palomino* (90%), *Pedro Ximénez, Moscatel, Palomino Fino, Palomino de Jerez.*

| | |
|---|---|
| Hectares of Vineyard | 10,000 |
| Nº Viticulturists | 2,540 |
| Nº of Bodegas | 74 |
| 2008 Harvest | Very Good |
| 2007 Production | 56,293,000 l. |
| Marketing | 20% domestic 80% export |

**CONSEJO REGULADOR**
Avda. Álvaro Domecq, 2
11405 Jerez de la Frontera (Cádiz)
☎: 956 332 050 - Fax: 956 338 908
@vinjerez@sherry.org
www.sherry.org

## GENERAL CHARACTERISTICS OF THE WINES:

| | |
|---|---|
| **MANZANILLA AND FINO** | These are straw yellow in colour. They are characterised by their salty notes, typical of the biological ageing under the Velo en Flor (more pronounced in the case of the Manzanilla), and by the bitter notes conferred by ageing. |
| **OLOROSO** | With completely oxidative ageing, the range can be varied depending on the higher or lower scale level (i.e. the number of sacas of Solera wine to be bottled) and, consequently, the greater or lesser refreshing with unaged wine for the first criadera.<br>In the very old wines, it is customary to tone them down with Mistela of *Pedro Ximénez* which provide notes of sweetness to mitigate the bitter tannins of the oak. |
| **PEDRO XIMÉNEZ** | These are characterised by their marked palate of raisin, although some have a small percentage of Oloroso to reduce the sweetness. On the palate they are flavourful and sweet. |
| **CREAM** | These combine the bitter notes of the Olorosos with hints of toast and the sweetness of the *Pedro Ximénez*. |

## 2008 VINTAGE RATING:

# EXCELLENT

## AECOVI-JEREZ

Urb. Pie de Rey, 3
11407 Jerez de la Frontera (Cádiz)
☎: 956 180 873 - Fax: 956 180 301
info@aecovi-jerez.com
www.aecovi-jerez.com

MIRA LA MAR MZ

**87** Colour: bright yellow. Nose: complex, expressive, pungent, saline, fine lees. Palate: rich, powerful, fresh, fine bitter notes, flavourful, great length.

ALFARAZ MOSCATEL DE PASAS

**90** Colour: old gold, amber rim. Nose: dried fruit, honeyed notes, floral. Palate: rich, flavourful, good structure, great length.

ALFARAZ MOSCATEL DULCE

**87** Colour: old gold, amber rim. Nose: warm, varietal, ripe fruit, honeyed notes, pattiserie. Palate: powerful, sweet, balanced.

ALFARAZ OL

**86** Colour: iodine, amber rim. Nose: medium intensity, toasty, spicy. Palate: fine bitter notes, rich, fine bitter notes.

ALFARAZ PX

**88** Colour: dark mahogany. Nose: complex, fruit liqueur notes, pattiserie, toasty, sun-drenched nuances, acetaldehyde. Palate: sweet, rich, unctuous, powerful.

## ALVARO DOMECQ S.L.

Alamos, 23
11401 Jerez de la Frontera (Cádiz)
☎: 956 339 634 - Fax: 956 340 402
j.sosa@alvarodomecq.com
www.alvarodomecq.com

ARANDA CREAM CR

**89** Colour: iodine, amber rim. Nose: iodine notes, acetaldehyde, fruit liqueur notes, candied fruit. Palate: flavourful, rich, good structure.

LA JANDA FI

**85** Colour: bright yellow. Nose: complex, expressive. Palate: rich, powerful, fresh, fine bitter notes, correct.

LA JACA MZ
palomino

**85** Colour: bright yellow. Nose: expressive, pungent, saline, medium intensity. Palate: fine bitter notes, light-bodied, fresh.

1730 VORS OL

**91** Colour: iodine, amber rim. Nose: powerful, complex, elegant, dry nuts, toasty, iodine notes. Palate: rich, fine bitter notes, fine solera notes, long, spicy.

ALBUREJO OL

**87** Colour: iodine, amber rim. Nose: complex, elegant, dry nuts, toasty. Palate: rich, fine bitter notes, fine solera notes, long, spicy.

1730 PX

**91** Colour: dark mahogany. Nose: complex, fruit liqueur notes, dried fruit, pattiserie, toasty. Palate: sweet, rich, unctuous, powerful.

## BODEGA SANATORIO

Olivo, 1
11130 Chiclana de la Frontera (Cádiz)
☎: 956 400 756 - Fax: 956 532 907
administracion@bodegamanuelaragon.com
www.bodegasanatorio.com

GLORIA MOSCATEL DULCE

**87** Colour: bright straw. Nose: floral, ripe fruit, fruit preserve. Palate: sweet, fruity, fresh.

FINO GRANERO FI

**83**

TÍO ALEJANDRO OL

**87** Colour: iodine, amber rim. Nose: pattiserie, candied fruit, honeyed notes. Palate: sweet, spicy, long.

VIEJO ARRUMBAO OL

**80**

EL NETO
LOS CUATRO
NARANJA
CREAM VIEJO A.

## BODEGAS 501 DEL PUERTO

Valdés, 7 y 9
11500 El Puerto de Sta. María (Cádiz)
☎: 956 855 511 - Fax: 956 873 053
info@bodegas501.com
www.bodegas501.com

GADES 501 30 AÑOS VORS AM

**91** Colour: iodine, amber rim. Nose: powerful, complex, dry nuts, toasty, acetaldehyde, warm. Palate: rich, fine bitter notes, fine solera notes, long, spicy.

501 ZURBARÁN CR

**86** Colour: iodine, amber rim. Nose: fruit liqueur notes, flor yeasts, saline, spicy. Palate: flavourful, balanced, fine bitter notes.

501 MARINERO FI

**83**

501 TERCIOS OL

**85** Colour: iodine, amber rim. Nose: candied fruit, fruit liqueur notes, spicy. Palate: flavourful, powerful, sweetness.

GADES 501 PX
pedro ximénez

**86** Colour: dark mahogany. Nose: pattiserie, tar, sun-drenched nuances, dried fruit. Palate: flavourful, powerful, sweet, unctuous.

## BODEGAS ALMOCADEN S.A.

Jardinillo, 16
11404 Jerez de la Frontera (Cádiz)
☎: 956 185 324 - Fax: 956 187 526
almocaden@bodegasalmocaden.com
www.bodegasalmocaden.com

## ALMOCADEN AM

**90** Colour: iodine, amber rim. Nose: caramel, roasted almonds, saline. Palate: flavourful, powerful, sweetness, good acidity.

## ALMOCADEN CR

**91** Colour: iodine, amber rim. Nose: roasted almonds, varnish, acetaldehyde. Palate: sweetness, flavourful, powerful, fleshy.

## PAQUIRO FI

**84**

## LA CALETERA MZ

**87** Colour: bright yellow. Nose: expressive, pungent, saline, medium intensity. Palate: rich, fresh, fine bitter notes, easy to drink.

## ALMOCADEN OL

**82**

## ALMOCADEN PX

**87** Colour: dark mahogany. Nose: complex, fruit liqueur notes, dried fruit, pattiserie, toasty. Palate: sweet, rich, unctuous, good finish.

## BODEGAS BARBADILLO

Luis de Eguilaz, 11
11540 Sanlúcar de Barrameda (Cádiz)
☎: 956 385 500 - Fax: 956 385 501
barbadillo@barbadillo.com
www.barbadillo.com

## RELIQUIA AM

**96** Colour: iodine, amber rim. Nose: powerful, complex, elegant, dry nuts, toasty, acetaldehyde. Palate: rich, fine bitter notes, fine solera notes, long, spicy, round.

## BARBADILLO AMONTILLADO 30 AÑOS AM

**94** Colour: iodine, amber rim. Nose: powerful, complex, elegant, dry nuts, toasty. Palate: rich, fine bitter notes, fine solera notes, long, spicy, great length.

## PRÍNCIPE AM

**90** Colour: iodine, amber rim. Nose: powerful, complex, elegant, dry nuts, toasty, saline. Palate: fine bitter notes, fine solera notes, long, spicy, great length.

## EVA CREAM CR

**90** Colour: iodine, amber rim. Nose: fruit liqueur notes, candied fruit, acetaldehyde. Palate: spicy, long, flavourful.

## MANZANILLA EN RAMA SACA DE INVIERNO MZ

**94** Colour: bright golden. Nose: powerful, complex, pungent, flor yeasts. Palate: flavourful, powerful, long, fine solera notes.

## SOLEAR MZ

**90** Colour: bright straw. Nose: complex, expressive, pungent, saline. Palate: rich, powerful, fresh, fine bitter notes.

## MUYFINA MZ

**87** Colour: bright yellow. Nose: expressive, pungent, saline, medium intensity. Palate: rich, fresh, fine bitter notes.

## LAURA MOSCATEL

**90** Colour: light mahogany. Nose: balanced, overripe fruit, floral. Palate: fine solera notes, rich, flavourful, great length.

## BARBADILLO VORS 30 AÑOS DULCE OL

**90** Colour: iodine, amber rim. Nose: powerful, complex, elegant, dry nuts, toasty. Palate: rich, fine bitter notes, fine solera notes, long, spicy, sweet.

## RELIQUIA OL

**90** Colour: iodine, amber rim. Nose: powerful, complex, elegant, dry nuts, toasty. Palate: rich, fine bitter notes, fine solera notes, long, spicy.

## BARBADILLO 30 AÑOS VORS SECO OL
palomino

**89** Colour: iodine, amber rim. Nose: complex, elegant, dry nuts, toasty, fruit liqueur notes. Palate: rich, fine bitter notes, fine solera notes, long, spicy.

## SAN RAFAEL OL

**88** Colour: iodine, amber rim. Nose: candied fruit, caramel. Palate: rich, sweetness, flavourful, great length, balanced.

## CUCO OLOROSO SECO OL

**88** Colour: iodine, amber rim. Nose: expressive, caramel. Palate: powerful, balanced, rich, spicy.

## RELIQUIA PC

**93** Colour: iodine, amber rim. Nose: acetaldehyde, fruit liqueur notes, dark chocolate, aged wood nuances, roasted almonds. Palate: flavourful, fleshy, powerful, long.

## BARBADILLO PALO CORTADO 30 VORS PC

**91** Colour: iodine, amber rim. Nose: acetaldehyde, candied fruit, fruit liqueur notes. Palate: spicy, flavourful, powerful, spirituous.

## OBISPO GASCÓN PC
palomino

**90** Colour: old gold, amber rim. Nose: dry nuts, acetaldehyde, roasted almonds. Palate: flavourful, powerful, fleshy, fine bitter notes.

## PX RELIQUIA PX

**93** Colour: dark mahogany. Nose: varietal, complex, elegant, dark chocolate, dried fruit. Palate: rich, flavourful, balanced, spicy, fine solera notes.

## LA CILLA PX

**87** Colour: dark mahogany. Nose: complex, fruit liqueur notes, dried fruit, pattiserie, toasty. Palate: sweet, rich, unctuous, powerful.

# BODEGAS BARÓN

Molinillo 2a 2 y 3
11540 Sanlúcar de Barrameda (Cádiz)
☎: 956 360 796 - Fax: 956 363 256
baron.as@terra.es
www.bodegasbaron.net

## MANZANILLA PASADA BARÓN MZ
palomino

**90** Colour: bright yellow. Nose: complex, expressive, pungent, saline. Palate: rich, powerful, fresh, fine bitter notes.

## MANZANILLA FINA BARÓN MZ
palomino

**84**

## MOSCATEL PASA BARÓN
moscatel

**87** Colour: iodine, amber rim. Nose: dried fruit, caramel, pattiserie. Palate: unctuous, sweet, great length.

## P.X. VIEJO BARÓN PX
pedro ximénez

**89** Colour: dark mahogany. Nose: complex, fruit liqueur notes, dried fruit, pattiserie, toasty. Palate: sweet, rich, unctuous, powerful.

# BODEGAS GARVEY

Ctra. Circunvalación, s/n
11407 Jerez de la Frontera (Cádiz)
☎: 956 319 650 - Fax: 956 319 824
marketing@grupogarvey.com
www.bodegasgarvey.com

## TIO GUILLERMO

**89** Colour: light mahogany, amber. Nose: powerful, expressive, pungent, toasty. Palate: rich, flavourful, complex, great length.

## OÑANA AM

**93** Colour: iodine, amber rim. Nose: powerful, complex, elegant, dry nuts, toasty, saline. Palate: rich, fine bitter notes, fine solera notes, long, spicy.

## FLOR DEL MUSEO CR

**87** Colour: iodine, amber rim. Nose: candied fruit, acetaldehyde, pungent. Palate: flavourful, powerful, sweet, spirituous.

## FLOR DE JEREZ CR

**87** Colour: iodine, amber rim. Nose: characterful, complex, acetaldehyde, fruit liqueur notes. Palate: flavourful, powerful, good structure.

## SAN PATRICIO FI

**92** Colour: bright straw. Nose: complex, expressive, pungent, saline, white flowers, flor yeasts. Palate: rich, powerful, fresh, fine bitter notes, great length.

## JUNCAL MZ

**88** Colour: bright yellow. Nose: complex, expressive, pungent, saline. Palate: rich, powerful, fresh, fine bitter notes.

## ASALTO AMOROSO OL
palomino, pedro ximénez

**90** Colour: iodine, amber rim. Nose: powerful, complex, elegant, dry nuts, toasty. Palate: rich, fine bitter notes, fine solera notes, long, spicy.

## GARVEY 1780 VOS OL

**90** Colour: old gold, amber rim. Nose: powerful, expressive, complex, caramel. Palate: sweetness, good structure, flavourful, great length.

## PUERTA REAL OL

**90** Colour: iodine, amber rim. Nose: powerful, complex, elegant, dry nuts, toasty. Palate: rich, fine bitter notes, fine solera notes, long, spicy.

## GARVEY 1780 VORS OL

**89** Colour: old gold, amber rim. Nose: roasted almonds, varnish, acetaldehyde. Palate: rich, sweetness, flavourful.

## OCHAVICO OL

**88** Colour: iodine, amber rim. Nose: iodine notes, acetaldehyde, candied fruit. Palate: good structure, rich, flavourful, fine solera notes, toasty.

## JAUNA PC

**90** Colour: old gold, amber rim. Nose: dry nuts, caramel. Palate: sweetness, spirituous, flavourful.

## GRAN ORDEN PX

**93** Colour: dark mahogany. Nose: pattiserie, cocoa bean, dried fruit, honeyed notes. Palate: flavourful, rich, balanced, fine solera notes.

## GARVEY 1780 VORS PX

**92** Colour: dark mahogany. Nose: complex, fruit liqueur notes, dried fruit, pattiserie, toasty, sun-drenched nuances. Palate: sweet, rich, unctuous, powerful.

## GARVEY 1780 VOS PX
pedro ximénez

**90** Colour: dark mahogany. Nose: complex, fruit liqueur notes, dried fruit, pattiserie, toasty. Palate: sweet, rich, unctuous, powerful.

## GARVEY PX

**88** Colour: dark mahogany. Nose: complex, fruit liqueur notes, dried fruit, pattiserie, toasty. Palate: sweet, rich, unctuous, powerful, fine solera notes.

## BODEGAS GUTIÉRREZ COLOSÍA

Avda. Bajamar, 40
11500 El Puerto de Sta. María (Cádiz)
☎: 956 852 852 - Fax: 956 542 936
info@gutierrezcolosia.com
www.gutierrezcolosia.com

## GUTIÉRREZ COLOSÍA SOLERA FAMILIAR DRY AM
palomino

**95** Colour: iodine, amber rim. Nose: powerful, complex, elegant, dry nuts, caramel. Palate: rich, fine bitter notes, fine solera notes, long, spicy.

## GUTIÉRREZ COLOSÍA AMONTILLADO VIEJO AM
palomino

**90** Colour: iodine, amber rim. Nose: powerful, complex, elegant, dry nuts, toasty, acetaldehyde, pungent. Palate: rich, fine bitter notes, fine solera notes, long, spicy.

## GUTIÉRREZ COLOSÍA CR

**88** Colour: iodine, amber rim. Nose: spicy, flor yeasts, pungent, roasted almonds. Palate: flavourful, powerful, fleshy.

## MARI PEPA CR

**86** Colour: iodine, amber rim. Nose: characterful, fruit liqueur notes, caramel, warm. Palate: powerful, complex, flavourful.

## GUTIÉRREZ COLOSÍA FI

**88** Colour: bright yellow. Nose: complex, expressive, pungent, saline, grassy. Palate: rich, powerful, fresh, fine bitter notes.

## CAMPO DE GUÍA FI

**88** Colour: bright yellow. Nose: complex, expressive, pungent, saline. Palate: rich, powerful, fresh, fine bitter notes.

## GUTIÉRREZ COLOSÍA MOSCATEL SOLEADO

**88** Colour: dark mahogany. Nose: varietal, expressive, floral, honeyed notes. Palate: rich, great length, correct.

## GUTIÉRREZ COLOSÍA SOLERA FAMILIAR DRY OL
palomino

**90** Colour: iodine, amber rim. Nose: powerful, complex, elegant, dry nuts, toasty. Palate: rich, fine bitter notes, fine solera notes, long, spicy.

## GUTIÉRREZ COLOSÍA OLOROSO VIEJO OL

**89** Colour: iodine, amber rim. Nose: powerful, complex, elegant, dry nuts, toasty, caramel. Palate: rich, fine bitter notes, fine solera notes, long, spicy.

## SANGRE Y TRABAJADERO OL

**86** Colour: iodine, amber rim. Nose: sweet spices, caramel, candied fruit. Palate: flavourful, fleshy, spirituous, sweetness.

### GUTIÉRREZ COLOSÍA PALO CORTADO VIEJO PC

**91** Colour: old gold, amber rim. Nose: acetaldehyde, pungent, roasted almonds, caramel. Palate: flavourful, powerful, balanced, fine solera notes.

### GUTIÉRREZ COLOSÍA PX

**90** Colour: mahogany. Nose: varietal, expressive, varnish, dark chocolate, honeyed notes. Palate: concentrated, fruity, rich, fine solera notes.

### GUTIÉRREZ COLOSÍA SOLERA FAMILIAR PX

**87** Colour: light mahogany. Nose: characterful, complex, dried fruit, sun-drenched nuances. Palate: flavourful, good structure, sweet, fine solera notes.

## BODEGAS HARVEYS

Pintor Muñoz Cebrián, s/n
11402 Jerez de la Frontera (Cádiz)
☎: 956 346 000 - Fax: 956 349 427
visitas@bodegasharveys.com
www.bodegasharveys.com

### HARVEYS VORS AM
palomino 100%

**91** Colour: iodine, amber rim. Nose: powerful, complex, elegant, dry nuts, toasty, smoky, acetaldehyde. Palate: rich, fine bitter notes, fine solera notes, long, spicy.

### HARVEYS BRISTOL CREAM CR
palomino 80%, pedro ximénez 20%

**87** Colour: iodine, amber rim. Nose: roasted almonds, candied fruit, fruit liqueur notes. Palate: flavourful, good structure, spirituous.

### HARVEYS RESERVE OLD CREAM SHERRY CR
palomino 80%, pedro ximénez 20%

**87** Colour: iodine, amber rim. Nose: characterful, candied fruit, fruit liqueur notes. Palate: powerful, flavourful, sweetness.

### HARVEYS FI
palomino 100%

**91** Colour: bright yellow. Nose: complex, expressive, pungent, saline, grassy. Palate: rich, powerful, fresh, fine bitter notes, great length.

### HARVEYS VORS RICH OLD OL
palomino 90%, pedro ximénez 10%

**92** Colour: iodine, amber rim. Nose: powerful, complex, elegant, dry nuts, toasty. Palate: rich, fine bitter notes, fine solera notes, long, spicy, sweetness.

### HARVEYS VORS PC
palomino 98%, pedro ximénez 2%

**92** Colour: iodine, amber rim. Nose: varnish, caramel, acetaldehyde, iodine notes. Palate: flavourful, powerful, fleshy, sweetness.

### HARVEYS VORS PX
pedro ximénez 100%

**90** Colour: dark mahogany. Nose: complex, fruit liqueur notes, dried fruit, pattiserie, toasty, acetaldehyde. Palate: sweet, rich, unctuous, powerful, fine solera notes.

## BODEGAS HIDALGO-LA GITANA

Banda de Playa, 42
11540 Sanlúcar de Barrameda (Cádiz)
☎: 956 385 304 - Fax: 956 363 844
bodegashidalgo@lagitana.es
www.lagitana.es

### NAPOLEON VORS AM
palomino 100%

**91** Colour: iodine, amber rim. Nose: powerful, complex, elegant, dry nuts, toasty, acetaldehyde. Palate: rich, fine bitter notes, fine solera notes, long, spicy.

### NAPOLEÓN AM
palomino 100%

**90** Colour: iodine, amber rim. Nose: powerful, complex, elegant, dry nuts, toasty, acetaldehyde. Palate: rich, fine bitter notes, fine solera notes, long, spicy.

### ALAMEDA CR
palomino 75%, pedro ximénez 25%

**86** Colour: iodine, amber rim. Nose: medium intensity, candied fruit, spicy. Palate: flavourful, sweetness.

### PASTRANA MANZANILLA PASADA MZ
palomino 100%

**94** Colour: bright golden. Nose: flor yeasts, pungent, roasted almonds. Palate: fine bitter notes, powerful, flavourful, long.

### LA GITANA MZ
palomino 100%

**92** Colour: bright yellow. Nose: complex, expressive, pungent, saline, characterful, fresh. Palate: rich, powerful, fresh, fine bitter notes.

### OLOROSO AÑADA 1986 OL
palomino 100%

**91** Colour: old gold, amber rim. Nose: powerful, characterful, expressive, fruit liqueur notes, acetaldehyde. Palate: flavourful, spirituous, warm, fine bitter notes.

**FARAÓN 30 AÑOS VORS OL**
palomino 100%

**89** Colour: old gold, amber rim. Nose: fruit liqueur notes, fruit liqueur notes, aged wood nuances, caramel. Palate: fine bitter notes, sweetness, spirituous.

**FARAÓN OL**
palomino 100%

**88** Colour: old gold, amber rim. Nose: dry nuts, spicy, caramel. Palate: flavourful, fine solera notes, great length.

**WELLINGTON 30 AÑOS VORS PC**
palomino 100%

**91** Colour: iodine, amber rim. Nose: sweet spices, varnish, fruit liqueur notes, fruit liqueur notes. Palate: flavourful, powerful, fleshy, sweetness, great length.

**JEREZ CORTADO WELLINGTON 20 AÑOS VOS PC**
palomino 100%

**88** Colour: iodine, amber rim. Nose: powerful, warm, iodine notes. Palate: flavourful, fleshy, complex.

**TRIANA PX**
pedro ximénez 100%

**90** Colour: light mahogany. Nose: powerful, caramel, varnish, characterful. Palate: balanced, rich, flavourful, concentrated.

**TRIANA 30 AÑOS VORS PX**
pedro ximénez 100%

**89** Colour: dark mahogany. Nose: tar, dark chocolate, sun-drenched nuances, candied fruit. Palate: powerful, full, sweet, unctuous, fine solera notes.

## BODEGAS LA CIGARRERA

Pza. Madre de Dios, s/n
11540 Sanlucar de Barrameda (Cádiz)
☎: 956 381 285 - Fax: 956 383 824
lacigarrera@bodegaslacigarrera.com
www.lacigarrera.com

**LA CIGARRERA MZ**

**90** Colour: bright yellow. Nose: saline, expressive, fresh, fine lees. Palate: fine bitter notes, balanced, great length, fresh.

## BODEGAS OSBORNE

Fernán Caballero, 7
11500 El Puerto de Sta. María (Cádiz)
☎: 956 869 000 - Fax: 956 869 026
comunicaciones@osborne.es
www.osborne.es

**OSBORNE RARE SHERRY AOS AM**
palomino

**94** Colour: iodine, amber rim. Nose: powerful, complex, elegant, dry nuts, toasty. Palate: rich, fine bitter notes, fine solera notes, long, spicy, sweetness.

**AMONTILLADO 51-1ª 30 AÑOS VORS AM**
palomino 100%

**93** Colour: iodine, amber rim. Nose: powerful, complex, elegant, dry nuts, toasty, saline. Palate: rich, fine bitter notes, fine solera notes, long, spicy.

**COQUINERO AM**
palomino

**90** Colour: bright straw. Nose: elegant, pungent, saline. Palate: flavourful, powerful, complex, fine bitter notes.

**SANTA MARÍA CREAM CR**
pedro ximénez, palomino

**87** Colour: iodine, amber rim. Nose: candied fruit, fruit liqueur notes, acetaldehyde. Palate: flavourful, sweet, spirituous.

**FINO QUINTA FI**
palomino 100%

**92** Colour: bright yellow. Nose: powerful, characterful, complex, saline, pungent. Palate: flavourful, powerful, fleshy, balanced, long.

**CARA DE GALLO MZ**
palomino

**86** Colour: bright straw. Nose: complex, pungent, saline, iodine notes. Palate: rich, powerful, fresh, fine bitter notes.

**SIBARITA VORS OL**
palomino 98%, pedro ximénez 2%

**95** Colour: iodine, amber rim. Nose: powerful, complex, elegant, dry nuts, toasty. Palate: rich, fine bitter notes, fine solera notes, long, spicy, sweetness.

**OSBORNE RARE SHERRY SOLERA BC 200 OL**
pedro ximénez, palomino

**95** Colour: iodine, amber rim. Nose: complex, elegant, dry nuts, toasty. Palate: rich, fine bitter notes, fine solera notes, long, spicy, sweetness, great length.

## OSBORNE SOLERA INDIA OL
pedro ximénez, palomino

**93** Colour: iodine, amber rim. Nose: powerful, complex, elegant, dry nuts, toasty. Palate: rich, fine bitter notes, fine solera notes, long, spicy, balanced.

## 10 RF OL
palomino, pedro ximénez

**88** Colour: iodine, amber rim. Nose: candied fruit, fruit liqueur notes, acetaldehyde. Palate: flavourful, powerful, fleshy, sweetness.

## BAILÉN OL
palomino

**88** Colour: iodine, amber rim. Nose: powerful, complex, elegant, dry nuts, candied fruit. Palate: rich, fine bitter notes, fine solera notes, long, spicy.

## CAPUCHINO VORS PC
palomino 100%

**94** Colour: iodine, amber rim. Nose: spicy, aged wood nuances, roasted almonds, candied fruit, fruit liqueur notes. Palate: flavourful, powerful, sweetness, fleshy, good acidity, warm.

## OSBORNE RARE SHERRY SOLERA PAP PC
pedro ximénez, palomino

**92** Colour: old gold, amber rim. Nose: powerful, complex, pungent, saline, roasted almonds. Palate: long, fine solera notes, flavourful.

## VENERABLE VORS PX
pedro ximénez 100%

**95** Colour: dark mahogany, yellow. Nose: complex, fruit liqueur notes, dried fruit, pattiserie, toasty, tar. Palate: sweet, rich, unctuous, powerful, roasted-coffee aftertaste.

## OSBORNE 1827 PX
pedro ximénez

**91** Colour: dark mahogany. Nose: varietal, warm, honeyed notes, sweet spices. Palate: flavourful, sweet, concentrated, balanced.

## OSBORNE RARE SHERRY PX PX
pedro ximénez

**90** Colour: dark mahogany. Nose: complex, fruit liqueur notes, pattiserie, toasty, sun-drenched nuances. Palate: sweet, rich, unctuous, powerful, fine solera notes.

## BODEGAS TERRY

Toneleros, s/n
11500 El Puerto de Santa María (Cádiz)
☎: 956 151 500 - Fax: 956 858 474
visitas@bodegasterry.com
www.bodegasterry.com

## TERRY AMONTILLADO AM
palomino 100%

**90** Colour: iodine, amber rim. Nose: powerful, complex, elegant, dry nuts. Palate: rich, fine bitter notes, fine solera notes, long, spicy.

## TERRY FINO FI
palomino 100%

**92** Colour: bright straw. Nose: complex, expressive, pungent, saline, grassy. Palate: rich, powerful, fresh, fine bitter notes.

## TERRY OLOROSO OL
palomino 100%

**90** Colour: iodine, amber rim. Nose: powerful, complex, elegant, dry nuts, toasty. Palate: rich, fine bitter notes, fine solera notes, long, spicy.

## TERRY PEDRO XIMENEZ PX
pedro ximénez 100%

**89** Colour: dark mahogany. Nose: complex, fruit liqueur notes, dried fruit, pattiserie, toasty, sun-drenched nuances. Palate: sweet, rich, unctuous, powerful.

## BODEGAS TRADICIÓN

Cordobeses, 3 y 5
11408 Jerez de la Frontera (Cádiz)
☎: 956 168 628 - Fax: 956 331 963
jerez@bodegastradicion.com
www.bodegastradicion.com

## TRADICIÓN MUY VIEJO 30 AÑOS VORS AM

**91** Colour: iodine, amber rim. Nose: powerful, complex, elegant, dry nuts, toasty, acetaldehyde. Palate: rich, fine bitter notes, fine solera notes, long, spicy.

## TRADICIÓN MUY VIEJO 30 AÑOS VORS OL

**91** Colour: iodine, amber rim. Nose: powerful, complex, elegant, toasty, acetaldehyde. Palate: rich, fine solera notes, long, spicy, fine bitter notes.

### TRADICIÓN VORS 30 AÑOS PC

**90** Colour: iodine, amber rim. Nose: roasted almonds, spicy, acetaldehyde, iodine notes. Palate: flavourful, rich, complex, fleshy.

### TRADICIÓN 20 AÑOS VOS PX

**91** Colour: dark mahogany. Nose: dark chocolate, varnish, sweet spices, expressive. Palate: good structure, flavourful, balanced.

## CÉSAR L. FLORIDO ROMERO

Padre Lerchundi, 35-37
11550 Chipiona (Cádiz)
☎: 956 371 285 - Fax: 956 370 222
florido@bodegasflorido.com
www.bodegasflorido.com

### CRUZ DEL MAR CR
palomino 75%, moscatel 25%

**81**

### FINO CÉSAR FI
palomino 100%

**89** Colour: bright yellow. Nose: complex, expressive, pungent, saline. Palate: rich, powerful, fresh, fine bitter notes.

### CÉSAR FLORIDO MOSCATEL ESPECIAL
moscatel 100%

**90** Colour: iodine, amber rim. Nose: fruit liqueur notes, candied fruit, pattiserie. Palate: spirituous, sweet, rich.

### CÉSAR FLORIDO MOSCATEL DORADO
moscatel 100%

**87** Colour: iodine, amber rim. Nose: aged wood nuances, pattiserie, dried fruit. Palate: sweet, spirituous, rich.

### CÉSAR FLORIDO MOSCATEL PASAS
moscatel pasificado 100%

**87** Colour: iodine, amber rim. Nose: toasty, dried fruit, sun-drenched nuances. Palate: sweet, powerful, flavourful.

## DELGADO ZULETA

Avda de Rocío Jurado s/n
11540 Sanlúcar de Barrameda (Cádiz)
☎: 956 360 133 - Fax: 956 360 780
comercial@delgadozuleta.com

### MONTEAGUDO AM
palomino 100%

**87** Colour: iodine, amber rim. Nose: powerful, acetaldehyde, pungent, iodine notes. Palate: long, spicy, rich, fine bitter notes.

### LA GOYA MZ
palomino 100%

**93** Colour: bright yellow. Nose: complex, expressive, pungent, saline. Palate: rich, powerful, fresh, fine bitter notes, great length, flavourful.

### ZULETA MOSCATEL
moscatel 100%

**88** Colour: light mahogany. Nose: dried fruit, medium intensity, honeyed notes. Palate: flavourful, rich, great length.

### MONTEAGUDO PC
palomino 100%

**85** Colour: light mahogany, amber. Nose: balanced, powerfull, fine lees, iodine notes. Palate: flavourful, fine bitter notes, balanced.

### QUO VADIS

## DIOS BACO

Tecnología, parcela A-14
Parque Empresarial de Jerez
11402 Jerez de la Frontera (Cádiz)
☎: 956 333 337 - Fax: 956 333 825
info@bodegasdiosbaco.com
www.bodegasdiosbaco.com

### DIOS BACO AM
palomino 100%

**91** Colour: iodine, amber rim. Nose: powerful, complex, elegant, dry nuts, toasty. Palate: rich, fine bitter notes, fine solera notes, long, spicy.

### BULERÍA CR
palomino 80%, pedro ximénez 20%

**82**

### DIOS BACO OL
palomino 100%

**91** Colour: iodine, amber rim. Nose: powerful, complex, elegant, dry nuts, toasty. Palate: rich, fine bitter notes, fine solera notes, long, spicy, sweetness.

### BACO IMPERIAL 30 AÑOS VORS OL
palomino 100%

**90** Colour: iodine, amber rim. Nose: powerful, complex, elegant, dry nuts, toasty. Palate: rich, fine bitter notes, fine solera notes, long, spicy.

**OXFORD 1970 PX**
pedro ximénez 100%

**89** Colour: dark mahogany. Nose: dark chocolate, pattiserie, varnish, dried fruit. Palate: good structure, flavourful, great length.

EMPERATRIZ
BACO IMPERIAL
ESNOBISTA
BACO DE ELITE

## EL MAESTRO SIERRA

Pza. de Silos, 5
11403 Jerez de la Frontera (Cádiz)
☎: 956 342 433 - Fax: 956 342 433
info@maestrosierra.com
www.maestrosierra.com

**EL MAESTRO SIERRA 12 AÑOS AM**
palomino 100%

**90** Colour: old gold, amber rim. Nose: powerful, spicy, roasted almonds, acetaldehyde. Palate: flavourful, fine bitter notes, balanced.

**EL MAESTRO SIERRA VIEJO 1830 AM**
palomino 100%

**90** Colour: iodine, amber rim. Nose: complex, elegant, dry nuts, toasty, acetaldehyde. Palate: rich, fine bitter notes, fine solera notes, long, spicy.

**EL MAESTRO SIERRA FI**
palomino 100%

**92** Colour: bright yellow. Nose: complex, expressive, pungent, saline, grassy. Palate: rich, powerful, fresh, fine bitter notes, great length.

**EL MAESTRO SIERRA VORS OL**

**89** Colour: iodine, amber rim. Nose: powerful, complex, toasty, acetaldehyde. Palate: rich, fine bitter notes, fine solera notes, long, spicy, spirituous, warm.

**EL MAESTRO SIERRA 15 AÑOS OL**
palomino

**86** Colour: iodine, amber rim. Nose: smoky, overripe fruit. Palate: spirituous, fine bitter notes, sweetness.

**EL MAESTRO SIERRA VIEJÍSIMO PX**
pedro ximénez 100%

**91** Colour: dark mahogany. Nose: complex, dried fruit, pattiserie, toasty, dark chocolate. Palate: sweet, rich, unctuous, powerful, varietal, great length.

**EL MAESTRO SIERRA PX**
pedro ximénez 100%

**86** Colour: light mahogany. Nose: balanced, dark chocolate, tar, acetaldehyde. Palate: varietal, sweet, balanced, rich.

## EMILIO HIDALGO

Clavel, 29
11402 Jerez de la Frontera (Cádiz)
☎: 956 341 078 - Fax: 956 320 922
emiliohidalgo@emiliohidalgo.es
www.emiliohidalgo.es

**EL TRESILLO 1874 ESPECIAL AM**

**91** Colour: iodine, amber rim. Nose: powerful, complex, elegant, dry nuts, toasty, pungent. Palate: rich, fine bitter notes, fine solera notes, long, spicy.

**LA PANESA ESPECIAL FINO FI**

**90** Colour: bright yellow. Nose: complex, expressive, pungent, saline. Palate: rich, powerful, fresh, fine bitter notes.

**GOBERNADOR OL**

**88** Colour: old gold, amber rim. Nose: roasted almonds, acetaldehyde. Palate: balanced, spirituous, fine bitter notes.

**MARQUÉS DE RODIL PC**

**88** Colour: old gold, amber rim. Nose: flor yeasts, medium intensity, roasted almonds. Palate: flavourful, powerful, complex, rich.

**HIDALGO PEDRO XIMÉNEZ PX**

**87** Colour: dark mahogany. Nose: dried fruit, dark chocolate, varnish. Palate: good structure, sweet, good finish.

MORENITA
CHARITO
PRIVILEGIO
PEDRO XIMÉNEZ SANTA ANA

## EMILIO LUSTAU

Arcos, 53
11402 Jerez de la Frontera (Cádiz)
☎: 956 341 597 - Fax: 956 347 789
lustau2@a2000.es
www.emilio-lustau.com

**LUSTAU ESCUADRILLA AM**
palomino

**90** Colour: iodine, amber rim. Nose: powerful, complex, elegant, toasty. Palate: rich, fine bitter notes, fine solera notes, long, spicy.

## BOTAINA AM

**89** Colour: iodine, amber rim. Nose: acetaldehyde, pungent, iodine notes, powerfull. Palate: good structure, rich, flavourful, spicy, great length.

## LUSTAU EAST INDIA SOLERA CR SOLERA
palomino, pedro ximénez

**88** Colour: iodine, amber rim. Nose: caramel, fruit liqueur notes, fruit liqueur notes. Palate: flavourful, powerful, sweetness, spicy.

## LUSTAU PUERTO FINO FI
palomino

**96** Colour: bright yellow. Nose: complex, pungent, saline, elegant, neat. Palate: rich, powerful, fresh, fine bitter notes, flavourful, great length.

## LA INA FI

**94** Colour: bright yellow. Nose: complex, expressive, pungent, saline. Palate: rich, powerful, fresh, fine bitter notes, great length.

## LUSTAU JARANA FI
palomino

**91** Colour: bright yellow. Nose: pungent, saline, grassy. Palate: unctuous, fine bitter notes, flavourful, powerful.

## LUSTAU PAPIRUSA MZ SOLERA
palomino

**94** Colour: bright straw. Nose: saline, fine lees, flor yeasts. Palate: long, complex, rich, great length, fine bitter notes.

## LUSTAU EMILÍN MOSCATEL SOLERA
moscatel 100%

**90** Colour: iodine, amber rim. Nose: complex, expressive, sweet spices, caramel. Palate: balanced, rich, fresh.

## RÍO VIEJO OL

**91** Colour: iodine, amber rim. Nose: powerful, complex, elegant, dry nuts, toasty. Palate: rich, fine bitter notes, fine solera notes, long, spicy.

## LUSTAU AÑADA 1990 OL
palomino

**90** Colour: iodine, amber rim. Nose: acetaldehyde, candied fruit, caramel. Palate: creamy, sweetness, flavourful, fine solera notes.

## LUSTAU DON NUÑO OL
palomino

**90** Colour: iodine, amber rim. Nose: powerful, complex, elegant, dry nuts, toasty. Palate: rich, fine bitter notes, fine solera notes, long, spicy, sweetness.

## EMPERATRIZ EUGENIA OL
palomino

**89** Colour: iodine, amber rim. Nose: powerful, complex, elegant, dry nuts, toasty. Palate: rich, fine bitter notes, fine solera notes, long, spicy.

## LUSTAU PENÍNSULA PC

**87** Colour: iodine, amber rim. Nose: candied fruit, powerfull. Palate: great length, spicy, balanced.

## LUSTAU SAN EMILIO PX
pedro ximénez

**92** Colour: dark mahogany. Nose: balanced, warm, varietal, dried fruit, dark chocolate, pattiserie. Palate: fine solera notes, rich, flavourful.

## VIÑA 25 PX
pedro ximénez

**89** Colour: dark mahogany. Nose: powerful, caramel, varnish, dried fruit. Palate: rich, varietal, spirituous, great length.

# EQUIPO NAVAZOS

Cartuja nº1 - módulo 6
11401 Jerez de la Frontera (Cádiz)
☎: 649 435 979
equipo@navazos.com
www.equiponavazos.com

## LA BOTA DE CREAM Nº 19 CR

**94** Colour: iodine, amber rim. Nose: aromatic coffee, roasted almonds, candied fruit, fruit liqueur notes, pattiserie, sweet spices. Palate: flavourful, powerful, sweet, concentrated, unctuous, spirituous, fine solera notes, creamy.

## LA BOTA DE FINO "MACHARNUDO ALTO" BOTA Nº 18 FI

**96** Colour: bright yellow. Nose: complex, characterful, expressive, medium intensity, dried flowers, wild herbs, flor yeasts, saline. Palate: round, complex, flavourful, fine bitter notes.

## LA BOTA DE MANZANILLA BOTA Nª 16 MZ

**99** Colour: bright yellow. Nose: complex, expressive, pungent, saline, spicy, powerfull. Palate: powerful, fresh, fine bitter notes, rich.

## LA BOTA DE OLOROSO Nº14, BOTA "NO" OL
palomino

**96** Colour: iodine, amber rim. Nose: powerful, expressive, elegant, dry nuts, fruit liqueur notes, aged wood nuances. Palate: flavourful, powerful, fleshy, rich, good structure, sweetness, long.

## LA BOTA DE PALO CORTADO "BOTA PUNTA" BOTA Nº 17 PC

**99** Colour: iodine, amber rim. Nose: powerful, expressive, candied fruit, dry nuts, roasted almonds, sweet spices, aged wood nuances, iodine notes. Palate: flavourful, fleshy, spirituous, good acidity, fine bitter notes, long.

## FEDERICO PATERNINA

Ctra. Morabita, km. 2
11407 Jerez de la Frontera (Cádiz)
☎: 956 186 112 - Fax: 956 303 500
paternina@paternina.com
www.paternina.com

### FINO IMPERIAL 30 AÑOS VORS AM

**91** Colour: iodine, amber rim. Nose: powerful, complex, elegant, dry nuts, toasty, iodine notes. Palate: rich, fine bitter notes, fine solera notes, long, spicy.

### BERTOLA 12 AÑOS AM

**88** Colour: iodine, amber rim. Nose: complex, elegant, dry nuts, toasty. Palate: rich, fine bitter notes, fine solera notes, long, spicy.

### BERTOLA CR

**85** Colour: iodine, amber rim. Nose: varnish, caramel, characterful. Palate: flavourful, powerful, spicy.

### BERTOLA FI

**90** Colour: bright straw. Nose: complex, expressive, pungent, saline, grassy. Palate: rich, powerful, fresh, fine bitter notes, great length.

### VICTORIA REGINA VORS OL

**90** Colour: old gold, amber rim. Nose: powerful, complex, elegant, toasty, acetaldehyde. Palate: rich, fine bitter notes, fine solera notes, long, spicy.

### BERTOLA 12 AÑOS OL

**87** Colour: old gold, amber rim. Nose: balanced, medium intensity, spicy, overripe fruit. Palate: good structure, fine solera notes, good finish.

## VIEJA SOLERA 30 AÑOS VORS PX

**90** Colour: dark mahogany. Nose: complex, fruit liqueur notes, dried fruit, pattiserie, toasty, tar, acetaldehyde. Palate: sweet, rich, unctuous, powerful, fine solera notes.

### BERTOLA 12 AÑOS PX

**88** Colour: dark mahogany. Nose: complex, fruit liqueur notes, dried fruit, pattiserie, toasty, aged wood nuances. Palate: sweet, rich, unctuous, powerful, fine solera notes.

PEMARTIN
VICTORIA

## GONZÁLEZ BYASS JEREZ

Manuel María González, 12
11403 Jerez de la Frontera (Cádiz)
☎: 956 357 000 - Fax: 956 357 043
elrincondegb@gonzalezbyass.es
www.gonzalezbyass.es

### AMONTILLADO DEL DUQUE V.O.R.S. AM
palomino 100%

**91** Colour: iodine, amber rim. Nose: powerful, complex, elegant, dry nuts, toasty, iodine notes. Palate: rich, fine bitter notes, fine solera notes, long, spicy.

### VIÑA AB AM
palomino 100%

**82**

### TÍO PEPE FI
palomino 100%

**93** Colour: bright yellow. Nose: fresh, grassy, saline, pungent. Palate: flavourful, fresh, great length.

### MATUSALEM V.O.R.S OL
palomino, pedro ximénez

**92** Colour: iodine, amber rim. Nose: powerful, complex, elegant, dry nuts, toasty. Palate: rich, fine bitter notes, fine solera notes, long, spicy, sweet.

### ALFONSO OL
palomino 100%

**87** Colour: old gold, amber rim. Nose: medium intensity, candied fruit, honeyed notes. Palate: sweetness, spirituous, flavourful, spicy.

### SOLERA 1847 OL
palomino, pedro ximénez

**86** Colour: iodine, amber rim. Nose: balanced, medium intensity, candied fruit. Palate: sweetness, rich, lacks balance.

### CROFT ORIGINAL PCR
palomino 100%

**88** Colour: bright straw. Nose: flor yeasts, pungent, expressive, fresh. Palate: flavourful, sweet, balanced.

### APÓSTOLES V.O.R.S. PC
palomino, pedro ximénez

**91** Colour: iodine, amber rim. Nose: acetaldehyde, iodine notes, caramel, aromatic coffee. Palate: flavourful, powerful, concentrated, sweetness, long.

### NOÉ V.O.R.S PX
pedro ximénez 100%

**93** Colour: dark mahogany. Nose: complex, fruit liqueur notes, dried fruit, pattiserie, toasty, acetaldehyde. Palate: sweet, rich, unctuous, powerful, fine solera notes.

### GONZALEZ BYASS
NÉCTAR

## HEREDEROS DE ARGÜESO S.A.

Mar, 8
11540 Sanlúcar de Barrameda (Cádiz)
☎: 956 385 116 - Fax: 956 368 169
argueso@argueso.es
www.argueso.es

### ARGÜESO AMONTILLADO VIEJO AM

**90** Colour: iodine, amber rim. Nose: powerful, complex, elegant, saline. Palate: rich, fine bitter notes, fine solera notes, long, spicy, good structure.

### SAN LEÓN "CLÁSICA" MZ

**93** Colour: bright yellow. Nose: complex, expressive, pungent, saline, elegant. Palate: rich, powerful, fresh, fine bitter notes, great length.

### SAN LEÓN RESERVA DE FAMILIA MZ

**93** Colour: bright yellow. Nose: powerful, characterful, pungent, iodine notes. Palate: flavourful, powerful, fresh, fleshy, complex.

### LAS MEDALLAS DE ARGÜESO MZ

**83**

## HIJOS DE RAINERA PÉREZ MARÍN

Ctra. Nacional IV, km. 640

11406 Jerez de la Frontera (Cádiz)
☎: 956 321 004 - Fax: 956 340 829
visitas@grupoestevez.com
www.grupoestevez.com

### LA GUITA MZ

**90** Colour: bright yellow. Nose: complex, expressive, pungent, saline, powerfull. Palate: rich, powerful, fresh, fine bitter notes.

### DE BANDERA

## LA ALACENA DE CARLOS HERRERA

Amapola, 2 Local 14 Edificio Notaria
41950 Castilleja de la Cuesta (Sevilla)
☎: 954 169 128 - Fax: 954 164 288
info@alacenach.com
www.laalacenadecarlosherrera.com

### ALACENA DE CARLOS HERRERA AM
palomino

**88** Colour: iodine, amber rim. Nose: acetaldehyde, pungent, fruit liqueur notes, roasted almonds. Palate: flavourful, good structure, fleshy.

### ALACENA DE CARLOS HERRERA FI
palomino

**88** Colour: bright yellow. Nose: complex, expressive, pungent, saline. Palate: rich, powerful, fresh, fine bitter notes.

### ALACENA DE CARLOS HERRERA MZ
palomino

**90** Colour: bright yellow. Nose: complex, expressive, pungent, saline. Palate: rich, powerful, fresh, fine bitter notes.

### ALACENA DE CARLOS HERRERA OL
palomino

**87** Colour: iodine, amber rim. Nose: caramel, toasty, fruit liqueur notes. Palate: flavourful, rich, sweetness.

### ALACENA DE CARLOS HERRERA PX

**88** Colour: dark mahogany. Nose: complex, fruit liqueur notes, dried fruit, pattiserie, toasty. Palate: sweet, rich, unctuous, powerful.

## LUIS CABALLERO

San Francisco, 32
11500 El Puerto de Sta. María (Cádiz)
☎: 956 851 751 - Fax: 956 853 802

marketing@caballero.es
www.caballero.es

## DON LUIS AM
palomino

**87** Colour: old gold, amber rim. Nose: candied fruit, flor yeasts, roasted almonds. Palate: flavourful, powerful, spicy, fine solera notes.

## MANOLA CREAM CR

**86** Colour: iodine, amber rim. Nose: powerful, fruit liqueur notes, roasted almonds. Palate: flavourful, sweet, fine solera notes.

## PAVÓN PUERTO FINO FI SOLERA

**89** Colour: bright yellow. Nose: complex, expressive, pungent, saline. Palate: rich, powerful, fresh, fine bitter notes, great length.

## MACARENA MZ
palomino

**90** Colour: bright yellow. Nose: complex, expressive, pungent, saline. Palate: rich, powerful, fresh, fine bitter notes.

## PADRE LERCHUNDI MOSCATEL

**89** Colour: light mahogany. Nose: dried fruit, floral. Palate: fine solera notes, fresh, flavourful, great length.

## CABALLERO OLOROSO REAL OL
palomino

**88** Colour: iodine, amber rim. Nose: elegant, dry nuts, toasty, medium intensity, candied fruit. Palate: rich, fine bitter notes, fine solera notes, long, spicy.

# REAL TESORO

Ctra. Nacional IV, km. 640
11406 Jerez de la Frontera (Cádiz)
☎: 956 321 004 - Fax: 956 340 829
visitas@grupoestevez.com
www.grupoestevez.es

## TÍO MATEO FI

**93** Colour: bright yellow. Nose: expressive, pungent, saline, powerfull. Palate: rich, powerful, fresh, fine bitter notes.

## PX VIEJO REAL TESORO

# REY FERNANDO DE CASTILLA

San Fco. Javier, 3

11404 Jerez de la Frontera (Cádiz)
☎: 956 182 454 - Fax: 956 182 222
bodegas@fernandodecastilla.com
www.fernandodecastilla.com

## ANTIQUE FERNANDO DE CASTILLA AM
palomino 100%

**93** Colour: iodine, amber rim. Nose: powerful, complex, elegant, dry nuts, toasty, pungent. Palate: rich, fine bitter notes, fine solera notes, long, spicy, great length.

## ANTIQUE FERNANDO DE CASTILLA FI
palomino 100%

**91** Colour: bright golden. Nose: complex, characterful, powerfull, roasted almonds. Palate: flavourful, powerful, fleshy, spicy.

## FERNANDO DE CASTILLA CLASIC DRY SEC FI
palomino 100%

**90** Colour: bright straw. Nose: flor yeasts, pungent, saline, powerfull. Palate: powerful, flavourful, fleshy, complex.

## ANTIQUE FERNANDO DE CASTILLA OL
palomino 100%

**92** Colour: iodine, amber rim. Nose: powerful, complex, elegant, dry nuts, toasty, spicy. Palate: rich, fine bitter notes, fine solera notes, long, spicy.

## ANTIQUE FERNANDO DE CASTILLA PC
palomino 100%

**94** Colour: old gold, amber rim. Nose: roasted almonds, pungent, acetaldehyde, sweet spices. Palate: flavourful, powerful, sweetness, fleshy.

## ANTIQUE FERNANDO DE CASTILLA PX
pedro ximénez 100%

**92** Colour: dark mahogany. Nose: overripe fruit, varietal, expressive, cocoa bean, toasty. Palate: fine solera notes, rich.

## CLASSIC FERNANDO DE CASTILLA PREMIUM SWEET PX
pedro ximénez 100%

**90** Colour: light mahogany. Nose: powerful, dried fruit, fruit liqueur notes. Palate: sweet, fruity, flavourful, spicy.

# SANCHEZ ROMATE HERMANOS

Lealas 26-30
11403 Jerez de la Frontera (Cádiz)
☎: 956 182 212 - Fax: 956 185 276
comercial@romate.com
www.romate.com

## NPU AM

**92** Colour: iodine, amber rim. Nose: complex, elegant, dry nuts, toasty, acetaldehyde, pungent. Palate: rich, fine bitter notes, fine solera notes, long, spicy.

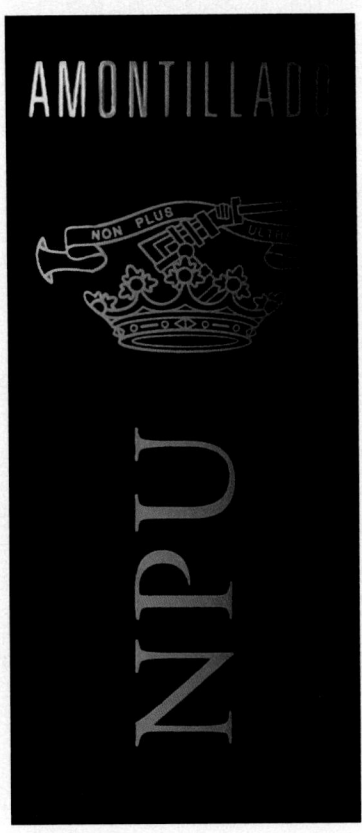

## LA SACRISTÍA DE ROMATE VORS AM

**90** Colour: iodine, amber rim. Nose: powerful, complex, elegant, dry nuts, toasty, acetaldehyde. Palate: rich, fine bitter notes, fine solera notes, long, spicy.

## IBERIA CR

**88** Colour: iodine, amber rim. Nose: elegant, complex, acetaldehyde, candied fruit. Palate: flavourful, good structure, sweet, fine bitter notes.

## FINO ROMATE FI

**88** Colour: yellow, bright golden. Nose: expressive, dry nuts, grassy, saline. Palate: dry, flavourful, good acidity, spirituous, long.

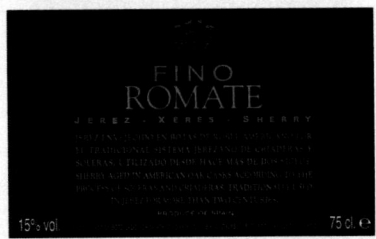

## MARISMEÑO FI

**87** Colour: bright straw. Nose: complex, expressive, pungent, saline. Palate: rich, powerful, fresh, fine bitter notes.

## AMBROSIA MOSCATEL

**90** Colour: dark mahogany. Nose: fresh, floral, honeyed notes, pattiserie, caramel. Palate: flavourful, rich, balanced, great length.

## LA SACRISTÍA DE ROMATE VORS OL

**93** Colour: old gold, amber rim. Nose: elegant, acetaldehyde, spicy, dry nuts, sweet spices. Palate: fine solera notes, rich, great length.

## DON JOSÉ OL
palomino
**90** Colour: iodine, amber rim. Nose: powerful, complex, elegant, dry nuts, toasty. Palate: rich, fine bitter notes, fine solera notes, long, spicy.

## REGENTE PC

**91** Colour: iodine, amber rim. Nose: expressive, balanced, sweet spices. Palate: rich, flavourful, spicy, fine bitter notes, great length.

## LA SACRISTÍA DE ROMATE PX

**90** Colour: dark mahogany. Nose: complex, fruit liqueur notes, dried fruit, pattiserie, toasty. Palate: sweet, rich, unctuous, powerful.

## DUQUESA PX

**89** Colour: dark mahogany. Nose: sun-drenched nuances, honeyed notes, expressive, floral. Palate: flavourful, spirituous, concentrated, fine bitter notes.

ROMATE VIVA LA PEPA
CARDENAL CISNEROS

## SANDEMAN JEREZ

Pizarro, 10
11403 Jerez de la Frontera (Cádiz)
☎: 956 151 700 - Fax: 956 300 007
visitors.jerez@sandeman.eu
www.sandeman.eu

### ROYAL ESMERALDA VOS AMONTILLADO 20 AÑOS AM
palomino 100%

**92** Colour: iodine, amber rim. Nose: powerful, complex, elegant, dry nuts, toasty, saline, acetaldehyde. Palate: rich, fine bitter notes, fine solera notes, long, spicy.

### CHARACTER MEDIUM DRY AM
palomino 95%, pedro ximénez 5%

**88** Colour: old gold, amber rim. Nose: caramel, elegant, fruit liqueur notes. Palate: flavourful, sweetness, balanced.

### DRY DON MEDIUM DRY AM
palomino 95%, pedro ximénez 5%

**87** Colour: iodine, amber rim. Nose: candied fruit, dried fruit, fruit liqueur notes. Palate: flavourful, sweetness, fine solera notes.

### RARE FINO SHERRY FI
palomino 100%

**91** Colour: bright golden. Nose: expressive, fresh, roasted almonds, pungent. Palate: flavourful, rich, complex.

### DON FINO SUPERIOR FI
palomino 100%

**88** Colour: bright straw. Nose: medium intensity, characterful, spicy. Palate: powerful, flavourful, fresh.

### ARMADA RICH CREAM OL
palomino 90%, pedro ximénez 10%

**90** Colour: iodine, amber rim. Nose: complex, elegant, dry nuts, toasty. Palate: rich, fine bitter notes, fine solera notes, long, spicy.

### ROYAL CORREGIDOR 20 AÑOS VOS OL
palomino 91%, pedro ximénez 9%

**90** Colour: old gold, amber rim. Nose: expressive, candied fruit, spicy. Palate: rich, flavourful, sweetness, fine solera notes.

### ROYAL AMBROSANTE 20 AÑOS PX
pedro ximénez 100%

**93** Colour: dark mahogany. Nose: complex, fruit liqueur notes, dried fruit, pattiserie, toasty, acetaldehyde. Palate: sweet, rich, unctuous, powerful, fine solera notes.

## VALDESPINO

Ctra. Nacional IV, km. 640
11406 Jerez de la Frontera (Cádiz)
☎: 956 321 004 - Fax: 956 340 829
visitas@grupoestevez.com

www.grupoestevez.es

### COLISEO VORS AM

**94** Colour: iodine, amber rim. Nose: acetaldehyde, iodine notes, roasted almonds, sweet spices. Palate: flavourful, powerful, full, warm, sweetness.

### TÍO DIEGO AM

**84**

### YNOCENTE FI
palomino

**93** Colour: bright yellow. Nose: complex, expressive, pungent, saline. Palate: rich, powerful, fresh, fine bitter notes.

### MOSCATEL VIEJÍSIMO TONELES

**97** Colour: light mahogany. Nose: powerful, complex, characterful, tar, dark chocolate, overripe fruit. Palate: sweet, fleshy, complex, unctuous, fine bitter notes.

### DON GONZALO VOS OL

**97** Colour: iodine, amber rim. Nose: powerful, complex, elegant, dry nuts, toasty, warm. Palate: rich, fine bitter notes, fine solera notes, long, spicy, sweetness.

### SOLERA 1842 OL

**97** Colour: iodine, amber rim. Nose: powerful, complex, elegant, toasty, candied fruit, roasted almonds, acetaldehyde. Palate: rich, fine bitter notes, fine solera notes, long, spicy, sweetness, flavourful.

### SOLERA SU MAJESTAD VORS OL

**96** Colour: iodine, amber rim. Nose: powerful, complex, elegant, dry nuts, toasty, caramel. Palate: rich, fine bitter notes, fine solera notes, long, spicy.

### CARDENAL PC

**96** Colour: iodine, amber rim. Nose: iodine notes, candied fruit, fruit liqueur notes, dark chocolate, roasted almonds. Palate: flavourful, spirituous, good structure, concentrated, long.

### EL CANDADO PX

**90** Colour: dark mahogany. Nose: complex, fruit liqueur notes, dried fruit, toasty. Palate: sweet, rich, unctuous, powerful, fine solera notes.

### NIÑOS

## VINÍCOLA SOTO (GRUPO GARVEY)

Cañada de la Loba, s/n (Finca Cerro Viejo)
11407 Jerez de la Frontera (Cádiz)
☎: 956 319 650 - Fax: 956 319 824
marketing@grupogarvey.com
www.vinicolasoto.com

### DON JOSÉ MARÍA OL

**91** Colour: old gold, amber rim. Nose: acetaldehyde, toasty, candied fruit. Palate: rich, flavourful, fine solera notes, great length.

### LA LIDIA
### LA ESPUELA
### SOTO

## WILLIAMS & HUMBERT S.A.

Ctra. N-IV, km. 641, 75
11408 Jerez de la Frontera (Cádiz)
☎: 956 353 400 - Fax: 956 353 412
secretaria@williams-humbert.com
www.williams-humbert.com

### JALIFA VORS "30 YEARS" AM

**90** Colour: iodine, amber rim. Nose: powerful, complex, elegant, dry nuts, toasty, iodine notes, acetaldehyde. Palate: rich, fine solera notes, long, spicy.

### DRY SACK MEDIUM DRY CR

**88** Colour: iodine, amber rim. Nose: candied fruit, overripe fruit, fruit liqueur notes. Palate: flavourful, sweet, fine solera notes.

### CANASTA CR

**85** Colour: iodine, amber rim. Nose: fruit liqueur notes, fruit liqueur notes, warm, varnish. Palate: flavourful, spicy, sweet, warm.

### DRY SACK "SOLERA ESPECIAL" 15 AÑOS OL

**87** Colour: old gold, amber rim. Nose: expressive, toasty, acetaldehyde. Palate: rich, balanced, spirituous, sweet.

### DOS CORTADOS PC
palomino

**92** Colour: iodine, amber rim. Nose: acetaldehyde, pungent, fruit liqueur notes, fruit liqueur notes. Palate: flavourful, powerful, fleshy, spicy.

DON GUIDO SOLERA ESPECIAL 20 AÑOS VOS PX

**94** Colour: dark mahogany. Nose: complex, fruit liqueur notes, dried fruit, pattiserie, toasty, tar, acetaldehyde. Palate: sweet, rich, unctuous, powerful, fine solera notes.

ALEGRÍA

SOME OTHER WINERIES WITHIN THE DO:

**AGROALIMENTARIA VIRGEN DEL ROCÍO**
**BODEGAS GASPAR FLORIDO**
**BODEGAS J. FERRIS M.**
**BODEGAS PEDRO ROMERO**
**BODEGAS GRANT**
**CARBAJO RUIZ**
**FAUSTINO GONZÁLEZ S.L.**
**HEREDEROS DE NICOLÁS MARTÍN S.L.**

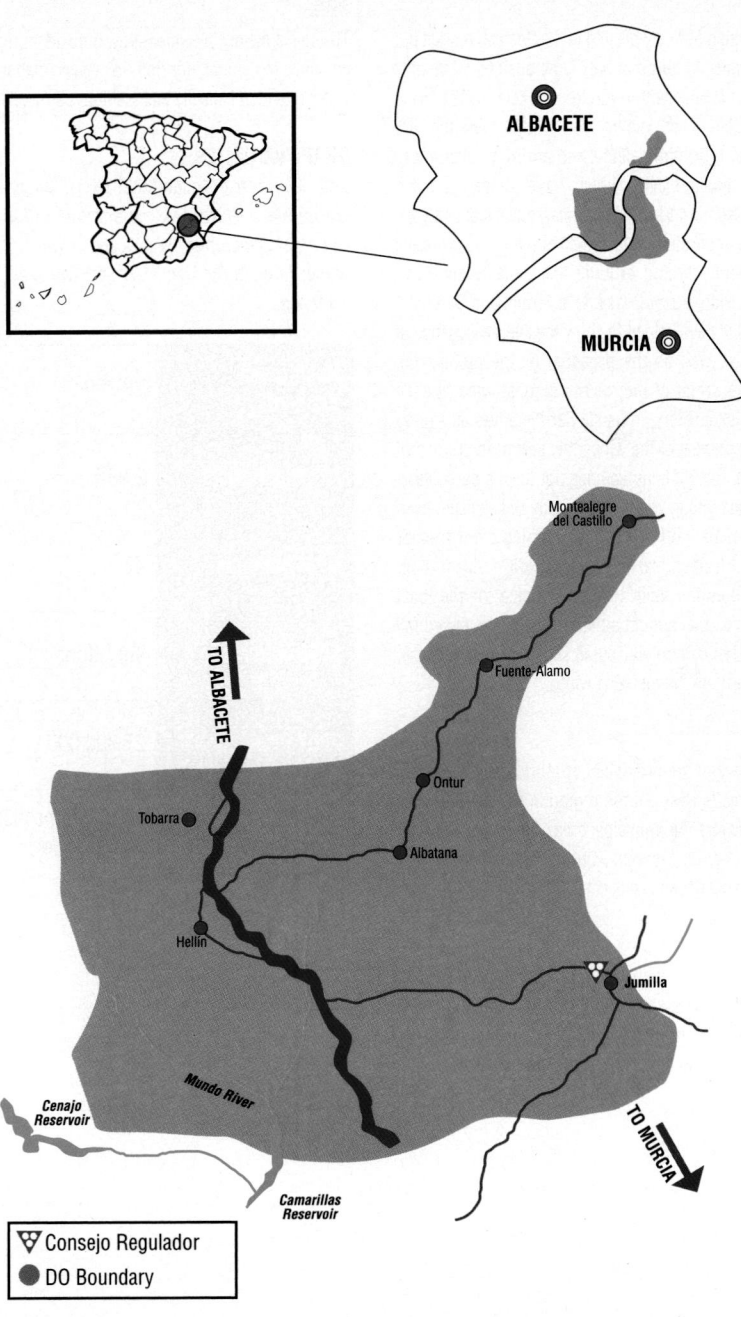

ALBACETE

MURCIA

Montealegre
del Castillo

TO ALBACETE

Fuente-Alamo

Ontur

Tobarra

Albatana

Hellín

Jumilla

Mundo River

Cenajo
Reservoir

Camarillas
Reservoir

TO MURCIA

▽ Consejo Regulador
● DO Boundary

## NEWS

Jumilla is losing not only ground in the Spanish market but also importance in terms of bulk wine business. The only and greatest chance within foreign markets for the DO is its formidable, well-known back label. Grapes are subjected to thorough selection to afford an even more formidable quality level, which have yielded a sales increase of around 11% in foreign markets in just one year. Ratings are accordingly high, thanks mainly to wineries with an openly foreign attitude like Julia Roch (Casa Castillo), El Nido, Luzón, Casa de la Ermita and Carchelo, properties that have helped to show the overall elegance of the region as well as the potential or the monastrell. Mayoral, the brand of one of the biggest wine houses within Spanish territory, J. García Carrión, gives us a good idea of the potential of the wines this part of the region of Murcia. Still, the 2008 vintage has not been a particularly good one, and young wines show pretty unbalanced, even just occasionally, although those coming from fresher soils yielded fruitier, fresher –more acidic– wines. Also, syrah becomes the main blending choice for the local varieties, given that almost a third of the wines tasted fall into that sort of pattern. The syrah seems to arise a juicier, more floral vein to the resulting wines.

## LOCATION

Midway between the provinces of Murcia and Albacete, this DO spreads over a large region in the southeast of Spain and covers the municipal areas of Jumilla (Murcia) and Fuente Álamo, Albatana, Ontur, Hellín, Tobarra and Montealegre del Castillo (Albacete).

## CLIMATE

Continental in nature with Mediterranean influences. It is characterized by its aridity and low rainfall (270 mm) which is mainly concentrated in spring and autumn. The winters are cold and the summers dry and quite hot.

## SOIL

The soil is mainly brownish-grey, brownish-grey limestone and limy. In general, it is poor in organic matter, with great water retention capacity and medium permeability.

## GRAPE VARIETIES:

**Red:** *Monastrell* (main 35,373 Ha), *Garnacha Tinta, Garnacha Tintorera, Cencibel (Tempranillo), Cabernet Sauvignon, Merlot* and *Syrah.*

**White:** *Airén* (3,751 Ha), *Macabeo, Malvasía* and *Pedro Ximénez.*

| | |
|---|---|
| Hectares of Vineyard | 28,200 |
| Nº Viticulturists | 2,987 |
| Nº of Bodegas | 43 |
| 2008 Harvest | Very Good |
| 2007 Production | 27,300,000 l. |
| Marketing | 45.4% domestic 54.6% export |

**CONSEJO REGULADOR**
San Roque, 15. Apdo Correos 66
30520 Jumilla (Murcia)
☎: 968 781 761 - Fax: 968 781 900
@ info@crdo-jumilla.com
www.crdo-jumilla.com

## GENERAL CHARACTERISTICS OF THE WINES:

| | |
|---|---|
| **WHITES** | Although they are not the most characteristic of the region, those produced from *Macabeo* are superior to those produced from Airen. In general, the white wines of Jumilla are straw yellow in colour; they have a moderate fruity character and a certain body on the palate; moreover, they are balanced and flavourful. |
| **ROSÉS** | These tend have a salmon pink colour; the nose is quite fruity and has a good aromatic intensity; on the palate they are flavourful, some with slightly more body and a bit warmer. |
| **REDS** | These are the region's wines par excellence, based on a variety, the *Monastrell* that, subject to the production techniques, provides wines with a lot of intense colour, with characteristic aromas of ripe black fruit and occasionally dried fruit; on the palate the best are very powerful with excellent tannin structure, flavourful and meaty. The Crianzas combine this fruity character with the contributions of the wood, and in the case of the older wines, although oxidation notes may still appear, the evolutionary trend of the variety is controlled more and more. |

## 2008 VINTAGE RATING:

## GOOD

## BARÓN DEL SOLAR

Barón del Solar, 8 Bajo
30520 Jumilla (Murcia)
☎: 968 756 136 - Fax: 968 716 197
info@barondelsolar.com
www.barondelsolar.com

BARÓN DEL SOLAR 2008 T
monastrell 80%, cabernet sauvignon 20%

**88** Colour: cherry, purple rim. Nose: red berry notes, ripe fruit. Palate: flavourful, fruity, good acidity, round tannins.

BARÓN DEL SOLAR MANOS 2007 T
monastrell 100%

**91** Colour: cherry, garnet rim. Nose: ripe fruit, spicy, creamy oak, toasty, complex. Palate: powerful, flavourful, toasty, round tannins.

BARÓN DEL SOLAR 2007 T
monastrell 80%, cabernet sauvignon 20%

**87** Colour: cherry, garnet rim. Nose: powerfull, dark chocolate, aromatic coffee, toasty, ripe fruit. Palate: powerful, flavourful, fleshy.

## BLEDA

Ctra. a Ontur, km. 16
30520 Jumilla (Murcia)
☎: 968 780 012 - Fax: 968 782 699
vinos@bodegasbleda.com

CASTILLO DE JUMILLA MACABEO 2008 B
macabeo 100%

**85** Colour: bright straw. Nose: fresh, fresh fruit, white flowers. Palate: flavourful, fruity, good acidity, balanced.

CASTILLO DE JUMILLA MONASTRELL 2008 RD
monastrell 100%

**86** Colour: rose, purple rim. Nose: ripe fruit, red berry notes, floral, expressive. Palate: fruity, fresh.

CASTILLO DE JUMILLA MONASTRELL 2008 T
monastrell 100%

**87** Colour: cherry, purple rim. Nose: expressive, fresh fruit, red berry notes, floral. Palate: flavourful, fruity, good acidity, round tannins, balsamic.

CASTILLO DE JUMILLA MONASTRELL - TEMPRANILLO 2008 T
monastrell 50%, tempranillo 50%

**87** Colour: cherry, purple rim. Nose: red berry notes, floral, ripe fruit. Palate: flavourful, fruity, good acidity, round tannins.

DIVUS 2007 T
monastrell 95%, merlot 5%

**91** Colour: cherry, garnet rim. Nose: spicy, creamy oak, toasty, complex, fruit preserve, dark chocolate. Palate: powerful, flavourful, toasty, round tannins.

DIVUS 2006 T
monastrell 95%, merlot 5%

**90** Colour: bright cherry. Nose: ripe fruit, sweet spices, expressive, dark chocolate. Palate: flavourful, fruity, toasty, round tannins.

CASTILLO DE JUMILLA 2005 TC
monastrell 90%, tempranillo 10%

**87** Colour: bright cherry. Nose: ripe fruit, sweet spices, creamy oak, expressive. Palate: flavourful, fruity, toasty, round tannins.

CASTILLO DE JUMILLA 2003 TR
monastrell 90%, tempranillo 10%

**87** Colour: cherry, garnet rim. Nose: ripe fruit, spicy, toasty, complex, aged wood nuances. Palate: powerful, flavourful, toasty, round tannins.

## BODEGA ARTESANAL VIÑA CAMPANERO

Ctra. de Murcia, s/n Apdo. 346
30520 Jumilla (Murcia)
☎: 968 780 754 - Fax: 968 780 754
bodegas@vinacampanero.com
www.vinacampanero.com

VEGARDAL MONASTRELL CEPAS VIEJAS 2008 T
monastrell 100%

**87** Colour: bright cherry. Nose: ripe fruit, sweet spices, expressive. Palate: flavourful, fruity, toasty, round tannins.

VEGARDAL CUCO DEL ARDAL SELECCIÓN 2007 T
monastrell 100%

**88** Colour: bright cherry. Nose: sweet spices, creamy oak, fruit preserve, fruit liqueur notes. Palate: flavourful, toasty, round tannins, warm.

VEGARDAL MONASTRELL Y TEMPRANILLO 2006 T
monastrell 80%, tempranillo 20%

**85** Colour: cherry, garnet rim. Nose: powerfull, fruit liqueur notes, fruit liqueur notes, aromatic coffee, aged wood nuances, spicy. Palate: powerful, spirituous, fine bitter notes.

## BODEGA HACIENDA DEL CARCHE

Ctra. de El Carche, km. 8,3  Apdo. correos 257
30520 Jumilla (Murcia)
☎: 968 108 248 - Fax: 968 975 935
fran@haciendadelcarche.com
www.haciendadelcarche.com

HACIENDA DEL CARCHE 2008 B
airén 33%, macabeo 33%, sauvignon blanc 33%

**86** Colour: bright straw. Nose: fresh, fresh fruit, white flowers. Palate: flavourful, fruity, good acidity, balanced.

TAVS 2007 T
monastrell 80%, syrah 20%

**88** Colour: bright cherry. Nose: sweet spices, ripe fruit. Palate: flavourful, toasty, round tannins.

TAVS SELECCIÓN 2007 T
monastrell 50%, syrah 25%, cabernet sauvignon 25%

**85** Colour: bright cherry. Nose: sweet spices, creamy oak, fruit liqueur notes, fruit preserve. Palate: flavourful, fruity, toasty, round tannins, warm, pruney.

HACIENDA DEL CARCHE CEPAS VIEJAS 2006 T
monastrell 50%, cabernet sauvignon 50%

**87** Colour: bright cherry. Nose: powerfull, fruit preserve, sweet spices. Palate: flavourful, toasty, powerful, round tannins, pruney.

## BODEGA SAN JOSÉ

Camino de Hellín, s/n
02652 Ontur (Albacete)
☎: 670 281 037 - Fax: 967 324 186
export@bodegasanjose.com
www.bodegasanjose.com

VILLA DE ONTUR 2008 B
airén 100%

**81**

VILLA DE ONTUR 2008 RD
garnacha 100%

**79**

DOMINIO DE ONTUR MONASTRELL 2008 T
monastrell 100%

**88** Colour: cherry, purple rim. Nose: floral, powerfull, varietal, red berry notes, ripe fruit. Palate: flavourful, good acidity, powerful tannins, ripe fruit.

DOMINIO DE ONTUR SYRAH 2008 T
syrah 100%

**88** Colour: cherry, purple rim. Nose: expressive, red berry notes, floral, ripe fruit, wild herbs. Palate: flavourful, fruity, good acidity, round tannins.

DOMINIO DE ONTUR GARNACHA 2008 T
garnacha 100%

**87** Colour: cherry, purple rim. Nose: red berry notes, floral, ripe fruit, powerfull. Palate: flavourful, round tannins, balanced.

DOMINIO DE ONTUR MERLOT 2008 T
merlot

**86** Colour: cherry, purple rim. Nose: expressive, red berry notes, floral, ripe fruit, fruit preserve. Palate: flavourful, fruity, good acidity, round tannins.

DOMINIO DE ONTUR MERLOT 2007 T
merlot 100%

**88** Colour: cherry, purple rim. Nose: expressive, fresh fruit, red berry notes, floral, mineral. Palate: flavourful, fruity, good acidity, round tannins.

## BODEGAS 1890

Ctra. Venta del Olivo, km. 2,5
30520 Jumilla (Murcia)
☎: 968 757 099 - Fax: 968 757 099
elisam@jgc.es
www.vinosdefamilia.com

MAYORAL COSECHA 2008 T JOVEN
monastrell 70%, syrah 20%, cabernet sauvignon 10%

**87** Colour: black cherry, purple rim. Nose: powerfull, fruit preserve, ripe fruit. Palate: powerful, fleshy, fruity.

MAYORAL SYRAH 2006 T
syrah 100%

**90** Colour: black cherry. Nose: ripe fruit, varietal, toasty, powerfull, characterful. Palate: powerful, fleshy, spicy, concentrated, round tannins.

MAYORAL 2006 TC
monastrell 70%, tempranillo 30%

**86** Colour: cherry, garnet rim. Nose: ripe fruit, spicy, creamy oak, toasty, complex. Palate: powerful, flavourful, toasty, round tannins.

MAYORAL CABERNET SAUVIGNON 2006 T
cabernet sauvignon 100%

## 83

MAYORAL 2003 TR
monastrell 40%, tempranillo 40%, cabernet sauvignon 20%

**90** Colour: cherry, garnet rim. Nose: spicy, toasty, complex, fruit preserve, new oak. Palate: powerful, round tannins, toasty, ripe fruit.

### BODEGAS CARCHELO

Casas de la Hoya, s/n
30520 Jumilla (Murcia)
☎: 968 435 137 - Fax: 968 435 200
administracion@carchelo.com
www.carchelo.com

CARCHELO 2007 T
monastrell 40%, syrah 40%, cabernet sauvignon 20%

**88** Colour: very deep cherry. Nose: fruit preserve, red berry notes, expressive, sweet spices, cocoa bean. Palate: flavourful, powerful, fruity, concentrated, round tannins.

ALTICO SYRAH 2006 T
syrah 100%

**90** Colour: bright cherry. Nose: sweet spices, creamy oak, expressive, fruit preserve, dried flowers. Palate: flavourful, fruity, toasty, round tannins, varietal.

CANALIZO FINCA SIERVA 2006 TC
monastrell 40%, syrah 40%, tempranillo 20%

**89** Colour: cherry, garnet rim. Nose: powerfull, spicy, aromatic coffee, fruit preserve, fruit liqueur notes. Palate: flavourful, powerful, spicy, round tannins.

AUTISTA 2006 TC

**88** Colour: cherry, garnet rim. Nose: powerfull, warm, fruit liqueur notes, ripe fruit, aromatic coffee, aged wood nuances. Palate: powerful, flavourful, fleshy, roasted-coffee aftertaste.

### BODEGAS GUARDIOLA

Avda. de Murcia, s/n
30520 Jumilla (Murcia)
☎: 968 781 711 - Fax: 968 781 030
info@bodegasguardiola.com
www.bodegasguardiola.com

DON GUARDIOLA 2008 RD FERMENTADO
EN BARRICA
syrah 100%

**90** Colour: rose, purple rim. Nose: powerfull, ripe fruit, red berry notes, floral, spicy. Palate: fleshy, powerful, fruity, fresh, long.

CASPER MONASTRELL 2007 T BARRICA
monastrell

**88** Colour: bright cherry. Nose: sweet spices, creamy oak, expressive, fruit preserve, overripe fruit. Palate: flavourful, fruity, toasty, round tannins.

DON GUARDIOLA SELECCIÓN 2007 T
monastrell 85%, syrah 15%

**85** Colour: cherry, garnet rim. Nose: closed, fruit preserve, red berry notes, sweet spices. Palate: powerful, fruity, spicy.

### BODEGAS LUZÓN

Ctra. Jumilla-Calasparra, km. 3,100
30520 Jumilla (Murcia)
☎: 968 784 135 - Fax: 968 781 911
info@bodegasluzon.com
www.bodegasluzon.com

LUZÓN 2008 BFB
macabeo 70%, chardonnay 30%

**85** Colour: bright yellow. Nose: ripe fruit, sweet spices, fragrant herbs, fresh. Palate: rich, smoky aftertaste, flavourful, fresh, good acidity.

FINCA LUZÓN 2008 RD
monastrell 70%, cabernet sauvignon 30%

**86** Colour: rose, purple rim. Nose: ripe fruit, red berry notes, floral, expressive, fragrant herbs. Palate: fleshy, fruity, fresh.

FINCA LUZÓN 2008 T
monastrell 70%, syrah 30%

**90** Colour: cherry, purple rim. Nose: expressive, red berry notes, floral, ripe fruit. Palate: flavourful, fruity, round tannins, balsamic.

LUZÓN SYRAH 2008 T
syrah 100%

**89** Colour: cherry, purple rim. Nose: red berry notes, rose petals, varietal, ripe fruit. Palate: flavourful, fruity, good acidity, round tannins.

LUZÓN 2008 T
monastrell 65%, syrah 35%

**88** Colour: very deep cherry, purple rim. Nose: powerfull, earthy notes, mineral, fruit preserve. Palate: powerful, fruity, concentrated, powerful tannins.

## LUZÓN PETIT VERDOT 2008 T
petit verdot 100%

**86** Colour: cherry, purple rim. Nose: powerfull, fruit preserve, red berry notes, scrubland. Palate: flavourful, fruity, good acidity, powerful, grainy tannins.

## LUZÓN MONASTRELL 2007 T
monastrell 100%

**87** Colour: cherry, purple rim. Nose: fresh fruit, red berry notes, varietal. Palate: flavourful, fruity, good acidity, round tannins.

## ALTOS DE LUZÓN 2006 T
monastrell 50%, cabernet sauvignon 25%, tempranillo 25%

**90** Colour: cherry, garnet rim. Nose: ripe fruit, spicy, toasty, complex, aromatic coffee. Palate: powerful, flavourful, toasty, round tannins.

## ALMA DE LUZÓN 2005 T
monastrell 70%, cabernet sauvignon 20%, syrah 10%

**93** Colour: dark-red cherry, very deep cherry. Nose: spicy, fruit preserve, complex, ripe fruit, fruit liqueur notes, cocoa bean. Palate: flavourful, toasty, good acidity, round tannins, full, long.

## CASTILLO DE LUZÓN 2005 TC
monastrell 50%, cabernet sauvignon 20%, tempranillo 20%, merlot 10%

**90** Colour: cherry, garnet rim. Nose: spicy, toasty, complex, fruit preserve. Palate: powerful, flavourful, toasty, round tannins.

## BODEGAS MÄHLER-BESSE

49, rue Camille Godard
33000 Bordeaux (Francia)
☎: 33- 556 560 - Fax: 33- 556 560
s.dechelotte@mahler-besse.com
www.mahler-besse.com

## TAJA MONASTRELL 2007 T
monastrell 100%

**84**

## TAJA EXCELENCIA 2005 T
tempranillo 75%, cabernet sauvignon 25%

**90** Colour: bright cherry. Nose: ripe fruit, sweet spices, creamy oak, expressive, mineral. Palate: flavourful, fruity, toasty, round tannins.

## TAJA 2005 TR
monastrell 50%, tempranillo 20%, cabernet sauvignon 20%, merlot 10%

**87** Colour: cherry, garnet rim. Nose: ripe fruit, spicy, toasty. Palate: powerful, flavourful, toasty, round tannins.

## TAJA 2003 TGR
monastrell 30%, tempranillo 20%, cabernet sauvignon 30%, merlot 20%

**82**

## BODEGAS PÍO DEL RAMO

Ctra. Almanza, s/n
02652 Ontur (Albacete)
☎: 967 323 230 - Fax: 967 323 230
info@piodelramo.com
www.piodelramo.com

## PÍO DEL RAMO CHARDONNAY 2008 B BARRICA
chardonnay 100%

**87** Colour: bright straw. Nose: fresh, white flowers, expressive, ripe fruit, varietal. Palate: flavourful, fruity, good acidity, balanced.

## PÍO DEL RAMO 2008 T ROBLE
monastrell, syrah, cabernet sauvignon

**87** Colour: bright cherry. Nose: sweet spices, expressive, fruit preserve, toasty. Palate: flavourful, fruity, toasty, round tannins.

## PÍO DEL RAMO 2007 TC
syrah, monastrell, cabernet sauvignon

**89** Colour: cherry, garnet rim. Nose: ripe fruit, spicy, creamy oak, toasty, complex. Palate: powerful, flavourful, toasty, round tannins.

## BODEGAS SALZILLO

Ctra. Nacional 344, km 57,2
30520 Jumilla (Murcia)
☎: 968 846 705 - Fax: 968 843 604
salzillo@bodegassalzillo.com
www.bodegassalzillo.com

## ZENIZATE MONASTRELL 2008 T
monastrell 100%

**86** Colour: cherry, purple rim. Nose: expressive, red berry notes, floral, ripe fruit. Palate: flavourful, fruity, good acidity, round tannins.

## MATIUS 2006 TC
monastrell 65%, syrah 25%, cabernet sauvignon 10%

**88** Colour: cherry, garnet rim. Nose: spicy, creamy oak, toasty, complex, fruit preserve. Palate: powerful, flavourful, toasty, round tannins.

## CAMELOT DULCE MONASTRELL 2007 T DULCE
monastrell 100%

**88** Colour: very deep cherry. Nose: varietal, characterful, candied fruit, overripe fruit. Palate: sweet, fruity, powerful.

## BODEGAS SAN DIONISIO S.C.

Ctra. Higuera, s/n
02651 Fuenteálamo (Albacete)
☎: 967 543 032 - Fax: 967 543 136
sandionisio@bodegassandinisio.es
www.bodegassandinisio.es

SEÑORÍO DE FUENTEÁLAMO MACABEO
SELECCIÓN B
macabeo

**85** Colour: bright straw. Nose: fresh, fresh fruit, tropical fruit. Palate: flavourful, fruity, good acidity, balanced.

SEÑORÍO DE FUENTEÁLAMO MONASTRELL RD
syrah

**87** Colour: rose, purple rim. Nose: powerfull, ripe fruit, red berry notes, floral, expressive. Palate: fleshy, powerful, fruity, fresh.

SEÑORIO DE FUENTEÁLAMO 2005 TC
monastrell, syrah

**88** Colour: cherry, garnet rim. Nose: complex, red berry notes, ripe fruit, toasty. Palate: fruity, powerful, flavourful, round tannins, roasted-coffee aftertaste.

MAINETES SELECCIÓN 2005 T
merlot, monastrell, syrah

**88** Colour: cherry, garnet rim. Nose: spicy, toasty, complex, fruit preserve, wet leather. Palate: powerful, flavourful, toasty, round tannins.

## BODEGAS SAN ISIDRO BSI

Ctra. Murcia, s/n
30520 Jumilla (Murcia)
☎: 968 780 700 - Fax: 968 782 351
bsi@bsi.es
www.bsi.es

SABATACHA 2008 B
airén 100%

**84**

SABATACHA 2007 BFB
airén 100%

**81**

SABATACHA 2008 RD
monastrell 100%

**83**

SABATACHA SYRAH 2008 T
syrah 100%

**87** Colour: cherry, purple rim. Nose: fresh fruit, red berry notes, floral, varietal. Palate: flavourful, fruity, good acidity, round tannins.

GÉMINA MONASTRELL 2008 T
monastrell 100%

**86** Colour: cherry, purple rim. Nose: fresh fruit, red berry notes, varietal. Palate: flavourful, fruity, good acidity, round tannins.

SABATACHA MONASTRELL 2008 T
monastrell 100%

**86** Colour: cherry, purple rim. Nose: expressive, fresh fruit, red berry notes, floral. Palate: flavourful, fruity, good acidity, round tannins.

SABATACHA MONASTRELL ECOLÓGICO 2008 T
monastrell 100%

**81**

SABATACHA 2008 T MACERACIÓN CARBÓNICA
monastrell 100%

**80**

SABATACHA MERLOT 2007 T
merlot 100%

**87** Colour: bright cherry. Nose: ripe fruit, sweet spices, creamy oak, expressive, varietal. Palate: flavourful, fruity, toasty, round tannins.

SABATACHA PETIT VERDOT 2007 T
petit verdot 100%

**85** Colour: cherry, purple rim. Nose: fresh fruit, floral, balsamic herbs. Palate: flavourful, fruity, good acidity, round tannins.

GÉMINA CUVÉE SELECCIÓN 2005 T
monastrell 100%

**89** Colour: cherry, garnet rim. Nose: spicy, creamy oak, toasty, ripe fruit, mineral. Palate: powerful, flavourful, toasty, round tannins.

**GÉMINA**

C U V É E   S E L E C C I Ó N

La tierra caliza de Jumilla recibe con agrado los rayos del dorado sol del mediterráneo para crear los frutos de la vida que se convertirán en vinos de exquisita calidad con un aroma y sabor inconfundibles.

Gémina Cuvée Selección es un vino elaborado a partir de viñas Monastrell de pié franco, con un corto paso por madera, obteniéndose así un vino con gran personalidad y elegancia.

**BODEGAS SAN ISIDRO**

**SABATACHA 2005 TC**
monastrell 100%

**86** Colour: cherry, garnet rim. Nose: ripe fruit, spicy, toasty, complex, roasted coffee, dark chocolate. Palate: powerful, flavourful, toasty, round tannins.

**SABATACHA ECOLÓGICO 2004 TC**
monastrell 100%

**83**

**GÉMINA PREMIUM 2003 TR**
monastrell 100%

**90** Colour: cherry, garnet rim. Nose: ripe fruit, spicy, creamy oak, toasty, complex. Palate: powerful, flavourful, toasty, round tannins.

**SABATACHA 2002 TR**
monastrell 100%

**87** Colour: cherry, garnet rim. Nose: ripe fruit, spicy, toasty, dark chocolate, aromatic coffee. Palate: powerful, flavourful, toasty, round tannins.

**SABATACHA 2000 TGR**
monastrell 100%

**88** Colour: pale ruby, brick rim edge. Nose: elegant, spicy, fine reductive notes, wet leather, aged wood nuances, fruit liqueur notes. Palate: spicy, fine tannins, elegant, long.

**GENUS MONASTRELL SYRAH T**
monastrell 80%, syrah 20%

**85** Colour: cherry, garnet rim. Nose: medium intensity, spicy, ripe fruit. Palate: spicy, ripe fruit, round tannins.

**GÉMINA DULCE 2006 TINTO DULCE**
monastrell 100%

**81**

LACRIMA CRISTI

## BODEGAS SILVANO GARCIA

Avda. de Murcia, 29
30520 Jumilla (Murcia)
☎: 968 780 767 - Fax: 968 916 125
export@silvanogarcia.com
www.silvanogarcia.com

**VIÑAHONDA 2008 B**
macabeo 100%

**87** Colour: bright straw. Nose: fresh, fresh fruit, white flowers. Palate: flavourful, fruity, good acidity, balanced.

**SILVANO GARCÍA MOSCATEL 2007 B**
moscatel 100%

**88** Colour: golden. Nose: powerfull, floral, honeyed notes, candied fruit, fragrant herbs. Palate: flavourful, sweet, fresh, fruity, good acidity, long.

**VIÑAHONDA 2008 RD**
monastrell 100%

**85** Colour: rose, purple rim. Nose: ripe fruit, red berry notes, floral, expressive. Palate: fleshy, powerful, fruity, fresh.

**SILVANO GARCÍA MONASTRELL 2007 T**
monastrell 100%

**88** Colour: cherry, purple rim. Nose: expressive, overripe fruit, sun-drenched nuances. Palate: flavourful, fruity, good acidity, sweet.

# DO JUMILLA

**VIÑAHONDA MONASTRELL 2007 T**
monastrell 100%

**84**

**VIÑAHONDA 2007 T**
monastrell 60%, tempranillo 20%, syrah 10%, merlot 10%

**83**

**VIÑAHONDA 2006 TC**
monastrell 50%, tempranillo 20%, cabernet sauvignon 30%

**87** Colour: cherry, garnet rim. Nose: ripe fruit, spicy, toasty. Palate: powerful, flavourful, toasty, round tannins.

**VIÑAHONDA ALLIER FINESSE 2006 T**
monastrell 60%, tempranillo 30%, syrah 10%

**87** Colour: bright cherry. Nose: ripe fruit, sweet spices, creamy oak, expressive. Palate: flavourful, fruity, toasty, round tannins.

## BODEGAS TORRECASTILLO

Ctra. de Bonete, s/n
02650 Montealegre del Castillo (Albacete)
☎: 967 582 188 - Fax: 967 582 339
bodega@torrecastillo.com
www.torrecastillo.com

**TORRECASTILLO 2008 T**
monastrell

**88** Colour: cherry, purple rim. Nose: expressive, fresh fruit, red berry notes, floral. Palate: flavourful, fruity, good acidity, round tannins.

**TORRECASTILLO SELECCIÓN 2008 T**
monastrell 50%, syrah 50%

**84**

**TORRECASTILLO ELLO 2007 T**
monastrell 70%, syrah 20%, cabernet sauvignon 10%

**85** Colour: black cherry. Nose: fruit preserve, overripe fruit, powerfull. Palate: concentrated, warm, round tannins.

**TORRECASTILLO 2005 TC**
monastrell 80%, syrah 20%

**88** Colour: very deep cherry. Nose: fruit liqueur notes, fruit liqueur notes, aromatic coffee, spicy. Palate: spicy, ripe fruit, round tannins.

**TORRECASTILLO 2004 TR**
monastrell 80%, cabernet sauvignon 20%

**87** Colour: cherry, garnet rim. Nose: ripe fruit, spicy, toasty, aromatic coffee. Palate: powerful, flavourful, toasty, round tannins.

## BODEGAS Y VIÑEDOS CASA DE LA ERMITA

Ctra. El Carche, km. 11 Aptdo. Correos 289
30520 Jumilla (Murcia)
☎: 968 783 035 - Fax: 968 716 063
bodega@casadelaermita.com
www.casadelaermita.com

**CASA DE LA ERMITA 2008 B**

**87** Colour: bright straw. Nose: fresh, fresh fruit, white flowers, expressive. Palate: flavourful, fruity, good acidity, balanced.

**CASA DE LA ERMITA 2008 RD**
monastrell

**83**

**CASA DE LA ERMITA 2008 T ROBLE**
monastrell, petit verdot

**86** Colour: bright cherry. Nose: ripe fruit, sweet spices, creamy oak, expressive. Palate: flavourful, fruity, toasty, round tannins.

**MONASTERIO DE SANTA ANA MONASTRELL 2008 T**
monastrell

**85** Colour: bright cherry. Nose: sweet spices, creamy oak, overripe fruit. Palate: flavourful, fruity, toasty, round tannins.

**CASA DE LA ERMITA DULCE MONASTRELL 2007 T**
monastrell

**85** Colour: cherry, garnet rim. Nose: spicy, candied fruit, overripe fruit. Palate: good acidity, pruney, long.

**CASA DE LA ERMITA 2006 TC**
monastrell, petit verdot

**88** Colour: cherry, garnet rim. Nose: ripe fruit, spicy, creamy oak, toasty, complex. Palate: powerful, flavourful, toasty, round tannins.

**CASA DE LA ERMITA PETIT VERDOT 2006 T**
petit verdot

**88** Colour: cherry, garnet rim. Nose: fruit preserve, ripe fruit, spicy, dark chocolate. Palate: fine bitter notes, spicy, flavourful, round tannins.

## PICO MADAMA 2006 T
monastrell, petit verdot

**86** Colour: cherry, garnet rim. Nose: ripe fruit, spicy, toasty, aromatic coffee. Palate: powerful, flavourful, toasty, round tannins.

## EL NIDO

Paraje de la Aragona, s/n
30520 Jumilla (Murcia)
☎: 968 435 022 - Fax: 968 435 653
info@bodegaselnido.com
www.bodegaselnido.com

### CLIO 2007 T
monastrell 70%, cabernet sauvignon 30%

**94** Colour: bright cherry. Nose: sweet spices, expressive, earthy notes, new oak, ripe fruit. Palate: flavourful, fruity, toasty, round tannins.

### EL NIDO 2007 T
cabernet sauvignon 70%, monastrell 30%

**95** Colour: bright cherry. Nose: ripe fruit, sweet spices, creamy oak, lactic notes, powerfull, varietal. Palate: flavourful, fruity, toasty, round tannins.

### CLIO 2006 T
monastrell 70%, cabernet sauvignon 30%

**95** Colour: cherry, garnet rim. Nose: mineral, powerfull, ripe fruit, fruit expression, dark chocolate, aromatic coffee, sweet spices. Palate: flavourful, powerful, fleshy, ripe fruit, round tannins.

### EL NIDO 2006 T
cabernet sauvignon 70%, monastrell 30%

**94** Colour: black cherry. Nose: powerfull, mineral, toasty, spicy, complex, aromatic coffee. Palate: flavourful, powerful, good structure, spicy, warm, powerful tannins.

## FINCA EL PASO

Avda. Diagonal, 590, 5 1
08021 Barcelona ()
☎: 660 445 464
montse@vinergia.com
www.vinergia.es

### FINCA EL PASO 2008 T
monastrell 100%

**89** Colour: bright cherry. Nose: floral, fruit preserve, lactic notes, wild herbs. Palate: flavourful, good structure, fruity aftestaste, fine bitter notes, long.

## FINCA OMBLANCAS

Ctra. Jumilla-Ontur, km. 3,3
30520 Jumilla (Murcia)
☎: 968 780 850 - Fax: 968 780 850
omblancas@fincaomblancas.com
www.fincaomblancas.com

### OMBLANCAS DELAÍN 2005 T
monastrell 100%

**87** Colour: cherry, garnet rim. Nose: medium intensity, fruit liqueur notes, fruit liqueur notes, dark chocolate. Palate: warm, powerful, round tannins.

### OMBLANCAS DENUÑO CABERNET SAUVIGNON 2005 T
cabernet sauvignon 100%

**87** Colour: cherry, garnet rim. Nose: ripe fruit, spicy, creamy oak, toasty, complex. Palate: powerful, flavourful, toasty, round tannins.

### OMBLANCAS DENUÑO MONASTRELL 2005 T
monastrell 100%

**87** Colour: cherry, garnet rim. Nose: fruit preserve, fruit liqueur notes, aromatic coffee, aged wood nuances. Palate: flavourful, spicy, classic aged character, long.

### OMBLANCAS DENUÑO PETIT VERDOT 2005 T
petit verdot 90%, syrah 5%, monastrell 5%

**85** Colour: bright cherry. Nose: fruit liqueur notes, aromatic coffee, spicy. Palate: flavourful, toasty, round tannins, warm.

### OMBLANCAS SELECCIÓN ESPECIAL 2004 T
monastrell 85%, cabernet sauvignon 15%

**90** Colour: cherry, garnet rim. Nose: expressive, elegant, fruit liqueur notes, aged wood nuances, aromatic coffee. Palate: flavourful, spicy, classic aged character, fine bitter notes, round tannins.

## JUAN GIL

Paraje de la Aragona
30520 Jumilla (Murcia)
☎: 968 435 022 - Fax: 968 716 051
info@juangil.es
www.juangil.es

### JUAN GIL 12 MESES 2007 T
monastrell 100%

**91** Colour: cherry, garnet rim. Nose: expressive, ripe fruit, fresh fruit, sweet spices, balsamic herbs, scrubland.

Palate: flavourful, powerful, balsamic, sweetness, round tannins.

**JUAN GIL 4 MESES 2007 T**
monastrell 100%

**91** Colour: cherry, garnet rim. Nose: powerfull, ripe fruit, balsamic herbs, spicy. Palate: flavourful, powerful, fleshy, balsamic.

## ORO WINES JUMILLA

Portillo de la Glorieta, 7 B
30520 Jumilla (Murcia)
☎: 968 435 022 - Fax: 968 716 051
info@orowines.com

**WRONGO DONGO 2008 T JOVEN**

**90** Colour: cherry, garnet rim. Nose: powerfull, ripe fruit, scrubland, sweet spices, fresh fruit. Palate: flavourful, good structure, powerful, spicy.

## PEDRO LUIS MARTÍNEZ

Barrio Iglesias, 55
30520 Jumilla (Murcia)
☎: 968 780 142 - Fax: 968 716 256
comercial@alceno.com
www.alceno.com

**ALCEÑO 2008 B**
macabeo 80%, airén 20%

**84**

**ALCEÑO 2008 RD**
monastrell 80%, syrah 20%

**82**

**ALCEÑO 2008 T**
monastrell 60%, syrah 20%, tempranillo 20%

**88** Colour: cherry, purple rim. Nose: expressive, fresh fruit, red berry notes, floral, varietal. Palate: flavourful, fruity, good acidity, round tannins.

**ROMEO 2007 T JOVEN**
monastrell 100%

**86** Colour: cherry, purple rim. Nose: fresh fruit, red berry notes, floral. Palate: flavourful, fruity, good acidity, round tannins.

**ALCEÑO MONASTRELL 2007 T ROBLE**
monastrell 60%, syrah 40%

**90** Colour: bright cherry. Nose: sweet spices, creamy oak, expressive, red berry notes. Palate: flavourful, fruity, toasty, round tannins.

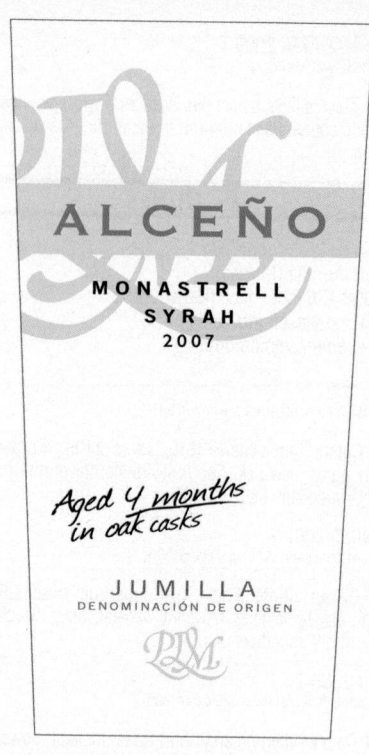

**ALCEÑO SYRAH PREMIUM 2006 T**
syrah 85%, monastrell 15%

**91** Colour: bright cherry. Nose: ripe fruit, sweet spices, creamy oak, expressive, powerfull, varietal, mineral. Palate: flavourful, fruity, toasty, round tannins.

**ALCEÑO DULCE 2006 T**
monastrell 100%

**90** Colour: cherry, garnet rim. Nose: powerfull, varietal, candied fruit, dried fruit, fruit liqueur notes. Palate: powerful, fleshy, spirituous, ripe fruit, sweet.

**ALCEÑO MONASTRELL 2006 T**
monastrell 80%, syrah 20%

**90** Colour: bright cherry. Nose: sweet spices, creamy oak, expressive, ripe fruit. Palate: flavourful, fruity, toasty, round tannins.

**ALCEÑO SELECCIÓN 2005 TC**
monastrell 50%, syrah 40%, tempranillo 10%

**88** Colour: cherry, garnet rim. Nose: ripe fruit, spicy, toasty, complex. Palate: powerful, flavourful, toasty, round tannins.

**ROMEO 2005 TC**
monastrell 100%

**87** Colour: cherry, garnet rim. Nose: ripe fruit, spicy, toasty. Palate: powerful, flavourful, toasty, round tannins.

## PROPIEDAD VITÍCOLA CASA CASTILLO

Ctra. Jumilla - Hellín, km. 15,7
30520 Jumilla (Murcia)
☎: 968 781 691 - Fax: 968 716 238
info@casacastillo.es
www.casacastillo.es

**VALTOSCA 2008 T**
syrah 100%

**94** Colour: bright cherry. Nose: sweet spices, creamy oak, expressive, earthy notes, ripe fruit. Palate: flavourful, fruity, toasty, round tannins, great length.

**CASA CASTILLO MONASTRELL 2008 T**
monastrell 100%

**90** Colour: cherry, purple rim. Nose: expressive, fresh fruit, red berry notes, floral. Palate: flavourful, fruity, good acidity, round tannins.

**VALTOSCA 2007 T**
syrah 100%

**93** Colour: cherry, purple rim. Nose: ripe fruit, red berry notes, scrubland, sweet spices, creamy oak. Palate: flavourful, fruity, spicy, long.

**CASA CASTILLO MONASTRELL 2007 T**
monastrell 100%

**88** Colour: cherry, purple rim. Nose: medium intensity, ripe fruit, spicy. Palate: flavourful, fruity, ripe fruit.

**CASA CASTILLO PIE FRANCO 2006 T**
monastrell 100%

**95** Colour: cherry, garnet rim. Nose: ripe fruit, spicy, creamy oak, toasty, complex, mineral. Palate: powerful, flavourful, toasty, round tannins, long.

**LAS GRAVAS 2006 T**
monastrell 55%, cabernet sauvignon 45%

**93** Colour: cherry, garnet rim. Nose: elegant, complex, ripe fruit, spicy, mineral, dry stone. Palate: flavourful, good structure, spicy, ripe fruit, long.

## VIÑA ELENA S.L.

Estrecho de Marín s/n
30520 Jumilla (Murcia)
☎: 968 781 340 - Fax: 968 435 275
info@vinaelena.com
www.vinaelena.com

**LOS CUCOS DE LA ALBERQUILLA 2007 T**
cabernet sauvignon 100%

**87** Colour: cherry, garnet rim. Nose: ripe fruit, spicy, toasty, complex, dark chocolate, aged wood nuances. Palate: powerful, flavourful, toasty, round tannins.

**PACHECO SELECCIÓN 2006 T**
monastrell 60%, merlot 20%, cabernet sauvignon 20%

**86** Colour: cherry, garnet rim. Nose: fruit liqueur notes, fruit liqueur notes, aromatic coffee, aged wood nuances. Palate: spirituous, spicy, ripe fruit.

**PACHECO 2005 TC**
monastrell 80%, merlot 10%, cabernet sauvignon 10%

**87** Colour: cherry, garnet rim. Nose: ripe fruit, spicy, creamy oak, toasty, aromatic coffee. Palate: powerful, flavourful, toasty, round tannins.

## VIÑAS CASA DEL RICO

Poeta Andrés Boralin, 1 5°d
30011 Murcia (Murcia)
☎: 676 460 808

**GORGOCIL MONASTRELL 2007 T**
monastrell

**91** Colour: cherry, purple rim. Nose: expressive, fresh fruit, red berry notes, floral, sweet spices. Palate: flavourful, fruity, good acidity, round tannins.

**GORGOCIL TEMPRANILLO 2007 T**
tempranillo

**90** Colour: bright cherry. Nose: ripe fruit, sweet spices, creamy oak, expressive, mineral. Palate: flavourful, fruity, toasty, round tannins.

## VIÑEDOS DEL QUÓRUM

Ctra. Jumilla-Albatana, km. 6
30520 Jumilla (Murcia)
☎: 968 757 508 - Fax: 968 108 253
gmartinez@vinedosdelquorum.com
www.vinedosdelquorum.com

NDQ 2008 T
monastrell

**84**

NDQ SELECCIÓN 2007 T

**88** Colour: bright cherry. Nose: ripe fruit, sweet spices, creamy oak. Palate: flavourful, fruity, toasty, round tannins.

## VIÑEDOS Y BODEGAS JM MARTÍNEZ VERDÚ

Valle Hoya de Torres
30520 Jumilla (Murcia)
☎: 968 756 240 - Fax: 968 756 240
info@xenysel.com
www.xenysel.com

XENYSEL 12 2007 T
monastrell 100%

**88** Colour: cherry, garnet rim. Nose: ripe fruit, spicy, toasty, complex, cocoa bean, mineral. Palate: powerful, flavourful, toasty, balsamic, varietal, powerful tannins.

CALZÁS PIE FRANCO 2006 T BARRICA
monastrell 100%

**91** Colour: cherry, garnet rim. Nose: ripe fruit, spicy, creamy oak, toasty, complex. Palate: powerful, flavourful, toasty, round tannins.

XENYSEL 2006 T
monastrell 100%

**85** Colour: cherry, garnet rim. Nose: candied fruit, fruit liqueur notes, dried fruit. Palate: warm, ripe fruit, spicy.

XENYSEL MONASTRELL 2006 T BARRICA
monastrell 100%

**85** Colour: deep cherry. Nose: fruit preserve, overripe fruit, sweet spices, dark chocolate. Palate: powerful, concentrated, round tannins.

SOME OTHER WINERIES WITHIN THE DO:

**ALTOS DEL CUADRADO**
**BODEGAS HUERTAS**
**BODEGAS OLIVARES**
**BODEGAS SIMÓN**
**COOP. NTRA. SRA .DE LA ENCARNACIÓN**
**DELAMPA S.L.**
**EL CARCHE**
**SEÑORÍO DEL CONDESTABLE**
**VIÑEDOS Y BODEGAS ASENSIO CARCELÉN**

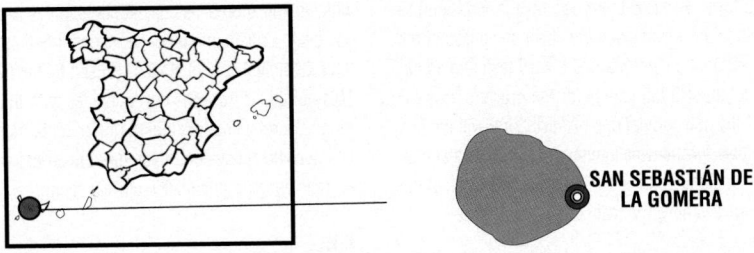

SAN SEBASTIÁN DE
LA GOMERA

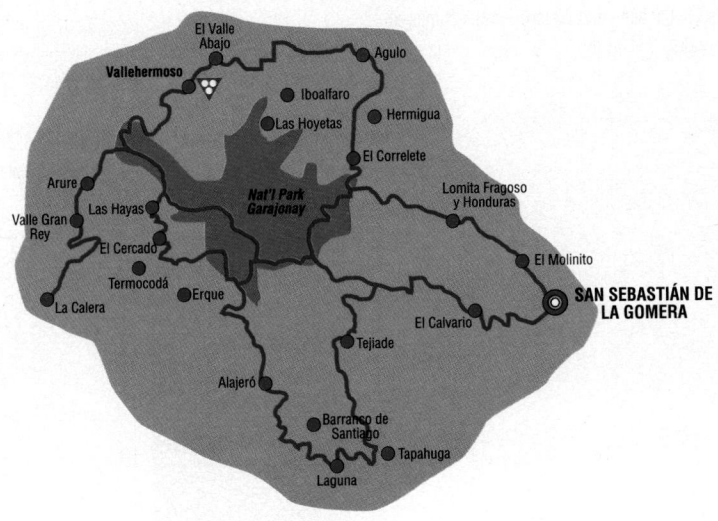

Consejo Regulador
DO Boundary

## NEWS

The wineries from La Gomera show little interest to send their wines for us to taste them. We take it is difficult to grow grapes in the island given the sheer steepness of the vineyards, rendering vine growing a hard task and an expensive one too, with high costs for the growers. It is expected that the new regulations of April 2009 will mean a brand new time for the wine industry in La Gomera and an opportunity to come up at last with great renderings of the forastera blanca variety, the main one in the region.

## LOCATION

The majority of the vineyards are found in the north of the island, in the vicinity of the towns of Vallehermoso (some 385 Ha) and Hermigua. The remaining vineyards are spread out over Agulo, Valle Gran Rey –near the capital city of La Gomera, San Sebastián– and Alajeró, on the slopes of the Garajonay peak.

## CLIMATE

The island benefits from a subtropical climate together with, as one approaches the higher altitudes of the Garajonay peak, a phenomenon of permanent humidity known as 'mar de nubes' (sea of clouds) caused by the trade winds. This humid air from the north collides with the mountain range, thereby creating a kind of horizontal rain resulting in a specific ecosystem made up of luxuriant valleys. The average temperature is 20°C all year round.

## SOIL

The most common soil in the higher mountain regions is deep and clayey, while, as one approaches lower altitudes towards the scrubland, the soil is more Mediterranean with a good many stones and terraces similar to those of the Priorat.

## GRAPE VARIETIES:

**White:** *Forastera* (90%), *Gomera Blanca*, *Listán Blanca* and *Marmajuelo*.
**Red:** *Listán Negra* (5%), *Negramoll* (2%); experimental: *Tintilla Castellana*, *Cabernet Sauvignon* and *Rubí Cabernet*.

| | |
|---|---|
| Hectares of Vineyard | 126 |
| Nº Viticulturists | 210 |
| Nº of Bodegas | 13 |
| 2008 Harvest | N/A |
| 2007 Production | 55,000 l. |
| Marketing | 100% domestic |

**CONSEJO REGULADOR**
Avda. Guillermo Ascanio, 16, 1º
38840 Vallehermoso (La Gomera)
☎: 922 800 801 - Fax: 922 801 146
@ crdolagomera@mixmail.com

**GENERAL CHARACTERISTICS OF THE WINES:**

| | |
|---|---|
| **WHITES** | Almost all the wines are based on the *Forastera*, and are produced according to traditional methods: they are usually a little overripe and have rustic and warm notes. The best examples are from the higher and less humid areas, with wild and scrubland notes. |
| **REDS** | The warm climate leaves its mark on most of the young red wines of the island, with a somewhat sweet taste with balsamic notes. The greenness that can be seen in many of them is the result of the high production that on occasions the varietal pattern of the *Listán Negra* and the *Negramoll* have, from which they are produced. |

## 2008 VINTAGE RATING:

## N/A

# DO LA GOMERA

SOME WINERIES WITHIN THE DO:

**BODEGA INSULAR DE LA GOMERA**
**COMUNIDAD DE BIENES MONTORO C.B.**
**FAUSTINO NIEBLA NEGRÍN**
**HUMBERTO ASCANIO MONTESINOS**
**JORGE SUÁREZ COELLO**
**RAMÓN MARICHAL FELIPE**

## NEWS

In a region where you can make wine with virtually every grape variety you can think of –37 altogether, including the experimental ones, as reflected in the new regulations– there are high probabilities of finding great differences in terms of quality, and such was the main outcome of our tasting in La Mancha this year. Wines made from grapes with shorter cycles –tempranillo (known locally as cencibel), syrah, merlot, airén and macabeo– fared much better in a unusually colder summer. The sauvignon blanc wines showed particularly expressive and had nothing to envy to more northerly renderings.

Considering the high percentage of short-cycle grape varieties planted in La Mancha (more than 90% of the DO) we can ascertain the quality of the vintage as opposed to those of 2005 and 2006, which show generally a warmer, even hot character. But it is evident that grape varieties with longer cycles such as garnacha, cabernet sauvignon and petit verdot did not fare well, with abundant herbaceous, green and astringent notes. The majority of cooperatives from La Mancha are ready to pay for quantity rather than quality, regardless of the grape variety and vine-growing standards. On the other hand, wines aged in wood even for shorter periods as well as reserva and gran reserva renderings get the best ratings, being the 14% new wine allowed by law in the final blend the reason behind their good performance, since they manage to show less woody, and aged notes, and had a more noticeable, fresher and asier character more in tune with modern market requirements. The wines from Fontana, Bodegas Volver and Finca Antigua are the best examples of the new and evidently better philosophy of an incredibly vast wine region.

## LOCATION

On the southern plateau in the provinces of Albacete, Ciudad Real, Cuenca and Toledo. It is the largest wine-growing region in Spain and in the world.

## CLIMATE

Extreme continental, with temperatures ranging between 40/45°C in summer and –10/12°C in winter. Rather low rainfall, with an average of about 375 mm per year.

## SOIL

The terrain is flat and the vineyards are situated at an altitude of about 700 m above sea level. The soil is generally sandy, limy and clayey.

## GRAPE VARIETIES:

**White:** *Airén* (majority), *Macabeo, Pardilla, Chardonnay, Sauvignon Blanc.*

**Red:** *Cencibel* (majority amongst red varieties), *Garnacha, Moravia, Cabernet Sauvignon, Merlot* and *Syrah.*

| | |
|---|---|
| Hectares of Vineyard | 184,509 |
| Nº Viticulturists | 20,086 |
| Nº of Bodegas | 281 |
| 2008 Harvest | Very Good |
| 2007 Production | 103,943,000 l. |
| Marketing | 33% domestic 67% export |

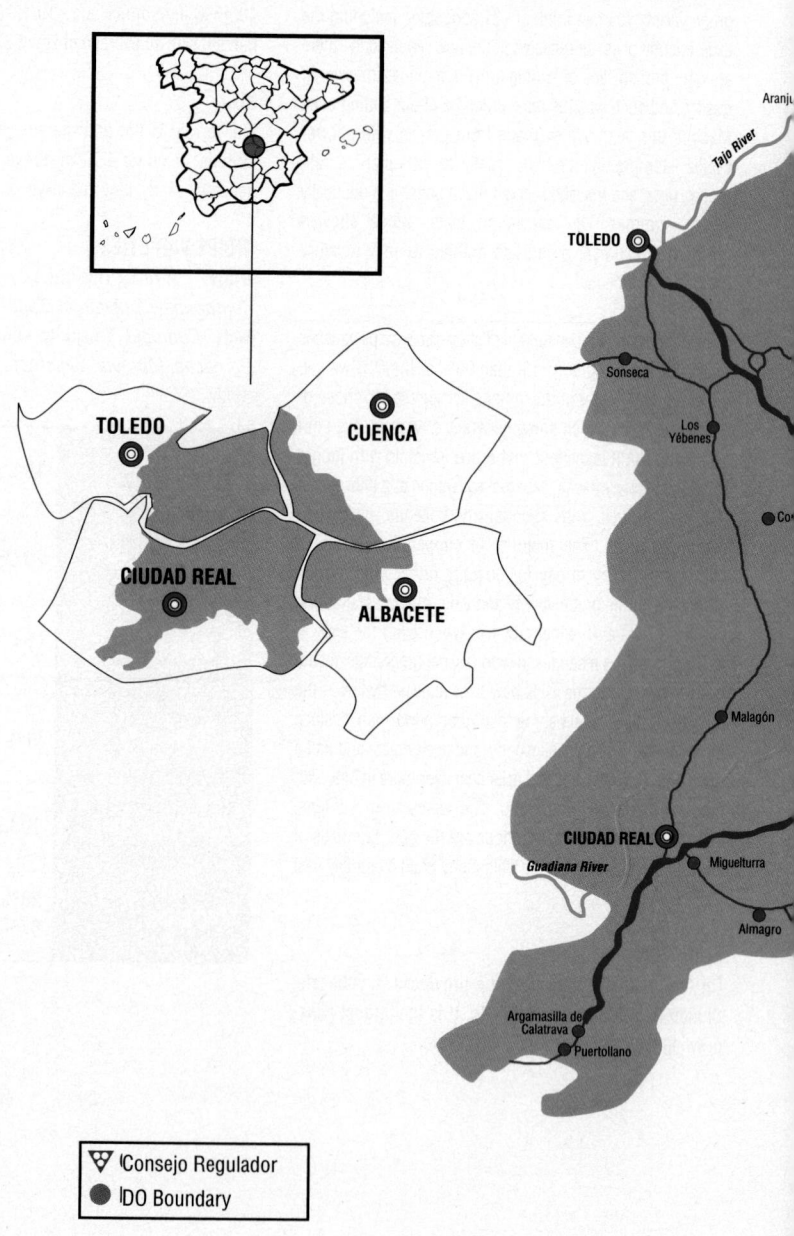

Consejo Regulador
DO Boundary

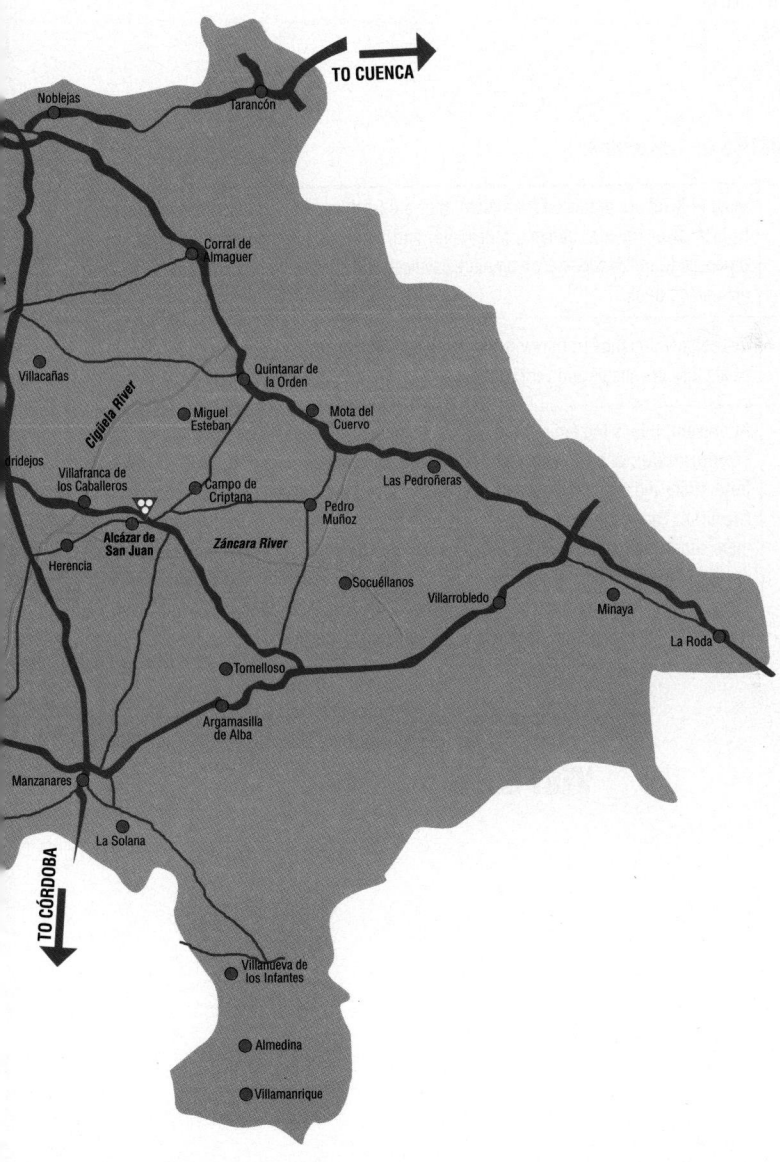

# DO LA MANCHA

**CONSEJO REGULADOR**
Avda. de Criptana, 73
13600 Alcázar de San Juan (Ciudad Real)
☎: 926 541 523 - Fax: 926 588 040
@ consejo@lamanchado.es
www.lamanchado.es
www.lamanchawines.com

## GENERAL CHARACTERISTICS OF THE WINES:

| | |
|---|---|
| **WHITES** | Most of them are produced from Airén; they are fresh and fruity, sometimes with notes of tropical fruit (melon, banana, pineapple) and somewhat limited on the palate. Those produced from *Macabeo* are a bit more balanced and intense, and are fruity, fresh and very pleasant to drink. |
| **ROSÉS** | The colour can range from onion skin to pink; on the nose they are fresh and fruity; on the palate they are supple and very light. |
| **REDS** | At present, this is the type of the highest quality in the region. Based on the *Cencibel* (*Tempranillo*), one can especially find young red wines with a good colour, which are fresh, fruity and with a varietal character on the nose; on the palate they are meaty and quite flavourful. Those aged in wood generally maintain these characteristics, although they are more supple due to the contribution of the barrel. The Reservas and Gran Reservas follow the line of the traditional wines from Rioja, as far as the conception of their ageing.<br>There are also single variety *Cabernet Sauvignon* wines that add to the characteristics of this variety, quite warm notes, typical of the sunshine of the region. |

## 2008 VINTAGE RATING:

# VERY GOOD

## ALEJANDRO FERNÁNDEZ TINTO PESQUERA "EL VINCULO"

Avda. Juan Carlos I s/n
13610 Campo de Criptana (Ciudad Real)
☎: 926 563 709 - Fax: 926 563 709
elvinculo@elvinculo.com
www.grupopesquera.com

EL VÍNCULO 2004 TR

**87** Colour: cherry, garnet rim. Nose: ripe fruit, spicy, toasty, dark chocolate. Palate: powerful, flavourful, toasty, round tannins.

## AMANCIO MENCHERO MÁRQUEZ

Legión, 27
13260 Bolaños de Calatrava (Ciudad Real)
☎: 926 870 076 - Fax: 926 871 558
amanciomenchero@hotmail.com

FINCA MORIANA 2008 B
airén 100%

**78**

FINCA MORIANA 2004 TC
cencibel 100%

**87** Colour: bright cherry. Nose: ripe fruit, sweet spices, creamy oak, expressive. Palate: flavourful, fruity, toasty, round tannins.

## BODEGA EL REMEDIO

Ctra. Cabezamesada, s/n
45370 Santa Cruz de la Zarza (Toledo)
☎: 925 143 233 - Fax: 925 143 233
elremedio@ucaman.es
www.bodegaelremedio.com

VIÑAS DE RIBOCHE MACABEO 2008 B
macabeo 100%

**77**

ENCAÑO TEMPRANILLO 2008 T
tempranillo 100%

**78**

ENCAÑO TEMPRANILLO 2007 T ROBLE
tempranillo 100%

**83**

VIÑAS DE RIBOCHE 2008 ROSADO SEMIDULCE
tempranillo 100%

**78**

## BODEGA LA DEFENSA

Avda. de Castilla La Mancha, 38
45370 Santa Cruz de la Zarza (Toledo)
☎: 925 143 234 - Fax: 925 125 154
bodegasladefensa@bodegasladefensa.es
www.bodegasladefensa.es

VELSINIA AIREN 2008 B
airén 100%

**77**

VELSINIA 2008 T
tempranillo 100%

**81**

## BODEGA LA TERCIA-VINOS ECOLÓGICOS

Pza. Santa Quiteria, 12
13600 Alcázar de San Juan (Ciudad Real)
☎: 926 541 512 - Fax: 926 550 104
bodegalatercia@terra.es
www.bodegalatercia.com

YEMANUEVA AIRÉN ECOLÓGICO 2008 B
airén 100%

**78**

YEMANUEVA AIRÉN 2007 B JOVEN
airén

**80**

YEMANUEVA TEMPRANILLO ECOLÓGICO 2007 T

**83**

YEMASERENA TEMPRANILLO SELECCIÓN LIMITADA 2004 T
tempranillo 100%

**84**

## BODEGA Y VIÑA ALDOBA

Ctra. Alcázar, s/n
13700 Tomelloso (Ciudad Real)
☎: 926 505 653 - Fax: 926 505 652
aldoba@allozo.com

ALDOBA 2008 B
macabeo 100%

**76**

ALDOBA SELECCIÓN TEMPRANILLO 2008 T
tempranillo 100%

**83**

ALDOBA 2005 TC
tempranillo 100%

**83**

ALDOBA 2004 TR
tempranillo 100%

**77**

## BODEGAS AYUSO

Miguel Caro, 6
02600 Villarrobledo (Albacete)
☎: 967 140 458 - Fax: 967 144 925
export@bodegasayuso.es
www.bodegasayuso.es

ARMIÑO 2008 B
airén 100%

**84**

FINCA LOS AZARES SAUVIGNON BLANC 2008 B
sauvignon blanc 100%

**84**

CASTILLO DE BENIZAR MACABEO 2008 B
macabeo

**79**

ESTOLA 2007 B
airén 80%, chardonnay 20%

**82**

CASTILLO DE BENIZAR CABERNET SAUVIGNON
2008 RD
cabernet sauvignon 100%

**83**

CASTILLO DE BENIZAR TEMPRANILLO 2008 T
tempranillo 100%

**83**

FINCA LOS AZARES PETIT VERDOT 2005 T
petit verdot 100%

**87** Colour: dark-red cherry, garnet rim. Nose: neat, expressive, balsamic herbs, toasty. Palate: full, powerful, flavourful, slightly dry, soft tannins.

ESTOLA 2005 TC
tempranillo 100%

**84**

ESTOLA 2004 TR
tempranillo 75%, cabernet sauvignon 25%

**85** Colour: cherry, garnet rim. Nose: medium intensity, ripe fruit, fruit liqueur notes, spicy. Palate: flavourful, spirituous, spicy.

FINCA LOS AZARES MERLOT CABERNET
SAUVIGNON 2004 T
cabernet sauvignon 50%, merlot 50%

**85** Colour: cherry, garnet rim. Nose: ripe fruit, spicy, creamy oak, toasty, complex. Palate: powerful, flavourful, toasty, round tannins.

ESTOLA 1999 TGR
tempranillo 65%, cabernet sauvignon 35%

**85** Colour: pale ruby, brick rim edge. Nose: elegant, spicy, fine reductive notes, wet leather, aged wood nuances, fruit liqueur notes. Palate: spicy, fine tannins, elegant, long.

## BODEGAS CAMPOS REALES (COOPERATIVA NUESTRA SEÑORA DEL ROSARIO)

Castilla La Mancha, 4
16670 El Provencio (Cuenca)
☎: 967 166 066 - Fax: 967 165 032
info@bodegascamposreales.com
www.bodegascamposreales.com

CANFORRALES ALMA VERDEJO 2008 B
verdejo 100%

**85** Colour: bright straw. Nose: fresh fruit, fruit expression, white flowers. Palate: fresh, fruity, easy to drink.

CANFORRALES GARNACHA 2008 RD
garnacha 100%

**85** Colour: rose, purple rim. Nose: expressive, red berry notes, candied fruit. Palate: fruity, fresh, light-bodied.

CANFORRALES CLÁSICO TEMPRANILLO 2008 T
tempranillo 100%

**89** Colour: bright cherry. Nose: ripe fruit, sweet spices, creamy oak, expressive. Palate: flavourful, fruity, toasty, round tannins.

CAMPOS REALES 2008 T
tempranillo 100%

**87** Colour: cherry, purple rim. Nose: expressive, fresh fruit, red berry notes, sweet spices. Palate: flavourful, fruity, good acidity, round tannins.

CANFORRALES SYRAH 2007 T ROBLE
syrah 100%

**86** Colour: very deep cherry. Nose: ripe fruit, roasted coffee, creamy oak, dark chocolate. Palate: fine bitter notes, powerful, fleshy, roasted-coffee aftertaste.

CANFORRALES SELECCIÓN 2007 T
tempranillo 100%

**84**

CÁNFORA "PIE FRANCO" 2003 T
tempranillo 100%

**91** Colour: bright cherry. Nose: ripe fruit, sweet spices, creamy oak, roasted coffee. Palate: flavourful, fruity, toasty, round tannins.

## BODEGAS CASTILLO DE CONSUEGRA

Ctra. Alcazar, km. 0,2
45700 Consuegra (Toledo)
☎: 925 481 036 - Fax: 925 480 393
sales@calderico.com
www.calderico.com

CALDERICO 2008 B JOVEN
airén

**82**

CALDERICO 2008 T
tempranillo

**84**

CALDERICO 2005 TC
tempranillo

**82**

CALDERICO 2004 TR

**85** Colour: cherry, garnet rim. Nose: medium intensity, ripe fruit, sweet spices, red berry notes. Palate: flavourful, fruity, spicy.

## BODEGAS CENTRO ESPAÑOLAS S.A.

Ctra. Alcázar, s/n
13700 Tomelloso (Ciudad Real)

☎: 926 505 654 - Fax: 926 505 652
allozo@allozo.com
www.allozo.com

ALLOZO V 2008 B
verdejo

**80**

FUENTE DEL RITMO 2008 B
airén 100%

**79**

ALLOZO FINCA DE LA FUENTE 2008 B
macabeo 100%

**78**

ALLOZO 2008 RD
tempranillo 100%

**78**

ALLOZO FINCA LA FUENTE 2008 T
tempranillo

**86** Colour: cherry, purple rim. Nose: expressive, fresh fruit, red berry notes, floral. Palate: flavourful, fruity, good acidity, grainy tannins.

ALLOZO MERLOT DE FINCA LOMA DE LOS FRAILES 2008 T
merlot 100%

**84**

ALLOZO FINCA LOS FRAILES CABERNET 2008 T
cabernet sauvignon 100%

**83**

ALLOZO SHYRAZ DE FINCA DE LA RAMA 2008 T
syrah 100%

**83**

FUENTE DEL RITMO TEMPRANILLO 2008 T
tempranillo 100%

**83**

ALLOZO 2005 TC
tempranillo 100%

**85** Colour: cherry, garnet rim. Nose: fruit preserve, spicy, aromatic coffee. Palate: flavourful, warm, fine bitter notes.

ALLOZO 927 2005 T
tempranillo, syrah, merlot

**82**

FUENTE DEL RITMO 2005 TC
tempranillo 100%

**81**

FUENTE DEL RITMO 2004 TR
tempranillo 100%

**81**

ALLOZO 2003 TR
tempranillo 100%

**78**

ALLOZO 2002 TGR
tempranillo 100%

**84**

ALLOZO FINCA LOS CANTOS 2002 T
tempranillo 100%

**82**

## BODEGAS CRISTO DE LA VEGA

General Goded, 6
13630 Socuéllamos (Ciudad Real)
☎: 926 530 388 - Fax: 926 530 024
dptotecnico@bodegascrisve.com
www.bodegascrisve.com

YUGO AIRÉN 2008 B
airén 100%

**81**

EL YUGO 2008 RD
garnacha 80%, tempranillo 20%

**83**

EL YUGO 2004 TC
tempranillo 100%

**83**

YUGO 50 ANIVERSARIO 2003 TR
tempranillo 100%

**79**

YUGO SYRAH-TEMPRANILLO-MERLOT T

**87** Colour: cherry, garnet rim. Nose: fresh fruit, expressive, floral. Palate: light-bodied, fruity, flavourful, good acidity, round tannins.

MARQUÉS DE CASTILLA

## BODEGAS ENTREMONTES (NUESTRA SEÑORA DE LA PIEDAD)

Circunvalación, s/n
45800 Quintanar de la Orden (Toledo)
☎: 925 180 930 - Fax: 925 180 480
comercial@bodegasentremontes.com

CLAVELITO AIRÉN 2008 B
airén 100%

**82**

CLAVELITO MACABEO 2008 B
macabeo 100%

**82**

CLAVELITO SAUVIGNON BLANC 2008 B JOVEN
sauvignon blanc

**80**

CLAVELITO VERDEJO 2008 B
verdejo 100%

**79**

CLAVELITO SAUVIGNON BLANC 2007 B
sauvignon blanc 100%

**82**

CLAVELITO 2008 RD
tempranillo 100%

**81**

ENTREMONTES TEMPRANILLO 2008 T
tempranillo 100%

**83**

ENTREMONTES CABERNET SAUVIGNON 2008 T
cabernet sauvignon 100%

**75**

ENTREMONTES TEMPRANILLO 2007 T

**82**

ENTREMONTES CABERNET SAUVIGNON 2007 T

**81**

ENTREMONTES GARNACHA 2007 T
garnacha 100%

**79**

ENTREMONTES TEMPRANILLO MERLOT SYRAH
2006 T
tempranillo 33%, merlot 33%, syrah 33%

**72**

ENTREMONTES 2004 TC
tempranillo 100%

**86** Colour: dark-red cherry, garnet rim. Nose: expressive,
ripe fruit, spicy. Palate: powerful, flavourful, great length,
slightly dry, soft tannins.

ENTREMONTES 2003 T ROBLE
tempranillo

**81**

ENTREMONTES 2002 T ROBLE
tempranillo 100%

**80**

ENTREMONTES 2002 TR
tempranillo 100%

**75**

ENTREMONTES 2000 TGR
tempranillo 100%

**83**

ENTREMONTES BN
macabeo 60%, verdejo 40%

**82**

ENTREMONTES SS
airén 100%

**82**

## BODEGAS HERMANOS RUBIO

Ctra. de Villamuelas, s/n
45740 Villasequilla (Toledo)
☎: 925 310 284 - Fax: 925 325 133
info@bhrubio.com
www.bodegashermanosrubio.com

VIÑA ALAMBRADA 2008 B
airén 100%

**85** Colour: yellow, bright straw. Nose: neat, white flowers,
grassy. Palate: flavourful, long, good finish.

ZOCODOVER SELECCIÓN SAUVIGNON BLANC 2007 B
sauvignon blanc 100%

**83**

ZOCODOVER SELECCIÓN 2002 TC
tempranillo 50%, cabernet sauvignon 50%

**84**

SEÑORÍO DE ZOCODOVER 2002 TR
tempranillo 100%

**83**

SEÑORÍO DE ZOCODOVER 2002 TC
tempranillo 100%

**83**

ZOCODOVER SELECCIÓN 2001 TR
tempranillo 50%, cabernet sauvignon 50%

**84**

## BODEGAS ISLA

Nuestra Señora de la Paz, 9
13210 Villarta San Juan (Ciudad Real)
☎: 926 640 004 - Fax: 926 640 062
b.isla@terra.es
www.bodegasisla.com

ISLA ORO AIRÉN 2008 B
airén 100%

**81**

ISLA ORO GARNACHA 2008 RD
garnacha 100%

**72**

ISLA ORO TEMPRANILLO 2008 T
tempranillo 100%

**78**

ISLA ORO TEMPRANILLO 2003 TC
tempranillo

**78**

ISLA ORO TEMPRANILLO MERLOT SYRAH 2005 T
tempranillo 33%, merlot 33%, syrah 33%

**83**

## Isla Oro

TEMPRANILLO
SYRAH-MERLOT

**LA MANCHA**
Denominación de Origen

LA MANCHA
DENOMINACIÓN DE ORIGEN

Embotellado por: Bodegas Isla, S.L.
Villarta de San Juan - Ciudad Real - ESPAÑA
R.E.: CLM - 559/CR

75 cl.                          12,5% vol.

### BODEGAS J. SANTOS

Sagunto, 6
45850 La Villa de Don Fadrique (Toledo)
☎: 925 195 120 - Fax: 925 195 650
exportjsantos@telefonica.net

JULIÁN SANTOS TEMPRANILLO 2003 T
tempranillo 100%

**75**

DON FADRIQUE 2000 TR
tempranillo 100%

**83**

---

DON FADRIQUE 1998 TGR
tempranillo 100%

**77**

MONTE DEL ALCALDE

### BODEGAS LA REMEDIADORA

Alfredo Atieza, 149-151
02630 La Roda (Albacete)
☎: 967 440 600 - Fax: 967 441 465
export@laremediadora.com
www.laremediadora.com

LA VILLA REAL VENDIMIA SELECCIONADA 2008 B
macabeo

**78**

LA VILLA REAL 2008 RD
tempranillo 100%

**82**

LA VILLA REAL VENDIMIA SELECCIONADA 2008 T
tempranillo 50%, syrah 50%

**86** Colour: cherry, purple rim. Nose: expressive, fresh fruit, red berry notes, floral, sweet spices. Palate: flavourful, fruity, good acidity, round tannins.

LA VILLA REAL 2003 TC
tempranillo 50%, cabernet sauvignon 50%

**89** Colour: cherry, garnet rim. Nose: expressive, ripe fruit, dark chocolate, sweet spices. Palate: fleshy, ripe fruit, long, great length.

LA VILLA REAL SUMILLER 2002 TR
tempranillo 100%

**82**

### BODEGAS LAHOZ

Ctra. N-310 (Tomelloso-Villarrobledo) km. 108,500
13630 Socuéllamos (Ciudad Real)
☎: 926 699 083 - Fax: 926 514 929
info@bodegaslahoz.com
www.bodegaslahoz.com

VEGA CÓRCOLES SAUVIGNON BLANC 2008 B
sauvignon blanc

**88** Colour: bright straw. Nose: fresh, fresh fruit, white flowers, varietal. Palate: flavourful, fruity, good acidity, balanced.

VEGA CÓRCOLES AIRÉN 2008 B
airén

**83**

VEGA CÓRCOLES 2008 RD
tempranillo

**87** Colour: rose, purple rim. Nose: powerfull, ripe fruit, red berry notes, floral, expressive. Palate: fleshy, powerful, fruity, fresh.

VEGA CÓRCOLES 2008 T
tempranillo

**84**

VEGA CÓRCOLES 2006 T ROBLE
tempranillo

**85** Colour: cherry, garnet rim. Nose: characterful, candied fruit, sweet spices. Palate: flavourful, powerful, harsh oak tannins.

## BODEGAS LATUE

Camino de la Esperilla, s/n
45810 Villanueva de Alcardete (Toledo)
☎: 925 166 350 - Fax: 925 166 673
export@latue.com
www.latue.com

LATÚE T

**86** Colour: bright cherry. Nose: ripe fruit, sweet spices, creamy oak, expressive. Palate: flavourful, fruity, toasty, round tannins.

LATÚE ESP

**85** Colour: bright straw. Nose: medium intensity, fresh fruit, dried herbs, floral. Palate: fresh, fruity, flavourful, good acidity.

## BODEGAS LEGANZA

Ctra. Madrid-Alicante, km. 121,700
45800 Quintanar de la Orden (Toledo)
☎: 925 564 452 - Fax: 925 564 021
info@bodegasleganza.com
www.bodegasleganza.com

FINCA LOS TRENZONES VERDEJO 2008 B
verdejo

**85** Colour: bright straw. Nose: fresh, fresh fruit, white flowers. Palate: flavourful, fruity, good acidity, balanced.

CONDESA DE LEGANZA VIURA 2008 B
viura

**82**

FINCA LOS TRENZONES 2008 B
sauvignon blanc

**82**

CONDESA DE LEGANZA VERDEJO 2008 B
verdejo

**80**

CONDESA DE LEGANZA SAUVIGNON BLANC 2008 B
sauvignon blanc

**77**

FINCA LOS TRENZONES CABERNET SAUVIGNON 2008 RD
cabernet sauvignon

**86** Colour: rose, purple rim. Nose: ripe fruit, candied fruit, red berry notes. Palate: flavourful, fruity, fresh.

CONDESA DE LEGANZA TEMPRANILLO ROSE 2008 RD

**84**

CONDESA DE LEGANZA MERLOT TEMPRANILLO 2007 T
merlot, tempranillo

**83**

FINCA LOS TRENZONES SHIRAZ 2006 T
syrah

**83**

CONDESA DE LEGANZA 2004 TC
tempranillo 100%

**85** Colour: cherry, garnet rim. Nose: powerfull, slightly evolved, scrubland, red berry notes. Palate: fleshy, balanced, round.

CONDESA DE LEGANZA 1998 TR

**84**

FINCA LOS TRENZONES TEMPRANILLO T

**80**

## BODEGAS LOZANO

Avda. Reyes Católicos, 156
02600 Villarrobledo (Albacete)
☎: 967 141 907 - Fax: 967 138 087
p.delacruz@bodegas-lozano.com
www.bodegas-lozano.com

AÑORANZA SAUVIGNON BLANC 2008 B

**86** Colour: bright straw. Nose: ripe fruit, tropical fruit, medium intensity, white flowers. Palate: rich, fruity, correct.

**87** Colour: deep cherry, bright ochre rim. Nose: fruit liqueur notes, fine reductive notes, tobacco, aged wood nuances. Palate: fruity, spicy, round tannins, classic aged character.

ORISTÁN 2004 TC

**86** Colour: cherry, garnet rim. Nose: ripe fruit, toasty, old leather. Palate: light-bodied, fruity, round tannins, spicy.

GRAN ORISTÁN 2000 TGR

**84**

ABANICO

## BODEGAS MARTÍNEZ SÁEZ

Finca San José, Ctra. Barrax km. 14,8
02600 Villarrobledo (Albacete)
☎: 967 443 088 - Fax: 967 440 204
avidal@bodegasmartinezsaez.es
www.bodegasmartinezsaez.es

VIÑA ORCE MACABEO 2008 B
macabeo
**82**

VIÑA ORCE MACABEO 2008 RD
merlot, syrah
**83**

VIÑA ORCE SYRAH 2008 T
syrah
**82**

VIÑA ORCE SYRAH 2007 T
tempranillo, syrah
**81**

MARQUÉS DE TOLEDO 2008 B
verdejo
**83**

AÑORANZA 2008 RD
tempranillo
**83**

AÑORANZA TEMPRANILLO 2008 T
tempranillo

**85** Colour: deep cherry, purple rim. Nose: red berry notes, fruit expression, ripe fruit. Palate: rich, flavourful, fruity.

AÑORANZA CABERNET SHIRAZ 2008 T
**82**

AÑORANZA TEMPRANILLO 2005 TC

**85** Colour: cherry, garnet rim. Nose: ripe fruit, spicy, medium intensity. Palate: good acidity, fresh, fruity.
ORISTÁN 2004 TR
tempranillo, cabernet sauvignon

VIÑA ORCE 2004 TC

**82**

VIÑA ORCE 2002 TR
cabernet sauvignon 60%, merlot 40%

**84**

VIÑA ESCAMEL ESP

**86** Colour: bright straw. Nose: medium intensity, fresh fruit, dried herbs, floral. Palate: fresh, fruity, flavourful, good acidity.

## BODEGAS NARANJO

Felipe II, 5
13150 Carrión de Calatrava (Ciudad Real)
☎: 926 814 155 - Fax: 926 815 335
info@bodegasnaranjo.com
www.bodegasnaranjo.com

VIÑA CUERVA AIRÉN 2008 B
airén

**82**

VIÑA CUERVA 2008 RD
tempranillo 100%

**83**

VIÑA CUERVA 2005 TC
tempranillo

**85** Colour: cherry, garnet rim. Nose: powerfull, ripe fruit, spicy, dark chocolate. Palate: flavourful, fleshy, round tannins.

VIÑA CUERVA MERLOT TEMPRANILLO 2005 T
tempranillo 30%, merlot 70%

**82**

CASA DE LA DEHESA 2004 TC
tempranillo 100%

**89** Colour: bright cherry. Nose: ripe fruit, sweet spices, creamy oak, expressive. Palate: flavourful, fruity, toasty, round tannins.

VIÑA CUERVA 2003 TR
tempranillo 100%

**84**

## BODEGAS ROMERO DE ÁVILA SALCEDO

Avda. Constitución, 4
13240 La Solana (Ciudad Real)
☎: 926 631 426 - Fax: 926 634 189

santi@bodegasromerodeavila.com
www.bodegasromerodeavila.com

PORTENTO TEMPRANILLO 2008 T
tempranillo

**87** Colour: dark-red cherry, purple rim. Nose: varietal, neat, violet drops, fresh fruit, raspberry. Palate: sweetness, varietal, full.

PORTENTO 2008 T ROBLE
tempranillo, syrah

**83**

PORTENTO 2004 TC
tempranillo, cabernet sauvignon

**83**

## BODEGAS SAN ISIDRO DE P. MUÑOZ

Ctra El Toboso, 1
13620 Pedro Muñoz (Ciudad Real)
☎: 926 586 057 - Fax: 926 568 380
jesusr@viacotos.com
www.viacotos.com

AMIGO SANCHO 2007 B JOVEN
macabeo

**73**

LA HIJUELA TEMPRANILLO 2007 T
tempranillo 100%

**79**

GRAN AMIGO SANCHO 2006 TC
tempranillo 100%

**87** Colour: cherry, purple rim. Nose: expressive, ripe fruit, red berry notes, sweet spices. Palate: fruity, fleshy, ripe fruit.

## BODEGAS VERDÚGUEZ S.A.T.

Los Hinojosos 1
45810 Villanueva de Alcardete (Toledo)
☎: 925 167 493 - Fax: 925 166 148
verduguez@bodegasverduguez.com
www.bodegasverduguez.com

VEREDA MAYOR 2008 B
chardonnay

**70**

PALACIOS REALES 2008 T
tempranillo

**85** Colour: dark-red cherry. Nose: ripe fruit, fruit preserve, roasted coffee. Palate: powerful, fleshy, round tannins.

IMPERIAL TOLEDO 2007 T

**85** Colour: bright cherry. Nose: ripe fruit, roasted coffee, smoky. Palate: flavourful, toasty, round tannins.

IMPERIAL TOLEDO 2007 T
syrah

**82**

PALACIOS REALES 2007 T
merlot

**78**

ESTILO 21

## BODEGAS VERUM

Ctra. de Argmasilla de Alba, km. 0,8
13700 Tomelloso (Ciudad Real)
☎: 926 511 404 - Fax: 926 515 047
info@bodegasverum.com
www.bodegasverum.com

VERUM GRAN CUEVA ESP
chardonnay

**88** Colour: bright straw. Nose: powerfull, candied fruit, ripe fruit, citrus fruit. Palate: flavourful, fruity, fresh, fleshy.

## BODEGAS VOLVER

Pza. de Grecia, 1 Local 1B
45005 Toledo (Toledo)
☎: 690 818 509 - Fax: 976 852 764
info@orowines.com

PASO A PASO VERDEJO 2008 B
verdejo 100%

**87** Colour: bright golden. Nose: fresh, ripe fruit, fruit expression, tropical fruit. Palate: flavourful, ripe fruit, fine bitter notes.

PASO A PASO TEMPRANILLO 2008 T
tempranillo 100%

**90** Colour: cherry, purple rim. Nose: powerfull, expressive, ripe fruit, fruit expression, lactic notes, floral. Palate: flavourful, powerful, ripe fruit, slightly dry, soft tannins.

VOLVER 2007 T
tempranillo 100%

**89** Colour: cherry, garnet rim. Nose: powerfull, roasted coffee, ripe fruit, warm. Palate: powerful, fleshy, warm, round tannins.

## BODEGAS Y VIÑEDOS LADERO

Ctra. Alcázar, s/n
13700 Tomelloso (Ciudad Real)
☎: 926 505 653 - Fax: 926 505 652

ladero@allozo.com
www.allozo.com

LADERO SELECCIÓN MACABEO 2008 B
macabeo 100%

**78**

LADERO SELECCIÓN TEMPRANILLO 2008 T
tempranillo 100%

**79**

LADERO 2004 TC
tempranillo 100%

**78**

LADERO 2003 TR
tempranillo 100%

**78**

## CASA GUALDA

Tapias, 8
16708 Pozoamargo (Cuenca)
☎: 969 387 173 - Fax: 969 387 202
info@casagualda.com
www.casagualda.com

CASA GUALDA 2008 B
macabeo

**82**

CASA GUALDA TEMPRANILLO 2008 T
tempranillo 90%, cabernet sauvignon 5%, merlot 5%

**85** Colour: cherry, purple rim. Nose: medium intensity, red berry notes. Palate: fruity, flavourful, good finish.

CASA GUALDA SELECCIÓN 2006 T
tempranillo, petit verdot, syrah

**87** Colour: cherry, garnet rim. Nose: ripe fruit, spicy, creamy oak, toasty, complex. Palate: powerful, flavourful, toasty, round tannins.

CASA GUALDA 2005 TC
tempranillo 50%, cabernet sauvignon 50%

**85** Colour: cherry, garnet rim. Nose: characterful, fruit liqueur notes, spicy. Palate: flavourful, full, toasty, warm.

CASA GUALDA SELECCIÓN C&J 2005 T
tempranillo

**83**

# Casa Gualda
Gran Vino para Guardar

SELECCIÓN C&J

UNFILTERED

RED WINE

Elaborado por
"Ntra. Sra. de la Cabeza" S. Coop.
POZOAMARGO 16708 Cuenca - España

## CERVANTINO

Grande, 66
13670 Villarubia de los Ojos (Ciudad Real)
☎: 926 898 018 - Fax: 926 266 514
cervantino@b-lozano.com

CERVANTINO 2008 B
airén 100%

**81**

CERVANTINO 2008 T
tempranillo 100%

**87** Colour: cherry, purple rim. Nose: expressive, fresh fruit, red berry notes, floral. Palate: flavourful, fruity, good acidity, round tannins.

CERVANTINO 2003 TC
tempranillo 100%

**86** Colour: cherry, garnet rim. Nose: medium intensity, ripe fruit. Palate: flavourful, fruity, powerful.

## COOPERATIVA LA UNIÓN

La Paz, s/n
13600 Alcazar de San Juan (Ciudad Real)
☎: 926 541 371 - Fax: 926 545 678
launion@ucaman.es

CAZ DE ALCAZAR 2008 B
macabeo

## 78

CAZ DE ALCAZAR 2008 B
airén

## 77

CAZ DE ALCAZAR 2008 B
verdejo

## 74

CAZ DE ALCAZAR 2008 RD
cencibel

## 82

CAZ DE ALCAZAR ELÍTE 2008 T

**87** Colour: cherry, purple rim. Nose: expressive, fresh fruit, red berry notes, floral. Palate: flavourful, fruity, good acidity, round tannins.

CAZ DE ALCAZAR 2008 T
cencibel

## 82

### COOPERATIVA NUESTRA SEÑORA DE LA MUELA

Real, 16
45880 Corral de Almaguer (Toledo)
☎: 925 190 161 - Fax: 925 207 434
cooplamuela@ozu.es
www.cooperativalamuela.com

PORTILLO 2008 B
airén 100%

## 80

CASTILLO DE LA MUELA 2008 B
airén 100%

## 72

CASTILLO DE LA MUELA 2008 T
cencibel 100%

**86** Colour: cherry, purple rim. Nose: expressive, fresh fruit, red berry notes, floral. Palate: flavourful, fruity, good acidity, round tannins.

### COOPERATIVA NUESTRA SEÑORA DE LA PAZ

Ctra. Madrid - Alicante km 99, 800
45880 Corral de Almaguer (Toledo)
☎: 925 190 269 - Fax: 925 190 268
cooplapaz@hotmail.com

ALTOVELA 2008 B
sauvignon blanc

## 81

CAMPO AMABLE
BRUT ALTOVELA

## COOPERATIVA NUESTRA SEÑORA DE LA SOLEDAD

Ctra. Tarancón, s/n
16411 Fuente de Pedro Naharro (Cuenca)
☎: 969 125 039 - Fax: 969 125 907
info@bodegasoledad.com
www.bodegasoledad.com

RIBERA DEL RIANSARES 2006 TC
tempranillo 100%

**87** Colour: bright cherry. Nose: ripe fruit, sweet spices, creamy oak, expressive. Palate: flavourful, fruity, toasty, round tannins.

## COOPERATIVA SAN ISIDRO

Camino Esperilla, s/n
45810 Villanueva de Alcardete (Toledo)
☎: 925 167 429 - Fax: 925 166 673
calidadsanisidro@telefonica.net

PINGOROTE 2008 B JOVEN
sauvignon blanc

**87** Colour: bright straw. Nose: fresh, fresh fruit, white flowers, expressive. Palate: flavourful, fruity, good acidity, balanced.

PINGOROTE CHARDONNAY B BARRICA
chardonnay

**89** Colour: yellow, bright golden. Nose: neat, expressive, candied fruit, smoky. Palate: round, unctuous, long.

PINGOROTE TC
tempranillo

**85** Colour: dark-red cherry, garnet rim. Nose: characterful, fruit liqueur notes, sweet spices. Palate: good structure, fleshy, spicy, long.

PINGOROTE TR
tempranillo

**85** Colour: cherry, garnet rim. Nose: powerfull, fruit liqueur notes, spicy. Palate: warm, powerful, flavourful, great length, slightly dry, soft tannins.

## DOMECQ BODEGAS + CINCO CASAS

Virgen de las Nieves, 2
13720 Cinco Casas (Ciudad Real)
☎: 926 529 010 - Fax: 926 526 070
jcutilla@domecqbodegas.com
www.domecqbodegas.com

VIÑA SANTA ELENA B

**82**

VIÑA SANTA ELENA 2006 TC
tempranillo 100%

**82**

VIÑA SANTA ELENA T

**81**

## EL PROGRESO SOCIEDAD COOP. CLM

Avda. de la Virgen, 89
13670 Villarubia de los Ojos (Ciudad Real)
☎: 926 896 088 - Fax: 926 896 135
elprogreso@cooprogres.com
www.bodegaselprogreso.com

OJOS DEL GUADIANA 2008 B
verdejo 100%

**81**

OJOS DEL GUADIANA AIRÉN JOVEN 2008 B
airén 100%

**79**

OJOS DEL GUADIANA TEMPRANILLO 2008 T
cencibel 100%

**88** Colour: cherry, purple rim. Nose: expressive, fresh fruit, red berry notes, floral. Palate: flavourful, fruity, good acidity, round tannins.

OJOS DEL GUADIANA SYRAH 2006 T ROBLE
syrah 100%

**85** Colour: bright cherry. Nose: ripe fruit, sweet spices, creamy oak. Palate: flavourful, fruity, toasty, round tannins.

OJOS DEL GUADIANA 2005 TC
cencibel 100%

**85** Colour: cherry, garnet rim. Nose: fruit preserve, red berry notes, sweet spices, creamy oak. Palate: flavourful, ripe fruit, spicy.

OJOS DEL GUADIANA 2004 TR
cencibel 100%

**87** Colour: cherry, garnet rim. Nose: dark chocolate, spicy, medium intensity, ripe fruit. Palate: spicy, flavourful, complex.

OJOS DEL GUADIANA 2002 TGR
cencibel 100%

**86** Colour: cherry, garnet rim. Nose: fruit preserve, ripe fruit, caramel, spicy. Palate: flavourful, spirituous, spicy, round tannins.

## EVARISTO MATEOS S.A.

Mayor, 62
45350 Noblejas (Toledo)
☎: 925 140 082 - Fax: 925 140 573
evaristomateos@telefonica.net
www.evaristomateos.com

EVARISTO I 2008 B
airén

**82**

EVARISTO I 2007 T
cencibel

**83**

EVARISTO I 2003 TC
cencibel

**85** Colour: cherry, garnet rim. Nose: ripe fruit, creamy oak, cocoa bean, sweet spices. Palate: flavourful, powerful, ripe fruit, toasty.

SEMBRADOR 1998 TR
cencibel

**78**

## FINCA ANTIGUA

Ctra. Quintanar - Los Hinojosos, km. 11,5
16417 Los Hinojosos (Cuenca)
☎: 969 129 700 - Fax: 969 129 496
info@fincaantigua.com
www.familiamartinezbujanda.com

FINCA ANTIGUA MOSCATEL NATURALMENTE DULCE 2008 B
moscatel

**87** Colour: bright straw. Nose: wild herbs, ripe fruit, citrus fruit, varietal. Palate: flavourful, fruity, sweet, fresh.

FINCA ANTIGUA 2008 B
viura 100%

**84**

FINCA ANTIGUA SYRAH 2007 T
syrah 100%

**90** Colour: cherry, purple rim. Nose: sweet spices, creamy oak, ripe fruit, fruit expression. Palate: flavourful, powerful, fleshy, round tannins.

FINCA ANTIGUA TEMPRANILLO 2007 T
tempranillo 100%

**88** Colour: bright cherry. Nose: ripe fruit, creamy oak, expressive, varietal. Palate: flavourful, fruity, toasty, round tannins.

FINCA ANTIGUA CABERNET SAUVIGNON 2007 T
cabernet sauvignon 100%

**87** Colour: cherry, garnet rim. Nose: medium intensity, ripe fruit, varietal, spicy, aromatic coffee. Palate: flavourful, powerful, fleshy.

FINCA ANTIGUA PETIT VERDOT 2006 T
petit verdot 100%

**90** Colour: bright cherry. Nose: ripe fruit, sweet spices, creamy oak, varietal. Palate: flavourful, fruity, toasty, round tannins.

FINCA ANTIGUA 2006 TC
tempranillo 50%, merlot 20%, cabernet sauvignon 20%, syrah 5%, petit verdot 5%

**88** Colour: cherry, garnet rim. Nose: ripe fruit, spicy, creamy oak, toasty, complex. Palate: powerful, flavourful, toasty, round tannins.

FINCA ANTIGUA MERLOT 2006 T
merlot 100%

**87** Colour: bright cherry. Nose: sweet spices, creamy oak, expressive. Palate: flavourful, fruity, toasty, round tannins.

CLAVIS VIÑEDO PICO GARBANZO 2004 TR

**91** Colour: dark-red cherry, bright ochre rim. Nose: elegant, scrubland, ripe fruit, spicy, dark chocolate. Palate: fleshy, round, slightly dry, soft tannins, toasty.

FINCA ANTIGUA 2004 TR
merlot 70%, syrah 10%, cabernet sauvignon 20%

**90** Colour: very deep cherry, brick rim edge. Nose: balanced, expressive, ripe fruit, scrubland, spicy. Palate: fleshy, long, great length, slightly dry, soft tannins.

## FINCA LA BLANCA S.L.

Princesa, 84
45840 Puebla de Almoradiel (Toledo)
☎: 925 178 437 - Fax: 925 178 432
montedonlucio@terra.es
www.capel-vinos.es

RIBERA DE LOS MOLINOS 2008 B
airén, macabeo, sauvignon blanc

## 79

MONTE DON LUCIO MACABEO 2008 B
macabeo 100%

## 78

MONTE DON LUCIO TEMPRANILLO 2008 T
tempranillo 100%

## 83

MONTE DON LUCIO CABERNET SAUVIGNON 2008 T
cabernet sauvignon 100%

## 76

RIBERA DE LOS MOLINOS 2008 T
tinto aragón 50%, tempranillo 25%, cabernet sauvignon 25%

## 70

---

## FONTANA

Extramuros, s/n
16411 Fuente de Pedro Naharro (Cuenca)
☎: 969 125 433 - Fax: 969 125 387
bf@bodegasfontana.com
www.bodegasfontana.com

FONTAL 2008 B
verdejo, sauvignon blanc

**90** Colour: bright straw. Nose: fresh, fresh fruit, white flowers, expressive. Palate: flavourful, fruity, good acidity, balanced.

FONTAL 2008 RD
merlot 70%, syrah 30%

## 83

FONTAL TEMPRANILLO 2007 T ROBLE
tempranillo

**85** Colour: deep cherry. Nose: medium intensity, ripe fruit, grassy, spicy. Palate: powerful, flavourful, round tannins.

FONTAL 2005 TC
tempranillo, cabernet sauvignon

**86** Colour: cherry, garnet rim. Nose: scrubland, spicy, fruit liqueur notes. Palate: round tannins, warm, fine bitter notes.

---

## JACINTO JARAMILLO E HIJOS S.L.

Calvario, 31
13160 Torralba de Calatrava (Ciudad Real)
☎: 926 811 332 - Fax: 926 811 340

bodegasjaramillo@vegazacatena.com
www.vegazacatena.com

VEGA ZACATENA B

## 77

VEGA ZACATENA 2005 TC
tempranillo, cabernet sauvignon

**87** Colour: cherry, garnet rim. Nose: medium intensity, ripe fruit, sweet spices. Palate: flavourful, fleshy, spicy.

VEGA ZACATENA 2003 TR

## 81

---

## JESÚS DEL PERDÓN - BODEGAS YUNTERO S.C.C.M.

Pol. Ind. Carretera, s/n
13200 Manzanares (Ciudad Real)
☎: 926 610 309 - Fax: 926 610 516
yuntero@yuntero.com
www.yuntero.com

YUNTERO MACABEO 2008 B
macabeo 100%

## 84

MUNDO DE YUNTERO AIRÉN ECOLÓGICO 2008 B
airén

## 80

YUNTERO TEMPRANILLO 2008 RD
tempranillo 100%

## 82

MUNDO DE YUNTERO TEMPRANILLO ECOLÓGICO 2008 T
tempranillo

**86** Colour: cherry, purple rim. Nose: expressive, fresh fruit, red berry notes, floral. Palate: flavourful, fruity, good acidity, round tannins.

MUNDO DE YUNTERO TEMPRANILLO ECOLÓGICO 2007 T ROBLE
tempranillo

**86** Colour: cherry, garnet rim. Nose: ripe fruit, spicy, creamy oak, toasty. Palate: powerful, flavourful, toasty, round tannins.

YUNTERO SYRAH 2007 T
syrah

# DO LA MANCHA

## 84

**YUNTERO 2004 TC**
tempranillo, cabernet sauvignon

**88** Colour: cherry, garnet rim. Nose: complex, scrubland, red berry notes, raspberry, toasty. Palate: fleshy, long, spicy, great length.

**YUNTERO SELECCIÓN 2003 TR**
tempranillo, cabernet sauvignon

## 84

**YUNTERO SELECCIÓN 2001 TR**
tempranillo 85%, syrah 15%

## 84

**LYRAE 2008 ESP**
macabeo

## 84

**CASA LA TEJA**
EPÍLOGO

## NTRA. SRA. DEL PILAR SOC. COOP. DE C-L-M

Extramuros, s/n
45810 Villanueva de Alcardete (Toledo)
☎: 925 166 375 - Fax: 925 166 611
alcardet@terra.es

**GRUMIER 2008 B**
airén 100%

## 79

**ALCARDET 2006 BR**
airén 100%

## 80

**ALCARDET BRUT 2006 ESP**
macabeo 100%

## 80

## NUESTRA SEÑORA DE MANJAVACAS SOC. COOP.

Camino del Campo de Criptana, s/n
16630 Mota del Cuervo (Cuenca)
☎: 967 180 025 - Fax: 967 181 120
info@zagarron.com
www.zagarron.com

**VERDINAL SAUVIGNON BLANC 2008 B**
sauvignon blanc 100%

## 81

**VERDINAL CHARDONNAY 2008 BFB**
chardonnay 100%

## 81

**SANDOGAL TEMPRANILLO 2006 TC**

**88** Colour: bright cherry. Nose: ripe fruit, sweet spices, creamy oak, expressive. Palate: flavourful, fruity, toasty, round tannins.

## PAGO DE LA JARABA

Ctra. Nacional 310, km. 142,7
02600 Villarrobledo (Albacete)
☎: 967 138 250 - Fax: 967 138 252
info@lajaraba.com
www.lajaraba.com

**PAGO DE LA JARABA MERLOT 2004 TC**
merlot 100%

**85** Colour: cherry, garnet rim. Nose: powerfull, fruit liqueur notes, fruit liqueur notes, spicy, earthy notes. Palate: powerful, fleshy, spicy, grainy tannins.

## S.C.V. DE C.L.M. VIRGEN DE LAS VIÑAS

Ctra. Argamasilla de Alba s/n
13700 Tomelloso (Ciudad Real)
☎: 926 510 865 - Fax: 926 512 130
atencion.cliente@vinostomillar.com
www.vinostomillar.com

**TOMILLAR CHARDONNAY 2008 B**
chardonnay 100%

## 84

**TOMILLAR 2003 TR**
cabernet sauvignon 80%, tempranillo 20%

**86** Colour: cherry, garnet rim. Nose: expressive, candied fruit, fruit liqueur notes, sweet spices, dark chocolate. Palate: fleshy, long, ripe fruit, slightly dry, soft tannins.

LORENZETE
ROCÍO LÓPEZ LÓPEZ
TOMILLAR
DON EUGENIO

## SANTA CATALINA

Cooperativa, 2

13240 La Solana (Ciudad Real)
☎: 926 632 194 - Fax: 926 631 085
compras@santacatalina.es

**LOS GALANES 2008 B**
airén

**84**

**LOS GALANES 2008 B**
verdejo

**84**

**CAMPECHANO 2008 B**
airén

**82**

**CAMPECHANO 2008 RD**
cencibel, cabernet sauvignon

**82**

**LOS GALANES 2008 T**
cencibel

**86** Colour: cherry, purple rim. Nose: fresh fruit, red berry notes, floral. Palate: flavourful, fruity, good acidity, grainy tannins.

**CAMPECHANO 2008 T**
cencibel

**78**

## SANTÍSIMO CRISTO DEL ESPÍRITU SANTO S.C.L.

Pol. Ind. Las Viñas
13420 Malagón (Ciudad Real)
☎: 926 802 640 - Fax: 926 801 040
malagon@grupomontesnorte.com

**QUINTANARES 2008 B**
airén

**80**

**QUINTANARES 2008 T**
merlot, syrah, cabernet sauvignon, tempranillo

**78**

## VIHUCAS DISTRIBUCIONES Y SERVICIOS

Mayor, 3
45860 Villacañas (Toledo)

☎: 925 160 309 - Fax: 925 160 176
info@vihucas.com
www.vihucas.com

**VIHUCAS DOBLE 0607 2007 T**
merlot 65%, cencibel 35%

**84**

**VIHUCAS COLECCIÓN FAMILIAR 2006 TC**
merlot 100%

**87** Colour: cherry, garnet rim. Nose: ripe fruit, spicy, creamy oak, toasty, complex. Palate: powerful, flavourful, toasty, round tannins.

**VIHUCAS COLECCIÓN FAMILIAR 2005 T**
merlot 100%

**82**

## VINÍCOLA DE CASTILLA

Pol. Ind. Calle I
13200 Manzanares (Ciudad Real)
☎: 926 647 800 - Fax: 926 610 466
nacional@vinicoladecastilla.com
www.vinicoladecastilla.com

**FINCA VIEJA TEMPRANILLO 2008 T**
tempranillo 100%

**81**

**SEÑORÍO DE GUADIANEJA 2004 TC**
tempranillo 100%

**85** Colour: cherry, garnet rim. Nose: fruit preserve, sweet spices, dark chocolate. Palate: rich, good structure, round tannins.

**SEÑORÍO DE GUADIANEJA 2002 TR**
tempranillo 100%

**85** Colour: pale ruby, brick rim edge. Nose: fruit liqueur notes, sweet spices, toasty. Palate: good structure, full, flavourful, long.

**CANTARES EXTRA BRUT ESP**
verdejo 100%

**76**

CASTILLO DE ALHAMBRA

## VINÍCOLA DE TOMELLOSO

Ctra. Toledo - Albacete, km. 130,8
13700 Tomelloso (Ciudad Real)

# DO LA MANCHA

☎: 926 513 004 - Fax: 926 538 001
vinicola@vinicolatomelloso.com
www.vinicolatomelloso.com

**GAZATE CHARDONNAY 2008 B**
chardonnay

**85** Colour: bright straw. Nose: floral, fresh fruit. Palate: flavourful, fruity, fresh.

**AÑIL 2008 B**
macabeo

**84**

**GAZATE SAUVIGNON BLANC 2008 B**
sauvignon blanc

**84**

**GAZATE VERDEJO 2008 B**
verdejo

**84**

**FINCA CERRADA 2008 B**

**81**

**TORRE DE GAZATE AIRÉN 2008 B**
airén

**77**

**TORRE DE GAZATE 2008 RD**

**84**

**FINCA CERRADA TEMPRANILLO 2008 T**
tempranillo 100%

**86** Colour: cherry, purple rim. Nose: red berry notes, fresh fruit, lactic notes. Palate: fresh, fruity, easy to drink.

**TORRE DE GAZATE 2005 TC**
cencibel, cabernet sauvignon

**85** Colour: cherry, garnet rim. Nose: scrubland, grassy, ripe fruit, red berry notes, dark chocolate. Palate: flavourful, powerful, round tannins.

**GAZATE MERLOT 2008 T**
merlot

**83**

**GAZATE SYRAH 2008 T**
syrah

**81**

TORRE DE GAZATE 2007 T ROBLE

**85** Colour: cherry, purple rim. Nose: expressive, neat, fruit expression, fresh fruit, spicy, toasty. Palate: good structure, flavourful, long, fine tannins.

TORRE DE GAZATE CENCIBEL 2007 T
cencibel

**80**

FINCA CERRADA 2005 TC
tempranillo, cabernet sauvignon, syrah

**81**

FINCA CERRADA 2002 TR
tempranillo, cabernet sauvignon

**83**

TORRE DE GAZATE 2000 TR

**85** Colour: cherry, garnet rim. Nose: fresh fruit, red berry notes, sweet spices. Palate: fresh, fruity, flavourful.

TORRE DE GAZATE 1999 TGR

**82**

MANTOLÁN BN
macabeo

**75**

---

## VINNICO EXPORT

De la Muela, 16
03730 Jávea (Alicante)
☎: 965 791 967 - Fax: 966 461 471
info@vinnico.com
www.vinnico.com

FLOR DEL MONTGÓ TEMPRANILLO 2007 T
tempranillo 100%

**87** Colour: deep cherry, garnet rim. Nose: spicy, powerfull, aromatic coffee, ripe fruit. Palate: flavourful, full, fruity, good acidity, toasty, round tannins.

---

## VINOS COLOMAN

Goya, 17
13620 Pedro Muñoz (Ciudad Real)
☎: 926 586 410 - Fax: 926 586 656
coloman@satcoloman.com
www.satcoloman.com

BESANA REAL MACABEO 2008 B
macabeo 100%

**73**

BESANA REAL 2008 RD
tempranillo 100%

**86** Colour: brilliant rose. Nose: rose petals, violets, red berry notes. Palate: fruity, fresh, flavourful.

BESANA REAL TEMPRANILLO 2008 T
tempranillo 100%

**84**

BESANA REAL MERLOT SYRAH 2007 T ROBLE
merlot 60%, syrah 40%

**86** Colour: cherry, purple rim. Nose: medium intensity, ripe fruit, red berry notes, floral, sweet spices. Palate: flavourful, fruity, fleshy.

COLOMÁN 2006 TC
tempranillo 100%

**86** Colour: bright cherry. Nose: sweet spices, creamy oak, fruit preserve. Palate: flavourful, fruity, toasty, round tannins.

BESANA REAL CABERNET SAUVIGNON 2006 T ROBLE
cabernet sauvignon 100%

**85** Colour: cherry, garnet rim. Nose: ripe fruit, spicy, creamy oak, toasty. Palate: powerful, flavourful, toasty, round tannins.

---

## VINOS Y BODEGAS

Ctra. de las Mesas, km. 1
13630 Socuéllanos (Ciudad Real)
☎: 926 531 067 - Fax: 926 532 249
roman@vinosybodegas.com
www.vinosybodegas.com

REAL BODEGA 2003 TC
tempranillo, cabernet sauvignon

**84**

REAL BODEGA 2002 TR
tempranillo, cabernet sauvignon

**82**

---

## VIÑEDOS MEJORANTES

Ctra. de Villafranca, km. 2
45860 Villacañas (Toledo)
☎: 925 201 036 - Fax: 925 200 023

---

portillejo@portillejo.com
www.portillejo.com

**PORTILLEJO VERDEJO 2008 B**
verdejo 100%

**82**

**PORTILLEJO MACABEO 2007 B**
macabeo 100%

**78**

**PORTILLEJO 6675 2006 TC**
cabernet sauvignon 100%

**84**

**PORTILLEJO CABERNET SAUVIGNON 2006 T ROBLE**
cabernet sauvignon 100%

**84**

**PORTILLEJO MERLOT 2006 T ROBLE**
merlot 100%

**84**

**PORTILLEJO CABERNET SAUVIGNON 2005 TC**
cabernet sauvignon 100%

**84**

**PORTILLEJO CABERNET SAUVIGNON 2004 TC**
cabernet sauvignon 100%

**84**

**PORTILLEJO CABERNET SAUVIGNON 2003 TR**
cabernet sauvignon 100%

**86** Colour: cherry, garnet rim. Nose: ripe fruit, spicy, creamy oak, toasty. Palate: powerful, flavourful, toasty, round tannins.

**PORTILLEJO CABERNET SAUVIGNON 2002 TR**
cabernet sauvignon 100%

**82**

## VIÑEDOS Y BODEGAS MUÑOZ

Ctra. Villarrubia, 11
45350 Noblejas (Toledo)
☎: 925 140 070 - Fax: 925 141 334
info@bodegasmunoz.com
www.bodegasmunoz.com

**ARTERO MACABEO 2008 B**
macabeo 100%

**81**

**BLAS MUÑOZ CHARDONNAY 2007 BFB**
chardonnay 100%

**87** Colour: bright yellow. Nose: powerfull, ripe fruit, sweet spices, creamy oak, fragrant herbs. Palate: rich, smoky aftertaste, flavourful, fresh, good acidity.

**ARTERO 2008 RD**
tempranillo 100%

**82**

**ARTERO TEMPRANILLO 2008 T**
tempranillo 100%

**82**

**ARTERO TEMPRANILLO MERLOT 2005 TC**
tempranillo 50%, merlot 50%

**87** Colour: bright cherry. Nose: ripe fruit, sweet spices, creamy oak, expressive. Palate: flavourful, fruity, toasty, round tannins.

**ARTERO MERLOT 2002 TR**
merlot 100%

**83**

## SOME OTHER WINERIES WITHIN THE DO:

**ALCASOR**
**ANTONIO BALLESTEROS**
**BACO, BODEGAS ASOCIADAS COOPERATIVAS**
**BERNAL GARCÍA-CHICOTE**
**BIBIANO S.L.**
**BODEGA FLORES ALCÁZAR**
**BODEGA MANUEL DE LA OSA (IRJIMPA, S.L.)**
**BODEGA Y VIÑEDOS LA CANDELARIA**
**BODEGAS ARVA VITIS**
**BODEGAS BONJORNE**
**BODEGAS CASA ANTONETE**
**BODEGAS DEL CARMEN S.L.**
**BODEGAS DON MAMBRINO**
**BODEGAS ENOMAR**
**BODEGAS GARRÓN S.A.**
**BODEGAS LÓPEZ MERCIER S.L.**
**BODEGAS LOZANO S.L.**
**BODEGAS NOBLEJAS**
**BODEGAS SALCEDO BALMASEDA**
**BODEGAS VIÑASORO**
**BODEGAS Y VIÑEDOS BRO VALERO**
**CASAGRANDE**
**COOP. AGRARIA NTRA. SRA. DE LAS NIEVES**
**COOP. AGRÍCOLA LA HUMILDAD**

COOP. NTRA. SRA DE LA ASUNCIÓN
COOP. NTRA. SRA DE LOS REMEDIOS
COOP. NTRA. SRA DEL EGIDO
COOP. NUESTRO PADRE JESÚS DE NAZARENO
COOP. SAN ISIDRO LABRADOR
COOP. SANTA QUITERIA
COOP. SANTO NIÑO DE LA BOLA
COSECHEROS EMBOTELLADORES S.A.
DEL SAZ
EXPLOTACIONES HERMANOS DELGADO S.L.
FINCA LABAJOS
HERMANOS CAÑADAS ZARRAUTE S.L.
INDUSTRIA VINÍCOLA LOS CANDEALES S.L.
J. GARCÍA CARRIÓN LA MANCHA
JESÚS FERNÁNDEZ VERDÚGUEZ
JOSÉ LUIS GUILLERMO MENDIETA S.L.
LA VID Y LA ESPIGA S.C., C-LM
LORETO
MARTÍN PUIG S.A.
MAZORRAL NCR
MUÑOZ MONTOYA E HIJOS
SAN FERNANDO
SANTA RITA S.A.T.
SDAD. COOP. AGRARÍA
  NTRA. SRA DE LA VEGA
SOCIEDAD COOP. AGRARIA
  NTRA. SRA DE ROSARIO
SDAD. COOP. AGRARIA NTRA. SRA DE RUS
SDAD. COOP. AGRARIA PEÑARROYA
SDAD. COOP. ANGEL DEL ALCAZAR
SDAD. COOP. DE CASTILLA LA MANCHA
CORZA DE LA SIERRA
SDAD. COOP. DEL CAMPO
  NTRA. SRA DE LA PAZ
SDAD. COOP. DEL CAMPO SAN ISIDRO
SDAD. COOP. NTRA. SRA DEL ESPINO
TRINIDAD FUENTES GARCÍA
VINOS ISIDORO DÍAZ-REGAÑÓN
VIÑEDOS Y RESERVAS

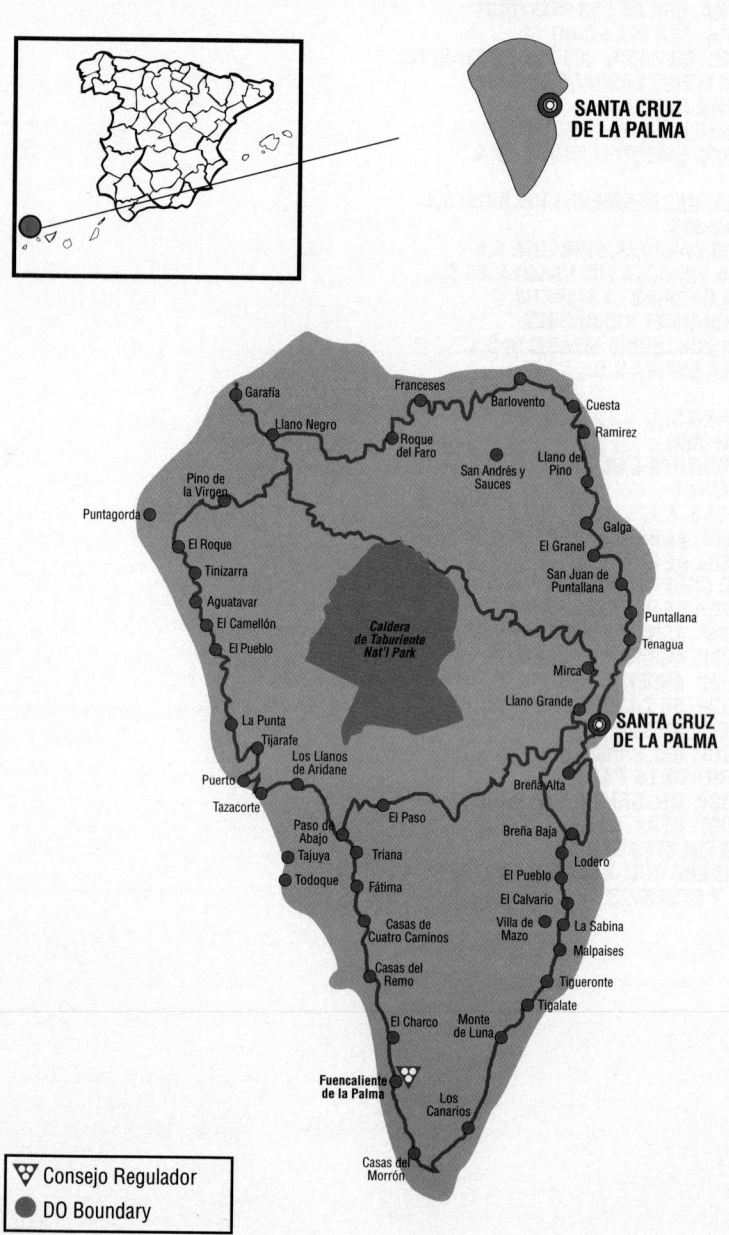

SANTA CRUZ
DE LA PALMA

Garafía
Franceses
Barlovento
Cuesta
Llano Negro
Roque del Faro
Ramirez
Pino de la Virgen
San Andrès y Sauces
Llano del Pino
Puntagorda
El Roque
Tinizarra
El Granel
Galga
Aguatavar
San Juan de Puntallana
El Camellón
Caldera de Taburiente Nat'l Park
Puntallana
El Pueblo
Tenagua
Mirca
La Punta
Llano Grande
Tijarafe
SANTA CRUZ DE LA PALMA
Los Llanos de Aridane
Puerto
Breña Alta
Tazacorte
Paso de Abajo
El Paso
Breña Baja
Tajuya
Triana
Lodero
Todoque
Fátima
El Pueblo
El Calvario
Casas de Cuatro Caminos
Villa de Mazo
La Sabina
Casas del Remo
Malpaises
Tigueronte
El Charco
Monte de Luna
Tigalate
Fuencaliente de la Palma
Los Canarios
Casas del Morrón

Consejo Regulador
DO Boundary

## NEWS

Malvasía wines from La Palma are still the best assets from the island as well as part of its identity, but they have to work hard to promote them. Although they may not be the richest or more complex wines in the world, in some occasions they can reach a level of elegance and complexity comparable to the best sweet wines from the Mosel region in Germany. The wines are made as "naturalmente dulces", i.e., unfortified, meaning that the alcohol comes exclusively from the fermentation of the sugars contained in the grapes, and reach their best aromatic expression (acetaldehydes, terpenes…) at least two years after being bottled. A recently bottled malvasía will hardly show its true potential, and the predominant notes are grapey and mineral (volcanic). Dry whites of the 2008 vintage show more subtle and floral as befits a textbook vintage, without the heat waves or hail storms of other years. Albillo is being increasingly made into single-varietal renderings and shows great potential in the wines of Eufrosina Pérez Rodríguez and Vega Norte. Red and rosé wines are few and far between, but to be honest we can do without the former, given that the excessive amount of bunches per vine does not promote a balanced maturation. As a sort of nostalgic note of former times we still find in the island the so called "vinos de Tea", with maybe far too prominent notes of pine resin where there should be herbal and eucalyptus ones on the nose, as well as a rounder palate to render them more 'drinkable'.

## LOCATION

The production area covers the whole island of San Miguel de La Palma, and is divided into three distinct sub-regions: Hoyo de Mazo, Fuencaliente and Northern La Palma.

## CLIMATE

Variable according to the altitude and the direction that the vineyards face. The relief is a fundamental aspect in La Palma, seeing as it gives rise to different climates and microclimates; one must not forget that it has the highest altitudes in relation to surface area of all the Canary Islands. Nevertheless, as it is situated in the Atlantic, it benefits from the effects of the trade winds (humid and from the northwest), which temper the temperatures and tone down the climatic contrasts.

## SOIL

The vineyards are situated at altitudes of between 200 m and 1,400 m above sea level in a coastal belt ranging in width which surrounds the whole island. Due to the ragged topography, the vineyards occupy the steep hillsides in the form of small terraces. The soil is mainly of volcanic origin.

## GRAPE VARIETIES:

**White:** *Malvasía, Güal and Verdello* (main); *Albillo, Bastardo Blanco, Bermejuela, Bujariego, Burra Blanca, Forastera Blanca, Listán Blanco, Moscatel, Pedro Ximénez, Sabro* and *Torrontés.*
**Red:** *Negramol* (main), *Listán Negro* (Almuñeco), *Bastardo Negro, Malvasía Rosada, Moscatel Negro, Tintilla, Castellana* and *Listán Prieto.*

## SUB REGIONS:

**Hoyo de Mazo:** It comprises the municipal districts of Villa de Mazo, Breña Baja, Breña Alta and Santa Cruz de La Palma, at altitudes of between 200 m and 700 m. The vines grow over the terrain on hillsides covered with volcanic stone ('Empedrados') or with volcanic gravel ('Picón Granado'). White and mainly red varieties are grown.
**Fuencaliente:** It comprises the municipal districts of Fuencaliente, El Paso, Los Llanos de Aridane and Tazacorte. The vines grow over terrains of volcanic ash at altitudes of between 200 m and 1900 m. The white varieties and the sweet Malvasia stand out.
**Northern La Palma:** Situated at an altitude of between 100 m and 200 m, It comprises the municipal areas of Puntallana, San Andrés and Sauces, Barlovento, Garafía, Puntagorda and Tijarafe. The region is richer in vegetation and the vines grow on trellises and using the goblet system. The traditional 'Tea' wines are produced here.

| Hectares of Vineyard | 755 |
|---|---|
| Nº Viticulturists | 1,253 |
| Nº of Bodegas | 18 |
| 2008 Harvest | N/A |
| 2007 Production | 870,000 l. |
| Marketing | 100% domestic |

**CONSEJO REGULADOR**
Dr. Acosta Gómez, 7
38740 Fuencaliente (La Palma)
☎: 922 444 432 / 04 - Fax: 922 444 404
@ cr.vinoslapalma@terra.es
www.malvasiadelapalma.com

## GENERAL CHARACTERISTICS OF THE WINES:

| | |
|---|---|
| **WHITES** | Produced mainly from *Bujariego* or combined with *Listán Blanco*. They are dry, fruity with certain rustic notes; on occasion they also display mineral and volcanic nuances. They are the most classic wines of the island; nevertheless, they are sweet wines from *Malvasía*, complex and original with notes that are reminiscent of fine herbs. |
| **ROSÉS** | The colour ranges from salmon to pink. The wines are light, fruity and delicate. |
| **REDS** | Produced mainly from *Negramol*, they usually have a deep cherry-red colour. As with the rosés, these wines are also fresh and light. |
| **TEA WINE** | A characteristic wine from La Palma, normally produced from *Negramol*, *Listán Prieto* and *Albillo*, and aged in tea (Canary oak), which gives it intense noses and palates of resin that combine with the fruity and herbaceous touches of the grape. |

## 2008 VINTAGE RATING:

## VERY GOOD

## BODEGAS CARBALLO

Ctra. Las Indias, 74
38740 Fuencaliente de La Palma
(Santa Cruz de Tenerife)
☎: 922 444 140 - Fax: 922 211 744
info@bodegascarballo.com
www.bodegascarballo.com

MALVASÍA DULCE CARBALLO 2001 B

**95** Colour: iodine, amber rim. Nose: dry nuts, honeyed notes, aged wood nuances, citrus fruit. Palate: flavourful, powerful, sweet, long.

BRISAS DEL SUR

## BODEGAS TAMANCA S.L.

Ctra. Gral. Tamanca, 75
38750 El Paso (La Palma)
☎: 922 494 155 - Fax: 922 494 296
bioaad@telefonica.net

TAMANCA PEDREGAL 2008 B
Bujariego 60%, albillo 40%

**86** Colour: pale. Nose: faded flowers, ripe fruit, candied fruit, fragrant herbs. Palate: flavourful, fleshy, ripe fruit.

TAMANCA MALVASÍA DULCE 2005 B BARRICA

**92** Colour: golden. Nose: powerfull, floral, honeyed notes, candied fruit, fragrant herbs. Palate: flavourful, sweet, fresh, fruity, good acidity, long.

TAMANCA PEDREGAL 2008 T BARRICA

**82**

TAMANCA MALVASÍA 2006 BLANCO DULCE

**92** Colour: bright straw. Nose: powerfull, honeyed notes, candied fruit, citrus fruit, floral. Palate: flavourful, sweet, fleshy, long.

## BODEGAS TENEGUÍA

Los Canarios, s/n
38740 Fuencaliente de La Palma (Tenerife)
☎: 922 444 078 - Fax: 922 444 394
enologia@vinosteneguia.com
www.vinosteneguia.com

TENEGUÍA LISTÁN BLANCO 2008 B
listán blanco 100%

**87** Colour: pale. Nose: fresh fruit, tropical fruit, grassy, smoky, earthy notes. Palate: flavourful, fruity, fresh.

TENEGUÍA LA GOTA 2008 B
listán blanco 30%, negramoll 23%, albillo 23%, bujariego 23%

**84**

TENEGUÍA SABRO DULCE 2006 B
sabro 85%, gual 15%

**92** Colour: bright golden. Nose: powerfull, characterful, complex, candied fruit, citrus fruit, honeyed notes. Palate: flavourful, sweetness, good acidity.

TENEGUÍA MALVASÍA DULCE 2005 B RESERVA
malvasia 100%

**92** Colour: bright golden. Nose: expressive, powerfull, citrus fruit, honeyed notes, candied fruit, aged wood nuances. Palate: flavourful, sweet, rich, fine bitter notes.

**TENEGUÍA MALVASÍA SECO 2006 B**
malvasia 100%

**88** Colour: bright golden. Nose: powerfull, expressive, honeyed notes, dry nuts, toasty. Palate: flavourful, sweetness, fleshy, fine bitter notes.

**TENEGUÍA MALVASÍA DULCE 2000 B RESERVA**
malvasia 100%

**90** Colour: iodine, amber rim. Nose: dry nuts, honeyed notes, tar, pattiserie. Palate: flavourful, fleshy, spirituous, fine bitter notes.

**TENEGUÍA VARIETALES 2008 T**
negramoll 50%, babos 50%, bastardo %, castellana %
**79**

**TENEGUÍA NEGRAMOLL 2008 T**
negramoll 100%
**78**

**TENEGUÍA MALVASÍA 2006 BLANCO DULCE**
malvasia 100%

**91** Colour: bright straw. Nose: mineral, honeyed notes, fruit liqueur notes, fruit liqueur notes, earthy notes. Palate: flavourful, sweetness, fleshy, round tannins.

**ZEUS NEGRAMOLL 2005 TINTO DULCE**
negramoll 100%

**92** Colour: cherry, garnet rim. Nose: expressive, complex, ripe fruit, fruit liqueur notes, sweet spices, cocoa bean. Palate: flavourful, sweetness, fleshy, fine bitter notes, spicy.

## CARLOS FERNÁNDEZ FELIPE

Las Ledas, 40
38710 Breña Baja (Canarias)
☎: 922 434 439 - Fax: 922 434 439

**VIÑA ETNA MALVASIA DULCE 2008 B**

**89** Colour: bright straw. Nose: powerfull, varietal, smoky, earthy notes. Palate: flavourful, sweet, spirituous, long.

**TION 2008 B**
albillo 30%, listán blanco 60%, malvasia 10%

**88** Colour: pale. Nose: expressive, floral, white flowers, fresh fruit, tropical fruit. Palate: flavourful, fruity, fresh.

**FONKA 2008 T**
**80**

## COOPERATIVA AGRÍCOLA VIRGEN DEL PINO

Camino de la Cooperativa, 6 El Pinar
38738 Puntagorda (La Palma)
☎: 922 493 211 - Fax: 922 493 211

**VIÑA TRAVIESA 2008 B**
**83**

**VIÑA TRAVIESA 2008 T**
**73**

## EUFROSINA PÉREZ RODRÍGUEZ

Briesta, 3 El Castillo
38788 Villa de Garafia (La Palma)
☎: 922 400 447 - Fax: 922 400 447
yeestan@m.s.n.com

**EL NÍSPERO 2008 B**
albillo 100%

**90** Colour: pale. Nose: earthy notes, smoky, fresh fruit, citrus fruit, grassy. Palate: flavourful, fruity, fresh.

## JUAN MATÍAS TORRES PÉREZ

Ciudad Real 10 Los Canarios
38740 Fuentecaliente de la Palma

# DO LA PALMA

(Santa Cruz de Tenerife)
☎: 922 444 219 - Fax: 922 444 219
bodegasjuanmatias@lapalmaenred.com
www.lapalmaenred.com/bodegasjuanmatias

VID SUR DULCE 2008 B

**87** Colour: bright golden. Nose: candied fruit, reduction notes, faded flowers. Palate: sweet, fine bitter notes.

VID SUR 2008 B

**77**

VID SUR DULCE 2006 B

**92** Colour: bright golden. Nose: varnish, aged wood nuances, pattiserie, honeyed notes, dry nuts. Palate: flavourful, powerful, sweet, fleshy, rich, long.

VID SUR 2008 T BARRICA

**67**

## ONÉSIMA PÉREZ RODRÍGUEZ

Las Tricias
38738 Garafia (La Palma)
☎: 922 463 481 - Fax: 922 463 481

VITEGA ALBILLO 2008 B
albillo

**87** Colour: pale. Nose: medium intensity, fresh fruit, floral. Palate: flavourful, fleshy, fruity.

VITEGA 2008 B
albillo ,listán blanco

**87** Colour: pale. Nose: white flowers, jasmine, fresh fruit, fruit expression. Palate: flavourful, fruity, fresh, good acidity.

VITEGA 2008 RD

**82**

VITEGA 2006 TC
listán negro ,prieto picudo

**70**

VITEGA 2005 TR
tintilla ,castellana

**81**

VITEGA TEA 2005 T

**74**

## S.A.T. BODEGAS NOROESTE DE LA PALMA

Bellido Alto, s/n
38780 Tijarafe (Santa Cruz de Tenerife)
☎: 922 491 075 - Fax: 922 491 075
satbellido@wanadoo.es
www.netpublicdir.com/bnoroeste

VEGA NORTE 2008 B
listán blanco ,albillo

**85** Colour: pale. Nose: candied fruit, earthy notes, powerfull. Palate: flavourful, fruity, fresh, fine bitter notes.

VEGA NORTE ALBILLO 2008 B
albillo

**83**

VEGA NORTE 2008 RD

**88** Colour: rose, purple rim. Nose: mineral, powerfull, ripe fruit, red berry notes. Palate: flavourful, sweetness, fruity, fleshy.

VEGA NORTE NEGRAMOLL 2008 T

**85** Colour: cherry, garnet rim. Nose: powerfull, ripe fruit, raspberry. Palate: flavourful, fleshy, fruity.

VEGA NORTE 2008 T FERMENTADO EN BARRICA
prieto picudo

**85** Colour: cherry, garnet rim. Nose: fruit expression, raspberry, earthy notes, balsamic herbs. Palate: flavourful, fruity, fine bitter notes. Personality.

VEGA NORTE "VINO DE TEA" 2008 T

**82**

SOME OTHER WINERIES WITHIN THE DO:

**AGRÍCOLA VELHOCO
BODEGA CASTRO Y MOGAN
BODEGA JOSÉ ALBERTO TABARES PÉREZ
BODEGA PERDOMO S.A.T.
BODEGAS EL HOYO
JORGE L. RODRÍGUEZ
LAS TOSCAS S.A.T.
MELQUIADES CAMACHO HERNÁNDEZ**

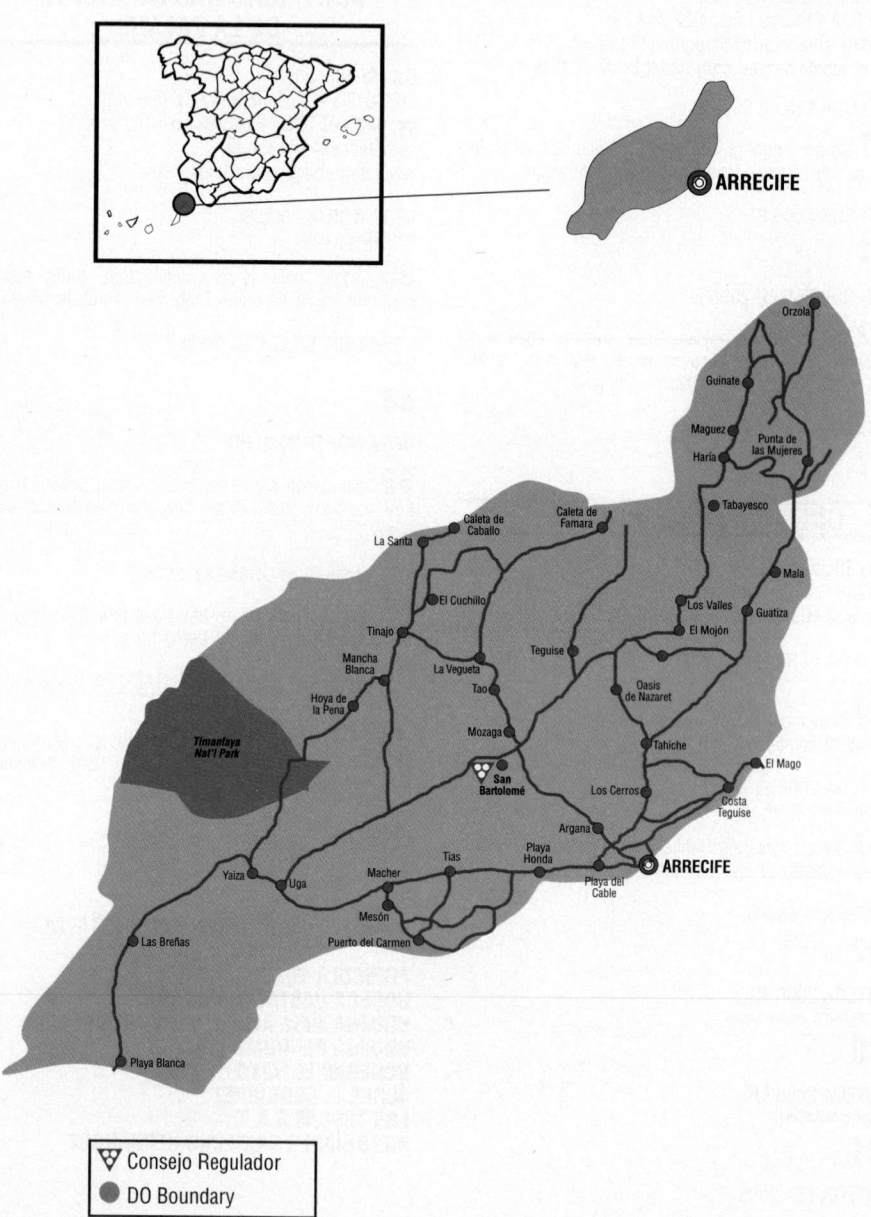

Consejo Regulador

DO Boundary

## NEWS

The malvasía and moscatel dry renderings from Lanzarote show in an amazingly good shape, with even fresher and more varietal fruit expression. Rosé wines have a deeper colour and are a little warmer and sweeter. Reds from Lanzarote, with their ashy, volcanic character are dropping their 'green' notes of old, given that vine growers tend to reduce the yields as a way to achieve a better quality. Stratvs (with listán negra and tinta conejera) and Bermejo are leading properties working with local varieties and short ageing spells. In the near future we will be able to taste in these wines foreign varieties recently approved by the new regulations, without a doubt, good news for a dry region with traditional –and costly– vine growing practices. In a lower step in terms of quality we find the semisweet renderings, which do not manage to find their place; they seem to lack nosetic expression as a result of wine making practices, for they are made by blending dry wines and frozen, unfermented must from the same vintage. Nevertheless, sweet wines are the real stars of the DO and probably of the whole Canary Islands. The best examples are the "naturalmente dulces", i.e. unfortified, meaning that the alcohol comes exclusively from the fermentation of the sugars contained in the overripe grapes. They are also very homogenous products, given that they resort to the same solera system from Jerez. Also unfortified is a great novelty and the top wine of the DO – rated at 94 points–, Stratvs Malvasía.

## LOCATION

On the island of Lanzarote. The production area covers the municipal areas of Tinajo, Yaiza, San Bartolomé, Haría and Teguise.

## CLIMATE

Dry subtropical in nature, with low rainfall (about 200 mm per year) which is spread out irregularly throughout the year. On occasions, the Levante wind (easterly), characterised by its low humidity and which carries sand particles from the African continent, causes a considerable increase in the temperatures.

## SOIL

Volcanic in nature (locally known as 'Picón'). In fact, the cultivation of vines is made possible thanks to the ability of the volcanic sand to perfectly retain the water from dew and the scant rainfall. The island is relatively flat (the maximum altitude is 670 m) and the most characteristic form of cultivation is in 'hollows' surrounded by semicircular walls which protect the plants from the wind. This singular trainig system brings about an extremaly low density.

## GRAPE VARIETIES:

**White:** *Malvasía* (majority 75%), *Pedro Ximénez, Diego, Listán Blanco, Moscatel, Burrablanca, Breval.*
**Red:** *Listán Negra* (15%) and *Negramoll.*

| Hectares of Vineyard | 1,986 |
|---|---|
| N° Viticulturists | 1,742 |
| N° of Bodegas | 15 |
| 2008 Harvest | Very Good |
| 2007 Production | 1,350,000 l. |
| Marketing | 90% domestic 10% export |

**CONSEJO REGULADOR**
Arrecife, 9. 35550 San Bartolomé (Lanzarote)
☎: 928 521 048 - Fax: 928 521 049
@ info@dolanzarote.com
www.dolanzarote.com

## GENERAL CHARACTERISTICS OF THE WINES:

| | |
|---|---|
| **WHITES** | The most characteristic wines of the island are the white *Malvasía* wines. They have vegetative noses with volcanic and mineral nuances. There are more classical and traditional wines, which have a yellow amber colour, with almond and mellow noses; the young white wines, which have a golden yellow colour, great varietal noses, sometimes with noses of fennel or mint, and are flavourful on the palate; and the semi-sec, with similar characteristics, but sweeter on the palate. |
| **ROSÉS** | In general, they have a pink or raspberry pink colour and are quite fresh and fruity. |
| **REDS** | These are usually mid-tone, with a deep cherry-red colour; they are somewhat warm and have a good structure on the palate. |

## 2008 VINTAGE RATING:

# GOOD

# DO LANZAROTE

## BODEGA LOS BERMEJOS

Camino a Los Bermejos, 7
35550 San Bartolomé de Lanzarote (Las Palmas)
☎: 928 522 463 - Fax: 928 522 641
bodega@losbermejos.com
www.losbermejos.com

BERMEJO MALVASÍA SECO 2008 B

**88** Color: bright straw. Nose: fresh, fresh fruit, white flowers, earthy notes. Palate: flavourful, fruity, good acidity, balanced.

BERMEJO DIEGO 2008 B

**86** Color: pale. Nose: scrubland, earthy notes, ripe fruit. Palate: flavourful, fruity, fleshy.

BERMEJO MALVASÍA NATURALMENTE DULCE B

**90** Color: bright golden. Nose: spicy, floral, candied fruit, citrus fruit. Palate: flavourful, sweet, fleshy.

ROSADO BERMEJO 2008 RD

**88** Color: onion pink. Nose: elegant, candied fruit, dried flowers, fragrant herbs, red berry notes. Palate: light-bodied, flavourful, good acidity, long, spicy.

BERMEJO 2008 T ROBLE

**88** Color: cherry, purple rim. Nose: powerfull, ripe fruit, red berry notes, sweet spices. Palate: flavourful, ripe fruit, spicy, round tannins.

BERMEJO TINTO MC 2008 T

**83**

BERMEJO MOSCATEL NATURALMENTE DULCE BLANCO DULCE

**90** Color: bright golden. Nose: fruit preserve, citrus fruit, varietal. Palate: flavourful, fleshy, sweet, ripe fruit.

BERMEJO 2007 BN
malvasia

**86** Color: bright straw. Nose: powerfull, fresh fruit, grassy, white flowers. Palate: flavourful, fruity, fresh.

## BODEGA STRATVS

Ctra. La Geria - Uga, km. 18
35570 Yaiza (Las Palmas)
☎: 928 809 977 - Fax: 928 524 651
bodega@stratvs.com

STRATVS MALVASIA SECO 2008 B
malvasia

**91** Colour: bright straw. Nose: fresh, fresh fruit, white flowers, expressive, mineral. Palate: flavourful, fruity, good acidity, balanced.

STRATVS DIEGO SEMIDULCE 2008 B
diego 90%, moscatel 10%

**87** Color: bright straw. Nose: candied fruit, citrus fruit, honeyed notes. Palate: flavourful, sweetness, ripe fruit.

STRATVS MALVASIA NATURALMENTE DULCE 2006 B
malvasia 100%

**94** Colour: bright golden. Nose: powerful, varietal, complex, fruit preserve. Palate: flavourful, concentrated, sweet, good acidity, balanced.

STRATVS MOSCATEL DULCE 2006 B
moscatel 100%

**94** Colour: old gold. Nose: powerful, varietal, characterful, fruit liqueur notes, fruit preserve. Palate: flavourful, powerful, fleshy, sweet, balanced.

STRATVS MOSCATEL LICOR 2006 B
moscatel 100%

**88** Colour: old gold. Nose: powerful, characterful, fruit preserve. Palate: flavourful, powerful, sweet, fine bitter notes.

STRATVS 2008 RD
HHHH7,5€

**86** Color: rose, purple rim. Nose: powerfull, raspberry, red berry notes, ripe fruit. Palate: flavourful, ripe fruit, good acidity.

STRATVS 2008 T
tinta conejera 50%, listán negro 50%

**87** Color: cherry, purple rim. Nose: powerfull, ripe fruit, balsamic herbs, scrubland. Palate: flavourful, powerful, balsamic.

STRATVS 2007 TC
tinta conejera 60%, listán negro 40%

**90** Colour: cherry, garnet rim. Nose: grassy, ripe fruit, smoky, spicy. Palate: flavourful, powerful, creamy, balanced.

STRATVS 2007 T

**89** Colour: cherry, purple rim. Nose: powerful, ripe fruit, mineral, grassy. Palate: flavourful, powerful, good structure, fruity.

## BODEGAS MALPAIS DE MAGUEZ

Cueva de los Verdes, 5
35542 Punta Mujeres - Haria (Las Palmas)
☎: 616 908 484 - Fax: 928 848 110
bodegamalpais@gmail.com

LA GRIETA MALVASÍA SECO 2008 B
malvasia

**82**

## EL GRIFO

El Islote, 121
35550 San Bartolomé (Las Palmas)
☎: 928 524 036 - Fax: 928 832 634
malvasia@elgrifo.com
www.elgrifo.com

EL GRIFO MALVASÍA COLECCIÓN 2008 B

**88** Color: bright straw. Nose: fresh, fresh fruit, white flowers, expressive. Palate: flavourful, fruity, good acidity, balanced.

EL GRIFO CANARI 1997 B

**92** Color: golden. Nose: powerfull, floral, honeyed notes, candied fruit, acetaldehyde. Palate: flavourful, sweet, fresh, fruity, good acidity, long, fine solera notes.

EL GRIFO 2008 RD

**87** Color: rose, purple rim. Nose: powerfull, ripe fruit, red berry notes, floral, expressive. Palate: fleshy, powerful, fruity, fresh.

CANARI
ANA

## MOZAGA S.A.

Ctra. Arrecife a Tinajo, 78
35562 Mozaga (Lanzarote)
☎: 928 520 485 - Fax: 928 521 409
bodegasmozaga@hotmail.com

TEIGA 2007 BFB
malvasia 100%

**87** Color: bright yellow. Nose: powerfull, ripe fruit, sweet spices, creamy oak. Palate: rich, smoky aftertaste, flavourful, fresh, good acidity.

MOZAGA 75 VINO DE LICOR B
moscatel 100%

**90** Color: golden. Nose: powerfull, honeyed notes, candied fruit, fragrant herbs, fruit liqueur notes. Palate: flavourful, sweet, fresh, fruity, good acidity, long.

DIEGO
GUARDAFIA

## VEGA DE YUCO

Camino del Cabezo s/n
35572 Masdache (Tías) (Lanzarote)
☎: 928 524 316 - Fax: 928 524 316
bodegavegadeyuco@hotmail.com
www.vegadeyuco.es

YAIZA 2008 B
malvasia 100%

**86** Color: pale. Nose: fresh fruit, grapey, floral. Palate: fruity, sweetness, flavourful.

VEGA DE YUCO 2008 B
malvasia 100%

**85** Color: pale. Nose: white flowers, fresh fruit. Palate: flavourful, sweetness, fruity.

YAIZA SEMI 2008 B
malvasia 100%

**85** Color: pale. Nose: medium intensity, candied fruit, white flowers. Palate: good acidity, sweetness, fruity.

PRINCESA ICO SEMIDULCE 2008 B
moscatel 50%, malvasia 50%

**84**

YAIZA 2008 RD
listán negro 100%

**83**

VEGA DE YUCO 2008 RD
listán negro 100%

**82**

YAIZA 2008 T
listán negro 100%

**83**

FAMARA DULCE 2008 T
listán negro 100%

**81**

VEGA DE YUCO 2008 T

**80**

SOME OTHER WINERIES WITHIN THE DO:

**BARRETO**
**BODEGA LA GERIA**
**BODEGAS ANAXCRÓN 2000**
**BODEGAS GERMÁN LÓPEZ FIGUERAS**
**BODEGAS GUIGUAN**
**BODEGAS LA MESETA**
**BODEGAS LA VEGUETA**
**CASTILLO DE GUANAPAY**
**FINCA LAS QUEMADAS S.L.**
**REYMAR**
**TIMANFAYA**
**TINACHE**

# DO MÁLAGA AND DO SIERRAS DE MÁLAGA

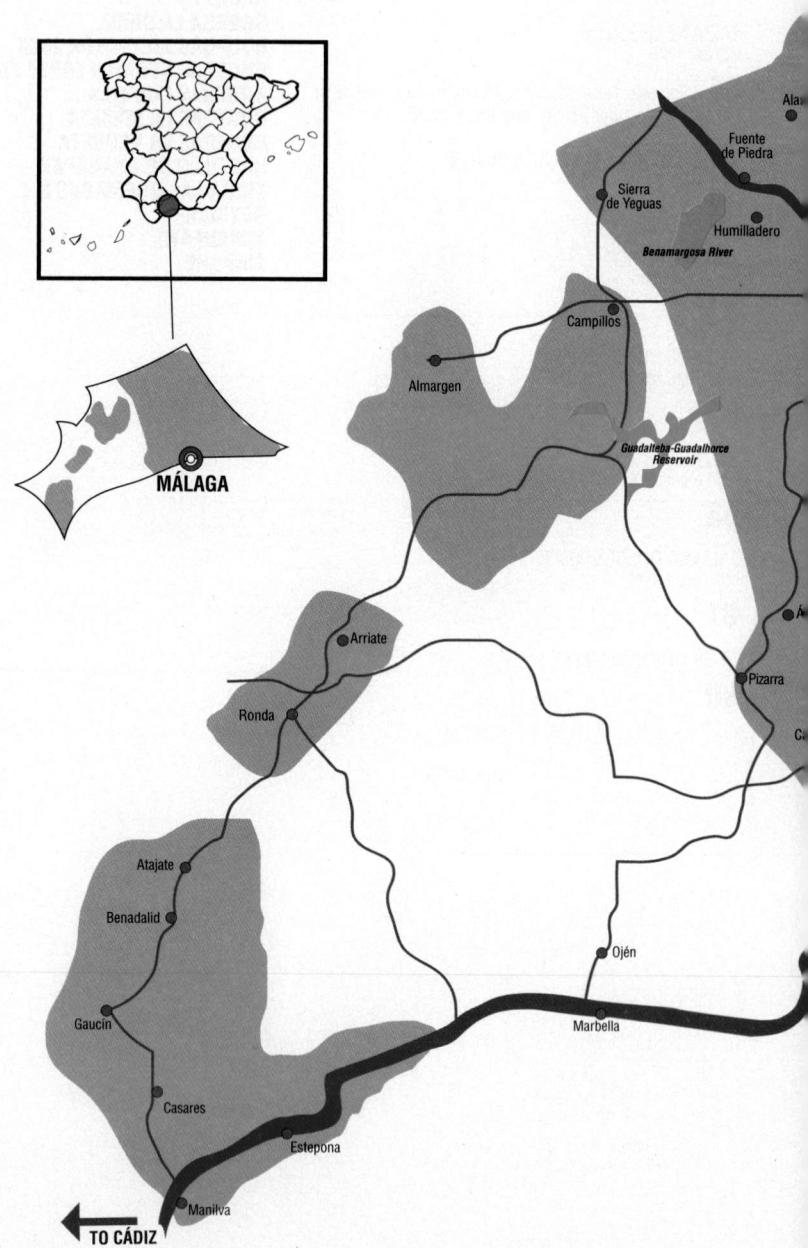

**MÁLAGA**

Alaa

Fuente de Piedra

Sierra de Yeguas

Humilladero

*Benamargosa River*

Campillos

Almargen

*Guadalteba-Guadalhorce Reservoir*

Arriate

Pizarra

Ronda

Ca

Atajate

Benadalid

Ojén

Gaucín

Marbella

Casares

Estepona

Manilva

← **TO CÁDIZ**

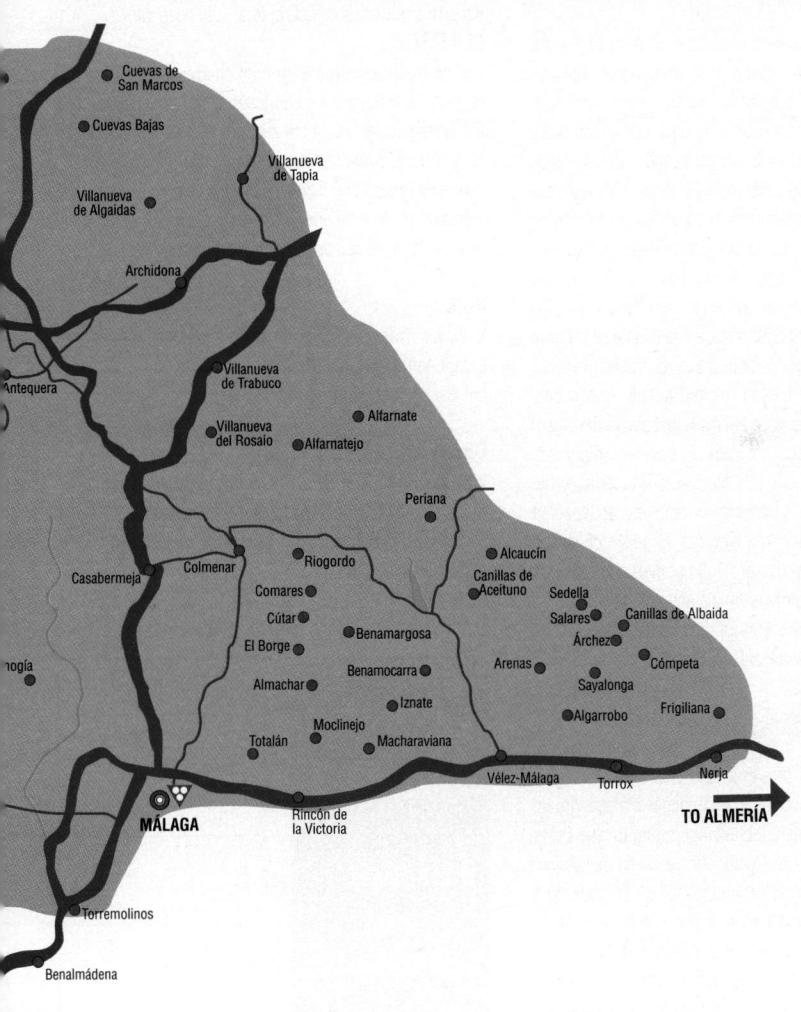

Cuevas de San Marcos
Cuevas Bajas
Villanueva de Tapia
Villanueva de Algaidas
Archidona
Antequera
Villanueva de Trabuco
Alfarnate
Villanueva del Rosaio
Alfarnatejo
Periana
Alcaucín
Casabermeja
Colmenar
Riogordo
Canillas de Aceituno
Comares
Sedella
Cútar
Salares
Canillas de Albaida
El Borge
Benamargosa
Árchez
nogía
Almachar
Benamocarra
Arenas
Cómpeta
Iznate
Sayalonga
Moclinejo
Algarrobo
Frigiliana
Totalán
Macharaviana
Vélez-Málaga
Torrox
Nerja
MÁLAGA
Rincón de la Victoria
TO ALMERÍA
Torremolinos
Benalmádena
ola

▽ Consejo Regulador
● DO Boundary

## NEWS

Málaga has five more wineries, three of them in Ronda, probably the most interesting area in a region that has become increasingly bipolar in recent years. And it is precisely in Ronda where risks of unbalanced vintages are higher as high are some of its vineyards and maturation gets particularly slow for long-cycle varieties. While white and rosé wines are few and far between, reds varieties seem to be better adapted to soil and climate and therefore yield more interesting wines. The stars of this new era are cabernet sauvignon and petit verdot. The more alcoholic examples come from the 2005 and 2006 vintages, and in those we have taste from 2007 we already notice a fresher, fruitier character hardly overshadowed by the toasted quality of the oak. Another interesting area is La Axarquía just above the city of Málaga, a primarily sweet –and naturally sweet– territory with wines made from moscatel de Alejandría, traditionally the flagship grape variety of the region reaching unexpected heights with the fantastic four labels of Jorge Ordóñez. The relatively cool temperatures of 2008 compared to previous vintages yielded even more aromatic and complex wines. In some areas hail destroyed 60% of the harvest, but it will not make much difference since most of that fruit was destined to the production of raisins.

As to the rest of traditional and generoso wines of the DO, they also show great character and even some modern features in the shape of some new labels with a highly commercial concept thought up by Bodegas Málaga Virgen. Thanks to all these wines, the average rating for the DO is going up every year in our Guide. The so-called trasañejos, one of the wine categories within the DO, which undergo a minimum ageing period of five years, show pretty much up to the high qualitative standards of old. Some of the highest ratings go to wines of limited edition promoted by the provincial government to commemorate its 75º anniversary through the art project Conarte. To this celebration, the wineries have brought their best renderings.

## LOCATION

In the province of Málaga. It covers 54 municipal areas along the coast (in the vicinity of Málaga and Estepona) and inland (along the banks of the river Genil), together with the new sub-region of Serranía de Ronda, a region to which the two new municipal districts of Cuevas del Becerro and Cortes de la Frontera have been added.

## CLIMATE

Varies depending on the production area. In the northern region, the summers are short with high temperatures, and the average rainfall is in the range of 500 mm; in the region of Axarquía, protected from the northerly winds by the mountain ranges and facing south, the climate is somewhat milder due to the influence of the Mediterranean; whilst in the west, the climate can be defined as dry subhumid.

## SOIL

It varies from red Mediterranean soil with limestone components in the northern region to decomposing slate on steep slopes of the Axarquía.

## GRAPE VARIETIES:

**White:** DO Málaga: *Pedro Ximénez* and *Moscatel*; DO Sierras de Málaga: *Chardonnay, Moscatel, Pedro Ximénez, Macabeo, Sauvignon Blanc* and *Colombard.*

**Red** (only DO Sierras de Málaga): *Romé, Cabernet Sauvignon, Merlot, Syrah, Tempranillo, Petit Verdot.*

| | |
|---|---|
| Hectares of Vineyard | 1,200 |
| Nº Viticulturists | 487 |
| Nº of Bodegas | 36 |
| 2008 Harvest | Good |
| 2007 Production | 4,300,000 l. |
| Marketing | 63% domestic 37% export |

## TYPOLOGY OF CLASSIC WINES:

**Liqueur wines:** from 15 to 22% vol.

**Natural sweet wines:** from 15 to 22 % vol. obtained from the *Moscatel* or *Pedro Ximénez* varieties, from musts with a minimum sugar content of 244 grams/litre.
**Naturally sweet wines** (with the same varieties, over 13% vol. and from musts with 300 grams of sugar/litre) and still wines (from 10 to 15% vol.).

Depending on their ageing:
**Málaga Joven:** Unaged still wines.
**Málaga Pálido:** Unaged non-still wines.
**Málaga:** Wines aged for between 6 and 24 months.
**Málaga Noble:** Wines aged for between 2 and 3 years.
**Málaga Añejo:** Wines aged for between 3 and 5 years.
**Málaga Trasañejo:** Wines aged for over 5 years.

**CONSEJO REGULADOR**
Fernando Camino, 2, 3° 3
29016 Málaga
☎: 952 228 493 - Fax: 952 227 990
@ info@vinomalaga.com
www.vinomalaga.com

**GENERAL CHARACTERISTICS OF THE WINES:**

| | |
|---|---|
| **TRADITIONAL WINES** | Their personality is marked by the grape syrup, the must that is concentrated or dehydrated by the heat that caramelises the wine and gives it its characteristic colour, sweetness and mellowness. There is a distinction between the 'Málaga', a sweet wine produced from the first must of the grape, the *Pedro Ximénez* and the *Moscatel*, which are produced from the grapes of the same name. |
| **MODERN WINES** | Produced from autochtonous and foreign varieties, they are marked by the heat of the climate, especially in the case of the red wines, which are very sunny with 'scorched' notes. The new natural sweet whites offer pleasant soft, mellow aromas and are very fresh on the palate, and sweet at the same time. |

## 2008 VINTAGE RATING:

## VERY GOOD

## BODEGA ANTIGUA CASA DE GUARDIA

Ctra. Olias, s/n. El Romerillo 29197 (Málaga)
☎: 952 030 714 - Fax: 952 252 150
info@casadeguardia.com
www.casadeguardia.com

VERDIALES CONARTE AÑEJO
pedro ximénez 60%, moscatel 40%

**91** Colour: light mahogany. Nose: powerfull, dried fruit, candied fruit, caramel, aromatic coffee. Palate: powerful, concentrated, spirituous.

VERDIALES SECO AÑEJO
pedro ximénez 100%

**87** Colour: iodine, amber rim. Nose: dried fruit, candied fruit, citrus fruit. Palate: flavourful, sweetness, spirituous.

MOSCATEL GUARDIA NOBLE
moscatel 90%, pedro ximénez 10%

**82**

PAJARETE 1908 TRASAÑEJO
pedro ximénez 100%

**87** Colour: iodine, amber rim. Nose: caramel, roasted almonds, pattiserie. Palate: flavourful, sweet, spirituous, long.

PEDRO XIMEN 1908 TRASAÑEJO
pedro ximénez 100%

**85** Colour: iodine, amber rim. Nose: powerfull, candied fruit, fruit liqueur notes, pattiserie. Palate: flavourful, concentrated, sweet.

EL CHAVEA
ISABEL II

## BODEGA CUESTA LA VIÑA

Antigua Ctra. Ronda-Sevilla, Pk. 3,3 A-2300
Montecorto, 29400 Ronda (Málaga)
☎: 629 589 336 - Fax: 952 870 719
bodega@vinosjorgebonet.es
www.vinosjorgebonet.es

JORGE BONET 2008 RD

**83**

JORGE BONET TSMC 2006 T

**89** Colour: bright cherry. Nose: ripe fruit, sweet spices, creamy oak, powerfull. Palate: flavourful, fruity, toasty, round tannins.

JORGE BONET TSMC 2005 T

**86** Colour: cherry, garnet rim. Nose: powerfull, overripe fruit, fruit liqueur notes, toasty. Palate: toasty, spicy, powerful, warm.

## BODEGA DESCALZOS VIEJOS

Partido de los Molinos del Tajo, s/n
29400 Ronda (Málaga)
☎: 952 874 696 - Fax: 952 875 501
info@descalzosviejos.com
www.descalzosviejos.com

DV DESCALZOS VIEJOS CHARDONNAY 2008 B
chardonnay 100%

**87** Colour: straw. Nose: fresh fruit, medium intensity, mineral, creamy oak. Palate: varietal, flavourful, creamy, smoky aftertaste.

DV DESCALZOS VIEJOS 2007 T
syrah 50%, merlot 35%, garnacha 15%

**89** Colour: cherry, purple rim. Nose: expressive, fresh, ripe fruit, scrubland. Palate: flavourful, fruity, fleshy.

DV CONARTE 2006 T
petit verdot 40%, syrah 30%, merlot 20%, cabernet sauvignon 20%

**91** Colour: bright cherry. Nose: ripe fruit, sweet spices, creamy oak, balsamic herbs. Palate: flavourful, fruity, toasty, round tannins.

DV DESCALZOS VIEJOS (+) 2005 T
syrah 30%, cabernet sauvignon 30%, merlot 20%, petit verdot 20%

**92** Colour: cherry, garnet rim. Nose: powerfull, ripe fruit, creamy oak, toasty. Palate: flavourful, fleshy, round tannins.

## BODEGA LOS BUJEOS

Ctra. Ronda El Burgo, Km 1
29400 Ronda (Málaga)
☎: 952 161 170 - Fax: 952 161 160
bodega@eljuncal.com
www.bodegapasoslargos.com

A PASOS 2006 T

**90** Colour: cherry, garnet rim. Nose: powerful, ripe fruit, creamy oak, sweet spices. Palate: flavourful, powerful, fleshy, round tannins, roasted-coffee aftertaste.

PASO
PASOS LARGOS

## BODEGA VETAS

Camino Nador. Finca El Baco
29350 Arriate (Málaga)
☎: 952 870 539 - Fax: 952 870 539
elbacoarriate@hotmail.com

VETAS PETIT VERDOT 2005 T
petit verdot 100%

**93** Colour: cherry, garnet rim. Nose: ripe fruit, spicy, creamy oak, complex, new oak, mineral. Palate: powerful, flavourful, toasty, round tannins.

VETAS SELECCIÓN 2003 T
petit verdot 60%, cabernet sauvignon 40%, cabernet franc %

**92** Colour: cherry, garnet rim. Nose: spicy, creamy oak, toasty, mineral, fruit preserve. Palate: powerful, flavourful, toasty, round tannins.

## BODEGA Y VIÑEDOS DE LA CAPUCHINA

Cortijo La Capuchina, Apartado Correos 26
29532 Mollina (Málaga)
☎: 679 153 639 - Fax: 952 031 583
bodegacapuchina@terra.es
www.bodegalacapuchina.es

CAPUCHINA VIEJA CONARTE 2006 T
cabernet franc 35%, syrah 35%, merlot 30%, cabernet sauvignon %

**91** Colour: cherry, garnet rim. Nose: ripe fruit, spicy, toasty, new oak. Palate: powerful, flavourful, toasty, round tannins.

CAPUCHINA VIEJA 2006 T
cabernet franc 45%, syrah 45%, merlot 10%, cabernet sauvignon %

**90** Colour: bright cherry. Nose: ripe fruit, sweet spices, creamy oak. Palate: flavourful, fruity, toasty, round tannins.

CAPUCHINA VIEJA SOL 2008 BLANCO DULCE
moscatel 100%

**88** Colour: bright golden. Nose: powerful, candied fruit, citrus fruit, honeyed notes. Palate: flavourful, sweet, warm, fine bitter notes.

## BODEGAS BENTOMIZ S.L.

Finca Almendro
Pago Cuesta Robano
29752 Sayalonga (Málaga)

☎: 952 115 939
info@bodegasbentomiz.com
www.bodegasbentomiz.com

ARIYANAS TERRUÑO PIZARROSO 2006 BC
moscatel 100%

**90** Colour: bright golden. Nose: powerful, varietal, fruit liqueur notes, honeyed notes. Palate: flavourful, fleshy, sweet, long.

ARIYANAS TINTO DE ENSAMBLAJE 2006 T
cabernet sauvignon 40%, tempranillo 40%, romé 20%

**92** Colour: cherry, garnet rim. Nose: fruit expression, ripe fruit, balsamic herbs, floral, elegant. Palate: flavourful, fleshy, ripe fruit, round tannins. Personality.

ARIYANAS NATURALMENTE DULCE 2007 B DULCE
moscatel 100%

**91** Colour: bright yellow. Nose: varietal, expressive, fresh fruit, citrus fruit, floral. Palate: flavourful, sweet, fruity, long.

## BODEGAS GOMARA

Diseminado Maqueda Alto, 59
29590 Campanillas (Málaga)
☎: 952 434 195 - Fax: 952 626 312
bodegas@gomara.com
www.gomara.com

SECO AÑEJO GOMARA AÑEJO

**85** Colour: iodine, amber rim. Nose: candied fruit, fruit liqueur notes, dry nuts. Palate: warm, sweetness, spirituous.

MÁLAGA TRASAÑEJO GOMARA MÁLAGA TRASAÑEJO
pedro ximénez 100%

**90** Colour: light mahogany. Nose: dark chocolate, caramel, aromatic coffee, pattiserie. Palate: fine bitter notes, unctuous, spirituous.

GOMARA MOSCATEL MÁLAGA
moscatel 100%

**87** Colour: old gold, amber rim. Nose: candied fruit, fruit preserve, fruit liqueur notes. Palate: sweet, spirituous, long.

MÁLAGA DULCE GOMARA MÁLAGA SOLERA
pedro ximénez 90%, moscatel 10%

**84**

LACRIMAE CHRISTI GOMARA NOBLE SOLERA
pedro ximénez 90%, moscatel 10%

# DO MÁLAGA AND DO SIERRAS DE MÁLAGA

**85** Colour: dark mahogany. Nose: powerful, warm, candied fruit, caramel. Palate: sweet, fine bitter notes, unctuous.

GOMARA PAJARETE NOBLE
pedro ximénez 100%

**84**

SECO GOMARA NOBLE
pedro ximénez 100%

**81**

GOMARA PEDRO XIMÉNEZ PX
pedro ximénez 100%

**81**

GRAN GOMARA TRASAÑEJO SOLERA
pedro ximénez 70%, moscatel 30%

**90** Colour: iodine, amber rim. Nose: expressive, candied fruit, honeyed notes, pattiserie. Palate: flavourful, spirituous, long.

## BODEGAS MÁLAGA VIRGEN

Autovía A-92, km. 132 Dirección Sevilla
(Camino de Servicio)
29520 Fuente de Piedra (Málaga)
☎: 952 319 454 - Fax: 952 359 819
marketing@bodegasmalagavirgen.com
www.bodegasmalagavirgen.com

BARÓN DE RIVERO 2008 B
moscatel, chardonnay

**87** Colour: bright straw. Nose: fresh fruit, floral, grassy. Palate: flavourful, fruity, fresh, light-bodied.

PERNALES SYRAH 2006 T
syrah

**89** Colour: cherry, garnet rim. Nose: powerful, ripe fruit, fruit preserve, toasty. Palate: flavourful, powerful, fleshy.

CHORRERA CREAM AÑEJO CR

**91** Colour: iodine, amber rim. Nose: varnish, roasted almonds, acetaldehyde. Palate: flavourful, fleshy, complex, rich.

SOL DE MÁLAGA MALAGA

**87** Colour: dark mahogany. Nose: powerful, dried fruit, fruit liqueur notes, dark chocolate. Palate: powerful, concentrated, sweet.

MOSCATEL IBERIA MALAGA

**87** Colour: light mahogany. Nose: powerful, sun-drenched nuances, dried fruit, dry nuts. Palate: powerful, concentrated, sweet.

MOSCATEL 30 AÑOS MOSCATEL

**91** Colour: light mahogany. Nose: powerful, overripe fruit, sun-drenched nuances, dark chocolate, aged wood nuances. Palate: sweet, fine bitter notes, unctuous.

MOSCATEL RESERVA DE FAMILIA MOSCATEL

**89** Colour: old gold, amber rim. Nose: powerful, candied fruit, fruit liqueur notes, varietal. Palate: flavourful, sweetness, good acidity.

TRES LEONES MOSCATEL

**86** Colour: bright yellow. Nose: medium intensity, candied fruit, fruit liqueur notes. Palate: sweet, flavourful, fine bitter notes.

TRAJINERO OL SOLERA

**88** Colour: iodine, amber rim. Nose: powerful, complex, elegant, dry nuts, toasty. Palate: rich, fine bitter notes, fine solera notes, long, spicy.

CARTOJAL PCR

**87** Colour: bright straw. Nose: powerful, varietal, floral, honeyed notes, ripe fruit. Palate: good acidity, flavourful, fruity, sweet.

PEDRO XIMENEZ 30 AÑOS PX

**92** Colour: dark mahogany. Nose: complex, fruit liqueur notes, dried fruit, pattiserie, toasty, warm. Palate: sweet, rich, unctuous, powerful.

PEDRO XIMÉNEZ RESERVA DE FAMILIA PX

**90** Colour: dark mahogany. Nose: complex, fruit liqueur notes, dried fruit, pattiserie, toasty. Palate: sweet, rich, unctuous, powerful.

MÁLAGA VIRGEN PX

**87** Colour: light mahogany. Nose: powerful, candied fruit, fruit liqueur notes, roasted almonds. Palate: powerful, sweet, fine bitter notes, unctuous.

SECO TRASAÑEJO 30 AÑOS TRASAÑEJO

**92** Colour: iodine, amber rim. Nose: powerful, fruit liqueur notes, candied fruit, caramel, roasted almonds. Palate: flavourful, powerful, spirituous.

BARÓN DE RIVERO
DON SALVADOR
DON JUAN

## BODEGAS QUITAPENAS

Ctra. de Guadalmar, 12 29004 Málaga (Málaga)
☎: 952 247 595 - Fax: 952 105 138
ventas@quitapenas.es
www.quitapenas.es

QUITAPENAS MOSCATEL PLATA 2008 B
moscatel 100%

**84**

GUADALVIN 2007 T
syrah 100%

**77**

QUITAPENAS MÁLAGA DULCE 2008 MALAGA
pedro ximénez 80%, moscatel 20%

**83**

MÁLAGA LAGAR 2008 MALAGA
pedro ximénez 80%, moscatel 20%

**82**

MÁLAGA VIÑA 2008 MÁLAGA
pedro ximénez 80%, moscatel 20%

**78**

MÁLAGA PX 2006 NOBLE
pedro ximénez 100%

**81**

MÁLAGA PAJARETE 2005 NOBLE
pedro ximénez 70%, moscatel 20%, rome 10%

**83**

QUITAPENAS MOSCATEL DORADO 2008 PÁLIDO
moscatel 100%

**85** Colour: bright golden. Nose: candied fruit, dried fruit, citrus fruit. Palate: sweet, concentrated, long.

MÁLAGA ORO VIEJO 5 AÑOS 2003 TRASAÑEJO
pedro ximénez 90%, moscatel 10%

**85** Colour: light mahogany. Nose: powerful, candied fruit, fruit liqueur notes, caramel, aromatic coffee. Palate: powerful, sweet, long.

MÁLAGA VIEJO ABUELO 10 AÑOS 1990 TRASAÑEJO
pedro ximénez 90%, moscatel 10%

**90** Colour: light mahogany. Nose: powerful, warm, candied fruit, dark chocolate. Palate: sweet, powerful, fine bitter notes, unctuous.

## COMPAÑÍA DE VINOS DE TELMO RODRÍGUEZ

El Monte s/n, 01308 Lanciego (Alava)
☎: 945 628 315 - Fax: 945 628 314
contact@telmorodriguez.com
www.telmorodriguez.com

MR 2007 B

**92** Colour: bright straw. Nose: candied fruit, citrus fruit, floral. Palate: flavourful, fleshy, sweet, fresh.

MOLINO REAL 2006 B

**97** Colour: bright straw. Nose: powerful, expressive, varietal, candied fruit, citrus fruit, white flowers. Palate: flavourful, fleshy, sweet, fresh, fruity.

## CORTIJO LOS AGUILARES

Puente de la Ventilla, Ctra. a Campillo Apartado 119
29400 Ronda (Málaga)
☎: 952 874 457 - Fax: 952 855 464
info@cortijolosaguilares.com
www.cortijolosaguilares.com

CORTIJO LOS AGUILARES 2008 RD

**88** Colour: rose, purple rim. Nose: fresh fruit, raspberry, floral. Palate: flavourful, fruity, fresh, fleshy.

CORTIJO LOS AGUILARES PINOT NOIR 2008 T
pinot noir

**88** Colour: bright cherry. Nose: elegant, candied fruit, fruit expression, spicy, balsamic herbs. Palate: flavourful, fresh, fruity.

CORTIJO LOS AGUILARES 2008 T
tempranillo, merlot

**85** Colour: cherry, purple rim. Nose: powerful, balsamic herbs, ripe fruit, scrubland. Palate: flavourful, fruity, good acidity.

CORTIJO LOS AGUILARES TADEO 2007 T

**92** Colour: bright cherry. Nose: ripe fruit, sweet spices, creamy oak, expressive, mineral. Palate: flavourful, toasty, round tannins, fleshy.

CORTIJO LOS AGUILARES PAGO EL ESPINO 2007 T

**89** Colour: cherry, garnet rim. Nose: powerful, ripe fruit, fruit expression, sweet spices, creamy oak. Palate: flavourful, fleshy, ripe fruit, round tannins.

## DIMOBE (BODEGA A. MUÑOZ CABRERA)

San Bartolomé, 5, 29738 Moclinejo (Málaga)
☎: 952 400 594 - Fax: 952 400 743
bodega@dimobe.es
www.dimobe.es

**EL LAGAR DE CABRERA SYRAH 2007 T JOVEN**
syrah 100%

**86** Colour: cherry, garnet rim. Nose: expressive, fresh fruit, floral. Palate: flavourful, fruity, fresh.

**EL LAGAR DE CABRERA 2006 TC**
syrah 100%

**82**

**RUJAQ ANDALUSI AÑEJO**
moscatel 100%

**84**

**VIÑA AXARKIA 2008 DULCE**
moscatel 100%

**83**

**SEÑORÍO DE BROCHES 2008 MOSCATEL**
moscatel 100%

**86** Colour: bright straw. Nose: powerful, candied fruit, fruit preserve. Palate: flavourful, fruity, sweet, fresh.

**EL LAGAR DE CABRERA 2008 MOSCATEL**
moscatel 100%

**84**

**ZUMBRAL CONARTE 2006 MOSCATEL**
moscatel 100%

**88** Colour: iodine, amber rim. Nose: powerful, candied fruit, dried fruit. Palate: flavourful, sweet, long.

**ZUMBRAL 2006 MOSCATEL**
moscatel 100%

**85** Colour: iodine, amber rim. Nose: candied fruit, citrus fruit, warm. Palate: spirituous, sweet, long.

**ARCOS DE MOCLINEJO 1975 PX**
pedro ximénez 100%

**87** Colour: iodine, amber rim. Nose: powerful, candied fruit, overripe fruit. Palate: flavourful, sweet, spicy, long.

## JORGE ORDÓÑEZ & CO

Pº de la Axarquia, 19, 29718 Almáchar (Málaga)
☎: 952 504 706 - Fax: 976 852 764
office@jorge-ordonez.es

**BOTANI 2008 B**
moscatel

**90** Colour: bright straw. Nose: powerful, ripe fruit, fresh fruit, fragrant herbs. Palate: powerful, flavourful, fleshy, ripe fruit, good acidity.

**VICTORIA CONARTE 2007 B**
moscatel

**95** Colour: bright straw. Nose: powerful, floral, scrubland, honeyed notes, candied fruit. Palate: sweet, full, great length.

**ORDÓÑEZ & CO. VIÑAS VIEJAS B**

**98** Colour: golden. Nose: powerful, floral, honeyed notes, candied fruit, fragrant herbs. Palate: flavourful, sweet, fresh, fruity, good acidity, long.

**Nº 2 VICTORIA 2007 BLANCO DULCE**
moscatel

**96** Colour: bright yellow. Nose: complex, wild herbs, candied fruit, honeyed notes. Palate: powerful, flavourful, good acidity, sweet.

**N 1 SELECCIÓN ESPECIAL 2007 BLANCO DULCE**
moscatel

**94** Colour: bright golden. Nose: powerful, elegant, candied fruit, honeyed notes, floral. Palate: flavourful, powerful, rich, sweet.

### SOME OTHER WINERIES WITHIN THE DO:

**BODEGA CONRAD/COTO DE LA VIÑA
SAN JACINTO
BODEGA DOÑA FELISA, S.L.
BODEGA KIENINGER
BODEGAS JOAQUÍN FERNÁNDEZ
BODEGAS LA SANGRE DE RONDA
BODEGAS PÉREZ HIDALGO C.B.
BODEGAS VILORIA
F. SCHATZ
GARCÍA ORDÓÑEZ S.L.
LÓPEZ GARCÍA S.A.
LÓPEZ-MADRID
R. Y F. ANGULO VARONA
RONDA LA VIEJA
TIERRAS DE MOLLINA**

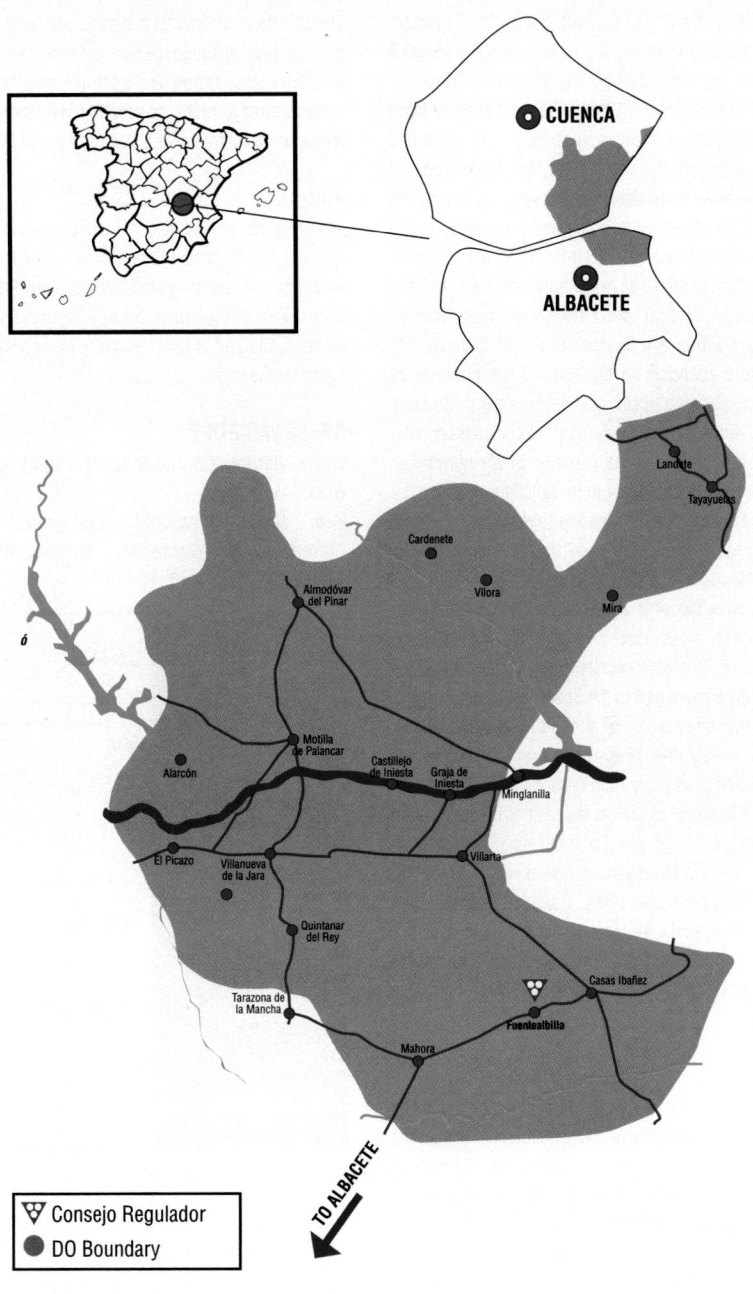

CUENCA

ALBACETE

Landete
Tayayuelas
Cardenete
Almodóvar del Pinar
Vilora
Mira
Motilla de Palancar
Castillejo de Iniesta
Graja de Iniesta
Alarcón
Minglanilla
El Picazo
Villanueva de la Jara
Villarta
Quintanar del Rey
Casas Ibañez
Tarazona de la Mancha
Fuentealbilla
Mahora

TO ALBACETE

Consejo Regulador
DO Boundary

## NEWS

Manchuela is showing much better in its 2007 vintage, when the most forward-looking varieties are in a splendid shape. On the top rankings we find Finca Sandoval, Altolandón and Bodegas y Viñedos Ponce. As for the 2008 vintage, the picture changes incredibly, with white and rosé wines leading the show and a rosé made from the local bobal by Altos del Cabriel at the very top. It is maybe a thing from the past, when bobal was the main variety in an area that was well known for rosé wines full of intense red fruit notes. In the white grape front, the main choice is macabeo and verdejo, wich have also been planted everywhere within the Spanish territory. Nevertheless bobal, more abundant in this part of the province of Cuenca and showing fresher and more elegant, has more followers within the new generation of winemakers, who tend to blend it with grape varieties of Mediterranean origins in order to come to a more refined expression. La Casilla de Bodegas and Viñedos Ponce is the leading name for this grape variety, with good balance and a terroir-driven style. As we go down the quality ladder, we find bobal examples higher in acidity and fruitier than the ones we get from the areas closer to the sea. We have to bear in mind that this DO enjoys excellent soils and a mild climate typical of the Eastern part of the Spanish peninsula, which, in addition to an exceptional altitude (over 700 meters), becomes simply the best terroir for varietal wines anywhere. The ones made from touriga nacional and syrah from Finca Sandoval as well as the malbec rendering from Altolandón are enough proof of it all, along with the new valiant tries like El Monegrillo, working with petit verdot, cabernet sauvignon and syrah. Outside the most solid bunch of Manchuela we have to mention wines with a lesser background and rating capabilities, but prices under the 6€ mark, which renders them a good choice for importers.

## LOCATION

The production area covers the territory situated in the southeast of the province of Cuenca and the northeast of Albacete, between the rivers Júcar and Cabriel. It comprises 70 municipal districts, 26 of which are in Albacete and the rest in Cuenca.

## CLIMATE

The climate is continental in nature, with cold winters and hot summers, although the cool and humid winds from the Mediterranean during the summer help to lower the temperatures at night, so creating favourable day-night temperature contrasts for a slow ripening of the grapes.

## SOIL

The vineyards are situated at an altitude ranging between 600 and 700 m above sea level. The terrain is mainly flat, except for the ravines outlined by the rivers. Regarding the composition of the terrain, below a clayey surface of gravel or sand, the soil is limy, which is an important quality factor for the region.

## GRAPE VARIETIES:

**White:** *Albillo, Chardonnay, Macabeo, Sauvignon Blanc, Verdejo.*

**Red:** *Bobal, Cabernet Sauvignon, Cencibel (Tempranillo), Garnacha, Merlot, Monastrell, Moravia Dulce, Syrah.*

| | |
|---|---|
| Hectares of Vineyard | 3,944 |
| Nº Viticulturists | 994 |
| Nº of Bodegas | 29 |
| 2008 Harvest | Very Good |
| 2007 Production | 1,546,479 l. |
| Marketing | 40% domestic 60% export |

**CONSEJO REGULADOR**
Matadero, 5. 02260 Fuentealbilla (Albacete)
☎: 967 477 535 - Fax: 967 477 505
@ domanchuela@lamanchuela.es
www.do-manchuela.com

## GENERAL CHARACTERISTICS OF THE WINES:

| | |
|---|---|
| **WHITES** | Normally produced from *Macabeo*, they have a straw yellow colour, apple fruity aromas, and are pleasant and easy drinking. |
| **ROSÉS** | These have a raspberry colour; the *Bobal* variety gives intense fruity aromas to raspberry, and on occasion hints of herbs; on the palate they are flavourful, fresh and balanced. |
| **REDS** | Cherry-coloured, they are very similar to the wines from La Mancha, with notes of blackberries and, on occasions, with an earthy background; they are supple, flavourful and warm on the palate. Those produced from *Bobal* have a better defined fruity expression (blackberry) and are very flavourful. |

## 2008 VINTAGE RATING:

## VERY GOOD

# DO MANCHUELA

## ALTOLANDON

Ctra. N-330, km. 242
16330 Landete (Cuenca)
☎: 677 228 974 - Fax: 962 300 662
altolandon@altolandon.com
www.altolandon.com

ALTOLANDON CHARDONNAY 2008 B
chardonnay 100%

**85** Colour: bright yellow. Nose: powerful, aged wood nuances, wild herbs. Palate: dry, fine bitter notes, harsh oak tannins.

ALTOLANDON 2006 T
syrah 50%, cabernet sauvignon 50%, garnacha %

**91** Colour: bright cherry. Nose: ripe fruit, sweet spices, creamy oak, mineral. Palate: flavourful, fruity, toasty, round tannins.

RAYUELO 2006 T
bobal 50%, malbec 40%, monastrell 10%

**91** Colour: bright cherry, garnet rim. Nose: complex, balanced, ripe fruit, cocoa bean. Palate: flavourful, elegant, fine bitter notes, round tannins.

ALTOLANDON 2005 T
syrah 50%, garnacha 50%, cabernet sauvignon %

**90** Colour: deep cherry. Nose: aged wood nuances, toasty, ripe fruit. Palate: powerful, spirituous, toasty.

## BODEGA EL MONEGRILLO

Finca El Monegrillo, Polígono 13, parcela 20
16235 Iniesta (Cuenca)
☎: 646 689 153

EL MONEGRILLO T

**90** Colour: very deep cherry. Nose: powerful, expressive, mineral, ripe fruit, roasted coffee. Palate: powerful, fleshy, round tannins, toasty.

## BODEGA SEÑORIO DEL JUCAR

Pol. Ind. Parc 64-70
02200 Casas Ibáñez (Albacete)
☎: 967 460 632 - Fax: 967 460 564
info@bsjucar.es
www.senoriodeljucar.com

SEÑORÍO DEL JÚCAR 2003 RESERVA
tempranillo 80%, cabernet sauvignon 20%

**85** Colour: cherry, garnet rim. Nose: wet leather, spicy, roasted almonds. Palate: flavourful, good structure, round tannins, easy to drink.

## BODEGA VITIVINOS

Camino de Cabezuelas, s/n
02270 Villamalea (Albacete)
☎: 967 483 114 - Fax: 967 483 964
info@vitivinos.com
www.vitivinos.com

VIÑA ALTABA 2008 B
macabeo 80%, verdejo 20%

**86** Colour: pale. Nose: ripe fruit, tropical fruit, warm. Palate: rich, fruity, full, fine bitter notes.

AZUA VERDEJO 2008 B
verdejo 100%

**82**

VIÑA ALTABA 2008 RD
bobal 100%

**86** Colour: rose, purple rim. Nose: fresh fruit, violet drops, expressive, floral. Palate: fruity, flavourful, fresh, spicy.

AZUA BOBAL 2008 T ROBLE
bobal 100%

**85** Colour: bright cherry, purple rim. Nose: medium intensity, red berry notes, fresh. Palate: fruity, flavourful, balanced.

AZUA SYRAH 2007 T ROBLE
syrah 100%

**84**

AZUA SELECCIÓN BOBAL VIEJO 2006 TC
bobal 100%

**84**

AZUA SELECCIÓN BOBAL VIEJO 2003 TC
bobal 100%

**84**

## BODEGAS SAN GREGORIO MAGNO SOC. COOP. DE CLM

Ctra. de Ledaña, s/n
02246 Navas de Jorquera (Albacete)
☎: 967 482 134 - Fax: 967 482 134
sangregorio@amialbacete.com

MONTE MIRÓN 2006 T FERMENTADO EN BARRICA
bobal 100%

**83**

MONTE MIRÓN 2001 TR

**85** Colour: cherry, garnet rim. Nose: candied fruit, fruit liqueur notes, sweet spices. Palate: spicy, toasty, flavourful.

## BODEGAS VILLAVID

Niño Jesús, 25
16280 Villarta (Cuenca)
☎: 962 189 006 - Fax: 962 189 125
info@villavid.com
www.villavid.com

VILLAVID MACABEO VERDEJO 2008 B
macabeo 50%, verdejo 50%

**82**

VILLAVID 2008 RD
bobal 100%

**85** Colour: light cherry. Nose: fresh fruit, fruit expression, red berry notes, violet drops. Palate: flavourful, fruity, good acidity.

VILLAVID 2005 TC
tempranillo 100%

**85** Colour: cherry, garnet rim. Nose: wet leather, toasty, ripe fruit, medium intensity. Palate: correct, balanced, good finish.

## BODEGAS Y VIÑEDOS PONCE

Ctra. San Clemente, s/n
16230 Villanueva de la Jara (Cuenca)
☎: 677 434 523 - Fax: 967 490 580
ponce@iniestahoy.com

CLOS LOJEN 2008 T
bobal 100%

**86** Colour: deep cherry, purple rim. Nose: fresh fruit, floral, wild herbs. Palate: fresh, flavourful, full, fruity, slightly dry, soft tannins.

P.F. 2007 T
bobal 100%

**91** Colour: deep cherry. Nose: powerful, mineral, scrubland, toasty. Palate: powerful, fleshy, good acidity, varietal.

LA CASILLA (ESTRECHA) 2007 T
bobal 100%

**91** Colour: bright cherry, garnet rim. Nose: red berry notes, medium intensity, balanced, varietal, earthy notes. Palate: flavourful, great length, balanced.

PINO 2007 T
bobal 100%

**90** Colour: very deep cherry. Nose: toasty, ripe fruit, varietal, aromatic coffee. Palate: powerful, fleshy, ripe fruit, mineral.

LA CASILLA 2007 T
bobal 100%

**88** Colour: bright cherry, purple rim. Nose: fresh, red berry notes. Palate: flavourful, fresh, good structure, easy to drink, round tannins.

## CHERUBINO VALSANGIACOMO S.A.

Ctra. Cheste-Godelleta, km. 1
46370 Chiva (Valencia)
☎: 962 510 451 - Fax: 962 511 361
cvalsangiacomo@cherubino.es
www.cherubino.es

EL MONEGRILLO 2006 T
syrah 30%, cabernet sauvignon 70%

**86** Colour: deep cherry, garnet rim. Nose: ripe fruit, spicy, warm. Palate: powerful, long, toasty, balanced, round tannins, balsamic.

## COOPERATIVA DEL CAMPO SAN ANTONIO ABAD

Valencia, 41
02270 Villamalea (Albacete)
☎: 967 483 023 - Fax: 967 483 536
gerencia@vinos-saac.com
www.vinos-saac.com

ALTOS DEL CABRIEL 2008 B
macabeo 100%

**85** Colour: bright straw. Nose: fresh, fresh fruit, white flowers, expressive, fine lees. Palate: flavourful, fruity, good acidity, balanced.

ALTOS DEL CABRIEL 2007 B
macabeo

**82**

ALTOS DEL CABRIEL 2008 RD
bobal 100%

**87** Colour: rose, purple rim. Nose: powerful, ripe fruit, red berry notes, floral, expressive. Palate: fleshy, powerful, fruity, fresh.

**ALTOS DEL CABRIEL 2007 T**
tempranillo 100%

**81**

**GREDAS VIEJAS 2006 T ROBLE**
syrah 100%

**84**

**VIÑAMALEA 2005 TC**
tempranillo 100%

**83**

**ALTOS DEL CABRIEL 2008 SEMIDULCE**
macabeo 100%

**84**

## COOPERATIVA UNIÓN CAMPESINA INIESTENSE

San Idefonso, 1
16235 Iniesta (Cuenca)
☎: 967 490 120 - Fax: 967 490 777
comercial@cooperativauci.com
www.cooperativauci.com

**REALCE VIURA 2008 B**
viura 100%

**80**

**REALCE 2008 RD**
bobal 100%

**86** Colour: light cherry. Nose: powerful, ripe fruit, red berry notes, floral, expressive. Taste fleshy, powerful, fruity, fresh.

**REALCE 2008 T**
tempranillo 100%

**82**

**REALCE TEMPRANILLO 2005 TC**
tempranillo 100%

**83**

**REALCE BOBAL 2003 TR**
bobal 100%

**83**

## FINCA SANDOVAL

Ctra. CM-3222, km. 26,800
16237 Ledaña (Cuenca)
☎: 616 444 805

fincasandoval@gmail.com
www.grandespagos.com/pagoshtml#

**FINCA SANDOVAL CUVEE TNS MAGNUM 2007 T**
touriga nacional, syrah

**94** Colour: cherry, purple rim. Nose: powerful, creamy oak, sweet spices, dark chocolate, ripe fruit. Palate: flavourful, fleshy, ripe fruit.

**FINCA SANDOVAL 2007 T**

**93** Colour: cherry, purple rim. Nose: lactic notes, red berry notes, fruit expression, creamy oak, sweet spices. Palate: flavourful, fleshy, fruity, round tannins.

**SALIA 2007 T**

**92** Colour: bright cherry. Nose: ripe fruit, sweet spices, creamy oak, red berry notes. Palate: flavourful, fruity, toasty, round tannins.

**SIGNO 2007 T**

**92** Colour: bright cherry. Nose: creamy oak, expressive, red berry notes, fresh fruit, undergrowth, floral. Palate: flavourful, fruity, toasty, round tannins, fleshy.

## NUESTRA SEÑORA DE LA CABEZA SOC. COOP.

Avda. del Vino, 10
02200 Casas Ibáñez (Albacete)
☎: 967 460 105 - Fax: 967 460 266
info@coop-cabeza.com
www.coop-cabeza.com

**VIARIL 2007 BFB**
macabeo

**86** Colour: bright yellow. Nose: powerful, ripe fruit, creamy oak, fragrant herbs. Taste rich, smoky aftertaste, flavourful, fresh, good acidity.

## PAGOS DE FAMILIA VEGA TOLOSA

Pol. Ind.
02200 Casas Ibáñez (Albacete)
☎: 617 379 328 - Fax: 967 461 331
info@vegatolosa.com
www.vegatolosa.com

**VEGA TOLOSA SELECCIÓN 2008 B**
macabeo 80%, sauvignon blanc 15%, chardonnay 5%

**86** Colour: bright straw. Nose: ripe fruit, dried herbs, mineral. Palate: flavourful, fruity, good finish.

**VEGA TOLOSA NATURE 2008 T**
syrah 50%, tempranillo 50%

**85** Colour: deep cherry. Nose: mineral, fresh, ripe fruit. Palate: fruity, flavourful, round tannins, spicy.

**VEGA TOLOSA VIÑAS VIEJAS 2007 T**
bobal 100%

**87** Colour: deep cherry. Nose: powerful, toasty, fruit preserve, earthy notes. Palate: powerful, fleshy, fine bitter notes, fine tannins.

**VEGA TOLOSA FINCA LOS HALCONES 2006 T FERMENTADO EN BARRICA**
cabernet sauvignon 100%

**88** Colour: deep cherry. Nose: toasty, ripe fruit, powerfull. Palate: round tannins, powerful, flavourful, concentrated.


## SOME OTHER WINERIES WITHIN THE DO:

**BODEGA SAN ISIDRO S.C.L.A.**
**BODEGAS RECIAL**
**BODEGAS ROBLEALTO**
**COOPERATIVA DEL CAMPO VIRGEN**
   **DE LAS NIEVES**
**SAN ISIDRO SC DE CLM**
**SAN ISIDRO SOC. COOP.**
**SOCIEDAD COOPERATIVA AGRARIA**
   **SANTA MARÍA MAGDALENA**
**SOCIEDAD COOPERATIVA SAN JORGE**

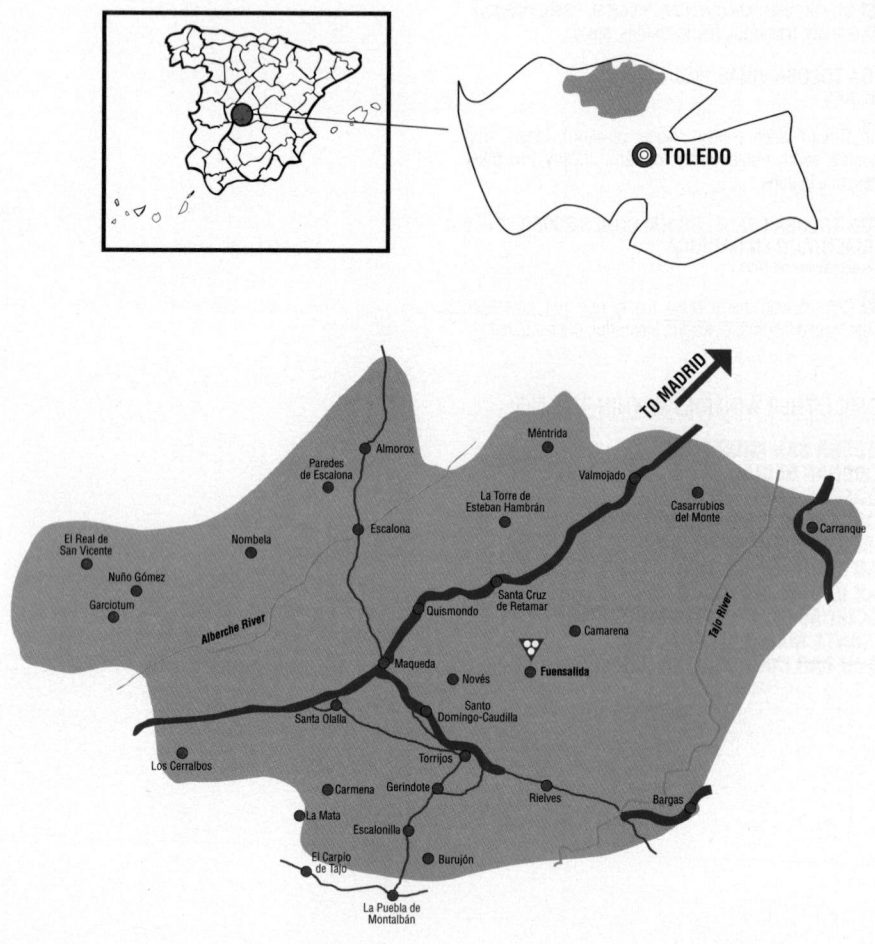

TOLEDO

TO MADRID

Méntrida

Almorox
Paredes
de Escalona

Valmojado

La Torre de
Esteban Hambrán

Casarrubios
del Monte

Carranque

El Real de
San Vicente

Nombela

Escalona

Nuño Gómez

Santa Cruz
de Retamar

Camarena

Garciotum

Alberche River

Quismondo

Maqueda

Novés

Fuensalida

Santo
Domingo-Caudilla

Tajo River

Santa Olalla

Los Cerralbos

Torrijos

Carmena

Gerindote

Rielves

Bargas

La Mata

Escalonilla

El Carpio
de Tajo

Burujón

La Puebla de
Montalbán

▽ Consejo Regulador
● DO Boundary

# DO MÉNTRIDA

## NEWS
A fresher vintage with lower production figures have provided a selective, overall better vintage. In this occasion we have focused mainly on those wineries that try to pamper the local garnacha, the main variety in the region. A usually warmer, more alcoholic variety in previous vintages, it yielded in 2008 rosé wines more spice and complexity. Nevertheless, we want to be realistic and in spite of our efforts to promote the local garnacha, at the top of our appreciation we find the qualitative blends of other varieties that make Alonso Cuesta and Arrayán.

## LOCATION
In the north of the province of Toledo. It borders with the provinces of Ávila and Madrid to the north, with the Tajo to the south, and with the Sierra de San Vicente to the west. It is made up of 51 municipal areas of the province of Toledo.

## CLIMATE
Continental, dry and extreme, with long, cold winters and hot summers. Late frosts in spring are quite common. The average rainfall is between 300 mm and 500 mm, and is irregularly distributed throughout the year.

## SOIL
The vineyards are at an altitude of between 400 m and 600 m, although some municipal districts of the Sierra de San Vicente reach an altitude of 800 m. The soil is mainly sandy-clayey, with a medium to loose texture.

## GRAPE VARIETIES:
**White:** *Albillo, Macabeo, Sauvignon Blanc, Chardonnay* and *Verdejo*.
**Red:** *Garnacha* (majority 85% of total), *Cencibel* (*Tempranillo*), *Cabernet Sauvignon, Merlot, Syrah* and *Petit Verdot*.

| Hectares of Vineyard | 8,500 |
|---|---|
| Nº Viticulturists | 1,557 |
| Nº of Bodegas | 23 |
| 2008 Harvest | Good |
| 2007 Production | N/A |
| Marketing | 93.2% domestic 6.8% export |

# DO MÉNTRIDA

## CONSEJO REGULADOR

Avda. Cristo del Amparo, 16
45510 Fuensalida (Toledo)
☎: 925 785 185 - Fax: 925 784 154
@ administracion@domentrida.es
www.domentrida.es

## GENERAL CHARACTERISTICS OF THE WINES:

| ROSÉS | Normally produced from *Garnacha*, they have a raspberry pink colour; they have a fruity aroma and are meaty and supple on the palate. |
|---|---|
| REDS | These have a dark cherry colour; on the nose, they are noticeable for their hints of ripe fruit typical of long ripening periods; on the palate they are meaty, warm and supple. |

## 2008 VINTAGE RATING:

# VERY GOOD

## ALONSO CUESTA

Pza. Constitución, 4
45920 La Torre de Esteban Hambrán (Toledo)
☎: 925 795 742 - Fax: 925 795 742
administracion@alonsocuesta.com

**ALONSO CUESTA 2005 T**
garnacha 60%, tempranillo 30%, cabernet sauvignon 10%

**91** Colour: dark-red cherry. Nose: characterful, powerfull, mineral, tar, aromatic coffee, balsamic herbs. Palate: powerful, good structure, concentrated, slightly dry, soft tannins, balsamic.

RC REUTERS

## BERBERANA

Ctra. de Vitoria, km. 182-183
26360 Cenicero (La Rioja)
☎: 941 453 100 - Fax: 941 450 101
info@berberana.com
www.berberana.com

**BERBERANA RESERVA CLÁSICO 1877 2004 RESERVA**

**86** Colour: bright cherry, garnet rim. Nose: red berry notes, fresh, spicy. Palate: ripe fruit, toasty, balsamic, round tannins, lacks balance.

## BODEGAS ARRAYÁN

Finca La Verdosa, s/n
45513 Santa Cruz del Retamar (Toledo)
☎: 916 633 131 - Fax: 916 632 796
comercial@arrayan.es
www.arrayan.es

**ARRAYÁN 2008 RD**
syrah, petit verdot, merlot, cabernet sauvignon

**86** Colour: rose, purple rim. Nose: powerful, ripe fruit, red berry notes. Palate: flavourful, powerful, fleshy, fruity, sweetness.

**ARRAYÁN PREMIUM 2007 T**
syrah 55%, cabernet sauvignon 15%, merlot 20%, petit verdot 10%

**91** Colour: cherry, garnet rim. Nose: ripe fruit, red berry notes, lactic notes, sweet spices, dark chocolate. Palate: flavourful, fleshy, fruity, good structure.

**ARRAYÁN PETIT VERDOT 2007 T**
petit verdot 100%

**90** Colour: bright cherry. Nose: ripe fruit, sweet spices, creamy oak, expressive. Palate: flavourful, fruity, toasty, round tannins.

**ESTELA DE ARRAYAN 2007 T**
syrah, petit verdot, cabernet sauvignon, merlot

**90** Colour: cherry, garnet rim. Nose: ripe fruit, spicy, creamy oak, toasty, complex, lactic notes. Palate: powerful, flavourful, toasty, round tannins.

**ARRAYÁN SYRAH 2007 T**
syrah 100%

**89** Colour: cherry, garnet rim. Nose: candied fruit, ripe fruit, sweet spices, cocoa bean. Palate: flavourful, fruity, fleshy.

**ARRAYÁN SELECCIÓN 2007 T**
syrah 35%, merlot 30%, cabernet sauvignon 30%, petit verdot 5%

**85** Colour: cherry, garnet rim. Nose: woody, toasty, ripe fruit. Palate: flavourful, powerful, fleshy, spicy.

## BODEGAS CANOPY

Avda. Barber, 71
45004 (Toledo)
☎: 619 244 878 - Fax: 925 283 681
achacon@masfuturo.com

**LA VIÑA ESCONDIDA 2007 T**
garnacha

**93** Colour: cherry, garnet rim. Nose: fresh, ripe fruit, scrubland, toasty. Palate: flavourful, fruity, fresh, balsamic, fruity aftestaste. Personality.

**TRES PATAS 2007 T**
garnacha 80%, syrah 20%

**91** Colour: cherry, garnet rim. Nose: expressive, mineral, ripe fruit, spicy, balanced. Palate: flavourful, powerful, fleshy, mineral.

**MALPASO 2007 T**
syrah 100%

**91** Colour: cherry, garnet rim. Nose: powerful, ripe fruit, red berry notes, lactic notes, toasty, sweet spices. Palate: flavourful, powerful, fleshy, ripe fruit, round tannins.

## BODEGAS JIMÉNEZ LANDI

Avda. Solana, 45
45930 Méntrida (Toledo)
☎: 918 178 213 - Fax: 918 178 213
jose@jimenezlandi.com
www.jimenezlandi.com

CANTOS DEL DIABLO 2007 T
garnacha 100%

**97** Colour: dark-red cherry. Nose: floral, acacia flower, fruit liqueur notes, fruit expression, dry stone, mineral, wild herbs, spicy, cocoa bean. Palate: fruity, flavourful, powerful, sweetness, spirituous, complex. Personality.

JIMÉNEZ-LANDI FIN DEL MUNDO 2007 T
garnacha tinta 100%

**95** Colour: dark-red cherry. Nose: mineral, dry stone, fruit expression, fruit liqueur notes, dried herbs. Palate: powerful, flavourful, fruity, complex, round, spirituous, balsamic, spicy. Personality.

PIÉLAGO 2007 T
garnacha 100%

**92** Colour: dark-red cherry. Nose: ripe fruit, mineral, dry stone, creamy oak. Palate: good structure, fruity, powerful, flavourful, ripe fruit, balsamic, creamy. Personality.

JIMÉNEZ-LANDI SOTORRONDERO 2007 T
syrah 90%, garnacha 10%

**92** Colour: dark-red cherry. Nose: mineral, undergrowth, fruit expression, wild herbs. Palate: spirituous, fruity, full, powerful, flavourful. Personality.

## COOPERATIVA AGRÍCOLA SANTO CRISTO DE LA SALUD

Ctra. Méntrida, s/n
45920 Torre de Esteban Hambrán (Toledo)
☎: 925 795 114 - Fax: 925 795 114
coopcrist@telefonica.net

SEÑORIO DE ESTEBAN HAMBRÁN 2008 RD

**86** Colour: brilliant rose. Nose: fruit expression, macerated fruit, floral, balsamic herbs. Palate: flavourful, full, fruity, sweetness.

SEÑORIO DE ESTEBAN HAMBRÁN 2008 T

**82**

TORRESTEBAN 2005 TC

**82**

## COOPERATIVA CONDES DE FUENSALIDA

Avda. San Crispín, 129
45510 Fuensalida (Toledo)

☎: 925 784 823 - Fax: 925 784 823
condesdefuensalida@hotmail.com
www.condesdefuensalida.iespana.es

CONDES DE FUENSALIDA 2007 T
garnacha, tempranillo

**86** Colour: bright cherry. Nose: fruit expression, macerated fruit, mineral, cocoa bean. Palate: creamy, good acidity, elegant, round.

## COOPERATIVA NUESTRA SEÑORA DE LA NATIVIDAD

Puente San Roque, 1
45930 Méntrida (Toledo)
☎: 918 177 004 - Fax: 918 177 004
natividad.3081@cajarural.com

VEGA BERCIANA 2008 RD

**72**

VEGA BERCIANA 2008 T

**79**

VALLE PEDROMORO 2005 T BARRICA

**77**

## COOPERATIVA NUESTRA SEÑORA DE LINARES

Inmaculada, 95
45920 Torre de Esteban Hambrán (Toledo)
☎: 925 795 452 - Fax: 925 795 452
cooplina@futurnet.es

FORTITUDO RD

**86** Colour: rose, purple rim. Nose: fresh fruit, red berry notes, citrus fruit, fragrant herbs, floral. Palate: flavourful, full, good acidity.

FORTITUDO 2008 T

**80**

## COOPERATIVA SANTA MARÍA MAGDALENA

Santa M. Magdalena, 2
45960 Chozas de Canales (Toledo)
☎: 918 176 142 - Fax: 918 176 191
csmagdalena.3081@cajarural.com

ROCANALES 2008 RD

**78**

ROCANALES 2008 T

**74**

## LA CERCA S.A.

Lepanto, s/n
45950 Casarrubios del Monte (Toledo)
☎: 918 172 456 - Fax: 916 905 046
bodegaslacerca@yahoo.es

MOLINO VIEJO TEMPRANILLO 2007 T BARRICA

**83**

DON CECILIO 2007 T

**80**

MOLINO VIEJO TEMPRANILLO 2006 CRIANZA

**84**

ORO BLANCO

PERLA NEGRA

## VIÑEDOS DE CAMARENA, SDAD. COOPERATIVA DE CLM

Ctra. Toledo - Valmojado, km.24,6
45180 Camarena (Toledo)
☎: 918 174 347 - Fax: 918 174 632
vdecamarena@hotmail.com
www.vdecamarena.com

BASTIÓN DE CAMARENA 2008 RD

**87** Colour: brilliant rose. Nose: fruit expression, candied fruit, citrus fruit, raspberry, balsamic herbs, spicy, floral. Palate: flavourful, full, fresh, fruity.

BASTIÓN DE CAMARENA 2007 T

**85** Colour: deep cherry. Nose: fruit expression, red berry notes, balsamic herbs. Palate: fleshy, full, flavourful, balsamic.

EL GARBOSO

## VIÑEDOS Y BODEGAS GONZÁLEZ

Real, 86
45180 Camarena (Toledo)

☎: 918 174 063 - Fax: 918 174 136
bodegasgonzalez@yahoo.es
www.vinobispo.com

VIÑA BISPO 2008 B

**86** Colour: bright yellow. Nose: fresh fruit, tropical fruit, scrubland, dry stone. Palate: powerful, full, flavourful, good acidity.

VIÑA BISPO 2008 RD

**85** Colour: rose, purple rim. Nose: fruit expression, fresh fruit, fragrant herbs. Palate: fruity, rich, good acidity.

VIÑA BISPO 2004 TC

**83**

SOME OTHER WINERIES WITHIN THE DO:

**COOPERATIVA NTRA. SRA. DE GRACIA
COOPERATIVA SANTO DOMINGO GUZMÁN
COOPERATIVA VIRGEN DEL CARMEN
LAS CAÑADAS DE CARTEMA
VIÑEDOS Y BODEGAS EL BARRO**

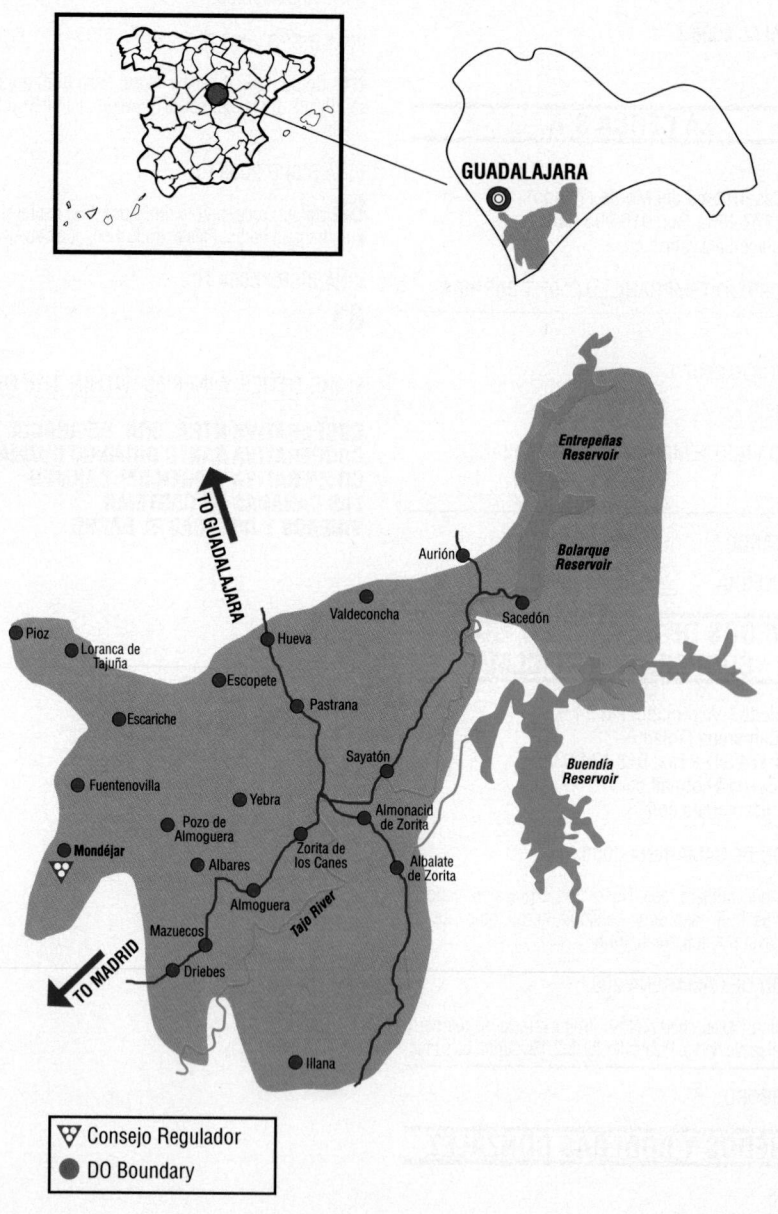

GUADALAJARA

Entrepeñas Reservoir

Bolarque Reservoir

Buendía Reservoir

TO GUADALAJARA

Aurión

Valdeconcha

Sacedón

Hueva

Pioz

Loranca de Tajuña

Escopete

Escariche

Pastrana

Sayatón

Fuentenovilla

Yebra

Pozo de Almoguera

Almonacid de Zorita

Mondéjar

Zorita de los Canes

Albares

Albalate de Zorita

Almoguera

Tajo River

Mazuecos

TO MADRID

Driebes

Illana

▽ Consejo Regulador
● DO Boundary

## NEWS

One of the youngest DOs within Spanish territory, it is nevertheless running out of wineries –from the four of the original plan to just two– and try to overcome those difficulties every year. The 2008 vintage was a poor one in terms of quantity, a terrible prospect for the local cooperatives. Bodeas Mariscal seems to have the future of the region in its hands, and has come up with a single-varietal syrah under the Tierra Rubia label as well as a more than correct white torrontés.

## LOCATION

In the southwest of the province of Guadalajara. It is made up of the municipal districts of Albalate de Zorita, Albares, Almoguera, Almonacid de Zorita, Driebes, Escariche, Escopete, Fuenteovilla, Illana, Loranca de Tajuña, Mazuecos, Mondéjar, Pastrana, Pioz, Pozo de Almoguera, Sacedón, Sayatón, Valdeconcha, Yebra and Zorita de los Canes.

## CLIMATE

Temperate Mediterranean. The average annual temperature is around 18°C and the average rainfall is 500 mm per year.

## SOIL

The south of the Denomination is characterized by red soil on lime-clayey sediments, and the north (the municipal districts of Anguix, Mondéjar, Sacedón, etc.) has brown limestone soil on lean sandstone and conglomerates.

## GRAPE VARIETIES:

**White (40%):** *Malvar* (majority 80% of white varieties), *Macabeo* and *Torrontés*.

**Red (60%):** *Cencibel* (*Tempranillo* – represents 95% of red varieties) and *Cabernet Sauvignon* (5%) and *Syrah*.

| Hectares of Vineyard | 1,300 |
|---|---|
| Nº Viticulturists | 700 |
| Nº of Bodegas | 2 |
| 2008 Harvest | Reds wine: Excellent Whites wine: Very Good |
| 2007 Production | 5,000,000 l. |
| Marketing | 80% domestic 20% export |

**CONSEJO REGULADOR**
Plaza Mayor, 10. 19110 Mondéjar (Guadalajara)
☎: 949 385 284 - Fax: 949 385 284
@ crdom@crdomondejar.com

## GENERAL CHARACTERISTICS OF THE WINES:

| | |
|---|---|
| **WHITES** | Those produced according to the more modern style tend to have a pale straw yellow colour; they have a fruity, fresh aroma and on the palate they are light and fruity; in the more traditional wines, however, there may appear notes of over-ripening. |
| **ROSÉS** | In general, they are light, supple and quite pleasant, although without excessive aromatic intensity. |
| **REDS** | These are probably the most interesting of the region. Produced mainly from *Cencibel*, their style resembles those from La Mancha: good aromatic intensity, with a presence of ripe fruit, supple and flavourful on the palate. |

## 2008 VINTAGE RATING:

# AVERAGE

## MARISCAL

Avda. Constitución, 37
19110 Mondejar (Guadalajara)
☎: 949 385 138 - Fax: 949 387 740
comex@mariscal.es
www.mariscal.es

PAGO DE ARIS TORRONTÉS 2007 B
torrontés 100%

**84**

TIERRA RUBIA 2006 T
syrah 100%

**86** Colour: deep cherry, garnet rim. Nose: floral, expressive, sweet spices, fresh fruit. Palate: full, flavourful, sweet tannins.

VEGA TAJUÑA
CUEVA DE LOS JUDÍOS
SEÑORÍO DE MARISCAL

## SOCIEDAD COOPERATIVA SANTA MARÍA MAGDALENA

Ctra. Perales - Albares, km. 71, 200
19110 Mondejar (Guadalajara)
☎: 949 385 139 - Fax: 949 387 727

JARDINILLO 2007 B

**70**

VALMORES

# DO MONTERREI

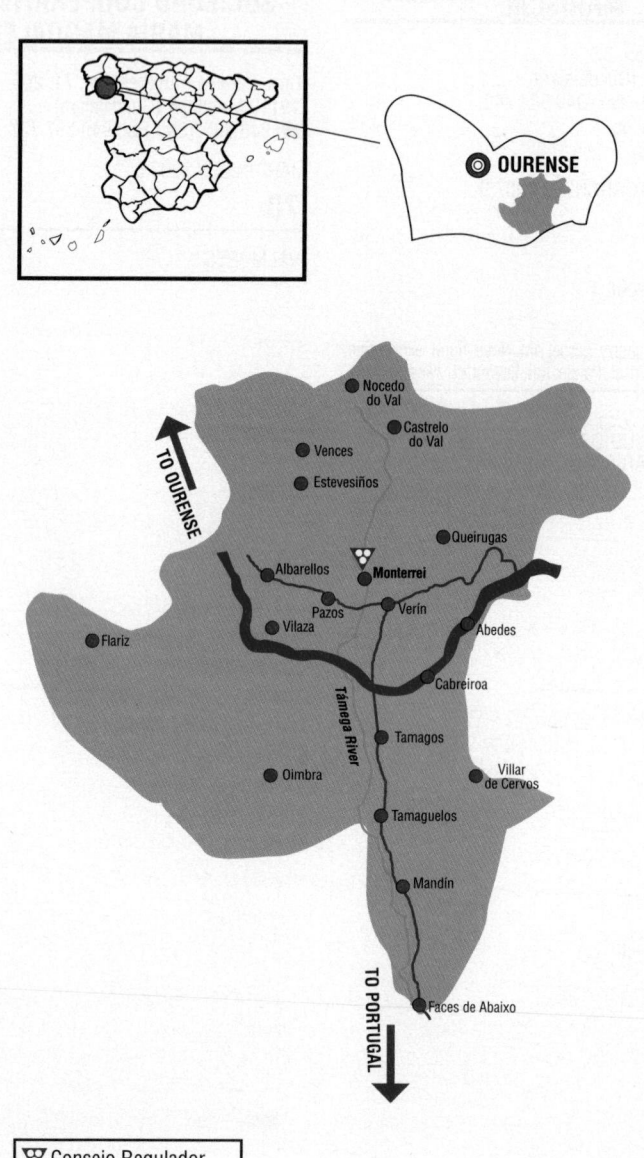

OURENSE

TO OURENSE

Nocedo do Val
Castrelo do Val
Vences
Estevesiños
Queirugas
Albarellos
**Monterrei**
Pazos
Verín
Viļaza
Abedes
Fariz
Cabreiroa
Támega River
Tamagos
Villar de Cervos
Oimbra
Tamaguelos
Mandín
TO PORTUGAL
Faces de Abaixo

▽ Consejo Regulador
● DO Boundary

## NEWS

Monterrei is on the rise, not only because of our interest – given their joined effort towards local varieties– but also because it is becoming popular. This inner region of Galicia has known a sales increase of over 20% just last year, mostly for the foreign markets and thanks to powerful wines with far more character and alcohol than its neighbouring Atlantic wine regions. We have not tasted many wines, but most of them reached the top ratings of our Guide, with a well-defined and varied character. To support all these investments in the varietal front, the Consejo Regulador has put into effect the Monterrei Superior back label for those wines containing at least 85% of the local grapes. Quinta de Muradella and Gargalo are the best defenders of patrimonial grapes like mencía, bastardo tinta or caíño. Precisely, the top wine from the region is the bastardo from Quinta da Muradella, a fruity, balsamic rendering full of supple and round tannins. From the same winery we have, for the very first time, a textbook rosé with notes of flint under the Mistal label. Whites are usually made from low-productive dona blanca, treixadura or godello plantings that yield elegant, very Burgundian renderings. The white Terra do Gargalo 'on the lees', one of the pioneers in the DO, gets the highest rating. It is more than evident that the wineries have managed to get the hang of the different varieties, as well as the more suitable ageing periods or soils for every variety, from granite to slate.

## LOCATION

In the east of the province of Orense, on the border with Portugal. The vineyards occupy the valley of Monterrei, and it is made up of the municipal districts of Verín, Monterrei, Oimbra and Castrelo do Vall.

## CLIMATE

Midway between the Atlantic and Continental influences. Drier than in the rest of Galicia, with maximum temperatures of 35°C in summer and minimum of –5°C in winter.

## SOIL

The vineyards cover the slopes of the mountains and valleys irrigated by the Támega river and its tributaries. The soil is quite clayey, deep, rather heavy and, in some places, somewhat sandy.

## GRAPE VARIETIES:

**White:** *Dona Blanca, Verdello* (*Godello*) and *Treixadura* (*Verdello Louro*).
**Red:** *Mencía, Bastardo* (or *María Ardoña*).

| | |
|---|---|
| Hectares of Vineyard | 370 |
| Nº Viticulturists | 333 |
| Nº of Bodegas | 23 |
| 2008 Harvest | Very Good |
| 2007 Production | 909,780 l. |
| Marketing | 70% domestic 30% export |

## SUB-REGIONS:

**Val de Monterrei.** Comprising the vineyards situated in the valley region (therefore, more level terrains) and covering the parishes and municipal districts belonging to the following city councils: Castrelo do Val (Castrelo do Val, Pepín and Nocedo); Monterrei (Albarellos, Infesta, Monterrei and Vilaza); Oimbra (Oimbra, Rabal, O Rosal and San Cibrao); Verín (Abedes, Cabreiroa, Feces da Baixo, Feces de Cima, Mandín, Mourazos, Pazos, Queizás, A Rasela, Tamagos, Tamaguelos, Tintores, Verín, Vilela and Vilamaior do Val).

**Ladeira de Monterrei.** These vineyards occupy the hills. The parishes and municipal districts that make up this sub-region are: Castrelo do Val (Gondulfes and Servoi), Oimbra (As Chas and A Granxa), Monterrey (Flariz, Medeiros, Mixós, Estevesiños and Vences) and Verín (Queirugas).

**CONSEJO REGULADOR**
Mercado Comarcal, 1. 32600 Verín (Orense)
☎: 988 590 007 - Fax: 988 410 634
@ info@domonterrei.com
www.domonterrei.com

## GENERAL CHARACTERISTICS OF THE WINES:

| | |
|---|---|
| **WHITES** | These have a straw yellow colour and are fresh and pleasant. Those produced from autochthonous grapes, as opposed to the flatter of the *Palomino* variety, are more intense and fruity, flavourful on the palate, with a good alcohol-acidity balance. |
| **REDS** | With a deep cherry-red colour, these are mainly young red wines which have a good fruity character, although, on occasions, there are herbaceous notes; on the palate they are light and fruity. |

## 2008 VINTAGE RATING:

# EXCELLENT

## ADEGAS PAZO DAS TAPIAS, S.L.

Pazos - Verin
32600 Verin (Ourense)
☎: 988 261 256 - Fax: 988 261 264
info@pazodomar.com
www.pazodastapias.com

ALMA DE BLANCO GODELLO 2008 B
godello

**88** Colour: straw, pale. Nose: fresh fruit, powerfull, scrubland. Palate: fruity, full, fresh.

ALMA DE TINTO 2008 T
mencía 100%

**85** Colour: cherry, purple rim. Nose: violets, red berry notes, fresh. Palate: fruity, correct, easy to drink, fresh.

## BODEGA PAZOS DEL REY

Carrero Blanco, 33 (Albarellos)
32618 Monterrei (Ourense)
☎: 988 425 959 - Fax: 988 425 949
informacion@pazodemonterrey.es
www.pazodemonterrey.es

PAZO DE MONTERREY 2008 B
godello 90%, treixadura 10%

**90** Colour: bright straw. Nose: white flowers, ripe fruit, fresh fruit, grassy, mineral. Palate: flavourful, fleshy, fruity, fresh.

## BODEGAS Y VIÑEDOS QUINTA DA MURADELLA

Avda. Luis Espada, 99. Entresuelo, dcha.
32600 Verín (Ourense)
☎: 988 411 724 - Fax: 988 590 427
muradella@verin.net

ALANDA 2008 B BARRICA
dona blanca 70%, treixadura 15%, godello 15%

**90** Colour: bright straw. Nose: fragrant herbs, complex, varietal. Palate: creamy, balsamic, fruity aftestaste, light-bodied, flavourful, fruity.

MISTAL RD
Bastardo 90%, mencia 10%

**88** Colour: rose, purple rim. Nose: fresh fruit, dry stone, characterful, varietal, expressive. Palate: fresh, fruity, flavourful, mineral.

ALANDA 2007 T BARRICA
bastardo 10%, mencía 90%

**88** Colour: bright cherry, bright ochre rim. Nose: fresh, fresh fruit, wild herbs, mineral, smoky. Palate: complex, varietal, fresh, fruity, balsamic.

GORVIA 2006 T
mencía 100%

**90** Colour: bright cherry, orangey edge. Nose: characterful, complex, varietal, fresh, undergrowth, mineral. Palate: balsamic, creamy, smoky aftertaste, mineral.

QUINTA DA MURADELLA
2006 T FERMENTADO EN BARRICA
bastardo 100%

**90** Colour: dark-red cherry. Nose: wild herbs, ripe fruit, balsamic herbs, spicy. Palate: flavourful, fruity, fresh.

DOÑA POLANCA
A TRABE
MURADELLA
BASTARDO

## CASTRO DE LOBARZÁN

Ctra. de Requeixo, 51 Villaza
32618 Monterrei (Ourense)
☎: 988 418 163 - Fax: 988 418 163
castrodelobarzan@wanadoo.es

CASTRO DE LOBARZÁN 2008 B
godello, treixadura

**89** Colour: bright straw. Nose: floral, elegant, dry stone, ripe fruit. Palate: light-bodied, powerful, fruity, good acidity, good finish.

CASTRO DE LOBARZÁN MENCÍA 2007 T
mencía, aranxa

**89** Colour: bright cherry, cherry, purple rim. Nose: expressive, fresh, red berry notes, violets. Palate: good structure, flavourful, good acidity, fine bitter notes.

## CREGO E MONAGUILLO S.L.

Rua Nova s/n Salgueira de Monterrei
32618 Salgueira de Monterrei (Ourense)
☎: 988 418 164 - Fax: 988 418 164
marketing@cregoemonaguillo.com
www.cregoemonaguillo.com

CREGO E MONAGUILLO 2008 B
godello 70%, treixadura 30%

**89** Colour: bright straw. Nose: fresh fruit, wild herbs, powerfull, floral. Palate: full, fruity, good acidity, good finish.

MAROVA
CREGO E MONAGUILLO

## GARGALO

Rua Do Castelo, 59
32619 Pazos Verín (Ourense)
☎: 988 590 203 - Fax: 988 590 295
gargalo@verino.es
www.gargalo.es

TERRA DO GARGALO 2008 B
godello 80%, treixadura 20%

**89** Colour: bright straw. Nose: fresh fruit, grassy, floral, expressive. Palate: fresh, fruity, easy to drink, good finish.

TERRA DO GARGALO GODELLO Y TREIXADURA
SOBRE LÍAS 2007 B
godello 50%, treixadura 50%

**91** Colour: straw, pale. Nose: ripe fruit, spicy, lees reduction notes, characterful. Palate: rich, full, flavourful, good acidity, elegant.

SOME OTHER WINERIES WITHIN THE DO:

**ADEGA COOPERATIVA TERRAS DO CIGARRÓN
S.C.G.
ADEGA VALDERELLO
ADEGAS LADAIRO
ADEGAS MADREVELLA
ADEGAS QUINTA DO BUBLE S.L.
ADEGAS TRIAY
BODEGAS MAGMUS**

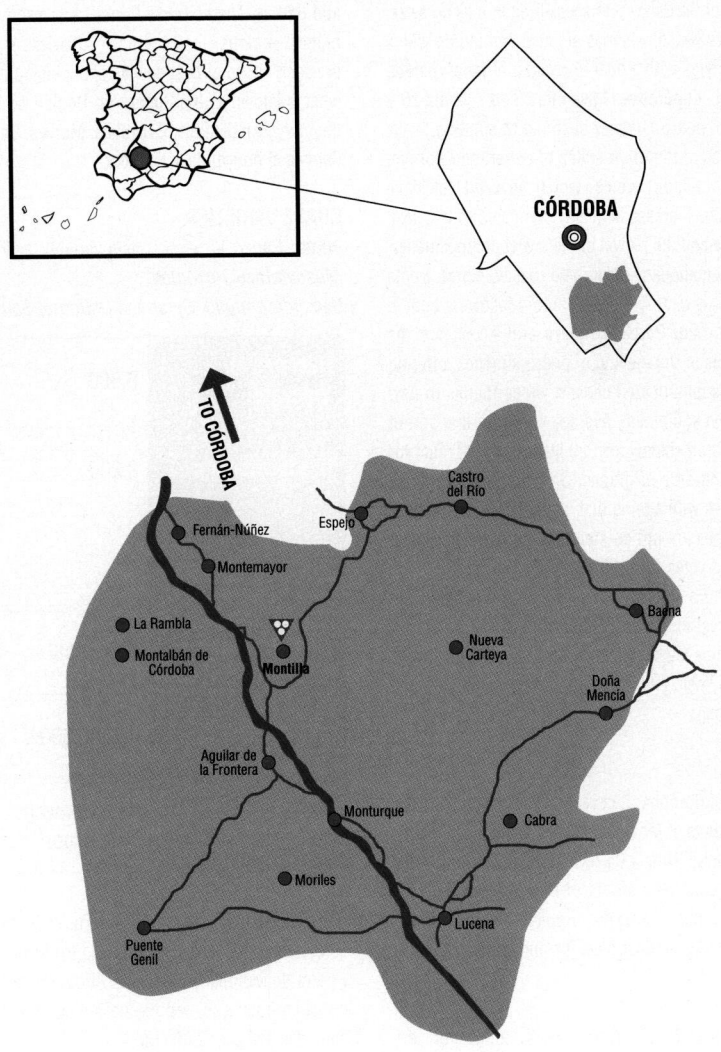

CÓRDOBA

TO CÓRDOBA

Castro del Río
Espejo
Fernán-Núñez
Montemayor
La Rambla
Baena
Montalbán de Córdoba
Nueva Carteya
Montilla
Doña Mencía
Aguilar de la Frontera
Monturque
Cabra
Moriles
Lucena
Puente Genil

▽ Consejo Regulador
● DO Boundary

# DO MONTILLA-MORILES

## NEWS

In this Andalousian region, around the town of Montilla –in the province of Córdoba– and specialized in making sweet pedro ximénez wines, wineries are also coming up with a diversity of styles with a goal to reach a broader market. Wineries and cooperatives have increased a whole 26% the amount of pedro ximénez destined to sunning, while they make less of the other styles of generoso (oloroso, fino and amontillado) wines, which nevertheless have known a serious increase in quality compared to last year. The reason behind the revival of the sweet pedro ximénez, with its lovely mahogany colour and roasted coffee aroma is the fact that is getting more and more followers both in Spain and abroad. Pérez Barquero and Alvear are the leading houses in the making of pedro ximénez, offering increasingly sophisticated dessert wines thanks to new technology and equipment. Average yields for that sort of product are astonishingly low: 29 litres of sweet must for every 100 kilograms of grapes. Only the best examples manage to lose with ageing that 'stalky' note –remember that here grapes are not de-stemmed– and the very best come from old vines (over 25 years of age) planted in the best white albero soils typical of the region, which yield iodine and limestone notes. We understand that the type of wood, humidity levels and physical conditions of the bodega greatly help pedro ximénez wines to get closer to 100 points ratings.

## LOCATION

To the south of Córdoba. It covers all the vineyards of the municipal districts of Montilla, Moriles, Montalbán, Puente Genil, Montruque, Nueva Carteya and Doña Mencía, and part of the municipal districts of Montemayor, Fernán-Núñez, La Rambla, Santaella, Aguilar de la Frontera, Lucena, Cabra, Baena, Castro del Río and Espejo.

## CLIMATE

Semi-continental Mediterranean, with long, hot, dry summers and short winters. The average annual temperature is 16.8°C and the average rainfall is between 500 mm and 1,000 mm per year.

## SOIL

The vineyards are situated at an altitude of between 125 m and 640 m. The soils are franc, franc-sandy and, in the higher regions, calcareous ('Albarizas'), which are precisely those of best quality, and which predominate in what is known as the Upper Sub-Region, which includes the municipal districts of Montilla, Moriles, Castro del Río, Cabra and Aguilar de la Frontera.

## GRAPE VARIETIES:

**White:** Pedro Ximénez (main variety), Lairén, Baladí, Moscatel and Torrontés.
**Red:** Tempranillo, Syrah and Cabernet Sauvignon.

| | |
|---|---|
| Hectares of Vineyard | 6,500 |
| N° Viticulturists | 3,200 |
| N° of Bodegas | 92 |
| 2008 Harvest | Very Good |
| 2007 Production | 22,000,000 l. |
| Marketing | 83% domestic 12% export |

**SUB-REGIONS:** There is a difference between the vineyards in the flatter regions and in the higher regions (Sierra de Montilla and Moriles Alto). The latter, situated on calcareous soil, are the best quality of the DO and comprise just over 2,000 Ha.

**CONSEJO REGULADOR**
Rita Pérez, s/n. 14550 Montilla (Córdoba)
☎: 957 699 957 - Fax: 957 652 866
@ crdo@montilla-moriles.org
www.montilla-moriles.org

## GENERAL CHARACTERISTICS OF THE WINES:

| | |
|---|---|
| **YOUNG WHITES** | Created relatively recently, they are light and fruity wines for rapid consumption. |
| **FINOS** | Produced following the classical biological procedure of 'velo en flor'. With saline aromas of yeast and bitter almonds, they differ from the Jerezanos in being less dry on the palate. |
| **OLOROSOS** | These are mahogany coloured, with aromas of confectionery; they are sweet and flavourful on the palate. |
| **AMONTILLADOS** | Amber or old gold in colour. Nutty aroma (almonds and hazelnut); on the palate they have sweet notes with certain notes of biological ageing due to their origin as Finos. |
| **PEDRO XIMÉNEZ** | This is the Montilla-Moriles wine par excellence. Produced from sun-dried grapes, the colour may range from mahogany to very dark browns, thoroughly dense and concentrated. Unmistakable due to its aroma of raisins and dates, with a hint of toast; on the palate it is sweet, mellow and flavourful. |

## 2008 VINTAGE RATING:

# VERY GOOD

## ALVEAR

María Auxiliadora, 1
14550 Montilla (Córdoba)
☎: 957 650 100 - Fax: 957 650 135
alvearsa@alvear.es
www.alvear.es

MARQUÉS DE LA SIERRA 2008 B
pedro ximénez, chardonnay, moscatel

**81**

CARLOS VII AM
pedro ximénez 100%

**89** Colour: iodine, amber rim. Nose: roasted almonds, varnish, dry nuts, saline, pungent. Palate: spicy, fine bitter notes, flavourful.

ALVEAR SOLERA CREAM CR
pedro ximénez 100%

**88** Colour: light mahogany. Nose: candied fruit, sun-drenched nuances, aged wood nuances. Palate: sweet, spicy, fine solera notes.

C.B. FI
pedro ximénez 100%

**91** Colour: bright yellow. Nose: complex, expressive, pungent, saline. Palate: rich, powerful, fresh, fine bitter notes.

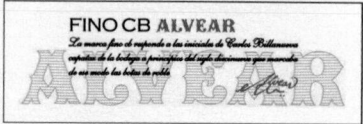

ALVEAR FINO EN RAMA 2004 FI
pedro ximénez 100%

**90** Colour: bright yellow. Nose: complex, expressive, pungent, saline. Palate: rich, powerful, fresh, fine bitter notes.

CAPATAZ FI
pedro ximénez 100%

**92** Colour: bright straw. Nose: characterful, pungent, saline, scrubland. Palate: flavourful, fleshy.

ASUNCIÓN OL
pedro ximénez 100%

**91** Colour: iodine, amber rim. Nose: roasted almonds, smoky, candied fruit, pattiserie. Palate: flavourful, powerful, spirituous, sweetness.

FESTIVAL PCR
pedro ximénez 100%

**87** Colour: pale. Nose: medium intensity, candied fruit, fruit preserve. Palate: flavourful, sweetness, fine bitter notes.

ALVEAR PEDRO XIMÉNEZ DE AÑADA 2005 PX
pedro ximénez 100%

**90** Colour: iodine, amber rim. Nose: sun-drenched nuances, fruit liqueur notes, overripe fruit. Palate: flavourful, concentrated, spicy.

ALVEAR PX COSECHA 2004 PX
pedro ximénez 100%

**92** Colour: dark mahogany. Nose: complex, fruit liqueur notes, dried fruit, pattiserie, toasty. Palate: sweet, rich, unctuous, powerful.

ALVEAR PX 1927 PX
pedro ximénez 100%

**90** Colour: iodine, amber rim. Nose: powerful, candied fruit, tar. Palate: flavourful, powerful, sweet.

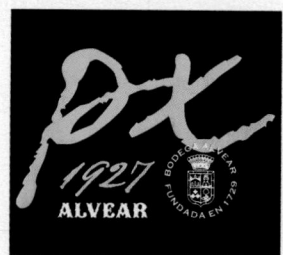

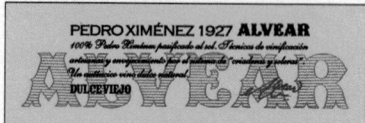

ALVEAR DULCE VIEJO 2000 PX RESERVA
pedro ximénez 100%

**91** Colour: dark mahogany. Nose: complex, fruit liqueur notes, dried fruit, pattiserie, toasty. Palate: sweet, rich, unctuous, powerful.

**ALVEAR PX 1830 PX RESERVA**
pedro ximénez 100%

**98** Colour: dark mahogany. Nose: complex, fruit liqueur notes, dried fruit, pattiserie, toasty, dark chocolate. Palate: sweet, rich, unctuous, powerful, fine solera notes.

## ARAGÓN Y COMPAÑIA

Camino de la Estación, 11 Aptdo. 534
14900 Lucena (Córdoba)
☎: 957 500 046 - Fax: 957 502 935
gerencia@aragonycia.com
www.aragonycia.com

**VIÑA JOVEN B JOVEN**
pedro ximénez, lairen, baladi

**78**

**LAGAR DE CAMPOARAS B JOVEN**
pedro ximénez, airén, baladí

**75**

**PACORRITO AM**
pedro ximénez 100%

**84**

**PATRICIA CR**
pedro ximénez 100%

**88** Colour: light mahogany. Nose: candied fruit, dry nuts, saline. Palate: fine solera notes, spirituous, good acidity.

**MORILES 47 FI**
pedro ximénez 100%

**85** Colour: bright yellow. Nose: complex, expressive, pungent, saline. Palate: rich, powerful, fresh, fine bitter notes.

**P.G. FI**
pedro ximénez 100%

**85** Colour: bright yellow. Nose: neat, candied fruit, saline, flor yeasts. Palate: fresh, easy to drink, thin.

**PILYCRIM PCR**
pedro ximénez 100%

**77**

**ARACELI PX VIEJO PX**
pedro ximénez 100%

**85** Colour: light mahogany. Nose: expressive, dried fruit, candied fruit. Palate: concentrated, sweet, roasted-coffee aftertaste, unctuous.

**ARACELI PX**
pedro ximénez 100%

**84**

## BODEGAS DELGADO

Cosano, 2
14500 Puente Genil (Córdoba)
☎: 957 600 085 - Fax: 957 604 571
fino@bodegasdelgado.com
www.bodegasdelgado.com

**DELGADO 1874 AMONTILLADO NATURAL MUY VIEJO AM**
pedro ximénez

**89** Colour: iodine, amber rim. Nose: roasted almonds, varnish, pungent, dry nuts, aged wood nuances. Palate: flavourful, fleshy, spirituous, spicy.

**SEGUNDA BOTA FI**
pedro ximénez

**85** Colour: pale. Nose: iodine notes, smoky, roasted almonds. Palate: powerful, fine bitter notes, good acidity.

**DELGADO 1874 OL**
pedro ximénez

**88** Colour: light mahogany. Nose: powerful, fruit liqueur notes, spicy. Palate: spicy, sweetness, balanced, fine solera notes.

**DELGADO 1874 PX**
pedro ximénez

**93** Colour: dark mahogany. Nose: complex, fruit liqueur notes, dried fruit, pattiserie, toasty, sun-drenched nuances. Palate: sweet, rich, unctuous, powerful, fine solera notes.

LAGAR DE BENAZOLA
LAGAR DE SAN ANTONIO
DON JOSÉ
OLD CREAMDEL
F.E.O.
MANOLO
D.H.
CALIFA
ELIO BERHANYER SELECCIÓN

## BODEGAS LA AURORA

Avda. de Europa, 7
14550 Montilla (Córdoba)
☎: 957 650 362 - Fax: 957 654 642
administracion@bodegaslaaurora.com
www.bodegaslaaurora.com

## FINO SIERRA FI

**89** Colour: pale. Nose: saline, candied fruit, smoky. Palate: flavourful, powerful, good acidity.

## FINO AMANECER FI

**77**

## SOLERA 1981 1981 PX
pedro ximénez

**90** Colour: light mahogany. Nose: grapey, candied fruit, aromatic coffee. Palate: sweet, full, flavourful.

## AMANECER PX
pedro ximénez

**87** Colour: light mahogany. Nose: dried fruit, honeyed notes, cocoa bean. Palate: sweet, flavourful, full.

## BODEGAS LUQUE

La Molinera, 3
14860 Doña Mencía (Córdoba)
☎: 957 676 029 - Fax: 957 676 029
bodegasluque@terra.es

## EL ABUELO SOLERA 1888 AM
pedro ximénez 100%

**86** Colour: iodine, amber rim. Nose: powerful, expressive, fruit liqueur notes, candied fruit. Palate: powerful, fine bitter notes, warm.

## FINO EL PATO FI
pedro ximénez 100%

**84**

## SOLERA ANDALUZA FI
pedro ximénez 100%

**82**

## PALE CREAM CHIPI
## LOS LUQUES (IMPERIAL)
## BODEGA LUQUE

## BODEGAS MORENO

Fuente de la Salud, 2
14006 Córdoba
☎: 957 767 605 - Fax: 957 279 907
moreno@morenosa.com
www.morenosa.com

## SIETE SABIOS AM

**90** Colour: iodine, amber rim. Nose: powerful, complex, elegant, dry nuts, toasty. Palate: rich, fine bitter notes, fine solera notes, long, spicy.

## CABRIOLA AMONTILLADO VIEJO AM

**89** Colour: iodine, amber rim. Nose: powerful, complex, dry nuts, toasty, sweet spices. Palate: rich, fine bitter notes, fine solera notes, long, spicy.

## MUSA AM

**84**

## MUSA FI

**79**

## BENAVIDES FI

**74**

## PLATINO SOLERA OLOROSA OL

**91** Colour: iodine, amber rim. Nose: elegant, roasted almonds, candied fruit, saline. Palate: flavourful, complex, round, spirituous.

## MUSA OLOROSO OL

**90** Colour: amber. Nose: dry nuts, dried fruit, honeyed notes. Palate: flavourful, roasted-coffee aftertaste, spirituous.

## FUNDACIÓN 1819 OL

**85** Colour: iodine, amber rim. Nose: warm, candied fruit, toasty. Palate: spirituous, unctuous, long.

## ALBOROQUE PC

**89** Colour: iodine, amber rim. Nose: sweet spices, fruit liqueur notes, fruit liqueur notes. Palate: flavourful, fleshy, spirituous, good structure.

## VIRGILIO 1925 PX
pedro ximénez

**90** Colour: dark mahogany. Nose: pattiserie, dried fruit, honeyed notes. Palate: sweet, roasted-coffee aftertaste, unctuous.

## UNA VIDA PX

**86** Colour: mahogany. Nose: warm, dry nuts, dried fruit. Palate: sweetness, concentrated, roasted-coffee aftertaste.

## MUSA PX
pedro ximénez

**85** Colour: iodine, amber rim. Nose: dry nuts, candied fruit. Palate: sweet, flavourful, roasted-coffee aftertaste.

## COMPAÑÍA VINÍCOLA DEL SUR S.A.

Burgueños, 9
14550 Montilla (Córdoba)
☎: 957 650 500 - Fax: 957 652 335
comercial@vinicoladelsur.com

MONTE CRISTO SELECTION AM
pedro ximénez 100%

**91** Colour: iodine, amber rim. Nose: powerful, complex, elegant, dry nuts, toasty. Palate: rich, fine bitter notes, fine solera notes, long, spicy.

VERBENERA FI
pedro ximénez 100%

**90** Colour: bright yellow. Nose: complex, expressive, pungent, saline. Palate: rich, powerful, fresh, fine bitter notes.

MONTE CRISTO SELECTION FI
pedro ximénez 100%

**88** Colour: bright yellow. Nose: complex, expressive, saline, candied fruit, grassy. Palate: rich, powerful, fresh, fine bitter notes.

MONTE CRISTO OL
pedro ximénez 100%

**92** Colour: iodine, amber rim. Nose: elegant, dry nuts, iodine notes, honeyed notes. Palate: flavourful, fresh, spirituous.

TOMÁS GARCÍA PX
pedro ximénez 100%

**90** Colour: iodine, amber rim. Nose: candied fruit, honeyed notes, caramel. Palate: sweet, unctuous, warm.

MONTE CRISTO SELECTION PX
pedro ximénez 100%

**87** Colour: dark mahogany. Nose: complex, fruit liqueur notes, dried fruit, pattiserie, toasty. Palate: sweet, rich, unctuous, powerful.

## COOPERATIVA AGRÍCOLA LA UNIÓN

Avda. de Italia, 1
14550 Montilla (Córdoba)
☎: 957 651 855 - Fax: 957 657 135
info@cooperativalaunion.com

ALGARABÍA AFRUTADO 2008 B
chardonnay 100%

**84**

TRES PALACIOS FI
pedro ximénez 100%

**85** Colour: bright yellow. Nose: pungent, saline, balanced. Palate: rich, powerful, fresh, fine bitter notes.

FINO 79 FI
pedro ximénez 100%

**80**

## GRACIA HERMANOS S.A.

Avda. Marqués de la Vega de Armijo, 103
14550 Montilla (Córdoba)
☎: 957 650 162 - Fax: 957 652 335
comercial@bodegasgracia.com
www.bodegasgracia.com

VIÑAVERDE 2008 B
pedro ximénez, verdejo, moscatel, macabeo, torrontés

**83**

TAUROMAQUIA AMONTILLADO VIEJO AM
pedro ximénez 100%

**88** Colour: iodine, amber rim. Nose: dry nuts, acetaldehyde, powerfull. Palate: flavourful, sweetness, fine bitter notes.

SOLERA FINA TAUROMAQUIA FI
pedro ximénez 100%

**92** Colour: bright yellow. Nose: complex, expressive, pungent, saline, smoky. Palate: rich, powerful, fresh, fine bitter notes.

FINO CORREDERA FI
pedro ximénez 100%

**87** Colour: bright yellow. Nose: expressive, pungent, saline. Palate: rich, powerful, fresh, fine bitter notes.

GRACIA FI
pedro ximénez 100%

**84**

TAUROMAQUIA OL
pedro ximénez 100%

**84**

TAUROMAQUIA PX
pedro ximénez 100%

**90** Colour: iodine, amber rim. Nose: sun-drenched nuances, dark chocolate, aged wood nuances. Palate: fleshy, sweet, powerful.

GRACIA PX

**88** Colour: dark mahogany. Nose: characterful, sun-drenched nuances, overripe fruit, candied fruit. Palate: correct, sweet, flavourful.

SOLERA FINA MARÍA DEL VALLE

## PÉREZ BARQUERO S.A.

Avda. Andalucía, 27
14550 Montilla (Córdoba)
☎: 957 650 500 - Fax: 957 650 208
info@perezbarquero.com
www.perezbarquero.com

VIÑA AMALIA 2008 B
pedro ximénez, moscatel, verdejo, torrontés

**83**

GRAN BARQUERO AM
pedro ximénez 100%

**91** Colour: iodine, amber rim. Nose: sweet spices, roasted almonds, pungent, candied fruit. Palate: flavourful, powerful, fine solera notes.

GRAN BARQUERO FI
pedro ximénez 100%

**90** Colour: bright yellow. Nose: complex, expressive, pungent, saline. Palate: rich, powerful, fresh, fine bitter notes.

FINO LOS AMIGOS FI
pedro ximénez 100%

**83**

GRAN BARQUERO OL
pedro ximénez 100%

**90** Colour: iodine, amber rim. Nose: powerful, complex, dry nuts, toasty. Palate: rich, fine bitter notes, fine solera notes, long, spicy.

PÉREZ BARQUERO PEDRO XIMÉNEZ DE COSECHA 2007 PX
pedro ximénez 100%

**89** Colour: amber. Nose: expressive, sun-drenched nuances, dried fruit. Palate: flavourful, sweet, unctuous.

P.X. LA CAÑADA
pedro ximénez 100%

**96** Colour: dark mahogany. Nose: complex, fruit liqueur notes, dried fruit, pattiserie, toasty, sun-drenched nuances. Palate: sweet, rich, unctuous, powerful, fine solera notes, long.

GRAN BARQUERO PX
pedro ximénez 100%

**90** Colour: dark mahogany. Nose: roasted almonds, grapey, overripe fruit. Palate: flavourful, sweet, unctuous, roasted-coffee aftertaste.

CASA VILLA ZEVALLOS
CORAZÓN LATINO

## TORO ALBALÁ

Avda. Antonio Sánchez Romero, 1
14920 Aguilar de la Frontera (Córdoba)
☎: 957 660 046 - Fax: 957 661 494
info@toroalbala.com
www.toroalbala.com

ELÉCTRICO FINO DEL LAGAR FI

**84**

DON PX 1979 1979 PX GRAN RESERVA

**92** Colour: dark mahogany. Nose: complex, dried fruit, honeyed notes, aromatic coffee. Palate: good structure, unctuous, roasted-coffee aftertaste.

DON P.X. PX

**89** Colour: iodine, amber rim. Nose: fruit liqueur notes, expressive, varietal, sun-drenched nuances. Palate: sweet, powerful, spicy.

LA NORIA

SOME OTHER WINERIES WITHIN THE DO:

**A. MIGUEL OJEDA CHACÓN
AGUERA
BODEGAS A. DOBLAS MARTOS
BODEGAS CRUZ CONDE
BODEGAS JESÚS NAZARENO, S.C.A.
BODEGAS LAMA
BODEGAS NAVARRO
BODEGAS ROBLES
CONCEPCIÓN SÁNCHEZ RODRÍGUEZ
CONDE DE LA CORTINA
COOPERATIVA VITIVINÍCOLA LA PURÍSIMA
CRISMONA S.A.
EQUIPO NAVAZOS
ESPEJO S.A.
HEREDEROS TORRES BURGOS S.L.
MAILLO E HIJOS S.L.
MARÍN S.L.
MORA CHACÓN DE LUCENA S.L.
NAVISA
SAN RAFAEL
SILLERO S.A.
SOC. DE SOCORROS MUTUOS DE
    ORIF. Y PLATEROS**

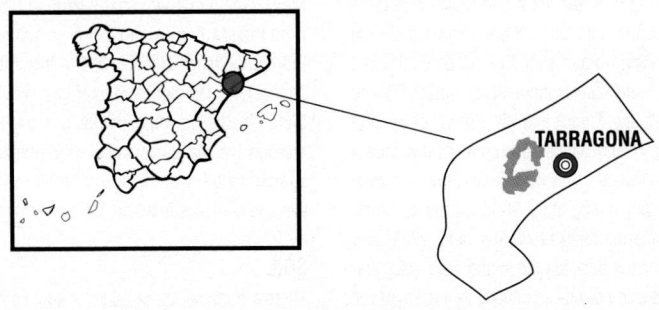

▽ Consejo Regulador
● DO Boundary

# DO MONTSANT

## NEWS
Montsant progresses through our latest editions of the guide as one of the DOs –along with Jerez and Rioja– with more wines reaching the 90 points rating. It has also become a big seller abroad, jumping from three to five million bottles in a single year, and a spectacular increase of almost 50% to countries like Germany, France and UK. Prices –starting at 6€– and an exceptional quality have become its best assets in the international markets. This whole qualitative landscape has a follow up in our tasting of the 2008 vintage, a shorter one in production terms thanks to winter rains. White and rosé renderings are top between the young ones: juicy and with a good sweet-acid balance so difficult to find anywhere else in Spain; and whites for connoisseurs from very ripe garnacha blanca and a fine, herbal macabeo made from the young winemaking promises of the region. The real aces in terms of expression come from wines of the 2007 vintage: ripe, concentrated, full of floral, balsamic and mineral notes. The 2006 renderings, putting aside the good –although mediocre– renderings, are top notch and get the highest ratings with names like Celler El Masroig, Ètim, Joan d'Anguera, Mas de Can Blau, Acústic and Venus La Universal with longer ageing periods and render the old vines from the region a solid bet for the future. The DO has underway a program to classify the soils, but what comes to the fore in our tasting is the fruity, fresher character of the wines from Cornudella, or the mineral one in those from Falset. The Montsant universe shows a great respect for vine and variety over ageing.

## LOCATION
In the region of Priorat (Tarragona). It is made up of Baix Priorat, part of Alt Priorat and various municipal districts of Ribera d'Ebre that were already integrated into the Falset sub-region. In total, 16 municipal districts: La Bisbal de Falset, Cabaces, Capçanes, Cornudella de Montsant, La Figuera, Els Guiamets, Marçà, Margalef, El Masroig, Pradell, La Torre de Fontaubella, Ulldemolins, Falset, El Molar, Darmós and La Serra d'Almos. The vineyards are located at widely variable altitudes, ranging between 200 m to 700 m above sea level.

## CLIMATE
Although the vineyards are located in a Mediterranean region, the mountains that surround the region isolate it from the sea to a certain extent, resulting in a somewhat more Continental climate. Due to this, it benefits from the contrasts in day/night temperatures, which is an important factor in the ripening of the grapes. However, it also receives the sea winds, laden with humidity, which help to compensate for the lack of rainfall in the summer. The average rainfall is between 500 and 600 mm per year.

## SOIL
There are mainly three types of soil: compact calcareous soils with pebbles on the borders of the DO; granite sands in Falset; and siliceous slate (the same stony slaty soil as Priorat) in certain areas of Falset and Cornudella.

## GRAPE VARIETIES:
**White:** *Chardonnay, Garnacha Blanca, Macabeo, Moscatel, Pansal, Parellada.*
**Red:** *Cabernet Sauvignon, Cariñena, Garnacha Tinta, Garnacha Peluda, Merlot, Monastrell, Picapoll, Syrah, Tempranillo* and *Mazuela.*

| Hectares of Vineyard | 1,926 |
|---|---|
| Nº Viticulturists | 897 |
| Nº of Bodegas | 54 |
| 2008 Harvest | Very Good |
| 2007 Production | 5,239,600 l. |
| Marketing | 30% domestic 70% export |

**CONSEJO REGULADOR**
Plaça de la Quartera, 6
43730 Falset (Tarragona)
☎: 977 831 742 - Fax: 977 830 676
@ info@domontsant.com
www.domontsant.com

## GENERAL CHARACTERISTICS OF THE WINES:

| | |
|---|---|
| **WHITES** | The most characteristic are the white wines based on *Garnacha Blanca*, which gives wines with body and a certain structure and the characteristic notes of herbs and hints of Mediterranean woodland, typical of the variety. The white wines from *Macabeo* are a little lighter and refined, fresh and fruity. |
| **ROSÉS** | There are not many examples, but in general they are produced from *Garnacha*. They are flavourful and fruity, maybe too full-bodied, but very pleasant with good red berry definition. |
| **REDS** | These are, without doubt, the most characteristic wines of the DO. They are produced almost exclusively from *Garnacha* or from a blend of this variety and *Mazuelo* with foreign varieties, especially *Cabernet Sauvignon* or *Syrah*. The young wines are fruity, meaty and flavourful. The best examples amongst those aged in barrels have high levels of fruitiness: they are powerful, meaty, with a high alcohol content. Mineral notes may also appear. They are reminiscent of Priorat wines, perhaps with less extraction and weight. |
| **TRADITIONAL WINES** | Liqueurs (sweet) are produced mainly from *Garnacha*. They are usually sticky and mellow on the palate, with aromas and a taste of raisins and preserved fruit. |

## 2008 VINTAGE RATING:

# EXCELLENT

## ACUSTIC CELLER

St. Lluís, 12, 43777 Els Guiamets (Tarragona)
☎: 629 472 988 - Fax: 977 678 149
acustic@acusticceller.com
www.acusticceller.com

ACÚSTIC 2008 B
garnacha blanca 60%, macabeo 25%, garnacha roja 10%, prensal 5%

**91** Colour: bright straw. Aroma:: balsamic herbs, scrubland, citrus fruit, mineral. Taste:: fresh, fruity, full, flavourful.

BRAÓ 2007 T
cariñena 55%, garnacha 45%

**92** Colour: bright cherry. Nose: ripe fruit, sweet spices, creamy oak, expressive, floral. Palate: flavourful, fruity, toasty, round tannins.

ACÚSTIC 2007 T
cariñena 60%, garnacha 40%

**91** Colour: bright cherry. Nose: fruit preserve, red berry notes, dark chocolate, sweet spices. Palate: powerful, spirituous, concentrated, sweet tannins.

AUDITORI 2007 T
garnacha

**90** Colour: cherry, purple rim. Nose: medium intensity, red berry notes, ripe fruit, spicy, scrubland. Palate: flavourful, fleshy, fruity, fresh.

## AGRICOLA D'ULLDEMOLINS SANT JAUME

Saltadora, 17, 43363 Ulldemolins (Tarragona)
☎: 977 561 613 - Fax: 977 561 613
ulldemolins@retemail.es

LES PEDRENYERES 2007 B
garnacha blanca, macabeo

**87** Colour: bright straw. Nose: grapey, white flowers, balsamic herbs, spicy. Palate: flavourful, full, fresh, spirituous.

LES PEDRENYERES 2005 T
garnacha

**90** Colour: cherry, garnet rim. Nose: fruit liqueur notes, fruit preserve, dry nuts, spicy. Palate: fine tannins, balsamic, full, classic aged character.

ULLDEMOLINS

## AGRÍCOLA I SC DE LA SERRA D'ALMOS

Avda. Cooperativa s/n
43746 La Serra D'Almos (Tarragona)
☎: 977 418 125 - Fax: 977 418 399
coopserra@telefonica.net
www.serradalmos.com

MUSSEFRES 2008 T
cariñena 30%, garnacha 30%, tempranillo 30%, cabernet sauvignon 10%

**84**

MUSSEFRES VIÑAS VIEJAS 2005 T
cariñena 60%, cabernet sauvignon 40%

**92** Colour: cherry, garnet rim. Nose: sweet spices, earthy notes, fruit liqueur notes, fruit liqueur notes, elegant. Palate: spicy, toasty, creamy, fine tannins.

MUSSEFRES 2002 T

**89** Colour: cherry, garnet rim. Nose: ripe fruit, spicy, creamy oak, toasty, complex, damp earth, tobacco. Palate: powerful, flavourful, toasty, round tannins.

## BODEGA VERMUNVER

Dalt, 29, 43775 Marçà (Tarragona)
☎: 977 178 288 - Fax: 977 178 288
vermunver@genesi.cat

GÈNESI SELECCIÓ 2006 T
garnacha 60%, cariñena 40%

**89** Colour: very deep cherry. Nose: characterful, fruit expression, mineral, dark chocolate. Palate: fleshy, good structure, full.

## BUIL & GINÉ

Ctra. de Gratallops - Vilella Baixa, km. 11,5
43737 Gratallops (Tarragona)
☎: 977 839 810 - Fax: 977 839 811
info@builgine.com
www.builgine.com

BABOIX 2006 T
garnacha, cariñena, cabernet sauvignon, merlot, tempranillo

**88** Colour: cherry, purple rim. Nose: expressive, fresh fruit, red berry notes, floral, undergrowth, cocoa bean. Palate: flavourful, fruity, good acidity, round tannins.

**17-XI 2006 T**
garnacha, cariñena, tempranillo

**88** Colour: cherry, purple rim. Nose: expressive, fresh fruit, red berry notes, floral. Palate: flavourful, fruity, good acidity, round tannins.

## CAN JUST VITICULTORS

Font Vella, 20, 43730 Falset (Tarragona)
☎: 666 355 356
eli@canjustviticultors.com
www.canjustviticultors.com

**NUBAC 2006 T**

**89** Colour: cherry, garnet rim. Nose: dark chocolate, tobacco, undergrowth, earthy notes. Palate: fleshy, good structure, full, good acidity.

IUSTA

## CELLER CEDÓ ANGUERA

Ctra. La Serra d'Almos-Darmós, km. 0,2
43746 La Serra d'Almos (Tarragona)
☎: 699 694 728 - Fax: 977 417 369
celler@cedoanguera.com
www.cedoanguera.com

**ANEXE 2008 T**
cariñena 40%, garnacha 40%, syrah 20%

**86** Colour: cherry, purple rim. Nose: fresh fruit, red berry notes, mineral. Palate: flavourful, fruity, good acidity, round tannins.

**CLÒNIC 2007 T**
cariñena 60%, syrah 20%, cabernet sauvignon 20%

**88** Colour: bright cherry. Nose: ripe fruit, sweet spices, expressive, mineral, red berry notes. Palate: flavourful, fruity, toasty, round tannins.

## CELLER COOPERATIVA CORNUDELLA

Comte de Rius, 2
43360 Cornudella de Montsant (Tarragona)
☎: 977 82 1 3 - Fax: 977 821 329
info@cornudella.net
www.cornudella.net

**EL CODOLAR B**
macabeo 85%, planta nova 10%, garnacha blanca 5%

**79**

**EL CODOLAR 2007 T**
garnacha 50%, cariñena 50%

**86** Colour: ruby red. Nose: fruit expression, fruit liqueur notes, macerated fruit. Palate: fleshy, flavourful, fruity.

**CASTELL DE SIURANA SELECCIÓ DE COSTERS 2005 T**
garnacha 70%, cariñena 30%

**89** Colour: bright cherry. Nose: fruit expression, macerated fruit, cocoa bean, sweet spices, balsamic herbs. Palate: round, elegant, good acidity.

**CASTELL DE SIURANA GARNATXA DEL MONTSANT 2004 T**
garnacha roja 100%

**87** Colour: pale ruby, brick rim edge. Nose: roasted almonds, sweet spices, rancio notes, faded flowers. Palate: flavourful, rich, creamy, toasty.

**CASTELLA DE SIURANA MISTELA 2008 VINO DE LICOR**
garnacha 100%

**88** Colour: ruby red, brick rim edge. Nose: fruit liqueur notes, dry nuts, aged wood nuances, dark chocolate. Palate: full, rich, flavourful, fine solera notes.

## CELLER DE CAPÇANES

Llebaria, s/n, 43776 Capçanes (Tarragona)
☎: 977 178 319 - Fax: 977 178 319
cellercapcanes@cellercapcanes.com

**MAS DONÍS 2008 B**

**84**

**MAS DONÍS 2008 RD**

**87** Colour: brilliant rose. Nose: elegant, dried flowers, red berry notes, earthy notes. Palate: light-bodied, flavourful, good acidity, long, spicy.

**NINOT 2008 RD**

**87** Colour: rose, purple rim. Nose: powerful, ripe fruit, red berry notes, floral, expressive. Palate: fleshy, powerful, fruity, fresh.

**MAS DONÍS 2008 T**

**86** Colour: ruby red. Nose: macerated fruit, mineral, dried herbs. Palate: full, fresh, flavourful.

**CABRIDA 2007 T**
garnacha

**91** Colour: deep cherry. Nose: complex, characterful, balsamic herbs, fresh fruit, cocoa bean. Palate: powerful, good structure, full, mineral.

LASENDAL GARNATXA 2007 T BARRICA

**89** Colour: cherry, purple rim. Nose: expressive, fresh fruit, red berry notes, floral, undergrowth. Palate: flavourful, fruity, good acidity, round tannins, mineral.

NINOT 2007 T

**89** Colour: bright cherry. Nose: expressive, fresh fruit, red berry notes, floral, mineral. Palate: flavourful, fruity, good acidity, round tannins.

MAS COLLET 2007 T BARRICA

**88** Colour: deep cherry. Nose: fresh fruit, red berry notes, characterful, scrubland, dry stone. Palate: fleshy, flavourful, full.

COSTERS DEL GRAVET 2006 T

**91** Colour: bright cherry. Nose: ripe fruit, sweet spices, creamy oak, expressive, mineral. Palate: fruity, toasty, round tannins.

VALL DEL CALÀS 2006 T

**90** Colour: bright cherry. Nose: ripe fruit, sweet spices, creamy oak, expressive, dried flowers. Palate: fruity, toasty, round tannins, fleshy.

MAS TORTÓ 2006 TC

**89** Colour: very deep cherry. Nose: expressive, fresh fruit, red berry notes, floral, dark chocolate. Palate: flavourful, fruity, good acidity, round tannins, fleshy.

NINOT SELECCIÓ 2004 TR

**87** Colour: cherry, garnet rim. Nose: ripe fruit, spicy, creamy oak, toasty. Palate: powerful, flavourful, toasty, round tannins.

PANSAL DEL CALÀS VINO DE LICOR

**92** Colour: black cherry, purple rim. Nose: complex, powerfull, fruit expression, aromatic coffee, cocoa bean, mineral. Palate: fleshy, fresh, powerful, concentrated.

CAPÇANES
FLOR DE PRIMAVERA PERAJ HA'ABIB
VALL DEL CALÀS

## CELLER DOSTERRAS

Ctra. Falset a Marça, km. 2, 43775 Marça (Tarragona)

☎: 678 730 596
jgrau@dosterras.com
www.dosterras.com

VESPRES 2007 T

**90** Colour: deep cherry. Nose: fruit liqueur notes, earthy notes, floral, sweet spices, dark chocolate. Palate: fleshy, good structure, full, good acidity.

DOSTERRAS 2006 T

**90** Colour: deep cherry. Nose: expressive, red berry notes, mineral, balsamic herbs. Palate: flavourful, fruity, good acidity, round tannins.

## CELLER EL MASROIG

Passeig de L'Arbre, 3, 43736 El Masroig (Tarragona)
☎: 977 825 026
celler@cellermasroig.com
www.cellermasroig.com

LES SORTS 2007 B
cariñena blanca 100%

**86** Colour: golden. Nose: characterful, expressive, macerated fruit, rancio notes, creamy oak. Palate: full, flavourful, fresh, creamy.

LES SORTS ROSAT 2008 RD
garnacha 90%, cariñena 10%

**90** Colour: rose, purple rim. Nose: powerful, ripe fruit, red berry notes, floral, rose petals. Palate: fleshy, powerful, fruity, fresh, flavourful.

ORTO 2008 T

**88** Colour: bright cherry. Nose: ripe fruit, sweet spices, creamy oak, expressive, earthy notes. Palate: flavourful, fruity, toasty, round tannins.

LES SORTS 2008 T
cariñena 50%, garnacha 30%, sumoll 20%

**87** Colour: deep cherry. Nose: floral, raspberry, mineral. Palate: fleshy, fresh, full, fine bitter notes.

MISTELA NEGRA DEL MONTSANT 2008 T
cariñena 100%

**87** Colour: dark-red cherry. Nose: fruit liqueur notes, spicy, dark chocolate, mineral. Palate: fleshy, good structure, full, confected.

ETNIC 2006 T
cariñena 85%, garnacha 15%

**94** Colour: bright cherry. Nose: ripe fruit, creamy oak, expressive, floral. Palate: flavourful, fruity, toasty, round tannins, great length.

## CASTELL DE LES PINYERES 2006 T
garnacha 45%, cariñena 35%, merlot 20%, cabernet sauvignon %

**92** Colour: bright cherry. Nose: ripe fruit, sweet spices, creamy oak, expressive, dry stone. Palate: flavourful, fruity, toasty, round tannins.

## LES SORTS SYCAR 2006 T
cariñena 60%, syrah 40%

**90** Colour: bright cherry. Nose: ripe fruit, sweet spices, creamy oak, expressive. Palate: flavourful, fruity, toasty, round tannins.

## LES SORTS VINYES VELLES 2005 TC
cariñena 50%, garnacha 40%, cabernet sauvignon 10%

**90** Colour: bright cherry. Nose: ripe fruit, sweet spices, creamy oak, expressive, smoky, aromatic coffee. Palate: flavourful, fruity, toasty, round tannins.

## MAS ROIG 2005 TC
cariñena 75%, garnacha 15%, cabernet sauvignon 10%

**90** Colour: bright cherry. Nose: fruit expression, aromatic coffee, sweet spices, roasted almonds. Palate: powerful, flavourful, round tannins, balsamic.

## MISTELA MOLT VELLA DEL MAISROIG VINO DE LICOR
cariñena 100%

**85** Colour: light mahogany. Nose: roasted almonds, aged wood nuances, sweet spices, pattiserie. Palate: creamy, confected.

SOLÀ FRED

## CELLER ELS GUIAMETS

Avinguda Ctra. nº 23, 43777 Els Guiamets (Tarragona)
☎: 977 413 018 - Fax: 977 413 113
comercial@cellerelsguiamets.com
www.cellerelsguiamets.com

## VALL SELLADA 2007 BFB
garnacha blanca

**86** Colour: yellow. Nose: fresh fruit, balsamic herbs, dried herbs. Palate: full, flavourful, fresh, creamy.

## GRAN METS 2005 T
cabernet sauvignon, merlot, ull de llebre

**89** Colour: dark-red cherry, orangey edge. Nose: aromatic coffee, aged wood nuances, wet leather. Palate: powerful, full, concentrated, creamy, mineral.

## ISIS 2005 T
syrah, garnacha, cariñena

**88** Colour: bright cherry. Nose: ripe fruit, sweet spices, creamy oak, expressive, fine reductive notes. Palate: fruity, toasty, round tannins, fleshy.

## CELLER LAURONA S.A.

Ctra. Bellmunt - Sort dels Capellans (Pol. 21)
43730 Falset (Tarragona)
☎: 977 831 712 - Fax: 977 831 797
laurona@cellerlaurona.com
www.cellerlaurona.com

## 6 VINYES DE LAURONA 2005 T

**91** Colour: bright cherry. Nose: sweet spices, creamy oak, expressive, floral, earthy notes, fruit expression. Palate: flavourful, fruity, toasty, round tannins.

## LAURONA 2005 T

**89** Colour: bright cherry. Nose: ripe fruit, sweet spices, creamy oak, expressive, cocoa bean, cedar wood. Palate: fruity, toasty, round tannins, powerful, creamy.

## CELLER LOS TROVADORES

Avda. de las Encinas, 25
28707 San Sebastian de los Reyes (Madrid)
☎: 679 459 074
cgomez@lostrovadores.com
www.lostrovadores.com

## CITAREUS 2005 T
garnacha 40%, mazuelo 30%, cabernet sauvignon 30%

**88** Colour: bright cherry. Nose: ripe fruit, sweet spices, creamy oak, mineral. Palate: flavourful, fruity, toasty, round tannins.

*Los Trovadores*

www.lostrovadores.com
info@lostrovadores.com
+34 679 459 074

## GALLICANT 2004 T
garnacha 60%, mazuelo 30%, syrah 10%

**90** Colour: bright cherry. Nose: ripe fruit, sweet spices, creamy oak, expressive, earthy notes, balsamic herbs. Palate: flavourful, fruity, toasty, round tannins, fresh.

## CELLER MALONDRO

Miranda, 27, 43360 Cornudella del Montsant (Tarragona)
☎: 636 595 736 - Fax: 977 821 451
jcestivill@malondro.es
www.malondro.es

MALONDRO B

**77**

MALONDRO 2006 TC

**89** Colour: bright cherry. Nose: ripe fruit, sweet spices, creamy oak, expressive, undergrowth. Palate: flavourful, fruity, toasty, round tannins.

LATRIA 2006 T

**89** Colour: bright cherry. Nose: ripe fruit, sweet spices, creamy oak. Palate: flavourful, fruity, toasty, round tannins.

## CELLER ORCELLA

Ctra. 1 - 3, 43736 La Figuera (Tarragona)
☎: 977 262 143 - Fax: 977 262 123
orcella@mixmail.com
www.orcella.net

ORCELLA MIMA 2008 T

**86** Colour: deep cherry. Nose: ripe fruit, balsamic herbs, earthy notes. Palate: flavourful, full, fruity.

ARDEA 2006 TC

**91** Colour: bright cherry. Nose: ripe fruit, creamy oak, expressive, sweet spices. Palate: flavourful, fruity, toasty, round tannins, mineral.

ORSUS

## CELLER PASCONA

Camí dels Fontals, s/n, 43730 Falset (Tarragona)
☎: 609 291 770 - Fax: 977 117 098
info@pascona.com
www.pascona.com

PASCONA SELECCIÓ 2008 T ROBLE
merlot 50%, syrah 50%

**87** Colour: cherry, purple rim. Nose: expressive, fresh fruit, red berry notes, floral, mineral. Palate: flavourful, fruity, good acidity, round tannins.

PASCONA EVOLUCIÓ 2006 TC
garnacha 50%, cabernet sauvignon 50%

**90** Colour: bright cherry. Nose: ripe fruit, sweet spices, creamy oak, expressive, dry stone. Palate: flavourful, fruity, toasty, round tannins, fresh.

PASCONA TRADICIÓ 2006 TC
garnacha 60%, mazuelo 30%, cabernet sauvignon 10%

**89** Colour: cherry, garnet rim. Nose: ripe fruit, spicy, creamy oak, toasty, complex. Palate: powerful, flavourful, toasty, round tannins.

## CELLERS BARONIA
## DEL MONTSANT S.L.

Comte de Rius, 1
43360 Cornudella de Montsant (Tarragona)
☎: 977 821 483 - Fax: 977 821 483
englora@baronia-m.com
www.baronia-m.com

ENGLORA 2005 TC

**90** Colour: cherry, purple rim. Nose: expressive, fresh fruit, red berry notes, floral, dry stone. Palate: flavourful, fruity, good acidity, round tannins.

CLOS D'ENGLORA AV 14 2004 T

**93** Colour: cherry, purple rim. Nose: expressive, floral, undergrowth, mineral. Palate: flavourful, fruity, good acidity, round tannins, powerful.

## CELLERS CAN BLAU

Ctra. Bellmunt s/n, 43730 Falset (Tarragona)
☎: 629 261 379 - Fax: 968 716 051
info@orowines.com

CAN BLAU 2007 T
cariñena, syrah, garnacha

**90** Colour: cherry, garnet rim. Nose: powerful, expressive, ripe fruit, red berry notes, mineral, toasty. Palate: warm, good acidity, flavourful, fruity aftestaste.

MAS DE CAN BLAU 2006 T
cariñena, syrah, garnacha

**93** Colour: cherry, garnet rim. Nose: mineral, roasted coffee, sweet spices, ripe fruit, fruit preserve. Palate: flavourful, powerful, fleshy, round tannins.

## CELLERS SANT RAFEL

Mas Sant Rafel, 43774 Pradell de la Teixeta (Tarragona)
☎: 689 792 305 - Fax: 977 323 078
cellerssantrafel@yahoo.es

**SOLPOST FRESC 2007 TC**
garnacha 80%, cabernet sauvignon 10%, syrah 10%

**89** Colour: deep cherry. Nose: expressive, fresh fruit, red berry notes, floral, cocoa bean. Palate: flavourful, fruity, good acidity, round tannins.

**SOLPOST 2006 TC**

**91** Colour: bright cherry. Nose: raspberry, mineral, cocoa bean, elegant. Palate: flavourful, full, round.

**SOLPOST 2005 T**
garnacha 50%, cariñena 35%, cabernet sauvignon 15%

**89** Colour: dark-red cherry, garnet rim. Nose: complex, fruit preserve, smoky, cocoa bean, mineral. Palate: fleshy, good structure, flavourful.

## CINGLES BLAUS

Finca Mas de les Moreres, Afueras de Cornudella, s/n
43360 Cornudella de Montsant (Tarragona)
☎: 977 326 080 - Fax: 977 323 928
info@cinglesblaus.com

**CINGLES BLAUS OCTUBRE 2007 T**
garnacha 60%, cariñena 20%, syrah 20%

**89** Colour: deep cherry. Nose: fresh fruit, red berry notes, violet drops, balsamic herbs, mineral. Palate: fleshy, fresh, fruity, full, fruity aftestaste.

**CINGLES BLAUS MAS DE LES MORERES 2006 T**
garnacha 50%, cariñena 15%, merlot 15%, cabernet sauvignon 10%, syrah 10%

**89** Colour: bright cherry. Nose: fruit expression, red berry notes, sweet spices, smoky. Palate: powerful, flavourful, spirituous, sweet tannins.

**CINGLES BLAUS SELECCIÓ T**
garnacha 80%, syrah 20%

**88** Colour: bright cherry. Nose: sweet spices, creamy oak, expressive, fruit liqueur notes, earthy notes. Palate: flavourful, fruity, toasty, round tannins, creamy.

**CINGLES BLAUS DOLÇ**

## COC & DELICATESSEN S.L.

Plaça Geroni Gelpi, 9-D
08340 Vilassar de Mar (Barcelona)
☎: 937 502 491
coc@clubcoc.com
www.clubcoc.com

TATI 2008 RD

**80**

## COCA I FITO

Portal, 18
43393 Almoster (Tarragona)
☎: 619 776 948
info@cellarwines.eu
www.cellarwines.eu

COCA I FITÓ 2006 T
syrah 50%, garnacha 30%, Samsó 20%                23€

**93** Colour: bright cherry. Nose: characterful, complex, fruit liqueur notes, dark chocolate, sweet spices. Palate: flavourful, fruity, fresh, toasty, round tannins, mineral.

## COOPERATIVA AGRICOLA AUBACS I SOLANS S.C.C.L.

Carretera, 1
43736 La Figuera (Tarragona)
☎: 977 825 228 - Fax: 977 825 201
aubacs.i.solans@wanadoo.es

PROSIT 2007 T

**86** Colour: deep cherry. Nose: fruit expression, fresh fruit, earthy notes, balsamic herbs. Palate: fleshy, flavourful, fruity.

AUBACS I SOLANS

## ETIM

Miquel Barceló, 31, 43730 Falset (Tarragona)
☎: 977 830 105 - Fax: 977 830 363
info@etim.es
www.etim.es

ETIM 2008 B

**90** Colour: pale. Nose: smoky, balsamic herbs, dried herbs. Palate: full, light-bodied, fresh, creamy.

ÈTIM VEREMA TARDANA 2007 B

**89** Colour: golden. Nose: powerful, candied fruit, fragrant herbs, balsamic herbs. Palate: flavourful, sweet, fresh, fruity, good acidity, long.

ETIM 2007 B BARRICA

**89** Colour: golden. Nose: fruit liqueur notes, candied fruit, dry nuts, faded flowers. Palate: warm, unctuous, fruity.

CASTELL DE FALSET 2007 B

**88** Colour: golden. Nose: fruit liqueur notes, fruit preserve, dry nuts, dried herbs. Palate: rich, full, flavourful, balsamic, toasty.

ETIM ROSAT 2008 RD

**88** Colour: rose, purple rim. Nose: powerful, ripe fruit, red berry notes, floral, expressive. Palate: fleshy, powerful, fruity, fresh, carbonic notes.

ETIM NEGRE 2007 T

**88** Colour: deep cherry, garnet rim. Nose: macerated fruit, creamy oak, spicy, mineral. Palate: powerful, good structure, complex, round tannins.

ÈTIM SELECTION SYRAH 2006 T

**91** Colour: bright cherry. Nose: ripe fruit, expressive, varietal, aromatic coffee, characterful. Palate: flavourful, fruity, toasty, round tannins.

CASTELL DE FALSET 2006 T

**90** Colour: deep cherry. Nose: fruit expression, smoky, cedar wood, earthy notes.

ETIM L'ESPARVER 2006 T

**90** Colour: very deep cherry. Nose: fruit expression, fresh fruit, red berry notes, dark chocolate, mineral.

ÈTIM VEREMA TARDANA 2006 T

**90** Colour: ruby red, orangey edge. Nose: sun-drenched nuances, fruit liqueur notes, spicy, cedar wood, tobacco. Palate: fleshy, full, flavourful, creamy, good acidity.

ÈTIM VEREMA SOBREMADURADA SELECCIÓ VINYES VELLES 2005 T

**92** Colour: black cherry, garnet rim. Nose: fruit liqueur notes, dry nuts, tobacco, aged wood nuances, aromatic coffee. Palate: flavourful, fine bitter notes, good acidity, balanced.

## ÈTIM OLD VINES GRENACHE 2005 T

**91** Colour: bright cherry. Nose: ripe fruit, sweet spices, creamy oak, expressive, roasted almonds, smoky. Palate: fruity, toasty, round tannins, powerful, good structure.

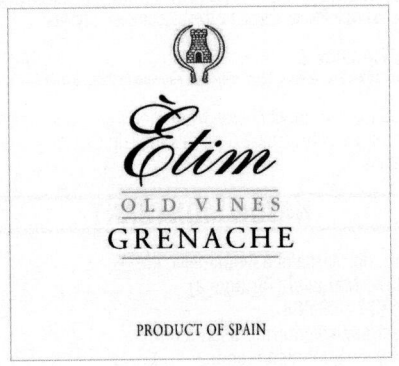

## ÈTIM SELECTION SYRAH 2005 T

**91** Colour: bright cherry. Nose: ripe fruit, sweet spices, creamy oak, expressive, fruit expression. Palate: flavourful, fruity, toasty, round tannins, complex, fresh.

## CASTELL DE FALSET 2005 T

**91** Colour: bright cherry. Nose: ripe fruit, sweet spices, creamy oak, expressive, damp earth. Palate: flavourful, fruity, toasty, round tannins.

## ETIM L'ESPARVER 2005 T

**89** Colour: cherry, purple rim. Nose: expressive, fresh fruit, red berry notes, floral, undergrowth, dark chocolate. Palate: flavourful, fruity, good acidity, round tannins, mineral.

## IMUS SELECCIÓ DE VINYES

---

# JOAN D'ANGUERA

Mayor 23, 43746 Darmós (Tarragona)
☎: 977 418 348 - Fax: 977 418 302
josep@cellersjoandanguera.com
www.cellerjoandanguera.com

JOAN D'ANGUERA 2008 T
syrah 45%, garnacha 35%, cabernet sauvignon 20%

**86** Colour: cherry, purple rim. Nose: expressive, fresh fruit, red berry notes, floral, undergrowth. Palate: flavourful, fruity, good acidity, round tannins.

FINCA L'ARGATA 2007 T
garnacha 45%, syrah 45%, cabernet sauvignon 10%

**90** Colour: deep cherry. Nose: fruit preserve, balsamic herbs, smoky, cocoa bean, floral. Palate: fleshy, full, flavourful, round tannins.

PLANELLA 2007 T
cariñena 40%, syrah 30%, garnacha 15%, cabernet sauvignon 15%

**90** Colour: bright cherry. Nose: ripe fruit, sweet spices, creamy oak, expressive. Palate: flavourful, fruity, toasty, round tannins, good acidity.

BUGADER 2006 T
syrah 85%, garnacha 15%

**92** Colour: dark-red cherry. Nose: varietal, characterful, fruit preserve, mineral, damp earth, aromatic coffee. Palate: fleshy, spirituous, full, round tannins, balsamic.

# LA COVA DELS VINS S.C.P.

Bosquet, 5 àtic 4, 43730 Falset (Tarragona)
☎: 977 83 1 1
covavins@wanadoo.es

OMBRA 2007 T BARRICA

**89** Colour: bright cherry. Nose: fruit expression, red berry notes, balsamic herbs, floral, cocoa bean. Palate: full, powerful, balsamic.

TERRÒS 2007 T

**88** Colour: dark-red cherry. Nose: fruit preserve, floral. Palate: fleshy, rich, flavourful, powerful tannins.

# MAS DE L'ABUNDÀNCIA VITICULTORS

Camí de Gratallops, s/n
43736 El Masroig (Tarragona)

☎: 637 415 263
info@masdelabundancia.com

**FLVMINIS 2007 T**

**89** Colour: cherry, purple rim. Nose: expressive, fresh fruit, red berry notes, floral. Palate: flavourful, fruity, good acidity, round tannins.

**MAS DE L'ABUNDÀNCIA 2006 T**

**91** Colour: cherry, garnet rim. Nose: macerated fruit, sweet spices, undergrowth, earthy notes, elegant. Palate: flavourful, rich, fine tannins.

## MAS DE LA CAÇADORA

Avinguda de la Carretera, 9
43777 Els Guiamets (Tarragona)
☎: 977 413 005 - Fax: 977 413 005
masdelacasadora@yahoo.es
www.masdelacasadora.com

**OREIG 2008 B**
garnacha blanca 60%, macabeo 20%, moscatel 20%

**78**

**TRETZE 2007 BFB**
garnacha blanca 100%

**79**

**U MAS DE LA CAÇADORA 2008 RD**
garnacha 50%, merlot 50%

**85** Colour: light cherry. Nose: powerful, ripe fruit, red berry notes, floral, expressive. Palate: fleshy, powerful, fruity, fresh, sweetness.

**LIMBEU 2006 T**
garnacha 60%, merlot 40%

**87** Colour: ruby red, garnet rim. Nose: roasted almonds, smoky, spicy. Palate: flavourful, full, fine tannins.

**QUOM 2005 T**
merlot 40%, garnacha 25%, cariñena 25%, cabernet sauvignon 10%

**86** Colour: cherry, garnet rim. Nose: ripe fruit, spicy, creamy oak, toasty, complex, cigar. Palate: flavourful, toasty, round tannins, mineral.

PANSES

## MAS PERINET (D.O. MONTSANT)

Finca Mas Perinet, s/n T-7402 km. 6,4
43660 Cornudella de Montsant (Tarragona)
☎: 977 827 113 - Fax: 977 827 180

info@masperinet.com
www.masperinet.com

**CLOS MARÍA 2007 B**
garnacha blanca 63%, chenin blanc 17%, moscatel 14%, macabeo 6%

**92** Colour: bright straw. Nose: ripe fruit, citrus fruit, sweet spices, cocoa bean. Palate: flavourful, fleshy, complex, ripe fruit.

**GOTIA 2006 T**
garnacha 36%, merlot 33%, cabernet sauvignon 22%, syrah 9%

**93** Colour: bright cherry. Nose: ripe fruit, sweet spices, creamy oak, dry stone. Palate: flavourful, fruity, toasty, round tannins.

## NATUR MONTSANT

Ctra. de Margalef a Granadella, km. 4
43371 Margalef (Tarragona)
☎: 977 088 888
masfranch@naturmontsant.com
www.naturmontsant.com

**MAS FRANCH NEGRE 2006 T**

**89** Colour: dark-red cherry. Nose: fruit preserve, dark chocolate, sweet spices. Palate: concentrated, full, rich.

**MAS FRANCH ÓPTIM T**

**90** Colour: bright cherry. Nose: ripe fruit, sweet spices, creamy oak, expressive. Palate: flavourful, fruity, toasty, round tannins.

## NOGUERALS S.C.P.

Tou, 5
43360 Cornudella de Montsant (TarragonaC)
☎: 650 033 546 - Fax: 934 419 879
noguerals@hotmail.com

**CORBATERA 2006 T**

**91** Colour: dark-red cherry. Nose: cocoa bean, dark chocolate, fruit preserve, mineral, floral. Palate: powerful, flavourful, concentrated, round tannins.

## PORTAL DEL MONTSANT

DaH, 74, 43775 Marça (Tarragona)
☎: 977 178 486 - Fax: 934 173 591
portal@portaldelmontsant.com
www.portaldelmontsant.com

**SANTBRU 2008 B**
garnacha blanca 80%, garnacha gris 10%, macabeo 10%

**92** Colour: straw. Nose: fresh fruit, wild herbs, fruit expression. Palate: fruity, flavourful, smoky aftertaste.

### BRUNUS ROSÉ 2008 RD
garnacha 100%

**90** Colour: rose, purple rim. Nose: violet drops, fruit expression, red berry notes. Palate: powerful, flavourful, fruity.

### SANTBRU CARINYENES VELLES 2007 T
cariñena 65%, syrah 20%, garnacha 15%

**91** Colour: deep cherry. Nose: ripe fruit, sweet spices, expressive, mineral, cocoa bean. Palate: flavourful, fruity, toasty, round tannins, sweetness, powerful.

### BRUNUS 2007 T
cariñena 55%, syrah 30%, garnacha 15%

**90** Colour: cherry, garnet rim. Nose: ripe fruit, spicy, creamy oak, toasty, complex. Palate: powerful, flavourful, toasty, round tannins.

### SANTBRU CARINYENES VELLES 2006 T
cariñena 65%, garnacha 20%, syrah 15%

**89** Colour: bright cherry. Nose: ripe fruit, sweet spices, creamy oak, expressive, dry stone, mineral. Palate: flavourful, fruity, toasty, round tannins, spirituous.

## UNIÓ CORPORACIÓ ALIMENTARIA - CELLERS UNIÓ

Joan Oliver, 16-24 , 43206 Reus (Tarragona)
☎: 977 330 055 - Fax: 977 330 070
reus@cellersunio.com
www.cellersunio.com

### DAIRO FLORAL 2008 T
garnacha 60%, tempranillo 20%, syrah 20%

**85** Colour: deep cherry. Nose: expressive, fresh fruit, red berry notes, mineral. Palate: flavourful, fruity, good acidity, round tannins.

### PERLAT 2007 T
garnacha 40%, cariñena 40%, syrah 20%

**86** Colour: bright cherry. Nose: raspberry, red berry notes, earthy notes, balsamic herbs. Palate: fleshy, full, fruity, fresh.

### PERLAT GARNATXA 2006 T
garnacha 90%, cariñena 10%

**90** Colour: bright cherry. Nose: ripe fruit, creamy oak, expressive, floral. Palate: flavourful, fruity, toasty, round tannins.

### PERLAT 2N ANY DE CRIANÇA 2006 T
garnacha 70%, cariñena 20%, syrah 10%

**89** Colour: cherry, garnet rim. Nose: ripe fruit, spicy, toasty, complex. Palate: powerful, flavourful, toasty, round tannins.

### PERLAT SYRAH 2006 T
syrah 90%, garnacha 10%

**87** Colour: bright cherry. Nose: ripe fruit, sweet spices, creamy oak, expressive. Palate: flavourful, fruity, toasty, round tannins.

### CLOS DE LA TERRA 2006 T
garnacha 50%, samso 25%, syrah 25%

**86** Colour: dark-red cherry. Nose: fruit liqueur notes, mineral. Palate: fleshy, spirituous, round tannins.

### ROCA BLANCA 2005 TC
garnacha 50%, mazuelo 30%, merlot 20%

**88** Colour: bright cherry. Nose: macerated fruit, fruit expression, cocoa bean, smoky, balsamic herbs. Palate: fruity, full, flavourful, round tannins.

### DAIRO 2005 TC
cariñena 50%, garnacha 30%, syrah 20%

**88** Colour: very deep cherry. Nose: fruit preserve, floral, mineral, dark chocolate. Palate: fleshy, spirituous, fruity, flavourful, good acidity.

### PERLAT SELECCIÓ 2005 T
cariñena 50%, garnacha 30%, syrah 20%

**87** Colour: bright cherry. Nose: ripe fruit, sweet spices, creamy oak, expressive, dark chocolate. Palate: fruity, toasty, round tannins, powerful.

## VENDRELL RIVED

Bassa, 10
43775 Marçà (Tarragona)
☎: 637 537 383 - Fax: 977 263 053
jmvendrell@gmail.com

### SERE 2007 T
garnacha 80%, cariñena 20%

**85** Colour: bright cherry. Nose: raspberry, characterful, expressive, mineral. Palate: fleshy, concentrated, round tannins.

### L'ALLEU SELECCIÓ 2006 T
garnacha 60%, cariñena 40%

**90** Colour: bright cherry. Nose: ripe fruit, sweet spices, expressive, fruit expression, smoky. Palate: flavourful, fruity, toasty, round tannins.

### L'ALLEU 2005 T
garnacha 60%, cariñena 40%

**88** Colour: cherry, purple rim. Nose: expressive, floral, macerated fruit, mineral. Palate: flavourful, fruity, good acidity, round tannins.

## VENUS LA UNIVERSAL

Ctra. Porrera, s/n, 43730 Falset (Tarragona)
☎: 629 238 236 - Fax: 639 121 244
info@venuslauniversal.com
www.venuslauniversal.com

DIDO 2008 B
garnacha blanca 60%, macabeo 40%

**92** Colour: golden. Nose: grapey, warm, smoky, white flowers, scrubland. Palate: fresh, flavourful, rich.

DIDO 2008 T
garnacha 55%, merlot 20%, cabernet sauvignon 20%, syrah 15%

**91** Colour: bright cherry. Nose: sweet spices, creamy oak, ripe fruit, red berry notes. Palate: flavourful, fruity, toasty, round tannins.

DIDO 2007 T
garnacha 55%, merlot 20%, cabernet sauvignon 20%, syrah 15%

**92** Colour: bright cherry. Nose: fruit liqueur notes, mineral, floral, dark chocolate. Palate: powerful, rich, flavourful, sweet tannins.

VENUS LA UNIVERSAL 2007 T
cariñena 50%, sumoll 40%, garnacha 10%

**93** Colour: deep cherry. Nose: warm, characterful, dark chocolate, fruit preserve, floral, mineral. Palate: powerful, flavourful, round tannins, balsamic.

## VINYES D'EN GABRIEL

Ctra. Darmós - La Serra s/n
43746 Darmós (Tarragona)
☎: 609 989 345
info@vinyesdengabriel.com
www.vinyesdengabriel.com

L´HERAVI 2008 T

**88** Colour: dark-red cherry. Nose: macerated fruit, smoky, floral. Palate: fleshy, fresh, fruity, flavourful, creamy.

L´HERAVI 2007 TC

**88** Nose: expressive, fresh fruit, red berry notes, floral, earthy notes, creamy oak. Palate: flavourful, fruity, good acidity, round tannins.

## VINYES DOMÈNECH

Camí de La Fou s/n Polígono 6
43776 Capçanes (Tarragona)
☎: 670 297 395 - Fax: 932 127 759
juanignasi@vinyesdomenech.com
www.vinyesdomenech.com

FURVUS 2007 T
garnacha 70%, merlot 30

**92** Colour: bright cherry. Nose: sweet spices, creamy oak, expressive, red berry notes, mineral. Palate: flavourful, fruity, toasty, round tannins.

TEIXAR 2006 T
garnacha 100%

**92** Colour: cherry, garnet rim. Nose: powerful, ripe fruit, warm, toasty, dark chocolate. Palate: flavourful, fleshy, spicy, ripe fruit, mineral, round tannins.

## VIÑAS DEL MONTSANT

Partida Coll de Mora, s/n, 43775 Marça (Tarragona)
☎: 977 831 309 - Fax: 977 831 356
fraguerau@fraguerau.com

FRA GUERAU 2006 T

**89** Colour: cherry, garnet rim. Nose: fruit expression, fruit preserve, warm, ripe fruit, sweet spices, elegant. Palate: fine tannins, flavourful, full.

SOME OTHER WINERIES WITHIN THE DO:

**AIBAR 1895 S.L.**
**CELLER CUBELLS I CUBELLS**
**CELLER FRANCESC MASDEU**
**CELLER MAS DE LES VINYES**
**CELLER RONADELLES**
**CELLERS CAPAFONS OSSÓ**
**CELLERS FOLCH S.L.**
**CELLERS GRIFOLL DECLARA**
**CLOS MOGADOR (SPECTACLE VINS)**
**EL CUCULLAR S.C.P.**
**ENRIC ANGUERA CEDÓ**
**ESCOLA D'ENOLOGIA IES PRIORAT**
**FINCA MORES S.C.P.**
**TERRASSES DEL MONTSANT**
**TERRES DE CODOLS I LICORELLA**

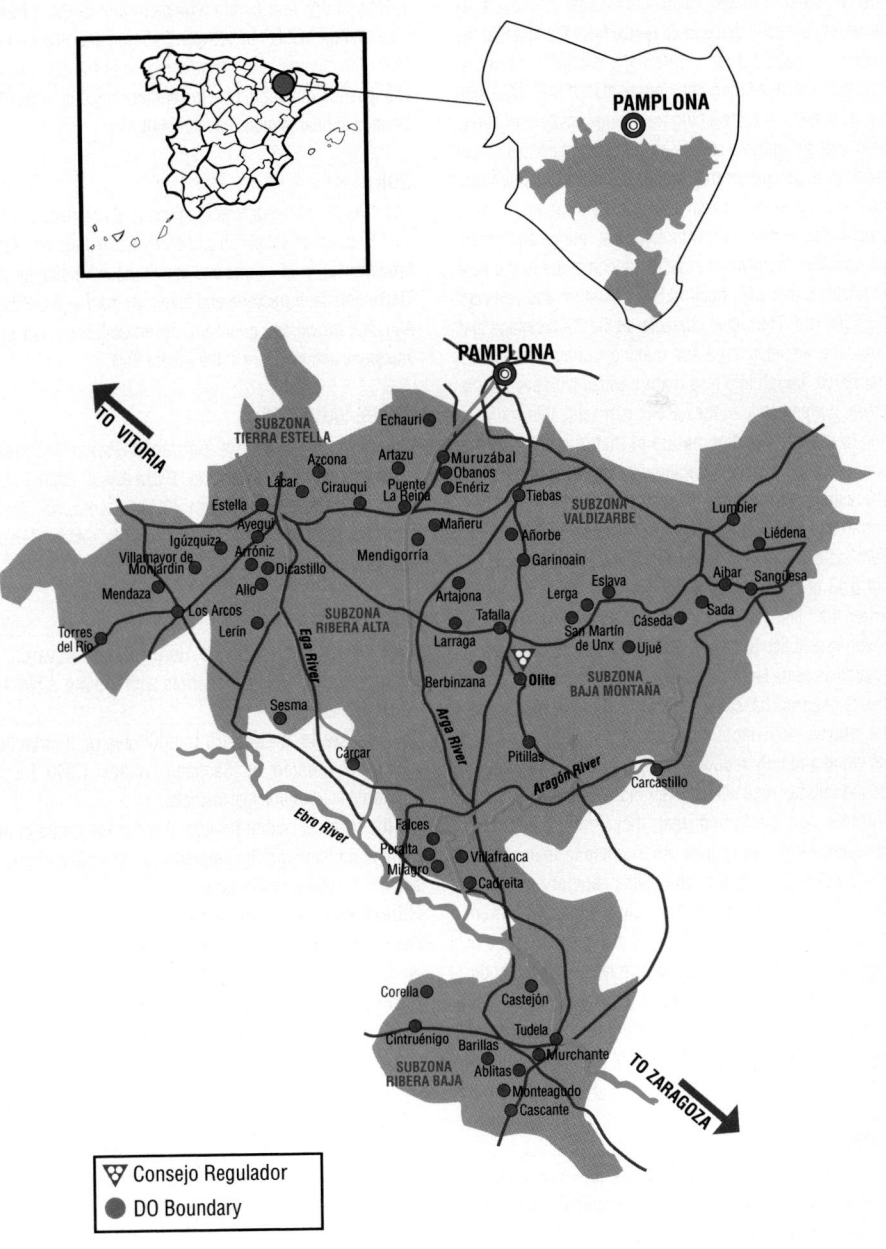

Consejo Regulador
DO Boundary

## NEWS

We should start to ask Navarra to be able to show in its wines the diversity that should derive from the fact that the region enjoys three different climatic patterns, mediterranean, atlantic and continental. If they managed so, its wines will be reaching top ratings easily, and surely we would be enjoying rosé wines of real stature that would work as flagships for the region. But unfortunately there are very few wines of real relevance, a huge lot of them languishing in mid table with mediocre ratings and hardly no novelties to speak of save those contained in the new regulations that will affect mainly viticulture and vineyard management. The cooler character of the 2008 vintage that could be an advantage for making young wines, has translated though into less mature wines with even some green, unripe notes. In the case of garnacha, this could be due to the late-ripening nature of that grape and to the poor selection practices traditionally shown by the coops, still responsible for the management of most of the 17.000 hectares of vineyard that Navarra has. Young wines made from tempranillo –a short-cycle variety– show some good red fruit character. The aged wines of 2007 are much better than last year's young ones, since it has become common practice to destine the best wines to oak ageing, regardless of its length. The safest bets come from varied blends of garnacha, cabernet, merlot and graciano. As for the reserva renderings, they show a worrying amount of old wood and ugly reductive notes. In 2008 the winners are indubitably rosé wines, even more so in a year when Brussels has confirmed that they should be made exclusively from red grapes. An example to follow: Gran Feudo Sobre Lías. In the white wine category we could look for young wines made from chardonnay, with more character than ever before. There is also a better range of barrel-fermented examples or aged in new oak, simply the great white hope for a region in great need of it. Also noteworthy are the sweet wines from moscatel made by wineries like Azpea, Castillo de Monjardín and Pago de Cirsus.

## LOCATION

In the province of Navarra. It draws together areas of different climates and soils, which produce wines with diverse characteristics.

## CLIMATE

Typical of dry, sub-humid regions in the northern fringe, with average rainfall of between 593 mm and 683 mm per year. The climate in the central region is transitional and changes to drier conditions in southern regions, where the average annual rainfall is a mere 448 mm.

## SOIL

The diversity of the different regions is also reflected in the soil. Reddish or yellowish and stony in the Baja Montaña, brownish-grey limestone and limestone in Valdizarbe and Tierra Estella, limestone and alluvium marl in the Ribera Alta, and brown and grey semi-desert soil, brownish-grey limestone and alluvium in the Ribera Baja.

## GRAPE VARIETIES:

**White:** *Chardonnay* (2%), *Garnacha Blanca, Malvasía, Moscatel de Grano Menudo, Viura* (6% of total).
**Red:** *Cabernet Sauvignon* (9%), *Garnacha Tinta* (majority 42% of total), *Graciano, Mazuela, Merlot, Tempranillo* (29%).

## SUB-REGIONS:

**Baja Montaña.** Situated northeast of Navarra, it comprises 22 municipal districts with around 2,500 Ha under cultivation.
**Tierra Estella.** In western central Navarra, it stretches along the Camino de Santiago. It has 1,800 Ha of vineyards in 38 municipal districts.
**Valdizarbe.** In central Navarra. It is the key centre of the Camino de Santiago. It comprises 25 municipal districts and has 1,100 Ha of vineyards.
**Ribera Alta.** In the area around Olite, it takes in part of central Navarra and the start of the southern region. There are 26 municipal districts and 3,300 Ha of vineyards.
**Ribera Baja.** In the south of the province, it is the most important in terms of size (4,600 Ha). It comprises 14 municipal districts.

| | |
|---|---|
| Hectares of Vineyard | 17,000 |
| N° Viticulturists | 4,930 |
| N° of Bodegas | 116 |
| 2008 Harvest | Very Good |
| 2007 Production | 56,000,000 l. |
| Marketing | 70% domestic 30% export |

**CONSEJO REGULADOR.**
Rúa Romana s/n. 31390 Olite (Navarra)
☎: 948 741 812 - Fax: 948 741 776
@ consejoregulador@vinonavarra.com
www.vinonavarra.com

## GENERAL CHARACTERISTICS OF THE WINES:

| | |
|---|---|
| **WHITES** | Although a minority product with respect to the red and rosé wines, young wines and wines fermented in barrels are also produced from the *Chardonnay* variety: golden yellow in colour, the best are characterised by their creamy and toasted aromas, which are well combined with fruit, and by their varietal character. Amongst the sweet wines, the whites from the *Moscatel de Grano Menudo*, a traditional variety which is slowly being recovered, stand out. There are few examples, although of high quality: grapey and honey aromas on the nose; flavourful, complex and fresh on the palate. |
| **ROSÉS** | Most are produced from *Garnacha*, although there are also examples from *Tempranillo* and *Cabernet Sauvignon*. Raspberry pink coloured, they are very fresh and fruity with a great character of red berries; on the palate they are balanced, flavourful and fruity. |
| **REDS** | These vary according to the varieties and the regions they are produced in. In the northern regions, where the Tempranillo predominates, the wines have a more Atlantic character; the aroma is more reminiscent of red berries; they are fresher with higher levels of acidity. In the south, the varietal character of the *Garnacha* stands out: the wines are warmer, with notes of ripe black fruit, round and supple on the palate. As well as these, there are the single variety wines from foreign varieties (mainly *Cabernet Sauvignon* and *Merlot*, with a marked varietal character), together with the red wines that combine autochthonous and foreign grape varieties. |

## 2008 VINTAGE RATING:

## GOOD

# DO NAVARRA

## ALEX

Ctra. Tudela, s/n
31591 Corella (Navarra)
☎: 948 782 014 - Fax: 948 782 164
info@vinosalex.com
www.vinosalex.com

ALEX VIURA 2008 B

**82**

ALEX GARNACHA 2008 RD

**87** Colour: rose, purple rim. Nose: powerful, ripe fruit, red berry notes, floral. Palate: fleshy, powerful, fruity, fresh.

ALEX TEMPRANILLO 2008 T

**85** Colour: dark-red cherry. Nose: ripe fruit, red berry notes, spicy. Palate: round tannins, fruity, flavourful.

ALEX 2006 TC

**86** Colour: deep cherry, garnet rim. Nose: fruit preserve, aged wood nuances, spicy. Palate: balanced, fruity, round tannins.

ALEX MERLOT 2006 T

**78**

ALEX 2000 TR

**88** Colour: deep cherry, bright ochre rim. Nose: fruit liqueur notes, elegant, sweet spices, cocoa bean, aromatic coffee. Palate: fruity, good acidity, slightly dry, soft tannins.

ALEX 2006 MOSCATEL

**87** Colour: old gold, amber rim. Nose: candied fruit, powerfull, fruit liqueur notes. Palate: sweetness, fruity, unctuous.

## ARDOA

Las Mercedes, 31, 4º Depto. 4 y 5
48930 Las Arenas-Getxo (Vizcaya)
☎: 944 315 872 - Fax: 944 315 875
info@ardoa.com
www.ardoa.com

AGA 2007 T
tempranillo 85%, cabernet sauvignon 10%, merlot 5%

**84**

AZCÚNAGA 2006 TC
tempranillo 85%, cabernet sauvignon 10%, merlot 5%

**84**

AZCÚNAGA SELECCIÓN PRIVADA 2001 TR
cabernet sauvignon 100%

**83**

## ARISTU

Ctra. N-240 Pamplona-Saca, km. 35
31440 Lumbier (Navarra)
☎: 948 398 098 - Fax: 948 880 290
baristu@teleline.es

ARISTU GARNACHA 2008 RD

**87** Colour: raspberry rose. Nose: fresh fruit, red berry notes, floral, expressive. Palate: flavourful, fresh, fruity.

MAZTEGI GARNACHA 2007 T

**84**

CAMPO MENDARTE 2007 T

**78**

ARISTU GARNACHA 2005 T

**78**

ARISTU 2004 TC
tempranillo, garnacha

**83**

ARISTU 2002 TR

**85** Colour: light cherry, bright ochre rim. Nose: fruit preserve, toasty, spicy, woody. Palate: light-bodied, harsh oak tannins, lacks fruit, good acidity.

## ARMENDARIZ

Avda. El Salvador, 11-Bajo
31370 Falces (Navarra)
☎: 948 734 135 - Fax: 948 714 902
josepueyo@teleline.es

ARMENDARIZ 2008 RD
garnacha 80%, tempranillo 20%

**82**

ARMENDARIX 2008 T JOVEN
tempranillo 80%, garnacha 20%

**78**

DON JUAN
JUANRON
VALDESANJUAN

## AROA BODEGAS

Apalaz 13
31292 Zurukoain (Navarra)
☎: 948 555 394 - Fax: 948 555 395
info@aroawines.com
www.aroawines.com

AROA TEMPRANILLO 2008 T
tempranillo 100%

## 77

OTARE 2007 TC

## 81

AROA DEIERRI 2006 T
merlot 40%, cabernet sauvignon 35%, tempranillo 25%

**88** Colour: very deep cherry. Nose: macerated fruit, dried flowers, spicy, cocoa bean, creamy oak. Palate: slightly dry, soft tannins, fruity, balanced, good acidity, great length.

AROA JAUNA 2005 TC
cabernet sauvignon 50%, merlot 40%, tempranillo 10%

**86** Colour: cherry, garnet rim. Nose: fruit liqueur notes, toasty. Palate: rich, fruity, pruney, sweet tannins.

OTARE 2005 TC

**86** Colour: cherry, garnet rim. Nose: ripe fruit, fruit liqueur notes, dark chocolate, toasty. Palate: spicy, long, round tannins.

AROA GORENA 2004 TR
cabernet sauvignon 70%, tempranillo 30%

**89** Colour: cherry, garnet rim. Nose: powerful, warm, varietal, scrubland, ripe fruit. Palate: flavourful, powerful, fleshy, spicy, round tannins.

## ASENSIO VIÑEDOS Y BODEGAS

Mayor, 84
31293 Sesma (Navarra)
☎: 948 698 078 - Fax: 948 698 097
info@bodegasasensio.com

JAVIER ASENSIO 2008 B
moscatel 50%, chardonnay 50%

**87** Colour: pale. Nose: fresh fruit, honeyed notes, citrus fruit. Palate: flavourful, fruity, fresh.

JAVIER ASENSIO 2008 RD
merlot 60%, tempranillo 40%

## 79

JAVIER ASENSIO CABERNET SAUVIGNON 2005 TR
cabernet sauvignon 100%

**89** Colour: dark-red cherry, garnet rim. Nose: ripe fruit, green pepper, elegant, sweet spices. Palate: fruity, powerful, good acidity, round tannins.

JAVIER ASENSIO MERLOT 2005 TR
merlot 100%

**86** Colour: cherry, garnet rim. Nose: powerful, fruit liqueur notes, fruit preserve, sweet spices.

JAVIER ASENSIO 2005 TC
tempranillo 50%, merlot 30%, cabernet sauvignon 20%

**85** Colour: cherry, garnet rim. Nose: powerful, fruit preserve, toasty. Palate: flavourful, powerful, fleshy.

JAVIER ASENSIO 2004 TR
merlot 75%, tempranillo 25%

**88** Colour: cherry, garnet rim. Nose: powerful, fruit liqueur notes, toasty, new oak. Palate: flavourful, powerful, fleshy, round tannins.

## AZUL Y GARANZA BODEGAS

San Juan, 19
31310 Carcastillo (Navarra)
☎: 659 857 979 - Fax: 948 725 677
info@azulygaranza.com
www.azulygaranza.com

ROSA DE AZUL Y GARANZA 2008 RD

**85** Colour: light cherry. Nose: fruit preserve, violet drops, expressive. Palate: unctuous, fruity, flavourful, correct.

ABRIL DE AZUL Y GARANZA 2008 T

**86** Colour: cherry, purple rim. Nose: powerful, balsamic herbs, grassy. Palate: flavourful, fruity, fresh.

SEIS DE AZUL Y GARANZA 2007 T

**88** Colour: cherry, garnet rim. Nose: fragrant herbs, ripe fruit, dark chocolate. Palate: flavourful, powerful, fleshy, round tannins.

DESIERTO DE AZUL Y GARANZA 2006 T

## 84

## BODEGA COSECHEROS REUNIDOS

Plaza San Antón, 1
31390 Olite (Navarra)
☎: 948 740 067 - Fax: 948 740 067

cosecheros@ucan.es
www.winenzezen.com

**VIÑA JUGUERA 2008 RD**
garnacha

**83**

**SECRETUM LEONARDI 2007 T**
tempranillo, garnacha, merlot

**83**

**VIÑA JUGUERA 2005 TC**
tempranillo, garnacha, merlot

**85** Colour: very deep cherry, garnet rim. Nose: ripe fruit, spicy, creamy oak, dark chocolate. Palate: fruity, flavourful, round tannins, balanced.

## BODEGA DE SADA

Arrabal, 2
31491 Sada (Navarra)
☎: 948 877 013 - Fax: 948 877 433
bodega@bodegadesada.com
www.bodegadesada.com

**PALACIO DE SADA 2008 RD**
garnacha 100%

**83**

**PALACIO DE SADA GARNACHA 2008 T**
garnacha 100%

**84**

**PALACIO DE SADA 2005 TC**
garnacha 90%, tempranillo 5%, cabernet sauvignon 5%  HHHHH5,5€

**86** Colour: cherry, garnet rim. Nose: fruit preserve, toasty, sweet spices, aromatic coffee. Palate: flavourful, powerful, spicy.

## BODEGA DE SARRÍA

Finca Señorío de Sarría, s/n
31100 Puente La Reina (Navarra)
☎: 948 202 200 - Fax: 948 202 202
info@bodegadesarria.com
www.bodegadesarria.com

**SEÑORÍO DE SARRÍA VIÑEDO Nº 3 2008 BFB**
chardonnay 100%

**87** Colour: bright straw. Nose: ripe fruit, creamy oak, aged wood nuances. Palate: rich, fruity, smoky aftertaste.

**SEÑORÍO DE SARRÍA CHARDONNAY 2008 B**
chardonnay 100%

**83**

**SEÑORÍO DE SARRÍA VIÑEDO Nº 5 2008 RD**
garnacha 100%

**89** Colour: light cherry. Nose: powerful, ripe fruit, red berry notes, floral, expressive. Palate: fleshy, powerful, fruity, fresh.

**SEÑORÍO DE SARRÍA 2008 RD**
garnacha 100%

**84**

**SEÑORÍO DE SARRÍA 2006 TC**
tempranillo

**85** Colour: deep cherry, garnet rim. Nose: ripe fruit, scrubland, spicy, dark chocolate. Palate: flavourful, round tannins, spicy.

**SEÑORÍO DE SARRÍA VIÑEDO Nº 7 GRACIANO 2005 T**
garnacha 100%

**88** Colour: cherry, garnet rim. Nose: balsamic herbs, scrubland, ripe fruit, sweet spices, dark chocolate. Palate: flavourful, fleshy, ripe fruit.

**SEÑORÍO DE SARRÍA VIÑEDO Nº 8 2005 T**
mazuelo 100%

**83**

**SEÑORÍO DE SARRÍA VIÑEDO Nº 4 2005 T**
merlot 100%

**81**

**SEÑORÍO DE SARRIA RESERVA ESPECIAL 2004 TR**
cabernet sauvignon

**89** Colour: black cherry, orangey edge. Nose: ripe fruit, cocoa bean, dark chocolate, sweet spices, creamy oak. Palate: fleshy, flavourful, powerful.

**SEÑORÍO DE SARRÍA MOSCATEL 2008 B DULCE**
moscatel 100%

**90** Colour: bright straw. Nose: powerful, candied fruit, honeyed notes, floral. Palate: flavourful, ripe fruit, sweet, good acidity.

**SEÑORÍO DE SARRÍA MOSCATEL 2007 BLANCO DULCE**
moscatel grano menudo

**90** Colour: bright yellow. Nose: expressive, balanced, varietal, fruit preserve, floral. Palate: flavourful, powerful, fleshy, fresh.

## BODEGA INURRIETA

Carretera Falces-Miranda de Arga, Km.30
31370 Falces (Navarra)
☎: 948 737 309 - Fax: 948 737 310
info@bodegainurrieta.com
www.bodegainurrieta.com

**INURRIETA ORCHÍDEA 2008 B**
chardonnay 85%, viura 15%

**90** Colour: yellow. Nose: ripe fruit, characterful, lees reduction notes, dried herbs. Palate: round, fruity, flavourful, fine bitter notes.

**INURRIETA ORCHÍDEA 2007 B**
chardonnay 85%, viura 15%

**90** Colour: bright straw. Nose: powerful, ripe fruit, sweet spices, cocoa bean. Palate: flavourful, fleshy, fruity, good acidity.

**INURRIETA MEDIODÍA 2008 RD**
garnacha 85%, merlot 10%, cabernet sauvignon 5%

**87** Colour: rose, purple rim. Nose: powerful, ripe fruit, red berry notes. Palate: flavourful, fruity, fresh.

**INURRIETA "SUR" 2007 T**
garnacha 50%, graciano 50%

**88** Colour: cherry, purple rim. Nose: expressive, lactic notes, red berry notes. Palate: flavourful, fruity, fresh.

**INURRIETA NORTE 2007 T**
cabernet sauvignon 50%, merlot 50%

**86** Colour: cherry, garnet rim. Nose: powerful, ripe fruit, red berry notes, creamy oak, toasty. Palate: flavourful, ripe fruit, round tannins.

**INURRIETA CUATROCIENTOS 2006 TC**
cabernet sauvignon 50%, merlot 25%, garnacha 25%

**87** Colour: cherry, garnet rim. Nose: powerful, ripe fruit, fine reductive notes, toasty, dark chocolate. Palate: flavourful, spicy, round tannins.

**LADERAS DE INURRIETA 2005 T**
graciano 100%

**90** Colour: cherry, garnet rim. Nose: powerful, ripe fruit, toasty, new oak, dark chocolate. Palate: flavourful, powerful, fleshy, round tannins.

**ALTOS DE INURRIETA 2006 TR**
cabernet sauvignon 50%, graciano 25%, garnacha 25%

**89** Colour: deep cherry, garnet rim. Nose: ripe fruit, tobacco, fine reductive notes. Palate: full, good acidity, fruity, powerful, slightly dry, soft tannins.

## BODEGA MÁXIMO ABETE

Ctra. Estella-Sangüesa, km. 43,5
31495 San Martín de Unx (Navarra)
☎: 948 738 330 - Fax: 948 738 343
info@bodegasmaximoabete.com
www.bodegasmaximoabete.com

**GUERINDA 2008 B**
chardonnay 100%

**82**

**CASTILLO DE SAN MARTÍN DE UNX 2008 B**
chardonnay 70%, viura 30%

**78**

**CASTILLO DE SAN MARTÍN DE UNX 2008 RD**
garnacha 100%

**82**

**GUERINDA 2008 RD**
garnacha 100%

**80**

CASTILLO DE SAN MARTÍN DE UNX 2008 T
tempranillo 55%, garnacha 45%

**77**

GUERINDA 2007 T ROBLE
garnacha 25%, tempranillo 25%, cabernet sauvignon 25%, merlot 25%

**84**

GUERINDA GRACINO SELECCIÓN 2007 T
graciano 100%

**83**

GUERINDA 2006 TC
garnacha, cabernet sauvignon, merlot

**85** Colour: deep cherry, garnet rim. Nose: fruit preserve, spicy, new oak. Palate: fruity, flavourful, round tannins.

CASTILLO DE SAN MARTÍN DE UNX 2005 TC
tempranillo 50%, merlot 30%, graciano 20%

**87** Colour: cherry, garnet rim. Nose: powerful, fruit preserve, fruit liqueur notes, toasty, sweet spices. Palate: flavourful, powerful, round tannins.

## BODEGA NUESTRA SEÑORA DEL ROMERO S.C.

Ctra. de Tarazona, 33 Apdo. de Correos, 24
31520 Cascante (Navarra)
☎: 948 851 411 - Fax: 948 844 504
info@bodegasdelromero.com
www.bodegasdelromero.com

MALÓN DE ECHAIDE VIURA 2008 B
viura 100%

**87** Colour: bright straw. Nose: fresh, fresh fruit, white flowers, expressive. Palate: flavourful, fruity, good acidity, balanced.

MALÓN DE ECHAIDE GARNACHA 2008 RD
garnacha 100%

**84**

MALÓN DE ECHAIDE TEMPRANILLO 2008 T
tempranillo 100%

**80**

MALÓN DE ECHAIDE GARNACHA VIEJA 2008 T
garnacha 100%

**78**

TORRECILLA 2008 T
tempranillo 70%, garnacha 30%

**78**

MALÓN DE ECHAIDE 2005 TC
tempranillo 80%, cabernet sauvignon 15%

**84**

TORRECILLA 2004 TC
tempranillo 85%, cabernet sauvignon 15%

**78**

PLANDENAS 2002 TR
tempranillo 80%, garnacha 10%, cabernet sauvignon 10%

**80**

MALÓN DE ECHAIDE CABERNET SAUVIGNON 2001 TR
cabernet sauvignon 100%

**86** Colour: deep cherry, orangey edge. Nose: fruit liqueur notes, sweet spices, aromatic coffee, tobacco. Palate: rich, fruity, good acidity, harsh oak tannins.

MALÓN DE ECHAIDE MERLOT 2001 TR
merlot 100%

**84**

SEÑOR DE CASCANTE 2000 TGR
tempranillo 85%, cabernet sauvignon 15%

**82**

## BODEGA OTAZU

Señorío de Otazu, s/n
31174 Echauri (Navarra)
☎: 948 329 200 - Fax: 948 329 353
otazu@otazu.com
www.otazu.com

PALACIO DE OTAZU CHARDONNAY 2007 B
chardonnay 100%

**88** Colour: bright straw. Nose: fresh, varietal, floral, grassy. Palate: flavourful, fruity, fresh, good acidity.

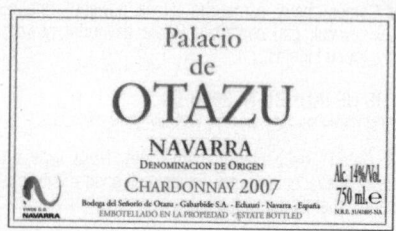

### PALACIO DE OTAZU CHARDONNAY 2006 BFB
chardonnay 100%

**90** Colour: bright yellow. Nose: powerful, ripe fruit, sweet spices, creamy oak, fragrant herbs, elegant. Palate: rich, smoky aftertaste, flavourful, fresh, good acidity.

### PALACIO DE OTAZU 2008 RD
merlot 100%

**86** Colour: rose, purple rim. Nose: fresh fruit, red berry notes, medium intensity. Palate: fruity, fleshy, fresh, flavourful.

### PALACIO DE OTAZU 2006 TC
tempranillo, merlot, cabernet sauvignon

**91** Colour: cherry, garnet rim. Nose: ripe fruit, spicy, creamy oak, toasty, complex, mineral. Palate: powerful, flavourful, toasty, round tannins.

### PALACIO DE OTAZU BERQUERA 2005 TR
tempranillo, merlot, cabernet sauvignon

**88** Colour: deep cherry. Nose: powerful, ripe fruit, sweet spices, toasty. Palate: flavourful, powerful, fleshy, ripe fruit.

### PALACIO DE OTAZU ALTAR 2004 TC
cabernet sauvignon, tempranillo

**92** Colour: cherry, garnet rim. Nose: medium intensity, ripe fruit, new oak, toasty, mineral. Palate: flavourful, ripe fruit, long, round tannins.

PALACIO DE
**OTAZU**
ALTAR

## BODEGA PAGO DE CIRSUS

Ctra. de Ablitas a Ribaforada, km. 5
31523 Ablitas (Navarra)
☎: 948 386 210 - Fax: 629 354 190
bodegasin@pagodecirsus.com
www.pagodecirsus.com

### PAGO DE CIRSUS CHARDONNAY 2008 B
chardonnay 100%

**87** Colour: bright straw. Nose: powerful, varietal, ripe fruit, citrus fruit. Palate: flavourful, fruity, fresh, fleshy.

### PAGO DE CIRSUS CHARDONNAY 2007 BFB
chardonnay 100%

**90** Colour: yellow. Nose: ripe fruit, pattiserie, creamy oak, characterful. Palate: round, unctuous, powerful, smoky aftertaste.

### PAGO DE CIRSUS MOSCATEL 2006 BFB
moscatel 100%

**92** Colour: golden. Nose: powerful, floral, honeyed notes, candied fruit, fragrant herbs. Palate: flavourful, sweet, fresh, fruity, good acidity, long.

### PAGO DE CIRSUS MOSCATEL VENDIMIA TARDÍA 2006 BFB
moscatel 100%

**90** Colour: bright yellow. Nose: fruit liqueur notes, candied fruit, honeyed notes, warm. Palate: sweet, fleshy, rich, good acidity.

### PAGO DE CIRSUS DE IÑAKI NUÑEZ VENDIMIA SELECCIONADA 2006 TC
tempranillo 55%, merlot 25%, cabernet sauvignon 20%

**89** Colour: bright cherry. Nose: ripe fruit, sweet spices, creamy oak, expressive. Palate: flavourful, fruity, toasty, round tannins.

### PAGO DE CIRSUS DE IÑAKI NÚÑEZ SELECCIÓN DE FAMILIA 2005 T
tempranillo 60%, merlot 25%, cabernet sauvignon 15%

**91** Colour: very deep cherry, garnet rim. Nose: ripe fruit, floral, elegant, sweet spices, warm. Palate: full, fleshy, fruity, round tannins.

### PAGO DE CIRSUS DE IÑAKI NÚÑEZ CUVEE ESPECIAL 2004 TR
tempranillo 40%, cabernet sauvignon 35%, merlot 25%

**87** Colour: cherry, garnet rim. Nose: powerful, ripe fruit, balsamic herbs, toasty, aged wood nuances. Palate: flavourful, powerful, fleshy, slightly dry, soft tannins.

## BODEGA SAN SALVADOR

Ctra. de Allo, 102
31243 Arróniz (Navarra)
☎: 948 537 128 - Fax: 948 537 662
galcibar.produccion@consebro.com

CASTIL HARRIA 2008 B

**85** Colour: bright straw. Nose: medium intensity, fresh, floral, ripe fruit, grassy. Palate: fruity, varietal, flavourful.

GALCÍBAR 2008 B
**82**

CASTILUZAR 2008 B
viura
**80**

CASTILUZAR 2008 RD

**85** Colour: brilliant rose. Nose: medium intensity, fresh, fresh fruit. Palate: good acidity, fruity, flavourful.

CASTIL HARRIA 2008 RD

**85** Colour: brilliant rose. Nose: red berry notes, dried flowers, expressive. Palate: flavourful, fruity, fresh.

GALCÍBAR RD
**83**

CASTILUZAR 2008 T
**83**

CASTIL HARRIA 2008 T
**81**

GALCÍBAR 2007 T
tempranillo
**82**

GALCÍBAR 2005 TC
tempranillo

**88** Colour: deep cherry, garnet rim. Nose: ripe fruit, earthy notes, complex, sweet spices, aromatic coffee. Palate: flavourful, unctuous, pruney, sweet tannins.

CASTILUZAR 2005 TC

**86** Colour: cherry, garnet rim. Nose: medium intensity, balsamic herbs, scrubland, ripe fruit. Palate: flavourful, spicy.

VIÑA ARNATA

## BODEGA VIÑAS DEL CAMINO

Avda. de los Fueros, 18
31522 Monteagudo (Navarra)
☎: 948 843 102 - Fax: 948 843 161
bodegadelcamino@bodegadelcamino.com
www.bodegadelcamino.com

CONDE DE ARTOIZ VIURA 2008 B
viura 100%
**79**

CONDE DE ARTOIZ ROSADO DE LÁGRIMA 2008 RD
garnacha 100%

**87** Colour: rose, purple rim. Nose: raspberry, red berry notes. Palate: flavourful, fruity, fresh, varietal.

CONDE DE ARTOIZ 2007 T
tempranillo 80%, garnacha 20%
**77**

CONDE DE ARTOIZ 2003 TC
tempranillo 80%, merlot 20%
**81**

PEDRO DE IVAR PRESTIGIO 2001 T
garnacha 60%, tempranillo 40%

**89** Colour: cherry, garnet rim. Nose: spicy, toasty, dark chocolate. Palate: flavourful, powerful, fleshy.

PEDRO DE IVAR 2001 TR
tempranillo 60%, merlot 40%

**85** Colour: deep cherry, bright ochre rim. Nose: fruit liqueur notes, spicy, sweet spices, tobacco. Palate: light-bodied, harsh oak tannins, spirituous.

## BODEGA Y VIÑAS VALDELARES

Ctra. Eje del Ebro, Km. 60
31579 Carcar (Navarra)
☎: 656 849 602 - Fax: 948 674 198
valdelares@terra.es
www.valdelares.com

VALDELARES CHARDONNAY 2008 B
**77**

VALDELARES 2008 RD

**85** Colour: brilliant rose. Nose: fresh, expressive, red berry notes. Palate: good acidity, fruity, fresh, easy to drink.

VALDELARES 2008 T

**87** Colour: cherry, garnet rim. Nose: expressive, red berry notes, ripe fruit. Palate: flavourful, fruity, fresh.

VALDELARES ALTA EXPRESIÓN 2007 T

**89** Colour: deep cherry. Nose: dark chocolate, sweet spices, caramel, ripe fruit. Palate: fleshy, powerful, flavourful, toasty.

VALDELARES 2006 TC

**84**

VALDELARES DULCE 2008 BLANCO DULCE

**81**

## BODEGAS 1877

Brisol 16 bis
28230 Las Rozas (Madrid)
☎: 917 104 880 - Fax: 916 343 830
federicol@swd.es
www.swd.es

MARQUÉS DE LUZ 2006 TC
merlot 80%, cabernet sauvignon 20%

**83**

## BODEGAS AYERRA

Ctra. de Olite, km. 2,5
31495 San Martín de Unx (Navarra)
☎: 948 738 190 - Fax: 948 730 198
bodegasayerra@yahoo.es
www.bodegasayerra.es

AYERRA LÁGRIMA 2008 RD
garnacha 100%

**85** Colour: rose, purple rim. Nose: red berry notes, floral. Palate: flavourful, fruity, fresh.

AYERRA JOVEN 2008 T
tempranillo 100%

**80**

AYERRA 2005 TR
tempranillo 33%, merlot 33%, cabernet sauvignon 33%

**87** Colour: deep cherry, garnet rim. Nose: fruit preserve, spicy, creamy oak, toasty. Palate: fruity, balanced, flavourful, round tannins.

AYERRA 2005 TC
tempranillo 33%, merlot 33%, cabernet sauvignon 33%

**84**

## BODEGAS AZPEA

Camino Itúrbero, s/n
31440 Lumbier (Navarra)
☎: 948 880 433 - Fax: 948 880 433
info@bodegasazpea.com
www.bodegasazpea.com

AZPEA JOVEN 2006 T

**77**

AZPEA SELECCIÓN 2005 T

**87** Colour: cherry, garnet rim. Nose: powerful, fruit liqueur notes, toasty, spicy. Palate: flavourful, ripe fruit, spicy.

AZPEA GARNACHA 2006

**81**

AZPEA VINO DULCE DE MOSCATEL 2006 BLANCO DULCE

**93** Colour: bright straw. Nose: powerful, varietal, candied fruit, citrus fruit, honeyed notes. Palate: flavourful, sweet, ripe fruit, good acidity.

## BODEGAS BERAMENDI

Ctra. Tafalla s/n
31495 San Martín de Unx (Navarra)
☎: 948 738 262 - Fax: 948 738 080
info@bodegasberamendi.com
www.bodegasberamendi.com

3F 2008 B
chardonnay 50%, moscatel 50%

**86** Colour: pale. Nose: floral, fresh fruit, expressive, grassy, honeyed notes. Palate: flavourful, fruity, fresh.

3F 2008 RD
garnacha 100%

**87** Colour: rose, purple rim. Nose: powerful, ripe fruit, floral. Palate: flavourful, fleshy, good acidity.

BERAMENDI

## BODEGAS CAMILO CASTILLA

Santa Bárbara, 40
31591 Corella (Navarra)
☎: 948 780 006 - Fax: 948 780 515

info@bodegascamilocastilla.com
www.bodegascamilocastilla.com

**PINK 2008 RD**
garnacha 100%

**87** Colour: rose, purple rim. Nose: powerful, ripe fruit, red berry notes. Palate: fruity, flavourful, fresh, fine bitter notes.

**MONTECRISTO MOSCATEL 2008 B DULCE**

**87** Colour: bright straw. Nose: ripe fruit, honeyed notes, expressive. Palate: creamy, fresh, sweet, long.

**CAPRICHO DE GOYA VINO DE LICOR**
moscatel 100%                                               22€

**91** Colour: old gold, amber rim. Nose: dry nuts, candied fruit, powerfull, sun-drenched nuances. Palate: powerful, full, good acidity, long.

RAYO DE SOL

## BODEGAS CAMPOS DE ENANZO

Mayor, 189
31521 Murchante (Navarra)
☎: 948 838 030 - Fax: 948 838 677
export@camposenanzo.com
www.camposenanzo.com

**BASIANO TEMPRANILLO 2008 T**

**86** Colour: deep cherry, purple rim. Nose: ripe fruit, warm, floral. Palate: fleshy, flavourful, fruity, good acidity, good finish.

**ENANZO TEMPRANILLO 2008 T**
tempranillo

**85** Colour: cherry, purple rim. Nose: powerful, varietal, ripe fruit, red berry notes. Palate: flavourful, fruity, fresh.

**REMONTE TEMPRANILLO 2008 T**
**83**

**ENANZO 2003 TC**
**84**

**REMONTE 2003 TC**
**83**

**REMONTE 2002 TR**

**88** Colour: deep cherry, orangey edge. Nose: fruit liqueur notes, aromatic coffee, cedar wood, expressive, complex. Palate: fine tannins, flavourful, good acidity, balanced.

**ENANZO 2002 TR**

**85** Colour: deep cherry, orangey edge. Nose: fruit liqueur notes, aromatic coffee, toasty. Palate: spicy, easy to drink, flavourful, soft tannins.

**REMONTE TEMPRANILLO 2006**
**83**

## BODEGAS CORELLANAS

Santa Bárbara, 29
31591 Corellana (Navarra)
☎: 948 780 029 - Fax: 948 781 542
jdaniel@bodegascorellanas.com
www.bodegascorellanas.com

**VIÑA RUBICÁN 2008 B**
viura 60%, moscatel 40
**80**

**VIÑA RUBICÁN TEMPRANILLO 2007 T**
tempranillo 100%
**83**

**VIÑA RUBICÁN UNICO 2005 T**
garnacha 85%, tempranillo 15%
**83**

**VIÑA RUBICÁN 2005 TC**
tempranillo 85%, cabernet sauvignon 15%
**83**

**VIÑA RUBICÁN 2003 TR**
cabernet sauvignon 33%, merlot 33%, tempranillo 33%

**85** Colour: deep cherry, garnet rim. Nose: ripe fruit, sweet spices, balanced, aromatic coffee. Palate: flavourful, fruity, round tannins, spicy.

**SARASATE EXPRESION 2008 BLANCO DULCE**

**88** Colour: bright straw. Nose: honeyed notes, overripe fruit. Palate: fleshy, sweet, good acidity.

CASTILLO DE BLENDO

## BODEGAS FINCA ALBRET

Ctra. Cadreita-Villafranca, s/n
31515 Cadreita (Navarra)
☎: 948 406 806 - Fax: 948 406 699
info@fincaalbret.com
www.fincaalbret.com

## ALBRET CHARDONNAY 2008 B
chardonnay 100%

**89** Colour: bright straw. Nose: ripe fruit, expressive, varietal, pattiserie, creamy oak. Palate: elegant, creamy, rich, fruity.

## ALBRET 2005 TC
tempranillo 50%, merlot 20%, cabernet sauvignon 30%

**83**

## ALBRET LA VIÑA DE MI MADRE 2004 TR
cabernet sauvignon 95%, merlot 5%

**91** Colour: cherry, garnet rim. Nose: powerful, ripe fruit, red berry notes, sweet spices, new oak. Palate: flavourful, fruity, fleshy, spicy, round tannins.

## ALBRET 2004 TR
tempranillo 85%, cabernet sauvignon 10%, merlot 5%

**88** Colour: deep cherry, garnet rim. Nose: ripe fruit, spicy, new oak, cocoa bean. Palate: unctuous, fruity, smoky aftertaste, toasty, round tannins, elegant.

## BODEGAS ITURBIDE

Término la Torre, s/n
31350 Peralta (Navarra)
☎: 948 750 537 - Fax: 647 742 368
bodegasiturbide@bodegasiturbide.com
www.bodegasiturbide.com

### 9 NOVEM 2008 RD
garnacha 100%

**84**

### 9 NOVEM SELECCIÓN 2007 T
garnacha 70%, tempranillo 30%

**85** Colour: cherry, garnet rim. Nose: ripe fruit, fruit preserve, dark chocolate, caramel. Palate: powerful, sweetness, fleshy.

### NOVEM 2007 T
tempranillo 60%, garnacha 30%, cabernet sauvignon 10%

**83**

## BODEGAS JULIÁN CHIVITE

Ribera, 34
31592 Cintruénigo (Navarra)
☎: 948 811 000 - Fax: 948 811 407
info@bodegaschivite.com
www.bodegaschivite.com

### GRAN FEUDO CHARDONNAY 2008 B
chardonnay

**90** Colour: bright straw. Nose: varietal, ripe fruit, citrus fruit, white flowers, fragrant herbs. Palate: flavourful, fruity, fresh, rich.

### GRAN FEUDO DULCE 2008 B
100% moscatel

**92** Colour: golden. Nose: powerful, floral, honeyed notes, fragrant herbs, fresh fruit. Palate: flavourful, sweet, fresh, fruity, good acidity, long.

### CHIVITE COLECCIÓN 125 VENDIMIA TARDÍA 2007 B
moscatel

**95** Colour: bright straw. Nose: powerful, ripe fruit, candied fruit, honeyed notes, sweet spices. Palate: flavourful, fleshy, sweet, good acidity.

### CHIVITE COLECCIÓN 125 2007 BFB

**91** Colour: bright straw. Nose: powerful, ripe fruit, citrus fruit, sweet spices, cocoa bean, toasty. Palate: flavourful, fleshy, ripe fruit, good acidity.

### GRAN FEUDO 2008 RD

**90** Colour: rose, purple rim. Nose: fresh fruit, red berry notes, floral. Palate: flavourful, fruity, fresh, good acidity.

### GRAN FEUDO "SOBRE LÍAS" 2007 RD
tempranillo, garnacha, merlot

**90** Colour: onion pink. Nose: elegant, candied fruit, dried flowers, fragrant herbs, red berry notes, sweet spices. Palate: flavourful, good acidity, long, spicy.

### CHIVITE COLECCIÓN 125 2006 RD

**92** Colour: raspberry rose. Nose: elegant, expressive, red berry notes, fragrant herbs. Palate: flavourful, fleshy, ripe fruit, good acidity, fine bitter notes.

### GRAN FEUDO 2006 TC

**88** Colour: cherry, garnet rim. Nose: ripe fruit, spicy, creamy oak, toasty, complex, earthy notes. Palate: powerful, flavourful, toasty, round tannins.

### CHIVITE COLECCIÓN 125 2005 TR

**92** Colour: deep cherry, garnet rim. Nose: powerful, toasty, dark chocolate, aromatic coffee, ripe fruit. Palate: flavourful, powerful, fleshy, fine bitter notes, round tannins.

### GRAN FEUDO 2005 TR

**88** Colour: cherry, garnet rim. Nose: ripe fruit, spicy, creamy oak, toasty, complex, old leather. Palate: powerful, flavourful, toasty, round tannins.

**GRAN FEUDO VIÑAS VIEJAS 2005 TR**

**88** Colour: cherry, garnet rim. Nose: ripe fruit, spicy, creamy oak, complex, earthy notes. Palate: powerful, flavourful, toasty, round tannins.

## BODEGAS LEZAUN

Egiarte, 1
31292 Lakar (Navarra)
☎: 948 541 339 - Fax: 948 536 055
info@lezaun.com
www.lezaun.com

**EGIARTE ROSADO 2008 RD**
garnacha 100%

**84**

**LEZAUN TEMPRANILLO 2008 T**
tempranillo 100%

**85** Colour: deep cherry, purple rim. Nose: ripe fruit, red berry notes, varietal, expressive. Palate: rich, fruity, flavourful, grainy tannins, fine bitter notes.

**LEZAUN EGIARTE 2008 T**
tempranillo 70%, merlot 30%

**76**

**LEZAUN GAZAGA 2007 T**
tempranillo 60%, cabernet sauvignon 25%, merlot 15%

**89** Colour: deep cherry, brick rim edge. Nose: fruit preserve, fragrant herbs, balsamic herbs, cocoa bean, sweet spices. Palate: fruity, flavourful, balanced, elegant, slightly dry, soft tannins, warm.

**EGIARTE 2006 TC**
tempranillo, cabernet sauvignon, merlot

**84**

**LEZAUN 2006 TC**
tempranillo 50%, cabernet sauvignon 30%, merlot 20%

**83**

**EGIARTE MERLOT SELECCIÓN 2006 T**
merlot 100%

**78**

**LEZAUN 2004 TR**
garnacha 33%, graciano 33%, tempranillo 33%

**88** Colour: deep cherry, bright ochre rim. Nose: ripe fruit, floral, complex, sweet spices, cocoa bean. Palate: rich, fruity, good acidity, slightly dry, soft tannins.

**EGIARTE 2005 RESERVA**
tempranillo, cabernet sauvignon, merlot

**84**

## BODEGAS LOGOS

Sor Mónica de Jesús, 2
31522 Monteagudo (Navarra)
☎: 941 398 008 - Fax: 941 398 070

**LOGOS 2007 RD**
garnacha 100%

**83** Colour: raspberry rose. Nose: ripe fruit, warm, closed. Palate: unctuous, fruity, easy to drink.

**LOGOS II 2005 TC**
garnacha 40%, cabernet sauvignon 40%, tempranillo 20%

**85** Colour: cherry, garnet rim. Nose: fruit preserve, toasty, dark chocolate. Palate: fruity, round tannins, roasted-coffee aftertaste, toasty.

**LOGOS I 2004 T**
garnacha 40%, cabernet sauvignon 30%, tempranillo 30%

**90** Colour: bright cherry. Nose: ripe fruit, sweet spices, creamy oak, dark chocolate. Palate: flavourful, fruity, toasty, round tannins.

## BODEGAS MACAYA

Ctra. Berbinzana, 74
31251 Larraga (Navarra)
☎: 948 711 549 - Fax: 948 711 788
info@bodegasmacaya.com
www.bodegasmacaya.com

**CONDADO DE ALMARA FINCA LINTE 2008 T**

**83**

**CONDADO DE ALMARA SELECCIÓN 2007 T**

**82**

**CONDADO DE ALMARA 2005 TC**

**86** Colour: cherry, garnet rim. Nose: powerful, ripe fruit, spicy, toasty. Palate: flavourful, spicy, ripe fruit, round tannins.

**CONDADO DE ALMARA 2003 TR**

**88** Colour: cherry, garnet rim. Nose: powerful, ripe fruit, sweet spices. Palate: flavourful, fleshy, spicy, round tannins.

**ALMARA CABERNET SAUVIGNON 2004 RESERVA**

**89** Colour: dark-red cherry, garnet rim. Nose: fruit liqueur notes, sweet spices. Palate: rich, full, fruity, smoky aftertaste, slightly dry, soft tannins.

## BODEGAS OCHOA

Alcalde Maillata, 2
31390 Olite (Navarra)
☎: 948 740 006 - Fax: 948 740 048
info@bodegasochoa.com
www.bodegasochoa.com

**OCHOA VIURA-CHARDONNAY 2008 B**
viura 70%, chardonnay 23%, moscatel 7%

**86** Colour: pale. Nose: fresh fruit, citrus fruit, floral. Palate: flavourful, fresh, fruity, easy to drink.

**MOSCATO DE OCHOA 2007 B**
moscatel 100%

**87** Colour: pale. Nose: medium intensity, varietal, citrus fruit, fresh fruit. Palate: fruity, fresh, sweetness, good acidity, fine bead.

**OCHOA MOSCATEL 2007 BLANCO DULCE**
moscatel 100%

**88** Colour: straw, pale. Nose: grapey, honeyed notes, white flowers. Palate: sweetness, flavourful, powerful, long.

**OCHOA ROSADO DE LÁGRIMA 2008 RD**
garnacha 50%, cabernet sauvignon 50%

**89** Colour: onion pink. Nose: elegant, candied fruit, dried flowers, fragrant herbs, red berry notes. Palate: light-bodied, flavourful, good acidity, long, spicy.

**OCHOA GARNACHA 2008 RD**
garnacha 100%

**86** Colour: light cherry. Nose: fresh fruit, expressive, dried flowers. Palate: fruity, flavourful, good finish, round.

**OCHOA GRACIANO-GARNACHA 2006 T**
graciano 50%, garnacha 50%

**88** Colour: deep cherry, garnet rim. Nose: ripe fruit, creamy oak, sweet spices, expressive. Palate: flavourful, fruity, slightly dry, soft tannins.

**OCHOA MIL GRACIAS 2006 TC**
graciano 100%

**83**

**OCHOA TEMPRANILLO 2005 TC**
tempranillo 100%

**86** Colour: cherry, garnet rim. Nose: sweet spices, new oak. Palate: flavourful, fruity, good acidity, round tannins.

**OCHOA MERLOT 2005 TC**
merlot 100%

**85** Colour: deep cherry, brick rim edge. Nose: ripe fruit, toasty, dark chocolate. Palate: pruney, flavourful, round tannins.

**OCHOA 2002 TR**
tempranillo 55%, cabernet sauvignon 30%, merlot 15%

**88** Colour: pale ruby, brick rim edge. Nose: elegant, ripe fruit, aromatic coffee. Palate: flavourful, spicy, round tannins.

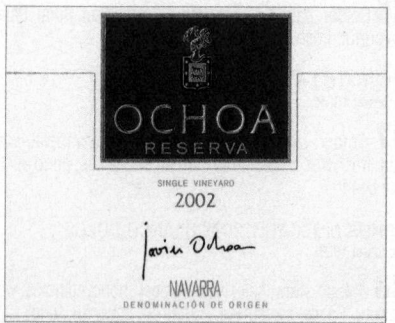

## OCHOA VENDIMIA SELECCIONADA 2001 TR
cabernet sauvignon 50%, merlot 50%

**90** Colour: cherry, garnet rim. Nose: powerful, fruit liqueur notes, spicy, aromatic coffee. Palate: flavourful, powerful, spicy, ripe fruit, long.

## BODEGAS ORVALAIZ

Ctra. Pamplona-Logroño s/n
31151 Obanos (Navarra)
☎: 948 344 437 - Fax: 948 344 401
bodega@orvalaiz.es
www.orvalaiz.es

**VIÑA ORVALAIZ 2008 B**
viura 90%, malvasia 10%

**83**

**ORVALAIZ ROSADO DE LÁGRIMA 2008 RD**
cabernet sauvignon 100%

**83**

**VIÑA ORVALAIZ 2008 T**
tempranillo 75%, cabernet sauvignon 25%

**83**

**ORVALAIZ GARNACHA 2007 T**
garnacha 100%

**87** Colour: bright cherry. Nose: ripe fruit, sweet spices, creamy oak, expressive. Palate: flavourful, fruity, toasty, round tannins.

**ORVALAIZ CABERNET SAUVIGNON 2007 T**
cabernet sauvignon 100%

**85** Colour: cherry, garnet rim. Nose: green pepper, medium intensity, spicy, aromatic coffee. Palate: spicy, ripe fruit, round tannins.

**ORVALAIZ TEMPRANILLO 2007 T**
tempranillo 100%

**85** Colour: cherry, garnet rim. Nose: powerful, expressive, ripe fruit, sweet spices. Palate: flavourful, ripe fruit, spicy, round tannins.

**ORVALAIZ MERLOT 2007 T ROBLE**
merlot 100%

**85** Colour: cherry, garnet rim. Nose: ripe fruit, scrubland, sweet spices. Palate: flavourful, spicy, ripe fruit.

**ORVALAIZ 2006 TC**
tempranillo 40%, cabernet sauvignon 30%, merlot 30%

**82**

**SEPTENTRIÓN 2005 TC**
tempranillo 85%, cabernet sauvignon 15%

**87** Colour: cherry, garnet rim. Nose: ripe fruit, fruit liqueur notes, toasty, dark chocolate. Palate: flavourful, fleshy, spicy, fine bitter notes.

SEPTENTRION

NAVARRA          crianza
                 2005

**ORVALAIZ 2004 TR**
tempranillo 50%, cabernet sauvignon 30%, merlot 20%

**88** Colour: very deep cherry, orangey edge. Nose: fruit preserve, toasty, creamy oak, dark chocolate, warm. Palate: good acidity, balanced, round tannins, fruity.

## BODEGAS PAGO DE LARRÁINZAR S.L.

Camino de la Corona s/n
31240 Ayegui (Navarra)
☎: 948 550 421 - Fax: 948 556 120
pagodelarrainzar@pagodelarrainzar.com
www.pagodelarrainzar.com

**PAGO DE LARRAINZAR 2006 T**
merlot 50%, cabernet sauvignon 30%, tempranillo 15%, garnacha 5%

**90** Colour: cherry, garnet rim. Nose: ripe fruit, spicy, creamy oak, toasty, complex. Palate: powerful, flavourful, toasty, round tannins, roasted-coffee aftertaste, mineral.

## BODEGAS PALACIO DE LA VEGA

Condesa de la Vega, s/n
31263 Dicastillo (Navarra)
☎: 948 527 009 - Fax: 948 527 333
cristina.perezganuza@pernod-ricard-espana.com
www.palaciodelavega.com

PALACIO DE LA VEGA CHARDONNAY 2008 BFB
**80**

PALACIO DE LA VEGA CHARDONNAY 2007 BFB
chardonnay 100%

**87** Colour: bright straw. Nose: fruit preserve, sweet spices, woody. Palate: rich, good acidity, smoky aftertaste, lacks fruit.

PALACIO DE LA VEGA CHARDONNAY 2007 B
chardonnay 100%

**86** Colour: yellow. Nose: fresh fruit, sweet spices, fresh, wild herbs. Palate: rich, fruity, easy to drink, flavourful.

PALACIO DE LA VEGA 2008 RD
cabernet sauvignon, garnacha

**86** Colour: brilliant rose. Nose: raspberry, red berry notes, floral, expressive. Palate: good acidity, fresh, fruity, fleshy.

PALACIO DE LA VEGA MERLOT 2004 TC
merlot 100%

**85** Colour: deep cherry, orangey edge. Nose: ripe fruit, sweet spices, aged wood nuances, creamy oak. Palate: creamy, long, spicy, good acidity, round tannins.

PALACIO DE LA VEGA CABERNET SAUVIGNON TEMPRANILLO 2004 TC
cabernet sauvignon, tempranillo

**85** Colour: deep cherry, bright ochre rim. Nose: ripe fruit, green pepper, sweet spices, balanced. Palate: light-bodied, fruity, sweetness, round tannins.

PALACIO DE LA VEGA CABERNET SAUVIGNON 2002 TR
cabernet sauvignon 100%

**85** Colour: pale ruby, brick rim edge. Nose: powerful, fruit liqueur notes, sweet spices. Palate: flavourful, spicy, ripe fruit.

CONDE DE LA VEGA DEL POZO 2002 TR
merlot, tempranillo, cabernet sauvignon

**85** Colour: deep cherry. Nose: powerful, fruit liqueur notes, toasty, dark chocolate. Palate: flavourful, spicy, round tannins.

## BODEGAS PRÍNCIPE DE VIANA

Mayor, 191
31521 Murchante (Navarra)
☎: 948 838 640 - Fax: 948 818 574
info@principedeviana.com
www.principedeviana.com

PRÍNCIPE DE VIANA CHARDONNAY 2008 B
chardonnay 100%
**84**

PRÍNCIPE DE VIANA VENDIMIA TARDÍA 2007 BFB
chardonnay 100%

**90** Colour: bright yellow. Nose: powerful, candied fruit, honeyed notes, citrus fruit. Palate: flavourful, fleshy, good acidity, ripe fruit.

PRÍNCIPE DE VIANA CABERNET SAUVIGNON 2008 RD
cabernet sauvignon 85%, merlot 15%

**87** Colour: light cherry. Nose: fresh fruit, red berry notes, lactic notes. Palate: fruity, fleshy, flavourful.

PRÍNCIPE DE VIANA GARNACHA 2008 RD
garnacha 100%
**79**

PRÍNCIPE DE VIANA 2006 TC
tempranillo 40%, merlot 30%, cabernet sauvignon 30%

**87** Colour: cherry, garnet rim. Nose: powerful, ripe fruit, spicy, toasty. Palate: flavourful, ripe fruit, spicy, long, round tannins.

PRÍNCIPE DE VIANA 2004 TR
tempranillo 60%, merlot 25%, cabernet sauvignon 15%

**88** Colour: cherry, garnet rim. Nose: powerful, ripe fruit, sweet spices. Palate: flavourful, powerful, ripe fruit, round tannins.

PRÍNCIPE DE VIANA 1423 2004 TR
tempranillo 75%, merlot 10%, cabernet sauvignon 10%, garnacha 5%

**88** Colour: cherry, garnet rim. Nose: powerful, fruit liqueur notes, sweet spices, wet leather. Palate: flavourful, spicy, ripe fruit.

## BODEGAS SAN MARTÍN

Ctra. de Sanguesa, s/n
31495 San Martín de Unx (Navarra)
☎: 948 738 294 - Fax: 948 738 297
admbodegasm@hotmail.com

**ILAGARES 2008 B**
viura 100%

**85** Colour: straw. Nose: medium intensity, varietal, ripe fruit, grassy. Palate: flavourful, fruity, great length.

**ILAGARES 2008 RD**
garnacha 100%

**81**

**ILAGARES 2008 T**
tempranillo 60%, garnacha 30%, merlot 10%, cabernet sauvignon %

**83**

**ALMA DE UNX 2006 T**
garnacha 100%

**85** Colour: deep cherry, garnet rim. Nose: macerated fruit, floral, varietal. Palate: warm, pruney, grainy tannins.

**SEÑORÍO DE UNX 2005 TC**
tempranillo 80%, garnacha 20%

**85** Colour: very deep cherry, garnet rim. Nose: fruit liqueur notes, spicy, creamy oak. Palate: flavourful, powerful, balanced, round tannins.

**SEÑORÍO DE UNX SELECCIÓN 2003 TR**
tempranillo 100%

**88** Colour: cherry, garnet rim. Nose: powerful, fruit liqueur notes, spicy, toasty. Palate: flavourful, fleshy, spicy, round tannins.

## BODEGAS URABAIN

Ctra. Estella, 21
31262 Allo (Navarra)
☎: 948 523 011 - Fax: 948 523 409
vinos@bodegasurabain.com
www.bodegasurabain.com

**F. URABAIN CHARDONNAY 2008 B**
chardonnay 100%

**87** Colour: bright straw. Nose: ripe fruit, wild herbs, varietal. Palate: fresh, fruity, easy to drink.

**F. URABAIN 2008 RD**

**87** Colour: light cherry. Nose: fresh fruit, floral, expressive. Palate: full, flavourful, fruity, good finish.

**F. URABAIN 2008 T**
cabernet sauvignon 60%, tempranillo 40%

**81**

**URABAIN "PRADO DE CHICA" 2007 T**
merlot 100%

**86** Colour: deep cherry. Nose: new oak, toasty, ripe fruit. Palate: flavourful, fleshy, fruity, round tannins.

**URABAIN FINCA SANTA BÁRBARA 2006 T**
merlot 80%, cabernet sauvignon 20%

**84**

## BODEGAS VALCARLOS

Ctra. Circunvalación, s/n
31210 Los Arcos (Navarra)
☎: 948 640 806 - Fax: 948 640 866
ignacio_vela@bodegasvalcarlossl.es
www.bodegasvalcarlos.com

**FORTIUS 2008 B**
viura, chardonnay

**83**

**FORTIUS CHARDONNAY 2008 B**
chardonnay

**82**

**MARQUÉS DE VALCARLOS 2008 B**
viura, chardonnay

**79**

**FORTIUS SELECCIÓN CABERNET SAUVIGNON 2008 RD**

**88** Colour: rose, purple rim. Nose: powerful, ripe fruit, red berry notes. Palate: fruity, fleshy, good acidity.

**MARQUÉS DE VALCARLOS 2008 RD**

**84**

**FORTIUS 2008 RD**

**83**

**FORTIUS TEMPRANILLO 2006 T**

**83**

**FORTIUS 2005 TC**

**88** Colour: deep cherry, garnet rim. Nose: fruit preserve, powerfull, creamy oak, cocoa bean. Palate: fruity, good acidity, elegant, balanced, round tannins, long.

**MARQUÉS DE VALCARLOS 2005 TC**

**84**

**ÉLITE DE FORTIUS 2004 T**

**90** Colour: cherry, garnet rim. Nose: powerful, fruit liqueur notes, cocoa bean, sweet spices. Palate: flavourful, spicy, round tannins, long.

FORTIUS MERLOT 2004 TC

**89** Colour: deep cherry, bright ochre rim. Nose: ripe fruit, sweet spices, dark chocolate, new oak. Palate: flavourful, fruity, powerful, slightly dry, soft tannins.

FORTIUS 2000 TR

**84**

FORTIUS 1999 TGR

**89** Colour: pale ruby, brick rim edge. Nose: spicy, aromatic coffee, fruit liqueur notes. Palate: flavourful, spicy, classic aged character.

MARQUÉS DE VALCARLOS 1999 TR

**80**

FORTIUS CABERNET TC

**86** Colour: deep cherry, garnet rim. Nose: ripe fruit, balanced, sweet spices. Palate: flavourful, fruity, good acidity, round tannins.

MARQUÉS DE VALCARLOS 2000 TR

**84**

## BODEGAS VEGA DEL CASTILLO

Rua Romana, 7
31390 Olite (Navarra)
☎: 948 740 012 - Fax: 948 741 074
info@vegadelcastillo.com
www.vegadelcastillo.com

VEGA DEL CASTILLO 2008 B
viura, chardonnay, moscatel

**87** Colour: straw. Nose: expressive, fresh, ripe fruit, grassy, floral. Palate: rich, fresh, flavourful, good acidity.

AUZOLAN 2008 RD
garnacha

**82**

VEGA DEL CASTILLO ROSADO DE LÁGRIMA 2008 RD
garnacha

**81**

VEGA DEL CASTILLO GARNACHA CEPAS VIEJAS 2008 T
garnacha

**84**

AUZOLAN ECOLÓGICO 2008 T
tempranillo, cabernet sauvignon, merlot

**84**

VEGA DEL CASTILLO TEMPRANILLO 2008 T
tempranillo

**83**

AUZOLÁN LLAVERO ECOLÓGICO 2006 TC
cabernet sauvignon

**87** Colour: deep cherry, orangey edge. Nose: ripe fruit, powerfull, spicy. Palate: warm, fruity, flavourful, round tannins, balsamic.

MARQUÉS DE LA REAL DEFENSA 2005 TC
tempranillo, cabernet sauvignon, merlot

**87** Colour: deep cherry, bright ochre rim. Nose: ripe fruit, sweet spices, balanced. Palate: flavourful, fruity, round tannins, good acidity.

MERAK VEGA DEL CASTILLO 2005 T
tempranillo, cabernet sauvignon, merlot

**86** Colour: deep cherry, orangey edge. Nose: fruit liqueur notes, sweet spices, aromatic coffee, warm. Palate: fruity, pruney, round tannins, spicy.

VEGA DEL CASTILLO 2005 TC
tempranillo, cabernet sauvignon, merlot

**85** Colour: cherry, garnet rim. Nose: medium intensity, ripe fruit, sweet spices. Palate: flavourful, spicy, round tannins.

VEGA DEL CASTILLO 2003 TR
tempranillo, cabernet sauvignon, merlot

**88** Colour: deep cherry, garnet rim. Nose: ripe fruit, toasty, aromatic coffee. Palate: flavourful, fruity, round tannins, easy to drink.

MARQUÉS DE LA REAL DEFENSA SELECCIÓN 2002 TC
tempranillo, cabernet sauvignon, merlot

**85** Colour: cherry, garnet rim. Nose: powerful, toasty, ripe fruit. Palate: flavourful, spicy, round tannins.

DUBHE

## BODEGAS Y VIÑEDOS ARTAZU S.A.

Mayor, 3
31109 Artazu (Navarra)
☎: 945 600 119 - Fax: 945 600 850
artazu@artadi.com

ARTAZURI 2008 RD

**86** Colour: raspberry rose. Nose: red berry notes, raspberry, fresh, expressive. Palate: fruity, flavourful, easy to drink, good acidity.

# DO NAVARRA

ARTAZURI 2008 T

**85** Colour: cherry, purple rim. Nose: ripe fruit, balsamic herbs, scrubland. Palate: flavourful, fruity, fresh.

SANTA CRUZ DE ARTAZU 2007 T

**93** Colour: bright cherry. Nose: varietal, powerfull, expressive, fresh fruit, cocoa bean. Palate: fresh, fruity, powerful, flavourful, varietal.

## BODEGAS Y VIÑEDOS NEKEAS

Las Huertas s/n
31154 Añorbe (Navarra)
☎: 948 350 296 - Fax: 948 350 300
nekeas@nekeas.com
www.nekeas.com

NEKEAS CHARDONNAY "CUVÉE ALLIER"
2008 BFB
chardonnay 100%

**89** Colour: straw. Nose: ripe fruit, sweet spices, creamy oak, balanced. Palate: rich, fruity, good acidity, concentrated, fruity aftestaste.

NEKEAS VIURA/ CHARDONNAY 2008 B
viura 70%, chardonnay 30%

**87** Colour: straw. Nose: ripe fruit, lactic notes, sweet spices. Palate: flavourful, fruity, fleshy, fresh.

ODAIZA DE VEGA SIDONIA 2007 B
chardonnay 100%

**92** Colour: bright yellow. Nose: powerful, ripe fruit, sweet spices, creamy oak, fragrant herbs. Palate: rich, smoky aftertaste, flavourful, fresh, good acidity.

NEKEAS 2008 RD
garnacha 50%, cabernet sauvignon 50%

**84**

EL CHAPARRAL DE VEGA SINDOA 2008 T
garnacha 100%

**86** Colour: cherry, purple rim. Nose: ripe fruit, red berry notes, balsamic herbs. Palate: flavourful, fruity, spicy.

NEKEAS 2006 TC
cabernet sauvignon 60%, tempranillo 40%

**85** Colour: deep cherry, garnet rim. Nose: medium intensity, green pepper, spicy, toasty. Palate: spicy, round tannins, good acidity, flavourful.

IZAR DE NEKEAS 2004 TR
cabernet sauvignon 50%, tempranillo 25%, merlot 25%

**86** Colour: pale ruby, brick rim edge. Nose: powerful, roasted coffee, dark chocolate, smoky. Palate: powerful, toasty, powerful tannins.

## CAMINO DEL VILLAR

Camino del Villar. N-161, km. 3
31591 Corella (Navarra)
☎: 948 401 321 - Fax: 948 781 414
sales@vinaaliaga.com
www.vinaaliaga.com

VIÑA ALIAGA MOSCATEL VENDIMIA TARDÍA 2008 B
moscatel

**87** Colour: bright straw. Nose: candied fruit, citrus fruit, honeyed notes. Palate: flavourful, fruity, sweet.

VIÑA ALIAGA ROSADO DE LÁGRIMA 2008 RD
garnacha 100%

**85** Colour: rose. Nose: fresh fruit, red berry notes, violet drops. Palate: carbonic notes, fruity, good acidity, easy to drink.

VIÑA ALIAGA GARNACHA VIEJA 2007 T
garnacha 100%

**88** Colour: cherry, garnet rim. Nose: powerful, ripe fruit, creamy oak, sweet spices, mineral, earthy notes. Palate: flavourful, powerful, fleshy, spicy.

VIÑA ALIAGA TEMPRANILLO 2007 T
tempranillo 100%

**83**

VIÑA ALIAGA 2005 TC
tempranillo 80%, cabernet sauvignon 20%

**85** Colour: cherry, garnet rim. Nose: powerful, toasty, smoky. Palate: spicy, ripe fruit, fine bitter notes, round tannins.

VIÑA ALIAGA CUVÉE 2005 T
tempranillo 85%, cabernet sauvignon 15%

**82**

VIÑA ALIAGA GRACIANO 2005 TC
graciano 100%

**82**

VIÑA ALIAGA ANTONIO CORPUS 2002 T
garnacha 100%

**85** Colour: cherry, garnet rim. Nose: spicy, tobacco, woody. Palate: flavourful, fruity, balsamic, round tannins.

VIÑA ALIAGA VENDIMIA SELECCIONADA 2001 T
tempranillo 70%, cabernet sauvignon 30%

**85** Colour: cherry, garnet rim. Nose: ripe fruit, spicy, toasty, complex, tobacco, balsamic herbs. Palate: flavourful, toasty, soft tannins.

VIÑA ALIAGA 2001 TR
tempranillo 75%, cabernet sauvignon 25%

**81**

VIÑA ALIAGA GRAN SELECCIÓN 2000 TR
cabernet sauvignon 70%, tempranillo 30%

**83**

## CASTILLO DE MONJARDÍN

Viña Rellanada, s/n
31242 Villamayor de Monjardín (Navarra)
☎: 948 537 412 - Fax: 948 537 436
sonia@monjardin.es
www.monjardin.es

CASTILLO DE MONJARDÍN CHARDONNAY 2008 B
chardonnay 100%

**84**

CASTILLO DE MONJARDÍN CHARDONNAY 2007 BFB
chardonnay 100%

**91** Colour: bright yellow. Nose: powerful, ripe fruit, sweet spices, creamy oak. Palate: rich, flavourful, fresh, good acidity.

CASTILLO DE MONJARDÍN CHARDONNAY 2005 B RESERVA
chardonnay 100%

**90** Colour: bright yellow. Nose: candied fruit, smoky, sweet spices. Palate: good acidity, flavourful, smoky aftertaste, ripe fruit.

ESENCIA MONJARDIN 2004 B
chardonnay 100%

**94** Colour: bright yellow. Nose: powerful, candied fruit, fruit liqueur notes, fruit liqueur notes, citrus fruit. Palate: flavourful, fleshy, ripe fruit, sweet.

CASTILLO DE MONJARDÍN MERLOT 2008 RD
merlot 100%

**85** Colour: rose, purple rim. Nose: faded flowers, ripe fruit. Palate: flavourful, fruity, fresh.

TINTICO 2008 T JOVEN
tempranillo

**84**

CASTILLO DE MONJARDÍN CABERNET SAUVIGNON MERLOT 2006 TC
merlot 50%, cabernet sauvignon 30%, tempranillo 20%

**86** Colour: cherry, garnet rim. Nose: ripe fruit, spicy, toasty, complex. Palate: powerful, flavourful, toasty, round tannins.

CASTILLO DE MONJARDÍN DEYO 2006 TC
merlot 100%

**86** Colour: deep cherry. Nose: powerful, ripe fruit, sweet spices, toasty, varietal. Palate: flavourful, fleshy, creamy, round tannins.

CASTILLO DE MONJARDÍN FINCA LOS CARASOLES 2005 TR
cabernet sauvignon 80%, tempranillo 20%

**84**

## COMPAÑÍA VITIVINÍCOLA TANDEM

Ctra. Pamplona - Logroño km. 35,9
31292 Lácar (Navarra)
☎: 948 536 031 - Fax: 948 536 068
bodega@tandem.es
www.tandem.es

ARS IN VITRO 2008 RD

**85** Colour: raspberry rose. Nose: ripe fruit, expressive, fresh. Palate: fruity, flavourful, easy to drink.

ARS IN VITRO 2006 T
tempranillo, merlot

**87** Colour: deep cherry, garnet rim. Nose: fruit liqueur notes, fruit preserve, spicy. Palate: flavourful, balanced, round tannins.

ARS NOVA 2005 T

**87** Colour: bright cherry. Nose: elegant, expressive, ripe fruit, sweet spices, cocoa bean. Palate: flavourful, spicy, ripe fruit.

ARS MÁCULA 2004 T

**88** Colour: black cherry. Nose: ripe fruit, sweet spices, creamy oak, dark chocolate, dried herbs. Palate: fleshy, powerful, flavourful, balanced, slightly dry, soft tannins.

ARS MEMORIA 2005

**87** Colour: deep cherry, brick rim edge. Nose: macerated fruit, aged wood nuances, spicy. Palate: fruity, powerful, slightly dry, soft tannins, good structure.

## CRIANZA Y VIÑEDOS R. REVERTE

Lejalde nº 43
31593 Fitero (Navarra)
☎: 948 366 031 - Fax: 948 183 487
comercial@rafaelreverte.es
www.rafaelreverte.es

ODIPUS VENDIMIA SELECCIONADA 2007 T

**90** Colour: bright cherry. Nose: ripe fruit, sweet spices, creamy oak, expressive, fragrant herbs. Palate: flavourful, fruity, toasty, round tannins.

ODIPUS GARNACHA 2007 T
garnacha

**88** Colour: cherry, garnet rim. Nose: powerful, warm, ripe fruit, sweet spices, creamy oak. Palate: flavourful, sweetness, fleshy.

## EMILIO VALERIO

Paraje de Argonga, s/n
31263 Dicastillo (Navarra)
☎: 625 440 755 - Fax: 935 083 737
info@laderasdemontejurra.com
www.laderasdemontejurra.com

EMILIO VALERIO VIÑAS DE AMBURZA 2006 T
graciano, garnacha, cabernet sauvignon

**90** Colour: cherry, garnet rim. Nose: ripe fruit, spicy, toasty, complex, dark chocolate. Palate: powerful, flavourful, toasty, round tannins.

EMILIO VALERIO. VIÑAS DEL PALOMAR
EN ARGONGA 2006 T
garnacha, merlot, graciano

**88** Colour: cherry, garnet rim. Nose: powerful, toasty, dark chocolate, smoky, ripe fruit. Palate: powerful, flavourful, fleshy, fine bitter notes, toasty.

VIÑAS DE AMBURZA
VIÑAS DEL PALOMAR

## FERNÁNDEZ DE ARCAYA

La Serna, 31
31210 Los Arcos (Navarra)
☎: 948 640 811 - Fax: 948 441 060
info@fernandezdearcaya.com
www.fernandezdearcaya.com

CONDESA DE GARIN 2007 T ROBLE
tempranillo 85%, cabernet sauvignon 10%, merlot 5%

**88** Colour: bright cherry. Nose: ripe fruit, sweet spices, creamy oak, expressive. Palate: flavourful, fruity, toasty, round tannins.

CONDESA DE GARIN 2006 TC
tempranillo 80%, cabernet sauvignon 15%, merlot 5%

**87** Colour: cherry, garnet rim. Nose: ripe fruit, sweet spices, dark chocolate. Palate: flavourful, powerful, fleshy.

VIÑA PERGUITA 2006 T ROBLE
tempranillo 85%, cabernet sauvignon 10%, merlot 5%

**84**

VIÑA PERGUITA 2005 TC
tempranillo 80%, cabernet sauvignon 15%, merlot 5%

**83**

FERNÁNDEZ DE ARCAYA 2004 TR
cabernet sauvignon 100%

**90** Colour: cherry, garnet rim. Nose: ripe fruit, spicy, creamy oak, toasty, complex. Palate: powerful, flavourful, toasty, round tannins.

FERNÁNDEZ DE ARCAYA 2001 TR
cabernet sauvignon 100%

**89** Colour: very deep cherry, bright ochre rim. Nose: sweet spices, aromatic coffee, warm, fruit liqueur notes. Palate: fruity, sweetness, round tannins, round.

CONDESA DE GARIN 1996 TR
cabernet sauvignon 100%

**88** Colour: light cherry, orangey edge. Nose: fruit liqueur notes, sweet spices, aromatic coffee, tobacco. Palate: classic aged character, spirituous, smoky aftertaste, round tannins.

## GARCIA BURGOS

Finca Cantera, s/n
31521 Murchante (Navarra)
☎: 948 847 734 - Fax: 948 847 734
info@bodegasgarciaburgos.com
www.bodegasgarciaburgos.com

SH 2007 T
syrah 100%

**89** Colour: cherry, garnet rim. Nose: powerful, ripe fruit, scrubland, toasty. Palate: flavourful, fleshy, pruney.

FINCA LA CANTERA DE SANTA ANA 2006 T
cabernet sauvignon 100%

**91** Colour: cherry, purple rim. Nose: powerful, mineral, ripe fruit, dark chocolate, sweet spices. Palate: flavourful, powerful, fleshy, ripe fruit.

GARCÍA BURGOS VENDIMIA SELECCIONADA 2005 T
cabernet sauvignon 60%, merlot 40%

**90** Colour: bright cherry. Nose: ripe fruit, sweet spices, creamy oak. Palate: flavourful, fruity, toasty, round tannins.

GARCÍA BURGOS RESERVA UNICA 2005 T
cabernet sauvignon 100%

**89** Colour: dark-red cherry, garnet rim. Nose: ripe fruit, green pepper, varietal, expressive. Palate: fruity, flavourful, toasty, round tannins.

RESERVA LOLA GARCÍA 2004 T
merlot 100%

**91** Colour: cherry, garnet rim. Nose: powerful, ripe fruit, fruit expression, sweet spices, cocoa bean. Palate: flavourful, ripe fruit, round tannins.

RESERVA LOLA GARCÍA 2004 TR
merlot 100%

**88** Colour: cherry, garnet rim. Nose: powerful, ripe fruit, sweet spices, toasty. Palate: flavourful, powerful, fleshy.

## IRACHE

Monasterio de Irache, 1
31240 Ayegui (Navarra)
☎: 948 551 932 - Fax: 948 554 954
irache@irache.com
www.irache.com

CASTILLO IRACHE 2008 B
chardonnay 100%

**86** Colour: pale. Nose: ripe fruit, tropical fruit, citrus fruit. Palate: flavourful, fruity, fresh.

CASTILLO IRACHE GARNACHA 2008 RD
garnacha 100%

**81**

CASTILLO IRACHE TEMPRANILLO 2008 T
tempranillo 100%

**82**

CASTILLO IRACHE 2004 TC
cabernet sauvignon 60%, merlot 40%

**88** Colour: cherry, garnet rim. Nose: ripe fruit, sweet spices, complex. Palate: flavourful, fruity, slightly dry, soft tannins, easy to drink.

FUENTE CERRADA

## JUAN SIMÓN ROSEL

Camino de Aspra, s/n
31521 Murchante (Navarra)
☎: 948 816 776
vinoscartan@hotmail.com

CARTÁN 2008 T
garnacha 40%, tempranillo 40%, mazuelo 20%

**77**

CARTÁN 2005 TC
tempranillo 50%, cabernet sauvignon 50%

**88** Colour: bright cherry. Nose: ripe fruit, sweet spices, creamy oak. Palate: flavourful, fruity, toasty, round tannins.

## LONG WINES

Avda. del Monte, 46
28120 Algete (Madrid)
☎: 916 221 305 - Fax: 916 220 029
william@william-long.com
www.longwines.com

PUERTO DEL MONTE VIURA 2008 B

**80**

PUERTO DEL MONTE GARNACHA 2008 RD

**88** Colour: light cherry. Nose: red berry notes, floral, expressive, ripe fruit. Palate: unctuous, flavourful, fruity, round.

PUERTO DEL MONTE GARNACHA 2008 T

**82**

## LUIS GURPEGUI MUGA

Ctra. Pamplona, s/n
31330 Villafranca (Navarra)
☎: 948 670 050 - Fax: 948 670 259
bodegas@gurpegui.es
www.gurpegui.es

MONTE ORY TEMPRANILLO - CABERNET SAUVIGNON 2008 T

**86** Colour: cherry, garnet rim. Nose: medium intensity, ripe fruit, toasty. Palate: flavourful, ripe fruit, spicy, round tannins.

PREEMY 2008 T

**85** Colour: cherry, purple rim. Nose: ripe fruit, scrubland, medium intensity. Palate: powerful, ripe fruit, round tannins.

MONTE ORY TEMPRANILLO-MERLOT 2008 T

**83**

MONTE ORY 2005 TC

**83**

MONTE ORY 2004 TR

**86** Colour: cherry, garnet rim. Nose: powerful, ripe fruit, toasty, creamy oak. Palate: flavourful, toasty, ripe fruit, round tannins.

SAN ASISCLO

## MARCO REAL

Ctra. Pamplona/Zaragoza, km. 38
31390 Olite (Navarra)
☎: 948 712 193 - Fax: 948 712 343
info@familiabelasco.com
www.familiabelasco.com

HOMENAJE 2008 B

**84**

HOMENAJE 2008 RD
garnacha, cabernet sauvignon

**90** Colour: rose, purple rim. Nose: ripe fruit, medium intensity, varietal, fruit expression, red berry notes. Palate: flavourful, fruity, fresh, good structure.

HOMENAJE 2008 T

**85** Colour: cherry, purple rim. Nose: powerful, ripe fruit, floral. Palate: flavourful, fleshy, fruity.

## MARCO REAL COLECCIÓN PRIVADA 2006 TC

**89** Colour: cherry, garnet rim. Nose: ripe fruit, spicy, creamy oak, toasty, complex. Palate: powerful, flavourful, toasty, round tannins.

## MARCO REAL COLECCIÓN PRIVADA 2005 TC

**90**

## HOMENAJE 2005 TC

**88** Colour: cherry, garnet rim. Nose: powerful, ripe fruit, toasty, sweet spices. Palate: flavourful, fleshy, spicy, long, round tannins.

## MARCO REAL RESERVA DE FAMILIA 2005 TR

**88** Colour: cherry, garnet rim. Nose: powerful, ripe fruit, sweet spices, creamy oak. Palate: flavourful, spicy, round tannins.

## MARQUES DE MONTECIERZO S.L.

San José, 62
31590 Castejón (Navarra)
☎: 948 814 414 - Fax: 948 814 420
info@marquesdemontecierzo.com
www.marquesdemontecierzo.com

### EMERGENTE 2008 B
chardonnay

**85** Colour: bright straw. Nose: fresh, fresh fruit, white flowers. Palate: flavourful, fruity, good acidity, balanced.

### EMERGENTE 2008 BFB

**85** Colour: bright straw. Nose: powerful, ripe fruit, smoky, toasty. Palate: fleshy, ripe fruit, creamy.

### EMERGENTE ROSADO DE LÁGRIMA 2008 RD

**83**

### EMERGENTE 2006 T ROBLE

**86** Colour: deep cherry. Nose: fruit preserve, fragrant herbs, sweet spices, dark chocolate. Palate: fruity, flavourful, warm, balanced, round tannins.

### EMERGENTE 2005 TC

**86** Colour: cherry, garnet rim. Nose: powerful, ripe fruit, spicy. Palate: flavourful, spicy, round tannins.

### EMERGENTE RESERVA NUMERADA 2004 TR

**83**

### MARQUES DE MONTECIERZO SELECCIÓN 2003 TC

**88** Colour: cherry, garnet rim. Nose: new oak, roasted coffee, aromatic coffee, ripe fruit. Palate: flavourful, powerful, fleshy, spicy.

## EMERGENTE 2007 BLANCO DULCE

**78**

## PAGO DE SAN GABRIEL S.L.

Paraje La Sarda, n-232, km. 84,4
31590 Castejón (Navarra)
☎: 629 443 316 - Fax: 944 911 146
psangabriel@terra.es

### ZUBIOLA 2007 T

**89** Colour: bright cherry. Nose: ripe fruit, sweet spices, creamy oak, expressive. Palate: flavourful, fruity, toasty, round tannins.

### PRADOMAYOR DE ZUBIOLA 2006

**89** Colour: very deep cherry. Nose: sweet spices, creamy oak, macerated fruit, dark chocolate. Palate: round tannins, balanced, elegant, good acidity, long, great length.

## PALACIO DE MURUZÁBAL

La Cruz, s/n
31152 Muruzábal (Navarra)
☎: 948 344 279 - Fax: 948 344 325
muruzabal1000@yahoo.es
www.palaciodemuruzabal.jimdo.es

### PALACIO DE MURUZÁBAL 2000 TR

**79**

### PALACIO DE MURUZÁBAL 1998 TGR

**91** Colour: pale ruby, brick rim edge. Nose: elegant, spicy, fine reductive notes, wet leather, aged wood nuances, fruit liqueur notes. Palate: spicy, fine tannins, elegant, long.

## PIEDEMONTE S.C.

Rua Romana, s/n
31390 Olite (Navarra)
☎: 948 712 406 - Fax: 948 740 090
bodega@piedemonte.com
www.piedemonte.com

### PIEDEMONTE CHARDONNAY 2008 B
chardonnay 100%

**87** Colour: bright yellow. Nose: fresh fruit, wild herbs, expressive. Palate: rich, fruity, flavourful.

### PIEDEMONTE GAMMA 2008 B
chardonnay, viura, moscatel

**82**

### PIEDEMONTE 2008 RD
garnacha 100%

**78**

### PIEDEMONTE GAMMA 2008 T
tempranillo, merlot, cabernet sauvignon

**84**

### PIEDEMONTE MERLOT 2008 T
merlot 100%

**84**

### QUINCE 2006 T
merlot 100%

**90** Colour: deep cherry. Nose: powerful, spicy, varietal, new oak, toasty. Palate: powerful, flavourful, spicy, creamy, round tannins.

### PIEDEMONTE CABERNET SAUVIGNON 2006 TC
cabernet sauvignon 100%

**86** Colour: cherry, garnet rim. Nose: ripe fruit, green pepper, varietal, spicy, balanced. Palate: light-bodied, fruity, toasty, warm, slightly dry, soft tannins.

### PIEDEMONTE 2006 TC
merlot, tempranillo, cabernet sauvignon

**85** Colour: deep cherry, garnet rim. Nose: stalky, herbaceous, fruit liqueur notes, sweet spices, warm. Palate: light-bodied, flavourful, fruity, round tannins, pruney.

### PIEDEMONTE 2005 TR
merlot, tempranillo, cabernet sauvignon

**88** Colour: deep cherry, orangey edge. Nose: ripe fruit, sweet spices, cocoa bean. Palate: light-bodied, fruity, flavourful, sweetness, round tannins.

### PIEDEMONTE MOSCATEL 2008 BLANCO DULCE
moscatel 100%

**86** Colour: straw. Nose: grapey, dry nuts, candied fruit. Palate: sweetness, good acidity, flavourful.

## SEÑORÍO DE ANDIÓN

Ctra. Pamplona-Zaragoza, km. 38
31390 Olite (Navarra)

☎: 948 712 193 - Fax: 948 712 343
info@familiabelasco.com
www.familiabelasco.com

### SEÑORÍO DE ANDIÓN 2005 T
cabernet sauvignon, merlot, tempranillo, graciano

**92** Colour: cherry, garnet rim. Nose: powerful, ripe fruit, sweet spices, dark chocolate. Palate: flavourful, fleshy, ripe fruit, round tannins.

### SEÑORÍO DE ANDIÓN 2002 T
cabernet sauvignon, merlot, tempranillo, graciano

**91** Colour: black cherry, brick rim edge. Nose: ripe fruit, fragrant herbs, sweet spices, cocoa bean, dark chocolate. Palate: balanced, elegant, warm, good acidity, fruity, flavourful, round tannins.

## SOCIEDAD COOPERATIVA SAN JOSÉ

Avda. Navarra, s/n
31591 Corella (Navarra)
☎: 948 780 058 - Fax: 948 780 058
coopsanjose@telefonica.net

### SEÑORÍO DE CORELLA 2008 RD

**84**

### SEÑORÍO DE CORELLA 2008 T JOVEN

**83**

### CONDE ALPERCHE

## VICENTE MALUMBRES

Santa Bárbara, 15
31591 Corella (Navarra)
☎: 948 401 920 - Fax: 948 401 653
info@malumbres.com
www.malumbres.com

### MALUMBRES 2008 RD

**84**

### MALUMBRES GARNACHA 2007 TC

**82**

### MALUMBRES 2005 TC

**86** Colour: deep cherry, bright ochre rim. Nose: fruit liqueur notes, toasty. Palate: fruity, flavourful, warm, round tannins, creamy.

MALUMBRES 2005 TR

**84**

MALUMBRES GRACIANO 2003 TC

**84**

MALUMBRES PRIMEROS VIÑEDOS 2002 TC

**84**

## VINICOLA CORELLANA S.A.

Ctra. del Villar, s/n
26341 Corella (Navarra)
☎: 948 780 617 - Fax: 948 401 894
info@vinicolacorellana.com
www.vinicolacorellana.com

VIÑA ZORZAL GARNACHAA 2008 RD
garnacha 100%

**80**

VIÑA ZORZAL 2008 T
tempranillo 100%

**78**

VIÑA ZORZAL GRACIANO 2007 T
graciano 100%

**80**

REYNOBLE PLATINUM 2006 T
merlot 85%, graciano 15%

**86** Colour: very deep cherry, garnet rim. Nose: ripe fruit, varietal, toasty, spicy, expressive. Palate: flavourful, fruity, harsh oak tannins, toasty.

REYNOBLE CABERNET SAUVIGNON 2006 T
cabernet sauvignon 100%

**86** Colour: deep cherry, brick rim edge. Nose: ripe fruit, green pepper, varietal, sweet spices. Palate: flavourful, fruity, pruney, grainy tannins.

REYNOBLE 2003 TC
tempranillo 80%, cabernet sauvignon 20%

**85** Colour: cherry, garnet rim. Nose: powerful, fruit preserve, toasty, sweet spices. Palate: flavourful, spicy, ripe fruit.

## VINICOLA NAVARRA

Avda. Pamplona, 25
31398 Tiebas (Navarra)

☎: 948 360 131 - Fax: 948 360 544
info@domecqbodegas.com
www.domecqbodegas.com

CASTILLO DE JAVIER GARNACHA 2008 RD
garnacha 100%

**85** Colour: brilliant rose. Nose: medium intensity, red berry notes, raspberry. Palate: fruity, fleshy, easy to drink.

LAS CAMPANAS GARNACHA 2008 RD
garnacha 100%

**85** Colour: raspberry rose. Nose: medium intensity, red berry notes, ripe fruit. Palate: flavourful, ripe fruit, fleshy.

LAS CAMPANAS TEMPRANILLO 2008 T
tempranillo 100%

**84**

CASTILLO DE JAVIER 2005 TC
tempranillo 80%, cabernet sauvignon 20%, merlot %

**84**

LAS CAMPANAS 2005 TC
tempranillo 80%, cabernet sauvignon 20%

**82**

CASTILLO DE JAVIER 2002 TR
tempranillo 75%, cabernet sauvignon 17%, merlot 8%

**87** Colour: cherry, garnet rim. Nose: powerful, ripe fruit, fruit liqueur notes. Palate: powerful, sweetness, warm.

## VINOS Y VIÑEDOS
## DOMINIO LASIERPE

Ribera, s/n
31592 Cintruénigo (Navarra)
☎: 948 811 033 - Fax: 948 815 160
info@bodegacirbonera.com
www.dominiolasierpe.com

FINCA LASIERPE ROSADO DE LÁGRIMA 2008 RD
garnacha 100%

**86** Colour: brilliant rose. Nose: fresh, expressive, floral, fresh fruit. Palate: fruity, flavourful, fresh.

FINCA LASIERPE TEMPRANILLO GARNACHA 2008 T
tempranillo 60%, garnacha 40%

**82**

69 LASIERPE GARNACHA CABERNET SAUVIGNON 2007 T
garnacha 50%, cabernet sauvignon 50%

**91** Colour: deep cherry, garnet rim. Nose: ripe fruit, dried herbs, creamy oak, cocoa bean, sweet spices. Palate: fruity, flavourful, good structure, fleshy, soft tannins, elegant.

## 69 LASIERPE TEMPRANILLO MERLOT 2007 T
tempranillo 50%, merlot 50%

**85** Colour: cherry, garnet rim. Nose: overripe fruit, medium intensity. Palate: flavourful, fleshy, fruity.

## SONORUS 2007 T
cabernet sauvignon 85%, tempranillo 15%

**85** Colour: cherry, garnet rim. Nose: warm, sweet spices, green pepper. Palate: flavourful, powerful, ripe fruit.

## FLOR DE LASIERPE GARNACHA VIÑAS VIEJAS 2007 T
garnacha 100%

**84**

## DOMINIO LASIERPE CUVÉE 2006 T
tempranillo 85%, cabernet sauvignon 15%

**88** Colour: deep cherry, brick rim edge. Nose: macerated fruit, fragrant herbs, cocoa bean, dark chocolate, sweet spices. Palate: good acidity, elegant, balanced, round tannins, spicy.

## DOMINIO LASIERPE 2005 TC
tempranillo 85%, cabernet sauvignon 15%

**87** Colour: cherry, garnet rim. Nose: scrubland, sweet spices, dark chocolate, toasty. Palate: flavourful, ripe fruit, spicy.

## SONORUS 2005 CRIANZA
cabernet sauvignon 40%, tempranillo 30%, garnacha 30%

**85** Colour: cherry, garnet rim. Nose: ripe fruit, green pepper, sweet spices. Palate: flavourful, fruity, correct, round tannins.

## SONORUS 2004 RESERVA
cabernet sauvignon 50%, tempranillo 40%, garnacha 10%

**88** Colour: very deep cherry. Nose: sweet spices, creamy oak, cocoa bean, ripe fruit. Palate: round tannins, flavourful, balanced, good acidity.

## VIÑA MAGAÑA

San Miguel, 9
31523 Barillas (Navarra)
☎: 948 850 034 - Fax: 948 851 536
bodegas@vinamagana.com
www.vinamagana.com

## MAGAÑA CALCHETAS 2006 T

**91** Colour: bright cherry. Nose: ripe fruit, sweet spices, creamy oak, expressive, dark chocolate, earthy notes. Palate: flavourful, fruity, toasty, round tannins.

## TORCAS 2004 T

**90** Colour: deep cherry. Nose: powerful, varietal, expressive, fruit preserve. Palate: spirituous, powerful, flavourful, varietal, sweetness, roasted-coffee aftertaste, toasty.

## DIGNUS

## VIÑA VALDORBA

Ctra. de la Estación, s/n
31395 Garinoain (Navarra)
☎: 948 720 505 - Fax: 948 720 505
bodegasvaldorba@bodegasvaldorba.com
www.bodegasvaldorba.com

## EOLO 2008 B
chardonnay 100%

**84**

## EOLO 2008 RD
garnacha 100%

**84**

## EOLO GARNACHA 2007 T
garnacha 100%

**80**

## EOLO GARNACHA 2006 TC
garnacha 100%

**87** Colour: black cherry, garnet rim. Nose: fruit preserve, creamy oak, sweet spices, fragrant herbs. Palate: flavourful, fruity, good acidity, balanced, round tannins.

## EOLO 2006 TC
cabernet sauvignon 25%, merlot 25%, garnacha 25%, graciano 25%

**87** Colour: deep cherry, garnet rim. Nose: macerated fruit, toasty, fragrant herbs, balsamic herbs. Palate: balanced, warm, good acidity, flavourful, long, round tannins.

## EOLO 2006 T ROBLE
garnacha 50%, cabernet sauvignon 50%

**80**

## EOLO GRACIANO 2003 TC
graciano 100%

**86** Colour: cherry, garnet rim. Nose: powerful, ripe fruit, sweet spices, toasty. Palate: flavourful, ripe fruit, spicy.

## CAURO GRAN EOLO 2002 TR
cabernet sauvignon 50%, graciano 50%

**90** Colour: cherry, garnet rim. Nose: powerful, fruit liqueur notes, sweet spices, toasty. Palate: flavourful, spicy, ripe fruit.

**GRAN EOLO 2002 TR**
cabernet sauvignon 35%, merlot 35%, graciano 30%

**86** Colour: pale ruby, brick rim edge. Nose: dark chocolate, aromatic coffee, tobacco, fruit liqueur notes. Palate: flavourful, spicy, ripe fruit.

## VIÑEDOS Y BODEGAS ALCONDE

Ctra. de Calahorra s/n
31260 Lerín (Navarra)
☎: 948 530 058 - Fax: 948 530 589
info@bodegavirgenblanca.com
www.bodegavirgenblanca.com

**VIÑA SARDASOL 2008 B**
chardonnay 75%, viura 25%

**83**

**VIÑA SARDASOL ROSADO DE LÁGRIMA 2008 RD**
garnacha 100%

**83**

**VIÑA SARDASOL MERLOT 2007 T ROBLE**
merlot 100%

**84**

**BODEGAS ALCONDE SELECCIÓN GARNACHA 2005 TR**
garnacha 85%, cabernet sauvignon 10%, merlot 5%

**84**

**BODEGAS ALCONDE SELECCIÓN TEMPRANILLO 2005 TR**
tempranillo 85%, merlot 10%, cabernet sauvignon 5%

**90** Colour: cherry, garnet rim. Nose: powerful, ripe fruit, sweet spices, toasty, new oak. Palate: flavourful, powerful, spicy, round tannins.

SOME OTHER WINERIES WITHIN THE DO:

**BODEGA COOPERATIVA SANTO CRISTO DEL AMPARO**
**BODEGA SAN RAMÓN S.C.**
**BODEGAS ADA S.L.**
**BODEGAS DE LA CASA DE LÚCULO**
**BODEGAS ESCALERA S.C.A.**
**BODEGAS HEREDEROS DE LUIS GARCÍA MARTÍNEZ**
**BODEGAS LOGOS**
**BODEGAS PAGOS DE ARAIZ**
**BODEGAS PALACIO DE AZCONA**
**BODEGAS PARRALDEA**
**BODEGAS ULLATE**
**BODEGAS Y VIÑEDOS ALZANIA**
**BODEGAS Y VIÑEDOS QUADERNA VIA**
**CARLOS MAGAÑA**
**CASTILLO DE ENERIZ**
**COOPERATIVA ANGEL DE LA GUARDA**
**COOPERATIVA LA CRUZ**
**COOPERATIVA SAN MIGUEL S.C.**
**COOPERATIVA SAN RAIMUNDO ABAD**
**COOPERATIVA VINÍCOLA DE TAFALLA S.C.L.**
**DÁMASO GARBAYO ALDUÁN**
**HEREDERO DEL CONDE DE NAVASQÜÉS**
**L. CARRICAS S.A.**
**MONASTERIO DE LA OLIVA VIÑEDOS Y BODEGAS**
**MONASTIR**
**TODA EUROPA INTERCOMERCIAL**
**VIÑA ARBEL S.L.**
**VITIVINÍCOLA DE CARCAR S.L.**

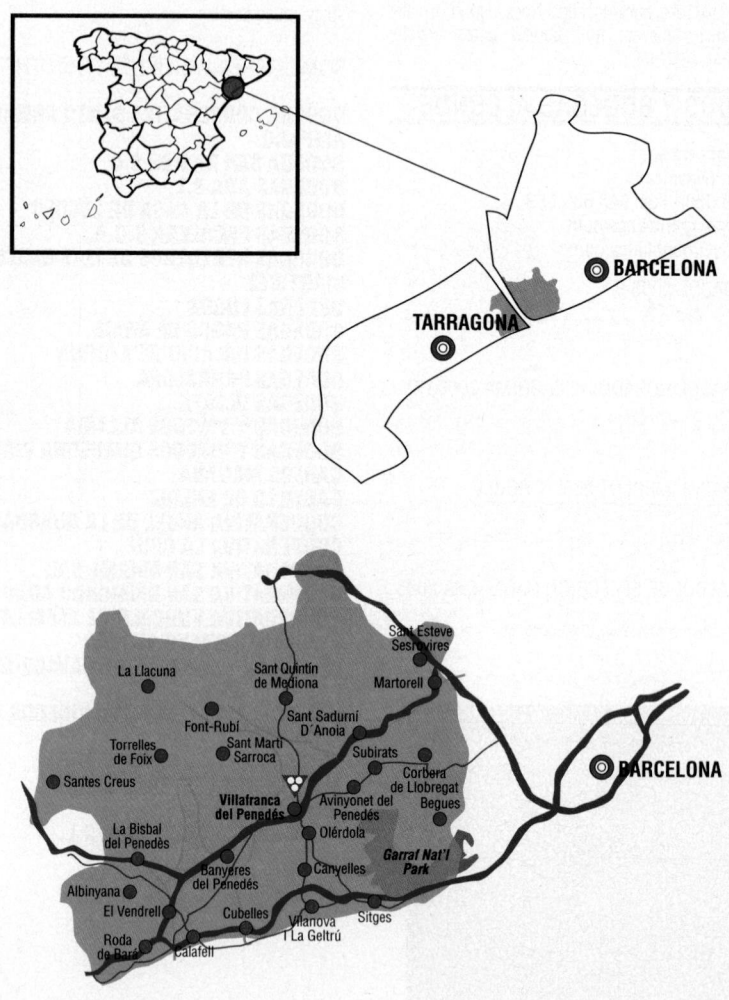

▽ Consejo Regulador
● DO Boundary

## NEWS

In a region with far too many wines of every sort and quality it is difficult to find a common denominator. Besides, the Consejo Regulador is continuously adding to their catalogue new varieties and styles. The last invention is an icewine with no alcohol addition. The best potential is appreciated in white wines made from xarel.lo, which manage to get the best ratings. With this variety, very suitable to barrel fermentation, Pardas and Avgvstvs come up with the best renderings. The young rosé wines are fruit bombs in terms of colour and aroma, very commercial but less elegant. A cooler vintage has given shape to grapes with optimal maturity, fruitier and with a more varietal edge. The experience the wineries have gained with all sorts of varieties becomes evident in a broader catalogue of brands, the best of which are made by houses like Can Ràfols dels Caus, Albet i Noya and Jané Ventura. Probably the most peculiar ones are the pinot noir Ad Fines and El Rocallís, made from the Italian variety incroccio manzoni, a cross between riesling and pinot blanc, all of which gives an overall impression of the region as a real experimental lab. With over seven hundred wines tasted, there is no other region offering such a range of wines, vintages and ratings, something that forced us to work even harder to come up with any sort of conclusions.

## LOCATION

In the province of Barcelona, between the pre-coastal Catalonian mountain range and the plains that lead to the Mediterranean coast. There are three different areas: Penedès Superior, Penedès Central or Medio and Bajo Penedès.

## CLIMATE

Mediterranean, in general warm and mild; warmer in the Bajo Penedés region due to the influence of the Mediterranean Sea, with slightly lower temperatures in Medio Penedés and Penedés Superior, where the climate is typically pre-coastal (greater contrasts between maximum and minimum temperatures, more frequent frosts and annual rainfall which at some places can reach 990 litres per square metre).

## SOIL

There is deep soil, not too sandy or too clayey, permeable, which retains the rainwater well. The soil is poor in organic matter and not very fertile.

## GRAPE VARIETIES:

**White:** *Macabeo* (6,622 Ha), *Xarel·lo* (7,833 Ha), *Parellada* (6,045 Ha), *Chardonnay* (1,038 Ha), *Riesling, Gewürztraminer, Chenin Blanc, Moscatel de Alejandría.*

**Red:** *Garnacha, Merlot* (1,554 Ha), *Cariñena, Ull de Llebre* (*Tempranillo* – 1,507 Ha), *Pinot Noir, Monastrell, Cabernet Sauvignon* (11,487 Ha) and *Syrah.*

| | |
|---|---|
| Hectares of Vineyard | 26,080 |
| Nº Viticulturists | 3,945 |
| Nº of Bodegas | 156 |
| 2008 Harvest | Very Good |
| 2007 Production | 162,453,943 l. |
| Marketing | 73.62% domestic 26.38% export |

# DO PENEDÈS

## SUB-REGIONS:

**Penedès Superior.** The vineyards reach an altitude of 800 m; the traditional, characteristic variety is the Parellada, which is better suited to the cooler regions.

**Penedès Central or Medio.** Cava makes up a large part of the production in this region; the most abundant traditional varieties are Macabeo and Xarel-lo.

**Bajo Penedès.** This is the closest region to the sea, with a lower altitude and wines with a markedly Mediterranean character.

## CONSEJO REGULADOR

Pol. Industrial Domenys II. Plaça Àgora
08720 Vilafranca del Penedés. Apdo. 226
☎: 938 904 811 - Fax: 938 904
@ dopenedes@dopenedes.es

## GENERAL CHARACTERISTICS OF THE WINES:

| | |
|---|---|
| **WHITES** | The classical wines of the region, produced with the *Macabeo, Xarel-lo, Parellada* varieties, which stand out for their fruity character and extreme lightness. They are fresh wines, and are pleasant to drink within the year. Barrel-fermented wines are also starting to appear, mainly single variety wines of *Xarel-lo* and *Macabeo*, with a greater capacity to age due to the contribution of the tannins of the wood. Another important group is the *Chardonnay* white wines, whether young (fruity, with lemony notes and fine varietal character) or fermented in barrels, which combine the fruity personality of *Chardonnay* with the creamy notes of the oak. |
| **ROSÉS** | Modern in style, raspberry pink coloured, powerful, aromatic and fresh. They are produced from varieties as diverse as *Tempranillo, Cabernet, Merlot* or *Pinot Noir*. |
| **REDS** | Those produced from autochthonous grapes, generally *Garnacha* and *Tempranillo*, are young red wines, and are pleasant and easy drinking, although, on occasions, they may be a bit light and have certain herbal notes due to overproduction in the vineyard. Regarding those aged in wood, they may come from foreign varieties (mainly *Cabernet* and *Merlot*) or combined with local grape varieties. They integrate the notes of fine wood with fruity aromas with a good intensity; on the palate they are concentrated and meaty. |

## 2008 VINTAGE RATING:

## VERY GOOD

## ALBET I NOYA

Can Vendrell de la Codina, s/n
08739 Sant Pau D'Ordal (Barcelona)
☎: 938 994 812 - Fax: 938 994 930
albetinoya@albetinoya.cat
www.albetinoya.cat

**ALBET I NOYA 3 MACABEUS 2008 B**
macabeo

**91** Colour: bright straw. Nose: white flowers, ripe fruit, sweet spices. Palate: flavourful, powerful, fleshy, fruity.

**ALBET I NOYA LIGNUM 2008 B**
sauvignon blanc, chardonnay

**90** Colour: bright straw. Nose: white flowers, spicy, ripe fruit, fruit expression. Palate: flavourful, fruity, fresh, good structure.

**ALBET I NOYA XAREL-LO CLÀSSIC 2008 B**
xarel.lo

**87** Colour: bright straw. Nose: elegant, medium intensity, ripe fruit, white flowers. Palate: flavourful, fleshy, complex.

**MARINA RION 2008 B**

**87** Colour: bright straw. Nose: fresh, fresh fruit, white flowers, expressive. Palate: flavourful, fruity, good acidity, balanced.

**ALBET I NOYA PETIT ALBET 2008 B**
chardonnay, xarel.lo

**85** Colour: bright straw. Nose: white flowers, fresh fruit, floral. Palate: flavourful, fruity, fresh.

**ALBET I NOYA DOLÇ LES TIMBES 2008 B**
viognier

**83**

**ALBET I NOYA COL.LECCIÓ CHARDONNAY 2007 B**
chardonnay 100%

**91** Colour: bright straw. Nose: powerful, varietal, ripe fruit, sweet spices. Palate: flavourful, fruity, rich.

**ALBET I NOYA EL BLANC XXV 2007 B**
viognier, experimentaes

**87** Colour: bright straw. Nose: ripe fruit, warm, spicy, toasty. Palate: flavourful, powerful, fleshy.

**ALBET I NOYA PINOT NOIR MERLOT CLÀSSIC 2008 RD**
pinot noir, merlot

**86** Colour: rose, purple rim. Nose: powerful, ripe fruit, red berry notes. Palate: flavourful, powerful, fleshy.

**ALBET I NOYA TEMPRANILLO CLÀSSIC 2008 T**
tempranillo

**88** Colour: cherry, purple rim. Nose: red berry notes, ripe fruit, floral. Palate: flavourful, fleshy, fruity.

**ALBET I NOYA LIGNUM 2007 T**
garnacha, cariñena, cabernet sauvignon

**89** Colour: deep cherry, orangey edge. Nose: powerful, earthy notes, toasty, new oak, ripe fruit. Palate: flavourful, spicy, ripe fruit, round tannins.

**ALBET I NOYA COL.LECCIÓ SYRAH 2006 T**
syrah 100%

**91** Colour: cherry, purple rim. Nose: creamy oak, new oak, toasty, ripe fruit. Palate: flavourful, powerful, fleshy, round tannins.

**BELAT 2006 T**

**90** Colour: cherry, garnet rim. Nose: ripe fruit, spicy, creamy oak. Palate: powerful, flavourful, toasty, round tannins.

**FINCA LA MILANA 2005 T**
cabernet sauvignon, tempranillo, merlot

**91** Colour: cherry, garnet rim. Nose: ripe fruit, spicy, creamy oak, toasty, complex, earthy notes. Palate: powerful, flavourful, toasty, round tannins.

**ALBET I NOYA RESERVA MARTÍ 2004 T**
tempranillo, syrah, cabernet sauvignon, merlot, syrah

**89** Colour: cherry, garnet rim. Nose: powerful, warm, spicy, toasty. Palate: flavourful, creamy, ripe fruit, spicy, round tannins.

**ALBET I NOYA DOLÇ ADRIÀ 2003 TINTO DULCE**
syrah, tempranillo

**86** Colour: cherry, garnet rim. Nose: powerful, warm, overripe fruit, fruit liqueur notes. Palate: full, fleshy, sweet.

## ALEMANY I CORRIO

Melió, 78
08720 Vilafranca del Penedés (Barcelona)
☎: 938 922 746 - Fax: 938 172 587
sotlefriec@totpenedes.com

PLOU I FA SOL 2008 B
xarel.lo, malvasia

**92** Colour: bright yellow. Nose: creamy oak, spicy, roasted almonds, dried herbs. Palate: smoky aftertaste, mineral, fruity, full, powerful, flavourful.

PAS CURTEI 2007 T

**93** Colour: very deep cherry. Nose: creamy oak, characterful, expressive, powerfull, damp earth, truffle notes. Palate: good acidity, powerful, flavourful, varietal, fruity, fresh, toasty, smoky aftertaste.

SOT LEFRIEC 2005 T

**94** Colour: deep cherry. Nose: ripe fruit, creamy oak, expressive, aromatic coffee, cedar wood. Palate: flavourful, fruity, toasty, round tannins, powerful, varietal.

## ALSINA & SARDÁ

Barrio Les Tarumbes, s/n
08733 Pla del Penedés (Barcelona)
☎: 938 988 132 - Fax: 938 988 671
alsina@alsinasarda.com
www.alsinasarda.com

ALSINA & SARDÁ CHARDONNAY XAREL.LO 2008 B

**81**

ALSINA & SARDÁ BLANC DE BLANCS 2008 B
macabeo, parellada

**81**

ALSINA & SARDÁ LA BOITANA 2008 B
xarel.lo

**78**

ALSINA & SARDÁ 2008 RD
merlot

**78**

ARNAU 2008 T
merlot

**84**

ALSINA & SARDÁ MERLOT 2006 TC

**86** Colour: cherry, garnet rim. Nose: powerful, varietal, ripe fruit, toasty, sweet spices. Palate: powerful, flavourful, fleshy, round tannins.

ALSINA & SARDÁ CABERNET SAUVIGNON 2003 TR

**83**

ALSINA & SARDA RESERVA DE FAMILIA 2001 T
merlot

**87** Colour: pale ruby, brick rim edge. Nose: powerful, caramel, aromatic coffee, pattiserie. Palate: spicy, classic aged character, round tannins.

## AVINYÓ CAVAS

Masia Can Fontanals
08793 Avinyonet del Penedés (Barcelona)
☎: 938 970 055 - Fax: 938 970 691
avinyo@avinyo.com
www.avinyo.com

AVINYÓ MERLOT S.C. T
merlot 100%

**84**

AVINYÓ CABERNET SAUVIGNON 2004 TC
cabernet sauvignon 100%

**85** Colour: very deep cherry, garnet rim. Nose: ripe fruit, candied fruit. Palate: flavourful, ripe fruit, fruity aftestaste.

ESTEVE I VIA FERMENTACIÓ NATURAL BLANCO DE AGUJA
macabeo, xarel.lo, moscatel

**87** Colour: bright straw. Nose: white flowers, citrus fruit, fresh fruit. Palate: flavourful, sweetness, good acidity.

## BODEGA CAN BONASTRE

Ctra. B 224, km. 13,2
08783 Masquefa (Barcelona)
☎: 937 726 167 - Fax: 937 727 929
export@canbonastre.com
www.canbonastre.com

CAN BONASTRE 2008 B
xarel.lo 60%, chardonnay 40%

**88** Colour: bright golden. Nose: varietal, fresh, balanced. Palate: good structure, fresh, flavourful, good acidity, great length.

**MAUREL 2007 B**
chardonnay 100%

**89** Colour: bright golden. Nose: varietal, medium intensity, expressive. Palate: flavourful, fleshy, good acidity, fine bitter notes.

**NARA 2006 TC**
cabernet sauvignon 85%, merlot 15%

**90** Colour: bright cherry. Nose: sweet spices, creamy oak, powerfull, ripe fruit. Palate: flavourful, fruity, toasty, round tannins.

**ERUMIR**

## BODEGAS CAPITÀ VIDAL

Ctra. Villafranca-Igualada, km. 30
08733 Pla del Penedés (Barcelona)
☎: 938 988 630 - Fax: 938 988 625
capitavidal@capitavidal.com
www.capitavidal.com

**CLOS VIDAL BLANC DE BLANCS 2008 B**
macabeo 50%, xarel.lo 28%, parellada 20%, moscatel 2%
**83**

**CLOS VIDAL ROSÉ CUVÉE 2008 RD**
syrah 45%, merlot 30%, garnacha 25%

**87** Colour: salmon. Nose: expressive, floral, red berry notes. Palate: flavourful, fruity, fresh, light-bodied.

**CLOS VIDAL MERLOT 2006 TC**
merlot 85%, tempranillo 15%
**81**

**CLOS VIDAL 2005 TR**
cabernet sauvignon 90%, tempranillo 10%

**87** Colour: cherry, garnet rim. Nose: powerful, ripe fruit, cocoa bean, creamy oak. Palate: good structure, flavourful, spicy.

## BODEGAS GRAMONA

Industria, 34-36
08770 Sant Sadurní D'Anoia (Barcelona)
☎: 938 910 113 - Fax: 938 183 284
comunicacion@gramona.com
www.gramona.com

**GRAMONA MAS ESCORPÍ CHARDONNAY 2008 B**
chardonnay 100%

**90** Colour: bright straw. Nose: ripe fruit, citrus fruit, fruit expression, white flowers. Palate: flavourful, fleshy, complex, fruity.

**GRAMONA SAUVIGNON BLANC 2008 BFB**
sauvignon blanc 100%

**89** Colour: bright yellow. Nose: powerful, ripe fruit, citrus fruit, white flowers. Palate: ripe fruit, flavourful, fleshy.

**VI DE GEL GEWÜRZTRAMINER 2008 B**
gewürztraminer 100%

**89** Colour: bright straw. Nose: fresh, fresh fruit, white flowers, expressive, varietal. Palate: flavourful, fruity, good acidity, balanced.

**GRAMONA MOUSTILLANT 2008 B**
parellada 100%

**86** Colour: bright straw. Nose: white flowers, ripe fruit, citrus fruit, grassy. Palate: flavourful, fruity, fresh, fine bead.

**GRAMONA GESSAMÍ 2007 B**
moscatel, sauvignon blanc

**90** Colour: bright straw. Nose: powerful, ripe fruit, wild herbs, fruit expression, citrus fruit, complex. Palate: flavourful, powerful, fruity, fresh, varietal.

**VI DE GEL GEWÜRZTRAMINER 2004 BC**
gewürztraminer 100%

**93** Colour: bright straw. Nose: powerful, candied fruit, honeyed notes, petrol notes. Palate: flavourful, powerful, fleshy, complex.

**PRIMEUR GRAMONA 2008 RD**
syrah 100%

**85** Colour: rose, purple rim. Nose: ripe fruit, red berry notes, powerfull. Palate: fleshy, flavourful, powerful.

**GRAMONA GRA A GRA 2003 BLANCO DULCE**
sauvignon blanc 50%, chardonnay 50%

**93** Colour: bright straw. Nose: candied fruit, honeyed notes, powerfull, warm. Palate: flavourful, good acidity, sweet, complex.

**GRAMONA AGRELLA ROSAT DE AGUJA**
**84**

## BODEGAS J. TRIAS

Comerç, 6
08720 Vilafranca del Penedés (Barcelona)
☎: 938 902 627 - Fax: 938 901 724
bodegas@jtrias.com
www.jtrias.com

## TRIAS BATLLE BLANC DE BLANCS 2008 B
macabeo 45%, xarel.lo 30%, parellada 15%, moscatel 10%

**84**

## TRIAS-BATLLE CHARDONNAY 2008 BC
chardonnay 100%

**82**

## TRIAS BATLLE 2008 RD
cabernet sauvignon 40%, merlot 40%, syrah 20%

**81**

## TRIAS-BATLLE 2008 T
tempranillo 85%, merlot 15%

**87** Colour: cherry, purple rim. Nose: red berry notes, fresh fruit, expressive. Palate: concentrated, fruity, fruity aftestaste, great length.

## TRIAS-BATLLE 2006 TC
merlot 70%, cabernet sauvignon 15%, tempranillo 15%

**89** Colour: cherry, garnet rim. Nose: ripe fruit, sweet spices, balanced. Palate: good structure, flavourful, fruity, round tannins.

## TRIAS-BATLLE CABERNET SAUVIGNON 2006 TC
cabernet sauvignon 100%

**86** Colour: very deep cherry, garnet rim. Nose: ripe fruit, spicy, balanced. Palate: fleshy, full, spicy, fruity, round tannins.

## BODEGAS MIGUEL TORRES

Miguel Torres i Carbó, 6
08203 Vilafranca del Penedés (Barcelona)
☎: 938 177 400 - Fax: 938 177 444
mailadmin@torres.es
www.torres.es

## FRANSOLA 2008 B

**91** Colour: bright straw. Nose: powerful, varietal, grassy, white flowers, fresh fruit. Palate: flavourful, fruity, fresh, fleshy, ripe fruit.

## WALTRAUD 2008 B
riesling

**91** Colour: bright straw. Nose: fresh fruit, citrus fruit, fragrant herbs, expressive, varietal. Palate: fresh, fruity, good acidity, fine bitter notes.

## GRAN VIÑA SOL CHARDONNAY 2008 B

**88** Colour: bright straw. Nose: varietal, fruit expression, ripe fruit, floral, fresh fruit. Palate: flavourful, fruity, fresh, fleshy.

## ATRIUM CHARDONNAY 2007 B
chardonnay

**89** Colour: bright yellow. Nose: balanced, ripe fruit, floral, varietal. Palate: good structure, flavourful, powerful, fine bitter notes.

## ATRIUM 2008 T

**88** Colour: cherry, garnet rim. Nose: powerful, varietal, ripe fruit, red berry notes. Palate: flavourful, ripe fruit, round tannins.

## ATRIUM 2007 T
merlot

**89** Colour: cherry, purple rim. Nose: fresh, red berry notes, scrubland, floral. Palate: flavourful, fleshy, fruity, correct.

## ATRIUM 2006 T

**87** Colour: cherry, garnet rim. Nose: varietal, grassy, fresh. Palate: flavourful, ripe fruit, spicy, balsamic, round tannins.

## MAS LA PLANA CABERNET SAUVIGNON 2005 T

**92** Colour: very deep cherry, garnet rim. Nose: varietal, creamy oak, cocoa bean. Palate: complex, fruity, fine bitter notes, smoky aftertaste, round tannins.

## RESERVA REAL 2004 T

**93** Colour: very deep cherry, garnet rim. Nose: complex, expressive, cocoa bean, dark chocolate, mineral, ripe fruit. Palate: rich, fruity, powerful, round tannins.

## GRAN CORONAS

## BODEGAS PINORD

Doctor Pasteur, 6
08720 Vilafranca del Penedés (Barcelona)
☎: 938 903 066 - Fax: 938 170 979
pinord@pinord.es
www.pinord.com

## PINORD CHARDONNAY 2008 B

**90** Colour: bright straw. Nose: varietal, powerfull, fruit expression, ripe fruit. Palate: flavourful, fleshy, fruity, good acidity.

## PINORD VIÑA MIREIA 2008 B

**85** Colour: bright straw. Nose: ripe fruit, white flowers, grassy. Palate: fruity, fleshy, ripe fruit.

## PINORD CLOS DE TORRIBAS 2008 B

**82**

+ NATURA BLANC DE BLANC 2008 B

**82**

GAUDIANA 2008 B

**78**

PINORD CHARDONNAY 2007 BFB

**81**

PINORD PREMIUM 2008 RD

**87** Colour: raspberry rose. Nose: elegant, candied fruit, red berry notes. Palate: flavourful, fruity, fresh.

PINORD CLOS DE TORRIBAS 2008 RD

**82**

GAUDIANA 2008 RD

**67**

PINORD LA NANSA RD

**84**

PINORD CLOS 15 MERLOT 2007 TC

**89** Colour: cherry, garnet rim. Nose: powerful, creamy oak, sweet spices. Palate: flavourful, powerful, fleshy, spicy, round tannins.

+ NATURA 2007 T

**87** Colour: cherry, garnet rim. Nose: ripe fruit, spicy, balsamic herbs, scrubland. Palate: flavourful, spicy, ripe fruit, round tannins.

PINORD CLOS DE TORRIBAS 2005 TC
tempranillo

**87** Colour: cherry, garnet rim. Nose: powerful, warm, toasty, caramel. Palate: powerful, fleshy, spicy.

PINORD CLOS DE TORRIBAS 2003 TR
tempranillo

**85** Colour: deep cherry, orangey edge. Nose: powerful, ripe fruit, sweet spices, toasty. Palate: flavourful, spicy, ripe fruit, classic aged character.

PINORD CHATELDON CABERNET SAUVIGNON 2002 TR

**91** Colour: pale ruby, brick rim edge. Nose: elegant, expressive, aromatic coffee, spicy, fruit liqueur notes. Palate: flavourful, spicy, classic aged character, round tannins.

PINORD PI DEL NORD CABERNET SAUVIGNON 2002 T

**88** Colour: cherry, garnet rim. Nose: powerful, ripe fruit, sweet spices, aged wood nuances. Palate: flavourful, powerful, fleshy, spicy.

PINORD CHATELDON CABERNET SAUVIGNON 2001 TGR

**89** Colour: deep cherry, orangey edge. Nose: powerful, fruit liqueur notes, ripe fruit, spicy, aromatic coffee. Palate: flavourful, fleshy, spicy, round tannins.

PINORD REYNAL T

**82**

PINORD LA NANSA BLANCO DE AGUJA

**85** Colour: pale. Nose: white flowers, fresh fruit, citrus fruit, grassy. Palate: sweetness, fruity, fresh, fine bead.

PINORD REYNAL BLANCO DE AGUJA

**81**

VIÑA CHATEL

## BODEGAS TORRE DEL VEGUER

Urb. Torre de Veguer, s/n
08810 Sant Pere de Ribes (Barcelona)
☎: 938 963 190 - Fax: 938 963 190
torredelveguer@torredelveguer.com
www.torredelveguer.com

TORRE DEL VEGUER DULCE VENDIMIA TARDÍA 2008 B
moscatel 100%

**92** Colour: bright straw. Nose: powerful, varietal, white flowers, ripe fruit, grassy. Palate: flavourful, fleshy, good acidity, long.

TORRE DEL VEGUER XAREL.LO 2008 B
xarel.lo 95%, sauvignon blanc 5%

**87** Colour: bright straw. Nose: powerful, grassy, floral, fresh fruit. Palate: flavourful, fruity, fresh.

TORRE DEL VEGUER MUSCAT 2008 B
moscatel 100%

**85** Colour: bright straw. Nose: powerful, white flowers, ripe fruit. Palate: sweetness, flavourful, great length.

TORRE DEL VEGUER SAUVIGNON BLANC 2008 B
sauvignon blanc 100%

**85** Colour: bright straw. Nose: powerful, ripe fruit, citrus fruit, white flowers. Palate: flavourful, fruity, fleshy.

**TORRE DEL VEGUER CABERNET SAUVIGNON 2006 T**
cabernet sauvignon 100%

**86** Colour: cherry, garnet rim. Nose: powerful, ripe fruit, toasty, aromatic coffee. Palate: powerful, sweetness, spicy, round tannins.

**TORRE DEL VEGUER RAÏMS DE LA INMORTALITAT 2 2001 TR**
merlot 60%, cabernet sauvignon 15%, cariñena 12,5%, tempranillo 12,5%

**81**

RAIM DE LA IMMORTALITAT

## BODEGUES SUMARROCA S.L.

Barrio El Rebato, s/n
08739 Subirats (Barcelona)
☎: 938 911 092 - Fax: 938 911 778
sumarroca@sumarroca.es
www.sumarroca.es

**SUMARROCA GRAN BLANC DE BLANCS 2008 B**
chardonnay, moscatel, riesling, sauvignon blanc, gewürztraminer

**88** Colour: bright straw. Nose: varietal, grapey, fresh, expressive, fragrant herbs. Palate: flavourful, rich, balanced.

**SUMARROCA MUSCAT 2008 B**
moscatel 100%

**88** Colour: bright straw. Nose: grapey, honeyed notes, floral, lactic notes. Palate: flavourful, rich, balanced, fine bitter notes.

**SUMARROCA BLANC DE BLANCS 2008 B**
macabeo, xarel.lo, parellada, chardonnay, moscatel

**88** Colour: bright straw. Nose: medium intensity, fragrant herbs, citrus fruit. Palate: easy to drink, flavourful, fine bitter notes, fruity.

**SUMARROCA CHARDONNAY 2008 B**
chardonnay 100%

**87** Colour: yellow, pale. Nose: lactic notes, ripe fruit, balanced. Palate: fleshy, great length, good acidity, fine bitter notes.

**SUMARROCA PINOT NOIR 2008 RD**
pinot noir

**88** Colour: rose, purple rim. Nose: floral, expressive, red berry notes. Palate: flavourful, fruity, fresh, fleshy.

**SUMARROCA 2008 RD**

**87** Colour: brilliant rose. Nose: elegant, candied fruit, dried flowers, fragrant herbs, red berry notes. Palate: light-bodied, flavourful, good acidity, long, spicy.

**LONIA 2008 T**
merlot 60%, tempranillo 20%, cabernet sauvignon 20%

**87** Colour: cherry, purple rim. Nose: powerful, ripe fruit, red berry notes, spicy. Palate: flavourful, powerful, fruity.

**BÒRIA 2006 T**
syrah 70%, cabernet sauvignon 15%, merlot 15%

**90** Colour: cherry, garnet rim. Nose: ripe fruit, spicy, creamy oak, toasty, complex. Palate: powerful, flavourful, toasty, round tannins.

**TERRAL 2006 T**
syrah 35%, cabernet franc 35%, tempranillo 25%, merlot 5%HHH12€

**88** Colour: cherry, garnet rim. Nose: mineral, powerfull, ripe fruit, sweet spices, toasty. Palate: flavourful, powerful, fleshy, spicy.

**SUMARROCA SANTA CREU DE CREIXÀ 2006 T**
merlot 40%, cabernet sauvignon 35%, cabernet franc 35%, syrah 10%

**87** Colour: cherry, garnet rim. Nose: fruit preserve, fruit liqueur notes, toasty, aromatic coffee. Palate: spicy, ripe fruit, concentrated.

## CA N'ESTELLA

Masia Can Estella
08635 Sant Esteve Sesrovires (Barcelona)
☎: 934 161 387 - Fax: 934 161 620
e.mallol@fincacanestella.com

**CLOT DELS OMS CHARDONNAY 2008 B**
chardonnay

**86** Colour: bright straw. Nose: balanced, fresh, medium intensity, ripe fruit. Palate: flavourful, ripe fruit, good finish.

**CLOT DELS OMS BS 2008 B**
macabeo, xarel.lo, chardonnay

**86** Colour: bright yellow. Nose: fresh, balanced, medium intensity. Palate: flavourful, fleshy, good structure.

**CLOT DELS OMS FINCA CA N'ESTELLA 2007 BFB**
xarel.lo

**90** Colour: bright yellow. Nose: varietal, medium intensity, ripe fruit, white flowers. Palate: easy to drink, spicy, fresh, fruity, good acidity.

**CLOT DELS OMS FINCA CA N'ESTELLA 2007 BFB**
chardonnay

**88** Colour: bright golden. Nose: varietal, medium intensity, ripe fruit. Palate: elegant, fine bitter notes, creamy, balanced.

### GRAN CLOT DELS OMS 2008 RD

**85** Colour: rose, purple rim. Nose: powerful, ripe fruit, red berry notes, floral, expressive. Palate: fleshy, powerful, fruity, fresh.

### CLOT DELS OMS 2008 RD

**81**

### CLOT DELS OMS FINCA CA N'ESTELLA RD

**87** Colour: rose, purple rim. Nose: powerful, ripe fruit, red berry notes, fruit expression. Palate: flavourful, fruity, sweetness, balanced.

### GRAN CLOT DELS OMS 2004 T

**85** Colour: cherry, garnet rim. Nose: toasty, aromatic coffee, ripe fruit, spicy, dark chocolate. Palate: spicy, toasty, round tannins.

### CLOT DELS OMS TS 2004 T
merlot, cabernet sauvignon

**84**

### CLOT DELS OMS CABERNET SAUVIGNON 2004 T

**83**

### CLOT DELS OMS MERLOT 2003 T

**85** Colour: cherry, garnet rim. Nose: toasty, dark chocolate, spicy, fruit liqueur notes. Palate: flavourful, spicy, ripe fruit.

## CAL RASPALLET VITICULTORS

Barri Sabanell, 11
08736 Font Rubí (Barcelona)
☎: 938 944 565 - Fax: 938 944 565
calraspallet@vinifera.cat
www.vinifera.info

### NUN VINYA DELS TAUS 2007 B

**92** Colour: bright straw. Nose: wild herbs, smoky, fruit expression. Palate: balanced, creamy, mineral, long, balsamic.

### IMPROVISACIÓ 2007 B

**89** Colour: straw. Nose: fresh fruit, grassy, dry stone, mineral. Palate: balsamic, fruity, fresh, flavourful.

## CAN CAMPS

Cam Camps s/n

08810 Olivella (Barcelona)
☎: 938 970 013

### PEDRADURA MASSÍS DEL GARRAF 2008 B
xarel.lo 54%, malvasia 26%, parellada 14%, moscatel 6%

**90** Colour: bright straw. Nose: fresh fruit, white flowers, grassy. Palate: fruity, fresh.

### PEDRADURA MASSÍS DEL GARRAF 2004 TR
marcelant 100%

**86** Colour: very deep cherry, garnet rim. Nose: ripe fruit, warm, toasty, old leather. Palate: fleshy, powerful, ripe fruit, good acidity.

## CAN DESCREGUT

Masia Can Descregut s/n
08735 Vilobi del Penedès (Barcelona)
☎: 938 978 273 - Fax: 938 170 786
candescregut@hotmail.com
www.montdarac.com

### DESCREGUT 30 2008 B
xarel.lo, macabeo, chardonnay

**84**

### EQUILIBRI 2006 B
xarel.lo, chardonnay

**85** Colour: bright straw. Nose: powerful, candied fruit, citrus fruit, sweet spices, smoky. Palate: flavourful, powerful, fleshy, fine bitter notes.

### DESCREGUT 100 MERLOT 2008 RD
merlot

**79**

### DESCREGUT 20/80 2005 T
merlot, syrah

**80**

## CAN RÀFOLS DELS CAUS

Can Rafols del Caus s/n
08739 Avinyonet del Penedés (Barcelona)
☎: 938 970 013 - Fax: 938 970 370
canrafolsdelscaus@canrafolsdelscaus.com
www.canrafolsdelscaus.com

### PETIT CAUS 2008 B
xarel.lo 45%, macabeo 20%, chardonnay 10%, parellada 10%, chenin blanc 10%, moscatel 5%

**88** Colour: bright straw. Nose: powerful, ripe fruit, citrus fruit, white flowers. Palate: flavourful, fruity, fresh.

**VINYA LA CALMA 2006 B**
chenin blanc 100%

**90** Colour: bright yellow. Nose: powerful, ripe fruit, sweet spices, creamy oak, fragrant herbs. Palate: rich, smoky aftertaste, flavourful, fresh, good acidity.

**GRAN CAUS 2006 B**
xarel.lo 50%, chardonnay 25%, chenin blanc 25%

**89** Colour: bright straw. Nose: ripe fruit, citrus fruit, white flowers. Palate: flavourful, fleshy, fruity.

**XAREL.LO PAIRAL 2005 B**

**87** Colour: bright yellow. Nose: candied fruit, citrus fruit, sweet spices, warm. Palate: powerful, fleshy, sweetness.

**EL ROCALLÍS 2004 BFB**
riesling 100%

**89** Colour: bright golden. Nose: powerful, ripe fruit, candied fruit, sweet spices, toasty. Palate: fleshy, flavourful, powerful, spicy.

**EL ROCALLÍS 2002 BFB**
riesling

**91** Colour: bright straw. Nose: powerful, candied fruit, fruit liqueur notes, dry nuts, toasty, cocoa bean. Palate: fleshy, complex, rich, warm, fine bitter notes.

**PETIT CAUS 2008 RD**
merlot 35%, tempranillo 35%, syrah 10%, cabernet sauvignon 10%, cabernet franc 10%

**88** Colour: brilliant rose. Nose: red berry notes, candied fruit, fruit expression, floral. Palate: flavourful, fruity, fresh.

**GRAN CAUS 2008 RD**
merlot 100%

**85** Colour: rose, purple rim. Nose: medium intensity, red berry notes, ripe fruit, violet drops. Palate: flavourful, fruity, fleshy.

**PETIT CAUS 2007 T**
merlot 57%, cabernet sauvignon 24%, syrah 19%

**87** Colour: cherry, purple rim. Nose: fresh, red berry notes, floral. Palate: fresh, fruity, good acidity, balanced.

**AD FINES 2003 T**
pinot noir 100%

**91** Colour: pale ruby, brick rim edge. Nose: candied fruit, woody, sweet spices, fruit liqueur notes, complex, elegant. Palate: easy to drink, balanced.

**GRAN CAUS 2002 T**
cabernet franc 38%, merlot 42%, cabernet sauvignon 20%

**88** Colour: light cherry, orangey edge. Nose: fine reductive notes, fruit liqueur notes, elegant. Palate: spicy, easy to drink, great length.

**CAUS LUBIS 2000 T**
merlot 100%

**91** Colour: deep cherry, garnet rim. Nose: closed, ripe fruit, elegant. Palate: fruity, good structure, full, complex, round tannins.

**EL ROCALLÍS FERMENTADO EN BARRICA**
incrocio manzoni 100%

**91** Colour: bright straw. Nose: faded flowers, scrubland, dry stone. Palate: powerful, flavourful, fruity, complex.

## CAN RAMON VITICULTORS DEL MONTGRÓS

Masia Can Climent, s/n
08810 Sant Pere de Ribes (Barcelona)
☎: 675 650 800 - Fax: 938 962 882
xavibar22@hotmail.com
www.eracancliment.com

**CLOS LENTISCUS XAREL.LO 2007 B**
xarel.lo 100%

**83**

**CAN RAMON ROSÉE 2008 RD**

**83**

**CLOS LENTISCUS SUMOLL 2004 T**
sumoll 100%

**79**

**CLOS LENTISCUS ROSÉE 2008 ESP**
sumoll 34%, samsó 33%, syrah 33%

**79**

**CLOS LENTISCUS ESP**

**78**

L'ERA DE CAN CLIMENT

## CANALS CANALS

Avda. Mare de Deu Montserrat, 9
08769 Castellví de Rosanes (Barcelona)
☎: 937 755 446 - Fax: 937 741 719
cava@canalscanals.com
www.canalscanals.com

MASIA SUBIRANA XAREL.LO MACERAT 2008 B
xarel.lo 100%

**87** Colour: bright straw, greenish rim. Nose: white flowers, fresh fruit. Palate: fruity, fresh, light-bodied.

MASIA SUBIRANA CHARDONNAY 2008 B

**86** Colour: bright straw. Nose: ripe fruit, citrus fruit, tropical fruit. Palate: flavourful, fleshy, fruity.

MASIA SUBIRANA MERLOT 2006 TC
merlot 100%

**84**

MASIA SUBIRANA CABERNET SAUVIGNON 2005 TC
cabernet sauvignon 100%

**86** Colour: cherry, garnet rim. Nose: ripe fruit, spicy, balsamic herbs, candied fruit. Palate: flavourful, fleshy, great length.

## CANALS NADAL

Ponent, 2
08733 El Pla del Penedés (Barcelona)
☎: 938 988 081 - Fax: 938 989 050
cava@canalsnadal.com
www.canalsnadal.com

CANALS NADAL GRAN XAREL.LO 2007 BFB
xarel.lo 100%

**82**

ANTONI CANALS NADAL CABERNET SAUVIGNON MERLOT 2004 TC
cabernet sauvignon 50%, merlot 50%

**84**

## CASA RAVELLA

Ctra. de Barcelona s/n
08739 Ordal (Barcelona)
☎: 938 179 173 - Fax: 938 179 245
bodega@condedeolzinellas.com
www.condedeolzinellas.com

HEREDEROS DEL CONDE DE OLZINELLAS 2008 B
xarel.lo 80%, chardonnay 20%

**88** Colour: bright straw. Nose: fresh, fresh fruit, white flowers, expressive. Palate: flavourful, fruity, good acidity, balanced.

CASA RAVELLA 2007 BFB
xarel.lo 70%, chardonnay 30%

**90** Colour: bright straw. Nose: fragrant herbs, creamy oak, sweet spices, ripe fruit, balanced. Palate: flavourful, fleshy, fruity.

CASA RAVELLA 2006 BFB
xarel.lo 70%, chardonnay 30%

**88** Colour: bright straw. Nose: ripe fruit, citrus fruit, sweet spices. Palate: flavourful, powerful, fine bitter notes.

CASA RAVELLA 2008 T
merlot 90%, cabernet sauvignon 10%

**78**

CASA RAVELLA TINTO SELECCIÓN 2006 T ROBLE
cabernet sauvignon 100%

**87** Colour: very deep cherry, garnet rim. Nose: cocoa bean, sweet spices, ripe fruit. Palate: flavourful, toasty, round tannins.

## CASTELLROIG - FINCA SABATÉ I COCA

Ctra. Sant Sadurní d'Anoia-Vilafranca del Penedés, km. 1
08739 Subirats (Barcelona)
☎: 938 911 927 - Fax: 938 914 055
info@castellroig.com
www.castellroig.com

CASTELLROIG SELECCIÓ 2008 B
xarel.lo, chardonnay

**90** Colour: bright straw. Nose: powerful, candied fruit, ripe fruit, sweet spices. Palate: flavourful, powerful, fleshy, ripe fruit.

CASTELLROIG XAREL.LO 2008 B
xarel.lo

**86** Colour: bright straw. Nose: expressive, citrus fruit, medium intensity. Palate: flavourful, unctuous, balanced, good acidity.

TERROJA DE SABATÉ I COCA 2007 B
xarel.lo

**90** Colour: bright straw. Nose: ripe fruit, citrus fruit, fragrant herbs, floral. Palate: flavourful, fruity, fleshy, ripe fruit.

CASTELLROIG ULL DE LIEBRE 2008 RD

**85** Colour: rose, purple rim. Nose: powerful, ripe fruit, red berry notes, floral, expressive, balsamic herbs. Palate: fleshy, powerful, fruity, fresh, carbonic notes.

CASTELLROIG ULL DE LLEBRE 2005 T
ull de llebre

**87** Colour: cherry, garnet rim. Nose: powerful, varietal, ripe fruit, warm. Palate: fleshy, ripe fruit, round tannins.

## CAVA JOSEP M. FERRET GUASCH

Barri L'alzinar, 68

08739 Font-Rubí (Barcelona)
☎: 938 979 037 - Fax: 938 979 414
ferretguasch@ferretguasch.com
www.ferretguasch.com

JOSEP M. FERRET GUASCH XAREL.LO 2008 B
xarel.lo 100%

**86** Colour: bright straw. Nose: medium intensity, fruit expression, floral. Palate: fresh, fruity, good acidity.

GEBRE CABERNET SAUVIGNON 2008 RD
cabernet sauvignon 100%

**85** Colour: rose, purple rim. Nose: grassy, ripe fruit, red berry notes. Palate: powerful, fleshy, sweetness.

## CAVA RECAREDO

Tamarit, 10
08770 Sant Sadurní D'Anoia (Barcelona)
☎: 938 910 214 - Fax: 938 911 697
cava@recaredo.es
www.recaredo.com

ELS RAUSTALS 2005 T
cabernet sauvignon 79%, ull de llebre 21%

**87** Colour: black cherry, orangey edge. Nose: woody, toasty, ripe fruit, fruit liqueur notes. Palate: flavourful, concentrated, round tannins.

## CAVAS FERRET

Avda. de Catalunya, 36
08736 Guardiola de FontRubí (Barcelona)
☎: 938 979 148 - Fax: 938 979 285
ferret@cavasferret.com
www.cavasferret.com

IGNEA 2008 B
parellada 40%, xarel.lo 30%, macabeo 30%

**90** Colour: bright straw. Nose: white flowers, balanced, ripe fruit, fruit expression, sweet spices, cocoa bean. Palate: flavourful, fleshy, good structure, spicy, round tannins.

ABAC 2008 B
xarel.lo 100%

**87** Colour: pale. Nose: fresh fruit, citrus fruit, wild herbs, fine lees. Palate: fruity, fresh, easy to drink.

FERRET BLANC SELECCIÓ DE BARRIQUES 2004 BFB
xarel.lo 50%, chardonnay 50%

**83**

IGNEA 2008 RD
merlot 30%, cabernet sauvignon 30%, tempranillo 40%

**85** Colour: rose, purple rim. Nose: fresh fruit, red berry notes, dried flowers, lactic notes. Palate: fruity, light-bodied, easy to drink.

EZEQUIEL FERRET Nº 1 S.C. T
merlot, cabernet sauvignon, tempranillo, syrah

**87** Colour: black cherry, orangey edge. Nose: powerful, ripe fruit, warm, toasty, spicy. Palate: flavourful, fleshy, spicy.

IGNEA 2007 T
merlot 40%, cabernet sauvignon 30%, tempranillo 20%

**88** Colour: bright cherry. Nose: ripe fruit, sweet spices, creamy oak. Palate: flavourful, fruity, toasty, round tannins.

FERRET BLANC SELECCIÓ DE BARRIQUES 2000 T
cabernet sauvignon 46%, tempranillo 30%, merlot 24%

**86** Colour: deep cherry, garnet rim. Nose: woody, toasty, wet leather. Palate: flavourful, powerful, fleshy, spicy.

## CAVAS HILL

Bonavista, 2
08734 Moja (Alt Penedès) (Barcelona)
☎: 938 900 588 - Fax: 938 170 246
cavashill@cavashill.com
www.cavashill.com

ORO PENEDÈS HILL 2008 B
moscatel, xarel.lo

**87** Colour: bright yellow. Nose: grapey, jasmine, floral, fruit expression. Palate: flavourful, rich, balanced, fruity, good acidity.

BLANC BRUC HILL 2008 BFB
xarel.lo, sauvignon blanc, chardonnay

**84**

CHARDONNAY HILL 2008 BFB
chardonnay 100%

**83**

MASIA HILL 2008 BFB
xarel.lo, macabeo

**81**

MASÍA HILL 2008 RD

**84**

MASÍA HILL 2008 T
tempranillo

**86** Colour: cherry, garnet rim. Nose: fresh, red berry notes, expressive. Palate: easy to drink, fruity, good acidity.

GRAN CIVET HILL 2004 TC

**84**

GRAN TOC HILL 2003 TR

**84**

CABERNET SAUVIGNON HILL 2003 TR

**82**

## CAVAS LAVERNOYA

Finca La Porchada
08729 Sant Marsal (Barcelona)
☎: 938 912 202 - Fax: 938 911 159
lavernoya@lavernoya.com
www.lavernoya.com

LÁCRIMA BACCUS BLANC DE BLANCS B

**82**

LAVERNOYA

## CAVAS MESTRES

Plaça Ajuntament, 8
08770 Sant Sadurní D'Anoia (Barcelona)
☎: 938 910 043 - Fax: 938 911 611
cava@mestres.es
www.mestres.es

MESTRES 1312 CUPATGE BLANC 2008 B
xarel.lo 60%, chardonnay 20%, sauvignon blanc 20%

**84**

MESTRES CUPATGE ROSAT 1312 2008 RD
cabernet sauvignon 80%, merlot 20%, garnacha %, syrah %

**85** Colour: rose, purple rim. Nose: candied fruit, red berry notes, expressive, warm. Palate: rich, fruity, flavourful, good finish.

## CELLER CAL COSTAS

Masia Cal Costas s/n
08736 Font Rubí (Barcelona)
☎: 934 140 948 - Fax: 934 140 948
info@jmiqueljane.com
www.jmiquel.com

J. MIQUEL JANÉ SAUVIGNON BLANC 2008 B
sauvignon blanc 100%

**88** Colour: bright straw. Nose: white flowers, varietal, ripe fruit, fruit expression. Palate: flavourful, fruity, fresh, fleshy.

J. MIQUEL JANÉ BLANC DE BLANCS 2008 B
xarel.lo 85%, parellada 10%, chardonnay 5%

**86** Colour: bright straw. Nose: ripe fruit, citrus fruit, white flowers. Palate: fruity, fresh, flavourful.

J. MIQUEL JANÉ CABERNET SAUVIGNON 2008 RD
cabernet sauvignon 100%

**82**

J. MIQUEL JANÉ 2005 T
merlot 70%, cabernet sauvignon 30%

**85** Colour: cherry, garnet rim. Nose: ripe fruit, balanced. Palate: fruity, easy to drink, good finish.

J. MIQUEL JANÉ 2000 TR

**86** Colour: cherry, garnet rim. Nose: powerful, ripe fruit, spicy, woody. Palate: sweetness, warm, fine bitter notes.

## CELLER JORDI LLUCH

Barrio Les Casetes, s/n
08777 Sant Quintí de Mediona (Barcelona)
☎: 938 988 138 - Fax: 938 988 138
vinyaescude@vinyaescude.com
www.vinyaescude.com

VINYA ESCUDÉ MAIOLES 2007 BFB
chardonnay 85%, xarel.lo 15%

**81**

VINYA ESCUDÉ NOGUERA 2005 TC
cabernet sauvignon 85%, merlot 15%

**85** Colour: cherry, garnet rim. Nose: powerful, fruit liqueur notes, dry nuts. Palate: flavourful, powerful, spicy, ripe fruit.

## CELLERS AVGVSTVS FORUM

Ctra. Sant Vicenç s/n
43700 El Vendrell (Tarragona)
☎: 977 666 910 - Fax: 977 666 590
avgvstvs@avgvstvs.es
www.avgvstvs.es

AVGVSTVS XAREL.LO 2008 BFB
xarel.lo 100%

**90** Colour: bright yellow. Nose: medium intensity, dried herbs, ripe fruit. Palate: fresh, fruity, balanced, fine bitter notes, elegant.

## AVGVSTVS CHARDONNAY 2007 BFB
chardonnay 100%

**89** Colour: bright golden. Nose: varietal, ripe fruit, sweet spices, fragrant herbs. Palate: flavourful, fruity, complex, balanced.

## AVGVSTVS XAREL.LO 2007 BFB
xarel.lo 100%

**88** Colour: bright yellow. Nose: smoky, spicy, fragrant herbs, ripe fruit. Palate: complex, good structure, good acidity, fine bitter notes.

## AVGVSTVS CABERNET SAUVIGNON ROSÉ 2008 RD
cabernet sauvignon 100%

**82**

## AVGVSTVS MERLOT SYRAH 2007 T
merlot 65%, syrah 35%

**88** Colour: bright cherry, garnet rim. Nose: fresh, red berry notes, ripe fruit, expressive. Palate: spicy, flavourful, good acidity.

## AVGVSTVS VI VARIETALES 2007 T FERMENTADO EN BARRICA
garnacha, cabernet franc, cabernet sauvignon, merlot, syrah, tempranillo

**86** Colour: black cherry, garnet rim. Nose: macerated fruit, powerfull, balanced. Palate: powerful, good acidity, fruity, good finish.

## AVGVSTVS CABERNET SAUVIGNON-MERLOT 2006 T ROBLE
cabernet sauvignon 50%, merlot 50%

**89** Colour: very deep cherry, garnet rim. Nose: warm, ripe fruit, toasty, spicy. Palate: powerful, concentrated, ripe fruit, round tannins.

## AVGVSTVS CABERNET FRANC 2006 T ROBLE
cabernet franc 100%

**86** Colour: very deep cherry, garnet rim. Nose: candied fruit, warm, expressive, varietal, spicy. Palate: fruity, flavourful, round tannins.

## AVGVSTVS TRAJANVS 2005 TR
cabernet sauvignon 40%, merlot 40%, cabernet franc 20%

**88** Colour: black cherry, garnet rim. Nose: ripe fruit, warm, spicy. Palate: flavourful, fleshy, ripe fruit, round tannins.

## EUDALD MASSANA NOYA

Finca El Maset s/n
08739 Sant Pau D'Ordal (Barcelona)
☎: 938 994 124 - Fax: 938 994 139

bodega@massananoya.com
www.massananoya.com

## CEPELL EUDALD MASSANA NOYA 2008 B

**84**

## EUDALD MASSANA NOYA " AVI TON" XAREL.LO 2007 BFB

**87** Colour: bright golden. Nose: fruit liqueur notes, fruit preserve, dry nuts, white flowers. Palate: fruity, full, powerful, warm.

## CEPELL 2008 RD

**79**

## LA CREUETA EUDALD MASSANA NOYA 2006 T FERMENTADO EN BARRICA

**86** Colour: cherry, garnet rim. Nose: varietal, neat, toasty, dark chocolate, fresh. Palate: fleshy, correct, round tannins.

## FERRE I CATASUS

Ctra. de Sant Sadurní, km. 8 Masia Can Gustems
08792 La Granada (Barcelona)
☎: 938 974 558 - Fax: 938 974 708
info@ferreicatasus.com
www.castelldelmirall.com

## FERRÉ I CATASÚS BLANC D'EXPRESSIÓ 2008 B
xarel.lo 40%, chardonnay 25%, chenin blanc 15%, moscatel 10%, sauvignon blanc 10%

**83**

## FERRÉ I CATASÚS XAREL.LO 3 VIÑAS 2008 B
xarel.lo

**82**

## FERRÉ I CATASÚS JOVE 2008 T
syrah 50%, cabernet sauvignon 30%, merlot 20%

**87** Colour: cherry, purple rim. Nose: powerful, ripe fruit, red berry notes. Palate: flavourful, fruity, fleshy.

## CAMERLOT 2005 TC
cabernet sauvignon 60%, merlot 40%

**84**

## GIRÓ DEL GORNER

Masia Giró del Gorner, s/n
08797 Puigdálber (Barcelona)
☎: 938 988 032
gorner@girodelgorner.com
www.girodelgorner.com

## BLANC GORNER 2008 B
xarel.lo 45%, macabeo 35%, parellada 20%

**85** Colour: bright straw. Nose: ripe fruit, fruit expression, citrus fruit. Palate: flavourful, fruity, fleshy.

## GORNER MERLOT 2008 RD
merlot 100%

**82**

## GORNER CABERNET-MERLOT 2004 TR
merlot 50%, cabernet sauvignon 50%

**82**

# GIRÓ RIBOT

Finca El Pont, s/n
08972 Santa Fe del Penedés (Barcelona)
☎: 938 974 050 - Fax: 938 974 311
comercial@giroribot.es
www.giroribot.es

## RAISSANT COUPAGE 2008 B
chardonnay 55%, xarel.lo 20%, macabeo 15%, parellada 10%

**87** Colour: bright yellow. Nose: varietal, ripe fruit, balanced. Palate: flavourful, fruity, good acidity.

## GIRÓ RIBOT BLANC FLOR 2008 B
moscatel 85%, gewürztraminer 15%

**86** Colour: bright yellow. Nose: grapey, floral, citrus fruit. Palate: flavourful, fresh, fruity, fruity aftestaste, good acidity.

## GIRÓ RIBOT MUSCAT DE FRONTIGNAC 2008 B
moscatel 100%

**85** Colour: bright straw. Nose: powerful, candied fruit, white flowers, varietal. Palate: flavourful, fruity, fresh.

## GIRÓ RIBOT BLANC DE BLANCS 2008 B
xarel.lo 50%, macabeo 30%, parellada 20%

**83**

# GRIMAU DE PUJADES

Castell de Les Pujades s/n
08732 La Munia (Barcelona)
☎: 938 918 031 - Fax: 938 918 426
grimau@grimau.com
www.grimau.com

## GRIMAU BLANC DE BLANCS 2008 B
macabeo, parellada, chardonnay, xarel.lo

**83**

## GRIMAU CHARDONNAY 2007 BC
chardonnay

**81**

## GRIMAU CABERNET SAUVIGNON 2005 TR
cabernet sauvignon

**82**

# HACIENDA MARQUÉS DE LA CONCORDIA

Ctra. El Ciego, s/n
26350 Cenicero (La Rioja)
☎: 914 365 900 - Fax: 914 365 932
iruiz@haciendas-espana.com
www.haciendas-espana.com

## HACIENDA ABASCAL 2005 TC

**88** Colour: cherry, garnet rim. Nose: medium intensity, ripe fruit, sweet spices, dark chocolate. Palate: powerful, flavourful, spicy, round tannins.

## MM RESERVA PRIVADA 2001 TR
cabernet sauvignon 40%, tempranillo 30%, merlot 30%

**88** Colour: cherry, garnet rim. Nose: ripe fruit, toasty, aromatic coffee, wet leather. Palate: flavourful, spicy, ripe fruit.

VINNATURE

# HERETAT MAS TINELL

Carretera de Vilafranca a St. Martí Sarroca, km. 0,5
08720 Vilafranca del Penedés (Barcelona)
☎: 938 170 586 - Fax: 938 170 500
oscar.re@mastinell.com
www.mastinell.com

## GISELE MAS TINELL 2008 BFB
xarel.lo 85%, moscatel 15%

**88** Colour: bright yellow. Nose: powerful, ripe fruit, sweet spices, creamy oak. Palate: rich, flavourful, fresh, good acidity.

## CLOS SANT PAU VENDIMIA TARDÍA 2008 B
moscatel 100%

**88** Colour: golden. Nose: floral, honeyed notes, candied fruit, fragrant herbs. Palate: flavourful, sweet, fresh, fruity, good acidity, long.

## HERETAT MAS TINELL CHARDONNAY 2008 B
chardonnay 100%

**87** Colour: bright straw. Nose: powerful, varietal, ripe fruit, citrus fruit. Palate: flavourful, fruity, fresh, fleshy.

## HERETAT MAS TINELL ALBA BLANC DE LLUNA 2008 B

**87** Colour: bright straw. Nose: fresh, fresh fruit, white flowers. Palate: flavourful, fruity, good acidity, balanced.

## ARTE MAS TINELL 2003 TR
cabernet sauvignon 85%, garnacha 10%, merlot 5%

**83**

## JANÉ VENTURA

Ctra. Calafell, 2
43700 El Vendrell (Tarragona)
☎: 977 660 118 - Fax: 977 661 239
janeventura@janeventura.com
www.janeventura.com

### JANÉ VENTURA "FINCA ELS CAMPS" MACABEU 2008 BFB
macabeo 95%, xarel.lo 5%

**91** Colour: bright straw. Nose: ripe fruit, complex, mineral, dry stone, scrubland, spicy. Palate: flavourful, fruity, good acidity, mineral, fine bitter notes.

### JANÉ VENTURA SELECCIÓ 2008 B
xarel.lo 65%, moscatel 15%, chardonnay 15%, malvasia 5%

**90** Colour: bright straw. Nose: fresh, fresh fruit, white flowers, expressive. Palate: flavourful, fruity, good acidity, balanced.

### JANÉ VENTURA SELECCIÓ 2008 RD
ull de llebre 50%, merlot 20%, syrah 20%, sumoll 10%

**85** Colour: rose, purple rim. Nose: powerful, ripe fruit, red berry notes, floral, expressive. Palate: fleshy, powerful, fruity, fresh.

### JANÉ VENTURA SELECCIÓ 2007 T
ull de llebre 40%, cabernet sauvignon 20%, merlot 20%, sumoll 10%, syrah 10%

**91** Colour: cherry, garnet rim. Nose: powerful, spicy, creamy oak, scrubland. Palate: flavourful, powerful, fleshy, spicy.

### JANÉ VENTURA "MAS VILELLA" 2006 T
cabernet sauvignon 100%

**92** Colour: bright cherry. Nose: ripe fruit, sweet spices, creamy oak, expressive, earthy notes. Palate: flavourful, fruity, toasty, round tannins.

### JANÉ VENTURA "FINCA ELS CAMPS" ULL DE LLEBRE 2005 T
ull de llebre 100%

**90** Colour: cherry, garnet rim. Nose: ripe fruit, spicy, creamy oak, toasty, complex. Palate: powerful, flavourful, toasty, round tannins.

## JAUME LLOPART ALEMANY

Font Rubí, 9
08736 Font-Rubí (Barcelona)
☎: 938 979 133 - Fax: 938 979 133
info@jaumellopartalemany.com
www.jaumellopartalemany.com

### JAUME LLOPART ALEMANY SAUVIGNON BLANC (VINYA D'EN LLUC) 2008 B
sauvignon blanc 100%

**89** Colour: bright straw. Nose: powerful, ripe fruit, citrus fruit, grassy, white flowers. Palate: flavourful, fruity, fresh.

### JAUME LLOPART ALEMANY 2008 B
parellada, xarel.lo

**85** Colour: bright straw. Nose: powerful, fresh fruit, citrus fruit, grassy. Palate: flavourful, fresh.

### JAUME LLOPART ALEMANY 2008 RD
merlot, tempranillo

**82**

### JAUME LLOPART ALEMANY MERLOT 2008 T
merlot 100%

**85** Colour: cherry, purple rim. Nose: red berry notes, grassy, balsamic herbs. Palate: powerful, fruity, fresh.

## JAUME SERRA

Ctra. de Vilanova, km. 2,5
08800 Vilanova i la Geltru (Barcelona)
☎: 938 936 404 - Fax: 938 142 262
jaumeserra@jgc.es
www.vinosdefamilia.com

### JAUME SERRA MERLOT 2008 RD
merlot 100%

**82**

### JAUME SERRA TEMPRANILLO 2006 T
tempranillo 100%

**80**

### JAUME SERRA CABERNET SAUVIGNON 2005 T ROBLE
cabernet sauvignon 100%

**84**

### JAUME SERRA MERLOT 2005 T ROBLE
merlot 100%

**81**

JAUME SERRA 2005 TC
cabernet sauvignon 65%, merlot 20%, tempranillo 15%

**79**

JAUME SERRA 2003 TR
cabernet sauvignon 50%, merlot 30%, tempranillo 20%

**82**

JAUME SERRA MACABEO 2008 BLANCO
macabeo 100%

**78**

JAUME SERRA XAREL.LO 2008 BLANCO SEMI-DULCE
xarel.lo 100%

**81**

## JEAN LEÓN

Pago Jean León
08775 Torrelavit (Barcelona)
☎: 938 995 512 - Fax: 938 995 517
jeanleon@jeanleon.com
www.jeanleon.com

JEAN LEÓN CHARDONNAY 2007 B

**92** Colour: bright straw. Nose: powerful, varietal, ripe fruit, citrus fruit, fine lees. Palate: flavourful, fruity, fleshy, complex.

JEAN LEÓN MERLOT 2006 T ROBLE
merlot

**90** Colour: deep cherry, garnet rim. Nose: earthy notes, red berry notes, ripe fruit, spicy. Palate: fleshy, concentrated, round tannins, balanced.

JEAN LEÓN CABERNET SAUVIGNON 2005 TR
cabernet sauvignon

**88** Colour: cherry, garnet rim. Nose: cocoa bean, sweet spices, ripe fruit, balanced. Palate: flavourful, balanced, ripe fruit, great length.

ZEMIS

## JOAN SARDÀ

Ctra. Vilafranca- St. Jaume dels Domenys, km. 8,1
08732 Castellvi de la Marca (Barcelona)
☎: 937 720 900 - Fax: 937 721 495
joansarda@joansarda.com
www.joansarda.com

JOAN SARDÀ CHARDONNAY 2008 B
chardonnay

**87** Colour: bright straw. Nose: ripe fruit, citrus fruit, fruit expression. Palate: flavourful, fleshy, fruity.

BLANC MARINER 2008 B
xarel.lo, chardonnay

**84**

JOAN SARDÀ CABERNET SAUVIGNON 2008 RD
cabernet sauvignon

**77**

JOAN SARDÀ MERLOT 2007 TC
merlot

**86** Colour: cherry, garnet rim. Nose: spicy, toasty, cocoa bean, ripe fruit. Palate: flavourful, powerful, fleshy.

GRAN VINYA SARDÀ 2005 TR
cabernet sauvignon, tempranillo, merlot

**87** Colour: cherry, garnet rim. Nose: ripe fruit, spicy, creamy oak, toasty, complex. Palate: powerful, flavourful, toasty, round tannins.

JOAN SARDÀ CABERNET SAUVIGNON 2005 TC
cabernet sauvignon

**86** Colour: cherry, garnet rim. Nose: powerful, ripe fruit, toasty, sweet spices. Palate: powerful, flavourful, fleshy, round tannins.

## JOSÉ MARIA ROSELL MIR

Masel de Can Ros.
08739 Subirats (Barcelona)
☎: 938 911 354 - Fax: 938 911 311
josep@rosellmir.com

PLA DE LA CREU 2008 B
xarel.lo

**84**

MARC MIR 2008 B
xarel.lo, chardonnay

**83**

PLA DE LA CREU 2008 RD
merlot, cabernet sauvignon

**84**

ROSELL MIR PLA DE LA CREU 2007 T
merlot

**86** Colour: cherry, garnet rim. Nose: powerful, balsamic herbs, scrubland, ripe fruit. Palate: spicy, ripe fruit, round tannins.

ROSELL MIR MASIA POSTA 2006 T
cabernet sauvignon, merlot

**78**

ROSELL MIR CABERNET SAUVIGNON 2005 TC
cabernet sauvignon

**83**

## JOSEP GUILERA RIAMBAU

Can Guilera, s/n
08739 Sant Pau D'Ordal (Barcelona)
☎: 938 993 094 - Fax: 938 993 094
canguilera@comaroma.net
www.comaroma.net

COMA ROMÀ 2008 RD
merlot 80%, ull de llebre 20%

**86** Colour: raspberry rose. Nose: powerful, red berry notes, fresh fruit. Palate: fruity, fresh, flavourful.

COMA ROMÀ 2007 T
merlot 100%

**88** Colour: cherry, purple rim. Nose: fresh fruit, red berry notes, varietal, balanced. Palate: flavourful, good structure, fresh, fruity.

## JUVÉ Y CAMPS

Sant Venat, 1
08770 Sant Sadurní D'Anoia (Barcelona)
☎: 938 911 000 - Fax: 938 912 100
comunicacio@juveycamps.com
www.juveycamps.com

MIRANDA D'ESPIELLS CHARDONNAY FLOR 2008 BFB
chardonnay 100%

**88** Colour: bright straw. Nose: ripe fruit, sweet spices, dried flowers. Palate: flavourful, fleshy, ripe fruit.

ERMITA D'ESPIELLS "BLANC FLOR" 2008 B
macabeo 30%, xarel.lo 30%, parellada 30%, chardonnay 10%

**85** Colour: bright straw. Nose: candied fruit, macerated fruit, dried herbs. Palate: flavourful, fine bitter notes, good acidity.

FLOR D'ESPIELLS CHARDONNAY 2008 BFB
chardonnay 100%

**84**

CASA VELLA D'ESPIELLS CABERNET SAUVIGNON 2006 T ROBLE
cabernet sauvignon 85%, merlot 15%

**91** Colour: bright cherry, garnet rim. Nose: complex, ripe fruit, earthy notes, dark chocolate. Palate: concentrated, balanced, round tannins, spicy.

VIÑA ESCARLATA MERLOT 2006 T
merlot 100%

**90** Colour: cherry, garnet rim. Nose: fresh, ripe fruit, mineral. Palate: complex, full, creamy, fruity aftestaste, great length.

CASA VELLA D'ESPIELLS CABERNET SAUVIGNON MAGNUM 2005 T ROBLE
cabernet sauvignon 85%, merlot 15%

**88** Colour: black cherry, garnet rim. Nose: powerful, balanced, ripe fruit, dark chocolate. Palate: fruity, round tannins.

## LLOPART

Ctra. de Sant Sadurni - Ordal, km. 4
08739 Subirats (Barcelona)
☎: 938 993 125 - Fax: 938 993 038
llopart@llopart.es
www.llopart.es

LLOPART CLOS DELS FÒSSILS CHARDONNAY 2008 B
chardonnay, xarel.lo

**89** Colour: bright straw. Nose: ripe fruit, fruit expression, citrus fruit. Palate: flavourful, fleshy, fruity, fresh.

LLOPART VITIS 2008 B
xarel.lo, moscatel, subirat parent

**86** Colour: bright straw. Nose: fresh, fresh fruit, white flowers. Palate: flavourful, fruity, good acidity, balanced.

LLOPART CASTELL DE SUBIRATS 2005 TR
merlot, cabernet sauvignon, tempranillo

**87** Colour: deep cherry, garnet rim. Nose: powerful, creamy oak, cocoa bean, dark chocolate. Palate: powerful, fleshy, sweetness, round tannins.

## LOXAREL

Masia Can Mayol, s/n
08735 Vilobí del Penedés (Barcelona)
☎: 938 978 001 - Fax: 938 978 111
loxarel@loxarel.com
www.loxarel.com

CORA DE LOXAREL 2008 B
moscatel, chardonnay, xarel.lo

**87** Colour: bright straw. Nose: honeyed notes, white flowers, varietal. Palate: good structure, easy to drink, good acidity, fine bitter notes.

GAIA DE LOXAREL 2008 B
sauvignon blanc

**84**

PETIT ARNAU DE LOXAREL 2008 RD
pinot noir, merlot

**82**

OPS DE LOXAREL 2008 T
cabernet sauvignon, merlot, tempranillo

**88** Colour: bright cherry. Nose: ripe fruit, sweet spices, creamy oak, expressive. Palate: flavourful, fruity, toasty, round tannins.

EOS DE LOXAREL SYRAH 2008 T
syrah

**86** Colour: cherry, purple rim. Nose: powerful, balsamic herbs, ripe fruit, scrubland. Palate: flavourful, balsamic, spicy, round tannins.

MAS CARGOLS DE LOXAREL 2007 T
pinot noir

**88** Colour: cherry, garnet rim. Nose: ripe fruit, spicy, creamy oak, toasty, complex. Palate: powerful, flavourful, toasty, round tannins.

OPS DE LOXAREL 2007 T
cabernet sauvignon, merlot, tempranillo

**86** Colour: cherry, garnet rim. Nose: ripe fruit, spicy, toasty. Palate: flavourful, ripe fruit, spicy, round tannins.

LOXAREL 2005 TR
cabernet sauvignon

**86** Colour: cherry, garnet rim. Nose: ripe fruit, sweet spices, toasty, new oak. Palate: flavourful, spicy, ripe fruit.

## MARTI SERDÀ

Ctra. D'Igualada a Vilafranca, km. 31.300
08792 Santa Fe del Penedés (Barcelona)
☎: 938 974 411 - Fax: 938 974 405
info@martiserda.com
www.martiserda.com

VINYET 2008 B JOVEN
parellada 60%, macabeo 20%, xarel.lo 20%

**83**

MARTÍ SERDA CHARDONNAY 2007 B JOVEN
chardonnay 100%

**84**

VINYET 2005 TC
tempranillo 75%, cabernet sauvignon 25%

**84**

MARTÍ SERDÁ MERLOT 2005 TC
merlot 100%

**82**

MARTÍ SERDÁ CABERNET SAUVIGNON 2003 TR
cabernet sauvignon 100%

**84**

MARTÍ SERDÁ MAS FARRENY 2001 TR
merlot 80%, cabernet sauvignon 20%

**86** Colour: cherry, garnet rim. Nose: ripe fruit, spicy, creamy oak, toasty, wet leather. Palate: powerful, flavourful, toasty, round tannins.

MARE NOSTRUM

## MAS CANDÍ

Ctra. de Les Gunyoles, s/n
08793 Les Gunyoles d'Avinyonet (Barcelona)
☎: 680 765 275 - Fax: 938 992 013
info@mascandi.com
www.mascandi.com

DESIG 2008 B
xarel.lo 100%

**88** Colour: bright straw. Nose: fresh, white flowers, ripe fruit. Palate: flavourful, fruity, good acidity, balanced.

MAS CANDÍ QX 2007 BFB
xarel.lo 100%

**87** Colour: bright yellow. Nose: powerful, expressive, candied fruit, ripe fruit, citrus fruit. Palate: flavourful, fruity, fleshy, sweetness.

LES FORQUES 2007 T
cabernet sauvignon

**87** Colour: black cherry, garnet rim. Nose: powerful, ripe fruit, sweet spices. Palate: spicy, pruney, round tannins.

## MAS CODINA

Barri El Gorner, s/n Mas Codina
08797 Puigdalber (Barcelona)
☎: 938 988 166 - Fax: 938 988 166
cavesmascodina@hotmail.com

MAS CODINA 2008 B
chardonnay 29%, macabeo 29%, xarel.lo 37%, moscatel 5%

# DO PENEDÈS

**86** Colour: bright straw. Nose: white flowers, ripe fruit, citrus fruit. Palate: flavourful, fleshy, sweetness, fruity.

**MAS CODINA 2008 RD**
merlot 40%, pinot noir 32%, cabernet sauvignon 28%

**79**

**MAS CODINA VINYA MIQUEL 2006 T**
syrah 100%

**86** Colour: cherry, garnet rim. Nose: balsamic herbs, scrubland, toasty, spicy. Palate: ripe fruit, flavourful, fleshy.

**MAS CODINA "VINYA FERRER" 2005 TC**
cabernet sauvignon 100%

**85** Colour: cherry, garnet rim. Nose: fruit preserve, creamy oak, dark chocolate. Palate: spicy, balsamic, fleshy, round tannins.

## MASET DEL LLEÓ

Avda.. Barcelona, 31 Pol.g Sant Pere Molanta
08734 Olerdola (Barcelona)
☎: 902 200 250 - Fax: 938 921 333
info@maset.com
www.maset.com

**MASET DEL LLEÓ XAREL.LO BLANC DE BLANCS 2008 B**

**85** Colour: bright straw. Nose: white flowers, fresh fruit, ripe fruit. Palate: flavourful, fruity, fresh.

**MASET DEL LLEÓ MERLOT 2008 RD**

**86** Colour: rose, purple rim. Nose: powerful, ripe fruit, red berry notes, floral, expressive. Palate: fleshy, powerful, fruity, fresh.

**MASET DEL LLEÓ 2006 TC**
cabernet sauvignon

**83**

**MASET DEL LLEÓ CABERNET SAUVIGNON 2003 TGR**

**85** Colour: black cherry, garnet rim. Nose: powerful, ripe fruit, fruit preserve, sweet spices. Palate: powerful, fleshy, ripe fruit, round tannins.

## MASIA BACH

Ctra. Martorell - Capellada, km. 20,5
08635 Sant Esteve de Sesrovires (Barcelona)
☎: 937 714 052 - Fax: 937 713 309
info@bach.es
www.bach.es

**BACH CHARDONNAY 2008 B**
chardonnay

**85** Colour: bright straw. Nose: ripe fruit, honeyed notes. Palate: flavourful, fruity, good acidity.

## MASÍA L'HEREU

Monistrol D'Anoia, s/n
08770 Sant Sadurni D'Anoia (Barcelona)
☎: 938 910 276 - Fax: 938 183 328
adelgado@haciendas-espana.com
www.haciendas-espana.com

**MASÍA L'HEREU MAS DE MONISTROL RESERVA PRIVADA 2004 TR**

**88** Colour: pale ruby, brick rim edge. Nose: expressive, fruit preserve, sweet spices, cocoa bean, aromatic coffee. Palate: round tannins, spicy, balanced, good acidity, warm.

**MM MASÍA L'HEREU 2000 T**

**90** Colour: deep cherry, bright ochre rim. Nose: ripe fruit, characterful, toasty, tobacco. Palate: light-bodied, spirituous, classic aged character, round tannins.

## MASÍA PUIGMOLTÓ

Barrio de Sant Marçal, 67
08732 Castellet i La Gornal (Barcelona)
☎: 938 186 119 - Fax: 938 918 169
avalles@emendis.es
www.emendis.es

**EMENDIS TRIO 2008 B**
macabeo 55%, chardonnay 30%, xarel.lo 25%

**89** Colour: bright straw. Nose: complex, fresh fruit, citrus fruit. Palate: flavourful, fruity, fresh, fleshy.

**GARBÍ 2008 B**
moscatel, parellada

**87** Colour: bright straw. Nose: fresh, expressive, ripe fruit, floral, citrus fruit. Palate: flavourful, fruity, sweetness, fine bead.

**EMENDIS 2007 BFB**
chardonnay 65%, xarel.lo 35%

**89** Colour: bright straw. Nose: sweet spices, cocoa bean, ripe fruit, dry nuts. Palate: flavourful, powerful, fleshy, sweetness.

**EMENDIS 2006 BFB**
chardonnay 65%, xarel.lo 35%

**86** Colour: bright yellow. Nose: powerful, ripe fruit, sweet spices, creamy oak, fragrant herbs. Palate: rich, smoky aftertaste, flavourful, fresh, good acidity.

EMENDIS NOX 2008 RD
merlot 90%, pinot noir 10%

**84**

EMENDIS DOLÇ MONASTRELL S.C. T

**86** Colour: cherry, garnet rim. Nose: overripe fruit, dried fruit, warm. Palate: powerful, fleshy, unctuous.

EMENDIS 2007 T BARRICA
tempranillo 90%, merlot 10%

**88** Colour: deep cherry, garnet rim. Nose: ripe fruit, medium intensity, fresh. Palate: fruity, easy to drink, balanced, good structure.

EMENDIS MATER 2006 TC
merlot 100%

**88** Colour: cherry, garnet rim. Nose: spicy, new oak, roasted coffee, ripe fruit. Palate: powerful, flavourful, ripe fruit, grainy tannins.

EMENDIS DOLÇ MOSCATEL MISTELA

**87** Colour: bright straw. Nose: floral, jasmine, varietal, ripe fruit. Palate: flavourful, fruity, sweetness.

## MATA D'ABELLÓ

Can Mata D'Abelló s/n
08790 Gélida (Barcelona)
☎: 699 392 049 - Fax: 933 713 279
jalemany@matadabello.com
www.matadabello.com

TOTTÓ 2008 BFB
xarel.lo 100%

**87** Colour: bright straw. Nose: expressive, ripe fruit, toasty, sweet spices, varietal. Palate: good structure, concentrated, long, good acidity.

FINCA AVELLÓ VINYES VELLES 2008 B
xarel.lo 100%

**85** Colour: bright straw. Nose: fresh, floral, dried herbs. Palate: good structure, fruity, fresh, good acidity.

TOIETES 2008 B JOVEN
xarel.lo 100%

**84**

FINCA AVELLÓ 50-50 2008 T ROBLE
merlot 100%

**79**

BALLÓ MERLOT 2006 TC
merlot 100%

**82**

## MONT MARÇAL

Finca Manlleu
08732 Castellví de la Marca (Barcelona)
☎: 938 918 281 - Fax: 938 919 045
mrivas@mont-marcal.com
www.mont-marcal.com

MONT MARÇAL 2008 T

**84**

## PARATÓ

Can Respall de Renardes
08733 (Barcelona)
☎: 938 988 182 - Fax: 938 988 510
info@parato.es
www.parato.es

PARATÓ ÁTICA TRES X TRES 2008 B
chardonnay, macabeo, xarel.lo

**83**

PARATÓ XAREL.LO 2008 B
xarel.lo 100%

**83**

PARATÓ FINCA RENARDES 2007 B
xarel.lo, parellada, macabeo, chardonnay

**89** Colour: bright straw. Nose: medium intensity, ripe fruit, fruit expression, scrubland. Palate: flavourful, fruity, fresh, fleshy.

PARATÓ 2008 RD
pinot noir 100%

**79**

FINCA RENARDES 2007 T ROBLE
tempranillo, cabernet sauvignon

**86** Colour: cherry, garnet rim. Nose: ripe fruit, floral, sweet spices. Palate: fresh, flavourful, easy to drink, fruity.

PARATÓ SAMSÓ 2006 T

**88** Colour: cherry, garnet rim. Nose: medium intensity, ripe fruit, sweet spices, dark chocolate. Palate: flavourful, long, round tannins.

### PARATÓ ÁTICA PINOT NOIR 2005 T
pinot noir 100%

**87** Colour: very deep cherry, garnet rim. Nose: ripe fruit, complex, balanced, wet leather. Palate: fleshy, warm, spicy, round tannins.

### PARATÓ NEGRE CLÀSSIC 2003 T
tempranillo, cabernet sauvignon

**86** Colour: cherry, garnet rim. Nose: candied fruit, woody. Palate: fleshy, powerful, ripe fruit, harsh oak tannins.

## PARDAS

Finca Can Comas, s/n
08775 Torrelavit (Barcelona)
☎: 938 995 005
pardas@cancomas.com
www.pardas.net

### PARDAS XAREL.LO 2007 B
xarel.lo 100%

**91** Colour: bright yellow. Nose: powerful, ripe fruit, sweet spices, creamy oak, fragrant herbs. Palate: rich, smoky aftertaste, flavourful, fresh, good acidity.

### PARDAS NEGRE FRANC 2006 T

**93** Colour: very deep cherry. Nose: creamy oak, toasty, fruit expression, damp earth. Palate: complex, good structure, fruity, powerful, flavourful.

### PARDAS ASPRIU 2005 T

**93** Colour: bright cherry. Nose: ripe fruit, creamy oak, expressive, spicy, cocoa bean, fruit expression, tobacco. Palate: flavourful, fruity, toasty, round tannins.

## PARÉS BALTA

Masía Can Baltá, s/n
08796 Pacs del Penedés (Barcelona)

☎: 938 901 399 - Fax: 938 901 143
paresbalta@paresbalta.com
www.paresbalta.com

### CALCARI XAREL.LO 2008 B

**91** Colour: bright straw. Nose: fresh, fresh fruit, white flowers, expressive, varietal. Palate: flavourful, fruity, good acidity, balanced.

### MAS DE CAROL 2008 B

**88** Colour: bright straw. Nose: white flowers, jasmine, fresh fruit, grassy. Palate: flavourful, fruity, fresh.

### PARÉS BALTA BLANC DE PANS 2008 B

**87** Colour: bright straw. Nose: ripe fruit, citrus fruit, floral. Palate: flavourful, powerful, light-bodied, fruity.

### GINESTA 2008 B

**86** Colour: bright straw. Nose: ripe fruit, fresh fruit, citrus fruit, floral. Palate: fruity, fresh, fleshy.

### PARÉS BALTA MAS PONS 2008 B
chardonnay

**85** Colour: bright straw. Nose: ripe fruit, spicy, dried flowers. Palate: flavourful, fleshy, sweetness.

### ELECTIO XAREL.LO 2007 B

**92** Colour: bright straw. Nose: powerful, varietal, dry stone, white flowers. Palate: flavourful, powerful, ripe fruit.

### PARÉS BALTA ROS DE PACS 2008 RD

**85** Colour: cherry, garnet rim. Nose: ripe fruit, raspberry, powerfull. Palate: flavourful, powerful, fleshy.

### HISENDA MIRET GARNATXA 2008 T

**90** Colour: cherry, purple rim. Nose: powerful, ripe fruit, red berry notes, spicy. Palate: powerful, fruity, fresh.

### PARÉS BALTA MAS PETIT 2007 T

**88** Colour: bright cherry. Nose: sweet spices, creamy oak, red berry notes, ripe fruit. Palate: flavourful, fruity, toasty, round tannins.

### MAS ELENA 2006 T

**91** Colour: cherry, garnet rim. Nose: ripe fruit, creamy oak, toasty, complex, red berry notes, sweet spices. Palate: powerful, flavourful, toasty, round tannins.

### MARTA DE BALTÀ 2006 T

**90** Colour: cherry, garnet rim. Nose: ripe fruit, spicy, creamy oak, toasty, complex, red berry notes. Palate: powerful, flavourful, toasty, round tannins.

## ABSIS 2005 T

**91** Colour: bright cherry. Nose: ripe fruit, sweet spices, creamy oak, expressive, red berry notes, earthy notes. Palate: flavourful, fruity, toasty, round tannins.

## MAS IRENE 2003 T

**88** Colour: cherry, garnet rim. Nose: powerful, varietal, ripe fruit, toasty, spicy. Palate: flavourful, powerful, fleshy, round tannins.

## ELECTIO XAREL.LO 2008 B
xarel.lo

**89** Colour: bright straw. Nose: ripe fruit, medium intensity, closed. Palate: concentrated, flavourful, powerful, balanced, good acidity.

## MAS IRENE 2005 T

**88** Colour: deep cherry, garnet rim. Nose: powerful, ripe fruit, red berry notes, spicy. Palate: flavourful, powerful, fleshy.

## RADIX

## PERE VENTURA

Ctra. de Vilafranca, km. 0,4
08770 Sant Sadurní D'Anoia (Barcelona)
☎: 938 183 371 - Fax: 938 912 679
info@pereventura.com
www.pereventura.com

## PERE VENTURA CHARDONNAY-XAREL.LO 2008 B
chardonnay 50%, xarel.lo 50%

**88** Colour: bright yellow. Nose: varietal, expressive, ripe fruit, sweet spices. Palate: fresh, flavourful, fleshy, good acidity.

## PERE VENTURA CHARDONNAY 2008 B
chardonnay 100%

**87** Colour: yellow, pale, greenish rim. Nose: varietal, fresh, citrus fruit, fruit expression. Palate: balanced, good acidity.

## INÈDIT MERLOT 2008 RD
merlot 100%

**83**

## PUIG ROMEU

Barri Piscina, 5
08779 La Llacuna (Barcelona)
☎: 938 976 206 - Fax: 938 977 087
info@puig-romeu.com
www.puig-romeu.com

## VINYA JORDINA 2008 B
viognier 50%, sauvignon blanc 30%, garnacha blanca 20%

**87** Colour: bright straw. Nose: floral, neat, fresh fruit, honeyed notes, dried herbs. Palate: flavourful, fruity, fresh, sweetness.

## 3 NEGRES CUPATGE 2006 T
merlot, tempranillo, syrah

**91** Colour: dark-red cherry. Nose: complex, powerfull, varietal, elegant, ripe fruit, dry stone, cocoa bean, creamy oak. Palate: complex, fruity, powerful, flavourful, balsamic, good finish, ripe fruit.

## BIEL.LO ESP
pinot noir 50%, parellada 50%

**83**

## RAVENTÓS I BLANC

Plaça del Roure
08770 Sant Sadurní D'Anoia (Barcelona)
☎: 938 183 262 - Fax: 938 912 500
raventos@raventos.com
www.raventos.com

## SILENCIS 2008 B
xarel.lo 62%, chardonnay 38%

**91** Colour: bright yellow. Nose: powerful, ripe fruit, sweet spices, creamy oak, fragrant herbs. Palate: rich, smoky aftertaste, flavourful, fresh, good acidity.

## PERFUM DE VI BLANC 2008 B
moscatel 50%, macabeo 50%

**87** Colour: bright straw. Nose: white flowers, varietal, powerfull, fresh fruit. Palate: fruity, fresh, sweetness, great length.

## MONTSERRAT BLANC 2007 B
chardonnay, xarel.lo

**87** Colour: bright yellow. Nose: smoky, dry nuts, sweet spices, spicy. Palate: full, powerful, flavourful, fruity.

## LA ROSA DE RAVENTÓS I BLANC 2008 RD
merlot 90%, pinot noir 10%

**85** Colour: rose, purple rim. Nose: powerful, ripe fruit, red berry notes, floral, expressive. Palate: fleshy, powerful, fruity, fresh.

## 11 2006 T
cabernet sauvignon 80%, monastrell 20%

**83**

# DO PENEDÈS

## ISABEL NEGRA 2005 T
merlot 50%, cabernet sauvignon 50%

**88** Colour: cherry, garnet rim. Nose: powerful, warm, ripe fruit, sweet spices, toasty. Palate: ripe fruit, concentrated, round tannins.

## RENÉ BARBIER

Partida Torre del Gall, s/n
08739 St. Cugat de Sesgarrigues (Barcelona)
☎: 938 917 090 - Fax: 938 917 099
renebarbier@renebarbier.es
www.renebarbier.es

RENÉ BARBIER KRALINER 2008 B
xarel.lo 40%, macabeo 30%, parellada 30%
**84**

RENÉ BARBIER CHARDONNAY SELECCIÓN 2007 BFB
chardonnay 100%

**86** Colour: bright straw. Nose: toasty, smoky, spicy, candied fruit, ripe fruit. Palate: flavourful, powerful, fleshy, fine bitter notes.

RENÉ BARBIER 2008 RD
tempranillo 60%, garnacha 20%, cariñena 20%
**79**

RENÉ BARBIER SELECCIÓN CABERNET SAUVIGNON 2006 TC
cabernet sauvignon 100%

**87** Colour: bright cherry, garnet rim. Nose: ripe fruit, medium intensity, varietal, balanced. Palate: good structure, spicy, good finish.

## ROCAMAR

Major, 80
08755 Castellbisbal (Barcelona)
☎: 937 711 205
info@rocamar.net

CASTELL DE RIBES SELECCIÓ 2007 B

**87** Colour: bright straw. Nose: white flowers, ripe fruit, grassy. Palate: flavourful, fruity, fresh, fleshy.

CASTELL DE RIBES SELECCIÓ 2008 RD
**78**

CASTELL DE RIBES SELECCIÓ 2007 T

**87** Colour: bright cherry. Nose: ripe fruit, sweet spices, creamy oak, new oak. Palate: flavourful, fruity, toasty, round tannins.

ROCAMAR

## ROS MARINA MAS UBERNI

Camino Puigdàlber a las Cases Noves
08739 Font-Rubí (Barcelona)
☎: 938 988 185 - Fax: 938 988 185
rosmarina@rosmarina.com

ROS MARINA XAREL.LO 2008 BFB
xarel.lo 100%

**85** Colour: bright straw. Nose: medium intensity, floral, short. Palate: fruity, flavourful.

ROS MARINA MERLOT 2007 T FERMENTADO EN BARRICA
merlot 100%

**88** Colour: bright cherry. Nose: ripe fruit, sweet spices, creamy oak, expressive. Palate: flavourful, fruity, toasty, round tannins.

ROS MARINA CABERNET MERLOT 2007 T FERMENTADO EN BARRICA
cabernet sauvignon 70%, merlot 30%

**85** Colour: cherry, garnet rim. Nose: powerful, ripe fruit, sweet spices, toasty. Palate: powerful, flavourful, fleshy.

## ROVELLATS

Pau Claris, 136
08009 (Barcelona)
☎: 934 880 575 - Fax: 934 880 819
rovellats@cavasrovellats.com
www.cavasrovellats.com

ROVELLATS BRUT DE TARDOR 2005 T
garnacha 42%, cabernet sauvignon 30%, merlot 23%, syrah 5%

**87** Colour: cherry, garnet rim. Nose: fresh, ripe fruit, sweet spices. Palate: powerful, flavourful, round tannins.

## SEGURA VIUDAS

Ctra. Sant Sadurní a St. Pere de Riudebitlles, km. 5
08775 Torrelavit (Barcelona)
☎: 938 917 070 - Fax: 938 996 006
seguraviudas@seguraviudas.es
www.seguraviudas.com

VIÑA HEREDAD 2008 B
xarel.lo 40%, parellada 35%, macabeo 25%

**85** Colour: bright straw. Nose: grassy, white flowers, fragrant herbs. Palate: flavourful, fresh, fruity.

**CREU DE LAVIT 2007 BFB**
xarel.lo 100%

**86** Colour: bright straw. Nose: powerful, varietal, expressive, ripe fruit. Palate: flavourful, fruity, fleshy, good acidity.

**CLOS JUVÈNCIA 2008 RD**
garnacha 45%, merlot 30%, syrah 20%

**81**

**VIÑA HEREDAD 2008 RD**
garnacha 45%, tempranillo 35%, cariñena 20%

**77**

**VIÑA HEREDAD CABERNET SAUVIGNON 2006 T**
cabernet sauvignon 100%

**87** Colour: bright cherry, garnet rim. Nose: warm, ripe fruit, varietal, grassy, sweet spices. Palate: concentrated, flavourful, round tannins.

**MAS D'ARANYÓ 2003 TR**
tempranillo 80%, cabernet sauvignon 20%

**84**

**SEGURA VIUDAS**

## TORELLÓ

Can Martí de Baix
08790 Sant Sadurni D'Anoia (Barcelona)
☎: 938 910 793 - Fax: 938 910 877
torello@torello.es
www.torello.es

**CRISALYS 2008 B**
xarel.lo 100%

**85** Colour: pale. Nose: grassy, ripe fruit, citrus fruit. Palate: flavourful, fruity, fleshy, fine bitter notes.

**PETJADES MERLOT 2008 RD**
merlot 100%

**83**

**RAIMONDA 2004 TR**
merlot, cabernet sauvignon

**86** Colour: cherry, garnet rim. Nose: powerful, woody, toasty, fruit liqueur notes. Palate: spicy, ripe fruit, fine bitter notes, warm.

## U MÉS U FAN TRES

Masia Navinés B Els Pujols

08736 Guardiola de Font-Rubí (Barcelona)
☎: 938 974 069 - Fax: 938 974 724
umesu@umesufan3.com
www.umesufan3.com

**DAHLIA 1 + 1 = 3 2008 B**
viognier 75%, xarel.lo 25%

**88** Colour: bright straw. Nose: grassy, white flowers, fresh fruit, tropical fruit. Palate: flavourful, fresh, good acidity, fleshy.

**SOLITERRA 1+1=3 2008 B**
xarel.lo 85%, sauvignon blanc 15%

**87** Colour: bright straw. Nose: white flowers, ripe fruit, citrus fruit. Palate: flavourful, fruity, fresh.

**CABERNET SAUVIGNON ROSÉ 1 + 1 = 3 2008 RD**
cabernet sauvignon 100%

**81**

**DÉFORA 1 + 1 = 3 2007 T**
garnacha 75%, cariñena 25%

**91** Colour: bright cherry, garnet rim. Nose: fresh, red berry notes, floral. Palate: full, good structure, fruity, round tannins, spicy, great length.

**DÉFORA 1 + 1 = 3 2006 T**
garnacha 75%, cariñena 25%

**91** Colour: cherry, garnet rim. Nose: balanced, ripe fruit, sweet spices, creamy oak. Palate: powerful, flavourful, ripe fruit, smoky aftertaste.

**CALIU 1 + 1 = 3**

## VALLFORMOSA

La Sala, 45
08735 Vilobi del Penedés (Barcelona)
☎: 938 978 286 - Fax: 938 978 355
vallformosa@vallformosa.es
www.vallformosa.com

**VALLFORMOSA CLOS MASET SELECCIÓN ESPECIAL 2005 T**
cabernet sauvignon 100%

**89** Colour: deep cherry, garnet rim. Nose: ripe fruit, toasty, sweet spices. Palate: creamy, ripe fruit, good acidity, round tannins.

**VALLFORMOSA SELECCIÓN ESPECIAL MERLOT MASIA FREYE 2005 T**

**88** Colour: bright cherry, garnet rim. Nose: ripe fruit, mineral, spicy, cocoa bean, varietal. Palate: flavourful, round tannins.

## CLAUDIA DE VALLFORMOSA 2008 B

**84**

## VALLFORMOSA CLOS MASET 2006 T

**90** Colour: cherry, garnet rim. Nose: ripe fruit, spicy, creamy oak, toasty, complex, mineral. Palate: powerful, flavourful, toasty, round tannins.

## VALLFORMOSA TEMPRANILLO CABERNET SAUVIGNON 2002 TR

**87** Colour: pale ruby, brick rim edge. Nose: powerful, fruit liqueur notes, spicy. Palate: flavourful, spicy, ripe fruit.

GEMMA DE VALLFORMOSA
MASIA FREYÉ MERLOT DE VALLFORMOSA
MARINA DE VALLFORMOSA

## VILADELLOPS VINÍCOLA

Finca Viladellops
08734 Olérdola (Barcelona)
☎: 938 188 371 - Fax: 938 188 371
md@viladellops.com
www.viladellops.com

FINCA VILADELLOPS 2007 BFB
xarel.lo 100%

**87** Colour: bright yellow. Nose: toasty, overripe fruit, warm. Palate: powerful, fleshy, sweetness.

FINCA VILADELLOPS 2006 T
garnacha 60%, syrah 40%

**87** Colour: cherry, garnet rim. Nose: ripe fruit, medium intensity, cocoa bean. Palate: flavourful, oaky, smoky aftertaste.

## VILARNAU

Carretera d'Espiells, km. 1,4
Finca "Can Petit"
08770 Sant Sadurní d'Anoia (Barcelona)
☎: 938 912 361 - Fax: 938 912 361
castelldevilarnau@castelldevilarnau.es
www.gonzalezbyass.com

DOMUS DE VILARNAU CHARDONNAY 2008 B

**83**

DOMUS DE VILARNAU PETIT BLANC 2008 B

**83**

LES PLANES DE VILARNAU PINOT NOIR 2008 RD
pinot noir 85%, merlot 15%

**83**

DOMUS DE VILARNAU CABERNET SAUVIGNON 2006 T
cabernet sauvignon 100%

**82**

## VINS EL CEP

Can Llopart de Les Alzines
08770 Sant Sadurní D'Anoia (Barcelona)
☎: 938 912 353 - Fax: 938 183 956
info@elcep.com
www.elcep.com

MARQUÉS DE GÉLIDA BLANC DE BLANCS 2008 B
macabeo 30%, xarel.lo 30%, parellada 20%, chardonnay 20%

**81**

L'ALZINAR BLANC SELECCIÓ 2008 B
macabeo 30%, parellada 15%, xarel.lo 40%, chardonnay 15%

**78**

L'ALZINAR CHARDONNAY 2008 BFB
chardonnay 100%

**77**

L'ALZINAR ULL DE LLEBRE 2005 TC
ull de llebre 100%

**90** Colour: cherry, garnet rim. Nose: ripe fruit, dark chocolate, cocoa bean. Palate: good structure, fleshy, creamy, round tannins.

## VINS I CAVES CUSCÓ BERGA

Esplugues, 7
08793 Avinyonet del Penedès (Barcelona)
☎: 938 970 164 - Fax: 938 970 164
cuscoberga@cuscoberga.com
www.cuscoberga.com

CUSCÓ BERGA CHARDONNAY SELECCIÓ 2008 B
chardonnay 100%

**83**

CUSCÓ BERGA MUSCAT 2008 B
moscatel 80%, macabeo 20%

**81**

CUSCÓ BERGA MERLOT SELECCIÓ 2008 RD
merlot 100%

**81**

CUSCÓ BERGA CABERNET SAUVIGNON - MERLOT 2006 T
cabernet sauvignon 80%, merlot 20%

**83**

CUSCÓ BERGA CABERNET SAUVIGNON MERLOT 2005 TC
cabernet sauvignon 80%, merlot 20%

**88** Colour: cherry, garnet rim. Nose: medium intensity, toasty, sweet spices, creamy oak. Palate: flavourful, ripe fruit, spicy, toasty.

## VINS I CAVES TUTUSAUS

Plaça de la Creu, 1
08795 Olesa de Bonesvalls (Barcelona)

☎: 938 984 181 - Fax: 938 984 181
info@cavestutusaus.com
www.cavestutusaus.com

VALL DOLINA 2008 RD
merlot 100%

**83**

VALL DOLINA MERLOT 2007 T
merlot 100%

**86** Colour: bright cherry, purple rim. Nose: varietal, grassy, red berry notes, sweet spices. Palate: flavourful, balsamic, correct.

## VIÑA TORREBLANCA

Finca Masia Torreblanca, s/n
08734 Miquel D'Olérdola (Barcelona)
☎: 938 915 066 - Fax: 938 900 102
info@vinatorreblanca.com
www.vinatorreblanca.com

TORREBLANCA LES ATZAVARES 2008 B

**85** Colour: bright straw. Nose: candied fruit, citrus fruit, white flowers. Palate: flavourful, fruity.

TORREBLANCA CHARDONNAY 2006 BFB

**84**

TORREBLANCA MERLOT 2008 RD

**81**

TORREBLANCA CABERNET SAUVIGNON 2005 TR

**80**

SOME OTHER WINERIES WITHIN THE DO:

**AMETLLER CIVILL
ANTONI VILAMAJÓ SAUMELL
ARVIC ARETEY
BLANCHER ESPUMOSOS DE CAVA
BOLET VINOS Y CAVAS
CAN FEIXES (HUGUET)
CAN QUETU
CAN RÀFOLS DELS CAUS
CANALS & MUNNÉ
CASTELL D'AGE
CAVA MIQUEL PONS
CAVA ROMAGOSA TORNÉ
CAVA XAMÓS
CAVAS PUIG MUNTS**

# DO PENEDÈS

CAVES M. BOSCH
CAVES MONASTELL
CAVES NAVERÁN
CELLER CAL SERRADOR
CELLER CAN PUJOL
CELLER COOPERATIU DE VILAFRANCA
S.C.C.L.
CELLERS DE CAN SURIOL DEL CASTELL
CELLERS DE L'ARBOÇ
CELLERS PLANAS ALBAREDA
COVIDES VIÑEDOS Y BODEGAS
CUSCOMAS
DURAN
FINCA ELS CUCONS
FRANCISCO DOMÍNGUEZ CRUCES - EL XAMFRÀ
HERETAT MAS JORNET
JAUME GIRÓ I GIRÓ
JOAN LLOPART PONS
JOAN RAVENTÓS ROSELL
JOSEP FERRET I MATEU
JOSEP MASACHS
MARTÍN SOLER
MAS COMTAL
MAS LLUET
MAS OLIVÉ
MAS RODÓ
MAS ROMANI
MASCARÓ
MASIA PAPIOL
MASOLIVÉ S.A.
MATA I COLOMA
MIL.LIARI SELECCIÓ
MONTAU DE SADURNÍ
MONTESQUIUS
MUNGUST
NADAL
OLIVELLA I BONET
ORIOL ROSSELL
PAGÉS ENTRENA
PERE RIUS
RAVENTÓS GUASCH
RAVENTÓS I BLANC
REFILAT
RIMARTS
SOLA RAVENTÓS
SOLER-JOVÉ
TORRENS MOLINER
VALLDOSERA
VALLORT VINYATERS
VEGA DE RIBES
WINNER WINES

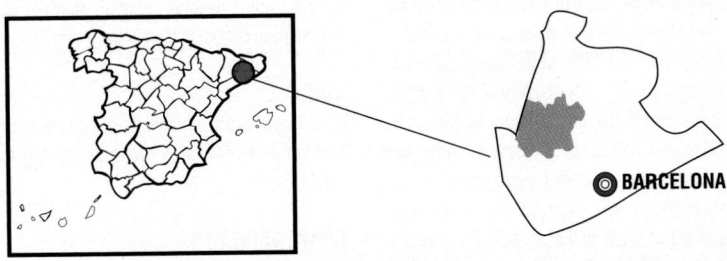

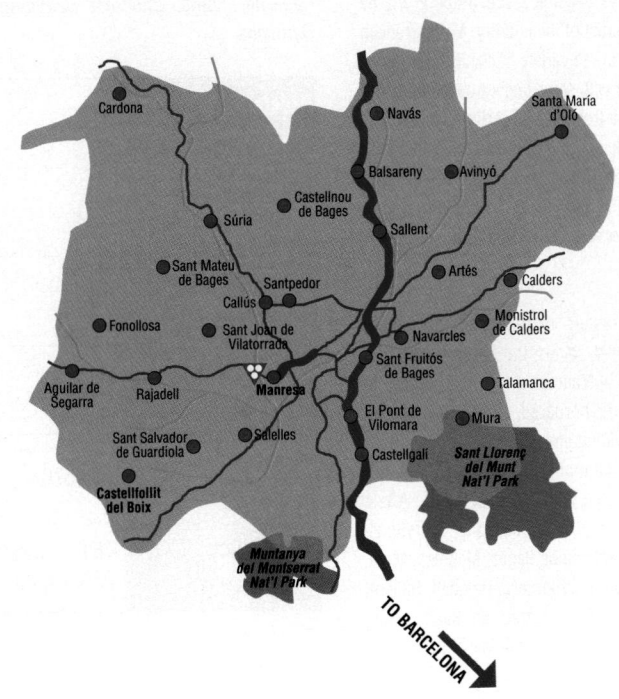

Cardona

Navás

Santa María
d'Oló

Balsareny

Avinyó

Castellnou
de Bages

Súria

Sallent

Sant Mateu
de Bages

Santpedor

Artés

Calders

Callús

Fonollosa

Sant Joan de
Vilatorrada

Navarcles

Monistrol
de Calders

Aguilar de
Segarra

Rajadell

Manresa

Sant Fruitós
de Bages

Talamanca

Sant Salvador
de Guardiola

Salelles

El Pont de
Vilomara

Mura

Castellgalí

Sant Llorenç
del Munt
Nat'l Park

Castellfollit
del Boix

Muntanya
del Montserrat
Nat'l Park

TO BARCELONA

BARCELONA

▽ Consejo Regulador

● DO Boundary

# DO PLA DE BAGES

## NEWS

To the light of the latest vintages, Pla de Bages is one of the best and safest buys in the whole of Spain, with increasing ratings from year to year and also white wines gaining in sophistication and elegance. The white variety picapoll, brought to notoriety a few years back by Abadal, has become the flagship grape for the DO, and is found nowadays in some other local houses with its rich and fresh character and lovely mineral and herbal nuances even when barrel-fermented. The sumoll, its red counterpart, does seem to be liked by vine growers as much as the picapoll, and therefore it is usually blended with French varieties or used to make rosé wines. The Consejo Regulador has put its eyes on other local varieties like mandó and picapoll negra, still experimental. Merlot has become a star grape in Pla de Bages, as well as in the rest of the country. Mediterranean climate seems to suit that red variety brilliantly, affording a lovely ripe fruit character with some undergrowth notes, and the best examples come from Abadal, Artium cooperative and Heretat Oller del Mas. The best wines from 2008 are white and rosé renderings, while the red of the 2006 vintage show still fresh and round and the 2005's are very easy to drink, have good structure and ageing potential.

## LOCATION

Covering one of the eastern extremes of the Central Catalonian Depression; it covers the natural region of Bages, of which the city of Manresa is the urban centre. To the south the region is bordered by the Montserrat mountain range, the dividing line which separates it from Penedés. It comprises the municipal areas of Fonollosa, Monistrol de Caldres, Sant Joan de Vilatorrada, Artés, Avinyó, Balsareny, Calders, Callús, Cardona, Castellgalí, Castellfollit del Boix, Castellnou de Bages, Manresa, Mura, Navarcles, Navàs, El Pont de Vilomara, Rajadell, Sallent, Sant Fruitós de Bages, Sant Mateu de Bages, Sant Salvador de Guardiola, Santpedor, Santa María d'Oló, Súria and Talamanca.

## LIMATE

Mid-mountain Mediterranean, with little rainfall (500 mm to 600 mm average annual rainfall) and greater temperature contrasts than in the Penedès.

## SOIL

The vineyards are situated at an altitude of about 400 m. The soil is franc-clayey, franc-sandy and franc-clayey-sandy.

## GRAPE VARIETIES:

**White:** *Chardonnay, Gewürztraminer, Macabeo, Picapoll, Parellada, Sauvignon Blanc.*
**Red:** *Sumoll, Ull de Llebre (Tempranillo), Merlot, Cabernet Franc, Cabernet Sauvignon, Syrah* and *Garnacha.*

| | |
|---|---|
| Hectares of Vineyard | 550 |
| Nº Viticulturists | 100 |
| Nº of Bodegas | 10 |
| 2008 Harvest | Good |
| 2007 Production | 537,570 l. |
| Marketing | 75% domestic 25% export |

**CONSEJO REGULADOR**
Casa de La Culla
La Culla, s/n. 08240 Manresa (Barcelona)
☎: 938 748 236 - Fax: 938 748 094
@ info@dopladebages.com
www.dopladebages.com

## GENERAL CHARACTERISTICS OF THE WINES:

| | |
|---|---|
| **WHITES** | These are of similar character to the Penedès white wines; they are young and fruity, and are the result of modern technology, both those that use autochtonous varieties and those based on *Chardonnay*. |
| **ROSÉS** | Produced mainly from *Merlot* and *Cabernet Sauvignon*, they have a raspberry pink colour and are clean and fruity on the nose with a good fruit expression of the grapes they are produced from. |
| **REDS** | Deep cherry-red coloured, fresh, with a pronounced character of the *viníferas* that they are based on. The fine varietal character of those produced from *Cabernet Sauvignon* stands out. |

## 2008 VINTAGE RATING:

## VERY GOOD

## ABADAL

Santa María d'Horta d'Avinyó
08279 Santa María D'Horta D'Avinyó (Barcelona)
☎: 938 757 525 - Fax: 938 748 326
info@abadal.net
www.abadal.net

**ABADAL PICAPOLL 2008 B**
picapoll 100%

**91** Color bright straw. Aroma citrus fruit, mineral, white flowers, fragrant herbs. Taste fruity, flavourful, good acidity, mineral.

**ABADAL BLANC 2008 B**
chardonnay 70%, sauvignon blanc 20%, picapoll 10%

**89** Colour: bright straw. Nose: fresh fruit, grapey, elegant, dried herbs, fine lees. Taste full, flavourful, fresh, good structure.

**ABADAL CHARDONNAY 2007 BFB**
chardonnay 100%

**87** Colour: bright golden. Nose: ripe fruit, expressive, caramel. Taste spirituous, rich, smoky aftertaste, flavourful.

**ABADAL CABERNET SAUVIGNON SUMOLL 2008 RD**
cabernet sauvignon 80%, sumoll 20%

**90** Colour: rose, purple rim. Nose: expressive, dried herbs, fresh fruit. Taste fruity, flavourful, fresh, good finish, full.

**ABADAL CABERNET FRANC TEMPRANILLO 2007 T**
cabernet franc 60%, tempranillo 40%

**87** Colour: bright cherry, purple rim. Nose: red berry notes, medium intensity. Taste easy to drink, fruity, balanced, good acidity.

**ABADAL 2006 TC**
cabernet sauvignon 50%, merlot 50%

**87** Colour: dark-red cherry. Nose: ripe fruit, warm, powerfull, spicy. Taste flavourful, fruity, balanced, round tannins.

**ABADAL SELECCIÓ 2005 T**
cabernet sauvignon 40%, cabernet franc 40%, syrah 20%

**91** Colour: dark-red cherry. Nose: elegant, fresh, complex, red berry notes, spicy, dark chocolate, mineral. Taste fruity, flavourful, spicy, round tannins.

**ABADAL 5 MERLOT 2005 TR**
merlot 100%

**89** Colour: deep cherry. Nose: varietal, expressive, mineral, spicy, elegant, fruit expression. Taste flavourful, good structure, great length, round tannins.

**ABADAL 3.9 2005 TR**
cabernet sauvignon 85%, syrah 15%

**89** Colour: deep cherry. Nose: spicy, mineral, fruit expression, varietal, expressive, balanced. Taste fruity, flavourful, spicy, good acidity, round tannins.

ABADAL
3.9
PLA DE BAGES
Denominació d'origen
2005
75 cl e   ELABORAT I EMBOTELLAT EN LA PROPIETAT PER:   14% vol.
MASIES D'AVINYÓ -R.E.6858-B-AVINYÓ-ESPANYA

## CELLER COOPERATIU D'ARTÉS SCCL - CAVES ARTIUM

Ctra. Rocafort, 44
08271 Artés (Barcelona)
☎: 938 305 325 - Fax: 938 306 289
artium@cavesartium.com
www.cavesartium.com

**ARTIUM PICAPOLL 2008 BFB**

**88** Colour: bright straw. Nose: powerfull, varietal, fresh fruit, white flowers. Palate: flavourful, fruity, fresh, fleshy.

**ARTIUM PICAPOLL 2008 B**

**87** Color bright straw. Aroma fresh, fresh fruit, white flowers, expressive. Taste flavourful, fruity, good acidity, balanced.

**ARTIUM VINYA ROCAS ALBAS 2006 TC**

**80**

**ARTIUM CABERNET SAUVIGNON 2005 TR**

**87** Colour: cherry, garnet rim. Nose: spicy, creamy oak, toasty, fruit liqueur notes. Palate: powerful, flavourful, toasty, round tannins.

ARTIUM MERLOT 2005 T
merlot

## 84

ARTIUM CABERNET SAUVIGNON 2004 TC

**86** Colour: pale ruby, brick rim edge. Nose: toasty, candied fruit, aromatic coffee, wet leather. Palate: powerful, flavourful, spicy.

ARTIUM CABERNET SAUVIGNON MAGNUM 2003 TC

## 83

## EL MOLI

Camí de Rajadell, km. 3
08241 Manresa (Barcelona)
☎: 931 021 965 - Fax: 931 021 965
collbaix@cellerelmoli.com
www.cellerelmoli.com

COLLBAIX 2008 B
macabeo 60%, picapoll 40%

**85** Colour: bright straw. Nose: ripe fruit, white flowers, expressive. Palate: rich, flavourful, fruity, pruney.

COLLBAIX 2006 T
cabernet sauvignon 100%

**87** Colour: deep cherry, brick rim edge. Nose: ripe fruit, floral, sweet spices, balanced. Palate: light-bodied, warm, spicy, flavourful.

COLLBAIX 2006 T
merlot 100%

**87** Colour: deep cherry, bright ochre rim. Nose: ripe fruit, spicy, elegant, floral. Palate: rich, flavourful, easy to drink, roasted-coffee aftertaste.

COLLBAIX 2006 T
merlot 60%, cabernet sauvignon 40%

**87** Colour: deep cherry, garnet rim. Nose: sweet spices, fruit preserve. Palate: fruity, light-bodied, easy to drink, spicy, round tannins, sweetness.

## HERETAT OLLER DEL MAS

Ctra. de Igualada, km. 3,4
08240 Manresa (Barcelona)
☎: 938 768 315 - Fax: 932 056 949
info@ollerdelmas.com
www.ollerdelmas.com

ARNAU OLLER SELECCIÓ DE LA FAMILIA 2006 T
merlot 100%

**89** Colour: bright cherry. Nose: balanced, expressive, varietal, cocoa bean, ripe fruit, mineral. Palate: flavourful, fruity, good structure, good acidity.

BERNAT OLLER 2006 T
merlot 100%

**88** Colour: bright cherry. Nose: ripe fruit, balanced, varietal, sweet spices. Palate: flavourful, fruity, good acidity, fruity aftetaste, round tannins.

## JAUMANDREU

Casa Jaumandreu Canet de Fals
08259 Fonollosa (Barcelona)
☎: 938 369 579 - Fax: 938 369 505
info@jaumandreu.com
www.jaumandreu.com

NISUS 2007 B
sauvignon blanc 60%, chardonnay 40%

## 81

IDAEUS 2005 T
merlot 70%, syrah 30%

**88** Colour: very deep cherry, bright ochre rim. Nose: fruit preserve, balanced, sweet spices, new oak. Palate: full, unctuous, grainy tannins, good structure.

CEDRUS MERLOT 2005 T
merlot 100%

**86** Colour: deep cherry, bright ochre rim. Nose: fruit preserve, warm, sweet spices, balanced. Palate: fruity, good acidity, round tannins, smoky aftertaste.

## JAUME GRAU - VINS GRAU

Ctra. C-37 de Igualada a Manresa, km. 75,5
08255 Maians (Barcelona)
☎: 938 356 002 - Fax: 938 356 812
info@vinsgrau.com
www.vinsgrau.com

JAUME GRAU AVRVM 2008 B
chardonnay 50%, sauvignon blanc 50%

**85** Colour: bright straw. Nose: tropical fruit, expressive, wild herbs, fresh fruit. Palate: flavourful, rich, fine bitter notes, good finish.

JAUME GRAU I GRAU PICAPOLL 2008 B
picapoll 100%

## 84

JAUME GRAU I GRAU MERLOT 2008 RD
merlot 100%

**85** Colour: rose, bright. Nose: fresh fruit, violet drops, lactic notes, powerfull. Palate: rich, fruity, flavourful, good acidity.

JAUME GRAU GRAU "GRATVS" 2005 TC
tempranillo 50%, merlot 50%

**87** Colour: deep cherry. Nose: ripe fruit, sweet spices, balsamic herbs. Palate: flavourful, long, slightly dry, soft tannins.

JAUME GRAU GRAU "GRATVS" 2004 TR
merlot 100%

**84**

SOME OTHER WINERIES WITHIN THE DO:

**CELLER COOPERATIU DE SALELLES**
**CELLER FARGAS-FARGAS**
**CELLER SOLERGIBERT**
**MAS DE SANT ISCLE S.A.T.**

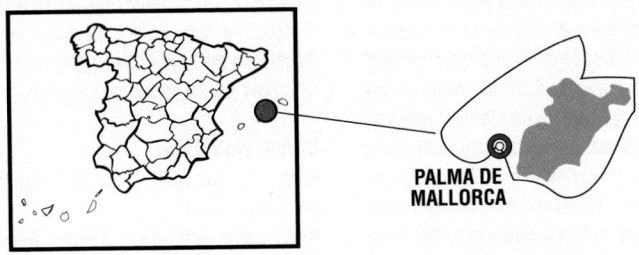

**PALMA DE MALLORCA**

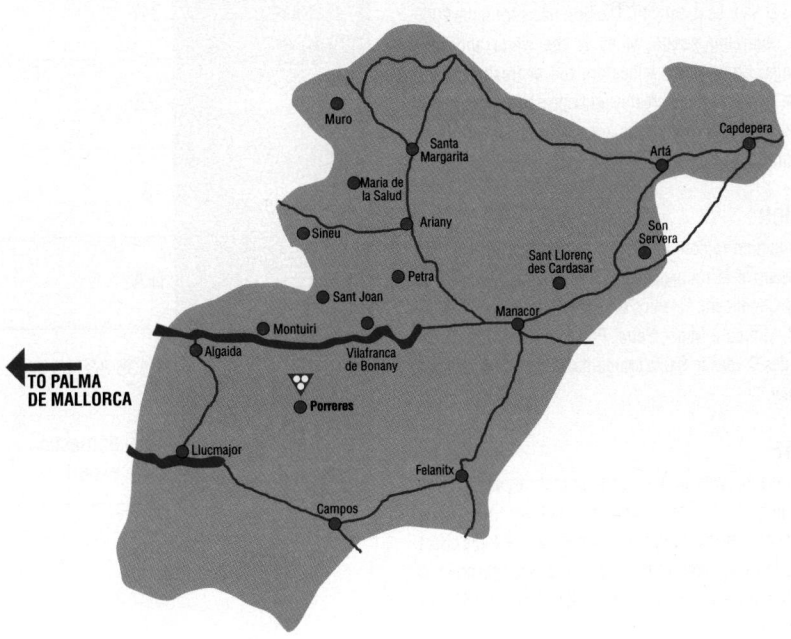

Muro
Santa Margarita
Maria de la Salud
Ariany
Sineu
Petra
Sant Joan
Montuiri
Algaida
Vilafranca de Bonany
TO PALMA DE MALLORCA
Porreres
Llucmajor
Campos
Felanitx
Manacor
Sant Llorenç des Cardasar
Son Servera
Artá
Capdepera

▽ Consejo Regulador
● DO Boundary

## NEWS

Every single year the wines from Pla I Llevant become a proper catalogue of novelties. From ugly ducks, white have become pretty merchandise and come shoulder to shoulder with 'international reds' made from French grape varieties. Probably the best example is the fact that a single-varietal merlot, Aia by Miquel Oliver, has become the best wine from the DO, something that tells a lot about singularity. Some other producers have started as well to blend callet and merlot, a style that, with age, has become a standard within the island, something between spice and the lovely confected Mediterranean touch that characterizes the fresh French grapes planted in the region. As we move along previous vintages, wines tend to loose their previous freshness, and the oxidative style takes in, not always showing at their best, though. The best news from the 2008 vintage regarding young wines is the white and rosé renderings. Chardonnay wines are full of freshness and elegance, away from the creamy and ripe notes of old, while the local moscatel renderings are pretty much 'up there' with the best.

## LOCATION

The production region covers the eastern part of Majorca and consists of 18 municipal districts: Algaida, Ariany, Artá, Campos, Capdepera, Felanitx, Lluchamajor, Manacor, Mª de la Salud, Montuiri, Muro, Petra, Porreres, Sant Joan, Sant Llorens des Cardasar, Santa Margarita, Sineu and Vilafranca de Bonany.

## CLIMATE

Mediterranean, with an average temperature of 16°C and with slightly cool winters and dry, hot summers. The constant sea breeze during the summer has a notable effect on these terrains close to the coast. The wet season is in autumn and the average annual rainfall is between 450 mm and 500 mm.

## SOIL

The soil is made up of limestone rocks, which give limy-clayey soils. The reddish Colour: of the terrain is due to the presence of iron oxide. The clays and calcium and magnesium carbonates, in turn, provide the whitish Colour: which can also be seen in the vineyards.

## GRAPE VARIETIES:

**White**: *Prensal Blanc, Macabeo, Parellada, Moscatel* and *Chardonnay.*

**Red**: *Callet* (majority), *Manto Negro, Fogoneu, Tempranillo, Monastrell, Cabernet Sauvignon, Merlot* and *Syrah.*

| | |
|---|---|
| Hectares of Vineyard | 347 |
| Nº Viticulturists | 109 |
| Nº of Bodegas | 13 |
| 2008 Harvest | N/A |
| 2007 Production | 1,135,800 l. |
| Marketing | 13% domestic 87% export |

**CONSEJO REGULADOR**
Molí de N'Amengual.
Dusai, 3. 07260 Porreres (Islas Baleares)
☎: 971 168 569 - Fax: 971 168 569
@ plaillevant@wanadoo.es

**GENERAL CHARACTERISTICS OF THE WINES:**

| | |
|---|---|
| **WHITES** | The characteristics of the white wines are conditioned by the peculiarities of the foreign varieties. The *Prensal* grape gives wines that singularly express the 'terruño' character of the region. |
| **ROSÉS** | These follow in the line of the rosés of Binissalem, although the distinction comes from those produced from French grape varieties. The sensorial definition of these varieties does not prevent them, in certain cases, from being a little heavy on the nose. |
| **REDS** | These share the style that characterises the Mediterranean adaptation of the French varieties they are produced from. Thus, they give off balsamic hints in the nose; on the Palate: they offer supple and ripe tannins; they are flavourful and full bodied. |

## 2008 VINTAGE RATING:

# VERY GOOD

## ARMERO I ADROVER

Camada Real s/n
07200 Mallorca (Balears)
☎: 971 827 103 - Fax: 971 580 305
luisarmero@armeroiadrover.com
www.armeroiadrover.com

ARMERO ADROVER CHARDONNAY PRENSAL 2008 B
chardonnay, prensal

**86** Colour: yellow, pale. Nose: fresh fruit, tropical fruit. Palate: flavourful, good structure, full.

ARMERO ADROVER 2006 B

**79**

ARMERO ADROVER SYRAH-CALLET ROSAT 2008 RD
syrah, merlot

**85** Colour: rose, purple rim. Nose: red berry notes, violets, lactic notes, medium intensity. Palate: flavourful, fruity, balanced.

ARMERO ADROVER CALLET-MERLOT 2007 T

**85** Colour: cherry, garnet rim. Nose: ripe fruit, spicy, toasty, complex, cocoa bean. Palate: powerful, flavourful, round tannins, fine bitter notes.

ARMERO I ADROVER COLLITA DE FRUITS 2006 T
callet

**83**

ARMERO I ADROVER COLLITA DE FRUITS 2004 T
callet, cabernet sauvignon, merlot

**84**

EL KUETO

## BODEGA JAUME MESQUIDA

Vileta, 7
07260 Porreres (Balears)
☎: 971 647 106 - Fax: 971 168 205
info@jaumemesquida.com
www.jaumemesquida.com

MOLÍ DE VENT 2008 B
prensal 80%, macabeo 10%, parellada 10%

**85** Colour: bright straw. Nose: fresh, fresh fruit, expressive, grassy. Palate: flavourful, fruity, balanced, good acidity.

CHARDONNAY BLANC 2008 B
chardonnay 100%

**84**

MOLÍ DE VENT 2008 RD
callet 80%, cabernet sauvignon 10%, syrah 10%

**85** Colour: light cherry. Nose: powerful, red berry notes, floral, expressive. Palate: fleshy, powerful, fruity, fresh.

ROSAT DE ROSA 2008 RD
merlot 50%, cabernet sauvignon 50%

**83**

JAUME MESQUIDA NEGRE 2007 T
callet, manto negro, cabernet sauvignon, syrah

**88** Colour: cherry, purple rim. Nose: white flowers, raspberry, sweet spices. Palate: flavourful, fruity, powerful tannins.

VIÑA DEL ALBARICOQUE 2005 T
cabernet sauvignon, merlot

**89** Colour: dark-red cherry. Nose: spicy, ripe fruit, sweet spices, toasty, mineral. Palate: flavourful, correct, round tannins.

JAUME MESQUIDA CABERNET SAUVIGNON 2005 TC
cabernet sauvignon 100%

**86** Colour: pale ruby, brick rim edge. Nose: fruit liqueur notes, wild herbs, toasty. Palate: powerful, fleshy, slightly dry, soft tannins.

## BODEGAS BORDOY

Cami de Muntanya, Ctra. Cala Blava - Lluchmajor
07690 Lluchmajor (Balears)
☎: 971 774 081
sarota@bodegasbordoy.es

SA ROTA BLANC CHARDONNAY 3 MESES 2008 BFB

**89** Colour: bright straw. Nose: fresh, fresh fruit, white flowers, expressive, varietal. Palate: flavourful, fruity, good acidity, balanced.

SA ROTA BLANC CHARDONNAY 2008 B
chardonnay

**82**

SA ROTA ROSAT 2008 RD

**76**

SA ROTA ANYADA 2007 T

**74**

SA ROTA SYRAH 2006 T
syrah

**85** Colour: cherry, garnet rim. Nose: powerful, ripe fruit, sweet spices, toasty. Palate: flavourful, powerful, fleshy, spicy.

SA ROTA 2005 TC

**84**

SA ROTA 2005 TR

**87** Colour: cherry, garnet rim. Nose: ripe fruit, spicy, creamy oak, toasty, wet leather. Palate: powerful, flavourful, toasty, round tannins.

## BODEGAS PERE SEDA

Cid Campeador, 22
07500 Manacor (Balears)
☎: 971 605 087 - Fax: 971 604 856
pereseda@pereseda.com
www.pereseda.com

PERE SEDA CHARDONNAY 2008 B
chardonnay 100%

**84**

PERE SEDA BLANC NOVELL 2008 B
macabeo, parellada

**83**

L'ARXIDUC PERE SEDA 2008 B
parellada, moscatel, chardonnay

**79**

L'ARXIDUC PERE SEDA 2008 RD
tempranillo 70%, merlot 30%

**78**

GVIVM MERLOT-CALLET 2007 T
merlot 70%, callet 30%

**86** Colour: cherry, purple rim. Nose: fruit liqueur notes, sweet spices, fine reductive notes. Palate: fleshy, powerful, slightly dry, soft tannins.

PERE SEDA NOVELL NEGRE 2007 T
cabernet sauvignon, merlot, callet, ull de llebre, manto negro

**85** Colour: light cherry. Nose: floral, red berry notes, sweet spices. Palate: flavourful, good finish.

L'ARXIDUC PERE SEDA 2006 T
callet, merlot, tempranillo, manto negro

**80**

MOSSÈN ALCOVER 2006 T
callet 60%, cabernet sauvignon 40%

**80**

PERE SEDA 2005 TC
merlot, syrah, cabernet sauvignon, callet

**82**

## VINS MIQUEL GELABERT

Carrer d'en Sales, 50
07500 Manacor (Balears)
☎: 659 502 662 - Fax: 971 821 444
vinsmg@vinsmiquelgelabert.com
www.vinsmiquelgelabert.com

CHARDONNAY ROURE 2008 B
chardonnay 100%

**87** Colour: bright yellow, greenish rim. Nose: fruit preserve, creamy oak. Palate: balanced, elegant, unctuous, long.

MUSCAT 2008 B
moscatel 100%

**85** Colour: bright yellow. Nose: varietal, grapey, fruit preserve. Palate: varietal, flavourful, long.

SA VALL SELECCIÓ PRIVADA 2007 BFB
chardonnay 50%, prensal 30%, moscatel 20%

**86** Colour: bright yellow. Nose: powerful, ripe fruit, sweet spices, creamy oak, fragrant herbs. Palate: rich, smoky aftertaste, flavourful, fresh, good acidity.

BLANC SA VALL 2007 B
riesling 100%

**82**

GOLOS 2006 T
callet, manto negro

**88** Colour: cherry, purple rim. Nose: spicy, toasty, dark chocolate, fruit expression. Palate: balanced, long, soft tannins.

TORRENT NEGRE SELECCIÓ PRIVADA
20 ANIVERSARI 2005 T

**89** Colour: dark-red cherry. Nose: spicy, mineral, wild herbs, toasty. Palate: powerful, flavourful, slightly dry, soft tannins.

TORRENT NEGRE CABERNET SELECCIÓ PRIVADA
2004 T
cabernet sauvignon

**87** Colour: light cherry. Nose: expressive, fruit expression, spicy, toasty. Palate: varietal, flavourful, soft tannins.

TORRENT NEGRE 2004 T
merlot 40%, cabernet sauvignon 30%, syrah 30%

**85** Colour: bright cherry. Nose: balsamic herbs, red berry notes, toasty. Palate: correct, flavourful, fine bitter notes, soft tannins.

GRAN VINYA SON CAULES 2004 T
callet

**84**

PETIT TORRENT 2004 T
cabernet sauvignon 60%, merlot 20%, callet 20%

**82**

VINYA DES MORÉ 2004 T
pinot noir 100%

**81**

## VINS TONI GELABERT

Camí dels Horts de Llodrá km. 1,3
07500 Manacor (Balears)
☎: 610 789 531 - Fax: 971 552 409
info@vinstonigelabert.com
www.vinstonigelabert.com

TONI GELABERT CHARDONNAY 2008 B
chardonnay 100%

**89** Colour: bright yellow. Nose: powerful, ripe fruit, sweet spices, creamy oak, fragrant herbs. Palate: rich, smoky aftertaste, flavourful, fresh, good acidity.

VINYA SON FANGOS 2008 B

**83**

NEGRE DE SA COLONIA 2007 T
callet 100%

**83**

TONI GELABERT PINOT NOIR 2006 T
pinot noir 100%

**86** Colour: light cherry. Nose: red berry notes, raspberry, wild herbs, creamy oak. Palate: flavourful, long, soft tannins.

TONI GELABERT COLONIA 2006 TC

**84**

TONI GELABERT FANGOS 2006 T
callet, merlot, cabernet sauvignon

**83**

SES HEREVES 2005 T
cabernet sauvignon, syrah, merlot

**84**

TONI GELABERT SYRAH 2005 T
syrah

**84**

TONI GELABERT MERLOT 2004 T
merlot

**84**

VINYA MACABEU

## VINYES I BODEGUES MIQUEL OLIVER

Font, 26
07520 Petra-Mallorca (Balears)
☎: 971 561 117 - Fax: 971 561 117
bodega@miqueloliver.com
www.miqueloliver.com

ORIGINAL MUSCAT MIQUEL OLIVER 2008 B
moscatel

**87** Colour: yellow, pale. Nose: varietal, grapey, fruit preserve. Palate: varietal, flavourful, fresh, great length.

SON CALÓ 2008 RD

**85** Colour: rose, purple rim. Nose: ripe fruit, red berry notes, floral. Palate: fleshy, powerful, fruity, fresh.

AIA 2007 T
merlot

**91** Colour: cherry, garnet rim. Nose: spicy, creamy oak, wild herbs, ripe fruit. Palate: good structure, flavourful, full, round tannins.

SYRAH NEGRE MIQUEL OLIVER 2006 T
syrah

**89** Colour: cherry, garnet rim. Nose: new oak, spicy, cocoa bean, fruit expression. Palate: good structure, roasted-coffee aftertaste, fine bitter notes, round tannins.

SES FERRITGES 2006 T
callet, cabernet sauvignon, merlot, syrah

**88** Colour: cherry, garnet rim. Nose: ripe fruit, spicy, toasty, complex, wet leather. Palate: powerful, flavourful, toasty, round tannins.

SOME OTHER WINERIES WITHIN THE DO:

**BODEGAS BORDOY
CAN MAJORAL
GALMÉS I FERRER**

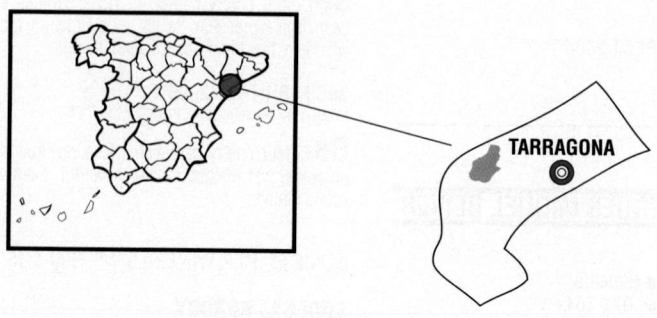

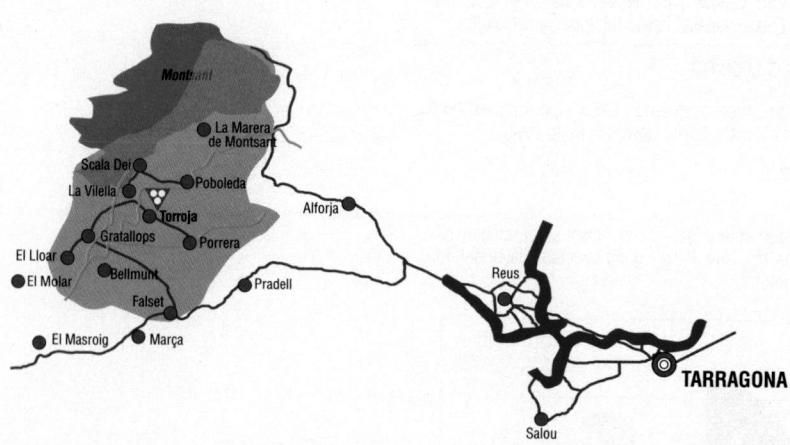

▽ Consejo Regulador
● DO Boundary

## NEWS

Soil, old vines, and the mastery of the best winemakers has brought to our tables a most than favourable vintage, similar in terms of quality to those of previous years. The 2008 vintage will not surely be the best one in the region, for even being a cool one, cariñena and garnacha grown on higher vineyards do not show at their best. Evidently, the best wines will be part of the future aged –crianza or else– wines. We get the feeling that some of the young wines are made for ageing, with great colour and fruit expression, although they seem too concentrated in character. In theory, young wines should be lighter and show a fleshier fruit expression, connatural to their nature. As a more refreshing counterpart we have rosé and white renderings. Compared to the Priorat wines of 2007, quite a hermetic bunch in any case, the wines are very juicy and exciting and far more developed than those of last year's. The 2005 are showing amazingly well on the nose, get good ratings, and have also a great ageing potential, even when we noticed, as young wines, notes of over-ripeness that have with time and bottle ageing disappear, becoming more elegant and with a mineral background. The best ratings go to complex, mineral and earthy garnachas that shove away from depth and huge extraction to show an overall finer, more elegant and fruity character, always with the goal to express also the character of small plots and the mineral –slate– nuances, the most characteristic feature of the region. The best novelties in terms of style come from some previous stars like Gran Cruor, Lo Mon, Elix or Dits del Terra.

Pretty soon, the Consejo Regulador will approve a new subcategory related to municipal names. The vi de vila (in catalan language "town wine") comes from plots within the same town –of a total of 12 towns or subzones– has the goal of achieving singularity but should not be mistaken with the "vinos de finca" or "vinos de pago" so common now in the rest of the country. The first aspirer to that category will be a label by Álvaro Palacios made exclusively with grapes from the town of Gratallops.

## LOCATION

In the province of Tarragona. It is made up of the municipal districts of La Morera de Montsant, Scala Dei, La Vilella, Gratallops, Bellmunt, Porrera, Poboleda, Torroja, Lloá, Falset and Mola.

## CLIMATE

Although with Mediterranean influences, it is temperate and dry. One of the most important characteristics is the practical absence of rain during the summer, which ensures very healthy grapes. The average rainfall is between 500 and 600 mm per year.

## SOIL

This is probably the most distinctive characteristic of the region and precisely what has catapulted it to the top positions in terms of quality, not only in Spain, but around the world. The soil, thin and volcanic, is composed of small pieces of slate (llicorella), which give the wines a markedly mineral character. The vineyards are located on terraces and very steep slopes.

## GRAPE VARIETIES:

**White**: *Chenin Blanc, Macabeo, Garnacha Blanca, Pedro Ximénez.*
**Red**: *Cariñena, Garnacha, Garnacha Peluda, Cabernet Sauvignon, Merlot, Syrah.*

| | |
|---|---|
| Hectares of Vineyard | 1,767 |
| Nº Viticulturists | 567 |
| Nº of Bodegas | 85 |
| 2008 Harvest | N/A |
| 2007 Production | 3,095,462 l. |
| Marketing | 48% domestic 52% export |

# DO Ca. PRIORAT

**CONSEJO REGULADOR**
Bassa, 9. 43737 Torroja del Priorat. (Tarragona)
☎: 977 839 495 - Fax: 977 839 495
@ info@doqpriorat.org
www.doqpriorat.org

## GENERAL CHARACTERISTICS OF THE WINES:

| | |
|---|---|
| **WHITES** | These are produced mainly from *Macabeo* and *Garnacha Blanca*. Straw yellow coloured, they have fruity noses and are reminiscent of mountain herbs; on the palate, they also show their Mediterranean character: they are somewhat warm with wild notes. |
| **ROSÉS** | These are maybe the least characteristic of the region. Due to the rather warm climate in which the grapes ripen, they are known for their ripe fruit notes; on the palate they are warm and flavourful. |
| **REDS** | The star product of the region. Produced from *Garnacha* and *Cariñena* combined in the high ranges with lesser percentages of foreign varieties; they are characterised by their very cloudy intense cherry colour. The best offer a nose with great complexity, with notes of very ripe fruit and the marked character of terruño (due to the effect of the slaty soil) that provide abundant mineral notes. On the palate, they have great character and structure; they are powerful, meaty, warm, and at the same time emphatically acidic, markedly tannic and very persistent. |
| **RANCIOS AND SWEET WINES** | The traditional Rancios of the region have noses of almonds and notes of mountain herbs; on the palate they are warm, flavourful with fine oxidative evolution.<br>There is also a range of sweet wines produced according to more traditional criteria. They have a cloudy cherry colour; the nose is of black fruit, almost raisin-like and notes of toast due to their ageing in oak; on the palate they are sweet, sticky, very fruity and well-balanced due to their good acidity. |

## 2008 VINTAGE RATING:

# VERY GOOD

## AIXALÀ I ALCAIT PARDELASSES

Balandra, 8
43737 Torroja del Priorat (Tarragona)
☎: 629 507 807 - Fax: 977 839 516
pardelasses@gmail.com
www.pardelasses.com

PARDELASSES 2007 T
garnacha, cariñena

**87** Colour: cherry, garnet rim. Nose: powerful, fruit preserve, dark chocolate, cocoa bean, creamy oak. Palate: powerful, concentrated, fleshy, spirituous.

PARDELASSES 2006 T
garnacha, cariñena

**89** Colour: dark-red cherry. Nose: powerful, characterful, fruit preserve, toasty, creamy oak. Palate: powerful, fleshy, spicy, ripe fruit, round tannins.

## ALVARO PALACIOS

Afores s/n
43737 Gratallops (Tarragona)
☎: 977 839 195 - Fax: 977 839 197
info@alvaropalacios.com

FINCA DOFÍ 2007 TC
garnacha 55%, cabernet sauvignon 45%, syrah %

**93** Colour: cherry, garnet rim. Nose: scrubland, sweet spices, toasty, ripe fruit, mineral. Palate: flavourful, good structure, powerful, fleshy, round tannins.

GRATALLOPS 2007 TC
garnacha 50%, samsó 35%, cabernet sauvignon 15%, syrah %

**92** Colour: cherry, garnet rim. Nose: expressive, elegant, complex, red berry notes, creamy oak, toasty. Palate: flavourful, powerful, fleshy, fruity, round tannins, fruity aftestaste.

CAMINS DEL PRIORAT 2007 TC
samsó 50%, garnacha 40%, cabernet sauvignon 10%, syrah %

**91** Colour: cherry, garnet rim. Nose: powerful, grassy, balsamic herbs, ripe fruit. Palate: flavourful, fleshy, fruity, round tannins.

LES TERRASSES VINYES VELLES 2007 TC
samsó 60%, garnacha 30%, cabernet sauvignon 10%, syrah %

**89** Colour: cherry, garnet rim. Nose: powerful, scrubland, balsamic herbs, toasty, aged wood nuances. Palate: flavourful, fruity, spicy, ripe fruit, slightly dry, soft tannins.

L'ERMITA 2006 TC
garnacha 100%

**96** Colour: cherry, garnet rim. Nose: elegant, expressive, candied fruit, ripe fruit, dry stone, citrus fruit. Palate: flavourful, fleshy, fruity, ripe fruit, creamy, round tannins.

## BLAI FERRÉ JUST

Piró, 28
43737 Gratallops (Tarragona)
☎: 647 217 751
blai@cellercecilio.com

BILLO 2008 T
garnacha 35%, syrah 35%, cariñena 20%, cabernet sauvignon 10%

**87** Colour: cherry, purple rim. Nose: powerful, ripe fruit, balsamic herbs, scrubland. Palate: ripe fruit, balsamic.

BILLO 2007 T
garnacha 35%, syrah 35%, cariñena 20%, cabernet sauvignon 10%

**90** Colour: deep cherry. Nose: characterful, complex, mineral, dry stone, aromatic coffee, toasty. Palate: powerful, flavourful, rich.

## BODEGA PARMI PRIORAT

Prat de la Riba, 20
43739 Porrera (Tarragona)
☎: 977 828 366 - Fax: 977 828 366
parmipriorat@yahoo.es

EL MAS DE LA SALUT 2006 T
cariñena 100%

**93** Colour: cherry, garnet rim. Nose: powerful, varietal, fruit liqueur notes, ripe fruit, creamy oak, sweet spices, dark chocolate. Palate: powerful, fleshy, complex, spicy.

LA COMA 2006 T
cariñena 100%

**91** Colour: cherry, garnet rim. Nose: powerful, warm, ripe fruit, sweet spices, creamy oak, toasty. Palate: flavourful, powerful, fleshy, spicy.

L'ESPERIT DE PORRERA 2006 T

**89** Colour: cherry, garnet rim. Nose: toasty, new oak, dark chocolate, earthy notes, ripe fruit. Palate: flavourful, powerful, fleshy, spirituous.

L'INFANT 2006 T
garnacha 80%, cariñena 20%

**93** Colour: cherry, garnet rim. Nose: powerful, ripe fruit, varietal, earthy notes. Palate: flavourful, powerful, fleshy, spicy, ripe fruit.

## BODEGAS MAS ALTA

Ctra. T-702, km. 16,8
43375 La Vilella Alta (Tarragona)
☎: 977 054 151 - Fax: 977 817 194
info@bodegasmasalta.com
www.bodegasmasalta.com

ARTIGAS 2008 BFB
garnacha blanca 50%, macabeo 40%, pedro ximénez 10%

**88** Colour: bright straw. Nose: fragrant herbs, macerated fruit. Palate: sweetness, spirituous, powerful, flavourful, spicy.

ARTIGAS 2007 T
garnacha 70%, cabernet sauvignon 18%, cariñena 12%

**90** Colour: cherry, garnet rim. Nose: powerful, fruit preserve, ripe fruit, toasty, new oak. Palate: powerful, flavourful, fleshy, complex.

LA CREU ALTA 2006 T
cariñena 50%, garnacha 35%, syrah 15%

**93** Colour: very deep cherry. Nose: complex, medium intensity, damp earth, mineral. Palate: fleshy, complex, spirituous, sweetness, powerful, flavourful.

LA BASSETA 2006 T
cariñena 45%, garnacha 40%, cabernet sauvignon 15%

**92** Colour: deep cherry. Nose: smoky, cocoa bean, ripe fruit, dry stone. Palate: complex, spirituous, fruity, powerful, flavourful, balanced.

ARTIGAS 2006 T
garnacha 80%, cabernet sauvignon 10%, cariñena 10%

**90** Colour: deep cherry. Nose: sweet spices, aromatic coffee, ripe fruit, medium intensity, expressive. Palate: fleshy, sweetness, fruity, flavourful, powerful.

## BODEGAS Y VIÑEDOS DEL CAL GRAU S.L.

Ctra. del Molar a El Lloar, km. 2,5
43736 El Molar (Tarragona)
☎: 900 505 855 - Fax: 956 852 339
vinos@gvitivinicola.com
www.grupohebe.com

LES ONES 2006 T

**91** Colour: cherry, garnet rim. Nose: powerful, mineral, ripe fruit, red berry notes, sweet spices. Palate: flavourful, fleshy, spicy, ripe fruit.

BADACELI 2005 T
samsó 55%, garnacha 35%, cabernet sauvignon 10%

**89** Colour: bright cherry. Nose: ripe fruit, sweet spices, creamy oak, toasty, mineral. Palate: flavourful, fruity, toasty, round tannins.

EPILEG
LA NINOTA

## BUIL & GINÉ

Ctra. de Gratallops - Vilella Baixa, km. 11,5
43737 Gratallops (Tarragona)
☎: 977 839 810 - Fax: 977 839 811
info@builgine.com
www.builgine.com

PLERET BLANC DOLÇ 2005 B
garnacha blanca, macabeo, pedro ximénez

**90** Colour: golden. Nose: powerful, floral, honeyed notes, candied fruit, fragrant herbs. Palate: flavourful, sweet, fresh, fruity, good acidity, long.

## GINÉ ROSAT 2008 RD
garnacha, merlot

**86** Colour: rose, purple rim. Nose: macerated fruit, fresh. Palate: fruity, fresh, powerful, flavourful.

## GINÉ GINÉ 2007 T
garnacha, cariñena

**85** Colour: cherry, garnet rim. Nose: medium intensity, ripe fruit, candied fruit. Palate: spicy, ripe fruit, round tannins.

## JOAN GINÉ 2006 T

**89** Colour: deep cherry. Nose: mineral, undergrowth, dry stone, ripe fruit. Palate: fruity, powerful, flavourful, varietal.

## PLERET 2004 T
garnacha, cabernet sauvignon, merlot, syrah

**86** Colour: cherry, garnet rim. Nose: spicy, dark chocolate, aromatic coffee, ripe fruit. Palate: spicy, flavourful, fleshy.

## PLERET NEGRE DOLÇ 2005 T DULCE
garnacha, cariñena, cabernet sauvignon

**90** Colour: cherry, garnet rim. Nose: powerful, overripe fruit, fruit liqueur notes. Palate: powerful, fleshy, sweet, good acidity, spirituous.

## BURGOS PORTA

Mas Sinén, s/n
43376 Poboleda (Tarragona)
☎: 696 094 509 - Fax: 977 321 339
burgos.porta@wanadoo.es

## MAS SINÉN COSTER 2006 TC
garnacha 35%, cabernet sauvignon 30%, cariñena 25%, syrah 10%

**90** Colour: deep cherry. Nose: complex, ripe fruit, fruit liqueur notes, cedar wood, creamy oak. Palate: fleshy, complex, sweetness, powerful, flavourful, toasty.

## CASA GRAN DEL SIURANA

Mayor, 3
43738 Bellmunt del Priorat (Tarragona)
☎: 932 233 022 - Fax: 932 231 370
perelada@castilloperelada.com
www.castilloperelada.com

## GRAN CRUOR 2006 T
syrah 80%, cabernet sauvignon 20%

**93** Colour: cherry, garnet rim. Nose: powerful, toasty, dark chocolate, aromatic coffee, ripe fruit. Palate: flavourful, powerful, fleshy, good structure, round tannins.

## CRUOR 2006 T
garnacha 30%, cabernet sauvignon 25%, syrah 20%, merlot 15%, cariñena 10%

**91** Colour: cherry, garnet rim. Nose: powerful, creamy oak, toasty, cocoa bean. Palate: flavourful, powerful, fleshy, spirituous, round tannins.

## GRAN CRUOR 2005 T
syrah 90%, cariñena 10%

**94** Colour: black cherry, garnet rim. Nose: powerful, expressive, ripe fruit, dry stone, aged wood nuances, creamy oak, cocoa bean. Palate: fleshy, complex, good structure, roasted-coffee aftertaste, long.

## CRUOR 2005 T
garnacha, cabernet sauvignon, cariñena, syrah, merlot

**89** Colour: cherry, garnet rim. Nose: earthy notes, mineral, ripe fruit, fruit liqueur notes, dark chocolate, aromatic coffee. Palate: flavourful, spicy, ripe fruit, good acidity, slightly dry, soft tannins.

## CELLER CASTELLET

Font de Dalt, 11
43739 Porrera (Tarragona)
☎: 977 828 044
cellercastellet@yahoo.es

## EMPIT 2007 T
garnacha 75%, cabernet sauvignon 15%, cariñena 10%

**89** Colour: cherry, purple rim. Nose: powerful, ripe fruit, sweet spices, toasty, varietal. Palate: fleshy, powerful, fruity, flavourful.

## FERRAL 2007 T
garnacha 48%, cabernet sauvignon 26%, syrah 17%, merlot 9%

**83**

## CELLER CECILIO

Piró, 28
43737 Gratallops (Tarragona)
☎: 977 839 181 - Fax: 977 839 507
celler@cellercecilio.com
www.cellercecilio.com

CELLER CECILIO BLANC 2008 B
garnacha blanca 100%

**86** Colour: bright straw. Nose: fresh, fresh fruit, white flowers, expressive, varietal. Palate: flavourful, fruity, good acidity, balanced.

CELLER CECILIO NEGRE 2007 T
garnacha 50%, cariñena 30%, cabernet sauvignon 20%

**87** Colour: cherry, garnet rim. Nose: powerful, toasty, expressive, earthy notes. Palate: powerful, flavourful, fleshy, complex.

L'ESPILL 2006 TC
garnacha 60%, cariñena 30%, cabernet sauvignon 10%

**85** Colour: cherry, garnet rim. Nose: powerful, fruit liqueur notes, toasty, aged wood nuances. Palate: fleshy, spirituous, powerful.

L'ESPILL 2005 TC
garnacha 60%, cariñena 30%, cabernet sauvignon 10%

**85** Colour: cherry, garnet rim. Nose: powerful, ripe fruit, sweet spices, toasty. Palate: flavourful, spicy, ripe fruit.

## CELLER DE L'ABADIA

De la Font, 38
43737 Gratallops (Tarragona)
☎: 977 054 078 - Fax: 977 054 078
jeroni@cellerabadia.com
www.cellerabadia.com

ALICE 2007 T
cariñena 40%, garnacha 30%, monastrell 20%, cabernet sauvignon 5%, syrah 5%

**90** Colour: dark-red cherry. Nose: complex, elegant, mineral, fruit expression. Palate: warm, round, powerful, flavourful.

CLOS CLARA 2006 T
cariñena 40%, garnacha 30%, cabernet sauvignon 15%, syrah 15%

**88** Colour: cherry, garnet rim. Nose: ripe fruit, spicy, creamy oak, toasty, complex. Palate: powerful, flavourful, toasty, round tannins.

## CELLER DE L'ENCASTELL

Castell, 13
43739 Porrera (Tarragona)
☎: 630 941 959 - Fax: 977 828 146
roquers@roquers.com
www.roquers.com

MARGE 2007 T
garnacha 60%, cabernet sauvignon 40%, merlot %, syrah %

**89** Colour: cherry, garnet rim. Nose: powerful, red berry notes, ripe fruit, earthy notes. Palate: flavourful, powerful, fleshy, good structure, round tannins.

ROQUERS DE PORRERA 2006 TC
garnacha 80%, cariñena %, merlot 20%, syrah %

**91** Colour: deep cherry. Nose: ripe fruit, mineral, damp earth, creamy oak. Palate: powerful, flavourful, fruity, spirituous, sweetness, complex, fleshy.

## CELLER DEL PONT S.L.

Del Riu, 1 Baixos
43374 La Vilella Baixa (Tarragona)
☎: 977 828 231 - Fax: 977 828 231
info@cellerdelpont.com
www.cellerdelpont.com

LO GIVOT 2006 T
garnacha 33%, mazuelo 32%, cabernet sauvignon 25%, syrah 10%

**89** Colour: cherry, garnet rim. Nose: powerful, ripe fruit, sweet spices, cedar wood. Palate: powerful, fleshy, ripe fruit, round tannins.

## CELLER DELS PINS VERS

Afores, s/n
43736 El Molar (Tarragona)
☎: 977 825 458 - Fax: 977 825 458
info@lafuina.com
www.lafuina.com

LA FUINA 2006 T

**90** Colour: cherry, garnet rim. Nose: powerful, warm, earthy notes, toasty, new oak, dark chocolate. Palate: flavourful, powerful, fleshy, spirituous, round tannins.

LA FUINA 2004 T

**90** Colour: cherry, garnet rim. Nose: ripe fruit, mineral, floral, expressive. Palate: full, powerful, good finish, round tannins, good structure.

## CELLER GENIUM S.L.

Nou, 92 Bajos
43376 Poboleda (Tarragona)
☎: 977 827 146 - Fax: 977 827 146
genium@geniumceller.com
www.geniumceller.com

GENIUM XIMENIS 2008 BFB
pedro ximénez 90%, otras 10%

**87** Colour: bright straw. Nose: medium intensity, ripe fruit, citrus fruit, spicy. Palate: flavourful, fleshy, fruity, ripe fruit.

GENIUM COSTERS 2006 TR
cariñena 50%, garnacha 30%, merlot 10%, syrah 10%

**90** Colour: deep cherry. Nose: candied fruit, fruit liqueur notes, complex, varietal, cocoa bean. Palate: complex, spirituous, fruity, powerful, flavourful.

GENIUM CELLER 2006 T
garnacha 60%, cariñena 20%, merlot 15%, syrah 5%

**89** Colour: deep cherry. Nose: ripe fruit, powerfull, complex, mineral, cedar wood, sweet spices. Palate: sweetness, good structure, powerful, flavourful, spicy, toasty.

GENIUM CELLER ECOLÒGIC 2006 T
garnacha 50%, cariñena 30%, merlot 10%, syrah 10%

**85** Colour: cherry, garnet rim. Nose: powerful, ripe fruit, sweet spices. Palate: spirituous, toasty, round tannins.

## CELLER JOAN SIMÓ

11 de Setembre, 7
43739 Porrera (Tarragona)
☎: 977 830 993 - Fax: 977 830 993
leseres@cellerjoansimo.com

LES ERES 2006 T
cariñena 55%, garnacha 30%, cabernet sauvignon 15%

**90** Colour: cherry, garnet rim. Nose: powerful, complex, warm, toasty, new oak, tar. Palate: flavourful, powerful, fleshy, spirituous.

LES ERES ESPECIAL DELS CARNERS 2006 T
garnacha 75%, cariñena 25%

**88** Colour: bright cherry. Nose: ripe fruit, sweet spices, creamy oak, expressive, mineral. Palate: flavourful, fruity, toasty, round tannins.

SENTIUS 2006 T
garnacha 55%, syrah 20%, cabernet sauvignon 20%, merlot 5%

**85** Colour: cherry, garnet rim. Nose: ripe fruit, red berry notes, sweet spices, creamy oak. Palate: powerful, flavourful, fleshy, spicy.

## CELLER MAS BASTÉ

De les Valls, 28
43737 Gratallops (Tarragona)
☎: 629 300 291 - Fax: 934 364 877
jacazurra@albagrup.com
www.cellerabadia.com

PEITES 2008 T
garnacha 75%, syrah 25%

**88** Colour: deep cherry. Nose: medium intensity, closed, ripe fruit. Palate: fruity, powerful, flavourful, concentrated, sweetness.

PEITES 2007 TC
cariñena 80%, syrah 10%, garnacha 10%

**90** Colour: cherry, garnet rim. Nose: powerful, expressive, characterful, new oak, toasty, ripe fruit. Palate: powerful, fleshy, flavourful.

## CELLER MAS DE LES PERERES

Mas de Les Pereres, s/n
43376 Poboleda (Tarragona)
☎: 977 827 257 - Fax: 977 827 257
dirk.hoet@village.uunet.be
www.nunci.com

# NUNCI
# PRIORAT
## fine wine

NUNCI BLANC 2007 BFB
garnacha blanca 65%, macabeo 35%

**88** Colour: bright straw. Nose: ripe fruit, citrus fruit, sweet spices, cocoa bean. Palate: flavourful, fruity, fresh, fleshy.

NUNCI ABOCAT 2007 B
macabeo 50%, garnacha blanca 30%, moscatel 20%

**87** Colour: bright straw. Nose: white flowers, fresh fruit, citrus fruit, varietal. Palate: flavourful, fruity, fresh, fleshy.

NUNCITO 2006 T BARRICA
garnacha 40%, syrah 40%, cariñena 20%

**84**

NUNCI NEGRE 2005 T
garnacha 40%, syrah 30%, cariñena 10%, cabernet franc 10%, merlot 5%, cabernet sauvignon 5%

**90** Colour: deep cherry. Nose: fruit liqueur notes, complex, expressive, mineral, aromatic coffee. Palate: complex, fleshy, full, powerful, flavourful, spirituous, balsamic, spicy, toasty.

NUNCI COSTERO 2005 T
cariñena 45%, garnacha 40%, cabernet franc 5%, cabernet sauvignon 5%, merlot 5%

**88** Colour: cherry, garnet rim. Nose: powerful, varietal, ripe fruit, red berry notes, sweet spices, toasty. Palate: ripe fruit, spicy, mineral, round tannins.

NUNCI NEGRE 2004 T
garnacha 40%, syrah 25%, cariñena 15%, cabernet franc 10%, merlot 5%, cabernet sauvignon 5%

**90** Colour: deep cherry. Nose: aromatic coffee, spicy, cedar wood, ripe fruit, mineral. Palate: complex, sweetness, spirituous, powerful, flavourful, fleshy, creamy, fruity aftestaste, mineral.

NUNCI COSTERO 2004 T
cariñena 45%, garnacha 40%, merlot 5%, cabernet franc 5%, cabernet sauvignon 5%

**86** Colour: cherry, garnet rim. Nose: powerful, fruit liqueur notes, spicy, new oak, toasty. Palate: flavourful, spirituous, spicy.

## CELLER MAS DOIX

Carme, 115
43376 Poboleda (Tarragona)
☎: 639 356 172 - Fax: 933 216 790
masdoix@bsab.com
www.masdoix.com

DOIX 2007 TC

**91** Colour: very deep cherry. Nose: ripe fruit, sweet spices, creamy oak, expressive, mineral. Palate: flavourful, fruity, toasty, round tannins, spirituous, fleshy, powerful.

SALANQUES T

**89** Colour: deep cherry. Nose: spicy, dark chocolate, earthy notes, mineral, ripe fruit. Palate: powerful, flavourful, spicy, roasted-coffee aftertaste, ripe fruit.

## CELLER MAS GARRIAN

Mas del Camperol, Camí Rieres, s/n
43736 El Molar (Tarragona)
☎: 977 262 118 - Fax: 977 262 118
masgarriansl@masgarrian.com
www.masgarrian.com

CLOS SEVERI 2005 TC
cariñena, cabernet sauvignon, garnacha, syrah

**88** Colour: cherry, garnet rim. Nose: powerful, ripe fruit, sweet spices. Palate: powerful, flavourful, fleshy, round tannins.

MAS DEL CAMPEROL 2005 TC
cariñena, cabernet sauvignon, garnacha, syrah

**84**

## CELLER MELIS

Balandra, 54
43737 Torroja del Priorat (Tarragona)
☎: 937 313 021 - Fax: 937 312 371
javier@melispriorat.com
www.melispriorat.com

ELIX 2007 T

**90** Colour: dark-red cherry. Nose: complex, varietal, fresh, damp undergrowth. Palate: powerful, flavourful, spicy.

ELIX 2006 T

**93** Colour: cherry, garnet rim. Nose: ripe fruit, toasty, new oak, creamy oak, scrubland. Palate: powerful, flavourful, fleshy, spicy, mineral.

MELIS 2006 T
garnacha 63%, cariñena 19%, syrah 6%, cabernet sauvignon 13%

**92** Colour: cherry, garnet rim. Nose: ripe fruit, sweet spices, aromatic coffee, tobacco, mineral. Palate: flavourful, powerful, fleshy, spicy, round tannins.

ELIX 2005 T

**93** Colour: deep cherry. Nose: mineral, dry stone, complex, characterful, expressive, spicy, cedar wood, roasted coffee. Palate: powerful, flavourful, rich, complex, fleshy.

MELIS 2005 T

**93** Colour: deep cherry. Nose: fruit expression, ripe fruit, powerfull, complex, damp earth, mineral, dark chocolate, aromatic coffee. Palate: sweetness, spirituous, good structure, powerful, flavourful.

## MELIS 2004 T

**92** Colour: deep cherry. Nose: ripe fruit, mineral, balanced, varietal, medium intensity, roasted coffee. Palate: powerful, flavourful, round, good acidity, sweetness.

## CELLER PASANAU

La Bassa, s/n
43361 La Morera de Montsant (Tarragona)
☎: 977 827 202 - Fax: 977 827 202
informacion@cellerpasanau.com
www.cellerpasanau.com

PASANAU CEPS NOUS 2007 T
garnacha 58%, mazuelo 19%, syrah 10%, cabernet sauvignon 7%, merlot 6%

**87** Colour: cherry, garnet rim. Nose: powerful, warm, fruit preserve, spicy. Palate: powerful, fleshy, sweetness, toasty.

PASANAU EL VELL COSTES 2006 T

**90** Colour: deep cherry. Nose: fruit expression, ripe fruit, complex, dry stone, mineral. Palate: flavourful, powerful, sweetness, spirituous, complex, creamy, spicy, toasty.

PASANAU LA MORERA DE MONTSANT 2006 T
garnacha 52%, merlot 28%, mazuelo 20%

**84**

PASANAU FINCA LA PLANETA 2005 T
cabernet sauvignon 75%, garnacha 25%

**85** Colour: cherry, garnet rim. Nose: scrubland, cedar wood, dark chocolate, overripe fruit. Palate: spicy, pruney, round tannins.

## CELLER PRIOR PONS

Rey, 4
43375 La Vilella Alta (Tarragona)
☎: 606 547 865
info@priorpons.com
www.priorpons.com

PRIOR PONS 2006 T
garnacha 40%, mazuelo 40%, cabernet sauvignon 20%

**91** Colour: cherry, garnet rim. Nose: ripe fruit, toasty, creamy oak, mineral. Palate: powerful, fleshy, spirituous, ripe fruit, round tannins.

ISARAL 2006 T
garnacha 35%, mazuelo 35%, cabernet sauvignon 30%

**82**

## CELLER SABATÉ

Nou, 6
43374 La Vilella Baixa (Tarragona)
☎: 977 839 209 - Fax: 977 839 209
cellersabate@cellersabate.com
www.cellersabate.com

MAS PLANTADETA 2007 BFB
garnacha blanca 100%

**88** Colour: bright straw. Nose: ripe fruit, earthy notes, spicy. Palate: fleshy, sweetness, flavourful.

MAS PLANTADETA 2008 RD
garnacha 100%

**88** Colour: onion pink. Nose: fresh fruit, fruit expression. Palate: sweetness, fresh, flavourful.

MAS PLANTADETA 2005 TC
garnacha 50%, cariñena 25%, cabernet sauvignon 25%

**80**

MAS D'EN BERNAT

## CELLER VALL-LLACH

Del Pont, 9
43739 Porrera (Tarragona)
☎: 977 828 244 - Fax: 977 828 325
celler@vallllach.com
www.vallllach.com

VALL-LLACH 2007 T

**91** Colour: very deep cherry. Nose: spicy, closed, characterful, complex. Palate: fleshy, complex, powerful, flavourful, roasted-coffee aftertaste, toasty, ripe fruit.

EMBRUIX DE VALL-LLACH 2007 T

**90** Colour: very deep cherry. Nose: caramel, creamy oak, candied fruit. Palate: complex, spirituous, powerful, flavourful, roasted-coffee aftertaste, toasty.

IDUS DE VALL-LLACH 2007 T

**89** Colour: deep cherry. Nose: macerated fruit, medium intensity, closed, spicy, creamy oak, mineral. Palate: ripe fruit, creamy, powerful, flavourful.

## CELLERS DE SCALA DEI

Rambla de la Cartoixa, s/n
43379 Scala Dei (Tarragona)

# DO Ca. PRIORAT

☎: 977 827 027 - Fax: 977 827 044
v.sanchez@codorniu.es
www.grupocodorniu.com

**CARTOIXA 2005 T**
garnacha, cariñena, syrah, cabernet sauvignon

**90** Colour: bright cherry, garnet rim. Nose: complex, elegant, candied fruit, citrus fruit, mineral. Palate: flavourful, good structure, elegant.

**SCALA DEI PRIOR 2005 TC**
garnacha, cabernet sauvignon, syrah

**86** Colour: cherry, garnet rim. Nose: spicy, creamy oak, complex, balsamic herbs, mineral, fruit preserve, tobacco. Palate: powerful, flavourful, toasty, round tannins, good acidity.

## CELLERS FUENTES S.L.

Montsant, 2
43738 Bellmunt del Priorat (Tarragona)
☎: 977 830 675 - Fax: 977 830 417
cellersfuentes@granclos.com
www.granclos.com

**GRAN CLOS 2003 B**
garnacha blanca 80%, macabeo 20%

**89** Colour: bright golden. Nose: powerful, candied fruit, petrol notes, honeyed notes, dry nuts. Palate: spirituous, flavourful, spicy.

**LES MINES SOLLUNA 2006 T**
garnacha 50%, cariñena 25%, merlot 25%

**88** Colour: cherry, garnet rim. Nose: powerful, characterful, ripe fruit, fruit liqueur notes, sweet spices, toasty. Palate: flavourful, powerful, fleshy, spicy.

**FINCA EL PUIG 2005 T**
garnacha 60%, otras 40%

**89** Colour: deep cherry. Nose: fruit expression, complex, dry stone, mineral, macerated fruit, candied fruit, dark chocolate, sweet spices. Palate: complex, spirituous, fruity, powerful, flavourful, mineral, spicy.

**GRAN CLOS 2004 T**
garnacha 55%, cariñena 35%, cabernet sauvignon 10%

**88** Colour: cherry, garnet rim. Nose: powerful, fruit liqueur notes, toasty, pattiserie. Palate: powerful, spirituous, spicy, round tannins.

**CARTUS 2004 T**
garnacha 76%, cariñena 24%

**86** Colour: black cherry. Nose: fruit liqueur notes, fruit liqueur notes, dark chocolate, toasty. Palate: powerful, fleshy, sweetness.

## CLOS BERENGUER

Ctra. T-734 del Masroig, PK 8,3
43735 El Molar (Tarragona)
☎: 977 361 390 - Fax: 977 361 390
info@closberenguer.com
www.closberenguer.com

**CLOS BERENGUER BLANC DE BÓTES 2006 B**
garnacha blanca 63%, xarel.lo 14%, pedro ximénez 23%

**81**

**CLOS BERENGUER FINCA LES SORTS 2006 T**
cabernet sauvignon 90%, syrah 10%

**90** Colour: deep cherry. Nose: dry stone, mineral, dark chocolate, cocoa bean, creamy oak. Palate: creamy, spicy, balsamic, powerful, flavourful, complex, good structure.

**CLOS BERENGUER VI DE GUARDA 2005 T**

**88** Colour: cherry, garnet rim. Nose: powerful, warm, ripe fruit, toasty. Palate: flavourful, spirituous, powerful, spicy.

## CLOS DE L'OBAC

Manyetes, s/n
43737 Gratallops (Tarragona)
☎: 977 839 276 - Fax: 977 839 371
info@costersdelsiurana.com
www.costersdelsiurana.com

**MISERERE 2005 TC**

**92** Colour: cherry, garnet rim. Nose: powerful, warm, ripe fruit, sweet spices, creamy oak. Palate: flavourful, powerful, fleshy, ripe fruit.

**CLOS DE L'OBAC 2005 TC**

**90** Colour: dark-red cherry. Nose: fruit expression, fine reductive notes, cigar. Palate: powerful, flavourful, round, full, rich.

**KYRIE**

## CLOS DOMINIC S.L.

Prat de la Riba, 3
43739 Porrera (Tarragona)
☎: 977 828 215 - Fax: 977 828 215
closdominic@closdominic.com
www.debrujasyvino.blogspot.com

**CLOS DOMINIC VINYES ALTES 2006 T**

**89** Colour: deep cherry. Nose: dark chocolate, sweet spices, fruit preserve. Palate: sweetness, spirituous, good structure, fleshy, powerful.

CLOS DOMINIC VINYES BAIXES 2006 T

**88** Colour: cherry, garnet rim. Nose: ripe fruit, spicy, creamy oak, toasty, complex. Palate: powerful, flavourful, toasty, round tannins.

## CLOS ERASMUS

La Font, 1
43737 Gratallops (Tarragona)
☎: 977 839 022 - Fax: 977 839 179
info@closerasmus.com

CLOS ERASMUS 2005 T

**95** Colour: cherry, garnet rim. Nose: powerful, fruit liqueur notes, ripe fruit, sweet spices, toasty. Palate: flavourful, spicy, fine bitter notes, toasty, sweet tannins.

## CLOS FIGUERAS

Carrer La Font, 38
43737 Gratallops (Tarragona)
☎: 977 831 712 - Fax: 977 831 797
laurona@cellerlaurona.com

CLOS FIGUERES 2007 T

**89** Colour: cherry, purple rim. Nose: powerful, ripe fruit, sweet spices, toasty. Palate: powerful, fleshy, good structure.

FONT DE LA FIGUERA 2007 T

**88** Colour: cherry, purple rim. Nose: powerful, ripe fruit, fruit liqueur notes, sweet spices, toasty. Palate: powerful, fleshy, flavourful.

## CLOS MOGADOR (SPECTACLE VINS)

Camí Manyetes s/n
43737 Gratallops (Tarragona)
☎: 977 839 171 - Fax: 977 839 426
closmogador@closmogador.com

CLOS MOGADOR 2007 T

**92** Colour: dark-red cherry. Nose: fresh fruit, complex, varietal, cocoa bean, spicy. Palate: complex, fresh, fruity, powerful, flavourful.

MANYETES 2007 T

**91** Colour: deep cherry. Nose: complex, expressive, powerfull, ripe fruit, fruit liqueur notes. Palate: powerful, flavourful, fruity, spirituous, fleshy.

CLOS MOGADOR 2006 T

**95** Colour: very deep cherry. Nose: cocoa bean, spicy, cedar wood, complex, undergrowth, mineral. Palate: powerful, flavourful, spirituous, sweetness, fleshy.

MANYETES 2006 T

**92** Colour: deep cherry. Nose: aromatic coffee, creamy oak, earthy notes, mineral, fruit preserve, fruit expression. Palate: sweetness, good structure, fruity, powerful, flavourful, roasted-coffee aftertaste.

NELIN

## COMBIER-FISCHER-GERIN S.L.

Baixa Font, 18
43737 (Torroja del Priorat)
☎: 977 839 403
yalellamaremos@yahoo.es

TRIO INFERNAL Nº 0/3 2007 BC

**91** Colour: bright golden. Nose: powerful, expressive, complex, spicy, wild herbs, aged wood nuances. Palate: complex, spirituous, powerful, flavourful, creamy, balsamic, smoky aftertaste.

RIU BY TRÍO INFERNAL 2007 T

**90** Colour: deep cherry. Nose: candied fruit, fruit liqueur notes, complex, varietal, sweet spices, creamy oak, dark chocolate. Palate: powerful, flavourful, fruity, fleshy.

TRIO INFERNAL Nº 2/3 2006 T

**93** Colour: deep cherry. Nose: powerful, complex, expressive, fruit expression, ripe fruit, dry stone, burnt matches, mineral. Palate: complex, fleshy, sweetness, powerful, flavourful, spirituous.

TRIO INFERNAL Nº 1/3 2005 TC

**87** Colour: cherry, garnet rim. Nose: ripe fruit, overripe fruit, dark chocolate, aromatic coffee. Palate: spicy, ripe fruit, round tannins.

## COSTERS DEL PRIORAT

Finca Sant Martí
43738 Bellmunt del Priorat (Tarragona)
☎: 618 203 473 - Fax: 938 921 333

info@costersdelpriorat.com
www.costersdelpriorat.com

CLOS CYPRES 2007 T

**91** Colour: cherry, garnet rim. Nose: powerful, varietal, characterful, earthy notes, ripe fruit. Palate: flavourful, powerful, fleshy, spicy, round tannins.

PISSARRES 2007 T
cariñena 55%, garnacha 30%, cabernet sauvignon 10%, syrah 5%

**87** Colour: cherry, garnet rim. Nose: fruit preserve, raspberry, creamy oak, pattiserie, sweet spices. Palate: powerful, flavourful, fleshy, spicy.

## DE MULLER

Camí Pedra Estela, 34
43205 Reus (Tarragona)
☎: 977 757 473 - Fax: 977 771 129
lab@demuller.es
www.demuller.es

LEGITIM 2005 TC
garnacha 50%, merlot 35%, syrah 10%, cariñena 5%

**86** Colour: cherry, garnet rim. Nose: fruit liqueur notes, candied fruit, sweet spices. Palate: flavourful, powerful, fleshy, spicy.

LES PUSSES DE MULLER 2004 TC
merlot 50%, syrah 50%

**89** Colour: pale ruby, brick rim edge. Nose: fruit liqueur notes, spicy, toasty. Palate: flavourful, powerful, fleshy, spirituous, fine bitter notes.

LO CABALÓ 2002 TR
garnacha 70%, merlot 10%, syrah 10%, cariñena 10%

**88** Colour: dark-red cherry, orangey edge. Nose: candied fruit, roasted coffee, cigar, wet leather. Palate: complex, good structure, powerful, flavourful.

DOM BERENGUER
DOM JOAN FORT

## DOMAINES MAGREZ ESPAGNE

Plaça Catalunya, 5
43739 Porrera (Tarragona)

☎: 977 828 016 - Fax: 977 828 016
trosdelpadri-bernardmagrez@hotmail.com

SINE NOMINE 2006 T
mazuelo, syrah, merlot, garnacha, cabernet sauvignon

**91** Colour: cherry, garnet rim. Nose: ripe fruit, spicy, creamy oak, toasty, complex, aged wood nuances. Palate: powerful, flavourful, toasty, round tannins.

HERÈNCIA DEL PADRÍ 2006 T
mazuelo, syrah, garnacha, merlot, cabernet sauvignon

**85** Colour: cherry, garnet rim. Nose: creamy oak, ripe fruit, sweet spices, earthy notes. Palate: flavourful, powerful, fleshy, round tannins.

## DOMINI DE LA CARTOIXA

Camino de la Solana s/n
43736 El Molar (Tarragona)
☎: 606 443 736 - Fax: 977 771 737
info@closgalena.com
www.closgalena.com

CLOS GALENA 2007 TC

**92** Colour: black cherry, dark-red cherry. Nose: powerful, ripe fruit, dark chocolate, creamy oak, mineral. Palate: flavourful, powerful, fleshy, spicy.

GALENA 2007 T

**90** Colour: cherry, garnet rim. Nose: powerful, earthy notes, ripe fruit, fruit liqueur notes, toasty. Palate: flavourful, powerful, fleshy, spicy.

## ELVIWINES S.L.

Granollers, 27 G
08173 Sant Cugat (Barcelona)
☎: 935 343 026 - Fax: 935 441 374
info@elviwines.com
www.elviwines.com

EL26 2006 TR
garnacha 20%, syrah 40%, cabernet sauvignon 40%

**92** Colour: deep cherry. Nose: complex, characterful, mineral, dry stone, aromatic coffee. Palate: complex, fleshy, spirituous, full, powerful, flavourful, spicy, smoky aftertaste, ripe fruit.

EL26 2005 T
merlot 30%, cabernet sauvignon 25%, cariñena 25%, garnacha 10%, syrah 10%

**86** Colour: cherry, garnet rim. Nose: powerful, toasty, spicy, ripe fruit, aromatic coffee. Palate: powerful, spicy, round tannins.

## FERRER BOBET

Ctra. Porrera a Falset (T-740), km. 7
43730 Falset (Tarragona)
☎: 609 945 532
eguerre@ferrerbobet.com
www.ferrerbobet.com

FERRER BOBET SELECCIÓ ESPECIAL 2006 T
cariñena 95 %, garnacha 5%

**94** Colour: very deep cherry. Nose: aromatic coffee, mineral, undergrowth, ripe fruit, elegant, complex. Palate: complex, powerful, flavourful, fruity, spirituous, sweetness.

FERRER BOBET 2006 T
cariñena 70%, garnacha 30%

**92** Colour: deep cherry. Nose: medium intensity, elegant, fruit expression, fruit liqueur notes, undergrowth, dry stone. Palate: complex, fleshy, powerful, flavourful, sweetness, sweet tannins.

## GRATAVINUM

Camí de la Vilella Baixa a El Lloar
Mas D'en Serres, s/n
43737 Gratallops (Tarragona)
☎: 938 901 399 - Fax: 938 901 143
gratavinum@gratavinum.com
www.gratavinum.com

2 PI R 2007 T
garnacha 60%, cariñena 25%, cabernet sauvignon 10%, syrah 5%

**92** Colour: very deep cherry. Nose: complex, expressive, mineral, cocoa bean, creamy oak. Palate: powerful, flavourful, fruity, complex.

GV5 2007 T
cariñena 55%, garnacha 20%, syrah 15%, cabernet sauvignon 10%

**91** Colour: deep cherry. Nose: slightly evolved, medium intensity, varietal, fruit liqueur notes. Palate: correct, fruity, toasty.

## JOAN AMETLLER

Ctra. La Morera de Monsant -Cornudella, Km.3, 2
43361 La Morera de Monsant (Tarragona)
☎: 933 208 439 - Fax: 933 208 437
ametller@ametller.com
www.ametller.com

CLOS CORRIOL 2008 B
garnacha blanca 45%, macabeo 45%, pedro ximénez 10%

**88** Colour: bright straw. Nose: fresh, fresh fruit, white flowers, expressive. Palate: flavourful, fruity, good acidity, balanced.

CLOS MUSTARDÓ 2007 B
garnacha blanca 60%, macabeo 30%, chardonnay %, pedro ximénez 10%

**88** Colour: bright straw. Nose: fresh, white flowers, fresh fruit. Palate: flavourful, fruity, good acidity, balanced.

CLOS MUSTARDÓ 2008 RD
cabernet sauvignon 80%, garnacha 20%

**88** Colour: rose. Nose: fresh, varietal, warm, ripe fruit. Palate: powerful, flavourful, fruity, easy to drink.

CLOS CORRIOL 2007 T
garnacha, cariñena

**86** Colour: cherry, garnet rim. Nose: powerful, ripe fruit, fruit preserve, toasty, new oak. Palate: spirituous, powerful, flavourful, fleshy.

CLOS MUSTARDÓ 2006 T
garnacha 55%, cariñena 25%, cabernet sauvignon 20%, merlot %

**89** Colour: very deep cherry. Nose: cocoa bean, fresh fruit, fruit expression. Palate: creamy, ripe fruit, toasty.

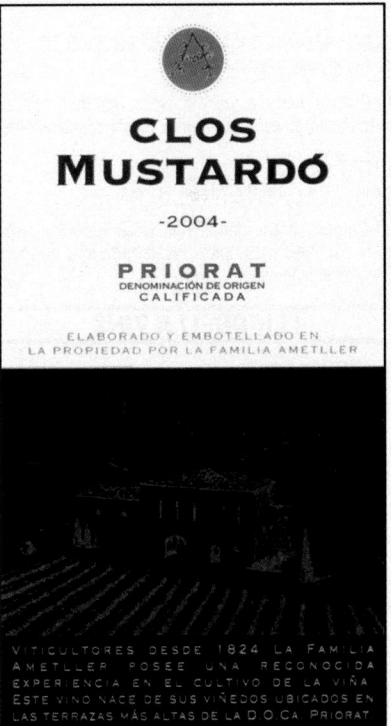

### ELS IGOLS 2005 TR
garnacha 60%, cariñena 30%, cabernet sauvignon 10%, merlot %

**86** Colour: cherry, garnet rim. Nose: fruit preserve, toasty, sweet spices. Palate: powerful, fleshy, spicy, pruney.

## LA CONRERIA D'SCALA DEI

Carrer Mitja Galta s/n (Finca Les Brugueres)
43379 Scala Dei (Tarragona)
☎: 977 827 055 - Fax: 977 827 055
laconreria@vinslaconreria.com
www.vinslaconreria.com

### LES BRUGUERES 2008 B

**88** Colour: bright straw. Nose: powerful, ripe fruit, citrus fruit, candied fruit. Palate: flavourful, fruity, sweetness.

### LA CONRERIA 2007 T
garnacha, syrah, merlot, cabernet sauvignon, cariñena

**86** Colour: cherry, garnet rim. Nose: powerful, complex, ripe fruit, creamy oak, toasty. Palate: powerful, flavourful, fruity, fleshy.

### IUGITER SELECCIÓ VINYES VELLES 2005 TC
garnacha, cariñena, cabernet sauvignon

**88** Colour: cherry, garnet rim. Nose: ripe fruit, spicy, wet leather. Palate: powerful, flavourful, toasty, round tannins.

### IUGITER 2005 T
garnacha, merlot, cabernet sauvignon, cariñena

**87** Colour: cherry, garnet rim. Nose: ripe fruit, spicy, creamy oak, toasty, complex. Palate: powerful, flavourful, toasty, round tannins.

## LLICORELLA VINS

Carrer de l'Era, 11
43737 Torroja del Priorat (Tarragona)
☎: 977 262 048 - Fax: 977 262 051
comercial@llicorellavins.com
www.llicorellavins.com

### AONIA 2007 T

**91** Colour: deep cherry. Nose: closed, varietal, complex, toasty, mineral. Palate: sweetness, fleshy, full, powerful, flavourful.

### GRAN NASARD 2005 T

**89** Colour: dark-red cherry. Nose: fruit liqueur notes, fruit expression, ripe fruit, dry stone, mineral. Palate: complex, spirituous, fruity, powerful, flavourful, balsamic, spicy.

### MAS SAURA 2004 T

**88** Colour: cherry, garnet rim. Nose: fruit preserve, aromatic coffee, dark chocolate. Palate: flavourful, powerful, fleshy, spicy.

## MAIUS VITICULTORS

Santa María, 17
08172 Sant Cugat del Vallès (Barcelona)
☎: 936 752 897 - Fax: 936 752 897
maius@maiusviticultors.com
www.maiusviticultors.com

### MAIUS BARRANC DE LA BRUIXA 2007 T

**83**

### MAIUS BARRANC DE LA BRUIXA 2006 T

**88** Colour: cherry, garnet rim. Nose: powerful, ripe fruit, fruit liqueur notes. Palate: flavourful, powerful, fleshy, spicy.

### INDRET 2006 T

**80**

## MARCO ABELLA S.L.

Ctra. de Porrera a Cornudella del Montsant, km. 0,7
43739 Porrera (Tarragona)
☎: 933 712 407 - Fax: 933 712 407
dmarco@marcoabella.com
www.marcoabella.com

### MAS MALLOLA 2007 T
garnacha 45%, cariñena 35%, cabernet sauvignon 10%, merlot 5%, syrah 5%

**90** Colour: cherry, garnet rim. Nose: ripe fruit, dark chocolate, sweet spices, expressive. Palate: round tannins, fruity, flavourful, good structure.

### CLOS ABELLA 2006 T
garnacha 40%, cariñena 40%, cabernet sauvignon 20%, syrah %

**90** Colour: dark-red cherry. Nose: mineral, undergrowth, ripe fruit, creamy oak. Palate: powerful, flavourful, sweetness, spirituous, fleshy, roasted-coffee aftertaste, toasty.

### CLOS ABELLA 2005 T
garnacha 40%, cariñena 40%, cabernet sauvignon 20%, syrah %

**90** Colour: cherry, garnet rim. Nose: powerful, ripe fruit, toasty, sweet spices, cocoa bean. Palate: flavourful, powerful, fleshy, spicy, round tannins.

## MAS BLANC

Ctra. Falset a Bellmunt del Priorat, km. 3

43730 Falset (Tarragona)
☎: 977 830 840 - Fax: 938 170 979
pinord@pinord.es

+ 7 2006 T

**89** Colour: cherry, garnet rim. Nose: creamy oak, toasty, dark chocolate, ripe fruit. Palate: flavourful, powerful, fleshy, spirituous.

BALCONS 2005 T

**88** Colour: cherry, garnet rim. Nose: powerful, warm, ripe fruit, toasty, aged wood nuances, aromatic coffee. Palate: spirituous, spicy, round tannins.

## MAS IGNEUS

Ctra. T-710, km. 11,1
43737 Gratallops (Tarragona)
☎: 977 262 259 - Fax: 977 054 027
celler@masigneus.com
www.masigneus.com

BARRANC DELS CLOSOS 2008 B

**89** Colour: bright straw. Nose: acacia flower, balsamic herbs, scrubland, expressive, fresh fruit. Palate: fresh, fruity, powerful, flavourful, complex.

BARRANC DELS CLOSOS 2006 T

**87** Colour: cherry, garnet rim. Nose: powerful, ripe fruit, sweet spices, aromatic coffee, dark chocolate. Palate: powerful, flavourful, fleshy, round tannins.

COSTERS DE MAS IGNEUS 2006 T

**86** Colour: cherry, garnet rim. Nose: dark chocolate, sweet spices, fruit preserve. Palate: powerful, fleshy, spicy.

MAS IGNEUS FA 206

## MAS LA MOLA

Raval, 4
43376 Poboleda ()
☎: 651 034 215
info@maslamola.com
www.maslamola.com

MAS LA MOLA 2007 B

**87** Colour: bright straw. Nose: powerful, ripe fruit, citrus fruit, toasty, creamy oak. Palate: flavourful, spicy, ripe fruit.

MAS LA MOLA 2006 T

**85** Colour: cherry, garnet rim. Nose: powerful, characterful, ripe fruit, sweet spices. Palate: flavourful, powerful, fleshy.

LA VINYETA VELLA 2005 T

**87** Colour: cherry, garnet rim. Nose: powerful, ripe fruit, sweet spices, toasty. Palate: flavourful, powerful, fleshy, spicy.

## MAS MARTINET

Ctra. Falset - Gratallops, km. 6
43730 Falset (Tarragona)
☎: 629 238 236 - Fax: 977 262 348
masmartinet@masmartinet.com
www.masmartinet.com

CLOS MARTINET 2007 T

**94** Colour: dark-red cherry, garnet rim. Nose: powerful, complex, mineral, cocoa bean, toasty. Palate: rich, powerful, flavourful, roasted-coffee aftertaste.

ELS ESCURÇONS 2007 T

**94** Colour: bright cherry. Nose: fruit expression, cocoa bean, elegant. Palate: fresh, fruity, fleshy, complex, fine tannins.

MARTINET BRU 2007 T

**92** Colour: cherry, purple rim. Nose: powerful, ripe fruit, red berry notes, sweet spices. Palate: flavourful, ripe fruit, fruity, fine tannins.

CAMI PESSEROLES 2007 T

**90** Colour: dark-red cherry, purple rim. Nose: powerful, mineral, fruit liqueur notes, dark chocolate. Palate: powerful, fleshy, warm, round tannins.

ELS ESCURÇONS 2006 T

**93** Colour: dark-red cherry, garnet rim. Nose: complex, warm, ripe fruit, fruit expression, cocoa bean. Palate: fleshy, flavourful, powerful, good acidity, sweetness, smoky aftertaste.

CAMI PESSEROLES 2006 T

**91** Colour: black cherry, garnet rim. Nose: medium intensity, elegant, complex, fruit liqueur notes, toasty. Palate: fleshy, warm, round, sweet tannins.

## MAS MARTINET ASSESSORAMENTS

Vidal i Barraquer, 8
43739 Porrera (Tarragona)
☎: 609 715 004 - Fax: 977 262 348
info@masmartinet-ass.com
www.masmartinet-ass.com

## MARTINET DEGUSTACIÓ 2 2005 T
syrah 50%, cabernet sauvignon 45%, garnacha 5%

**92** Colour: dark-red cherry. Nose: aromatic coffee, spicy, complex, expressive, mineral, earthy notes. Palate: complex, sweetness, full, powerful, flavourful, roasted-coffee aftertaste.

## MARTINET DEGUSTACIÓ 1 2004 T
merlot 40%, garnacha 25%, syrah 20%, cabernet sauvignon 15%

**94** Colour: very deep cherry. Nose: complex, expressive, powerfull, damp earth, mineral, macerated fruit, aromatic coffee, spicy, creamy oak. Palate: spirituous, complex, powerful, flavourful, full.

## MAS PERINET (D.O. PRIORAT)

Finca Mas Perinet, s/n T-702 km. 1,6
43361 La Morera de Montsant (Tarragona)
☎: 977 827 113 - Fax: 977 827 180
info@masperinet.com
www.masperinet.com

PERINET + PLUS 2006 T
cariñena 51%, garnacha 41%, syrah 8%

**92** Colour: bright cherry. Nose: sweet spices, creamy oak, new oak, ripe fruit, dark chocolate. Palate: flavourful, fruity, toasty, round tannins.

PERINET 2006 T
cariñena 36%, syrah 19%, garnacha 16%, cabernet sauvignon 15%, merlot 14%

**91** Colour: cherry, garnet rim. Nose: spicy, creamy oak, toasty, complex, fine reductive notes, undergrowth. Palate: powerful, flavourful, toasty, round tannins.

## MASET DEL LLEÓ

Avda. Barcelona, 31 Pol.Ind. Sant Pere Molanta
08734 Olerdola (Barcelona)
☎: 902 200 250 - Fax: 938 921 333
info@maset.com
www.maset.com

MAS VILÓ 2007 T

**90** Colour: deep cherry. Nose: fruit liqueur notes, fruit expression, complex, elegant, creamy oak, mineral. Palate: powerful, flavourful, fruity, complex.

CLOS VILÓ 2006 T

**87** Colour: cherry, garnet rim. Nose: powerful, varietal, ripe fruit, sweet spices. Palate: spicy, ripe fruit, toasty, round tannins.

CLOS GRAN VILÓ 2005 T

**90** Colour: cherry, garnet rim. Nose: powerful, ripe fruit, dark chocolate, sweet spices, creamy oak. Palate: flavourful, powerful, fleshy, spicy, round tannins.

## MAYOL VITICULTORS

De la Bassa, 24
43737 Torroja del Priorat (Tarragona)
☎: 977 839 395 - Fax: 977 839 317
celler@mayol.eu
www.mayol.eu

ROSER 2007 B
macabeo 95%, garnacha blanca 4%

**90** Colour: bright straw. Nose: fresh, fresh fruit, white flowers, expressive, sweet spices. Palate: flavourful, fruity, good acidity, balanced.

BROGIT 2006 TC
garnacha 50%, cabernet sauvignon 20%, syrah 15%, cariñena 10%, merlot 5%

**89** Colour: bright cherry. Nose: ripe fruit, sweet spices, creamy oak, expressive. Palate: flavourful, fruity, toasty, round tannins.

TORROJA DES DE DINS 2006 T
garnacha 65%, cabernet sauvignon 15%, syrah 15%, cariñena 5%

**88** Colour: cherry, garnet rim. Nose: ripe fruit, spicy, creamy oak, toasty, complex. Palate: powerful, flavourful, toasty, round tannins.

BROGIT 2005 TC
garnacha 50%, cabernet sauvignon 20%, syrah 15%, cariñena 10%, merlot 5%

**88** Colour: cherry, garnet rim. Nose: powerful, mineral, earthy notes, ripe fruit. Palate: flavourful, powerful, fleshy, complex.

## MERUM PRIORATI S.L.

Ctra. de Falset, km. 9,3
42739 Porrera (Tarragona)
☎: 977 828 307 - Fax: 977 828 324
info@merumpriorati.com
www.merumpriorati.com

OSMIN 2006 T
garnacha, cariñena, syrah, cabernet sauvignon, merlot

**89** Colour: cherry, garnet rim. Nose: powerful, varietal, ripe fruit, sweet spices, creamy oak, toasty. Palate: powerful, fleshy, fruity, spicy, round tannins.

ARDILES 2006 T
garnacha 45%, cariñena 34%, cabernet sauvignon 3%

**88** Colour: cherry, garnet rim. Nose: powerful, ripe fruit, sweet spices, cedar wood. Palate: powerful, flavourful, fleshy.

## NOGUERALS S.C.P.

Tou, 5
43360 Cornudella de Montsant (TarragonaC)
☎: 650 033 546 - Fax: 934 419 879
noguerals@hotmail.com

ABELLARS 2006 TC

**87** Colour: cherry, purple rim. Nose: powerful, ripe fruit, red berry notes, sweet spices, dark chocolate. Palate: flavourful, powerful, fleshy, spicy.

## PORTAL DEL PRIORAT

Clos del Portal. Pista del Lloar a Bellmunt
43736 El Molar (Tarragona)
☎: 977 178 486 - Fax: 934 173 591
portal@portaldelmontsant.com
www.portaldelpriorat.com

N D N 2007 T
garnacha, cariñena, cabernet sauvignon, syrah

**90** Colour: bright cherry. Nose: ripe fruit, sweet spices, creamy oak, expressive, candied fruit, fruit preserve. Palate: flavourful, fruity, toasty, round tannins, sweetness, spirituous, powerful.

SOMNI 2007 T
garnacha, syrah, cariñena

**90** Colour: deep cherry. Nose: powerful, fruit preserve, spicy, dark chocolate. Palate: fleshy, spirituous, powerful, flavourful.

## ROSA M. BARTOLOMÉ VERNET

Major, 23
43738 Bellmunt del Priorat (Tarragona)
☎: 977 320 448 - Fax: 977 320 448
antonio@primitiudebellmunt.com
www.primitiudebellmunt.com

PRIMITIU DE BELLMUNT 2007 T

**89** Colour: deep cherry, orangey edge. Nose: powerful, warm, overripe fruit, toasty, pattiserie. Palate: spicy, warm, fine bitter notes, fine tannins.

FINCA EL MIRADOR 2007 T

**89** Colour: bright cherry. Nose: sweet spices, creamy oak, expressive, red berry notes. Palate: flavourful, fruity, toasty, round tannins.

PRIMITIU DE BELLMUNT 2005 T

**90** Colour: cherry, garnet rim. Nose: powerful, fruit liqueur notes, overripe fruit, dark chocolate, aromatic coffee, varnish. Palate: powerful, fleshy, concentrated, round tannins.

CLOS BARTOLOMÉ

## ROTLLAN TORRA

Balandra, 6
43737 Torroja del Priorat (Tarragona)
☎: 902 177 000 - Fax: 933 050 112
comercial@rotllantorra.com
www.rotllantorra.com

BALANDRA 2005 TR
garnacha, cariñena, cabernet sauvignon

**87** Colour: dark-red cherry. Nose: spicy, smoky, fruit preserve. Palate: spirituous, sweetness, powerful, flavourful, fleshy.

ROTLLAN TORRÁ 2003 TR
garnacha, cariñena, cabernet sauvignon

**86** Colour: cherry, garnet rim. Nose: powerful, warm, fruit liqueur notes, sweet spices. Palate: sweetness, fleshy, spirituous, round tannins.

AMADIS
TIRANT

## SANGENIS I VAQUÉ

Pl. Catalunya, 3
43739 Porrera (Tarragona)
☎: 977 828 238
celler@sangenisivaque.com
www.sangenisivaque.com

SANGENIS I VAQUÉ 2006 T
garnacha 45%, cariñena 45%, syrah 10%

**89** Colour: bright cherry. Nose: ripe fruit, sweet spices, creamy oak, expressive. Palate: flavourful, fruity, toasty, round tannins.

DARA 2006 TR
garnacha 45%, cariñena 45%, merlot 10%

**82**

CORANYA 2005 T
garnacha 50%, cariñena 50%

**91** Colour: cherry, garnet rim. Nose: powerful, fruit liqueur notes, ripe fruit, sweet spices, creamy oak. Palate: flavourful, fleshy, spicy, creamy.

LO COSTER
CLOS MONLLEÓ
VALL POR

## SOLA CLASSIC

Nou, 15
43738 Bellmunt del Priorat (Tarragona)
☎: 977 831 134
info@solaclassic.com
www.solaclassic.com

SOLÀ CLASSIC 2007 T
garnacha 53%, samsó 47%

**89** Colour: cherry, garnet rim. Nose: powerful, red berry notes, ripe fruit, mineral, creamy oak, toasty. Palate: powerful, fleshy, flavourful, toasty.

VINYES JOSEP 2005 T
garnacha 53%, samsó 47%

**86** Colour: cherry, garnet rim. Nose: powerful, fruit preserve, fruit liqueur notes, creamy oak, toasty. Palate: spicy, ripe fruit, powerful tannins.

SOLÀ CLASSIC 2004 T
garnacha 50%, samsó 50%

**83**

## TERRA DE VEREMA

Córcega, 335 3-planta
08037 (Barcelona)
☎: 932 385 731 - Fax: 934 159 698
rfmarti@hotmail.com
www.terradeverema.com

TRIUMVIRAT 2007 T
garnacha 60%, cariñena 30%, syrah 10%

**88** Colour: black cherry. Nose: powerful, ripe fruit, fruit liqueur notes, sweet spices, cedar wood. Palate: flavourful, fleshy, powerful.

CORELIUM 2005 T
cariñena 90%, garnacha 10%

**89** Colour: cherry, garnet rim. Nose: powerful, spicy, toasty, new oak. Palate: flavourful, powerful, fleshy, round tannins.

## TERRES DE VIDALBA

Terme de les Foreses
43376 Poboleda (Tarragona)
☎: 616 413 722 - Fax: 977 128 027
info@terresdevidalba.com

TOCS 2005 T
garnacha 28%, syrah 30%, cabernet sauvignon 40%, merlot 2%

**88** Colour: cherry, garnet rim. Nose: powerful, ripe fruit, spicy, toasty, creamy oak. Palate: flavourful, powerful, spicy, ripe fruit.

TOCS 2004 T
garnacha 35%, syrah 30%, cabernet sauvignon 30%, merlot 5%

**87** Colour: cherry, garnet rim. Nose: powerful, ripe fruit, sweet spices. Palate: flavourful, powerful, fleshy, spicy.

## TERROIR AL LIMIT

Baixa Font, 12
43737 Torroja del Priorat (Tarragona)
☎: 977 828 057 - Fax: 977 828 380
dominik@terroir-al-limit.com
www.terroir-al-limit.com

TORROJA 2006 T
grenache 50%, garignan 50%

**93** Colour: dark-red cherry. Nose: powerful, ripe fruit, sweet spices, creamy oak, toasty. Palate: flavourful, powerful, fleshy, mineral.

DITS DEL TERRA 2006 T

**93** Colour: cherry, garnet rim. Nose: creamy oak, toasty, mineral, ripe fruit. Palate: fleshy, complex, fruity, powerful, mineral, toasty.

ARBOSSAR 2006 T
garignan 100%

**91** Colour: cherry, garnet rim. Nose: powerful, ripe fruit, earthy notes, creamy oak. Palate: flavourful, powerful, fleshy, good structure.

## TORRES PRIORAT

Finca La Soleta s/n
43737 El Lloar (Tarragona)
☎: 938 177 400 - Fax: 938 177 444
mailadmin@torres.es
www.torres.es

SALMOS 2007 T

**88** Colour: cherry, garnet rim. Nose: powerful, expressive, toasty, aged wood nuances. Palate: spicy, ripe fruit, powerful, round tannins.

PERPETUAL SALMOS 2006 TR

**90** Colour: cherry, garnet rim. Nose: powerful, ripe fruit, sweet spices, creamy oak. Palate: powerful, flavourful, fleshy, spirituous.

## TROSSOS DEL PRIORAT

Ctra. Gratallops a La Vilella Baixa, km. 10,65
43737 Gratallops (Tarragona)
☎: 670 590 788
celler@trossosdelpriorat.com
trossosdelpriorat.com

### LO MON 2006 T
garnacha 60%, cabernet sauvignon 15%, cariñena 15%, syrah 10%

**94** Colour: cherry, garnet rim. Nose: powerful, varietal, ripe fruit, sweet spices, toasty, mineral. Palate: flavourful, powerful, fleshy, complex.

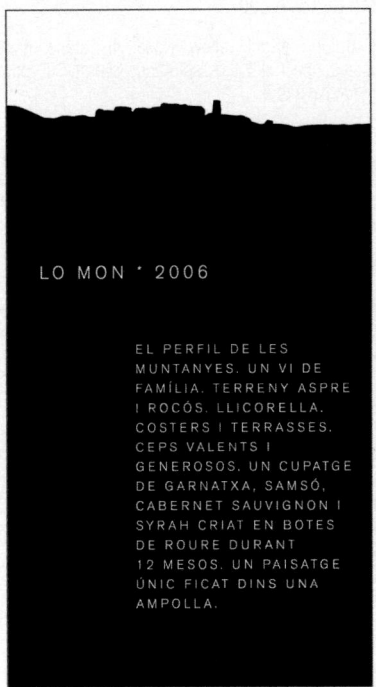

LO MON ' 2006

EL PERFIL DE LES MUNTANYES. UN VI DE FAMÍLIA. TERRENY ASPRE I ROCÓS. LLICORELLA. COSTERS I TERRASSES. CEPS VALENTS I GENEROSOS. UN CUPATGE DE GARNATXA, SAMSÓ, CABERNET SAUVIGNON I SYRAH CRIAT EN BOTES DE ROURE DURANT 12 MESOS. UN PAISATGE ÚNIC FICAT DINS UNA AMPOLLA.

## UNIÓ CORPORACIÓ ALIMENTARIA - CELLERS UNIÓ

Joan Oliver, 16-24
43206 Reus (Tarragona)
☎: 977 330 055 - Fax: 977 330 070
reus@cellersunio.com
www.cellersunio.com

### LLICORELLA BLANC PEDRO XIMÉNEZ 2007 B
pedro ximénez 90%, garnacha blanca 10%

**88** Colour: bright yellow. Nose: powerful, ripe fruit, sweet spices, fragrant herbs. Palate: rich, smoky aftertaste, flavourful, fresh, good acidity.

### TENDRAL SELECCIÓN 2007 T
garnacha 65%, cariñena 35%

**85** Colour: cherry, garnet rim. Nose: powerful, creamy oak, toasty, fruit liqueur notes. Palate: flavourful, powerful, fleshy.

### SEÑORÍO DE CONVEY 2006 T
garnacha 40%, cariñena 30%, syrah 30%

**87** Colour: cherry, garnet rim. Nose: powerful, warm, ripe fruit, creamy oak, toasty, dark chocolate. Palate: flavourful, powerful, fleshy.

### LLICORELLA ANYADA 2005 T
garnacha 30%, cariñena 30%, cabernet sauvignon 20%, merlot 10%, tempranillo 10%

**87** Colour: cherry, garnet rim. Nose: powerful, ripe fruit, fruit expression, raspberry, creamy oak, toasty. Palate: balsamic, ripe fruit, round tannins.

### LLICORELLA SELECCIÓ ESPECIAL 2004 T
garnacha 30%, cariñena 30%, cabernet sauvignon 20%, syrah 20%

**91** Colour: cherry, garnet rim. Nose: powerful, creamy oak, new oak, ripe fruit. Palate: flavourful, spicy, toasty, round tannins.

## VINÍCOLA DEL PRIORAT

Piró, s/n
43737 Gratallops (Tarragona)
☎: 977 839 167 - Fax: 977 839 201
info@vinicoladelpriorat.com
www.vinicoladelpriorat.com

### ÒNIX CLÀSSIC 2008 T

**87** Colour: very deep cherry. Nose: complex, medium intensity, varietal, dry stone, mineral, ripe fruit. Palate: correct, fruity, flavourful.

### ÒNIX FUSIÓ 2007 T

**90** Colour: bright cherry. Nose: ripe fruit, sweet spices, creamy oak, expressive. Palate: flavourful, fruity, toasty, round tannins.

### CLOS GEBRAT 2007 TC

**88** Colour: dark-red cherry. Nose: powerful, warm, ripe fruit, earthy notes. Palate: flavourful, powerful, fleshy, round tannins.

**ÒNIX FUSIÓ 2006 T**

**88** Colour: cherry, garnet rim. Nose: powerful, varietal, spicy, dark chocolate, caramel. Palate: powerful, flavourful, fleshy, sweetness.

**ÒNIX EVOLUCIÓ 2005 T**

**88** Colour: cherry, garnet rim. Nose: powerful, ripe fruit, wet leather, tobacco. Palate: flavourful, powerful, fleshy, spicy.

**ÒNIX SELECCIÓ 2005 TC**

**88** Colour: cherry, garnet rim. Nose: powerful, varietal, ripe fruit, creamy oak, aged wood nuances, dark chocolate. Palate: powerful, spirituous, spicy, round tannins.

MAS DELS FRARES

## VINNICO EXPORT

Muela, 16
03730 Jávea (Alicante)
☎: 965 791 967 - Fax: 966 461 471
info@vinnico.com
www.vinnico.com

**TOSALET 2007 T**
grenache 50%, carignan 26%, cabernet sauvignon 24%          15,9€

**87** Colour: cherry, garnet rim. Nose: ripe fruit, dark chocolate, sweet spices, creamy oak. Palate: flavourful, powerful, fleshy, spirituous.

## VITICULTORS DEL PRIORAT

Partida Palells, Mas Subirat
43738 Bellmunt del Priorat (Tarragona)
☎: 977 262 268 - Fax: 977 262 268
morlanda@inicia.es
www.morlanda.com

**MORLANDA 2008 B**

**91** Colour: bright straw. Nose: elegant, complex, varietal, scrubland, fruit liqueur notes. Palate: complex, spirituous, rich, powerful, flavourful.

**MORLANDA 2005 T**

**89** Colour: cherry, garnet rim. Nose: ripe fruit, characterful, dark chocolate, roasted coffee. Palate: powerful, flavourful, good structure, complex, creamy, roasted-coffee aftertaste, toasty, round tannins.

## VITICULTORS MAS D'EN GIL S.L.

Finca Mas d'en Gil, s/n
43738 Bellmunt del Priorat (Tarragona)
☎: 977 830 192 - Fax: 977 830 152
mail@masdengil.com
www.masdengil.com

**COMA ALTA 2008 B**

**90** Colour: bright straw. Nose: ripe fruit, wild herbs. Palate: sweetness, fruity, powerful, flavourful, complex, balsamic, fruity aftestaste.

**COMA BLANCA 2007 B**

**94** Colour: bright yellow. Nose: dry stone, mineral, scrubland, ripe fruit. Palate: spirituous, sweetness, complex, powerful, flavourful.

**CLOS FONTÀ 2007 TC**

**92** Colour: cherry, garnet rim. Nose: ripe fruit, fruit expression, earthy notes, toasty, creamy oak. Palate: powerful, fleshy, spicy, round tannins.

**COMA VELLA 2007 T**

**89** Colour: cherry, garnet rim. Nose: ripe fruit, red berry notes, sweet spices, toasty, new oak. Palate: powerful, flavourful, fleshy, spicy, round tannins.

GRAN BUIG

SOME OTHER WINERIES WITHIN THE DO:

**AINAT**
**BODEGAS BG RAFAEL BORDALAS GARCÍA**
**CELLER ARDÈVOL I ASSOCIATS**
**CELLER CAL PLA**
**CELLER DEVINSSI**
**CELLER MAS D'EN JUST S.L.**
**CELLER ROTLLAN & MARQUÉS**
**CELLERS CAPAFONS OSSÓ**
**CELLERS CARTOIXA DE MONTSALVAT**
**CELLERS RIPOLL SANS**
**CESCA VICENT PRIORAT**
**LA PERLA DEL PRIORAT**
**MASDEU I CAMPOS**
**MASIA DUCH**
**MERITXELL PALLEJÀ**
**SAÓ DEL COSTER**
**VALSANZO**
**VIÑEDOS DE ITHACA**

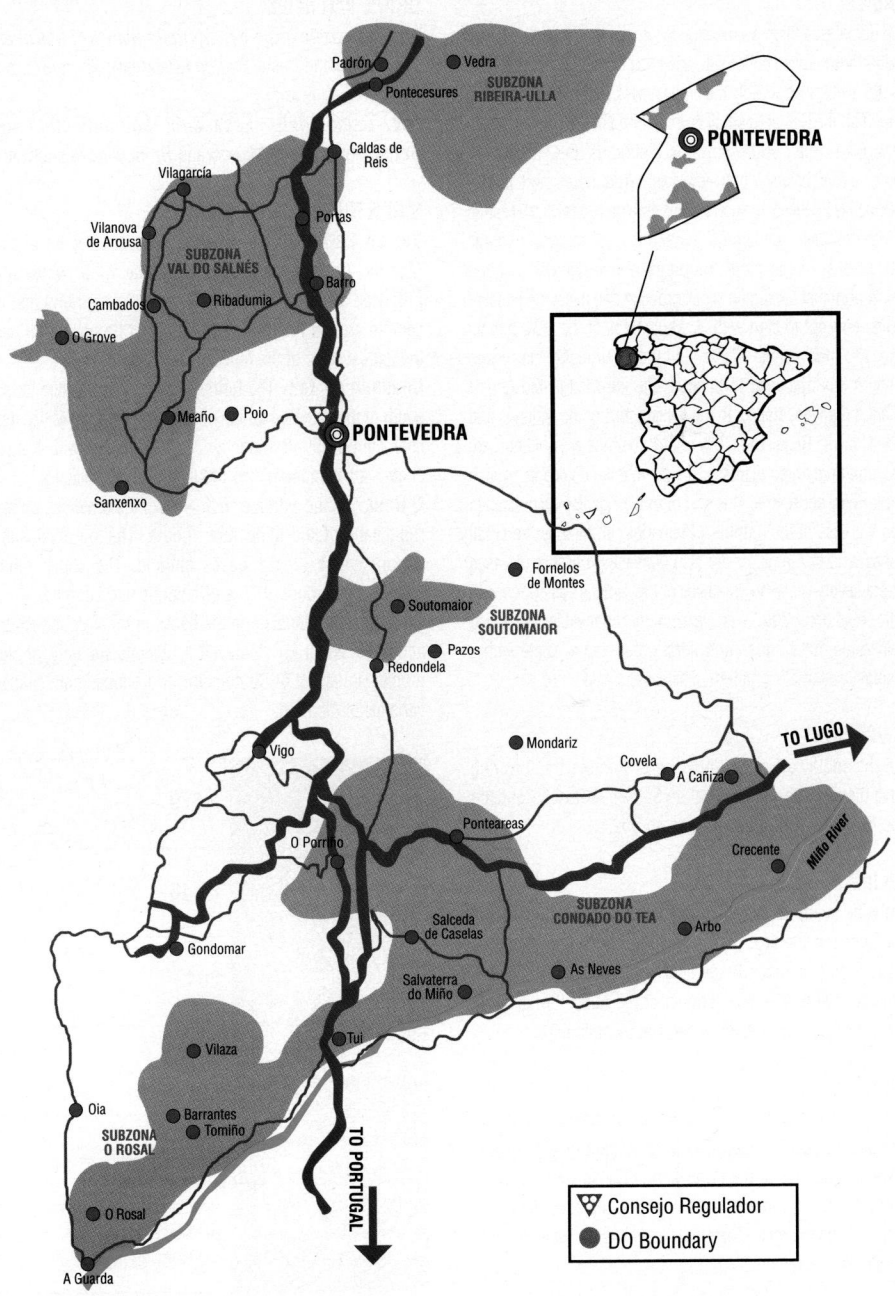

Padrón
Vedra
Pontecesures
SUBZONA
RIBEIRA-ULLA

PONTEVEDRA

Caldas de
Reis

Vilagarcía

Portas

Vilanova
de Arousa
SUBZONA
VAL DO SALNÉS

Barro

Cambados
Ribadumia

O Grove

Meaño
Poio

PONTEVEDRA

Sanxenxo

Fornelos
de Montes

Soutomaior
SUBZONA
SOUTOMAIOR

Pazos
Redondela

Mondariz

TO LUGO

Vigo

Covela
A Cañiza

Ponteareas

Crecente
Miño River

O Porriño

SUBZONA
CONDADO DO TEA

Salceda
de Caselas
Arbo

Gondomar

Salvaterra
do Miño
As Neves

Vilaza
Tui

Oia

Barrantes
Tomiño

SUBZONA
O ROSAL

TO PORTUGAL

O Rosal

A Guarda

Consejo Regulador
DO Boundary

## NEWS

In our latest edition we mentioned already the fact that the best albariños showed better with age once bottled. Ratings for the 2007 vintage are simply the highest ever, particularly for those aged on the lees or in small barrels for a short period. There is even an "old" 2004 Pazo de Señorans that shows an impressive balance between fresh fruit notes and bottle-reductive nuances. In such a short time quite a few new brands and complex renderings have hit the market (vintage selections, single plots, Burgundian-style wines), a good symptom that the region is still growing and has a magnificent wine concept to start with. A whole 64% of the DO's budget goes to promotional events, and that is probably the reason why it has managed to conquer the knowledgeable Anglo-Saxon markets. Thanks to the joined effort of the wineries and the Consejo Regulador, 18% of the albariños are sold abroad, an amazingly high increase of over 420% in sales in an also amazingly short time. This sort of move can also be noticed in an increase in the number of wineries, in the way the small ones tend to merge, or the also increasing number of wines tasted every year. The greatness of this vintage –as opposed to the mediocre 2007– is particularly noticeable in young albariños, full of fresh and floral notes and a palate with a fantastic alternating pattern of sweet and acid notes.

## LOCATION

In the southwest of the province of Pontevedra, covering five distinct sub-regions: Val do Salnés, O Rosal, Condado do Tea, Soutomaior and Ribeira do Ulla.

## CLIMATE

Atlantic, with moderate, mild temperatures due to the influence of the sea, high relative humidity and abundant rainfall (the annual average is around 1600 mm). There is less rainfall further downstream of the Miño (Condado de Tea), and as a consequence the grapes ripen earlier.

## SOIL

Sandy, shallow and slightly acidic, which makes fine soil for producing quality wines. The predominant type of rock is granite, and only in the Concellos of Sanxenxo, Rosal and Tomillo is it possible to find a narrow band of metamorphic rock. Quaternary deposits are very common in all the sub-regions.

## GRAPE VARIETIES:

**White:** *Albariño* (majority), *Loureira Blanca* or *Marqués*, *Treixadura* and Caíño *Blanco* (preferred); *Torrontés* and *Godello* (authorized).

**Red:** *Caíño Tinto, Espadeiro, Loureira Tinta* and *Sousón* (preferred); *Mencía* and *Brancellao* (authorized).

## SUB-REGIONS:

**Val do Salnés.** This is the historic sub-region of the Albariño (in fact, here, almost all the white wines are produced as single-variety wines from this variety) and is centred around the municipal district of Cambados. It has the flattest relief of the four sub-regions.

**Condado do Tea.** The furthest inland, it is situated in the south of the province on the northern bank of the Miño. It is characterized by its mountainous terrain. The wines must contain a minimum of 70% of Albariño and Treixadura.

**O Rosal.** In the extreme southwest of the province, on the right bank of the Miño river mouth. The warmest sub-region, where river terraces abound. The wines must contain a minimum of 70% of Albariño and Loureira.

**Soutomaior.** Situated on the banks of the Verdugo River, about 10 km from Pontevedra, it consists only of the municipal district of Soutomaior. It produces only single-varietals of Albariño.

| Hectares of Vineyard | 3,679 |
|---|---|
| Nº Viticulturists | 6,546 |
| Nº of Bodegas | 204 |
| 2008 Harvest | Good |
| 2007 Production | 13,327,730 l. |
| Marketing | 80.50% domestic 19.50% export |

**Ribeira do Ulla.** A new sub-region along the Ulla River, which forms the landscape of elevated valleys further inland. It comprises the municipal districts of Vedra and part of Padrón, Deo, Boquixon, Touro, Estrada, Silleda and Vila de Cruce. Red wines predominate.

## CONSEJO REGULADOR

Centro de Apoyo de Cabanas
36143 Salcedo (Pontevedra)
☎: 986 854 850 / 864 530 - Fax: 986 864 546
@ consejo@igatel.net
www.doriasbaixas.com

## GENERAL CHARACTERISTICS OF THE WINES:

| | |
|---|---|
| **WHITES** | Marked by the personality of the *Albariño*. They have a colour that ranges from pale yellow to greenish yellow. The nose is of herbs and flowers with excellent intensity that may be reminiscent of rather ripe apples, apricot, fennel or mint. On the palate they stand out for their oily and glycerine-like mouthfeel, their fruity character and persistence (the best examples have good doses of complexity and elegance). |
| **REDS** | At present there is very limited production. The first examples reveal a marked Atlantic character; the wines are a very brilliant violet cherry colour; they stand out for their notes of red berries and herbs reminiscent of eucalyptus and, on the palate, for their high acidity. |

## 2008 VINTAGE RATING:

# EXCELLENT

# DO RÍAS BAIXAS

## A. PAZOS DE LUSCO S.L.

Grixó - Alxen
36458 Salvaterra do Miño (Pontevedra)
☎: 986 658 519 - Fax: 987 514 570
info@lusco.es
www.lusco.com

ZIOS DE LUSCO 2008 B
albariño 100%

**90** Colour: bright straw. Nose: complex, varietal, characterful, fragrant herbs, medium intensity. Palate: powerful, flavourful, fruity, full, complex.

LUSCO 2007 B
albariño 100%

**88** Colour: bright yellow. Nose: varietal, fresh, complex. Palate: powerful, fresh, good structure, good acidity, great length, fruity.

LUSCO PAZO DE PIÑEIRO 2006 B
albariño 100%

**89** Colour: bright yellow. Nose: dried herbs, balsamic herbs, fine reductive notes. Palate: full, powerful, flavourful, varietal, rich.

## ADEGA CONDES DE ALBAREI

Lg. A Bouza, 1
36639 Castrelo Cambados (Pontevedra)
☎: 986 543 535 - Fax: 986 524 251
inf@condesdealbarei.com
www.condesdealbarei.com

CONDES DE ALBAREI 2008 B
albariño 100%

**90** Colour: bright straw. Nose: fresh, varietal, characterful, fruit expression. Palate: powerful, flavourful, fruity, fresh, good acidity, elegant.

ENXEBRE VENDIMIA SELECCIONADA 2008 B
albariño 100%

**88** Colour: straw. Nose: medium intensity, closed, fresh fruit. Palate: fruity, fresh, flavourful.

CONDES DE ALBAREI CARBALLO GALEGO 2007 BFB
albariño 100%

**88** Colour: straw. Nose: complex, smoky, fine lees, fresh fruit. Palate: powerful, flavourful, sweetness, complex, toasty.

CONDES DE ALBAREI EN RAMA 2005 B
albariño 100%

**90** Colour: bright yellow. Nose: expressive, balanced, ripe fruit, fragrant herbs, fine lees, medium intensity. Palate: flavourful, fleshy, good structure, sweetness, fresh, long, balsamic.

## ADEGA DURÁN S.L.

Rua Pardo Bazán, 1
36630 Cambados (Pontevedra)
☎: 986 542 354 - Fax: 986 716 312
duran@ventomareiro.com
www.ventomareiro.com

VENTO MAREIRO ALBARIÑO 2008 B

**81**

## ADEGA EIDOS

Padriñán, 65
36960 Sanxenxo (Pontevedra)
☎: 986 690 009 - Fax: 986 720 307
info@adegaeidos.com
www.adegaeidos.com

VEIGAS DE PADRIÑÁN 2008 B
albariño 100%

**90** Colour: bright straw. Nose: varietal, expressive, fresh, fresh fruit, floral. Palate: good acidity, balanced, fresh, fruity, fleshy, flavourful.

CONTRAAPAREDE 2005 B
albariño 100%

**91** Colour: bright yellow. Nose: powerful, sweet spices, creamy oak, fragrant herbs, citrus fruit. Palate: rich, smoky aftertaste, flavourful, fresh, good acidity.

EIDOS DE PADRIÑÁN

## ADEGA STELLA

Besomaño Bouza
36636 Ribadumia (Pontevedra)
☎: 609 149 716
adegastella@hotmail.com

CAMPUS STELLA 2007 B
albariño

**88** Colour: bright straw. Nose: medium intensity, ripe fruit, tropical fruit. Palate: flavourful, fruity, fresh, fleshy, fine bitter notes.

## ADEGA VALDÉS S.L.

As Regas s/n Santa Cruz de Rivadulla,
15885 Vedra (A Coruña)
☎: 981 512 439 - Fax: 981 509 226
comercial@gundian.com
www.adegavaldes.com

ALBARIÑO GUNDIAN 2008 B
albariño 100%

**88** Colour: bright straw. Nose: medium intensity, varietal, fresh. Palate: fresh, flavourful, easy to drink, good acidity, great length.

PAZO VILADOMAR 2008 B
treixadura 80%, albariño 20%

**88** Colour: pale. Nose: white flowers, fresh fruit, varietal, powerfull. Palate: fresh, fruity, powerful, flavourful.

GUNDIAN

## ADEGAS AROUSA

Tirabao, 15 Baión
36614 Vilanova de Arousa (Pontevedra)
☎: 986 506 113 - Fax: 986 715 454
adegasarousacvs@gmail.com
www.adegasarousa.com

PAZO DA BOUCIÑA 2008 B
albariño

**88** Colour: bright yellow. Nose: fruit expression, medium intensity, dried herbs. Palate: flavourful, varietal, good acidity, great length.

VAL DE MONXES 2008 B
albariño

**85** Colour: bright straw. Nose: medium intensity, fresh, floral. Palate: powerful, good structure, balanced, good acidity, good finish.

PAZO DA BOUCIÑA ARTE 2007 B
albariño

**87** Colour: bright straw. Nose: medium intensity, balanced, fresh. Palate: fruity, fresh, fine bitter notes, good acidity, great length.

## ADEGAS CASTROBREY

Camanzo s/n
36587 Vila de Cruces (Pontevedra)

☎: 986 583 643 - Fax: 986 583 722
bodegas@castrobrey.com
www.castrobrey.com

SIN PALABRAS 2008 B
albariño 100%

**91** Colour: straw. Nose: powerful, varietal, floral, fragrant herbs, fresh fruit. Palate: elegant, good acidity, complex, fruity, flavourful.

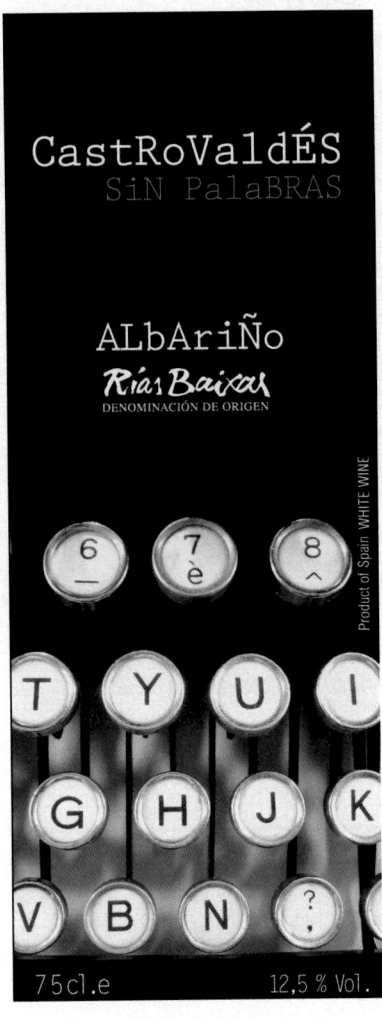

## SEÑORÍO DE REGAS 2008 B
albariño, treixadura, godello, torrontés

**90** Colour: bright yellow. Nose: medium intensity, fresh, neat, varietal. Palate: powerful, flavourful, good acidity, great length.

## SEÑORÍO DE CRUCES 2008 B
albariño 100%

**90** Colour: bright straw. Nose: medium intensity, varietal, fragrant herbs. Palate: flavourful, fresh, great length, good acidity, fine bitter notes.

## CASTRO BREY 2007 B
albariño 100%

**90** Colour: bright yellow. Nose: medium intensity, fragrant herbs, fresh fruit. Palate: good acidity, powerful, flavourful, fruity, fresh, full, complex.

## ADEGAS D'ALTAMIRA

Altamira - Dena s/n
36967 Meaño (Pontevedra)
☎: 986 746 046 - Fax: 986 745 725
central@adegasdaltamira.es
www.adegasdaltamira.es

### BRANDAL ALBARIÑO 2008 B
albariño 100%

**89** Colour: straw. Nose: fresh, varietal, expressive, floral. Palate: fruity, flavourful, good structure, fresh, good acidity, fine bitter notes.

### ADEGAS D'ALTAMIRA SELECCIÓN 2007 B
albariño 100%

**88** Colour: bright straw. Nose: medium intensity, fresh, scrubland. Palate: varietal, flavourful, fruity, good acidity, fine bitter notes.

### BRANDAL ALBARIÑO 2006 B BARRICA
albariño 100%

**89** Colour: bright straw. Nose: complex, smoky, scrubland, varietal, elegant. Palate: powerful, full, flavourful, varietal, rich, smoky aftertaste.

## ADEGAS GALEGAS

Meder, s/n
36457 Salvaterra de Miño (Pontevedra)
☎: 986 657 400 - Fax: 986 657 371
galiciano@galiciano.com
www.galiciano.com

## VEIGADARES 2008 B JOVEN

**93** Colour: bright straw. Nose: fresh fruit, wild herbs, varietal, mineral. Palate: full, powerful, fruity, good acidity, round.

## O DEUS DIONISOS 2008 B

**89** Colour: bright straw. Nose: fresh fruit, wild herbs, varietal. Palate: full, powerful, flavourful, fresh.

## VEIGADARES 2007 BFB

**89** Colour: bright yellow. Nose: smoky, ripe fruit, creamy oak. Palate: flavourful, rich, fruity, smoky aftertaste.

## GRAN VEIGADARES 2005 BFB

**88** Colour: bright yellow. Nose: fruit preserve, creamy oak, sweet spices, balanced. Palate: fruity, elegant, smoky aftertaste.

## DON PEDRO SOUTOMAIOR TEMPO B ROBLE

**90** Colour: bright yellow. Nose: creamy oak, balanced, grassy, ripe fruit. Palate: fleshy, powerful, fruity, long, spicy.

## DON PEDRO SOUTOMAIOR B

**87** Colour: bright straw. Nose: fresh fruit, grassy, expressive. Palate: rich, powerful, good acidity, fruity.

## BOUZA GRANDE 2007
albariño, treixadura, loureiro

**87** Colour: bright straw. Nose: grassy, ripe fruit, medium intensity, varietal. Palate: unctuous, fruity, flavourful.

RUBINES

## ADEGAS GRAN VINUM

Fermín Bouza Brey, 9 5ºB
36600 Vilagarcía de Arousa (Pontevedra)
☎: 986 555 742 - Fax: 986 555 742
info@adegasgranvinum.com
www.adegasgranvinum.com

### ESENCIA DIVIÑA 2008 B
albariño 100%

**90** Colour: pale. Nose: varietal, elegant, floral, fresh fruit, fragrant herbs. Palate: flavourful, powerful, fruity, fresh, carbonic notes, complex.

### GRAN VINUM 2008 B
albariño 100%

**89** Colour: straw. Nose: varietal, powerfull, fresh, complex, fragrant herbs. Palate: powerful, flavourful, fruity, fresh, complex.

MAR DE VIÑAS 2008 B
albariño 100%

**86** Colour: bright straw. Nose: floral, fresh fruit, medium intensity. Palate: fresh, fruity, flavourful, correct, great length.

## ADEGAS MORGADIO

Albeos - Creciente
36429 Creciente (Pontevedra)
☎: 988 261 212 - Fax: 988 261 213
info@morgadio.com
www.morgadio.com

MORGADÍO ALBARIÑO 2008 B
albariño 100%

**87** Colour: straw. Nose: balsamic herbs, fresh fruit, medium intensity. Palate: fresh, fruity, powerful, flavourful.

CAPRICHO DE MORGADÍO 2005 BFB
albariño 100%

**88** Colour: bright yellow. Nose: short, medium intensity, candied fruit. Palate: flavourful, balsamic, smoky aftertaste.

## ADEGAS TERRA SANTA S.L.

Avenida de Villagarcía, 100
36630 Cambados (Pontevedra)
☎: 986 542 947
terrasanta@adegasterrasanta.com
www.adegasterrasanta.com

TERRA SANTA ALBARIÑO 2008 B

**82**

VIÑA DOZO
PAZO SAN ANTON

## ADEGAS TOLLODOURO

Ctra. Tui-A Guarda, km. 45
36760 O Rosal (Pontevedra)
☎: 986 609 810 - Fax: 986 609 811
bodega@tollodouro.com
www.tollodouro.com

TOLLODOURO ROSAL 2008 B
albariño, treixadura, loureiro, caiño

**86** Colour: bright yellow. Nose: medium intensity, fruit expression, citrus fruit, fresh, balanced. Palate: flavourful, fruity, good acidity.

PONTELLÓN ALBARIÑO 2008 B
albariño 100%

**85** Colour: bright straw. Nose: medium intensity, short, fresh, fruit expression. Palate: correct, balanced, good acidity.

## ADEGAS VALMIÑOR

A Portela, s/n San Juan de Tabagón
36760 O'Rosal (Pontevedra)
☎: 986 609 060 - Fax: 986 609 313
valminor@adegasvalminor.com
www.adegasvalminor.com

VALMIÑOR 2008 B
albariño 100%

**91** Colour: bright yellow. Nose: white flowers, acacia flower, fresh fruit, fragrant herbs. Palate: powerful, flavourful, full, fruity, fresh, sweetness, good acidity.

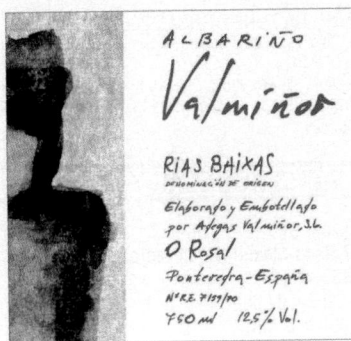

TORROXAL 2008 B
albariño 100%

**85** Colour: straw. Nose: medium intensity, varietal, fresh, fruit expression, honeyed notes. Palate: balanced, easy to drink.

DÁVILA 2007 B
albariño, loureiro, treixadura

**90** Colour: golden. Nose: fruit preserve, powerfull, fine reductive notes, dry stone, ripe fruit. Palate: powerful, flavourful, full, complex, reductive nuances, great length.

DÁVILA L.100 2007 B
loureiro 100%

**89** Colour: bright yellow. Nose: acacia flower, faded flowers, scrubland, fruit preserve. Palate: full, flavourful, complex, spicy.

DÁVILA M.100 2007 B
loureiro, caiño blanco, albariño

**88** Colour: bright straw. Nose: fine reductive notes, faded flowers, mineral, dried herbs. Palate: powerful, good structure, pruney, balsamic.

## ALDEA DE ABAIXO

Novas s/n
36778 O'Rosal (Pontevedra)
☎: 986 626 121 - Fax: 986 626 121
senoriodatorre@grannovas.com
www.grannovas.com

GRAN NOVAS ALBARIÑO 2007 B
albariño 100%

**90** Colour: bright straw. Nose: fine reductive notes, scrubland, balsamic herbs, candied fruit. Palate: powerful, flavourful, fruity, complex, full.

SEÑORÍO DA TORRE ROSAL 2007 B
albariño 80%, caiño 20%, loureiro %

**89** Colour: straw. Nose: powerful, varietal, complex, fresh fruit, fragrant herbs. Palate: powerful, flavourful, sweetness, good acidity.

## ATTIS BODEGAS Y VIÑEDOS

Morouzos, 21
36967 Dena-Meaño (Pontevedra)
☎: 986 744 164
info@penaguda.com
www.attisbyv.com

ATTIS 2008 B
albariño 100%

**88** Colour: bright yellow. Nose: grassy, ripe fruit, powerfull. Palate: flavourful, powerful, good structure, fruity, ripe fruit.

XIÓN 2008 B
albariño 100%

**87** Colour: straw. Nose: medium intensity, short, ripe fruit. Palate: good acidity, fruity, flavourful, fresh.

NANA 2007 B
albariño 100%

**86** Colour: bright golden. Nose: ripe fruit, creamy oak, closed, scrubland. Palate: fresh, fruity, spicy, balanced.

## BENITO SANTOS

Currás, 46 Caleiro
36628 Vilanova de Arousa (Pontevedra)
☎: 986 554 435 - Fax: 986 554 200
info@sucesoresdebenitosantos.com
www.sucesoresdebenitosantos.com

BENITO SANTOS IGREXARIO DE SAIAR 2007 B

**87** Colour: bright straw. Nose: fresh, fresh fruit, white flowers, expressive, varietal. Palate: flavourful, fruity, good acidity, balanced.

BENITO SANTOS TERRA DE CÁLAGO 2007 B
albariño

**86** Colour: bright straw. Nose: fresh, expressive, fruit preserve. Palate: flavourful, fruity, good acidity, balanced.

BENITO SANTOS PAGO DE XOAN 2006 B
albariño

**90** Colour: bright straw. Nose: fresh, fresh fruit, white flowers, expressive. Palate: flavourful, fruity, good acidity, balanced.

BENITO SANTOS PAGO DE BEMIL 2005 B
albariño 100%

**87** Colour: bright golden. Nose: characterful, ripe fruit, sweet spices. Palate: powerful, flavourful, fine bitter notes, spicy.

## BENJAMÍN MIGUEZ NOVAL

Porto de Abaixo, 10 Porto
36458 Salvaterra de Miño (Pontevedra)
☎: 986 122 705 - Fax: 986 122 705
info@mariabargiela.com
www.mariabargiela.com

MARÍA BARGIELA 2007 B
albariño 90%, treixadura 8%, loureiro 2%

**83**

## BODEGA GRANBAZÁN

Tremoedo, 46
36628 Vilanova de Arousa (Pontevedra)
☎: 986 555 562 - Fax: 986 555 799
export@agrodebazansa.es
www.agrodebazansa.es

GRANBAZÁN ÁMBAR 2008 B

**89** Colour: straw. Nose: medium intensity, varietal, fresh, fresh fruit. Palate: fruity, fresh, flavourful, balsamic.

GRANBAZÁN VERDE 2008 B

**89** Colour: straw. Nose: medium intensity, fresh, varietal, fresh fruit. Palate: powerful, flavourful, fruity, good acidity.

CONTRAPUNTO 2008 B
albariño

**86** Colour: straw. Nose: short, medium intensity, fresh, fresh fruit. Palate: fresh, fruity, flavourful, lacks expression.

GRANBAZÁN LIMOUSIN 2007 B ROBLE

**91** Colour: bright yellow. Nose: smoky, fragrant herbs, fruit preserve, complex, varietal, powerfull. Palate: powerful, flavourful, full, fresh, fruity, rich.

GRANBAZÁN DON ALVARO DE BAZÁN 2006 B

**89** Colour: bright yellow. Nose: faded flowers, ripe fruit, scrubland, fine reductive notes. Palate: complex, powerful, rich, creamy.

## BODEGA JOSÉ CARLOS QUINTAS PÉREZ

Fonte, 20
36492 Quintela - Crecente (Pontevedra)
☎: 669 485 271 - Fax: 986 267 145
info@josecarlosquintasperez.es
www.oreidecampoverde.es

O REI DE CAMPOVERDE 2007 B
albariño

**88** Colour: straw, pale. Nose: varietal, elegant, floral, fresh fruit. Palate: balanced, flavourful, fruity, good acidity, good finish.

DAINSUA 2007 B
albariño 35%, treixadura 35%, loureiro 30%

**87** Colour: bright yellow. Nose: medium intensity, fresh, grassy, floral, balanced. Palate: flavourful, balanced, fruity aftestaste, great length.

## BODEGA LAGAR DE PINTOS

Cabanelas, s/n
36636 Ribadumia (Pontevedra)
☎: 986 710 001 - Fax: 986 710 203
lagar@lagardepintos.com
www.lagardepintos.com

LAGAR DE PINTOS 2008 B

**82**

CASTIÑEIRA
VIZCONDE DE BARRANTES

## BODEGAS AGUIUNCHO

Las Pedreiras, 1
36990 Sanxenxo (Pontevedra)
☎: 986 720 980 - Fax: 986 727 063
info@aguiuncho.com
www.aguiuncho.com

AGUIUNCHO 2008 B

**87** Colour: bright straw. Nose: medium intensity, short. Palate: fine bitter notes, balanced, fresh, good acidity.

AGUIUNCHO BARRICA 2007 BFB

**85** Colour: bright yellow. Nose: reduction notes, varietal, ripe fruit, expressive. Palate: flavourful, good structure, fruity, spicy, creamy, good acidity.

## BODEGAS ALBAMAR S.L.N.E.

O Adro, 11
36639 Cambados (Pontevedra)
☎: 986 543 830 - Fax: 986 520 048
info@bodegasalbamar.com

ALBAMAR 2008 B
albariño 100%

**89** Colour: bright straw. Nose: medium intensity, fresh, fresh fruit, grassy. Palate: powerful, flavourful, fresh, fruity.

## BODEGAS ALTOS DE TORONA

Ctra. de Puxeiros a Peinador, 59
36416 Tameiga - Mos (Pontevedra)
☎: 986 403 086 - Fax: 986 403 086
ventas@hgabodegas.com
www.hgabodegas.com

TORRES DE ERMELO 2008 B

**89** Colour: bright straw. Nose: medium intensity, neat, fresh, varietal, fresh fruit. Palate: powerful, flavourful, full, fruity, complex.

ALBANTA 2007 B
albariño

**89** Colour: bright yellow, greenish rim. Nose: ripe fruit, fruit expression, scrubland, varietal. Palate: flavourful, fleshy, varietal, rich, long.

ALBANTA 2008

**90** Colour: bright straw. Nose: varietal, fresh, complex, fragrant herbs. Palate: fruity, full, balanced, fine bitter notes, good acidity.

## BODEGAS AQVITANIA

Bauza, 17 Castrelo
36639 Cambados (Pontevedra)
☎: 986 520 895 - Fax: 986 520 895
info@bodegasaquitania.com
www.bodegasaquitania.com

ALBARIÑO AQVITANIA 2008 B
albariño 100%

**90** Colour: bright straw. Nose: expressive, varietal, fragrant herbs, elegant. Palate: flavourful, varietal, balanced, great length, good acidity.

ALBARIÑO BERNON 2008 B
albariño 100%

**90** Colour: straw. Nose: varietal, powerfull, fresh, expressive, fresh fruit. Palate: powerful, flavourful, fruity, fresh, complex, balsamic.

## BODEGAS AS LAXAS

As Laxas, 16
36430 Arbo (Pontevedra)
☎: 986 665 444 - Fax: 986 665 554
info@bodegasaslaxas.com
www.bodegasaslaxas.com

LAXAS 2008 B
albariño 100%

**90** Colour: bright straw. Nose: fresh fruit, grassy, expressive. Palate: fresh, fruity, powerful, flavourful, sweetness, good acidity.

VAL DO SOSEGO 2008 B
albariño 100%

**89** Colour: straw. Nose: medium intensity, fresh, varietal, fragrant herbs, fresh fruit. Palate: powerful, flavourful, fruity, fresh, sweetness, good acidity.

BÁGOA DO MIÑO 2008 B
albariño 100%

**88** Colour: straw. Nose: fragrant herbs, fresh fruit. Palate: good structure, fruity, powerful, flavourful.

CONDADO LAXAS 2007 B
albariño 55%, treixadura 30%, loureiro 15%

**86** Colour: straw. Nose: scrubland, ripe fruit, herbaceous. Palate: fresh, fruity, flavourful, balsamic, lacks expression.

## BODEGAS CASTRO MARTÍN

Puxafeita, 3.
36636 Ribadumia (Pontevedra)
☎: 986 710 202 - Fax: 986 710 607
info@bodegascastromartin.com
www.bodegascastromartin.com

CASAL CAEIRO ALBARIÑO 2008 B
albariño 100%

**88** Colour: straw. Nose: medium intensity, fresh, varietal, grassy. Palate: powerful, flavourful, sweetness, good acidity.

BODEGA CASTRO MARTÍN ALBARIÑO 2007 B
albariño 100%

**89** Colour: bright straw. Nose: fresh, varietal, balanced, grassy. Palate: full, fresh, varietal, good acidity, great length.

## BODEGAS CHAVES

Condesa, 3
36636 Barrantes-Ribadumia (Pontevedra)
☎: 986 710 015 - Fax: 986 718 240
bodegaschaves@yahoo.es

CASTEL DE FORNOS 2008 B
albariño 100%

**85** Colour: bright straw. Nose: medium intensity, varietal, fresh, fragrant herbs. Palate: fruity, flavourful.

AÑO 2008

**CASTEL de FORNOS**
*Albariño*
Selección de uva Albariña
Elaborado y Embotellado por:
Bodegas Chaves S.L.
Ribadumia-Pontevedra-España
Produce of Spain

RÍAS BAIXAS
Denominación de Origen

White Wine
Alc 12,5% By Vol.
Contents 750 Ml.
R.E. Nº 4719-PO

## BODEGAS COTO REDONDO

Bouza do Rato, s/n Rubiós
36449 As Neves (Pontevedra)
☎: 986 667 212 - Fax: 986 648 279
info@bodegas-cotoredondo.com
www.bodegas-cotoredondo.com

SEÑORÍO DE RUBIÓS CONDADO BLANCO 2008 B
treixadura 75%, loureiro 20%, albariño 5%

**92** Colour: bright straw. Nose: varietal, elegant, fragrant herbs, fresh, expressive. Palate: flavourful, fruity, good acidity, fine bitter notes.

VAL DO XULIANA 2008 B
albariño 100%

**88** Colour: straw. Nose: white flowers, expressive, fresh, varietal, fresh fruit, citrus fruit. Palate: fruity, fresh, flavourful, great length, good acidity.

SEÑORÍO DE RUBIÓS ALBARIÑO 2008 B
albariño 100%

**87** Colour: straw. Nose: closed, lacks fruit, short. Palate: powerful, flavourful, fruity, fresh, fruity aftertaste.

SEÑORÍO DE RUBIÓS CONDADO BLANCO 2006 B ROBLE
treixadura 85%, albariño 10%, godello 5%

**92** Colour: bright straw. Nose: fresh, powerfull, elegant, complex, fragrant herbs, white flowers. Palate: powerful, flavourful, full, fruity, complex, creamy, smoky aftertaste.

SAN NOMEDIO 2007 T
mencia 100%

**83**

SEÑORÍO DE RUBIOS SOUSÓN 2007 T
souson 100%

**83**

SEÑORÍO DE RUBIOS 2007 T
souson 90%, espadeiro 10%

**81**

TERRA DO XULIANA 2007 T
souson 100%

**79**

SEÑORÍO DE RUBIÓS 2005 T ROBLE
souson 85%, espadeiro 10%, caiño 5%

**79**

## BODEGAS COUTO

Porto s/n
36760 O'Rosal (Pontevedra)
☎: 986 609 060 - Fax: 986 609 313
couto@bodegascouto.com
www.bodegascouto.com

SERRA DA ESTRELA 2008 B
albariño 100%

**87** Colour: bright yellow. Nose: fresh fruit, grassy, fresh, varietal. Palate: fresh, fruity, flavourful, fruity aftestaste.

## BODEGAS DEL PALACIO DE FEFIÑANES

Pza. de Fefiñanes, s/n
36630 Cambados (Pontevedra)
☎: 986 542 204 - Fax: 986 524 512
fefinanes@fefinanes.com
www.fefinanes.com

ALBARIÑO DE FEFIÑANES 2008 B
albariño 100%

**92** Colour: straw. Nose: varietal, expressive, fresh, fragrant herbs. Palate: fruity, flavourful, fruity aftestaste, good finish, complex.

1583 ALBARIÑO DE FEFIÑANES 2007 BFB
albariño 100%

**90** Colour: bright straw. Nose: complex, medium intensity, expressive, fine lees, smoky. Palate: elegant, round, fruity, powerful, flavourful, balsamic, creamy.

ALBARIÑO DE FEFIÑANES III AÑO 2005 B
albariño 100%

**93** Colour: bright yellow. Nose: mineral, fragrant herbs, macerated fruit. Palate: powerful, flavourful, full, fruity, fresh, elegant.

## BODEGAS FILLABOA

Lugar de Fillaboa, s/n
36459 Salvaterra do Miño (Pontevedra)
☎: 986 658 132 - Fax: 986 664 212
info@bodegasfillaboa.com
www.bodegasfillaboa.com

ALBARIÑO FILLABOA 2008 B
albariño 100%

**91** Colour: bright straw. Nose: complex, fresh, expressive, varietal, fragrant herbs, floral. Palate: powerful, flavourful, fruity, fresh, complex.

ALBARIÑO FILLABOA SELECCIÓN FINCA MONTE ALTO 2007 B
albariño 100%

**93** Colour: bright straw. Nose: medium intensity, complex, varietal, fine lees, damp earth, undergrowth, candied fruit. Palate: powerful, flavourful, fruity, rich, full.

FILLABOA FERMENTADO EN TINO

## BODEGAS FORJAS DEL SALNÉS

As Lovas, 5
36968 Xil (Santa Eulalia) (Pontevedra)
☎: 699 446 113 - Fax: 986 742 131
rodri@movistar.net

LEIRANA 2008 B

**93** Colour: bright straw. Nose: fragrant herbs, fresh fruit. Palate: powerful, flavourful, fruity, fresh, complex.

LEIRANA A ESCUSA 2008 B
albariño 100%

**90** Colour: straw. Nose: fresh fruit, grassy, fresh, complex. Palate: good acidity, balanced, elegant.

LEIRANA BARRICA 2007 B

**93** Colour: bright yellow. Nose: powerful, fresh, complex, creamy oak. Palate: complex, fresh, full, flavourful, powerful, rich, mineral, smoky aftertaste.

GOLIARDO CAIÑO 2007 T
caiño 100%

**93** Colour: dark-red cherry, orangey edge. Nose: fresh fruit, fruit expression, wild herbs, fresh, expressive, varietal. Palate: astringent, elegant, complex, flavourful, balsamic, mineral, smoky aftertaste.

GOLIARDO LOUREIRO 2007 T
loureiro 100%

**92** Colour: deep cherry. Nose: fresh fruit, cedar wood, toasty, aromatic coffee, fruit expression. Palate: powerful, flavourful, fruity, complex, balsamic, good acidity, varietal.

## BODEGAS LA CANA

36636 Sisan Ribadumia (Pontevedra)
☎: 968 435 022 - Fax: 968 716 051

info@orowines.com

LA CANA 2008 B
albariño 100%

**93** Colour: bright straw. Nose: fresh, neat, ripe fruit, spicy. Palate: fruity, fresh, mineral, good acidity, fleshy.

## BODEGAS MARQUÉS DE VIZHOJA

Finca La Moreira
36438 Arbo (Pontevedra)
☎: 986 665 825 - Fax: 986 665 960
marquesdevizhoja@marquesdevizhoja.com
www.marquesdevizhoja.com

TORRE LA MOREIRA 2008 B
albariño 100%

**87** Colour: straw. Nose: medium intensity, short, varietal. Palate: powerful, flavourful, fruity.

SEÑOR DA FOLLA VERDE 2007 B
albariño 70%, loureiro 15%, treixadura 15%

**87** Colour: straw. Nose: grassy, fresh fruit, fresh, balanced. Palate: fresh, fruity, powerful, flavourful.

MARQUÉS DE VIZHOJA B

**83**

## BODEGAS NANCLARES

Castriño, 13 - Castrelo
36639 Cambados (Pontevedra)
☎: 986 520 763 - Fax: 986 524 958
bodega@bodegasnanclares.com
www.bodegasnanclares.com

ALBERTO NANCLARES ALBARIÑO 2008 B
albariño 100%

**90** Colour: bright straw. Nose: fresh, fresh fruit, expressive, fragrant herbs. Palate: flavourful, fruity, good acidity, balanced.

SOVERRIBAS DE NANCLARES 2008 BFB
albariño 100%

**86** Colour: yellow, pale. Nose: expressive, varietal, floral, acacia flower. Palate: fine bitter notes, flavourful, fruity, slightly acidic, great length.

TEMPUS VIVENDI 2008 B
albariño 100%

**86** Colour: bright straw. Nose: fresh, fresh fruit, expressive, fragrant herbs. Palate: flavourful, fruity, slightly acidic.

## BODEGAS NÚÑEZ

Iglesia, 12 Tremoedo
36628 Villanueva (Pontevedra)
☎: 986 524 374 - Fax: 986 543 331
bodegas@bodegasandion.com
www.bodegasandion.com

ANDIÓN S.C. B

**90** Colour: straw. Nose: powerful, varietal, complex, fresh fruit, fragrant herbs. Palate: complex, powerful, flavourful, fruity, fresh.

GENUINO 2008 B
albariño

**91** Colour: straw. Nose: fresh, white flowers, expressive. Palate: flavourful, fruity, balanced, good structure, varietal, complex.

## BODEGAS PABLO PADÍN

Ameiro, 24 - Dena
36967 Meaño (Pontevedra)
☎: 986 743 231 - Fax: 986 745 791
info@pablopadin.com
www.pablopadin.com

ALBARIÑO SEGREL ÁMBAR 2008 B
albariño 100%

**90** Colour: bright straw. Nose: grassy, varietal, complex, fresh fruit. Palate: powerful, flavourful, fruity, fresh, complex.

EIRAL ALBARIÑO 2008 B
albariño 100%

**90** Colour: straw. Nose: medium intensity, varietal, fruit expression, fresh. Palate: fresh, flavourful, elegant, fine bitter notes, good acidity.

SEGREL ALBARIÑO 2008 B
albariño 100%

**86** Colour: straw. Nose: medium intensity, fresh, floral. Palate: correct, easy to drink, good finish, good acidity, fresh.

## BODEGAS RECTORAL DE AMANDI

Amandi
27423 Sober (Lugo)
☎: 988 384 200 - Fax: 988 384 068

MIUDIÑO ALBARIÑO 2008 B
albariño

**89** Colour: bright straw. Nose: fresh, fresh fruit, white flowers, expressive. Palate: flavourful, fruity, good acidity, balanced.

## BODEGAS SANTIAGO ROMA

Catariño, 5 Besomaño
36636 Ribadumia (Pontevedra)
☎: 986 718 477 - Fax: 986 718 477
bodega@santiagoroma.com
www.santiagoroma.com

ALBARIÑO SANTIAGO ROMA 2008 B
albariño 100%

**88** Colour: bright straw. Nose: fresh, white flowers, citrus fruit, elegant. Palate: flavourful, fruity, good acidity, balanced.

ALBARIÑO SANTIAGO ROMA SELECCIÓN 2008 B
albariño 100%

**87** Colour: bright straw. Nose: medium intensity, floral, balanced, fresh. Palate: flavourful, full, varietal, great length, good acidity.

## BODEGAS SEÑORÍO DE VALEI S.L.

Rua Touzosas, 22
36883 Valeixe - A Cañiza (Pontevedra)
☎: 626 532 634 - Fax: 988 370 704
info@bodegasenoriodevalei.com
www.bodegasenoriodevalei.com

SEÑORÍO DE VALEI 2008 B

**90** Colour: bright straw. Nose: fresh, white flowers, expressive, grassy. Palate: flavourful, fruity, good acidity, balanced.

ESTELA 2008 B

**87** Colour: bright straw. Nose: medium intensity, varietal, fresh, fresh fruit. Palate: powerful, flavourful, fruity, correct.

## BODEGAS TERRAS GAUDA

Ctra. Tui - A Guarda, km. 46
36760 As Eiras- O´Rosal (Pontevedra)
☎: 986 621 001 - Fax: 986 621 084
terrasgauda@terrasgauda.com
www.terrasgauda.com

TERRAS GAUDA 2008 B
albariño 70%, loureiro 18%, caiño 12%

# DO RÍAS BAIXAS

**90** Colour: bright yellow. Nose: medium intensity, expressive, complex, white flowers, fragrant herbs. Palate: powerful, flavourful, full, sweetness, good acidity.

ABADÍA DE SAN CAMPIO 2008 B
albariño 100%

**87** Colour: straw. Nose: powerful, short, fresh, neat, balsamic herbs. Palate: flavourful, fruity, fruity aftestaste, elegant.

TERRAS GAUDA ETIQUETA NEGRA 2007 BFB
albariño 70%, loureiro 20%, caíño 10%

**89** Colour: bright yellow. Nose: smoky, fruit preserve, medium intensity. Palate: powerful, flavourful, fruity, complex.

## BODEGAS VINUM TERRAE

Lgar. de Axis - Simes s/n
36968 Meaño (Pontevedra)
☎: 986 747 566 - Fax: 986 747 621
comercial@vinumterrae.com
www.vinumterrae.com

AGNUSDEI ALBARIÑO 2008 B
albariño 100%

**89** Colour: bright straw. Nose: elegant, varietal, fresh, fresh fruit, fragrant herbs. Palate: powerful, flavourful, fruity, complex.

## BODEGAS VIÑA NORA

Bruñeiras, 7
36440 As Neves (Pontevedra)
☎: 986 667 210 - Fax: 986 664 610
info@vinanora.com

NORA 2008 B
albariño

**93** Colour: bright straw. Nose: fresh fruit, citrus fruit, grassy, balsamic herbs, white flowers. Palate: flavourful, fruity, fresh, fleshy, balanced, long.

NORA DA NEVE 2007 BFB
albariño 100%

**95** Colour: bright yellow. Nose: powerful, ripe fruit, warm, toasty, creamy oak. Palate: fleshy, powerful, flavourful, spicy.

## BODEGAS Y VIÑEDOS DON OLEGARIO S.L.

Refoxos s/n - Corvillón
36634 Cambados (Pontevedra)
☎: 986 520 886 - Fax: 986 520 886

info@donolegario.com
www.donolegario.com

DON OLEGARIO ALBARIÑO 2008 B

**90** Colour: bright straw. Nose: powerful, expressive, white flowers, ripe fruit. Palate: flavourful, fleshy, ripe fruit.

## BOUZA DE CARRIL S.L.

Avenida Caponiñas, 14 - Barrantes
36636 Ribadumia (Pontevedra)
☎: 986 710 471 - Fax: 986 710 471
bodega@bouzacarril.com

BOUZA DE CARRIL ALBARIÑO 2008 B
albariño 100%

**87** Colour: yellow, straw. Nose: varietal, floral, medium intensity, fresh, fragrant herbs. Palate: flavourful, balanced, good acidity, fresh.

## BOUZA DO REI

Lugar de Puxafeita, s/n
36636 Ribadumia (Pontevedra)
☎: 986 710 257 - Fax: 986 718 393
bouzadorei@terra.es

BOUZA DO REI 2008 B
albariño 100%

**89** Colour: bright straw. Nose: white flowers, varietal, expressive, fragrant herbs. Palate: fruity, powerful, fruity aftestaste, good acidity.

CASTEL DE BOUZA 2008 B
albariño 100%

**89** Colour: bright straw. Nose: complex, elegant, fresh, varietal, fragrant herbs. Palate: flavourful, powerful, fruity, fresh, complex.

## CASTRO BAROÑA

Cabeiro - San Martín s/n
36637 Meis (Pontevedra)
☎: 981 134 847 - Fax: 981 174 030
castrobarona@castrobarona.com
www.castrobarona.com

CASTRO BAROÑA ALBARIÑO 2008 B
albariño 100%

**90** Colour: straw. Nose: medium intensity, varietal, fresh, grassy. Palate: fresh, varietal, flavourful, good structure, complex, fine bitter notes.

## BRUXA 2008 B
albariño 100%

**89** Colour: bright straw. Nose: fresh, fresh fruit, expressive. Palate: flavourful, fruity, good acidity, balanced, great length, fruity aftestaste.

## LAGAR DE CASTELO 2008 B
albariño 100%

**88** Colour: straw. Nose: varietal, medium intensity, expressive, fresh fruit, grassy. Palate: flavourful, powerful, fruity aftestaste.

## COMERCIAL GRUPO FREIXENET S.A.

Joan Sala, 2
08770 Sant Sadurní d'Anoia (Barcelona)
☎: 938 917 000 - Fax: 938 183 095
freixenet@freixenet.es
www.freixenet.es

## VIONTA 2008 B
albariño

**89** Colour: pale. Nose: acacia flower, floral, fresh fruit. Palate: flavourful, light-bodied, fruity, fruity aftestaste.

## COMPAÑIA DE VINOS TRICÓ

Rua A Caleira, 2 Bajo
36210 Vigo (Pontevedra)
☎: 637 50 7 3
j.lopez@espaciovital.es

## TRICÓ 2007 B
albariño

**92** Colour: bright straw. Nose: powerful, fresh, fresh fruit, fragrant herbs. Palate: flavourful, fresh, sweetness, balanced, fine bitter notes.

## CONSTANTINA SOTELO ARES

Castriño, 9-Castelo
36639 Cambados (Pontevedra)
☎: 986 524 704 - Fax: 986 524 704
adegasotelo@yahoo.es

## ROSALÍA 2008 B

**87** Colour: bright straw. Nose: candied fruit, ripe fruit, citrus fruit. Palate: flavourful, fruity, fleshy.

ADEGA SOTELO

## COVA SERODIA

Curras, 1 bis Romai Portas
36658 Romai (Pontevedra)
☎: 986 536 099 - Fax: 986 536 099
info@covaserodia.com
www.covaserodia.com

## GRAN COVA 2008 B
albariño

**87** Colour: bright yellow. Nose: varietal, elegant, powerfull, fragrant herbs. Palate: powerful, flavourful, sweetness, good acidity.

## COVA SERODIA 2008 B
albariño

**76**

## ESCUDEIRO S.L.

Avenida Rosalia de Castro-Barrantes
36636 Ribadumia (Pontevedra)
☎: 986 710 777 - Fax: 986 710 777
bodegasescudeiro@yahoo.es

## ALBARIÑO VIÑA ROEL 2008 B
albariño 100%

**85** Colour: bright straw. Nose: medium intensity, short, fresh, neat. Palate: fruity, flavourful, good acidity, good finish.

RIBERA DEL UMIA
VERDÍA

## EULOGIO POMARES ZÁRATE E HIJOS S.L.

Bouza, 23
36668 Padrenda - Meaño (Pontevedra)
☎: 986 718 503 - Fax: 986 718 549
info@albarino-zarate.com
www.albarino-zarate.com

## ZÁRATE 2008 B

**89** Colour: straw. Nose: medium intensity, fresh, expressive, varietal, fresh fruit. Palate: fresh, fruity, flavourful, balsamic.

## FUERA DE CARTA

Avda. Escondite, 5

28250 Torrelodones (Madrid)
☎: 912 976 089 - Fax: 912 977 414
monica@fueradcarta.com
www.fueradcarta.com

DE SAA 2007 B
albariño

**85** Colour: bright yellow. Nose: dry nuts, fruit preserve, fine lees, fragrant herbs. Palate: flavourful, powerful, fleshy, complex, rich, sweetness.

## GERARDO MÉNDEZ S.L.

Galiñanes - Lores, 10
36968 Meaño (Pontevedra)
☎: 986 747 046 - Fax: 986 747 046
info@bodegasgerardomendez.com
www.bodegasgerardomendez.com

ALBARIÑO DO FERREIRO 2008 B

**90** Colour: straw. Nose: medium intensity, varietal, grassy, mineral. Palate: fresh, fruity, good structure, flavourful.

DO FERREIRO CEPAS VELLAS 2007 B
albariño

**93** Colour: bright straw. Nose: dried flowers, macerated fruit, fragrant herbs, fine reductive notes, complex. Palate: powerful, flavourful, fruity, rich, good structure, complex.

## JULIÁN GONZÁLEZ AREAL

Finca Lavandeira - Rebordans, 1
36712 Tui (Pontevedra)
☎: 986 601 414 - Fax: 986 601 414
canonigoareal@canonigoareal.com

CANÓNIGO AREAL 2008 B
100% albariño

**84**

## LA VAL

Muguiña s/n Arantei
36450 Salvaterra de Miño (Pontevedra)
☎: 986 610 728 - Fax: 986 611 635
laval@bodegaslaval.com
www.bodegaslaval.com

LA VAL ALBARIÑO 2008 B
albariño 100%

**89** Colour: bright straw. Nose: powerful, varietal, fresh, complex, fresh fruit, fragrant herbs. Palate: powerful, flavourful, fruity, fresh, complex, fruity aftestaste.

ALBARIÑO ORBALLO 2008 B
albariño 100%

**88** Colour: yellow, straw. Nose: medium intensity, fresh, fruit expression. Palate: good structure, balanced, good acidity, full.

FINCA DE ARANTEI 2008 B
albariño 100%

**88** Colour: pale. Nose: fresh, floral, fresh fruit. Palate: fresh, fruity, light-bodied, flavourful, fruity aftestaste.

LA VAL ALBARIÑO 2007 BFB
albariño 100%

**89** Colour: bright yellow. Nose: elegant, fresh, varietal, smoky. Palate: balsamic, creamy, smoky aftertaste, flavourful, varietal, fruity.

VIÑA LUDY 2007 B
albariño 60%, loureiro 30%, treixadura 5%, caiño 5%

**86** Colour: bright straw. Nose: wild herbs, fine reductive notes, candied fruit. Palate: powerful, flavourful, varietal, balsamic, reductive nuances.

LA VAL CRIANZA SOBRE LÍAS 2004 BC
albariño 100%

**90** Colour: bright straw. Nose: faded flowers, fine reductive notes, smoky, creamy oak, medium intensity. Palate: fresh, fruity, flavourful, complex, balsamic, creamy.

## LAGAR DA CONDESA

Maran Arcos da Condesa
36650 Caldas de Reis (Pontevedra)
☎: 986 541 422 - Fax: 986 540 213
lagardacondesa@lagardacondesa.com
www.lagardacondesa.com

LAGAR DA CONDESA 2008 B
albariño 100%

**87** Colour: bright yellow. Nose: medium intensity, citrus fruit, floral, balanced, varietal. Palate: good structure, powerful, flavourful.

VÍA XIX 2007 B ROBLE
albariño 100%

**88** Colour: bright yellow. Nose: creamy oak, fine lees, fruit expression. Palate: varietal, good structure, flavourful, good acidity, great length.

LAGAR DA CONDESA 2007 B
albariño 100%

## 84

## LAGAR DE BESADA

Pazo, 11
36968 Xil-Meaño (Pontevedra)
☎: 986 747 473 - Fax: 986 747 826
info@lagardebesada.com
www.lagardebesada.com

EX-LIBRIS 2008 B
albariño 100%

**88** Colour: bright straw. Nose: fragrant herbs, white flowers, fresh, medium intensity. Palate: varietal, powerful, good structure, good acidity.

LAGAR DE BESADA 2008 B
albariño 100%

**88** Colour: bright straw. Nose: fresh fruit, grassy, varietal, fresh. Palate: powerful, flavourful, varietal, balsamic.

BALADIÑA 2007 B
albariño 100%

**88** Colour: straw. Nose: closed, short, fresh, fresh fruit. Palate: powerful, flavourful, fruity, fresh.

AÑADA DE BALADIÑA 2002 B
albariño 100%

**87** Colour: bright golden. Nose: honeyed notes, toasty, petrol notes. Palate: ripe fruit, spicy, fruity aftestaste, good structure.

BURBUJA DE BALADIÑA

## LAGAR DE COSTA

Sartaxes, 8 Castrelo
36639 Cambados (Pontevedra)
☎: 986 543 526 - Fax: 986 543 526
contacto@lagardecosta.com
www.lagardecosta.com

LAGAR DE COSTA 2008 B

**90** Colour: bright straw. Nose: varietal, powerfull, fresh, complex, fragrant herbs. Palate: fresh, fruity, powerful, flavourful, complex.

## LAGAR DE FORNELOS S.A.

Barrio de Cruces Fornelos

36778 La Guardia (Pontevedra)
☎: 986 625 875 - Fax: 986 625 011
lagar@riojalta.com
www.riojalta.com

LAGAR DE CERVERA 2008 B
albariño 100%

**92** Colour: bright straw. Nose: fresh, fresh fruit, white flowers, expressive. Palate: flavourful, fruity, good acidity, balanced.

## LAGAR DO REI

Carballoso - Xil
36968 Meaño (Pontevedra)
☎: 986 743 189 - Fax: 986 745 287
marisaconf@yahoo.es
www.ecogalicia.com/lagarderei

LAGAR DE REI 2008 B
albariño 100%

## 82

## MAIOR DE MENDOZA

Rúa de Xiabre, 58 Carril
36610 Villagarcía (Pontevedra)
☎: 986 508 896 - Fax: 986 507 924
maiordemendoza@terra.es
www.maiordemendoza.com

FULGET 2008 B

**91** Colour: straw. Nose: fresh, fragrant herbs, expressive, varietal. Palate: flavourful, fruity, balanced, fine bitter notes, fruity aftestaste, great length.

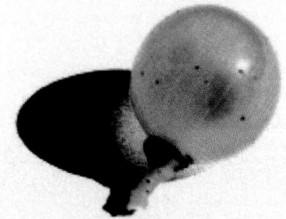

12,5% vol.                    75 Cl.

**MAIOR DE MENDOZA "SOBRE LÍAS" 2008 B**

**90** Colour: straw. Nose: complex, varietal, medium intensity, fragrant herbs. Palate: powerful, flavourful, sweetness, complex, varietal.

**MAIOR DE MENDOZA MACERACIÓN CARBÓNICA 2008 B**

**88** Colour: pale. Nose: grassy, fresh fruit, complex, varietal. Palate: powerful, flavourful, fresh, fruity, light-bodied.

**MAIOR DE MENDOZA 3 CRIANZAS 2006 B**
albariño

**87** Colour: bright yellow. Nose: fruit expression, varietal, medium intensity. Palate: balanced, fruity, flavourful, good acidity, great length, spicy.

## MAR DE ENVERO S.L.

Lugar Quintàns, 17

36638 Ribadumia (Pontevedra)
☎: 981 577 083 - Fax: 981 569 552
bodega@mardeenvero.es
www.mardeenvero.es

**MAR DE ENVERO 2007 B**
albariño 100%

**88** Colour: bright yellow. Nose: medium intensity, floral. Palate: flavourful, varietal, balsamic, good acidity, fine bitter notes, fruity aftestaste.

## MAR DE FRADES

Lg. Arosa, 16 Finca Valiñas
36637 Meis (Pontevedra)
☎: 986 680 911 - Fax: 986 680 926
mardefrades@mardefrades.com
www.mardefrades.com

**FINCA VALIÑAS "CRIANZA SOBRE LÍAS" 2008 B**

**84**

**MAR DE FRADES B**
albariño

**91** Colour: bright straw. Nose: fresh, fresh fruit, white flowers, varietal, fragrant herbs. Palate: flavourful, fruity, powerful, fresh, varietal.

ALGAREIRO

## MARÍA VICTORIA DOVALO MÉNDEZ

Villarreis, 21 Dena
36967 Meaño (Pontevedra)
☎: 610 705 205 - Fax: 986 745 036
veiganaum@gmail.com

**VEIGA NAÚM 2008 B**
albariño 100%

**87** Colour: yellow, straw. Nose: fresh, medium intensity, balanced, fruit expression, floral. Palate: good structure, varietal, easy to drink.

## MARTIN CODAX S.A.U.

Burgans, 91
36663 Vilariño-Cambados (Pontevedra)
☎: 986 526 040 - Fax: 986 526 901
comercial@martincodax.com
www.martincodax.com

**MARTÍN CÓDAX 2008 B**
albariño 100%

**88** Colour: straw. Nose: medium intensity, elegant, varietal, fresh fruit. Palate: good acidity, fruity, flavourful, fresh.

### BURGÁNS ALBARIÑO 2008 B
albariño 100%

**87** Colour: bright straw. Nose: fresh, varietal, medium intensity, fresh fruit, floral. Palate: flavourful, balanced, varietal.

### ORGANISTRUM 2007 B
albariño 100%

**90** Colour: straw. Nose: medium intensity, varietal, elegant, fresh fruit. Palate: powerful, flavourful, fresh, fruity, complex.

### MARTIN CODAX "PE REDONDO LÍAS" 2006 B
albariño 100%

**89** Colour: yellow, bright golden. Nose: medium intensity, neat, tropical fruit, grassy, floral, fine lees. Palate: fresh, fruity, correct, balanced.

### GALLAECIA MARTIN CÓDAX 2004 B
albariño 100%

**90** Colour: bright golden. Nose: powerful, characterful, honeyed notes, smoky, fine reductive notes. Palate: fleshy, sweetness, fine bitter notes, pruney, reductive nuances.

## O AFORADO

As Eiras
36778 O'Rosal (Pontevedra)
☎: 627 558 188 - Fax: 986 565 339
dalonso@dalonso.com
www.aforado.com

### AFORADO ROSAL 2007 B
albariño 80%, caiño 15%, marques 5%

**91** Colour: bright yellow. Nose: fine lees, scrubland, fine reductive notes, candied fruit. Palate: powerful, flavourful, full, rich, complex.

### AFORADO 2008 B
albariño 100%

**87** Colour: bright straw. Nose: fresh, fresh fruit, white flowers. Palate: flavourful, fruity, good acidity, balanced.

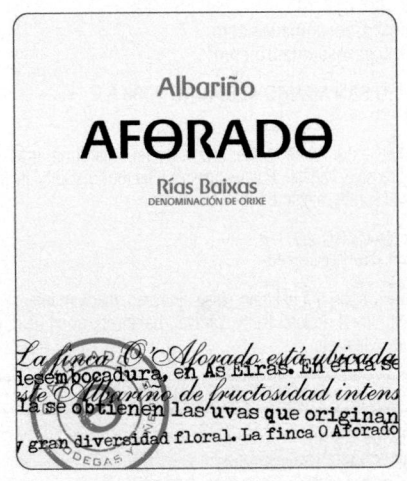

## PAZO DE BARRANTES

Finca Pazo de Barrantes, Barrantes
36636 Ribadumia (Pontevedra)
☎: 986 718 211 - Fax: 986 710 424
bodega@pazodebarrantes.com
www.marquesdemurrieta.com

### PAZO DE BARRANTES ALBARIÑO 2008 B
albariño

**93** Colour: bright yellow. Nose: citrus fruit, balsamic herbs, grassy, fine lees. Palate: elegant, round, good acidity.

### PAZO DE BARRANTES ALBARIÑO 2007 B
albariño

**92** Colour: bright straw. Nose: fresh, fresh fruit, white flowers, mineral. Palate: flavourful, fruity, good acidity, balanced.

## PAZO DE SAN MAURO

Pombal, 3 Porto
36458 Salvaterra de Miño (Pontevedra)
☎: 986 658 285 - Fax: 986 664 208
info@pazosanmauro.com
www.pazosanmauro.com

PAZO SAN MAURO ALBARIÑO 2008 B
albariño 100%

**90** Colour: straw. Nose: acacia flower, fresh fruit, grassy, expressive, varietal. Palate: powerful, flavourful, fruity, fresh, good acidity, elegant.

SANAMARO 2007 B
albariño 95%, loureiro 5%

**90** Colour: bright straw. Nose: fine lees, medium intensity, fresh, floral. Palate: fruity, varietal, balanced, good acidity, fruity aftestaste.

## PAZO DE SEÑORANS

Vilanoviña, 50
36616 Meis (Pontevedra)
☎: 986 715 373 - Fax: 986 715 569
info@pazodesenorans.com
www.pazodesenorans.com

PAZO DE SEÑORANS 2008 B
albariño 100%

**93** Colour: bright straw. Nose: floral, fresh fruit, macerated fruit, fragrant herbs. Palate: powerful, flavourful, full, fresh, complex, elegant.

SOL DE SEÑORANS 2006 B ROBLE
albariño 100%

**94** Colour: bright straw. Nose: smoky, scrubland, fine reductive notes, fine lees. Palate: complex, powerful, flavourful, full, balsamic, smoky aftertaste.

PAZO DE SEÑORANS SELECCIÓN DE AÑADA 2004 B
albariño 100%

**94** Colour: bright yellow. Nose: fine reductive notes, grassy, fresh fruit, mineral. Palate: round, powerful, flavourful, complex, balsamic, long.

## PAZO DE VILLAREI

Vía Rápida del Salnés, km. 5
36637 San Martiño de Meis (Pontevedra)
☎: 986 710 827 - Fax: 986 710 827
info@domecqbodegas.com
www.allieddomecqbodegas.com

CADOIRO DE TESELAS 2008 B
albariño

**90** Colour: bright straw. Nose: fresh, fresh fruit, white flowers, expressive. Palate: flavourful, fruity, good acidity, balanced.

TERRA D'OURO 2008 B
albariño

**90** Colour: bright straw. Nose: varietal, fresh, powerfull, complex. Palate: rich, powerful, flavourful, good acidity, balsamic, fruity aftestaste.

TERRA D'OURO 2007 B
albariño

**84**

PAZO DE VILLAREI

## PAZO PONDAL S.L.

Coto s/n Cabeiras
36436 Arbo (Pontevedra)
☎: 986 665 551 - Fax: 986 665 949
info@pazopondal.com
www.pazopondal.com

LEIRA 2008 B
albariño 100%

**87** Colour: straw. Nose: expressive, varietal, fragrant herbs, balanced. Palate: fresh, varietal, fruity, good acidity, confected.

PAZO PONDAL ALBARIÑO 2008 B
albariño 100%

**85** Colour: straw. Nose: fresh, balanced, fruit expression, neat, medium intensity. Palate: balanced, easy to drink, good finish.

## PAZO QUINTEIRO DA CRUZ S.L.

Lois
36636 Ribadumia (Pontevedra)
☎: 986 712 448 - Fax: 986 501 011
pedropinheirolago@yahoo.es
www.quinteirodacruz.webcindario.com

QUINTEIRO DA CRUZ 2007 B
albariño 100%

**77**

QUINTEIRO DA CRUZ ALLIER 2006 BFB
albariño 100%

**79**

QUINTEIRO DA CRUZ VENDIMIA TARDÍA
COLECCIÓN PRIVADA 2005 B
albariño 100%

**78**

## QUINTA COUSELO

Barrio de Couselo nº 13
36770 O'Rosal (Pontevedra)
☎: 986 625 051 - Fax: 986 626 267
quintacouselo@quintacouselo.com
www.quintacouselo.com

QUINTA DE COUSELO 2008 B
albariño, loureiro, caiño, treixadura

**89** Colour: bright yellow. Nose: varietal, fragrant herbs, balanced, fresh. Palate: good structure, flavourful, fruity, good acidity.

TURONIA 2008 B
albariño 100%

**85** Colour: bright yellow. Nose: medium intensity, fresh fruit. Palate: good acidity, light-bodied, fresh.

## ROSALIA DE CASTRO

Xil, 18
36968 Meaño (Pontevedra)
☎: 986 747 779 - Fax: 986 748 940
administracion@rosaliadecastro.eu
www.rosaliadecastro.eu

PACO & LOLA 2008 B

**92** Colour: bright yellow. Nose: powerful, fresh, expressive, varietal, fragrant herbs, balsamic herbs, fresh fruit. Palate: flavourful, powerful, fruity, fresh.

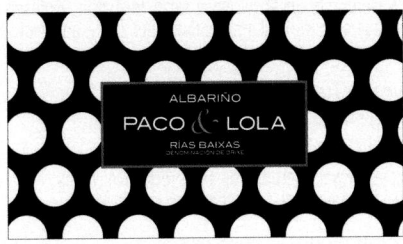

ROSALÍA DE CASTRO 2008 B

**88** Colour: bright yellow. Nose: varietal, fragrant herbs, fresh, medium intensity. Palate: balanced, fresh, flavourful, great length.

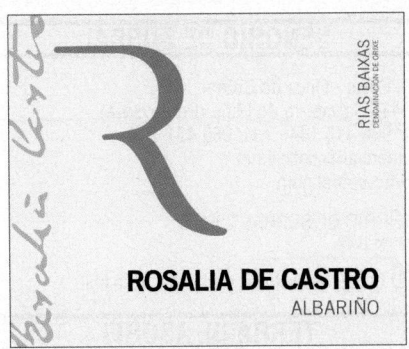

PACO & LOLA 2007 B
albariño

**91** Colour: bright straw. Nose: fruit expression, fresh fruit, fragrant herbs. Palate: powerful, fruity, fresh, long.

## SANTIAGO RUIZ

Rua do Vinicultor Santiago Ruiz
36760 San Miguel de Tabagón-O Rosal (Pontevedra)
☎: 986 614 083 - Fax: 986 614 142
info@bodegasantiagoruiz.com
www.bodegasantiagoruiz.com

SANTIAGO RUIZ 2008 B

**88** Colour: straw. Nose: short, fresh, fresh fruit. Palate: fresh, fruity, dry, varietal.

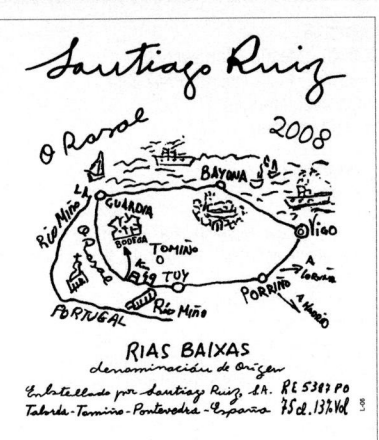

# DO RÍAS BAIXAS

## SEÑORIO DE SOBRAL

Lg. Porto - Finca do Sobral
36458 Salvaterra do Miño (Pontevedra)
☎: 986 415 144 - Fax: 986 421 744
comercial@ssobral.net
www.ssobral.com

SEÑORÍO DE SOBRAL 2008 B
albariño 100%

**86** Colour: straw. Nose: fresh, neat, fresh fruit.

## TERRA DE ASOREI

Rúa San Francisco, 2 - 1 ofic. C-D
36630 Cambados (Pontevedra)
☎: 608 117 451 - Fax: 986 520 813
info@terradeasorei.com
www.terradeasorei.com

PAZO TORRADO 2008 B
albariño 100%

**88** Colour: bright yellow. Nose: medium intensity, short. Palate: balanced, fresh, flavourful.

TERRA DE ASOREI 2008 B
albariño 100%

**87** Colour: bright yellow. Nose: fresh fruit, citrus fruit, dried herbs. Palate: correct, fresh, balanced, fine bitter notes, great length.

## VALDAMOR

Valdamor, 8
36968 Xil - Meaño (Pontevedra)
☎: 986 747 111 - Fax: 986 747 743
clientes@valdamor.es
www.valdamor.es

VALDAMOR 2008 B
albariño 100%

**90** Colour: straw. Nose: varietal, powerfull, elegant, fresh fruit, fragrant herbs. Palate: fresh, fruity, flavourful, complex.

VALDAMOR SELECCIÓN 2007 B
albariño 100%

**86** Colour: straw. Nose: reduction notes, varietal, fresh, grassy. Palate: good acidity, good structure, fruity, powerful, flavourful.

VALDAMOR BARRICA 2006 B
albariño 100%

**90** Colour: bright straw. Nose: fresh fruit, fragrant herbs, balsamic herbs, smoky. Palate: elegant, round, rich, flavourful, balsamic, smoky aftertaste.

## VALDUMIA

Camino Novo s/n - Zamar Rubianes
36619 Vilagarcía de Arousa (Pontevedra)
☎: 986 507 040 - Fax: 986 565 142
info@valdumia.com
www.valdumia.com

VALDUMIA PREMIUM 2008 B
albariño 100%

**86** Colour: straw. Nose: medium intensity, fresh, grassy, fruit expression. Palate: correct, balanced, easy to drink, light-bodied, good acidity.

VALDUMIA 2008 B
albariño 100%

**81**

VALDUMIA SELECCIÓN DE AÑADA 2008
albariño 100%

**84**

## VILARVIN ADEGAS VALTEA

Rua Portela, 14
36429 Creciente (Pontevedra)
☎: 986 666 344 - Fax: 986 644 914
vilarvin@vilarvin.com
www.vilarvin.com

VALTEA 2008 B
albariño 100%

**91** Colour: bright straw. Nose: fresh, fresh fruit, expressive, fragrant herbs, varietal. Palate: flavourful, fruity, good acidity, balanced.

FINCA GARABATO 2007 B
albariño 100%

**90** Colour: bright yellow. Nose: powerful, varietal, complex, acacia flower, scrubland, fine reductive notes. Palate: powerful, flavourful, fruity, good structure, complex.

PEDRAS RUBRAS- LIAS 2006 B
albariño 100%

**89** Colour: bright yellow. Nose: white flowers, fragrant herbs, smoky, creamy oak. Palate: powerful, flavourful, complex, smoky aftertaste, spicy, fruity.

## VIÑA ALMIRANTE

Peroxa, 5
36658 Portas (Pontevedra)
☎: 620 294 293 - Fax: 986 541 471
info@vinaalmirante.com
www.vinaalmirante.com

ELAS 2008 B
albariño 100%

**90** Colour: bright yellow. Nose: fresh, varietal, floral, expressive, fruit expression, fragrant herbs. Palate: flavourful, good structure, fine bitter notes.

PIONERO MUNDI 2008 B
albariño 100%

**89** Colour: bright yellow. Nose: fragrant herbs, fresh, elegant, varietal. Palate: good structure, flavourful, good acidity, fine bitter notes.

PIONERO MACCERATO 2008 B
albariño 100%

**88** Colour: straw. Nose: fragrant herbs, white flowers, medium intensity. Palate: fruity, balanced, good acidity, fine bitter notes.

VANIDADE 2008 B

**88** Colour: bright straw. Nose: fresh, white flowers, expressive, medium intensity. Palate: flavourful, fruity, balanced, great length.

ELAS 2007 B
albariño 100%

**93** Colour: bright yellow. Nose: powerful, varietal, neat, ripe fruit, fragrant herbs. Palate: fresh, fruity, good acidity, rich, great length.

SOME OTHER WINERIES WITHIN THE DO:

**ADEGA ARRAIANA
ADEGA DA SERRA
ADEGA RUBÉN
ADEGA VIEITES S.L.
ADEGAS BEIRAMAR
ADEGAS GÁNDARA
ALBARIÑO ADEGA DOSAN
ANTONIO ABALO MÉNDEZ
ARAGUNDE S.L.
BARREIRO AMADO S.L.
BELISARDO RODRÍGUEZ ROMERO
BENITO AMIL PADÍN
BODEGA EULOGIO GONDAR GALIÑANES
BODEGA MARTINEZ SERANTES
BODEGA MONTE SACRO
BODEGAS ADONIS
BODEGAS ROBALIÑO
C.B. PINTOS
CARBALLAL C.B.
CODORNÍU
CONCEPCIÓN BOULLOSA GASTAÑADUY
COSECHEROS REUNIDOS DE SOUTOMAIOR
DAVID MARTÍNEZ SOBRAL
DIVINA FERNÁNDEZ GIL
ENOTURISMO ACHA S.L.U.
FELICIANO DOPAZO PADÍN
FERNANDO DIÉGUEZ OTERO
FRANCISCO LAMEIRO FERREIRA
GALLAECIA PREMIUM / DELISPAIN BODEGAS
GIL ARMADA
JOSÉ ALVAREZ REY
JOSÉ ANGEL BOADO CHAVES
JOSÉ DOMÍNGUEZ POMBO
LAGAR DO FREIXO
LUIS PADÍN REY
M. DEL CARMEN VARELA TORRES
PABLO LÓPEZ FRANCO
PAZO AS BARREIRAS
PEDRALONGA (FCO. ALFONSO REBOREDA)
PORTA DO RIO MIÑO S.C.G.
QUINTA DO LOBELLE
ROSA GONZÁLEZ GONZÁLEZ
ROSA TORRES VARELA
TOMADA DE CASTRO
VEIGA SERANTES
VIEITOMAR
VIÑA BLANCA DO SALNES S.A.
VIÑA CARTIN**

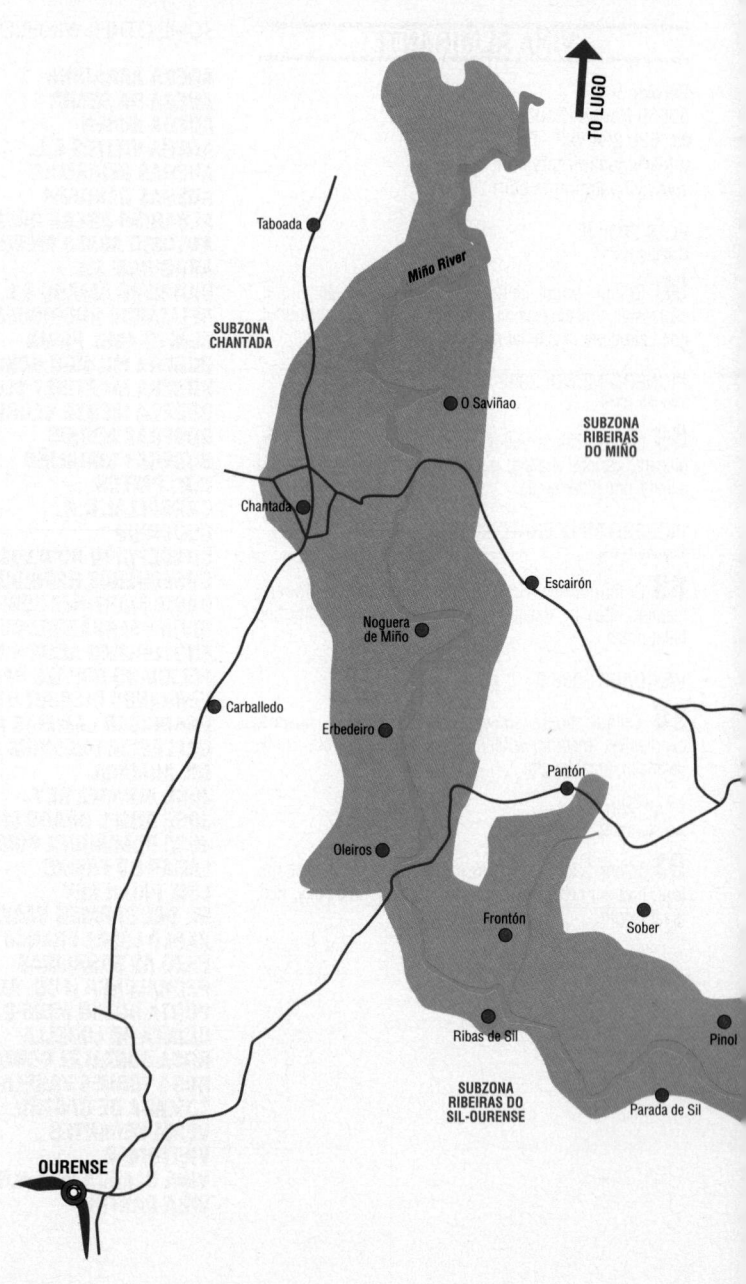

TO LUGO

Taboada

Miño River

SUBZONA
CHANTADA

O Saviñao

SUBZONA
RIBEIRAS
DO MIÑO

Chantada

Escairón

Noguera
de Miño

Carballedo

Erbedeiro

Pantón

Oleiros

Frontón

Sober

Ribas de Sil

Pinol

SUBZONA
RIBEIRAS DO
SIL-OURENSE

Parada de Sil

OURENSE

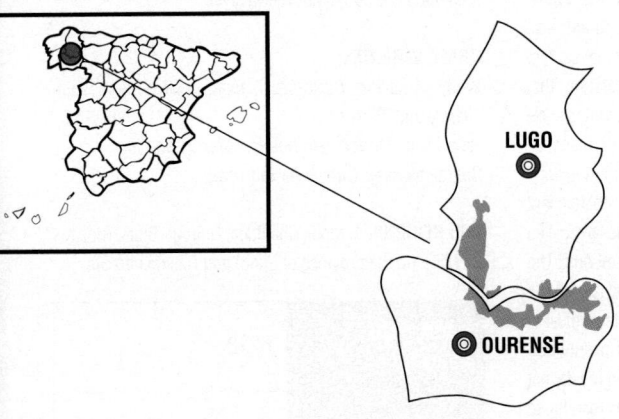

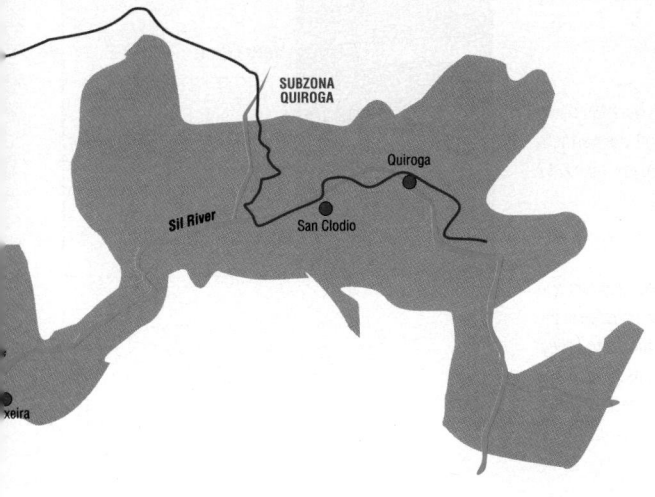

LUGO

OURENSE

SUBZONA
QUIROGA

Quiroga

Sil River

San Clodio

xeira

▽ Consejo Regulador
● DO Boundary

## NEWS

You have to be in quite a daring and almost surgical mood to cultivate vines on the terraces of the rivers Sil and Miño; to the sheer difficulty provided by the steepness of the vineyards we have to add that of finding the aptest microclimate. To those two reasons you have to add also the diversity of soils, altitude and sun-exposition of each of the five subzones to understand the expectation that surrounds the wines from the region every new vintage. We have to remember that, although they do not reach an extreme altitude, the vineyards are considered 'of mountain' in nature, given their steepness. Some of the most valiant vine growers have set their eyes on extreme areas like Quiroga or Manzaneda given their cooler conditions. The 2008 vintage has yielded wines more mature and expressive in character, which preserve well the varietal notes typical of the local grapes. Although lower in terms of production given some springtime setbacks, grapes reached mostly full maturity and yielded rounder and healthier wines than those from the previous vintage. Also godello wines are on an upward trend and will surely show the potential of the white wines from the region. Almost all wines from Ribeira Sacra have managed to reach the 'Summum' quality seal, a label born to promote the use of indigenous grapes such as mencía in the blend.

## LOCATION

The region extends along the banks of the rivers Miño and Sil in the south of the province of Lugo and the northern region of the province of Orense; it is made up of 17 municipal districts in this region.

## CLIMATE

Quite variable depending on the specific area. Less rain and slightly cooler climate and greater Continental influence in the Sil valley, and greater Atlantic character in the Miño valley. Altitude, on the other hand, also has an effect, with the vineyards closer to the rivers and with a more favourable orientation (south-southeast) being slightly warmer.

## SOIL

In general, the soil is highly acidic, although the composition varies greatly from one area to another. The vineyards are located on steep terraces and are no higher than 400 m to 500 m above sea level.

## GRAPE VARIETIES:

**White**: *Albariño, Loureira, Treixadura, Godello, Dona Blanca* and *Torrontés*.
**Red**: Main: *Mencía, Brancellao Merenzao.*
Complimentary: *Garnacha Tintorera.*

**SUB-REGIONS:** Amandi, Chantada, Quiroga-Bibei, Ribeiras do Miño (in the province of Lugo) and Ribeiras do Sil.

| Hectares of Vineyard | 1,228 |
|---|---|
| Nº Viticulturists | 2,836 |
| Nº of Bodegas | 98 |
| 2008 Harvest | Very Good |
| 2007 Production | 2,656,500 l. |
| Marketing | 90% domestic 10% export |

**CONSEJO REGULADOR**
Rua Pescadeías, 1, (Antiguo Torreón)
27400 Monforte de Lemos (Lugo)
☎: 982 410 968 - Fax: 982 411 265
@ info@ribeirasacra.org
www.ribeirasacra.org

## GENERAL CHARACTERISTICS OF THE WINES:

| | |
|---|---|
| **WHITES** | Single variety wines are produced from *Albariño* and *Godello*. The former have a greenish yellow colour with a fruity character and potency typical of *Albariño*; the latter are somewhat fresher than those of Valdeorras and less glycerine-like on the palate. There are also other white wines, the result of the blending of different varieties; these have a straw yellow colour and a fruity nose. |
| **REDS** | The single variety wines of *Mencía*, the most characteristic of the region, have a deep-red mid-tone colour; on the nose they are very fresh and roasted; on the palate, they are dry, fruity and without a pronounced structure. |

## 2008 VINTAGE RATING:

# VERY GOOD

## ADEGA DO MOLLON

Casanova Viñoás
Nogueira de Ramuín (Ourense)
☎: 988 222 272 - Fax: 988 226 641
pombares@mundo-r.com
www.pombares.com

POMBARES GODELLO 2008 B
godello 85%, treixadura 10%, albariño 5%

**79**

POMBARES SELECCIÓN 2008 T
mencia 90%, garnacha 10%

**86** Colour: very deep cherry. Nose: fruit expression, fresh fruit, mineral, balsamic herbs. Palate: flavourful, full, fruity, fresh.

## ADEGA PONTE DA BOGA S.L.

Couto Sampaio
32704 Castro Caldelas (Orense)
☎: 988 203 306 - Fax: 988 203 299
ponteboga@yahoo.es

PONTE DA BOGA 2008 B

**86** Colour: bright straw. Nose: fresh fruit, expressive, grassy. Palate: flavourful, fruity, good acidity, balanced.

PONTE DA BOGA 2008 T
mencía

**86** Colour: cherry, purple rim. Nose: expressive, fresh fruit, red berry notes, floral. Palate: flavourful, fruity, good acidity.

CAPRICHO DE MENCÍA 2007 T BARRICA

**87** Colour: dark-red cherry, purple rim. Nose: characterful, ripe fruit, floral, dark chocolate. Palate: fleshy, good structure, full, sweet tannins.

CAPRICHO DE MERENZAO 2007 T

**84**

## ADEGAS MOURE

Buenos Aires, 12 Bajo
27540 Escairón (Lugo)
☎: 982 452 031 - Fax: 982 452 700
abadiadacova@adegasmoure.com
www.adegasmoure.com

ABADÍA DA COVA ALBARIÑO 2008 B
albariño 100%

**87** Colour: yellow, bright golden. Nose: ripe fruit, wild herbs, complex. Palate: fresh, round, unctuous.

ABADIA DA COVA MENCÍA 2008 T
mencía 100%

**86** Color bright cherry. Aroma floral, fruit expression, red berry notes. Taste fruity, fresh, flavourful.

A FUGA 2008 T
mencía

**85** Colour: bright cherry. Nose: varietal, expressive, red berry notes, floral, fragrant herbs. Palate: fruity, fresh, fresh fruit tannins.

ABADIA DA COVA 2007 T BARRICA
mencía 100%

**84**

## ALGUEIRA

Doade s/n
27460 Sober (Lugo)
☎: 629 208 917 - Fax: 982 410 299
info@adegaalgueira.com
www.adegaalgueira.com

BRANDÁN GODELLO 2008 B
**84**

ALGUEIRA 2008 B
godello, albariño, treixadura
**84**

ALGUEIRA 2008 T
mencía
**82**

ALGUEIRA 2006 T ROBLE
**86** Colour: deep cherry. Nose: ripe fruit, creamy oak, faded flowers. Palate: fleshy, good acidity, round.

## BODEGA VICTORINO ÁLVAREZ

Luis Carballo, 74
32765 A Teixeira (Ourense)
☎: 988 207 418
solliomencia@terra.es

SOLLÍO MENCÍA 2008 T
mencía 100%
**87** Colour: deep cherry. Nose: fruit expression, ripe fruit, earthy notes, floral. Palate: fleshy, fruity, fresh, good structure.

## BODEGAS COSTOYA

Boga, 26 - A Abeleda
32764 A Teixeira (Ourense)
☎: 600 417 273 - Fax: 988 601 332
carlos_costoya@temera.com

ALODIO T
mencía, merenzao
**86** Colour: very deep cherry. Nose: fresh fruit, red berry notes, floral, characterful. Palate: fruity, fresh, good acidity.

## BODEGAS RECTORAL DE AMANDI

Amandi
27423 Sober (Lugo)
☎: 988 384 200 - Fax: 988 384 068

RECTORAL DE AMANDI 2008 T
**85** Colour: very deep cherry. Nose: varietal, fruit expression, raspberry, floral. Palate: flavourful, fleshy, round.

## CARLOS DÍAZ DÍAZ

Vilachá - Doabe
27424 Sober (Lugo)
☎: 982 152 425

ESTRELA 2008 T
mencía 98%, garnacha 2%
**85** Colour: very deep cherry. Nose: macerated fruit, red berry notes, floral. Palate: fleshy, fruity, fresh, balsamic.

## CASA MOREIRAS

San Martín de Siós
27430 Pantón (Lugo)
☎: 982 456 174 - Fax: 986 480 209
bodega@casamoreiras.com
www.casamoreiras.com

CASA MOREIRAS GODELLO 2008 B
godello
**87** Colour: bright straw. Nose: fresh, fresh fruit, white flowers, expressive. Palate: flavourful, fruity, balanced, unctuous.

CASA MOREIRAS MENCÍA 2008 T
mencía
**82**

## CÉSAR ENRÍQUEZ DIEGUEZ

Eirexe - Abeleda
32764 A Texeira (Ourense)
☎: 988 203 450

PEZA DO REI 2008 B
godello, treixadura, albariño
**83**

PEZA DO REI 2008 T
**87** Colour: very deep cherry. Nose: ripe fruit, cocoa bean, floral, earthy notes. Palate: fleshy, spirituous, balsamic, round tannins.

PEZA DO REI 2006 T ROBLE
mencía

**87** Colour: cherry, garnet rim. Nose: elegant, expressive, ripe fruit, wild herbs, balsamic herbs. Palate: complex, good structure, flavourful, round tannins.

## CONDADO DE SEQUEIRAS

Sequeiras - Camporramiro
27500 Chantada (Lugo)
☎: 944 732 516 - Fax: 944 120 227
condadodesequeiras@grupopeago.com

CONDADO DE SEQUEIRAS 2008 B
treixadura 50%, godello 50%

**84**

CONDADO DE SEQUEIRAS 2008 T
mencía 100%

**80**

CONDADO DE SEQUEIRAS 2006 T ROBLE
mencía 100%

**84**

## DOMINGO LÓPEZ FERNÁNDEZ

Doade, 54
27424 Sober (Lugo)
☎: 982 152 458

VIÑA CICHÓN 2008 T

**79**

## ERNESTO RODRÍGUEZ PÉREZ

Barrio, 13 Figueiroá
27460 Sober (Lugo)
☎: 982 152 410

VIÑA PEÓN 2008 T

**85** Colour: purple rim. Nose: expressive, raspberry, floral. Palate: fleshy, good structure, fruity, fresh, balsamic.

## JAVIER SEOANE NOVELLE

A Peroxa, 68
32150 A Peroxa (Ourense)
☎: 626 554 003 - Fax: 988 206 898
pradio.rs@gmail.com
www.pradio.org

PRÁDIO DE SEOANE 2008 T
mencía 85%, merenzao 15%, brancellao %

**83**

## JOSÉ MANUEL RODRÍGUEZ GONZÁLEZ

Vilachá - Doade
27424 Sober (Lugo)
☎: 982 460 613

DÉCIMA 2008 T
mencia

**87** Colour: bright cherry. Nose: fruit expression, red berry notes, floral, complex. Palate: full, fruity, fresh.

PRISCILLVS

## JOSÉ RODRÍGUEZ PRIETO

Barantes de Riba
27421 Sober (Lugo)
☎: 982 152 570

VIÑA REGUEIRAL 2008 T
mencía

**82**

## LEIRABELLA S.L.

Leirabella - Sacardebois
32747 Parada do Sil (Ourense)
☎: 988 290 003 - Fax: 988 290 003

BELLALEIRA 2008 T
mencía 90%, tempranillo 10%

**83**

## MARÍA ESTHER TEIJEIRO LEMOS

Pincelo - A Sariña
27517 Chantada (Lugo)
☎: 982 171 666 - Fax: 982 441 281

DIEGO DE LEMOS 2008 T
mencía

**86** Colour: cherry, purple rim. Nose: dried flowers, fruit expression. Palate: flavourful, light-bodied, good finish.

## PEDRO MANUEL RODRÍGUEZ PÉREZ

Sanmil, 41 Santa Cruz de Brosmos
27425 Sober (Lugo)
☎: 982 152 508 - Fax: 982 402 000
adegasguimaro@gmail.com

EL PECADO 2007 T

**91** Colour: dark-red cherry. Nose: closed, macerated fruit, fruit expression. Palate: powerful, flavourful, sweetness, fine bitter notes.

GUIMARO

## REGINA VIARUM

Doade, s/n
27424 Sober (Lugo)
☎: 619 009 777 - Fax: 986 227 129
info@reginaviarum.es
www.reginaviarum.es

REGINA VIARUM GODELLO 2008 B

**82**

REGINA VIARUM 2008 T
mencía

**85** Colour: cherry, purple rim. Nose: expressive, floral, wild herbs. Taste fresh, full, long.

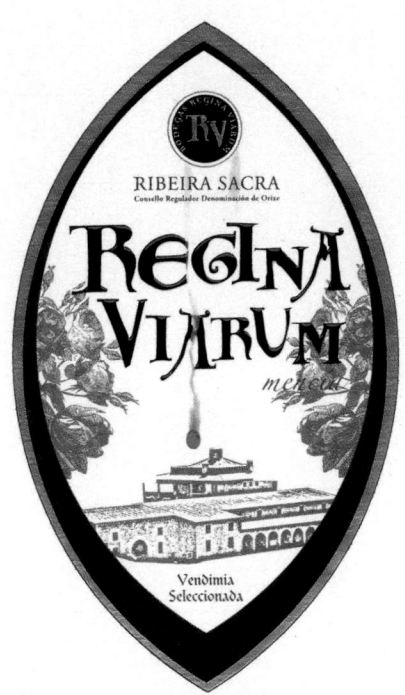

VÍA IMPERIAL 2008 T

**83**

REGINA EXPRESIÓN 2007 T BARRICA
mencía

**79**

VÍA APPIA

## ROSA MARÍA PUMAR RODRÍGUEZ

Salgueiros, 8 Rozabales
27413 Monforte de Lemos (Lugo)
☎: 689 175 981

SAN MAMED 2008 T

**86** Colour: cherry, purple rim. Nose: floral, fresh fruit, raspberry. Palate: fresh, fruity, long.

## VÍA ROMANA

A Ermida - Belesar, s/n
27500 Chantada (Lugo)
☎: 982 454 005 - Fax: 982 454 094
viaromana@viaromana.es
www.viaromana.es

VÍA ROMANA MENCÍA 2007 T BARRICA
mencía

**87** Colour: cherry, purple rim. Nose: balsamic herbs, wild herbs, ripe fruit, candied fruit. Palate: fleshy, great length, flavourful, fresh.

VÍA ROMANA SELECCIÓN DE AÑADA MAGNUM 2006 T

**87** Colour: bright cherry. Nose: sweet spices, expressive, undergrowth. Palate: flavourful, fruity, toasty, round tannins.

VÍA ROMANA MENCÍA 2006 T BARRICA

**87** Colour: ruby red. Nose: varietal, sweet spices, macerated fruit. Palate: balsamic, fresh, flavourful.

SOME OTHER WINERIES WITHIN THE DO:

**ADEGA DON RAMÓN S.L.
ADEGA PONTE MOURULLE
ADEGAS E VIÑEDOS LAREU
ADEGAS SAN JOSÉ
ADEGAS VIÑA GAROÑA S.L.
AMEDO**

AMELIA LEDO VENCE
AS OUBENZAS
BODEGA LOSADA FERNÁNDEZ
BODEGA SOUTELO
BODEGAS BOURIZA
BODEGAS SANTA MARÍA DE NOGUEIRA S.L.
CABO DO MUNDO
CASA NOGUEDO C.B.
CHAO DO COUSO
EDELMIRO DOMÍNGUEZ GONZÁLEZ
ELADIO MARTÍNEZ FERNÁNDEZ
EMILIO RODRÍGUEZ DÍAZ
ILDEFONSO FERNÁNDEZ RODRÍGUEZ
JAVIER FERNÁNDEZ GONZÁLEZ
JESÚS CONDE RODRÍGUEZ
JORGE CARNERO FIUZA
JORGE FEIJOO GONZÁLEZ
JOSÉ ANTONIO FORTES LÓPEZ
JOSÉ BLANCO LÓPEZ
JOSÉ M. CASTRO SESSE
JOSÉ MANUEL OTERO CASTRO
JOSÉ MANUEL VIDAL LÓPEZ
JOSÉ PÉREZ LÓPEZ
JOSÉ VÁZQUEZ ÁLVAREZ
LAURA LÓPEZ LÓPEZ
M. DEL CARMEN PRADO FERREIRO
M. ISOLINA MOREIRAS MÉNDEZ
MANUEL CALVO MÉNDEZ
MANUEL FERNÁNDEZ RODRÍGUEZ
MANUEL LÓPEZ LÓPEZ
MANUEL MONDELO RODRÍGUEZ
MANUEL VÁZQUEZ PÁRAMO
MANUELA VALDÉS PÉREZ
MARCELINO ALVAREZ GONZÁLEZ
MARÍA DEL CARMEN RODRÍGUEZ RODRÍGUEZ
MARÍA JESÚS LÓPEZ CRISTÓBAL
MARIBEL RODRÍGUEZ GONZÁLEZ
MAXIMINO LÓPEZ VÁZQUEZ
OSCAR FIGUEIRAS SÁNCHEZ
PEDRO PÉREZ FERNÁNDEZ
PENA DAS DONAS
PINCELO
RABELAS S.L.
RAMÓN MARCOS FERNÁNDEZ
SAT OS ERMITAÑOS
TOMÁS ARIAS FERNÁNDEZ
TOMÁS RODRÍGUEZ GONZÁLEZ
VAL DE QUIROGA S.L.
VIRXEN DOS REMEDIOS S.A.T.

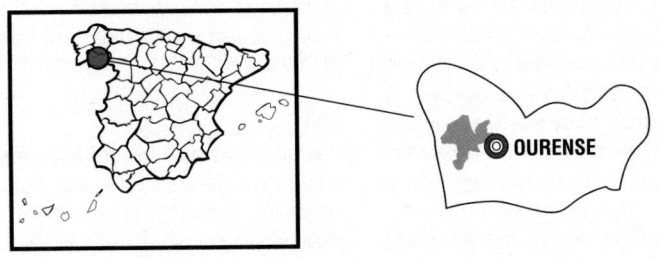

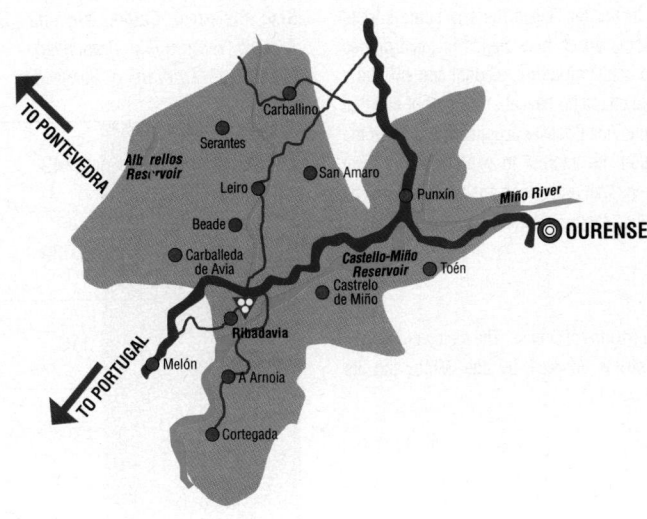

Consejo Regulador
DO Boundary

## NEWS

When Ribeiro seemed overshadowed by the sheer stardom of the albariño grape variety in Rías Baixas or the new and qualitative single-varietal renderings from Monterrei, the region is back to life like phoenix thanks to some lone rangers, small wineries of a truly international reach. A region with a vast vineyard, a little over 30 wineries and almost 90 vine-growers that do not own the vineyards they tend, Ribeiro is more prone to the defence of single varieties in its renderings, as well as copious blends of treixadura, torrontés, loureira, godello and lado and winemaking methods like barrel fermenting or ageing on the lees. The 2007 vintage still shows a fresh, youthful character, as well as some excellent ageing potential, not in vain it got a prize that recognized its excellence last year. As for the 2008, wines are richer, neater, and are a faithful expression of a warmer vintage. In the red wines there is some sort of generational relief based on new blends of local grapes which show good acidic structure, alcohol content and a fantabulous granite character typical of the sort of soil that Ribeiro enjoys. Only Viña Costeira accounts for 35% of the DO total production; its interest to work with the local varieties in single-varietal renderings has been imitated by newer houses like Casanova, Manuel Formigo, Sameirás and Cuñas Davia.

## LOCATION

In the west of the province of Orense. The region comprises 13 municipal districts marked by the Miño and its tributaries.

## CLIMATE

Atlantic, with low temperatures in winter, a certain risk of spring frosts, and high temperatures in the summer months. The average annual rainfall varies between 800 mm and 1,000 mm.

## SOIL

Predominantly granite, deep and rich in organic matter, although in some areas clayey soils predominate. The vineyards are on the slopes of the mountains (where higher quality wines are produced) and on the plains.

## GRAPE VARIETIES:

**White:** Preferred: *Treixadura, Torrontés, Palomino, Godello, Macabeo, Loureira* and *Albariño*. Authorized: *Albilla, Macabeo, Jerez*. Experimental: *Lado*.
**Red:** Preferred: *Caíño, Alicante, Sousón, Ferrón, Mencía, Tempranillo, Brancellao*.
Authorized: *Tempranillo, Garnacha*.

| | |
|---|---|
| **Hectares of Vineyard** | 2,749 |
| **Nº Viticulturists** | 6,029 |
| **Nº of Bodegas** | 119 |
| **2008 Harvest** | Excellent |
| **2007 Production** | 7,296,125 l. |
| **Marketing** | 95% domestic 5% export |

**CONSEJO REGULADOR**
Salgado Moscoso, 9
32400 Ribadavia (Orense).
☎: 988 477 200 - Fax: 988 477 20
@ info@ribeiro.es
www.ribeiro.es

## GENERAL CHARACTERISTICS OF THE WINES:

| | |
|---|---|
| **WHITES** | These are the most characteristic of the DO. The wines, produced from the autochtonous varieties (mainly *Treixadura* and *Torrontés*, although *Lairo*, *Loureira* and *Godello* are also used), are characterised by their fresh and fruity nose with notes of green apple, fennel and hints of flowers; on the palate they have good acidity, which makes them very fresh. Those produced from *Palomino*, however, are much more neutral, nosetically limited and less expressive on the palate. |
| **REDS** | The production is limited compared to the white wines. The most common are based on a non-local grape variety, the *Alicante*, exported after the phylloxera outbreak, which gives wines of medium quality and which are somewhat aggressive and acidic. Those of *Mencía*, on the other hand, have greater nosetic potency; they are fresh, light and pleasant to drink. Another line, still quite new, are the reds that experiment with other autochthonous grapes (*Brancellao*, *Caiño*, *Sousón* and *Ferrón*), which are more characteristic, but which, on some occasions, provide slight vegetative and herb sensations. |

## 2008 VINTAGE RATING:

### VERY GOOD

## A PORTELA S.A.T.

Piñeiros, s/n
32431 Beade (Orense)
☎: 988 480 050 - Fax: 988 480 201
beade@beadeprimacia.com
www.beadeprimacia.com

BEADE PRIMACÍA 2008 B
treixadura

**88** Colour: yellow, pale. Nose: fresh fruit, tropical fruit. Palate: fruity, flavourful, full.

SEÑORÍO DE BEADE

## ADEGA CASAL DE ARMÁN

Cotiño- San Andres-Ribadavia
32415 Ribadavia (Orense)
☎: 699 060 464 - Fax: 988 484 801
hotel@casaldearman.net
www.casaldearman.net

ARMÁN 2007 BFB
treixadura, albariño, godello

**86** Colour: bright yellow. Nose: ripe fruit, creamy oak, tropical fruit. Palate: fruity, flavourful, creamy, spicy.

CASAL DE ARMÁN 2007 B

**84**

## ADEGA DO MOUCHO

Trasmesones, 13
32400 Rivadavia (Ourense)
☎: 650 105 723
adegadomoucho@terra.es
www.adegadomoucho.com

ADEGA DO MOUCHO 2007 B

**87** Colour: bright straw. Nose: spicy, rancio notes, balsamic herbs. Palate: flavourful, fruity, good acidity, balanced.

## ADEGA DOS HECTÁREAS

San Francisco, 12 Bajo
32400 Ribadavia (Orense)
☎: 988 470 591
doshectareas@yahoo.es

DOS HECTÁREAS 2007 B
Treixadura, albariño, lado, godello

**83**

## ADEGA MANUEL FORMIGO

Cabo de Vila, 49
32431 Beade (Ourense)
☎: 627 569 885
info@fincateira.com
www.fincateira.com

FINCA TEIRA 2008 B

**88** Colour: straw. Nose: ripe fruit, balsamic herbs, spicy, white flowers. Palate: fresh, fruity, full, balsamic.

TEIRA X 2007 B
treixadura, alvilla, loureira, albariño

**86** Colour: bright straw. Nose: fruit expression, fresh fruit, balsamic herbs, damp earth. Palate: full, fruity, powerful, balsamic, long.

FINCA TEIRA 2007 B

**85** Colour: yellow. Nose: balsamic herbs, citrus fruit, tropical fruit, spicy. Palate: fruity, fresh, flavourful, good acidity.

TOSTADO DE TEIRA 2006 B

**90** Colour: old gold, amber rim. Nose: fruit liqueur notes, dry nuts, fine reductive notes, roasted almonds, aged wood nuances. Palate: powerful, flavourful, spirituous, creamy.

FINCA TEIRA 2008 T

**84**

## ADEGA MANUEL ROJO

Os Chaos
32417 Arnoia ()
☎: 670 309 688

MANUEL ROJO 2007 B

**82**

## ADEGA MARÍA DO PILAR

Casardeita, 14
32430 Castrelo de Miño (Ourense)
☎: 988 475 236 - Fax: 988 475 236
adega@adegamariadopilar.com
www.adegamariadopilar.com

SENLLEIRO SELECCIÓN 2007 B
godello 70%, treixadura 30%

## 70

RECHAMANTE 2007 T
mencía 50%, tempranillo 50%

**85** Colour: cherry, purple rim. Nose: red berry notes, raspberry, lactic notes, floral. Palate: flavourful, fruity, great length.

### ADEGA PAZO DO MAR

Ctra. Ourense-Castrelo, km. 12,5
32940 Feá (Ourense)
☎: 988 261 256 - Fax: 988 261 264
info@pazodomar.com
www.pazodomar.com

EXPRESIÓN DE PAZO DO MAR 2008 B
treixadura 100%

## 83

PAZO DO MAR 2008 B
treixadura, torrontés, godello

## 82

EXPRESIÓN DE PAZO DO MAR B BARRICA
treixadura

**89** Colour: bright yellow. Nose: expressive, fruit expression, smoky. Palate: flavourful, balanced, great length.

NEREIDA
TORRE DO OLIVAR

### ADEGAS AUREA LUX

Esposende
32415 Cenlle (Ourense)
☎: 988 470 368
info@aurealux.com
www.aurealux.com

LEIVE 2007 B
treixadura

## 82

PARADIGMA LEIVE 2007 B

## 78

AUREA LUX

### ADEGAS FRANCISCO FERNÁNDEZ

Prado, 14
32430 Castrelo do Miño (Ourense)

☎: 986 272 148 - Fax: 986 272 148
info@terraminei.com
www.terraminei.com

LAGAR DE BRAIS 2008 B
palomino 80%, torrontés 20%

## 79

TERRA MINEI 2007 B
treixadura 100%

**87** Colour: bright straw. Nose: fresh fruit, scrubland, fresh. Palate: flavourful, fruity, unctuous.

### ADEGAS PARENTE GARCÍA, S.L.PONTEVEDRA

As Chabolas, 22
32454 Cenlle (Ourense)
☎: 660 411 350 - Fax: 986 330 443
adegasparente@yahoo.es

QUINTA DO AVELINO 2008 B

**88** Colour: bright straw. Nose: fresh, fresh fruit, white flowers, expressive. Palate: flavourful, fruity, good acidity, balanced.

QUINTA DO AVELINO 2007 B

## 84

PAZO DOS FONDÁS

### ADEGAS VALDAVIA

Lugar de Puzos s/n Cuñas
32454 Cenlle (Ourense)
☎: 669 892 681
www.adegasvaldavia.com

CUÑAS DAVIA 2008 B JOVEN
treixadura, albariño, loureiro, lado, torrontés

**87** Colour: straw. Nose: citrus fruit, balsamic herbs, dried herbs, mineral. Palate: flavourful, full, good acidity.

CUÑAS DAVIA 2007 BFB
treixadura 80%, albariño 20%

**87** Colour: straw. Nose: elegant, dried herbs, balsamic herbs, sweet spices. Palate: good acidity, rich.

### ALEMPARTE

Lg. Gomariz, s/n
32429 Leiro (Ourense)
☎: 988 488 295 - Fax: 988 271 223
gestrico@telefonica.net

# DO RIBEIRO

AIRÓN 2007 B

## 82

### ALFONSO ALBOR RODRÍGUEZ

Coedo Cenlle
32454 (Ourense)
☎: 626 903 725

PAZOS DE ALBOR B
treixadura

## 77

### ANTONIO MONTERO SOBRINO

Santa María
32430 Castrelo do Miño (Ourense)
☎: 988 471 132

ANTONIO MONTERO "AUTOR" 2008 B
treixadura 70%, torrontés 20%, lado 10%, loureiro %

**88** Colour: straw. Nose: fruit expression, citrus fruit, balsamic herbs, dry stone. Palate: flavourful, rich, balsamic.

### ARCO DA VELLA A ADEGA DE ELADIO

Plaza de España, 1
32431 Beade (Ourense)
☎: 607 487 060 - Fax: 986 376 800
bodega@bodegaeladio.com
www.bodegaeladio.com

TORQUE DO CASTRO 2007 B
treixadura, godello, albariño, loureiro, torrontés

## 77

TARABELO 2006 T
caíño, brancellao, souson, ferron

## 79

### BODEGA CASTRO REI S.L.

Sampaio
32400 Ribadavia (Ourense)
☎: 988 472 069 - Fax: 988 472 069
castrorei@hotmail.com
www.castrorei.com

DIVINO REI 2008 B

## 82

CASTRO REI

### BODEGA COOP. SAN ROQUE

Ctra. Ribadavia - Carballiño, km. 4
32431 Beade (Ourense)
☎: 988 471 522 - Fax: 988 471 502
adegas@terradocastelo.com
www.terradocastelo.com

TERRA DO CASTELO TREIXADURA B
treixadura

## 82

TERRA DO CASTELO TREIXADURA SELECCIÓN B
treixadura

## 81

PARDIÑEIRO B

## 79

CARAVEL
FLORAVIA
TERRA DE CORCRES
TERRA DO AVIA

### BODEGAS CAMPANTE

Finca Reboreda, s/n
32941 Puga (Ourense)
☎: 988 261 212 - Fax: 988 261 213
info@campante.com
www.campante.com

GRAN REBOREDA 2008 B
treixadura 80%, godello 10%, loureiro 10%

## 84

VIÑA REBOREDA 2008 B
treixadura 80%, palomino 20%

## 81

ALMA DE REBOREDA TOSTADO 2005 B
treixadura 100%

**94** Colour: old gold, amber rim. Nose: grapey, candied fruit, honeyed notes, dry stone, scrubland, pattiserie, varnish. Palate: full, flavourful, good acidity, unctuous.

VIÑA REBOREDA 2008 T
mencía 100%

## 82

### BODEGAS DOCAMPO S.A.

32414 Ribadavia (Ourense)

☎: 988 470 258 - Fax: 988 470 421
admin@bodegasdocampo.com
www.bodegasdocampo.com

VIÑA DO CAMPO 2008 B
torrontés, treixadura

**81**

VIÑA DO CAMPO 2007 B BARRICA

**85** Colour: bright yellow. Nose: ripe fruit, sweet spices, fragrant herbs. Palate: rich, smoky aftertaste, flavourful, fresh, good acidity.

VENDIMIA ORO 2007 B
treixadura, torrontés, lado, loureiro

**81**

## BODEGAS NAIROA S.L.

A Ponte
32417 Arnoia (Ourense)
☎: 988 492 867 - Fax: 988 107 007
info@bodegasnairoa.com

ALBERTE 2008 B
treixadura 80%, torrontés 20%

**84**

VAL DE NAIROA 2008 B
treixadura 70%, albariño 20%, lado 10%

**82**

GRAN NAIROA
TERRALONGA

## BODEGAS O'VENTOSELA

Ctra. N-120, s/n
32574 Grova-Rivadabia (Ourense)
☎: 988 471 947 - Fax: 988 471 205
bodegas@oventosela.es

VIÑA LEIRIÑA 2008 B

**84**

GRAN LEIRIÑA 2007 B

**78**

O'VENTOSELA

## CUNQUEIRO S.L.

Prado, 4

32430 Castrelo de Miño (Orense)
☎: 988 489 023 - Fax: 988 489 082
info@bodegascunqueiro.es
www.bodegascunqueiro.es

CUNQUEIRO III MILENIUM 2008 B
treixadura, godello, loureiro, albariño

**87** Colour: bright yellow. Nose: elegant, fresh fruit, tropical fruit, floral. Palate: fresh, good structure, complex.

CUQUEIRA 2008 B
torrontés 40%, treixadura 60%, godello %

**82**

## EDUARDO PEÑA

Carrero Blanco s/n Barral
Castelo de Miño (Ourense)
☎: 629 872 130
eduardo@cafelatino.es

EDUARDO PEÑA 2008 B

**86** Colour: bright yellow, pale. Nose: neat, citrus fruit, tropical fruit. Palate: fresh, fruity, balanced, good acidity.

## EMILIO DOCAMPO DIÉGUEZ

San Andrés, 57
32400 Ribadavia (Ourense)
☎: 988 491 804 - Fax: 988 275 318
emilioddieguez@mixmail.com

CASAL DE PAULA 2008 B BARRICA
treixadura 100%

**88** Colour: yellow. Nose: neat, powerfull, elegant, fresh fruit, balsamic herbs, spicy, floral. Palate: fresh, fruity, creamy.

CASAL DE PAULA 2007 B
treixadura 75%, torrontés 15%, albariño 10%

**82**

SENSO VADÍO 2008 T
souson 33%, ferrón 33%, mencía 33%

**85** Colour: deep cherry. Nose: fruit expression, macerated fruit, raspberry, floral, undergrowth. Palate: complex, flavourful, easy to drink.

VIÑA DIÉGUEZ

## EMILIO ROJO

Lugar de Remoiño, s/n

32233 Arnoia (Orense)
☎: 988 488 050

EMILIO ROJO 2008 B

**90** Colour: yellow, straw. Nose: powerful, fruit expression, grassy, fresh. Palate: rich, fresh, complex, flavourful.

## JAVIER MONSALVE ALVAREZ

Villa Paz - A Ponte s/n
32417 Arnoia (Ourense)
☎: 677 457 614
eloilorenzo.es

ELOI LORENZO B
**83**

## JOSÉ ESTÉVEZ FERNÁNDEZ

Ponte
32417 Arnoia (Ourense)
☎: 696 402 970

MAURO E. ALVAREZ 2008 B
**82**

## JOSÉ GONZÁLEZ ALVAREZ

32427 Gomariz - Leiro (Ourense)
☎: 988 488 223

EDUARDO BRAVO PARAJE FLOR DE VIDES 2007 B
treixadura, albariño, torrontés

**85** Colour: yellow, pale, greenish rim. Nose: fresh fruit, tropical fruit, grassy. Palate: fruity, flavourful.

PAZO LALÓN 2007 B
treixadura
**79**

## JOSÉ MERENS MARTÍNEZ

Chaos
32417 Arnoia (Ourense)
☎: 607 533 314

LAGAR DO MERENS 2008 B
treixadura, lado

**89** Colour: bright straw, greenish rim. Nose: expressive, ripe fruit, tropical fruit, scrubland, dry stone. Palate: fruity, rich, powerful, balsamic.

LAGAR DO MERENS 2007 BFB

**90** Colour: yellow. Nose: spicy, dried herbs, balsamic herbs. Palate: flavourful, good acidity, elegant.

## MENTINI & MENTINI

Area Portuaria de Bouzas, s/n
36208 Vigo (Pontevedra)
☎: 986 246 608 - Fax: 986 246 664
mentini@mentini.es
www.mentini.es

MENTINI 2008 B
treixadura 80%, albariño 10%, lado 10%

**88** Colour: straw, pale. Nose: fresh fruit, fresh, grassy. Palate: rich, full, long, fine bitter notes.

De la unión de dos almas gemelas, se crea la fusión armoniosa, completa, de piel delicada la una, elegante y distinguida la otra . Nace así un vino natural y fresco, con toda la esencia y el carácter de la tierra Gallega.

Producción limitada a 5900 botellas

## PAZO CASANOVA

Camiño Souto do Río, 1
Santa Cruz de Arrabaldo
32990 Ourense (Ourense)
☎: 988 384 196 - Fax: 988 384 196
casanova@pazocasanova.com
www.pazocasanova.com

CASANOVA 2008 B
treixadura 80%, loureira 20%, albariño %, godello %

**87** Colour: straw. Nose: balsamic herbs, mineral, white flowers, complex. Palate: rich, fruity, balsamic, good acidity.

CASANOVA MÁXIMA 2008 B
treixadura 60%, godello 40%

**86** Colour: straw. Nose: grapey, white flowers, dried herbs. Palate: fresh, fruity.

## PAZO DE VIEITE

Ctra. Ribadavia Carbadiño, km. 6
32419 Vieite Leiro (Ourense)
☎: 988 488 229 - Fax: 988 488 229
info@pazodevieite.es

VIÑA FARNADAS 2008 B
treixadura 85%, godello 15%, albariño %, loureiro %, torrontés %

**78**

## PAZO LODEIRO
## (XULIO VÁZQUEZ QUINTELA)

O Barón Carvalliño
32500 (Ourense)
☎: 988 243 426

SEÑORÍO DO BARÓN 2007 B

**80**

PAZO LODEIRO 2007 B

**79**

## PAZO TIZÓN

Pol. Ind. Aimayor c/ Estaño, 4
28330 San Martín de la Vega (Madrid)
☎: 639 788 788
admon@pazotizon.com
www.pazotizon.com

EXTRAMUNDI 2007 B
albariño 50%, treixadura 50%

**80**

## PEÑA S.C.

Rua da Igrexa, 4 Vide
32430 Castrelo de Miño (Ourense)
☎: 988 489 094 - Fax: 988 489 094
info@lancero.es

VIÑA ENXIDO 2008 B
palomino 75%, autóctonas 25%

**80**

SEÑORÍO DO LANCERO 2008 B
treixadura, torrontés, godello

**79**

## PRODUCCIONES AMODIÑO, S.L.

32420 Cubilledo-Gomariz-Leiro (Ourense)
☎: 669 855 755
sanclodiovino@gmail.com

SANCLODIO 2008 B

**85** Colour: straw. Nose: grapey, white flowers, characterful, expressive. Palate: fresh, fruity, flavourful.

## SAMEIRAS

San Andrés, 98
32415 Ribadavia (Ourense)
☎: 988 491 812 - Fax: 988 470 591
sameiras@terra.es

1040 SAMEIRÁS 2008 B
treixadura, lado, godello, albariño

**90** Colour: bright straw. Nose: fresh, fresh fruit, white flowers, expressive. Palate: flavourful, fruity, good acidity, balanced.

SAMEIRÁS 2008 B
treixadura, albariño, lado, godello

**89** Colour: bright yellow. Nose: fresh fruit, citrus fruit, grassy. Palate: flavourful, full, long.

1040 SAMEIRÁS 2007 B
treixadura, lado, godello, albariño

**91** Colour: bright yellow, greenish rim. Nose: characterful, candied fruit, smoky, complex. Palate: flavourful, fruity, good structure.

SAMEIRÁS 2007 B

**79**

VIÑA DO AVÓ

## VALDEPUGA S.L.

Ctra. de Ourense a Cortegada, km 10
32940 Alongos -Toén (Ourense)
☎: 988 222 772 - Fax: 988 222 561
valdepuga@grupopuga.com
www.bodegasvaldepuga.com

TERRABOA 2008 B
treixadura, albariño, godello

**78**

VALDEPUGA 2008 B
treixadura, albariño, godello, loureiro

**77**

## VICENTE GIRALDEZ FERNÁNDEZ

Cenlle
32454 Cenlle (Ourense)
☎: 988 404 030

ALECRIN 2007 B

**83**

## VILERMA

Villerma - Gomariz
32429 Leiro (Ourense)
☎: 988 228 702 - Fax: 988 248 580

VILERMA 2008 B

**88** Colour: bright straw. Nose: fresh, fresh fruit, white flowers, expressive. Palate: flavourful, fruity, good acidity, balanced.

## VIÑA MEIN S.L.

Mein, s/n
32420 Leiro (Ourense)
☎: 617 326 248 - Fax: 988 488 732
info.bodega@vinamein.com
www.vinamein.com

VIÑA MEIN 2008 B
godello, loureira, torrontes, albariño, lado, albilla

**92** Colour: bright straw. Nose: fresh, fresh fruit, white flowers, expressive, dried herbs. Palate: flavourful, fruity, good acidity, balanced, balsamic.

VIÑA MEIN 2007 BFB

**92** Colour: bright yellow. Nose: balsamic herbs, smoky, candied fruit. Palate: good structure, elegant, unctuous, long.

## VITIVINÍCOLA DEL RIBEIRO S.C.G.

Valdepereira
32415 Ribadavia (Ourense)
☎: 902 636 466 - Fax: 988 470 330
comercial@pazoribeiro.com
www.vinoribeiro.com

VIÑA COSTEIRA 2008 B

**85** Colour: yellow. Nose: macerated fruit, floral, mineral. Palate: flavourful, light-bodied, fresh, balsamic.

ENTRA EN www.vinoribeiro.com Y EN CATAS ONLINE

PAZO 2008 B

**84**

COLECCIÓN COSTEIRA ALBARIÑO DO RIBEIRO 2008 B

**80**

PAZOS DE ULLOA 2007 B
palomino, otras

**85** Colour: bright straw. Nose: fresh, fresh fruit, expressive, scrubland, spicy. Palate: flavourful, fruity, good acidity, balanced.

COLECCIÓN COSTEIRA TREIXADURA BARRICA
2007 BFB

## 82

COLECCIÓN COSTEIRA TREIXADURA DO RIBEIRO B

**88** Colour: bright straw. Nose: citrus fruit, dry stone, scrubland, floral. Palate: flavourful, fruity, fresh.

ALÉN DA ISTORIA 2008 T

## 84

PAZO 2008 T

## 78

TOSTADO DE COSTEIRA 2006 VINO
NATURALMENTE DULCE

**89** Colour: amber. Nose: balsamic herbs, candied fruit, citrus fruit, dry nuts, varnish, smoky. Palate: powerful, flavourful, concentrated, balsamic.

SOME OTHER WINERIES WITHIN THE DO:

**ADEGAS RIVERA**
**ALANÍS S.A.**
**ANA MARTÍNEZ GONZÁLEZ**
**ANTONIO GARCÍA VÁZQUEZ**
**AURORA LÓPEZ GONZÁLEZ**
**BARBANTIÑO S.L.**
**BODEGA ALFREDO ALVARADO PIRES**
**BODEGA MERLOT IBÉRICA**
**BODEGAS UCEIRA S.C.**
**ELISA COLLARTE BERNÁRDEZ**
**FERNÁNDEZ RODRÍGUEZ S.C.**
**FREIJIDO**
**HEREDEROS DE JESÚS FREIJIDO S.L.**
**JAIME LÓPEZ VÁZQUEZ**
**JOSÉ ARMANDO BANGUESES LÓPEZ**
**JOSÉ CAMILO LÓPEZ RODRÍGUEZ**
**JOSÉ CARLOS GARCÍA FERNÁNDEZ**
**JOSÉ MANUEL BLANCO PÉREZ**
**LOEDA**
**LUIS A. RODRÍGUEZ VÁZQUEZ**
**LUIS BOCIJA CARNERO**
**MARÍA ALVAREZ SERRANO**
**PRADOMINIO**
**REY LAFUENTE**
**RODRÍGUEZ MÉNDEZ**
**XOSE VILLAR FERNÁNDEZ**

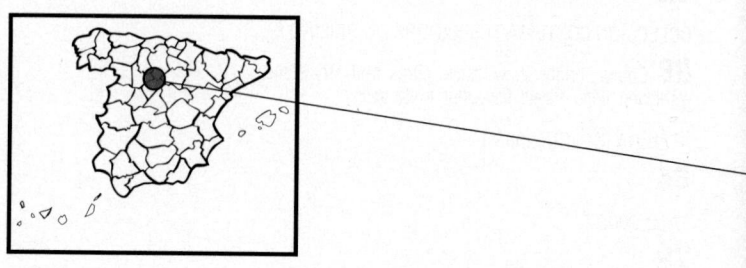

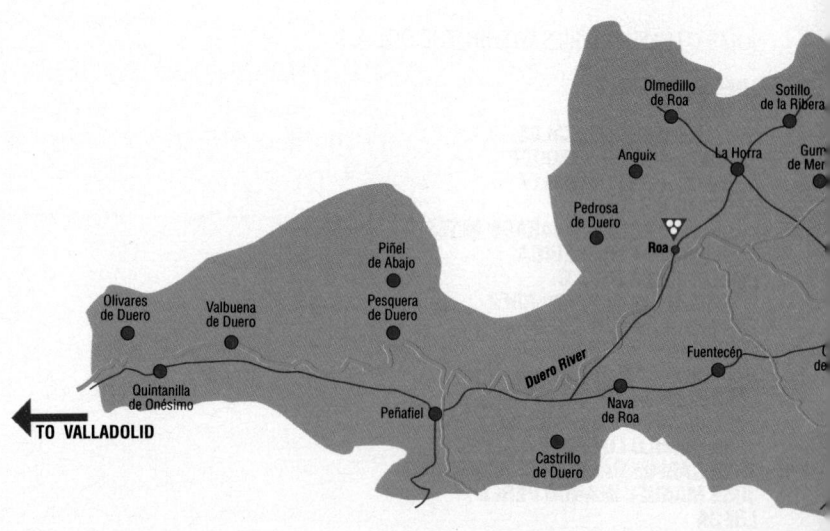

Olmedillo de Roa

Sotillo de la Ribera

Anguix

La Horra

Gum de Mer

Pedrosa de Duero

Roa

Piñel de Abajo

Olivares de Duero

Valbuena de Duero

Pesquera de Duero

Duero River

Fuentecén

Quintanilla de Onésimo

Peñafiel

Nava de Roa

TO VALLADOLID

Castrillo de Duero

▽ Consejo Regulador
● DO Boundary

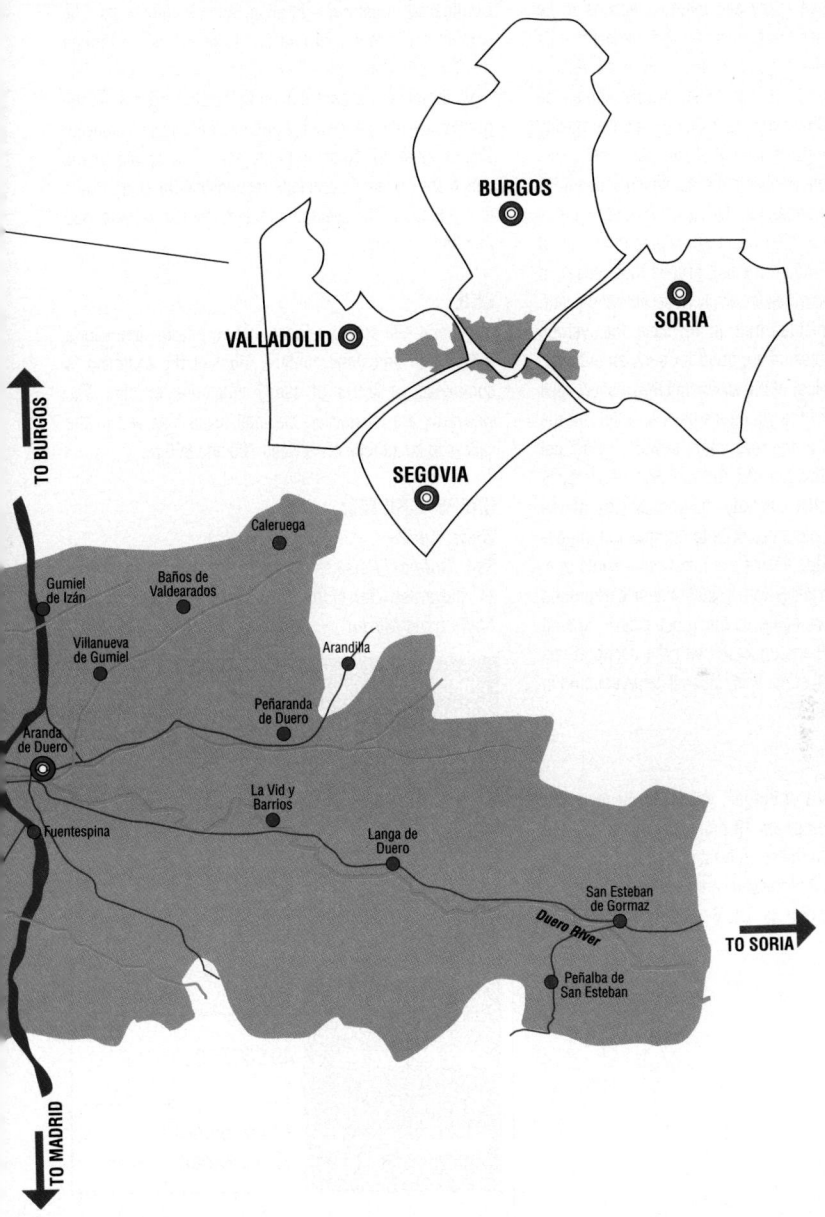

## NEWS

Ribera del Duero has many and various reasons to be jubilant: more wineries, more hectares and the fact that its young wines are the biggest sellers –over 43 million bottles– of a whole 66 million. Still, tasters should be vigilant over the 2008 vintage, renown by the sheer quality of its young renderings, it has not shown yet –obviously– the potential of its longer aged crianzas, which account for most of the international reputation of Ribera. From a climatic point of view, 2008 had a dry winter and a humid springtime, with abundant rainfall, grapes took longer to ripen and some green notes are easily noticeable along with those of heavily confected fruit. In any case, the average colour and fruit expression are good for such an extreme, continental region. Most of the wines undergo a short spell of oak ageing and, of the young we have to point out the excellent expression of the rosé, more powerful and floral than in previous vintages. As for the rest of vintages available in the market, mostly the top cuvées of the wineries made from old vines of tinto fino planted in poor soils, the 2004 vintage seems the most remarkable one, some elegant reserva wines with a solid mineral background that make us believe again in the most classic ageing methods. Protos is back up again with the best and has apparently left behind some wild, inconsistent years. All in all, Ribera remains Ribera.

## LOCATION

Between the provinces of Burgos, Valladolid, Segovia and Soria. This region comprises 19 municipal districts in the east of Valladolid, 5 in the north west of Segovia, 59 in the south of Burgos (most of the vineyards are concentrated in this province with 10,000 Ha) and 6 in the west of Soria.

## CLIMATE

Continental in nature, with slight Atlantic influences. The winters are rather cold and the summers hot, although mention must be made of the significant difference in day-night temperatures contributing to the slow ripening of the grapes, enabling excellent acidity indexes to be achieved. The greatest risk factor in the region is the spring frosts, which are on many occasions responsible for sharp drops in production. The average annual rainfall is between 450 mm and 500 mm.

## SOIL

In general, the soils are loose, not very fertile and with a rather high limestone content. Most of the sediment is composed of layers of sandy limestone or clay. The vineyards are located on the interfluvial hills and in the valleys at an altitude of between 700 and 850 m.

## GRAPE VARIETES:

**White:** *Albillo.*
**Red:** *Tinta del País* (*Tempranillo* – majority with 81% of all vineyards), *Garnacha Tinta, Cabernet Sauvignon, Malbec* and *Merlot.*

| | |
|---|---|
| Hectares of Vineyard | 20,905 |
| Nº Viticulturists | 8,386 |
| Nº of Bodegas | 250 |
| 2008 Harvest | Very Good |
| 2007 Production | 49,000,000 l. |
| Marketing | 72.5% domestic 27.5% export |

**CONSEJO REGULADOR**
Hospital, 6. 09300 Roa (Burgos).
☎: 947 541 221 - Fax: 947 541 116
@ info@doriberadelduero.es
www.riberadelduero.es

## GENERAL CHARACTERISTICS OF THE WINES:

| | |
|---|---|
| **ROSÉS** | They are onion skin coloured, fruity and flavourful, although on occasions they may be a little alcoholic and heavy. |
| **REDS** | These are the top wines of the DO. Produced mainly from a red grape variety of the country (*Tempranillo*), they are an intense cherry colour. On the nose, they are characterised by their noses of very ripe fruit, with the great character of the skins which is normally reminiscent of the smell of ink, although there are also young wines with rustic notes. Ageing in barrels allows these powerful wines to mellow and to acquire greater elegance. Their solid tannins and fine structure make them exceptional products for ageing in wood and in the bottle. On the palate, the red wines from Ribera are powerful, with body and a good balance between alcohol and acidity. |

## 2008 VINTAGE RATING:

# VERY GOOD

# DO RIBERA DEL DUERO

## AALTO, BODEGAS Y VIÑEDOS, S.A.

Paraje Vallejo de Carril, s/n
47360 Quintanilla de Arriba (Valladolid)
☎: 620 351 182 - Fax: 983 683 165
aalto@aalto.es
www.aalto.es

AALTO PS 2005 T

**93** Colour: cherry, garnet rim. Nose: cocoa bean, dark chocolate, sweet spices, toasty, ripe fruit. Palate: flavourful, powerful, fleshy, fruity, spicy, round tannins.

AALTO 2005 T

**92** Colour: cherry, garnet rim. Nose: ripe fruit, lactic notes, fruit preserve. Palate: flavourful, fleshy, powerful, round tannins.

## ABADÍA DE ACÓN

Ctra. Hontangas, km. 0,4
09400 Castrillo de la Vega (Burgos)
☎: 947 509 292 - Fax: 947 508 586
abadiadeacon@abadiadeacon.com
www.abadiadeacon.com

ACÓN 2008 T
tempranillo 100%

**86** Colour: cherry, purple rim. Nose: red berry notes, ripe fruit, lactic notes. Palate: flavourful, warm, fine bitter notes, great length.

ACÓN 2006 T ROBLE
tempranillo 100%

**88** Colour: cherry, garnet rim. Nose: ripe fruit, spicy, creamy oak, toasty, complex, tobacco. Palate: powerful, flavourful, toasty, round tannins.

ACÓN 2005 TC
tempranillo 100%

**90** Colour: cherry, garnet rim. Nose: ripe fruit, spicy, creamy oak, toasty, warm. Palate: powerful, flavourful, toasty, round tannins.

TARGÚM DE AUTOR 2005 TC
tempranillo 100%

**88** Colour: bright cherry. Nose: ripe fruit, sweet spices, creamy oak, expressive, fruit liqueur notes, undergrowth. Palate: flavourful, fruity, toasty, round tannins.

ACÓN 2004 TR
tempranillo 85%, cabernet sauvignon 15%

**90** Colour: cherry, garnet rim. Nose: ripe fruit, spicy, creamy oak, toasty, complex, fine reductive notes, damp earth. Palate: powerful, flavourful, toasty, round tannins, round.

## ALEJANDRO FERNÁNDEZ TINTO PESQUERA

Real nº 2
47315 Pesquera de Duero (Valladolid)
☎: 983 870 037 - Fax: 983 870 088
pesquera@pesqueraafernandez.com
www.grupopesquera.com

TINTO PESQUERA 2006 TC

**88** Colour: cherry, garnet rim. Nose: ripe fruit, spicy, creamy oak, toasty, complex. Palate: powerful, flavourful, toasty, round tannins.

## ALVARO ARRANZ

Ctra. de Valoria, s/n
47315 Pesquera ()
☎: 983 339 581 - Fax: 983 339 581
info@alvaroarranz.com
www.alvaroarranz.com

DÉCIMA TABLA 2006 T ROBLE
tempranillo 100%

**86** Colour: cherry, garnet rim. Nose: powerful, ripe fruit, smoky, earthy notes. Palate: flavourful, powerful, fleshy, round tannins.

DÉCIMA TABLA 2005 TC
tempranillo 100%

**89** Colour: cherry, garnet rim. Nose: ripe fruit, spicy, creamy oak, toasty, dark chocolate. Palate: powerful, flavourful, toasty, round tannins.

## ANTA BANDERAS

Ctra. Palencia-Aranda, km. 68
09443 Villalba de Duero (Burgos)
☎: 947 613 050 - Fax: 947 613 051
natura@antaempresas.com
www.antabodegas.com

ANTA 2008 RD
tempranillo 80%, merlot 20%

**85** Colour: raspberry rose. Nose: powerful, red berry notes, grassy. Palate: fleshy, powerful, fruity, fresh

ANTA A4 NUESTRO EQUILIBRIO 2007 T ROBLE
tempranillo 100%

**83**

ANTA A16 NUESTRA EXCELENCIA 2006 T
tempranillo 80%, cabernet sauvignon 17%, merlot 3%

**86** Colour: bright cherry. Nose: ripe fruit, sweet spices, expressive, grassy, cedar wood. Palate: flavourful, fruity, toasty, round tannins.

ANTA A10 BANDERAS 2006 T

**85** Colour: bright cherry. Nose: ripe fruit, creamy oak, grassy. Palate: flavourful, fruity, toasty, round tannins.

A DE ANTA MAGNUM 2005 T
tempranillo 80%, cabernet sauvignon 20%

**84**

## ARCO DE CURIEL

Calvario, s/n
47316 Curiel del Duero (Valladolid)
☎: 983 880 481 - Fax: 983 881 766
info@arcocuriel.com
www.arcocuriel.com

ARCO DE CURIEL 2008 T
tempranillo 100%

**84**

ARCO DE CURIEL 2007 T
tempranillo 100%

**84**

ARCO DE CURIEL ESPECIAL 2006 T
tempranillo 100%

**85** Colour: dark-red cherry. Nose: sweet spices, toasty, overripe fruit. Palate: flavourful, long, round tannins.

## ARZUAGA NAVARRO

Ctra. N-122, km. 325
47350 Quintanilla de Onésimo (Valladolid)
☎: 983 681 146 - Fax: 983 681 147
bodeg@arzuaganavarro.com
www.arzuaganavarro.com

VIÑEDOS Y BODEGAS LA PLANTA 2008 T ROBLE
tinto fino 100%

**90** Colour: bright cherry. Nose: ripe fruit, toasty, roasted coffee, red berry notes. Palate: flavourful, round tannins, roasted-coffee aftertaste.

TINTO ARZUAGA 2006 TC
tinto fino 90%, cabernet sauvignon 7%, merlot 3%

**89** Colour: very deep cherry. Nose: red berry notes, fruit expression, sweet spices, creamy oak, balanced, toasty. Palate: flavoured, powerful, fruity, roasted-coffee aftertaste.

AMAYA ARZUAGA "COLECCIÓN" 2006 TC
tinto fino 100%

**89** Colour: bright cherry. Nose: ripe fruit, sweet spices, creamy oak, expressive. Palate: flavourful, fruity, toasty, round tannins.

TINTO ARZUAGA 2005 TR
tinto fino 98%, merlot 2%

**90** Colour: deep cherry. Nose: caramel, cedar wood, fruit liqueur notes, ripe fruit. Palate: round tannins, powerful, sweetness, ripe fruit.

ARZUAGA RESERVA ESPECIAL 2005 TR
tinto fino 100%

**88** Colour: deep cherry. Nose: expressive, balanced, spicy, creamy oak, elegant. Palate: powerful, flavourful, fleshy, fruity aftestaste.

GRAN ARZUAGA 2004 T
tinto fino 100%

**92** Colour: cherry, garnet rim. Nose: cedar wood, dark chocolate, sweet spices, fruit expression. Palate: flavourful, good structure, full, round tannins.

TINTO ARZUAGA 2001 TGR
tinto fino 90%, cabernet sauvignon 5%, merlot 5%

**90** Colour: cherry, garnet rim. Nose: expressive, neat, candied fruit, toasty, dark chocolate. Palate: flavourful, spicy, ripe fruit, round tannins.

## ATALAYAS DE GOLBAN S.L.

Ctra. a Montejo, s/n
42345 Atauta (Soria)
☎: 913 020 247 - Fax: 917 661 941
atalayasdegolban@arrakis.es

ATALAYAS DE GOLBAN 2006 T

**89** Colour: bright cherry. Nose: ripe fruit, sweet spices, creamy oak, expressive. Palate: flavourful, fruity, toasty, round tannins.

VIRIDIANA

## BADEN NUMEN S.L.

Carreterilla s/n

47359 San Bernardo Valbuena de Duero (Valladolid)
☎: 615 995 552 - Fax: 983 683 041
bodega@badennumen.es
www.badennumen.es

**BADEN NUMEN "B" 2007 T**
tinto fino 100%

## 84

**BADEN NUMEN "N" 2006 TC**
tinto fino 100%

## 91 Colour: light cherry. Nose: fruit liqueur notes, sweet spices, toasty, complex. Palate: good structure, flavourful, elegant, soft tannins, round

**BADEN NUMEN ORO "AU" 2006 T**
tinto fino 100%

## 91 Colour: cherry, garnet rim. Nose: sweet spices, dark chocolate, fruit liqueur notes. Palate: flavourful, long, great length.

## BODEGA CONVENTO SAN FRANCISCO

Calvario, 22
47300 Peñafiel (Valladolid)
☎: 983 878 052 - Fax: 983 873 052
bodega@bodegaconvento.com
www.bodegaconvento.com

**CONVENTO SAN FRANCISCO 2006 T**
tinta del país 92%, merlot 8%

## 89 Colour: bright cherry. Nose: ripe fruit, sweet spices, creamy oak, expressive. Palate: flavourful, fruity, toasty, round tannins.

**CONVENTO SAN FRANCISCO 2005 T**
tinta del país 90%, merlot 10%

## 85 Colour: cherry, garnet rim. Nose: ripe fruit, spicy, toasty. Palate: powerful, flavourful, toasty, slightly dry, soft tannins, fine bitter notes.

**CONVENTO SAN FRANCISCO SELECCIÓN ESPECIAL 2004 T BARRICA**
tinta del país 90%, merlot 10%

## 91 Colour: cherry, garnet rim. Nose: ripe fruit, spicy, creamy oak, toasty, complex, undergrowth, fruit expression. Palate: powerful, flavourful, toasty, round tannins.

## BODEGA COOP. SAN PEDRO REGALADO

Ctra. de Aranda, s/n
09370 La Aguilera (Burgos)
☎: 947 545 017 - Fax: 947 545 017
bspregalado@terra.es

www.bodegaspregalado.com

**EMBOCADERO 2006 T**
tinta del país 100%

## 85 Colour: bright cherry. Nose: ripe fruit, sweet spices, creamy oak. Palate: flavourful, fruity, toasty, round tannins.

**LLANO DE ELENA SELECCIÓN 2004 T**
tinta del país 100%

## 87 Colour: cherry, garnet rim. Nose: ripe fruit, spicy, toasty, complex, fine reductive notes. Palate: powerful, flavourful, toasty, round tannins.

**EMBOCADERO 2003 T**
tinta del país 100%

## 87 Colour: deep cherry, bright ochre rim. Nose: damp earth, wet leather, fruit preserve, sweet spices. Palate: unctuous, fruity, powerful, round tannins.

## BODEGA COOPERATIVA SANTA ANA

Ctra. De Salas s/n
09410 Peñaranda de Duero (Burgos)
☎: 947 552 011
bodega@bodegasantana.com
www.bodegasantaana.com

**MONTE NEGRO T**

## 84

**CASTILLO DE PEÑARANDA VALDEPISÓN**

## BODEGA COOPERATIVA VIRGEN DE LA ASUNCIÓN

Las Afueras, s/n
09311 La Horra (Burgos)
☎: 947 542 057 - Fax: 947 542 057
nacional@virgendelaasuncion.com
www.virgendelaasuncion.com

**ZARZUELA 2008 RD**
tempranillo 100%

## 85 Colour: onion pink. Nose: elegant, candied fruit, dried flowers, fragrant herbs, red berry notes. Palate: light-bodied, flavourful, good acidity, long, spicy.

**VIÑA VALERA 2007 T**

## 84

**ZARZUELA 6 MESES BARRICA 2007 T BARRICA**
tempranillo 100%

## 82

**ZARZUELA 2006 TC**
tempranillo 100%

**88** Colour: cherry, garnet rim. Nose: ripe fruit, spicy, creamy oak, toasty, complex, balsamic herbs. Palate: powerful, flavourful, toasty, round tannins, good acidity.

**ZARZUELA 2004 TR**
tempranillo 95%, cabernet sauvignon 5%

**89** Colour: bright cherry. Nose: sweet spices, creamy oak, expressive, macerated fruit, undergrowth. Palate: flavourful, fruity, toasty, round tannins, elegant.

## BODEGA DE BLAS SERRANO

Ctra. Santa Cruz s/n
09472 Fuentelcésped (Burgos)
☎: 606 338 632
edb@bodegasdeblasserrano.com

**PHYLOS 2007 T**
tinta del país 100%

## 81

**MATHIS 2006 T**
tinta del país 100%

**91** Colour: cherry, garnet rim. Nose: ripe fruit, spicy, creamy oak, toasty, complex. Palate: powerful, flavourful, toasty, slightly dry, soft tannins.

**DE BLAS SERRANO BODEGAS 2006 T**
tinta del país 100%

**87** Colour: dark-red cherry. Nose: fruit liqueur notes, sweet spices, toasty. Palate: flavourful, full, great length, round tannins.

## BODEGA DOMINIO ROMANO

Los Lagares, s/n
47319 Rábano (Valladolid)
☎: 983 871 515 - Fax: 983 871 515
dominioromano@dominioromano.com

**DOMINIO ROMANO 2006 T**

**89** Colour: cherry, garnet rim. Nose: ripe fruit, spicy, creamy oak, toasty, complex. Palate: powerful, flavourful, toasty, round tannins.

**DOMINIO ROMANO RDR 2006 T**

**88** Colour: cherry, garnet rim. Nose: ripe fruit, spicy, creamy oak, toasty, complex, aromatic coffee. Palate: powerful, flavourful, toasty, round tannins.

## BODEGA MATARROMERA

Ctra. Renedo-Pesquera, km. 30
47359 Valbuena de Duero (Valladolid)
☎: 983 107 100 - Fax: 902 430 189
matarromera@matarromera.es
www.grupomatarromera.com

**MATARROMERA 2006 TC**
tempranillo 100%

**88** Colour: deep cherry. Nose: cocoa bean, fruit preserve. Palate: flavourful, full, round tannins.

**MATARROMERA 2004 TR**
tempranillo 100%

**88** Colour: cherry, garnet rim. Nose: ripe fruit, spicy, creamy oak, toasty, mineral. Palate: powerful, flavourful, toasty, round tannins.

**MATARROMERA PRESTIGIO 2003 TC**
tempranillo 100%

**89** Colour: cherry, garnet rim. Nose: powerful, candied fruit, ripe fruit, caramel, aromatic coffee. Palate: good structure, spirituous, spicy, round tannins.

**MATARROMERA PRESTIGIO PAGO DE LAS SOLANAS 2001 T ROBLE**
tempranillo 100%

**92** Colour: cherry, garnet rim. Nose: ripe fruit, spicy, creamy oak, toasty, complex, wet leather. Palate: powerful, flavourful, toasty, round tannins, spicy.

**MATARROMERA 2001 TGR**
tempranillo 100%

**90** Colour: cherry, garnet rim. Nose: medium intensity, ripe fruit, spicy, varnish. Palate: flavourful, good structure, easy to drink, spicy, classic aged character.

MATARROMERA

Gran Reserva

RIBERA DEL DUERO
RED WINE
BODEGA MATARROMERA, S.A.
ALC. 13.5% By VOL VALBUENA DE DUERO (España) 118 N° 78593. PRODUCT OF SPAIN
750 ML

# DO RIBERA DEL DUERO

MELIOR 2007 T
tempranillo 95%, cabernet sauvignon 5%

**82**

## BODEGA PAGO DE CIRSUS

Ctra. de Ablitas a Ribaforada, km. 5
31523 Ablitas (Navarra)
☎: 948 386 210 - Fax: 629 354 190
bodegasin@pagodecirsus.com
www.pagodecirsus.com

SENDA DE LOS OLIVOS VENDIMIA SELECCIONADA
2007 T
tempranillo 100%

**88** Colour: cherry, garnet rim. Nose: roasted coffee, fruit preserve, overripe fruit, lactic notes, wet leather. Palate: flavourful, powerful, round tannins.

SENDA DE LOS OLIVOS FINCA LA CARRASCA 2005 T
tempranillo 100%

**86** Colour: cherry, garnet rim. Nose: dark chocolate, spicy, creamy oak. Palate: powerful, fleshy, harsh oak tannins.

## BODEGA PÁRAMO ARROYO

Ctra. de Roa Pedrosa, km. 4
09314 Pedrosa de Duero (Burgos)
☎: 947 530 041 - Fax: 947 530 036
bodega@paramoarroyo.com
www.paramoarroyo.com

VIÑA EREMOS 2007 T ROBLE
tempranillo 100%

**87** Colour: cherry, garnet rim. Nose: mineral, ripe fruit, sweet spices, scrubland. Palate: flavourful, ripe fruit, spicy.

EREMUS 2005 TC
tempranillo 100%

**88** Colour: very deep cherry. Nose: aromatic coffee, cocoa bean, candied fruit, creamy oak. Palate: fleshy, full, slightly dry, soft tannins.

PÁRAMO ARROYO 2004 T
tempranillo 100%

**86** Colour: cherry, garnet rim. Nose: sweet spices, toasty, cocoa bean, fruit expression. Palate: flavourful, powerful, harsh oak tannins.

## BODEGA RENTO

Santa María, 36
47359 Olivares de Duero (Valladolid)

☎: 902 430 170 - Fax: 902 430 189
emina@emina.es
www.bodegarento.es

RENTO 2004 T
tempranillo 100%

**90** Colour: cherry, garnet rim. Nose: spicy, toasty, complex. Palate: powerful, flavourful, toasty, round tannins.

RENTO 2002 T
tempranillo 100%

**90** Colour: dark-red cherry. Nose: red berry notes, ripe fruit, sweet spices, mineral, aromatic coffee. Palate: flavourful, powerful, rich, spicy, round tannins.

## BODEGA S. ARROYO

Avda. del Cid, 99
09441 Sotillo de la Ribera (Burgos)
☎: 947 532 444 - Fax: 947 532 444
info@tintoarroyo.com
www.tintoarroyo.com

VIÑARROYO 2008 RD
tempranillo 70%, albillo 30%

**80**

ARROYO 2008 T
tempranillo 100%

**84**

TINTO ARROYO 2007 T ROBLE
tempranillo 100%

**82**

TINTO ARROYO VENDIMIA SELECCIONADA 2005 T
tempranillo 100%

**89** Colour: bright cherry. Nose: ripe fruit, sweet spices, creamy oak, expressive, mineral, floral. Palate: flavourful, fruity, toasty, round tannins.

**TINTO ARROYO 2006 TC**
tempranillo 100%

**89** Colour: cherry, garnet rim. Nose: ripe fruit, spicy, complex, dark chocolate. Palate: powerful, flavourful, toasty, round tannins.

**TINTO ARROYO 2005 TR**
tempranillo 100%

**86** Colour: bright cherry. Nose: sweet spices, creamy oak, expressive, fruit preserve, ripe fruit, smoky. Palate: flavourful, fruity, toasty, round tannins.

SEÑORÍO DE SOTILLO
CORNESA

## BODEGA SAN MAMÉS

Ctra. Valladolid, s/n
09315 Fuentecén (Burgos)
☎: 947 532 653 - Fax: 947 532 653
bodegasanmames@wanadoo.es
www.bodegasanmames.com

**VIÑA EL GUIJARRAL 2008 RD**
tempranillo 100%

**80**

**CUESTA ALTA 2007 T**
tempranillo 100%

**81**

**VIÑA EL GUIJARRAL 2007 T**
tempranillo 100%

**80**

**VIÑA EL GUIJARRAL 2006 T ROBLE**
tempranillo 100%

**83**

**VIÑA EL GUIJARRAL VENDIMIA SELECCIONADA 2005 T**
tempranillo 100%

**87** Colour: bright cherry. Nose: ripe fruit, sweet spices, creamy oak, expressive, fruit preserve, dark chocolate. Palate: flavourful, fruity, toasty, round tannins.

**VIÑA EL GUIJARRAL 2005 TC**
tempranillo 100%

**84**

## BODEGA VIÑA VILANO

Ctra. de Anguix, 10
03314 Pedrosa de Duero (Burgos)
☎: 947 530 029 - Fax: 947 530 037
info@vinavilano.com
www.vinavilano.com

# DO RIBERA DEL DUERO

**VIÑA VILANO 2008 RD**
tempranillo 100%

## 83

**VIÑA VILANO 2008 T**
tempranillo 100%

## 84

**VIÑA VILANO 2008 T ROBLE**
tempranillo 100%

## 83

**VIÑA VILANO 2006 TC**
tempranillo 100%

**87** Colour: bright cherry. Nose: ripe fruit, sweet spices, creamy oak, expressive, red berry notes. Palate: flavourful, fruity, toasty, round tannins.

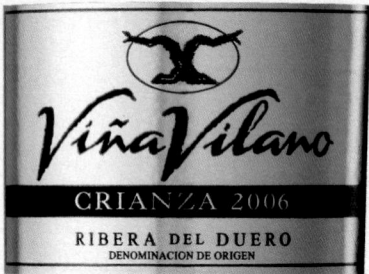

**VIÑA VILANO 2005 TR**
tempranillo 100%

**89** Colour: cherry, garnet rim. Nose: ripe fruit, spicy, toasty, warm. Palate: powerful, flavourful, toasty, round tannins, fine bitter notes.

**TERRA INCÓGNITA 2004 T**
tempranillo 100%

**88** Colour: bright cherry. Nose: ripe fruit, sweet spices, creamy oak, expressive, fruit liqueur notes. Palate: flavourful, fruity, toasty, round tannins, fruity aftertaste.

## BODEGA Y VIÑEDO FUENTECÉN

Cl. La Iglesia, 31
09315 Fuentecén (Burgos)
☎: 947 532 718 - Fax: 947 532 768
info@bodegahemar.com
www.bodegahemar.com

**HEMAR 2008 RD**
tempranillo 100%

**85** Colour: onion pink. Nose: elegant, candied fruit, dried flowers, fragrant herbs, red berry notes. Palate: light-bodied, flavourful, good acidity, long, spicy.

**HEMAR 2007 T ROBLE**
tempranillo 100%

## 82

**HEMAR 2006 TC**
tempranillo 100%

**89** Colour: deep cherry. Nose: fruit liqueur notes, spicy, toasty. Palate: flavourful, powerful, great length, slightly dry, soft tannins.

**LLANUM VENDIMIA SELECCIONADA 2006 T**
tempranillo 100%

**87** Colour: very deep cherry. Nose: toasty, spicy, fruit expression. Palate: flavourful, powerful, long.

## BODEGAS ABADÍA LA ARROYADA

c/La Tejera, s/n
09442 Terradillos de Esgueva (Burgos)
☎: 947 545 309 - Fax: 947 545 309
bodegas@abadialaarroyada.es
www.abadialaarroyada.es

**ABADÍA LA ARROYADA 2007 T ROBLE**
tempranillo 100%

**85** Colour: dark-red cherry. Nose: ripe fruit, dark chocolate, toasty. Palate: flavourful, full, great length.

**ABADÍA LA ARROYADA 2005 TC**
tempranillo 100%

**90** Colour: cherry, garnet rim. Nose: floral, ripe fruit, sweet spices, elegant. Palate: flavourful, good structure, long, fine tannins.

ABBATIA VENDIMIA SELECCIONADA 2004 T
tempranillo 100%

**87** Colour: cherry, garnet rim. Nose: ripe fruit, spicy, toasty, aged wood nuances. Palate: powerful, flavourful, toasty, round tannins.

## BODEGAS ARROCAL S.L.

Eras de Santa María, s/n
09443 Gumiel de Mercado (Burgos)
☎: 947 561 290 - Fax: 947 561 290
arrocal@arrocal.com
www.arrocal.com

ROSA DE ARROCAL 2008 RD
tempranillo 60%, albillo 40%

**83**

ARROCAL 2007 T
tempranillo 100%

**89** Colour: cherry, purple rim. Nose: expressive, fresh fruit, red berry notes, floral, sweet spices. Palate: flavourful, fruity, good acidity, round tannins.

ARROCAL MÁXIMO 2005 T
tempranillo 100%

**91** Colour: cherry, garnet rim. Nose: ripe fruit, spicy, creamy oak, toasty, complex, powerfull. Palate: powerful, flavourful, toasty, round tannins.

ARROCAL SELECCIÓN 2005 T
tempranillo 100%

**87** Colour: deep cherry. Nose: spicy, creamy oak, fruit liqueur notes. Palate: flavourful, great length, powerful tannins.

## BODEGAS ASENJO & MANSO

Ctra. Palencia-Aranda, km. 58,200
09311 La Horra (Burgos)
☎: 636 972 421 - Fax: 947 505 269
info@asenjo-manso.com
www.asenjo-manso.com

CERES 2006 T

**86** Colour: cherry, garnet rim. Nose: spicy, creamy oak, fruit liqueur notes, fruit preserve. Palate: sweet tannins, warm, toasty, ripe fruit, spicy.

SILVANUS TC

**92** Colour: cherry, garnet rim. Nose: ripe fruit, creamy oak, complex, sweet spices. Palate: flavourful, toasty, round tannins.

A&M TC

**90** Colour: very deep cherry. Nose: ripe fruit, sweet spices, creamy oak, expressive. Palate: flavourful, fruity, toasty, round tannins.

## BODEGAS BALBÁS

La Majada s/n
09311 La Horra (Burgos)
☎: 947 542 111 - Fax: 947 542 112
bodegas@balbas.es
www.balbas.es

BALBAS 2006 TC
tempranillo 90%, cabernet sauvignon 10%

**86** Colour: bright cherry. Nose: ripe fruit, sweet spices, creamy oak, expressive. Palate: flavourful, fruity, toasty, round tannins.

BALBAS 2005 TR
tempranillo 90%, cabernet sauvignon 10%

**88** Colour: cherry, garnet rim. Nose: ripe fruit, spicy, creamy oak, toasty, complex. Palate: powerful, flavourful, toasty, round tannins.

RITUS 2004 T
tempranillo 75%, merlot 25%

**89** Colour: bright cherry. Nose: ripe fruit, sweet spices, creamy oak, expressive. Palate: flavourful, fruity, toasty, round tannins.

ALITUS 2001 TR
tempranillo 75%, cabernet sauvignon 20%, merlot 5%

**92** Colour: cherry, garnet rim. Nose: medium intensity, candied fruit, fruit preserve, creamy oak, sweet spices. Palate: flavourful, powerful, fleshy, round tannins.

## BODEGAS BOHORQUEZ

Ctra. Peñafiel, s/n
47315 Pesquera de Duero (Valladolid)
☎: 915 640 508 - Fax: 915 643 751
info@bodegasbohorquez.com
www.bodegasbohorquez.com

BOHORQUEZ MMII 2005 T

**91** Colour: deep cherry, garnet rim. Nose: macerated fruit, floral, powerfull, sweet spices, new oak. Palate: flavourful, full, good acidity, roasted-coffee aftertaste, round tannins.

BOHORQUEZ MMII 2004 T

**91** Colour: deep cherry, brick rim edge. Nose: ripe fruit, red berry notes, sweet spices, cocoa bean, balanced. Palate: powerful, flavourful, rich, fleshy, round, soft tannins.

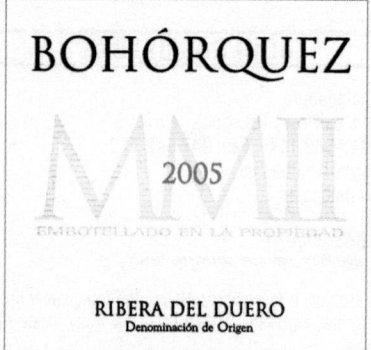

BOHÓRQUEZ
MMII
2005
EMBOTELLADO EN LA PROPIEDAD
RIBERA DEL DUERO
Denominación de Origen

## BODEGAS BRIEGO

Ctra. de Cuellar, s/n
47311 Fompedraza (Valladolid)
☎: 983 892 156 - Fax: 983 892 156
info@bodegasbriego.com
www.bodegasbriego.com

NOVA 2006 TC
tempranillo 100%

**91** Colour: cherry, garnet rim. Nose: sweet spices, dark chocolate, candied fruit, mineral. Palate: flavourful, long, round tannins.

BRIEGO 2006 TC
tempranillo 100%

**85** Colour: bright cherry. Nose: ripe fruit, sweet spices, creamy oak, expressive, cedar wood. Palate: flavourful, fruity, toasty, round tannins.

BRIEGO ADALID 2005 TR
tempranillo 100%

**90** Colour: bright cherry. Nose: ripe fruit, sweet spices, expressive, dark chocolate. Palate: flavourful, fruity, toasty, round tannins.

BRIEGO FIEL 2004 TR
tempranillo 100%

**90** Colour: cherry, garnet rim. Nose: ripe fruit, spicy, toasty, complex. Palate: powerful, flavourful, toasty, round tannins.

OYADA BRIEGO 2004 T
tempranillo 100%

**86** Colour: bright cherry. Nose: ripe fruit, sweet spices, expressive, fruit liqueur notes. Palate: flavourful, fruity, toasty, round tannins, pruney.

BRIEGO 2003 TR
tempranillo 100%

**88** Colour: cherry, garnet rim. Nose: spicy, toasty, tar, fruit preserve. Palate: powerful, flavourful, toasty, round tannins, warm.

Briego
RESERVA
Ribera del Duero
Denominación de Origen
2003
Elaborado y embotellado en la propiedad por Alberto y Benito, s.a.
en Fompedraza (Valladolid) España
750 ml.
13,5% Vol.
Product of Spain
Contiene Sulfitos  Contains Sulphites

NOVA 2003 TR
tempranillo 100%

**88** Colour: cherry, garnet rim. Nose: ripe fruit, spicy, toasty. Palate: powerful, flavourful, toasty, round tannins.

NOVA 1999 TGR
tempranillo 100%

**88** Colour: pale ruby, brick rim edge. Nose: elegant, spicy, fine reductive notes, wet leather, aged wood nuances, fruit liqueur notes. Palate: spicy, fine tannins, long, round.

TIEMPO BRIEGO

## BODEGAS BRIONES BANIANDRÉS

Camino Valdeguzmán, s/n
09314 Quintanamanvirgo (Burgos)
☎: 947 561 385 - Fax: 947 561 386
bodegas@apricus.es
www.apricus.es

APRICUS 2007 T
tinta del país

**87** Colour: cherry, garnet rim. Nose: expressive, red berry notes, white flowers, spicy, toasty. Palate: flavourful, fruity, long, good finish.

## BODEGAS CASTILLO DE GUMIEL

Avda. de Extremadura 55
09400 Aranda de Duero (Burgos)
☎: 947 510 839 - Fax: 947 510 839
castillodegumiel@hotmail.com
www.silenciovaldiruela.com

SILENCIO DE VALDIRUELA 2008 RD
tinta del país 50%, albillo 50%

**86** Colour: onion pink. Nose: elegant, candied fruit, dried flowers, red berry notes. Palate: flavourful, good acidity, long, spicy, unctuous.

SILENCIO DE VALDIRUELA 2008 T
tinta del país 100%

**84**

SILENCIO DE VALDIRUELA 2006 T ROBLE
tinta del país 100%

**86** Colour: bright cherry. Nose: ripe fruit, sweet spices, creamy oak, expressive, undergrowth. Palate: flavourful, fruity, toasty, sweet tannins.

SILENCIO DE VALDIRUELA 2006 TC
tinta del país 100%

**82**

SILENCIO DE VALDIRUELA 2004 TR
tinta del país 100%

**88** Colour: cherry, garnet rim. Nose: spicy, creamy oak, complex, candied fruit. Palate: powerful, flavourful, toasty, round tannins.

## BODEGAS CEPA 21

Ctra. N-122, km. 297
47318 Castrillo de Duero (Valladolid)
☎: 983 484 083 - Fax: 983 480 017
bodega@cepa21.com
www.cepa21.com

CEPA 21 2006 T

**91** Colour: deep cherry, garnet rim. Nose: creamy oak, sweet spices, dark chocolate, ripe fruit. Palate: fleshy, complex, great length.

## BODEGAS CRUZ DE ALBA

Síndico, 4 y 5
47350 Quintanilla de Onésimo (Valladolid)
☎: 941 310 295 - Fax: 941 310 832
www.cruzdealba.es

CRUZ DE ALBA 2006 TC
tempranillo 100%

**90** Colour: bright cherry. Nose: ripe fruit, sweet spices, creamy oak, expressive, fruit liqueur notes. Palate: flavourful, fruity, toasty, round tannins, fruity aftestaste.

CRUZ DE ALBA 2005 TC
tempranillo 100%

**90** Colour: deep cherry. Nose: fruit liqueur notes, fruit preserve, powerfull, warm, aromatic coffee, creamy oak. Palate: powerful, fleshy, sweetness, flavourful, spicy, mineral.

## BODEGAS CUEVAS JIMÉNEZ S.L.

Ctra. Madrid-Irún, N-I Km.165
09370 Gumiel de Izán (Burgos)
☎: 638 007 140 - Fax: 638 010 311
bodega@ferratus.es
www.ferratus.es

FERRATUS 2006 T
tempranillo 100%

**93** Colour: bright cherry. Nose: ripe fruit, sweet spices, creamy oak, expressive. Palate: flavourful, fruity, toasty, round tannins.

FERRATUS SENSACIONES 2005 T
tempranillo 100%

**93** Colour: dark-red cherry. Nose: ripe fruit, sweet spices, creamy oak, expressive, cocoa bean. Palate: flavourful, fruity, mineral, soft tannins.

FERRATUS SENSACIONES 2004 T
tempranillo 100%

**93** Colour: cherry, garnet rim. Nose: ripe fruit, spicy, creamy oak, toasty, complex, raspberry, undergrowth. Palate: powerful, flavourful, toasty, round tannins, balsamic.

## BODEGAS DE LOS RÍOS PRIETO

Ctra. Pesquera-Renedo s/n
47315 Pesquera de Duero (Valladolid)
☎: 983 880 383 - Fax: 983 878 032
info@bodegasdelosriosprieto.com
www.bodegasdelosriosprieto.com

PRIOS MAXIMUS 2008 T ROBLE
tempranillo 100%

**87** Colour: dark-red cherry. Nose: sweet spices, creamy oak, cocoa bean. Palate: flavourful, full, great length, fine tannins.

PRIOS MAXIMUS 2006 TC
tempranillo 95%, cabernet sauvignon 5%

**86** Colour: cherry, garnet rim. Nose: ripe fruit, spicy, toasty, complex, fruit liqueur notes. Palate: powerful, flavourful, round tannins.

PRIOS MAXIMUS 2005 TR
tempranillo 100%

**86** Colour: cherry, garnet rim. Nose: spicy, creamy oak, toasty, complex, fruit preserve, warm. Palate: powerful, flavourful, toasty, round tannins.

LARA PRIOS MAXIMUS VINO DE AUTOR 2005 T
tempranillo 100%

**85** Colour: bright cherry. Nose: ripe fruit, sweet spices, creamy oak, expressive, red berry notes. Palate: flavourful, fruity, toasty, round tannins.

## BODEGAS DIEZ LLORENTE

Ctra. Circunvalación, s/n
09300 Roa (Burgos)
☎: 947 540 341 - Fax: 947 540 341
bodegas@diezllorente.com
www.diezllorente.com

SEÑORÍO DE BRENDA CUATRO MESES EN BARRICA 2008 T
tempranillo 100%

**85** Colour: bright cherry. Nose: ripe fruit, sweet spices, creamy oak, roasted coffee. Palate: flavourful, fruity, toasty, round tannins.

DÍEZ LLORENTE 2008 T ROBLE
tempranillo 100%

**85** Colour: bright cherry. Nose: ripe fruit, sweet spices, creamy oak, expressive. Palate: flavourful, fruity, toasty, round tannins.

SEÑORÍO DE BRENDA COSECHA 2008 T
tempranillo 100%

**78**

DÍEZ LLORENTE 2005 TC
tempranillo 100%

**88** Colour: cherry, garnet rim. Nose: fruit preserve, toasty, floral. Palate: flavourful, fine tannins, great length.

SEÑORÍO DE BRENDA 2005 TC
tempranillo 100%

**85** Colour: cherry, garnet rim. Nose: ripe fruit, spicy, creamy oak, toasty. Palate: powerful, flavourful, toasty, round tannins.

SEÑORÍO DE BRENDA 2004 TR
tempranillo 100%

**88** Colour: cherry, garnet rim. Nose: ripe fruit, spicy, creamy oak, toasty, complex, balsamic herbs. Palate: powerful, flavourful, toasty, round tannins.

## BODEGAS DOMINIO DE ATAUTA

Ctra. a Morcuera s/n
42345 Atauta (Soria)
☎: 913 020 247 - Fax: 917 661 941
dominiodeatauta.ribera@arrakis.es
www.dominiodeatauta.com

DOMINIO DE ATAUTA VALDEGATILES 2007 T

**97** Colour: cherry, garnet rim. Nose: elegant, expressive, balanced, ripe fruit, mineral. Palate: flavourful, fleshy, complex, spicy, ripe fruit, fine tannins.

DOMINIO DE ATAUTA LLANOS DEL ALMENDRO 2007 T

**95** Colour: deep cherry. Nose: elegant, expressive, spicy, cocoa bean, mineral. Palate: flavourful, powerful, fleshy, spicy, ripe fruit, round tannins.

DOMINIO DE ATAUTA LA MALA 2007 T

**94** Colour: cherry, garnet rim. Nose: powerful, ripe fruit, spicy, toasty. Palate: flavourful, fleshy, spicy, ripe fruit, fine tannins.

DOMINIO DE ATAUTA 2006 T
tempranillo

**93** Colour: cherry, garnet rim. Nose: powerful, mineral, ripe fruit, cocoa bean, sweet spices. Palate: flavourful, fruity, spicy, round tannins, fine bitter notes.

## BODEGAS EMILIO MORO

Ctra. Peñafiel - Valoria, s/n
47315 Pesquera de Duero (Valladolid)
☎: 983 878 400 - Fax: 983 870 195
bodega@emiliomoro.com
www.emiliomoro.com

FINCA RESALSO 2007 T

**86** Colour: cherry, purple rim. Nose: floral, red berry notes, sweet spices. Palate: good structure, flavourful, long.

MALLEOLUS DE SANCHO MARTÍN 2006 T

**93** Colour: cherry, garnet rim. Nose: ripe fruit, creamy oak, toasty, complex, new oak. Palate: powerful, flavourful, toasty, round tannins.

MALLEOLUS DE VALDERRAMIRO 2006 T

**92** Colour: cherry, garnet rim. Nose: ripe fruit, spicy, creamy oak, toasty, aromatic coffee, complex. Palate: powerful, flavourful, toasty, round tannins, sweetness.

EMILIO MORO 2006 T

**89** Colour: cherry, garnet rim. Nose: ripe fruit, spicy, creamy oak, toasty, complex, earthy notes. Palate: powerful, flavourful, toasty, round tannins.

MALLEOLUS 2006 T

**88** Colour: cherry, garnet rim. Nose: ripe fruit, spicy, creamy oak, toasty, complex, aged wood nuances. Palate: powerful, flavourful, toasty, harsh oak tannins.

## BODEGAS EPIFANIO RIVERA S.L.

Onésimo Redondo, 1
47315 Pesquera de Duero (Valladolid)
☎: 983 870 109 - Fax: 983 870 109
comercial@epifaniorivera.com
www.epifaniorivera.com

ERIAL 2007 T
tinto fino 100%

**88** Colour: bright cherry. Nose: ripe fruit, sweet spices, creamy oak, expressive. Palate: flavourful, fruity, toasty, round tannins.

ERIAL TF 2006 T
tinto fino 100%

**89** Colour: bright cherry. Nose: ripe fruit, sweet spices, expressive, fresh fruit. Palate: flavourful, fruity, toasty, round tannins.

ERIAL 2006 T
tinto fino 100%

**86** Colour: bright cherry. Nose: sweet spices, creamy oak, expressive, red berry notes. Palate: flavourful, fruity, toasty, round tannins.

## BODEGAS FÉLIX CALLEJO

Avda. del Cid, km. 16,400
09441 Sotillo de la Ribera (Burgos)
☎: 947 532 312 - Fax: 947 532 304
callejo@bodegasfelixcallejo.com
www.bodegasfelixcallejo.com

VIÑA PILAR 2008 RD
tinto fino 100%

**85** Colour: rose, purple rim. Nose: powerful, ripe fruit, red berry notes, floral, expressive, violets. Palate: fleshy, powerful, fruity, fresh.

CALLEJO CUATRO MESES EN BARRICA 2007 T
tinto fino 100%

**87** Colour: cherry, purple rim. Nose: fresh fruit, floral. Palate: flavourful, fruity, good acidity, round tannins.

CALLEJO 2006 TC
tinto fino 100%

**88** Colour: bright cherry. Nose: ripe fruit, sweet spices, creamy oak, expressive, red berry notes. Palate: flavourful, fruity, toasty, round tannins.

FÉLIX CALLEJO SELECCIÓN VIÑEDOS 2005 TC
tinto fino 100%

**90** Colour: deep cherry. Nose: ripe fruit, sweet spices, creamy oak, expressive, cocoa bean. Palate: flavourful, fruity, toasty, round tannins, sweetness, powerful.

CALLEJO 2005 TR
tinto fino 100%

**89** Colour: cherry, garnet rim. Nose: spicy, toasty, complex, fruit preserve. Palate: powerful, flavourful, toasty, round tannins.

GRAN CALLEJO 2004 TGR
tinto fino 100%

**89** Colour: cherry, garnet rim. Nose: spicy, creamy oak, toasty, complex, ripe fruit. Palate: powerful, flavourful, toasty, round tannins.

## BODEGAS FÉLIX SANZ S.L.

Ronda Aradillas, s/n
47490 Rueda (Valladolid)
☎: 983 868 044 - Fax: 983 868 133
info@bodegasfelixsanz.es
www.bodegasfelixsanz.es

MONTENEGRO 2005 TC
tempranillo 100%

**82**

MONTENEGRO 2003 TR
tempranillo 100%

**83**

## BODEGAS GARCÍA DE ARANDA

Ctra. de Soria, s/n
09400 Aranda de Duero (Burgos)
☎: 947 501 817 - Fax: 947 506 355
bodega@bodegasgarcia.com
www.bodegasgarcia.com

SEÑORÍO DE LOS BALDÍOS 2008 T
tempranillo 100%

**82**

SEÑORÍO DE LOS BALDÍOS 2007 T ROBLE
tempranillo 100%

**82**

SEÑORÍO DE LOS BALDÍOS 2006 TC
tempranillo 100%

**83**
SEÑORÍO DE LOS BALDÍOS 2004 TR
tempranillo 100%

**87** Colour: cherry, garnet rim. Nose: spicy, creamy oak, toasty, fine reductive notes. Palate: powerful, flavourful, toasty, round tannins.

## BODEGAS HACIENDA MONASTERIO

Ctra. Pesquera - Valbuena, s/n
47315 Pesquera de Duero (Valladolid)
☎: 983 484 002 - Fax: 983 484 079
bmonasterio@haciendamonasterio.com
www.haciendamonasterio.com

HACIENDA MONASTERIO 2005 T

**93** Colour: cherry, garnet rim. Nose: ripe fruit, spicy, creamy oak, toasty, complex, mineral. Palate: powerful, flavourful, toasty, round tannins, fleshy.

HACIENDA MONASTERIO 2004 TR

**93** Colour: cherry, garnet rim. Nose: ripe fruit, spicy, creamy oak, toasty, complex, damp earth, undergrowth. Palate: powerful, flavourful, toasty, round tannins, reductive nuances.

## BODEGAS HERMANOS PÉREZ PASCUAS

Ctra. Roa, s/n
09314 Pedrosa de Duero (Burgos)
☎: 947 530 100 - Fax: 947 530 002
vinapedrosa@perezpascuas.com
www.perezpascuas.com

VIÑA PEDROSA 2007 TC

**90** Colour: cherry, garnet rim. Nose: ripe fruit, spicy, creamy oak, toasty, complex. Palate: powerful, flavourful, toasty, round tannins.

VIÑA PEDROSA 2006 TR

**92** Colour: bright cherry, garnet rim. Nose: fruit preserve, mineral, creamy oak, cocoa bean, balanced. Palate: fruity, good acidity, elegant, round tannins.

VIÑA PEDROSA 2006 TC

**89** Colour: cherry, garnet rim. Nose: fruit preserve, sweet spices, dry stone, cocoa bean. Palate: creamy, pruney, round tannins, flavourful.

PÉREZ PASCUAS GRAN SELECCIÓN 2004 TGR

**93** Colour: cherry, garnet rim. Nose: ripe fruit, spicy, creamy oak, toasty, complex, mineral. Palate: powerful, flavourful, toasty, round tannins.

VIÑA PEDROSA 2004 TGR

**90** Colour: cherry, garnet rim. Nose: ripe fruit, spicy, creamy oak, toasty, wet leather. Palate: powerful, flavourful, toasty, round tannins.

CEPA GAVILÁN 2007 T

**89** Colour: bright cherry. Nose: ripe fruit, sweet spices, creamy oak, expressive. Palate: flavourful, fruity, toasty, round tannins.

## BODEGAS HERMANOS SASTRE

San Pedro, s/n
09311 La Horra (Burgos)
☎: 947 542 108 - Fax: 947 542 108
sastre@vinasastre.com
www.vinasastre.com

VIÑA SASTRE 2007 T ROBLE
tinta del país 100%

**90** Colour: cherry, garnet rim. Nose: fruit preserve, spicy, cocoa bean, creamy oak. Palate: flavourful, good structure, long, fine tannins.

VIÑA SASTRE PESUS 2006 T
tinta del país 80%, merlot and cabernet sauvignon 20%

**95** Colour: very deep cherry. Nose: ripe fruit, sweet spices, creamy oak, expressive, roasted coffee, powerfull. Palate: flavourful, fruity, round tannins, powerful, sweetness.

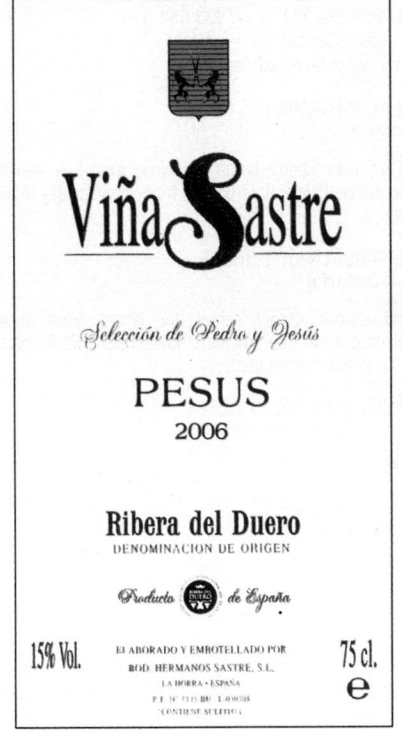

VIÑA SASTRE 2006 TC
tinta del país 100%

**95** Colour: deep cherry. Nose: ripe fruit, spicy, creamy oak, toasty, complex. Palate: powerful, flavourful, toasty, round tannins.

ACOS 2006 T
tinta del país 100%

**90** Colour: cherry, garnet rim. Nose: ripe fruit, creamy oak, complex, floral. Palate: powerful, flavourful, toasty, round tannins.

REGINA VIDES 2005 T
tinta del país 100%

**95** Colour: deep cherry. Nose: ripe fruit, creamy oak, expressive, cocoa bean, dark chocolate, caramel. Palate: flavourful, fruity, round tannins, creamy, toasty.

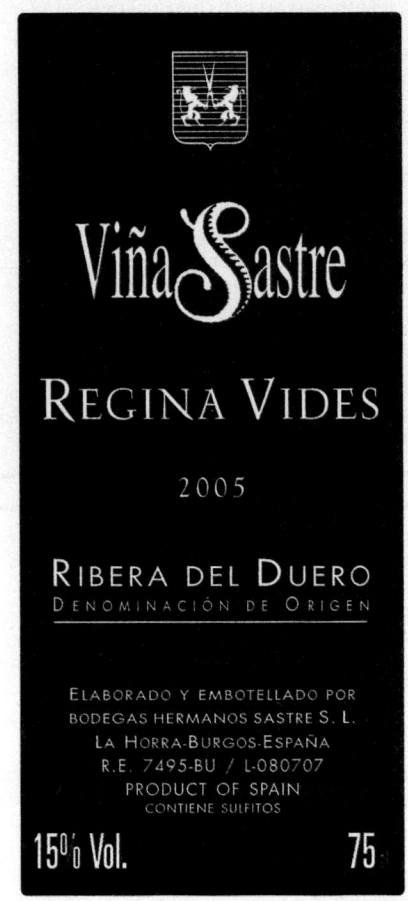

# DO RIBERA DEL DUERO

## BODEGAS IMPERIALES S.L.

Ctra. Madrid - Irun, km. 171
09370 Gumiel de Izán (Burgos)
☎: 947 544 070 - Fax: 947 525 759
direccion@bodegasimperiales.com
www.bodegasimperiales.com

ABADÍA DE SAN QUIRCE 2006 TC
tempranillo 100%

**90** Colour: very deep cherry. Nose: sweet spices, dark chocolate, candied fruit. Palate: flavourful, full, great length, slightly dry, soft tannins.

ABADÍA DE SAN QUIRCE FINCA HELENA
DE AUTOR 2005 T
tempranillo 100%

**90** Colour: cherry, garnet rim. Nose: ripe fruit, spicy, creamy oak, complex, dark chocolate. Palate: powerful, flavourful, toasty, round tannins.

ABADÍA DE SAN QUIRCE 2004 TR
tempranillo 100%

**90** Colour: cherry, garnet rim. Nose: ripe fruit, spicy, creamy oak, toasty, complex, floral, elegant. Palate: powerful, flavourful, toasty, round tannins.

ABADÍA DE SAN QUIRCE 2001 TGR
tempranillo 100%

**90** Colour: cherry, garnet rim. Nose: powerful, ripe fruit, candied fruit, roasted coffee, toasty. Palate: flavourful, powerful, spicy, round tannins.

## BODEGAS ISMAEL ARROYO

Los Lagares, 71
09441 Sotillo de la Ribera (Burgos)
☎: 947 532 309 - Fax: 947 532 487
bodega@valsotillo.com
www.valsotillo.com

MESONEROS DE CASTILLA 2008 RD
tinta del país 93%, albillo 7%

**80**

MESONEROS DE CASTILLA 2006 T
tinta del país 100%

**84**

VALSOTILLO 2005 TC
tinta del país 100%

**87** Colour: bright cherry. Nose: ripe fruit, sweet spices, creamy oak, expressive, fruit expression. Palate: flavourful, fruity, toasty, round tannins.

VALSOTILLO VS 2004 TR
tinta del país 100%

**90** Colour: cherry, garnet rim, garnet rim. Nose: ripe fruit, spicy, creamy oak, toasty, complex, fruit expression. Palate: powerful, flavourful, toasty, round tannins.

VALSOTILLO 2004 TR
tinta del país 100%

**89** Colour: bright cherry. Nose: ripe fruit, sweet spices, creamy oak, expressive, red berry notes, mineral. Palate: flavourful, fruity, toasty, round tannins, balsamic.

## BODEGAS LA CEPA ALTA

Ctra. de Quintanilla, 28
47359 Olivares de Duero (Valladolid)
☎: 983 294 381 - Fax: 983 681 010
laveguilla@gmail.com
www.vinoslaveguilla.com

CEPA ALTA 2008 T
tempranillo

**85** Colour: cherry, purple rim. Nose: fresh fruit, varietal, expressive. Palate: light-bodied, fruity, good acidity, grainy tannins.

CEPA ALTA 2007 T ROBLE
tempranillo 100%

**86** Colour: cherry, garnet rim. Nose: sweet spices, balanced, fresh fruit, red berry notes. Palate: light-bodied, fruity, grainy tannins, toasty.

LAVEGUILLA 2007 T ROBLE
tempranillo, cabernet sauvignon

**84**

CEPA ALTA 2006 TC
tempranillo 100%

**84**

LAVEGUILLA 2006 TC

**87** Colour: bright cherry. Nose: ripe fruit, sweet spices, creamy oak, expressive. Palate: flavourful, fruity, toasty, round tannins.

RIBERA DEL DUERO
DENOMINACIÓN DE ORIGEN

LAVEGUILLA

Crianza 2006

13,5% vol.                                    75 cl.

Elaborado y embotellado por:
Bodegas la Cepa Alta, S.L.
47359 Olivares de Duero (Valladolid) España

## BODEGAS LAMBUENA

Ctra. Fuentecén, s/n
09300 Roa (Burgos)
☎: 947 540 034 - Fax: 947 540 614
lambuena@bodegaslambuena.com
www.bodegaslambuena.com

LAMBUENA SELECCIÓN 2008 RD
tempranillo 100%

**84**

LAMBUENA 2007 T BARRICA
tempranillo 100%

**87** Colour: cherry, garnet rim. Nose: medium intensity, ripe fruit, balsamic herbs, sweet spices. Palate: flavourful, powerful, fleshy.

LAMBUENA 2005 TC
tempranillo 90%, cabernet sauvignon 10%, merlot %

**84**

LAMBUENA VIÑAS VIEJAS 2004 TC
tempranillo 100%

**85** Colour: cherry, garnet rim. Nose: ripe fruit, spicy, toasty, complex, closed. Palate: powerful, flavourful, toasty, round tannins, harsh oak tannins.

LAMBUENA 2004 TR
tempranillo 90%, cabernet sauvignon 10%, merlot %

**84**

## BODEGAS LÓPEZ CRISTÓBAL

Barrio Estación s/n
09300 Roa de Duero (Burgos)
☎: 947 561 139 - Fax: 947 540 606
bodega@lopezcristobal.com
www.lopezcristobal.com

LÓPEZ CRISTOBAL 2008 T ROBLE

**88** Colour: deep cherry, purple rim. Nose: expressive, ripe fruit, rose petals, sweet spices. Palate: good structure, flavourful, sweet tannins.

BAGÚS VENDIMIA SELECCIONADA 2005 T

**90** Colour: deep cherry. Nose: ripe fruit, sweet spices, creamy oak, expressive. Palate: flavourful, fruity, toasty, round tannins.

LÓPEZ CRISTOBAL 2004 TR

**89** Colour: cherry, garnet rim. Nose: ripe fruit, spicy, creamy oak, toasty, complex, red berry notes, floral. Palate: powerful, flavourful, toasty, round tannins, balsamic.

LÓPEZ CRISTOBAL TC

**90** Colour: bright cherry. Nose: ripe fruit, sweet spices, creamy oak, expressive, fruit liqueur notes. Palate: flavourful, fruity, toasty, round tannins, powerful, spirituous, mineral.

LÓPEZ CRISTOBAL SELECCIÓN T

**87** Colour: bright cherry. Nose: ripe fruit, sweet spices, creamy oak, expressive, smoky. Palate: flavourful, fruity, toasty, round tannins.

## BODEGAS LOS ASTRALES S.L.

Ctra. Olmedillo s/n
09313 Anguix (Burgos)
☎: 979 744 626 - Fax: 979 703 095

astrales2001@hotmail.com
www.astrales.es

**ASTRALES CHRISTINA 2006 T**
tempranillo 100%

**93** Colour: bright cherry. Nose: ripe fruit, sweet spices, creamy oak, expressive. Palate: flavourful, fruity, toasty, round tannins, fruity aftestaste.

**ASTRALES 2006 T**
tempranillo 100%

**91** Colour: bright cherry. Nose: ripe fruit, sweet spices, creamy oak, expressive, balsamic herbs. Palate: flavourful, fruity, toasty, round tannins.

## BODEGAS MUÑOZ Y MAZÓN

Avda. Valle Esgueva, 12
09310 Villatuelda (Burgos)
☎: 947 551 297

**AZUEL ROBLE 2008 T**
tempranillo 100%

**87** Colour: cherry, garnet rim. Nose: spicy, fresh fruit. Palate: fleshy, fruity, spicy, round tannins, easy to drink.

**AZUEL VENDIMIA SELECCIONADA 2007 T**
tempranillo 100%

**84**

**AZUEL 2005 TC**
tempranillo 100%

**86** Colour: cherry, garnet rim. Nose: ripe fruit, varietal, creamy oak. Palate: light-bodied, fruity, harsh oak tannins, toasty.

## BODEGAS PAGOS DE MOGAR

Ctra. Pesquera Km. 0,2
47359 Valbuena de Duero (Valladolid)
☎: 983 683 011 - Fax: 983 683 011
comercial@bodegaspagosdemogar.com
www.bodegaspagosdemogar.com

**MOGAR 2007 T ROBLE**
tinta del país 100%

**87** Colour: bright cherry. Nose: ripe fruit, sweet spices, dark chocolate. Palate: flavourful, fruity, toasty, round tannins.

**MOGAR VENDIMIA SELECCIONADA 2006 TC**
tinta del país 100%

**88** Colour: deep cherry. Nose: ripe fruit, sweet spices, creamy oak, expressive. Palate: flavourful, fruity, toasty, round tannins.

## BODEGAS PAGOS DE QUINTANA

Camino Fuentenavares, s/n
09443 Quintana del Pidío (Burgos)
☎: 947 561 034 - Fax: 947 561 038
bodegas@pagosdequintana.com
www.pagosdequintana.com

**PAGOS DE QUINTANA ROBLE 2007 T**
tinto fino 100%

**87** Colour: cherry, garnet rim. Nose: fragrant herbs, ripe fruit, spicy. Palate: flavourful, fruity, ripe fruit, round tannins.

**PAGOS DE QUINTANA 2006 TC**
tinto fino 100%

**85** Colour: cherry, garnet rim. Nose: ripe fruit, spicy, creamy oak, toasty, complex. Palate: powerful, flavourful, toasty, round tannins.

**PAGOS DE QUINTANA 2004 TR**
tinto fino 100%

**89** Colour: cherry, garnet rim. Nose: toasty, aromatic coffee, spicy. Palate: flavourful, powerful, harsh oak tannins.

## BODEGAS PASCUAL

Ctra. de Aranda, km. 5
09471 Fuentelcesped (Burgos)
☎: 947 557 351 - Fax: 947 557 312
tinto@bodegaspascual.com
www.bodegaspascual.com

**HEREDAD DE PEÑALOSA 2008 RD**
tempranillo 100%

**83**

**HEREDAD DE PEÑALOSA 2008 T ROBLE**
tempranillo 100%

**84**

**CASTILDIEGO 2008 T**
tempranillo 100%

**82**

**BURÓ DE PEÑALOSA 2005 TC**
tempranillo 100%

**86** Colour: dark-red cherry. Nose: ripe fruit, warm, spicy. Palate: fleshy, powerful, harsh oak tannins.

**BURÓ 2004 TR**
tempranillo 100%

**90** Colour: cherry, garnet rim. Nose: elegant, dried flowers, mineral, fine reductive notes. Palate: fleshy, complex, roasted-coffee aftertaste, powerful tannins.

**DIODORO AUTOR 2004 T**
tempranillo 100%

**87** Colour: cherry, garnet rim. Nose: ripe fruit, spicy, creamy oak, toasty, complex. Palate: powerful, flavourful, toasty, round tannins.

## BODEGAS PEÑAFALCÓN

Pisuerga, P. 42
47300 Peñafiel (Valladolid)
☎: 983 881 251 - Fax: 983 880 541
info@bodegaspenafalcon.com
www.bodegaspenafalcon.com

**PEÑAFALCÓN 2007 T ROBLE**
tempranillo 100%

**86** Colour: cherry, garnet rim. Nose: roasted coffee, characterful, powerfull, ripe fruit. Palate: flavourful, powerful, ripe fruit.

**PEÑAFALCÓN VENDIMIA SELECCIÓN 2005 TC**
tempranillo 100%

**89** Colour: cherry, garnet rim. Nose: ripe fruit, spicy, creamy oak, toasty, complex, balsamic herbs. Palate: powerful, flavourful, toasty, round tannins.

**PEÑAFALCÓN 2004 TR**
tempranillo 100%

**85** Colour: cherry, garnet rim. Nose: ripe fruit, spicy, creamy oak, toasty, complex, tobacco. Palate: powerful, flavourful, toasty, round tannins.

## BODEGAS PEÑAFIEL

Ctra. N-122, km. 311
47300 Peñafiel (Valladolid)
☎: 983 881 622 - Fax: 983 881 944
bodegaspenafiel@bodegaspenafiel.com
www.bodegaspenafiel.com

**ROSA DE MIROS 2008 RD**
tempranillo, merlot, cabernet sauvignon

**88** Colour: onion pink. Nose: elegant, candied fruit, dried flowers, fragrant herbs, red berry notes. Palate: light-bodied, flavourful, good acidity, long, spicy.

**MIROS 2006 T BARRICA**
tempranillo, merlot, cabernet sauvignon

**87** Colour: cherry, garnet rim. Nose: spicy, dark chocolate, fruit expression. Palate: good structure, flavourful, full, slightly dry, soft tannins.

**MIROS DE RIBERA SELECCIÓN BARRICAS 2004 T**
tempranillo 100%

**90** Colour: cherry, garnet rim. Nose: ripe fruit, spicy, toasty, complex, lactic notes, fine reductive notes. Palate: powerful, flavourful, toasty, round tannins.

**MIROS DE RIBERA 2004 TC**
tempranillo 100%

**88** Colour: cherry, garnet rim. Nose: ripe fruit, spicy, toasty, complex, earthy notes. Palate: powerful, flavourful, toasty, round tannins, reductive nuances.

**MIROS DE RIBERA COLECCIÓN PRIVADA 2003 TR**
tempranillo 100%

**89** Colour: cherry, garnet rim. Nose: ripe fruit, spicy, creamy oak, toasty, complex, fine reductive notes. Palate: powerful, flavourful, toasty, round tannins.

**MIROS DE RIBERA SELECCIÓN BARRICAS 2003 T**

**87** Colour: cherry, garnet rim. Nose: fruit preserve, fruit liqueur notes, toasty, old leather. Palate: spicy, pruney, round tannins.

**MIROS DE RIBERA 2002 TR**
tempranillo 100%

**88** Colour: cherry, garnet rim. Nose: ripe fruit, spicy, creamy oak, toasty, complex, tobacco, earthy notes. Palate: powerful, flavourful, toasty, round tannins, good acidity.

## BODEGAS PEÑALBA HERRAIZ S.L.

Sol de las Moreras, 3 2º dcha.
09400 Aranda de Duero (Burgos)
☎: 947 511 145 - Fax: 947 511 145
miguelpma@ono.com

**APTUS 2007 T**
tinta del país 95%, garnacha 5%

**87** Colour: cherry, garnet rim. Nose: creamy oak, sweet spices, ripe fruit, fruit preserve. Palate: flavourful, powerful, ripe fruit, round tannins.

**CARRAVID 2007 T**
tinta del país 95%, garnacha 5%

**86** Colour: cherry, purple rim. Nose: sweet spices, creamy oak, expressive, overripe fruit. Palate: flavourful, fruity, toasty, round tannins.

## BODEGAS PIEDRAS DE SAN PEDRO S.L.

Eras, 40
47315 Pesquera de Duero (Valladolid)
☎: 983 870 186
bodegas@piedrasdesanpedro.com
www.piedrasdesanpedro.com

**LOCULTO 2005 TC**
tempranillo 100%

**87** Colour: dark-red cherry. Nose: balsamic herbs, toasty, ripe fruit. Palate: fleshy, full, powerful, toasty.

**PIEDRAS DE SAN PEDRO 2004 TR**
tempranillo 100%

**90** Colour: cherry, garnet rim. Nose: ripe fruit, spicy, toasty, roasted coffee. Palate: powerful, flavourful, toasty, round tannins.

## BODEGAS PIGÓN

Ctra. de Burgos, s/n
09441 Sotillo de la Ribera (Burgos)
☎: 947 532 450 - Fax: 947 532 476
info@bodegaspigon.com
www.bodegaspigon.com

**VALDAYA 2006 T ROBLE**
tinto fino 100%

**88** Colour: bright cherry. Nose: ripe fruit, sweet spices, creamy oak, expressive. Palate: flavourful, fruity, toasty, round tannins.

**VALDAYA 2006 TC**
tinto fino 100%

**87** Colour: cherry, garnet rim. Nose: closed, creamy oak, toasty, ripe fruit. Palate: powerful, flavourful, toasty, fruity, round tannins, spicy, long.

**VALDAYA VENDIMIA SELECCIONADA 2006 TC**
tinto fino 100%

**84**

## BODEGAS PINGÓN

Ctra. N-122, km. 311
47300 Peñafiel (Valladolid)
☎: 983 880 623 - Fax: 983 880 623
carramimbre@bodegaspingon.com

www.bodegaspingon.com

**CARRAMIMBRE 2005 TC**
tempranillo 90%, cabernet sauvignon 10%

**88** Colour: cherry, garnet rim. Nose: spicy, toasty, fruit preserve. Palate: powerful, flavourful, toasty, round tannins.

**CARRAMIMBRE 2004 TR**
tempranillo 90%, cabernet sauvignon 10%

**87** Colour: cherry, garnet rim. Nose: ripe fruit, spicy, creamy oak, toasty, complex, fruit preserve, damp earth, old leather. Palate: powerful, flavourful, toasty, round tannins.

**ALTAMIMBRE 2005 T**
tempranillo 100%

# DO RIBERA DEL DUERO

**89** Colour: bright cherry. Nose: ripe fruit, sweet spices, expressive, aromatic coffee, floral. Palate: flavourful, fruity, toasty, round tannins.

## BODEGAS PINNA FIDELIS

Camino Llanillos, s/n
47300 Peñafiel (Valladolid)
☎: 983 878 034 - Fax: 983 878 035
comercial@pinnafidelis.com
www.pinnafidelis.com

PINNA FIDELIS 2007 T ROBLE
tinta del país 100%

**87** Colour: bright cherry. Nose: ripe fruit, sweet spices, creamy oak, expressive. Palate: flavourful, fruity, toasty, fine tannins.

PINNA FIDELIS 2005 TC
tinta del país 100%

**84**

PINNA FIDELIS VENDIMIA SELECCIONADA 2004 T
tinta del país 100%

**89** Colour: cherry, garnet rim. Nose: spicy, creamy oak, toasty, complex, fruit preserve. Palate: powerful, flavourful, toasty, round tannins.

PINNA FIDELIS 2004 TR
tinta del país 100%

**87** Colour: cherry, garnet rim. Nose: ripe fruit, spicy, toasty, complex, dark chocolate. Palate: powerful, flavourful, toasty, round tannins, varietal.

## BODEGAS PORTIA S.L.

Montecillo
09400 Allendeduero (Aranda de Duero)
☎: 945 622 500
info@bodegasfaustino.es
www.bodegasfaustino.es

PORTIA PRIMA 2006 T

**88** Colour: cherry, garnet rim. Nose: ripe fruit, spicy, creamy oak, toasty, complex. Palate: powerful, flavourful, toasty, round tannins.

PORTIA 2005 T

**87** Colour: bright cherry. Nose: ripe fruit, sweet spices, creamy oak, expressive, earthy notes. Palate: flavourful, fruity, toasty, round tannins.

## BODEGAS PRADO DE OLMEDO

Paraje El Salegar, s/n
09443 Quintana del Pidío (Burgos)
☎: 947 546 960 - Fax: 947 546 960
pradodeolmedo@pradodeolmedo.com
www.pradodeolmedo.com

VALDESANTOS 2008 RD

**81**

MONASTERIO DE SAN MIGUEL 2007 T
tinta del país 100%

**80**

MONASTERIO DE SAN MIGUEL 2005 TC
tinta del país 100%

**85** Colour: cherry, garnet rim. Nose: ripe fruit, spicy, toasty, scrubland. Palate: powerful, flavourful, toasty, round tannins, varietal.

VALDESANTOS 2005 TC
tinta del país 100%

**85** Colour: cherry, garnet rim. Nose: spicy, toasty, complex, fruit preserve. Palate: powerful, flavourful, toasty, round tannins.

MONASTERIO DE SAN MIGUEL 2004 TR
tinta del país 100%

**85** Colour: cherry, garnet rim. Nose: ripe fruit, spicy, toasty, complex. Palate: powerful, flavourful, toasty, grainy tannins.

## BODEGAS RESALTE DE PEÑAFIEL

Ctra. N-122, km. 312
47300 Peñafiel (Valladolid)
☎: 983 878 160 - Fax: 983 880 601
info@resalte.com
www.resalte.com

GRAN RESALTE 2000 TR
tempranillo 100%

**87** Colour: deep cherry, brick rim edge. Nose: fruit liqueur notes, toasty, varnish, aged wood nuances, complex. Palate: light-bodied, fruity, good acidity, grainy tannins, roasted-coffee aftertaste.

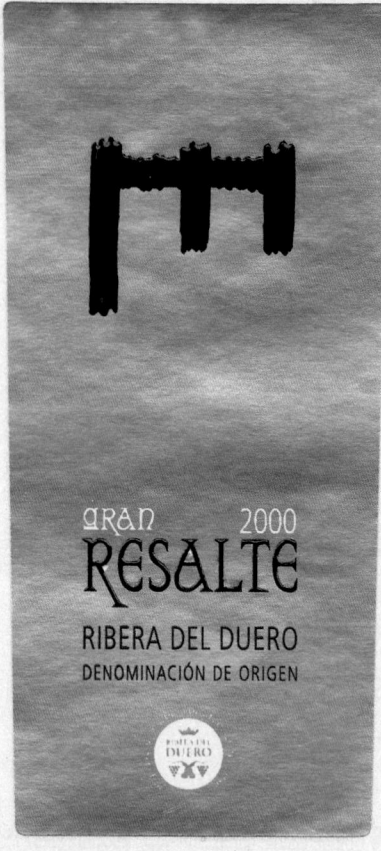

RESALTE VENDIMIA SELECCIONADA 2007 T
tempranillo 100%

**86** Colour: cherry, garnet rim. Nose: fruit preserve, sweet spices, creamy oak, balanced. Palate: flavourful, good acidity, toasty, sweet tannins.

PEÑA ROBLE 2007 T ROBLE
tempranillo 100%

**81**

RESALTE 2004 TC
tempranillo 100%

**88** Colour: deep cherry, garnet rim. Nose: lactic notes, sweet spices, new oak, fruit liqueur notes. Palate: fleshy, powerful, fruity, grainy tannins, good structure.

PEÑA ROBLE 2004 TC
tempranillo 100%

**84**

## BODEGAS REYES

Ctra. Va-So, km. 54, 300 Apdo. 41
47300 Peñafiel (Valladolid)
☎: 983 873 015 - Fax: 983 873 017
info@teofiloreyes.com
www.bodegasreyes.com

TEÓFILO REYES 2006 TC

**88** Colour: bright cherry. Nose: ripe fruit, sweet spices, creamy oak, expressive, balsamic herbs. Palate: flavourful, fruity, toasty, round tannins, good acidity.

TEÓFILO REYES 2005 TR

**87** Colour: cherry, garnet rim. Nose: ripe fruit, spicy, toasty, complex. Palate: powerful, flavourful, toasty, harsh oak tannins.

TAMIZ

## BODEGAS RODERO

Ctra. Boada, s/n
09314 Pedrosa de Duero (Burgos)
☎: 947 530 046 - Fax: 947 530 097
rodero@bodegasrodero.com
www.bodegasrodero.com

CARMELO RODERO 2008 T ROBLE

**87** Colour: dark-red cherry, purple rim. Nose: toasty, sweet spices, red berry notes. Palate: good structure, flavourful, great length.

CARMELO RODERO 2008 T

## 84

CARMELO RODERO 2007 TC

**92** Colour: cherry, garnet rim. Nose: ripe fruit, spicy, creamy oak, toasty, complex. Palate: powerful, flavourful, toasty, round tannins.

CARMELO RODERO 2006 TC

**91** Colour: cherry, garnet rim. Nose: ripe fruit, spicy, creamy oak, toasty, complex. Palate: powerful, flavourful, toasty, round tannins.

CARMELO RODERO TSM 2005 T

**94** Colour: cherry, garnet rim. Nose: ripe fruit, spicy, creamy oak, toasty, complex, scrubland. Palate: powerful, flavourful, toasty, round tannins.

CARMELO RODERO "VIÑAS DE VALTARREÑA" 2005 T

**90** Colour: deep cherry. Nose: ripe fruit, sweet spices, creamy oak, expressive, cocoa bean. Palate: flavourful, fruity, toasty, round tannins, warm, spirituous, powerful.

CARMELO RODERO 2004 TR

**91** Colour: bright cherry. Nose: sweet spices, creamy oak, expressive, new oak, ripe fruit. Palate: flavourful, fruity, toasty, round tannins.

## BODEGAS SANTA EULALIA

Malpica, s/n
09311 La Horra (Burgos)
☎: 983 586 868 - Fax: 947 580 180
bodegasfrutosvillar@bodegasfrutosvillar.com
www.bodegasfrutosvillar.com

CONDE DE SIRUELA 2006 TC
tinta del país 100%

**89** Colour: bright cherry. Nose: ripe fruit, sweet spices, creamy oak, expressive, undergrowth. Palate: flavourful, fruity, toasty, round tannins.

CONDE DE SIRUELA 2005 TR

**89** Colour: cherry, garnet rim. Nose: spicy, toasty, complex, fruit preserve. Palate: powerful, flavourful, toasty, round tannins.

CONDE DE SIRUELA 2005 T
tinta del país 100%

**88** Colour: cherry, garnet rim. Nose: ripe fruit, spicy, creamy oak, toasty. Palate: powerful, flavourful, toasty, round tannins.

LA HORRA
RIBERAL

## BODEGAS SEÑORIO DE NAVA

Ctra. Valladolid - Soria, 62
09318 Nava de Roa (Burgos)
☎: 987 209 790 - Fax: 987 209 808
c.puente@senoriodenava.es
www.senoriodenava.es

VEGA CUBILLAS 2007 T
tinta del país 100%

**85** Colour: cherry, purple rim. Nose: powerful, ripe fruit, balsamic herbs. Palate: flavourful, fruity, spicy.

VEGA CUBILLAS 2007 T ROBLE
tinta del país 100%

## 82

SEÑORÍO DE NAVA 2007 T ROBLE
tinta del país 100%

## 79

SEÑORÍO DE NAVA 2006 TC
tinta del país 100%

**89** Colour: deep cherry, garnet rim. Nose: macerated fruit, creamy oak, sweet spices, warm, aromatic coffee. Palate: full, rich, fruity, flavourful, good acidity, round tannins.

VEGA CUBILLAS 2006 TC
tinta del país 100%

**87** Colour: very deep cherry, garnet rim. Nose: ripe fruit, spicy, dark chocolate. Palate: round, fruity, powerful, toasty, round tannins.

SEÑORÍO DE NAVA 2004 TR
tinta del país 100%

**88** Colour: light cherry. Nose: fresh fruit, red berry notes, lactic notes, expressive, creamy oak, dark chocolate. Palate: good acidity, fruity, easy to drink, fleshy, good structure.

SEÑORÍO DE NAVA FINCA SAN COBATE 2001 TR
tinta del país 100%

**88** Colour: dark-red cherry, bright ochre rim. Nose: fruit liqueur notes, sweet spices, aged wood nuances, aromatic coffee. Palate: flavourful, rich, fruity, round tannins.

## BODEGAS SURCO S.L. (VALDRINAL)

Picote 19
09400 Aranda de Duero (Burgos)
☎: 915 480 232 - Fax: 915 477 476
info@valdrinal.com
www.valdrinal.com

VALDRINAL 2007 TC

**87** Colour: bright cherry. Nose: ripe fruit, sweet spices, creamy oak, expressive. Palate: flavourful, fruity, toasty, round tannins.

VALDRINAL 2004 TR

**86** Colour: cherry, garnet rim. Nose: powerful, toasty, aromatic coffee. Palate: powerful, fleshy, toasty.

## BODEGAS TARSUS

Ctra. De Roa-Anguix, km. 3
09313 Anguix (Burgos)
☎: 947 554 218 - Fax: 947 541 804
tarsus@domecqbodegas.com
www.domecqbodegas.com

QUINTA DE TARSUS 2006 TC
tempranillo 100%

**86** Colour: cherry, garnet rim. Nose: sweet spices, warm, fruit preserve. Palate: flavourful, fruity, round tannins, easy to drink.

TARSUS 2003 TR
tempranillo 98%, cabernet sauvignon 2%

**87** Colour: dark-red cherry, bright ochre rim. Nose: fruit liqueur notes, sweet spices, balanced, warm. Palate: flavourful, fruity, slightly dry, soft tannins, classic aged character, toasty.

## BODEGAS THESAURUS

Ctra. Quintanilla - Olivares de Duero
47359 Olivares de Duero (Valladolid)
☎: 983 250 319 - Fax: 983 250 329
exportacion@ciadevinos.com
www.ciadevinos.com

CASTILLO DE PEÑAFIEL S/C T ROBLE
tempranillo

**85** Colour: deep cherry, garnet rim. Nose: fruit liqueur notes, sweet spices, balanced, warm. Palate: flavourful, good acidity, spicy, round tannins.

FLUMEN DORIVM 2007 T ROBLE

**88** Colour: deep cherry, garnet rim. Nose: fruit preserve, fruit expression, sweet spices, balanced. Palate: fruity, good acidity, round tannins, spicy, easy to drink.

FLUMEN DORIVM 2007 T JOVEN

**81**

FLUMEN DORIVM 2006 TC

**88** Colour: deep cherry, garnet rim. Nose: fruit liqueur notes, toasty, caramel. Palate: full, fruity, powerful, good acidity, round tannins.

CASTILLO DE PEÑAFIEL 2003 TR
tempranillo

**85** Colour: cherry, garnet rim. Nose: medium intensity, toasty, spicy, fruit preserve. Palate: flavourful, fleshy, fine bitter notes.

VEGA LATORRE

## BODEGAS TIONIO

Tionio - Austum
47315 Pesquera de Duero (Valladolid)
☎: 933 950 811 - Fax: 983 870 185
info@parxet.es
www.parxet.es

AUSTUM TIONIO 2007 T
tinto fino 100%

**85** Colour: bright cherry. Nose: ripe fruit, sweet spices, expressive, balsamic herbs. Palate: flavourful, fruity, toasty, round tannins.

TIONIO 2005 TC
tinto fino 100%

**89** Colour: cherry, garnet rim. Nose: ripe fruit, spicy, toasty. Palate: flavourful, toasty, round tannins.

## BODEGAS TORREDEROS

Ctra. Valladolid, km. 289,300
09318 Fuentelisendo (Burgos)
☎: 947 532 627 - Fax: 947 532 731
administracion@torrederos.com
www.torrederos.com

TORREDEROS 2008 T
tempranillo 100%

**83**

**TORREDEROS 2007 T ROBLE**
tempranillo 100%

**85** Colour: cherry, purple rim. Nose: fresh fruit, red berry notes, sweet spices. Palate: flavourful, fruity, good acidity, round tannins.

**TORREDEROS 2005 TC**

**88** Colour: cherry, garnet rim. Nose: spicy, toasty, complex, fruit preserve. Palate: powerful, flavourful, toasty, round tannins.

**TORREDEROS 2004 TR**
tempranillo 100%

**92** Colour: cherry, garnet rim. Nose: toasty, fine reductive notes, sweet spices. Palate: complex, flavourful, round tannins.

## BODEGAS TORREMORÓN

Ctra. Boada, s/n
09314 Quintanamanvirgo (Burgos)
☎: 947 554 075 - Fax: 947 554 036
torremoron@wanadoo.es
www.torremoron.com

**TORREMORÓN 2006 TC**
tinta de toro 100%

**87** Colour: bright cherry. Nose: ripe fruit, sweet spices, creamy oak, expressive, macerated fruit. Palate: flavourful, fruity, toasty, round tannins.

**SENDERILLO 2005 TC**

**89** Colour: cherry, garnet rim. Nose: cocoa bean, sweet spices, fruit preserve. Palate: flavourful, full, round tannins.

**TORREMORÓN 2008 T**
tempranillo 100%

**83**

**SENDERILLO 2007 T ROBLE**
tinta de toro 100%

**86** Colour: bright cherry. Nose: ripe fruit, sweet spices, creamy oak, expressive, mineral. Palate: flavourful, fruity, toasty, round tannins.

**TORREMORÓN VENDIMIA SELECCIONADA 2005 T**
tinta de toro 100%

**88** Colour: cherry, garnet rim. Nose: spicy, toasty, ripe fruit. Palate: flavourful, good structure, harsh oak tannins.

## BODEGAS TRUS

Ctra. Pesquera Duero - Encinas, km. 3
47316 Piñel de Abajo (Valladolid)
☎: 902 302 330 - Fax: 902 302 340
trus@bodegastrus.com
www.bodegastrus.com

**TRUS 2004 T**
tinto fino 100%

**90** Colour: bright cherry. Nose: ripe fruit, sweet spices, creamy oak, expressive, smoky, mineral. Palate: flavourful, fruity, toasty, round tannins, fruity aftertaste.

## BODEGAS VALLE DE MONZÓN

Paraje El Salegar, s/n
09370 Quintana del Pidío (Burgos)
☎: 947 545 694 - Fax: 947 545 694
bodega@vallemonzon.com
www.vallemonzon.com

**HOYO DE LA VEGA 2008 RD**

**83**

**EL SALEGAR 2008 T**
tinta del país 100%

**84**

**HOYO DE LA VEGA 2007 T**
tinta del país 100%

**78**

**HOYO DE LA VEGA 2005 TR**
tinta del país 100%

**90** Colour: cherry, garnet rim. Nose: ripe fruit, spicy, creamy oak, toasty, lactic notes, mineral. Palate: powerful, flavourful, toasty, round tannins.

**EL SALEGAR 2005 TC**
tinta del país 100%

**88** Colour: bright cherry. Nose: sweet spices, creamy oak, expressive, undergrowth, red berry notes. Palate: flavourful, fruity, toasty, round tannins.

**HOYO DE LA VEGA 2005 TC**
tinta del país 100%

**86** Colour: deep cherry. Nose: ripe fruit, creamy oak, spicy, scrubland. Palate: flavourful, great length, slightly dry, soft tannins.

**GROMEJÓN**

## BODEGAS VALPINCIA

Ctra. de Melida a Peñafiel, km. 3,5
47300 Peñafiel (Valladolid)
☎: 983 878 007 - Fax: 983 880 620
penafiel@bodegasvalpincia.com
www.bodegasvalpincia.com

**VALPINCIA 2008 T**

**82**

**PAGOS DE VALCERRACIN 2008 T**

**81**

**PAGOS DE VALCERRACÍN 2007 T ROBLE**

**86** Colour: light cherry. Nose: varietal, expressive, spicy, fruit preserve. Palate: creamy, fruity, good acidity, toasty.

**VALPINCIA 2007 T ROBLE**

**83**

**GLORIA MAYOR 2006 TR**

**87** Colour: cherry, garnet rim. Nose: ripe fruit, spicy, creamy oak, toasty, neat. Palate: powerful, flavourful, toasty, round tannins, balsamic.

**VALPINCIA 2006 TC**

**84**

**PAGOS DE VALCERRACIN VENDIMIA SELECCIONADA 2004 TC**

**86** Colour: cherry, garnet rim. Nose: spicy, toasty, candied fruit, pattiserie. Palate: powerful, flavourful, toasty, round tannins, spicy, warm.

**VALPINCIA 2003 TR**

**84**

## BODEGAS VEGA SICILIA

Ctra. N-122, km. 323
47359 Valbuena de Duero (Valladolid)
☎: 983 680 147 - Fax: 983 680 263
vegasicilia@vega-sicilia.com
www.vega-sicilia.com

**VEGA SICILIA RESERVA ESPECIAL AÑADAS 89-90-94 89/90/94 T**

**98** Colour: pale ruby, brick rim edge. Nose: elegant, expressive, aromatic coffee, spicy, wet leather, waxy notes. Palate: flavourful, spicy, long, fine bitter notes, balanced, soft tannins.

**VALBUENA 5° 2005 T**
tinto fino 88%, merlot 12%, malbec %

**95** Colour: cherry, garnet rim. Nose: powerful, toasty, dark chocolate, ripe fruit, warm. Palate: flavourful, fleshy, powerful, spicy, ripe fruit, round tannins.

**VALBUENA 5° 2004 T**
tinto fino 88%, merlot 12%, malbec %

**96** Colour: cherry, garnet rim. Nose: elegant, expressive, ripe fruit, sweet spices, toasty. Palate: flavourful, fleshy, ripe fruit, soft tannins.

**VEGA SICILIA ÚNICO 2000 T**
tinto fino 93%, cabernet sauvignon 7%

**96** Colour: pale ruby, brick rim edge. Nose: elegant, ripe fruit, aged wood nuances, spicy, fine reductive notes. Palate: flavourful, good structure, spicy, long, soft tannins.

**VEGA SICILIA ÚNICO 1999 T**
tinto fino 93%, cabernet sauvignon 7%

**94** Colour: pale ruby, brick rim edge. Nose: powerful, ripe fruit, toasty, dark chocolate. Palate: flavourful, complex, ripe fruit, round tannins, fine bitter notes.

## BODEGAS VEGANZONES

c/Rosario, 4
47311 Fompedraza (Valladolid)
☎: 618 675 995 - Fax: 983 036 010
clete@bodegasveganzones.com
www.bodegasveganzones.com

**912 DE ALTITUD 2007 T ROBLE**
tempranillo 100%

**88** Colour: very deep cherry, purple rim. Nose: sweet spices, creamy oak, fruit preserve, expressive. Palate: rich, fruity, good finish, round tannins.

**912 DE ALTITUD 2006 T ROBLE**
tempranillo, merlot

**87** Colour: bright cherry. Nose: ripe fruit, sweet spices, creamy oak, expressive. Palate: flavourful, fruity, toasty, round tannins.

## BODEGAS VINUM TERRAE

Lgar. de Axis - Simes s/n
36968 Meaño (Pontevedra)
☎: 986 747 566 - Fax: 986 747 621
comercial@vinumterrae.com
www.vinumterrae.com

**VALDUNES 2004 T**
tinto fino 100%

**87** Colour: cherry, garnet rim. Nose: ripe fruit, spicy, woody, smoky. Palate: powerful, flavourful, toasty, round tannins.

## BODEGAS VITULIA S.L.

Avda. Montecillo, P- 63
09400 Aranda de Duero (Burgos)
☎: 947 515 051 - Fax: 947 515 051
vitulia@bodeasvitulia.com
www.bodegasvitulia.com

**VITULIA 2008 RD**
tempranillo 90%, albillo 10%

**85** Colour: onion pink. Nose: elegant, candied fruit, fragrant herbs, red berry notes, tropical fruit. Palate: light-bodied, flavourful, good acidity, long, spicy.

**VITULIA 2007 T**
tempranillo 100%

**85** Colour: cherry, purple rim. Nose: red berry notes, white flowers, lactic notes. Palate: flavourful, full, great length.

**VITULIA 2007 T ROBLE**
tempranillo 100%

**81**

**VITULIA 2005 TC**
tempranillo 100%

**79**

**VITULIA 2004 TR**
tempranillo 100%

**87** Colour: cherry, garnet rim. Nose: ripe fruit, spicy, creamy oak, toasty, complex, new oak. Palate: powerful, flavourful, toasty, round tannins.

## BODEGAS VIYUELA

Ctra. de Quintanamanvirgo, s/n
09314 Boada de Roa (Burgos)
☎: 947 530 072 - Fax: 947 530 075
viyuela@bodegasviyuela.com
www.bodegasviyuela.com

**VIYUELA 2008 T**
tempranillo 100%

**79**

**VIYUELA MALOLÁCTICA EN BARRICA 2007 T**
tempranillo 100%

**84**

**VIYUELA 10 2006 T**
tempranillo 100%

**90** Colour: bright cherry. Nose: ripe fruit, sweet spices, creamy oak, expressive. Palate: flavourful, fruity, toasty, round tannins.

**VIYUELA ROBLE BLEND 2006 T BARRICA**
tempranillo 100%

**87** Colour: bright cherry. Nose: sweet spices, creamy oak, expressive, fresh fruit. Palate: flavourful, fruity, toasty, round tannins.

**VIYUELA SELECCIÓN 2005 T**
tempranillo 100%

**89** Colour: cherry, garnet rim. Nose: ripe fruit, spicy, creamy oak, toasty, complex, earthy notes. Palate: flavourful, toasty, round tannins.

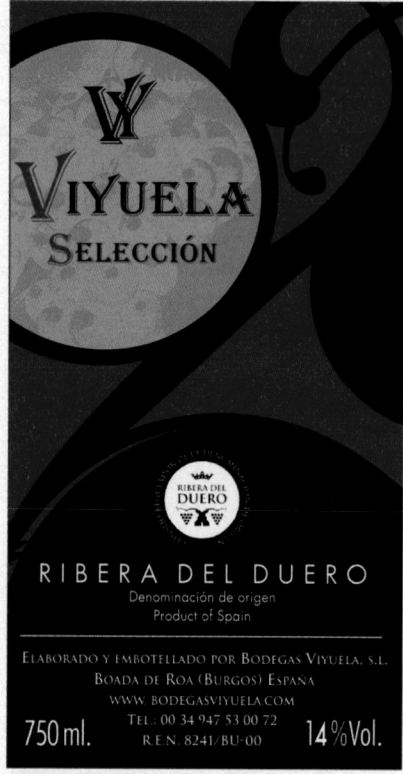

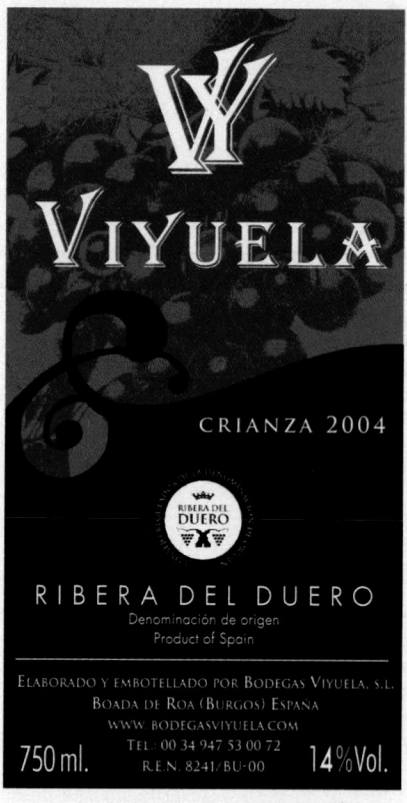

**VIYUELA 2005 TC**
tempranillo 100%

**86** Colour: cherry, garnet rim. Nose: ripe fruit, spicy, toasty, complex, warm. Palate: powerful, flavourful, toasty, round tannins.

**VIYUELA 2004 TR**
tempranillo 100%

**89** Colour: cherry, garnet rim. Nose: ripe fruit, spicy, creamy oak, toasty, complex, wet leather, earthy notes. Palate: powerful, flavourful, toasty, round tannins.

**VIYUELA 2004 TC**
tempranillo 100%

**89** Colour: cherry, garnet rim. Nose: ripe fruit, spicy, creamy oak, toasty, complex, fine reductive notes. Palate: powerful, flavourful, toasty, round tannins.

## BODEGAS VIZCARRA

Finca Chirri s/n
09317 Mambrilla de Castrejón (Burgos)
☎: 947 540 340 - Fax: 947 540 340
bodegas@vizcarra.es
www.vizcarra.es

**VIZCARRA SENDA DEL ORO 2008 T ROBLE**
tinto fino 100%

**88** Colour: cherry, purple rim. Nose: expressive, fresh fruit, red berry notes, floral, mineral. Palate: flavourful, fruity, good acidity, round tannins.

**VIZCARRA 2007 T**
tinto fino 100%

**91** Colour: bright cherry. Nose: ripe fruit, sweet spices, creamy oak, expressive, complex, floral. Palate: flavourful, fruity, toasty, round tannins, good acidity.

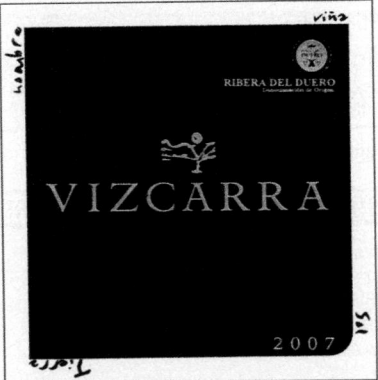

## BODEGAS Y VIÑAS LAS PINZAS

Ctra. Peñafiel-Pesquera, km. 6
47316 Curiel de Duero (Valladolid)
☎: 983 880 489 - Fax: 983 880 489
valdecuriel@yahoo.es
www.valdecuriel.es

CVRELVS VS 2006 T

**88** Colour: bright cherry. Nose: sweet spices, creamy oak, expressive, macerated fruit, fruit liqueur notes. Palate: flavourful, fruity, toasty, round tannins, spirituous.

VALDECURIEL 2006 TC

**85** Colour: bright cherry. Nose: ripe fruit, sweet spices, creamy oak, expressive, red berry notes. Palate: flavourful, fruity, toasty, round tannins.

VALDECURIEL 2004 TR
tempranillo

**86** Colour: dark-red cherry. Nose: toasty, spicy, dark chocolate, fine reductive notes. Palate: fleshy, powerful, harsh oak tannins.

## BODEGAS Y VIÑEDOS ALIÓN

Ctra. N-122, km. 312,4
Aptdo. 73 Padilla de Duero
47300 Peñafiel (Valladolid)
☎: 983 881 236 - Fax: 983 881 246

alion@bodegasalion.com
www.bodegasalion.com

ALIÓN 2006 T
tinto fino 100%

**94** Colour: cherry, garnet rim. Nose: powerful, ripe fruit, scrubland, sweet spices. Palate: flavourful, fleshy, ripe fruit, toasty, mineral.

ALIÓN 2005 T
tinto fino 100%

**96** Colour: deep cherry, garnet rim. Nose: elegant, sweet spices, dark chocolate, complex. Palate: flavourful, fleshy, toasty, round tannins.

## BODEGAS Y VIÑEDOS CONDE - NEO

Ctra. N-122, km. 274,5
09391 Castrillo de la Vega (Burgos)
☎: 947 514 393 - Fax: 947 514 393
info@bodegasconde.com
www.bodegasconde.com

DISCO 2007 T
tempranillo 100%

**91** Colour: cherry, garnet rim. Nose: spicy, floral, balsamic herbs, ripe fruit, cedar wood. Palate: flavourful, fruity, good structure, ripe fruit, round tannins.

SENTIDO 2007 T
tempranillo 100%

**90** Colour: cherry, garnet rim. Nose: ripe fruit, spicy, creamy oak, toasty, complex, warm. Palate: powerful, flavourful, toasty, round tannins.

OBRA 2007 T JOVEN
tempranillo 100%

**87** Colour: cherry, purple rim. Nose: expressive, fresh fruit, red berry notes, creamy oak. Palate: flavourful, fruity, good acidity, round tannins.

EL ARTE DE VIVIR 2007 T
tempranillo 100%

**87** Colour: bright cherry. Nose: ripe fruit, sweet spices, creamy oak, expressive. Palate: flavourful, fruity, toasty, round tannins.

OBRA 2007 T ROBLE
tempranillo 100%

**87** Colour: bright cherry. Nose: sweet spices, creamy oak, expressive, fruit preserve. Palate: toasty, round tannins, spicy, great length.

## CUARTO MOTIVO 4 MESES 2007 T ROBLE
tempranillo 100%

**87** Colour: bright cherry. Nose: ripe fruit, sweet spices, creamy oak, expressive. Palate: flavourful, fruity, toasty, round tannins.

## VIVIR, VIVIR 2007 T
tempranillo 100%

**81**

## NEO PUNTA ESENCIA 2006 T
tempranillo 100%

**90** Colour: bright cherry. Nose: ripe fruit, sweet spices, creamy oak, expressive. Palate: flavourful, fruity, toasty, round tannins.

## NEO 2006 T
tempranillo 100%

**89** Colour: bright cherry. Nose: ripe fruit, sweet spices, creamy oak, expressive, powerfull. Palate: flavourful, fruity, toasty, round tannins.

## OBRA 2005 TC
tempranillo 100%

**85** Colour: bright cherry. Nose: sweet spices, expressive, macerated fruit. Palate: flavourful, fruity, toasty, round tannins, soft tannins.

## BODEGAS Y VIÑEDOS DEL CONDE SAN CRISTÓBAL

Ctra. Valladolid a Soria, km. 303
47300 Peñafiel (Valladolid)
☎: 983 878 055 - Fax: 983 878 196
bodega@condesancristobal.com
www.condesancristobal.com

## CONDE DE SAN CRISTÓBAL 2006 T
tinta del país 80%, merlot 10%, cabernet sauvignon 10%

**90** Colour: bright cherry. Nose: ripe fruit, sweet spices, creamy oak, expressive. Palate: flavourful, fruity, toasty, round tannins.

## BODEGAS Y VIÑEDOS DEL JARO

Ctra. Pesquera - Valbuena, s/n. Finca El Quiñón
47315 Pesquera de Duero (Valladolid)
☎: 900 505 855 - Fax: 956 852 339
vinos@gvitivinicola.com
www.grupohebe.com

## CHAFANDÍN 2007 T
**91** Colour: bright cherry. Nose: ripe fruit, sweet spices, creamy oak, expressive, mineral. Palate: flavourful, fruity, toasty, round tannins.

## SED DE CANÁ 2007 T

**89** Colour: very deep cherry, garnet rim. Nose: macerated fruit, balanced, sweet spices, new oak, mineral. Palate: full, fruity, smoky aftertaste.

## JAROS 2006 T

**89** Colour: deep cherry, garnet rim. Nose: ripe fruit, sweet spices, new oak, balanced, red berry notes. Palate: powerful, full, good acidity, fruity, toasty.

SEMBRO

## BODEGAS Y VIÑEDOS ESCUDERO

Camino El Ramo, s/n
09311 Olmedillo de Roa (Burgos)
☎: 629 857 575 - Fax: 947 551 070
info@costaval.com
www.costaval.com

## COSTAVAL 2007 T ROBLE
tempranillo 100%

**83**

## COSTAVAL 2007 T
tempranillo 100%

**81**

## COSTAVAL 2006 TC
tempranillo 100%

**85** Colour: bright cherry. Nose: ripe fruit, sweet spices, creamy oak, expressive, red berry notes. Palate: flavourful, fruity, toasty, round tannins.

## ELOY ESCUDERO 2006 T
tempranillo 100%

**85** Colour: dark-red cherry. Nose: spicy, herbaceous, fruit preserve. Palate: spirituous, warm, balsamic, lacks expression.

## COSTAVAL 2004 TR
tempranillo 100%

**90** Colour: cherry, garnet rim. Nose: ripe fruit, spicy, creamy oak, toasty, complex, mineral, undergrowth. Palate: powerful, flavourful, toasty, round tannins, fruity aftertaste.

## BODEGAS Y VIÑEDOS GALLEGO ZAPATERO

Segunda Travesía de la Olma, 4
09312 Anguix (Burgos)
☎: 648 180 777
info@bodegasgallegozapatero.com

**YOTUEL 2007 T**
tempranillo 100%

**87** Colour: cherry, purple rim. Nose: powerful, varietal, expressive, red berry notes. Palate: flavourful, fruity, fresh, good structure.

**YOTUEL VIÑAS VIEJAS 2006 T**
tempranillo 100%

**91** Colour: deep cherry. Nose: spicy, cedar wood, ripe fruit. Palate: fine tannins, powerful, flavourful, toasty, ripe fruit, mineral.

**YOTUEL SELECCIÓN 2006 T**
tempranillo 100%

**88** Colour: bright cherry. Nose: ripe fruit, sweet spices, creamy oak. Palate: flavourful, fruity, toasty, round tannins.

**YOTUEL VIÑAS VIEJAS 2005 T**
tempranillo 100%

**91** Colour: cherry, garnet rim. Nose: characterful, varietal, mineral, earthy notes, cedar wood, dark chocolate. Palate: flavourful, powerful, fleshy, spicy, slightly dry, soft tannins.

## BODEGAS Y VIÑEDOS JUAN MANUEL BURGOS

Aranda, 39
09471 Fuentelcesped (Burgos)
☎: 947 55 744 - Fax: 947 557 443
www.byvjuanmanuelburgos.com

**AVAN CEPAS CENTENARIAS S/N T**

**87** Colour: dark-red cherry, garnet rim. Nose: fruit liqueur notes, floral, creamy oak, aged wood nuances, fruit preserve. Palate: flavourful, grainy tannins, fruity, spicy.

**AVAN NACIMIENTO 2007 T**

**90** Colour: bright cherry. Nose: ripe fruit, sweet spices, creamy oak, expressive, complex, red berry notes, lactic notes. Palate: flavourful, fruity, toasty, round tannins.

**AVAN CONCENTRACIÓN 2006 T**

**93** Colour: cherry, garnet rim. Nose: spicy, toasty, complex, mineral, ripe fruit, new oak. Palate: powerful, flavourful, toasty, round tannins.

**AVAN TERRUÑO DE VALDEHERNANDO 2006 T**

**93** Colour: cherry, garnet rim. Nose: expressive, ripe fruit, red berry notes, mineral, creamy oak, toasty. Palate: flavourful, powerful, fleshy, fruity, round tannins.

**AVAN VIÑEDO DEL TORRUBIO 2006 T**

**89** Colour: cherry, garnet rim. Nose: powerful, fruit preserve, creamy oak, dark chocolate, sweet spices. Palate: powerful, fleshy, sweetness.

## BODEGAS Y VIÑEDOS LLEIROSO

Ctra. Monasterio s/n
47359 Valbuena del Duero (Valladolid)
☎: 983 683 300 - Fax: 983 683 301
bodega@bodegaslleiroso.com
www.bodegaslleiroso.com

**LLEIROSO 2006 T**

**88** Colour: bright cherry. Nose: ripe fruit, sweet spices, creamy oak, expressive. Palate: flavourful, fruity, toasty, round tannins.

**LVZMILLAR 2006 T ROBLE**

**84**

LVZMILLAR 2006 TC

**87** Colour: cherry, garnet rim. Nose: ripe fruit, spicy, creamy oak, toasty, complex, undergrowth. Palate: flavourful, toasty, round tannins.

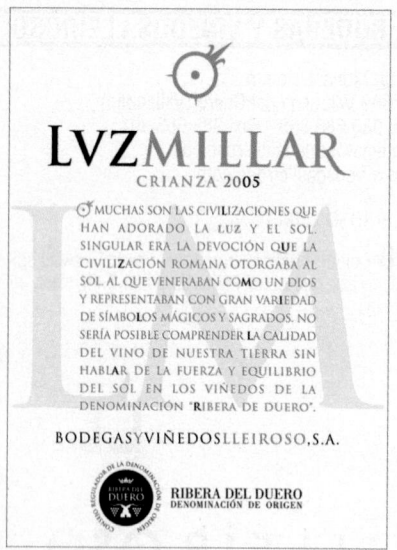

LVZMILLAR 2004 TR

**89** Colour: cherry, garnet rim. Nose: ripe fruit, spicy, creamy oak, toasty, complex, earthy notes, fine reductive notes. Palate: powerful, flavourful, toasty, round tannins, balsamic.

## BODEGAS Y VIÑEDOS MARTÍN BERDUGO

Ctra. de la Colonia, s/n
09400 Aranda de Duero (Burgos)
☎: 947 506 331 - Fax: 947 506 602
bodega@martinberdugo.com
www.martinberdugo.com

MARTÍN BERDUGO 2008 RD
tempranillo 100%

**83**

MARTÍN BERDUGO 2008 T
tempranillo 100%

**83**

MARTÍN BERDUGO 2007 T BARRICA
tempranillo 100%

**89** Colour: bright cherry. Nose: ripe fruit, sweet spices, creamy oak, expressive, balsamic herbs. Palate: flavourful, fruity, toasty, round tannins.

MARTÍN BERDUGO 2006 TC
tempranillo 100%

**90** Colour: deep cherry. Nose: ripe fruit, spicy, creamy oak, toasty, complex, fruit expression, mineral. Palate: powerful, flavourful, toasty, round tannins, sweetness, fruity.

MB MARTÍN BERDUGO 2005 T
tempranillo 100%

**88** Colour: cherry, garnet rim. Nose: ripe fruit, spicy, creamy oak, toasty, complex, floral. Palate: powerful, flavourful, toasty, round tannins.

## BODEGAS Y VIÑEDOS MONTEABELLÓN

Calvario s/n
09318 Nava de Roa (Burgos)
☎: 947 550 000 - Fax: 947 550 219
info@monteabellon.com
www.monteabellon.com

MONTEABELLÓN 5 MESES EN BARRICA 2007 T
tempranillo 100%

**88** Colour: cherry, garnet rim. Nose: ripe fruit, spicy, creamy oak, toasty, mineral. Palate: powerful, flavourful, toasty, round tannins.

MONTEABELLÓN 2006 TC
tempranillo 100%

**84**

MONTEABELLÓN 2004 TR
tempranillo 100%

**89** Colour: cherry, garnet rim. Nose: ripe fruit, spicy, creamy oak, toasty, complex, damp earth, fine reductive notes. Palate: powerful, flavourful, toasty, round tannins.

## BODEGAS Y VIÑEDOS MONTECASTRO

Ctra. VA-130, s/n
47318 Castrillo de Duero (Valladolid)
☎: 983 484 013 - Fax: 983 443 939
info@bodegasmontecastro.es
www.bodegasmontecastro.com

MONTECASTRO Y LLANAHERMOSA 2006 T
tempranillo 95%, cabernet sauvignon 2%, merlot 2%, garnacha 1%

**85** Colour: bright cherry. Nose: ripe fruit, sweet spices, creamy oak, expressive, balsamic herbs. Palate: flavourful, fruity, toasty, round tannins.

## BODEGAS Y VIÑEDOS ORTEGA FOURNIER

Finca El Pinar, s/n
09316 Berlangas de Roa (Burgos)
☎: 947 533 006 - Fax: 947 533 010
jmortega@ofournier.com
www.ofournier.com

URBAN RIBERA 2007 T ROBLE
tinta del país 100%

**85** Colour: bright cherry. Nose: ripe fruit, sweet spices. Palate: flavourful, fruity, toasty, round tannins.

URBAN RIBERA 2006 T ROBLE
tinta del país 100%

**88** Colour: bright cherry. Nose: ripe fruit, sweet spices, creamy oak, expressive. Palate: flavourful, fruity, toasty, round tannins.

SPIGA 2005 T
tinta del país 100%

**91** Colour: cherry, garnet rim. Nose: ripe fruit, spicy, creamy oak, toasty, complex, caramel. Palate: powerful, flavourful, toasty, round tannins, elegant.

ALFA SPIGA 2004 T
tinta del país 100%

**93** Colour: cherry, garnet rim. Nose: ripe fruit, spicy, creamy oak, toasty, complex. Palate: powerful, flavourful, toasty, round tannins, fresh, fine bitter notes.

O. FOURNIER 2004 T
tinta del país 100%

**92** Colour: cherry, garnet rim. Nose: spicy, creamy oak, toasty, complex, dark chocolate, raspberry. Palate: powerful, flavourful, toasty, round tannins, fleshy, mineral.

SPIGA 2004 T
tinta del país 100%

**90** Colour: cherry, garnet rim. Nose: ripe fruit, spicy, creamy oak, toasty, complex, varietal. Palate: powerful, flavourful, toasty, round tannins, mineral.

ALFA SPIGA 2003 T
tinta del país 100%

**91** Colour: cherry, garnet rim. Nose: ripe fruit, spicy, creamy oak, toasty, complex. Palate: powerful, flavourful, toasty, round tannins.

## BODEGAS Y VIÑEDOS RAUDA

Ctra. de Pedrosa s/n

09300 Roa (Burgos)
☎: 947 540 224 - Fax: 947 541 811
informacion@vinosderauda.com
www.vinosderauda.com

RAUDA 2008 RD
tinta del país 95%, albillo 5%

**83**

TINTO ROA 2008 T
tinta del país 100%

**81**

MUSAI DE TINTO ROA 2005 TR
tinta del país 100%

**90** Colour: bright cherry. Nose: ripe fruit, sweet spices, creamy oak, expressive, red berry notes, dry stone. Palate: flavourful, fruity, toasty, round tannins.

## BODEGAS Y VIÑEDOS RECOLETAS

Ctra. Quintanilla, s/n
47359 Olivares de Duero (Valladolid)
☎: 983 687 017 - Fax: 983 687 017
bodegas@gruporecoletas.com
www.bodegasrecoletas.com

RECOLETAS 2007 T ROBLE
tempranillo

**87** Colour: cherry, garnet rim. Nose: fruit preserve, sweet spices, caramel. Palate: fleshy, concentrated, sweetness.

RECOLETAS VENDIMIA SELECCIONADA 2005 T ROBLE
tempranillo

**91** Colour: cherry, garnet rim. Nose: ripe fruit, spicy, creamy oak, toasty, lactic notes, new oak. Palate: powerful, flavourful, toasty, round tannins.

RECOLETAS 2005 TC
tempranillo

**90** Colour: bright cherry. Nose: ripe fruit, sweet spices, creamy oak, roasted coffee. Palate: flavourful, fruity, toasty, round tannins, fleshy.

RECOLETAS 2004 TR
tempranillo

**87** Colour: bright cherry. Nose: ripe fruit, sweet spices, creamy oak, expressive, fruit preserve. Palate: flavourful, fruity, toasty, round tannins.

RECOLETAS VENDIMIA SELECCIONADA 2004 T
tempranillo

**86** Colour: very deep cherry. Nose: roasted coffee, overripe fruit, spicy. Palate: flavourful, powerful, round tannins.

VALDECAMPAÑA

## BODEGAS Y VIÑEDOS ROBEAL S.A.

Ctra. Anguix, s/n
09300 Roa (Burgos)
☎: 947 484 706 - Fax: 947 482 817
info@bodegasrobeal.com
www.bodegasrobeal.com

VALNOGAL 2007 T ROBLE
tempranillo 100%

**83**

LA CAPILLA 2005 TR
tempranillo 100%

**90** Colour: cherry, garnet rim. Nose: ripe fruit, spicy, creamy oak, toasty, complex. Palate: powerful, flavourful, toasty, round tannins.

LA CAPILLA VENDIMIA SELECCIONADA 2005 T

**89** Colour: cherry, garnet rim. Nose: ripe fruit, spicy, creamy oak, toasty, complex, elegant. Palate: powerful, flavourful, toasty, round tannins.

LA CAPILLA 2005 TC
tempranillo 100%

**84**

VALNOGAL 16 MESES 2005 T BARRICA
tempranillo 100%

**84**

## BODEGAS Y VIÑEDOS TABULA

Ctra. de Valbuena km. 2
47359 Olivares de Duero (Valladolid)
☎: 608 219 019 - Fax: 983 395 472
armando@bodegastabula.es
www.bodegastabula.es

DAMANA 2006 TC

**91** Colour: cherry, garnet rim. Nose: ripe fruit, spicy, creamy oak, toasty, complex. Palate: powerful, flavourful, toasty, slightly dry, soft tannins.

# DAMANA

CRIANZA

### RIBERA DEL DUERO
denominación de origen

TÁBULA 2006 T

**90** Colour: deep cherry. Nose: sweet spices, caramel, fruit liqueur notes, ripe fruit, warm, powerfull. Palate: warm, spirituous, toasty.

# Tábula

### RIBERA DEL DUERO
denominación de origen

CLAVE DE TÁBULA 2007 T

**93** Colour: bright cherry. Nose: mineral, fresh fruit, varietal, expressive, complex, cocoa bean. Palate: powerful, flavourful, fresh, fruity.

DAMANA 5 2007 T

**89** Colour: bright cherry. Nose: sweet spices, creamy oak, expressive, fresh fruit. Palate: flavourful, fruity, toasty, round tannins, fresh.

GRAN TÁBULA 2005 T

**93** Colour: bright cherry. Nose: ripe fruit, sweet spices, creamy oak, expressive. Palate: flavourful, fruity, toasty, round tannins.

## BODEGAS Y VIÑEDOS TAMARAL

Ctra. N-122 Valladolid-Soria, km. 310, 6
47314 Peñafiel (Valladolid)
☎: 983 878 017 - Fax: 983 878 089
info@tamaral.com
www.tamaral.com

TAMARAL 2007 T ROBLE
tempranillo 100%

**86** Colour: cherry, purple rim. Nose: fruit preserve, sweet spices, toasty. Palate: powerful, flavourful, fine bitter notes.

TAMARAL 2006 TC
tempranillo 100%

**86** Colour: bright cherry. Nose: ripe fruit, sweet spices, creamy oak, red berry notes. Palate: flavourful, fruity, toasty, round tannins, fruity aftestaste.

TAMARAL FINCA LA MIRA 2005 TR
tempranillo 100%

**85** Colour: cherry, garnet rim. Nose: ripe fruit, spicy, toasty. Palate: powerful, flavourful, toasty, harsh oak tannins.

TAMARAL 2004 TR
tempranillo 100%

**89** Colour: cherry, garnet rim. Nose: ripe fruit, spicy, creamy oak, toasty, complex, undergrowth. Palate: powerful, flavourful, toasty, round tannins, elegant.

## BODEGAS Y VIÑEDOS VALDERIZ S.L.

Ctra. Pedrosa, km 1
09300 Roa (Burgos)
☎: 947 540 460 - Fax: 947 541 032
bodega@valderiz.com

VALDEHERMOSO 2007 T ROBLE
tinto fino 100%

**87** Colour: cherry, garnet rim. Nose: medium intensity, ripe fruit, sweet spices, fragrant herbs. Palate: flavourful, powerful, fleshy, fruity.

VALDERIZ 2006 T

**91** Colour: bright cherry. Nose: ripe fruit, sweet spices, creamy oak, expressive, cocoa bean, mineral. Palate: fruity, toasty, round tannins, fleshy.

VALDEHERMOSO 2006 TC
tinto fino 100%

**88** Colour: bright cherry. Nose: ripe fruit, sweet spices, creamy oak, expressive, undergrowth. Palate: flavourful, fruity, toasty, round tannins.

VALDERIZ 2005 T
tinto fino 100%

**92** Colour: bright cherry. Nose: sweet spices, creamy oak, expressive, macerated fruit, damp earth, faded flowers. Palate: flavourful, fruity, toasty, round tannins, soft tannins.

VALDERIZ TOMÁS ESTEBAN 2005 T
tinto fino 100%

**92** Colour: deep cherry. Nose: ripe fruit, sweet spices, creamy oak, expressive, fruit liqueur notes. Palate: flavourful, fruity, toasty, round tannins, burning notes, spirituous.

VALDERIZ TOMÁS ESTEBAN 1999 T

**93** Colour: cherry, garnet rim. Nose: spicy, creamy oak, complex, macerated fruit, cocoa bean, aged wood nuances, mineral. Palate: powerful, flavourful, toasty, round tannins.

## BODEGAS Y VIÑEDOS VEGA DE YUSO S.L.

Basilón, 9 Cañada Real s/n
47350 Quintanilla de Onésimo (Valladolid)
☎: 983 680 054 - Fax: 983 680 294
bodega@vegadeyuso.com
www.vegadeyuso.com

VEGANTIGUA 10 MESES 2007 T BARRICA
tinto fino 100%

**87** Colour: cherry, garnet rim. Nose: medium intensity, ripe fruit, fruit preserve, sweet spices. Palate: flavourful, powerful, ripe fruit, round tannins.

TRES MATAS 2005 TC

**88** Colour: cherry, garnet rim. Nose: spicy, creamy oak, toasty, fruit preserve. Palate: powerful, flavourful, toasty, round tannins.

# DO RIBERA DEL DUERO

TRESMATAS 2004 TR
tinto fino 100%

**84**

## BODEGAS Y VIÑEDOS VIÑA MAYOR

Ctra. Valladolid - Soria, km. 325,6
47350 Quintanilla de Onésimo (Valladolid)
☎: 983 680 461 - Fax: 983 027 217
barcelo@habarcelo.es
www.vina-mayor.es

VIÑA MAYOR 2008 RD
tinta del país 100%

**82**

VIÑA MAYOR 2008 T ROBLE
tinta del país 100%

**84**

SECRETO 2007 T ROBLE
tinta del país 100%

**90** Colour: bright cherry. Nose: ripe fruit, sweet spices, new oak. Palate: flavourful, fruity, toasty, round tannins.

VIÑA MAYOR 2006 TC
tinta del país 100%

**87** Colour: cherry, garnet rim. Nose: powerful, varietal, ripe fruit, sweet spices, cocoa bean. Palate: flavourful, fruity, fleshy, spicy.

SECRETO 2005 TR
tinta del país 100%

**91** Colour: cherry, garnet rim. Nose: ripe fruit, spicy, creamy oak, toasty, complex, powerfull. Palate: powerful, flavourful, toasty, round tannins.

VIÑA MAYOR 2004 TR
tinta del país 100%

**90** Colour: cherry, garnet rim. Nose: ripe fruit, red berry notes, expressive, sweet spices. Palate: flavourful, fruity, fleshy, complex.

VIÑA MAYOR 2002 TGR
tinta del país 100%

**88** Colour: cherry, garnet rim. Nose: ripe fruit, fruit expression, powerfull, sweet spices, cocoa bean. Palate: ripe fruit, spicy, creamy.

## BODEGAS ZIFAR

Afueras de D. Juan Manuel, 9-11
47300 Peñafiel (Valladolid)

☎: 983 873 147 - Fax: 983 880 287
bodegaszifar@zifar.com
www.zifar.com

ZIFAR SELECCIÓN 2006 T
tempranillo 100%

**89** Colour: bright cherry. Nose: ripe fruit, sweet spices, creamy oak, expressive. Palate: flavourful, fruity, toasty, round tannins.

ZIFAR 2006 TC
tempranillo 100%

**86** Colour: bright cherry. Nose: ripe fruit, sweet spices, creamy oak, cedar wood. Palate: flavourful, fruity, toasty, round tannins.

ZIFAR 2005 TC
tinto fino

**86** Colour: deep cherry. Nose: fruit preserve, dark chocolate, spicy, aromatic coffee. Palate: concentrated, warm, grainy tannins, powerful.

## CEPAS Y BODEGAS

Pº de Zorrilla 77-3º
47007 Valladolid
☎: 983 355 543 - Fax: 983 340 824
info@cepasybodegas.com
www.cepasybodegas.com

ARCO DE GUÍA 2006 TC
tempranillo 100%

**86** Colour: bright cherry. Nose: sweet spices, creamy oak, expressive, fruit preserve. Palate: flavourful, fruity, toasty, round tannins.

CASTILLO DE DOIRAS 2004 T

**87** Colour: bright cherry. Nose: ripe fruit, sweet spices, creamy oak, expressive, balsamic herbs. Palate: flavourful, fruity, toasty, round tannins.

VILLACAMPA DEL MARQUÉS
COLECCIÓN VINOS DE GUARDA

## CILLAR DE SILOS

Paraje El Soto s/n
09370 Quintana del Pidio (Burgos)
☎: 947 545 126 - Fax: 947 545 605
bodega@cillardesilos.es
www.cillardesilos.es

CILLAR DE SILOS 2007 T
tempranillo 100%

**89** Colour: cherry, purple rim. Nose: expressive, red berry notes, violets, sweet spices, creamy oak. Palate: flavourful, full, long, round tannins.

**TORRESILO 2006 T**
tempranillo 100%

**90** Colour: bright cherry. Nose: ripe fruit, sweet spices, creamy oak, expressive. Palate: flavourful, fruity, toasty, round tannins.

## COMENGE BODEGAS Y VIÑEDOS

Camino del Castillo, s/n
47316 Curiel de Duero (Valladolid)
☎: 983 880 363 - Fax: 983 880 717
admin@comenge.com
www.comenge.com

**COMENGE 2006 T**
tempranillo 100%

**90** Colour: cherry, garnet rim. Nose: ripe fruit, spicy, creamy oak, toasty, complex. Palate: powerful, flavourful, toasty, round tannins.

**COMENGE "DON MIGUEL" 2005 T**
tempranillo 90%, cabernet sauvignon 10%

**90** Colour: cherry, garnet rim. Nose: ripe fruit, spicy, creamy oak, toasty, complex, mineral, fruit liqueur notes. Palate: powerful, flavourful, toasty, round tannins, creamy, balsamic, pruney.

## COMPAÑIA DE VINOS DE TELMO RODRÍGUEZ

El Monte s/n
01308 Lanciego (Alava)
☎: 945 628 315 - Fax: 945 628 314
contact@telmorodriguez.com
www.telmorodriguez.com

**MATALLANA 2006 T**

**94** Colour: cherry, garnet rim. Nose: ripe fruit, spicy, creamy oak, toasty, complex, earthy notes. Palate: powerful, flavourful, toasty, round tannins, fleshy.

**M2 DE MATALLANA 2006 T**

**89** Colour: cherry, garnet rim. Nose: ripe fruit, toasty, dark chocolate, sweet spices. Palate: flavourful, ripe fruit, balanced, round tannins.

GAZUR

## CONDADO DE HAZA S.L.

Ctra. La Horra, s/n
09300 Roa (Burgos)
☎: 947 525 254 - Fax: 947 525 262
info@condadodehaza.com
www.condadodehaza.com

CONDADO DE HAZA 2006 T

**87** Colour: cherry, garnet rim. Nose: spicy, creamy oak, toasty, ripe fruit. Palate: powerful, flavourful, toasty, round tannins.

ALENZA

## CONVENTO DE OREJA

Avda. Palecia, 1 - 9 L
47010 (Valladolid)
☎: 685 990 596 - Fax: 913 710 098
convento@conventooreja.com
www.conventooreja.com

CONVENTO OREJA 2007 T ROBLE
tinta del país 100%

**85** Colour: cherry, garnet rim. Nose: medium intensity, ripe fruit, lactic notes. Palate: flavourful, powerful, fruity.

CONVENTO OREJA 2006 TC
tinta del país 100%

**85** Colour: cherry, garnet rim. Nose: overripe fruit, sweet spices, creamy oak. Palate: powerful, fleshy, harsh oak tannins.

CONVENTO OREJA 2005 TC
tinta del país 100%

**87** Colour: cherry, garnet rim. Nose: spicy, creamy oak, toasty, complex, fruit liqueur notes. Palate: powerful, flavourful, toasty, round tannins, sweetness.

CONVENTO OREJA MEMORIA 2004 TR
tinta del país 100%

**88** Colour: cherry, garnet rim. Nose: ripe fruit, spicy, creamy oak, toasty, complex, wet leather. Palate: powerful, flavourful, toasty, round tannins, reductive nuances.

## DEHESA DE LOS CANÓNIGOS S.A.

Ctra. Renedo-Pesquera, km. 39
47315 Pesquera de Duero (Valladolid)
☎: 983 484 001 - Fax: 983 484 040

bodega@dehesacanonigos.com
www.bodegadehesadeloscanonigos.com

DEHESA DE LOS CANÓNIGOS 2006 TC

**87** Colour: deep cherry, orangey edge. Nose: medium intensity, toasty, creamy oak, aromatic coffee. Palate: spicy, balsamic, fleshy.

DEHESA DE LOS CANÓNIGOS 2001 TGR

**90** Colour: pale ruby, brick rim edge. Nose: elegant, spicy, fine reductive notes, wet leather, aged wood nuances, fruit liqueur notes. Palate: spicy, fine tannins, elegant, long.

## DEHESA VALDELAGUNA

Ctra. Valoria, km. 16
Pesquera de Duero (Valladolid)
☎: 699 940 955 - Fax: 921 142 325
montelaguna@montelaguna.es
www.montelaguna.es

MONTELAGUNA 2007 T
tempranillo 100%

**88** Colour: very deep cherry, purple rim. Nose: ripe fruit, elegant, warm, varietal. Palate: unctuous, fruity, powerful, ripe fruit.

MONTELAGUNA 2007 TC
tempranillo 100%

**88** Colour: bright cherry. Nose: ripe fruit, sweet spices, new oak. Palate: flavourful, fruity, toasty, round tannins.

RA 2006 T
tempranillo 100%

**90** Colour: very deep cherry. Nose: powerful, ripe fruit, fruit preserve, sweet spices, cocoa bean, scrubland. Palate: flavourful, fleshy, ripe fruit, creamy, round tannins.

## DÍAZ BAYO HERMANOS

Camino de los Anarinos, s/n
09471 Fuentelcésped (Burgos)
☎: 947 561 020 - Fax: 947 561 204
info@bodegadiazbayo.com
www.bodegadiazbayo.com

NUESTRO 10 MESES 2006 T BARRICA
tempranillo 100%

**92** Colour: dark-red cherry. Nose: powerful, ripe fruit, expressive, toasty. Palate: flavourful, powerful, fleshy, round tannins, creamy, roasted-coffee aftertaste, complex.

NUESTRO CRIANZA 2006 TC
tempranillo 100%

**92** Colour: cherry, garnet rim. Nose: ripe fruit, spicy, creamy oak, toasty, complex. Palate: powerful, flavourful, toasty, round tannins.

NUESTRO 20 MESES 2005 T BARRICA
tinta del país

**92** Colour: deep cherry. Nose: closed, ripe fruit, spicy, creamy oak. Palate: sweet tannins, flavourful, fleshy, full, spirituous, mineral.

## DOMINIO BASCONCILLOS

Condado de Treviño, 55
09001 (Burgos)
☎: 947 473 300 - Fax: 947 473 360
info@dominiobasconcillos.com
www.dominiobasconcillos.com

DOMINIO BASCONCILLOS 2006 T ROBLE

**87** Colour: cherry, garnet rim. Nose: ripe fruit, spicy, creamy oak, toasty, complex, floral. Palate: powerful, flavourful, toasty, round tannins.

VIÑA MAGNA 2005 TC
tinta del país 100%

**88** Colour: bright cherry. Nose: ripe fruit, sweet spices, creamy oak, expressive. Palate: flavourful, fruity, toasty, round tannins.

VIÑA MAGNA 2004 TR
tinta del país 100%

**85** Colour: pale ruby, brick rim edge. Nose: spicy, toasty, complex, fine reductive notes. Palate: powerful, flavourful, toasty, grainy tannins.

## DOMINIO DE PINGUS S.L.

Hospital s/n (Apdo. 93, Peñafiel)

47350 Quintanilla de Onésimo (Valladolid)
☎: 639 833 854

PINGUS 2007 T

**97** Colour: cherry, purple rim. Nose: powerful, fresh fruit, red berry notes, mineral, creamy oak. Palate: flavourful, fleshy, balsamic, round tannins.

FLOR DE PINGUS 2007 T

**95** Colour: cherry, purple rim. Nose: elegant, fresh fruit, red berry notes, sweet spices, creamy oak. Palate: flavourful, fruity, fresh, spicy.

PINGUS 2006 T

**97** Colour: cherry, garnet rim. Nose: elegant, ripe fruit, cocoa bean, sweet spices. Palate: fleshy, complex, flavourful, toasty, sweet tannins.

FLOR DE PINGUS 2006 T

**95** Colour: cherry, garnet rim. Nose: powerful, ripe fruit, toasty, dark chocolate, sweet spices. Palate: flavourful, fleshy, ripe fruit, sweet tannins.

## DOMINIO DE SAN ANTONIO

Ctra. Madrid-Irún (Camino Sinovas), Km. 163
09400 Aranda de Duero (Burgos)
☎: 661 328 504 - Fax: 985 310 010
grblanco@raraderaro.com

LA SOLEDAD 2007 TC
tempranillo

**92** Colour: cherry, garnet rim. Nose: ripe fruit, spicy, creamy oak, toasty, complex, mineral. Palate: powerful, flavourful, toasty, round tannins.

DOMINIO DE SAN ANTONIO 2007 T
tempranillo

**91** Colour: cherry, garnet rim. Nose: ripe fruit, spicy, creamy oak, toasty, complex. Palate: powerful, flavourful, toasty, round tannins.

LAS FAVORITAS 2007 T
tempranillo

**88** Colour: cherry, garnet rim. Nose: ripe fruit, spicy, creamy oak, toasty, complex. Palate: powerful, flavourful, toasty, round tannins.

## DURÓN S.A.

Ctra. Roa-La Horra km. 3,800
09300 Roa (Burgos)
☎: 902 227 700 - Fax: 902 227 701
bodega@cofradiasamaniego.com
www.bodegasduron.com

DURÓN 2005 TC

**87** Colour: deep cherry, brick rim edge. Nose: fruit liqueur notes, warm, spicy, aromatic coffee. Palate: light-bodied, fruity, good acidity, grainy tannins.

DURÓN 2003 TR

## 83

OPTIMO DE DURÓN

## ÉBANO VIÑEDOS Y BODEGAS S.L.

Ctra. Palencia, km. 15,5
09440 Gumiel de Mercado (Burgos)
☎: 986 609 060 - Fax: 986 609 313
ebano@ebanovinedosybodegas.com
www.ebanovinedosybodegas.com

ÉBANO 2007 T
tempranillo 100%

**85** Colour: bright cherry. Nose: ripe fruit, sweet spices, creamy oak. Palate: flavourful, fruity, toasty, round tannins.

ÉBANO 2005 TC
tempranillo 100%

**92** Colour: cherry, garnet rim. Nose: ripe fruit, spicy, toasty, complex, mineral. Palate: powerful, flavourful, toasty, round tannins, spicy.

## EL LAGAR DE ISILLA

Antigua Ctra. N-122 s/n
09471 La Vid (Burgos)
☎: 947 504 316 - Fax: 947 504 316
bodegas@lagarisilla.es
www.lagarisilla.es

EL LAGAR DE ISILLA 2007 T ROBLE
tinta del país 93%, cabernet sauvignon 7%

**86** Colour: cherry, garnet rim. Nose: medium intensity, balsamic herbs, fragrant herbs. Palate: flavourful, powerful, fleshy, ripe fruit, slightly dry, soft tannins.

EL LAGAR DE ISILLA 2007 T
tinta del país

## 84

EL LAGAR DE ISILLA 2006 TC

**89** Colour: bright cherry. Nose: ripe fruit, sweet spices, creamy oak, expressive, red berry notes. Palate: flavourful, fruity, toasty, round tannins.

EL LAGAR DE ISILLA VENDIMIA SELECCIONADA 2006 T
tinta del país

**89** Colour: bright cherry. Nose: ripe fruit, sweet spices, creamy oak, expressive, characterful. Palate: flavourful, fruity, toasty, round tannins.

EL LAGAR DE ISILLA 2004 TR
tinta del país

**89** Colour: cherry, garnet rim. Nose: ripe fruit, spicy, creamy oak, toasty, complex. Palate: powerful, flavourful, toasty, round tannins.

## EMINA

Ctra. San Bernardo s/n
47359 Valbuena de Duero (Valladolid)
☎: 902 430 170 - Fax: 902 430 189
emina@emina.es
www.emina.es

EMINA 12 MESES 2006 T
tempranillo 100%

**89** Colour: cherry, garnet rim. Nose: ripe fruit, spicy, toasty, complex, dark chocolate. Palate: powerful, flavourful, toasty, slightly dry, soft tannins.

EMINA PRESTIGIO 2006 T
tempranillo 100%

**89** Colour: bright cherry. Nose: ripe fruit, sweet spices, creamy oak, expressive. Palate: flavourful, fruity, toasty, round tannins.

**EMINA ATIO 2005 T**
tempranillo 100%

**90** Colour: cherry, garnet rim. Nose: ripe fruit, spicy, creamy oak, complex, cocoa bean. Palate: powerful, flavourful, toasty, round tannins, fresh.

**EMINA 400 2005 T**
tempranillo 100%

**90** Colour: cherry, garnet rim. Nose: ripe fruit, spicy, creamy oak, toasty, complex. Palate: powerful, flavourful, toasty, round tannins.

**EMINA 3 BARRICAS SPANISH 2005 T**
tempranillo 100%

**90** Colour: cherry, garnet rim. Nose: ripe fruit, spicy, creamy oak, toasty, complex, undergrowth. Palate: powerful, flavourful, toasty, round tannins.

**EMINA 3 BARRICAS FRENCH 2005 T**
tempranillo 100%

**89** Colour: bright cherry. Nose: ripe fruit, sweet spices, creamy oak, expressive, damp earth, undergrowth. Palate: flavourful, fruity, toasty, round tannins.

**EMINA 3 BARRICAS AMERICAN 2005 T**
tempranillo 100%

**88** Colour: bright cherry. Nose: ripe fruit, sweet spices, creamy oak, expressive, roasted coffee. Palate: flavourful, fruity, toasty, round tannins.

## FINCA TORREMILANOS
## BODEGAS PEÑALBA LÓPEZ

Finca Torremilanos
09400 Aranda de Duero (Burgos)
☎: 947 512 852 - Fax: 947 572 856
torremilanos@torremilanos.com
www.torremilanos.com

**MONTE CASTRILLO 2008 RD**
tempranillo

**87** Colour: rose. Nose: powerful, red berry notes, floral, expressive, ripe fruit. Palate: fruity, fresh, flavourful.

**CYCLO 2006 T**
tempranillo 100%

**92** Colour: deep cherry. Nose: ripe fruit, sweet spices, creamy oak, expressive. Palate: flavourful, fruity, toasty, slightly dry, soft tannins.

**TORREMILANOS 2005 TC**
tempranillo 90%, cabernet sauvignon 7%, merlot 3%

**87** Colour: very deep cherry. Nose: new oak, spicy, fruit preserve. Palate: flavourful, full, slightly dry, soft tannins.

**TORRE - ALBENIZ 2004 TR**
tempranillo

**88** Colour: bright cherry. Nose: ripe fruit, sweet spices, creamy oak, expressive, floral. Palate: flavourful, fruity, toasty, round tannins.

**TORREMILANOS 2004 TR**
tempranillo 85%, cabernet sauvignon 15%

**87** Colour: cherry, garnet rim. Nose: ripe fruit, spicy, toasty, complex, fine reductive notes. Palate: flavourful, toasty, powerful tannins.

**FINCA TORREMILANOS**

## FINCA VILLACRECES, S.L.

Ctra. Soria, km. 322
47350 Quintanilla de Onésimo (Valladolid)
☎: 983 680 437 - Fax: 983 683 314
villacreces@villacreces.com
www.villacreces.com

**FINCA VILLACRECES 2006 T**
tinto fino 86%, cabernet sauvignon 10%, merlot 4%

**90** Colour: cherry, garnet rim. Nose: ripe fruit, spicy, creamy oak, toasty, complex, cocoa bean, earthy notes. Palate: powerful, flavourful, toasty, round tannins.

## FUENTENARRO

Cruce
09311 La Horra (Burgos)
☎: 947 542 092 - Fax: 947 542 083
bodegas@fuentenarro.com
www.fuentenarro.com

**VIÑA FUENTENARRO 2008 RD**
tempranillo 100%

**83**

**VIÑA FUENTENARRO VENDIMIA SELECCIONADA 2007 T**
tempranillo 100%

**90** Colour: bright cherry. Nose: ripe fruit, sweet spices, creamy oak, expressive, balsamic herbs. Palate: flavourful, fruity, toasty, round tannins.

**VIÑA FUENTENARRO 2007 T**
tempranillo 100%

**88** Colour: bright cherry. Nose: ripe fruit, sweet spices, creamy oak, expressive, powerfull. Palate: flavourful, fruity, toasty, round tannins.

VIÑA FUENTENARRO 2006 T BARRICA
tempranillo 100%

**88** Colour: cherry, garnet rim. Nose: ripe fruit, toasty, complex, sweet spices. Palate: powerful, flavourful, toasty, slightly dry, soft tannins.

VIÑA FUENTENARRO 2005 TC
tempranillo 100%

**90** Colour: cherry, garnet rim. Nose: ripe fruit, spicy, creamy oak, toasty, complex, scrubland. Palate: powerful, flavourful, toasty, round tannins.

VIÑA FUENTENARRO 2004 TR
tempranillo 100%

**92** Colour: cherry, garnet rim. Nose: ripe fruit, spicy, creamy oak, toasty, mineral, fragrant herbs. Palate: powerful, flavourful, toasty, round tannins.

## FUENTESPINA

Camino Cascajo, s/n
09470 Fuentespina (Burgos)
☎: 921 596 002 - Fax: 921 596 035
ana@avelinovegas.com
www.avelinovegas.com

FUENTESPINA 2007 T ROBLE
tempranillo 100%

**87** Colour: bright cherry. Nose: ripe fruit, sweet spices, creamy oak, expressive. Palate: flavourful, fruity, toasty, round tannins.

CORONA DE CASTILLA PRESTIGIO 2006 T ROBLE
tempranillo 100%

**89** Colour: deep cherry. Nose: ripe fruit, spicy, complex. Palate: powerful, flavourful, toasty, round tannins.

FUENTESPINA 2006 TC
tempranillo 100%

**85** Colour: bright cherry. Nose: ripe fruit, sweet spices, creamy oak, expressive. Palate: flavourful, fruity, toasty, round tannins.

F DE FUENTESPINA 2004 T
tempranillo 100%

**91** Colour: cherry, garnet rim. Nose: ripe fruit, spicy, creamy oak, toasty, complex, characterful, mineral. Palate: powerful, flavourful, toasty, good structure, slightly dry, soft tannins.

FUENTESPINA 2004 TR
tempranillo 100%

**87** Colour: cherry, garnet rim. Nose: ripe fruit, spicy, toasty, caramel. Palate: powerful, flavourful, toasty, round tannins.

CORONA DE CASTILLA ÉLITE 2003 TR
tempranillo 100%

**86** Colour: cherry, garnet rim. Nose: spicy, fruit liqueur notes, toasty. Palate: flavourful, long, round tannins.

FUENTESPINA RESERVA ESPECIAL 2003 TR
tempranillo 100%

**86** Colour: cherry, garnet rim. Nose: overripe fruit, toasty, spicy. Palate: flavourful, great length, fine bitter notes, round tannins.

VIÑA CARPIO
ARCO VIEJO

## GRANDES BODEGAS

Ctra. de Sotillo, s/n
09311 La Horra (Burgos)
☎: 947 542 166 - Fax: 947 542 165
marketing@marquesdevelilla.com
www.marquesdevelilla.es

MARQUÉS DE VELILLA 2008 T JOVEN
tinta del país 100%

**84**

MARQUÉS DE VELILLA 2005 T
tinta del país 100%

**90** Colour: very deep cherry. Nose: creamy oak, toasty, fruit preserve, mineral. Palate: flavourful, elegant, fine tannins.

MARQUÉS DE VELILLA FINCA LA MARÍA 2005 T
tinta del país 100%

**87** Colour: bright cherry. Nose: ripe fruit, sweet spices, creamy oak, expressive, grassy, fruit liqueur notes. Palate: flavourful, fruity, toasty, round tannins.

DONCEL DE MATAPERRAS 2004 TC
tinta del país 100%

**91** Colour: cherry, garnet rim. Nose: spicy, creamy oak, toasty, fruit preserve, powerfull. Palate: powerful, flavourful, toasty, round tannins.

## GRUPO ALGAR

Carpinteros, 13
28670 Villaviciosa de Odón (Madrid)

☎: 916 169 122 - Fax: 916 166 724
info@grupoalgar.com
www.grupoalgar.com

**ABILIA 2006 T ROBLE**
tinta del país

**83**

**ABILIA 2005 TC**
tinta del país

**86** Colour: deep cherry, garnet rim. Nose: fruit preserve, balanced, creamy oak, dark chocolate. Palate: flavourful, powerful, good acidity, grainy tannins.

**ABILIA 2003 TR**
tinta del país

**88** Colour: light cherry, orangey edge. Nose: fruit liqueur notes, sweet spices, new oak, dark chocolate, balanced. Palate: flavourful, good acidity, round tannins, classic aged character.

## GRUPO YLLERA

Ctra. Madrid - Coruña, km. 173, 5
47490 Rueda (Valladolid)
☎: 983 868 097 - Fax: 983 868 177
grupoyllera@grupoyllera.com
www.grupoyllera.com

**BRACAMONTE 2007 T ROBLE**

**88** Colour: bright cherry. Nose: ripe fruit, sweet spices, creamy oak, red berry notes. Palate: flavourful, fruity, toasty, round tannins.

**BRACAMONTE 2001 TR**

**87** Colour: cherry, garnet rim. Nose: ripe fruit, spicy, toasty, aged wood nuances. Palate: powerful, flavourful, toasty, round tannins.

VIÑA DEL VAL

## HACIENDA SOLANO

La Solana, 6
09370 La Aguilera (Burgos)
☎: 947 545 582 - Fax: 947 545 582
hacienda_solano@yahoo.es
www.haciendasolano.com

**HACIENDA SOLANO 6 MESES 2007 T ROBLE**
tempranillo 100%

**82**

**HACIENDA SOLANO 12 MESES 2006 TC**
tempranillo 100%

**91** Colour: cherry, garnet rim. Nose: ripe fruit, spicy, creamy oak, toasty, complex. Palate: powerful, flavourful, toasty, round tannins.

## HERMANOS ESPINOSA RIVERA

Plazuela del Postigo, 10
47315 Pesquera de Duero (Valladolid)
☎: 983 870 137 - Fax: 983 870 201
hesvera@hesvera.es
www.hesvera.es

**HESVERA 2007 T ROBLE**
tinta del país 100%

**84**

**HESVERA 2006 TC**
tinta del país 100%

**87** Colour: cherry, garnet rim. Nose: ripe fruit, spicy, creamy oak, toasty. Palate: powerful, flavourful, toasty, round tannins.

**HESVERA COSECHA LIMITADA 2006 T ROBLE**
tinta del país 100%

**86** Colour: cherry, garnet rim. Nose: ripe fruit, spicy, creamy oak, toasty, complex, aged wood nuances, tobacco. Palate: powerful, flavourful, toasty, round tannins.

## HORNILLOS BALLESTEROS

Camino Tenerías, 9
09300 Roa de Duero (Burgos)
☎: 947 541 071 - Fax: 947 541 071
hornillosballesteros@telefonica.net

**MIBAL 2008 T**

**87** Colour: cherry, garnet rim. Nose: fresh fruit, red berry notes, animal reductive notes. Palate: full, fruity, flavourful, good acidity, round tannins.

**MIBAL 2006 T**

**87** Colour: bright cherry. Nose: ripe fruit, sweet spices, expressive, fruit liqueur notes. Palate: flavourful, toasty, sweet tannins.

**MIBAL SELECCIÓN 2005 T**

**91** Colour: cherry, garnet rim. Nose: ripe fruit, spicy, creamy oak, toasty, complex. Palate: powerful, flavourful, toasty, round tannins.

**PERFIL 2005 T**

**90** Colour: very deep cherry. Nose: ripe fruit, sweet spices, creamy oak, expressive, dark chocolate, cocoa bean. Palate: flavourful, fruity, toasty, round tannins, spirituous, fleshy, sweetness.

**MIBAL SELECCIÓN 2004 T**

**88** Colour: cherry, garnet rim. Nose: ripe fruit, spicy, toasty, creamy oak. Palate: powerful, flavourful, toasty, round tannins.

## J.A. CALVO CASAJÚS S.L.

Cercados s/n
09443 Quintana del Pidío (Burgos)
☎: 947 545 699 - Fax: 947 545 626
info@bodegascasajus.com
www.bodegascasajus.com

**CASAJÚS 2007 T BARRICA**
tinta del país 100%

**86** Colour: bright cherry. Nose: ripe fruit, expressive, scrubland. Palate: flavourful, fruity, round tannins, fine bitter notes.

**CASAJÚS 2005 TC**
tinta del país 100%

**91** Colour: very deep cherry. Nose: ripe fruit, spicy, creamy oak, toasty, complex, aromatic coffee. Palate: powerful, flavourful, toasty, round tannins, spirituous, creamy.

## LA COLECCIÓN D.C.E., S.L.

Domingo Martínez, 6
47007 (Valladolid)
☎: 983 271 595 - Fax: 983 271 608
exportacion@lacoacciondevinos.com
www.lacoacciondevinos.com

**VALLIS TOLITUM 2007 T**
tempranillo 80%, cabernet sauvignon 20%

**82**

**VALLIS 2007 T ROBLE**
tempranillo 100%

**82**

**1492 SANTAFÉ 2006 TC**
tempranillo 100%

**85** Colour: bright cherry. Nose: ripe fruit, sweet spices, creamy oak, expressive. Palate: flavourful, fruity, toasty, round tannins.

**PALACIO DE SANTA CRUZ VENDIMIA SELECCIONADA 2004 T**
tempranillo 100%

**88** Colour: cherry, garnet rim. Nose: spicy, toasty, complex, lactic notes, creamy oak, ripe fruit. Palate: powerful, flavourful, toasty, round tannins.

**1492 SANTAFÉ 2004 TR**
tempranillo 100%

**87** Colour: cherry, garnet rim. Nose: ripe fruit, spicy, creamy oak, toasty, complex. Palate: powerful, flavourful, toasty, round tannins.

## LEGARIS

Ctra. Peñafiel Encinas de Esgueva km. 2,5
47316 Curiel de Duero (Valladolid)
☎: 983 878 088 - Fax: 983 881 034
v.sanchez@codorniu.es
www.legaris.es

**LEGARIS 2006 TC**
tempranillo

**86** Colour: cherry, garnet rim. Nose: ripe fruit, spicy, creamy oak, toasty. Palate: powerful, flavourful, toasty, round tannins.

**LEGARIS 2005 TR**
tempranillo

**89** Colour: very deep cherry, garnet rim. Nose: ripe fruit, toasty, aromatic coffee, expressive. Palate: ripe fruit, powerful, grainy tannins, concentrated.

## LYNUS VIÑEDOS Y BODEGAS

Camino de las Pozas s/n
47350 Quintanilla de Onésimo (Valladolid)
☎: 661 879 016
rodrigo.pons@lynus.es

**PAGOS DEL INFANTE 2007 T ROBLE**
tempranillo 100%

**85** Colour: bright cherry. Nose: ripe fruit, sweet spices, creamy oak, expressive. Palate: flavourful, fruity, toasty, round tannins.

**LYNUS 2006 TC**
tempranillo 100%

**89** Colour: cherry, garnet rim. Nose: ripe fruit, spicy, creamy oak, toasty, complex. Palate: powerful, flavourful, toasty, round tannins, fine bitter notes.

**PAGOS DEL INFANTE 2006 TC**

**87** Colour: cherry, garnet rim. Nose: balanced, warm, cocoa bean, pattiserie, candied fruit. Palate: spicy, fruity, balanced.

**LYNUS ÁUREA 2005 TR**
tempranillo 100%

**91** Colour: cherry, garnet rim. Nose: ripe fruit, spicy, creamy oak, toasty, complex, cedar wood, undergrowth. Palate: powerful, flavourful, toasty, round tannins.

## MARQUÉS DE VALPARAISO

Paraje los Llanillos s/n
09370 Quintana del Pidío (Burgos)
☎: 947 545 286 - Fax: 947 545 163
m.valparaiso@fer.es
www.paternina.com

**FINCA EL ENCINAL 2007 T ROBLE**

**87** Colour: cherry, garnet rim. Nose: medium intensity, ripe fruit, spicy. Palate: flavourful, powerful, round tannins.

**MARQUÉS DE VALPARAÍSO 2007 T ROBLE**
tinta del país 100%

**82**

**MARQUÉS DE VALPARAÍSO 2006 TC**
tinta del país, cabernet sauvignon

**84**

**FINCA EL ENCINAL 2004 TC**

**87** Colour: cherry, garnet rim. Nose: ripe fruit, spicy, toasty, complex. Palate: powerful, flavourful, toasty, round tannins.

**MARQUÉS DE VALPARAÍSO 2002 TR**
tinta del país, cabernet sauvignon, merlot

**85** Colour: cherry, garnet rim. Nose: spicy, creamy oak, toasty, complex, fruit liqueur notes. Palate: powerful, flavourful, toasty, round tannins, sweetness.

**FINCA EL ENCINAL TR**

**83**

## MONTEBACO

Finca MonteAlto
47359 Valbuena de Duero (Valladolid)
☎: 983 485 128 - Fax: 983 485 033
montebaco@bodegasmontebaco.com
www.bodegasmontebaco.com

**MONTEBACO 2007 T**
tinto fino 100%

**90** Colour: cherry, purple rim. Nose: ripe fruit, creamy oak, spicy, cocoa bean. Palate: spicy, elegant, round tannins, ripe fruit.

**SEMELE 2007 T**
tinto fino 90%, merlot 10%

**82**

**MONTEBACO VENDIMIA SELECCIONADA 2006 TC**
tinto fino 100%

**90** Colour: bright cherry. Nose: ripe fruit, sweet spices, creamy oak, expressive, dark chocolate. Palate: flavourful, fruity, toasty, round tannins.

## MONTEGAREDO S.L.

Ctra. Boada - Pedrosa, km. 1
09314 Boada de Roa (Burgos)
☎: 947 530 003 - Fax: 947 530 017

info@montegaredo.com
www.montegaredo.com

MONTEGAREDO 2007 TC
tinto fino 100%

**83**

PIRÁMIDE 2006 T
tinto fino

**88** Colour: deep cherry. Nose: ripe fruit, powerfull, mineral, sweet spices, cocoa bean. Palate: flavourful, fleshy, powerful, fruity, long.

## MONTEVANNOS

Santiago, s/n
09450 Baños de Valdearados (Burgos)
☎: 947 534 277 - Fax: 947 534 016
bodega@montevannos.es
www.montevannos.es

MONTEVANNOS 2007 T ROBLE
tempranillo 89%, merlot 11%

**86** Colour: deep cherry. Nose: sweet spices, overripe fruit, dark chocolate. Palate: flavourful, fruity, toasty, slightly dry, soft tannins.

OPIMIUS SELECCIÓN ESPECIAL 2005 T
tempranillo 100%

**88** Colour: bright cherry. Nose: ripe fruit, sweet spices, creamy oak, fruit preserve, mineral. Palate: flavourful, fruity, toasty, round tannins.

MONTEVANNOS 2004 TC
tempranillo 90%, merlot 10%

**89** Colour: cherry, garnet rim. Nose: ripe fruit, spicy, creamy oak, toasty, complex. Palate: powerful, flavourful, toasty, round tannins.

MONTEVANNOS 2004 TR
tempranillo 85%, merlot 15%

**88** Colour: cherry, garnet rim. Nose: spicy, creamy oak, toasty, complex, macerated fruit, faded flowers. Palate: powerful, flavourful, toasty, round tannins.

## MUNTRA BODEGAS

Ctra. de Castillejo, s/n
09471 Santa Cruz de la Salceda (Burgos)
☎: 947 561 456 - Fax: 947 561 456
muntra@grupomiral.es
www.bodegasmuntra.es

MUNTRA 2006 T ROBLE
tempranillo 100%

**85** Colour: cherry, garnet rim. Nose: powerful, varietal, ripe fruit. Palate: flavourful, fruity, fleshy.

MUNTRA 2006 TC

**83**

## PAGO DE CARRAOVEJAS

Camino de Carraovejas, s/n
47300 Peñafiel (Valladolid)
☎: 983 878 020 - Fax: 983 878 022
administracion@pagodecarraovejas.com
www.pagodecarraovejas.com

PAGO DE CARRAOVEJAS 2007 TC

**92** Colour: bright cherry. Nose: ripe fruit, sweet spices, creamy oak, expressive, floral, undergrowth. Palate: flavourful, fruity, toasty, round tannins, creamy.

PAGO DE CARRAOVEJAS 2006 TC

**91** Colour: cherry, garnet rim. Nose: ripe fruit, complex, sweet spices, cocoa bean, lactic notes, red berry notes. Palate: powerful, fruity, good acidity, roasted-coffee aftertaste.

PAGO DE CARRAOVEJAS "CUESTA DE LAS LIEBRES" VENDIMIA SELECCIONADA 2005 TR

**93** Colour: dark-red cherry, orangey edge. Nose: ripe fruit, expressive, pattiserie, cocoa bean, earthy notes, scrubland. Palate: fruity, flavourful, powerful, soft tannins, elegant, full.

PAGO DE CARRAOVEJAS "CUESTA DE LAS LIEBRES" VENDIMIA SELECCIONADA 2004 TR

**92** Colour: very deep cherry, brick rim edge. Nose: ripe fruit, earthy notes, characterful, sweet spices, creamy oak, red berry notes. Palate: powerful, flavourful, fruity, round tannins, toasty.

## PAGO DE LOS CAPELLANES

Camino de la Ampudia s/n
09314 Pedrosa de Duero (Burgos)
☎: 947 530 068 - Fax: 947 530 111
bodega@pagodeloscapellanes.com
www.pagodeloscapellanes.com

PAGO DE LOS CAPELLANES 2008 T ROBLE
tinta del país

**89** Colour: cherry, purple rim. Nose: fresh, expressive, ripe fruit, scrubland, sweet spices. Palate: flavourful, fruity, powerful.

PAGO DE LOS CAPELLANES 2006 TC

**90** Colour: cherry, garnet rim. Nose: expressive, ripe fruit, mineral, sweet spices, creamy oak, dark chocolate. Palate: flavourful, fleshy, spicy, round tannins.

### PAGO DE LOS CAPELLANES PARCELA EL PICÓN 2005 TC

**92** Colour: cherry, garnet rim. Nose: earthy notes, mineral, ripe fruit, expressive, complex. Palate: flavourful, good structure, fleshy, spicy, long, round tannins.

### PAGO DE LOS CAPELLANES PARCELA EL NOGAL 2005 T

**92** Colour: very deep cherry. Nose: powerful, fruit preserve, overripe fruit, toasty, dark chocolate. Palate: flavourful, sweetness, fleshy, round tannins.

### PAGO DE LOS CAPELLANES 2005 TR

**90** Colour: cherry, garnet rim. Nose: ripe fruit, fruit expression, spicy, new oak. Palate: flavourful, spicy, round tannins.

## PAGOS DEL REY

Ctra. Palencia-Aranda, km. 53
09311 Olmedillo de Roa (Burgos)
☎: 947 551 111 - Fax: 947 551 311
administracion@pagosdelrey.com
www.pagosdelrey.com

### CONDADO DE ORIZA 2007 T JOVEN

**85** Colour: very deep cherry, purple rim. Nose: varietal, red berry notes, rose petals. Palate: flavourful, full, long, slightly dry, soft tannins.

### CONDADO DE ORIZA 2007 T ROBLE

**85** Colour: bright cherry. Nose: ripe fruit, toasty. Palate: flavourful, fruity, toasty, round tannins.

### ALTOS DE TAMARÓN FUEGO Y HIELO 2007 T JOVEN

**85** Colour: very deep cherry, purple rim. Nose: expressive, red berry notes, floral, sweet spices. Palate: flavourful, full, great length, fine bitter notes, harsh oak tannins.

### ALTOS DE TAMARÓN 2007 T ROBLE

**84**

### CONDADO DE ORIZA 2005 TC

**88** Colour: bright cherry. Nose: ripe fruit, sweet spices, creamy oak, expressive, raspberry, smoky. Palate: flavourful, fruity, toasty, round tannins, balsamic.

### ALTOS DE TAMARÓN 2005 TC

**87** Colour: bright cherry. Nose: ripe fruit, sweet spices, creamy oak, expressive, earthy notes. Palate: flavourful, fruity, toasty, round tannins.

### CONDADO DE ORIZA 2004 TR

**87** Colour: cherry, garnet rim. Nose: ripe fruit, spicy, creamy oak, toasty, complex, earthy notes, undergrowth. Palate: powerful, flavourful, toasty, round tannins.

### ALTOS DE TAMARÓN 2003 TR

**88** Colour: cherry, garnet rim. Nose: ripe fruit, spicy, toasty. Palate: powerful, flavourful, toasty, round tannins.

### ALTOS DE TAMARÓN 2002 TGR

**87** Colour: cherry, garnet rim. Nose: fine reductive notes, fruit expression, spicy, toasty. Palate: flavourful, powerful, lacks fruit.

### CONDADO DE ORIZA 2002 TGR

**86** Colour: cherry, garnet rim. Nose: old leather, fruit preserve, aged wood nuances. Palate: flavourful, full, long.

## PÁRAMO DE GUZMÁN

Ctra. Circunvalación, R-30
09300 Roa (Burgos)
☎: 947 541 191 - Fax: 947 541 192
paramodeguzman@paramodeguzman.es
www.paramodeguzman.es

### PÁRAMO DE GUZMÁN 2008 RD

**87** Colour: rose, purple rim. Nose: ripe fruit, red berry notes, floral. Palate: flavourful, light-bodied, fruity, fresh.

### PÁRAMO DE GUZMÁN 2007 T BARRICA

**87** Colour: cherry, garnet rim. Nose: powerful, ripe fruit, sweet spices, mineral. Palate: flavourful, powerful, spicy, round tannins.

### RAÍZ DE GUZMÁN 2006 T
tempranillo

**92** Colour: deep cherry. Nose: ripe fruit, sweet spices, mineral, characterful, expressive. Palate: flavourful, fleshy, spicy, creamy, round tannins.

### PÁRAMO DE GUZMÁN 2006 TC

**88** Colour: dark-red cherry. Nose: earthy notes, ripe fruit, caramel, reduction notes. Palate: fleshy, sweet tannins, lacks expression.

### PÁRAMO DE GUZMÁN 2004 TR

**90** Colour: cherry, garnet rim. Nose: elegant, fine reductive notes, aged wood nuances, dark chocolate, sweet spices. Palate: spicy, long, elegant, fine tannins.

## PARÍS TRIMIÑO MORENO

Barrio San Roque, s/n
09300 Roa de Duero (Burgos)
☎: 947 540 033 - Fax: 947 540 033
bodegaparis@bodegaparis.com
www.bodegaparis.com

TRIMIÑO 2008 T JOVEN

**86** Colour: cherry, purple rim. Nose: expressive, fresh fruit, red berry notes, floral. Palate: flavourful, fruity, good acidity, round tannins.

PARÍS TRIMIÑO 2005 TC

**85** Colour: bright cherry. Nose: ripe fruit, sweet spices, creamy oak, fruit preserve. Palate: flavourful, fruity, toasty, round tannins, pruney.

## PEPE LÓPEZ VINOS Y VIÑEDOS

Avda. Soria nº 53 Bajo
Buzón 136
47300 Peñafiel (Valladolid)
☎: 983 106 207 - Fax: 916 048 322
pepelopezvinos@yahoo.es
www.arrotos.es

ARROTOS 2008 T ROBLE

**84**

ARROTOS 2006 TC

**84**

ARROTOS 2005 TR

**88** Colour: cherry, garnet rim. Nose: spicy, toasty, complex, fruit preserve. Palate: powerful, flavourful, toasty, round tannins.

## PROTOS BODEGAS RIBERA DUERO DE PEÑAFIEL

Bodegas Protos, 24-28
47300 Peñafiel (Valladolid)
☎: 983 878 011 - Fax: 983 878 012
bodega@bodegasprotos.com
www.bodegasprotos.com

PROTOS 2006 TC
tinta fina 100%

**92** Colour: cherry, garnet rim. Nose: ripe fruit, spicy, creamy oak, toasty, complex, cedar wood, undergrowth. Palate: powerful, flavourful, toasty, round tannins, fruity aftestaste.

PROTOS SELECCIÓN 2006 T
tinta fina 100%

**91** Colour: bright cherry. Nose: ripe fruit, sweet spices, creamy oak, expressive. Palate: flavourful, fruity, toasty, round tannins.

**PROTOS 2004 TR**
tinta fina 100%

**91** Colour: cherry, garnet rim. Nose: ripe fruit, spicy, creamy oak, toasty, lactic notes. Palate: powerful, flavourful, toasty, round tannins.

## REAL SITIO DE VENTOSILLA

Ctra. Aranda-Palencia, km. 66
09443 Gumiel del Mercado (Burgos)
☎: 947 546 900 - Fax: 947 546 999
bodega@pradorey.com
www.pradorey.com

**PRADOREY 2008 RD FERMENTADO EN BARRICA**

**87** Colour: onion pink. Nose: elegant, candied fruit, dried flowers, red berry notes. Palate: light-bodied, flavourful, good acidity, long, spicy.

**PRADOREY 2007 T ROBLE**

**85** Colour: cherry, garnet rim. Nose: balsamic herbs, ripe fruit, red berry notes. Palate: good structure, flavourful, long, great length.

**PRADOREY ÉLITE 2006 T**

**88** Colour: bright cherry. Nose: ripe fruit, sweet spices, creamy oak, expressive. Palate: flavourful, fruity, toasty, round tannins.

**PRADOREY 2005 TC**

**88** Colour: bright cherry. Nose: ripe fruit, sweet spices, creamy oak, scrubland. Palate: flavourful, fruity, toasty, round tannins.

**PRADOREY 2004 TGR**

**90** Colour: cherry, garnet rim. Nose: ripe fruit, spicy, creamy oak, toasty, complex, undergrowth. Palate: powerful, flavourful, toasty, round tannins.

**PRADOREY 2004 TR**

**89** Colour: cherry, garnet rim. Nose: ripe fruit, spicy, creamy oak, toasty, complex, fruit expression, balsamic herbs. Palate: powerful, flavourful, toasty, round tannins, spicy.

**RECORBA**

## REGOSTO

Ctra. Villaverde Vallecas, km. 3,800
Mercamadrid Módulo 21
28053 (Madrid)
☎: 915 079 861 - Fax: 915 079 863
regosto@regosto.es

**REGOSTO 2006 TC**
tinta del país 100%

**87** Colour: bright cherry. Nose: ripe fruit, sweet spices, creamy oak, expressive, dried flowers. Palate: flavourful, fruity, toasty, round tannins.

**REGOSTO VENDIMIA SELECCIONADA 2004 T**
tinta del país 100%

**87** Colour: cherry, garnet rim. Nose: spicy, creamy oak, toasty, complex, scrubland. Palate: powerful, flavourful, toasty, ripe fruit, round tannins.

## SELECCIÓN CÉSAR MUÑOZ

Acera de Recoletos, 14
47004 (Valladolid)
☎: 666 548 751
magallanes@cesarmunoz.es
www.bodegasmagallanes.es

**MAGALLANES 2005 TC**
tempranillo

**91** Colour: cherry, garnet rim. Nose: powerful, ripe fruit, cocoa bean, sweet spices, mineral. Palate: flavourful, fleshy, ripe fruit, spicy, round tannins.

## SELECCIÓN DE TORRES

Calle Rosario, 56
47311 Fompedraza (Valladolid)
☎: 983 892 121 - Fax: 938 177 444
mailadmin@torres.es
www.torres.es

**CELESTE 2006 TC**

**88** Colour: cherry, garnet rim. Nose: powerful, ripe fruit, earthy notes, toasty, creamy oak. Palate: flavourful, fleshy, ripe fruit, round tannins.

## SEÑORIO DE BOCOS

Camino La Canaleja s/n
47317 Bocos de Duero (Valladolid)
☎: 983 880 988 - Fax: 983 880 988
bodegas@senoriodebocos.com
www.senoriodebocos.com

SEÑORIO DE BOCOS 2007 T ROBLE
tinta del país

**89** Colour: deep cherry, purple rim. Nose: medium intensity, balanced, red berry notes, sweet spices, cocoa bean. Palate: flavourful, fruity, fresh, round tannins.

AUTOR DE BOCOS 2006 T
tinta del país

**91** Colour: dark-red cherry. Nose: ripe fruit, fruit preserve, spicy, dark chocolate, mineral. Palate: flavourful, powerful, concentrated, good finish, round tannins.

SEÑORIO DE BOCOS 2006 TC
tinta del país

**86** Colour: deep cherry, garnet rim. Nose: powerful, dark chocolate, toasty, ripe fruit. Palate: flavourful, powerful, concentrated, round tannins.

## SEÑORIO DE LA SERNA

Ctra. Nacional 122, km. 291
09318 Valdezate (Burgos)
☎: 947 550 329 - Fax: 947 550 327
bodegadelaserna@hotmail.com
www.bodegadelaserna.com

GRAN JERARQUÍA 2004 TC
tempranillo 100%

**83**

GRAN JERARQUÍA 2003 TC
tempranillo 100%

**84**

GRAN JERARQUÍA 2000 TR
tempranillo 100%

**88** Colour: pale ruby, brick rim edge. Nose: aged wood nuances, fruit liqueur notes, fruit liqueur notes, spicy, pattiserie, fine reductive notes. Palate: flavourful, spicy, classic aged character.

GRAN JERARQUÍA 2000 TGR
tempranillo 100%

**86** Colour: pale ruby, brick rim edge. Nose: spicy, fine reductive notes, aged wood nuances, fruit liqueur notes, fruit expression. Palate: spicy, long, fine tannins.

GRAN JERARQUÍA 1999 TGR
tempranillo 100%

**87** Colour: pale ruby, brick rim edge. Nose: wet leather, aged wood nuances, spicy, fruit liqueur notes. Palate: spicy, long, elegant, fine tannins.

GRAN JERARQUÍA 1999 TR
tempranillo 100%

**84**

GRAN JERARQUÍA 1996 TGR
tempranillo 100%

**82**

## TORRES DE ANGUIX

Camino La Tejera s/n
09312 Anguix (Burgos)
☎: 947 554 008 - Fax: 947 554 129
bodega@torresdeanguix.com
www.torresdeanguix.com

TORRES DE ANGUIX 2008 RD
tinta del país 100%

**83**

ADMIRACIÓN 2007 T
tempranillo 100%

**88** Colour: deep cherry, garnet rim. Nose: ripe fruit, varietal, creamy oak, balanced. Palate: rich, powerful, good acidity, toasty, round tannins.

TORRES DE ANGUIX 2007 T BARRICA
tinta del país 100%

**87** Colour: bright cherry. Nose: ripe fruit, sweet spices, creamy oak, expressive. Palate: flavourful, fruity, toasty, round tannins.

GALLERY 101 2007 TC
tinta del país 100%

**87** Colour: cherry, garnet rim. Nose: powerful, ripe fruit, sweet spices. Palate: flavourful, powerful, fleshy, ripe fruit, round tannins.

A D'ANGUIX 2005 T
tinta del país 100%

**90** Colour: bright cherry. Nose: ripe fruit, sweet spices, creamy oak, expressive, fragrant herbs, fruit preserve. Palate: flavourful, fruity, toasty, round tannins.

## D'ANGUIX 2004 T
tinta del país 100%

**91** Colour: cherry, garnet rim. Nose: ripe fruit, spicy, creamy oak, toasty, complex. Palate: powerful, flavourful, toasty, round tannins.

## TORRES DE ANGUIX 2004 TC

**87** Colour: cherry, garnet rim. Nose: ripe fruit, spicy, toasty. Palate: powerful, flavurful, toasty, round tannins.

## TORRES DE ANGUIX 2003 TR
tinta del país 100%

**88** Colour: cherry, garnet rim. Nose: ripe fruit, spicy, toasty, complex. Palate: powerful, flavourful, toasty, round tannins.

## TORRES DE ANGUIX 2001 TR

**90** Colour: cherry, garnet rim. Nose: creamy oak, dark chocolate, aromatic coffee, ripe fruit. Palate: flavourful, powerful, fleshy, balanced.

## TORRES DE ANGUIX 2001 TGR
tinta del país 100%

**88** Colour: cherry, garnet rim. Nose: ripe fruit, spicy, toasty, old leather. Palate: powerful, flavourful, toasty, round tannins.

## TORRES DE ANGUIX 2000 TGR
tinta del país 100%

**86** Colour: cherry, garnet rim. Nose: ripe fruit, spicy, toasty, dark chocolate. Palate: powerful, flavourful, toasty, round tannins.

## REAL DE ANGUIX

## VALDUBÓN

Antigua N-I, km. 151
09460 Milagros (Burgos)
☎: 947 546 251 - Fax: 947 546 250
valdubon@valdubon.es
www.valdubon.com

## VALDUBÓN 2007 T ROBLE
tempranillo 100%

**86** Colour: cherry, garnet rim. Nose: medium intensity, ripe fruit, spicy, toasty. Palate: flavourful, powerful, spicy, round tannins.

## VALDUBÓN 2007 T
tempranillo 100%

**85** Colour: bright cherry. Nose: ripe fruit, sweet spices, grassy. Palate: flavourful, fruity, round tannins.

## HONORIS DE VALDUBON 2005 T
tempranillo 85%, merlot 9%, cabernet sauvignon 6%

**91** Colour: cherry, garnet rim. Nose: ripe fruit, spicy, creamy oak, toasty, complex, roasted coffee. Palate: powerful, flavourful, toasty, round tannins.

## VALDUBÓN 2004 TC
tempranillo 100%

**88** Colour: bright cherry. Nose: ripe fruit, sweet spices, creamy oak, expressive, smoky. Palate: flavourful, fruity, toasty, round tannins, balsamic.

## VALDUBÓN 2003 TR
tempranillo 100%

**87** Colour: cherry, garnet rim. Nose: ripe fruit, spicy, toasty, dark chocolate. Palate: powerful, flavourful, toasty, round tannins.

## VALLEBUENO

Ctra. Valbuena, 20
47315 Pesquera de Duero (Valladolid)
☎: 983 868 336 - Fax: 983 868 432
bodegasbccv@interbook.net
www.bodegasdecastilla.com

## VALLEBUENO 2003 TC
tempranillo 100%

**86** Colour: bright cherry. Nose: sweet spices, creamy oak, expressive, macerated fruit. Palate: flavourful, fruity, toasty, round tannins, sweet tannins.

## VALSANZO

Manuel Azaña, 9
Edificio Ambassador, Local 15
47014 (Valladolid)
☎: 983 150 150 - Fax: 983 150 151
valsanzo@valsanzo.com
www.valsanzo.com

## VALL SANZO 2005 TC
tempranillo 100%

**89** Colour: cherry, purple rim. Nose: creamy oak, sweet spices. Palate: flavourful, fruity, fine tannins.

## VINCE JOHN

Ctra. Roa Peñafiel, km. 8,3
09317 San Martín de Rubiales (Burgos)
☎: 947 550 121
bodegavicentesanjuan.es
www.bodegavicentesanjuan.com

**BLASÓN DE ROMERA TEMPRANILLO 2008 T**
tempranillo

**83**

**BLASÓN DE ROMERA 2007 T ROBLE**
tinta del país

**82**

**BLASÓN DE ROMERA 2006 TC**
tempranillo

**86** Colour: very deep cherry, bright ochre rim. Nose: creamy oak, balanced, fruit liqueur notes, fruit liqueur notes. Palate: unctuous, full, sweetness, grainy tannins.

**HEREDAD DE SAN JUAN 2005 TC**

**87** Colour: bright cherry. Nose: ripe fruit, dark chocolate, toasty. Palate: flavourful, fruity, toasty, round tannins.

## VINNICO EXPORT

Muela, 16
03730 Jávea (Alicante)
☎: 965 791 967 - Fax: 966 461 471
info@vinnico.com
www.vinnico.com

**AVENTINO 200 BARRELS 2006 T**
tempranillo 100%

**89** Colour: cherry, garnet rim. Nose: ripe fruit, spicy, creamy oak, complex, dark chocolate. Palate: powerful, flavourful, round tannins.

**AVENTINO 2006 T ROBLE**
tempranillo 100%

**89** Colour: bright cherry. Nose: ripe fruit, sweet spices, creamy oak, expressive. Palate: flavourful, fruity, toasty, round tannins.

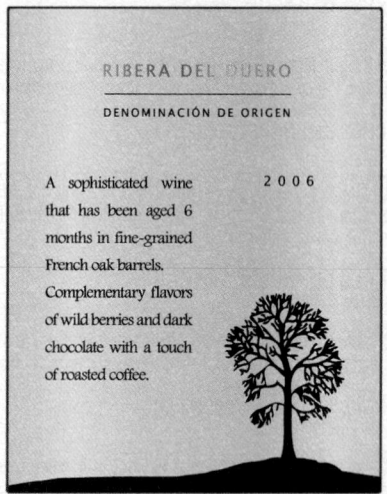

RIBERA DEL DUERO

DENOMINACIÓN DE ORIGEN

A sophisticated wine that has been aged 6 months in fine-grained French oak barrels. Complementary flavors of wild berries and dark chocolate with a touch of roasted coffee.

2006

## VINOS HERCAL

Pza. del Estudio, 7
09300 Roa (Burgos)
☎: 947 541 281
ventas@somanilla.es
www.somanilla.es

**BOCCA 2007 T ROBLE**
tempranillo

**87** Colour: cherry, garnet rim. Nose: pattiserie, sweet spices, ripe fruit. Palate: flavourful, powerful, spicy, ripe fruit.

**SOMANILLA VENDIMIA SELECCIONADA 2007 T**
tempranillo

**84**

**SOMANILLA VENDIMIA SELECCIONADA 2006 T**
tempranillo

**85** Colour: cherry, garnet rim. Nose: characterful, fruit preserve, toasty. Palate: flavourful, easy to drink.

## VINOS SANTOS ARRANZ (LÁGRIMA NEGRA)

Ctra. de Valbuena s/n
47315 Pesquera de Duero (Valladolid)
☎: 983 870 008 - Fax: 983 870 008
lagrimanegra82@hotmail.com
www.lagrima-negra.com

**LAGRIMA NEGRA 2007 T BARRICA**
tempranillo

**86** Colour: cherry, purple rim. Nose: expressive, fresh fruit, red berry notes, floral, balsamic herbs. Palate: flavourful, fruity, good acidity, round tannins.

**LÁGRIMA NEGRA 2006 TC**
tempranillo

**83**

**LÁGRIMA NEGRA 2004 TR**
tempranillo

**89** Colour: cherry, garnet rim. Nose: ripe fruit, spicy, toasty, complex, mineral. Palate: powerful, flavourful, toasty, round tannins.

## VIÑA ARNAIZ

Ctra. N-122 Km. 281
09316 Haza (Burgos)
☎: 914 355 556 - Fax: 915 766 607
rarevalo@jgc.es
www.vinosdefamilia.com

**MAYOR DE CASTILLA 2008 RD**
tempranillo 100%

**80**

**MAYOR DE CASTILLA 2008 T**
tempranillo 100%

**83**

**VIÑA ARNÁIZ 2007 T ROBLE**
tempranillo 95%, cabernet sauvignon 3%, merlot 2%

**87** Colour: bright cherry. Nose: ripe fruit, sweet spices, creamy oak, expressive. Palate: flavourful, toasty, round tannins.

**MAYOR DE CASTILLA 2007 T ROBLE**
tempranillo 100%

**84**

**MAYOR DE CASTILLA 2006 TC**
tempranillo 100%

**85** Colour: cherry, garnet rim. Nose: ripe fruit, spicy, toasty, complex. Palate: powerful, flavourful, toasty, round tannins.

**VIÑA ARNÁIZ 2004 TC**
tempranillo 100%

**83**

**VIÑA ARNÁIZ 2003 TR**
tempranillo 85%, cabernet sauvignon 10%, merlot 5%

**85** Colour: cherry, garnet rim. Nose: ripe fruit, spicy, creamy oak, toasty, complex, wet leather. Palate: powerful, flavourful, toasty, round tannins, creamy.

## VIÑA BUENA S.A.

Avda. Portugal, parcela 96
09400 Aranda de Duero (Burgos)
☎: 947 546 414 - Fax: 947 506 694
bodega@vinabuena.com

**FUERO REAL 2008 T**
tempranillo 100%

**86** Colour: cherry, purple rim. Nose: expressive, fresh fruit, red berry notes, floral. Palate: flavourful, fruity, good acidity, round tannins.

**VIÑA BUENA TEMPRANILLO 2008 T**
tempranillo 100%

**81**

**FUERO REAL 2005 TC**
tempranillo 100%

**84**

**VIÑA BUENA 2005 TC**
tempranillo 100%

**81**

**VAL ARANDA**
FORO

## VIÑA SOLORCA

Ctra. Circunvalación, s/n
09300 Roa (Burgos)

☎: 947 541 823 - Fax: 947 540 035
info@bodegassolorca.com
www.bodegassolorca.com

BARÓN DEL VALLE 2006 T BARRICA
tempranillo 100%

**87** Colour: bright cherry. Nose: ripe fruit, sweet spices, expressive, warm. Palate: flavourful, fruity, toasty, round tannins.

VIÑA SOLORCA 2004 TC
tempranillo 100%

**87** Colour: cherry, garnet rim. Nose: ripe fruit, spicy, toasty, wet leather. Palate: powerful, flavourful, toasty, round tannins.

GRAN SOLORCA 2003 TR
tempranillo 100%

**88** Colour: cherry, garnet rim. Nose: ripe fruit, spicy, toasty, wet leather. Palate: powerful, flavourful, toasty, round tannins.

ZARÚS

## VIÑA TUELDA

Camino de las Bodegas, 23
09310 Villatuelda (Burgos)
☎: 947 551 145 - Fax: 947 551 145
maurogh@terra.es
www.vintuelda.com

VIÑA TVELDA 2005 TR
tinto fino 95%

**88** Colour: cherry, garnet rim. Nose: ripe fruit, spicy, creamy oak, toasty, complex, roasted almonds. Palate: powerful, flavourful, toasty, round tannins.

VIÑA TVELDA 2006 TC
tinto fino 100%

**85** Colour: bright cherry. Nose: ripe fruit, sweet spices, creamy oak, expressive, fruit liqueur notes. Palate: flavourful, fruity, toasty, round tannins.

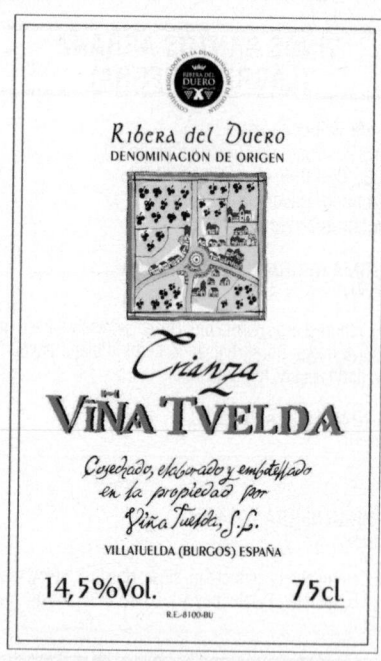

## VIÑAS Y VINOS EL MARQUÉS

Ctra. Pesquera, km. 1,5
47300 Peñafiel (Valladolid)
☎: 983 880 150 - Fax: 983 880 150
bodegaelmarques@telefonica.net
www.bodegaelmarques.com

VIÑAS Y VINOS EL MARQUÉS 2008 T ROBLE
tempranillo 100%

**88** Colour: cherry, purple rim. Nose: expressive, red berry notes, floral, creamy oak, complex. Palate: flavourful, fruity, good acidity, round tannins.

VIÑAS Y VINOS EL MARQUÉS 2005 TR
tempranillo 100%

**88** Colour: dark-red cherry, garnet rim. Nose: ripe fruit, elegant, balanced, sweet spices, cocoa bean. Palate: light-bodied, fruity, flavourful, spirituous, sweet tannins.

## VIÑAYTIA

Paraje El Soto s/n
09370 Quintana del Pidio (Burgos)
☎: 947 545 126 - Fax: 947 545 605
bodega@cillardesilos.es

EL QUINTANAL 2007 T
tempranillo 100%

**86** Colour: dark-red cherry. Nose: red berry notes, floral, wild herbs. Palate: flavourful, long, great length.

## VIÑEDOS ALONSO DEL YERRO

Finca Santa Marta, Ctra. Roa-Anguix, km. 1,8
09300 Roa (Burgos)
☎: 913 160 121 - Fax: 913 160 121
mariadelyerro@vay.es
www.alonsodelyerro.com

ALONSO DEL YERRO 2007 T
tempranillo 100%

**93** Colour: cherry, garnet rim. Nose: powerful, ripe fruit, red berry notes, sweet spices, cocoa bean. Palate: flavourful, fleshy, fruity, ripe fruit, round tannins, long.

"MARÍA" ALONSO DEL YERRO 2006 T
tempranillo 100%

**94** Colour: cherry, garnet rim. Nose: complex, aromatic coffee, sweet spices, fruit expression. Palate: good structure, flavourful, elegant, sweet tannins.

ALONSO DEL YERRO 2006 T

**92** Colour: cherry, garnet rim. Nose: complex, spicy, mineral, earthy notes, ripe fruit. Palate: flavourful, fleshy, fruity, fresh, round tannins.

## VIÑEDOS Y BODEGAS ÁSTER

Km. 55 Ctra. Palencia-Aranda (Término El Caño)
09313 Anguix (Burgos)
☎: 947 522 700 - Fax: 947 522 701
aster@riojalta.com
www.riojalta.com

ÁSTER FINCA EL OTERO 2006 T FERMENTADO EN BARRICA

**92** Colour: cherry, garnet rim. Nose: ripe fruit, spicy, creamy oak, toasty, complex, balsamic herbs. Palate: powerful, flavourful, toasty, round tannins.

ÁSTER 2003 TC
tinta del país 100%

**87** Colour: pale ruby, brick rim edge. Nose: spicy, aged wood nuances, fruit liqueur notes, old leather. Palate: spicy, fine tannins, elegant, long.

## VIÑEDOS Y BODEGAS GARCÍA FIGUERO S.L.

Ctra. La Horra-Roa, km. 2,2
09311 La Horra (Burgos)
☎: 947 542 127
bodega@tintofiguero.com
www.tintofiguero.com

FIGUERO TINUS 2006 T

**91** Colour: bright cherry. Nose: sweet spices, creamy oak, expressive, ripe fruit, mineral. Palate: flavourful, fruity, toasty, round tannins, fleshy.

TINTO FIGUERO 12 MESES BARRICA
2006 T BARRICA

**88** Colour: bright cherry. Nose: ripe fruit, expressive, new oak, aged wood nuances. Palate: flavourful, fruity, toasty, round tannins.

FIGUERO NOBLE 2005 T

**90** Colour: cherry, garnet rim. Nose: ripe fruit, spicy, creamy oak, toasty, complex. Palate: powerful, flavourful, toasty, round tannins.

TINTO FIGUERO 15 MESES BARRICA 2005 TR

**85** Colour: cherry, garnet rim. Nose: powerful, ripe fruit, sweet spices, dark chocolate, toasty. Palate: flavourful, fleshy, powerful.

TINTO FIGUERO VENDIMIA SELECCIONADA 2005 T

**84**

## VIÑEDOS Y BODEGAS GORMAZ

Ctra. de Soria, s/n
42330 San Esteban de Gormaz (Soria)
☎: 975 350 404 - Fax: 975 351 313
info@hispanobodegas.com
www.hispanobodegas.com

CATANIA 2007 T

**88** Colour: dark-red cherry, garnet rim. Nose: floral, fruit expression, spicy. Palate: flavourful, full, great length, slightly dry, soft tannins.

VIÑA GORMAZ 2007 T

**83**

12 LINAJES 2006 T ROBLE

**84**

CATANIA 2005 TC

**86** Colour: bright cherry. Nose: ripe fruit, sweet spices, creamy oak, expressive, smoky. Palate: flavourful, fruity, toasty, round tannins.

12 LINAJES 2005 TC

**85** Colour: cherry, garnet rim. Nose: ripe fruit, spicy, creamy oak, toasty, complex. Palate: powerful, flavourful, toasty, harsh oak tannins.

12 LINAJES 2004 TR

**83**

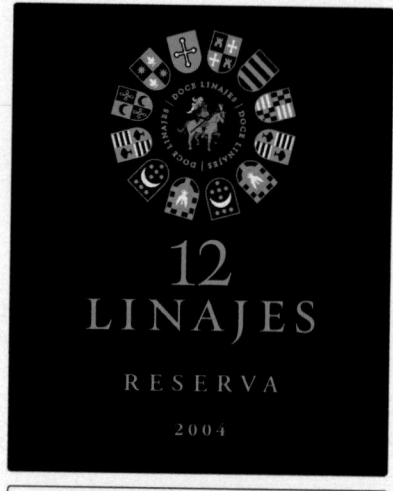

VIÑA GORMAZ TC

**87** Colour: bright cherry. Nose: ripe fruit, sweet spices, creamy oak, expressive, earthy notes. Palate: flavourful, fruity, toasty, round tannins.

## VIÑEDOS Y BODEGAS RIBÓN

Basilón, 15

47350 Quintanilla de Onésimo (Valladolid)
☎: 983 680 015 - Fax: 983 680 015
info@bodegasribon.com
www.bodegasribon.com

**RIBÓN 2006 TC**
tempranillo 100%

**87** Colour: cherry, garnet rim. Nose: ripe fruit, spicy, creamy oak, toasty, complex, dried herbs. Palate: powerful, flavourful, toasty, round tannins.

## WINNER WINES

Avda. del Mediterráneo, 38
28007 Madrid (Madrid)
☎: 915 019 042 - Fax: 915 017 794
winnerwines@ibernoble.com
www.ibernoble.com

**IBERNOBLE 2007 T ROBLE**
tempranillo 90%, cabernet sauvignon 10%

**82**

**IBERNOBLE 2006 TC**
tempranillo 90%, cabernet sauvignon 10%

**87** Colour: cherry, garnet rim. Nose: ripe fruit, sweet spices, cocoa bean, toasty. Palate: flavourful, long, harsh oak tannins.

**IBERNOBLE 2004 TR**
tempranillo 90%, cabernet sauvignon 10%

**89** Colour: cherry, garnet rim. Nose: ripe fruit, spicy, toasty. Palate: flavourful, long, slightly dry, soft tannins.

### SOME OTHER WINERIES WITHIN THE DO:

**ADRADA ECOLÓGICA**
**ALIZÁN BODEGAS Y VIÑEDOS**
**ARDOA**
**AVELINO VEGAS**
**BODEGA CACHOPA S.A.**
**BODEGA COMARCAL COOP. LA MILAGROSA S.C.**
**BODEGA DEL PALACIO DE LOS FRONTAURA Y VICTORIA**
**BODEGA COOP. LA ASUNCIÓN DE NTRA. SRA. S.C.**
**BODEGA RAUL CALVO BELTRÁN**
**BODEGA SAN GABRIEL**
**BODEGA SAN ROQUE DE LA ENCINA, SDAD. COOP.**
**BODEGAS SERVILIO - ARRANZ S.L.**
**BODEGAS CARRALBA**
**BODEGAS CASTILLALTA S.L.**
**BODEGAS CASTILLEJO DE ROBLEDO, S.A.**
**BODEGAS CASTILLO DE PEÑAFIEL S.L.**

**BODEGAS COOP. NTRA. SRA.DE LA ASUNCIÓN**
**BODEGAS COOP.VIRGEN DE LAS VIÑAS**
**BODEGAS FEDERICO S.L.**
**BODEGAS ITURRIA - MORAL S.L.**
**BODEGAS JOSÉ CABESTRERO S.L.**
**BODEGAS MARTÍN MEDINA**
**BODEGAS ONTAÑÓN**
**BODEGAS PÁRAMO DE CORCOS**
**BODEGAS REQUIEM S.L.**
**BODEGAS RIBERALTA**
**BODEGAS TIERRAS DE PEÑAFIEL**
**BODEGAS VALDEBILLA**
**BODEGAS VALDEVIÑAS**
**BODEGAS VALSARDO DE PEÑAFIEL S.L.**
**BODEGAS Y VIÑEDOS BURLÓN**
**BODEGAS Y VIÑEDOS DE HOZ SUALDEA**
**BODEGAS Y VIÑEDOS FRUTOS ARAGÓN**
**BODEGAS Y VIÑEDOS MONTE AIXA S.L.**
**BODEGAS Y VIÑEDOS SANTO DOMINGO**
**BODEGAS Y VIÑEDOS VALDUERO**
**BODEGAS Y VIÑEDOS VALTRAVIESO**
**BODEGAS Y VIÑEDOS VEGA REAL**
**CASADO ALVIDES**
**FINCA CAMPOS GÓTICOS**
**HIJOS DE ANTONIO POLO**
**JESÚS LEANDRO RIVERA FERNÁNDEZ**
**MARÍA ASCENSIÓN REPISO BOCOS**
**OSBORNE RIBERA DEL DUERO SELECCIÓN**
**PEDRO JAVIER MARTÍN SOLA**
**POMAR VIÑEDOS**
**S.A.T. SAN PABLO**
**SANCIUS BODEGAS Y VIÑEDOS**
**SOLIRA 2002 S.L.**
**TIERRAS EL GUIJARRAL**
**UVAGUILERA**
**VALLFORMOSA**
**VALTOÑAR S.L.**
**VIÑA MAMBRILLA S.L.**
**VITIVINÍCOLA DE VALBUENA**

# DO RIBERA DEL GUADIANA

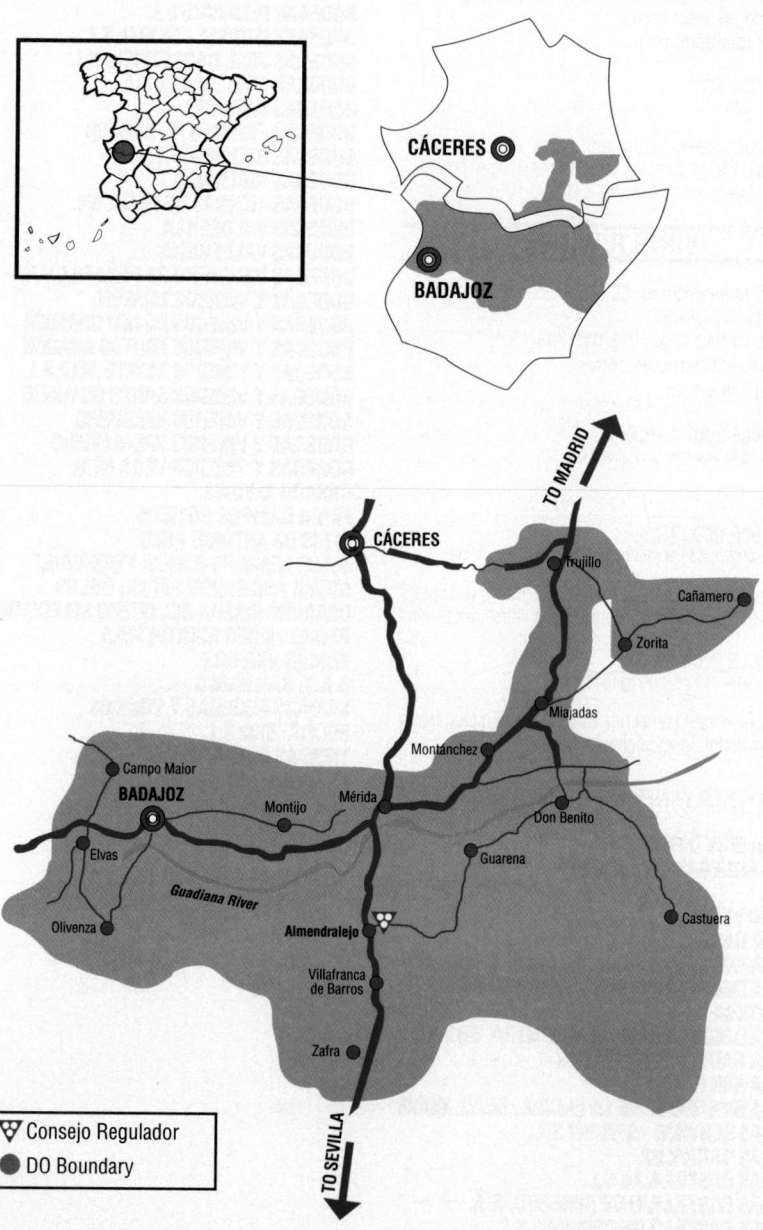

# DO RIBERA DEL GUADIANA

## NEWS

As a rule, the vintage rating given by the Consejo Regulador does not correspond to our own one, for they include in their rating wines too young to be rated properly given that they have not been in the bottle for a long enough period. Precisely, the wine law, applicable from this year on, will put an end to this sort of approach, obviously far from certain. As for our ratings, and given the milder and overall cooler nature of the 2008 vintage, which has delayed the ripening cycle of most varieties, the first conclusion is one of high fruit expression. White wines made from local grapes like eva, pardina and dona blanca are also on the rise in terms of quality. Earlier-ripening varieties like chardonnay and macabeo suffered greatly, and the overripe, confected notes appear, although there are also great examples of chardonnay like those from Viña Puebla from Bodegas Toribio and Pago Los Balancines, both of them from young wineries that bear the banner of modernity within the region. Also new is Bodega Carabal, from the Banús family, with the red wine Macareno and excellent and quality prospects. It is weird we do not see in this cooler vintage white and rosé wines of a more open aromatic character. The most numerous renderings are the red ones, based on tempranillo and cabernet sauvignon although without consistency, with an alternating pattern, depending on the producer, of warm and fresh notes. We have liked a lot wines with a short barrel-ageing period from the 2006 vintage, far more expressive and balanced than those from other vintages and pretty much in tune with the modern consumers. Reserva wines from hot vintages like 2005 and 2006 show pretty alcoholic and woody.

## LOCATION

Covering the 6 wine-growing regions of Extremadura, with a total surface of more than 87,000 Ha as described below.

## SUB-REGIONS:

**Cañamero.** To the south east of the province of Cáceres, in the heart of the Sierra de Guadalupe. It comprises the municipal districts of Alia, Berzocana, Cañamero, Guadalupe and Valdecaballeros. The vineyards are located on the mountainside, at altitudes of between 600 m to 800 m. The terrain is rugged and the soil is slaty and loose. The climate is mild without great temperature contrasts, and the average annual rainfall is 750 mm to 800 mm. The main grape variety is the white Alarije.

**Montánchez.** Comprising 27 municipal districts. It is characterised by its complex terrain, with numerous hills and small valleys. The vineyards are located on brown acidic soil. The climate is Continental in nature and the average annual rainfall is between 500 mm and 600 mm. The white grape variety Borba occupies two thirds of the vineyards in the region.

**Ribera Alta.** This covers the Vegas del Guadiana and the plains of La Serena and Campo de Castuera and comprises 38 municipal districts. The soil is very sandy. The most common varieties are Alarije, Borba (white), Tempranillo and Garnacha (red).

**Ribera Baja.** Comprising 11 municipal districts. The vineyards are located on clayey-limy soil. The climate is Continental, with a moderate Atlantic influence and slight contrasts in temperature. The most common varieties are: Cayetana Blanca and Pardina among the whites, and Tempranillo among the reds.

**Matanegra.** Rather similar to Tierra de Barros, but with a milder climate. It comprises 8 municipal districts, and the most common grape varieties are Beba, Montua (whites), Tempranillo, Garnacha and Cabernet Sauvignon (reds).

**Tierra de Barros.** Situated in the centre of the province of Badajoz and the largest (4475 Ha and 37 municipal districts). It has flat plains with fertile soils which are rich in nutrients and have great water retention capacity (Rainfall is

| | |
|---|---|
| Hectares of Vineyard | 26,000 |
| Nº Viticulturists | 2,897 |
| Nº of Bodegas | 63 |
| 2008 Harvest | Very Good |
| 2007 Production | 6,903,690 l. |
| Marketing | 20% domestic 80% export |

low: 350 mm to 450 mm per year). The most common varieties are the white Cayetana Blanca and Pardina, and the red Tempranillo, Garnacha and Cabernet Sauvignon.

## GRAPE VARIETES:

White: *Alarije, Borba, Cayetana Blanca, Pardina, Macabeo, Chardonnay, Chelva or Montua, Malvar, Parellada, Pedro Ximénez, Verdejo, Eva, Cigüente, Perruno, Moscatel de Alejandría, Moscatel de Grano Menudo* and *Sauvignon Blanc.*
Red: *Garnacha Tinta, Tempranillo, Bobal, Cabernet Sauvignon, Garnacha Tintorera, Graciano, Mazuela, Merlot, Monastrell, Syrah, Pinot Noir* and *Jaén Tinto.*

## CONSEJO REGULADOR

Ctra. Sevilla-Gijón, Km 114
06200 Almendralejo (Badajoz)
Apdo. Correos 299
☎: 924 671 302 - Fax: 924 664 703.
@ informacion@riberadelguadiana.org

## GENERAL CHARACTERISTICS OF THE WINES:

| WHITES | With the differences that may appear between the different sub-regions, the white wines are substantial, with a Mediterranean character (mountain herbs, undergrowth, supple on the palate, but at the same time, persistent and very flavourful). |
|---|---|
| ROSÉS | Except for some modern wine production with the usual raspberry flavour, they are, in general, warm, very fruity and with a point of sweetness produced by the high alcohol content. |
| REDS | The red wines are powerful, warm, supple, with sweet tannins and smoothness, even those based on the *Tempranillo.* Flavours of sunny vineyards with *Garnacha* that provide the ripe and fruity nuance characteristic of this grape variety. |

## 2008 VINTAGE RATING:

## VERY GOOD

## BODEGAS CAÑALVA

Coto, n° 54
10136 Cañamero (Cáceres)
☎: 927 369 405 - Fax: 927 369 405
info@bodegascanalva.com
www.bodegascañalva.com

FUENTE CORTIJO 2005 TC
tempranillo 100%

**87** Colour: deep cherry, orangey edge. Nose: powerful, ripe fruit, sweet spices, caramel, aromatic coffee. Palate: flavourful, fleshy, spicy, creamy.

## BODEGAS MEDINA

Ctra. N-432, km. 76
06310 Puebla de Sancho Pérez (Badajoz)
☎: 924 575 060 - Fax: 924 575 076
info@bodegasmedina.net
www.bodegasmedina.net

JALOCO 2008 B
eva 30%, alarije 70%

**75**

JALOCO 2008 RD
cabernet sauvignon 100%

**78**

JALOCO 2008 T ROBLE
cabernet sauvignon 100%

**78**

JALOCO 2008 T
merlot 56%, cabernet sauvignon 24%, syrah 20%

**76**

DIFERENTE 2008 T
merlot, cabernet sauvignon

**68**

DIFERENTE 2007 T ROBLE

**74**

JALOCO 2006 TC
cabernet sauvignon 100%

**78**

## BODEGAS ORTIZ

Ctra. de Sevilla 34

06200 Almendralejo (Badajoz)
☎: 924 662 811 - Fax: 924 665 406
info@bodegasortiz.com
www.bodegasortiz.com

SEÑORÍO DE ORÁN 2008 B
pardina

**79**

VIÑA ROJA TEMPRANILLO 2008 T
tempranillo

**80**

VIÑA ROJA COUPAGE 2005 TC
tempranillo 84%, cabernet sauvignon 16%

**87** Colour: cherry, garnet rim. Nose: powerful, ripe fruit, toasty, spicy. Palate: flavourful, sweetness, spicy, round tannins.

CASTILLO DE FERIA 2005 TC
tempranillo

**78**

VIÑA ROJA SELECCIÓN 2004 TR
tempranillo

**82**

## BODEGAS PARADELLS

Finca El Charro
06002 Badajoz
☎: 924 105 006 - Fax: 924 105 007
bodega@bodegasparadells.com
www.bodegasparadells.com

ZAOS VENDIMIA SELECCIONADA 2008 T
tempranillo 90%

**80**

ZAOS VENDIMIA SELECCIONADA 2007 T ROBLE
tempranillo 90%, cabernet sauvignon 10%

**83**

## BODEGAS ROMALE

Pol. Ind. Parc. 6 Manz. D
06200 Almendralejo (Badajoz)
☎: 924 667 255 - Fax: 924 665 877
romale@romale.com
www.romale.com

PRIVILEGIO DE ROMALE 2004 TC
tempranillo 100%

## 80

PRIVILEGIO DE ROMALE 2003 TR
tempranillo 100%

## 79

VIÑA ROMALE

### BODEGAS RUIZ TORRES

Ctra. EX 116, KM-33,8
10136 Cañamero (Cáceres)
☎: 927 369 024 - Fax: 927 369 302
info@ruiztorres.com
www.ruiztorres.com

ATTELEA 2008 B
macabeo 100%

## 79

ATTELEA 2007 T ROBLE
tempranillo 100%

## 83

ATTELEA 2003 TC
tempranillo 80%, cabernet sauvignon 20%

## 78

EX DE EXTREMADURA 2007 BN ESPUMOSO
chardonnay 70%, macabeo 30%

## 83

### BODEGAS TORIBIO

Luis Chamizo, 12 - 21
06310 Puebla de Sancho Pérez (Badajoz)
☎: 924 551 449 - Fax: 924 551 449
info@bodegastoribio.com
www.bodegastoribio.com

VIÑA PUEBLA CHARDONNAY 2008 B

**90** Colour: bright straw. Nose: ripe fruit, citrus fruit, expressive, sweet spices, cocoa bean. Palate: flavourful, fruity, fresh, fleshy.

VIÑA PUEBLA 2008 BFB

**88** Colour: bright straw. Nose: powerful, ripe fruit, citrus fruit, cocoa bean, spicy. Palate: flavourful, fleshy, ripe fruit, spicy.

VIÑA PUEBLA MACABEO 2008 B

**86** Colour: pale. Nose: ripe fruit, citrus fruit, white flowers. Palate: flavourful, fruity, fresh.

VIÑA PUEBLA SELECCIÓN 2008 T

**89** Colour: cherry, garnet rim. Nose: powerful, ripe fruit, sweet spices, cedar wood, red berry notes. Palate: flavourful, powerful, fleshy, spicy.

VIÑA PUEBLA TEMPRANILLO 2008 T
tempranillo

## 81

VIÑA PUEBLA ESENZIA 2006 TC

**87** Colour: cherry, garnet rim. Nose: powerful, ripe fruit, sweet spices, creamy oak. Palate: flavourful, powerful, fleshy.

VIÑA PUEBLA 2006 TC

## 84

### BODEGAS VENTURA DE VEGA

Badajoz, 70
06200 Almendralejo (Badajoz)
☎: 924 671 105 - Fax: 924 677 205
bodegas@vegaesteban.com
www.vegaesteban.com

VEGA ESTEBAN 2008 B
viura

## 82

CADENCIAS DE VEGA ESTEBAN TEMPRANILLO
2008 T
syrah, tempranillo

## 81

VEGA ESTEBAN 2008 T
tempranillo

## 77

LEYENDAS SELECCIÓN 2005 TC
tempranillo

## 83

VEGA ESTEBAN 2005 TC
tempranillo

## 78

### BODEGAS VITICULTORES DE BARROS

Ctra. de Badajoz, s/n
06200 Almendralejo (Badajoz)
☎: 924 664 852 - Fax: 924 664 852

export@vbarros.com
www.viticultoresdebarros.com

**EMPERADOR DE BARROS CAYETANA 2008 B**
cayetana blanca

**84**

**EMPERADOR DE BARROS MACABEO 2008 B**

**76**

**EMPERADOR DE BARROS TEMPRANILLO 2008 T**

**78**

**VIZANA 2005 TC**

**82**

## HIJOS DE FRANCISCO ESCASO

Ctra. Villafranca, 15
06360 Fuente del Maestre (Badajoz)
☎: 924 530 012 - Fax: 924 531 703
bodegasescaso@infonegocio.com
www.vallarcal.com

**VALLARCAL 2006 B**

**82**

**VALLARCAL 2008 T ROBLE**
tempranillo

**83**

**VALLARCAL 2004 TC**

**83**

**VALLARCAL 2004 TR**

**77**

## LAR DE BARROS - INVIOSA

Apdo. de Correos 291
Ctra. Ex-300, p.k. 55,9
Pol. Ind. Dehesa del Pedregal, Naves 4-5-6
06200 Almendralejo (Badajoz)
☎: 924 671 235 - Fax: 924 687 231
info@lardebarros.com
www.lardebarros.com

**LAR DE BARROS 2008 B**
macabeo 85%, chardonnay 10%, sauvignon blanc 5%

**81**

**LAR DE BARROS 2008 RD**
syrah 100%

**77**

**LAR DE BARROS TEMPRANILLO 2008 T**
tempranillo 100%

**76**

**LAR DE BARROS 2006 T ROBLE**
tempranillo 100%

**78**

**LAR DE BARROS 2005 TC**
tempranillo 100%

**77**

**LAR DE LARES 2004 TR**
tempranillo 100%

**81**

## MARCELINO DIAZ

Mecánica, s/n
06200 Almendralejo (Badajoz)
☎: 924 677 548 - Fax: 924 660 977
bodega@madiaz.com
www.madiaz.com

**PUERTA PALMA 2008 B**
pardina

**83**

**PUERTA PALMA 2008 T**
tempranillo 80%, cabernet sauvignon 15%, graciano 5%

**82**

**PUERTA PALMA FINCA LAS TENDERAS 2005 TC**

**82**

**PUERTA PALMA FINCA LAS TENDERAS 2004 TC**
tempranillo 85%, cabernet sauvignon 15%

**84**

**PUERTA PALMA FINCA EL CAMPILLO 2002 TR**
tempranillo 80%, graciano 20%

**83**

## MARTÍNEZ PAYVA

Ctra. Gijón - Sevilla, N-630, km. 646
Apdo. Correos 87

06200 Almendralejo (Badajoz)
☎: 924 671 130 - Fax: 924 663 056
info@payva.es
www.payva.es

PAYVA 2008 B

**83**

PAYVA MOSCATEL DULCE 2008 B

**78**

PAYVA CAYETANA BLANCA 2007 BFB

**85** Colour: bright golden. Nose: pattiserie, creamy oak, honeyed notes, dry nuts. Palate: flavourful, fleshy, spicy, roasted-coffee aftertaste.

PAYVA 2008 T
tempranillo

**85** Colour: cherry, purple rim. Nose: ripe fruit, creamy oak, sweet spices, cocoa bean. Palate: flavourful, powerful, fleshy, ripe fruit.

PAYVA TEMPRANILLO DULCE 2008 T

**80**

PAYVA 2006 TC

**84**

PAYVA SELECCIÓN 2005 TC

**82**

PAYVA 2003 TR

**82**

DOÑA FRANCISQUITA

## PAGO LOS BALANCINES

Paraje la Agraria
06475 Oliva de Mérida (Badajoz)
☎: 636 999 266
info@bodegastoribio.com

ALUNADO 2008 BFB
chardonnay

**92** Colour: bright straw. Nose: candied fruit, citrus fruit, lactic notes, cocoa bean, sweet spices, tropical fruit. Palate: flavourful, fleshy, complex, fresh, spicy, ripe fruit.

HUNO MATANEGRA 2007 TC
cabernet sauvignon, tempranillo, merlot

**93** Colour: cherry, garnet rim. Nose: powerful, spicy, creamy oak, toasty, aromatic coffee, ripe fruit. Palate: flavourful, fleshy, fruity, powerful, round tannins.

HUNO 2007 TC
cabernet sauvignon, tempranillo, merlot, syrah

**91** Colour: bright cherry, purple rim. Nose: powerful, balanced, ripe fruit, fruit expression, sweet spices. Palate: flavourful, powerful, fleshy, balanced, good acidity, powerful tannins.

## S. COOP. SAN ISIDRO DE ENTRIN

El Mirador
06197 Entrín Bajo (Badajoz)
☎: 924 481 105 - Fax: 924 481 017
info@coopsanisidroentrin.es

VEGA HERRERA 2008 B
eva

**89** Colour: pale. Nose: white flowers, fresh fruit, citrus fruit. Palate: flavourful, fruity, fresh.

VEGA HERRERA 2008 T
tempranillo

**86** Colour: cherry, purple rim. Nose: powerful, ripe fruit, raspberry. Palate: flavourful, fleshy, fruity.

VEGA HERRERA 2007 T ROBLE
tempranillo

**87** Colour: cherry, purple rim. Nose: medium intensity, fresh fruit, red berry notes. Palate: flavourful, fruity, fleshy, spicy, round tannins.

## SOCIEDAD COOP. MONTEVIRGEN

Hermano Rocha, 18
06208 Villalba de los Barros (Badajoz)
☎: 924 685 025 - Fax: 924 685 050
cooperativa@montevirgen.com
www.montevirgen.com

MARQUÉS M. DE VILLALBA 2008 B
pardina

**81**

SEÑORÍO DE VILLALBA 2008 RD

**78**

MARQUÉS M. DE VILLALBA 2008 T

**83**

MARQUÉS M. DE VILLALBA 2006 TC

**84**

MARQUÉS DE MONTEVIRGEN TR

## SDAD. COOP. SAN ISIDRO DE VILLAFRANCA DE LOS BARROS

Ctra. Fuente del Mestre, 12
06220 Villafranca de los Barros (Badajoz)
☎: 924 524 136 - Fax: 924 524 020
info@cooperativasanisidro.com
www.cooperativasanisidro.com

VALDEQUEMAO MACABEO 2008 B
macabeo 100%

**79**

VALDEQUEMAO CHARDONNAY 2008 B
chardonnay 100%

**70**

VALDEQUEMAO CABERNET SAUVIGNON 2008 T
cabernet sauvignon 100%

**82**

VALDEQUEMAO TEMPRANILLO 2008 T
tempranillo 100%

**81**

VALDEQUEMAO SHIRAZ 2008 T
syrah 100%

**81**

VALDEQUEMAO 2004 TC
tempranillo 100%

**81**

TAMUJITO

## SOCIEDAD COOPERATIVA VIÑAOLIVA

Pol. Ind., Parcela 4-17
06200 Almendralejo (Badajoz)
☎: 924 677 321
info@vinaoliva.com
www.vinaoliva.com

ZALEO PARDINA 2008 B

**83**

ZALEO MACABEO 2008 B

**78**

ZALEO TEMPRANILLO 2008 T

**84**

ZALEO SELECCIÓN 2007 T
tempranillo 100%

**88** Colour: cherry, purple rim. Nose: lactic notes, red berry notes, ripe fruit, sweet spices, cocoa bean. Palate: flavourful, fruity, fleshy.

## SOCIEDAD COOPERATIVA VIRGEN DE LA ESTRELLA

Mérida, 1
06230 Los Santos de Maimona (Badajoz)
☎: 924 544 094 - Fax: 924 572 490
export@maimona.com
www.maimona.com

VIÑA MAIMONA BEBA DE LOS SANTOS 2008 B
eva 100%

**86** Colour: bright straw. Nose: grassy, white flowers, ripe fruit. Palate: flavourful, fruity, fresh.

VIÑA MAIMONA 2008 T
tempranillo

**81**

VIÑA MAIMONA 2006 TC
tempranillo

**81**

## VINICOLA GUADIANA

Barjola, 15
06200 Almendralejo (Badajoz)
☎: 924 661 080 - Fax: 924 671 413
vigua@vinicolaguadiana.com
www.vinicolaguadiana.com

VIGUA 2008 T
tempranillo 100%

**83**

BASANGUS 2006 TC
tempranillo 100%

**82**

## VIÑA SANTA MARINA

Ctra. N-630, km. 634 - Apdo. 714
06800 Mérida (Badajoz)
☎: 902 506 364 - Fax: 924 027 675
bodega@vsantamarina.com
www.vsantamarina.com

TORREMAYOR 2006 TC
tempranillo 100%

**84**

TORREMAYOR 2003 TR
tempranillo 100%

**87** Colour: cherry, garnet rim. Nose: powerful, warm, candied fruit, aromatic coffee, toasty. Palate: flavourful, powerful, fleshy.

## VIÑAS DE ALANGE S.A.

Ctra. Almendralejo-Palomas, km 6,900
Apdo. Correos 231
06200 Almendralejo (Badajoz)
☎: 924 120 082 - Fax: 924 120 028
palacioquemado@alvear.es
www.palacioquemado.com

SEÑORÍO DE ALANGE 2008 B
pardina 100%

**80**

SEÑORÍO DE ALANGE TEMPRANILLO 2008 T
tempranillo 100%

**87** Colour: cherry, purple rim. Nose: ripe fruit, red berry notes, lactic notes, sweet spices. Palate: flavourful, fleshy, ripe fruit.

SEÑORÍO DE ALANGE SYRAH 2008 T
syrah 100%

**87** Colour: cherry, purple rim. Nose: powerful, ripe fruit, red berry notes, raspberry. Palate: flavourful, fleshy, spicy, ripe fruit.

"PQ" PALACIO QUEMADO 2006 T
syrah, otras

**86** Colour: cherry, garnet rim. Nose: toasty, smoky, roasted coffee, ripe fruit. Palate: spicy, toasty, slightly dry, soft tannins.

PALACIO QUEMADO 2005 TC
tempranillo 100%

**85** Colour: cherry, garnet rim. Nose: overripe fruit, warm, spicy, toasty. Palate: sweetness, spirituous, fleshy, round tannins.

PALACIO QUEMADO 2003 TR
tempranillo 100%

**84**

## VIÑEDOS Y BODEGA CARABAL

Ctra. Alía - Castilblanco, km. 10
10137 Alía (Cáceres)
☎: 917 346 152 - Fax: 913 720 440
jiglesias@bodega-carabal.es
www.bodega-carabal.es

MACARENO 2006 TC
syrah 53%, cabernet sauvignon 22%, tempranillo 15%, graciano 10%

**90** Colour: cherry, garnet rim. Nose: powerful, ripe fruit, creamy oak, new oak. Palate: flavourful, powerful, fleshy, good structure.

RASGO 2006 T ROBLE
syrah 40%, cabernet sauvignon 42%, tempranillo 18%

**87** Colour: cherry, garnet rim. Nose: powerful, toasty, dark chocolate, ripe fruit. Palate: flavourful, powerful, fleshy, round tannins.

SOME OTHER WINERIES WITHIN THE DO:

**BODEGA LAS GRANADAS
BODEGA SAN MARCOS
BODEGAS AGAPITA RUBIO BRAVO
BODEGAS PEÑA DEL VALLE
BODEGAS PUENTE AJUDA
BODEGAS VIÑA VEGA
CASTELAR S.A.
DOLORES MORENAS
EXAGRAVIN
JUAN LEANDRO ROMERO LÓPEZ
   (BODEGAS ROMERO)
S.A.T. SAN ANTONIO
SANTA MARTA VIRGEN
SDAD. COOP. AGRÍCOLA NTRA. SRA.
   DE VINÍCOLA EXTREMEÑA "SAN JOSÉ"
SDAD. COOP. DE OLIVAREROS
SDAD. COOP. NTRA. SRA. DE LA SOLEDAD
SDAD. COOP. SANTA MARÍA EGIPCIACA**

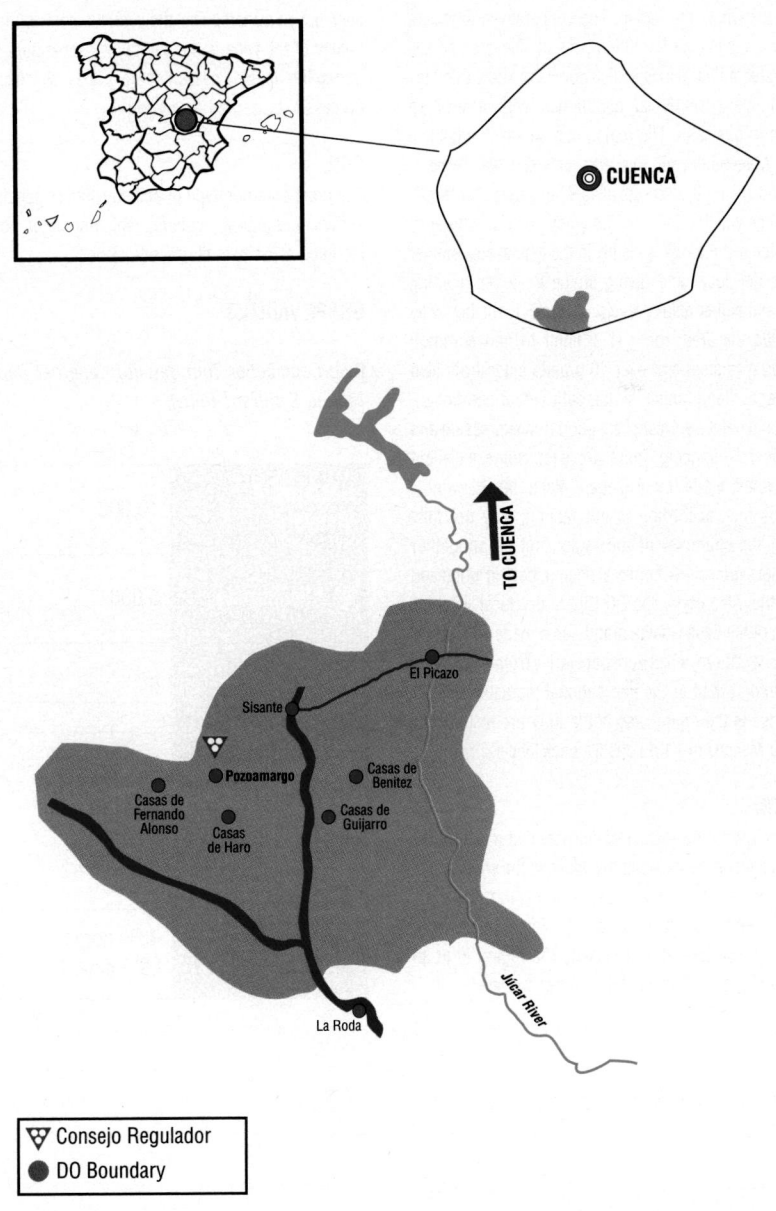

CUENCA

TO CUENCA

El Picazo

Sisante

Pozoamargo

Casas de
Benitez

Casas de
Fernando
Alonso

Casas
de Haro

Casas de
Guijarro

Júcar River

La Roda

▽ Consejo Regulador
● DO Boundary

# DO RIBERA DEL JÚCAR

## NEWS

Another safe bet within La Mancha, and surely the most modern one within the region. The cooperatives of Ribera del Júcar manage over 9.000 hectares of vineyard and sell abroad most of their wines, which comes to show that they have become commercial companies with a modern approach to business. The region can be easily mistaken with DO Manchuela, for this area between two rivers – Cabriel and Júcar– is also known as 'Manchuela de Cuenca', the province which comprises its vineyard. The difference between the two regions is mainly in the type of soil, stonier in Ribera del Júcar and giving shape to better ripening patterns and higher acidity levels. Diversity is the best way to describe the area, for it is difficult to find common features in a catalogue of over 40 brands made from also varied grapes (tempranillo, syrah, petit verdot and bobal), but we could point out freshness, good fruit expression and some mineral nuances. There are even some excellent kosher wines made by Bodegas Illana for Elviwines, renderings that, according to our tasting, may not fully represent the character of the region but an altogether exceptional expression of optimal ageing, both in wood and in the bottle. Also under the DO Ribera del Júcar label we find most of the Casa Gualda brand name made by Nuestra Señora de la Cabeza, a pioneer cooperative from La Mancha and a leading brand in the international markets. Most of the wineries in the region also bottle their products under the DO La Mancha or VT de Castilla back labels..

## LOCATION

The 7 wine producing municipal districts that make up the DO are located on the banks of the Júcar, in the south of the province of Cuenca. They are: Casas de Benítez, Casas de Guijarro, Casas de Haro, Casas de Fernando Alonso, Pozoamargo, Sisante and El Picazo. The region is at an altitude of between 650 and 750 m above sea level.

## CLIMATE

Continental in nature, dry, and with very cold winters and very hot summers. The main factor contributing to the quality of the wine is the day-night temperature contrasts during the ripening season of the grapes, which causes the process to be carried out slowly.

## SOIL

The most common type of soil consists of pebbles on the surface and a clayey subsoil, which provides good water retention capacity in the deeper levels.

## GRAPE VARITES

**Red:** *Cencibel* or *Tempranillo, Cabernet Sauvignon, Merlot, Syrah* and *Bobal.*

| | |
|---|---|
| **Hectares of Vineyard** | 10,000 |
| **Nº Viticulturists** | 5,000 |
| **Nº of Bodegas** | 9 |
| **2008 Harvest** | Very Good |
| **2007 Production** | 900,000 l. |
| **Marketing** | 40% domestic 60% export |

**CONSEJO REGULADOR**
Pza. Ayuntamiento, s/n. 16708 Pozoamargo (Cuenca)
Tel: 969 387 182. Fax: 969 387 208
do@vinosriberadeljucar.com
www.vinosriberadeljucar.com

## GENERAL CHARACTERISTICS OF THE WINES:

| | |
|---|---|
| **REDS** | With an intense cherry colour and violet edge when they are young, they resemble the wines of the peripheral regions of La Mancha, characterised by less rusticity. On the nose, the notes of blackberries, red berries and earthy nuances stand out. On the palate, they are expressive, with tannins which are flavourful and liverly; freshly acidic with varietal reminders of the principal grape variety, the *Cencibel*. |

### 2008 VINTAGE RATING:

## VERY GOOD

## BODEGA SAN GINÉS

Virgen del Carmen, 6
16707 Casas de Benitez (Cuenca)
☎: 969 382 037 - Fax: 969 382 449
cincoalmudes@cincoalmudes.es
www.cincoalmudes.es

CINCO ALMUDES TEMPRANILLO 2008 T

**88** Colour: cherry, purple rim. Nose: expressive, fresh fruit, red berry notes, floral, rose petals, dry stone. Palate: flavourful, fruity, round tannins.

CINCO ALMUDES TRADICIÓN JÚCAR 2007 T

**88** Colour: bright cherry. Nose: ripe fruit, sweet spices, expressive, undergrowth, tobacco. Palate: flavourful, fruity, toasty, round tannins.

CINCO ALMUDES 2005 TC

**80**

ALMUDES 5 DÉCADAS 2003 TR

**85** Colour: cherry, garnet rim. Nose: ripe fruit, spicy, creamy oak, toasty, complex, fine reductive notes. Palate: powerful, flavourful, toasty, round tannins.

CINCO ALMUDES 2006 CRIANZA
tempranillo

**82**

## BODEGAS Y VIÑEDOS ILLANA

Finca Buenavista s/n
16708 Pozoamargo (Cuenca)
☎: 969 147 039 - Fax: 969 147 057
info@bodegasillana.com
www.bodegasillana.com

CASA DE ILLANA BLANCO CARMEN 2007 BFB
sauvignon blanc 90%, moscatel 10%

**83**

CASA DE ILLANA 2008 T
tempranillo 100%

**85** Colour: cherry, purple rim. Nose: expressive, fresh fruit, red berry notes, floral, balsamic herbs, undergrowth. Palate: flavourful, fruity, good acidity, round tannins, slightly acidic.

CASA DE ILLANA SELECCIÓN 2006 T
petit verdot 50%, syrah 50%

**85** Colour: bright cherry. Nose: sweet spices, creamy oak, expressive, fruit liqueur notes, red berry notes, fresh. Palate: flavourful, fruity, toasty, round tannins.

CASA DE ILLANA TRADICIÓN 2006 T
bobal, tempranillo, syrah

**85** Colour: bright cherry. Nose: sweet spices, creamy oak, expressive, fine reductive notes, fresh fruit. Palate: flavourful, toasty, round tannins, fruity aftestaste.

CASA DE ILLANA TRESDECINCO 2004 T
tempranillo 35%, bobal 25%, syrah 20%, merlot 20%

**85** Colour: cherry, garnet rim. Nose: ripe fruit, spicy, creamy oak, toasty, complex. Palate: powerful, flavourful, toasty, round tannins.

## CASA GUALDA

Tapias, 8
16708 Pozoamargo (Cuenca)
☎: 969 387 173 - Fax: 969 387 202
info@casagualda.com
www.casagualda.com

CASA GUALDA 2008 B
sauvignon blanc

## 84

CASA GUALDA 2008 B
chardonnay

## 80

LÁGRIMAS DE CASA GUALDA B

## 78

CASA GUALDA SYRAH 2007 T

**86** Colour: cherry, purple rim. Nose: expressive, fresh fruit, red berry notes, floral, fruit expression, earthy notes. Palate: flavourful, fruity, round tannins.

CASA GUALDA PLUS ULTRA 2006 T
petit verdot, bobal

## 84

### COOPERATIVA PURÍSIMA CONCEPCIÓN

Ctra. Minaya-San Clemente, km. 10
16610 Casas de Fernando Alonso (Cuenca)
☎: 969 383 043 - Fax: 969 383 153
info@vinoteatinos.com
www.vinoteatinos.com

TEATINOS TEMPRANILLO 2008 T

**87** Colour: cherry, purple rim. Nose: expressive, fresh fruit, red berry notes, floral, earthy notes. Palate: flavourful, fruity, good acidity, round tannins, good structure.

TEATINOS CLAROS DE CUBA 2005 TR

**88** Colour: bright cherry. Nose: ripe fruit, sweet spices, expressive, mineral. Palate: flavourful, fruity, toasty, round tannins, fruity aftestaste.

TEATINOS SELECCIÓN 40 BARRICAS TEMPRANILLO 2005 TR

## 84

TEATINOS 40 BARRICAS SIGNVM 2004 TC

## 80

### ECOBODEGA LA MORENILLA

Calvario, 8
16707 Casas de Benítez (Cuenca)
☎: 609 382 251 - Fax: 969 382 251
bodega@lamorenilla.com
www.lamorenilla.com

AMADOR PARREÑO 2007 T
tempranillo

## 77

### ELVIWINES S.L.

Granollers, 27 G
08173 Sant Cugat (Barcelona)
☎: 935 343 026 - Fax: 935 441 374
info@elviwines.com
www.elviwines.com

NESS 2008 B
moscatel 50%, sauvignon blanc 50%

**86** Colour: bright straw. Nose: fresh, fresh fruit, white flowers, expressive, citrus fruit. Palate: flavourful, fruity, good acidity, balanced.

NESS 2008 T
merlot 39%, bobal 32%, tempranillo 25%, cabernet sauvignon 4%

**87** Colour: cherry, garnet rim. Nose: ripe fruit, spicy, creamy oak, toasty, complex, dry nuts. Palate: powerful, flavourful, toasty, round tannins.

ADAR 2007 T

**88** Colour: cherry, purple rim. Nose: expressive, fresh fruit, red berry notes, floral, undergrowth. Palate: flavourful, fruity, good acidity, round tannins.

VIÑA ENCINA DE ELVIWINES 2007 T
bobal 33%, merlot 26%, cabernet sauvignon 21%, tempranillo 20%

**85** Colour: cherry, garnet rim. Nose: ripe fruit, spicy, creamy oak, complex, fine reductive notes. Palate: powerful, flavourful, toasty, round tannins.

ALBAK 2007 T

## 84

CLASICO ELVIWINES 2007 T
tempranillo 88%, merlot 12%

## 84

FURIA DE ELVIWINES 2005 TC

**87** Colour: cherry, garnet rim. Nose: ripe fruit, spicy, creamy oak, toasty, complex, wet leather. Palate: powerful, flavourful, toasty, round tannins, good acidity.

ALBAK 2005 T

**87** Colour: pale ruby, brick rim edge. Nose: spicy, fine reductive notes, wet leather, aged wood nuances, fruit liqueur notes. Palate: spicy, elegant, long, good acidity.

ADAR 2005 T

**85** Colour: cherry, garnet rim. Nose: ripe fruit, spicy, creamy oak, toasty, wet leather, balsamic herbs. Palate: powerful, flavourful, toasty, round tannins, pruney.

## LA MAGDALENA SOCIEDAD COOPERATIVA

Ctra. de la Roda, s/n
16611 Casas de Haro (Cuenca)
☎: 969 380 722 - Fax: 969 380 722
vmoragona@ucaman.es
www.vegamoragona.com

VEGA MORAGONA MOSCATEL DE GRANO MENUDO 2007 B
moscatel 100%

**84**

VEGA MORAGONA TEMPRANILLO 2007 T JOVEN
tempranillo 100%

**87** Colour: cherry, purple rim. Nose: expressive, fresh fruit, red berry notes, floral, mineral, damp earth. Palate: flavourful, fruity, good acidity, round tannins, good structure, balsamic.

VEGA MORAGONA SYRAH 2007 T
syrah 100%

**85** Colour: bright cherry. Nose: ripe fruit, sweet spices, creamy oak, expressive, undergrowth. Palate: flavourful, fruity, toasty, round tannins, creamy.

VEGA MORAGONA CABERNET SAUVIGNON 2007 T
cabernet sauvignon 100%

**77**

VEGA MORAGONA 2006 TC
tempranillo 100%

**86** Colour: cherry, garnet rim. Nose: ripe fruit, spicy, creamy oak, toasty, complex, fruit liqueur notes, damp earth. Palate: powerful, flavourful, toasty, round tannins, full.

## LA PAÑOLETA ROJA

Octavio Cuartero, 97 2
02004 Albacete ()
☎: 967 232 268
info@lapanoletaroja.com
www.lapanoletaroja.com

QUO 2005 TR

**79**

SOME OTHER WINERIES WITHIN THE DO:

**COOPERJÚCAR S.C.L.**

## NEWS

We have to adjust our analysis on Rioja to the fact that it represents a whole 40%! of the Spanish wine industry. On the pyramid of its wines, no other DO compares to it in terms of average ratings and homogenous quality. After the sheer excellence of the 2007 vintage, the quality of the 2008 seems to be a wee bit lower but very positive altogether. The quality of the grapes used to make young wines was good, although late rains affected some areas and plots, a circumstance that is reflected in our tasting, where different ripening levels were pretty evident, showing the wines from Rioja Baja more mature, warm and clean overall, while in those from Rioja Alta and Rioja Alavesa the slow and cold nature of the vintage gave as a result a two-track quality pattern, with differentiated results depending on the patience of vine growers at harvest, and the best results coming from the most experienced ones, used to cooler vintages. Besides the usual suspects, brands which are performing consistently well year after year and every now and then come up with the odd single-plot rendering, Rioja is gaining reputation for its whites, which are increasing both sales and aromatic character compared to the rest of the national whites. Of our list, the best 2008 are Mártires (the new wine from Allende), Plácet, Conde de Valdemar Finca Alto Cantabria, Campillo and Muga. With them, the local viura has been brought to its ultimate expression, a success that has made the Consejo Regulador to approve the inclusion in its regulations of other white varieties like chardonnay, verdejo and sauvignon blanc, when we deem the present catalogue of malvasía, torrontés, tempranillo blanca, garnacha blanca and even maturana blanca was more than enough to promote Riojan wines to ratings over 90 points. Of the local varieties, graciano seems the best partner for tempranillo and works wonders even on its own. Of the red maturana ¬–there is a white version, too–, Viña Ijalba has come up with a wine that broadens the varietal catalogue of the region. As to sales figures of the different styles, some years ago young wines meant 60% of the total production of the DO, a percentage that goes now to the crianza and reserva wines, simply the most preferred choice for modern consumers. Oak-aged wines of 2007 are a great buy, as they gather the virtues of a top vintage in terms of maturity with also great ageing potential. As for the 2005 and 2006 vintages and of a richer, warmer character, they are still showing great concentration and a rich, chocolaty nose, while some reserva wines of 2004 exhibit wonderful attributes of 'vino de guarda', while they still have good ageing potential. The gran reserva wines show great attributes of good, classic oxidative ageing when there were fears not long ago the seal could disappear for lack of excellence.

## LOCATION

Occupying the Ebro valley. To the north it borders with the Sierra de Cantabria and to the south with the Sierra de la Demanda, and is made up of different municipal districts of La Rioja, the Basque Country and Navarra. The most western region is Haro and the easternmost, Alfaro, with a distance of 100 km between the two. The region is 40 km wide.

## CLIMATE

Quite variable depending on the different sub-regions. In general, there is a combination of Atlantic and Mediterranean influences, the latter becoming more dominant as the terrain descends from west to east, becoming drier and hotter. The average annual rainfall is slightly over 400 mm.

## SOIL

Various types: the clayey calcareous soil arranged in terraces and small plots which are located especially in Rioja Alavesa, la Sonsierra and some regions of Rioja Alta; the clayey ferrous soil, scattered throughout the region, with vineyards located on reddish, strong soil with hard, deep rock; and the alluvial soil in the area close to the rivers; these are the most level vineyards with larger plots; here the soil is deeper and has pebbles.

| | |
|---|---|
| Hectares of Vineyard | 63,592 |
| Nº Viticulturists | 18,258 |
| Nº of Bodegas | 1,203 |
| 2008 Harvest | Very Good |
| 2007 Production | 272,000,000 l. |
| Marketing | 68.2% domestic 31.8% export |

# DO Ca. RIOJA

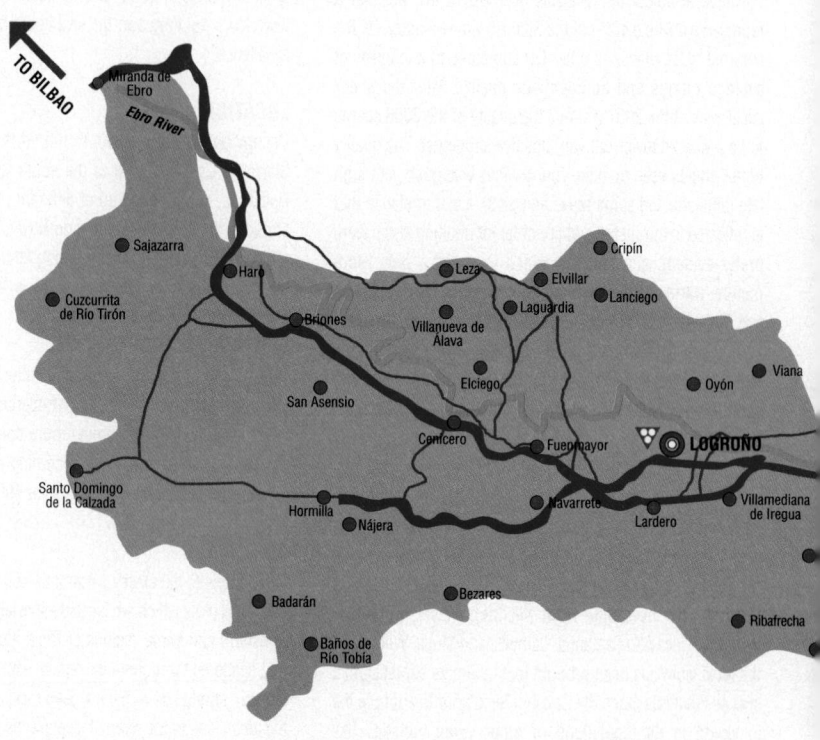

TO BILBAO

Miranda de Ebro

Ebro River

Sajazarra

Cuzcurrita de Río Tirón

Haro

Cripín

Leza

Elvillar

Lanciego

Briones

Laguardia

Villanueva de Álava

San Asensio

Elciego

Oyón

Viana

Cenicero

Fuenmayor

LOGROÑO

Santo Domingo de la Calzada

Hormilla

Navarrete

Lardero

Villamediana de Iregua

Nájera

Badarán

Bezares

Ribafrecha

Baños de Río Tobía

▽ Consejo Regulador

● DO Boundary

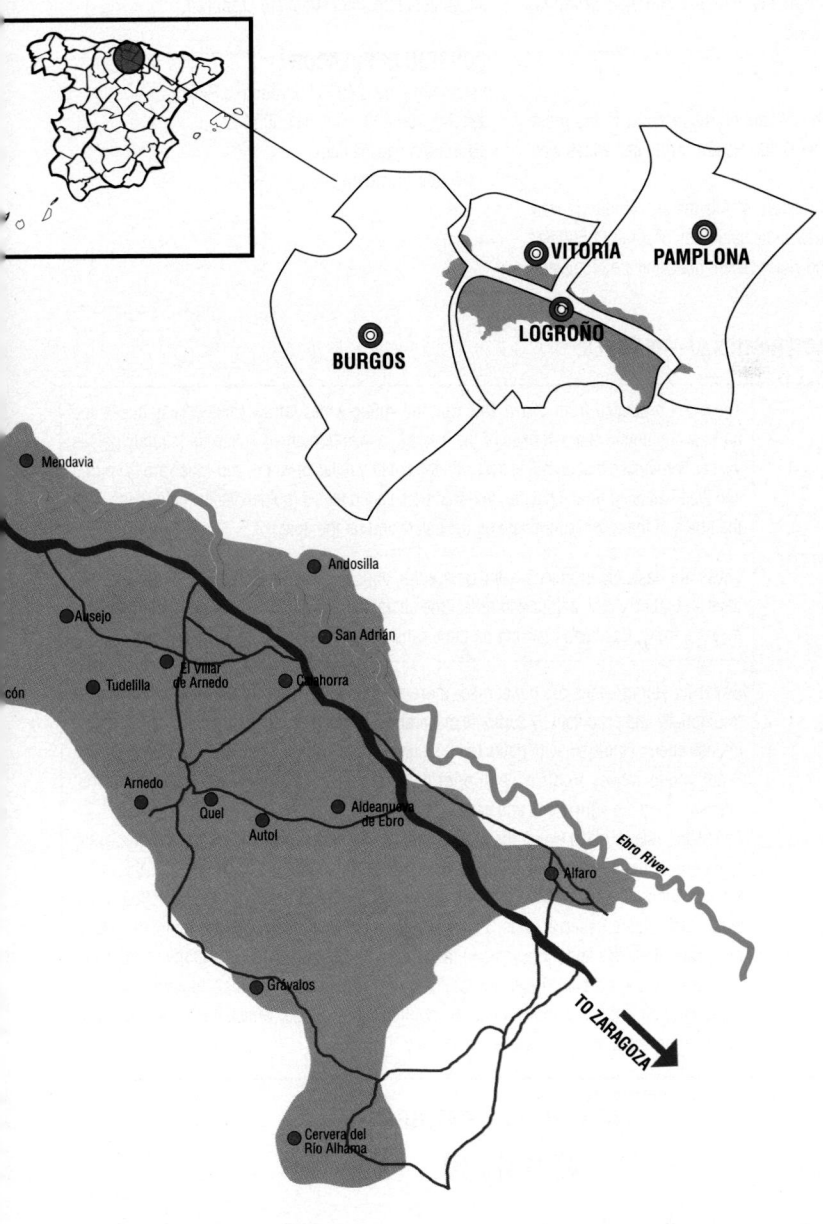

Mendavia

Andosilla

Ausejo

San Adrián

El Villar de Arnedo

Tudelilla

Calahorra

cón

Arnedo

Quel

Aldeanueva de Ebro

Autol

Ebro River

Alfaro

Grávalos

TO ZARAGOZA

Cervera del Río Alhama

VITORIA

PAMPLONA

LOGROÑO

BURGOS

**GRAPE VARITIES:**
White: *Viura* (7,045 Ha), *Malvasía* and *Garnacha Blanca*.
Red: *Tempranillo* (majority with 38,476 Ha), *Garnacha*, *Graciano* and *Mazuelo*.

**SUB-REGIONS:**
**Rioja Alta.** This has Atlantic influences; it is the most extensive with some 20,500 Ha and produces wines well suited for ageing.
**Rioja Alavesa.** A mixture of Atlantic and Mediterranean influences, with an area under cultivation of some 11,500 Ha; both young wines and wines suited for ageing are produced.

**Rioja Baja.** With approximately 18,000 Ha, the climate is purely Mediterranean; white wines and rosés with a higher alcohol content and extract are produced.

## CONSEJO REGULADOR
Estambrera, 52. 26006 Logroño (La Rioja)
☎: 941 500 400 - Fax: 941 500 672
@ info@riojawine.com
www.riojawine.com

**GENERAL CHARACTERISTICS OF THE WINES:**

| | |
|---|---|
| **WHITES** | These are produced from *Viura*. One can find young wines (straw yellow, fruity noses and herbaceous notes, characteristic of the variety), wines fermented in barrels (slightly golden yellow, with noses that combine fruit with the creamy notes of wood, and which are flavourful and well-balanced on the palate), and traditional aged wines (golden yellow colour, in which the notes of the oak predominate on the palate and on the nose). |
| **ROSÉS** | These are basically produced from *Garnacha*, almost always cultivated in Rioja Baja. The have a raspberry pink colour and reflect the character of the variety they are produced from they are fruity, fresh and pleasant on the palate. |
| **REDS** | As far as young wines are concerned, there are the wines from Rioja Alavesa, harvested traditionally and produced by carbonic maceration, which gives them great roasted strength: intense cherry coloured, with notes of ripe, sunny fruit (they are to be drunk within the year). Other young wines, produced with prior destemming, have slightly less colour and fruit intensity: they are light, fresh and easy drinking. As for the wines aged in wood, their characteristics are determined by the length of time they remain in contact with the oak, which determines the intensity of their colour. So, in the Crianza wines, the fruity notes of the grapes are slightly toned down by the action of the wood, while in the Reserva wines, and especially in the Gran Reserva wines (aged for at least two years in barrels and three years in the bottle), the roundness and harmony of the wines increases. On the nose, noses of vanilla, toast and tobacco appear, together with the complexity typical of the reduction in the bottle. In the younger wines, it is common to find notes reminiscent of leather and animal noses. |

## 2008 VINTAGE RATING:
# VERY GOOD

## AGRÍCOLA LABASTIDA

El Olmo, 8-9-10
01330 Labastida (Alava)
☎: 945 331 230 - Fax: 945 331 257
bodega@agricolalabastida.com
www.agricolalabastida.com

TIERRA DE FERNÁNDEZ GÓMEZ 2008 B
viura 60%, garnacha 30%, malvasia 10%

**82**

TIERRA DE FERNÁNDEZ GÓMEZ 2007 B
viura 60%, garnacha 30%, malvasia 10%

**79**

NUMEROS 2008 T

**90** Colour: cherry, purple rim. Nose: powerful, fruit preserve, lactic notes, red berry notes. Palate: flavourful, fruity, round tannins.

EL PRIMAVERA 2008 T
tempranillo 100%

**88** Colour: cherry, purple rim. Nose: powerful, varietal, ripe fruit, red berry notes, scrubland. Palate: flavourful, fruity, fleshy, good acidity, round tannins.

FERNÁNDEZ GÓMEZ 2008 T
tempranillo 90%, viura 10%

**87** Colour: cherry, purple rim. Nose: powerful, varietal, red berry notes. Palate: flavourful, powerful, fleshy, fruity.

LETRAS 2006 T
tempranillo

**93** Colour: bright cherry. Nose: ripe fruit, sweet spices, creamy oak, expressive, earthy notes. Palate: flavourful, fruity, toasty, round tannins.

TIERRA FIDEL 2006 T
graciano 50%, garnacha 50%

**91** Colour: deep cherry, garnet rim. Nose: complex, expressive, spicy, ripe fruit, balsamic herbs. Palate: complex, fleshy, flavourful.

EL BELISARIO 2006 T
tempranillo 100%

**87** Colour: black cherry, purple rim. Nose: roasted coffee, warm, balsamic herbs. Palate: spicy, harsh oak tannins.

LETRAS 2005 T

**91** Colour: cherry, garnet rim. Nose: mineral, powerfull, ripe fruit, sweet spices. Palate: flavourful, powerful, fleshy, round tannins.

EL BELISARIO 2005 T
tempranillo 100%

**90** Colour: cherry, purple rim. Nose: powerful, ripe fruit, scrubland. Palate: flavourful, ripe fruit, good acidity, fine bitter notes.

TIERRA DE FERNÁNDEZ GÓMEZ 2005 T
tempranillo 100%

**90** Colour: cherry, garnet rim. Nose: ripe fruit, floral, powerfull, sweet spices. Palate: flavourful, fruity, good acidity, round tannins.

TIERRA FIDEL 2005 T
graciano 50%, garnacha 50%

**89** Colour: cherry, garnet rim. Nose: powerful, ripe fruit, sweet spices, dark chocolate. Palate: flavourful, fleshy, ripe fruit, round tannins.

## AGUIRRE VITERI

Camino del Soto, 19
01306 La Puebla de Labarca (Alava)
☎: 945 607 148 - Fax: 945 607 148

AGUIRRE-VITERI 2008 T
tempranillo 95%, viura 5%

**85** Colour: dark-red cherry. Nose: fresh fruit, macerated fruit, varietal, powerfull. Palate: flavourful, fruity, sweetness.

AGUIRRE-VITERI SELECCIÓN 2007 T
tempranillo 100%

**85** Colour: cherry, garnet rim. Nose: powerful, ripe fruit, dark chocolate, sweet spices, toasty. Palate: flavourful, powerful, ripe fruit, round tannins.

AGUIRRE-VITERI 2005 TC
tempranillo 97%, graciano 3%

**83**

AGUIRRE-VITERI 2002 TR
tempranillo 100%

**83**

## ALADRO

El Barco, 23
01340 Elciego (Alava)
☎: 679 822 754

aladro@aladro.es
www.aladro.es

ALADRO 2008 T

**88** Colour: cherry, purple rim. Nose: fruit expression, fresh, expressive. Palate: fresh, fruity, flavourful, good acidity, round tannins.

## AMADOR GARCÍA

Avda. Río Ebro, 68 - 70
01307 Baños de Ebro (Álava)
☎: 945 290 583 - Fax: 945 290 373
bodegasamadorgarcia@gmail.com
www.bodegasamadorgarcia.com

PEÑAGUDO 2008 B
viura 100%

**86** Colour: bright straw. Nose: medium intensity, varietal, candied fruit, fruit expression. Palate: rich, fruity, flavourful.

AMADOR GARCÍA 2008 BFB
viura 100%

**86** Colour: straw. Nose: fruit expression, candied fruit, pattiserie. Palate: fruity, flavourful, spirituous.

PEÑAGUDO 2008 RD
tempranillo 85%, viura 15%

**84**

PEÑAGUDO 2008 T
tempranillo 90%, viura 10%

**86** Colour: cherry, purple rim. Nose: warm, medium intensity, red berry notes. Palate: fruity, flavourful, good finish, round tannins.

PEÑAGUDO 2005 TC
tempranillo 95%, graciano 2%, garnacha 3%

**87** Colour: deep cherry, garnet rim. Nose: ripe fruit, spicy, dark chocolate. Palate: balanced, concentrated, fruity, flavourful.

AMADOR GARCÍA VENDIMIA SELECCIONADA
2005 TC
tempranillo 95%, mazuelo 3%, graciano 2%

**87** Colour: black cherry, garnet rim. Nose: ripe fruit, dark chocolate, sweet spices, balanced. Palate: fruity, rich, round tannins.

BALCORRE

## AMURRIO BASTIDA S.C.

El Otero, 23
01330 Labastida (Rioja)
☎: 945 331 210 - Fax: 945 331 210
amurriobarroeta@yahoo.es

AMURRIO BARROETA 2008 T
tempranillo 90%, viura 10%

**86** Colour: deep cherry. Nose: floral, fresh fruit, red berry notes. Palate: fruity, flavourful, full.

ILUSIÓN DE AMURRIO BARROETA 2007 T
tempranillo 90%, viura 5%, garnacha 5%

**88** Colour: cherry, garnet rim. Nose: macerated fruit, ripe fruit, sweet spices, creamy oak. Palate: good acidity, round tannins, spicy, flavourful.

## ARABARTE

Ctra. Samaniego, s/n
01307 Villabuena (Alava)
☎: 945 609 408 - Fax: 945 609 409
arabarte@arabarte.es
www.arabarte.es

ARABARTE 2008 B

**85** Colour: straw. Nose: citrus fruit, ripe fruit, sweet spices. Palate: flavourful, fruity, fresh.

ARABARTE VINO DE AUTOR VENDIMIA
SELECCIONADA 2007 T

**84**

ARABARTE 2005 TC

**87** Colour: cherry, garnet rim. Nose: ripe fruit, spicy, creamy oak. Palate: balsamic, creamy, round tannins.

ARABARTE 2003 TR

**87** Colour: pale ruby, brick rim edge. Nose: fruit preserve, creamy oak, aged wood nuances, fine reductive notes. Palate: balsamic, creamy, round tannins, spicy.

ARABARTE 2001 TGR

**88** Colour: pale ruby, brick rim edge. Nose: fine reductive notes, sweet spices, aromatic coffee, tobacco, fruit preserve.

Palate: aged character, good structure, classic aged character, fine tannins.

## ARABARTE TEMPRANILLO T MACERACIÓN CARBÓNICA

**86** Colour: deep cherry. Nose: fresh fruit, ripe fruit. Palate: good acidity, fruity, flavourful.

## ARRIAGA Y MIMÉNDEZ COMPAÑIA DE VINOS

Capitán Cortés, 6 Piso 4 Puerta 3
26003 Logroño (La Rioja)
☎: 941 287 072 - Fax: 941 287 072
info@arriagaymimendez.com
www.arriagaymimendez.com

LA INVIERNA 2006 TC

**86** Colour: cherry, garnet rim. Nose: sweet spices, earthy notes, spicy, smoky. Palate: flavourful, fruity, toasty, round tannins, good acidity.

## ARTUKE BODEGAS Y VIÑEDOS

La Serna, 24
01307 Baños de Ebro (Alava)
☎: 945 623 323 - Fax: 945 623 323
artuke@artuke.com
www.artuke.com

ARTUKE SELECCIÓN 2008 T
tempranillo 90%, graciano 10%

**90** Colour: cherry, purple rim. Nose: expressive, fresh fruit, red berry notes, floral. Palate: flavourful, fruity, good acidity, round tannins.

ARTUKE 2008 T MACERACIÓN CARBÓNICA
tempranillo 95%, viura 5%

**88** Colour: cherry, purple rim. Nose: expressive, fresh fruit, red berry notes, floral. Palate: flavourful, fruity, good acidity, round tannins.

ARTUKE 2006 TC
tempranillo 90%, graciano 10%

**91** Colour: cherry, purple rim. Nose: balsamic herbs, grassy, ripe fruit, sweet spices. Palate: flavourful, fruity, spicy.

## BAIGORRI

Ctra. Vitoria-Logroño, km. 53
01307 Samaniego (Alava)

☎: 945 609 420 - Fax: 945 609 407
mail@bodegasbaigorri.com
www.bodegasbaigorri.com

BAIGORRI 2005 BFB
viura 50%, malvasia 50%

**90** Colour: bright straw. Nose: ripe fruit, sweet spices, expressive, cocoa bean. Palate: ripe fruit, flavourful, fleshy, spicy.

BAIGORRI 2008 RD
tempranillo 50%, garnacha 50%

**88** Colour: brilliant rose. Nose: red berry notes, raspberry, fresh, rose petals. Palate: flavourful, fruity, good acidity, fine bitter notes.

BAIGORRI 2008 T MACERACIÓN CARBÓNICA
tempranillo 100%

**85** Colour: cherry, garnet rim. Nose: fresh fruit, stalky, grassy. Palate: fresh, fruity, flavourful.

BAIGORRI 2005 TC
tempranillo 90%, garnacha 10%, others %

**91** Colour: cherry, garnet rim. Nose: ripe fruit, caramel, sweet spices. Palate: fleshy, powerful, ripe fruit, round tannins.

BAIGORRI DE GARAGE 2005 T
tempranillo 100%

**90** Colour: deep cherry, garnet rim. Nose: ripe fruit, cocoa bean, creamy oak. Palate: flavourful, complex, fleshy, ripe fruit, spicy.

BAIGORRI 2004 TR
tempranillo 100%

**89** Colour: cherry, garnet rim. Nose: balanced, powerfull, ripe fruit, sweet spices. Palate: fleshy, balsamic, fruity, round tannins.

## BARÓN DE LEY

Ctra. Mendavia - Lodosa, km. 5,5
31587 Mendavia (Navarra)
☎: 948 694 303 - Fax: 948 694 304
info@barondeley.com
www.barondeley.com

BARÓN DE LEY FINCA MONASTERIO 2007 T

**90** Colour: bright cherry. Nose: sweet spices, creamy oak, ripe fruit. Palate: flavourful, fruity, toasty, round tannins.

**BARON DE LEY 7 VIÑAS 2004 TR**
tempranillo 55%, graciano 15%, garnacha 15%, mazuelo 7%, viura 5%, others 3%

**91** Colour: deep cherry. Nose: fresh, fruit expression, ripe fruit, aromatic coffee, complex. Palate: flavourful, complex, ripe fruit, soft tannins.

**BARÓN DE LEY 2004 TR**

**88** Colour: cherry, garnet rim. Nose: powerful, ripe fruit, wet leather, toasty. Palate: spicy, classic aged character, ripe fruit.

## BERBERANA

Ctra. de Vitoria, km. 182-183
26360 Cenicero (La Rioja)
☎: 941 453 100 - Fax: 941 450 101
info@berberana.com
www.berberana.com

**VIÑA ALARDE 2005 TC**
tempranillo 100%

**87** Colour: cherry, garnet rim. Nose: ripe fruit, creamy oak, spicy, medium intensity. Palate: balanced, flavourful, fruity aftestaste, round tannins.

**BERBERANA CARTA DE ORO 2005 TR**
tempranillo 80%, garnacha 20%

**85** Colour: deep cherry, orangey edge. Nose: ripe fruit, expressive, pattiserie, sweet spices. Palate: warm, balanced, round tannins, spicy.

**VIÑA ALARDE 2004 TR**
tempranillo 80%, garnacha 20%

**87** Colour: cherry, garnet rim. Nose: fine reductive notes, tobacco, spicy. Palate: flavourful, warm, ripe fruit, round tannins.

## BERONIA

Ctra. Ollauri - Nájera, km. 1,8
26220 Ollauri (La Rioja)
☎: 941 338 000 - Fax: 941 338 266
elrincondegb@gonzalezbyass.es
www.beronia.es

**BERONIA VIURA 2008 B**
viura 100%

**84**

**BERONIA VIURA 2007 BFB**
viura 100%

**87** Nose: medium intensity, ripe fruit, smoky, pattiserie. Palate: rich, flavourful, fruity.

**BERONIA TEMPRANILLO 2007 T**
tempranillo 100%

**88** Colour: cherry, garnet rim. Nose: powerful, ripe fruit, red berry notes, lactic notes. Palate: flavourful, fruity, spicy, ripe fruit.

**BERONIA GRACIANO 2007 T**
graciano 100%

**88** Colour: cherry, garnet rim. Nose: powerful, ripe fruit, red berry notes, sweet spices. Palate: flavourful, powerful, fleshy, ripe fruit.

**BERONIA 2006 TC**
tempranillo 84%, garnacha 13%, mazuelo 3%

**86** Colour: deep cherry, orangey edge. Nose: ripe fruit, spicy, creamy oak. Palate: fruity, easy to drink, flavourful, round tannins.

**BERONIA ECOLÓGICO 2005 TC**
tempranillo

**89** Colour: dark-red cherry, garnet rim. Nose: powerful, ripe fruit, wild herbs, toasty, complex. Palate: correct, creamy, spicy, roasted-coffee aftertaste, round tannins.

**III A.C., BERONIA 2004 T**
tempranillo 90%, graciano 6%, mazuelo 4%

**90** Colour: very deep cherry, garnet rim. Nose: elegant, expressive, ripe fruit, sweet spices, cocoa bean. Palate: good structure, powerful, round tannins.

**BERONIA 2004 TR**
tempranillo 90%, graciano 4%, mazuelo 6%

**89** Colour: bright cherry, garnet rim. Nose: ripe fruit, cocoa bean, expressive. Palate: fruity, powerful, full, fine bitter notes, fruity aftestaste, toasty.

**BERONIA MAZUELO 2004 TR**
mazuelo 100%

**86** Colour: cherry, garnet rim. Nose: complex, varietal, scrubland, spicy. Palate: flavourful, classic aged character, fine tannins.

**BERONIA SELECCIÓN 198 BARRICAS 2001 TR**
tempranillo 87%, mazuelo 7%, graciano 6%

**88** Colour: deep cherry, orangey edge. Nose: expressive, powerfull, elegant, fruit liqueur notes, toasty, aromatic coffee. Palate: classic aged character, elegant, flavourful, round tannins.

**BERONIA 2001 TGR**
tempranillo 88%, mazuelo 8%, graciano 4%

**87** Colour: deep cherry, orangey edge. Nose: powerful, fruit liqueur notes, dark chocolate, spicy, pattiserie. Palate: flavourful, spicy, round tannins.

## BODEGA ABEL MENDOZA MONGE

Ctra. Peñacerrada, 7
26338 San Vicente de la Sonsierra (La Rioja)
☎: 941 308 010 - Fax: 941 308 010
jarrarte.abelmendoza@gmail.com

**ABEL MENDOZA MALVASÍA 2008 BFB**
malvasia 100%

**89** Colour: old gold. Nose: ripe fruit, pattiserie, medium intensity. Palate: flavourful, fruity, rich, creamy.

**ABEL MENDOZA VIURA 2008 BFB**
viura 100%

**86** Colour: bright straw. Nose: ripe fruit, grassy, toasty. Palate: powerful, flavourful, fleshy.

**ABEL MENDOZA TEMPRANILLO GRANO A GRANO 2006 T**
tempranillo 100%

**92** Colour: cherry, garnet rim. Nose: ripe fruit, spicy, creamy oak, toasty, complex, mineral. Palate: powerful, flavourful, toasty, round tannins.

**ABEL MENDOZA GRACIANO GRANO A GRANO 2006 T**
graciano 100%

**92** Colour: bright cherry. Nose: ripe fruit, sweet spices, creamy oak, expressive, red berry notes, lactic notes, balsamic herbs. Palate: flavourful, fruity, toasty, round tannins.

**ABEL MENDOZA SELECCIÓN PERSONAL 2006 T**
tempranillo 100%

**90** Colour: cherry, garnet rim. Nose: ripe fruit, red berry notes, sweet spices, lactic notes. Palate: flavourful, fleshy, spicy, round tannins.

**JARRARTE 2006 TC**
tempranillo 100%

**87** Colour: bright cherry. Nose: ripe fruit, sweet spices, creamy oak. Palate: flavourful, fruity, toasty, round tannins.

## BODEGA ANTIGUA USANZA

Camino Garugele, s/n
26338 San Vicente de la Sonsierra (La Rioja)
☎: 941 334 156 - Fax: 941 334 254
antiguausanza@antiguausanza.com
www.antiguausanza.com

**BALTHUS 2006 T**
tempranillo 100%

**88** Colour: cherry, garnet rim. Nose: ripe fruit, spicy, creamy oak, toasty, complex. Palate: powerful, flavourful, toasty, round tannins.

**BAU 2005 TC**
tempranillo 90%, graciano 5%, garnacha 5%

**86** Colour: cherry, garnet rim. Nose: ripe fruit, spicy, creamy oak, toasty, complex. Palate: powerful, flavourful, toasty, round tannins.

**CARMELO 2004 T**
tempranillo 100%

**91** Colour: cherry, garnet rim. Nose: ripe fruit, spicy, creamy oak, toasty, complex. Palate: powerful, flavourful, toasty, round tannins.

**BAU 2001 TR**
tempranillo 90%, graciano 5%, garnacha 5%

**90** Colour: very deep cherry. Nose: fruit preserve, expressive, cocoa bean, sweet spices, aromatic coffee. Palate: balanced, elegant, long, full, fine tannins.

## BODEGA BASAGOITI

Mas Parxet, s/n
08391 Tiana (Barcelona)
☎: 933 950 811 - Fax: 933 955 500
info@parxet.es

**BASAGOITI 2005 TC**
tempranillo 100%

**88** Colour: cherry, garnet rim. Nose: ripe fruit, expressive, spicy, creamy oak, cocoa bean. Palate: balanced, elegant, fruity, round tannins.

## BODEGA CONTADOR

Ctra. Baños de Ebro, km. 1,8
41927 San Vicente de la Sonsierra (La Rioja)
☎: 941 334 572
benjamin@bodegacontador.com

**QUÉ BONITO CACAREABA 2008 B**

**93** Colour: bright yellow. Nose: powerful, sweet spices, creamy oak, fragrant herbs, ripe fruit, cocoa bean. Palate: rich, smoky aftertaste, flavourful, fresh, good acidity.

**PREDICADOR 2008 B**
viura, garnacha blanca, malvasia

**92** Colour: bright yellow. Nose: powerful, ripe fruit, creamy oak, fragrant herbs, smoky. Palate: rich, smoky aftertaste, flavourful, fresh, good acidity.

**PREDICADOR 2007 B**
viura, garnacha blanca, malvasia

**91** Colour: bright yellow. Nose: powerful, fruit expression, cocoa bean, spicy, scrubland. Palate: flavourful, fleshy, smoky aftertaste, toasty, harsh oak tannins.

**CONTADOR 2007 T**

**97** Colour: very deep cherry. Nose: complex, expressive, aromatic coffee, spicy, fruit expression, ripe fruit. Palate: powerful, fleshy, round tannins, roasted-coffee aftertaste.

**LA VIÑA DE ANDRÉS ROMEO 2007 T**

**96** Colour: dark-red cherry. Nose: cocoa bean, creamy oak, fresh fruit, ripe fruit. Palate: flavourful, fleshy, good acidity, ripe fruit, spicy, round tannins.

**LA CUEVA DEL CONTADOR 2007 T**

**94** Colour: very deep cherry. Nose: expressive, neat, fresh fruit, ripe fruit, sweet spices, mineral. Palate: powerful, flavourful, fruity, fruity aftestaste, balsamic.

**PREDICADOR 2007 T**

**92** Colour: dark-red cherry. Nose: mineral, fresh fruit, ripe fruit, scrubland, spicy. Palate: fresh, fruity, flavourful, mineral.

## BODEGA DEL MONGE-GARBATI

Ctra. Rivas de Tereso, s/n
26338 San Vicente de la Sonsierra (La Rioja)
☎: 659 167 653 - Fax: 941 311 870
bodegamg@yahoo.es
www.vinaane.com

**VIÑA ANE 2005 T**

**85** Colour: deep cherry. Nose: aged wood nuances, spicy, ripe fruit. Palate: powerful, good structure, fine bitter notes.

**VIÑA ANE VENDIMIA SELECCIONADA 2005 T**

**85** Colour: very deep cherry. Nose: powerful, woody, smoky, ripe fruit, fruit liqueur notes. Palate: powerful, good structure, spirituous, fine bitter notes.

**VIÑA ANE VENDIMIA SELECCIONADA 2004 T**

**88** Colour: deep cherry. Nose: ripe fruit, expressive, neat, sweet spices, toasty, mineral. Palate: flavourful, powerful, concentrated, good structure.

## BODEGA FINCA DE LOS ARANDINOS

Ctra. de Entrena a Nalda, km. 1
26375 Entrena (La Rioja)
☎: 941 273 234 - Fax: 941 235 715
bodega@fincadelosarandinos.com
www.fincadelosarandinos.com

**FINCA DE LOS ARANDINOS 2007 T**
tempranillo 90%, garnacha 10%

**87** Colour: dark-red cherry. Nose: ripe fruit, creamy oak, spicy, balsamic herbs. Palate: good acidity, fleshy, flavourful, fruity, slightly dry, soft tannins.

## BODEGA HERMANOS BERRUECO

Herrería, Travesía 2, nº 2
01307 Villabuena (Alava)
☎: 945 609 034 - Fax: 945 623 344
info@berrueco.com
www.berrueco.com

**BERRUECO 2008 T**

**88** Colour: deep cherry. Nose: varietal, fresh, fresh fruit. Palate: fruity, full, flavourful, good acidity.

**BERRUECO 2004 TC**

**87** Colour: very deep cherry, garnet rim. Nose: fruit preserve, creamy oak, sweet spices, cocoa bean. Palate: fruity, elegant, good acidity.

**BERRUECO 2001 TR**

**87** Colour: light cherry, bright ochre rim. Nose: toasty, cocoa bean, aromatic coffee. Palate: elegant, long, slightly dry, soft tannins.

## BODEGA HERMANOS CASTILLO PÉREZ

Camino de la Estación, 15
26330 Briones (La Rioja)
☎: 667 730 651 - Fax: 941 301 006
arrostillo@hotmail.com

**ZURBAL 2008 B**
viura 100%

**87** Colour: bright straw. Nose: varietal, expressive, macerated fruit. Palate: rich, fruity, flavourful.

**ZURBAL 2008 T**
tempranillo 100%

**82**

**ZURBAL VITICULTURA ECOLÓGICA 2008 T**
tempranillo 100%

**82**

**ZURBAL 2006 TC**
tempranillo 100%

**86** Colour: dark-red cherry, garnet rim. Nose: fruit preserve, spicy, creamy oak. Palate: flavourful, round tannins, easy to drink, spicy.

**ZURBAL VENDIMIA SELECCIONADA 2006 T**
tempranillo 100%

**86** Colour: dark-red cherry, garnet rim. Nose: fruit preserve, spicy, creamy oak, balsamic herbs. Palate: flavourful, spicy, round tannins.

**ZURBAL 2004 TR**
tempranillo 100%

**88** Colour: deep cherry, orangey edge. Nose: fruit preserve, sweet spices, toasty, new oak, creamy oak. Palate: balanced, elegant, full, spicy, soft tannins.

## BODEGA MIGUEL MERINO

Calle Logroño, 16
26330 Briones (La Rioja)
☎: 941 322 263 - Fax: 941 322 294
info@miguelmerino.com
www.miguelmerino.com

**UNNUM 2005 TC**
tempranillo 100%

**87** Colour: cherry, garnet rim. Nose: ripe fruit, warm, creamy oak. Palate: spicy, fruity aftestaste, flavourful, fruity, round tannins.

**MIGUEL MERINO 2004 TR**
tempranillo 100%

**87** Colour: cherry, garnet rim. Nose: macerated fruit, creamy oak, sweet spices. Palate: fruity, flavourful, round tannins, spicy.

**MAZUELO DE LA QUINTA CRUZ**

## BODEGA PEDRO BENITO URBINA

Campillo, 33-35
26214 Cuzcurrita de Río Tirón (La Rioja)
☎: 941 224 272 - Fax: 941 224 272
urbina@fer.es
www.urbinavinos.com

**URBINA TEMPRANILLO 2007 T**
tempranillo 100%

**83**

**URBINA 1995 TGR**
tempranillo

**87** Colour: cherry, garnet rim. Nose: ripe fruit, expressive, medium intensity, caramel. Palate: flavourful, fruity, great length, round tannins.

## BODEGA SAN PRUDENCIO

Ctra. Viana, km. 1
01322 Moreda (Alava)
☎: 945 601 034 - Fax: 945 622 451
info@bodegasanprudencio.com
www.bodegasanprudencio.com

**ENVITE SEDUCCIÓN 2008 B**
viura 90%, malvasia 10%

**86** Colour: bright straw. Nose: fresh, white flowers, expressive, candied fruit, citrus fruit. Palate: flavourful, fruity, good acidity, sweetness.

**ENVITE 2008 B**
viura, malvasia

**82**

**CONCLAVE ESENCIA 2007 BFB**

**85** Colour: old gold. Nose: fruit expression, ripe fruit, pattiserie, fragrant herbs. Palate: fruity, fresh, light-bodied.

**ENVITE 2008 RD**

**83**

**CONCLAVE ESENCIA 2006 T**

**87** Colour: cherry, purple rim. Nose: powerful, ripe fruit, red berry notes, lactic notes. Palate: flavourful, powerful, fleshy, round tannins.

ENVITE 2006 TC

**86** Colour: cherry, garnet rim. Nose: ripe fruit, aromatic coffee, medium intensity. Palate: good structure, complex, spicy, round tannins.

## BODEGA SEÑORÍO DE LA ESTRELLA

Ctra. Logroño, s/n
26340 San Asensio (La Rioja)
☎: 941 457 133 - Fax: 941 457 133
bodegas@senoriodelaestrella.es
www.senoriodelaestrella.es

ARICHETA 2006 T

**88** Colour: dark-red cherry, garnet rim. Nose: ripe fruit, sweet spices, creamy oak. Palate: flavourful, fruity, ripe fruit, round tannins.

## BODEGA Y VIÑEDOS SOLABAL

Camino San Bartolomé, 6
26339 Abalos (La Rioja)
☎: 941 334 492 - Fax: 941 308 164
solabal@terra.es

MUÑARRATE DE SOLABAL 2008 B
viura 100%

**87** Colour: bright straw. Nose: fresh fruit, floral, grassy. Palate: fruity, flavourful, good structure, fine bitter notes.

MUÑARRATE DE SOLABAL 2008 RD
tempranillo 30%, viura 30%, garnacha 40%

**87** Colour: brilliant rose. Nose: red berry notes, ripe fruit, scrubland. Palate: flavourful, fruity, fleshy.

MUÑARRATE 2008 T
tempranillo 90%, viura 10%

**88** Colour: cherry, purple rim. Nose: expressive, fresh fruit, red berry notes, floral. Palate: flavourful, fruity, good acidity, round tannins.

SOLABAL 2006 TC
tempranillo 100%

**85** Colour: cherry, garnet rim. Nose: powerful, fruit preserve, toasty, sweet spices. Palate: flavourful, powerful, spicy.

SOLABAL 2005 TR
tempranillo 100%

**89** Colour: cherry, garnet rim. Nose: sweet spices, toasty, creamy oak, ripe fruit. Palate: flavourful, powerful, ripe fruit, round tannins.

ESCULLE DE SOLABAL 2005 TC
tempranillo 100%

**87** Colour: cherry, garnet rim. Nose: powerful, sweet spices, creamy oak, ripe fruit. Palate: flavourful, fleshy, spicy.

## BODEGAS AGE

Barrio de la Estación, s/n
26360 Fuenmayor (La Rioja)
☎: 941 293 500 - Fax: 941 293 501
bodegasage@domecqbodegas.com
www.bodegasage.com

SIGLO C.V.C. T JOVEN
tempranillo, garnacha

**81**

ROMERAL 2007 T JOVEN
tempranillo, garnacha

**78**

SIGLO SACO 2006 TC
tempranillo, garnacha, mazuelo

**85** Colour: cherry, garnet rim. Nose: medium intensity, ripe fruit, dark chocolate, sweet spices. Palate: flavourful, ripe fruit, spicy, round tannins.

SIGLO 2004 TR
tempranillo, mazuelo, graciano

**88** Colour: cherry, garnet rim. Nose: powerful, ripe fruit, cocoa bean, dark chocolate. Palate: flavourful, powerful, fleshy, spicy.

## BODEGAS ALABANZA

Polígono Industrial El Sequero, Avda. Cameros, 27
26150 Agoncillo (La Rioja)
☎: 941 437 051
bodegasalabanza@bodegasalabanza.com
www.bodegasalabanza.com

ALABANZA 2008 T
tempranillo 100%

**78**

VALDEGUINEA 2007 T

**88** Colour: cherry, garnet rim. Nose: ripe fruit, lactic notes, creamy oak. Palate: flavourful, powerful, fleshy, round tannins.

VALDEGUINEA 2006 T

**86** Colour: cherry, garnet rim. Nose: powerful, ripe fruit, sweet spices, cocoa bean. Palate: flavourful, powerful, fleshy, round tannins.

## ALABANZA 2006 TC
tempranillo 85%, garnacha 15%

**85** Colour: cherry, garnet rim. Nose: powerful, fruit preserve, smoky, toasty. Palate: powerful, fleshy, sweetness.

## ALABANZA SELECCIÓN 2005 T
tempranillo 75%, mazuelo 15%, graciano 10%

**87** Colour: cherry, garnet rim. Nose: ripe fruit, spicy, creamy oak, toasty, complex. Palate: powerful, flavourful, toasty, round tannins.

## ALABANZA 2005 TR
tempranillo 70%, garnacha 30%

**85** Colour: cherry, garnet rim. Nose: powerful, fruit preserve, warm, dark chocolate. Palate: powerful, fleshy, spicy, ripe fruit.

## BODEGAS ALAVESAS

Ctra. De Elciego s/n
01300 Laguardia (Alava)
☎: 902 227 700 - Fax: 902 227 701
bodega@cofradiasamaniego.com
www.solardesamaniego.com

### SOLAR DE SAMANIEGO 2005 TC
tempranillo 95%, graciano 5%

**86** Colour: cherry, garnet rim. Nose: ripe fruit, sweet spices, dark chocolate. Palate: spicy, ripe fruit, round tannins.

### VALCAVADA 2004 TR
tempranillo 75%, graciano 25%

**89** Colour: dark-red cherry. Nose: expressive, medium intensity, elegant, fruit expression, balsamic herbs, aged wood nuances. Palate: flavourful, rich, spicy, round tannins.

### SOLAR DE SAMANIEGO 2003 TR
tempranillo 92%, graciano 8%

**86** Colour: cherry, garnet rim. Nose: spicy, dark chocolate, ripe fruit. Palate: fruity, spicy, fleshy.

## BODEGAS ALTANZA

Ctra. Nacional 232, km. 419,5
26360 Fuenmayor (Rioja)
☎: 941 450 860 - Fax: 941 450 804
altanza@bodegasaltanza.com
www.bodegasaltanza.com

### LEALTANZA 2008 RD
tempranillo 100%

**85** Colour: brilliant rose. Nose: red berry notes, floral. Palate: flavourful, fresh, fruity, fine bitter notes, good acidity.

### LEALTANZA 2005 T
tempranillo 100%

**86** Colour: cherry, garnet rim. Nose: red berry notes, balanced, sweet spices. Palate: fruity, flavourful, good acidity, round tannins.

### EDULIS 2005 TC
tempranillo 100%

**83**

### LEALTANZA ARTISTAS ESPAÑOLES DALÍ 2004 TR
tempranillo 100%

**90** Colour: cherry, garnet rim. Nose: powerful, tar, toasty, ripe fruit, fruit preserve, cigar. Palate: powerful, ripe fruit, spicy.

### CLUB LEALTANZA SELECCIÓN 2004 TR
tempranillo 100%

**90** Colour: bright cherry, garnet rim. Nose: expressive, fresh, ripe fruit, balanced, spicy. Palate: good structure, round tannins, fine bitter notes.

### ALTANZA RESERVA ESPECIAL 2001 TR
tempranillo 100%

**87** Colour: cherry, garnet rim. Nose: powerful, smoky, aromatic coffee, ripe fruit. Palate: flavourful, powerful, spicy.

### LEALTANZA 2001 TR
tempranillo 100%

**87** Colour: cherry, garnet rim. Nose: powerful, ripe fruit, woody, toasty. Palate: powerful, spicy, ripe fruit.

## BODEGAS ALTOS DEL MARQUÉS

Ctra. de Navarrete, 232, salida 10, Vía de Servicio
26006 Logroño (La Rioja)
☎: 941 286 728 - Fax: 941 286 729
info@altosdelmarques.com
www.altosdelmarques.com

### ALTOS DEL MARQUÉS 2008 T
tempranillo, garnacha, mazuelo

**87** Colour: cherry, purple rim. Nose: red berry notes, balanced, fresh. Palate: flavourful, fruity, balanced, round tannins, great length.

### ATICUS 2005 TC

**87** Colour: cherry, garnet rim. Nose: powerful, fruit liqueur notes, toasty, caramel. Palate: flavourful, powerful, fleshy, spicy, round tannins.

ALTOS DEL MARQUÉS 2005 TC

**87** Colour: cherry, garnet rim. Nose: powerful, ripe fruit, red berry notes, sweet spices. Palate: flavourful, spicy, ripe fruit, round tannins.

ATICUS 2004 TR
tempranillo

**90** Colour: pale ruby, brick rim edge. Nose: powerful, expressive, fruit preserve, creamy oak, fine reductive notes, mineral. Palate: fleshy, fine tannins, flavourful.

ATICUS VENDIMIA SELECCIONADA 2004 T

**89** Colour: cherry, garnet rim. Nose: powerful, toasty, dark chocolate, wet leather. Palate: powerful, spicy, round tannins.

## BODEGAS ALTÚN

Las Piscinas, s/n
01307 Baños de Ebro (Alava)
☎: 945 609 317 - Fax: 945 609 309
altun@bodegasaltun.com

ALBIKER 2008 T
tempranillo 95%, viura 5%

**90** Colour: dark-red cherry. Nose: varietal, powerfull, expressive, red berry notes, fresh fruit. Palate: fresh, fruity, powerful, round tannins.

EVEREST 2006 T
tempranillo 100%

**90** Colour: cherry, garnet rim. Nose: expressive, powerfull, ripe fruit, cocoa bean, spicy. Palate: elegant, balanced, round, round tannins, full.

ALTÚN 2004 TR
tempranillo 100%

**89** Colour: cherry, garnet rim. Nose: ripe fruit, sweet spices, powerfull, expressive. Palate: powerful, flavourful, spicy, round tannins.

ALTÚN 2006 TC
tempranillo 100%

**87** Colour: cherry, garnet rim. Nose: ripe fruit, mineral, expressive, spicy. Palate: fruity, easy to drink, spicy, round tannins, balanced.

RIOJA

DENOMINACION DE ORIGEN CALIFICADA

ALTÚN

CRIANZA

BODEGAS ALTÚN, S.L.

## BODEGAS AMAREN

Ctra. Baños de Ebro, s/n,
01307 Villabuena (Alava)
☎: 945 175 240 - Fax: 945 174 566
bodegas@bodegasamaren.com
www.luiscanas.com

AMAREN GRACIANO 2005 TC
graciano 100%

**90** Colour: deep cherry. Nose: medium intensity, characterful, varietal, fresh fruit, cocoa bean, creamy oak, cedar wood. Palate: spirituous, fleshy, powerful, flavourful, good acidity.

AMAREN GRACIANO 2006 TC
graciano 100%

**92** Colour: very deep cherry. Nose: roasted coffee, aromatic coffee, ripe fruit, fruit expression, damp earth. Palate: good acidity, complex, fleshy, powerful, flavourful, fruity aftertaste, balsamic.

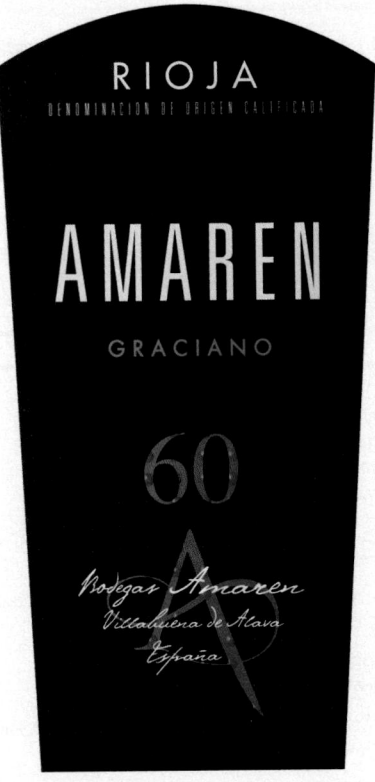

**AMAREN TEMPRANILLO 2002 TR**
tempranillo 100%

**90** Colour: dark-red cherry. Nose: ripe fruit, expressive, varietal, complex, creamy oak, cocoa bean. Palate: fruity, complex, flavourful, powerful, toasty, roasted-coffee aftertaste.

**AMAREN TEMPRANILLO 2004 TR**
tempranillo 100%

**91** Colour: deep cherry. Nose: red berry notes, cocoa bean, creamy oak, powerfull, characterful. Palate: fruity, powerful, flavourful, complex.

## BODEGAS AMÉZOLA DE LA MORA S.A.

Paraje Viña Vieja, s/n
26359 Torremontalbo (La Rioja)
☎: 941 454 532 - Fax: 941 454 537
info@bodegasamezola.es
www.bodegasamezola.net

**IÑIGO AMÉZOLA 2008 B**
viura 100%

**88** Colour: bright straw. Nose: fresh fruit, creamy oak. Palate: flavourful, rich, good acidity, easy to drink.

**IÑIGO AMÉZOLA 2007 T**
tempranillo 100%

**90** Colour: very deep cherry. Nose: expressive, fruit preserve, creamy oak, new oak, sweet spices, mineral. Palate: elegant, creamy, great length, fine tannins.

# DO Ca. RIOJA

**VIÑA AMÉZOLA 2006 TC**
tempranillo 85%, mazuelo 10%, graciano 5%

**87** Colour: very deep cherry, garnet rim. Nose: fruit preserve, mineral, spicy, creamy oak. Palate: full, flavourful, warm, fine tannins.

**SEÑORÍO AMÉZOLA 2002 TR**
tempranillo 85%, mazuelo 10%, garnacha 5%

**88** Colour: cherry, garnet rim. Nose: powerful, sweet spices, cocoa bean, aromatic coffee, dark chocolate, ripe fruit. Palate: flavourful, rich, sweetness, spicy, round tannins.

**SOLAR AMÉZOLA 1999 TGR**
tempranillo 85%, mazuelo 10%, graciano 5%

**87** Colour: light cherry, brick rim edge. Nose: macerated fruit, fine reductive notes, sweet spices, cocoa bean. Palate: aged character, good structure, fine tannins.

## BODEGAS ANTION

Manuel Iradier, 13
01340 Elciego (Alava)
☎: 902 122 211 - Fax: 945 622 229
marketing@grupoproconsol.com
www.bodegantion.com

**ANTIÓN VARIETAL TEMPRANILLO 2006 T**
tempranillo 100%

**90** Colour: cherry, garnet rim. Nose: ripe fruit, expressive, creamy oak, cocoa bean, sweet spices. Palate: round tannins, powerful, spicy, flavourful, balanced.

**BARON DE OJA 2006 TC**
tempranillo 100%

**90** Colour: cherry, garnet rim. Nose: ripe fruit, cocoa bean, spicy. Palate: elegant, balanced, round, flavourful, round tannins.

**ANTIÓN PREMIUM 2005 T**
tempranillo 100%

**92** Colour: cherry, garnet rim. Nose: ripe fruit, expressive, varietal, elegant, cocoa bean, sweet spices, balsamic herbs. Palate: creamy, round tannins, powerful, full, flavourful, elegant.

**ANTIÓN SELECCIÓN 2005 T**
tempranillo 100%

**91** Colour: cherry, garnet rim. Nose: varietal, powerfull, expressive, elegant, ripe fruit, cocoa bean, balsamic herbs. Palate: full, flavourful, balanced, elegant, round, round tannins.

## BODEGAS ARACO

Ctra. Lapuebla, s/n
01300 Laguardia (Alava)
☎: 945 600 209 - Fax: 945 600 067
araco@bodegasaraco.com
www.bodegasaraco.com

**ARACO 2008 T**
tempranillo 100%

**85** Colour: very deep cherry. Nose: ripe fruit, medium intensity. Palate: balsamic, fruity, flavourful.

**ARACO 2005 TC**
tempranillo 100%

**85** Colour: dark-red cherry. Nose: macerated fruit, creamy oak. Palate: round tannins, creamy, flavourful.

**ARACO 2004 TR**
tempranillo 100%

**84**

## BODEGAS BAGORDI

Ctra. de Estella, km. 32
31261 Andosilla (Navarra)
☎: 948 674 860 - Fax: 948 674 238
info@bagordi.com
www.bagordi.com

**USOA DE BAGORDI 2005 TC**
tempranillo 50%, graciano 30%, merlot 20%

**85** Colour: cherry, garnet rim. Nose: fruit preserve, creamy oak, spicy. Palate: good acidity, spicy, round tannins.

**BAGORDI GRACIANO 2004 TR**
graciano 100%

**85** Colour: cherry, garnet rim. Nose: fruit preserve, warm, creamy oak. Palate: flavourful, fruity, round tannins.

**BAGORDI GARNACHA 2001 TR**
garnacha 100%

**84**

## BODEGAS BERCEO

Cuevas, 32-34-36
26200 Haro (La Rioja)
☎: 941 310 744 - Fax: 941 310 744
bodegas@gurpegui.es
www.gurpegui.es

**PRIMI 2008 T**

**86** Colour: cherry, purple rim. Nose: ripe fruit, spicy. Palate: flavourful, fruity, spicy, round tannins.

## LOS DOMINIOS DE BERCEO PREFILOXÉRICO 2006 TC

**92** Colour: bright cherry. Nose: sweet spices, creamy oak, expressive, mineral, ripe fruit. Palate: flavourful, fruity, toasty, round tannins.

## VIÑA BERCEO 2005 TC

**88** Colour: bright cherry, garnet rim. Nose: fruit expression, fresh, red berry notes, medium intensity. Palate: good structure, flavourful, fruity.

## GONZALO DE BERCEO 2004 TR

**90** Colour: cherry, garnet rim. Nose: medium intensity, balanced, spicy. Palate: balanced, fruity, flavourful, fine bitter notes.

## LOS DOMINIOS DE BERCEO 2004 TR

**90** Colour: very deep cherry, garnet rim. Nose: dark chocolate, sweet spices, creamy oak, ripe fruit. Palate: fleshy, full, balsamic, round tannins.

## VIÑADRIA

# BODEGAS BILBAÍNAS

Estación, 3
26200 Haro (La Rioja)
☎: 941 310 147 - Fax: 941 310 706
v.sanchez@codorniu.es
www.bodegasbilbainas.com

## VIÑA ZACO 2006 T
tempranillo

**89** Colour: bright cherry. Nose: ripe fruit, sweet spices, creamy oak, expressive. Palate: flavourful, fruity, toasty, round tannins.

## LA VICALANDA 2004 TR
tempranillo

**93** Colour: cherry, garnet rim. Nose: ripe fruit, spicy, creamy oak, toasty, complex, earthy notes. Palate: powerful, flavourful, toasty, round tannins.

## VIÑA POMAL 2004 TR
tempranillo, mazuelo, graciano

**90** Colour: pale ruby, brick rim edge. Nose: fruit preserve, fine reductive notes, tobacco, damp earth, aromatic coffee, cocoa bean. Palate: spicy, aged character, fine tannins, balanced.

## VIÑA POMAL SELECCIÓN CENTENARIO 2004 TR
tempranillo

**89** Colour: dark-red cherry. Nose: elegant, expressive, fruit liqueur notes, ripe fruit, old leather, dark chocolate. Palate: flavourful, good structure, ripe fruit, soft tannins.

## VIÑA POMAL CEPA BORGOÑA 2004 TR
tempranillo

**88** Colour: cherry, garnet rim. Nose: neat, medium intensity, fruit liqueur notes, ripe fruit, wet leather, aromatic coffee. Palate: flavourful, good acidity, fine bitter notes, round tannins.

## LA VICALANDA 2001 TGR
tempranillo

**88** Colour: cherry, garnet rim. Nose: sweet spices, caramel, ripe fruit, wet leather. Palate: flavourful, good structure, complex, spicy, round tannins.

# BODEGAS BRETÓN CRIADORES

Ctra. de Fuenmayor, km. 1,5
26370 Navarrete (La Rioja)
☎: 941 440 840 - Fax: 941 440 812
info@bodegasbreton.com
www.bodegasbreton.com

## LORIÑÓN 2007 B
viura 100%

**87** Colour: bright straw. Nose: fresh, citrus fruit, white flowers, ripe fruit, tropical fruit. Palate: flavourful, fleshy, balanced, fine bitter notes.

## L 5 LORIÑÓN 2006 TC
tempranillo 100%

**89** Colour: deep cherry, garnet rim. Nose: fruit liqueur notes, earthy notes, cocoa bean. Palate: fleshy, good structure, round tannins, fruity aftestaste.

## LORIÑÓN 2006 TC
tempranillo 85%, mazuelo 15%, graciano %, garnacha %

**88** Colour: very deep cherry, garnet rim. Nose: ripe fruit, balanced, spicy, old leather. Palate: flavourful, good acidity, round tannins.

## ALBA DE BRETÓN 2005 TR
tempranillo 100%

**90** Colour: bright cherry, garnet rim. Nose: elegant, varietal, expressive, fruit expression, cocoa bean, creamy oak. Palate: fruity, round, fine bitter notes, round tannins.

## DOMINIO DE CONTE 2005 TR
tempranillo 90%, graciano 10%

**90** Colour: deep cherry, garnet rim. Nose: dark chocolate, sweet spices, ripe fruit, earthy notes. Palate: fruity, concentrated, fine bitter notes.

**PAGOS DEL CAMINO 2005 T**
garnacha 100%

**89** Colour: deep cherry, garnet rim. Nose: fresh, ripe fruit, varnish, balsamic herbs, medium intensity. Palate: flavourful, fruity, round tannins.

**LORIÑÓN 2005 TR**
tempranillo 85%, mazuelo 15%, graciano %, garnacha %

**87** Colour: cherry, garnet rim. Nose: fine reductive notes, caramel, ripe fruit, tobacco. Palate: flavourful, spicy, ripe fruit.

**ALBA DE BRETÓN 2004 TR**

**92** Colour: cherry, garnet rim. Nose: ripe fruit, spicy, creamy oak, toasty, complex, floral, undergrowth. Palate: flavourful, toasty, round tannins, classic aged character, good acidity.

**DOMINIO DE CONTE 2004 TR**

**91** Colour: cherry, garnet rim. Nose: ripe fruit, spicy, creamy oak, toasty, complex, characterful, elegant. Palate: flavourful, toasty, round tannins, round, classic aged character.

**LORIÑÓN 2004 TR**

**87** Colour: cherry, garnet rim. Nose: ripe fruit, spicy, creamy oak, toasty, complex. Palate: flavourful, toasty, soft tannins.

**LORIÑÓN 2001 TGR**
tempranillo 85%, garnacha 5%, graciano 5%, mazuelo 5%

**88** Colour: cherry, garnet rim. Nose: fine reductive notes, ripe fruit, medium intensity, spicy. Palate: long, flavourful, balanced, great length.

## BODEGAS CADARSO CIORDIA

Mayor,17
31239 Aras (Navarra)
☎: 948 644 040 - Fax: 948 644 040
bodegas_cadarso_ciordia@telefonica.net

**TRESARAS 2008 BFB**
viura 100%

**87** Colour: bright straw. Nose: powerful, ripe fruit, sweet spices, creamy oak. Palate: flavourful, fleshy, powerful.

**TRESARAS 2008 T**
tempranillo 100%

**83**

**TRESARAS 2005 TC**
tempranillo 80%, graciano 15%, garnacha 5%

**86** Colour: cherry, garnet rim. Nose: medium intensity, balanced, ripe fruit, wet leather. Palate: correct, spicy, easy to drink, classic aged character.

**TRESARAS 2005 T**

**85** Colour: dark-red cherry, garnet rim. Nose: roasted coffee, dark chocolate. Palate: flavourful, roasted-coffee aftertaste, round tannins.

**TRESARAS 2003 TR**
tempranillo 80%, graciano 20%

**85** Colour: dark-red cherry, brick rim edge. Nose: fine reductive notes, tobacco, old leather. Palate: spicy, easy to drink, classic aged character, fine tannins.

## BODEGAS CASA PRIMICIA

Camino de la Hoya, 1
01300 Laguardia (Alava)
☎: 945 600 296 - Fax: 945 621 252
info@bodegascasaprimicia.com
www.bodegasprimicia.com

**VIÑA DIEZMO 2006 TC**
tempranillo 100%

**88** Colour: deep cherry, orangey edge. Nose: fruit preserve, creamy oak, smoky. Palate: flavourful, fruity, round tannins.

**CASA PRIMICIA MAZUELO 2005 TC**
mazuelo 100%

**89** Colour: cherry, garnet rim. Nose: fruit expression, ripe fruit, varietal, creamy oak, spicy. Palate: fruity, flavourful, round tannins, spicy.

**CASA PRIMICIA GARNACHA 2005 TC**
garnacha 100%

**89** Colour: cherry, garnet rim. Nose: expressive, varietal, fruit preserve, warm, sweet spices. Palate: fruity, slightly dry, soft tannins, balanced.

**CASA PRIMICIA GRACIANO 2005 T**
graciano 100%

**88** Colour: cherry, garnet rim. Nose: ripe fruit, warm, varietal, balsamic herbs, spicy, creamy oak. Palate: balanced, flavourful, round tannins, fruity.

**JULIÁN MADRID 2004 TR**
tempranillo 80%, others 20%

**84**

**VIÑA DIEZMO**

CARRAVALSECA
CURIUM

## BODEGAS CASTILLO DE MENDOZA, S.L.

Paraje San Juan
26338 San Vicente de la Sonsierra (La Rioja)
☎: 941 334 496 - Fax: 941 334 566
bodegas@castillodemendoza.com

MOMILDE VENDIMIA SELECCIÓN 2007 TC
tempranillo 100%

**90** Colour: cherry, purple rim. Nose: mineral, powerfull, ripe fruit, cocoa bean, sweet spices. Palate: flavourful, fleshy, powerful.

NORALBA AGRICULTURA ECOLÓGICA 2007 TC
tempranillo 90%, garnacha 10%

**89** Colour: bright cherry. Nose: ripe fruit, sweet spices, creamy oak, expressive, lactic notes. Palate: flavourful, fruity, toasty, round tannins.

VIÑA VITARÁN 2006 TC
tempranillo 100%

**88** Colour: cherry, garnet rim. Nose: powerful, red berry notes, ripe fruit, lactic notes, cocoa bean, creamy oak. Palate: flavourful, fleshy, powerful.

EVENTO CASTILLO DE MENDOZA 2005 T
tempranillo 100%

**89** Colour: bright cherry, garnet rim. Nose: balanced, ripe fruit, caramel. Palate: concentrated, fruity, spicy, round tannins.

CASTILLO DE MENDOZA 2005 TR
tempranillo 100%

**88** Colour: bright cherry, garnet rim. Nose: balanced, ripe fruit, sweet spices. Palate: flavourful, good acidity, round tannins.

CHIRIMENDO

## BODEGAS CASTILLO DE SAJAZARRA

Del Río, s/n
26212 Sajazarra (La Rioja)
☎: 941 320 066 - Fax: 941 320 251
bodega@castillo-de-sajazarra.com
www.castillo-de-sajazarra.com

DIGMA 2006 T
tempranillo 100%

**94** Colour: bright cherry. Nose: ripe fruit, sweet spices, creamy oak, expressive, mineral. Palate: flavourful, fruity, toasty, round tannins.

SOLAR DE LÍBANO 2006 TC

**90** Colour: cherry, garnet rim. Nose: fruit expression, fresh fruit, varietal, aromatic coffee, cedar wood. Palate: creamy, fruity aftestaste, balanced.

DIGMA 2005 T
tempranillo 100%

**95** Colour: cherry, garnet rim. Nose: powerful, ripe fruit, dark chocolate, sweet spices, mineral. Palate: flavourful, spicy, ripe fruit, round tannins.

CASTILLO DE SAJAZARRA 2004 TR
tempranillo

**90** Colour: deep cherry, orangey edge. Nose: ripe fruit, sweet spices, aromatic coffee. Palate: flavourful, spicy, classic aged character, round tannins.

SOLAR DE LÍBANO 2004 TR
tempranillo

**90** Colour: cherry, garnet rim. Nose: ripe fruit, spicy, creamy oak, toasty, complex. Palate: powerful, flavourful, toasty, round tannins.

SOLAR DE LÍBANO 2003 TR
tempranillo

**89** Colour: pale ruby, brick rim edge. Nose: powerful, ripe fruit, sweet spices, dark chocolate. Palate: flavourful, ripe fruit, spicy, classic aged character.

## BODEGAS CORRAL

Ctra. de Logroño, km. 10
26370 Logroño (La Rioja)
☎: 941 440 193 - Fax: 941 440 195
info@donjacobo.es
www.donjacobo.es

DON JACOBO 2008 B
viura 100%

**83**

DON JACOBO 2008 RD
garnacha 50%, tempranillo 50%

**85** Colour: raspberry rose, coppery red. Nose: medium intensity, fresh, raspberry, dried herbs. Palate: flavourful, fruity.

ALTOS DE CORRAL 2005 T FERMENTADO EN BARRICA
tempranillo 100%

**88** Colour: bright cherry, garnet rim. Nose: fruit preserve, sweet spices, dark chocolate. Palate: fleshy, powerful, good acidity.

DON JACOBO 2004 TC
tempranillo 85%, garnacha 10%, mazuelo 5%, graciano %

**85** Colour: pale ruby, brick rim edge. Nose: ripe fruit, fine reductive notes. Palate: flavourful, classic aged character, round tannins.

ALTOS DE CORRAL SINGLE STATE 2002 TR
tempranillo 100%

**90** Colour: deep cherry. Nose: varietal, fresh, elegant, fruit expression, cocoa bean, creamy oak. Palate: round, balanced, elegant, good acidity, powerful, flavourful, fruity, toasty, fine tannins.

DON JACOBO 2002 TR
tempranillo 95%, garnacha 5%, mazuelo %

**87** Colour: cherry, garnet rim. Nose: ripe fruit, fine reductive notes, cocoa bean. Palate: flavourful, full, spicy, soft tannins.

DON JACOBO 1995 TGR
tempranillo 85%, garnacha 15%

**89** Colour: pale ruby, brick rim edge. Nose: complex, fine reductive notes, tobacco, cedar wood, spicy. Palate: powerful, flavourful, round, elegant, smoky aftertaste.

## BODEGAS COVILA

Camino del Soto, 26
01306 La Puebla de Labarca (Álava)
☎: 945 627 232 - Fax: 945 627 295
comercial@covila.es
www.covila.es

COVILA 2006 TC
tempranillo 100%

**86** Colour: cherry, garnet rim. Nose: medium intensity, ripe fruit, spicy. Palate: flavourful, spicy, ripe fruit.

PAGOS DE LABARCA AEX 2005 T
tempranillo 100%

**91** Colour: cherry, garnet rim. Nose: ripe fruit, powerfull, toasty, dark chocolate. Palate: flavourful, powerful, round tannins.

COVILA 2004 TR
tempranillo 100%

**85** Colour: cherry, garnet rim. Nose: medium intensity, sweet spices, dark chocolate. Palate: flavourful, ripe fruit, spicy, round tannins.

PAGOS DE LABARCA 2001 TGR
tempranillo 100%

**87** Colour: cherry, garnet rim. Nose: powerful, fruit preserve, dark chocolate. Palate: powerful, fleshy, spicy, pruney.

FINCA LABARCA
VIÑA GURIA
MESA MAYOR

## BODEGAS DARIEN

Ctra. Logroño-Zaragoza, km. 7
26006 Logroño (La Rioja)
☎: 941 258 130 - Fax: 941 270 352
info@darien.es
www.darien.es

DARIEN 2006 TC
tempranillo 80%, mazuelo 13%, garnacha 7%

**86** Colour: cherry, garnet rim. Nose: medium intensity, ripe fruit, sweet spices, toasty. Palate: flavourful, fleshy, spicy, round tannins.

DARIEN 2005 TR
tempranillo 85%, graciano 8%, mazuelo 7%

**88** Colour: cherry, garnet rim. Nose: ripe fruit, spicy, creamy oak, toasty, complex. Palate: powerful, flavourful, toasty, round tannins.

DELIUS 2004 T
tempranillo 80%, graciano 20%

**89** Colour: cherry, garnet rim. Nose: ripe fruit, spicy, toasty, wet leather. Palate: powerful, flavourful, toasty, round tannins.

DARIEN SELECCIÓN 2003 T
tempranillo 68%, mazuelo 32%

**88** Colour: light cherry, garnet rim. Nose: sweet spices, fruit liqueur notes, woody. Palate: powerful, toasty.

## BODEGAS DAVID MORENO

Ctra. de Villar de Torre s/n
26310 Badarán (La Rioja)
☎: 941 367 338 - Fax: 941 418 685
davidmoreno@davidmoreno.es
www.davidmoreno.es

DAVID MORENO 2008 B
viura 100%

**82**

DAVID MORENO 2008 T
tempranillo 80%, garnacha 20%

**79**

DAVID MORENO 2006 TC
tempranillo 85%, garnacha 15%

**83**

DAVID MORENO SELECCIÓN DE LA FAMILIA
2005 TC
tempranillo 90%, garnacha 10%

**86** Colour: cherry, garnet rim. Nose: ripe fruit, spicy, aged wood nuances, new oak. Palate: round tannins, flavourful, fruity.

DAVID MORENO 2004 TR
tempranillo 90%, garnacha 10%

**85** Colour: pale ruby, brick rim edge. Nose: medium intensity, aged wood nuances, woody, spicy. Palate: easy to drink, classic aged character, round tannins.

VOBISCUM

## BODEGAS DE CRIANZA MARQUÉS DE GRIÑÓN S.A.V.

Avda. del Ebro, s/n
26540 Alfaro (La Rioja)
☎: 941 453 100 - Fax: 941 453 114
www.marquesdegrinon.com

MARQUÉS DE GRIÑÓN COLECCIÓN PRIVADA 2005 TC
tempranillo 100%

**88** Colour: cherry, garnet rim. Nose: ripe fruit, toasty, spicy. Palate: balanced, fruity, full, powerful, round tannins.

## BODEGAS DE FAMILIA BURGO VIEJO

Concordia, 8
26540 Alfaro (La Rioja)
☎: 941 183 405 - Fax: 941 181 603
bodegas@burgoviejo.com
www.burgoviejo.com

BURGO VIEJO 2008 T
tempranillo 85%, garnacha 10%, mazuelo 5%

**82**

BURGO VIEJO GARNACHA 2008 T JOVEN
garnacha 100%

**79**

BURGO VIEJO 2006 TC
tempranillo 90%, graciano 10%

**86** Colour: cherry, garnet rim. Nose: ripe fruit, warm, creamy oak, spicy. Palate: balanced, fruity, classic aged character, round tannins.

BURGO VIEJO 2000 TGR
tempranillo 100%

**84**

## BODEGAS DE LOS HEREDEROS DEL MARQUÉS DE RISCAL

Torrea, 1
01340 Elciego (Alava)
☎: 945 606 000 - Fax: 945 606 023
marquesderiscal@marquesderiscal.com
www.marquesderiscal.com

FINCA TORREA 2006 TR

**93** Colour: deep cherry, garnet rim. Nose: ripe fruit, expressive, sweet spices, cedar wood. Palate: flavourful, spicy, ripe fruit, fine tannins.

MARQUÉS DE RISCAL 2005 TR

**90** Colour: cherry, garnet rim. Nose: spicy, cocoa bean, dark chocolate, toasty, ripe fruit. Palate: flavourful, spicy, easy to drink, fine bitter notes.

BARÓN DE CHIREL 2004 TR
tempranillo 85%, others 15%

**90** Colour: cherry, garnet rim. Nose: ripe fruit, spicy, toasty, complex, aged wood nuances. Palate: powerful, flavourful, toasty, round tannins.

MARQUÉS DE RISCAL 2003 TGR

**93** Colour: very deep cherry. Nose: damp earth, undergrowth, spicy, cedar wood, candied fruit. Palate: round, complex, good structure, powerful, flavourful, sweetness, round tannins.

MARQUES DE RISCAL SELECCIÓN GEHRY 2001 T

**93** Colour: very deep cherry, orangey edge. Nose: cedar wood, sweet spices, complex, fine reductive notes, tobacco, damp earth, truffle notes, powerfull. Palate: concentrated, powerful, flavourful, complex.

MARQUÉS DE RISCAL 150 ANIVERSARIO
2001 TGR

**91** Colour: deep cherry, orangey edge. Nose: expressive, elegant, dark chocolate, sweet spices, cocoa bean, fruit liqueur notes. Palate: flavourful, fleshy, ripe fruit, spicy, sweet tannins.

## BODEGAS DE SANTIAGO

Avda. del Ebro, 50
01307 Baños de Ebro (Alava)
☎: 945 601 209 - Fax: 945 601 209
b.desantiago@telefonica.net

LAGAR DE SANTIAGO 2008 BFB
viura 100%

**88** Colour: bright straw. Nose: expressive, fresh, white flowers, grassy. Palate: flavourful, good structure, good acidity.

LAGAR DE SANTIAGO 2007 TC
tempranillo 100%

**88** Colour: bright cherry. Nose: sweet spices, creamy oak, fruit liqueur notes, toasty. Palate: flavourful, fruity, toasty, round tannins.

## BODEGAS DEL MEDIEVO

Circunvalación San Roque s/n
26559 Aldeanueva de Ebro (La Rioja)
☎: 941 163 141 - Fax: 941 144 204
info@bodegasdelmedievo.com
www.bodegasdelmedievo.com

COFRADE 2008 B
viura 100%

**87** Colour: pale. Nose: powerful, ripe fruit, citrus fruit, tropical fruit. Palate: flavourful, fruity, fresh.

MEDIEVO 2008 BFB
viura 100%

**87** Colour: bright straw. Nose: powerful, fruit preserve, citrus fruit, tropical fruit. Palate: flavourful, powerful, fleshy.

COFRADE 2008 RD
garnacha 100%

**87** Colour: brilliant rose. Nose: ripe fruit, fruit expression, varietal. Palate: ripe fruit, full, flavourful, creamy, rich.

COFRADE 2008 T MACERACIÓN CARBÓNICA
tempranillo 100%

**87** Colour: cherry, purple rim. Nose: expressive, fresh fruit, red berry notes, floral. Palate: flavourful, fruity, good acidity, round tannins.

MEDIEVO 2006 TC
tempranillo 80%, garnacha 10%, graciano 5%, mazuelo 5%

**87** Colour: cherry, garnet rim. Nose: powerful, characterful, dark chocolate, smoky. Palate: powerful, fleshy, spicy, round tannins.

MDV 2005 T
graciano 100%

**89** Colour: very deep cherry. Nose: powerful, toasty, dark chocolate, smoky. Palate: flavourful, spicy, round tannins.

MEDIEVO 2004 TR
tempranillo 80%, garnacha 10%, graciano 5%, mazuelo 5%

**87** Colour: cherry, garnet rim. Nose: ripe fruit, toasty, creamy oak. Palate: flavourful, powerful, fleshy, spicy, round tannins.

## BODEGAS DINASTIA VIVANCO

Ctra. Nacional 232
26330 Briones (La Rioja)
☎: 941 322 360 - Fax: 941 322 316
infobodega@dinastiavivanco.es
www.dinastiavivanco.com

VIVANCO 2008 B
viura 80%, malvasia 20%

**85** Colour: bright straw. Nose: medium intensity, ripe fruit, fruit expression. Palate: rich, fruity, fresh.

VIVANCO 2008 RD
tempranillo 85%, garnacha 15%

**87** Colour: rose. Nose: powerful, expressive, raspberry, ripe fruit. Palate: flavourful, fruity, full.

COLECCIÓN VIVANCO PARCELAS DE MAZUELO 2007 T
mazuelo 100%

**89** Colour: cherry, garnet rim. Nose: varietal, expressive, ripe fruit, cocoa bean, sweet spices, creamy oak. Palate: elegant, balanced, good acidity, warm, fine tannins.

COLECCIÓN VIVANCO PARCELAS DE GARNACHA 2006 T
garnacha 100%

**91** Colour: cherry, garnet rim. Nose: ripe fruit, red berry notes, sweet spices, creamy oak. Palate: flavourful, ripe fruit, creamy, round tannins.

COLECCIÓN VIVANCO PARCELAS DE GRACIANO 2006 T
graciano 100%

**90** Colour: cherry, garnet rim. Nose: fruit preserve, expressive, cocoa bean, creamy oak, sweet spices, varietal. Palate: elegant, balanced, good acidity, fine tannins, flavourful.

COLECCIÓN VIVANCO 4 VARIETALES 2005 T
tempranillo 70%, graciano 15%, garnacha 10%, mazuelo 5%

**90** Colour: cherry, garnet rim. Nose: ripe fruit, spicy, mineral, cocoa bean. Palate: flavourful, round tannins, powerful, spicy.

DINASTÍA VIVANCO 2005 TC
tempranillo 100%

**86** Colour: cherry, garnet rim. Nose: ripe fruit, medium intensity, toasty, spicy. Palate: easy to drink, round tannins, flavourful.

DINASTÍA VIVANCO 2004 TR
tempranillo 90%, graciano 10%

**87** Colour: cherry, garnet rim. Nose: ripe fruit, sweet spices, cocoa bean, creamy oak. Palate: spicy, soft tannins, flavourful, full.

## BODEGAS DOMECO DE JARAUTA

Camino Sendero Royal, 5
26559 Aldeanueva de Ebro (La Rioja)
☎: 941 163 078 - Fax: 941 163 078
luis@bodegasdomecodejarauta.com
www.bodegasdomecodejarauta.com

VIÑA MARRO 2008 T
tempranillo 100%

**85** Colour: cherry, purple rim. Nose: red berry notes, warm, powerfull. Palate: fruity, flavourful, great length.

VIÑA MARRO VENDIMIA SELECCIONADA 2007 T
tempranillo 100%

**86** Colour: black cherry, purple rim. Nose: ripe fruit, caramel. Palate: powerful, fine bitter notes, great length, fleshy.

VIÑA MARRO ECOLÓGICO 2007 T
tempranillo 100%

**83**

VIÑA MARRO 2005 TC
tempranillo 100%

**86** Colour: cherry, garnet rim. Nose: medium intensity, ripe fruit, dark chocolate, damp earth. Palate: powerful, good structure, fruity, round tannins, spicy.

VIÑA MARRO 2003 TR
tempranillo 100%

**88** Colour: dark-red cherry, garnet rim. Nose: candied fruit, fine reductive notes, sweet spices, pattiserie. Palate: good structure, powerful, spicy, fruity.

LAR DE SOTOMAYOR
SANCHO BARÓN

## BODEGAS DOMECQ

Ctra. de Villabuena, 9
01340 Elciego (Alava)
☎: 945 606 001 - Fax: 945 606 235
info@domecqbodegas.com
www.domecqbodegas.com

MARQUÉS DE ARIENZO VENDIMIA SELECCIONADA 2006 T RESERVA ESPECIAL
tempranillo 100%

**93** Colour: cherry, garnet rim. Nose: powerful, expressive, ripe fruit, sweet spices, toasty. Palate: flavourful, powerful, fleshy, spicy, round tannins.

VIÑA EGUÍA 2006 TC
tempranillo 95%, graciano 5%, mazuelo %

**87** Colour: deep cherry, orangey edge. Nose: powerful, fruit liqueur notes, ripe fruit, toasty, dark chocolate. Palate: flavourful, spicy, classic aged character.

MARQUÉS DE ARIENZO 2006 TC
tempranillo 95%, graciano 5%, mazuelo %

**86** Colour: bright cherry, orangey edge. Nose: powerful, ripe fruit, spicy, dark chocolate. Palate: flavourful, fleshy, spicy, round tannins.

MARQUÉS DE ARIENZO 2004 TR
tempranillo 95%, graciano 5%, mazuelo %

**88** Colour: cherry, garnet rim. Nose: ripe fruit, spicy, creamy oak, toasty. Palate: powerful, flavourful, toasty, round tannins.

MARQUÉS DE ARIENZO 2001 TGR
tempranillo 100%

**88** Colour: cherry, garnet rim. Nose: ripe fruit, spicy, toasty, wet leather. Palate: powerful, flavourful, toasty, round tannins.

## BODEGAS EDUARDO GARRIDO S.L.

Pza. de la Constitución, 2
26339 Abalos (La Rioja)
☎: 941 334 187 - Fax: 941 334 010

EDUARDO GARRIDO GARCÍA 2005 TC

**81**

EDUARDO GARRIDO GARCIA 2001 TGR

**87** Colour: pale ruby, brick rim edge. Nose: elegant, fine reductive notes, old leather, fruit liqueur notes. Palate: good structure, good acidity, fine tannins.

## BODEGAS EL CIDACOS

Ctra. de Carbonera, s/n
26512 Tudelilla (La Rioja)
☎: 941 152 058 - Fax: 941 152 303
info@bodegaselcidacos.com
www.bodegaselcidacos.com

MARQUÉS DE TUDELILLA 2006 TC
tempranillo 80%, garnacha 20%

**82**

MARQUÉS DE TUDELILLA 2002 TR
tempranillo 80%, garnacha 15%, graciano 5%

**85** Colour: deep cherry, orangey edge. Nose: fruit preserve, mineral, toasty. Palate: balanced, classic aged character, spicy, round tannins.

MARQUÉS DE TUDELILLA EDICIÓN LIMITADA
2005 T
tempranillo 90%, garnacha 5%, mazuelo 3%, graciano 2%

**85** Colour: deep cherry, orangey edge. Nose: fruit liqueur notes, toasty, creamy oak, spicy. Palate: full, fruity, spicy, round tannins.

## BODEGAS ESCUDERO

Ctra. de Arnedo, s/n
26587 Gravalos (La Rioja)
☎: 941 398 008 - Fax: 941 398 070
info@bodegasescudero.com
www.bodegasescudero.com

BECQUER 2008 B
chardonnay 60%, viura 40%

**84**

BECQUER 2007 T
tempranillo 70%, garnacha 30%

**88** Colour: bright cherry. Nose: sweet spices, fruit preserve, toasty, tobacco. Palate: flavourful, fruity, toasty, round tannins.

ARVUM 2005 T
garnacha 40%, tempranillo 40%, others 20%

**90** Colour: dark-red cherry. Nose: expressive, ripe fruit, elegant, balanced, sweet spices, creamy oak. Palate: flavourful, rich, fruity, good structure, round tannins.

SOLAR DE BECQUER 2005 TC
tempranillo 70%, mazuelo 20%, garnacha 10%

**85** Colour: cherry, garnet rim. Nose: ripe fruit, spicy, creamy oak, toasty. Palate: powerful, flavourful, toasty, round tannins.

SOLAR DE BÉCQUER 2001TR
tempranillo 70%, mazuelo 20%, garnacha 10%

**86** Colour: light cherry, orangey edge. Nose: spicy, fine reductive notes, wet leather, aged wood nuances, fruit liqueur notes. Palate: spicy, fine tannins, elegant, long.

VIDAU 2005 T
tempranillo 70%, garnacha 30%

**90** Color cherry, garnet rim. Nose: ripe fruit, spicy, creamy oak, toasty, complex. Palate: powerful, flavourful, toasty, round tannins.

## BODEGAS EXOPTO

Polígono Industrial Carravillar, 26
01300 Laguardia (Alava)
☎: 650 213 993 - Fax: 941 287 822

info@exopto.net
www.exopto.net

**HORIZONTE DE EXOPTO 2007 T**
tempranillo 80%, graciano 10%, garnacha 10%

**88** Colour: cherry, purple rim. Nose: cocoa bean, creamy oak, ripe fruit, balsamic herbs. Palate: fruity, flavourful, round tannins.

**BIG BANG DE EXOPTO 2007 T**
garnacha 50%, tempranillo 30%, graciano 20%

**83**

**EXOPTO 2006 T**
graciano 60%, tempranillo 30%, garnacha 10%

**88** Colour: cherry, garnet rim. Nose: powerful, ripe fruit, sweet spices, cocoa bean. Palate: flavourful, fleshy, spicy.

## BODEGAS FAUSTINO

Ctra. de Logroño, s/n
01320 Oyón (Alava)
☎: 945 622 500 - Fax: 945 622 106
info@bodegasfaustino.es
www.bodegasfaustino.es

**FAUSTINO V 2008 BFB**

**86** Colour: bright straw. Nose: medium intensity, candied fruit, dried herbs. Palate: fruity, flavourful, good acidity.

**FAUSTINO V 2008 B**
viura

**83**

**FAUSTINO V 2008 RD**

**87** Colour: rose, purple rim. Nose: fresh, ripe fruit, red berry notes. Palate: flavourful, fruity, fresh, easy to drink.

**FAUSTINO 2006 TC**

**85** Colour: cherry, garnet rim. Nose: caramel, dark chocolate, aromatic coffee, ripe fruit, warm. Palate: spicy, classic aged character, ripe fruit.

**FAUSTINO 9 MIL 2004 T**

**90** Colour: bright cherry. Nose: ripe fruit, sweet spices, creamy oak, expressive, medium intensity. Palate: flavourful, fruity, toasty, round tannins.

**FAUSTINO V 2004 TR**

**89** Colour: deep cherry, garnet rim. Nose: powerful, spicy, toasty, fruit liqueur notes. Palate: flavourful, spicy, classic aged character, round tannins.

**FAUSTINO EDICIÓN ESPECIAL 2001 T**

**91** Colour: pale ruby, brick rim edge. Nose: elegant, spicy, fine reductive notes, wet leather, aged wood nuances, fruit liqueur notes. Palate: spicy, fine tannins, elegant, long.

**FAUSTINO DE AUTOR RESERVA ESPECIAL 2001 TR**

**90** Colour: cherry, garnet rim. Nose: mineral, toasty, spicy, wet leather. Palate: classic aged character, spicy, fine bitter notes.

**FAUSTINO I 1998 TGR**

**88** Colour: dark-red cherry, garnet rim. Nose: aromatic coffee, fine reductive notes, tobacco. Palate: fleshy, classic aged character, good acidity, fine bitter notes, elegant.

## BODEGAS FERNÁNDEZ EGUILUZ

Los Morales, 7 bajo
26339 Abalos (La Rioja)
☎: 941 334 166 - Fax: 941 308 055
p.larosa@hotmail.es
www.penalarosa.com

**PEÑA LA ROSA 2008 B**
viura 80%, malvasia 20%

**81**

**PEÑA LA ROSA 2008 T**
tempranillo 100%

**86** Colour: cherry, purple rim. Nose: expressive, fresh fruit, red berry notes, floral. Palate: flavourful, fruity, good acidity, round tannins.

**PEÑA LA ROSA VENDIMIA SELECCIONADA 2005 T**
tempranillo 100%

**87** Colour: cherry, garnet rim. Nose: powerful, fruit expression, red berry notes, lactic notes, toasty. Palate: flavourful, ripe fruit, round tannins.

## BODEGAS FERNANDO REMÍREZ DE GANUZA

Constitución, 1
01307 Samaniego (Alava)
☎: 945 609 022 - Fax: 945 623 335

fernando@remirezdeganuza.com
www.remirezdeganuza.com

**ERRE PUNTO 2008 T MACERACIÓN CARBÓNICA**

**87** Colour: cherry, purple rim. Nose: expressive, fresh fruit, floral, balsamic herbs. Palate: flavourful, fruity, good acidity, round tannins.

**TRASNOCHO 2006 T**
tempranillo 90%, graciano 10%

**91** Colour: deep cherry. Nose: sweet spices, dark chocolate, ripe fruit, powerfull. Palate: complex, concentrated, fruity, powerful, flavourful, fleshy.

**FINCAS DE GANUZA 2004 TR**
tempranillo 90%, graciano 10%

**89** Colour: dark-red cherry. Nose: fruit preserve, fine reductive notes, damp earth, creamy oak, spicy, dark chocolate. Palate: good structure, spirituous, powerful, flavourful, roasted-coffee aftertaste, ripe fruit.

GRAVITY

## BODEGAS FINCA MANZANOS

Ctra. San Adrian-Azagra NA-134 Km. 49
31560 Azagra (Navarra)
☎: 948 692 500 - Fax: 948 692 700
info@fincamanzanos.com
www.fincamanzanos.com

**FINCA MANZANOS 2008 T JOVEN**
tempranillo 80%, garnacha 10%, mazuelo 10%

**80**

**FINCA MANZANOS 2006 TC**
tempranillo 90%, garnacha 5%, mazuelo 5%

**86** Colour: cherry, garnet rim. Nose: ripe fruit, tobacco. Palate: flavourful, ripe fruit, balanced, round tannins.

**SEÑORIO DE ARNEDO 2005 TC**
tempranillo 90%, garnacha 5%, mazuelo 5%

**85** Colour: bright cherry. Nose: ripe fruit, sweet spices, expressive, toasty, dark chocolate. Palate: flavourful, good structure, spicy.

**SEÑORIO DE ARNEDO 2004 TR**
tempranillo 90%, garnacha 5%, mazuelo 5%

**TRASNOCHO 2005 T**
tempranillo 90%, graciano 10%

**90** Colour: deep cherry. Nose: cedar wood, aged wood nuances, spicy, toasty. Palate: powerful, flavourful, fleshy, roasted-coffee aftertaste, toasty, harsh oak tannins.

**REMÍREZ DE GANUZA 2004 TR**
tempranillo 90%, graciano 10%

**94** Colour: deep cherry. Nose: complex, expressive, undergrowth, ripe fruit, cocoa bean, aromatic coffee, creamy oak. Palate: powerful, flavourful, full, spirituous, fleshy, toasty, roasted-coffee aftertaste, spicy.

# 84

VIÑA MARICHALAR
VIÑA BERRI
V. FERNÁNDEZ DE MANZANOS

## BODEGAS FOS

Término de Vialba, s/n
01340 Elciego (Alava)
☎: 945 606 681 - Fax: 945 606 608
fos@bodegasfos.com
www.bodegasfos.com

FOS 2008 B
viura 100%

**88** Colour: bright straw. Nose: floral, fruit expression, citrus fruit, fine lees. Palate: flavourful, complex, spicy, fine bitter notes.

FOS 2005 TC

**89** Colour: cherry, garnet rim. Nose: powerful, ripe fruit, sweet spices, dark chocolate. Palate: flavourful, powerful, fleshy, spicy, round tannins.

FOS 2004 TR
tempranillo 75%, graciano 25%

**89** Colour: cherry, garnet rim. Nose: powerful, ripe fruit, sweet spices, new oak, toasty. Palate: flavourful, powerful, spicy, round tannins.

## BODEGAS GARCÍA DE OLANO

Ctra. Vitoria s/n
01309 Paganos - La Guardia (Alava)
☎: 945 621 146 - Fax: 945 621 146
garciadeolano@telefonica.net
www.bodegasgarciadeolano.com

HEREDAD GARCÍA DE OLANO 2008 T
tempranillo 95%, viura 5%

**86** Colour: cherry, purple rim. Nose: fresh fruit, red berry notes, balanced. Palate: flavourful, fresh, good acidity, round tannins.

3 DE OLANO 2007 T
tempranillo 100%

**87** Colour: cherry, garnet rim. Nose: powerful, ripe fruit, red berry notes, sweet spices, cocoa bean. Palate: flavourful, powerful, fleshy, round tannins.

OLANUM 2006 T BARRICA
tempranillo 100%

**86** Colour: cherry, garnet rim. Nose: powerful, fruit preserve, new oak, toasty. Palate: flavourful, fleshy, spicy, pruney.

HEREDAD GARCÍA DE OLANO 2005 TC
tempranillo 100%

**88** Colour: cherry, garnet rim. Nose: powerful, ripe fruit, sweet spices, creamy oak. Palate: flavourful, fruity, ripe fruit.

MAULEÓN MACERACIÓN CARBÓNICA 2001 TR
tempranillo 100%

**85** Colour: pale ruby, brick rim edge. Nose: medium intensity, slightly evolved, sweet spices, pattiserie. Palate: spicy, classic aged character, round tannins.

## BODEGAS GÓMEZ CRUZADO

Avda. Vizcaya, 6
26200 Haro (La Rioja)
☎: 941 312 502 - Fax: 941 303 567
bodega@gomezcruzado.com
www.gomezcruzado.com

HONORABLE TEMPRANILLO 2005 T
tempranillo 100%

**90** Colour: cherry, garnet rim. Nose: sweet spices, powerfull, ripe fruit, toasty. Palate: flavourful, ripe fruit, spicy, round tannins.

GÓMEZ CRUZADO 2005 T
tempranillo 100%

**89** Colour: deep cherry, garnet rim. Nose: cocoa bean, sweet spices, creamy oak, ripe fruit. Palate: fleshy, complex, powerful, roasted-coffee aftertaste, round tannins.

PREDILECTO
VIÑA ANDREA

## BODEGAS GÓMEZ DE SEGURA IBÁÑEZ

Barrio El Campillar, 7
01300 Laguardia (Alava)
☎: 615 929 828 - Fax: 945 600 227
info@gomezdesegura.com
www.gomezdesegura.com

GÓMEZ DE SEGURA 2008 T
tempranillo 100%

**86** Colour: cherry, purple rim. Nose: expressive, red berry notes, floral, ripe fruit. Palate: flavourful, fruity, good acidity, round tannins.

GÓMEZ DE SEGURA 2006 TC
tempranillo 100%

**87** Colour: cherry, garnet rim. Nose: powerful, ripe fruit, sweet spices, toasty. Palate: flavourful, balanced, fine bitter notes, round tannins.

GÓMEZ DE SEGURA 2004 TR
tempranillo 100%

**88** Colour: cherry, garnet rim. Nose: sweet spices, cocoa bean, new oak, ripe fruit. Palate: flavourful, fruity, spicy.

## BODEGAS GREGORIO MARTÍNEZ

Polígono 1. Parcela 12
26190 Nalda (La Rioja)
☎: 941 220 266 - Fax: 941 203 849
bodegas@gregoriomartinez.com
www.gregoriomartinez.com

GREGORIO MARTÍNEZ VENDIMIA SELECCIONADA 2005 TC
tempranillo 100%

**87** Colour: cherry, garnet rim. Nose: ripe fruit, spicy, creamy oak, toasty, complex. Palate: powerful, flavourful, toasty, round tannins.

GREGORIO MARTÍNEZ 2005 TC
tempranillo 100%

**86** Colour: cherry, garnet rim. Nose: powerful, fruit liqueur notes, spicy, pattiserie. Palate: flavourful, spicy, ripe fruit, round tannins.

GREGORIO MARTÍNEZ 2001 TR
tempranillo 100%

**85** Colour: cherry, garnet rim. Nose: toasty, dark chocolate, fruit preserve. Palate: flavourful, sweetness, spicy, classic aged character.

## BODEGAS HEREDAD BAÑOS BEZARES S.L.

Solana, s/n
26290 Briñas (La Rioja)
☎: 941 312 423 - Fax: 941 303 020
bodega@banosbezares.com
www.banosbezares.com

BOHEDAL 2008 B
viura 100%

**84**

GRAN BOHEDAL 2006 BFB
viura 100%

**89** Colour: bright yellow. Nose: ripe fruit, floral, expressive, creamy oak. Palate: flavourful, fruity, concentrated, great length.

BOHEDAL 2008 T
tempranillo 100%

**85** Colour: cherry, purple rim. Nose: medium intensity, red berry notes. Palate: balanced, fresh, fruity, flavourful, round tannins.

HEBABE 2007 T
graciano 100%

**87** Colour: cherry, purple rim. Nose: powerful, varietal, ripe fruit, grassy. Palate: flavourful, fruity, fresh, spicy.

GRAN BOHEDAL 2005 TC
tempranillo 100%

**85** Colour: cherry, garnet rim. Nose: medium intensity, woody, ripe fruit. Palate: powerful, flavourful, good acidity.

GRAN BOHEDAL 2002 TR
tempranillo 100%

**86** Colour: cherry, garnet rim. Nose: ripe fruit, warm, fine reductive notes, tobacco. Palate: spicy, balsamic, round tannins, great length.

GRAN BOHEDAL 2001 TGR
tempranillo 100%

**85** Colour: cherry, garnet rim. Nose: old leather, ripe fruit, aromatic coffee, tobacco. Palate: powerful, good structure, round tannins, classic aged character.

## BODEGAS HEREDAD DE ADUNA

Matarredo, 39
01307 Samaniego (Alava)

☎: 945 623 343 - Fax: 945 609 290
baduna@arrakis.es
www.heredadaduna.com

## ADUNA 2008 T

**87** Colour: very deep cherry. Nose: ripe fruit, varietal, red berry notes. Palate: good acidity, flavourful, fruity, powerful, round tannins.

### RETVM 2008 T
termpranillo 100%

**83**

### RETVM 2006 TC

**83**

## ADUNA 2006 TC
**83**

## ADUNA VENDIMIA SELECCIONADA 2005 T

**88** Colour: cherry, garnet rim. Nose: fruit preserve, powerfull, creamy oak, spicy. Palate: unctuous, round tannins, flavourful, powerful.

## ADUNA 2004 TR

**85** Colour: pale ruby, brick rim edge. Nose: fruit preserve, medium intensity, spicy, creamy oak. Palate: flavourful, balanced, long, round tannins.

### RETVM 2004 TR
tempranillo 100%

**83**

## BODEGAS HERENCIA FONTEMAYORE

Polg. 6 parcela 266-352
26360 Fuenmayor (La Rioja)

## HERENCIA FONTEMAYORE 2005 TC

**85** Colour: cherry, garnet rim. Nose: ripe fruit, spicy, creamy oak, toasty. Palate: powerful, flavourful, toasty, round tannins.

## CASTILLO DE BARQUERA

## BODEGAS HERMANOS PECIÑA

Ctra. de Vitoria, km. 47
26338 San Vicente de la Sonsierra (La Rioja)
☎: 941 334 366 - Fax: 941 334 180

info@bodegashermanospecina.com
www.bodegashermanospecina.com

## CHOBEO DE PECIÑA 2005 T
tempranillo 100%

**89** Colour: cherry, garnet rim. Nose: warm, fruit preserve, wet leather, toasty, dark chocolate. Palate: flavourful, powerful, round tannins.

## SEÑORÍO DE P. PECIÑA 2005 TC
tempranillo 95%, graciano 3%, garnacha 2%

**85** Colour: dark-red cherry, garnet rim. Nose: spicy, scrubland, ripe fruit, wet leather. Palate: flavourful, balanced, round tannins.

## SEÑORÍO DE P. PECIÑA 2001 TR
tempranillo 95%, graciano 3%, garnacha 2%

**90** Colour: pale ruby, brick rim edge. Nose: fine reductive notes, tobacco, elegant, spicy, fruit liqueur notes. Palate: flavourful, good structure, easy to drink, fine bitter notes, fine tannins.

## PECIÑA VENDIMIA SELECCIONADA 2001 TR
tempranillo 100%

**85** Colour: deep cherry, garnet rim. Nose: fruit liqueur notes, toasty, dark chocolate. Palate: flavourful, spicy, round tannins.

## SEÑORÍO DE P. PECIÑA 1998 TGR
tempranillo 95%, graciano 3%, garnacha 2%

**86** Colour: pale ruby, brick rim edge. Nose: medium intensity, balanced, tobacco, old leather. Palate: classic aged character, easy to drink, good acidity.

## BODEGAS IZADI

Herrería Travesia II, nº5
01307 Villabuena de Álava (Álava)
☎: 945 609 086 - Fax: 945 609 261
marketing@izadi.com
www.izadi.com

## IZADI 2008 B

**89** Colour: bright straw. Nose: fresh, fresh fruit, white flowers, expressive, sweet spices. Palate: flavourful, fruity, good acidity, balanced.

## IZADI MAGNUM 2005 TC
tempranillo

**88** Colour: cherry, garnet rim. Nose: powerful, creamy oak, fine reductive notes, aromatic coffee. Palate: powerful, good structure, flavourful, spicy, fine tannins.

IZADI 2005 TC
tempranillo 100%

**87** Colour: cherry, garnet rim. Nose: ripe fruit, creamy oak, spicy. Palate: good acidity, fruity, full, flavourful, round tannins.

IZADI EL REGALO 2004 TR
tempranillo 100%

**90** Colour: deep cherry. Nose: complex, powerfull, fine reductive notes, spicy, aromatic coffee, candied fruit. Palate: powerful, flavourful, good structure, roasted-coffee aftertaste, ripe fruit, spicy.

## BODEGAS LA EMPERATRIZ

Ctra. Santo Domingo - Haro, km. 31,500
26241 Baños de Rioja (La Rioja)
☎: 941 300 105 - Fax: 941 300 231
correo@bodegaslaemperatriz.com
www.bodegaslaemperatriz.com

FINCA LA EMPERATRIZ VIURA CEPAS
VIEJAS 2008 B
viura 100%

**88** Colour: bright straw. Nose: expressive, fruit expression, dried herbs. Palate: flavourful, rich, spicy.

FINCA LA EMPERATRIZ VIURA CEPAS VIEJAS
2007 B

**90** Colour: bright yellow. Nose: ripe fruit, sweet spices, fragrant herbs, smoky, fine lees. Palate: rich, smoky aftertaste, flavourful, fresh, good acidity.

FINCA LA EMPERATRIZ TERRUÑO 2007 T
tempranillo 100%

**88** Colour: very deep cherry, garnet rim. Nose: fruit expression, characterful, spicy. Palate: flavourful, full, good structure, slightly dry, soft tannins.

ZENON 2007 TR
tempranillo 100%

**88** Colour: very deep cherry, garnet rim. Nose: fruit preserve, medium intensity, new oak. Palate: powerful, roasted-coffee aftertaste, great length.

## BODEGAS LAGAR DE ZABALA

Pza. Mayor s/n
26338 San Vicente de la Sonsierra (La Rioja)
☎: 941 334 435 - Fax: 941 334 435
bodegaslagardezabala@hotmail.com
www.bodegaslagardezabala.com

LAGAR DE ZABALA VENDIMIA SELECCIONADA
2008 T
tempranillo 100%

**86** Colour: deep cherry. Nose: red berry notes, fresh fruit, varietal. Palate: fruity, flavourful.

LAGAR DE ZABALA 2005 TC
tempranillo 100%

**86** Colour: cherry, garnet rim. Nose: sweet spices, fruit preserve. Palate: fruity, full, fruity aftestaste.

LAGAR DE ZABALA 2004 TC
tempranillo 100%

**87** Colour: cherry, garnet rim. Nose: macerated fruit, spicy, creamy oak. Palate: balanced, round tannins, fruity, flavourful.

## BODEGAS LAGUNILLA

Ctra. de El Ciego, s/n
26350 Cenicero (La Rioja)
☎: 941 453 100 - Fax: 941 453 114
info@lagunilla.com
www.lagunilla.com

LAGUNILLA CASA DEL COMENDADOR 2005 TC
tempranillo 80%, garnacha 20%

**87** Colour: cherry, garnet rim. Nose: medium intensity, elegant, ripe fruit, spicy, creamy oak. Palate: round tannins, good acidity, classic aged character, balanced.

LAGUNILLA CASA DEL COMENDADOR 2004 TR
tempranillo 80%, garnacha 20%

**88** Colour: cherry, garnet rim. Nose: elegant, balanced, medium intensity, ripe fruit. Palate: flavourful, concentrated, fine bitter notes, fine tannins, classic aged character.

LAGUNILLA OPTIMUS 2004 T
tempranillo, syrah, merlot, cabernet sauvignon

**87** Colour: black cherry, garnet rim. Nose: macerated fruit, fine reductive notes, tobacco. Palate: powerful, warm, fruity, round tannins, fine bitter notes.

## BODEGAS LANDALUCE

Ctra. Los Molinos s/n
01300 Laguardia (Alava)
☎: 944 571 250 - Fax: 944 571 260
asier@bodegaslandaluce.es

ELLE DE LANDALUCE 2008 B
viura, malvasia

**88** Colour: bright yellow. Nose: fresh, grassy, floral, powerfull. Palate: flavourful, fresh, fruity, good acidity, balanced.

ELLE DE LANDALUCE 2006 TC

**86** Colour: cherry, garnet rim. Nose: sweet spices, fruit preserve, dark chocolate. Palate: fruity, flavourful, easy to drink, round tannins, spicy.

CAPRICHO DE LANDALUCE 2006 T

**85** Colour: cherry, garnet rim. Nose: ripe fruit, warm, creamy oak. Palate: good acidity, round tannins, fruity, flavourful.

## BODEGAS LAR DE PAULA S.L.

Coscojal, s/n
01309 Elvillar (Alava)
☎: 945 604 068 - Fax: 945 604 105
info@lardepaula.com
www.lardepaula.com

LAR DE PAULA 2008 T

**86** Colour: very deep cherry. Nose: varietal, fresh fruit, red berry notes. Palate: flavourful, fruity, good acidity.

MERUS.4 2005 T
tempranillo 100%

**91** Colour: cherry, garnet rim. Nose: elegant, expressive, fruit preserve, ripe fruit. Palate: round tannins, flavourful, full, balanced, elegant.

LAR DE PAULA 2005 TC
tempranillo 100%

**88** Colour: cherry, garnet rim. Nose: ripe fruit, creamy oak, spicy. Palate: good acidity, balanced, round tannins, fruity, flavourful.

LAR DE PAULA CEPAS VIEJAS 2005 T
tempranillo 100%

**87** Colour: cherry, garnet rim. Nose: fruit preserve, sweet spices, creamy oak, cocoa bean. Palate: round tannins, flavourful, full, powerful.

LAR DE PAULA 2004 TR
tempranillo 100%

**87** Colour: cherry, garnet rim. Nose: spicy, candied fruit, fine reductive notes. Palate: round tannins, flavourful, spicy.

## BODEGAS LAUNA

Ctra. Vitoria-Logroño, km. 57
01300 Laguardia (Alava)
☎: 946 824 108 - Fax: 946 824 108

info@bodegaslauna.com
www.bodegaslauna.com

ALTEA DE ANTONIO ALCARAZ 2008 B
viura 100%

**83**

ALTEA DE ANTONIO ALCARAZ 2008 RD
garnacha, tempranillo

**84**

ALTEA DE ANTONIO ALCARAZ 2008 T
MACERACIÓN CARBÓNICA
tempranillo

**87** Colour: cherry, purple rim. Nose: expressive, fresh fruit, red berry notes, floral. Palate: flavourful, fruity, good acidity, round tannins.

GLORIA ANTONIO ALCARAZ 2006 TC
tempranillo

**89** Colour: very deep cherry. Nose: sweet spices, aged wood nuances, expressive, ripe fruit, fresh fruit. Palate: fresh, fruity, fine bitter notes, grainy tannins.

ANTONIO ALCARAZ 2006 TC

**88** Colour: bright cherry. Nose: ripe fruit, sweet spices, creamy oak, expressive. Palate: flavourful, fruity, toasty, round tannins.

ANTONIO ALCARAZ 2004 TR

**88** Colour: cherry, garnet rim. Nose: ripe fruit, spicy, creamy oak, toasty, complex, dark chocolate. Palate: powerful, flavourful, toasty, round tannins.

## BODEGAS LOLI CASADO

Avda. de la Poveda, 46
01306 Lapuebla de Labarca (Alava)
☎: 945 607 096 - Fax: 945 607 412
loli@bodegaslolicasado.com
www.bodegaslolicasado.com

POLUS 2008 B
viura 100%

**88** Colour: bright straw. Nose: fresh, fresh fruit, white flowers. Palate: flavourful, fruity, good acidity, balanced.

COVARA 2008 T
tempranillo 90%, others 10%

**87** Colour: very deep cherry. Nose: red berry notes, ripe fruit, varietal. Palate: flavourful, powerful, fruity, fresh.

POLUS TEMPRANILLO 2007 T
tempranillo 100%

**86** Colour: cherry, garnet rim. Nose: ripe fruit, balsamic herbs, creamy oak. Palate: round tannins, flavourful, powerful, spicy.

POLUS GRACIANO 2006 T
graciano 85%, tempranillo 15%

**88** Colour: cherry, garnet rim. Nose: varietal, ripe fruit, balsamic herbs, spicy. Palate: flavourful, mineral, round tannins, elegant.

POLUS 2005 TC
tempranillo 90%, graciano 10%, mazuelo %

**88** Colour: cherry, garnet rim. Nose: ripe fruit, creamy oak, sweet spices. Palate: round tannins, balanced, flavourful, long.

JAUN DE ALZATE 2005 TC
tempranillo 90%, graciano 10%, mazuelo %

**84**

JAUN DE ALZATE 2004 TR
tempranillo 90%, graciano 10%, mazuelo %

**84**

JAUN DE ALZATE 2001 TGR
tempranillo 90%, graciano 10%, mazuelo %

**85** Colour: brick rim edge, deep cherry. Nose: fruit preserve, caramel, sweet spices. Palate: flavourful, soft tannins, aged character.

## BODEGAS LUIS ALEGRE

Ctra. Navaridas, s/n
01300 Laguardia (Alava)
☎: 945 600 089 - Fax: 945 600 729
luisalegre@bodegasluisalegre.com
www.bodegasluisalegre.com

LUIS ALEGRE SELECCIÓN DE ROBLES EUROPA 2007 BFB
viura 90%, malvasia 10%

**89** Colour: golden, greenish rim. Nose: fruit expression, acacia flower, balsamic herbs, ripe fruit, smoky. Palate: creamy, ripe fruit, flavourful, rich.

LUIS ALEGRE 2006 TC
tempranillo 85%, garnacha 15%, mazuelo %, graciano %

**86** Colour: cherry, garnet rim. Nose: ripe fruit, sweet spices, fruit liqueur notes. Palate: flavourful, full, fruity, round tannins.

PONTAC 2005 T
tempranillo 95%, graciano 5%

**89** Colour: cherry, garnet rim. Nose: ripe fruit, creamy oak, spicy. Palate: round tannins, creamy, flavourful, powerful, concentrated.

LUIS ALEGRE SELECCIÓN ESPECIAL 2005 TR
tempranillo 95%, garnacha 5%, mazuelo %

**88** Colour: cherry, garnet rim. Nose: medium intensity, ripe fruit, toasty, spicy. Palate: flavourful, fleshy, round tannins.

RESERVA LUIS ALEGRE 2005 TR
tempranillo 90%, garnacha 10%, mazuelo %

**88** Colour: cherry, garnet rim. Nose: ripe fruit, fruit liqueur notes, creamy oak, sweet spices. Palate: flavourful, round tannins, spicy, ripe fruit.

## BODEGAS LUIS CAÑAS

Ctra. Samaniego, 10
01307 Villabuena (Alava)
☎: 945 623 373 - Fax: 945 609 289
bodegas@luiscanas.com

HIRU 3 RACIMOS 2005 T
tempranillo 95%, graciano 15%

**91** Colour: deep cherry, garnet rim. Nose: complex, varietal, ripe fruit, balanced, spicy. Palate: flavourful, fine bitter notes.

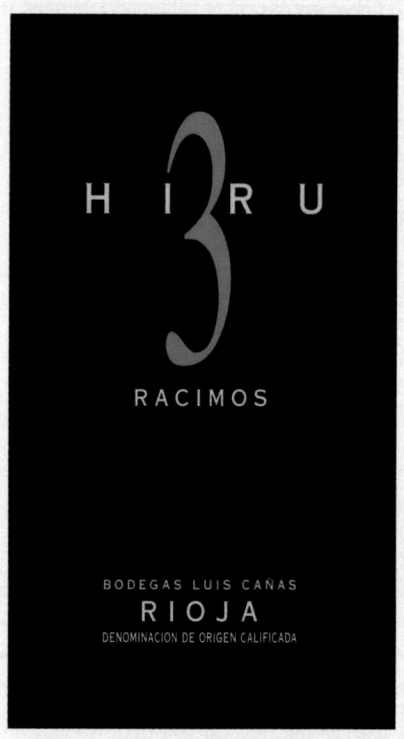

H I R U
3
RACIMOS

BODEGAS LUIS CAÑAS
RIOJA
DENOMINACION DE ORIGEN CALIFICADA

## LUIS CAÑAS 2008 BFB
viura 95%, malvasia 15%

**88** Colour: straw, greenish rim. Nose: smoky, scrubland. Palate: fruity, flavourful, smoky aftertaste.

## HIRU 3 RACIMOS 2006 T
tempranillo 100%

**92** Colour: bright cherry, garnet rim. Nose: ripe fruit, expressive, elegant, complex, cocoa bean, sweet spices. Palate: flavourful, good structure, round tannins.

## LUIS CAÑAS 2006 TC
tempranillo 95%, garnacha 5%

**86** Colour: cherry, garnet rim. Nose: balanced, medium intensity, ripe fruit. Palate: balanced, round tannins.

## LUIS CAÑAS SELECCIÓN DE FAMILIA 2003 TR
tempranillo 85%, others 15%

**89** Colour: deep cherry, garnet rim. Nose: powerful, ripe fruit, toasty, dark chocolate, smoky. Palate: flavourful, powerful, fleshy, spicy, round tannins.

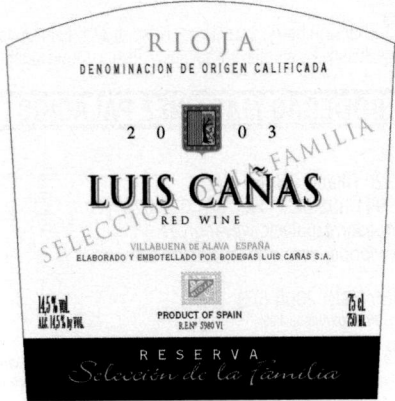

## LUIS CAÑAS 2003 TR
tempranillo 95%, graciano 5%

**86** Colour: cherry, garnet rim. Nose: powerful, fruit preserve, toasty, pattiserie. Palate: flavourful, powerful, fleshy, sweetness.

## LUIS CAÑAS 2001 TGR
tempranillo 95%, graciano 5%

**88** Colour: cherry, garnet rim. Nose: powerful, toasty, dark chocolate. Palate: flavourful, concentrated, ripe fruit, round tannins.

# BODEGAS MARQUÉS DE VARGAS

Ctra. Zaragoza, km. 6
26006 Logroño (La Rioja)
☎: 941 261 401 - Fax: 941 238 696
bodega@marquesdevargas.com
www.marquesdevargas.com

## MARQUÉS DE VARGAS RESERVA PRIVADA 2005 TR

**92** Colour: dark-red cherry. Nose: aromatic coffee, spicy, creamy oak, ripe fruit, undergrowth, truffle notes. Palate: unctuous, elegant, powerful, flavourful, complex, full.

## MARQUÉS DE VARGAS HACIENDA PRADOLAGAR 2004 TR

**92** Colour: deep cherry. Nose: varietal, damp undergrowth, aromatic coffee, creamy oak. Palate: powerful, flavourful, complex, roasted-coffee aftertaste, mineral, powerful tannins.

## MARQUÉS DE VARGAS 2004 T

**90** Colour: dark-red cherry, orangey edge. Nose: fine reductive notes, tobacco, damp earth, aromatic coffee, cocoa bean, expressive, powerfull, elegant, spicy, toasty.

# BODEGAS MARTÍNEZ CORTA

Ctra. Cenicero, s/n
26313 Uruñuela (La Rioja)
☎: 670 937 520 - Fax: 941 362 120
enologia@bodegasmartinezcorta.com

## MARTÍNEZ CORTA CEPAS ANTIGUAS 2008 T
tempranillo 100%

**88** Colour: very deep cherry. Nose: varietal, expressive, fresh fruit, red berry notes. Palate: fruity, flavourful, fleshy, slightly dry, soft tannins.

## MARTÍNEZ CORTA 2008 T
tempranillo 100%

**87** Colour: deep cherry. Nose: varietal, fresh fruit, red berry notes. Palate: round tannins, fruity, flavourful, fresh.

## SOROS 2006 T
tempranillo 100%

**89** Colour: cherry, garnet rim. Nose: expressive, elegant, fruit preserve, warm, spicy, creamy oak. Palate: round tannins, fruity, flavourful, spirituous, balanced, spirituous.

## SOROS PREMIUM 2006 T
tempranillo 90%, garnacha 10%

**89** Colour: cherry, garnet rim. Nose: expressive, fruit preserve, creamy oak, spicy. Palate: balanced, elegant, spicy, round tannins, fruity.

**MARTÍNEZ CORTA 33 2006 T**
tempranillo 33%, graciano 33%, garnacha 33%

**89** Colour: cherry, garnet rim. Nose: expressive, fresh, ripe fruit, sweet spices, creamy oak, cocoa bean. Palate: fruity, flavourful, balanced, round tannins.

**MARTÍNEZ CORTA 2006 TC**
tempranillo 100%

**87** Colour: cherry, garnet rim. Nose: ripe fruit, sweet spices, creamy oak. Palate: balanced, round tannins, spicy, easy to drink.

**SOROS 2006 TC**
tempranillo 100%

**85** Colour: cherry, garnet rim. Nose: ripe fruit, spicy, toasty. Palate: warm, round tannins, flavourful.

**MARTÍNEZ CORTA 2005 TR**
tempranillo 100%

**90** Colour: cherry, garnet rim. Nose: expressive, ripe fruit, spicy, creamy oak. Palate: balanced, round tannins, fruity aftetaste, flavourful.

**MARTÍNEZ CORTA SELECCIÓN ESPECIAL 2005 T**
tempranillo 100%

**88** Colour: cherry, garnet rim. Nose: ripe fruit, mineral, smoky, creamy oak. Palate: flavourful, powerful, fruity aftetaste.

**LA VIÑA DEL CORTA**

## BODEGAS MARTÍNEZ LAORDEN

Ctra. Huércanos, s/n
26350 Cenicero (La Rioja)
☎: 941 454 446 - Fax: 941 454 766
administracion@martinezlaorden.com
www.martinezlaorden.com

**A & A DE MARTÍNEZ LAORDEN 2007 B**
viura 80%, malvasia 15%, garnacha 5%

**80**

**EL TALUD 2008 RD**
tempranillo 100%

**85** Colour: brilliant rose. Nose: medium intensity, red berry notes, fresh. Palate: easy to drink, good acidity.

**EL TALUD 2008 T**
tempranillo 100%

**87** Colour: cherry, purple rim. Nose: powerful, ripe fruit, scrubland, floral. Palate: flavourful, fruity, fleshy.

**MARTÍNEZ LAORDEN GRACIANO 2006 T**
graciano 100%

**89** Colour: bright cherry, garnet rim. Nose: expressive, varietal, ripe fruit, balsamic herbs. Palate: powerful, ripe fruit, good acidity, fine bitter notes.

**LANZADO 2005 TC**
tempranillo 100%

**87** Colour: cherry, garnet rim. Nose: medium intensity, ripe fruit, dark chocolate, cocoa bean, creamy oak. Palate: flavourful, fleshy, spicy.

**MARTÍNEZ LAORDEN GARNACHA 2005 T**
garnacha 100%

**86** Colour: cherry, purple rim. Nose: powerful, ripe fruit, sweet spices. Palate: flavourful, fruity, ripe fruit.

**LA ORBE 2004 T**
tempranillo 100%

**88** Colour: cherry, garnet rim. Nose: fruit liqueur notes, spicy, toasty. Palate: flavourful, spicy, fleshy, round tannins.

## BODEGAS MARTÍNEZ PALACIOS

Real, 22
26220 Ollauri (Rioja)
☎: 941 338 023 - Fax: 941 338 023
bodegasmtzpalacios@yahoo.es
www.bodegasmartinezpalacios.com

**ORMAEGUI 2008 BFB**
viura 90%, garnacha 10%

**88** Colour: bright straw. Nose: expressive, ripe fruit, sweet spices, creamy oak. Palate: flavourful, powerful, fleshy, round tannins.

**MARTÍNEZ PALACIOS 2005 TC**
tempranillo 100%

**82**

**MARTÍNEZ PALACIOS PAGO CANDELA 2004 T**
tempranillo 90%, graciano 10%

**84**

**MARTÍNEZ PALACIOS 2004 TR**
tempranillo 100%

## 83

FAMILIA VILLAR SANTAMARÍA

### BODEGAS MEDRANO IRAZU S.L.

San Pedro, 14
01309 Elvillar (Alava)
☎: 945 604 066 - Fax: 945 604 126
amador@bodegasmedranoirazu.com
www.bodegasmedranoirazu.com

MEDRANO IRAZU 2008 BFB
viura 100%

## 84

ARDENS 2007 BFB
viura 100%

**88** Colour: old gold. Nose: ripe fruit, balsamic herbs, scrubland. Palate: fresh, fruity, flavourful, full.

MEDRANO-IRAZU SELECCIÓN 2008 T
tempranillo 100%

**87** Colour: bright cherry, garnet rim. Nose: red berry notes, fresh, lactic notes. Palate: fruity, balanced, good acidity, round tannins.

LUIS MEDRANO GRACIANO 2007 T
graciano 100%

**93** Colour: black cherry, garnet rim. Nose: ripe fruit, spicy, creamy oak, toasty, complex, cocoa bean. Palate: powerful, flavourful, toasty, round tannins.

LUIS MEDRANO 2007 T
tempranillo 100%

**90** Colour: bright cherry. Nose: ripe fruit, sweet spices, creamy oak, expressive, earthy notes, warm. Palate: flavourful, fruity, toasty, round tannins.

ARDENS 2006 T
tempranillo 100%

**86** Colour: bright cherry, garnet rim. Nose: ripe fruit, warm. Palate: flavourful, fruity, round tannins, good acidity, correct.

MEDRANO IRAZU 2004 TR
tempranillo 100%

**88** Colour: cherry, garnet rim. Nose: powerful, ripe fruit, spicy, warm. Palate: flavourful, powerful, fleshy, spicy, ripe fruit.

MEDRANO IRAZU 2006 TC
tempranillo 100%

**87** Colour: very deep cherry, garnet rim. Nose: ripe fruit, warm, balanced, varietal, cocoa bean. Palate: fleshy, powerful, spicy.

### BODEGAS MENTOR

San Antón, 4 Entpta. Dcha.
26002 Logroño (La Rioja)
☎: 941 270 795 - Fax: 941 244 577
info@puertagotica.es
www.puertagotica.es

MENTOR ROBERTO TORRETTA 2005 T
tempranillo 100%

**93** Colour: deep cherry, garnet rim. Nose: powerful, expressive, mineral, fruit expression, ripe fruit, sweet spices, toasty. Palate: flavourful, fleshy, complex, round tannins.

**MENTOR 2005 TR**
tempranillo 100%

**91** Colour: bright cherry. Nose: creamy oak, expressive, ripe fruit, sweet spices. Palate: flavourful, fruity, toasty, round tannins.

## BODEGAS MITARTE S.L.

Avda. San Ginés, 19
01330 Labastida (Alava)
☎: 945 331 069 - Fax: 945 331 069
bodegas@mitarte.com

**MITARTE 2008 BFB**
viura 100%

**86** Colour: bright straw. Nose: fresh, varietal, candied fruit. Palate: fresh, fruity, flavourful.

**MITARTE 2008 BFB**

**84**

**MITARTE 2008 T**
tempranillo 70%, garnacha 20%, viura 10%

**87** Colour: deep cherry. Nose: fresh fruit, red berry notes, varietal. Palate: flavourful, fruity, fresh, concentrated.

**MITARTE 3 HOJA 2008 T**
tempranillo 100%

**85** Colour: deep cherry. Nose: varietal, fresh fruit, red berry notes. Palate: flavourful, fruity, good finish.

**MITARTE MAZUELO 2006 T**
mazuelo 100%

**85** Colour: cherry, garnet rim. Nose: medium intensity, fruit preserve, spicy, ripe fruit. Palate: flavourful, fruity, fruity aftestaste, round tannins.

**MITARTE VENDIMIA SELECCIONADA 2005 TC**
tempranillo 85%, graciano 15%

**85** Colour: cherry, garnet rim. Nose: ripe fruit, spicy. Palate: fruity, slightly dry, soft tannins, powerful.

**S Y C (SANTIAGO Y CARMEN) DE MITARTE 2004 T**
tempranillo 100%

**87** Colour: cherry, garnet rim. Nose: fruit preserve, sweet spices, powerfull. Palate: spicy, flavourful, powerful, round tannins.

**MITARTE 2004 TR**
tempranillo 100%

**86** Colour: cherry, garnet rim. Nose: spicy, aged wood nuances, ripe fruit. Palate: fruity, flavourful, long, good finish, round tannins.

**DE FAULA 2004 TR**
tempranillo 100%

**85** Colour: cherry, garnet rim. Nose: warm, fruit liqueur notes, spicy, creamy oak. Palate: flavourful, full, spicy, round tannins.

## BODEGAS MUGA

Barrio de la Estación, s/n
26200 Haro (La Rioja)
☎: 941 310 498 - Fax: 941 312 867
info@bodegasmuga.com
www.bodegasmuga.com

**MUGA 2008 B**
viura 90%, malvasia 10%

**91** Colour: bright straw. Nose: ripe fruit, creamy oak, balanced, elegant. Palate: fresh, fruity, easy to drink, creamy.

**MUGA 2008 RD**
viura 90%, malvasia 10%

**89** Colour: coppery red. Nose: fresh fruit, dried herbs, elegant. Palate: light-bodied, fruity, flavourful, good structure, good acidity.

**ARO 2005 T**

**94** Colour: dark-red cherry, garnet rim. Nose: earthy notes, ripe fruit, characterful, varietal, sweet spices, aromatic coffee, old leather. Palate: powerful, good structure, good acidity, grainy tannins, toasty.

**TORRE MUGA 2005 T**
tempranillo 75%, mazuelo 15%, graciano 10%

**92** Colour: bright cherry, garnet rim. Nose: smoky, spicy, scrubland, dark chocolate. Palate: fleshy, powerful, ripe fruit, round tannins.

**MUGA SELECCIÓN ESPECIAL 2005 TR**
tempranillo 70%, garnacha 20%, mazuelo 10%, graciano %

**91** Colour: cherry, garnet rim. Nose: powerful, ripe fruit, toasty, dark chocolate, aged wood nuances. Palate: flavourful, powerful, fleshy, spicy, round tannins.

**MUGA 2005 TC**
tempranillo 70%, garnacha 20%, mazuelo 10%, graciano %

**88** Colour: cherry, garnet rim. Nose: powerful, ripe fruit, sweet spices, tar. Palate: flavourful, spicy, ripe fruit, round tannins.

**MUGA SELECCIÓN ESPECIAL 2004 TR**
tempranillo 70%, garnacha 20%, mazuelo 10%, graciano %

**90** Colour: deep cherry, garnet rim. Nose: complex, caramel, ripe fruit. Palate: flavourful, spicy, good acidity, fine bitter notes.

**PRADO ENEA 2001 TGR**
tempranillo 80%, garnacha 20%, mazuelo %, graciano %

**91** Colour: pale ruby, brick rim edge. Nose: expressive, elegant, fine reductive notes, spicy, macerated fruit. Palate: flavourful, spicy, fine tannins.

ENEAS

## BODEGAS MURILLO VITERI

La Majadilla, s/n
26350 Cenicero (La Rioja)
☎: 944 495 839 - Fax: 944 263 725
imurillo@bodegasmurilloviteri.com
www.bodegasmurilloviteri.com

**MURILLO VITERI EXPRESIÓN 2005 T**

**86** Colour: cherry, garnet rim. Nose: ripe fruit, elegant, spicy, creamy oak. Palate: flavourful, concentrated, round tannins, great length.

ARANZUBIA

## BODEGAS MURUA

Ctra. Laguardia s/n
01340 Elciego (Alava)
☎: 945 606 260 - Fax: 945 606 326
info@bodegasmurua.com
www.bodegasmurua.com

**MURUA 2006 BFB**
viura 50%, malvasia 30%, garnacha 20%

**87** Colour: bright straw. Nose: sweet spices, toasty, fruit preserve, fruit liqueur notes. Palate: powerful, fleshy, spicy, fine bitter notes.

**MURUA M 2004 T**
tempranillo 99%, graciano 1%

**90** Colour: cherry, garnet rim. Nose: powerful, ripe fruit, sweet spices, mineral. Palate: flavourful, fleshy, powerful, round tannins.

**MURUA 2003 TR**
tempranillo 90%, graciano 8%, mazuelo 2%

**87** Colour: pale ruby, brick rim edge. Nose: medium intensity, fruit preserve, sweet spices, cocoa bean. Palate: flavourful, round tannins, spicy, creamy.

**VEGUIN DE MURUA 1996 TR**
tempranillo 95%, graciano 5%

**89** Colour: pale ruby, brick rim edge. Nose: spicy, fine reductive notes, fruit liqueur notes. Palate: fine tannins, classic aged character, aged character, balanced.

## BODEGAS NAVA-RIOJA S.A.T.

Ctra. Eje del Ebro, s/n
31261 Andosilla (Navarra)
☎: 948 690 454 - Fax: 948 674 491
info@bodegasnavarioja.com
www.bodegasnavarioja.com

**PARDOÑO 2004 TC**
tempranillo 90%, graciano 10%

**85** Colour: cherry, garnet rim. Nose: powerful, fruit liqueur notes, spicy, toasty. Palate: flavourful, spicy, round tannins.

**PARDOÑO 2008 T JOVEN**
tempranillo 100%

**85** Colour: cherry, purple rim. Nose: red berry notes, medium intensity. Palate: flavourful, fruity, good acidity, round tannins.

**OTIS TARDA ECOLÓGICO 2008 T**
tempranillo 100%

**85** Colour: bright cherry, purple rim. Nose: red berry notes, balanced. Palate: fruity, flavourful, balanced, great length, round tannins.

**OTIS TARDA 2007 T BARRICA**
tempranillo 100%

**88** Colour: cherry, garnet rim. Nose: medium intensity, fruit liqueur notes, spicy, toasty. Palate: flavourful, powerful, fleshy, spicy, round tannins.

**PARDOÑO 2006 TC**
tempranillo 85%, graciano 15%

**87** Colour: cherry, garnet rim. Nose: sweet spices, toasty, ripe fruit. Palate: flavourful, spicy, fleshy, round tannins.

BARÓN DE PARDO

## BODEGAS NAVAJAS

Camino Balgarauz, 2
26370 Navarrete (La Rioja)
☎: 941 440 140 - Fax: 941 440 657
bodegasnavajas@terra.es
www.bodegasnavajas.com

**NAVAJAS 2008 B**
viura 100%

**86** Colour: straw. Nose: floral, candied fruit, varietal. Palate: fresh, fruity, flavourful.

**NAVAJAS 2005 BC**
viura 100%

**86** Colour: bright straw. Nose: powerful, ripe fruit, tropical fruit, sweet spices. Palate: flavourful, balanced, fruity.

**NAVAJAS 2005 RD**
viura 50%, tempranillo 50%

**88** Colour: onion pink. Nose: lactic notes, sweet spices, cocoa bean, ripe fruit. Palate: flavourful, fleshy, sweetness, ripe fruit.

**NAVAJAS 2006 TC**
tempranillo 95%, mazuelo 5%

**86** Colour: cherry, garnet rim. Nose: ripe fruit, balsamic herbs, dark chocolate, balanced. Palate: fleshy, toasty, round tannins, spicy, ripe fruit.

**NAVAJAS GRACIANO 2005 TC**
graciano 100%

**88** Colour: cherry, garnet rim. Nose: ripe fruit, varietal, balanced, complex. Palate: concentrated, warm, toasty, fruity aftestaste.

**NAVAJAS 2004 TR**
tempranillo 90%, graciano 5%, mazuelo 5%

**87** Colour: cherry, garnet rim. Nose: ripe fruit, cocoa bean, sweet spices. Palate: flavourful, full, round tannins, great length, easy to drink.

GENTES DE FORASTIA
VEGA DEL RÍO

## BODEGAS OLARRA

Avda. de Mendavia, 30
26009 Logroño (La Rioja)
☎: 941 235 299 - Fax: 941 253 703
bodegasolarra@bodegasolarra.es
www.bodegasolarra.es

**CERRO AÑÓN 2005 TC**
tempranillo 80%, garnacha 10%, mazuelo 10%, graciano %

**86** Colour: dark-red cherry, garnet rim. Nose: fruit liqueur notes, powerfull, expressive, dark chocolate. Palate: flavourful, round tannins, good acidity.

**CERRO AÑÓN 2002 TR**
tempranillo 80%, garnacha 5%, mazuelo 15%, graciano %

**90** Colour: pale ruby, brick rim edge. Nose: spicy, aromatic coffee, aged wood nuances, fruit liqueur notes. Palate: spicy, easy to drink, ripe fruit.

**SUMMA 2001 TR**
tempranillo 60%, mazuelo 25%, graciano 15%

**88** Colour: cherry, garnet rim. Nose: ripe fruit, medium intensity, spicy. Palate: flavourful, good finish, slightly dry, soft tannins.

RECIENTE
OTOÑAL
AÑARES

## BODEGAS ONDALÁN

Ctra. de Logroño nº 22
01320 Oyón (Alava)
☎: 945 622 537 - Fax: 945 622 538
ondalan@ondalan.es
www.ondalan.es

**LAUDO 2008 T**
tempranillo 100%

**83**

**ONDALÁN SELECCIÓN 2006 T**
tempranillo 100%

**88** Colour: cherry, garnet rim. Nose: powerful, ripe fruit, spicy. Palate: flavourful, powerful, fleshy.

**100 ABADES SELECCIÓN 2006 T**
graciano 100%

**87** Colour: cherry, garnet rim. Nose: powerful, ripe fruit, sweet spices. Palate: flavourful, powerful, fleshy, round tannins.

**ONDALÁN 2006 TC**
tempranillo 80%, graciano 20%

**86** Colour: bright cherry. Nose: ripe fruit, sweet spices, creamy oak. Palate: flavourful, fruity, toasty, round tannins.

**ONDALÁN 2004 TR**
tempranillo 100%

**85** Colour: cherry, garnet rim. Nose: powerful, ripe fruit, spicy. Palate: flavourful, fleshy, spicy, ripe fruit.

## BODEGAS ONDARRE

Ctra. de Aras, s/n
31230 Viana (Navarra)
☎: 948 645 300 - Fax: 948 646 002
bodegasondarre@bodegasondarre.es
www.bodegasondarre.es

**MAYOR DE ONDARRE 2004 TR**
tempranillo, mazuelo

**90** Colour: cherry, garnet rim. Nose: powerful, fruit liqueur notes, creamy oak. Palate: spicy, flavourful, ripe fruit.

**ORDEN DE ONDARRE 2004 TR**
tempranillo 75%, garnacha 10%, mazuelo 15%

**89** Colour: cherry, garnet rim. Nose: powerful, warm, ripe fruit, spicy, toasty. Palate: fine bitter notes, ripe fruit, spicy.

## BODEGAS ONTAÑON

Avda. de Aragón, 3
26006 Logroño (La Rioja)
☎: 941 234 200 - Fax: 941 270 482
comunicacion@ontanon.es
www.ontanon.es

**ONTAÑÓN 2001 TR**      ·

**91** Colour: dark-red cherry. Nose: powerful, complex, cocoa bean, roasted coffee. Palate: powerful, flavourful, complex, fleshy, ripe fruit, balsamic, roasted-coffee aftertaste.

**ONTAÑÓN 2006 TC**

**89** Colour: cherry, garnet rim. Nose: ripe fruit, fruit liqueur

notes, creamy oak. Palate: warm, powerful, flavourful, slightly dry, soft tannins.

**ONTAÑÓN 2001 TGR**
tempranillo 90%, graciano 10%

**86** Colour: pale ruby, brick rim edge. Nose: overripe fruit, fine reductive notes, cocoa bean, aged wood nuances, tobacco. Palate: aged character, spicy, creamy, soft tannins.

**LINAJE DE VETIVER**
**ARTESO**

## BODEGAS ORBEN

Ctra. laguardia, km. 60
01340 (Álava)
☎: 945 609 086 - Fax: 945 609 261
marketing@izadi.com
www.bodegasorben.com

**MALPUESTO 2007 T**

**95** Colour: bright cherry. Nose: ripe fruit, sweet spices, creamy oak, earthy notes. Palate: flavourful, fruity, toasty, round tannins, fleshy.

**ORBEN 2006 T**
tempranillo 97%, graciano 3%

**89** Colour: cherry, garnet rim. Nose: expressive, elegant, ripe fruit, spicy, cocoa bean. Palate: fruity, balanced, spicy, round tannins.

## BODEGAS OSTATU

Ctra. Vitoria, 1
01307 Samaniego (Álava)

☎: 945 609 133 - Fax: 945 623 338
ostatu@ostatu.com
www.ostatu.com

**OSTATU 2008 B**
viura 90%, malvasia 10%

**88** Colour: bright straw. Nose: expressive, elegant, complex, fruit expression, floral. Palate: fruity, good acidity, flavourful.

**OSTATU LADERAS DEL PORTILLO 2007 T**
tempranillo 98%, viura 2%

**91** Colour: bright cherry. Nose: ripe fruit, sweet spices, expressive, toasty, dark chocolate, new oak. Palate: flavourful, fruity, toasty, round tannins.

**GLORIA DE OSTATU 2006 T**
tempranillo 100%

**92** Colour: dark-red cherry. Nose: powerful, ripe fruit, sweet spices, toasty, dark chocolate, aged wood nuances. Palate: flavourful, powerful, fleshy, spicy, round tannins.

**OSTATU LADERAS DEL PORTILLO 2006 T**
tempranillo 98%, viura 2%

**91** Colour: cherry, garnet rim. Nose: ripe fruit, powerfull, toasty, creamy oak. Palate: flavourful, powerful, fleshy, fruity, round tannins.

**OSTATU 2006 T**
tempranillo 90%, mazuelo 10%, graciano %, garnacha %

**87** Colour: deep cherry. Nose: fruit expression, ripe fruit, cocoa bean, creamy oak. Palate: fruity, powerful, flavourful, fleshy, soft tannins, roasted-coffee aftertaste.

**MAZARREDO DE OSTATU 2006 T**
tempranillo 90%, mazuelo 10%, graciano %, garnacha %

**86** Colour: cherry, garnet rim. Nose: powerful, ripe fruit, scrubland, toasty, creamy oak. Palate: flavourful, ripe fruit, spicy, round tannins.

**GLORIA DE OSTATU 2005 T**
tempranillo 100%

**94** Colour: black cherry, garnet rim. Nose: elegant, expressive, fruit expression, earthy notes, creamy oak. Palate: round, rich, complex, round tannins.

**OSTATU 2005 TR**
tempranillo 100%

**92** Colour: cherry, garnet rim. Nose: fresh, ripe fruit, cocoa bean, elegant. Palate: ripe fruit, great length, spicy, round tannins, fruity aftestaste.

## BODEGAS PALACIO S.A.

San Lázaro, 1
01300 Laguardia (Álava)
☎: 945 600 151 - Fax: 945 600 297
cosme@bodegaspalacio.com
www.bodegaspalacio.es.es

**COSME PALACIO 2007 BC**
viura 100%

**85** Colour: bright straw. Nose: grassy, ripe fruit, citrus fruit. Palate: flavourful, fruity.

**MILFLORES 2008 T**

**86** Colour: cherry, purple rim. Nose: fresh fruit, red berry notes, lactic notes, medium intensity. Palate: fresh, easy to drink, good finish.

**COSME PALACIO 2007 TC**
tempranillo 100%

**91** Colour: deep cherry. Nose: creamy oak, toasty, ripe fruit, undergrowth. Palate: concentrated, fruity, powerful, flavourful, fleshy, toasty, roasted-coffee aftertaste.

**GLORIOSO 2007 TC**
tempranillo 100%

**85** Colour: dark-red cherry. Nose: ripe fruit, reduction notes, toasty. Palate: fleshy, flavourful, toasty, ripe fruit.

**PALACIO 2005 T RESERVA ESPECIAL**
tempranillo 100%

**90** Colour: very deep cherry, garnet rim. Nose: fresh, ripe fruit, expressive, complex. Palate: flavourful, fruity, fine bitter notes, round tannins.

**GLORIOSO 2005 TR**
tempranillo 100%

**87** Colour: deep cherry, orangey edge. Nose: powerful, ripe fruit, toasty. Palate: powerful, fleshy, round tannins.

**COSME PALACIO 2005 TR**
tempranillo 100%

**87** Colour: dark-red cherry. Nose: reduction notes, ripe fruit, creamy oak, toasty. Palate: good structure, powerful, flavourful, fleshy, toasty, lacks expression.

## BODEGAS PATROCINIO

Ctra. Cenicero
26313 Uruñuela (La Rioja)
☎: 941 371 319 - Fax: 941 371 435
info@bodegaspatrocinio.com

**SEÑORIO DE UÑUELA 2008 B**
viura 100%

**85** Colour: bright straw. Nose: white flowers, medium intensity. Palate: flavourful, fruity, good acidity.

**SEÑORIO DE UÑUELA 2007 BFB**
viura 100%

**83**

**SEÑORIO DE UÑUELA 2008 RD**
tempranillo 100%

**85** Colour: rose, bright. Nose: medium intensity, fresh, red berry notes. Palate: flavourful, fruity, good acidity.

**ZINIO 2008 T**
tempranillo 100%

**85** Colour: very deep cherry. Nose: ripe fruit, red berry notes. Palate: spicy, fruity, flavourful.

**SEÑORIO DE UÑUELA 2008 T**
tempranillo 100%

**84**

**ZINIO 2007 T**
tempranillo 70%, garnacha 30%

**87** Colour: cherry, garnet rim. Nose: ripe fruit, medium intensity, creamy oak, spicy. Palate: round tannins, spicy, flavourful, fruity.

**ZINIO VENDIMIA SELECCIONADA 2006 T**
tempranillo 85%, graciano 15%

**87** Colour: cherry, garnet rim. Nose: ripe fruit, red berry notes, lactic notes, creamy oak, toasty. Palate: flavourful, fruity, fleshy, round tannins.

**SEÑORIO DE UÑUELA 2006 TC**
tempranillo 100%

**87** Colour: cherry, garnet rim. Nose: powerful, ripe fruit, sweet spices, toasty, new oak. Palate: flavourful, powerful, round tannins.

**ZINIO VENDIMIA SELECCIONADA 2005 TC**
tempranillo 100%

**87** Colour: cherry, garnet rim. Nose: ripe fruit, medium intensity, spicy, creamy oak. Palate: easy to drink, round tannins, flavourful, rich.

**ZINIO VENDIMIA SELECCIONADA 2004 TR**
tempranillo 100%

**87** Colour: cherry, garnet rim. Nose: medium intensity, ripe fruit, spicy, creamy oak. Palate: flavourful, fruity aftestaste, round tannins, warm.

**SEÑORIO DE UÑUELA 2002 TR**
tempranillo 100%

**84**

**SEÑORIO DE UÑUELA ED. LIMITADA 2001 TR**
tempranillo 100%

**85** Colour: pale ruby, brick rim edge. Nose: fruit preserve, toasty, fine reductive notes. Palate: warm, fruity, round tannins, spicy.

## BODEGAS PEDRO MARTÍNEZ ALESANCO

José García, 20
26310 Badarán (La Rioja)
☎: 941 367 075 - Fax: 941 367 075
info@bodegasmartinezalesanco.com
www.bodegasmartinezalesanco.com

**PEDRO MARTÍNEZ ALESANCO 2008 BFB**
viura 100%

**82**

**PEDRO MARTÍNEZ ALESANCO 2008 T**
tempranillo 100%

**87** Colour: bright cherry. Nose: ripe fruit, sweet spices, creamy oak, expressive. Palate: flavourful, fruity, toasty, round tannins.

**PEDRO MARTÍNEZ ALESANCO 2006 TC**
tempranillo 80%, garnacha 20%

**90** Colour: cherry, garnet rim. Nose: powerful, ripe fruit, lactic notes, creamy oak, cocoa bean, sweet spices. Palate: flavourful, creamy, spicy.

**PEDRO MARTÍNEZ ALESANCO 2005 TR**
tempranillo 90%, garnacha 10%

**90** Colour: cherry, garnet rim. Nose: powerful, ripe fruit, red berry notes, sweet spices, creamy oak. Palate: flavourful, powerful, fleshy, round tannins.

**PEDRO MARTÍNEZ ALESANCO SELECCIÓN 2005 TC**
tempranillo 40%, garnacha 30%, others 30%

**87** Colour: cherry, garnet rim. Nose: powerful, fruit expression, ripe fruit, sweet spices, creamy oak. Palate: flavourful, powerful, fleshy, spicy.

**PEDRO MARTÍNEZ ALESANCO 2001 TGR**
tempranillo 80%, garnacha 20%

**85** Colour: cherry, garnet rim. Nose: medium intensity, ripe fruit, sweet spices, cocoa bean. Palate: flavourful, spicy, classic aged character.

## BODEGAS PERICA

Avda. de la Rioja, 59
26340 San Asensio (La Rioja)
☎: 941 457 152 - Fax: 941 457 240
correo@bodegasperica.net
www.bodegasperica.net

**OLAGOSA 2008 BFB**
viura 100%

**86** Colour: bright straw. Nose: ripe fruit, sweet spices, expressive. Palate: flavourful, sweetness, fruity.

**VIÑA OLAGOSA 2006 TC**
tempranillo 90%, garnacha 5%, mazuelo 5%

**86** Colour: cherry, garnet rim. Nose: ripe fruit, sweet spices, creamy oak. Palate: flavourful, fruity, balanced, good acidity, round tannins.

**PERICA ORO RESERVA ESPECIAL 2004 TR**
tempranillo 95%, graciano 5%

**88** Colour: orangey edge, deep cherry. Nose: expressive, powerfull, fruit preserve, spicy, toasty. Palate: round tannins, flavourful, powerful.

**VIÑA OLAGOSA 2004 TR**
tempranillo 90%, garnacha 5%, mazuelo 5%

**84**

MI VILLA

## BODEGAS PUELLES

Camino de los Molinos, s/n
26339 Abalos (La Rioja)
☎: 941 334 415 - Fax: 941 334 132
informacion@bodegaspuelles.com
www.bodegaspuelles.com

**PUELLES 2006 TC**
tempranillo

**85** Colour: cherry, garnet rim. Nose: medium intensity, short, fruit expression, sweet spices. Palate: flavourful, balanced.

**EL MOLINO DE PUELLES ECOLÓGICO 2005 T**
tempranillo 100%

**86** Colour: cherry, garnet rim. Nose: varietal, ripe fruit. Palate: fine bitter notes, spicy, round tannins.

**PUELLES ZENUS 2004 T**
tempranillo

**87** Colour: bright cherry, garnet rim. Nose: fruit preserve, spicy, warm, toasty. Palate: powerful, fruity aftestaste, round tannins.

**PUELLES 2003 TR**
tempranillo

**87** Colour: cherry, garnet rim. Nose: ripe fruit, lactic notes, balanced. Palate: flavourful, fruity, good structure, spicy, fine bitter notes.

## BODEGAS RAMIREZ DE LA PISCINA

Ctra. Vitoria-Laguardia s/n
26338 San Vicente de la Sonsierra (La Rioja)
☎: 941 334 505 - Fax: 941 334 506
rampiscina@knet.es
www.ramirezdelapiscina.com

**RAMÍREZ DE LA PISCINA 2005 TC**
tempranillo 100%

**85** Colour: cherry, garnet rim. Nose: medium intensity, ripe fruit. Palate: good structure, easy to drink, fine bitter notes.

**RAMÍREZ DE LA PISCINA 2001 TR**
tempranillo 100%

**85** Colour: pale ruby, brick rim edge. Nose: fruit liqueur notes, ripe fruit, spicy. Palate: flavourful, good structure, good acidity, fine bitter notes.

**RAMÍREZ DE LA PISCINA SELECCIÓN 2005 TC**
tempranillo 100%

**90** Colour: dark-red cherry, garnet rim. Nose: ripe fruit, sweet spices, expressive, varietal. Palate: creamy, great length, fruity aftestaste, mineral.

ENTARI

## BODEGAS RAMÓN BILBAO

Avda. Santo Domingo, 34
26200 Haro (La Rioja)
☎: 941 310 295 - Fax: 941 310 832
info@bodegasramonbilbao.es
www.bodegasramonbilbao.es

RAMÓN BILBAO TEMPRANILLO EDICIÓN LIMITADA 2007 TC

**91** Colour: bright cherry. Nose: ripe fruit, sweet spices, creamy oak, expressive, mineral. Palate: flavourful, fruity, toasty, round tannins.

RAMÓN BILBAO 2007 TC

**90** Colour: bright cherry. Nose: ripe fruit, sweet spices, toasty. Palate: flavourful, fruity, toasty, round tannins.

MIRTO DE RAMÓN BILBAO 2006 T

**91** Colour: cherry, garnet rim. Nose: ripe fruit, spicy, creamy oak, complex, mineral. Palate: powerful, flavourful, toasty, round tannins.

RAMÓN BILBAO 2005 TR

**88** Colour: cherry, garnet rim. Nose: ripe fruit, spicy, creamy oak, toasty. Palate: powerful, flavourful, toasty, round tannins.

RAMÓN BILBAO 2004 TGR

**88** Colour: cherry, garnet rim. Nose: ripe fruit, toasty, sweet spices. Palate: flavourful, toasty, easy to drink.

VIÑA TURZABALLA 2001 TGR

**88** Colour: pale ruby, brick rim edge. Nose: medium intensity, ripe fruit, toasty, spicy. Palate: flavourful, spicy, easy to drink, classic aged character.

## BODEGAS REGALIA DE OLLAURI

Ctra. de Nájera, km. 1
26220 Ollauri (La Rioja)
☎: 941 338 373 - Fax: 941 338 374
info@bodegasregalia.es
www.bodegasregalia.es

MARQUÉS DE TERÁN COSECHA ESPECIAL 2007 T
tempranillo 100%

**90** Colour: bright cherry. Nose: sweet spices, creamy oak, expressive, powerfull, ripe fruit. Palate: flavourful, fruity, toasty, round tannins.

MARQUÉS DE TERÁN 2005 TC
tempranillo 95%, mazuelo 5%

**88** Colour: cherry, garnet rim. Nose: powerful, ripe fruit, sweet spices, toasty. Palate: flavourful, spicy, ripe fruit, round tannins.

MARQUÉS DE TERÁN 2002 TR
tempranillo 90%, mazuelo 5%, garnacha 5%

**84**

## BODEGAS RIOJANAS

Estación, 1 - 21
26350 Cenicero (La Rioja)
☎: 941 454 050 - Fax: 941 454 529
bodega@bodegasriojanas.com
www.bodegasriojanas.com

PUERTA VIEJA 2008 B
viura 100%

**82**

VIÑA ALBINA 2008 BFB
viura 90%, malvasia 10%

**78**

VIÑA ALBINA SEMIDULCE 2001 B RESERVA
viura 90%, malvasia 10%

**91** Colour: golden. Nose: powerful, floral, honeyed notes, candied fruit, fragrant herbs, petrol notes. Palate: flavourful, sweet, fresh, fruity, good acidity, long.

**ARTACHO 4M 2008 T**
tempranillo 100%

**87** Colour: cherry, purple rim. Nose: powerful, varietal, sweet spices, lactic notes. Palate: flavourful, fruity, easy to drink.

**CANCHALES 2008 T**
tempranillo 100%

**85** Colour: cherry, purple rim. Nose: ripe fruit, spicy, scrubland. Palate: flavourful, fruity, fresh.

**MONTE REAL 2006 TC**
tempranillo 100%

**86** Colour: cherry, garnet rim. Nose: sweet spices, dark chocolate, ripe fruit. Palate: flavourful, fleshy, pruney, round tannins.

**PUERTA VIEJA 2006 TC**
tempranillo 80%, mazuelo 15%, graciano 5%

**82**

**GRAN ALBINA 2005 TR**
tempranillo 34%, mazuelo 33%, graciano 33%

**87** Colour: pale ruby, brick rim edge. Nose: fruit liqueur notes, spicy, toasty. Palate: spicy, classic aged character, round tannins.

**VIÑA ALBINA 2004 TR**
tempranillo 80%, mazuelo 15%, graciano 5%

**88** Colour: pale ruby, brick rim edge. Nose: medium intensity, fruit liqueur notes, spicy, pattiserie. Palate: flavourful, spicy, classic aged character, easy to drink.

**GRAN ALBINA 2004 TR**
tempranillo 34%, mazuelo 33%, graciano 33%

**87** Colour: cherry, garnet rim. Nose: powerful, ripe fruit, spicy, aromatic coffee. Palate: flavourful, spicy, fleshy, balsamic.

**MONTE REAL 2004 TR**
tempranillo 80%, mazuelo 15%, graciano 5%

**84**

**MONTE REAL 2001 TGR**
tempranillo 80%, mazuelo 15%, graciano 5%

**88** Colour: light cherry, brick rim edge. Nose: fruit preserve, aged wood nuances, varnish. Palate: light-bodied, fruity, grainy tannins, aged character.

**VIÑA ALBINA 2001 TGR**
tempranillo 80%, mazuelo 15%, graciano 5%

**86** Colour: pale ruby, brick rim edge. Nose: powerful, fruit liqueur notes, spicy, aromatic coffee. Palate: flavourful, sweetness, spicy, fine tannins.

**VIÑA ALBINA 2008 SEMIDULCE**

**85** Colour: bright straw. Nose: candied fruit, floral, honeyed notes. Palate: ripe fruit, fruity, sweetness.

## BODEGAS RIOLANC

Curillos, 36
01308 Lanciego (Alava)
☎: 945 608 140 - Fax: 945 608 140
riolanc@riolanc.com
www.riolanc.com

**RIOLANC VENDIMIA SELECCIONADA 2008 T**
tempranillo 85%, mazuelo 15%

**85** Colour: dark-red cherry. Nose: fresh fruit, red berry notes, raspberry. Palate: fruity, flavourful, full.

**RIOLANC VENDIMIA SELECCIONADA 2006 T**
tempranillo 100%

**86** Colour: cherry, garnet rim. Nose: ripe fruit, spicy, creamy oak. Palate: warm, round tannins, fruity, flavourful.

## BODEGAS RODA

Avda. de Vizcaya, 5
26200 Haro (La Rioja)
☎: 941 303 001 - Fax: 941 312 703
rodarioja@roda.es
www.roda.es

**CIRSION 2007 T**
tempranillo 100%

**96** Colour: dark-red cherry, purple rim. Nose: powerful, ripe fruit, macerated fruit, creamy oak, new oak, cocoa bean. Palate: flavourful, fleshy, spicy, round tannins.

**CIRSION 2006 T**
tempranillo 100%

**94** Colour: deep cherry, garnet rim. Nose: ripe fruit, cocoa bean, aromatic coffee, sweet spices, creamy oak. Palate: flavourful, fleshy, complex, spicy, round tannins.

**RODA I 2005 TR**
tempranillo 100%

**93** Colour: bright cherry. Nose: ripe fruit, sweet spices, creamy oak, expressive, powerfull, mineral. Palate: flavourful, fruity, toasty, fine tannins.

RODA 2005 TR
tempranillo 85%, graciano 9%, garnacha 6%

**91** Colour: bright cherry. Nose: ripe fruit, sweet spices, creamy oak, mineral, warm. Palate: flavourful, fruity, toasty, round tannins.

## BODEGAS SEÑORIO DE YERGA S.A.

Barrio Bodegas, s/n
26142 Villamediana (La Rioja)
☎: 941 435 003 - Fax: 941 435 003
info@senoriodeyerga.com

CASTILLO DE YERGA 2005 TC
tempranillo 90%, garnacha 10%

**85** Colour: cherry, garnet rim. Nose: ripe fruit, spicy, complex. Palate: powerful, flavourful, toasty, round tannins.

CASTILLO YERGA 2004 TR
tempranillo 90%, mazuelo 10%

**86** Colour: cherry, garnet rim. Nose: spicy, fruit expression, toasty. Palate: flavourful, classic aged character, round tannins.

CASTILLO YERGA 2001 TGR
tempranillo 85%, graciano 10%, mazuelo 5%

**86** Colour: pale ruby, brick rim edge. Nose: caramel, fruit liqueur notes, tobacco, old leather. Palate: flavourful, balanced, light-bodied, classic aged character.

## BODEGAS SOLANA DE RAMIREZ RUIZ

Arana 24
26339 Abalos (La Rioja)
☎: 941 308 049 - Fax: 941 308 049
consultas@solanaderamirez.com
www.valsarte.com

VALSARTE VENDIMIA SELECCIONADA 2007 TC
tempranillo 100%

**86** Colour: bright cherry, garnet rim. Nose: aromatic coffee, roasted coffee, smoky. Palate: spicy, roasted-coffee aftertaste, good acidity, harsh oak tannins.

SOLANA DE RAMÍREZ 2008 T
tempranillo 90%, viura 5%, garnacha 5%

**88** Colour: cherry, purple rim. Nose: grassy, floral, ripe fruit. Palate: flavourful, powerful, fleshy.

VALSARTE 2006 TC
tempranillo 100%

**83**

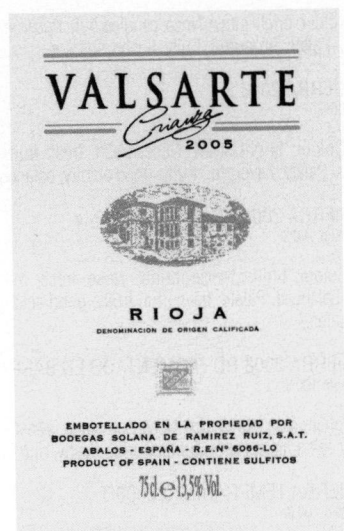

VALSARTE 2005 TC
tempranillo 85%, graciano 15%

## 84

**VALSARTE 2004 TR**
tempranillo 85%, graciano 10%, others 5%

**87** Colour: deep cherry, orangey edge. Nose: powerful, ripe fruit, sweet spices. Palate: flavourful, fleshy, spicy.

**SOLANA DE RAMÍREZ 2004 TC**
tempranillo 85%, graciano 15%

## 84

**VALSARTE 2001 TR**
tempranillo 85%, graciano 10%, others 5%

**87** Colour: cherry, garnet rim. Nose: toasty, dark chocolate, sweet spices, ripe fruit. Palate: flavourful, powerful, fleshy, round tannins.

## BODEGAS SONSIERRA

El Remedio, s/n
26338 San Vicente de la Sonsierra (La Rioja)
☎: 941 334 031 - Fax: 941 334 245
administracion@sonsierra.com
www.sonsierra.com

**SONSIERRA 2008 BFB**
viura 100%

**86** Colour: bright straw. Nose: candied fruit, ripe fruit, sweet spices. Palate: flavourful, fruity, fleshy, spicy.

**SONSIERRA 2008 B**
viura 100%

**85** Colour: bright straw. Nose: fresh, fresh fruit, white flowers. Palate: flavourful, fruity, good acidity, balanced.

**SONSIERRA 2008 RD**
tempranillo 100%

**86** Colour: brilliant rose, bright. Nose: fresh, red berry notes, balanced. Palate: flavourful, fruity, good acidity, fine bitter notes.

**SONSIERRA 2008 RD FERMENTADO EN BARRICA**
tempranillo 100%

**86** Colour: rose, purple rim. Nose: scrubland, sweet spices, creamy oak. Palate: flavourful, powerful, fleshy, ripe fruit.

**SONSIERRA TEMPRANILLO 2008 T**
tempranillo 100%

**87** Colour: cherry, purple rim. Nose: powerful, varietal, fresh fruit, red berry notes, lactic notes. Palate: flavourful, fruity, fresh.

**SONSIERRA VENDIMIA SELECCIONADA 2006 TC**
tempranillo 100%

**90** Colour: bright cherry. Nose: ripe fruit, sweet spices, creamy oak, expressive, lactic notes. Palate: flavourful, fruity, toasty, round tannins.

**PAGOS DE LA SONSIERRA EDICCION ESPECIAL DAVID DELFIN 2006 T**
tempranillo 100%

**90** Colour: cherry, garnet rim. Nose: powerful, ripe fruit, fruit preserve, toasty, dark chocolate. Palate: flavourful, powerful, spicy, round tannins, mineral.

**SONSIERRA 2006 TC**
tempranillo 100%

**87** Colour: deep cherry, garnet rim. Nose: ripe fruit, balanced, spicy, elegant. Palate: flavourful, full, good acidity, spicy, harsh oak tannins.

**IPOROS 2005 T**
tempranillo 100%

**88** Colour: cherry, garnet rim. Nose: powerful, ripe fruit, sweet spices, toasty. Palate: flavourful, powerful, fleshy, ripe fruit.

**SONSIERRA 2005 TC**

**88** Colour: cherry, garnet rim. Nose: ripe fruit, balanced, sweet spices, new oak. Palate: flavourful, good acidity, round tannins, smoky aftertaste.

**PAGOS DE LA SONSIERRA 2004 TR**
tempranillo 100%

**90** Colour: deep cherry, garnet rim. Nose: scrubland, balsamic herbs, expressive. Palate: flavourful, complex, spicy, fruity.

**SONSIERRA 2004 TR**
tempranillo 100%

**88** Colour: cherry, garnet rim. Nose: powerful, toasty, aromatic coffee, dark chocolate. Palate: flavourful, powerful, fleshy, spicy, round tannins.

**SONSIERRA 2001 TGR**
tempranillo 100%

**88** Colour: pale ruby, brick rim edge. Nose: ripe fruit, spicy, pattiserie. Palate: easy to drink, fruity, light-bodied, round tannins, classic aged character.

## BODEGAS TARÓN

Ctra. de Miranda, s/n
26211 Tirgo (La Rioja)
☎: 941 301 650 - Fax: 941 301 817
info@bodegastaron.com
www.bodegastaron.com

**TARÓN 2008 B**
viura 100%

**87** Colour: old gold. Nose: expressive, varietal, fresh, ripe fruit, white flowers. Palate: fruity, rich, full.

**TARÓN 2008 RD**
tempranillo 50%, garnacha 50%

**87** Colour: salmon. Nose: candied fruit, red berry notes, elegant. Palate: flavourful, fruity.

**TARÓN 2006 TC**
tempranillo 90%, mazuelo 10%

**87** Colour: deep cherry, garnet rim. Nose: fruit preserve, sweet spices. Palate: flavourful, fleshy, spicy.

**TARÓN TEMPRANILLO 2008 T**
tempranillo 100%

**86** Colour: cherry, purple rim. Nose: fruit preserve, fruit liqueur notes, dark chocolate. Palate: flavourful, spicy, round tannins.

**TARÓN 4MB 2007 T**
tempranillo 95%, mazuelo 5%

**86** Colour: cherry, garnet rim. Nose: warm, fruit preserve, sweet spices. Palate: flavourful, powerful, fleshy, toasty.

**TARÓN 2004 TR**
tempranillo 75%, graciano 15%, mazuelo 10%

**88** Colour: cherry, garnet rim. Nose: powerful, ripe fruit, dark chocolate, sweet spices. Palate: flavourful, powerful, fleshy, spicy, round tannins.

## BODEGAS TOBÍA

Ctra. Nac. 232, km. 438, s/n
26340 San Asensio (La Rioja)
☎: 941 457 425 - Fax: 941 457 401
tobia@bodegastobia.com
www.bodegastobia.com

**ALMA DE TOBÍA 2008 RD FERMENTADO EN BARRICA**

**90** Colour: rose, purple rim. Nose: powerful, ripe fruit, red berry notes, expressive, sweet spices. Palate: fleshy, powerful, fruity, fresh.

**TOBIA GRACIANO 2007 TC**

**90** Colour: bright cherry. Nose: sweet spices, creamy oak, expressive, floral, varietal, macerated fruit. Palate: flavourful, fruity, toasty, round tannins.

OSCAR TOBÍA
VIÑA TOBÍA

## BODEGAS VALDELACIERVA

Ctra. Burgos, km. 13
26370 Navarrete (La Rioja)
☎: 941 440 620 - Fax: 941 440 787
info@hispanobodegas.com
www.hispanobodegas.com

**VALDELAMILLO 2008 T**

**85** Colour: deep cherry. Nose: ripe fruit, sweet spices, lactic notes. Palate: flavourful, fruity, spicy, round tannins.

**CAMPO ALTO 2008 T**
tempranillo

## 80

VALDELAMILLO 2006 TC

**85** Colour: cherry, garnet rim. Nose: powerful, ripe fruit, sweet spices, toasty. Palate: flavourful, spicy, round tannins.

CAMPO ALTO 2006 TC

## 79

VALDELAMILLO 2004 TR

## 83

CAMPO ALTO 2004 TR
tempranillo

## 83

---
### BODEGAS VALDELANA
---

Puente Barricuelo, 67/69
01340 Elciego (Álava)
☎: 945 606 055 - Fax: 945 606 587
ana@bodegasvaldelana.com
www.bodegasvaldelana.com

BARÓN LADRÓN DE GUEVARA 2008 B
viura 100%

**88** Colour: old gold, amber rim. Nose: expressive, varietal, ripe fruit, floral, dried herbs. Palate: flavourful, rich, fruity, full.

VALDELANA 2008 B
viura 100%

**87** Colour: bright straw. Nose: fresh, fresh fruit, white flowers, tropical fruit, powerfull. Palate: flavourful, fruity, good acidity, balanced.

VALDELANA 2008 T
tempranillo 95%, viura 5%

**90** Colour: cherry, purple rim. Nose: fresh, expressive, red berry notes, lactic notes. Palate: fruity, flavourful, great length, round tannins.

BARÓN LADRÓN DE GUEVARA 2008 T
tempranillo 95%, viura 5%

**89** Colour: cherry, purple rim. Nose: ripe fruit, red berry notes, lactic notes, floral. Palate: flavourful, fruity, round tannins.

BARÓN LADRÓN DE GUEVARA DE AUTOR 2006 TC
tempranillo 95%, graciano 5%

**92** Colour: cherry, garnet rim. Nose: ripe fruit, spicy, creamy oak, toasty, complex, mineral, cocoa bean. Palate: powerful, flavourful, toasty, round tannins.

VALDELANA 2006 TC
tempranillo 95%, mazuelo 5%

**88** Colour: cherry, garnet rim. Nose: cocoa bean, spicy, creamy oak, balsamic herbs. Palate: ripe fruit, fine bitter notes, round tannins, complex.

AGNUS D VALDELANA 2006 TC
tempranillo 95%, graciano 5%

**87** Colour: cherry, purple rim. Nose: cocoa bean, aromatic coffee, powerfull, new oak. Palate: lacks fruit, harsh oak tannins.

BARÓN LADRÓN DE GUEVARA 2006 TC
tempranillo 95%, mazuelo 5%

**85** Colour: cherry, garnet rim. Nose: powerful, ripe fruit, warm. Palate: flavourful, fruity, ripe fruit.

BARÓN LADRÓN DE GUEVARA 2004 TR
tempranillo 95%, graciano 5%

**90** Colour: cherry, garnet rim. Nose: toasty, new oak, ripe fruit, sweet spices. Palate: flavourful, powerful, fleshy, round tannins.

VALDELANA 2004 TR
tempranillo 95%, graciano 5%

## 84

---
### BODEGAS VALDEMAR
---

Camino Viejo, s/n
01320 Oyón (Alava)
☎: 945 622 188 - Fax: 945 622 111
info@valdemar.es
www.valdemar.es

VALDEMAR VIURA 2008 B
viura 90%, malvasia 10%

**88** Colour: straw. Nose: medium intensity, fresh, ripe fruit, floral, grassy. Palate: flavourful, fruity, fresh, easy to drink.

CONDE DE VALDEMAR FINCA ALTO CANTABRIA 2008 BFB
viura 100%

**88** Colour: bright straw. Nose: powerful, ripe fruit, candied fruit, sweet spices. Palate: powerful, fleshy, creamy, round tannins.

CONDE DE VALDEMAR 2008 B
viura 100%

## 83

**VALDEMAR GARNACHA 2008 RD**
garnacha 100%

**85** Colour: rose, purple rim. Nose: powerful, ripe fruit, red berry notes, floral. Palate: fleshy, powerful, fruity, fresh.

**CONDE DE VALDEMAR 2008 RD**
garnacha 85%, tempranillo 15%

**82**

**VALDEMAR TEMPRANILLO 2008 T**
tempranillo 100%

**89** Colour: very deep cherry. Nose: expressive, powerfull, varietal, fresh fruit, grassy. Palate: fresh, fruity, powerful, flavourful.

**CONDE DE VALDEMAR GARNACHA 2007 T**
garnacha 100%

**88** Colour: cherry, garnet rim. Nose: expressive, fruit preserve, dark chocolate, sweet spices. Palate: elegant, balanced, round tannins.

**INSPIRACIÓN VALDEMAR 2006 T**
tempranillo 90%, graciano 10%

**90** Colour: garnet rim. Nose: expressive, elegant, medium intensity, sweet spices, cocoa bean, creamy oak, mineral, fruit preserve. Palate: flavourful, elegant, balanced, round tannins.

**CONDE DE VALDEMAR 2006 TC**
tempranillo 90%, mazuelo 10%

**89** Colour: cherry, garnet rim. Nose: ripe fruit, warm, expressive, sweet spices, creamy oak. Palate: balanced, elegant, round tannins, spicy.

**INSPIRACIÓN VALDEMAR COLECCIÓN VARIETALES 2005 T**
experimental 100%

**93** Colour: cherry, garnet rim. Nose: powerful, characterful, ripe fruit, dark chocolate, toasty, creamy oak. Palate: flavourful, powerful, fleshy, spicy, round tannins.

**INSPIRACIÓN VALDEMAR GRACIANO 2005 T**
graciano 100%

**91** Colour: cherry, garnet rim. Nose: expressive, varietal, powerfull, creamy oak, cocoa bean, ripe fruit. Palate: flavourful, powerful, round tannins, balsamic.

**CONDE DE VALDEMAR 2005 TR**
tempranillo 90%, mazuelo 10%

**89** Colour: cherry, garnet rim. Nose: powerful, expressive, ripe fruit, fruit liqueur notes, sweet spices, creamy oak. Palate: round tannins, good structure, balanced, elegant.

**INSPIRACIÓN VALDEMAR EDICIÓN LIMITADA 2004 T**
tempranillo 70%, graciano 15%, experimental 15%

**93** Colour: cherry, garnet rim. Nose: powerful, expressive, complex, fruit preserve, sweet spices, dark chocolate, aromatic coffee. Palate: balanced, round tannins, elegant, flavourful.

**CONDE DE VALDEMAR 2003 TGR**
tempranillo 85%, mazuelo 10%, graciano 5%

**88** Colour: dark-red cherry, orangey edge. Nose: expressive, medium intensity, fruit liqueur notes, creamy oak, cocoa bean. Palate: good structure, fruity aftestaste, round tannins, balanced.

# BODEGAS VALLEMAYOR

Ctra. Logroño-Vitoria 38
26360 Fuenmayor (La Rioja)
☎: 941 450 142 - Fax: 941 450 376
vallemayor@fer.es
www.vallemayor.com

**VALLE MAYOR WHITE RIOJA 2008 B**
viura, malvasia

**85** Colour: bright straw. Nose: fresh, fresh fruit, white flowers. Palate: flavourful, fruity, good acidity.

**VALLE MAYOR RIOJA 2008 RD**
garnacha, tempranillo, viura

# DO Ca. RIOJA

**84**

COLECCIÓN VALLE MAYOR VIÑA ENCINEDA
VENDIMIA SELECCIONADA 2006 T
tempranillo

**84**

VALLEMAYOR 2005 TC
tempranillo

**82**

COLECCIÓN VALLE MAYOR VIÑA CERRADILLA
VENDIMIA SELECCIONADA 2004 TC
tempranillo

**88** Colour: cherry, garnet rim. Nose: ripe fruit, spicy, creamy oak, toasty, complex, fruit liqueur notes. Palate: powerful, flavourful, toasty, round tannins.

VALLEMAYOR 2001 TGR
tempranillo

**86** Colour: dark-red cherry, orangey edge. Nose: fruit liqueur notes, sweet spices, caramel, tobacco, fine reductive notes. Palate: sweet tannins, balanced, aged character, spicy.

VALLEMAYOR 2001 TR
tempranillo

**86** Colour: pale ruby, brick rim edge. Nose: fruit liqueur notes, caramel, aged wood nuances, fine reductive notes. Palate: sweet tannins, classic aged character, aged character, balanced.

## BODEGAS VALSACRO

Ctra. N-232, km. 364
26510 Pradejón (La Rioja )
☎: 941 398 008 - Fax: 941 398 070
ventas@valsacro.com
www.valsacro.com

VALSACRO 2005 T
vidau 40%, tempranillo 50%, mazuelo 10%

**89** Colour: deep cherry, garnet rim. Nose: sweet spices, mineral, creamy oak, ripe fruit. Palate: good structure, flavourful, round tannins.

## BODEGAS VARAL

San Vicente, 40
01307 Baños de Ebro (Alava)
☎: 945 623 321 - Fax: 945 623 321
bodegasvaral@bodegasvaral.com
www.bodegasvaral.com

ESENCIAS DE VARAL 2008 B
viura 100%

**86** Colour: bright straw. Nose: ripe fruit, floral, expressive. Palate: fruity, fresh, easy to drink.

TRUJALERO 2008 T
tempranillo 90%, viura 6%, garnacha 4%

**84**

ESENCIAS DE VARAL 2006 T
tempranillo 100%

**90** Colour: cherry, garnet rim. Nose: powerful, sweet spices, mineral, ripe fruit. Palate: flavourful, fruity, fresh.

VARAL VENDIMIA SELECCIONADA 2006 T
tempranillo 100%

**90** Colour: cherry, garnet rim. Nose: powerful, sweet spices, cocoa bean, ripe fruit, red berry notes. Palate: flavourful, ripe fruit, round tannins.

MAYOR TRUJALERO 2005 TC
tempranillo 100%

**87** Colour: cherry, garnet rim. Nose: dark chocolate, creamy oak, toasty, ripe fruit. Palate: flavourful, spicy, toasty, round tannins.

## BODEGAS VIÑA BERNEDA

Ctra. Somalo, 59
26313 Uruñuela (La Rioja)
☎: 941 371 304 - Fax: 941 371 304
berneda@vinaberneda.com
www.vinaberneda.com

VIÑA BERNEDA 2007 BFB

**90** Colour: bright yellow. Nose: powerful, ripe fruit, sweet spices, creamy oak, fragrant herbs. Palate: rich, smoky aftertaste, flavourful, fresh, good acidity.

VIÑA BERNEDA 2008 T MACERACIÓN CARBÓNICA

**85** Colour: deep cherry. Nose: fruit expression, fresh fruit, raspberry. Palate: fruity, flavourful, fresh.

VIÑA BERNEDA 2006 TC

**86** Colour: cherry, garnet rim. Nose: ripe fruit, toasty, spicy. Palate: good acidity, round tannins, balsamic, spicy.

## BODEGAS VIÑA LAGUARDIA

Ctra. Laguardiaa, s/n
01309 Elvillar (Alava)

☎: 945 604 143 - Fax: 945 604 150
bodegas@vinalaguardia.es
www.vinalaguardia.es

URTEKO 2008 T
tempranillo 85%, viura 15%

**87** Colour: bright cherry. Nose: ripe fruit, sweet spices, creamy oak. Palate: flavourful, fruity, toasty, round tannins.

ECANIA 2004 TC
tempranillo

**85** Colour: cherry, garnet rim. Nose: fruit liqueur notes, sweet spices, pattiserie. Palate: flavourful, spicy, classic aged character.

ECANIA 1998 TR

**85** Colour: cherry, garnet rim. Nose: medium intensity, ripe fruit, warm, spicy. Palate: spirituous, classic aged character, spicy.

BROTON

## BODEGAS VIRGEN DEL VALLE

Ctra. a Villabuena, 3
01307 Samaniego (Alava)
☎: 945 609 033 - Fax: 945 609 106
cincel@cincel.net
www.cincel.net

CINCEL 2005 T
tempranillo 95%, mazuelo 5%, graciano %

**85** Colour: cherry, garnet rim. Nose: medium intensity, spicy, woody, dark chocolate. Palate: powerful, spicy, ripe fruit.

CINCEL SELECCIÓN 2004 T
tempranillo 90%, mazuelo 10%, graciano %

**81**

CINCEL 2001 TC
tempranillo 95%, mazuelo 5%, graciano %

**86** Colour: cherry, garnet rim. Nose: warm, powerfull, toasty, dark chocolate. Palate: flavourful, fleshy, warm.

## BODEGAS Y VIÑAS SENDA GALIANA

Barrio Bodegas, s/n
26142 Villamediana (La Rioja)
☎: 941 435 375 - Fax: 941 436 072
info@sendagaliana.es

SENDA GALIANA 2005 TC
tempranillo 90%, garnacha 10%

**82**

SENDA GALIANA 2004 TR
tempranillo 90%, mazuelo 10%

**83**

SENDA GALIANA 2001 TGR
tempranillo 85%, graciano 10%, mazuelo 5%

**84**

## BODEGAS Y VIÑEDOS ALICIA ROJAS

Ctra. Nacional 232, km. 376 - 377
26513 Ausejo (La Rioja)
☎: 941 430 010 - Fax: 941 430 286
info@bodegasaliciarojas.com
www.bodegasaliciarojas.es

FINCA ALICIA ROJAS 2005 TC

**84**

ALICIA ROJAS 2001 TR

**86** Colour: cherry, garnet rim. Nose: fine reductive notes, wet leather, tobacco, spicy, dark chocolate. Palate: fleshy, good acidity, round tannins.

SOLARCE

## BODEGAS Y VIÑEDOS ALUÉN

Robledal, 18
26320 Baños de Río Tobia (La Rioja)
☎: 607 166 152 - Fax: 941 374 851
javierssm@telefonica.net
www.bodegasaluen.com

ALUÉN 2006 TC
tempranillo 92%, graciano 8%

**85** Colour: cherry, garnet rim. Nose: ripe fruit, medium intensity, sweet spices, creamy oak. Palate: flavourful, concentrated, slightly dry, soft tannins, spirituous.

## BODEGAS Y VIÑEDOS ALVAR

Gran Vía 39 Ent. 3 Of. 11
26002 Logroño (La Rioja)
☎: 941 588 068 - Fax: 941 588 068
alvar@bodegasalvar.com
www.bodegasalvar.com

LIVIUS 2007 BFB
viura 70%, malvasia 30%

**89** Colour: old gold, amber rim. Nose: expressive, ripe fruit, pattiserie, creamy oak. Palate: good acidity, fruity, fruity aftestaste.

LIVIUS TEMPRANILLO 2006 T
tempranillo 100%

**90** Colour: cherry, garnet rim. Nose: expressive, ripe fruit, red berry notes, mineral, sweet spices, creamy oak. Palate: full, flavourful, long, ripe fruit, powerful tannins.

LIVIUS GRACIANO 2006 T
graciano 100%

**90** Colour: dark-red cherry, garnet rim. Nose: varietal, ripe fruit, spicy, creamy oak, cocoa bean. Palate: slightly dry, soft tannins, flavourful, elegant, balanced.

MILETO

## BODEGAS Y VIÑEDOS ARRANZ-ARGOTE

Mayor Alta, 43
26370 Navarrete (La Rioja)
☎: 699 046 043
bodega@vinoarar.com
www.vinoarar.com

ARAR 2004 T
tempranillo, graciano, mazuelo, maturana

**86** Colour: cherry, garnet rim. Nose: fruit preserve, spicy, toasty. Palate: round tannins, flavourful, fruity aftestaste.

## BODEGAS Y VIÑEDOS ARTADI S.A.

Ctra. de Logroño, s/n
01300 Laguardia (Alava)
☎: 945 600 119 - Fax: 945 600 850
info@artadi.com
www.artadi.com

ARTADI 2008 T

**88** Colour: deep cherry. Nose: varietal, fresh, fresh fruit. Palate: powerful, flavourful, fruity, sweetness, fruity aftestaste.

VIÑA EL PISÓN 2007 T

**98** Colour: deep cherry. Nose: ripe fruit, sweet spices, creamy oak, expressive, complex, varietal. Palate: flavourful, fruity, toasty, round tannins, powerful, complex.

ARTADI PAGOS VIEJOS 2007 T

**95** Colour: bright cherry. Nose: ripe fruit, sweet spices, creamy oak, expressive, cocoa bean, fruit expression, complex. Palate: fruity, toasty, round tannins, complex, powerful, fresh.

ARTADI VIÑAS DE GAIN 2007 T
tempranillo 100%

**90** Colour: dark-red cherry. Nose: varietal, powerfull, complex, fresh fruit, undergrowth. Palate: powerful, flavourful, rich, fresh, toasty, slightly dry, soft tannins.

## BODEGAS Y VIÑEDOS CASADO MORALES

Avda. de la Pobeda, 12-14
01306 La Puebla de Labarca (Alava)
☎: 945 607 017 - Fax: 945 063 173
info@casadomorales.es
www.casadomorales.es

CASADO MORALES 2008 B

**84**

CASADO MORALES 2005 BC
viura

**81**

CASADO MORALES 2004 B RESERVA

**86** Colour: yellow, golden. Nose: candied fruit, ripe fruit, pattiserie. Palate: balanced, flavourful, powerful.

CASADO MORALES 2008 RD

**88** Colour: brilliant rose. Nose: fresh fruit, red berry notes, rose petals. Palate: fresh, fruity, flavourful, good acidity, balanced.

NOBLEZA 2008 T

**85** Colour: very deep cherry. Nose: fresh fruit, red berry notes, raspberry. Palate: fruity, sweetness, good acidity.

NOBLEZA DIMIDIUM 2007 T
tempranillo

**84**

EME DE CASADO MORALES 2007 T

**84**

CASADO MORALES 2006 TC

**87** Nose: ripe fruit, spicy, creamy oak, expressive. Palate: balanced, full, concentrated, flavourful, round tannins.

CASADO MORALES 2005 TR

**87** Colour: cherry, garnet rim. Nose: ripe fruit, creamy oak, sweet spices. Palate: good acidity, long, spicy, round tannins, fleshy.

LADERAS SUR CASADO MORALES CARÁCTER 2005 TR

**86** Colour: cherry, garnet rim. Nose: fruit preserve, spicy. Palate: good acidity, slightly dry, soft tannins, flavourful, full.

## BODEGAS Y VIÑEDOS GAUDUSSON

Avda. Zamudio, 2
26221 Gimileo (La Rioja)
☎: 941 311 947 - Fax: 941 312 231
comercial@gaudusson.com
www.gaudusson.com

GAVDVSSON 2005 TC
tempranillo 100%
**84**

MARQUÉS DE MATAFLORIDA 2001 TR
tempranillo 100%
**78**

## BODEGAS Y VIÑEDOS GONZÁLEZ TESO, S.C.

Olmo, 34-36
01330 Labastida (Alava)
☎: 945 331 321
j.gontes@hotmail.com
www.gontes.com

GONTÉS 2008 T FERMENTADO EN BARRICA
tempranillo 100%
**83**

OLMO 34 2007 T
tempranillo 50%, garnacha 30%, graciano 20%

**88** Colour: bright cherry. Nose: sweet spices, creamy oak, expressive, red berry notes. Palate: flavourful, fruity, toasty, round tannins.

GONTÉS EXPRESIÓN 2006 T
tempranillo 100%

**91** Colour: bright cherry. Nose: sweet spices, creamy oak, expressive, red berry notes, ripe fruit. Palate: flavourful, fruity, toasty, round tannins.

GONTÉS 2006 TC
tempranillo 85%, garnacha 15%

**87** Colour: cherry, garnet rim. Nose: ripe fruit, spicy, creamy oak, toasty. Palate: powerful, flavourful, toasty, round tannins.

GONTÉS 2005 TC
tempranillo 100%

**89** Colour: deep cherry, orangey edge. Nose: ripe fruit, sweet spices, creamy oak. Palate: fruity, flavourful, good structure, round tannins.

GONTÉS EXPRESIÓN 2005 T
tempranillo 100%

**86** Colour: dark-red cherry, orangey edge. Nose: macerated fruit, fruit liqueur notes, creamy oak, sweet spices. Palate: flavourful, fruity.

GONTÉS 2004 TC
tempranillo 85%, garnacha 15%

**85** Colour: bright cherry. Nose: ripe fruit, sweet spices, creamy oak. Palate: flavourful, fruity, toasty, round tannins.

GONTÉS EXPRESIÓN 2003 T
tempranillo 100%

**88** Colour: cherry, garnet rim. Nose: powerful, toasty, creamy oak, cocoa bean. Palate: flavourful, fleshy, ripe fruit, round tannins.

## BODEGAS Y VIÑEDOS HERAS CORDÓN

Ctra. Lapuebla, km.2
26360 Fuenmayor (La Rioja)
☎: 941 451 413 - Fax: 941 450 265
bodegas@herascordon.com
www.herascordon.com

HERAS CORDÓN VENDIMIA SELECCIONADA 2005 TC
tempranillo 85%, graciano 10%, mazuelo 5%

**86** Colour: cherry, garnet rim. Nose: powerful, ripe fruit, spicy, toasty. Palate: flavourful, spicy, ripe fruit, round tannins.

HERAS CORDÓN RESERVA EXCELENTE 2004 T
tempranillo 85%, graciano 10%, mazuelo 5%
**84**

## BODEGAS Y VIÑEDOS ILURCE

Avda. de Logroño, 7
26540 Alfaro (La Rioja)

☎: 941 180 829 - Fax: 941 183 897
info@ilurce.com
www.ilurce.com

**ILURCE 2008 RD**

**85** Colour: brilliant rose. Nose: raspberry, fresh, balanced. Palate: fresh, fruity, good acidity, fine bitter notes.

**ILURCE 2008 T**
garnacha 100%

**87** Colour: cherry, purple rim. Nose: expressive, fresh fruit, red berry notes, floral. Palate: flavourful, fruity, good acidity, round tannins.

**ILURCE 2006 TC**
graciano 100%

**85** Colour: very deep cherry, garnet rim. Nose: varietal, grassy. Palate: flavourful, powerful, correct, varietal.

**ILURCE VENDIMIA SELECCIONADA 2005 TC**
garnacha 60%, tempranillo 40%

**89** Colour: cherry, garnet rim. Nose: powerful, ripe fruit, sweet spices, creamy oak. Palate: flavourful, powerful, fleshy, round tannins.

**ILURCE 2002 TC**
tempranillo 70%, garnacha 15%, graciano 15%

**87** Colour: cherry, garnet rim. Nose: toasty, creamy oak, aged wood nuances. Palate: flavourful, good structure, sweetness, spicy, classic aged character.

**ILURCE VENDIMIA SELECCIONADA 2001 TR**
tempranillo 60%, garnacha 40%

**83**

## BODEGAS Y VIÑEDOS LABASTIDA

Avda. Diputación, 22
01330 Labastida (Alava)
☎: 945 331 161 - Fax: 945 331 118
info@bodegaslabastida.com
www.bodegaslabastida.com

**SOLAGÜEN CEPAS VIEJAS 2005 T**
tempranillo 62%, garnacha 38%

**87** Nose: ripe fruit, spicy. Palate: flavourful, fruity, round tannins, powerful.

**SOLAGÜEN 2004 TR**
tempranillo 100%

**87** Colour: pale ruby, brick rim edge. Nose: ripe fruit, creamy oak, spicy. Palate: flavourful, powerful, round tannins, spicy.

**MANUEL QUINTANO 2004 TR**
tempranillo 70%, garnacha 30%

**86** Colour: cherry, garnet rim. Nose: medium intensity, fruit liqueur notes, aged wood nuances, spicy. Palate: round tannins, flavourful.

## BODEGAS Y VIÑEDOS PUENTE DEL EA

La Fuente, 8
26212 Sajazarra (La Rioja)
☎: 941 320 405 - Fax: 941 320 406
puentedea@terra.es

**PUENTE DEL EA 2008 BFB**

**88** Colour: bright straw. Nose: fragrant herbs, white flowers, ripe fruit, candied fruit, citrus fruit. Palate: flavourful, fruity, fleshy, good acidity.

**ERIDANO VENDIMIA SLECCIONADA 2008 T JOVEN**
tempranillo 90%, garnacha 10%

**88** Colour: cherry, garnet rim. Nose: red berry notes, ripe fruit, spicy, dry stone. Palate: flavourful, fleshy, fruity, spicy.

**ERIDANO 2008 T JOVEN**
tempranillo

**85** Colour: cherry, garnet rim. Nose: grassy, ripe fruit, red berry notes. Palate: flavourful, fruity, fresh.

**ERIDANO CRIANZA PLATA 2006 TC**
tempranillo

**90** Colour: cherry, garnet rim. Nose: spicy, creamy oak, toasty, mineral, ripe fruit. Palate: powerful, flavourful, toasty, round tannins.

**ERIDANO 2006 TC**
tempranillo

**88** Colour: cherry, garnet rim. Nose: ripe fruit, spicy, creamy oak, toasty, complex. Palate: powerful, flavourful, toasty, round tannins.

**ERIDANO 2004 TR**
tempranillo

**88** Colour: cherry, garnet rim. Nose: creamy oak, toasty, ripe fruit, red berry notes. Palate: flavourful, powerful, fleshy, fruity, fresh.

## BODEGAS Y VIÑEDOS PUJANZA S.L.

Ctra. del Villar s/n
01300 Laguardia (Alava)
☎: 945 600 548 - Fax: 945 600 522
gerencia@bodegaspujanza.com
www.bodegaspujanza.com

**PUJANZA NORTE 2006 T**
tempranillo 100%

**91** Colour: deep cherry. Nose: elegant, complex, aromatic coffee, roasted coffee, fruit expression, undergrowth. Palate: complex, spirituous, fruity, powerful, flavourful.

**PUJANZA 2006 T**
tempranillo 100%

**89** Colour: dark-red cherry. Nose: characterful, ripe fruit, creamy oak, dark chocolate. Palate: flavourful, fruity, creamy, balsamic.

## BODEGAS Y VIÑEDOS TRITIUM S.L.

Dr. Estanislao del Campo 28, Bajo
26350 Cenicero (La Rioja)
☎: 941 232 160 - Fax: 941 270 629
ibervin@fer.es
www.tritium.es

**TRITIUM GARNACHA 2007 T**

**90** Colour: cherry, garnet rim. Nose: varietal, expressive, ripe fruit. Palate: fruity, balanced, great length, round tannins.

**TRITIUM TINTO JOVEN 2007 T**
tempranillo

**87** Colour: cherry, garnet rim. Nose: ripe fruit, expressive, red berry notes. Palate: round, flavourful, fruity, grainy tannins.

**TRITIUM VENDIMIA SELECCIONADA 2006 T**
tempranillo

**84**

**TRITIUM TEMPRANILLO 2005 T**

**85** Colour: cherry, garnet rim. Nose: fruit liqueur notes, toasty, spicy. Palate: flavourful, balanced, good acidity, great length.

## BODEGAS Y VIÑEDOS ZUAZO GASTÓN

Las Norias, 2
01320 Oyón (Alava)
☎: 945 601 526 - Fax: 945 622 917
zuazogaston@zuazogaston.com
www.zuazogaston.com

**ZUAZO GASTÓN 2008 T**
tempranillo

**86** Colour: cherry, purple rim. Nose: varietal, red berry notes, lactic notes. Palate: flavourful, fruity, light-bodied, correct, good finish.

**ZUAZO GASTÓN 2006 TC**

**88** Colour: dark-red cherry. Nose: powerful, ripe fruit, toasty, sweet spices, caramel, dark chocolate. Palate: flavourful, sweetness, spicy, round tannins.

**FINCA COSTANILLAS 2006 T**

**88** Colour: cherry, garnet rim. Nose: powerful, fruit liqueur notes, sweet spices, toasty. Palate: flavourful, ripe fruit, spicy, round tannins.

**ZUAZO GASTÓN 2004 TR**

**87** Colour: cherry, garnet rim. Nose: ripe fruit, dark chocolate, sweet spices. Palate: flavourful, fleshy, spicy.

## BODEGAS YSIOS

Camino de la Hoya s/n
01300 Laguardia (Alava)
☎: 945 600 640 - Fax: 945 600 520
ysios@domecqbodegas.com
www.bodegasysios.com

**YSIOS EDICIÓN LIMITADA 2002 TR**
tempranillo 100%

**90** Colour: cherry, garnet rim. Nose: powerful, ripe fruit, sweet spices, dark chocolate. Palate: fleshy, powerful, spicy, fine bitter notes.

**YSIOS 2004 T**
tempranillo 100%

**89** Colour: cherry, garnet rim. Nose: expressive, complex, powerfull, ripe fruit, aromatic coffee, cocoa bean. Palate: elegant, round tannins, balanced.

## BODEGAS ZUGOBER

Tejerías, 13-15
01306 Lapuebla de Labarca (Alava)
☎: 945 627 228 - Fax: 945 627 281
zugober@zugober.com
www.zugober.com

BELEZOS ACUARELA 2008 T
tempranillo 100%

**87** Colour: deep cherry, purple rim. Nose: grassy, fruit expression, red berry notes. Palate: flavourful, fruity, fresh.

BELEZOS VENDIMIA SELECCIONADA 2006 T
tempranillo 100%

**89** Colour: cherry, garnet rim. Nose: expressive, sweet spices, cocoa bean, ripe fruit, lactic notes. Palate: flavourful, powerful, ripe fruit, round tannins.

BELEZOS 2006 TC
tempranillo 100%

**84**

## CAMPILLO S.L.

Ctra. de Logroño, s/n

01300 Laguardia (Alava)
☎: 945 600 826 - Fax: 945 600 837
info@bodegascampillo.es

CAMPILLO 2008 BFB

**91** Colour: bright yellow. Nose: powerful, ripe fruit, sweet spices, creamy oak, fragrant herbs. Palate: rich, smoky aftertaste, flavourful, fresh, good acidity.

CAMPILLO 2008 RD

**86** Colour: rose. Nose: fruit expression, fresh fruit, red berry notes. Palate: fruity, powerful, flavourful.

CAMPILLO 2005 TC

**88** Colour: dark-red cherry. Nose: fresh fruit, complex, varietal, powerfull, caramel, creamy oak. Palate: powerful, flavourful, complex, fleshy, rich.

CAMPILLO FINCA CUESTA CLARA 2004 T

**93** Colour: deep cherry. Nose: fresh fruit, undergrowth, creamy oak, dark chocolate. Palate: complex, powerful, flavourful, ripe fruit, toasty.

CAMPILLO 2001 TR

**90** Colour: deep cherry. Nose: complex, ripe fruit, fine reductive notes, tobacco, damp earth, macerated fruit, cocoa bean, creamy oak. Palate: complex, fruity, powerful, flavourful, smoky aftertaste, toasty.

CAMPILLO RESERVA ESPECIAL 2001 TR

**90** Colour: dark-red cherry. Nose: powerful, complex, sweet spices, cocoa bean, macerated fruit. Palate: good structure, powerful, flavourful, fruity.

CAMPILLO 1995 TGR

**89** Colour: cherry, garnet rim. Nose: fine reductive notes, ripe fruit, spicy, dark chocolate. Palate: flavourful, powerful, spicy, round tannins.

## CARLOS SAMPEDRO PÉREZ DE VIÑASPRE

Páganos, 44 Bajo
01300 Laguardia (Alava)
☎: 945 600 146 - Fax: 945 600 146
info@bodegascarlossampedro.com
www.bodegascarlossampedro.com

BRILLADOR 2007 T
tempranillo 95%, viura 5%

**83**

VIÑASPERI 2006 TC
tempranillo 100%

**84**

VIÑASPERI 2005 TR
tempranillo 100%

**88** Colour: cherry, garnet rim. Nose: fruit liqueur notes, spicy, toasty. Palate: round tannins, flavourful, fruity aftestaste.

VIÑA CONSTANTINA
CARLOS SAN PEDRO PÉREZ DE VIÑASPRE

## CARLOS SERRES S.A.

Avda. Santo Domingo, 40
26200 Haro (La Rioja)
☎: 941 310 294 - Fax: 941 310 418
info@carlosserres.com
www.carlosserres.com

SERRES VIURA 2008 B

**86** Colour: bright straw. Nose: fresh, fresh fruit, white flowers, expressive. Palate: flavourful, fruity, good acidity, balanced.

SERRES 2008 RD
tempranillo 80%, garnacha 20%

**83**

SERRES TEMPRANILLO GARNACHA 2008 T
tempranillo 100%

**85** Colour: bright cherry, purple rim. Nose: red berry notes, balanced. Palate: fruity, fresh, easy to drink, good finish.

CARLOS SERRES 2005 TC
tempranillo 85%, garnacha 15%

**83**

ONOMÁSTICA 2004 TR
tempranillo 80%, graciano 10%, mazuelo 10%

**90** Colour: deep cherry, garnet rim. Nose: ripe fruit, complex, spicy, expressive. Palate: flavourful, balanced, fruity, great length, round tannins.

CARLOS SERRES 2004 TR
tempranillo 90%, mazuelo 10%

**84**

CARLOS SERRES 2001 TGR
tempranillo 85%, graciano 10%, mazuelo 5%

**87** Colour: cherry, garnet rim. Nose: spicy, aromatic coffee, ripe fruit. Palate: complex, powerful, fine bitter notes, good acidity, round tannins.

## CASTILLO DE CUZCURRITA

San Sebastián, 1
26214 Cuzcurrita del Río Tirón (La Rioja)
☎: 941 328 022 - Fax: 941 301 620
info@castillodecuzcurrita.com

CERRADO DEL CASTILLO 2005 T
tempranillo 100%

**92** Colour: cherry, garnet rim. Nose: powerful, ripe fruit, red berry notes, lactic notes, sweet spices, cocoa bean. Palate: flavourful, fleshy, spicy, ripe fruit, round tannins.

SEÑORÍO DE CUZCURRITA

## COMPAÑIA BODEGUERA DE VALENCISO

Ctra. Ollauri-Najera, km. 0,4
26220 Ollauri (La Rioja)
☎: 941 304 724 - Fax: 941 304 728
valenciso@valenciso.com
www.valenciso.com

VALENCISO 2004 TR

**89** Colour: cherry, garnet rim. Nose: ripe fruit, spicy, creamy oak, toasty, complex, tobacco. Palate: flavourful, toasty, fine tannins, smoky aftertaste.

## COMPAÑIA DE VINOS DE TELMO RODRÍGUEZ

El Monte s/n
01308 Lanciego (Alava)
☎: 945 628 315 - Fax: 945 628 314
contact@telmorodriguez.com
www.telmorodriguez.com

LZ 2008 T

**88** Colour: cherry, purple rim. Nose: powerful, grassy, red berry notes, wild herbs. Palate: flavourful, powerful, fruity, round tannins.

ALTOS DE LANZAGA 2006 T

**94** Colour: black cherry, garnet rim. Nose: powerful, dark chocolate, aromatic coffee, toasty, ripe fruit. Palate: flavourful, fleshy, powerful, roasted-coffee aftertaste, round tannins.

LANZAGA 2006 T

**92** Colour: cherry, garnet rim. Nose: ripe fruit, spicy, creamy oak, complex, fine reductive notes. Palate: powerful, flavourful, toasty, round tannins.

## CONDE DEL DONADÍO DE CASASOLA

Ctra. de Logroño, s/n
26220 Ollauri (La Rioja)
☎: 917 104 880 - Fax: 917 104 881
anap@swd.es
www.bodegascondedeldonadio.com

CONDE DEL DONADÍO BERTÍN OSBORNE 2005 TC
tempranillo 100%

**86** Colour: cherry, garnet rim. Nose: medium intensity, ripe fruit, spicy. Palate: flavourful, spicy, fine tannins.

## CÓRDOBA MARTÍNEZ S.C.

La Poveda, 64
01306 Lapuebla de Labarca (Alava)
☎: 945 627 212 - Fax: 945 607 364
info@bodegasjosecordoba.com
www.bodegasjosecordoba.com

JOSÉ CÓRDOBA 2008 B
viura 90%, malvasia 10%

**85** Nose: scrubland, fresh fruit, fruit expression, citrus fruit. Palate: flavourful, fleshy, fruity.

JOSÉ CÓRDOBA 2008 T
tempranillo 100%

**86** Colour: very deep cherry. Nose: varietal, powerfull, red berry notes. Palate: flavourful, fruity, round tannins.

## CRIADORES DE RIOJA

Ctra. de Clavijo, s/n
26141 Alberite (La Rioja)
☎: 941 436 702 - Fax: 941 436 430
info@criadoresderioja.com
www.criadoresderioja.com

CASTILLO DE CLAVIJO 2008 BFB
viura 100%

**87** Colour: bright straw. Nose: medium intensity, ripe fruit, smoky, dried herbs. Palate: fruity, flavourful, full, good acidity.

CASTILLO DE CLAVIJO 2005 TC
tempranillo 90%, garnacha 10%

**84**

CASTILLO DE CLAVIJO 2004 TR
tempranillo 90%, mazuelo 10%

**83**

CASTILLO DE CLAVIJO TGR
tempranillo 80%, graciano 10%, mazuelo 10%

**84**

## CVNE - COMPAÑÍA VINÍCOLA DEL NORTE DE ESPAÑA

Barrio de la Estacion s/n
26200 Haro (La Rioja)
☎: 941 304 800 - Fax: 941 304 815
marketing@cvne.com
www.cvne.com

MONOPOLE 2008 B
viura 100%

**87** Colour: bright straw. Nose: fruit expression, white flowers, grassy, fresh. Palate: easy to drink, correct.

CUNE 2008 B
viura 100%

**85** Colour: straw. Nose: ripe fruit, fruit expression, grassy. Palate: fruity, flavourful, rich.

CORONA SEMIDULCE 2005 B
viura 90%, malvasia 10%

**90** Colour: yellow, greenish rim. Nose: petrol notes, candied fruit. Palate: balanced, good acidity, sweetness, rich, flavourful.

CUNE 2008 RD
tempranillo 100%

**84**

CUNE 2007 TC
tempranillo 80%, garnacha 20%, mazuelo %

**87** Colour: deep cherry. Nose: medium intensity, varietal, fresh fruit, fruit expression, aromatic coffee, creamy oak. Palate: fresh, fruity, flavourful.

CUNE 2006 TR
tempranillo 80%, mazuelo 10%, garnacha 5%, graciano 5%

**87** Colour: deep cherry. Nose: medium intensity, sweet spices, toasty, ripe fruit. Palate: good structure, flavourful, powerful, fleshy, creamy.

IMPERIAL 2005 TR
tempranillo 85%, graciano 10%, mazuelo 5%

**89** Colour: deep cherry. Nose: ripe fruit, toasty, dark chocolate, spicy. Palate: fruity, powerful, flavourful, complex.

IMPERIAL 2004 TR
tempranillo 85%, graciano 10%, mazuelo 5%

**93** Colour: cherry, garnet rim. Nose: ripe fruit, spicy, creamy oak, toasty, complex, cocoa bean. Palate: powerful, flavourful, toasty, complex, fine tannins.

REAL DE ASÚA 2004 T
tempranillo 100%

**93** Colour: deep cherry. Nose: undergrowth, ripe fruit, fine reductive notes, tobacco. Palate: round, elegant, flavourful, complex, smoky aftertaste, toasty, round tannins.

IMPERIAL 2000 TGR
tempranillo 85%, graciano 10%, mazuelo 5%

**87** Colour: dark-red cherry, brick rim edge. Nose: old leather, cigar, fine reductive notes, waxy notes, complex, spicy. Palate: good acidity, round, elegant, powerful, complex, spicy.

## DIEZ-CABALLERO

Barrihuelo, 73
01340 Elciego (Alava)
☎: 944 807 295 - Fax: 944 630 938
diez-caballero@diez-caballero.es
www.diez-caballero.com

DÍEZ-CABALLERO 2008 BFB
viura 70%, malvasia 30%

**83**

DÍEZ-CABALLERO VICTORIA 2008 T
tempranillo 100%

**90** Colour: bright cherry, garnet rim. Nose: cocoa bean, dark chocolate, red berry notes, ripe fruit. Palate: flavourful, complex, spicy, round tannins.

DIEZ-CABALLERO TEMPRANILLO 2006 TC
tempranillo 100%

**88** Colour: bright cherry. Nose: sweet spices, creamy oak, lactic notes. Palate: flavourful, fruity, toasty, round tannins.

DÍEZ-CABALLERO 2004 TR
tempranillo 100%

**88** Colour: cherry, garnet rim. Nose: powerful, ripe fruit, dark chocolate, cocoa bean. Palate: flavourful, powerful, spicy, round tannins.

DÍEZ-CABALLERO VENDIMIA SELECCIONADA 2004 TR
tempranillo 100%

**87** Colour: cherry, garnet rim. Nose: fruit preserve, powerfull, warm, dark chocolate. Palate: flavourful, powerful, fleshy.

## DOMINIO DE BERZAL

Término Río Salado s/n
01307 Baños de Ebro (Alava)
☎: 945 623 368 - Fax: 945 623 368

info@dominioberzal.com
www.dominioberzal.com

**DOMINIO DE BERZAL 2008 B**
viura 97%, malvasia 3%

**88** Colour: bright straw. Nose: floral, varietal, fruit expression. Palate: rich, fruity, powerful, full, flavourful.

**DOMINIO DE BERZAL 2008 T**
tempranillo 90%, viura 10%

**86** Colour: light cherry, purple rim. Nose: fresh, fruit expression, balanced. Palate: easy to drink, round tannins.

**DOMINIO DE BERZAL 2006 TC**
tempranillo 95%, graciano 5%

**87** Colour: deep cherry, garnet rim. Nose: red berry notes, ripe fruit, expressive, varietal. Palate: flavourful, fruity, good acidity, spicy.

**DOMINIO DE BERZAL SELECCIÓN PRIVADA 2005 T**
tempranillo 100%

**88** Colour: deep cherry, garnet rim. Nose: cocoa bean, tobacco, dark chocolate, ripe fruit. Palate: fleshy, creamy, round tannins.

## EL COTO DE RIOJA

Camino Viejo de Logroño, 26
01320 Oyón (Alava)
☎: 945 622 216 - Fax: 945 622 315
cotorioja@elcoto.com
www.elcoto.com

**EL COTO 2008 B**
viura 100%

**84**

**EL COTO RD**
garnacha 80%, tempranillo 20%

**88** Colour: brilliant rose. Nose: fresh fruit, fruit expression. Palate: fruity, flavourful, fresh.

**EL COTO 2006 TC**
tempranillo 100%

**83**

**COTO MAYOR 2005 TC**
tempranillo 90%, graciano 10%

**88** Colour: cherry, garnet rim. Nose: candied fruit, spicy, dark chocolate, toasty. Palate: flavourful, spicy, round tannins.

**COTO REAL VINO DE AUTOR 2004 TR**
tempranillo 70%, garnacha 20%, graciano 10%

**88** Colour: cherry, garnet rim. Nose: fine reductive notes, cigar, caramel, spicy. Palate: flavourful, spicy, classic aged character.

**COTO DE IMAZ 2004 TR**
tempranillo 100%

**88** Colour: cherry, garnet rim. Nose: sweet spices, dark chocolate, fruit preserve. Palate: fleshy, spicy, fine bitter notes, good acidity.

**COTO DE IMAZ 2000 TGR**
tempranillo 100%

**90** Colour: pale ruby, brick rim edge. Nose: elegant, spicy, fine reductive notes, wet leather, aged wood nuances, fruit liqueur notes. Palate: spicy, fine tannins, elegant, long.

**COTO DE IMAZ ANIVERSARIO 2000 TR**
tempranillo 100%

**87** Colour: bright cherry, orangey edge. Nose: wet leather, tobacco, fruit liqueur notes. Palate: flavourful, spicy, classic aged character.

## EMPATÍA

Pza. Fermín Gurbindo, 2
26339 Abalos (La Rioja)
☎: 941 334 302 - Fax: 941 308 023
direccion@hotelvilladeabalos.com
www.hotelvilladeabalos.com

**EMPATÍA 2007 BFB**
viura, malvasia, garnacha blanca

**88** Colour: bright straw. Nose: fresh fruit, characterful, creamy oak, dried herbs. Palate: rich, fruity, good acidity, confected, spicy.

**EMPATÍA VENDIMIA SELECCIONADA 2006 T**

**89** Colour: cherry, garnet rim. Nose: powerful, ripe fruit, sweet spices, creamy oak, mineral. Palate: flavourful, fleshy, ripe fruit, spicy, round tannins.

**EMPATÍA 2006 T**
tempranillo, garnacha

**87** Colour: cherry, garnet rim. Nose: fruit preserve, fruit liqueur notes, warm, sweet spices. Palate: full, fruity, flavourful, sweet tannins, toasty.

## ESTRAUNZA

Avda. La Poveda, 25
01306 Lapuebla de Labarca (Álava)
☎: 945 627 245 - Fax: 945 627 293

v.medrano@euskalnet.net
www.bodegasestraunza.com

**BLAS DE LEZO 2008 T**
tempranillo 100%

**86** Colour: very deep cherry. Nose: varietal, fresh, expressive, fresh fruit. Palate: round tannins, flavourful, fruity.

**SOLAR DE ESTRAUNZA 2008 T**
tempranillo 100%

**85** Colour: deep cherry. Nose: fresh fruit, varietal, fresh. Palate: fruity, flavourful, round tannins.

**SOLAR DE ESTRAUNZA 2006 TC**
tempranillo 100%

**85** Colour: cherry, garnet rim. Nose: ripe fruit, creamy oak, spicy. Palate: spicy, round tannins, flavourful.

**BLAS DE LEZO 2006 TC**
tempranillo 100%

**83**

**SOLAR DE ESTRAUNZA VENDIMIA SELECCIONADA 2004 T**
tempranillo 100%

**86** Colour: cherry, garnet rim. Nose: ripe fruit, toasty, sweet spices. Palate: round tannins, flavourful, powerful, spicy.

**SOLAR DE ESTRAUNZA 2004 TR**
tempranillo 100%

**85** Colour: orangey edge, deep cherry. Nose: fruit preserve, spicy, toasty. Palate: powerful, flavourful, round tannins.

## FERNÁNDEZ DE PIÉROLA

Ctra. Logroño s/n Finca El Somo
01322 Moreda (Alava)
☎: 945 622 480 - Fax: 945 622 489
comercial@pierola.com
www.pierola.com

**FERNÁNDEZ DE PIÉROLA 2008 BFB**

**84**

**FERNÁNDEZ DE PIÉROLA 2005 TC**

**83**

**FERNÁNDEZ DE PIÉROLA 2003 TR**

**87** Colour: cherry, garnet rim. Nose: ripe fruit, spicy, creamy oak, toasty. Palate: powerful, flavourful, toasty, round tannins.

**VITIUM 2003 TR**

**87** Colour: cherry, garnet rim. Nose: toasty, smoky, ripe fruit. Palate: flavourful, fleshy, spirituous.

## FINCA ALLENDE

Pza. Ibarra, 1
26330 Briones (La Rioja)
☎: 941 322 301 - Fax: 941 322 302
info@finca-allende.com
www.finca-allende.com

**MARTIRES 2008 B**
viura 100%

**95** Colour: bright straw. Nose: powerful, ripe fruit, fresh fruit, fruit expression, sweet spices, creamy oak, mineral. Palate: flavourful, powerful, fleshy, complex, spicy.

**ALLENDE 2007 B**
viura 80%, malvasia 20%

**93** Colour: bright straw. Nose: powerful, fresh, ripe fruit, citrus fruit, candied fruit. Palate: flavourful, powerful, fleshy, fruity, long.

**CALVARIO 2007 T**
tempranillo 90%, garnacha 8%, graciano 2%

**94** Colour: deep cherry, garnet rim. Nose: powerful, fruit expression, ripe fruit, sweet spices, creamy oak, cocoa bean. Palate: flavourful, fleshy, spicy, toasty, elegant, soft tannins.

**ALLENDE 2007 T**
tempranillo 100%

**92** Colour: very deep cherry. Nose: powerful, creamy oak, roasted coffee, fresh fruit, red berry notes. Palate: powerful, fleshy, flavourful, good structure, slightly dry, soft tannins.

**CALVARIO 2006 T**
tempranillo 90%, garnacha 8%, graciano 2%

**94** Colour: cherry, garnet rim. Nose: powerful, earthy notes, balsamic herbs, toasty, new oak, dark chocolate, ripe fruit. Palate: flavourful, powerful, fleshy, spicy, balsamic.

**AVRVS 2006 T**
tempranillo 85%, graciano 15%

**93** Colour: deep cherry, garnet rim. Nose: ripe fruit, powerfull, damp earth, spicy, fruit liqueur notes. Palate: powerful, fleshy, spicy, full, toasty, slightly dry, soft tannins.

**ALLENDE 2006 T**
tempranillo 100%

**89** Colour: deep cherry. Nose: powerful, spicy, ripe fruit, toasty. Palate: spicy, warm, fine bitter notes, round tannins.

**AVRVS 2005 T**
tempranillo 85%, graciano 15%

**96** Colour: cherry, garnet rim. Nose: powerful, ripe fruit, sweet spices, cedar wood, mineral, balsamic herbs, creamy oak. Palate: flavourful, fleshy, complex, spicy, long, round tannins.

**ALLENDE 2005 T**
tempranillo 100%

**91** Colour: bright cherry. Nose: ripe fruit, sweet spices, creamy oak, elegant, complex, mineral. Palate: flavourful, fruity, round tannins, toasty.

## FINCA EGOMEI

Ctra. Corella s/n
26240 Alfaro (La Rioja)
☎: 941 741 003 - Fax: 941 741 003
info@egomei.es
www.egomei.es

**EGOMEI 2006 T**
tempranillo 85%, graciano 15%

**90** Colour: cherry, garnet rim. Nose: ripe fruit, toasty, dark chocolate. Palate: flavourful, fleshy, spicy, round tannins.

**EGOMEI ALMA 2005 T**
tempranillo 75%, graciano 15%

**93** Colour: deep cherry, garnet rim. Nose: powerful, characterful, ripe fruit, dark chocolate, toasty. Palate: flavourful, fleshy, spicy, fine bitter notes, round tannins.

## FINCA NUEVA

Calle Las Eras, 14
26330 Briones (La Rioja)
fincanuevabriones@gmail.com

**FINCA NUEVA 2008 BFB**
viura 100%

**89** Colour: bright straw. Nose: powerful, ripe fruit, citrus fruit, floral, sweet spices. Palate: flavourful, fruity, fresh, fleshy.

**FINCA NUEVA 2008 B**
viura 100%

**88** Colour: pale. Nose: medium intensity, expressive, white flowers, fresh fruit, citrus fruit. Palate: flavourful, fruity, fresh.

**FINCA NUEVA 2008 RD**
garnacha 50%, tempranillo 50%

**89** Colour: rose, purple rim. Nose: red berry notes, fresh fruit, floral. Palate: flavourful, fleshy, fruity, sweetness, fine bitter notes.

**FINCA NUEVA 2008 T**
tempranillo 100%

**90** Colour: black cherry, purple rim. Nose: powerful, ripe fruit, warm. Palate: flavourful, fleshy, ripe fruit, good acidity.

**FINCA NUEVA 2006 TC**
tempranillo 100%

**88** Colour: cherry, garnet rim. Nose: ripe fruit, powerfull, honeyed notes. Palate: flavourful, fleshy, sweetness, round tannins.

**FINCA NUEVA 2004 TR**
tempranillo 100%

**90** Colour: cherry, garnet rim. Nose: balanced, expressive, ripe fruit, sweet spices, cocoa bean. Palate: flavourful, fleshy, long, round tannins.

## FINCA VALPIEDRA S.L.

Término El Montecillo, s/n
26360 Fuenmayor (La Rioja)
☎: 941 450 876 - Fax: 941 450 875
info@bujanda.com
www.familiamartinezbujanda.com

**FINCA VALPIEDRA 2006 TR**
tempranillo 100%

**90** Colour: dark-red cherry. Nose: powerful, spicy, toasty, new oak, ripe fruit. Palate: flavourful, powerful, fleshy, round tannins.

**CANTOS DE VALPIEDRA 2006 T**
tempranillo 94%, experimental 3%, graciano 3%

**90** Colour: bright cherry. Nose: ripe fruit, sweet spices, creamy oak, expressive. Palate: flavourful, fruity, toasty, round tannins.

**FINCA VALPIEDRA 2005 TR**

**90** Colour: deep cherry, garnet rim. Nose: cocoa bean, dark chocolate, ripe fruit, sweet spices, mineral. Palate: good structure, powerful, flavourful.

## FLORENTINO DE LECANDA

Cuevas, 36
26200 Haro (La Rioja)
☎: 941 303 477 - Fax: 941 312 707
florentinodelecanda@fer.es
www.bodegaslecanda.com

FLORENTINO DE LECANDA 2006 TC
tempranillo 85%, garnacha 15%

**83**

FLORENTINO DE LECANDA 2001 TR
tempranillo 85%, garnacha 15%

**87** Colour: pale ruby, brick rim edge. Nose: fine reductive notes, old leather, tobacco, caramel, macerated fruit. Palate: elegant, easy to drink, spicy.

CASUNE

## FLORENTINO MARTÍNEZ C.B.

Ermita, 33
26311 Cordovín (La Rioja)
☎: 941 418 614 - Fax: 941 418 614
bod.florentino@teleline.es
www.florentinomartinez.com

FLORENTINO MARTÍNEZ 2008 B
viura 85%, malvasia 15%

**83**

FLORENTIUS 2008 B

**80**

FLORENTINO MARTÍNEZ 2008 T
tempranillo 100%

**74**

FLORENTINO MARTÍNEZ 2005 TC
tempranillo 100%

**84**

TANKA 2004 T
tempranillo 100%

**90** Colour: cherry, garnet rim. Nose: powerful, mineral, ripe fruit, varietal. Palate: flavourful, powerful, fleshy, complex, long, toasty.

FLORENTINO MARTÍNEZ VENDIMIA SELECCIONADA 2001 TR
tempranillo 100%

**85** Colour: cherry, garnet rim. Nose: warm, fruit liqueur notes, spicy, creamy oak. Palate: balanced, aged character, round tannins, great length.

FLORENTINO MARTÍNEZ 2008 CLARETE
garnacha 80%, viura 20%

**82**

## FRANCO ESPAÑOLAS

Cabo Noval, 2
26009 Logroño (La Rioja)
☎: 941 251 300 - Fax: 941 262 948
francoespanolas@francoespanolas.com
www.paternina.com

BARBARO 2005 T

**87** Colour: cherry, garnet rim. Nose: medium intensity, fruit liqueur notes, spicy, aromatic coffee, caramel. Palate: flavourful, spicy, round tannins.

RIOJA BORDÓN 2005 TC

**84**

BARON D'ANGLADE 2004 TR

**91** Colour: cherry, garnet rim. Nose: powerful, ripe fruit, spicy, toasty, aromatic coffee. Palate: flavourful, spicy, round tannins.

RIOJA BORDÓN 2004 TR

**86** Colour: deep cherry, orangey edge. Nose: spicy, fruit liqueur notes, toasty, caramel. Palate: spicy, classic aged character, fine bitter notes.

RIOJA BORDÓN 2001 TGR

**87** Colour: pale ruby, brick rim edge. Nose: elegant, fruit liqueur notes, spicy, toasty, aromatic coffee, tobacco. Palate: spicy, classic aged character, fine bitter notes.

RINSOL
DIAMANTE
VIÑA SOLEDAD
ROYAL
EXCELSO

## GAILUR

Avda. Puente del Ebro, 76
01307 Baños del Ebro (Alava)
☎: 945 609 158 - Fax: 943 835 952
bodegasgailur@euskalnet.net
www.bodegasgailur.com

SOLAR GAILUR 2008 B
viura 100%

## 82

SOLAR GAILUR 2008 T
tempranillo 100%

## 79

ARDANDEGI 2006 TC
tempranillo 100%

**87** Colour: cherry, garnet rim. Nose: ripe fruit, creamy oak, spicy. Palate: balanced, flavourful, fruity, round tannins.

GAILUR 2006 TC
tempranillo 100%

**86** Colour: cherry, garnet rim. Nose: ripe fruit, creamy oak, spicy. Palate: balanced, warm, round tannins.

SEÑORÍO DE LAURGAIN

## GIL BERZAL

Ctra. Elvillar, 2
01300 Laguardia (Alava)
☎: 945 600 735 - Fax: 945 600 735
gilberzal@telefonica.net
www.recoveco.es

RECOVECO 2008 T
tempranillo 90%, viura 10%

## 84

RECOVECO VENDIMIA SELECCIONADA 2004 TC

**85** Colour: cherry, garnet rim. Nose: ripe fruit, spicy, toasty. Palate: round tannins, fruity, flavourful.

RECOVECO COLECCIÓN PRIVADA 2003 TC
tempranillo 90%, graciano 10%

## 84

## GRANJA NUESTRA SEÑORA DE REMELLURI

Ctra. Rivas, s/n
01330 Labastida (Alava)
☎: 943 631 710 - Fax: 943 630 874
info@remelluri.com
www.remelluri.com

REMELLURI 2007 B
moscatel, garnacha blanca, sauvignon blanc, viognier, chardonnay, rousanne

**93** Colour: bright straw. Nose: powerful, ripe fruit, elegant, floral, citrus fruit, sweet spices. Palate: flavourful, fleshy, fruity, rich.

REMELLURI 2005 TR
tempranillo, graciano, garnacha

**94** Colour: very deep cherry. Nose: elegant, complex, ripe fruit, cocoa bean, creamy oak, undergrowth, mineral. Palate: complex, rich, full, powerful, fruity aftestaste, spicy, fine tannins.

REMELLURI COLECCIÓN JAIME RODRÍGUEZ 2004 T
tempranillo

**92** Colour: deep cherry, orangey edge. Nose: powerful, complex, candied fruit, fine reductive notes, dark chocolate, aromatic coffee, creamy oak. Palate: powerful, flavourful, fruity, sweetness, spicy, round tannins.

LA GRANJA REMELLURI 1999 TGR
tempranillo, graciano, garnacha

**88** Nose: old leather, tobacco, spicy, cedar wood, dark chocolate, fruit preserve. Palate: unctuous, elegant, flavourful, powerful, rich, smoky aftertaste, soft tannins.

## GRUPO ALGAR

Carpinteros, 13
28670 Villaviciosa de Odón (Madrid)
☎: 916 169 122 - Fax: 916 166 724
info@grupoalgar.com
www.grupoalgar.com

SEÑORÍO DE GARDI 2005 TC
tempranillo 80%, garnacha 20%

**85** Colour: bright cherry, orangey edge. Nose: cocoa bean, dark chocolate, creamy oak, ripe fruit. Palate: flavourful, spicy, ripe fruit, round tannins.

SEÑORÍO DE GARDI 2001 TR
tempranillo 80%, garnacha 20%

## 83

## GRUPO YLLERA

Ctra. Madrid - Coruña, km. 173, 5
47490 Rueda (Valladolid)
☎: 983 868 097 - Fax: 983 868 177
grupoyllera@grupoyllera.com
www.grupoyllera.com

COELUS JOVEN 2008 T

**87** Colour: cherry, purple rim. Nose: floral, macerated fruit, spicy. Palate: flavourful, fruity, good acidity, round tannins.

**COELUS 2005 TC**
tempranillo

**85** Colour: deep cherry, orangey edge. Nose: ripe fruit, sweet spices, cocoa bean, balanced. Palate: fruity, sweetness, flavourful, spicy, round tannins.

**COELUS 2003 TR**
tempranillo

**83**

## HACIENDA MARQUÉS DE LA CONCORDIA

Ctra. El Ciego, s/n
26350 Cenicero (La Rioja)
☎: 914 365 900 - Fax: 914 365 932
info@haciendas-espana.com
www.haciendas-espana.com

**HACIENDA SUSAR 2005 T**
tempranillo 50%, merlot 20%, cabernet sauvignon 20%, syrah 10%

**91** Colour: bright cherry, cherry, garnet rim. Nose: expressive, elegant, earthy notes, ripe fruit. Palate: fleshy, fruity, fine bitter notes, creamy.

**MARQUÉS DE LA CONCORDIA 2005 TC**
tempranillo 100%

**88** Colour: cherry, garnet rim. Nose: expressive, powerfull, ripe fruit, spicy, toasty. Palate: balanced, flavourful, round tannins, fruity aftestaste.

**MARQUÉS DE LA CONCORDIA 2004 TR**
tempranillo 100%

**90** Colour: cherry, garnet rim. Nose: medium intensity, elegant, ripe fruit, sweet spices, creamy oak. Palate: fruity, flavourful, fruity aftertaste, round tannins.

## HACIENDA URBIÓN

Santiago Aldaz, s/n
26120 Albelda de Iregua (Rioja)
☎: 941 444 233 - Fax: 941 444 427
info@vinicolareal.com

**URBION 2005 TC**
tempranillo 100%

**87** Colour: cherry, garnet rim. Nose: ripe fruit, sweet spices, creamy oak. Palate: round tannins, ripe fruit, spicy, flavourful.

## HEREDAD DE BAROJA S.L.

Cercas Altas, 6

01309 Elvillar (Alava)
☎: 945 604 068 - Fax: 945 604 105
info@heredadbaroja.com
www.heredadbaroja.com

**CAUTIVO VARIETAL TEMPRANILLO 2008 T**
tempranillo 100%

**88** Colour: cherry, purple rim. Nose: ripe fruit, mineral, spicy. Palate: good structure, flavourful, fruity, good acidity, fresh.

**CAUTIVO 2005 TC**

**86** Colour: cherry, garnet rim. Nose: fruit preserve, creamy oak, sweet spices. Palate: flavourful, spicy, good acidity.

**CAUTIVO 2004 TR**
tempranillo 100%

**88** Colour: cherry, garnet rim. Nose: ripe fruit, spicy. Palate: powerful, flavourful, spicy, balanced, round tannins.

**CAUTIVO 2001 TGR**
tempranillo 100%

**88** Colour: pale ruby, brick rim edge. Nose: fruit preserve, fine reductive notes, cocoa bean, cedar wood. Palate: elegant, classic aged character, fine tannins, balanced.

RINCÓN DE BAROJA
GRAN BAROJA
CAUTUM

## HEREDAD GUZMÁN ALDAZÁBAL

Madrid, 10
01309 Navaridas (Álava)
☎: 945 605 172 - Fax: 945 605 172
guzmanaldazabal@euskalnet.net

**GUZMÁN ALDAZÁBAL GRACIANO 2007 T**
graciano 100%

**88** Colour: cherry, purple rim. Nose: ripe fruit, scrubland, balsamic herbs, sweet spices. Palate: flavourful, fruity, good acidity.

**GUZMÁN ALDAZÁBAL 2006 T**
tempranillo 100%

**83**

## HEREDAD UGARTE

Ctra. A-124 - Paganos
01309 Laguardia (Álava)

☎: 945 282 844 - Fax: 945 271 319
info@heredadugarte.com
www.herredadugarte.com

**DOMINIO DE UGARTE 2005 TR**
tempranillo 95%, graciano 5%

**87** Colour: cherry, garnet rim. Nose: medium intensity, fruit preserve, spicy, creamy oak. Palate: round tannins, flavourful, easy to drink.

**MARTÍN CENDOYA 2005 TR**
tempranillo 80%, graciano 5%, mazuelo 5%

**87** Colour: cherry, garnet rim. Nose: ripe fruit, aged wood nuances, spicy. Palate: easy to drink, spicy, round tannins, balanced.

**HEREDAD UGARTE 2006 TC**
tempranillo 92%, garnacha 8%

**87** Colour: cherry, garnet rim. Nose: ripe fruit, spicy, creamy oak. Palate: round tannins, fruity, flavourful, easy to drink.

**ANASTASIO 2005 T**
tempranillo

**89** Colour: dark-red cherry. Nose: powerful, spicy, aged wood nuances, ripe fruit. Palate: powerful, flavourful, harsh oak tannins, toasty, fine bitter notes.

**TÉRMINO DE UGARTE**
**UGARTE**
**CEDULA REAL**

## HERMANOS FERNÁNDEZ

Pza. Nueva, 3
01309 Laserna - Laguardiaa (Alava)
☎: 945 621 103 - Fax: 945 621 103

**CASTILLO LA SERNA 2008 B**

**82**

**CASTILLO LA SERNA VENDIMIA SELECCIONADA 2008 T**

**89** Colour: cherry, purple rim. Nose: powerful, ripe fruit, red berry notes. Palate: flavourful, fruity, fleshy, round tannins.

**CASTILLO LA SERNA 2006 T**

**83**

## HERMANOS FRÍAS DEL VAL

Herrerías, 13
01307 Villabuena (Álava)
☎: 945 609 172 - Fax: 945 609 172
friasdelval@euskalnet.net

**HERMANOS FRÍAS DEL VAL 2008 BFB**
viura 100%

**88** Colour: bright golden. Nose: fruit expression, ripe fruit, pattiserie, smoky. Palate: elegant, flavourful, fruity, full.

**HERMANOS FRÍAS DEL VAL 2008 B**
viura 100%

**80**

**DON PEDUZ SELECCIÓN 2008 T**
tempranillo 100%

**86** Colour: cherry, garnet rim. Nose: fresh fruit, red berry notes. Palate: fleshy, warm, flavourful.

**HERMANOS FRÍAS DEL VAL 2008 T**
tempranillo 85%

**83**

**HERMANOS FRÍAS DEL VAL ALTA EXPRESIÓN 2006 T**
tempranillo 100%

**88** Colour: cherry, garnet rim. Nose: sweet spices, toasty, ripe fruit. Palate: round tannins, spicy, flavourful, powerful.

**HERMANOS FRÍAS DEL VAL 2006 TC**
tempranillo 100%

**84**

## HERMANOS LAREDO VILLANUEVA C.B.

Mayor, 18
01309 Leza (Alava)
☎: 945 605 018 - Fax: 945 605 178
bodegaslaredo@telefonica.net
www.bodegaslaredo.com

**LAREDO ANAIAK 2008 B**
viura 80%, malvasia 20%

**78**

**SEÑORÍO DE LAREDO 2003 B RESERVA**
viura 50%, malvasia 50%

**83**

**LAREDO ANAIAK 2008 RD**
garnacha 50%, tempranillo 50%

**85** Colour: brilliant rose. Nose: fruit expression, fresh fruit, raspberry. Palate: fresh, fruity, flavourful.

**LAREDO ANAIAK 2008 T**
tempranillo 95%, others 5%

**84**

**SEÑORÍO DE LAREDO 2004 TC**
tempranillo 90%, graciano 5%, garnacha 5%

**82**

**SEÑORÍO DE LAREDO 1999 TR**
tempranillo 80%, graciano 10%, graciano 10%

**83**

## JOSE MARÍA SÁENZ COSECHEROS Y CRIADORES

Ctra. LR-123, km.61
26511 El Villar de Arnedo (La Rioja)

☎: 941 159 034 - Fax: 941 159 034
bodegajmsaenz@hotmail.com

**PRESAGIO 2008 T**
tempranillo 70%, garnacha 30%

**87** Colour: very deep cherry. Nose: fresh fruit, red berry notes, stalky. Palate: flavourful, fruity, fresh, powerful.

**PRESAGIO VENDIMIA SELECCIONADA 2007 T**
tempranillo 90%, graciano 10%

**87** Colour: cherry, garnet rim. Nose: powerful, ripe fruit, spicy, creamy oak. Palate: fruity, powerful, flavourful, round tannins.

**PRESAGIO 2006 TC**
tempranillo 80%, graciano 15%, mazuelo 5%

**84**

## JUAN ALCORTA

Camino de la Puebla, 50
26006 Logroño (La Rioja)
☎: 941 279 900 - Fax: 941 279 901
juanalcorta@domecqbodegas.com
www.allieddomecqbodegas.com

**DOMINIO CAMPO VIEJO 2006 T**

**91** Colour: cherry, garnet rim. Nose: powerful, ripe fruit, dark chocolate, sweet spices. Palate: flavourful, fleshy, complex, spicy, ripe fruit.

**AZPILICUETA 2006 TC**
tempranillo, graciano, mazuelo

**90** Colour: bright cherry. Nose: ripe fruit, sweet spices, creamy oak, expressive. Palate: flavourful, fruity, toasty, round tannins.

**ALCORTA 2006 TC**
tempranillo

**87** Colour: cherry, garnet rim. Nose: powerful, ripe fruit, spicy, toasty. Palate: flavourful, fleshy, ripe fruit, round tannins.

**AZPILICUETA 2005 TR**
tempranillo, mazuelo, graciano

**89** Colour: cherry, garnet rim. Nose: powerful, ripe fruit, sweet spices, toasty. Palate: flavourful, powerful, fleshy, round tannins.

**CAMPO VIEJO 2006 TC**
tempranillo, garnacha, mazuelo

**87** Colour: cherry, garnet rim. Nose: ripe fruit, sweet spices, toasty. Palate: ripe fruit, round tannins.

**CAMPO VIEJO 2005 TR**
tempranillo, graciano, mazuelo

**87** Colour: cherry, garnet rim. Nose: cigar, wet leather, fruit liqueur notes. Palate: flavourful, spicy, ripe fruit.

**ALCORTA 2005 TR**
tempranillo

**87** Colour: cherry, garnet rim. Nose: powerful, ripe fruit, sweet spices, toasty. Palate: flavourful, powerful, fleshy, round tannins.

**MARQUÉS DE VILLAMAGNA 2004 TGR**
tempranillo, graciano, mazuelo

**91** Colour: very deep cherry. Nose: spicy, sweet spices, ripe fruit. Palate: flavourful, rich, fleshy, complex.

**AZPILICUETA 2004 TR**
tempranillo 85%, mazuelo 10%, graciano 5%

**90** Colour: deep cherry. Nose: expressive, elegant, ripe fruit, spicy, sweet spices. Palate: flavourful, fleshy, spicy, round tannins.

**CAMPO VIEJO 2002 TGR**
tempranillo, graciano, mazuelo

**90** Colour: cherry, garnet rim. Nose: powerful, ripe fruit, sweet spices, toasty. Palate: flavourful, powerful, fine bitter notes.

**CAMPO VIEJO SEMIDULCE**

**78**

## LA COLECCIÓN D.C.E., S.L.

Domingo Martínez, 6
47007 (Valladolid)
☎: 983 271 595 - Fax: 983 271 608
exportacion@lacolecciondevinos.com
www.lacolecciondevinos.com

**ALDERAN 2004 TC**
tempranillo 100%

**84**

## LA ENCINA BODEGAS Y VIÑEDOS

Ctra. N 124, km. 45
26290 Briñas (La Rioja)
☎: 941 305 630 - Fax: 941 313 028
laencinabodegas@tobelos.com
www.tobelos.com

**TOBELOS 2008 BFB**
viura 80%, garnacha blanca 20%

**88** Colour: bright golden, bright straw. Nose: ripe fruit, smoky, pattiserie. Palate: creamy, flavourful, rich, full.

**TAHÓN DE TOBELOS 2005 TR**
tempranillo 100%

**91** Colour: bright cherry. Nose: ripe fruit, sweet spices, creamy oak, expressive, mineral. Palate: flavourful, fruity, toasty, round tannins.

**TOBELOS 2005 TC**
tempranillo 100%

**88** Colour: cherry, garnet rim. Nose: powerful, ripe fruit, red berry notes, sweet spices. Palate: flavourful, ripe fruit, spicy.

LEUKADE

## LA RIOJA ALTA

Avda. Vizcaya, 8
26200 Haro (La Rioja)
☎: 941 310 346 - Fax: 941 312 854
riojalta@riojalta.com
www.riojalta.com

VIÑA ARANA 2004 TR
tempranillo 95%, mazuelo 5%

**92** Colour: bright cherry, orangey edge. Nose: elegant, expressive, spicy, aromatic coffee, fruit liqueur notes. Palate: flavourful, complex, spicy, classic aged character.

VIÑA ALBERDI 2003 TC
tempranillo 100%

**89** Colour: cherry, garnet rim. Nose: expressive, ripe fruit, spicy, aromatic coffee. Palate: flavourful, fresh, spicy, long.

VIÑA ARDANZA 2001 TR
tempranillo 90%, garnacha 10%

**93** Colour: bright cherry, orangey edge. Nose: elegant, complex, fruit liqueur notes, aromatic coffee, cigar, fine reductive notes. Palate: flavourful, spicy, fine bitter notes, round tannins.

GRAN RESERVA 904 RIOJA ALTA 1997 TGR
tempranillo 90%, graciano 10%

**94** Colour: pale ruby, brick rim edge. Nose: elegant, fine reductive notes, wet leather, aged wood nuances, fruit liqueur notes, characterful, fruit liqueur notes, sweet spices. Palate: spicy, fine tannins, elegant, long.

LA RIOJA ALTA GRAN RESERVA 890 1995 TGR
tempranillo 96%, graciano 3%, mazuelo 1%

**89** Colour: pale ruby, brick rim edge. Nose: elegant, spicy, fine reductive notes, wet leather, aged wood nuances, fruit liqueur notes. Palate: spicy, fine tannins, elegant, long.

## LAN

Paraje del Buicio, s/n
26360 Fuenmayor (La Rioja)
☎: 941 450 950 - Fax: 941 450 567
info@bodegaslan.com
www.bodegaslan.com

LAN EDICIÓN LIMITADA 2006 T

**92** Colour: very deep cherry, garnet rim. Nose: spicy, scrubland, fruit preserve. Palate: fleshy, complex, spicy.

CULMEN 2005 TR

**94** Colour: cherry, garnet rim. Nose: ripe fruit, spicy, creamy oak, toasty, complex, earthy notes. Palate: powerful, flavourful, toasty, round tannins.

LAN 2005 TC

**85** Colour: cherry, garnet rim. Nose: wet leather, toasty, sweet spices, aged wood nuances. Palate: flavourful, spicy, round tannins.

LAN 2004 TR

**85** Colour: cherry, garnet rim. Nose: powerful, ripe fruit, sweet spices, toasty. Palate: flavourful, fleshy, spicy, round tannins.

**VIÑA LANCIANO 2004 TR**

**88** Colour: cherry, garnet rim. Nose: powerful, toasty, cedar wood. Palate: spicy, ripe fruit, round tannins.

**LAN TGR**

**88** Colour: cherry, garnet rim. Nose: ripe fruit, sweet spices. Palate: fleshy, complex, good structure, spicy, round tannins.

## LAVALLE

Mayor, 51
01309 Navaridas (Alava)
☎: 945 605 032 - Fax: 945 605 032

**LAVALLE 2008 T**
tempranillo 92%, others 8%

**86** Colour: very deep cherry. Nose: red berry notes, maceration notes, fresh fruit. Palate: fruity, flavourful, good acidity.

## LEZA GARCÍA

San Ignacio, 26
26313 Uruñuela (La Rioja)
☎: 941 371 142 - Fax: 941 371 035
bodegasleza@bodegasleza.com
www.bodegasleza.com

**LG DE LEZA GARCÍA 2006 T**
tempranillo 100%

**83**

**LEZA GARCÍA 2005 T**
tempranillo 100%

**87** Colour: cherry, garnet rim. Nose: dark chocolate, aged wood nuances, toasty. Palate: flavourful, spicy, ripe fruit, round tannins.

**VALDEPALACIOS 2005 TC**
tempranillo 90%, garnacha 10%

**85** Colour: cherry, garnet rim. Nose: ripe fruit, sweet spices, aged wood nuances. Palate: round tannins, spicy, easy to drink, flavourful.

**VALDEPALACIOS VENDIMIA SELECCIONADA 2005 T**
tempranillo 95%, garnacha 5%

**84**

**BARÓN DE VILLACAMPA 2004 T**
tempranillo 90%, garnacha 10%

**87** Colour: cherry, garnet rim. Nose: fruit preserve, creamy oak, toasty, spicy. Palate: sweetness, round tannins, easy to drink, classic aged character.

**BARÓN DE VILLACAMPA 2001 TR**
tempranillo 90%, garnacha 10%

**88** Colour: cherry, garnet rim. Nose: sweet spices, toasty. Palate: spicy, ripe fruit, classic aged character.

**LEZA GARCÍA 2001 TR**
tempranillo 90%, garnacha 10%

**87** Colour: cherry, garnet rim. Nose: powerful, fruit liqueur notes, wet leather, spicy. Palate: flavourful, spicy, ripe fruit.

## LONG WINES

Avda. del Monte, 46
28120 Algete (Madrid)
☎: 916 221 305 - Fax: 916 220 029
william@william-long.com
www.longwines.com

**FINCA AMALIA TEMPRANILLO 2007 T**
tempranillo 100%

**86** Colour: cherry, garnet rim. Nose: powerful, ripe fruit, red berry notes, sweet spices. Palate: flavourful, powerful, fleshy.

**FINCA AMALIA 2006 TC**

**87** Colour: bright cherry, orangey edge. Nose: powerful, ripe fruit, spicy, toasty. Palate: flavourful, spicy, round tannins.

**FINCA AMALIA 2004 TR**

**86** Colour: cherry, garnet rim. Nose: powerful, ripe fruit, spicy, toasty. Palate: flavourful, spicy, round tannins.

## LUBERRI MONJE AMESTOY

Camino de Rehoyos, s/n
01340 Elciego (Alava)
☎: 945 606 010 - Fax: 945 606 482
luberri@luberri.com

**LUBERRI 2008 T**
tempranillo 95%, viura 5%

**87** Colour: cherry, purple rim. Nose: expressive, fresh fruit, red berry notes, floral. Palate: flavourful, fruity, good acidity, round tannins.

**SEIS DE LUBERRI 2007 T**
tempranillo 100%

**86** Colour: cherry, purple rim. Nose: toasty, smoky, stalky. Palate: flavourful, spicy, good acidity.

**BIGA 2006 TC**
tempranillo 100%

**87** Colour: cherry, garnet rim. Nose: medium intensity, ripe fruit, spicy, toasty. Palate: ripe fruit, spicy, round tannins.

**LUBERRI CEPAS VIEJAS 2005 TC**
tempranillo 100%

**90** Colour: bright cherry. Nose: ripe fruit, sweet spices, creamy oak, powerfull. Palate: flavourful, fruity, toasty, round tannins.

**MONJE AMESTOY 2005 T**
tempranillo 95%, cabernet sauvignon 5%

**87** Colour: cherry, garnet rim. Nose: powerful, fruit preserve, fruit liqueur notes, toasty, sweet spices. Palate: fleshy, flavourful, spicy, round tannins.

## MARQUÉS CAMPO NUBLE

Avda. del Ebro, s/n
26540 Alfaro (La Rioja)
☎: 941 183 502 - Fax: 941 183 157
camponuble@camponuble.com
www.camponuble.com

**CAMPO BURGO 2008 B**
viura 100%

**83**

**CAMPO BURGO 2008 RD**
garnacha 100%

**86** Colour: brilliant rose. Nose: candied fruit, spicy, expressive. Palate: fruity, fresh, flavourful.

**CAMPO BURGO 2008 T**
tempranillo 90%, garnacha 10%

**87** Colour: cherry, garnet rim. Nose: red berry notes, fresh, varietal. Palate: easy to drink, fruity, fresh, fine bitter notes, flavourful.

**CAMPO BURGO 2006 TC**
tempranillo 100%

**83**

**MARQUÉS DE CAMPO NUBLE 2005 TC**

**81**

**MARQUÉS DE CAMPO NUBLE 2004 TR**

**85** Colour: pale ruby, brick rim edge. Nose: toasty, fruit preserve, powerfull. Palate: classic aged character, creamy, round tannins, flavourful.

**CAMPO BURGO 2004 TR**
tempranillo 100%

**83**

**CONDE DE ROMANONES 2003 TR**
tempranillo 100%

**89** Colour: pale ruby, brick rim edge. Nose: medium intensity, spicy, ripe fruit. Palate: round tannins, spicy, rich, classic aged character.

## MARQUÉS DE CÁCERES

Ctra. Logroño, s/n
26350 Cenicero (La Rioja)
☎: 941 454 000 - Fax: 941 454 400
marquesdecaceres@fer.es
www.marquesdecaceres.com

**MARQUÉS DE CÁCERES 2008 B**
viura 100%

**86** Colour: pale. Nose: floral, ripe fruit, grassy, medium intensity. Palate: flavourful, fruity, fresh.

**MARQUÉS DE CÁCERES ANTEA 2008 BFB**
viura 93%, malvasia 7%

**86** Colour: bright straw. Nose: medium intensity, fruit expression, grassy. Palate: flavourful, fruity, good acidity.

**SATINELA SEMI-DULCE 2008 B**
viura 95%, malvasia 5%

**85** Colour: straw. Nose: candied fruit, grassy. Palate: flavourful, powerful, fruity.

**MARQUÉS DE CÁCERES 2008 RD**
tempranillo 80%, garnacha 20%

**87** Colour: rose, purple rim. Nose: ripe fruit, varietal. Palate: powerful, flavourful, fruity, sweetness, ripe fruit.

**MC MARQUÉS DE CÁCERES 2006 T**
tempranillo 100%

**93** Colour: very deep cherry. Nose: roasted coffee, creamy oak, undergrowth, truffle notes, ripe fruit. Palate: fleshy, complex, powerful, flavourful.

**MARQUÉS DE CÁCERES 2006 TC**
tempranillo 85%, garnacha 10%, graciano 5%

**88** Colour: dark-red cherry. Nose: smoky, ripe fruit, balanced, cocoa bean, creamy oak. Palate: fruity, powerful, flavourful, toasty, smoky aftertaste.

**GAUDIUM GRAN VINO 2004 TR**
tempranillo 95%, graciano 5%

**94** Colour: deep cherry. Nose: sweet spices, cocoa bean, ripe fruit, spicy. Palate: fruity, complex, powerful, flavourful, soft tannins.

**MARQUÉS DE CÁCERES 2004 TR**
tempranillo 85%, garnacha 10%, graciano 5%

**93** Colour: dark-red cherry. Nose: complex, expressive, cocoa bean, toasty, elegant. Palate: complex, flavourful, elegant, round, soft tannins.

**MARQUÉS DE CÁCERES 2001 TGR**
tempranillo 85%, garnacha 10%, graciano 5%

**92** Colour: dark-red cherry, brick rim edge. Nose: complex, fine reductive notes, tobacco, elegant, spicy. Palate: elegant, round, complex, flavourful, rich, fine tannins.

## MARQUÉS DE MURRIETA

Finca Ygay, Ctra. Logroño-Zaragoza, km. 5
26006 Logroño (La Rioja)
☎: 941 271 370 - Fax: 941 251 606
rrpp@marquesdemurrieta.com
www.marquesdemurrieta.com

DALMAU 2005 TR

**96** Colour: cherry, garnet rim. Nose: spicy, creamy oak, toasty, complex, damp earth. Palate: powerful, flavourful, toasty, round tannins.

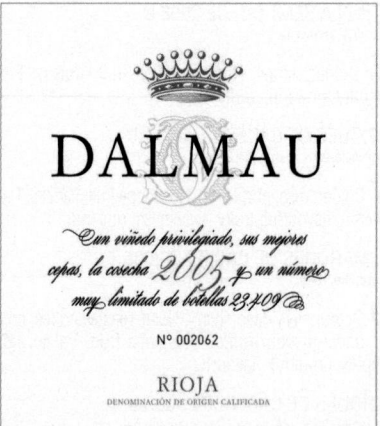

CAPELLANIA 2005 B
viura

**94** Colour: bright golden. Nose: expressive, wild herbs, ripe fruit, sweet spices, smoky. Palate: flavourful, fleshy, ripe fruit, fine bitter notes.

CAPELLANIA 2004 B
viura

**94** Colour: bright golden. Nose: expressive, powerfull, ripe fruit, creamy oak, toasty, sweet spices, fragrant herbs. Palate: flavourful, fleshy, ripe fruit, great length.

DALMAU 2004 TR

**95** Colour: cherry, garnet rim. Nose: expressive, ripe fruit, sweet spices. Palate: flavourful, powerful, spicy, ripe fruit, round tannins.

MARQUÉS DE MURRIETA 2004 TR

**92** Colour: cherry, garnet rim. Nose: complex, elegant, ripe fruit, toasty, spicy. Palate: flavourful, spicy, soft tannins.

MARQUÉS DE MURRIETA 2005 TR

**91** Colour: cherry, garnet rim. Nose: elegant, expressive, ripe fruit, toasty, aromatic coffee. Palate: flavourful, spicy, ripe fruit, round tannins.

CASTILLO YGAY 2001 TGR
tempranillo, mazuelo

**97** Colour: pale ruby, brick rim edge. Nose: elegant, spicy, fine reductive notes, wet leather, fruit liqueur notes, cigar. Palate: spicy, fine tannins, elegant, long.

CASTILLO YGAY 2000 TGR

**95** Colour: pale ruby, brick rim edge. Nose: expressive, waxy notes, wet leather, fruit preserve, dry nuts. Palate: flavourful, spicy, ripe fruit, soft tannins.

## MARQUÉS DE REINOSA

Ctra. Rincón de Soto, s/n
26560 Autol (La Rioja)
☎: 941 401 327 - Fax: 941 390 065
bodegas@marquesdereinosa.com
www.marquesdereinosa.com

MARQUÉS DE REINOSA 2008 RD

**84**

MARQUÉS DE REINOSA TEMPRANILLO 2008 T
tempranillo 100%

**87** Colour: deep cherry. Nose: varietal, fresh fruit, expressive, fresh. Palate: round tannins, fruity, powerful.

MARQUÉS DE REINOSA 2006 TC
tempranillo 100%

**85** Colour: cherry, garnet rim. Nose: macerated fruit, spicy, sweet spices, powerfull. Palate: round tannins, flavourful, spicy.

VIÑESTRAL 2006 TC
tempranillo 85%, garnacha 10%, mazuelo 5%

**84**

MARQUÉS DE REINOSA 2004 TR
tempranillo 95%, mazuelo 5%

**85** Colour: cherry, garnet rim. Nose: fruit preserve, creamy oak, sweet spices. Palate: flavourful, classic aged character, long, round tannins.

## MARQUÉS DE TOMARES, UNIÓN DE VITICULTORES RIOJANOS

Ctra. de Cenicero, s/n. Apdo. Correo, 3
26360 Fuenmayor (La Rioja)
☎: 941 451 129 - Fax: 941 450 297
info@marquesdetomares.com
www.marquesdetomares.es

MARQUÉS DE TOMARES DOÑA CARMEN 2002 TR
tempranillo 90%, graciano 10%

**89** Colour: pale ruby, brick rim edge. Nose: medium intensity, toasty, warm, fruit liqueur notes. Palate: flavourful, fine tannins, aged character, balanced, elegant, classic aged character.

MARQUÉS DE TOMARES RESERVA DE FAMILIA 2001 TR
tempranillo 80%, graciano 15%, mazuelo 5%

**88** Colour: pale ruby, brick rim edge. Nose: medium intensity, cocoa bean, spicy, fine reductive notes. Palate: balanced, elegant, fine tannins, classic aged character.

## MARQUÉS DE VITORIA

Camino de Santa Lucía, s/n
01320 Oyón (Alava)

# DO Ca. RIOJA

☎: 945 622 134 - Fax: 945 601 496
info@bodegasmarquesdevitoria.es
www.marquesdevitoria.com

MARQUÉS DE VITORIA 2008 B

**86** Colour: bright straw. Nose: varietal, fresh, medium intensity. Palate: rich, fruity, flavourful.

MARQUÉS DE VITORIA 2008 RD

**88** Colour: rose. Nose: fresh fruit, raspberry, fresh, varietal. Palate: flavourful, fresh.

ORIGINAL MARQUES DE VITORIA 2008 T

**90** Colour: bright cherry. Nose: ripe fruit, sweet spices, creamy oak, expressive. Palate: flavourful, fruity, toasty, round tannins.

MARQUÉS DE VITORIA ECCO 2008 T

**82**

MARQUÉS DE VITORIA 2006 TC

**89** Colour: cherry, garnet rim. Nose: ripe fruit, creamy oak, sweet spices, dark chocolate. Palate: elegant, round tannins, classic aged character, fruity.

MARQUÉS DE VITORIA 2004 TR

**89** Colour: cherry, garnet rim. Nose: fruit expression, ripe fruit, creamy oak, dark chocolate, sweet spices. Palate: elegant, flavourful, fruity, round tannins.

MARQUÉS DE VITORIA 1998 TGR

**87** Colour: pale ruby, brick rim edge. Nose: fruit preserve, warm, fine reductive notes, spicy. Palate: creamy, aged character, classic aged character, fine tannins.

ECCO

## MARQUÉS DEL PUERTO

Ctra. de Logroño, s/n
26360 Fuenmayor (La Rioja)
☎: 941 450 001 - Fax: 941 450 051
c.parejo@mbrizard.com
www.mariebrizard.com

MARQUÉS DEL PUERTO 2008 B JOVEN
viura 100%

**83**

MARQUÉS DEL PUERTO 2008 RD
tempranillo 50%, garnacha 50%

**87** Colour: rose. Nose: red berry notes, raspberry, varietal, powerfull, fresh. Palate: fresh, fruity, powerful, flavourful.

MARQUÉS DEL PUERTO 2006 TC
tempranillo 90%, mazuelo 10%

**80**

BENTUS "VENDIMIA SELECCIONADA" 2004 TR
tempranillo 80%, mazuelo 20%, garnacha %, graciano %

**82**

MARQUÉS DEL PUERTO 2004 TR
tempranillo 90%, mazuelo 10%

**81**

MARQUÉS DEL PUERTO 2001 TGR

**87** Colour: pale ruby, brick rim edge. Nose: fine reductive notes, old leather, tobacco, elegant, balanced. Palate: reductive nuances, spicy, long, balsamic, soft tannins.

## MARTÍNEZ LACUESTA S.A.

Paraje de Ubieta
26200 Haro (La Rioja)
☎: 941 310 050 - Fax: 941 303 748
info@martinezlacuesta.com
www.martinezlacuesta.com

MARTÍNEZ LACUESTA 2006 TC
tempranillo 85%, graciano 10%, mazuelo 5%

**88** Colour: cherry, garnet rim. Nose: powerful, ripe fruit, sweet spices, cocoa bean. Palate: flavourful, fleshy, spicy.

FELIX MARTÍNEZ LACUESTA 2005 TR
tempranillo 75%, graciano 20%, mazuelo 5%

**88** Colour: cherry, garnet rim. Nose: powerful, ripe fruit, lactic notes, sweet spices, creamy oak. Palate: flavourful, spicy, ripe fruit, round tannins.

MARTÍNEZ LACUESTA 2004 TR
tempranillo 85%, graciano 10%, mazuelo 5%

**86** Colour: cherry, garnet rim. Nose: medium intensity, ripe fruit, sweet spices, dark chocolate, aromatic coffee. Palate: flavourful, spicy, fine bitter notes.

VENTILLA 71
CAMPEADOR

## MIGUEL ÁNGEL MURO

Avda. Diputación, 4
01306 Lapuebla de Labarca (Alava)

☎: 627 434 726 - Fax: 945 607 081
info@bodegasmiguelangel.com
www.jexba7.com

MIGUEL ÁNGEL MURO 2008 T

# 84

AMENITAL 2007 TC

**89** Colour: black cherry, garnet rim. Nose: ripe fruit, warm, dark chocolate. Palate: fleshy, good structure, complex, good acidity, round tannins.

MURO BUJANDA 2006 TC

# 83

MURO BUJANDA 2004 TR

**87** Colour: black cherry. Nose: powerful, fruit preserve, toasty, cocoa bean. Palate: powerful, concentrated, round tannins.

## MONTECILLO

Ctra. Navarrete-Fuenmayor, km. 2
26360 Fuenmayor (La Rioja)
☎: 956 869 000 - Fax: 956 869 026
comunicacion@osborne.es
www.osborne.es

VIÑA MONTY 2006 TC
tempranillo 90%, mazuelo 10%

**88** Colour: bright cherry, garnet rim. Nose: creamy oak, expressive, scrubland, fine reductive notes. Palate: flavourful, fruity, toasty, soft tannins.

CUMBRE MONTECILLO 2005 TR
tempranillo 80%, graciano 20%

**91** Colour: cherry, garnet rim. Nose: powerful, varietal, ripe fruit, red berry notes, creamy oak, dark chocolate. Palate: powerful, flavourful, fleshy, creamy, round tannins.

MONTECILLO 2005 TC
tempranillo 100%

**88** Colour: bright cherry, garnet rim. Nose: red berry notes, ripe fruit, cocoa bean. Palate: flavourful, fruity, balanced, good acidity, soft tannins.

MONTECILLO 2005 TR
tempranillo 90%, mazuelo 10%

**85** Colour: bright cherry, orangey edge. Nose: smoky, toasty, aged wood nuances, fruit liqueur notes. Palate: spicy, ripe fruit, classic aged character.

VIÑA CUMBRERO 2004 TC
tempranillo 100%

**85** Colour: light cherry, garnet rim. Nose: ripe fruit, aged wood nuances, old leather. Palate: good structure, classic aged character, easy to drink.

VIÑA MONTY 2003 TR
tempranillo 90%, graciano 10%

**87** Colour: ruby red, orangey edge. Nose: spicy, toasty, cigar, fine reductive notes. Palate: flavourful, full, fine tannins.

MONTECILLO 2001 TGR
tempranillo 90%, graciano 10%

**88** Colour: light cherry, orangey edge. Nose: wet leather, animal reductive notes, fruit liqueur notes. Palate: classic aged character, spicy, elegant, balanced.

MONTECILLO 130 ANIVERSARIO 1994 TGR
tempranillo 100%

**88** Colour: light cherry, orangey edge. Nose: old leather, tobacco, fruit liqueur notes, spicy. Palate: elegant, balanced, easy to drink, soft tannins.

## MONTELATURCE

Pasada del Cristo
26140 Lardero (La Rioja)
☎: 941 449 368 - Fax: 941 449 369
info@montelaturce.com
www.montelaturce.com

CUETO 2008 B
viura, malvasia

# 80

CUETO 2008 RD

# 80

CUETO 2008 T

# 84

CUETO 2006 TC

**88** Colour: cherry, garnet rim. Nose: cocoa bean, sweet spices, complex, ripe fruit. Palate: flavourful, fruity, great length, spicy.

CUETO SELECCIÓN 2006 T
tempranillo

**87** Colour: cherry, garnet rim. Nose: toasty, old leather, tobacco, powerfull. Palate: flavourful, fruity, good acidity, fine bitter notes.

## PAGO DE LARREA

Ctra. Cenicero - Elciego, km. 1,2
01340 Elciego (Alava)
☎: 945 606 063 - Fax: 945 606 063
bodega@pagodelarrea.com
www.pagodelarrea.com

**CAECUS 2008 T**
tempranillo 95%, garnacha 5%

**86** Colour: deep cherry. Nose: fresh fruit, red berry notes, medium intensity, varietal. Palate: fruity, flavourful, easy to drink.

**CAECUS 2006 TC**
tempranillo 100%

**86** Colour: cherry, garnet rim. Nose: ripe fruit, spicy, fruit liqueur notes. Palate: flavourful, fleshy, good finish, round tannins.

**CAECUS 2005 TR**
tempranillo 100%

**87** Colour: cherry, garnet rim. Nose: ripe fruit, spicy, creamy oak, warm. Palate: round tannins, flavourful, fleshy, easy to drink.

## PAGO DE VISTAHERMOSA S.L.

Finca Vistahermosa
 Molino de Ocón (La Rioja)
☎: 915 905 591 - Fax: 915 642 498
herrero.clara@gmail.com

**CONVERSA 2006 T**
garnacha

**89** Colour: cherry, garnet rim. Nose: ripe fruit, expressive, sweet spices, cocoa bean. Palate: round tannins, fruity, flavourful, spicy.

## PAGOS DEL REY S.L.

Polígono Buicio Parcela, 1
26360 Fuenmayor (La Rioja)
☎: 941 450 818 - Fax: 941 450 818
jlmartinez@felixsolisavantis.com
www.pagosdelrey.com

**ARNEGUI 2008 B**
viura 100%

**88** Colour: bright straw. Nose: varietal, fresh, fresh fruit. Palate: rich, fruity, flavourful, powerful.

**ARNEGUI 2008 RD**
garnacha 100%

**87** Colour: brilliant rose. Nose: raspberry, fruit expression, ripe fruit. Palate: flavourful, fruity, full.

**EL CIRCULO 2008 T JOVEN**
tempranillo 95%, garnacha 5%

**87** Nose: varietal, fresh, ripe fruit, red berry notes. Palate: good acidity, astringent, fruity, flavourful.

**ARNEGUI 2008 T**
tempranillo 95%, garnacha 5%

**87** Colour: deep cherry. Nose: ripe fruit, red berry notes. Palate: flavourful, easy to drink, fruity.

**CASTILLO DE ALBAI 2008 T JOVEN**
tempranillo 95%, garnacha 5%

**87** Colour: cherry, purple rim. Nose: red berry notes, floral, ripe fruit, sweet spices. Palate: flavourful, fruity, good acidity, round tannins.

**EL CIRCULO 2006 TC**
tempranillo 100%

**88** Colour: cherry, garnet rim. Nose: ripe fruit, sweet spices, creamy oak. Palate: flavourful, spicy, ripe fruit, round tannins.

**CASTILLO DE ALBAI 2006 TC**
tempranillo 100%

**88** Colour: bright cherry. Nose: ripe fruit, sweet spices, creamy oak, lactic notes. Palate: flavourful, fruity, toasty, round tannins.

**ARNEGUI 2006 TC**
tempranillo 100%

**82**

**CASTILLO DE ALBAI 2005 TR**
tempranillo 100%

**88** Colour: cherry, garnet rim. Nose: powerful, ripe fruit, sweet spices, aromatic coffee. Palate: flavourful, powerful, fleshy, round tannins.

**EL CIRCULO 2005 TR**
tempranillo 100%

**88** Colour: cherry, garnet rim. Nose: powerful, ripe fruit, sweet spices, cocoa bean, lactic notes. Palate: flavourful, fleshy, ripe fruit, round tannins.

**ARNEGUI 2005 TR**
tempranillo 100%

**79**

## PAISAJES Y VIÑEDOS

Pza. Ibarra, 1
26330 Briones (La Rioja)
☎: 941 322 301 - Fax: 941 322 302

PAISAJES VIII LA PASADA 2006 T

**93** Colour: very deep cherry. Nose: spicy, aromatic coffee, creamy oak, fruit expression. Palate: fresh, fruity, powerful, flavourful.

PAISAJES V VALSALADO 2006 T

**89** Colour: dark-red cherry. Nose: sweet spices, creamy oak, ripe fruit. Palate: complex, powerful, flavourful, fleshy, ripe fruit.

PAISAJES VII CECIAS 2006 T

**88** Colour: deep cherry. Nose: expressive, aromatic coffee, caramel, ripe fruit. Palate: spirituous, good structure, flavourful.

## PALACIOS REMONDO

Avda. Zaragoza, 8
26540 Alfaro (La Rioja)
☎: 941 180 207 - Fax: 941 181 628
info@palaciosremondo.com

PLÁCET VALTOMELLOSO 2008 B
viura

**94** Colour: bright straw. Nose: fragrant herbs, grassy, ripe fruit, sweet spices. Palate: flavourful, fleshy, fruity, good acidity.

PROPIEDAD 2007 T

**90** Colour: cherry, garnet rim. Nose: ripe fruit, spicy, creamy oak, toasty, complex, balsamic herbs, mineral. Palate: powerful, flavourful, toasty, round tannins.

LA MONTESA 2007 TC

**90** Colour: cherry, garnet rim. Nose: powerful, ripe fruit, sweet spices, cocoa bean. Palate: flavourful, fleshy, ripe fruit, round tannins.

LA MONTESA 2006 TC

**90** Colour: bright cherry. Nose: ripe fruit, sweet spices, creamy oak. Palate: flavourful, fruity, toasty, round tannins.

## PATERNINA

Avda. Santo Domingo, 11
26200 Haro (La Rioja)

☎: 941 310 550 - Fax: 941 312 778
paternina@paternina.com
www.paternina.com

MONTE HARO "TEMPRANILLO" 2008 T
tempranillo

**85** Colour: cherry, garnet rim. Nose: powerful, ripe fruit, spicy, toasty. Palate: flavourful, spicy, round tannins.

PATERNINA BANDA ORO 2005 TC
tempranillo, mazuelo, garnacha

**86** Colour: cherry, garnet rim. Nose: powerful, aromatic coffee, spicy, toasty. Palate: spicy, fine bitter notes, round tannins.

PATERNINA BANDA AZUL 2005 TC
tempranillo, mazuelo, garnacha

**81**

CONDES DE LOS ANDES 2004 TR
tempranillo, mazuelo, garnacha

**89** Colour: cherry, garnet rim. Nose: toasty, dark chocolate, caramel, dry nuts. Palate: fine bitter notes, spicy, fine tannins.

PATERNINA VIÑA VIAL 2004 TR
tempranillo, garnacha, mazuelo

**84**

CONDES DE LOS ANDES 2001 TGR
tempranillo, mazuelo

**87** Colour: pale ruby, brick rim edge. Nose: elegant, medium intensity, fruit liqueur notes, spicy. Palate: flavourful, spicy, fine bitter notes.

CLOS PATERNINA 2001 TR
tempranillo, mazuelo, experimental

**85** Colour: pale ruby, brick rim edge. Nose: powerful, ripe fruit, sweet spices, toasty. Palate: flavourful, powerful, fleshy, round tannins.

GRACIELA 2003 BLANCO DULCE RESERVA
viura, malvasia

**82**

BANDA DORADA
BANDA ROSA
BANDA VERDE
PATERNINA BANDA ROJA

## R. LÓPEZ DE HEREDIA VIÑA TONDONIA

Avda. Vizcaya, 3

26200 Haro (La Rioja)
☎: 941 310 244 - Fax: 941 310 788
bodega@lopezdeheredia.com
www.tondonia.com

**VIÑA GRAVONIA 1999 BC**
viura 100%

**87** Colour: bright golden. Nose: sweet spices, caramel, medium intensity, overripe fruit. Palate: flavourful, balanced.

**VIÑA TONDONIA 1990 B RESERVA**
viura 90%, malvasia 10%

**90** Colour: bright golden. Nose: candied fruit, roasted almonds, elegant, expressive, fine reductive notes. Palate: ripe fruit, flavourful.

**VIÑA TONDONIA 1987 B GRAN RESERVA**
viura 90%, malvasia 10%

**89** Colour: bright golden. Nose: candied fruit, spicy, smoky, rancio notes, petrol notes. Palate: fleshy, fine bitter notes, confected, spicy.

**VIÑA TONDONIA 1998 RD**
garnacha 60%, tempranillo 30%, viura 10%

**86** Colour: onion pink. Nose: fine reductive notes, waxy notes, old leather, candied fruit, spicy, aged wood nuances. Palate: powerful, flavourful, smoky aftertaste, spicy.

**VIÑA CUBILLO 2003 TC**
tempranillo 65%, mazuelo 25%, garnacha 10%

**89** Colour: pale ruby, brick rim edge. Nose: medium intensity, old leather, tobacco, elegant. Palate: classic aged character, light-bodied, balanced.

**VIÑA BOSCONIA 2001 TR**
tempranillo 80%, garnacha 15%, graciano and mazuelo 5%

**89** Colour: bright cherry, orangey edge. Nose: medium intensity, complex, spicy, pattiserie. Palate: spicy, classic aged character, good acidity, elegant.

**VIÑA TONDONIA 2000 TR**
tempranillo 75%, garnacha 15%, graciano and mazuelo 10%

**89** Colour: pale ruby, brick rim edge. Nose: medium intensity, fruit liqueur notes, spicy, pattiserie. Palate: flavourful, spicy, ripe fruit, fine tannins.

**VIÑA TONDONIA 1991 TGR**
tempranillo 70%, garnacha 20%, graciano and mazuelo 10%

**88** Colour: pale ruby, brick rim edge. Nose: spicy, pattiserie, wet leather, tobacco, fruit liqueur notes. Palate: flavourful, spicy, classic aged character, easy to drink.

**VIÑA BOSCONIA 1991 TGR**
tempranillo 80%, garnacha 15%, graciano and mazuelo 5%

**84**

## RIOJA VEGA

Ctra. Logroño-Mendavia, km. 92
31230 Viana (Navarra)
☎: 948 646 263 - Fax: 948 645 612
info@riojavega.com
www.riojavega.com

**RIOJA VEGA 2006 TC**
tempranillo 80%, garnacha 15%, mazuelo 5%

**87** Colour: cherry, garnet rim. Nose: powerful, fruit liqueur notes, spicy, dark chocolate. Palate: flavourful, spicy, ripe fruit.

**RIOJA VEGA 2005 TR**
tempranillo 85%, graciano 10%, mazuelo 5%

**87** Colour: cherry, garnet rim. Nose: powerful, fruit liqueur notes, spicy, dark chocolate. Palate: spicy, ripe fruit, round tannins.

## SAN ASENSIO

Pº de Urumea, 21
20014 San Sebastián (Guipúzcoa)
☎: 943 468 455

**CASTILLO DE SAN ASENSIO S.C. T**

**81**

## SANTAMARÍA LÓPEZ

Ctra. Elvillar s/n
01300 Laguardia (Alava)
☎: 945 621 212 - Fax: 945 621 222
santamaria@santamarialopez.com
www.santamarialopez.com

**ANGEL SANTAMARÍA VENDIMIA SELECCIONADA 2007 B**
viura 75%, malvasia 25%

**86** Colour: bright straw. Nose: smoky, varietal, medium intensity, ripe fruit, creamy oak. Palate: flavourful, rich, creamy.

**ANGEL SANTAMARÍA VENDIMIA SELECCIONADA 2005 TC**
tempranillo 100%

**88** Colour: black cherry, garnet rim. Nose: ripe fruit, powerfull, varietal, sweet spices, dark chocolate, roasted coffee. Palate: balanced, spicy.

## EDITOR 2005 TC
tempranillo 100%

**87** Colour: garnet rim. Nose: balanced, ripe fruit, spicy, lactic notes. Palate: fruity, easy to drink, varietal.

## SDAD. COOP. BODEGA SAN MIGUEL

Ctra. de Zaragoza, 7
26513 Ausejo (La Rioja)
☎: 941 430 005 - Fax: 941 430 209
info@bodegasanmiguel.com

### CAMPOLOSA 2008 RD
garnacha 100%

**87** Colour: rose, purple rim. Nose: powerful, ripe fruit, red berry notes, floral, expressive. Palate: fleshy, powerful, fruity, fresh.

### CAMPOLOSA 2008 T
tempranillo 100%

**85** Colour: very deep cherry. Nose: ripe fruit, varietal, expressive. Palate: fruity, flavourful, good acidity.

### HEBE 2005 TC
tempranillo 100%

**87** Colour: black cherry, garnet rim. Nose: fruit preserve, creamy oak, pattiserie. Palate: good acidity, balanced, flavourful, fruity, slightly dry, soft tannins.

### CAMPOLOSA 2005 TC
tempranillo 100%

**85** Colour: dark-red cherry, garnet rim. Nose: ripe fruit, pattiserie, creamy oak, spicy. Palate: good acidity, flavourful, round tannins.

## SENDERO ROYAL

Ctra. LR 384 Nac. 232 Km. 0,08
26559 Aldeanueva de Ebro (La Rioja)
☎: 941 743 999 - Fax: 941 743 031
info@senderoroyal.com
www.senderoroyal.com

### GRACIARTE 2008 T JOVEN
graciano 100%

**87** Colour: dark-red cherry. Nose: medium intensity, ripe fruit, red berry notes. Palate: balsamic, flavourful, fruity.

VALLAROSO
SENDERO ROYAL

## SEÑORÍO DE ARANA

La Cadena, 20
01330 Labastida (Alava)
☎: 945 331 150 - Fax: 944 212 738
senoriodearana@infonegocio.com
www.senoriodearana.com

### VIÑA DEL OJA 2008 T
tempranillo 100%
**81**

### VIÑA DEL OJA 2005 TC
**84**

### VIÑA DEL OJA 2001 TR
**89** Colour: pale ruby, brick rim edge. Nose: elegant, expressive, macerated fruit, fine reductive notes, tobacco. Palate: good structure, fine bitter notes, fine tannins.

## SEÑORÍO DE SAN VICENTE

Los Remedios, 27
26338 San Vicente de la Sonsierra (La Rioja)
☎: 902 334 080 - Fax: 945 600 885
info@eguren.com
www.eguren.com

### SAN VICENTE 2006 T
**92** Nose: cedar wood, creamy oak, roasted coffee, ripe fruit. Palate: fleshy, powerful, flavourful, good structure, toasty, slightly dry, soft tannins.

## SEÑORÍO DE SOMALO S.L.

Ctra. de Baños, 62
26321 Bobadilla (La Rioja)
☎: 941 202 351 - Fax: 941 202 351
info@bodegasomalo.com
www.bodegasomalo.com

### SEÑORÍO DE J.A. SOMALO 2008 B
viura 95%, malvasia 5%
**83**

### SEÑORÍO DE J.A. SOMALO 2008 RD
garnacha 60%, viura 40%
**77**

### SEÑORÍO DE J.A. SOMALO 2008 T
tempranillo 85%, garnacha 15%

## 80

SEÑORÍO DE J.A. SOMALO 2005 TC
tempranillo 90%, garnacha 10%

## 81

SEÑORÍO DE J.A. SOMALO 2001 TR
tempranillo 90%, garnacha 10%

## 84

### SEÑORÍO DE ULÍA

Paraje del Buicio, s/n
26360 Fuenmayor (La Rioja)
☎: 941 450 567 - Fax: 941 450 567
info@marquesdeulia.com

MARQUÉS DE ULÍA 2005 TC

**88** Colour: cherry, garnet rim. Nose: powerful, ripe fruit, sweet spices. Palate: flavourful, ripe fruit, round tannins.

MARQUÉS DE ULÍA 2004 TR

**87** Colour: cherry, garnet rim. Nose: fruit liqueur notes, sweet spices, toasty, fine reductive notes. Palate: flavourful, spicy, round tannins.

LA VENDIMIA MARQUÉS DE ULÍA 2004 T

**87** Colour: cherry, garnet rim. Nose: powerful, ripe fruit, spicy, toasty. Palate: flavourful, spicy, round tannins.

### SIERRA CANTABRIA

Amorebieta, 3
26338 San Vicente de la Sonsierra (La Rioja)
☎: 902 334 080 - Fax: 941 334 371
info@eguren.com
www.eguren.com

SIERRA CANTABRIA ORGANZA 2007 B

**93** Colour: bright straw. Nose: ripe fruit, mineral, elegant, dried herbs, sweet spices. Palate: powerful, good structure, spicy, mineral.

MURMURÓN 2008 T

**88** Colour: deep cherry. Nose: varietal, fresh, expressive. Palate: powerful, flavourful, fresh.

FINCA EL BOSQUE 2007 T

**96** Colour: very deep cherry. Nose: creamy oak, spicy, cedar wood, fruit expression, fresh fruit. Palate: complex, fleshy, fruity, powerful, flavourful, powerful tannins.

SIERRA CANTABRIA COLECCIÓN PRIVADA 2007 T

**95** Colour: deep cherry. Nose: macerated fruit, fresh fruit, aromatic coffee, creamy oak, fruit expression. Palate: creamy, toasty, mineral, varietal, flavourful, powerful.

SIERRA CANTABRIA 2007 T

**91** Colour: dark-red cherry, bright cherry. Nose: powerful, varietal, expressive, smoky. Palate: powerful, flavourful, fruity, fresh, toasty, fruity aftertaste.

AMANCIO 2006 T

**94** Colour: deep cherry. Nose: cocoa bean, dark chocolate, cedar wood, sweet spices, ripe fruit, dry stone. Palate: powerful, flavourful, fleshy, full, spirituous, complex, toasty, smoky aftertaste.

SIERRA CANTABRIA CUVÈE ESPECIAL 2006 T

**91** Colour: very deep cherry. Nose: spicy, aromatic coffee, dark chocolate, cedar wood, aged wood nuances. Palate: powerful, flavourful, fruity, good structure.

SIERRA CANTABRIA 2006 TC

**91** Colour: deep cherry, bright ochre rim. Nose: ripe fruit, sweet spices, cocoa bean, warm, earthy notes. Palate: creamy, full, round tannins.

SIERRA CANTABRIA 2005 TR

**92** Colour: deep cherry. Nose: complex, expressive, ripe fruit, cocoa bean, mineral. Palate: creamy, spicy, flavourful, fruity, toasty, powerful tannins.

SIERRA CANTABRIA 2004 TGR

**94** Colour: dark-red cherry. Nose: complex, undergrowth, cocoa bean, smoky. Palate: elegant, balanced, round, mineral, spicy.

### SOLAR VIEJO DE LA GUARDIA

Camino de la Hoya, s/n
01300 Laguardia (Alava)
☎: 945 600 113 - Fax: 945 600 600
solarviejo@solarviejo.com
www.solarviejo.com

SOLAR VIEJO 2008 T
tempranillo

## 84

SOLAR VIEJO VENDIMIA SELECCIONADA 2006 T
tempranillo

**87** Colour: cherry, garnet rim. Nose: ripe fruit, warm, medium intensity, creamy oak, spicy. Palate: flavourful, spicy, fleshy, round tannins.

**SOLAR VIEJO 2006 TC**
tempranillo

**85** Colour: dark-red cherry. Nose: ripe fruit, creamy oak. Palate: spicy, round tannins, flavourful, fruity.

**SOLAR VIEJO 2004 TR**
tempranillo 90%, graciano 10%

**88** Colour: cherry, garnet rim. Nose: ripe fruit, fruit liqueur notes, cocoa bean, sweet spices. Palate: flavourful, classic aged character, round tannins, balanced.

## SOTO DE TORRES

Alto Otero
01330 Labastida (Alava)
www.ibericosvino.com

**IBÉRICOS 2006 TC**
tempranillo 100%

**87** Colour: cherry, garnet rim. Nose: ripe fruit, spicy, toasty, complex. Palate: powerful, flavourful, toasty, round tannins.

## TIERRA ANTIGUA

Urbanización Monje Vigilia, 7
26120 Albelda de Iregua (La Rioja)
☎: 941 444 233 - Fax: 941 444 427
info@tierrantigua.com

**ETHOS PRIVADO 2005 T**
tempranillo 100%

**89** Colour: deep cherry, purple rim. Nose: spicy, cocoa bean, creamy oak, fruit preserve. Palate: flavourful, good acidity, fine bitter notes, round tannins.

**TIERRA ANTIGUA 2004 TR**
tempranillo 85%, graciano 15%, garnacha %

**90** Colour: cherry, garnet rim. Nose: powerful, ripe fruit, sweet spices, toasty, dark chocolate. Palate: flavourful, spicy, fine bitter notes, fleshy, round tannins.

**TIERRA ANTIGUA 2003 TR**

**89** Colour: cherry, garnet rim. Nose: powerful, ripe fruit, warm, sweet spices, dark chocolate. Palate: flavourful, powerful, fleshy, spicy, round tannins.

## TORRE DE OÑA

Finca San Martín
01309 Páganos - Laguardia (Álava)
☎: 945 621 154 - Fax: 945 621 171
baron@riojalta.com
www.riojalta.com

**BARÓN DE OÑA 2005 TR**
tempranillo 95%, mazuelo 5%

**87** Colour: cherry, garnet rim. Nose: expressive, ripe fruit, pattiserie, aromatic coffee. Palate: flavourful, powerful, good structure, great length.

## VALENTIN PASCUAL WEIGAND

Dr. Azcárraga, 23
26350 Cenicero (La Rioja)
☎: 941 454 053

**VALENTIN PASCUAL 2008 T**

**87** Colour: very deep cherry. Nose: varietal, fresh, fresh fruit, red berry notes. Palate: fruity, flavourful, fresh.

## VALLFORMOSA RIOJA

La Sala, 45
08735 Vilobi del Penedés (Barcelona)
☎: 938 978 286 - Fax: 938 978 355
vallformosa@vallformosa.es
www.vallformosa.com

**PRIMUM VITAE TEMPRANILLO 2003 TR**

**88** Colour: light cherry, bright ochre rim. Nose: aged wood nuances, varnish, old leather, fruit liqueur notes. Palate: light-bodied, flavourful, pruney, classic aged character, easy to drink.

## VALORIA S.A.

Ctra. de Burgos, km. 5
26006 Logroño (La Rioja)
☎: 941 204 059 - Fax: 941 204 155
inf@vina-valoria.es
www.vina-valoria.es

VIÑA VALORIA 2007 BFB
viura 100%

**82**

VIÑA VALORIA 2004 BC
viura 100%

**85** Colour: bright straw. Nose: powerful, ripe fruit, citrus fruit, sweet spices. Palate: flavourful, powerful, fleshy, fine bitter notes.

VIÑA VALORIA 2007 T
tempranillo 80%, mazuelo 10%, graciano 10%

**84**

VIÑA VALORIA 2005 TC
tempranillo 80%, mazuelo 10%, graciano 10%

**86** Colour: cherry, garnet rim. Nose: fruit liqueur notes, spicy, aromatic coffee. Palate: flavourful, spicy, ripe fruit, long.

## VIÑA VALORIA VENDIMIA SELECCIONADA 2004 T
tempranillo 100%

**85** Colour: cherry, garnet rim. Nose: powerful, fruit liqueur notes, sweet spices, dark chocolate. Palate: flavourful, spicy, fleshy.

VIÑA VALORIA 1999 TR
tempranillo 80%, mazuelo 10%, graciano 10%

**86** Colour: pale ruby, brick rim edge. Nose: fruit liqueur notes, spicy, aromatic coffee. Palate: flavourful, spicy, classic aged character, long.

VIÑA VALORIA 1992 TGR
tempranillo 80%, mazuelo 10%, graciano 10%

**88** Colour: pale ruby, brick rim edge. Nose: elegant, fruit liqueur notes, pattiserie. Palate: easy to drink, spicy, classic aged character.

## VALSANZO

Manuel Azaña, 9
Edificio Ambassador, Local 15
47014 Valladolid
☎: 983 150 150 - Fax: 983 150 151
valsanzo@valsanzo.com
www.valsanzo.com

LACRIMUS 2005 TC
tempranillo 85%, graciano 15%

**87** Colour: cherry, garnet rim. Nose: ripe fruit, powerfull, sweet spices. Palate: flavourful, fleshy, spicy, round tannins.

## VINÍCOLA REAL

Santiago Aldaz, s/n
26120 Albelda de Iregua (La Rioja)
☎: 941 444 233 - Fax: 941 444 427
info@vinicolareal.com
www.vinicolareal.com

CUEVA DEL MONGE 2007 BFB

**89** Colour: bright straw. Nose: powerful, overripe fruit, fruit preserve, sweet spices. Palate: flavourful, powerful, fleshy.

VIÑA LOS VALLES ECOLÓGICO 2007 TC

**91** Colour: ruby red. Nose: undergrowth, mineral, fresh fruit, wild herbs. Palate: powerful, flavourful, fruity, balsamic, spicy.

CUEVA DEL MONGE 2006 T
tempranillo 100%
ç

**89** Colour: dark-red cherry. Nose: ripe fruit, complex, spicy, cedar wood, cocoa bean. Palate: good acidity, fruity, powerful, flavourful.

### VIÑA LOS VALLES 50 & 50 2005 TC
garnacha 50%, graciano 50%

**89** Colour: cherry, garnet rim. Nose: damp undergrowth, ripe fruit, balsamic herbs. Palate: flavourful, ripe fruit, spicy, round tannins.

### VIÑA LOS VALLES 70 & 30 2005 TC
tempranillo 70%, graciano 30%

**88** Colour: cherry, garnet rim. Nose: medium intensity, ripe fruit, scrubland, toasty. Palate: flavourful, ripe fruit, spicy, round tannins.

### VIÑA LOS VALLES 80 & 20 2005 TC
tempranillo 80%, mazuelo 20%

**87** Colour: cherry, garnet rim. Nose: powerful, sweet spices, toasty, balsamic herbs. Palate: flavourful, spicy, balsamic.

### CONFESOR 2004 T
tempranillo 85%, graciano 8%, garnacha 2%, mazuelo 5%

**91** Colour: cherry, garnet rim. Nose: ripe fruit, spicy, creamy oak, toasty, complex. Palate: powerful, flavourful, toasty, round tannins.

### 200 MONGES SELECCIÓN ESPECIAL 2004 TR
tempranillo 100%

**91** Colour: deep cherry. Nose: expressive, powerfull, complex, undergrowth, truffle notes, fine reductive notes, cigar, fresh fruit. Palate: complex, powerful, flavourful, spirituous, ripe fruit, creamy.

### 200 MONGES 2004 TR
tempranillo 85%, graciano 10%, mazuelo 5%

**89** Colour: dark-red cherry, orangey edge. Nose: closed, elegant, expressive, creamy oak. Palate: fleshy, fruity, powerful, flavourful.

### 200 MONGES 2003 TGR
tempranillo 85%, graciano 10%, mazuelo 5%

**91** Colour: dark-red cherry. Nose: complex, ripe fruit, fine reductive notes, old leather. Palate: powerful, flavourful, spicy, toasty, ripe fruit.

### 200 MONGES 1999 TGR

**89** Colour: pale ruby, brick rim edge. Nose: elegant, spicy, fine reductive notes, wet leather, aged wood nuances, fruit liqueur notes. Palate: spicy, fine tannins, elegant, long.

## VINÍCOLA RIOJANA DE ALCANADRE S.C.

San Isidro, 46
26509 Alcanadre (La Rioja)
☎: 941 165 036 - Fax: 941 165 289
f.saenz@riojanadealcanadre.com
www.vinicolariojanadealcanadre.com

### ARADÓN 2008 B
viura 100%

**82**

### ARADÓN 2008 RD
garnacha 100%

**82**

### ARADÓN 2008 T
tempranillo 90%, garnacha 10%

**85** Colour: bright cherry, purple rim. Nose: red berry notes, ripe fruit, lactic notes. Palate: fruity, flavourful, balanced.

### ARADÓN 2004 TC
tempranillo 90%, garnacha 5%, mazuelo 5%

**86** Colour: cherry, garnet rim. Nose: toasty, aromatic coffee, powerfull, warm. Palate: flavourful, spicy, classic aged character, round tannins.

VIÑA ROMITA
BARZAGOSO
SILVAL

## VIÑA EGUILUZ S.L.

Camino de San Bartolomé, 10
26339 Abalos (La Rioja)
☎: 941 334 064 - Fax: 941 583 022
info@bodegaseguiluz.es
www.bodegaseguiluz.es

### EGUILUZ 2008 T
tempranillo 100%

**87** Colour: very deep cherry. Nose: ripe fruit, varietal, expressive. Palate: flavourful, fruity, round tannins, great length.

### EGUILUZ 2005 TC
tempranillo 100%

**85** Colour: dark-red cherry, garnet rim. Nose: fruit liqueur notes, sweet spices, toasty, cocoa bean. Palate: creamy, easy to drink, flavourful, slightly dry, soft tannins.

# DO Ca. RIOJA

## VIÑA HERMINIA

Camino de los Agudos, 1
26559 Aldeanueva de Ebro (La Rioja)
☎: 941 142 305 - Fax: 941 142 303
vherminia@vherminia.es
www.vherminia.es

**VIÑA HERMINIA EXCELSUS 2006 T**
tempranillo 60%, garnacha 40%

**88** Colour: bright cherry, garnet rim. Nose: elegant, balanced, ripe fruit. Palate: flavourful, fruity, balanced, fruity aftestaste, round tannins.

**VIÑA HERMINIA 2005 TC**
tempranillo 85%, garnacha 15%

**85** Colour: cherry, garnet rim. Nose: powerful, warm, ripe fruit, spicy. Palate: flavourful, spicy, good acidity, round tannins.

**VIÑA HERMINIA 2001 TR**

**85** Colour: deep cherry, orangey edge. Nose: powerful, ripe fruit, dark chocolate. Palate: flavourful, spicy, round tannins.

## VIÑA HERMOSA

Avda. de la Rioja, s/n
26221 Gimileo (La Rioja)
☎: 941 304 231 - Fax: 941 304 326
santiagoijalba@fer.es
www.santiagoijalba.com

**ABANDO 2008 BFB**
viura

**86** Colour: straw. Nose: ripe fruit, smoky, pattiserie. Palate: flavourful, fruity, fresh.

**ABANDO 2008 RD FERMENTADO EN BARRICA**
tempranillo

**87** Colour: rose, purple rim. Nose: toasty, aromatic coffee, sweet spices, ripe fruit. Palate: flavourful, ripe fruit, fruity.

**VIÑA HERMOSA 2006 TC**
tempranillo

**84**

**ABANDO VENDIMIA SELECCIONADA 2004 TC**
tempranillo

**87** Colour: cherry, garnet rim. Nose: warm, ripe fruit, sweet spices, toasty. Palate: flavourful, good structure, spicy, good acidity.

**IREP TEMPRANILLO 2004 T**
tempranillo

**87** Colour: cherry, garnet rim. Nose: powerful, ripe fruit, warm, toasty, dark chocolate. Palate: flavourful, spicy, round tannins.

**OGGA 2004 TR**
tempranillo

**87** Colour: cherry, garnet rim. Nose: powerful, fruit preserve, dark chocolate, toasty. Palate: powerful, sweetness, spicy.

**JARRERO**

## VIÑA IJALBA

Ctra. Pamplona, km. 1
26006 Logroño (La Rioja)
☎: 941 261 100 - Fax: 941 261 128
vinaijalba@ijalba.com
www.ijalba.com

**GENOLI 2008 B**
viura 100%

**84**

**DIONISIO RUIZ IJALBA 2005 T**
maturana 100%

**90** Colour: cherry, garnet rim. Nose: ripe fruit, lactic notes, aged wood nuances, cedar wood, new oak. Palate: flavourful, powerful, fleshy, spicy, round tannins.

**IJALBA 2005 TC**
tempranillo 90%, graciano 10%

**88** Colour: cherry, garnet rim. Nose: powerful, ripe fruit, sweet spices, scrubland. Palate: flavourful, powerful, fleshy, round tannins.

**IJALBA 2005 TR**
tempranillo 80%, graciano 20%

**85** Colour: cherry, garnet rim. Nose: medium intensity, ripe fruit, warm. Palate: flavourful, powerful, spicy, round tannins.

**IJALBA GRACIANO 2005 TC**
graciano 100%

**85** Colour: cherry, garnet rim. Nose: tar, toasty, aromatic coffee, fruit liqueur notes. Palate: flavourful, spicy, classic aged character.

**IJALBA SELECCIÓN ESPECIAL 2001 TR**
tempranillo 50%, graciano 50%

**87** Colour: cherry, garnet rim. Nose: powerful, ripe fruit, dark chocolate, aged wood nuances. Palate: flavourful, powerful, fleshy, spicy.

ALOQUE
LIVOR
MÚRICE

## VIÑA OLABARRI

Ctra. Haro-Anguciana, s/n
26200 Haro (La Rioja)
☎: 941 310 937 - Fax: 941 311 602
info@bodegasolabarri.com
www.bodegasolabarri.com

VIÑA OLABARRI 2007 TC

**86** Colour: cherry, garnet rim. Nose: ripe fruit, toasty, sweet spices, cocoa bean. Palate: fleshy, flavourful, smoky aftertaste.

VIÑA OLABARRI 2005 TR

**87** Colour: cherry, garnet rim. Nose: medium intensity, spicy, ripe fruit, fruit liqueur notes. Palate: classic aged character, creamy, smoky aftertaste, flavourful.

VIÑA OLABARRI 2004 TGR

**87** Colour: pale ruby, brick rim edge. Nose: fruit liqueur notes, sweet spices, cocoa bean, fine reductive notes. Palate: elegant, fine tannins, pruney, great length.

BIKANDI VENDIMIA SELECCIONADA 2004 TC

**86** Colour: cherry, garnet rim. Nose: ripe fruit, dark chocolate, spicy. Palate: flavourful, fruity, round tannins.

BIKANDI VENDIMIA SELECCIONADA 2001 TR

**90** Colour: bright cherry. Nose: ripe fruit, sweet spices, creamy oak, powerfull. Palate: flavourful, fruity, toasty, round tannins.

## VIÑA REAL

Ctra. Logroño - Laguardia, km. 4,8
01300 Laguardia (Alava)
☎: 945 625 255 - Fax: 945 625 211
marketing@cvne.com
www.cvne.com

VIÑA REAL 2007 BFB
viura 90%, malvasia 10%

**89** Colour: bright straw. Nose: powerful, ripe fruit, spicy, new oak. Palate: flavourful, fruity, fresh, fleshy.

VIÑA REAL 2007 TC
tempranillo 85%, garnacha 15%, mazuelo %

**90** Colour: deep cherry. Nose: fresh fruit, cocoa bean, smoky, fruit expression. Palate: fruity, powerful, flavourful, fleshy.

PAGOS DE VIÑA REAL 2005 T
tempranillo 100%

**90** Colour: deep cherry. Nose: ripe fruit, undergrowth, sweet spices, creamy oak, toasty. Palate: spicy, powerful, good structure, flavourful, round, spirituous, round tannins.

VIÑA REAL 2005 TR
tempranillo 90%, garnacha 5%, graciano 5%

**90** Colour: deep cherry. Nose: medium intensity, complex, ripe fruit, cocoa bean, spicy. Palate: round, fruity, powerful, flavourful, toasty, reductive nuances.

VIÑA REAL 2001 TGR
tempranillo 95%, graciano 5%

**91** Colour: dark-red cherry, brick rim edge. Nose: elegant, waxy notes, fine reductive notes, ripe fruit, spicy, aromatic coffee. Palate: round, elegant, powerful, flavourful, toasty, round tannins.

## VIÑA SALCEDA

Ctra. de Cenicero, km. 3
01340 Elciego (Alava)
☎: 945 606 125 - Fax: 945 606 069
info@vinasalceda.com

VIÑA SALCEDA 2006 TC

**89** Colour: bright cherry. Nose: ripe fruit, sweet spices, creamy oak, expressive, floral. Palate: flavourful, fruity, toasty, round tannins.

**VIÑA SALCEDA 2005 TR**

**90** Colour: cherry, garnet rim. Nose: ripe fruit, toasty, complex, undergrowth, sweet spices. Palate: flavourful, toasty, fresh, complex, classic aged character.

**CONDE DE LA SALCEDA 2005 TR**

**91** Colour: cherry, garnet rim. Nose: powerful, ripe fruit, cocoa bean, sweet spices, creamy oak. Palate: flavourful, fleshy, spicy, round tannins.

## VIÑEDOS DE ALDEANUEVA S. COOP.

Avda. Juan Carlos I, 100
26559 Aldeanueva de Ebro (La Rioja)
☎: 941 163 039 - Fax: 941 163 585
va@aldeanueva.com
www.aldeanueva.com

**AZABACHE 2008 RD**
garnacha 100%

**88** Colour: onion pink. Nose: elegant, candied fruit, dried flowers, fragrant herbs, red berry notes. Palate: light-bodied, flavourful, good acidity, long, spicy.

**AZABACHE TEMPRANILLO 2008 T**
tempranillo 100%

**88** Colour: very deep cherry. Nose: fresh fruit, red berry notes, varietal. Palate: flavourful, fruity, round tannins.

**CULTO 2005 T**
graciano 60%, tempranillo 40%

**87** Colour: cherry, garnet rim. Nose: fruit preserve, spicy, mineral. Palate: slightly dry, soft tannins, flavourful, powerful.

**AZABACHE VENDIMIA SELECCIONADA 2005 TC**
tempranillo 70%, garnacha 20%, mazuelo 10%

**83**

AZABACHE GRACIANO 2004 TR
graciano 100%

**84**

## VIÑEDOS DE PÁGANOS

Ctra. Navaridas, s/n
01309 Páganos (Alava)
☎: 945 600 590 - Fax: 945 600 885
info@eguren.com
www.eguren.com

LA NIETA 2007 T

**94** Colour: very deep cherry. Nose: fruit expression, red berry notes, fresh fruit, roasted coffee, creamy oak. Palate: powerful tannins, good structure, powerful, flavourful, complex, fruity aftestaste, toasty.

EL PUNTIDO 2006 T BARRICA

**91** Colour: deep cherry. Nose: powerful, complex, smoky, cocoa bean, spicy, sweet spices, roasted coffee. Palate: powerful, flavourful, fruity, good structure, fleshy.

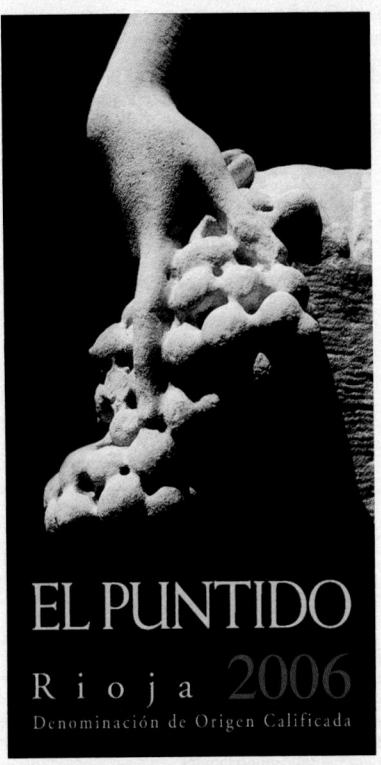

## VIÑEDOS DEL CONTINO

Finca San Rafael, s/n
01321 Laserna (Álava)
☎: 945 600 201 - Fax: 945 621 114
jesus.madrazo@contino.es
www.cvne.com

CONTINO VIÑA DEL OLIVO 2007 T
tempranillo 88%, graciano 12%

**94** Colour: cherry, purple rim. Nose: powerful, ripe fruit, red berry notes, fruit expression, creamy oak, sweet spices, cocoa bean. Palate: flavourful, ripe fruit, spicy, fleshy.

CONTINO GRACIANO 2006 T
graciano 100%

**92** Colour: bright cherry. Nose: ripe fruit, sweet spices, creamy oak, expressive, varietal, balsamic herbs. Palate: flavourful, fruity, toasty, round tannins.

**CONTINO VIÑA DEL OLIVO 2005 T**
tempranillo 90%, graciano 9%, mazuelo 1%

**93** Colour: cherry, garnet rim. Nose: ripe fruit, spicy, creamy oak, complex, earthy notes, toasty, dark chocolate. Palate: powerful, flavourful, toasty, round tannins.

**CONTINO 2005 TR**
tempranillo 85%, graciano 10%, mazuelo 5%

**90** Colour: cherry, garnet rim. Nose: ripe fruit, spicy, creamy oak, toasty, complex, lactic notes. Palate: powerful, flavourful, toasty, round tannins.

## VIÑEDOS DEL TERNERO

Finca El Ternero
09200 Miranda de Ebro (Burgos)
☎: 941 320 021 - Fax: 941 302 729
egisto@vinedosdelternero.com
www.vinedosdelternero.com

**MIRANDA 2005 T**
tempranillo 95%, mazuelo 5%

**91** Colour: dark-red cherry. Nose: roasted coffee, ripe fruit. Palate: good structure, powerful, flavourful, complex, full.

**SEL DE SU MERCED 2005 TR**
tempranillo 95%, mazuelo 5%

**91** Colour: deep cherry. Nose: powerful, ripe fruit, red berry notes, spicy, creamy oak. Palate: flavourful, fleshy, spicy, ripe fruit, round tannins.

**MIRANDA 2005 TC**
tempranillo 95%, mazuelo 5%

**90** Colour: dark-red cherry. Nose: varietal, damp earth, creamy oak, roasted coffee. Palate: powerful, flavourful, rich, fruity, round.

**PICEA 650 2005 T**
tempranillo 95%, mazuelo 5%

**89** Colour: dark-red cherry. Nose: spicy, creamy oak, ripe fruit, aged wood nuances. Palate: spirituous, powerful, complex, toasty, roasted-coffee aftertaste.

## VIÑEDOS MONTALVILLO S.L.

Ctra. N-232, km. 351
26559 Aldeanueva de Ebro (La Rioja)
☎: 941 743 035 - Fax: 941 743 118
info@montalvillo.com

**MONTALVILLO 2005 TC**
tempranillo, mazuelo, garnacha

**81**

## VIÑEDOS RUIZ JIMÉNEZ

Ctra. Comarcal LR-115 Km. 43,5
26559 Aldeanueva de Ebro (La Rioja)
☎: 941 163 577 - Fax: 941 163 577
info@vinedosruiz-jimenez.es
www.vinedosruiz-jimenez.es

**PERSEUS JOVEN 2008 T**
tempranillo 70%, garnacha 30%

**80**

**VALCALIENTE 2005 TC**
tempranillo 90%, graciano 10%

**88** Colour: cherry, garnet rim. Nose: ripe fruit, dark chocolate, sweet spices, balanced, balsamic herbs. Palate: fleshy, concentrated, round tannins.

**VALCALIENTE 2005 TR**
garnacha 100%

**87** Colour: cherry, garnet rim. Nose: ripe fruit, expressive, spicy. Palate: balanced, flavourful, round tannins, fine bitter notes.

## VIÑEDOS Y BODEGAS DE LA MARQUESA

Herrería, 76
01307 Villabuena de Alava (Alava)
☎: 945 609 085 - Fax: 945 623 304
info@valserrano.com
www.valserrano.com

**VALSERRANO 2008 BFB**
viura 95%, malvasia 5%

**88** Colour: straw. Nose: ripe fruit, varietal, creamy oak, smoky. Palate: fruity, elegant, flavourful, rich.

**VALSERRANO 2006 TC**
tempranillo 90%, mazuelo 10%

**88** Colour: bright cherry. Nose: sweet spices, creamy oak, ripe fruit. Palate: flavourful, fruity, toasty, round tannins.

**VALSERRANO FINCA MONTEVIEJO 2005 T**
tempranillo 95%, garnacha 5%, graciano %

**90** Colour: cherry, garnet rim. Nose: ripe fruit, spicy, creamy oak, toasty, complex, earthy notes. Palate: powerful, flavourful, toasty, round tannins, long.

**VALSERRANO 2005 TR**
tempranillo 90%, graciano 10%

**89** Colour: cherry, garnet rim. Nose: ripe fruit, spicy, creamy oak, toasty, complex. Palate: powerful, flavourful, toasty, round tannins.

**VALSERRANO MAZUELO 2005 T**
mazuelo 100%

**89** Colour: cherry, garnet rim. Nose: balanced, dark chocolate, sweet spices, ripe fruit. Palate: fruity, flavourful, balanced.

**VALSERRANO GARNACHA 2005 T**
garnacha 100%

**89** Colour: bright cherry. Nose: ripe fruit, sweet spices, expressive, dark chocolate, varietal. Palate: flavourful, fruity, toasty, round tannins, good acidity.

**VALSERRANO GRACIANO 2005 T**
graciano 100%

**88** Colour: deep cherry, garnet rim. Nose: cocoa bean, spicy, fine reductive notes. Palate: flavourful, good structure, round tannins.

**VALSERRANO 2003 TGR**
tempranillo 90%, graciano 10%

**87** Colour: cherry, garnet rim. Nose: ripe fruit, elegant, fruit liqueur notes, spicy. Palate: ripe fruit, powerful, warm, round tannins.

## VIÑEDOS Y BODEGAS XXI

Avda. de Mendavia, 29
26006 Logroño (La Rioja)
☎: 917 104 880 - Fax: 917 104 881
anap@swd.es
www.swd.es

**ENTRECEPAS TEMPRANILLO 2008 T**
tempranillo 100%

**85** Colour: cherry, purple rim. Nose: expressive, fresh fruit, red berry notes, floral. Palate: flavourful, fruity, good acidity, round tannins.

**ENTRECEPAS 2004 TC**
tempranillo 57%, graciano 20%, garnacha 13%, mazuelo 10%

**85** Colour: cherry, garnet rim. Nose: sweet spices, aromatic coffee, cocoa bean, ripe fruit. Palate: flavourful, spicy, ripe fruit, easy to drink.

**ENTRECEPAS SELECCIÓN 2002 T**
tempranillo 75%, graciano 10%, mazuelo 8%, garnacha 7%

**88** Colour: cherry, garnet rim. Nose: powerful, ripe fruit, spicy, aromatic coffee. Palate: flavourful, spicy, ripe fruit, round tannins.

**ENTRECEPAS 2002 TR**
tempranillo 54%, garnacha 30%, mazuelo 12%, graciano 4%

**83**

## VOCARRAJE

Ctra. San Román s/n
49810 Moral de Toro (Zamora)
☎: 630 084 080
belensegovia@wanadoo.es

ABDON SEGOVIA 2007 T

**88** Colour: cherry, garnet rim. Nose: ripe fruit, spicy, creamy oak, toasty, complex, mineral. Palate: powerful, flavourful, toasty, fresh fruit tannins.

## WINNER WINES

Avda. del Mediterráneo, 38
28007 Madrid (Madrid)
☎: 915 019 042 - Fax: 915 017 794
winnerwines@ibernoble.com
www.ibernoble.com

VIÑA SASETA 2008 T
tempranillo 100%

**86** Colour: very deep cherry. Nose: varietal, green pepper, ripe fruit, red berry notes. Palate: good acidity, ripe fruit, round tannins.

VIÑA SASETA 2005 TC
tempranillo 90%, mazuelo 5%, graciano 5%

**87** Colour: cherry, garnet rim. Nose: macerated fruit, warm, creamy oak, pattiserie. Palate: spicy, round tannins, fruity, full.

VIÑA SASETA 2003 TR
tempranillo 90%, graciano 5%, mazuelo 5%

**85** Colour: deep cherry, bright ochre rim. Nose: macerated fruit, fine reductive notes, sweet spices, creamy oak, tobacco. Palate: balanced, long, classic aged character, round tannins.

SOME OTHER WINERIES WITHIN THE DO :

ABEICA
ANTONIO RAMÍREZ-PECIÑA
ARIBAU CUVÉE
ARNÁEZ GONZALO, SEGUNDO Y B.
AYESA S.C.
BENIGNO BASOCO S.C.
BIURKO GORRI
BOD. PEDRO Y JAIME MARTÍNEZ PRADO
BODEGA 1102
BODEGA CLÁSSICA
BODEGA EL FABULISTA S.L.
BODEGA SAN ROQUE S. COOP.
BODEGAS 501 DEL PUERTO
BODEGAS AFERSA
BODEGAS ALDONIA
BODEGAS ALONSO GONZÁLEZ
BODEGAS CASTILLO DE FUENMAYOR
BODEGAS CONSEJO DE LA ALTA
BODEGAS CUNA DE REYES
BODEGAS D. MATEOS S.L.

BODEGAS DON BALBINO
BODEGAS FIN DE SIGLO
BODEGAS FORCADA S.L.
BODEGAS FUENMAYOR S.A.
BODEGAS HERMOSILLA
BODEGAS J.E.R.
BODEGAS KEFRÉN
BODEGAS LAS ORCAS (ABANDO SAN PEDRO)
BODEGAS MORAZA
BODEGAS NAVARRSOTILLO
BODEGAS OLARTIA
BODEGAS PASTOR DÍAZ
BODEGAS REAL DIVISA S.A.
BODEGAS REY DE VIÑAS
BODEGAS RUCONIA
BODEGAS VALLOBERA S.L.
BODEGAS VÉLEZ
BODEGAS VILLARNEDO
BODEGAS Y VIÑEDOS RUYAVÍ S.L.
BONIFACIO MARTÍNEZ BOBADILLA
CÁNDIDO BESA S.C.
CARDEMA S.L.
CARLOS OLASOLO
CASA GUALDA
CASA JUAN
COOP. SAN JUSTO Y SAN ISIDRO
COOP. SAN SIXTO
COVIAL
DUNVIRO S.C.
EL SANTUARIO VINÍCOLA RIOJANO
ELVIWINES S.L.
ESPADA OJEDA S.C.
FAUSTINO RIVERO ULECIA S.A.
FÉLIX IBÁÑEZ BUJANDA S.C.
FÉLIX SOLÍS
FERVIÑO
FINCA ESTARIJO
FINCA LA GRAJERA
GERARDO VITERI VICENTE
HERMANOS OTERO MUÑOZ S.C.
HONORIO RUBIO VILLAR
IDIAQUEZ S.C.
IRONDA S.L.
JON ZAMALLOA, S.C.
JOSÉ BASOCO BASOCO
JUAN JOSÉ URARTE ESPINOSA
LARCHAGO
LECEA
LÓPEZ MORENAS
LOS ARLOS
LUIS GURPEGUI MUGA
LUIS MARÍA PALACIOS SÁEZ
LUIS MARÍN DIEZ
M. A. PASCUAL LARRIETA

MAETIERRA DOMINUM
MARIANO ANTÓN SAENZ
MARQUÉS DE CARRIÓN
MAYOR DE MIGUELOA S.L.
MURIEL
NUESTRA SEÑORA DEL VICO
PÉREZ BASOCO S.C.
PROPIEDAD GRIAL
RAMÓN DE AYALA E HIJOS
REAL JUNTA S.A.
RIOJA SANTIAGO
RODOLFO GARCÍA MARTELO
SÁENZ DE SANTAMARÍA S.L.
SEÑORÍO DE LAS VIÑAS S.L.
SEÑORÍO DE LOS ARCOS
SEÑORÍO DE URARTE, S.L.
SDAD COOP. LIMITADA COMARCAL
   DE NAVARRETE
TODA EUROPA INTERCOMERCIAL
TREVIÑO RUIZ DE LAS HERAS
VALFORJA, PROPIEDAD VITIVINÍCOLA
VALGRANDE S.A.
VINOS IRADIER
VINOS MERINO S.L.
VIÑA ALMUDENA S.L.
VIÑA EL FUSTAL
VIÑEDOS REAL RUBIO
VIÑEGRA DON TEÓFILO 1º
VITIS VINICOR

# DO RUEDA

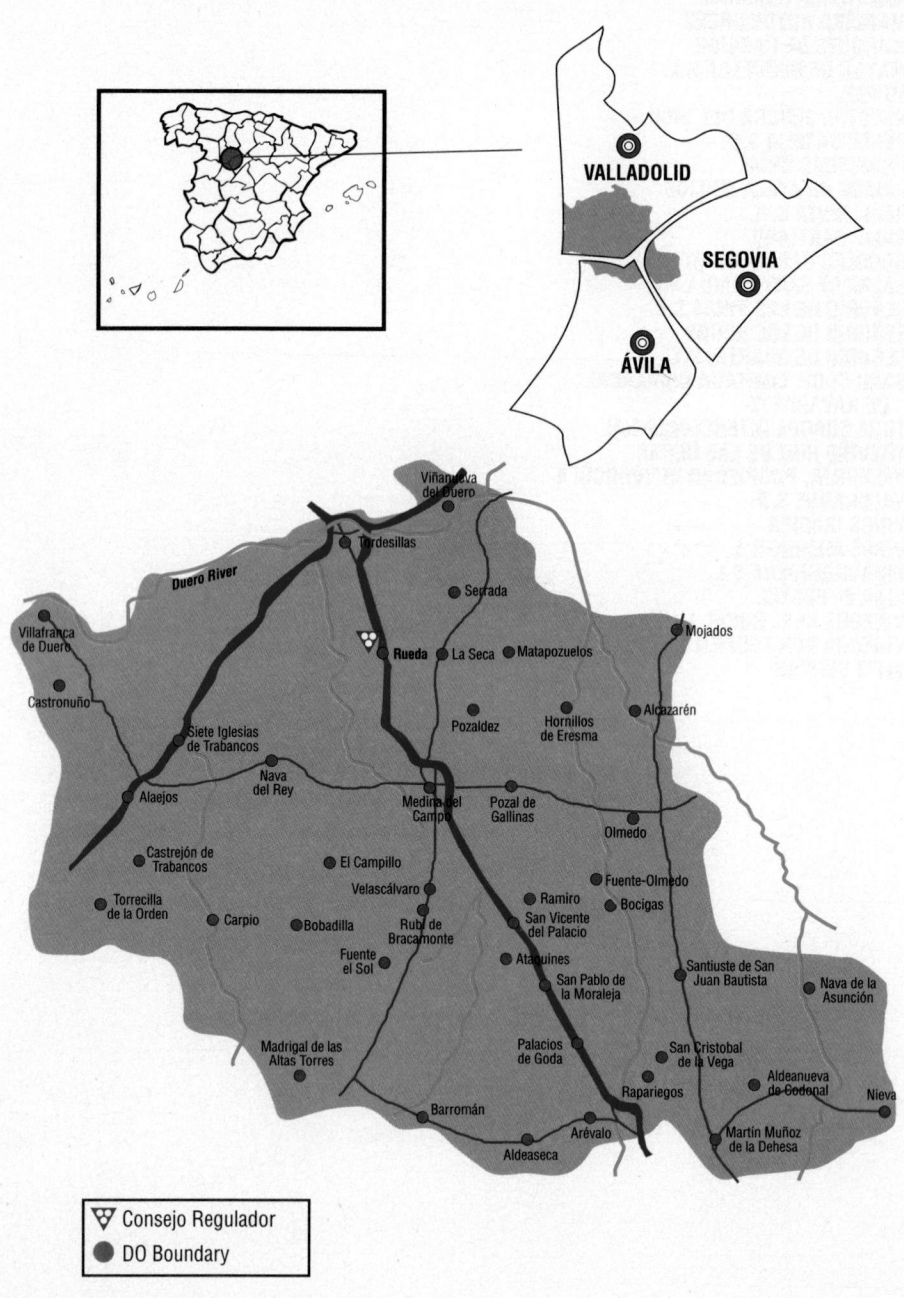

VALLADOLID

SEGOVIA

ÁVILA

Viñanueva
del Duero

Tordesillas

Duero River

Serrada

Villafranca
de Duero

Mojados

Rueda   La Seca   Matapozuelos

Castronuño

Alcazarén

Siete Iglesias
de Trabancos

Pozaldez   Hornillos
de Eresma

Nava
del Rey

Alaejos

Medina del
Campo   Pozal de
Gallinas

Olmedo

Castrejón de
Trabancos

El Campillo

Velascálvaro

Fuente-Olmedo

Torrecilla
de la Orden   Carpio   Bobadilla

Ramiro   Bocigas

Rubí de
Bracamonte

San Vicente
del Palacio

Fuente
el Sol

Ataquines

Santiuste de San
Juan Bautista

Nava de la
Asunción

San Pablo de
la Moraleja

Madrigal de las
Altas Torres

Palacios
de Goda

San Cristobal
de la Vega

Aldeanueva
de Codonal

Nieva

Rapariegos

Barromán

Arévalo

Martín Muñoz
de la Dehesa

Aldeaseca

▽ Consejo Regulador
● DO Boundary

**704** *Peñín Guide to Spanish Wine*

## NEWS

There are in Rueda more hectares than ever before, and new plantings seem to put their money on... verdejo!. All the recent investments still trust their financial and commercial future to this flagship grape, planted abundantly over 2005 and 2006, and which accounts for more than 41% of the whine wines from the region. The success of this variety even in international markets and thanks to the promotional campaigns of the DO, has meant a 20% export increase. Red and rosé wines from 2009 can carry again the Rueda back label, but they will hardly manage to be up to the quality standard of the white renderings. The vast tasting we conducted allows us to conclude that there is not only great diversity of soils and grape varieties in the region, but also different qualities. Rains at the beginning of October happened when around 80% of the harvest had already being picked. Cooler than average summer temperatures delayed ripening and helped to secure a better balance of sugars and acidity, yielding wines with better structure and longer bottle life. According to our tasting, this is surely one the best vintages of the last fifteen years, with a verdejo that shows brilliant character and singularity, with notes of fresh white fruit, herbs and its typical bitter nuance; a vintage which overshadows the 2007 barrel-fermented renderings, significantly lower in terms of quality. Some 2006's like V3 and Náiades bear evidence of the benefits of age. In the sort of inner fight between verdejo and sauvignon blanc, the latter is showing an increasing creaminess, less tropical and very appealing aromas in the hands of those producers than lean towards the more traditional methods.

## LOCATION

In the provinces of Valladolid (53 municipal districts), Segovia (17 municipal districts) and Ávila (2 municipal districts). The vineyards are situated on the undulating terrain of a plateau and are conditioned by the influence of the river Duero that runs through the northern part of the region.

## CLIMATE

Continental in nature, with cold winters and short hot summers. Rainfall is concentrated in spring and autumn. The average altitude of the region is between 600 m and 700 m, and only in the province of Segovia does it exceed 800 m.

## SOIL

Many pebbles on the surface. The terrain is stony, poor in organic matter, with good aeration and drainage. The texture of the soil is variable although, in general, sandy limestone and limestone predominate.

## GRAPE VARIETIES:

**White:** *Verdejo* (52%), *Viura* (22%), *Sauvignon Blanc* (7%) and *Palomino Fino* (19%).
**Red:** *Tempranillo, Cabernet Sauvignon, Merlot* and *Garnacha.*

| | |
|---|---|
| Hectares of Vineyard | 9,944 |
| Nº Viticulturists | 1,350 |
| Nº of Bodegas | 54 |
| 2008 Harvest | Very Good |
| 2007 Production | 40,571,472 l. |
| Marketing | 80.64% domestic 19.35% export |

# DO RUEDA

**CONSEJO REGULADOR**
Real, 8. 47490 Rueda (Valladolid)
☎: 983 868 248 - Fax: 983 868 135
@ crdo.rueda@dorueda.com
www.dorueda.com.

## GENERAL CHARACTERISTICS OF THE WINES:

| | |
|---|---|
| **WHITES** | These are produced mainly from *Verdejo*. As the percentage of this grape variety increases (from Rueda to Rueda Verdejo), a more characteristic style is obtained. Greenish straw coloured, they offer fine and elegant noses, fruity, with hints of fennel, mint and apple. On the palate they are fresh, fruity and with a characteristic bitter aftertaste, which contrasts with the sensation of ripe grapes, sweetness and freshness. Those produced from *Sauvignon Blanc* offer good roasted potency, with floral notes and, in most cases, notes of tropical fruit. They are flavourful with a certain oily character. |
| **ESPUMOSOS** | These are produced according to the traditional method of a second fermentation in the bottle. They are fresh with hints of yeast, although, in general, they are slightly heavier than the Cavas. |
| **REDS** | These are based mainly on the *Tempranillo*, with the participation of especially *Cabernet Sauvignon*. They have a quite intense cherry colour and are fruity, meaty and flavourful; they may be reminiscent of the red wines of Cigales. |
| **CLASSIC WHITES** | The so-called 'Dorado' fits the pattern of the traditional Generoso wines. Produced from a minimum of 40% Verdejo and an alcohol content not less than 15°, they have a golden colour and a slightly toasted palate due to the long oxidation process they are subjected to in the wooden barrels. There is also a 'Palido' labelling for wines of this style with shorter ageing in wood. |

## 2008 VINTAGE RATING:

# EXCELLENT

## AGRICOLA CASTELLANA S.C.L.

Ctra. Rodilana, s/n
47491 La Seca (Valladolid)
☎: 983 816 320 - Fax: 983 816 562
info@agricolacastellana.com
www.agricolacastellana.com

### VISIGODO VERDEJO 2008 B
verdejo

**91** Colour: bright straw. Nose: fresh, fresh fruit, white flowers, expressive, varietal. Palate: flavourful, fruity, good acidity, balanced.

### PALACIO DE VIVERO 2008 B
verdejo 100%

**89** Colour: straw. Nose: neat, fresh, varietal, fragrant herbs. Palate: powerful, flavourful, fruity, complex.

### AZUMBRE SAUVIGNON 2008 B
sauvignon blanc 100%

**88** Colour: bright straw. Nose: ripe fruit, tropical fruit. Palate: fruity, fresh, flavourful.

### CUATRO RAYAS VERDEJO 2008 B
verdejo 100%

**88** Colour: bright straw. Nose: medium intensity, grassy, fresh fruit. Palate: flavourful, fresh, easy to drink.

### VELITERRA 2008 B
verdejo 50%, viura 50%

**83**

### VACCEOS 2008 RD
tempranillo 100%

**82**

### CUATRO RAYAS 2008 B
sauvignon blanc 100%

**88** Colour: bright straw. Nose: fresh, fresh fruit, white flowers, grassy. Palate: flavourful, fruity, good acidity, balanced.

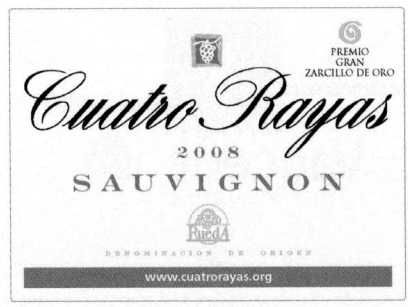

### AZUMBRE VERDEJO VENDIMIA SELECCIONADA 2008 B
verdejo 100%

**86** Colour: bright straw. Nose: fresh fruit, citrus fruit, tropical fruit. Palate: flavourful, fruity, fresh.

### PAMPANO 2008 SEMIDULCE B
verdejo 100%

**87** Colour: straw. Nose: medium intensity, candied fruit, floral. Palate: fresh, fruity, sweetness.

### VACCEOS 2005 TC
tempranillo 100%

**88** Colour: bright cherry. Nose: ripe fruit, sweet spices, creamy oak, expressive. Palate: flavourful, fruity, toasty, round tannins.

### VACCEOS TEMPRANILLO 2008 T ROBLE
tempranillo 100%

**88** Colour: deep cherry. Nose: powerful, roasted almonds, aged wood nuances, roasted coffee. Palate: powerful, flavourful, toasty, roasted-coffee aftertaste.

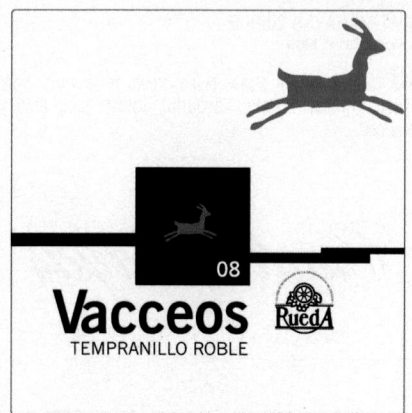

**Vacceos** RuedA
TEMPRANILLO ROBLE

## ALTAENCINA

Cañada Real, 30
47008 Valladolid (Valladolid)
☎: 639 780 716 - Fax: 983 868 905
pablo@altaencina.com
www.altaencina.com

QUIVIRA VERDEJO 2008 B
verdejo 100%

**88** Colour: bright straw. Nose: fresh, fresh fruit, white flowers, balanced, varietal. Palate: flavourful, fruity, good acidity, balanced.

## ÁLVAREZ Y DÍEZ S.A.

Juan Antonio Carmona, 12
47500 Nava del Rey (Valladolid)
☎: 983 850 136 - Fax: 983 850 761
bodegas@alvarezydiez.com
www.alvarezydiez.com

MANTEL BLANCO RUEDA VERDEJO 2008 B

**89** Colour: bright straw. Nose: grassy, fresh fruit, neat, fresh, varietal. Palate: light-bodied, powerful, flavourful, fruity.

MANTEL BLANCO SAUVIGNON BLANC 2008 B

**89** Colour: bright straw. Nose: fresh, fresh fruit, white flowers, grassy. Palate: flavourful, fruity, good acidity, balanced.

MONTE ALINA 2008 B

**85** Colour: bright straw. Nose: ripe fruit, grassy, citrus fruit. Palate: rich, flavourful, fruity, sweetness.

MANTEL BLANCO 2007 BFB

**90** Colour: bright straw. Nose: sweet spices, cocoa bean, ripe fruit. Palate: flavourful, fruity, fleshy.

## ÁNGEL RODRÍGUEZ VIDAL

Torcido, 1
47491 La Seca (Valladolid)
☎: 983 816 302 - Fax: 983 816 302
martinsancho@martinsancho.com

MARTINSANCHO VERDEJO 2008 B
verdejo 100%

**90** Colour: bright yellow. Nose: characterful, varietal, fresh fruit, grassy. Palate: powerful, flavourful, fruity, full, complex.

## AURA (DOMECQ BODEGAS)

Autovía del Noroeste, km. 175
47490 Rueda (Valladolid)
☎: 983 868 286 - Fax: 983 868 168
mcarreir@domecqbodegas.com
www.domecqbodegas.com

AURA VERDEJO 2008 B
verdejo 87%, sauvignon blanc 13%

**89** Colour: bright straw. Nose: ripe fruit, fruit expression, grassy. Palate: flavourful, ripe fruit, easy to drink.

AURA SAUVIGNON BLANC 2008 B
sauvignon blanc 100%

**89** Colour: straw. Nose: fresh fruit, fragrant herbs, powerfull, varietal, elegant, complex. Palate: powerful, flavourful, fresh, complex, fruity.

## AVELINO VEGAS

Real del Pino, 36
40460 Santiuste (Segovia)
☎: 921 596 002 - Fax: 921 596 035
ana@avelinovegas.com
www.avelinovegas.com

MONTESPINA VERDEJO 2008 B JOVEN
verdejo 100%

**91** Colour: bright straw. Nose: fresh fruit, white flowers, expressive, varietal, grassy. Palate: flavourful, fruity, good acidity, balanced.

MONTESPINA SAUVIGNON 2008 B JOVEN
sauvignon blanc 100%

**90** Colour: bright straw. Nose: powerful, ripe fruit, tropical fruit, grassy. Palate: flavourful, fruity, fresh.

CASA DE LA VEGA SAUVIGNON 2008 B JOVEN
sauvignon blanc 100%

**88** Colour: bright straw. Nose: fresh, white flowers, expressive, tropical fruit. Palate: flavourful, fruity, good acidity, balanced.

CASA DE LA VEGA VERDEJO 2008 B JOVEN
verdejo 100%

**87** Colour: bright straw. Nose: fresh, fresh fruit, white flowers. Palate: flavourful, fruity, good acidity, balanced.

## BELONDRADE

Camino del Puerto
47491 La Seca (Valladolid)
☎: 983 481 001 - Fax: 600 590 024
info@belondradeylurton.com
www.belondradeylurton.com

BELONDRADE Y LURTON 2007 BFB
verdejo 100%

**92** Colour: bright yellow. Nose: varietal, powerfull, elegant, creamy oak, smoky. Palate: powerful, rich, complex, fresh.

## BODEGA EMINA MEDINA

Ctra. Medina del Campo - Olmedo, km. 1,2
47400 Medina del Campo (Valladolid)

☎: 902 430 170 - Fax: 902 430 189
eminarueda@emina.es
www.eminarueda.es

SELECCIÓN PERSONAL CARLOS MORO EMINA
VERDEJO 2008 B
verdejo 100%

**91** Colour: bright straw. Nose: fresh, fresh fruit, white flowers, expressive, sweet spices. Palate: flavourful, fruity, good acidity, balanced.

MELIOR VERDEJO 2008 B
verdejo 100%

**89** Colour: bright straw. Nose: fresh fruit, fruit expression, grassy. Palate: powerful, flavourful, fruity, good acidity.

EMINA VERDEJO 2008 B
verdejo

**88** Colour: bright straw. Nose: white flowers, grassy, varietal. Palate: powerful, flavourful, fleshy, good acidity.

MELIOR RUEDA 2008 B
verdejo 90%, viura 10%

**87** Colour: bright straw. Nose: balanced, powerfull, varietal. Palate: fruity, light-bodied.

EMINA RUEDA 2008 B

**86** Colour: straw. Nose: fresh fruit, varietal, grassy. Palate: light-bodied, flavourful, fruity, fresh.

EMINA RUEDA SEMIDULCE 2007 B

**85** Colour: bright straw. Nose: powerful, fresh fruit, floral. Palate: flavourful, sweetness, good acidity.

EMINA BN
verdejo 100%

**84**

EMINA 2008 SS
verdejo 100%

**85** Colour: bright straw. Nose: white flowers, fresh fruit. Palate: good acidity, balanced, varietal.

## BODEGA FRANÇOIS LURTON

Camino Magarin s/n
47529 Villafranca del Duero (Valladolid)
☎: 983 034 030 - Fax: 983 034 040
bodega@jflurton.es
www.jflurton.es

HERMANOS LURTON 2008 B
verdejo 85%, sauvignon blanc 15%

**87** Colour: bright straw. Nose: fresh, fresh fruit, expressive, fragrant herbs. Palate: flavourful, fruity, good acidity, balanced, varietal.

HERMANOS LURTON CUESTA DE ORO 2007 BFB
verdejo 100%

**90** Colour: bright golden. Nose: ripe fruit, dry nuts, dried herbs, dry stone. Palate: flavourful, fruity, spicy, long.

DE PUTA MADRE 2006 B
verdejo 100%

**89** Colour: bright golden. Nose: dry nuts, spicy, aged wood nuances, toasty. Palate: good structure, rich, flavourful, fine bitter notes, round.

## BODEGA GÓTICA

Ctra. Rueda-La Seca, km. 1,2
47490 Rueda (Valladolid)
☎: 983 868 387 - Fax: 983 868 387
mjhmonsalve@ya.com
www.trascampanas.com

MONSALVE VERDEJO 2008 B
verdejo 100%

**90** Colour: bright straw. Nose: powerful, varietal, grassy, ripe fruit. Palate: flavourful, fruity, fresh.

POLÍGONO 10 VERDEJO 2008 B
verdejo 100%

**90** Colour: bright straw. Nose: grassy, fresh, fruit expression. Palate: flavourful, fruity, fleshy.

TRASCAMPANAS VERDEJO 2008 B
verdejo 100%

**92** Colour: bright straw. Nose: ripe fruit, fruit expression, tropical fruit, floral. Palate: flavourful, fleshy, varietal, good acidity.

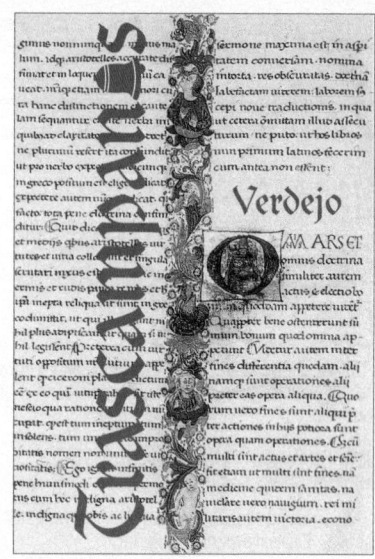

TRASCAMPANAS SELECCIÓN 2008 B
verdejo 100%

**89** Colour: bright straw. Nose: ripe fruit, tropical fruit, honeyed notes. Palate: flavourful, fleshy, ripe fruit.

TRASCAMPANAS SAUVIGNON 2008 B
sauvignon blanc 100%

**91** Colour: bright yellow. Nose: macerated fruit, fragrant herbs, undergrowth. Palate: powerful, flavourful, fresh, fruity, complex, balsamic.

POLÍGONO 10 SAUVIGNON 2008 B
sauvignon blanc 100%

**89** Colour: straw. Nose: fresh fruit, varietal, powerfull, fresh. Palate: powerful, flavourful, varietal, fruity, sweetness, good acidity.

BADAJO RUEDA 2008 B
verdejo 70%, viura 30%

**88** Colour: straw. Nose: fresh fruit, grassy. Palate: good acidity, sweetness, fresh, fruity.

MOYORIDO VERDEJO 2008 B
verdejo 100%

**88** Colour: bright straw. Nose: fresh fruit, varietal, floral. Palate: flavourful, fresh, fruity.

## BODEGA HERMANOS DEL VILLAR

Zarcillo, s/n
47490 Rueda (Valladolid)
☎: 983 868 904 - Fax: 983 868 905
pablo@orodecastilla.com
www.orodecastilla.com

ORO DE CASTILLA VERDEJO 2008 B
verdejo 100%

**89** Colour: bright straw. Nose: macerated fruit, fresh, varietal. Palate: powerful, flavourful, fruity, fresh, complex.

ORO DE CASTILLA SAUVIGNON BLANC 2008 B
sauvignon blanc

**87** Colour: straw. Nose: fresh fruit, varietal, powerfull, fresh, wild herbs. Palate: easy to drink, powerful, flavourful, fresh.

## BODEGA JAVIER SANZ VITICULTOR

San Judas, 2
47491 La Seca (Valladolid)
☎: 983 816 669 - Fax: 983 816 639
bodega@jsviticultor.com
www.jsviticultor.com

VILLA NARCISA RUEDA VERDEJO 2008 B
verdejo 100%

**90** Colour: bright straw. Nose: powerful, varietal, expressive, fresh, characterful, fresh fruit, fruit expression, fragrant herbs. Palate: powerful, flavourful, fruity, complex, full.

VILLA NARCISA SAUVIGNON BLANC 2008 B JOVEN
sauvignon blanc 100%

**90** Colour: bright straw. Nose: varietal, powerfull, complex, fragrant herbs, balsamic herbs. Palate: powerful, flavourful, fruity, fresh, balsamic, mineral.

REY SANTO 2008 B JOVEN
verdejo 50%, viura 50%

**88** Colour: bright straw. Nose: ripe fruit, powerfull, white flowers. Palate: flavourful, fruity, good acidity.

# DO RUEDA

VILLA NARCISA 2007 BFB
verdejo 100%

**86** Colour: bright yellow. Nose: powerful, candied fruit, pattiserie, sweet spices. Palate: fleshy, flavourful, warm.

## BODEGA PALACIO DE BORNOS

Ctra. Madrid-Coruña km. 170,7
47490 Rueda (Valladolid)
☎: 983 868 336 - Fax: 983 868 432
bodegasbccv@interbook.net
www.bodegasdecastilla.com

PALACIO DE BORNOS SAUVIGNON BLANC
VENDIMIA SELECCIONADA 2008 B
sauvignon blanc

**90** Colour: bright straw. Nose: fresh, fresh fruit, white flowers, expressive, tropical fruit. Palate: flavourful, fruity, good acidity, balanced.

BORNOS SAUVIGNON BLANC DULCE 2008 B
sauvignon blanc 100%

**88** Colour: bright straw. Nose: fresh, fresh fruit, white flowers, expressive. Palate: flavourful, good acidity, balanced, sweetness, fruity.

PALACIOS DE BORNOS VERDEJO 2008 B
verdejo 100%

**87** Colour: bright straw. Nose: fresh fruit, varietal, mineral, wild herbs. Palate: fresh, fruity, powerful, flavourful.

PALACIOS DE BORNOS VERDEJO 2007 BFB
verdejo

**90** Colour: bright straw. Nose: ripe fruit, expressive, sweet spices. Palate: flavourful, fleshy, good acidity.

PALACIO DE BORNOS VERDEJO VENDIMIA
SELECCIONADA 2004 BFB
verdejo

**92** Colour: bright yellow. Nose: smoky, ripe fruit, fine reductive notes. Palate: fresh, fruity, rich, flavourful.

PALACIOS DE BORNOS BR
verdejo

**84**

## BODEGA REINA DE CASTILLA

Ctra. Serrada - La Seca Camino La Moya
47491 La Seca (Valladolid)
☎: 983 816 667 - Fax: 983 816 663
bodega@reinadecastilla.es
www.reinadecastilla.es

REINA DE CASTILLA VERDEJO 2008 B
verdejo 100%

**91** Colour: bright straw. Nose: fresh fruit, fruit expression, floral, grassy. Palate: flavourful, fleshy, fresh, fruity.

EL BUFÓN 2008 B
verdejo 100%

**90** Colour: bright straw. Nose: fresh fruit, grassy, varietal, powerfull, fresh. Palate: powerful, flavourful, light-bodied, fresh, fruity.

REINA DE CASTILLA SAUVIGNON BLANC 2008 B
sauvignon blanc 100%

**90** Colour: bright straw. Nose: ripe fruit, white flowers, powerfull, grassy. Palate: flavourful, fleshy, powerful, good acidity.

ISABELINO 2008 B
verdejo 65%, viura 35%

**88** Colour: bright straw. Nose: fresh, white flowers, ripe fruit. Palate: flavourful, fruity, good acidity, balanced.

## BODEGA SOLAR DE MUÑOSANCHO

Plaza de La Olma, 3
47491 La Seca (Valladolid)
☎: 983 372 221 - Fax: 983 372 221
bprius@terra.es
www.solarmsancho.com

PRIUS DE MORAÑA VERDEJO 2008 B

**86** Colour: straw. Nose: fresh fruit, fresh, neat, varietal. Palate: powerful, flavourful, fruity.

## BODEGA VIÑA VILANO

Ctra. de Anguix, 10
03314 Pedrosa de Duero (Burgos)
☎: 947 530 029 - Fax: 947 530 037
info@vinavilano.com
www.vinavilano.com

VIÑA VILANO VERDEJO 2008 B
verdejo 100%

**87** Colour: bright straw. Nose: fresh, fresh fruit, expressive, balsamic herbs. Palate: flavourful, fruity, good acidity, balanced.

## BODEGAS ANTAÑO

Arribas, 7-9
47490 Rueda (Valladolid)
☎: 983 868 533 - Fax: 983 868 514
comercial@bodegasantano.com
www.bodegasantano.com

LEGUILLÓN VERDEJO 2008 B
verdejo 100%

**91** Colour: bright straw. Nose: floral, fresh fruit, grassy, complex, elegant, fresh, varietal. Palate: powerful, flavourful, fruity, fresh, complex.

ALTA PLATA RUEDA 2008 B
verdejo 100%

**90** Colour: bright straw. Nose: powerful, varietal, ripe fruit, grassy. Palate: flavourful, fruity, good acidity.

VIÑA MOCÉN SAUVIGNON BLANC 2008 B
sauvignon blanc 100%

**89** Colour: bright straw. Nose: powerful, fresh fruit, grassy. Palate: flavourful, fruity, fresh.

VIÑA MOCÉN VERDEJO 2008 B
verdejo 100%

**89** Colour: bright straw. Nose: ripe fruit, fruit expression, floral. Palate: flavourful, fleshy, fruity, good acidity.

MOCÉN VERDEJO 2006 BFB
verdejo 100%

**86** Colour: bright yellow. Nose: sweet spices, cocoa bean, candied fruit. Palate: sweetness, fine bitter notes, ripe fruit.

## BODEGAS CASTELO DE MEDINA

Ctra. CL-602, km. 48
47465 Villaverde de Medina (Valladolid)
☎: 983 831 932 - Fax: 983 831 857
comercial@castelodemedina.es
www.castelodemedina.es

CASTELO DE MEDINA VERDEJO 2008 B
verdejo 100%

**88** Colour: bright straw. Nose: fresh fruit, ripe fruit, floral, grassy. Palate: flavourful, fruity, fresh.

REAL CASTELO RUEDA VERDEJO 2008 B
verdejo 85%, sauvignon blanc 15%

**88** Colour: bright straw. Nose: grassy, fresh, expressive, fresh fruit. Palate: flavourful, fruity, fresh.

CASTELO DE LA DEHESA 2008 B
verdejo 50%, viura 50%, sauvignon blanc %

**86** Colour: bright straw. Nose: fresh fruit, grassy, medium intensity. Palate: flavourful, fruity, fresh.

CASTELO DE MEDINA SAUVIGNON BLANC 2008 B
sauvignon blanc 100%

**86** Colour: bright straw. Nose: fresh, fresh fruit, white flowers, expressive. Palate: flavourful, fruity, good acidity, balanced.

CASTELO ÁMBAR SEMIDULCE 2007 B
sauvignon blanc 100%

**83**

CASTELBURGO

## BODEGAS DE LOS HEREDEROS DEL MARQUÉS DE RISCAL

Torrea, 1
01340 Elciego (Alava)
☎: 945 606 000 - Fax: 945 606 023
marquesderiscal@marquesderiscal.com
www.marquesderiscal.com

FINCA MONTICO 2008 B
verdejo

**90** Colour: bright yellow. Nose: complex, expressive, fresh, varietal, grassy, undergrowth, mineral. Palate: powerful, flavourful, rich, fruity, complex, good structure.

MARQUÉS DE RISCAL RUEDA 2008 B

**89** Colour: bright yellow. Nose: fresh fruit, macerated fruit, fragrant herbs. Palate: fresh, fruity, rich, powerful, flavourful.

MARQUÉS DE RISCAL SAUVIGNON BLANC 2008 B
sauvignon blanc 100%

**88** Colour: straw. Nose: candied fruit, wild herbs, fresh fruit. Palate: fruity, powerful.

MARQUÉS DE RISCAL LIMOUSIN 2007 B

**92** Colour: bright straw. Nose: powerful, characterful, smoky, creamy oak, ripe fruit. Palate: creamy, smoky aftertaste, powerful, flavourful, full.

## BODEGAS FÉLIX LORENZO CACHAZO S.L.

Ctra. Medina del Campo, km. 9
47220 Pozáldez (Valladolid)
☎: 983 822 176 - Fax: 983 822 008
bodegas@cachazo.com
www.cachazo.com

GRAN CARDIEL RUEDA VERDEJO 2008 B
verdejo 100%

**90** Colour: straw. Nose: fresh fruit, varietal, balsamic herbs, grassy. Palate: balanced, powerful, flavourful, fruity.

CARRASVIÑAS VERDEJO 2008 B
verdejo 100%

**90** Colour: bright straw. Nose: fresh fruit, white flowers, expressive, varietal, grassy. Palate: flavourful, fruity, good acidity, balanced.

**MANIA RUEDA VERDEJO 2008 B**
verdejo 100%

**90** Colour: bright straw. Nose: powerful, varietal, fresh, complex, balsamic herbs, fragrant herbs. Palate: powerful, flavourful, fresh, fruity, complex.

**QUIETUS VERDEJO 2008 B**
verdejo 100%

**CARRASVIÑAS ESPUMOSO 2007 BR**
verdejo 100%

**87** Colour: bright straw. Nose: medium intensity, fresh fruit, dried herbs, fine lees, floral. Palate: fresh, fruity, flavourful, good acidity.

**LARRUA**

## BODEGAS FÉLIX SANZ S.L.

Ronda Aradillas, s/n
47490 Rueda (Valladolid)
☎: 983 868 044 - Fax: 983 868 133
info@bodegasfelixsanz.es
www.bodegasfelixsanz.es

**VIÑA CIMBRÓN RUEDA 2008 B**
verdejo 50%, viura 50%

**89** Colour: straw. Nose: powerful, varietal, complex, fragrant herbs, fresh fruit. Palate: fresh, fruity, powerful, flavourful.

**VIÑA CIMBRÓN RUEDA SAUVIGNON 2008 B**
sauvignon blanc 100%

**89** Colour: bright straw. Nose: fresh, fresh fruit, expressive, varietal. Palate: flavourful, fruity, good acidity, balanced.

**VIÑA CIMBRÓN RUEDA VERDEJO 2008 B**
verdejo 100%

**89** Colour: pale. Nose: powerful, ripe fruit, fruit expression, floral. Palate: flavourful, fruity, fleshy.

**VIÑA CIMBRÓN 2007 BFB**
verdejo 85%, viura 15%

**90** Colour: bright yellow. Nose: powerful, ripe fruit, sweet spices, creamy oak, fragrant herbs. Palate: rich, smoky aftertaste, flavourful, fresh, good acidity.

## BODEGAS GARCÍA DE ARANDA

Ctra. de Soria, s/n
09400 Aranda de Duero (Burgos)
☎: 947 501 817 - Fax: 947 506 355
bodega@bodegasgarcia.com
www.bodegasgarcia.com

**ORO BLANCO VERDEJO 2008 B**
verdejo 100%

**86** Colour: bright straw. Nose: fresh, fresh fruit, white flowers. Palate: flavourful, fruity, good acidity.

**ORO BLANCO RUEDA 2008 B**
viura 50%, verdejo 50%

**85** Colour: bright straw. Nose: ripe fruit, floral. Palate: flavourful, fruity, fleshy.

## BODEGAS GARCIGRANDE

Aradillas, s/n
47490 Rueda (Valladolid)
☎: 983 868 561 - Fax: 983 868 449
info@hispanobodegas.com
www.hispanobodegas.com

**ANIER 2008 B**

**89** Colour: straw. Nose: fragrant herbs, fresh fruit, powerfull, varietal. Palate: fruity, complex, powerful, flavourful.

**SEÑORÍO DE GARCI GRANDE RUEDA 2008 B**

**88** Colour: bright straw. Nose: fresh fruit, dry stone, mineral, fragrant herbs. Palate: good acidity, good structure, powerful, flavourful, complex.

# DO RUEDA

SEÑORÍO DE GARCI GRANDE VERDEJO 2008 B

**90** Colour: bright straw. Nose: varietal, expressive, ripe fruit, grassy, white flowers. Palate: good acidity, fruity, fresh.

12 LINAJES 2008 B

**90** Colour: bright straw. Nose: powerful, varietal, neat, fresh fruit, fragrant herbs. Palate: powerful, flavourful, fresh, fruity.

SEÑORÍO DE GARCI GRANDE SAUVIGNON BLANC 2008 B
sauvignon blanc

**85** Colour: bright straw. Nose: powerful, tropical fruit, ripe fruit, grassy. Palate: flavourful, powerful.

MOZARES

## BODEGAS JOSÉ PARIENTE

Ctra. Rueda, km. 2.5
47491 La Seca (Valladolid)
☎: 983 816 600 - Fax: 983 816 620
info@josepariente.com
www.josepariente.com

JOSÉ PARIENTE VERDEJO 2008 B

**90** Colour: bright straw. Nose: fresh fruit, varietal, expressive, powerfull. Palate: powerful, flavourful, fruity, complex, fruity aftestaste.

JOSÉ PARIENTE SAUVIGNON BLANC 2008 B

**89** Colour: bright straw. Nose: medium intensity, macerated fruit, candied fruit. Palate: fruity, powerful, flavourful, complex.

JOSÉ PARIENTE 2007 BFB

**88** Colour: bright yellow. Nose: ripe fruit, sweet spices, creamy oak. Palate: rich, flavourful, fresh, good acidity.

## BODEGAS NAIA

Camino San Martín s/n
47491 La Seca (Valladolid)
☎: 628 434 933 - Fax: 676 643 369
info@bodegasnaia.com

NAIA 2008 B

**91** Colour: bright straw. Nose: fresh fruit, floral, varietal, characterful, expressive. Palate: powerful, flavourful, full, fruity, fresh.

**K-NAIA 2008 B**
verdejo 85%, sauvignon blanc 10%, viura 5%

**89** Colour: bright straw. Nose: fresh, varietal, grassy, fresh fruit. Palate: fresh, fruity, light-bodied, flavourful.

**LAS BRISAS 2008 B**
verdejo

**88** Colour: bright straw. Nose: ripe fruit, grassy, floral. Palate: flavourful, fruity, fresh, fleshy.

**NAIADES 2007 BFB**
verdejo

**93** Color bright yellow. Aroma powerfull, ripe fruit, sweet spices, creamy oak, fragrant herbs. Taste rich, smoky aftertaste, flavourful, fresh, good acidity.

**NAIADES 2006 BFB**
verdejo

**93** Colour: bright yellow. Nose: smoky, creamy oak, ripe fruit, fruit expression, complex, powerfull. Palate: complex, fruity, powerful, flavourful, full.

## BODEGAS NILO

Federico García Lorca, 7
47490 Rueda (Valladolid)
☎: 690 068 682 - Fax: 983 868 366
info@bodegasnilo.com
www.bodegasnilo.com

**BIANCA 2008 B**
verdejo 100%

**88** Colour: bright straw. Nose: ripe fruit, floral, warm, expressive. Palate: powerful, flavourful, good acidity, fruity, good finish.

NAT

## BODEGAS PEÑAFIEL

Ctra. N-122, km. 311
47300 Peñafiel (Valladolid)
☎: 983 881 622 - Fax: 983 881 944
bodegaspenafiel@bodegaspenafiel.com
www.bodegaspenafiel.com

**ALBA MIROS 2008 B**
verdejo 100%

**90** Colour: bright straw. Nose: fresh, fresh fruit, white flowers, expressive, varietal. Palate: flavourful, fruity, good acidity, balanced.

## BODEGAS PRADOREY

Ctra. Nacional VI, km. 172,5
47490 Rueda (Valladolid)
☎: 983 444 048 - Fax: 983 868 564
bodega@pradorey.com
www.pradorey.com

**PRADOREY VERDEJO 2008 B**
verdejo 100%

**90** Colour: bright straw. Nose: powerful, ripe fruit, floral, grassy. Palate: flavourful, powerful, fleshy.

**PRADOREY SAUVIGNON BLANC 2008 B**
sauvignon blanc 100%

**88** Colour: bright straw. Nose: ripe fruit, floral, grassy. Palate: flavourful, fruity, sweetness, rich.

PR 3 BARRICAS 2007 BFB
verdejo 100%

**92** Colour: bright yellow. Nose: smoky, creamy oak, ripe fruit, fruit expression, scrubland. Palate: fresh, fruity, full, powerful, flavourful.

BIRLOCHO

## BODEGAS PROTOS

Ctra. CL 610, km. 32,5
47491 La Seca (Valladolid)
☎: 983 878 011 - Fax: 983 878 012
bodega@bodegasprotos.com
www.bodegasprotos.com

PROTOS VERDEJO 2008 B
verdejo 100%

**88** Colour: bright straw. Nose: ripe fruit, dried flowers, fragrant herbs. Palate: fruity, fresh, flavourful.

## BODEGAS RUEDA PÉREZ

Calle Boyón
47220 Pozaldez (Valladolid)
☎: 650 454 657 - Fax: 983 822 049
satruedaperez@terra.es
www.bodegasruedaperez.es

VIÑA BURÓN VERDEJO 2008 B
verdejo 100%

**90** Colour: bright straw. Nose: varietal, fresh fruit, fruit expression, floral. Palate: flavourful, powerful, fruity, fresh.

ZAPADORADO VERDEJO 2008 B
verdejo 100%

**88** Colour: straw. Nose: fresh fruit, fragrant herbs, powerfull, varietal. Palate: fruity, fresh, flavourful, good acidity.

JOSÉ GALO VERDEJO SELECCIÓN 2008 B
verdejo 100%

**86** Colour: straw. Nose: fresh fruit, varietal, fresh, medium intensity. Palate: fruity, flavourful, good structure, fruity aftestaste.

## BODEGAS SEÑORIO DE NAVA

Ctra. Valladolid - Soria, 62
09318 Nava de Roa (Burgos)
☎: 987 209 790 - Fax: 987 209 808
c.puente@senoriodenava.es
www.senoriodenava.es

VIÑA MARIAN VERDEJO SAUVIGNON 2008 B
sauvignon blanc 60%, verdejo 40%

**89** Colour: bright straw. Nose: fresh fruit, expressive, neat, fresh, varietal. Palate: powerful, flavourful, fruity, complex.

VIÑA MARIAN VERDEJO 2008 B
verdejo 100%

**85** Colour: bright straw. Nose: fresh, fresh fruit, white flowers. Palate: flavourful, fruity, good acidity, balanced.

SEÑORÍO DE NAVA VERDEJO 2008 B
verdejo 100%

**83**

## BODEGAS SURCO S.L. (VALDRINAL)

Picote 19
09400 Aranda de Duero (Burgos)
☎: 915 480 232 - Fax: 915 477 476
info@valdrinal.com
www.valdrinal.com

VALDRINAL DE SANTAMARÍA 2008 B
verdejo 100%

**90** Colour: bright straw. Nose: fresh, fresh fruit, white flowers, expressive. Palate: flavourful, fruity, good acidity, balanced.

## BODEGAS VAL DE VID

Ctra. Valladolid - Medina del Campo, km. 23,6
47239 Serrada (Valladolid)
☎: 983 559 914 - Fax: 983 559 914
valdevid@valdevid.com

CONDESA EYLO VERDEJO 2008 B

**90** Colour: bright straw. Nose: powerful, ripe fruit, fruit expression, citrus fruit. Palate: flavourful, fruity, fresh, fleshy.

VAL DE VID 2008 B

**90** Colour: bright straw. Nose: fresh, fresh fruit, white flowers, expressive. Palate: flavourful, fruity, good acidity, balanced.

EYLO RUEDA B

**89** Colour: bright straw. Nose: fresh, powerfull, varietal, fresh fruit, grassy. Palate: good acidity, balanced, powerful, flavourful, fruity, fresh, varietal.

## BODEGAS VALPINCIA

Ctra. de Melida a Peñafiel, km. 3,5
47300 Peñafiel (Valladolid)
☎: 983 878 007 - Fax: 983 880 620

penafiel@bodegasvalpincia.com
www.bodegasvalpincia.com

VALPINCIA VERDEJO 2008 B

**85** Colour: bright straw. Nose: fresh, white flowers, expressive, candied fruit. Palate: flavourful, fruity, good acidity, balanced.

VALPINCIA RUEDA 2008 B

**85** Colour: bright straw. Nose: fresh fruit, white flowers, expressive. Palate: flavourful, fruity, good acidity, balanced.

## BODEGAS VERACRUZ S.L.

Juan A. Carmona, 1
47500 Nava del Rey (Valladolid)
☎: 983 850 136 - Fax: 983 850 761
j.benito@alvarezydiez.com

ERMITA VERACRUZ VERDEJO 2008 B

**91** Colour: bright straw. Nose: ripe fruit, varietal, citrus fruit, scrubland, white flowers. Palate: round, fleshy, fruity.

## BODEGAS VERDEAL S.L.

Nueva, 8
40200 Cuellar (Segovia)
☎: 921 140 125 - Fax: 921 142 421
e.poza@bodegasverdeal.com

VERDEAL 2008 B
verdejo 100%

**88** Colour: bright straw. Nose: wild herbs, ripe fruit, tropical fruit, expressive. Palate: rich, fruity, flavourful.

## BODEGAS Y VIÑEDOS
## ÁNGEL LORENZO CACHAZO S.L.

Estación, 53

47220 Pozaldez (Valladolid)
☎: 983 822 481 - Fax: 983 822 012
bodegamartivilli@jet.es
www.martivilli.com

MARTIVILLÍ VERDEJO 2008 B
verdejo 100%

**90** Colour: bright straw. Nose: fragrant herbs, burnt matches, fruit expression, fresh fruit, varietal, powerfull, characterful. Palate: powerful, flavourful, fruity, full, sweetness.

MARTIVILLÍ SAUVIGNON BLANC 2008 B
sauvignon blanc 100%

**90** Colour: bright straw. Nose: fresh, fresh fruit, white flowers, tropical fruit. Palate: flavourful, fruity, good acidity, balanced.

EL PERRO VERDE 2008 B

**90** Colour: bright yellow. Nose: fresh fruit, macerated fruit, complex, expressive, varietal, grassy. Palate: fruity, full, powerful, flavourful.

MARTIVILLÍ BN
verdejo 100%

**84**

LORENZO CACHAZO
CACHAZO

## BODEGAS Y VIÑEDOS
## MARTÍN BERDUGO

Ctra. de la Colonia, s/n
09400 Aranda de Duero (Burgos)
☎: 947 506 331 - Fax: 947 506 602
bodega@martinberdugo.com
www.martinberdugo.com

## MARTÍN BERDUGO VERDEJO 2008 B
verdejo 100%

**87** Colour: bright straw. Nose: fresh, fresh fruit, white flowers, expressive. Palate: flavourful, fruity, good acidity, balanced, balsamic.

## BODEGAS Y VIÑEDOS MONTEABELLÓN

Calvario s/n
09318 Nava de Roa (Burgos)
☎: 947 550 000 - Fax: 947 550 219
info@monteabellon.com
www.monteabellon.com

MONTEABELLÓN VERDEJO 2008 B
verdejo 100%

**88** Colour: bright straw. Nose: fresh, fresh fruit, white flowers, expressive. Palate: flavourful, fruity, good acidity, balanced.

## BODEGAS Y VIÑEDOS SHAYA

40462 Aldeanueva del Codonal (Segovia)
☎: 968 435 022
info@orowines.com

SHAYA 2008 B
verdejo 100%

**91** Colour: bright straw. Nose: powerful, varietal, fresh fruit, grassy, mineral. Palate: flavourful, fruity, fresh, good acidity.

## BODEGAS Y VIÑEDOS VIÑA MAYOR

Ctra. Valladolid - Soria, km. 325,6
47350 Quintanilla de Onésimo (Valladolid)
☎: 983 680 461 - Fax: 983 027 217
barcelo@habarcelo.es
www.vina-mayor.es

VIÑA MAYOR VERDEJO 2008 B
verdejo

**89** Colour: bright straw. Nose: ripe fruit, floral, varietal, grassy. Palate: flavourful, powerful, fleshy, fruity.

## BUIL & GINÉ

Ctra. de Gratallops - Vilella Baixa, km. 11,5
43737 Gratallops (Tarragona)
☎: 977 839 810 - Fax: 977 839 811
info@builgine.com

www.builgine.com

NOSIS 2008 B
verdejo 100%

**90** Colour: bright straw. Nose: fresh, fresh fruit, expressive, grassy, ripe fruit. Palate: flavourful, fruity, good acidity.

## COMPAÑIA DE VINOS MIGUEL MARTÍN

Ctra. Burgos - Portugal, km. 101
47290 Cubillas de Santa María (Valladolid)
☎: 983 250 319 - Fax: 983 250 329
exportacion@ciadevinos.com
www.ciadevinos.com

CASTICAL VERDEJO-VIURA 2008 B

**88** Colour: bright straw. Nose: fresh, fresh fruit, white flowers, powerfull. Palate: flavourful, fruity, good acidity, balanced.

DOMINE 2008 B
verdejo, sauvignon blanc

**85** Colour: straw, pale. Nose: fresh fruit, expressive, fragrant herbs. Palate: fruity, flavourful, easy to drink, correct, fine bitter notes.

## CUEVAS DE CASTILLA

Ctra. Madrid-Coruña, km. 171
47490 Rueda (Valladolid)
☎: 983 868 336 - Fax: 983 868 432
bodegasbccv@interbook.net
www.bodegasdecastilla.com

ESPADAÑA SAUVIGNON 2008 B
sauvignon blanc

**88** Colour: bright straw. Nose: candied fruit, floral, grassy. Palate: flavourful, fruity, fresh.

ESPADAÑA VERDEJO 2008 B
verdejo 98%, sauvignon blanc 2%

**88** Colour: bright straw. Nose: medium intensity, expressive, fresh fruit. Palate: flavourful, fruity, fresh.

COLAGÓN 2008 B
verdejo 60%, viura 40%

**87** Colour: straw. Nose: medium intensity, neat, fresh, varietal. Palate: fresh, fruity, flavourful.

SEÑORÍO DE ILLESCAS 2004 TC
tempranillo 85%, cabernet sauvignon 15%

**86** Colour: cherry, garnet rim. Nose: medium intensity, ripe fruit, balsamic herbs, green pepper. Palate: ripe fruit, spicy, toasty.

## DE ALBERTO

Ctra. de Valdestillas, 2
47239 Serrada (Valladolid)
☎: 983 559 107 - Fax: 983 559 084
info@dealberto.com
www.dealberto.com

DE ALBERTO VERDEJO SELECCIÓN 2008 B
verdejo 100%

**92** Colour: bright straw. Nose: fresh fruit, fragrant herbs, expressive, varietal, complex. Palate: powerful, flavourful, fruity, full, mineral.

MONASTERIO DE PALAZUELOS VERDEJO 2008 B
verdejo 100%

**89** Colour: straw. Nose: fresh, neat, varietal, fresh fruit. Palate: flavourful, powerful, fresh, rich.

MONASTERIO DE PALAZUELOS RUEDA 2008 B
verdejo 70%, viura 30%

**88** Colour: bright straw. Nose: expressive, ripe fruit, floral. Palate: flavourful, fruity, good acidity.

MONASTERIO DE PALAZUELOS SAUVIGNON BLANC 2008 B
sauvignon blanc 100%

**79**

DE ALBERTO VERDEJO SELECCIÓN 2007 BFB
verdejo 100%

**90** Colour: bright straw. Nose: powerful, expressive, ripe fruit, sweet spices. Palate: flavourful, fruity, sweetness, good acidity.

## ESTANCIA PIEDRA S.L.

Ctra. Toro Salamanca, km 5
49800 Toro (Zamora)
☎: 980 693 900 - Fax: 980 693 901
info@estanciapiedra.com
www.estanciapiedra.com

PIEDRA VERDEJO 2008 B
verdejo 100%

**88** Colour: bright yellow. Nose: ripe fruit, expressive, tropical fruit, white flowers. Palate: unctuous, good acidity, fruity, flavourful, good finish.

## FINCA CASERÍO DE DUEÑAS

Ctra. Cl. 602
(Medina del Campo - Nava del Rey), km. 50,2
47465 Villaverde de Medina (Valladolid)
☎: 915 006 000 - Fax: 915 006 006
barcelo@habarcelo.es
www.habarcelo.es

VIÑA MAYOR VERDEJO 2008 B
verdejo 100%

**86** Colour: bright straw. Nose: fresh, fresh fruit, white flowers, grassy. Palate: flavourful, fruity, good acidity, balanced.

## GARCIAREVALO

Pza. San Juan, 4
47230 Matapozuelos (Valladolid)
☎: 983 832 914 - Fax: 983 832 986
garciarevalo@garciarevalo.com
www.garciarevalo.com

TRES OLMOS LÍAS 2008 B
verdejo 100%

**90** Colour: bright straw. Nose: fresh, fresh fruit, white flowers, expressive. Palate: flavourful, fruity, good acidity, balanced.

VIÑA ADAJA VERDEJO 2008 B
verdejo 100%

**87** Colour: bright straw. Nose: grassy, fresh fruit, floral. Palate: flavourful, fruity, fresh, fleshy.

CASAMARO
LA TORREVIEJA

## GRANDES BODEGAS

Ctra. de Sotillo, s/n
09311 La Horra (Burgos)
☎: 947 542 166 - Fax: 947 542 165
marketing@marquesdevelilla.com
www.marquesdevelilla.es

VIÑA DE MERCADO RUEDA VERDEJO 2008 B
verdejo

**88** Colour: bright straw. Nose: ripe fruit, grassy. Palate: flavourful, fruity, fresh, long.

CATALINA DE MERCADO

## GRUPO ALGAR

Carpinteros, 13
28670 Villaviciosa de Odón (Madrid)
☎: 916 169 122 - Fax: 916 166 724
info@grupoalgar.com
www.grupoalgar.com

ABILIA VERDEJO 2008 B
verdejo

**85** Colour: bright straw. Nose: varietal, fresh, balanced, tropical fruit. Palate: flavourful, fruity, easy to drink.

ABILIA 2008 B
verdejo, viura

**83**

## GRUPO YLLERA

Ctra. Madrid - Coruña, km. 173, 5
47490 Rueda (Valladolid)
☎: 983 868 097 - Fax: 983 868 177
grupoyllera@grupoyllera.com
www.grupoyllera.com

TIERRA BUENA 2008 B

**90** Colour: bright straw. Nose: fresh, fruit expression, fresh fruit, floral. Palate: flavourful, fleshy, fruity.

VIÑA CANTOSÁN VARIETAL VERDEJO 2008 B

**90** Colour: bright straw. Nose: powerful, varietal, ripe fruit, fruit expression. Palate: flavourful, fruity, fresh, good acidity.

BRACAMONTE VERDEJO 2008 B

**89** Colour: bright straw. Nose: powerful, varietal, grassy, ripe fruit. Palate: flavourful, fruity, fresh, good acidity.

BRACAMONTE RUEDA 2008 B JOVEN

**88** Colour: bright straw. Nose: powerful, ripe fruit, fruit expression, floral. Palate: flavourful, fruity, fleshy.

VIÑA CANTOSÁN 2006 BFB

**86** Colour: bright straw. Nose: candied fruit, citrus fruit, jasmine. Palate: flavourful, fruity, sweetness.

CANTOSÁN BR
**83**

CANTOSÁN BN
**83**

CANTOSÁN SS
**82**

## HACIENDA MARQUÉS DE LA CONCORDIA

Ctra. El Ciego, s/n
26350 Cenicero (La Rioja)
☎: 914 365 900 - Fax: 914 365 932
iruiz@haciendas-espana.com
www.haciendas-espana.com

VEGA DE LA REINA VERDEJO 2008 B
verdejo 85%, sauvignon blanc 15%

**91** Colour: bright straw. Nose: powerful, varietal, ripe fruit, fruit expression, floral. Palate: flavourful, fruity, fresh, good acidity.

VEGA DE LA REINA SAUVIGNON BLANC 2008 B
sauvignon blanc 100%

**91** Colour: bright straw. Nose: powerful, varietal, ripe fruit, tropical fruit. Palate: flavourful, fruity, fresh.

## JAVIER SANZ CANTALAPIEDRA

San Judas, 2

47191 La Seca (Valladolid)
☎: 983 816 669 - Fax: 983 816 639
bodega@jsviticultor.com
www.jsviticultor.com

**ORDEN TERCERA RUEDA VERDEJO 2008 B JOVEN**
verdejo 100%

**91** Colour: straw. Nose: powerful, varietal, complex, fragrant herbs, mineral. Palate: powerful, flavourful, rich, fresh, complex.

## LA COLECCIÓN D.C.E., S.L.

Domingo Martínez, 6
47007 Valladolid
☎: 983 271 595 - Fax: 983 271 608
exportacion@lacoleccciondevinos.com
www.lacoleccciondevinos.com

**OTER DE CILLAS VERDEJO 2008 B**
verdejo 100%

**88** Colour: bright straw. Nose: fresh, fresh fruit, grassy. Palate: flavourful, fruity, good acidity, balanced.

**OTER DE CILLAS SAUVIGNON BLANC 2008 B**
sauvignon blanc 100%

**88** Colour: bright straw. Nose: fresh, fresh fruit, white flowers, tropical fruit. Palate: flavourful, fruity, good acidity, balanced.

**OTER DE CILLAS 2006 BFB**
verdejo 85%, sauvignon blanc 15%

**88** Colour: bright golden. Nose: powerful, candied fruit, ripe fruit, citrus fruit, toasty, sweet spices. Palate: flavourful, fleshy, ripe fruit.

**FUENTESCLARAS ESP FERMENTADO EN BARRICA**
verdejo 85%, sauvignon blanc 15%

**85** Colour: pale. Nose: fresh fruit, floral, grassy. Palate: flavourful, fruity, fresh.

**OTER DE CILLAS SAUVIGNON BLANC 2007 SEMIDULCE**
sauvignon blanc 100%

**90** Colour: bright straw. Nose: fresh, expressive, ripe fruit, white flowers. Palate: flavourful, fleshy, fruity, sweetness.

## LA SOTERRAÑA

Ctra. Valladolid Madrid, N-601, km. 151
47410 Olmedo (Valladolid)
☎: 983 601 026 - Fax: 983 601 026
info@bodegaslasoterrana.com
www.bodegaslasoterrana.com

**ERESMA SAUVIGNON 2008 B**
sauvignon blanc 100%

**91** Colour: straw. Nose: varietal, powerfull, fresh, complex, floral, acacia flower. Palate: powerful, flavourful, varietal, mineral, fruity.

**V&R 2008 B**
verdejo 85%, viura 15%

**90** Colour: straw. Nose: rose petals, fresh fruit, balanced, powerfull, varietal, neat, fresh. Palate: powerful, flavourful, fresh, fruity, complex.

**ERESMA VERDEJO 2008 B**
verdejo 100%

**89** Colour: bright straw. Nose: powerful, fresh fruit, fruit expression, grassy. Palate: flavourful, fruity, fresh.

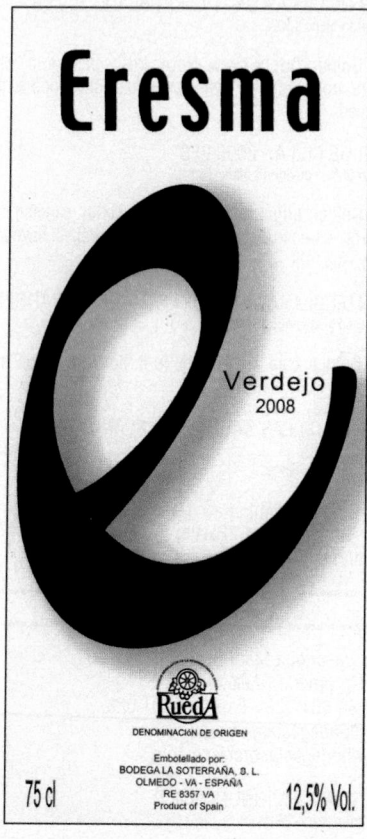

**Eresma**

Verdejo
2008

RuedA
DENOMINACIÓN DE ORIGEN

Embotellado por:
BODEGA LA SOTERRAÑA, S. L.
OLMEDO - VA - ESPAÑA
RE 8357 VA
Product of Spain

75 cl          12,5% Vol.

## LIBERALIA ENOLÓGICA

Camino del Palo, s/n
49800 Toro (Zamora)
☎: 980 692 571 - Fax: 980 692 571
byvliberalia@hotmail.com
www.liberalia.es

ENEBRAL 2008 B
verdejo

**91** Colour: bright straw. Nose: ripe fruit, powerfull, varietal, dried herbs. Palate: flavourful, varietal, good acidity, fruity, fine bitter notes.

## LONG WINES

Avda. del Monte, 46

28120 Algete (Madrid)
☎: 916 221 305 - Fax: 916 220 029
william@william-long.com
www.longwines.com

CALAMAR VERDEJO 2008 B
verdejo

**88** Colour: bright straw. Nose: fresh, fresh fruit, white flowers. Palate: flavourful, fruity, good acidity, balanced.

## MONTEBACO

Finca MonteAlto
47359 Valbuena de Duero (Valladolid)
☎: 983 485 128 - Fax: 983 485 033
montebaco@bodegasmontebaco.com
www.bodegasmontebaco.com

MONTEBACO VERDEJO 2008 B
verdejo 100%

**89** Colour: pale. Nose: citrus fruit, grassy, expressive, ripe fruit. Palate: round, unctuous, good acidity, good finish, fine bitter notes, fruity.

## PAGOS DEL REY

Camino La Barbera, s/n
47490 Rueda (Valladolid)
☎: 983 868 182 - Fax: 983 868 182
rueda@pagosdelrey.com
www.pagosdelrey.com

ANALIVIA SAUVIGNON BLANC 2008 B

**92** Colour: bright straw. Nose: complex, fresh, powerfull, varietal, dry stone. Palate: fruity, full, powerful, flavourful, great length, mineral, fruity aftestaste.

ANALIVIA VERDEJO 2008 B
verdejo

**88** Colour: bright straw. Nose: fresh fruit, white flowers, citrus fruit. Palate: flavourful, fleshy, fruity.

BLUME VERDEJO 2008 B

**88** Colour: bright straw. Nose: powerful, varietal, ripe fruit, citrus fruit, floral. Palate: flavourful, powerful, fleshy.

BLUME SAUVIGNON BLANC 2008 B
sauvignon blanc

**88** Colour: bright straw. Nose: floral, grassy, ripe fruit. Palate: fruity, fresh, flavourful.

ANALIVIA 2008 B

**87** Colour: bright straw. Nose: grassy, floral, ripe fruit. Palate: flavourful, fruity, fresh.

BLUME 2008 B

**86** Colour: bright straw. Nose: dried herbs, fresh fruit, citrus fruit, ripe fruit. Palate: flavourful, fruity, fresh.

## PREDIO DE VASCARLÓN S.L.

Ctra. Rueda s/n
47491 La Seca (Valladolid)
☎: 983 816 325 - Fax: 983 816 326
vascarlon@prediodevascarlon.com
www.prediodevascarlon.com

ATELIER VERDEJO 2008 B
verdejo 100%

**89** Colour: straw. Nose: fresh, varietal, fresh fruit, candied fruit. Palate: fresh, fruity, flavourful, fruity aftestaste.

TARDEVIENES 2008 B
verdejo 50%, viura 50%

**89** Colour: bright straw. Nose: ripe fruit, expressive, floral. Palate: flavourful, ripe fruit, good acidity.

## SITIOS DE BODEGA

Cuatro Calles s/n
47491 La Seca (Valladolid)
☎: 983 103 223 - Fax: 983 816 561
oficina@sitiosdebodega.com
www.sitiosdebodega.com

PALACIO DE MENADE SAUVIGNON BLANC 2008 B
sauvignon blanc 100%

**91** Colour: bright straw. Nose: fresh, fresh fruit, white flowers, expressive, fragrant herbs. Palate: flavourful, fruity, good acidity, balanced.

CONCLASS 2008 B

**89** Colour: bright straw. Nose: neat, fresh, varietal, powerfull. Palate: fruity, fresh, flavourful, powerful.

PALACIO DE MENADE SAUVIGNON BLANC DULCE 2008 BLANCO DULCE
sauvignon blanc 100%

**91** Colour: bright straw. Nose: fresh fruit, fruit expression, fragrant herbs, mineral. Palate: powerful, flavourful, fruity, fresh, complex, fruity aftestaste, mineral.

## SOLANA ARCO IRIS

Ginebra, 24

40468 Montejo de Arévalo (Segovia)
☎: 609 122 978
info@hoyodelaprieta.es

HOYO DE LA PRIETA 2008 B
verdejo

**88** Colour: bright straw. Nose: powerful, varietal, ripe fruit. Palate: flavourful, fruity, fresh, fleshy.

## TERA Y CASTRO

Serrano, 222 - Local
28016 Madrid
☎: 915 902 529 - Fax: 915 644 431
info@teraycastro.com
www.teraycastro.com

PENTIO 2008 B

**90** Colour: bright straw. Nose: ripe fruit, fragrant herbs, varietal, expressive. Palate: rich, fruity, flavourful, ripe fruit.

DILECTUM 2006 BFB
verdejo

**92** Colour: bright yellow. Nose: ripe fruit, powerfull, toasty, creamy oak, dried herbs. Palate: round, good acidity, good structure, spicy.

## TERNA BODEGAS

Cuatro Calles s/n
47491 La Seca (Valladolid)
☎: 983 103 223 - Fax: 983 816 561
oficina@sitiosdebodega.com
www.sitiosdebodega.com

V3 VIÑAS VIEJAS VERDEJO 2007 BFB
verdejo 100%

**89** Colour: bright straw. Nose: medium intensity, fresh fruit, floral, sweet spices. Palate: fruity, fresh, flavourful.

V3 VIÑAS VIEJAS VERDEJO 2006 BFB
verdejo 100%

**95** Colour: bright yellow. Nose: sweet spices, creamy oak, fragrant herbs, fresh fruit. Palate: rich, smoky aftertaste, flavourful, fresh, good acidity.

SAXUM (TERRENOS PEDREGOSOS) SAUVIGNON BLANC 2006 B
sauvignon blanc 100%

**92** Colour: bright yellow. Nose: powerful, expressive, ripe fruit, citrus fruit, sweet spices, creamy oak. Palate: flavourful, fleshy, rich, ripe fruit.

## VALSANZO

Manuel Azaña, 9, Edificio Ambassador, Local 15
47014 Valladolid
☎: 983 150 150 - Fax: 983 150 151
valsanzo@valsanzo.com
www.valsanzo.com

VIÑA SANZO VERDEJO 2008 B
verdejo 100%

**90** Colour: bright straw. Nose: fresh fruit, complex, varietal, fresh, fragrant herbs. Palate: powerful, flavourful, fresh, fruity.

## VINOS SANZ

Ctra. Madrid-La Coruña, km. 170,5
47490 Rueda (Valladolid)
☎: 916 408 730 - Fax: 916 408 731
vinossanz@vinossanz.com
www.vinossanz.com

FINCA LA COLINA SAUVIGNON BLANC 2008 B
sauvignon blanc 100%

**91** Colour: bright straw. Nose: grassy, floral, fresh fruit, powerfull. Palate: flavourful, powerful, sweetness, fruity.

SANZ CLÁSICO 2008 B
verdejo 70%, viura 30%

**90** Colour: bright straw. Nose: powerful, varietal, fresh fruit, floral, grassy. Palate: fruity, fresh, flavourful, fleshy.

FINCA LA COLINA VERDEJO 2008 B
verdejo 100%

**92** Colour: bright yellow. Nose: fresh fruit, macerated fruit, fragrant herbs, mineral. Palate: powerful, flavourful, fruity, complex, full.

SANZ SAUVIGNON BLANC 2008 B
sauvignon blanc 100%

**89** Colour: bright straw. Nose: powerful, expressive, ripe fruit, tropical fruit. Palate: flavourful, powerful, fleshy.

## VIÑEDOS DE NIEVA S.L.

Camino Real s/n
40447 Nieva (Segovia)
☎: 921 594 628 - Fax: 921 595 409
admon@vinedosdenieva.com
www.vinedosdenieva.com

BLANCO NIEVA PIE FRANCO 2008 B
verdejo 100%

**91** Colour: bright straw. Nose: powerful, fresh fruit, ripe fruit, grassy. Palate: fruity, fresh, flavourful.

LOS NAVALES 2008 B
verdejo 100%

**90** Colour: bright straw. Nose: powerful, varietal, complex, fragrant herbs. Palate: powerful, flavourful, fruity, complex, balsamic, fruity aftestaste.

BLANCO NIEVA 2008 B
verdejo 100%

**88** Colour: bright straw. Nose: fresh, fresh fruit, white flowers, varietal. Palate: flavourful, fruity, good acidity, balanced.

BLANCO NIEVA SAUVIGNON 2008 B
sauvignon blanc 100%

**88** Colour: bright straw. Nose: fresh, fresh fruit, white flowers. Palate: flavourful, fruity, good acidity, balanced.

BLANCO NIEVA 2007 BFB
verdejo 100%

**88** Colour: bright yellow. Nose: candied fruit, honeyed notes, spicy, pattiserie. Palate: flavourful, sweetness, ripe fruit.

SOME OTHER WINERIES WITHIN THE DO:

**ALDOR
ARDOA
BODEGA VALDEHERMOSO
BODEGAS CERROSOL
BODEGAS TORRESMANUR, S.L.
BODEGAS VIDAL SOBLECHERO
CAMPOS GÓTICOS
COMERCIAL GRUPO FREIXENET S.A.
COMPAÑÍA DE VINOS DE TELMO RODRÍGUEZ
DELISPAJN BODEGAS
J. GARCIA CARRIÓN
MARQUÉS DE IRÚN
MONTE PEDROSO RICARDO RODRÍGUEZ
OSBORNE RIBERA DEL DUERO
PALACIO DE VILLACHICA
QUINTA DE LA QUIETUD
TARDENCUBA BODEGAS Y VIÑEDOS
TONELERÍA BURGOS S.L.
VICENTE SANZ
VIÑA DEL SOPIÉ
VIÑEDOS SECA S.L.**

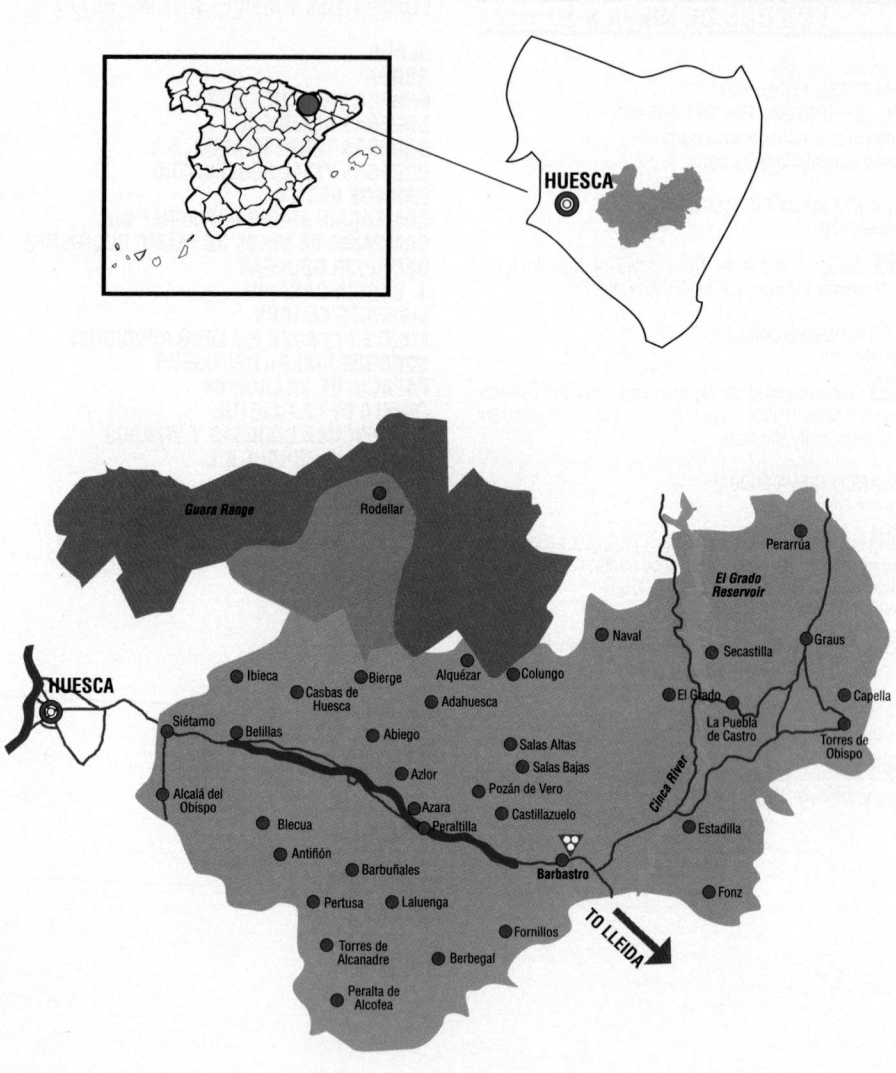

Guara Range
Rodellar
Perarrúa
El Grado Reservoir
Naval
Secastilla
Graus
HUESCA
Ibieca
Bierge
Alquézar
Colungo
El Grado
Capella
Casbas de Huesca
Adahuesca
La Puebla de Castro
Siétamo
Belillas
Abiego
Torres de Obispo
Salas Altas
Alcalá del Obispo
Azlor
Salas Bajas
Blecua
Azara
Pozán de Vero
Estadilla
Antiñón
Peraltilla
Castillazuelo
Barbuñales
Barbastro
Fonz
Pertusa
Laluenga
Fornillos
TO LLEIDA
Torres de Alcanadre
Berbegal
Peralta de Alcofea
Cinca River

▽ Consejo Regulador
● DO Boundary

## NEWS

In the analysis of all the vintages put forward by Somontano for our tasting, with wines as old as of the 2001 vintage, the general impression is one of consistency, with balanced, mature and expressive renderings. To this overall bonanza we have to add the fact that the problems derived from the climatic conditions of the year 2008 are hardly evident in the final wines given the level of technical development that has taken place both in the vineyard and in the wineries over the last few years. The total grape production for the DO, a 30% lower, has resulted in an equally lower figure of young wines, though there has been a rise in the white and rosé categories. The key factor has been the optimal harvesting time for every variety, so the best wines of the 2008 vintage are part of ageing crianza or reserva blends which will be released over the next few years. In the white wine front there has happened a sort of revival of the gewürztraminer and the chardonnay, which show richer and more aromatic than ever. The rosé renderings are also an excellent buy. And to this positive picture we have to add two new varieties, riesling and sauvignon blanc, and the question arises: are they no Spanish varieties suitable to the climate and soils of this region? We cannot forget the way Somontano pioneered plantings of French varieties in Spain, even when it could translate in a drawback in foreign markets tired of the superabundance of those grapes and willing to discover the real Spanish ones. Like Secastilla, one of the latest renderings from Viñas del Vero, made solely from garnacha. The Consejo Regulador has given the green light to sweet and fortified wine making in its new regulations. Somontano has gained a solid reputation for single-variety renderings of French grapes like chardonnay, merlot, syrah and pinot noir. All in all, reds are showing pretty well in terms of quality, but the ones that really made the grade were the white renderings from Enate and Viñas del Vero.

## LOCATION

In the province of Huesca, around the town of Barbastro. The region comprises 43 municipal districts, mainly centred round the region of Somontano and the rest of the neighbouring regions of Ribagorza and Monegros.

## CLIMATE

Characterised by cold winters and hot summers, with sharp contrasts in temperature at the end of spring and autumn. The average annual rainfall is 500 mm, although the rains are scarcer in the south and east.

## SOIL

The soil is mainly brownish limestone, not very fertile, with a good level of limestone and good permeability.

## GRAPE VARIETIES:

**White:** *Macabeo, Garnacha Blanca, Alcañón, Chardonnay* and *Gewürztraminer.*
**Red:** *Tempranillo, Garnacha Tinta, Cabernet Sauvignon, Merlot, Moristel, Parraleta, Pinot Noir* and *Syrah.*

| | |
|---|---|
| **Hectares of Vineyard** | 4,737 |
| **Nº Viticulturists** | 515 |
| **Nº of Bodegas** | 32 |
| **2008 Harvest** | Very Good |
| **2007 Production** | 11,325,300 l. |
| **Marketing** | 77% domestic 23% export |

# DO SOMONTANO

**CONSEJO REGULADOR**
Avda. de la Merced, 64
22300 Barbastro (Huesca)
☎: 974 313 031 - Fax: 974 315 132
@ somontano@dosomontano.com
www.dosomontano.com

## GENERAL CHARACTERISTICS OF THE WINES:

| | |
|---|---|
| **WHITES** | The traditional wines of the region, they are based on the *Macabeo* variety, giving young wines with a straw yellow colour, which are fresh and easy drinking (worthy of mention is the only existing example of late harvest *Macabeo*, which has revealed a complexity uncommon to this variety). Although of higher quality, they are generally produced from *Chardonnay*, whether for young wines or wines fermented in barrels, which gives white wines with powerful aromas, with good varietal definition, oily and flavourful on the palate. |
| **ROSÉS** | Produced from autochthonous or foreign grapes, they follow the line of the modern rosés: raspberry pink in colour, good fruit intensity, light, fresh and easy drinking. |
| **REDS** | The traditional red wine of the region, produced from *Moristel* and *Tempranillo*, is notably fruity and intense. There have also been very interesting experiences with single variety wines produced from local grapes, specifically *Moristel* and *Parraleta*, of notable quality; both produced as young wines and characterised by an excellent fruity character and a certain complexity of notes. In the rest of the red wines the foreign varieties impose themselves, blended with the local grapes or presented separately. The aged *Cabernet* and *Merlot* wines stand out for their Atlantic influence, varietal character, aromatic potency and fine blend with the wood due to not excessive ageing periods; they have a good structure on the palate. |

## 2008 VINTAGE RATING:

# VERY GOOD

## ALDAHARA BODEGA

Ctra. Barbastro, 10
22423 Estadilla (Huesca)
☎: 974 305 236 - Fax: 974 305 236
bodega@aldahara.es
www.aldahara.es

ALDAHARA 2008 B
chardonnay 100%

**83**

ALDAHARA TEMPRANILLO 2007 T
tempranillo 100%

**86** Colour: cherry, garnet rim. Nose: medium intensity, ripe fruit, fruit preserve, sweet spices, creamy oak. Palate: flavourful, fruity, fleshy, round tannins.

ALDAHARA 2007 T
cabernet sauvignon, merlot, tempranillo

**85** Colour: cherry, garnet rim. Nose: fresh, expressive, ripe fruit, red berry notes. Palate: flavourful, fruity, fresh.

MONTEAGUARÉS 2007 T
cabernet sauvignon, merlot, tempranillo

**84**

ALDAHARA RASÉ 2007 T
syrah 100%

**83**

ALDAHARA 2005 TC
cabernet sauvignon, merlot

**88** Colour: cherry, garnet rim. Nose: toasty, dark chocolate, candied fruit. Palate: flavourful, good structure, spicy.

## BAL D'ISABENA BODEGAS

Ctra. A-1605, km. 11,2
22587 Laguarres (Huesca)
☎: 974 544 302 - Fax: 974 310 151
info@baldisabena.com
www.baldisabena.com

ISABENA 2008 RD
merlot

**87** Colour: rose, purple rim. Nose: powerful, ripe fruit, red berry notes, floral, expressive. Palate: fleshy, powerful, fruity, fresh.

COJÓN DE GATO 2007 T
syrah 50%, merlot 50%

**90** Colour: bright cherry. Nose: ripe fruit, sweet spices, creamy oak, expressive, fruit preserve. Palate: flavourful, fruity, toasty, round tannins.

ISABENA 2007 T
merlot 40%, syrah 40%, garnacha 20%

**87** Colour: cherry, garnet rim. Nose: fruit liqueur notes, wild herbs, spicy. Palate: fleshy, great length, slightly dry, soft tannins.

REIS D'ISABENA 2006 T
merlot

**85** Colour: cherry, garnet rim. Nose: powerful, warm, fruit preserve. Palate: spicy, round tannins.

## BLECUA

Naval, km. 3, 7
22300 Barbastro (Huesca)
☎: 974 302 216 - Fax: 974 302 098
marketing@vinasdelvero.es
www.bodegablecua.com

BLECUA 2004 TR

**92** Colour: cherry, garnet rim. Nose: expressive, ripe fruit, wild herbs, spicy, toasty. Palate: good structure, flavourful, long, roasted-coffee aftertaste.

## BODEGA OTTO BESTUÉ

Ctra. A-138, km. 0,5
22312 Enate (Huesca)
☎: 976 78 01 - Fax: 974 305 157
info@bodega-ottobestue.com
www.bodega-ottobestue.com

BESTUÉ DE OTTO BESTUÉ CHARDONNAY 2008 B
chardonnay

**88** Colour: bright straw. Nose: fresh, fresh fruit, white flowers. Palate: flavourful, fruity, good acidity, balanced.

BESTUÉ DE OTTO BESTUÉ TEMPRANILLO CABERNET SAUVIGNON 2008 RD

**87** Colour: brilliant rose. Nose: floral, rose petals, red berry notes. Palate: fruity, fresh.

BESTUÉ DE OTTO BESTUÉ FINCA SANTA SABINA 2007 T
cabernet sauvignon, tempranillo

**89** Colour: cherry, garnet rim. Nose: sweet spices, creamy oak, fruit preserve. Palate: flavourful, fleshy, fruity.

# DO SOMONTANO

BESTUÉ DE OTTO BESTUÉ FINCA RABLEROS 2007 T
tempranillo, cabernet sauvignon

**88** Colour: cherry, garnet rim. Nose: raspberry, wild herbs, fruit liqueur notes. Palate: powerful, flavourful, full, slightly dry, soft tannins.

## BODEGA PIRINEOS

Ctra. Barbastro-Naval, km. 3,5
22300 Barbastro (Huesca)
☎: 974 311 289 - Fax: 974 306 688
info@bodegapirineos.com
www.bodegapirineos.com

PIRINEOS GEWÜRZTRAMINER 2008 B
gewürztraminer 100%

**88** Colour: bright golden. Nose: ripe fruit, powerfull, white flowers. Palate: flavourful, rich, good acidity, fruity.

PIRINEOS MESACHE 2008 B
chardonnay, gewürztraminer, macabeo

**87** Colour: bright golden. Nose: fresh fruit, fragrant herbs, medium intensity. Palate: fresh, fruity, rich, good finish.

MONTESIERRA MACABEO-CHARDONNAY 2008 B
macabeo, chardonnay

**83**

ALQUÉZAR 2008 RD
moristel, tempranillo, garnacha

**88** Colour: onion pink. Nose: elegant, candied fruit, dried flowers, fragrant herbs, red berry notes. Palate: flavourful, good acidity, long, spicy.

MONTESIERRA TEMPRANILLO-GARNACHA 2008 RD
tempranillo, garnacha

**86** Colour: raspberry rose. Nose: floral, rose petals, fresh fruit. Palate: light-bodied, fresh.

PIRINEOS MERLOT-CABERNET 2008 RD
merlot, cabernet sauvignon

**85** Colour: coppery red. Nose: elegant, candied fruit, dried flowers, fragrant herbs, red berry notes. Palate: light-bodied, flavourful, good acidity, long, spicy.

PIRINEOS MESACHE 2008 T
tempranillo, garnacha, syrah, parraleta

**89** Colour: deep cherry, purple rim. Nose: fresh fruit, violet drops, lactic notes. Palate: flavourful, elegant, fruity aftestaste, great length.

MONTESIERRA ECOLÓGICO 2008 T
merlot, tempranillo

**87** Colour: cherry, purple rim. Nose: ripe fruit, red berry notes, fragrant herbs. Palate: flavourful, fruity, fresh.

MARBORÉ 2005 TC
tempranillo, cabernet sauvignon, merlot, moristel, parraleta

**90** Colour: cherry, garnet rim. Nose: elegant, balanced, red berry notes, ripe fruit, wild herbs, sweet spices. Palate: good structure, flavourful, long, round tannins.

BODEGA PIRINEOS MERLOT- CABERNET 2005 TC
merlot, cabernet sauvignon

**88** Colour: cherry, purple rim. Nose: fruit preserve, spicy, creamy oak. Palate: long, flavourful, slightly dry, soft tannins.

SEÑORÍO DE LAZÁN 2004 TR
tempranillo, cabernet sauvignon, moristel

**84**

## BODEGAS ABINASA

Ctra. Tarragona San Sebastián, km. 180
22124 Lascellas (Huesca)
☎: 974 319 156 - Fax: 974 319 156
info@bodegasabinasa.com
www.bodegasabinasa.com

ANA 2008 B
macabeo 100%

**86** Colour: bright straw. Nose: fresh fruit, wild herbs, citrus fruit, creamy oak. Palate: rich, fruity, flavourful, balanced, smoky aftertaste.

ANA 2006 T ROBLE
cabernet sauvignon 60%, merlot 40%

**80**

ANA 2004 TC
merlot 60%, cabernet sauvignon 40%

**84**

ANA 2005 ROBLE
cabernet sauvignon, merlot

**83**

## BODEGAS ALODIA

Ctra. A-1229, km. 11,3
22147 Adahuesca (Huesca)
☎: 974 318 265 - Fax: 974 318 265

info@alodia.es
www.alodia.es

**ALODIA TINTO SEDUCCIÓN 2006 T**
syrah 75%, parraleta 25%

**87** Colour: bright cherry. Nose: ripe fruit, sweet spices, creamy oak, expressive. Palate: flavourful, fruity, toasty, round tannins.

**ALODIA CRUS DE LOS 2005 T**
cabernet sauvignon 50%, garnacha 50%

**87** Colour: cherry, garnet rim. Nose: toasty, powerfull, ripe fruit. Palate: spicy, toasty, round tannins.

**LUXURIA 2006 ESP**

**83**

## BODEGAS CHESA

Corona de Aragón, 35 A-3 3-A
22300 Barbastro (Huesca)
☎: 649 870 637 - Fax: 974 313 552
bodegaschesa@hotmail.com
www.bodegaschesa.com

**CHESA 2007 T ROBLE**
merlot 65%, cabernet sauvignon 35%

**88** Colour: bright cherry. Nose: ripe fruit, sweet spices, expressive. Palate: flavourful, fruity, toasty, round tannins.

**CHESA MERLOT CABERNET 2007 T**
merlot 65%, cabernet sauvignon 35%

**84**

## BODEGAS ESTADA S.L.

Ctra. Barbastro-Alquézar, Km. 6,4
22313 Castillazuelo (Huesca)
☎: 628 430 823
info@bodegasestada.com
www.bodegasestada.es

**ESTADA SAN CARBÁS 2008 B**
chardonnay

**89** Colour: bright straw. Nose: fresh, fresh fruit, white flowers, expressive. Palate: flavourful, fruity, good acidity, balanced.

**ESTADA 2008 RD**

**86** Colour: rose, purple rim. Nose: medium intensity, red berry notes. Palate: flavourful, fruity, fresh.

**VILLA ESTATA 2006 T**

**89** Colour: cherry, garnet rim. Nose: powerful, fruit liqueur notes, fragrant herbs, spicy. Palate: flavourful, powerful, spicy.

**ESTADA "EL BRECO" 2006 T**
cabernet sauvignon, tempranillo, merlot

**84**

**ESTADA 2005 TR**
cabernet sauvignon, tempranillo, merlot, garnacha

**89** Colour: pale ruby, brick rim edge. Nose: ripe fruit, cocoa bean, sweet spices, toasty. Palate: good structure, full, flavourful, long, creamy, great length.

## BODEGAS FÁBREGAS

Cerler, s/n
22300 Barbastro (Huesca)
☎: 974 310 498 - Fax: 974 310 498
info@bodegasfabregas.com
www.bodegasfabregas.com

**FÁBREGAS PURO MERLOT 2007 T**
merlot 100%

**88** Colour: cherry, garnet rim. Nose: powerful, varietal, ripe fruit, raspberry, spicy. Palate: flavourful, powerful, fleshy.

**MINGUA 2007 T ROBLE**

**87** Colour: cherry, garnet rim. Nose: medium intensity, fruit preserve, warm, toasty. Palate: flavourful, fruity, fresh.

**FÁBREGAS PURO SYRAH 2006 T**
syrah

**86** Colour: cherry, garnet rim. Nose: spicy, creamy oak, toasty, fruit liqueur notes. Palate: powerful, flavourful, toasty, round tannins.

**VEGA FERRERA 2006 TC**
merlot, cabernet sauvignon, syrah

**86** Colour: cherry, garnet rim. Nose: medium intensity, ripe fruit, spicy. Palate: flavourful, powerful, spicy.

**VEGA ZICONIA 2003 TR**

**87** Colour: pale ruby, brick rim edge. Nose: ripe fruit, toasty, old leather. Palate: flavourful, long, great length.

## BODEGAS IRIUS

Ctra. Barbastro a Monzón, N-240 km. 155
22300 Barbastro (Huesca)

☎: 974 269 900 - Fax: 945 622 229
visitairius@bodegairius.com
www.bodegairius.com

## ABSUM COLECCIÓN GEWÜRZTRAMINER 2007 B
gewürztraminer

**87** Colour: bright straw. Nose: dried flowers, fruit preserve. Palate: flavourful, fruity, fresh.

## DISUPERI GEWÜRZTRAMINER CHARDONNAY 2008 B
chardonnay, gewürztraminer

**87** Colour: bright straw. Nose: fragrant herbs, floral, fresh fruit. Palate: flavourful, fruity, fresh.

## ABSUM VARIETALES 2007 B
chardonnay 60%, gewürztraminer 25%, pinot noir 15%

**89** Colour: bright straw. Nose: expressive, fresh fruit, fruit expression, sweet spices. Palate: flavourful, fruity, fresh, fleshy.

## ABSUM COLECCIÓN CHARDONNAY ECOLÓGICO 2007 B
chardonnay

**88** Colour: bright straw. Nose: fresh, fresh fruit, white flowers, expressive. Palate: flavourful, fruity, good acidity, balanced.

## ABSUM VARIETALES 2007 T
tempranillo 50%, merlot 35%, cabernet sauvignon 10%, syrah 5%

**92** Colour: bright cherry. Nose: ripe fruit, sweet spices, creamy oak, expressive. Palate: flavourful, fruity, toasty, round tannins.

## ABSUM COLECCIÓN MERLOT 2006 T
merlot

**93** Colour: cherry, garnet rim. Nose: neat, new oak, toasty, fruit preserve. Palate: flavourful, powerful, fleshy, spicy, round tannins.

## ABSUM COLECCIÓN TEMPRANILLO 2006 T
tempranillo

**90** Colour: bright cherry. Nose: ripe fruit, sweet spices, creamy oak, expressive. Palate: flavourful, fruity, toasty, round tannins.

## DISUPERI MERLOT 2006 T
merlot

**86** Colour: cherry, purple rim. Nose: powerful, fruit preserve, candied fruit. Palate: flavourful, powerful, spicy.

## IRIUS PREMIUM 2004 T
tempranillo, cabernet sauvignon, merlot

**95** Colour: bright cherry. Nose: ripe fruit, sweet spices, creamy oak, expressive, lactic notes. Palate: flavourful, fruity, toasty, round tannins.

## IRIUS SELECCIÓN 2004 T
tempranillo, cabernet sauvignon, merlot

**92** Colour: cherry, garnet rim. Nose: ripe fruit, powerfull, warm, creamy oak, dark chocolate. Palate: flavourful, powerful, spicy, round tannins.

## DISUPERI 2004 TC
tempranillo 85%, cabernet sauvignon 15%

**87** Colour: cherry, garnet rim. Nose: fruit liqueur notes, spicy. Palate: spicy, ripe fruit, round tannins.

## DISUPERI 2003 TR
tempranillo 85%, cabernet sauvignon 15%

**89** Colour: cherry, garnet rim. Nose: ripe fruit, spicy, creamy oak, toasty. Palate: powerful, flavourful, toasty, round tannins.

# BODEGAS LALANNE

Castillo San Marcos, s/n
22300 Barbastro (Huesca)
☎: 974 310 689 - Fax: 974 310 689
lalanne@bodegaslalanne.com
www.bodegaslalanne.com

## LALANNE GEWÜRZTRAMINER 2008 B
chardonnay, gewürztraminer

**87** Colour: yellow, bright straw. Nose: medium intensity, neat, fresh fruit, floral. Palate: flavourful, easy to drink, good acidity, unctuous.

## LALANNE SYRAH 2008 T
syrah

**86** Colour: cherry, purple rim. Nose: ripe fruit, lactic notes, earthy notes. Palate: flavourful, fresh, fruity.

## LALANNE CLASSIC 2006 TC
cabernet sauvignon, merlot

**83**

## LALANNE 2001 TR

**88** Colour: cherry, garnet rim. Nose: ripe fruit, spicy, creamy oak, toasty. Palate: powerful, flavourful, toasty, round tannins.

LEONOR LALANNE
LAURA LALANNE

# DO SOMONTANO

## BODEGAS LASIERRA

Baja, 12
22133 Bespén (Huesca)
☎: 974 260 365 - Fax: 974 260 365
info@bodegaslasierra.es
www.bodegaslasierra.es

BESPÉN 2008 B
macabeo
**83**

BESPÉN 2008 RD
tempranillo
**83**

BESPÉN VENDIMIA SELECCIONADA 2007 TC
merlot
**88** Colour: cherry, garnet rim. Nose: medium intensity, expressive, ripe fruit, candied fruit. Palate: flavourful, fruity, spicy.

## BODEGAS LAUS

Ctra. N-240, km 154,8
22300 Barbastro (Huesca)
☎: 974 269 708 - Fax: 974 269 715
info@bodegaslaus.com
www.bodegaslaus.com

LAUS FLOR DE CHARDONNAY 2008 B
chardonnay 100%
**88** Colour: bright straw. Nose: ripe fruit, fruit expression, fragrant herbs, sweet spices. Palate: flavourful, fruity, fresh.

LAUS FLOR DE GEWÜRZTRAMINER 2008 B
**88** Colour: yellow, bright straw. Nose: candied fruit, white flowers, dried herbs. Palate: fresh, flavourful, great length.

LAUS 700 ALT 2006 B
chardonnay 65%, gewürztraminer 35%
**90** Colour: bright straw. Nose: ripe fruit, fruit expression, floral. Palate: flavourful, fruity, fresh.

LAUS FLOR DE MERLOT 2008 RD
merlot 85%, cabernet sauvignon 15%
**90** Colour: rose, purple rim. Nose: powerful, ripe fruit, red berry notes, floral, expressive. Palate: fleshy, powerful, fruity, fresh.

LAUS 2005 T ROBLE
merlot 40%, cabernet sauvignon 30%, tempranillo 30%
**86** Colour: cherry, garnet rim. Nose: sweet spices, ripe fruit, earthy notes. Palate: flavourful, fruity, ripe fruit.

LAUS 700 ALT 2004 TC
syrah 40%, cabernet sauvignon 35%, merlot 25%
**88** Colour: cherry, garnet rim. Nose: expressive, fruit preserve, cocoa bean, cedar wood. Palate: flavourful, balanced, great length.

LAUS 2004 TC
merlot 50%, cabernet sauvignon 50%
**86** Colour: pale ruby, brick rim edge. Nose: characterful, fruit liqueur notes, wild herbs, dark chocolate. Palate: flavourful, toasty, harsh oak tannins.

LAUS 2003 TR
cabernet sauvignon 100%
**88** Colour: pale ruby, brick rim edge. Nose: fruit preserve, spicy, old leather. Palate: powerful, fleshy, great length.

## BODEGAS MELER

Luis Buñuel, 15 4ª A
22300 Barbastro (Huesca)
☎: 974 312 964 - Fax: 974 306 871
bodegasmeler@yahoo.es
www.bodegasmeler.com

MELER CHARDONNAY 2008 B
chardonnay 100%
**88** Colour: bright yellow. Nose: candied fruit, tropical fruit, white flowers. Palate: fruity, unctuous, long.

MELER SYRAH 2008 T
syrah 100%
**88** Colour: dark-red cherry, purple rim. Nose: violet drops, red berry notes, lactic notes, varietal. Palate: powerful, flavourful, long, great length.

LUMBRETA 2006 T
cabernet sauvignon, garnacha, tempranillo
**88** Colour: cherry, garnet rim. Nose: spicy, creamy oak, toasty, macerated fruit. Palate: powerful, flavourful, toasty, round tannins.

ANDRÉS MELER 2005 T
cabernet sauvignon 100%

**90** Colour: cherry, garnet rim. Nose: ripe fruit, spicy, creamy oak, toasty, complex. Palate: powerful, flavourful, toasty, round tannins.

MELER 2005 TC
merlot, cabernet sauvignon

**89** Colour: cherry, garnet rim. Nose: ripe fruit, spicy, creamy oak, toasty. Palate: powerful, flavourful, toasty, round tannins.

## BODEGAS MONCLUS

Ctra. Radiquero - Alquezar s/n
22145 Radiquero (Huesca)
☎: 974 315 231 - Fax: 974 315 231
comercial@inesdemonclus.com
www.inesdemonclus.com

INÉS DE MONCLUS CHARDONNAY
GEWÜRZTRAMINER 2008 B
chardonnay 50%, gewürztraminer 50%

**86** Colour: bright golden. Nose: medium intensity, fresh fruit, wild herbs. Palate: unctuous, good acidity, fruity, light-bodied.

INÉS DE MONCLÚS RESERVA DE FAMILIA 2004 TR
tempranillo 60%, merlot 20%, cabernet sauvignon 20%

**88** Colour: cherry, garnet rim. Nose: ripe fruit, spicy, creamy oak, toasty, complex, candied fruit, fragrant herbs. Palate: powerful, flavourful, toasty, round tannins.

INÉS DE MONCLÚS MERLOT 2003 TR
merlot 90%, cabernet sauvignon 10%

**88** Colour: cherry, garnet rim. Nose: ripe fruit, spicy, creamy oak, toasty, complex. Palate: powerful, flavourful, toasty, round tannins.

VIÑAS DE RADIQUERO

## BODEGAS MONTE ODINA

Monte Odina, s/n
22415 Ilche (Huesca)
☎: 974 343 480 - Fax: 974 343 484
bodega@monteodina.com
www.monteodina.com

MONTE ODINA 2008 RD
cabernet sauvignon 100%

**87** Colour: brilliant rose. Nose: medium intensity, ripe fruit, fragrant herbs. Palate: flavourful, fresh.

MONTE ODINA 2007 T
merlot

**87** Colour: cherry, garnet rim. Nose: powerful, ripe fruit, sweet spices. Palate: flavourful, fleshy, round tannins.

MONTE ODINA 2006 TC
cabernet sauvignon 50%, merlot 50%

**86** Colour: cherry, garnet rim. Nose: ripe fruit, wild herbs, spicy. Palate: flavourful, fruity, fine bitter notes, harsh oak tannins.

MONTE ODINA 2006 T ROBLE
cabernet sauvignon 50%, merlot 50%

**83**

## BODEGAS OBERGO

Ctra. La Puebla, km. 0.6
22439 Ubiergo (Huesca)
☎: 699 357 866
bodegasobergo@obergo.es
www.obergo.es

LAGRIMAS DE OBERGO 2008 RD
garnacha 60%, syrah 40%

**88** Colour: brilliant rose. Nose: elegant, candied fruit, dried flowers, fragrant herbs, red berry notes. Palate: light-bodied, flavourful, good acidity, long, spicy.

OBERGO CARAMELOS 2008 T JOVEN
garnacha

**90** Colour: cherry, purple rim. Nose: ripe fruit, fruit preserve, red berry notes, scrubland, sweet spices. Palate: creamy, flavourful, fruity, fresh.

OBERGO VARIETALES 2007 T
merlot

**91** Colour: cherry, garnet rim. Nose: powerful, dark chocolate, roasted coffee, ripe fruit. Palate: flavourful, powerful, fleshy, round tannins.

OBERGO "FINCA DE LA MATA" 2007 T
merlot 40%, cabernet sauvignon 40%, garnacha 20%

**90** Colour: bright cherry. Nose: ripe fruit, sweet spices, creamy oak, expressive. Palate: flavourful, fruity, toasty, round tannins.

## BODEGAS RASO HUETE

Joaquín Costa, 23
22423 Huesca
☎: 974 305 447

info@bodegasrasohuete.com
www.bodegasrasohuete.com

## PARTIDA ARNAZAS CABERNET-MERLOT 2007 T
cabernet sauvignon, merlot

**89** Colour: cherry, garnet rim. Nose: expressive, elegant, sweet spices, ripe fruit. Palate: flavourful, fruity, fresh, spicy.

## ARNAZAS SELECCIÓN 2006 TC
syrah, merlot, tempranillo

**82**

## ARNAZAS MERLOT 2005 T ROBLE
merlot

**88** Colour: bright cherry. Nose: sweet spices, creamy oak, expressive, fruit preserve. Palate: flavourful, fruity, toasty, round tannins.

## ARNAZAS CABERNET-MERLOT 2004 TC
cabernet sauvignon, merlot

**90** Colour: cherry, garnet rim. Nose: ripe fruit, spicy, creamy oak, toasty, complex. Palate: powerful, flavourful, toasty, round tannins.

## ARNAZAS 2004 TR
cabernet sauvignon, merlot

**89** Colour: bright cherry. Nose: ripe fruit, sweet spices, creamy oak, expressive. Palate: flavourful, fruity, toasty, round tannins.

## BODEGAS SIERRA DE GUARA

Ctra. A-1229, Km. 0,2
22124 Lascellas (Huesca)
☎: 974 319 363 - Fax: 974 319 010
idrias@bodegassierradeguara.es
www.bodegassierradeguara.es

## IDRIAS CHARDONNAY 2008 B
chardonnay 100%

**87** Colour: bright straw. Nose: fresh, fresh fruit, white flowers, expressive. Palate: flavourful, fruity, good acidity, balanced.

## IDRIAS CHARDONNAY EDICIÓN ESPECIAL 2007 BFB
chardonnay 100%

**90** Colour: bright yellow. Nose: powerful, ripe fruit, sweet spices, creamy oak, fragrant herbs. Palate: rich, smoky aftertaste, flavourful, fresh, good acidity.

## IDRIAS MERLOT 2008 RD
merlot 100%

**86** Colour: rose, purple rim. Nose: powerful, ripe fruit, red berry notes, floral, expressive. Palate: fleshy, powerful, fruity, fresh.

## IDRIAS ABIEGO 2007 T ROBLE
merlot, cabernet sauvignon, tempranillo

**85** Colour: cherry, garnet rim. Nose: fresh fruit, raspberry, wild herbs. Palate: flavourful, long, stalky, slightly dry, soft tannins.

## IDRIAS SEVIL 2005 T
merlot 50%, cabernet sauvignon 50%

**88** Colour: bright cherry. Nose: ripe fruit, sweet spices, creamy oak, expressive, roasted coffee. Palate: flavourful, fruity, toasty, round tannins.

## ALIUS

## BODEGAS Y VIÑEDOS OLVENA S.L.

Ctra. Nacional 123, km. 5
22300 Barbastro (Huesca)
☎: 974 308 481 - Fax: 974 308 482
info@bodegasolvena.com
www.bodegasolvena.com

## OLVENA CHARDONNAY 2008 B
chardonnay 100%

**88** Colour: bright yellow. Nose: fresh fruit, tropical fruit, floral. Palate: fresh, flavourful, long.

## OLVENA GEWÜRZTRAMINER 2007 B
gewürztraminer 100%

**90** Colour: yellow, bright straw. Nose: elegant, white flowers, dried herbs, ripe fruit. Palate: flavourful, fresh, long, fine bitter notes.

## OLVENA 2008 RD
merlot 100%

**87** Colour: rose, purple rim. Nose: powerful, ripe fruit, red berry notes, floral, expressive. Palate: fleshy, powerful, fruity, fresh.

## OLVENA HACHE 2006 T
garnacha 40%, syrah 60%

**86** Colour: cherry, purple rim. Nose: characterful, ripe fruit, candied fruit, wild herbs. Palate: flavourful, spicy, good finish.

## OLVENA 2005 TC
cabernet sauvignon 100%

**90** Colour: cherry, garnet rim. Nose: ripe fruit, spicy, creamy oak, toasty, complex. Palate: powerful, flavourful, toasty, round tannins, good acidity.

OLVENA CUATRO O EL PAGO DE LA LIBÉLULA 2005 T
tempranillo 45%, cabernet sauvignon 25%, merlot 15%, syrah 15%

**89** Colour: cherry, garnet rim. Nose: fruit liqueur notes, wild herbs, sweet spices, toasty. Palate: good structure, balanced, round, fruity aftestaste, round tannins.

## DALCAMP

Constitución, 4
22415 Monesma de San Juan (Lleida)
☎: 973 760 018 - Fax: 973 760 523
rdalfo@mixmail.com
www.castillodemonesma.com

CASTILLO DE MONESMA GEWÜRZTRAMINER 2008 B
gewürztraminer

**85** Colour: bright straw. Nose: floral, ripe fruit. Palate: flavourful, fresh, fruity.

CASTILLO DE MONESMA 2006 T ROBLE
cabernet sauvignon, merlot, syrah, garnacha

**84**

CASTILLO DE MONESMA 2005 TC
cabernet sauvignon, merlot

**89** Colour: bright cherry. Nose: ripe fruit, sweet spices, creamy oak, expressive. Palate: flavourful, fruity, toasty, round tannins.

CASTILLO DE MONESMA 2004 TR

**86** Colour: cherry, garnet rim. Nose: sweet spices, fruit liqueur notes, toasty. Palate: flavourful, spicy, round tannins.

CASTILLO DE MONESMA CABERNET SAUVIGNON 2002 TR

**87** Colour: pale ruby, brick rim edge. Nose: ripe fruit, fruit liqueur notes, toasty. Palate: flavourful, good finish.

CASTILLO DE MONESMA 2002 TC

**87** Colour: cherry, garnet rim. Nose: ripe fruit, spicy, toasty, complex, fine reductive notes. Palate: powerful, flavourful, toasty, round tannins.

## ENATE

Avda. de las Artes, 1
22314 Salas Bajas (Huesca)
☎: 974 302 580 - Fax: 974 300 046
bodega@enate.es
www.enate.es

ENATE CHARDONNAY-234 2008 B
chardonnay 100%

**90** Colour: bright yellow. Nose: powerful, varietal, complex, ripe fruit, dried flowers. Palate: flavourful, fruity, rich, balanced, good acidity.

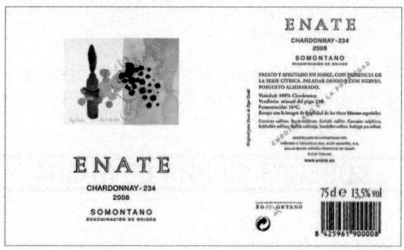

ENATE GEWÜRZTRAMINER 2008 B
gewürztraminer 100%

**89** Colour: bright straw. Nose: floral, ripe fruit, expressive. Palate: flavourful, powerful, fruity.

ENATE CHARDONNAY 2007 BFB
chardonnay 100%

**93** Colour: bright yellow. Nose: powerful, ripe fruit, sweet spices, creamy oak, fragrant herbs. Palate: rich, smoky aftertaste, flavourful, fresh, good acidity.

ENATE UNO CHARDONNAY 2006 BFB
chardonnay 100%

**94** Colour: bright golden. Nose: sweet spices, ripe fruit, citrus fruit. Palate: flavourful, fruity, spicy, spirituous, great length.

### ENATE CABERNET SAUVIGNON 2008 RD
cabernet sauvignon 100%

**88** Colour: rose, purple rim. Nose: powerful, ripe fruit, red berry notes, floral, expressive. Palate: powerful, fruity, fresh.

### ENATE CABERNET SAUVIGNON MERLOT 2007 TC
cabernet sauvignon 50%, merlot 50%

**87** Colour: cherry, garnet rim. Nose: fresh fruit, raspberry, varietal. Palate: fleshy, fruity, long, slightly dry, soft tannins.

### ENATE SYRAH-SHIRAZ 2006 T
syrah 100%

**90** Colour: cherry, garnet rim. Nose: ripe fruit, spicy, creamy oak, toasty, complex. Palate: powerful, flavourful, toasty, round tannins.

### ENATE RESERVA ESPECIAL 2005 TR
cabernet sauvignon, merlot

**94** Colour: cherry, garnet rim. Nose: ripe fruit, spicy, creamy oak, toasty, complex, elegant, mineral. Palate: powerful, flavourful, toasty, round tannins.

### ENATE UNO 2005 T
cabernet sauvignon, merlot

**92** Colour: black cherry. Nose: creamy oak, dark chocolate, toasty, ripe fruit, earthy notes. Palate: flavourful, powerful, fleshy, roasted-coffee aftertaste.

### ENATE MERLOT-MERLOT 50CL. 2005 T
merlot

**91** Colour: black cherry. Nose: fresh fruit, complex, varietal, cocoa bean, toasty, new oak. Palate: balanced, elegant, round, complex, fruity, powerful, flavourful, smoky aftertaste.

### ENATE MERLOT-MERLOT 2005 T
merlot 100%

**91** Colour: cherry, garnet rim. Nose: ripe fruit, spicy, complex, earthy notes. Palate: powerful, flavourful, toasty, round tannins.

### ENATE TEMPRANILLO CABERNET SAUVIGNON 2005 TC
tempranillo 70%, cabernet sauvignon 30%

**87** Colour: cherry, garnet rim. Nose: ripe fruit, fruit liqueur notes, spicy, toasty. Palate: flavourful, spicy, ripe fruit, soft tannins.

### ENATE VARIETALES DEL DOS MIL CUATRO 2004 T
cabernet sauvignon, merlot, tempranillo, syrah

**90** Colour: cherry, garnet rim. Nose: ripe fruit, spicy, creamy oak, toasty, complex, dark chocolate. Palate: powerful, flavourful, toasty, round tannins.

### ENATE TEMPRANILLO CABERNET SAUVIGNON 2004 TC
tempranillo, cabernet sauvignon

**88** Colour: cherry, garnet rim. Nose: sweet spices, ripe fruit, fruit liqueur notes. Palate: flavourful, spicy, round tannins.

### ENATE CABERNET SAUVIGNON 2003 TR
cabernet sauvignon 100%

**90** Colour: cherry, garnet rim. Nose: ripe fruit, candied fruit, sweet spices. Palate: flavourful, good structure, round tannins.

## OSCA

La Iglesia, 1
22124 Ponzano (Huesca)
☎: 974 319 017 - Fax: 974 319 175
bodega@bodegasosca.com
www.bodegasosca.com

## OSCA GARNACHA BLANCA 2008 B
garnacha blanca

**85** Colour: yellow, pale. Nose: medium intensity, white flowers, wild herbs. Palate: fresh, flavourful, fruity aftestaste.

## OSCA 2008 B
**82**

## OSCA 2008 RD
**82**

## OSCA 2008 T
tempranillo, moristel

**83**

## MASCÚN SYRAH 2006 T
syrah

**87** Colour: cherry, garnet rim. Nose: ripe fruit, toasty, sweet spices, warm. Palate: flavourful, spicy, ripe fruit.

## OSCA 2005 TC
**86** Colour: cherry, garnet rim. Nose: spicy, aromatic coffee, ripe fruit, fruit liqueur notes. Palate: spicy, classic aged character.

## OSCA MORISTEL 2005 TC
moristel

**85** Colour: cherry, garnet rim. Nose: ripe fruit, fruit liqueur notes, spicy, toasty. Palate: flavourful, powerful, spicy.

## OSCA GRAN EROLES 2004 TR
**89** Colour: cherry, garnet rim. Nose: ripe fruit, sweet spices, toasty. Palate: flavourful, spicy, ripe fruit.

## CASTILLO DE L'AINSA 2004 TC
**87** Colour: cherry, garnet rim. Nose: ripe fruit, sweet spices, toasty. Palate: flavourful, spicy, round tannins.

## MASCÚN GARNACHA 2003 T
garnacha

**87** Colour: cherry, garnet rim. Nose: characterful, candied fruit, wild herbs, fine reductive notes. Palate: fleshy, spicy, powerful tannins.

## MASCÚN MERLOT T
**87** Colour: cherry, garnet rim. Nose: powerful, expressive, ripe fruit, sweet spices. Palate: flavourful, powerful.

## SENTIF

Baja, 4
22133 Bespén (Huesca)
☎: 646 779 926 - Fax: 974 260 363
sentif@bespenvinos.com

### SENTIF 2006 T
garnacha 15%, moristel 5%, tempranillo 35%, cabernet sauvignon 20%, merlot 25%

**89** Colour: cherry, garnet rim. Nose: ripe fruit, fruit preserve, cedar wood, sweet spices. Palate: flavourful, powerful, fleshy, good structure, long.

## VIÑAS DEL VERO

Naval, km. 3,7
22300 Barbastro (Huesca)
☎: 974 302 216 - Fax: 974 302 098
marketing@vinasdelvero.es
www.vinasdelvero.es

### VIÑAS DEL VERO CLARIÓN 2008 B
**92** Colour: bright straw. Nose: fresh fruit, wild herbs. Palate: fresh, fruity, flavourful.

### VIÑAS DEL VERO GEWÜRZTRAMINER COLECCIÓN EL ENEBRO 2008 B
gewürztraminer

**90** Colour: bright straw. Nose: fresh, fresh fruit, white flowers, expressive. Palate: flavourful, fruity, good acidity, balanced.

### VIÑAS DEL VERO CHARDONNAY 2008 B
chardonnay

**90** Colour: bright straw. Nose: fresh, fresh fruit, white flowers, expressive. Palate: flavourful, fruity, good acidity, balanced.

### VIÑAS DEL VERO CHARDONNAY COLECCIÓN "SAN MIGUEL" 2007 B
chardonnay

**93** Colour: bright straw. Nose: powerful, ripe fruit, fruit preserve, expressive, tropical fruit. Palate: flavourful, fleshy, rich, balanced.

### VIÑAS DEL VERO PINOT NOIR COLECCIÓN LAS ALMUNIAS 2007 T
pinot noir

**90** Colour: cherry, garnet rim. Nose: medium intensity, red berry notes, fruit expression, scrubland. Palate: flavourful, spicy, easy to drink, fine tannins.

LA MIRANDA DE SECASTILLA 2006 T
garnacha

**91** Colour: deep cherry. Nose: neat, expressive, ripe fruit, red berry notes, sweet spices. Palate: flavourful, fruity, fresh, fleshy, mineral.

VIÑAS DEL VERO SYRAH COLECCIÓN
LAS CANTERAS 2006 T
syrah

**90** Colour: cherry, garnet rim. Nose: toasty, new oak, sweet spices. Palate: flavourful, spicy, round tannins.

SECASTILLA 2005 T

**91** Colour: cherry, garnet rim. Nose: ripe fruit, raspberry, wild herbs, creamy oak, balanced. Palate: complex, flavourful, spicy, long, mineral, great length.

VIÑAS DEL VERO MERLOT COLECCIÓN
EL ARIÑO 2005 T
merlot

**90** Colour: cherry, garnet rim. Nose: spicy, creamy oak, toasty, complex. Palate: powerful, flavourful, toasty, round tannins.

VIÑAS DEL VERO CABERNET SAUVIGNON
COLECCIÓN LOS SASOS 2005 T
cabernet sauvignon

**88** Colour: cherry, garnet rim. Nose: ripe fruit, spicy, creamy oak, toasty, complex. Palate: powerful, flavourful, toasty, round tannins.

VIÑAS DEL VERO GRAN VOS 2004 TR

**90** Colour: cherry, garnet rim. Nose: expressive, red berry notes, wild herbs, spicy. Palate: flavourful, good structure, long, good finish.

SOME OTHER WINERIES WITHIN THE DO:

**BODEGAS BALLABRIGA**
**BODEGAS VALDOVINOS**
**BODEGAS VILLA D'ORTA**
**FUERA DE CARTA**
**MONTESA VINÍCOLA**
**SERS**

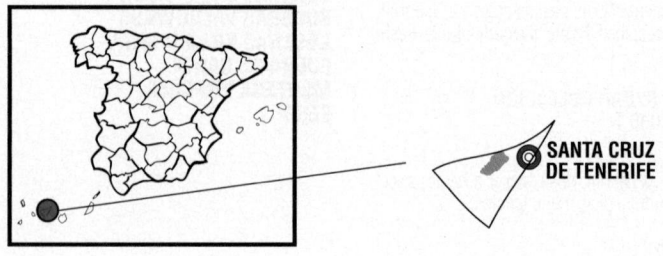

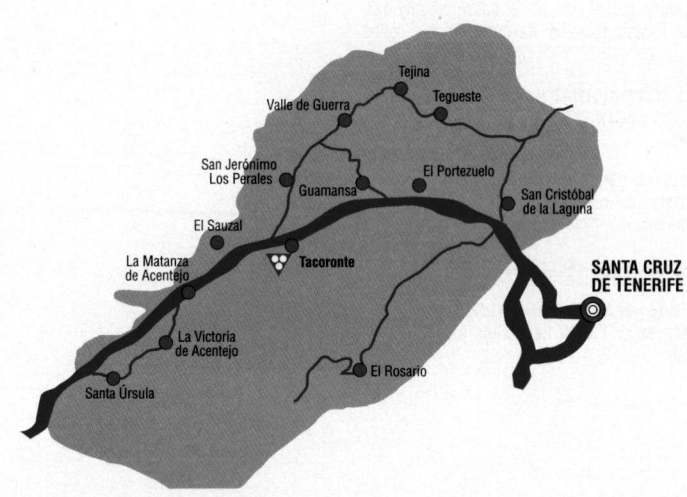

▽ Consejo Regulador
● DO Boundary

## NEWS
The most numerous wines within the Canary Islands are those from Tacoronte, a region mainly known through the efforts and commercial success of a consolidated brand name, Viña Norte. Of unique climatic conditions, with high humidity levels given the proximity of the Atlantic Ocean, it keeps a mild temperature climatic pattern and the volcanic soils provide very original, singular wines. The 2008 vintage had no major incidences from the climatic point of view and the only differences come from altitude. Young whites and reds are the best renderings from the DO, with a handful of brands performing consistently well and the same also consistent difficulties for the local grapes to ripen fully. The real flagship of the region is Viña Norte Maceración Carbónica, a powerful wine with a lot of fresh fruit expression, as well as herbs and minerals that put it amongst the best Spanish young wines. Tacoronte also has a couple of novelties in the red wine category from Buten – Cráter and Magma–, a house that is working on terroir and a blend of mantonegro with French varieties. There is no need to repeat once again that the sweet wines –whites and reds– from Humboldt get all the medals.

## LOCATION
Situated in the north of Tenerife, stretching for 23 km and is composed of 9 municipal districts: Tegueste, Tacoronte, El Sauzal, La Matanza de Acentejo, La Victoria de Acentejo, Santa Úrsula, La Laguna, Santa Cruz de Tenerife and El Rosario.

## CLIMATE
Typically Atlantic, affected by the orientation of the island and the relief which give rise to a great variety of microclimates. The temperatures are in general mild, thanks to the influence of the trade winds, which provide high levels of humidity, around 60%, although the rains are scarce.

## SOIL
The soil is volcanic, reddish, and is made up of organic matter and trace elements. The vines are cultivated both in the valleys next to the sea and higher up at altitudes of up to 1,000 m.

## GRAPE VARIETIES:
**White:** Preferred: *Güal, Malvasía, Listán Blanco* and *Marmajuelo*.
Authorized: *Pedro Ximénez, Moscatel, Verdello, Vijariego, Forastera Blanca* and *Torrontés*.
**Red:** Preferred: *Listán Negra* and *Negramoll*.
Authorized: *Tintilla, Moscatel Negro* and *Malvasía Rosada*.

## SUB-REGIONS:
**Anaga** (covering the municipal areas of La Laguna, Santa Cruz de Tenerife and Tegueste) which falls within the limits of the Anaga Rural Park.

| | |
|---|---|
| Hectares of Vineyard | 1,563 |
| Nº Viticulturists | 2,277 |
| Nº of Bodegas | 52 |
| 2008 Harvest | Good |
| 2007 Production | 1,175,000 l. |
| Marketing | 99% domestic 1% export |

# DO TACORONTE-ACENTEJO

**CONSEJO REGULADOR**
Ctra. General del Norte, 97. 38350 Tacoronte.
☎: 922 560 107 - Fax: 922 561 155
@ consejo@tacovin.com
www.tacovin.com

**GENERAL CHARACTERISTICS OF THE WINES:**

| WHITES | These are light and fruity; they are produced in small quantities. |
|---|---|
| ROSÉS | Produced mainly from *Listán Negro*, they maintain the varietal character of this stock and are fresh and pleasant to drink. |
| REDS | These are the most characteristic wines of the DO. The young red wines have a deep cherry-red or deep red ruby colour; on the nose they develop aromas with a good intensity; they are fresh and fruity and transmit a somewhat wild character, but are original from the *Listán* grape. Recently, Crianza wines aged in barrels have also been produced. |

## 2008 VINTAGE RATING:

## GOOD

## AFECAN, S.A. (BODEGA "EL LOMO")

Ctra. El Lomo, 18
38280 Tegueste (Tenerife)
☎: 922 545 254 - Fax: 922 546 453
oficina@bodegaellomo.com
www.bodegaellomo.com

EL LOMO MALVASÍA DULCE 2008 B
malvasia 100%

**88** Colour: pale. Nose: powerful, fresh fruit, fruit expression, citrus fruit, grassy, sweet spices. Palate: flavourful, fruity, fresh.

EL LOMO 2008 B
listán blanco 95%, Vigiriego 5%, otras

**84**

EL LOMO 2008 T
listán negro 95%, negramoll 5%

**82**

EL LOMO 2007 TC
listán negro 95%, negramoll 5%, otras

**85** Colour: cherry, garnet rim. Nose: powerful, toasty, spicy, warm. Palate: flavourful, spicy, ripe fruit.

## AGRYENCA

Fray Diego, 2 Los Perales
38350 Tacoronte (Tenerife)
☎: 922 564 013 - Fax: 922 564 013
bodega@agryenca.com
www.agryenca.com

TABAIBAL 2008 T BARRICA

**72**

## BODEGA ACEVEDO

Camino El Guincho, 140
38270 Valle Guerra (Santa Cruz de Tenerife)
☎: 922 540 808 - Fax: 922 545 212
info@bodegaacevedo.com

ACEVEDO CASTELLANA 2008 T
castellana 100%

**86** Colour: dark-red cherry. Nose: powerful, sweet spices, toasty, ripe fruit, earthy notes. Palate: flavourful, powerful, ripe fruit, spicy.

EL GUINCHO 2 MESES 2008 T
listán negro 50%, negramoll 30%, baboso 20%, Vigiriego %, tintilla %

**84**

EL GUINCHO 2008 T
listán negro 80%, negramoll 20%

**82**

ACEVEDO 2008 T
listán negro 70%, negramoll 30%

**81**

## BODEGA INSERCASA

Finca El Fresal/Camino Juan Fernandez, s/n
38270 La Laguna (Santa Cruz de Tenerife)
☎: 922 285 316 - Fax: 922 270 626
info@vinobronce.com
www.vinobronce.com.com

BRONCE SYRAH 2008 T
syrah

**83**

## BODEGA LA PALMERA

Camino La Herrera nº83
38369 El Sauzal (Tenerife)
☎: 922 573 485 - Fax: 922 573 485
info@bodegalapalmera.com
www.bodegalapalmera.com

LA PALMERA 2008 B
listán blanco, gual, malvasia

**84**

LA PALMERA AFRUTADO 2008 B
listán blanco 100%

**82**

LA PALMERA 2008 T MACERACIÓN CARBÓNICA
listán negro

**82**

LA PALMERA 2008 T

**78**

LA PALMERA 2007 T BARRICA
listán negro, castellana

**81**

L´ANGELET 2005 TC

**85** Colour: cherry, garnet rim. Nose: warm, fruit liqueur notes, fruit liqueur notes, sweet spices, toasty. Palate: powerful, flavourful, great length.

## BODEGAS DOMÍNGUEZ CUARTA GENERACIÓN

Calvario, 79
38350 Tacoronte (Tenerife)
☎: 922 572 435 - Fax: 922 572 435
correo@bodegasdominguez.com
www.bodegasdominguez.com

DOMINGUEZ ESPECIAL 2008 B

**82**

DOMINGUEZ MALVASÍA CLÁSICO 2006 B

**89** Colour: bright golden. Nose: pattiserie, spicy, honeyed notes, fruit expression. Palate: flavourful, fleshy, powerful, good acidity.

DOMINGUEZ SELECCIÓN NEGRAMOLL 2006 T

**84**

## BODEGAS INSULARES TENERIFE

Vereda del Medio, 48
38350 Tacoronte (Tenerife)
☎: 922 570 617 - Fax: 922 570 043
bitsa@bodegasinsularestenerife.es
www.bodegasinsularestenerife.es

VIÑA NORTE 2008 B MACERACIÓN CARBÓNICA

**78**

VIÑA NORTE 2008 RD

**85** Colour: rose, purple rim. Nose: fragrant herbs. Palate: ripe fruit, flavourful, fruity.

VIÑA NORTE 2008 T MACERACIÓN CARBÓNICA

**90** Colour: cherry, purple rim. Nose: powerful, red berry notes, raspberry, fruit expression. Palate: flavourful, fruity, fresh, balsamic.

VIÑA NORTE 2008 T

**82**

VIÑA NORTE 2006 TC
listán negro, negramoll

**90** Colour: dark-red cherry. Nose: fruit expression, aromatic coffee, creamy oak, complex, balsamic herbs. Palate: fruity, fresh, complex, elegant.

VIÑA NORTE VENDIMIA SELECCIONADA 2005 T

**85** Colour: cherry, garnet rim. Nose: powerful, toasty, dark chocolate. Palate: flavourful, powerful, fleshy.

VIÑA NORTE 2005 TC

**84**

HUMBOLDT VERDELLO 2005 BLANCO DULCE

**94** Colour: bright straw. Nose: sweet spices, creamy oak, ripe fruit, honeyed notes, citrus fruit. Palate: flavourful, fleshy, good acidity, fine bitter notes, long.

HUMBOLDT VENDIMIA TARDÍA 2005 B DULCE

**90** Colour: bright straw. Nose: balsamic herbs, fruit preserve, candied fruit, dry nuts, pattiserie. Palate: flavourful, fleshy, complex, sweet.

HUMBOLDT 1997 B DULCE

**92** Colour: bright golden. Nose: powerful, dry nuts, candied fruit, citrus fruit, honeyed notes, acetaldehyde. Palate: flavourful, rich, fleshy, sweet, fine bitter notes.

HUMBOLDT 2001 T DULCE

**95** Colour: cherry, garnet rim. Nose: powerful, characterful, complex, candied fruit, dark chocolate. Palate: flavourful, powerful, fleshy, sweet, long.

## BODEGAS TEXIMAR S.L.

Ctra. General El Socorro, 53 San Luis
38292 Tegueste (Tenerife)
☎: 922 542 605 - Fax: 922 542 790
teximar@teximar.com
www.teximar.com

VALLE MOLINA GUAL 2008 B BARRICA

**77**

VALLE MOLINA MOSCATEL 2007 B

**82**

VIÑA SANTO DOMINGO 2008 T

**83**

## BUTEN

San Nicolás, 122
38360 El Sauzal (Santa Cruz de Tenerife)
☎: 922 573 272 - Fax: 922 573 225
crater@bodegasbuten.com

MAGMA DE CRÁTER 2006 TC
negramoll, syrah

**90** Colour: cherry, garnet rim. Nose: ripe fruit, characterful, earthy notes, toasty. Palate: flavourful, powerful, fleshy, round tannins.

CRÁTER 2005 T BARRICA
listán negro, negramoll

**89** Colour: cherry, garnet rim. Nose: elegant, candied fruit, ripe fruit, sweet spices, creamy oak. Palate: flavourful, fleshy, spicy, round tannins.

## C.B. HERMANOS PÍO HERNÁNDEZ

Real, 42
38370 La Matanza de Acenjo (Tenerife)
☎: 922 577 828 - Fax: 922 578 761
emiliopio@ferreteriahnospio.es

FUENTECILLA 2008 T
listán negro, listán blanco, negramoll
**78**

## CHÁVEZ SAN DIEGO S.L.

Botello, 2
38370 La Matanza de Acentejo (Tenerife)
☎: 922 579 029

SAN DIEGO 2008 B
**78**

SAN DIEGO 2008 T

**87** Colour: cherry, purple rim. Nose: ripe fruit, raspberry, powerfull. Palate: flavourful, fleshy, ripe fruit.

## EL GRANILETE

Torreón s/n
38350 Tacoronte (Santa Cruz de Tenerife)
☎: 922 211 414 - Fax: 922 209 945
jgescuela@terra.es

EL GRANILETE 2008 T

**81**

## EL MOCANERO S.L.

Ctra. General, 347
38350 Tacoronte (Santa Cruz de Tenerife)
☎: 922 560 762 - Fax: 922 560 762
elmocanerosl@hotmail.com

EL MOCANERO 2008 T MACERACIÓN CARBÓNICA

**86** Colour: deep cherry. Nose: red berry notes, fresh fruit, scrubland. Palate: flavourful, fruity, fresh.

EL MOCANERO 2008 T
negramoll
**83**

EL MOCANERO 2008 T
**78**

ZERAFINA

## HOYA DEL NAVÍO

Camino Hacienda el Pino, 42
38350 Tacoronte ()
☎: 616 396 923
info@hoyadelnavio.com

HOYA DEL NAVÍO 2008 T
listán negro 50%, negramoll 50%
**83**

## IGNACIO DÍAZ GONZÁLEZ

Capitan Brotons, 1 ATICO
38200 La Laguna (Santa Cruz de Tenerife)
☎: 922 252 610 - Fax: 922 252 088
arq_idg@hotmail.com

VIÑA ORLARA 2008 T
**83**

## J.A. FLORES S.L.

Cuchareras Bajas, 2
38370 La Matanza de Acentejo (Tenerife)
☎: 922 577 194 - Fax: 922 577 194

VIÑA FLORES 2008 T
**84**

VIÑA FLORES 2008 T MACERACIÓN CARBÓNICA

**68**

## LA BALDESA

El Calvario, 67
38360 El Sauzal (Santa Cruz de Tenerife)
☎: 922 330 557
miguel@pacheco.as
www.baldesa.com

LA BALDESA 2008 B

**79**

LA BALDESA 2008 T
listán blanco

**82**

## M. CRISTINA GONZÁLEZ GARCÍA

Barranco de San Juan, s/n
38350 Tacoronte (Tenerife)
☎: 922 284 084 - Fax: 922 284 084
carbajalestf@yahoo.es

CARBAJALES 2008 T

**85** Colour: bright cherry. Nose: ripe fruit, sweet spices, creamy oak. Palate: flavourful, fruity, toasty, round tannins.

## MARBA

Ctra. del Socorro, 253 Portezuelo
38280 Tegueste (Tenerife)
☎: 639 065 015 - Fax: 922 638 400
bodegas_marba@telefonica.net

MARBA BLANCO BARRICA 2008 B
listán blanco 85%, varietal 15%

**86** Colour: bright yellow. Nose: powerful, ripe fruit, sweet spices, creamy oak, fragrant herbs, tropical fruit. Palate: fresh, good acidity, sweetness.

MARBA 2008 B
listán blanco 85%, otras 15%

**84**

MARBA 2008 RD

**84**

## MONJE

Camino Cruz de Leandro, 36
38359 El Sauzal (Santa Cruz de Tenerife)
☎: 922 585 027 - Fax: 922 585 027
monje@bodegasmonje.com
www.bodegasmonje.com

MONJE DRAGOBLANCO 2008 B

**83**

EVENTO 2008 BFB

**81**

HOLLERA MONJE 2008 RD

**82**

HOLLERA MONJE 2008 T MACERACIÓN CARBÓNICA

**87** Colour: cherry, purple rim. Nose: floral, ripe fruit, red berry notes, scrubland. Palate: fruity, fresh, flavourful.

MONJE 2008 T

**84**

TINTILLA MONJE 2006 T FERMENTADO EN BARRICA

**82**

MONJE LISTAN NEGRO 2006 T FERMENTADO EN BARRICA

**81**

MONJE DE AUTOR 2000 TR

**86** Colour: pale ruby, brick rim edge. Nose: wet leather, candied fruit, dry nuts, spicy, aged wood nuances. Palate: fine bitter notes, spicy, classic aged character.

MONJE MOSCATEL 2005 DULCE

**82**

VINO PADRE MIGUEL MONJE 2002 TINTO DULCE

**86** Colour: deep cherry, orangey edge. Nose: candied fruit, dried fruit, fruit liqueur notes. Palate: sweet, powerful.

DRAGOBLANCO

## REJANERO

Rejanero, 5 - El Socorro
38280 Tegueste (Tenerife)
☎: 922 540 120 - Fax: 922 544 773
info@bodegas-rejanero.com

REJANERO 2008 B
**82**
REJANERO TRADICIONAL 2008 T
**77**
REJANERO 2006 T BARRICA
**83**

## TROPICAL MAR

Ctra. Los Angeles, 69
38360 Sauzal (Tenerife)
☎: 922 575 184

DON GUSTAVO 2008 B
**82**
DON GUSTAVO 2008 T
**82**

## VIÑA EL MATO

Calvario, 270
38350 Tacoronte (Tenerife)
☎: 922 561 752 - Fax: 922 561 752
jose.sarabia@navegalia.com

VIÑA EL MATÓ 2008 B
**79**
VIÑA EL MATÓ 2008 T
**78**
VIÑA EL MATÓ 2008 T MACERACIÓN CARBÓNICA
**70**

SOME OTHER WINERIES WITHIN THE DO:

**BODEGA JUAN FUENTES TABARES
BODEGAS TAGOROR
BODEGAS Y VIÑEDOS 2005 S.L.
CALDOS DE ANAGA
CÁNDIDO HERNÁNDEZ PÍO
EDUARDO HERNÁNDEZ TORRES
GUAYONGE C.B.
HIMACOPASA
JUAN GUTIERREZ LEÓN
LA ISLETA
MODAS EL ARCA S.L.
PRESAS OCAMPO S.A.T.
RUIZ**

# DO TARRAGONA

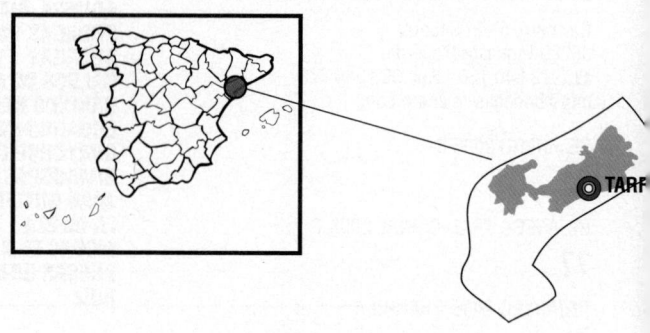

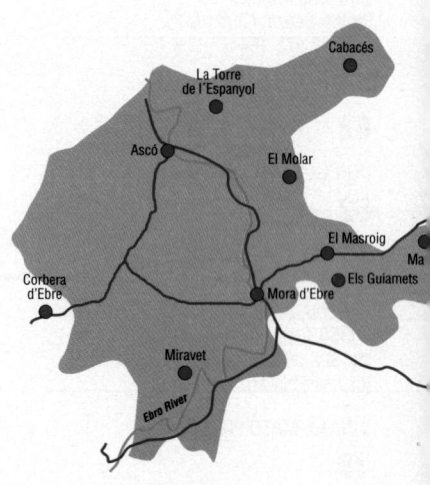

▽ Consejo Regulador
● DO Boundary

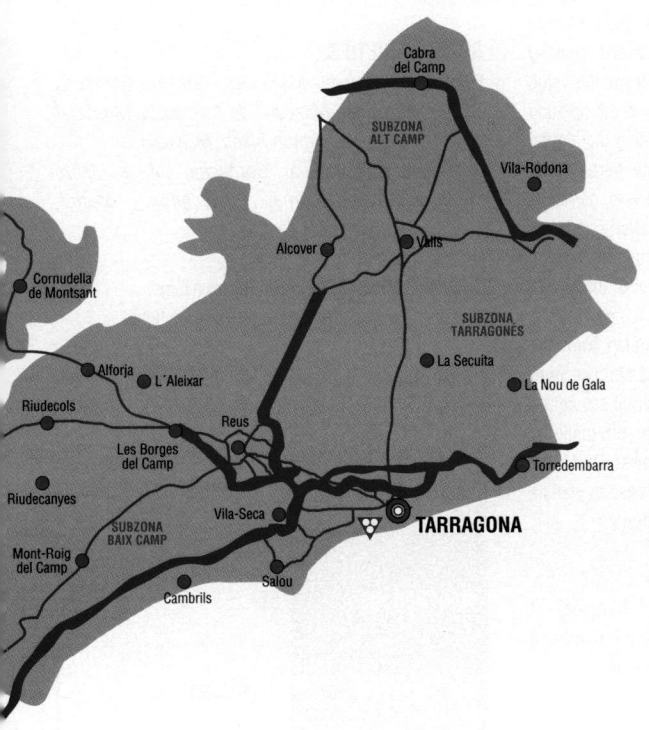

# DO TARRAGONA

## NEWS

Of Tarragona one could say that there is not a homogenous wine pattern, particularly from the varietal point of view. But we have to remember, or to remind the consumer, that there is a huge effort on the part of the wineries to bottle their wines under that DO label, considering that 70% of the total production goes to cava base wines. Only De Muller seems to be brave enough to bottle their sparkling renderings under the DO's label. It is difficult though to understand the DO's grape choice and their blends, although the vine growers have managed to get the hang of every imaginable grape. The wines from the 2008 vintage are fruitier in style given the delay in the ripening period and the white renderings representing the almost 'official lean' of the vintage: fresh, rich, herbaceous, particularly those from de chardonnay, xarel.lo, garnacha blanca, moscatel... The rosé wines are offering a more powerful and acidic profile, save the one offered by Adernats, more French and oxidized. Likewise, the barrel-aged wines are achieving a more complex and Mediterranean style based on toasted notes from the heavily sunned grape skins. Alto to be taken into account al the single-variety renderings from cabernet sauvignon and garnacha and the first ever 100% sumoll, made by Rondoya coop. The likes of Vinyes del Terrer, De Muller and Vinos Padró reached the highest ratings, as well as the usual suspects, the rich sweet and licoreux.

## LOCATION

The region is situated in the province of Tarragona. It comprises two different wine-growing regions: El Camp and Ribera d'Ebre, with a total of 72 municipal areas.

## CLIMATE

Mediterranean in the region of El Camp, with an average annual rainfall of 500 mm. The region of the Ribera has a rather harsh climate with cold winters and hot summers; it also has the lowest rainfall in the region (385 mm per year).

## SOIL

El Camp is characterized by its calcareous, light terrain, and the Ribera has calcareous terrain and also some alluvial terrain.

## GRAPE VARIETIES:

**White:** *Chardonnay, Macabeo, Xarel·lo, Garnacha Blanca, Parellada, Moscatel de Alejandría, Moscatel de Frontignan, Sauvignon Blanc, Malvasía.*

**Red:** *Samsó (Cariñena), Garnacha, Ull de Llebre (Tempranillo), Cabernet Sauvignon, Merlot, Monastrell, Pinot Noir, Syrah.*

**SUB-REGIONS:** El Camp and Ribera d'Ebre (See specific characteristics in previous sections).

| | |
|---|---|
| Hectares of Vineyard | 6,147 |
| Nº Viticulturists | 1,853 |
| Nº of Bodegas | 58 |
| 2008 Harvest | Very Good |
| 2007 Production | 4,000,000 l. |
| Marketing | 60% domestic 40% export |

**CONSEJO REGULADOR**
Avda. Catalunya, 50. 43002 Tarragona
☎: 977 217 931 - Fax: 977 229 102
@ dotarragona@ctmail.net

## GENERAL CHARACTERISTICS OF THE WINES:

| | |
|---|---|
| **WHITES** | These have a markedly Mediterranean character, with notes reminiscent of mountain herbs. Yellow straw in colour, they are fresh, fruity and flavourful on the palate. |
| **ROSÉS** | Most of these have a colour that ranges from salmon to raspberry. They are fresh, fruity, light and pleasant to drink. |
| **REDS** | The young wines are the most characteristic. They have a cherry colour and are fruity, flavourful, with a slightly warm hint due to the Mediterranean influence, although much less meaty and powerful than those of Montsant. |
| **TRADITIONAL WINES** | These are the Licorosos (sweet) and the so-called Rancios Secos, with an alcohol content of between 13.5° and 23°, and the Generosos (dry), with an alcohol content of between 14° and 23°. Some also undergo the traditional processes. |

## 2008 VINTAGE RATING:

## VERY GOOD

## AGRIC. I CAIXA AGRÀRIA I SECCIÓ DE CREDIT DE BRAFIM S.C.C.L.

Major, 50
43812 Brafim (Tarragona)
☎: 977 620 061 - Fax: 977 620 061
oficina@agricolabrafim.com
www.agricolabrafim.com

PUIG RODÓ MACABEU 2008 B
macabeo 100%

**78**

PUIG RODÓ XAREL.LO 2008 B
xarel.lo 100%

**74**

PUIG RODÓ 2008 RD
ull de llebre 100%

**84**

PUIG RODÓ NEGRA 2008 T
ull de llebre 80%, merlot 20%

**87** Colour: cherry, garnet rim. Nose: powerful, ripe fruit, red berry notes, sweet spices, cocoa bean. Palate: powerful, flavourful, fleshy.

## AGRIC. Y CAIXA NOVA DE RODONYA

St. Sebastia, 3
43812 Rodonya ()
☎: 977 608 010
crodonya@telefonica.es

SUMOI CAPVESPRE 2008 T

**90** Colour: cherry, garnet rim. Nose: expressive, toasty, new oak, ripe fruit. Palate: good acidity, fine bitter notes, spicy, slightly dry, soft tannins.

CAPVESPRE 2008 T

**87** Colour: deep cherry. Nose: red berry notes, ripe fruit, lactic notes. Palate: flavourful, ripe fruit, fleshy.

## BODEGA COOPERATIVA VILA-RODONA

Ctra. Santes Creus, s/n
43814 Vila-Rodona (Tarragona)
☎: 977 638 004 - Fax: 977 639 075
copvilar@copvilar.e.telefonica.net
www.coopvila-rodona.com

FLAMA ROJA 2008 B

**72**

MOSCATELL VILA-RODONA B

**82**

FLAMA ROJA 2007 TR

**81**

FLAMA ROJA 2001 TR

**83**

VI RANCI VILA-RODONA RANCIO

**87** Colour: light mahogany. Nose: powerful, fruit liqueur notes, fruit liqueur notes, dry nuts, spicy, cocoa bean. Palate: powerful, sweetness, fine bitter notes, good acidity.

VILA-RODONA VINO DE LICOR

**78**

## BODEGAS J. M. BACH I FILLS

Camí Vell de Cambrils 180
43480 Vilaseca (Tarragona)
☎: 977 353 099 - Fax: 977 353 154
closbarenys@closbarenys.com
www.closbarenys.com

CLOS BARENYS MUSCAT 2008 B
moscatel 100%

**72**

CLOS BARENYS MERLOT/SYRAH 2007 T
merlot 50%, syrah 50%

**85** Colour: cherry, garnet rim. Nose: medium intensity, ripe fruit, scrubland, balsamic herbs. Palate: flavourful, spicy, ripe fruit.

CLOS BARENYS MERLOT/MERLOT 2007 T
merlot 100%

**84**

CLOS BARENYS 2004 TC
merlot 50%, cabernet sauvignon 50%

**86** Colour: cherry, garnet rim. Nose: powerful, toasty, dark chocolate. Palate: flavourful, spirituous, spicy, warm.

CLOS BARENYS 2003 TR
merlot 50%, cabernet sauvignon 50%

**85** Colour: cherry, garnet rim. Nose: ripe fruit, toasty, warm, wet leather. Palate: flavourful, powerful, fleshy, spicy.

## CELLER MAS LA BOELLA

Autovía Reus-Tarragona, (T-11) km. 12
43110 La Canonja (Tarragona)
☎: 977 771 515 - Fax: 977 300 306
celler@laboella.com
www.laboella.com

MAS LA BOELLA 2008 T
cabernet sauvignon 80%, monastrell 20%

**86** Colour: cherry, purple rim. Nose: powerful, ripe fruit, red berry notes. Palate: flavourful, fleshy, ripe fruit.

MAS LA BOELLA VI DE GUARDA 2007 T
cabernet sauvignon 100%

**89** Colour: cherry, garnet rim. Nose: ripe fruit, spicy, creamy oak, toasty, complex, mineral. Palate: powerful, flavourful, toasty, round tannins.

MAS LA BOELLA SELECCIÓ MAGNUM 2007 T
cabernet sauvignon 100%

**88** Colour: cherry, garnet rim. Nose: ripe fruit, spicy, toasty, complex, aromatic coffee, warm. Palate: powerful, flavourful, toasty, round tannins.

## DE MULLER

Camí Pedra Estela, 34
43205 Reus (Tarragona)
☎: 977 757 473 - Fax: 977 771 129
lab@demuller.es
www.demuller.es

DE MULLER CHARDONNAY 2008 BFB
chardonnay 100%

**90** Colour: bright yellow. Nose: powerful, ripe fruit, sweet spices, creamy oak, fragrant herbs. Palate: rich, smoky aftertaste, flavourful, fresh, good acidity.

DE MULLER MUSCAT 2008 B
moscatel 100%

**87** Colour: pale. Nose: fresh fruit, white flowers, powerfull, varietal. Palate: flavourful, fruity, fresh.

SOLIMAR 2008 B
moscatel 35%, macabeo 50%, sauvignon blanc 15%

**86** Colour: pale. Nose: fresh fruit, fruit expression, tropical fruit. Palate: flavourful, fruity, fresh.

DE MULLER MOSCATEL AÑEJO B
moscatel 100%

**90** Colour: golden. Nose: powerful, floral, honeyed notes, candied fruit, fragrant herbs. Palate: flavourful, sweet, fresh, fruity, good acidity, long.

SOLIMAR 2008 RD
garnacha 35%, tempranillo 35%, syrah 18%, pinot noir 12%

**84**

DE MULLER PINOT NOIR 2008 RD
pinot noir 100%

**79**

DE MULLER SYRAH 2008 T
syrah 100%

**86** Colour: bright cherry. Nose: ripe fruit, sweet spices, creamy oak, expressive. Palate: flavourful, fruity, toasty, round tannins.

DE MULLER CABERNET SAUVIGNON 2006 TC
cabernet sauvignon 100%

**88** Colour: cherry, garnet rim. Nose: ripe fruit, spicy, creamy oak, toasty, complex. Palate: powerful, flavourful, toasty, round tannins.

DE MULLER MERLOT 2006 T BARRICA
merlot 100%

**87** Colour: cherry, garnet rim. Nose: scrubland, powerfull, warm, ripe fruit, creamy oak, sweet spices. Palate: spicy, ripe fruit, round tannins.

SOLIMAR 2006 TC
cabernet sauvignon 60%, merlot 40%

**84**

PORPORES DE MULLER 2003 TR
cabernet sauvignon 40%, merlot 40%, tempranillo 20%

**88** Colour: deep cherry, orangey edge. Nose: fruit liqueur notes, spicy, aromatic coffee, toasty. Palate: flavourful, spicy, ripe fruit.

DE MULLER AVREO SEMIDULCE 1954 AÑEJO

**89** Colour: light mahogany. Nose: powerful, fruit preserve, candied fruit, dry nuts, fruit liqueur notes, toasty. Palate: flavourful, powerful, sweetness.

MAS DE VALLS 2007 BN
macabeo 55%, chardonnay 35%, parellada 10%

**87** Colour: bright straw. Nose: medium intensity, fresh fruit, dried herbs, fine lees, floral. Palate: fresh, fruity, flavourful, good acidity.

**RESERVA REINA VIOLANT 2006 ESP**
chardonnay 50%, pinot noir 50%

**88** Colour: bright straw. Nose: dried herbs, fine lees, floral, ripe fruit. Palate: fresh, fruity, flavourful, good acidity.

**DE MULLER RANCIO SECO RANCIO**
garnacha , cariñena

**89** Colour: iodine, amber rim. Nose: powerful, complex, elegant, dry nuts, toasty. Palate: rich, fine bitter notes, fine solera notes, long, spicy.

**PAJARETE SOLERA 1851 VINO DE LICOR**
moscatel , garnacha , garnacha blanca

**92** Colour: dark mahogany. Nose: toasty, dark chocolate, aged wood nuances, powerfull, fruit liqueur notes. Palate: powerful, fleshy, spicy.

**AUREO SECO VINO DE LICOR**
garnacha 70%, garnacha blanca 30%

**90** Colour: iodine, amber rim. Nose: roasted almonds, aged wood nuances, pattiserie, fruit liqueur notes, fruit liqueur notes. Palate: fleshy, complex, spicy.

**MISA DULCE SUPERIOR VINO DE LICOR**
garnacha blanca 60%, macabeo 40%

**87** Colour: iodine, amber rim. Nose: powerful, fruit liqueur notes, citrus fruit, honeyed notes. Palate: sweetness, unctuous, good acidity.

A. MULLER

## MAS DEL BOTÓ

Camí de Porrera a Alforja, s/n
43365 Alforja (Tarragona)
☎: 630 982 747 - Fax: 977 236 396
pep@masdelboto.cat
www.masdelboto.cat

**GANAGOT 2006 T**
garnacha 85%, cariñena 10%, cabernet sauvignon 5%

**83**

**GANAGOT 2005 T**
garnacha 85%, cariñena 10%, cabernet sauvignon 5%

**84**

## MAS VICENÇ

Mas Vicenç, s/n
43811 Cabra de Camp (Tarragona)
☎: 977 630 024 - Fax: 977 630 134
masvicens@gmail.com

www.masvicenç.com

**MAS VICENÇ 2008 B**
chardonnay , garnacha blanca

**85** Colour: bright straw. Nose: powerful, ripe fruit, citrus fruit, candied fruit. Palate: flavourful, fruity, fresh, fine bitter notes.

**MAS VICENÇ 2008 B**
macabeo

**84**

**MAS VICENÇ DOLÇ 2008 B**
moscatel

**83**

**MAS VICENÇ 2007 T**
ull de llebre , cabernet sauvignon

**88** Colour: cherry, garnet rim. Nose: spicy, creamy oak, toasty, macerated fruit. Palate: powerful, flavourful, toasty, round tannins.

## SERRA DE LLABERIA

Avda. Vidal i Barraquer, 12, 8º, 4ª
43005 Tarragona (Tarragona)
☎: 977 824 122 - Fax: 977 824 122
info@serradellaberia.com
www.serradellaberia.com

**SERRA DE LLABERIA ELISABETH 2007 B**
garnacha blanca 80%, chardonnay 20%

**85** Colour: bright straw. Nose: powerful, fruit liqueur notes, fruit liqueur notes, citrus fruit. Palate: powerful, fine bitter notes, warm.

**SERRA DE LLABERIA ELISABETH 2004 TR**
cabernet sauvignon 60%, merlot 30%, garnacha 10%, syrah %

**87** Colour: cherry, garnet rim. Nose: ripe fruit, spicy, toasty, cedar wood, aged wood nuances. Palate: powerful, flavourful, toasty, round tannins.

**SERRA DE LLABERIA ELISABETH 2003 TC**
cabernet sauvignon 60%, merlot 30%, garnacha 10%, syrah %

**89** Colour: bright cherry. Nose: ripe fruit, sweet spices, creamy oak, expressive, dark chocolate. Palate: flavourful, fruity, toasty, round tannins.

## UNIÓ CORPORACIÓ ALIMENTARIA - CELLERS UNIÓ

Joan Oliver, 16-24
43206 Reus (Tarragona)
☎: 977 330 055 - Fax: 977 330 070

reus@cellersunio.com
www.unio.coop.com

**ROUREDA BLANC DE BLANCS 2008 B**
macabeo 33%, xarel.lo 33%, chardonnay 33%

**84**

**ROCA MORA 2008 B**
macabeo 50%, garnacha 30%, parellada 20%

**83**

**ROCA MORA 2008 RD**
syrah 40%, merlot 40%, ull de llebre 20%

**85** Colour: rose, purple rim. Nose: powerful, ripe fruit, red berry notes, floral, expressive. Palate: fleshy, powerful, fruity, fresh.

**ROUREDA RUBÍ 2008 RD**
merlot 40%, tempranillo 30%, sumoll 30%

**82**

**ROUREDA NEGRE 2008 T**
garnacha 40%, mazuelo 40%, syrah 20%

**86** Colour: cherry, garnet rim. Nose: powerful, ripe fruit, red berry notes. Palate: flavourful, fruity, fleshy, ripe fruit.

**ROCA MORA 2008 T**
garnacha 50%, ull de llebre 30%, cariñena 20%

**83**

**ROUREDA 2005 TC**
garnacha 40%, tempranillo 40%, cabernet sauvignon 20%

**87** Colour: cherry, garnet rim. Nose: expressive, ripe fruit, red berry notes, creamy oak. Palate: flavourful, ripe fruit, spicy, round tannins.

**ROUREDA 2003 TR**
tempranillo 40%, mazuelo 30%, cabernet sauvignon 30%

**82**

**ROCA MORA 2002 TGR**
tempranillo 40%, garnacha 30%, cariñena 30%

**80**

## VINETUM IBERI

Nou, 21
43748 Ginestar (Tarragona)
☎: 977 409 018 - Fax: 932 152 775
info@vinetumiberi.es
www.lestires.es

**BARRANC DE NORIA 2006 B**

**85** Colour: bright straw. Nose: new oak, toasty, woody, dry nuts, ripe fruit. Palate: flavourful, powerful, fine bitter notes.

**LES TIRES 2006 T**
merlot , garnacha , tempranillo , petit verdot

**87** Colour: cherry, garnet rim. Nose: powerful, smoky, caramel, ripe fruit. Palate: spicy, ripe fruit, round tannins.

**COMUNS DEL L'HEREU 2005 T**
merlot , garnacha , tempranillo

**89** Colour: bright cherry, garnet rim. Nose: neat, expressive, toasty, balsamic herbs. Palate: flavourful, light-bodied, good structure, long, balsamic.

## VINICOLA I SECCIÓ DE CRÉDIT SANT ISIDRE DE NULLES

Estació, s/n
43887 Nulles (Tarragona)
☎: 977 614 965 - Fax: 977 602 622
casinulles@casinulles.com
www.vinicoladenulles.com

**ADERNATS 2008 BFB**
xarel.lo 100%

**90** Colour: bright straw. Nose: sweet spices, cocoa bean, citrus fruit, candied fruit, ripe fruit. Palate: flavourful, fruity, ripe fruit.

**ADERNATS SEDUCCIÓN 2008 B**
xarel.lo 30%, moscatel 37%, chardonnay 33%

**85** Colour: bright straw. Nose: fresh, fresh fruit, white flowers, grassy. Palate: flavourful, fruity, good acidity, balanced.

**ADERNATS BLANC 2008 B**
macabeo 30%, xarel.lo 50%, moscatel 3%, chardonnay 17%

**84**

**ADERNATS ROSAT 2008 RD**
tempranillo 55%, merlot 45%

**89** Colour: coppery red. Nose: candied fruit, red berry notes, citrus fruit, fragrant herbs. Palate: spicy, flavourful, sweetness.

**ADERNATS NEGRE JOVE 2008 T**
tempranillo 100%

**84**

**ADERNATS ANGELUS 2008 T**
merlot 19%, tempranillo 81%

**82**

**ADERNATS 2005 TC**
tempranillo 75%, merlot 25%

**85** Colour: cherry, garnet rim. Nose: powerful, ripe fruit, dark chocolate. Palate: flavourful, fleshy, sweetness.

## VINOS PADRÓ

Avda. Catalunya, 64-70
43812 Brafim (Tarragona)
☎: 977 620 012 - Fax: 977 620 486
info@vinspadro.com
www.vinspadro.com

IPSIS XAREL.LO 2008 B

**90** Colour: bright straw. Nose: fresh, fresh fruit, white flowers, expressive, sweet spices. Palate: flavourful, fruity, good acidity, balanced.

IPSIS BLANCO FLOR 2008 B

**87** Colour: pale, greenish rim. Nose: grassy, floral, fresh fruit, citrus fruit. Palate: flavourful, fruity, fresh.

IPSIS CHARDONNAY 2008 B

**87** Colour: bright straw. Nose: fragrant herbs, white flowers, ripe fruit, citrus fruit. Palate: flavourful, fruity, fresh.

IPSIS ROSADO DE LÁGRIMA 2008 RD

**85** Colour: rose, purple rim. Nose: powerful, ripe fruit, red berry notes, floral. Palate: fleshy, powerful, fruity, fresh.

IPSIS 2005 TC
tempranillo , merlot

**91** Colour: bright cherry. Nose: sweet spices, creamy oak, expressive, ripe fruit. Palate: flavourful, fruity, toasty, round tannins.

IPSIS TEMPRANILLO MERLOT 2008 T
tempranillo , merlot

**88** Colour: cherry, purple rim. Nose: expressive, red berry notes, floral, ripe fruit. Palate: flavourful, fruity, good acidity,

round tannins.
CRINEL 2006 TC

**85** Colour: cherry, garnet rim. Nose: creamy oak, sweet spices, ripe fruit. Palate: flavourful, fleshy, ripe fruit.

BACANAL 2006 TC

**85** Colour: cherry, garnet rim. Nose: spicy, creamy oak, toasty, fruit liqueur notes. Palate: powerful, flavourful, toasty, round tannins.

CAPITOL
DON SEVERO

## VINYA JANINE

Anselm Clavé, 1
43812 Rodonyá (Tarragona)
☎: 977 628 305 - Fax: 977 628 305
vjanine@tinet.org
www.vinyajanine.com

VINYA JANINE CABERNET SAUVIGNON MERLOT 2006 T

**81**

## VINYES DEL TERRER

Camí del Terrer s/n
43480 Vila-Seca (Tarragona)
☎: 977 269 229 - Fax: 977 269 229
info@terrer.net
www.terrer.net

TERRER D'AUBERT 2006 T
cabernet sauvignon 100%

**92** Colour: cherry, garnet rim. Nose: powerful, ripe fruit, earthy notes, toasty, new oak. Palate: flavourful, fleshy, spicy, round tannins.

NUS DEL TERRER 2006 T
cabernet sauvignon 72%, garnacha 28%

**91** Colour: cherry, garnet rim. Nose: spicy, toasty, mineral, ripe fruit. Palate: concentrated, powerful, flavourful.

SOME OTHER WINERIES WITHIN THE DO:

**AGRÀRIA TOUS VALLS S.L.
AGRÍCOLA I S.C. MONTBRIÓ DEL CAMP
CELLER BOSCOS DE VALLS
COOP. AGRÍCOLA SANT JAUME DE BENISSANET**

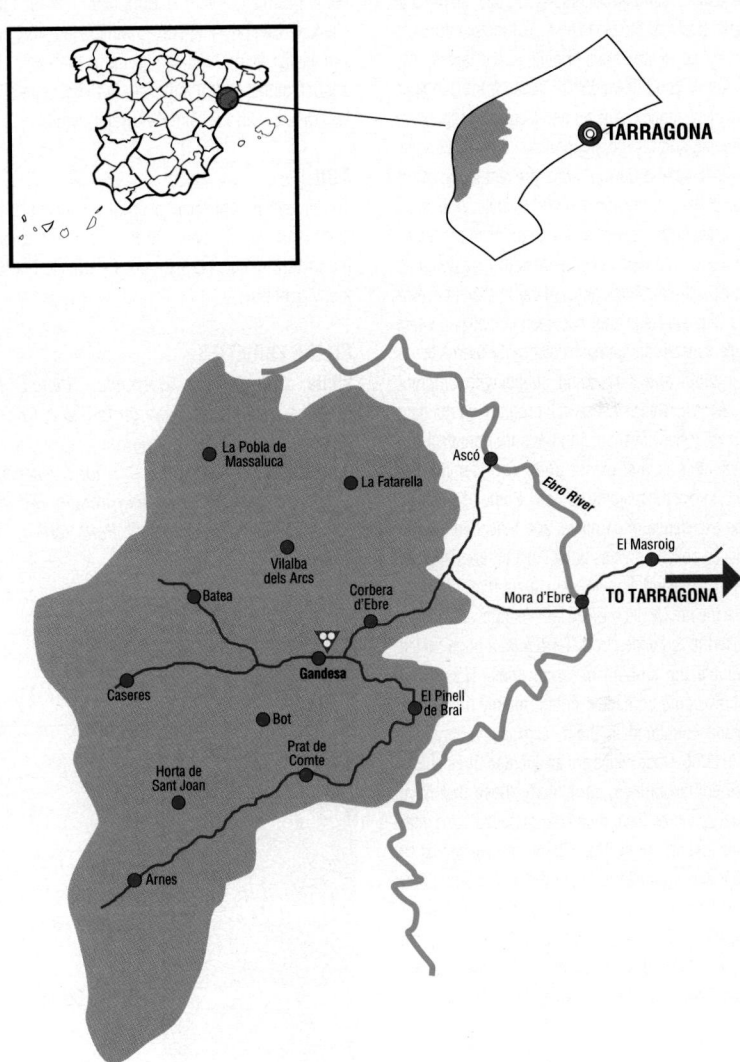

TARRAGONA

La Pobla de Massaluca

La Fatarella

Ascó

Ebro River

Vilalba dels Arcs

El Masroig

Batea

Corbera d'Ebre

Mora d'Ebre

TO TARRAGONA

Gandesa

Caseres

El Pinell de Brai

Bot

Prat de Comte

Horta de Sant Joan

Arnes

Consejo Regulador
DO Boundary

## NEWS

In spite of the difficult climatic conditions of 2008, so dry that provoked water stress in the vines and mild temperatures to the end of the cycle, which delayed ripening, our tasting was nevertheless full of good news. White wines from garnacha blanca are full of aromatic character and elegance, capable of good bottle ageing and far more expressive when oak-aged. The wineries Edètaria and Celler Piñol represent some of the best examples of that variety and that sort of style, with some mineral and herbal notes as well as those of finely confected fruit, and the former manage to come up with a golden, ripe and mature 2005 with fine aging notes of oak and great overall elegance. The Consejo Regulador has seen in labelling white garnacha single-varietals as "garnacha blanca de Terra Alta" as an exciting product and it is going ahead with different promotional events as well as a research program on ripening patterns and quality classification. Another important decision line for the wineries is that of not bottling under the DO Catalunya label, in fact the majority of them. Some of the basic factors for the excellence of garnacha and macabeo are the quaternary clayey soils known as panal, sea breezes and the northerly dry, cool wind known as cierzo that helps to counterbalance the hot Mediterranean sun, features all of them that benefit also the red wines from Terra Alta, a huge bunch that easily double the amount of white ones. The young renderings show some confected notes, mainly due to the garnacha peluda contained in them, a grape variety that suffered a lot in 2008. Rosé wines are an average three points over the 2009 edition ratings, particularly those that have syrah. The crianza wines have mostly a garnacha base with French varieties, mainly syrah. The 2007 wines are similar to those of 2008 in terms of freshness, and the 2005 and 2006 are ageing well within the warm –verging on sweet– pattern of the region. Mistela and sweet wines, including the typical rancio renderings of the area, which follow the solera ageing pattern typical of Jerez, are the best wines from the region.

## LOCATION

In the southeast of Catalonia, in the province of Tarragona. It covers the municipal districts of Arnes, Batea, Bot, Caseres, Corbera d´Ebre, La Fatarella, Gandesa, Horta de Sant Joan, Pinell de Brai, La Pobla de Massaluca, Prat de Comte and Vilalba dels Arcs.

## CLIMATE

Mediterranean, with continental influences. It is characterized by its hot, dry summers and very cold winters, especially in the higher regions in the east. The average annual rainfall is 400 mm. Another vital aspect is the wind: the 'Cierzo' and the 'Garbi' (Ábrego) winds.

## SOIL

The vineyards are located on an extensive plateau at an altitude of slightly over 400 m. The soil is calcareous and the texture mainly clayey, poor in organic matter and with many pebbles.

## GRAPE VARIETIES:

**White:** *Chardonnay, Garnacha Blanca, Parellada, Macabeo, Moscatel, Sauvignon Blanc, Chenin, Pedro Ximénez.* Experimental: *Viognier.*

**Red:** *Cabernet Sauvigon, Cariñena, Garnacha Tinta, Garnacha Peluda, Syrah, Tempranillo, Merlot, Samsó, Cabernet Franc.* Experimental: *Petit Verdot, Marselane, Caladoc.*

| | |
|---|---|
| **Hectares of Vineyard** | 6,210 |
| **N° Viticulturists** | 1,662 |
| **N° of Bodegas** | 42 |
| **2008 Harvest** | White wines: Very Good The rest: Good |
| **2007 Production** | 13,400,054 l. |
| **Marketing** | 85% domestic 15% export |

**CONSEJO REGULADOR**
Avinguda Catalunya, 31
43780 Gandesa (Tarragona)
☎: 977 421 278 - Fax: 977 421 623
@ info@doterraalta.com
www.doterraalta.com

## GENERAL CHARACTERISTICS OF THE WINES:

| | |
|---|---|
| **WHITES** | These are the most interesting products of the region. They are produced from the Garnacha Blanca variety, and have a purely Mediterranean character. With yellowish nuances, they have moses of ripe fruit and mountain herbs; they are supple, warm, complex and very expressive on the palate. |
| **ROSÉS** | Mainly produced from Garnacha, they offer all the fruitiness and tastiness on the palate, that one expects from this variety. |
| **REDS** | Cherry-coloured, they are characterised by their ripe fruit nose; they are quite flavourful on the palate. |
| **GENEROSOS** | This is another of the traditional wines of the region, whether in its Rancio or Mistela versions. |

## 2008 VINTAGE RATING:

# GOOD

## AGRICOLA ST JOSEP DE BOT

Estació, 2
43785 Bot (Tarragona)
☎: 977 428 035 - Fax: 977 428 192
info@coopbot.com
www.coopbot.com

**CLOT D'ENCÍS 2008 B**
garnacha blanca 85%, otras 15%

**88** Colour: bright straw. Nose: ripe fruit, floral, grassy. Palate: flavourful, fruity, fresh.

**BRAU DE BOT 2008 B**
garnacha blanca 60%, macabeo 40%

**84**

**LLÀGRIMES DE TARDOR 2007 BFB**
garnacha blanca 100%

**92** Colour: bright straw. Nose: ripe fruit, candied fruit, citrus fruit, sweet spices, aged wood nuances. Palate: flavourful, powerful, fleshy.

**CLOT D'ENCIS 2008 RD**
syrah 100%

**83**

**LA PLANA D'EN FONOLL 2008 T**
ull de llebre, samsó, syrah, merlot

**88** Colour: cherry, purple rim. Nose: toasty, creamy oak, cocoa bean, ripe fruit. Palate: flavourful, powerful, fleshy, spicy.

**CLOT D'ENCÍS 2008 T**
garnacha, syrah, samsó, merlot

**85** Colour: cherry, purple rim. Nose: ripe fruit, fruit expression, red berry notes. Palate: powerful, flavourful, fruity.

**LLÀGRIMES DE TARDOR 2007 TC**
garnacha, samsó, syrah, cabernet sauvignon, merlot

**85** Colour: cherry, garnet rim. Nose: creamy oak, toasty, dark chocolate, ripe fruit. Palate: spicy, slightly overripe, round tannins.

**LLÀGRIMES DE TARDOR SELECCIÓ 2006 TC**
samsó, syrah, merlot, cabernet sauvignon

**90** Colour: cherry, garnet rim. Nose: powerful, sweet spices, cocoa bean, creamy oak. Palate: flavourful, spicy, ripe fruit.

**LLÀGRIMES DE TARDOR MISTELA BLANCA 2008 VINO DE LICOR**
garnacha blanca 100%

**87** Colour: old gold, amber rim. Nose: powerful, expressive, fruit liqueur notes, fruit liqueur notes, roasted almonds, varnish. Palate: sweet, flavourful, good acidity, fine bitter notes.

**LLÀGRIMES DE TARDOR MISTELA NEGRA 2007 VINO DE LICOR**
garnacha

**88** Colour: cherry, garnet rim. Nose: powerful, ripe fruit, sweet spices, toasty, candied fruit. Palate: flavourful, powerful, fleshy, spirituous.

## ALTAVINS VITICULTORS S.L.

Tarragona, 42
43786 Batea (Tarragona)
☎: 977 430 596 - Fax: 977 430 371
altavins@altavins.com
www.altavins.com

**ILERCAVONIA 2008 B**
garnacha blanca

**81**

**ALMODÍ 2008 T**
garnacha

**88** Colour: cherry, purple rim. Nose: ripe fruit, red berry notes, lactic notes. Palate: flavourful, fleshy, fruity.

**TEMPUS SIS MESOS 2006 T**
garnacha, syrah, samso, cabernet sauvignon

**86** Colour: cherry, garnet rim. Nose: powerful, warm, dark chocolate, toasty. Palate: flavourful, powerful, fleshy, round tannins.

**DOMUS PENSI 2004 TC**
cabernet sauvignon, syrah, garnacha, merlot

**88** Colour: deep cherry, orangey edge. Nose: candied fruit, aged wood nuances, pattiserie. Palate: flavourful, spirituous, spicy.

JORN NOU

## CATERRA AGRICOLA I SEC DE CRÈDIT TERRA ALTA SCCL

Glorieta s/n
43783 La Pobla de Massaluca (Tarragona)
☎: 977 439 765 - Fax: 977 439 765
catapoma@telefonica.net
www.caterra.es

**FONT CALENTA 2007 B**
macabeo 80%, garnacha blanca 20%

**85** Colour: bright straw. Nose: slightly evolved, petrol notes, citrus fruit, honeyed notes. Palate: flavourful, fleshy, sweetness.

HEREUS CATERRA 2007 B
garnacha blanca 100%

**85** Colour: bright golden. Nose: petrol notes, citrus fruit, ripe fruit. Palate: flavourful, fleshy, spicy.

L'ESPERIT DEL CERÇ 2007 BFB
garnacha blanca 100%

**82**

HEREUS CATERRA 2008 T
garnacha 50%, cariñena 50%

**83**

L'ESPERIT DEL CERÇ 2007 TC
garnacha 50%, cariñena 50%

**83**

FONT CALENTA NEGRO 2007 T
cariñena 50%, garnacha 50%

**81**

## CELLER AGRÍCOLA FUSTER

Méndez Núñez, 15
43780 Gandesa (Tarragona)
☎: 678 036 487 - Fax: 977 234 665
dardell@dardell.es
www.dardell.es

DARDELL GARNACHA & VIOGNIER 2008 B

**85** Colour: bright straw, coppery red. Nose: fragrant herbs, candied fruit, elegant. Palate: fruity, spicy.

PROHOM 2008 B

**77**

DARDELL GARNACHA Y SYRAH 2008 T

**85** Colour: cherry, purple rim. Nose: floral, grassy, red berry notes. Palate: flavourful, fruity, fine bitter notes.

DARDELL 10 MESES BARRICA 2007 T BARRICA
garnacha, syrah, cabernet sauvignon

**85** Colour: cherry, garnet rim. Nose: ripe fruit, aromatic coffee, caramel, warm. Palate: spicy, ripe fruit, long.

PROHOM 2007 T

**81**

## CELLER BÁRBARA FORÉS

Santa Anna, 28
43780 Gandesa (Tarragona)
☎: 977 420 160 - Fax: 977 421 399
info@cellerbarbarafores.com
www.cellerbarbarafores.com

BÀRBARA FORÉS 2008 B
garnacha blanca 90%, viognier 10%

**88** Colour: bright straw. Nose: fresh, white flowers, expressive, ripe fruit. Palate: flavourful, fruity, good acidity, balanced.

EL QUINTÀ BÁRBARA FORÉS 2007 BFB
garnacha blanca 100%

**90** Colour: bright yellow. Nose: powerful, ripe fruit, sweet spices, creamy oak, fragrant herbs. Palate: rich, smoky aftertaste, flavourful, fresh, good acidity.

VI DOLÇ NATURAL BÁRBARA FORÉS 2006 B
garnacha blanca 100%

**92** Colour: golden. Nose: powerful, floral, honeyed notes, candied fruit, fragrant herbs. Palate: flavourful, sweet, fresh, fruity, good acidity, long.

BÀRBARA FORÉS 2008 RD
garnacha 38%, syrah 53%, cariñena 9%

**85** Colour: rose, purple rim. Nose: powerful, ripe fruit, red berry notes, floral, expressive. Palate: fleshy, powerful, fruity, fresh.

EL TEMPLARI 2007 T
garnacha 60%, morenillo 40%

**84**

BÁRBARA FORÉS NEGRE 2006 T
garnacha 30%, syrah 55%, cariñena 15%

**88** Colour: dark-red cherry. Nose: ripe fruit, candied fruit, dark chocolate, toasty, scrubland. Palate: fleshy, sweetness, powerful, round tannins.

COMA D'EN POU BÀRBARA FORÉS 2004 T
garnacha 33%, cabernet sauvignon 33%, syrah 17%, merlot 17%

**90** Colour: cherry, garnet rim. Nose: ripe fruit, spicy, creamy oak, toasty, complex, earthy notes. Palate: powerful, flavourful, toasty, round tannins.

FOSCANT

## CELLER CAL MENESCAL

Joan Amades, 2
43785 Bot (Tarragona)

☎: 977 428 095 - Fax: 977 428 261
info@cellermenescal.com
www.cellermenescal.com

VALL DEL RACÓ 2008 B
garnacha blanca 65%, otras 35%

**83**

AVUS DOLÇ 2007 T
garnacha 100%

**87** Colour: cherry, garnet rim. Nose: dark chocolate, cocoa bean, overripe fruit, raspberry. Palate: flavourful, sweet, fleshy.

AVUS 2007 T ROBLE
garnacha 60%, syrah 20%, ull de llebre 20%

**86** Colour: cherry, garnet rim. Nose: powerful, candied fruit, fruit preserve, toasty, sweet spices. Palate: powerful, spirituous, spicy.

## CELLER COOPERATIU GANDESA S.C.C.L.

Avda. Catalunya, 28
43780 Gandesa (Tarragona)
☎: 977 420 017 - Fax: 977 420 403
gandesadevins@coopgandesa.com
www.coopgandesa.com

GANDESA 2008 B

**87** Colour: pale. Nose: fresh fruit, ripe fruit, citrus fruit. Palate: flavourful, fruity, fresh, sweetness.

SOMDINOU 2007 B

**89** Colour: bright yellow. Nose: powerful, ripe fruit, sweet spices, creamy oak, fragrant herbs. Palate: rich, smoky aftertaste, flavourful, fresh, good acidity.

ANTIC CASTELL 2007 B

**83**

CÉSAR MARTINELL 2007 BFB

**81**

GANDESA 2008 RD

**85** Colour: coppery red. Nose: medium intensity, candied fruit, red berry notes. Palate: flavourful, fruity, fresh.

GANDESA 2008 T

**83**

PURESA 2006 T

**88** Colour: cherry, garnet rim. Nose: powerful, characterful, fruit liqueur notes, toasty, dark chocolate. Palate: powerful, fleshy, sweetness.

SOMDINOU 2006 T
cariñena 35%, garnacha 65%

**86** Colour: very deep cherry. Nose: spicy, aged wood nuances, roasted almonds, fruit liqueur notes. Palate: flavourful, powerful, spirituous.

ANTIC CASTELL 2006 T

**81**

VARVALL 2005 TR

**83**

GANDESA TINTA MISTELA

**85** Colour: cherry, garnet rim. Nose: powerful, warm, candied fruit, dried fruit, overripe fruit. Palate: flavourful, powerful, sweet, concentrated, warm.

VI DE LICOR 1919 VINO DE LICOR

**90** Colour: iodine, amber rim. Nose: powerful, warm, fruit liqueur notes, sweet spices, pattiserie, roasted almonds. Palate: powerful, fine bitter notes, spirituous.

MISTELA GANDESA VINO DE LICOR

**85** Colour: bright straw. Nose: candied fruit, citrus fruit, floral. Palate: flavourful, sweet, fruity, good acidity.

PUIG VENTOS

## CELLER LA BOLLIDORA

Tacons, 8
43782 Vilalba dels Arcs (Tarragona)
☎: 630 888 588
info@cellerlabollidora.com
www.cellerlabollidora.com

CALITJA 2008 B

**86** Colour: bright straw. Nose: ripe fruit, varietal, grassy. Palate: flavourful, fruity, easy to drink.

FLOR DE GARNATXA 2007 BFB

**87** Colour: bright straw. Nose: medium intensity, ripe fruit, sweet spices, toasty. Palate: flavourful, fleshy, spicy, ripe fruit.

SAÓ 2008 T
garnacha, cariñena, syrah

**84**

PLAN B 2006 T

**85** Colour: cherry, garnet rim. Nose: overripe fruit, dried fruit, fruit liqueur notes, toasty. Palate: concentrated, sweetness, fine bitter notes.

## CELLER MARIOL

Joan Miro, s/n
43786 Batea (Tarragona)
☎: 934 367 628 - Fax: 934 500 281
celler@cellermariol.es
www.cellermariol.es

VINYA SEDOSA BLANC DE BLANCS 2008 B

**84**

AH! 2007 TC

**89** Colour: cherry, garnet rim. Nose: ripe fruit, spicy, creamy oak, toasty, complex. Palate: powerful, flavourful, toasty, round tannins.

MAS MONTASELL SYRAH 2001 TR

**86** Colour: cherry, garnet rim. Nose: elegant, ripe fruit, warm, spicy, aromatic coffee. Palate: flavourful, fresh, spicy, easy to drink.

VI DE PAGÉS
VINYA PUBILLA
CELLER MARIOL
LA CLAU
MAS MONTASELL

## CELLER PIÑOL

Algars, 7
43786 Batea (Tarragona)
☎: 977 43 0 5 - Fax: 977 430 498
info@cellerpinol.com
www.vinospinol.com

L'AVI ARRUFÍ 2008 B
garnacha blanca 95%, viognier 5%

**91** Colour: bright straw. Nose: creamy oak, cocoa bean, ripe fruit, tropical fruit. Palate: fleshy, complex, spicy.

PORTAL N. SRA PORTAL 2008 B
garnacha blanca 75%, sauvignon blanc 15%, macabeo 5%, viognier 5%

**90** Colour: bright straw. Nose: fresh, fresh fruit, white flowers, expressive, mineral. Palate: flavourful, fruity, good acidity, balanced.

JOSEFINA PIÑOL 2008 B
garnacha blanca 100%

**88** Colour: light mahogany, coppery red. Nose: powerful, floral, honeyed notes, candied fruit, fragrant herbs. Palate: flavourful, sweet, fresh, fruity, good acidity, long.

L'AVI ARRUFÍ 2006 T
garnacha, syrah, cabernet sauvignon, merlot, tempranillo

**92** Colour: cherry, garnet rim. Nose: powerful, expressive, ripe fruit, toasty, new oak. Palate: powerful, flavourful, fleshy, spicy.

l'Avi Arrufi
Vi de guarda 2005
D.O.Terra Alta
Celler Piñol

PORTAL N. SRA PORTAL 2007 T ROBLE
garnacha, cabernet sauvignon, merlot, syrah, tempranillo

**91** Colour: bright cherry. Nose: sweet spices, creamy oak, expressive, earthy notes, ripe fruit. Palate: flavourful, fruity, toasty, round tannins.

MATHER TERESINA SELECCIÓN DE VIÑAS VIEJAS 2006-07 T
garnacha, morenillo, cabernet sauvignon, syrah, merlot

**92** Colour: cherry, garnet rim. Nose: creamy oak, toasty, new oak, ripe fruit, expressive. Palate: flavourful, powerful, fleshy, good structure.

JOSEFINA PIÑOL 2007 T DULCE
garnacha 90%, syrah 10%

**91** Colour: black cherry, orangey edge. Nose: powerful, dried fruit, overripe fruit, citrus fruit. Palate: powerful, sweet, good structure, concentrated.

RAIG DE RAÏM
SACRA NATURA

## CELLER XAVIER CLUA

Vall de Sant Isidre, 41
43782 Vilalba dels Arcs (Tarragona)
☎: 977 263 069 - Fax: 977 439 003
info@cellerclua.com
www.cellerclua.com

MAS D'EN POL 2008 B
garnacha blanca, sauvignon blanc, moscatel

**87** Colour: bright straw. Nose: ripe fruit, fruit expression, floral. Palate: fruity, fresh, flavourful, fleshy.

MAS D'EN POL 2008 T
garnacha, syrah, merlot, cabernet sauvignon

**86** Colour: cherry, purple rim. Nose: powerful, warm, ripe fruit. Palate: flavourful, powerful, fleshy.

CLUA MIL.LENNIUM 2006 T
garnacha, syrah, merlot, cabernet sauvignon, pinot noir

**88** Colour: cherry, garnet rim. Nose: powerful, warm, overripe fruit, dark chocolate, sweet spices. Palate: flavourful, powerful, fleshy, spicy.

MAS D'EN POL 2006 T
garnacha, syrah, merlot, cabernet sauvignon

**85** Colour: cherry, garnet rim. Nose: powerful, fruit liqueur notes, scrubland, toasty. Palate: powerful, fine bitter notes, spicy.

MIL.LENNIUM DOLÇ 2005 T DULCE
garnacha 100%

**89** Colour: black cherry. Nose: overripe fruit, dried fruit, fruit liqueur notes, smoky, dark chocolate. Palate: powerful, fleshy, unctuous.

## CELLERS TARRONÉ

Calvari, 22
43786 Batea (Tarragona)
☎: 977 430 109 - Fax: 977 430 183
info@cellerstarrone.com
www.cellerstarrone.com

MERIAN 2008 B
garnacha blanca 90%, sauvignon blanc 10%

**87** Colour: bright straw. Nose: ripe fruit, fresh fruit, citrus fruit, grassy. Palate: flavourful, fruity, fresh.

MERIAN DULCE NATURAL 2008 T
garnacha 100%

**89** Colour: black cherry. Nose: powerful, warm, dried fruit, overripe fruit. Palate: fleshy, powerful, sweet, fine bitter notes, unctuous.

MERIAN 2008 T
garnacha, cabernet sauvignon, syrah, merlot

**88** Colour: deep cherry. Nose: powerful, characterful, ripe fruit, mineral. Palate: flavourful, powerful.

TORREMADRINA 2006 TC
garnacha, cabernet sauvignon, syrah, merlot

**87** Colour: cherry, garnet rim. Nose: powerful, warm, fruit liqueur notes, red berry notes. Palate: fine bitter notes, spicy, round tannins.

TORREMADRINA ROBLE 2006 T
garnacha, cabernet sauvignon, merlot, ull de llebre

**87** Colour: cherry, garnet rim. Nose: ripe fruit, spicy, creamy oak, toasty, new oak. Palate: powerful, flavourful, toasty, round tannins.

TORREMADRINA SELECCIÓN 2005 TC
garnacha, cabernet sauvignon, merlot, syrah

**90** Colour: cherry, garnet rim. Nose: ripe fruit, spicy, creamy oak, toasty, complex. Palate: powerful, flavourful, toasty, round tannins.

MAS TARRONÈ

## COOPERATIVA AGRÍCOLA CELLER BATEA

Moli, 30
43786 Batea (Tarragona)
☎: 977 430 056 - Fax: 977 430 589
enolegs@cellerbatea.com
www.cellerbatea.com

**LAS COLINAS DEL EBRO 2008 B**
garnacha blanca 95%, moscatel 5%

**88** Colour: bright straw. Nose: fresh, fresh fruit, white flowers, expressive. Palate: flavourful, fruity, good acidity, balanced.

**EQUINOX BATEA BLANC 2008 B**
garnacha blanca 100%

**85** Colour: light mahogany, coppery red. Nose: dried fruit, overripe fruit, honeyed notes. Palate: sweet, fleshy, powerful.

**CASTELL D'ALGARS 2008 B**

**85** Colour: bright straw. Nose: grassy, ripe fruit, fruit expression, citrus fruit. Palate: flavourful, powerful, sweetness.

**VALL MAJOR 2008 B**
garnacha blanca 95%, moscatel 5%

**83**

**PRIMICIA BOTA 2008 BFB**
garnacha blanca 100%

**74**

**LAS COLINAS DEL EBRO 2008 RD**
garnacha 50%, syrah 50%

**84**

**VALL MAJOR 2008 RD**
garnacha, syrah

**81**

**VALL MAJOR NEGRE 2008 T**
garnacha 100%

**89** Colour: cherry, purple rim. Nose: expressive, fresh fruit, red berry notes, floral. Palate: flavourful, fruity, good acidity, round tannins.

**LAS COLINAS DEL EBRO 2008 T**
syrah 50%, garnacha 50%

**89** Colour: cherry, garnet rim. Nose: ripe fruit, red berry notes, spicy, creamy oak. Palate: flavourful, fleshy, fruity, spicy.

**LAS COLINAS DEL EBRO SELECCION 2006 T**

**82**

**L'AUBE SELECCIÓ DE VINYES VELLES 2005 TC**
merlot 50%, garnacha 30%, cabernet sauvignon 20%

**87** Colour: cherry, garnet rim. Nose: powerful, dark chocolate, toasty. Palate: flavourful, powerful, fleshy, spicy.

**VIVERTELL 2005 TC**
garnacha 60%, tempranillo 40%, cabernet sauvignon %, syrah %

**84**

**EQUINOX BATEA NEGRE 2008 VINO DULCE NATURAL**
garnacha 100%

**87** Colour: cherry, garnet rim. Nose: powerful, fruit preserve, fruit liqueur notes, dried fruit. Palate: flavourful, powerful, fleshy, sweet.

## COOPERATIVA AGRÍCOLA DE CORBERA D'EBRE

Ponent, 21
43784 Corbera D'Ebre (Tarragona)
☎: 977 420 432 - Fax: 977 420 432
coop@corbera.tinet.org

**MIRMIL-LÓ 2008 B**
garnacha blanca, macabeo

**87** Colour: bright straw. Nose: ripe fruit, fresh fruit. Palate: flavourful, sweetness, fruity.

**MIRMIL-LÓ BLANC BRISAT 2008 B**
garnacha blanca

**78**

**MIRMIL-LÓ NEGRE 2008 T**
garnacha, cariñena, cabernet sauvignon

**81**

**NAKENS 2007 T**
garnacha, cariñena, syrah

**84**

**POBLE VELL BLANCO VINO DE LICOR BLANCO**
pedro ximénez

**84**

**VALL EXCELS**

## COVILALBA

Cervantes, 1-5
43782 Vilalba dels Arcs (Tarragona)
☎: 977 438 010 - Fax: 977 438 294
covilalba@covilalba.com
www.covilalba.com

**SUPREM 2008 B**
macabeo 50%, garnacha blanca 50%

**70**

**RANEI 1928 B**
garnacha blanca 100%

**92** Colour: iodine, amber rim. Nose: candied fruit, roasted almonds, varnish, caramel. Palate: flavourful, fleshy, complex, spirituous.

**FARISTOL 2007 T**
garnacha 100%

**75**

**2 FINQUES "VI DE GUARDA" 2006 T**
cariñena 100%

**87** Colour: cherry, garnet rim. Nose: powerful, fruit preserve, sweet spices, toasty. Palate: powerful, fleshy, toasty.

**FILL DEL TEMPS 2004 TC**
garnacha 60%, cariñena 40%

**85** Colour: deep cherry. Nose: powerful, tar, varnish, fruit liqueur notes. Palate: spicy, powerful.

**FILL DEL TEMPS SELECCIÓ 2004 T**
garnacha 50%, cariñena 40%, cabernet sauvignon 5%

**84**

**VALL DE BERRVS**

## ECOVITRES

Verge, 6
43782 Vilalba dels Arcs (Tarragona)
☎: 977 438 196
info@ecovitres.com
www.ecovitres.com

**ASPIRALL 2008 T**
garnacha 100%

**87** Colour: cherry, purple rim. Nose: powerful, ripe fruit, raspberry. Palate: fruity, fleshy, sweetness.

**GRAN GOTANYA 2004 T**
garnacha 60%, merlot 30%, morenillo 10%

**87** Colour: deep cherry, garnet rim. Nose: ripe fruit, candied fruit, balsamic herbs, toasty, spicy. Palate: spirituous, spicy, round tannins.

**BLANC DE MESIES**
**CATXAP**

## EDETÀRIA

Ctra. Gandesa - Villalba, s/n
43780 Gandesa (Tarragona)
☎: 977 421 534 - Fax: 977 421 534

celler@edetaria.com
www.edetaria.com

**VIA EDETANA 2008 B**
55% garnacha blanca, 45% viognier

**90** Colour: bright straw. Nose: white flowers, fresh fruit, grassy. Palate: flavourful, fruity, fresh.

**VINYA D'IRTO 2008 B**
50% garnacha, 40% macabeo, 10% moscatel

**86** Colour: bright straw. Nose: powerful, ripe fruit, grassy. Palate: flavourful, fleshy, fruity, fresh.

**EDETÀRIA 2007 B**
garnacha blanca, macabeo

**91** Colour: bright straw. Nose: ripe fruit, citrus fruit, white flowers, cocoa bean, sweet spices. Palate: flavourful, fleshy, spicy, ripe fruit.

**EDETÀRIA 2006 B**
85% garnacha blanca, 15% macabeo

**90** Colour: bright golden. Nose: toasty, fruit liqueur notes, citrus fruit, candied fruit. Palate: powerful, fleshy, ripe fruit, fine bitter notes.

**EDETÀRIA 2005 B**
85% garnacha blanca, 15% macabeo

**94** Colour: bright golden. Nose: powerful, expressive, candied fruit, citrus fruit, toasty, aged wood nuances. Palate: fleshy, powerful, ripe fruit, long.

**EDETÀRIA DOLÇ 2007 T**
70% garnacha, 30% cabernet sauvignon

**90** Colour: cherry, garnet rim. Nose: red berry notes, raspberry, grapey. Palate: powerful, fleshy, fruity, sweet.

**VINYA D'IRTO 2006 T**
60% garnacha, 20% caberner sauvignon, 10% merlot

**85** Colour: cherry, garnet rim. Nose: balsamic herbs, scrubland, toasty, dark chocolate. Palate: spicy, ripe fruit, oaky.

**EDETÀRIA 2005 T**
40% garnacha, 35% syrah, 25% cabernet sauvignon

**92** Colour: cherry, garnet rim. Nose: powerful, sweet spices, toasty, ripe fruit, mineral. Palate: flavourful, powerful, fleshy, round tannins.

**VIA EDETANA 2005 T**
33% garnacha fina, 33% garnacha peluda, 33% cariñena

**88** Colour: bright cherry. Nose: ripe fruit, sweet spices, creamy oak, expressive. Palate: flavourful, fruity, toasty, round tannins.

EDETÀRIA 2004 T
garnacha, syrah, cabernet sauvignon

**90** Colour: cherry, garnet rim. Nose: spicy, creamy oak, toasty, complex, overripe fruit, earthy notes. Palate: powerful, flavourful, toasty, round tannins.

## JOSE SANTIAGO VICENS VALLESPI

Avda. Aragó, 20
43780 Gandesa (Tarragona)
☎: 977 421 080 - Fax: 977 421 080
josepvicensv@wanadoo.es
www.vinsjosepvicens.com

VINYES DEL GRAU 2008 B
macabeo 70%, garnacha 25%, moscatel 5%

**84**

VINYES DEL GRAU SYRAH 2008 T
syrah 100%

**90** Colour: deep cherry. Nose: ripe fruit, red berry notes, raspberry, fruit expression. Palate: flavourful, powerful, fleshy, sweetness.

VINYES DEL GRAU NEGRO 2008 T
garnacha 70%, syrah 30%

**85** Colour: cherry, garnet rim. Nose: warm, scrubland, ripe fruit. Palate: flavourful, fruity, fleshy.

VINYES DEL GRAU SYRAH 2007 T
syrah 100%

**89** Colour: cherry, purple rim. Nose: powerful, red berry notes, raspberry, cocoa bean, creamy oak. Palate: flavourful, fleshy, fruity, spicy.

VINYES DEL GRAU 2006 TC
garnacha 45%, syrah 35%, cabernet sauvignon 20%

**85** Colour: cherry, garnet rim. Nose: powerful, warm, fruit liqueur notes, toasty. Palate: powerful, sweetness, spicy.

## SERRA DE CAVALLS

Bonaire, 1
43594 El Pinell de Brai (Tarragona)
☎: 977 426 049 - Fax: 977 426 049
sat@serradecavalls.com
www.serradecavalls.com

SERRA DE CAVALLS 1938 2006 T FERMENTADO EN BARRICA
merlot, cabernet sauvignon, syrah

**85** Colour: bright cherry. Nose: ripe fruit, sweet spices, creamy oak, toasty. Palate: flavourful, fruity, toasty, round tannins.

## TIERRA ANTIGUA

Urbanización Monje Vigilia, 7
26120 Albelda de Iregua (La Rioja)
☎: 941 444 233 - Fax: 941 444 427
info@tierrantigua.com

ROMASANTA 2007 T
garnacha 100%

**88** Colour: cherry, garnet rim. Nose: powerful, sweet spices, overripe fruit, sun-drenched nuances. Palate: flavourful, fleshy, ripe fruit, spirituous.

## UNIO CORPORACIO ALIMENTARIA - CELLERS UNIÓ

Joan Oliver, 16-24
43206 Reus (Tarragona)
☎: 977 330 055 - Fax: 977 330 070
reus@cellersunio.com
www.cellersunio.com

BLANC COPOS 2008 B
garnacha 90%, macabeo 10%

**86** Colour: bright straw. Nose: varietal, ripe fruit, fruit expression, citrus fruit. Palate: flavourful, fruity, fresh.

CLOS DEL PINELL 2008 B
garnacha 90%, macabeo 10%

**85** Colour: bright straw. Nose: candied fruit, citrus fruit, honeyed notes. Palate: flavourful, sweetness, fleshy.

COPOS NATURE 2008 B
garnacha 70%, macabeo 30%

**85** Colour: bright straw. Nose: candied fruit, citrus fruit, fragrant herbs. Palate: flavourful, fruity, fleshy.

CLOS DEL PINELL 2008 RD
syrah 75%, merlot 25%

**81**

COPOS NATURE 2008 T
cabernet sauvignon 50%, mazuelo 30%, tempranillo 20%

**87** Colour: bright cherry. Nose: ripe fruit, balsamic herbs, scrubland, earthy notes. Palate: flavourful, fleshy, spicy.

CLOS DEL PINELL 2008 T
garnacha 60%, samso 30%, syrah 10%

# DO TERRA ALTA

## 84

GRAN COPOS 2005 TR
garnacha 60%, mazuelo 25%, cabernet sauvignon 15%

**88** Colour: deep cherry. Nose: powerful, earthy notes, toasty, sweet spices. Palate: flavourful, fleshy, spicy, ripe fruit.

REINA ELIONOR 2005 TR
garnacha 60%, ull de llebre 20%, cabernet sauvignon 20%

## 81

CLOS DEL PINELL 2004 TC
garnacha 50%, garnacha peludo 30%, cariñena 20%

**85** Colour: cherry, garnet rim. Nose: powerful, warm, overripe fruit, toasty. Palate: spicy, round tannins.

MIL CEPAS 2003 TGR
garnacha 50%, tempranillo 25%, cabernet sauvignon 25%

## 84

VIÑA AGUSTINA 2002 TGR
garnacha 55%, cariñena 25%, tempranillo 20%

**85** Colour: deep cherry. Nose: powerful, ripe fruit, red berry notes, sweet spices, cocoa bean. Palate: flavourful, fleshy, fruity.

## VINOS LA BOTERA

Sant Roc, 26
43786 Batea (Tarragona)
☎: 977 430 009 - Fax: 977 430 801
labotera@labotera.com
www.labotera.com

VILA-CLOSA CLARDONNAY 2008 B
chardonnay 100%

**88** Colour: bright yellow. Nose: ripe fruit, sweet spices, creamy oak, fragrant herbs. Palate: rich, smoky aftertaste, flavourful, fresh, good acidity.

VILA-CLOSA 2008 B
garnacha 100%

## 84

L'ARNOT 2008 RD
garnacha 50%, syrah 50%

## 75

LA BOTERA 2008 T
cariñena, merlot

**88** Colour: deep cherry. Nose: fruit expression, macerated fruit, cocoa bean, creamy oak. Palate: fruity, fresh, powerful, flavourful.

VILA-CLOSA 2008 T
garnacha 50%, syrah 50%

## 84

MUDÈFER 2006 T
garnacha 40%, syrah 40%, cariñena 20%

## 79

SOME OTHER WINERIES WITHIN THE DO:

**AGRARIA SANT SALVADOR D'HORTA
ANDREU ROCA VAQUE
BODEGAS CORTIELLA
CELLER MASBLANCH
CELLER VINS FRISACH
COOPERATIVA AGRARIA DE EL
PINELL DE BRAI**

# DO TIERRA DE LEÓN

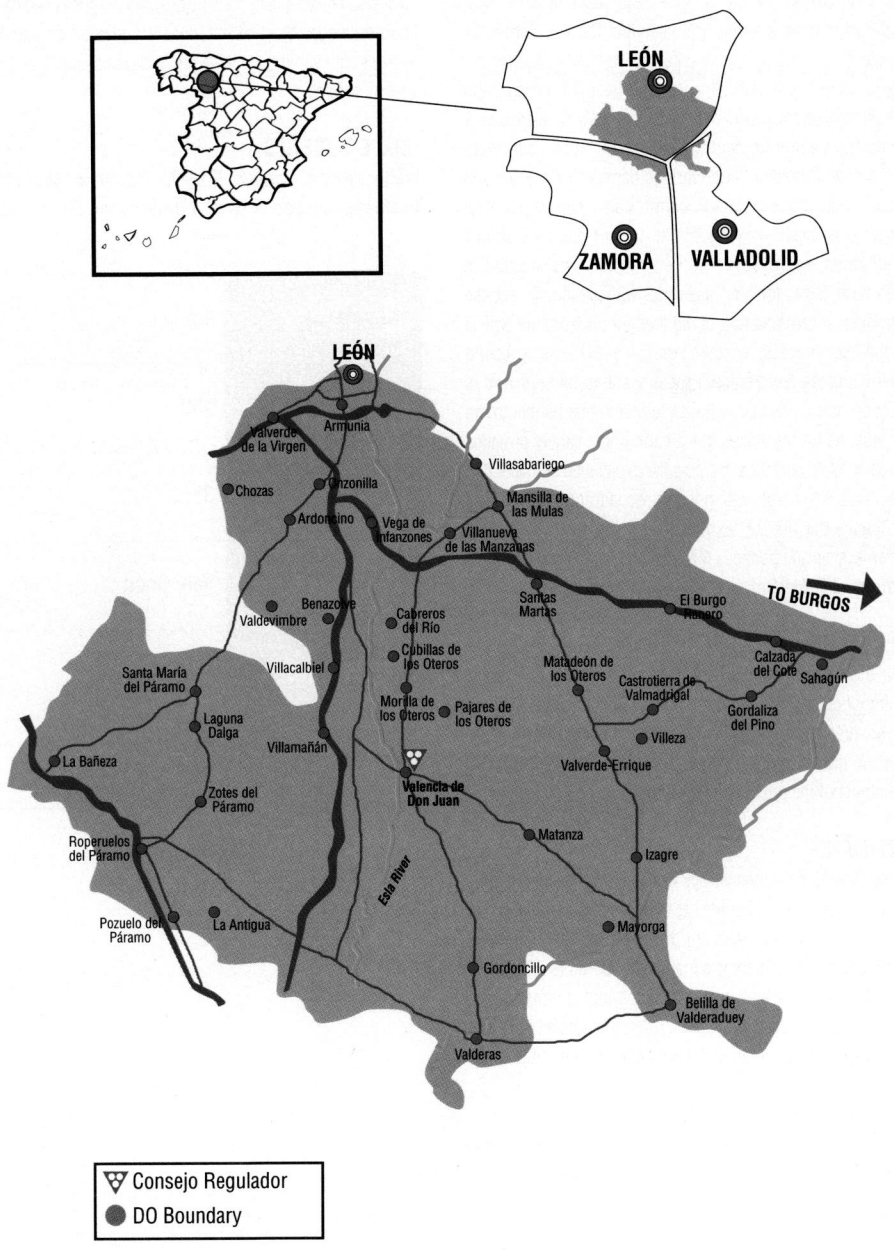

- ▽ Consejo Regulador
- ● DO Boundary

## NEWS

A new DO where cooperatives still have it their way, although some wineries are defending the singularity and potential of local grape varieties like the red prieto picudo and the white albarín. In just one year the wines from Valdevimbre and Ribera del Cea have greatly developed their character and fruit identity. Red wines made from prieto picudo and bottled under various names that reel around that of the grape (Preto, Pricum…) have shown powerful fruit expression as long as the use of oak was simply 'judicious'. For rosé drinkers Tierra de León is also paradise on earth, if they look for rosé wines with personality and the traditional carbonic trait of old that comes from the typical "madreo" process: by adding grapes to the wine, a second fermentation takes place. Probably still to be improved is the technical practice to translate that subtle bubble to the bottle. As for the whites, the albarín grape variety provides wines with character and a singular expression of macerated fruit and fine herbs, with good prices starting at 3€. Those fringing the title of 'extraordinary' are the wines from Pardevalles and Bodegas Margón, under the consultancy of the great Raúl Pérez.

## LOCATION

In the south of the province of León with the vineyard almost exclusively around the municipality of Valencia de Don Juan in a sort of triangle with the rivers Cea and Esla taking the other two corners. It includes also 19 municipal districts of the province of Valladolid.

## CLIMATE

The climate of the river valleys would follow a milder Atlantic continental pattern, but the high plateau of that part of León where most of the vines are planted turns the conditions into cooler ones. There is a marked temperature differential all through the year, winters are harsh and summers mild, there is always the risk of spring frosts and rainfall (500 mm average) happens mainly during the autumn months.

## SOIL

They are of great quality for vine growing purposes and have good drainage. Most of the vines are planted on alluvial terraces with varying percentages of clay and limestone and a rocky subsoil.

## GRAPE VARIETIES:

**White:** *Albarín, Verdejo, Godello, Palomino, Malvasía.*
**Red:** *Prieto picudo, Mencía, Garnacha* and *Tempranillo.*

| | |
|---|---|
| Hectares of Vineyard | 1,500 |
| Nº Viticulturists | 450 |
| Nº of Bodegas | 35 |
| 2008 Harvest | Very Good |
| 2007 Production | 1,200,000 l. |
| Marketing | 87% domestic 13% export |

**CONSEJO REGULADOR**
Alonso Castrillo, 29
24200 Valencia de Don Juan (León)
☎: 987 751 089 - Fax: 987 751 089
www.dotierradeleon.es

## GENERAL CHARACTERISTICS OF THE WINES:

| | |
|---|---|
| **WHITES** | Fully ripe local Albarín is the grape used to make some fine toasty wines which feature white fruit notes, roasted herbs and a fairly high alcohol content. |
| **ROSÉS** | The traditional and slightly carbonic –de aguja– rosé wines from the region are still made, although they have improved their quality with the best varietal values of the *Prieto Picudo* grape. |
| **REDS** | The majority are made from *Prieto Picudo* and are similar to those made from Mencía but an altogether fuller body and marked tannins. They are also very intense in colour, with a nose of fresh fruit and herbal nuances. |

## 2008 VINTAGE RATING:

# GOOD

## BARCILLO

Manuel Cadenas
24230 Valdevimbre (León)
☎: 680 214 589
administracion@barcillo.es
www.barcillo.es

BARCILLO 2008 B
verdejo 85%, albarin 15%

**88** Colour: bright yellow. Nose: varietal, powerfull, fresh, expressive, characterful. Palate: powerful, flavourful, sweetness, complex.

BARCILLO 2008 RD
prieto picudo 100%

**74**

BARCILLO B3 2007 T
prieto picudo 100%

**79**

BARCILLO 6 2007 T ROBLE
prieto picudo 100%

**78**

BARCILLO LAS MORANAS 2005 TC
prieto picudo 100%

**83**

## BODEGAS MARCOS MIÑAMBRES

Camino de Pobladura, s/n
24234 Villamañan (León)
☎: 987 767 038 - Fax: 987 767 371
satvined@picos.com

LOS SILVARES 2004 T ROBLE
prieto picudo 100%

**87** Colour: deep cherry. Nose: medium intensity, dry stone, wild herbs, red berry notes, spicy, toasty. Palate: good acidity, slightly dry, soft tannins, fruity, toasty.

## BODEGAS MARGÓN

Isaac García de Quirós, 6 - 1
24200 Valencia de Don Juan (León)
☎: 609 374 611 - Fax: 987 750 481
margon@gruporesnova.com
www.bodegasmargon.com

PRICUM ALBARÍN VALDEMUZ 2007 B
albarín 80%

**87** Colour: golden. Nose: complex, slightly evolved, new oak, damp earth, scrubland. Palate: flavourful, powerful, sweetness.

PRICUM 2008 RD
prieto picudo 100%

**89** Colour: rose, purple rim, bright. Nose: red berry notes, powerfull, violet drops, lactic notes. Palate: fleshy, fruity, good structure, fruity aftestaste.

RARA AVIS 2007 T BARRICA
prieto picudo 100%

**93** Colour: dark-red cherry. Nose: fruit expression, varietal, complex, mineral. Palate: fruity, powerful, flavourful, mineral, fruity aftestaste, toasty.

PRICUM PRIETO PICUDO 2007 T

**92** Colour: bright cherry. Nose: expressive, creamy oak, spicy, undergrowth, red clay notes, wild herbs. Palate: flavourful, fruity, fresh, mineral, good acidity, grainy tannins.

PRICUM PARAJE DE EL SANTO 2007 T
prieto picudo 100%

**90** Colour: deep cherry. Nose: ripe fruit, sweet spices, creamy oak, expressive. Palate: flavourful, fruity, toasty, round tannins.

PRICUM VALDEMUZ 2007
prieto picudo 100%

**91** Colour: dark-red cherry. Nose: complex, fresh fruit, fruit expression, cedar wood, creamy oak. Palate: good acidity, fresh, fruity, flavourful, toasty, smoky aftertaste.

## BODEGAS MELWA

Calvo Sotelo 4
24230 Valdevimbre (León)
☎: 987 304 149 - Fax: 987 304 149

VALLE GUDIN 2008 RD
prieto picudo 100%

**87** Colour: salmon. Nose: raspberry, fruit expression, red berry notes. Palate: fruity, full, powerful, flavourful.

VALLE GUDIN 2008 T
prieto picudo 100%

**87** Colour: dark-red cherry. Nose: varietal, powerfull, fresh, fresh fruit. Palate: powerful, flavourful, varietal, good acidity.

VALLE GUDIN 2005 TC
prieto picudo 100%

**85** Colour: dark-red cherry. Nose: spicy, toasty, wild herbs. Palate: flavourful, powerful, fruity, toasty.

## BODEGAS PELÁEZ

Calabozo, 12 Grajal de la Ribera
24796 La Antigua (León)
☎: 987 202 350 - Fax: 987 202 350
bodegaspelaez@ono.com

AIRAD 2008 B
verdejo 100%

**86** Colour: straw. Nose: characterful, neat, fresh, powerfull, white flowers. Palate: fresh, fruity, powerful, flavourful.

SENOEL 2008 RD
prieto picudo

**86** Colour: rose. Nose: fruit expression, fresh fruit, powerfull, expressive. Palate: powerful, flavourful, sweetness, fresh, fruity.

SENOEL 2008 T JOVEN
prieto picudo

**87** Colour: deep cherry. Nose: powerful, varietal, fresh, mineral, undergrowth. Palate: flavourful, powerful, varietal, fruity, fresh.

TRES ALMAS 2005 TC
prieto picudo

**88** Colour: deep cherry. Nose: spicy, creamy oak, macerated fruit, maceration notes. Palate: powerful, flavourful, fruity, toasty, mineral, grainy tannins.

## BODEGAS RIBERA DEL ORNIA

Madrid, 11
24765 Castrotierra de la Valduerna (León)
☎: 692 385 980 - Fax: 983 247 472
comercial@riberadelornia.es
www.riberadelornia.es

BAÑEIZA 2008 RD

**86** Colour: light cherry. Nose: fresh fruit, characterful, lactic notes. Palate: rich, good acidity, fruity, fine bitter notes.

VAL D'ORNIA 2006 TC
prieto picudo 100%

**87** Colour: cherry, garnet rim. Nose: ripe fruit, balanced, varietal, mineral. Palate: flavourful, balanced, round tannins.

VAL D'ORNIA 2005 T
prieto picudo 100%

**87** Colour: deep cherry. Nose: fresh, neat, expressive, fresh fruit, mineral, earthy notes. Palate: powerful, flavourful, fruity, spicy, great length.

VENDIMIARIO

## BODEGAS VINOS DE LEÓN

La Vega, s/n
24190 Armunia (León)
☎: 987 209 712 - Fax: 987 209 800
info@bodegasvinosdeleon.es
www.bodegasvinosdeleon.es

VALJUNCO 2008 B
verdejo 100%

**77**

VALJUNCO 2008 RD
prieto picudo 100%

**85** Colour: rose. Nose: red berry notes, fresh fruit, medium intensity, expressive, varietal. Palate: fresh, fruity, powerful, flavourful, sweetness.

VALJUNCO 2004 TC
prieto picudo 100%

**87** Colour: dark-red cherry. Nose: fresh fruit, creamy oak, spicy. Palate: flavourful, fruity, toasty, fruity aftestaste.

DON SUERO 2004 TR
prieto picudo 100%

**84**

DON SUERO 2000 TR

**83**

## BODEGAS Y VIÑEDOS LA SILVERA

Ctra. de Pajares de los Oteros, s/n
24209 Pajares de los Oteros (León )
☎: 987 753 018 - Fax: 987 429 790
gregory@estadopuro.es

PRETO 2008 RD

**87** Colour: onion pink. Nose: rose petals, fresh fruit, red berry notes. Palate: sweetness, powerful, fruity, fresh.

PRETO 12 MESES 2007 T
prieto picudo 100%

**88** Colour: deep cherry. Nose: fresh fruit, smoky, aromatic coffee. Palate: good acidity, fruity, flavourful, varietal, toasty.

PRETO 2007 T JOVEN

**85** Colour: dark-red cherry. Nose: varietal, fresh, fresh fruit. Palate: fruity, fresh, good acidity.

VEGA SILVERA

# DO TIERRA DE LEÓN

## BODEGAS Y VIÑEDOS PEDRO CASIS

Las Bodegas, s/n
24325 Gordaliza del Pino (León)
☎: 987 699 618 - Fax: 987 699 618
correo@bodegascasis.com
www.bodegascasis.com

CASIS 2006 TC

**87** Colour: dark-red cherry. Nose: ripe fruit, cedar wood, spicy, creamy oak. Palate: fresh, fruity, flavourful, smoky aftertaste, toasty.

## COOP. VINÍCOLA DE VALDEVIMBRE

Ctra. de León, s/n
24230 Valdevimbre (León)
☎: 987 304 195 - Fax: 987 304 195
valdevim@urcacyl.es

ABADÍA DE BALDEREDO 2008 RD
prieto picudo 100%

**72**

ABADÍA DE BALDEREDO 2005 TC
prieto picudo 100%

**79**

SEÑORÍO DE VALDÉS

## COOP. VINÍCOLA UNIÓN DEL PÁRAMO

Ctra. Sahagún, s/n
24325 Gordaliza del Pino (León)
☎: 987 784 057 - Fax: 987 784 057
cooperativa_launion@wanadoo.es

EL TESORO DEL PÁRAMO 2005 TC

**81**

## FRANCISCO GONZÁLEZ

La Fragua, s/n
24324 Villeza (León)
☎: 987 263 710 - Fax: 987 263 710
info@villeza.com
www.villeza.com

LAGRIMA DE VILLEZA 2008 B
albarín 100%

**83**

LAGRIMA DE VILLEZA 2008 RD
prieto picudo 80%, mencía 20%

**80**

TINTO VILLEZA 12 MESES 2006 TC
prieto picudo 100%

**88** Colour: deep cherry. Nose: powerful, varietal, fresh, red berry notes, dry stone, creamy oak, cocoa bean. Palate: fresh, fruity, powerful, flavourful, fleshy, smoky aftertaste, varietal.

TINTO VILLEZA 6 MESES 2006 T
prieto picudo 50%, mencía 50%

**88** Colour: dark-red cherry. Nose: fresh fruit, red berry notes, wild herbs, varietal. Palate: complex, fresh, fruity, flavourful, powerful, great length, fruity aftestaste, toasty.

TINTO VILLEZA 6 MESES 2006 T
prieto picudo 50%, mencía 50%

**87** Colour: dark-red cherry. Nose: varietal, fresh fruit, red clay notes, undergrowth, smoky. Palate: powerful, flavourful, fruity, balsamic, toasty.

## GORDONZELLO

Alto de Santa Marina, s/n
24294 Gordoncillo (León)
☎: 987 758 030 - Fax: 987 757 201
comercial@gordonzello.com
www.gordonzello.com

PEREGRINO 2008 B
verdejo 100%

**87** Colour: straw. Nose: fresh fruit, fragrant herbs. Palate: fruity, powerful, flavourful, full.

PEREGRINO 2008 RD
prieto picudo 100%

**86** Colour: rose. Nose: dry stone, fruit expression, fresh fruit, red berry notes. Palate: fruity, powerful, flavourful, sweetness.

GURDOS 2008 RD

**76**

PEREGRINO 2007 T
prieto picudo 100%

**85** Colour: deep cherry. Nose: unripe grapeskin notes, new oak, toasty, macerated fruit. Palate: creamy, balsamic, fruity aftestaste, toasty.

PEREGRINO TINTO 14 2006 TC
prieto picudo 100%

**88** Colour: deep cherry. Nose: ripe fruit, expressive, varietal, creamy oak, spicy. Palate: powerful, flavourful, fruity, creamy, toasty, mineral.

PEREGRINO 2006 T ROBLE
prieto picudo 100%

**86** Colour: dark-red cherry. Nose: expressive, varietal, red berry notes, red clay notes, smoky, creamy oak. Palate: fruity, powerful, flavourful, toasty.

PEREGRINO 2005 TC
prieto picudo 100%

**85** Colour: deep cherry. Nose: ripe fruit, wild herbs, reduction notes, varietal. Palate: powerful, flavourful, fruity, spicy, roasted-coffee aftertaste.

PEREGRINO 2004 TR
prieto picudo 100%

**80**

## SOCIEDAD COOPERATIVA VINOS DE LA RIBERA DEL CEA

Avda. Panduro y Villafañe, s/n
24220 Valderas (León)
☎: 987 762 191 - Fax: 987 762 191
info@riberacea.e.telefonica.net

VIÑA TRASDERREY 2007 T
prieto picudo 100%

**82**

VIÑA TRASDERREY 2005 TC
prieto picudo 100%

**83**

VIÑA CUESTASBUENAS

## TAMPESTA

La Socollada, s/n
24230 Valdevimbre (León)
☎: 987 351 025 - Fax: 987 351 025
bodegastampesta@terra.com

TAMPESTA 2008 RD
prieto picudo 100%

**85** Colour: rose. Nose: complex, varietal, red clay notes, raspberry. Palate: powerful, flavourful, fruity.

TAMPESTA 2007 T ROBLE
prieto picudo 60%, tempranillo 40%

**82**

TAMPESTA GOLÁN 2007 T ROBLE
prieto picudo 100%

**75**

## VILLACEZÁN

San Juan, 10
24294 Gordoncillo (León)
☎: 987 758 031 - Fax: 987 758 031
villacezan@villacezan.com
www.villacezan.com

ELVERITE 2008 B
verdejo 100%

**85** Colour: straw. Nose: fragrant herbs, ripe fruit, fresh fruit. Palate: fresh, fruity, full, flavourful, sweetness.

MOLENDORES 2008 RD
prieto picudo 86%, tempranillo 9%, mencía 5%

**85** Colour: onion pink. Nose: powerful, varietal, expressive, fresh, fresh fruit. Palate: powerful, flavourful, sweetness, fruity aftestaste.

DEHESA DE VILLACEZÁN 2008 T
prieto picudo 93%, tempranillo 7%

**84**

VILLACEZÁN SEIS MESES 2007 T
prieto picudo 40%, mencía 30%, tempranillo 30%

**88** Colour: cherry, garnet rim. Nose: undergrowth, red clay notes, fresh fruit, aromatic coffee, spicy. Palate: powerful, flavourful, fruity, varietal.

GALIO 2006 T
prieto picudo

**88** Colour: deep cherry. Nose: woody, creamy oak, fresh fruit. Palate: flavourful, fresh, correct, fruity.

VILLACEZÁN DOCE MESES 2006 T
prieto picudo 100%

**87** Colour: deep cherry. Nose: smoky, spicy, creamy oak, varietal, expressive. Palate: powerful, flavourful, varietal, toasty, mineral.

## VINÍCOLA VALMADRIGAL S.L.

Constitución, 16
24323 Castrotierra de Valmadrigal (León)
☎: 987 784 249 - Fax: 987 784 249
vinicolavalmadrigal@correoleon.com

# DO TIERRA DE LEÓN

CASTRO IUVARA 2008 B
verdejo 100%

**84**

CASTILLO DE VALMADRIGAL 2008 RD
prieto picudo 100%

**85** Colour: onion pink, rose. Nose: fruit liqueur notes, red berry notes, expressive, varietal, fresh. Palate: powerful, flavourful, fruity.

CASTRO IUVARA 2005 TR
prieto picudo 100%

**86** Colour: dark-red cherry. Nose: fruit preserve, sweet spices, creamy oak. Palate: toasty, flavourful, powerful, fruity.

## VIÑEDOS DE MEORIGA

Ctra. de Alberite s/n
47680 Mayorga (Valladolid)
☎: 983 751 182 - Fax: 983 751 182
bodegas@meoriga.com

SEÑORÍO DE MOGROVEJO 2008 B
verdejo 100%

**88** Colour: straw. Nose: fresh fruit, citrus fruit, fruit expression. Palate: powerful, flavourful, rich, fresh, sweetness.

SEÑORÍO DE MOGROVEJO 2008 RD
prieto picudo 100%

**84**

SEÑORÍO DE MOGROVEJO 2008 T
prieto picudo 100%

**80**

SEÑORÍO DE MOGROVEJO 2006 TC
prieto picudo 100%

**80**

SEÑORÍO DE MOGROVEJO 2005 T ROBLE
prieto picudo 100%

**87** Colour: dark-red cherry. Nose: medium intensity, ripe fruit, cocoa bean, aromatic coffee, sweet spices, toasty. Palate: flavourful, powerful, fleshy, round tannins.

## VIÑEDOS Y BODEGA PARDEVALLES

Ctra. de León, s/n
24230 Valdevimbre (León)
☎: 987 304 222 - Fax: 987 304 222

info@pardevalles.es
www.pardevalles.com

PARDEVALLES ALBARIN 2008 B
albarín 100%

**90** Colour: bright yellow. Nose: fresh fruit, fruit expression, macerated fruit, fragrant herbs, scrubland. Palate: good acidity, unctuous, fine bitter notes, balsamic.

PARDEVALLES 2008 RD
prieto picudo 100%

**87** Colour: rose, purple rim. Nose: red berry notes, raspberry, varietal, powerfull. Palate: powerful, flavourful, fruity, fresh, sweetness.

PARDEVALLES 2007 T
prieto picudo 100%

**87** Colour: dark-red cherry. Nose: fresh fruit, varietal, damp earth, spicy. Palate: fleshy, good structure, fruity.

PARDEVALLES GAMONAL 2006 T
prieto picudo 100%

**89** Colour: deep cherry. Nose: fresh fruit, red berry notes, fruit expression, aromatic coffee, smoky, caramel. Palate: powerful, flavourful, varietal, fruity.

PARDEVALLES CARROLEÓN 2005 T
prieto picudo 100%

**87** Colour: deep cherry. Nose: spicy, smoky, slightly evolved, undergrowth, fresh fruit. Palate: powerful, flavourful, fruity, balsamic, mineral, toasty.

SOME OTHER WINERIES WITHIN THE DO:

**BODEGA ARTURO ALVAREZ**
**BODEGA COOPERATIVA LOS OTEROS**
**BODEGA JORGE ROBLES**
**COOPERATIVA VINÍCOLA UNIÓN DEL VALLE**
**FERNÁNDEZ LLAMAZARES S.L.**
**NICOLÁS REY E HIJOS S.L.**
**SEÑORÍO DE CHOZAS**
**SEÑORÍO DE LOS ARCOS**

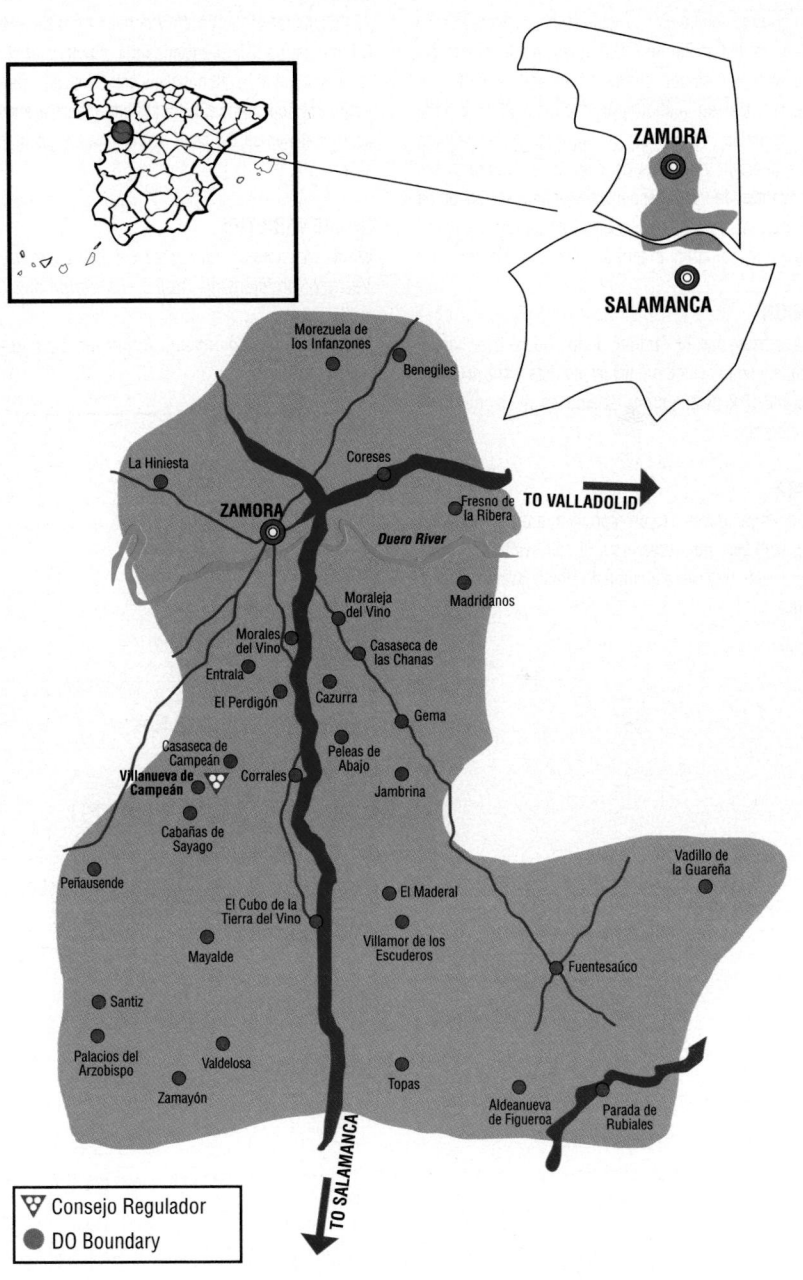

## NEWS

It is not crazy to point out once again at the excellence of the local tempranillo of Zamora. Old vines, poor soils and a climate with a dramatic contrast and very suitable for altitude wine making. A shorter production in 2008, but the quality remains very high in almost every winery. Improvements in vine growing have been started in the region by Viñas del Cénit, responsible for almost 40% of the export figures of the DO. Their conceptual approach is based on single-plots, different in terms of soil and vine age.

## LOCATION

In the southeast part of Zamora, on the Duero river banks. This region comprises 46 municipal districts in the province Zamora and 10 in neighbouring Salamanca. Average altitude is 750 meters.

## CLIMATE

Extreme temperatures as correspond to a dry continental pattern, with very hot summers and cold winters. It does not rain much and average annual rainfall hardly reaches 400 mm.

## SOIL

The character of the territory derives from the river Duero tributaries, so it is predominantly alluvial and clay in the lower strata that might not allow great drainage, though they vary a lot depending on the altitude. There are also some sandy patches on the plain land and stony ones on the hill side.

## GRAPE VARIETIES:

**White:** *Malvasía, Moscatel de grano menudo* and *Verdejo* (preferential); *Albillo, Palomino* and *Godello* (authorized).

**Red:** *Tempranillo* (main), *Cabernet Sauvignon* and *Garnacha*.

| | |
|---|---|
| Hectares of Vineyard | 760 |
| Nº Viticulturists | 234 |
| Nº of Bodegas | 8 |
| 2008 Harvest | N/A |
| 2007 Production | 4,534,770 l. |
| Marketing | 60.5% domestic 39.5% export |

**CONSEJO REGULADOR**
Plaza Mayor, 1
49708 Villanueva de Campeán (Zamora)
☎: 980 560 055 - Fax: 980 560 055
@ info@tierradelvino.net
www.tierradelvino.net

## GENERAL CHARACTERISTICS OF THE WINES:

| WHITES | They are fresh wines wines a slight herbal *Malvasía* character, full, flavoursome, with good alcohol content and a refreshing acidity. |
|---|---|
| REDS | They are very intense in colour, with a powerful nose and some complexity given by the great percentage of old vines found in the region. They also have higher acidity levels compared to Toro, thanks to the likewise higher altitude and the retention properties of the soil. |

## 2008 VINTAGE RATING:

## VERY GOOD

## ALTER EGO BODEGA DE CRIANZA

Larga, 4
49709 Cabañas de Sayago (Zamora)
☎: 670 095 149

ALTER ENOS 2006 B
verdejo

**86** Colour: bright yellow. Nose: toasty, woody, fruit liqueur notes. Palate: rich, fruity, warm, spicy, smoky aftertaste.

DOMINIO DE SEXMIL

## BODEGAS VIÑAS ZAMORANAS

Ctra. La Estación, s/n
49530 Coreses (Zamora)
☎: 980 500 995 - Fax: 980 500 611
bvz@bodegaszamoranas.es
www.bodegaszamoranas.es

NOVO 2005 T ROBLE
tempranillo 100%

**87** Colour: cherry, garnet rim. Nose: medium intensity, ripe fruit, sweet spices, creamy oak, toasty. Palate: flavourful, fruity, fresh.

VÍA AUGUSTA

## VIÑAS DEL CÉNIT

Ctra. de Circunvalación, s/n
49708 Villanueva de Campeán (Zamora)
☎: 609 11 9 2 - Fax: 976 852 764
vinasdelcenit@hotmail.com

CENIT 2007 T
tempranillo

**93** Colour: bright cherry. Nose: ripe fruit, expressive, creamy oak, fruit liqueur notes, earthy notes. Palate: flavourful, fruity, toasty, round tannins.

VENTA MAZARRÓN 2007 T

**91** Colour: bright cherry. Nose: ripe fruit, sweet spices, creamy oak, expressive, balsamic herbs, dark chocolate. Palate: flavourful, fruity, toasty, round tannins, powerful.

DEMORA 2007 T

**91** Colour: bright cherry. Nose: ripe fruit, sweet spices, creamy oak, expressive. Palate: flavourful, fruity, toasty, round tannins.

CENIT 2006 T

**93** Colour: cherry, garnet rim. Nose: ripe fruit, spicy, creamy oak, toasty, complex. Palate: powerful, flavourful, toasty, fine tannins.

DEMORA 2006 T
tempranillo

**91** Colour: cherry, garnet rim. Nose: powerful, ripe fruit, earthy notes, mineral, toasty, sweet spices. Palate: flavourful, fleshy, spicy, ripe fruit, round tannins.

SOME OTHER WINERIES WITHIN THE DO:

**ALIZÁN BODEGAS Y VIÑEDOS
BODEGAS EL SOTO
BODEGAS SELECCIONADAS ARMANDO S.L.
JUAN MIGUEL FUENTES SARDÓN
VIÑA ESCUDEROS S. COOP.**

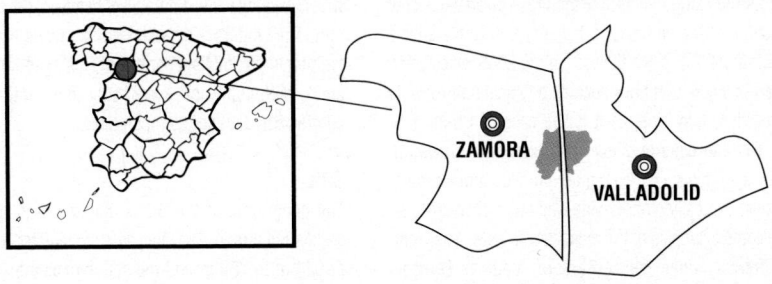

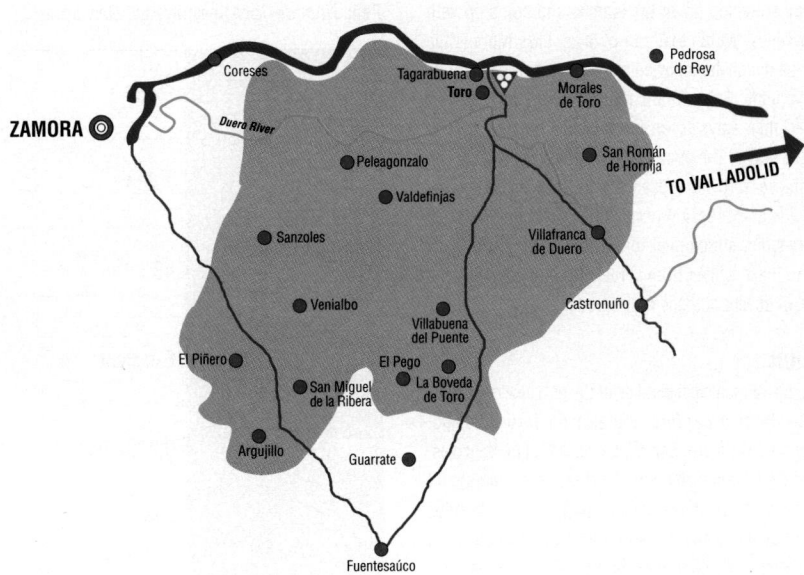

- ▽ Consejo Regulador
- ⬤ DO Boundary

# DO TORO

## NEWS

This year, Toro has become a safe bet for aged reds –both in the roble and longer crianza renderings– given the overall high quality of the vintage, particularly noticeable after a disappointing 2007. Nevertheless, young 2008 wines show the overripe notes that have become a typical trait for tinta de Toro when fully ripe, as it is the case of Primero de Fariña. Reds in general show pretty deep and powerful, features again typical of the region, but also more mineral as a proper expression of old-vine viticulture; there are also some elegant examples of the most classic style, when long aged. French winemakers (Bernard Magrez, François Lurton, Dominio Bendito and Quinta de la Quietud) have got the hang of the variety and understood the real essence of Toro, so there is no wonder they get the best ratings. As in the case of Priorat, they have managed to 'conquer' the region by softening down the tannins and come up with rounder wines. Within that sort of style, Elías Mora is the best of the nationals, followed closely by some old brands like Peñamonte, Sobreño and Muruve, which have greatly improved their ways to an international sort of style at affordable prices. The attempts to blend garnacha or syrah with tinta de Toro have been abandoned, favouring the single varietal expression of the latter. To counterbalance the heavy tannic structure of Toro reds, some wineries have started to make whites from verdejo that do not reach yet the level of quality of those from Rueda.

## LOCATION

Comprising 12 municipal districts of the province of Zamora (Argujillo, Boveda de Toro, Morales de Toro, El Pego, Peleagonzalo, El Piñero, San Miguel de la Ribera, Sanzoles, Toro, Valdefinjas, Venialbo and Villanueva del Puente) and three in the province of Valladolid (San Román de la Hornija, Villafranca de Duero and the vineyards of Villaester de Arriba and Villaester de Abajo in the municipal district of Pedrosa del Rey), which practically corresponds to the agricultural region of Bajo Duero. The production area is to the south of the course of the Duero, which crosses the region from east to west.

## CLIMATE

Extreme continental, with Atlantic influences and quite arid, with an average annual rainfall of between 350 mm and 400 mm. The winters are harsh (which means extremely low temperatures and long periods of frosts) and the summers short, although not excessively hot, with significant contrasts in day-night temperatures.

## SOIL

The geography of the DO is characterised by a gently-undulating terrain. The vineyards are situated at an altitude of 620 m to 750 m and the soil is mainly brownish-grey limestone. However, the stony alluvial soil is better.

## GRAPE VARIETIES:

**White:** *Malvasía* and *Verdejo*.
**Red:** *Tinta de Toro* (majority) and *Garnacha*.

| Hectares of Vineyard | 5,869 |
|---|---|
| Nº Viticulturists | 1,284 |
| Nº of Bodegas | 48 |
| 2008 Harvest | Excellent |
| 2007 Production | 9,900,000 l. |
| Marketing | 60% domestic 40% export |

**CONSEJO REGULADOR**
De la Concepción, 3
Palacio de los Condes de Requena
49800 Toro (Zamora).
☎: 980 690 335 - Fax: 980 693 201
@ consejo@dotoro.es
www.dotoro.es

## GENERAL CHARACTERISTICS OF THE WINES:

| | |
|---|---|
| **WHITES** | Produced mainly from the *Malvasía* variety, they have a colour ranging from pale yellow to greenish yellow; on the nose, rustic notes may appear, and on the palate, they have a slightly bitter aftertaste. |
| **ROSÉS** | The *Tinta de Toro* and *Garnacha* varieties are used, and are blended or used alone to produce single variety wines. Rosy coloured, they have notes of ripe red berries; they are meaty and fruity on the palate. |
| **REDS** | These are the most characteristic of the region. They have an astringency typical of the *Tinta de Toro* variety, and a high alcohol content (13° or more) and good acidity levels. When the wines are young, they have a dark cherry colour with violet nuances; on the nose they have good intensity with notes reminiscent of blackberries and black berry fruit in general; on the palate, they are powerful, flavourful, meaty, slightly overripe and have a good persistency.<br>Those aged in wood maintain the notes of ripe fruit together with the contribution of the oak and the meatiness on the palate. |

## <u>2008 VINTAGE RATING:</u>

# EXCELLENT

## ÁLVAREZ Y DÍEZ S.A.

Juan Antonio Carmona, 12
47500 Nava del Rey (Valladolid)
☎: 983 850 136 - Fax: 983 850 761
bodegas@alvarezydiez.com
www.alvarezydiez.com

MONTE ALINA 2008 T
tinta de toro

**88** Colour: bright cherry. Nose: ripe fruit, sweet spices, creamy oak, dark chocolate. Palate: flavourful, fruity, toasty, round tannins.

VALMORO 2006 T

**91** Colour: cherry, garnet rim. Nose: ripe fruit, spicy, creamy oak, complex. Palate: flavourful, good structure, fine tannins.

## ANGEL LÓPEZ MEDINA

Avda. de los Comuneros, 92
49810 Morales de Toro (Zamora)
☎: 980 698 082

LAGUNAMATA 2007 T

**87** Colour: cherry, purple rim. Nose: expressive, red berry notes, floral, candied fruit. Palate: flavourful, fruity, good acidity, round tannins.

## BODEGA CYAN

Ctra. Valdefinjas - Venialbo, km. 9,2 Finca La Calera
49800 Toro (Zamora)
☎: 902 430 170 - Fax: 902 430 189
cyan@matarromera.es
www.bodegacyan.es

CYAN PRESTIGIO 2003 T ROBLE
tinta de toro 100%

**90** Colour: cherry, garnet rim. Nose: ripe fruit, spicy, creamy oak, toasty, complex, damp earth. Palate: powerful, flavourful, toasty, round tannins.

CYAN PAGO DE LA CALERA 2001 TR
tinta de toro 100%

**93** Colour: cherry, garnet rim. Nose: ripe fruit, spicy, creamy oak, toasty, complex, mineral, tobacco, warm. Palate: powerful, flavourful, toasty, round tannins.

## BODEGA DEL PALACIO DE LOS FRONTAURA Y VICTORIA

Santiago, 17 - 4º

47001 Valladolid
☎: 983 360 284 - Fax: 983 345 546
cpardo@bodegasfrontaura.es
www.bodegasfrontaura.es

### DOMINIO DE VALDELACASA 2006 T
tinta de toro 100%

**92** Colour: bright cherry. Nose: ripe fruit, sweet spices, creamy oak, expressive, dark chocolate. Palate: flavourful, fruity, toasty, round tannins.

### FRONTAURA 2005 TR
tinta de toro 100%

**90** Colour: very deep cherry, purple rim. Nose: macerated fruit, cocoa bean, toasty. Palate: concentrated, fleshy, harsh oak tannins.

### FRONTAURA 2005 TC
tinta de toro 100%

**89** Colour: cherry, garnet rim. Nose: fruit preserve, wild herbs. Palate: fruity, flavourful, correct.

## BODEGA ELIAS MORA

Juan Mora, s/n
47530 San Román de Hornija (Valladolid)
☎: 983 784 029 - Fax: 983 784 029
comercial@victoriabenavides.com
www.bodegaseliasmora.com

### ELÍAS MORA 2006 TC

**93** Colour: cherry, garnet rim. Nose: fruit preserve, cocoa bean, toasty. Palate: flavourful, long, full, mineral.

### GRAN ELÍAS MORA 2005 T

**94** Colour: bright cherry. Nose: ripe fruit, creamy oak, expressive, complex, powerfull, mineral. Palate: flavourful,

fruity, toasty, round tannins.

### VIÑAS ELÍAS MORA 2007 T

**88** Colour: deep cherry. Nose: spicy, toasty, wild herbs. Palate: powerful, flavourful, slightly dry, soft tannins.

### ELÍAS MORA 2004 TR

**94** Colour: dark-red cherry. Nose: ripe fruit, spicy, creamy oak, toasty, complex, mineral. Palate: powerful, flavourful, toasty, round tannins.

### 2V PREMIUM

## BODEGA FRANÇOIS LURTON

Camino Magarin s/n
47529 Villafranca del Duero (Valladolid)
☎: 983 034 030 - Fax: 983 034 040
bodega@jflurton.es
www.jflurton.es

### EL ALBAR EXCELENCIA 2006 T
tinta de toro 100%

**93** Colour: bright cherry. Nose: ripe fruit, sweet spices, creamy oak, expressive, mineral. Palate: flavourful, fruity, toasty, round tannins.

### EL ALBAR BARRICAS 2006 T

**93** Colour: cherry, garnet rim. Nose: spicy, creamy oak, toasty, complex, mineral, fruit expression. Palate: powerful, flavourful, toasty, fruity aftestaste, fine tannins.

### CAMPO ELISEO 2004 T
tinta de toro 100%

**91** Colour: cherry, garnet rim. Nose: ripe fruit, spicy, creamy oak, toasty, powerfull, earthy notes. Palate: powerful, flavourful, toasty, round tannins.

## BODEGA MARXUACH

Autovía Tordesilla - Zamora, salida 438
Toro (Zamora)
☎: 923 541 050 - Fax: 923 568 425
info@marxuach.es

MARXUACH 2007 T ROBLE
tinta de toro 100%

**88** Colour: cherry, garnet rim. Nose: ripe fruit, spicy, creamy oak, toasty, complex. Palate: powerful, flavourful, toasty, round tannins.

MARXUACH 2004 TR
tinta de toro 100%

**85** Colour: cherry, garnet rim. Nose: ripe fruit, spicy, toasty, complex, cedar wood. Palate: powerful, flavourful, toasty, round tannins.

## BODEGA NUMANTHIA

Real, s/n
49882 Valdefinjas (Zamora)
☎: 980 699 147 - Fax: 980 699 147
pjutrera@moet-hennessy.com

TERMANTHIA 2006 T
tinta de toro 100%

**95** Colour: cherry, garnet rim. Nose: spicy, creamy oak, complex, fruit expression, dry stone. Palate: powerful, flavourful, toasty, round tannins.

NVMANTHIA 2006 T
tinta de toro 100%

**94** Colour: cherry, garnet rim. Nose: ripe fruit, spicy, creamy oak, complex, fruit preserve, elegant, powerfull, balsamic herbs, cocoa bean. Palate: powerful, flavourful, toasty, round tannins, good structure, fruity aftestaste.

## BODEGA RAMÓN RAMOS

Pozo, 35
49153 Venialbo (Zamora)
☎: 980 573 080 - Fax: 980 573 241
info@bodegaramonramos.com
www.bodegaramonramos.com

MONTETORO 2008 RD
tinta de toro 100%

**84**

MONTETORO 2008 T
tinta de toro 100%

**85** Colour: bright cherry. Nose: ripe fruit, sweet spices, expressive, floral. Palate: flavourful, fruity, toasty, round tannins, fine bitter notes.

MONTETORO 2007 T ROBLE
tinta de toro 100%

**87** Colour: cherry, purple rim. Nose: red berry notes, floral. Palate: flavourful, fruity, good acidity, round tannins.

MONTETORO 1998 TR
tinta de toro 100%

**86** Colour: cherry, garnet rim. Nose: ripe fruit, spicy, creamy oak, toasty, complex, fine reductive notes. Palate: powerful, flavourful, toasty, round tannins.

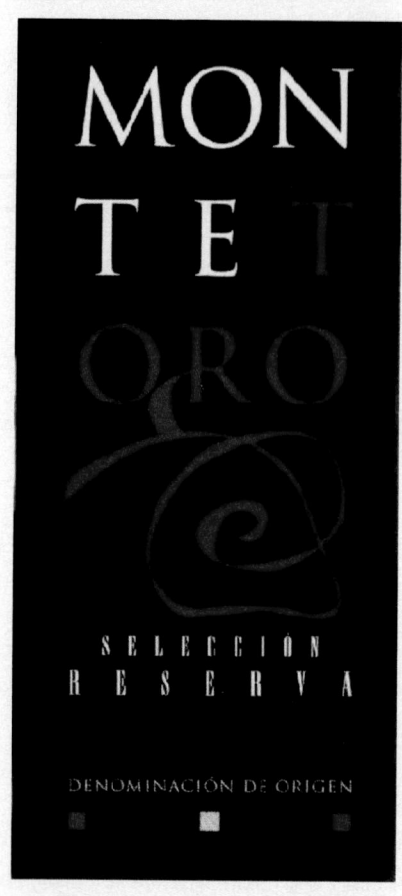

## MONTETORO SELECCIÓN 2006 TC
tinta de toro 100%

**86** Colour: bright cherry. Nose: sweet spices, creamy oak, expressive, macerated fruit, fruit liqueur notes. Palate: flavourful, fruity, toasty, round tannins.

## MONTETORO RESERVA DE FAMILIA VINO DE AUTOR 2001 TR
tinta de toro 100%

**89** Colour: cherry, garnet rim. Nose: ripe fruit, spicy, creamy oak, toasty, complex, roasted almonds, fruit expression. Palate: powerful, flavourful, toasty, round tannins.

## BODEGAS A. VELASCO E HIJOS S.L.

Ctra. Tordesillas, Pol. Ind. Norte, Parc. 17-18
49800 Toro (Zamora)
☎: 980 692 455 - Fax: 980 692 455
tecnico@bodegasvelascoehijos.com
www.bodegasvelascoehijos.com

PEÑA REJAS 2008 RD

**78**

GARABITAS SELECCIÓN VIÑAS VIEJAS 2006 T ROBLE

**89** Colour: deep cherry. Nose: fruit liqueur notes, spicy, toasty. Palate: powerful, flavourful, round tannins.

PEÑA REJAS 2004 TR

**91** Colour: very deep cherry, garnet rim. Nose: fruit liqueur notes, sweet spices, toasty, complex. Palate: flavourful, powerful, slightly dry, soft tannins.

## BODEGAS ALINDE

Miguel Iscar 5, 5 Dcha.
47401 (Valladolid)
☎: 650 581 558 - Fax: 983 246 158
alinde2004@yahoo.es
www.cellarwines.eu

ALINDE VENDIMIA SELECCIONADA 2006 T
tinta de toro

**85** Colour: cherry, garnet rim. Nose: spicy, creamy oak, toasty, complex, cedar wood, aromatic coffee. Palate: powerful, flavourful, toasty, round tannins.

ALINDE 2005 T
tinta de toro

**87** Colour: black cherry. Nose: fruit preserve, sweet spices. Palate: powerful, flavourful, long.

## BODEGAS ALTA CRIANZA

Avda. España, 10 2 B
26033 Logroño (La Rioja)
☎: 941 205 756
rdecarlos@wanadoo.es

ABIOS 2004 TC
tinta de toro

**88** Colour: cherry, garnet rim. Nose: ripe fruit, spicy, creamy oak, toasty, complex, undergrowth. Palate: powerful, flavourful, toasty, round tannins, fruity aftestaste.

## BODEGAS COVITORO

Ctra. de Tordesillas, 13
49800 Toro (Zamora)
☎: 980 690 347 - Fax: 980 690 143
santiago@covitoro.com
www.covitoro.com

CERMEÑO 2008 B
malvasia 100%

**77**

CERMEÑO 2008 RD
tinta de toro 80%, garnacha 20%

**85** Colour: rose, bright. Nose: ripe fruit, dried herbs. Palate: spicy, easy to drink, good finish.

CERMEÑO 2008 T
tinta de toro 100%

**87** Colour: cherry, purple rim. Nose: expressive, fresh fruit, red berry notes, floral. Palate: flavourful, fruity, good acidity, round tannins.

BACO 2007 T ROBLE
tinta de toro 100%

**85** Colour: cherry, garnet rim. Nose: ripe fruit, spicy, creamy oak, toasty. Palate: powerful, flavourful, toasty, round tannins.

GRAN CERMEÑO 2006 TC
tinta de toro 100%

**88** Colour: bright cherry. Nose: ripe fruit, sweet spices, expressive, red berry notes, smoky. Palate: flavourful, fruity, toasty, fine tannins.

CAÑUS VERUS 2005 T
tinta de toro 100%

**89** Colour: dark-red cherry. Nose: sweet spices, dark chocolate, toasty. Palate: powerful, fleshy, harsh oak tannins.

**BACO 2005 TC**
tinta de toro 100%

**86** Colour: bright cherry. Nose: ripe fruit, sweet spices, creamy oak, expressive. Palate: flavourful, fruity, toasty, round tannins.

**MARQUÉS DE LA VILLA 2003 TR**
tinta de toro 100%

**86** Colour: cherry, garnet rim. Nose: ripe fruit, spicy, creamy oak, toasty, complex. Palate: powerful, flavourful, toasty, round tannins.

## BODEGAS FARIÑA

Camino del Palo, s/n
49800 Toro (Zamora)
☎: 980 577 673 - Fax: 980 577 720
comercial@bodegasfarina.com
www.bodegasfarina.com

**GRAN COLEGIATA CAMPUS 2004 TC**
tinta de toro 100%

**90** Colour: dark-red cherry, garnet rim. Nose: sweet spices, toasty, wet leather. Palate: flavourful, full, round tannins, great length.

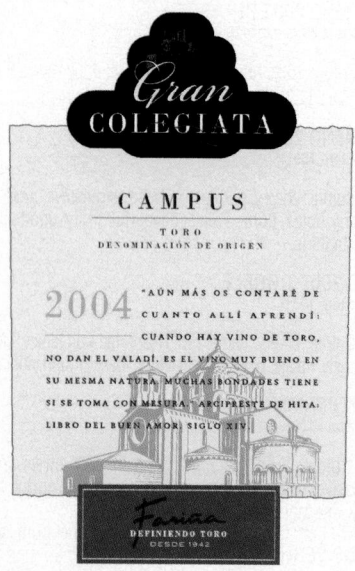

**COLEGIATA MALVASÍA 2008 B**
malvasia 100%

**82**

**PRIMERO 2008 T MACERACIÓN CARBÓNICA**
tinta de toro 100%

**90** Colour: cherry, purple rim. Nose: red berry notes, expressive, fresh. Palate: flavourful, fruity, fresh, round tannins.

**COLEGIATA 2007 T BARRICA**
tinta de toro 100%
**81**

**GRAN COLEGIATA ROBLE FRANCÉS 2004 TC**
tinta de toro 100%

**86** Colour: black cherry. Nose: sweet spices, fine reductive notes. Palate: flavourful, roasted-coffee aftertaste, fine tannins.

## BODEGAS FRANCISCO CASAS S.A.

Pº de San Cosme, 6
28600 Navalcarnero (Madrid)
☎: 918 110 207 - Fax: 918 110 798
f.casas@bodegascasas.com
www.bodegascasas.com

**CAMPARRÓN B**

**80**

**CAMPARRÓN 2008 RD**

**82**

**CAMPARRÓN SELECCION 2008 T**

**88** Colour: cherry, purple rim. Nose: ripe fruit, sweet spices, creamy oak, expressive. Palate: flavourful, fruity, toasty, round tannins, balsamic.

**CAMPARRÓN NOVUM 2008 T**

**86** Colour: cherry, purple rim. Nose: expressive, red berry notes, floral, balsamic herbs. Palate: flavourful, fruity, good acidity, round tannins.

**CAMPARRÓN 2006 TC**

**86** Colour: bright cherry. Nose: ripe fruit, sweet spices, creamy oak, expressive. Palate: flavourful, fruity, toasty, round tannins.

**CAMPARRÓN 2004 TR**

**86** Colour: cherry, garnet rim. Nose: ripe fruit, spicy, creamy oak, toasty, complex. Palate: powerful, flavourful, toasty, round tannins.

**GAMAZO**

## BODEGAS GIL LUNA

Ctra. Toro - Salamanca, km. 2
49800 Toro (Zamora)
☎: 980 698 509 - Fax: 980 698 294
pbgiluna@giluna.com
www.giluna.com

TRES LUNAS 2007 T
tinta de toro 95%, garnacha 5%

**84**

GIL LUNA 2005 T
tinta de toro 95%, garnacha 5%

**89** Colour: bright cherry. Nose: ripe fruit, sweet spices, creamy oak, expressive, faded flowers, fine reductive notes. Palate: flavourful, fruity, toasty, round tannins.

TRES LUNAS 2005 T
tinta de toro 95%, garnacha 5%

**89** Colour: cherry, garnet rim. Nose: ripe fruit, spicy, creamy oak, toasty, complex, undergrowth. Palate: powerful, flavourful, toasty, round tannins.

GIL LUNA 2004 T
tinta de toro 95%, garnacha 5%

**87** Colour: cherry, garnet rim. Nose: old leather, roasted coffee. Palate: fleshy, long, great length.

## BODEGAS MONTE LA REINA S.C.L.

Ctra. Toro - Zamora, km. 436,7
49881 Toro (Zamora)
☎: 980 082 011 - Fax: 980 082 012
bodega@montelareina.es
www.montelareina.es

TERTIUS VERDEJO 2008 B

**87** Colour: bright straw. Nose: fresh fruit, varietal, scrubland, floral, expressive. Palate: light-bodied, fruity, flavourful, good acidity.

CASTILLO MONTE LA REINA 2007 BFB
verdejo 100%

**85** Colour: bright yellow. Nose: powerfull, sweet spices, cocoa bean, ripe fruit, tropical fruit. Palate: flavourful, fleshy, good structure, fruity, toasty.

CASTILLO MONTE LA REINA 2008 B
verdejo 100%

**87** Colour: bright straw. Nose: varietal, wild herbs, citrus fruit, fresh fruit. Palate: fruity, flavourful, fresh, long.

TERTIUS 2008 T
tinta de toro 100%

**84**

CASTILLO MONTE LA REINA 2006 T FERMENTADO EN BARRICA
tinta de toro 100%

**88** Colour: cherry, garnet rim. Nose: ripe fruit, spicy, creamy oak, toasty, red berry notes. Palate: powerful, flavourful, toasty, round tannins.

CASTILLO MONTE LA REINA 2007 T ROBLE
tinta de toro 100%

**90** Colour: cherry, garnet rim. Nose: ripe fruit, spicy, toasty. Palate: flavourful, full, fine tannins.

INARAJA 2005 T
tinta de toro 100%

**91** Colour: cherry, garnet rim. Nose: ripe fruit, spicy, creamy oak, toasty, complex, mineral. Palate: powerful, flavourful, toasty, round tannins.

CASTILLO MONTE LA REINA VENDIMIA SELECCIONADA 2005 T
tinta de toro 100%

**90** Colour: cherry, garnet rim. Nose: spicy, creamy oak, toasty, complex, fruit liqueur notes, undergrowth. Palate: powerful, flavourful, toasty, round tannins.

TERTIUS 2007 T ROBLE
tinta de toro 100%

**87** Colour: bright cherry. Nose: ripe fruit, sweet spices, creamy oak, expressive. Palate: flavourful, fruity, toasty, round tannins.

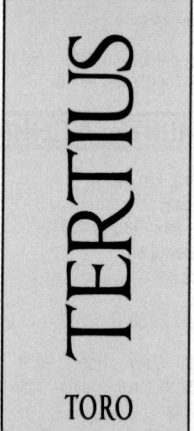

## BODEGAS REJADORADA S.L.

Rejadorada, 11
49800 Toro (Zamora)
☎: 980 693 089 - Fax: 980 693 089
rejadorada@rejadorada.com
www.rejadorada.com

## REJADORADA ROBLE 2007 T ROBLE
tinta de toro 100%

**87** Colour: bright cherry. Nose: ripe fruit, sweet spices, creamy oak, expressive. Palate: flavourful, fruity, toasty, round tannins.

## NOVELLUM REJADORADA 2006 TC
tinta de toro 100%

**91** Colour: cherry, garnet rim. Nose: toasty, earthy notes, complex. Palate: powerful, good structure, long.

## SANGO DE REJADORADA 2005 TR
tinta de toro 100%

**90** Colour: cherry, garnet rim. Nose: ripe fruit, spicy, creamy oak, toasty, complex, floral, aromatic coffee. Palate: powerful, flavourful, toasty, round tannins.

## BODEGAS SIETECERROS

Finca Villaester -Villaester de Arriba
47540 Pedrosa del Rey (Valladolid)
☎: 983 784 083 - Fax: 983 784 083
sietecerros@bodegasietecerros.com
www.bodegasietecerros.com

## QUEBRANTARREJAS 2007 T
tinta de toro 100%

**85** Colour: cherry, garnet rim. Nose: fruit preserve, spicy, warm. Palate: flavourful, fruity, balanced.

## PANÉ 2007 T
tinta de toro 100%

**85** Colour: cherry, garnet rim. Nose: ripe fruit, spicy, creamy oak, toasty. Palate: flavourful, toasty, round tannins, lacks balance.

## VALDELAZARZA 2006 T ROBLE
tinta de toro 100%

**86** Colour: cherry, garnet rim. Nose: overripe fruit, spicy, toasty. Palate: flavourful, long, great length.

## VALDELAZARZA SELECCIÓN 2005 T
tinta de toro 100%

**89** Colour: dark-red cherry. Nose: overripe fruit, wild herbs, spicy. Palate: good structure, flavourful, great length.

## VALDELAZARZA 2005 T
tinta de toro 100%

**84**

## VALDELAZARZA 2004 TR
tinta de toro 100%

**86** Colour: dark-red cherry. Nose: overripe fruit, sweet spices, toasty, wild herbs. Palate: flavourful, full, great length.

## BODEGAS SOBREÑO

Ctra. N-122, km. 423
49800 Toro (Zamora)
☎: 980 693 417 - Fax: 980 693 416
sobreno@sobreno.com
www.sobreno.com

## FINCA SOBREÑO ECOLÓGICO 2008 T
tinta de toro 100%

**89** Colour: cherry, purple rim. Nose: expressive, floral, fruit preserve. Palate: flavourful, fruity, good acidity, round tannins.

## FINCA SOBREÑO ECOLÓGICO 2008 T JOVEN
tinta de toro 100%

**88** Colour: bright cherry. Nose: ripe fruit, sweet spices, expressive, cocoa bean. Palate: flavourful, fruity, toasty, round tannins.

## FINCA SOBREÑO 2005 TC
tinta de toro 100%

**91** Colour: cherry, garnet rim. Nose: ripe fruit, spicy, creamy oak, toasty, complex, dried flowers. Palate: powerful, flavourful, toasty, round tannins.

**FINCA SOBREÑO RESERVA FAMILIAR 2004 TR**
tinta de toro 100%

**88** Colour: cherry, garnet rim. Nose: ripe fruit, spicy, creamy oak, toasty, complex, fruit liqueur notes, floral. Palate: powerful, flavourful, toasty, round tannins.

**FINCA SOBREÑO SELECCIÓN ESPECIAL 2003 TR**
tinta de toro 100%

**88** Colour: bright cherry. Nose: ripe fruit, sweet spices, creamy oak, expressive, violet drops. Palate: flavourful, fruity, toasty, round tannins.

## BODEGAS TORESANAS

Ctra. N-122 s/n Polígono Carabizal
49800 Toro (Zamora)
☎: 983 868 336 - Fax: 983 868 432
bodegasbccv@interbook.net
www.bodegasdecastilla.com

**AMANT NOVILLO 2007 T**
tinta de toro 100%

**88** Colour: dark-red cherry. Nose: ripe fruit, wild herbs, spicy. Palate: flavourful, good structure, balanced.

**AMANT 2007 T ROBLE**
tinta de toro 100%

**87** Colour: bright cherry. Nose: ripe fruit, sweet spices, creamy oak, expressive. Palate: flavourful, fruity, toasty, round tannins.

**OROT 2004 TC**
tinta de toro 100%

**87** Colour: cherry, garnet rim. Nose: toasty, spicy, fine reductive notes. Palate: flavourful, full, round tannins.

## BODEGAS TORREDUERO

Pol. Ind. Norte, Parcela 5
49800 Toro (Zamora)
☎: 980 693 421 - Fax: 980 693 422
bodega@bodegastorreduero.com
www.bodegastorreduero.com

**PEÑAMONTE 2008 B**
verdejo 70%, malvasia 30%

**81**

**PEÑAMONTE 2008 RD**
tinta de toro 100%

**84**

**PEÑAMONTE 2008 T**
tinta de toro 100%

**82**

**PEÑAMONTE 2006 T BARRICA**
tinta de toro 100%

**90** Colour: cherry, garnet rim. Nose: fruit liqueur notes, toasty. Palate: flavourful, full, long, balsamic.

**PEÑAMONTE 2005 TC**
tinta de toro 100%

**88** Colour: deep cherry. Nose: toasty, dark chocolate, spicy. Palate: complex, flavourful, round tannins.

**MARQUÉS DE PEÑAMONTE 2005 TC**
tinta de toro 100%

**84**

**MARQUÉS DE PEÑAMONTE 2003 TR**
tinta de toro 100%

**87** Colour: cherry, garnet rim. Nose: ripe fruit, spicy, creamy oak, toasty. Palate: powerful, flavourful, toasty, round tannins, fruity aftestaste.

## BODEGAS VEGA SAUCO

Avda. Comuneros, 108
49810 Morales de Toro (Zamora)
☎: 980 698 294 - Fax: 980 698 294
vegasauco@vegasauco.com
www.vegasauco.com

**VEGA SAÚCO "TO" 2005 TC**
tinta de toro 100%

**92** Colour: cherry, garnet rim. Nose: ripe fruit, spicy, creamy oak, toasty, complex, floral. Palate: powerful, flavourful, toasty, round tannins, fruity aftestaste.

ADOREMUS 2004 TR
tinta de toro 100%

**91** Colour: cherry, garnet rim. Nose: spicy, creamy oak, toasty, complex, characterful, elegant, fruit expression. Palate: powerful, flavourful, toasty, round tannins.

VEGA SAÚCO "TO" 2004 TC
tinta de toro 100%

**86** Colour: cherry, garnet rim. Nose: old leather, roasted coffee. Palate: flavourful, full, great length.

WENCES 2004 T
tinta de toro 80%, otras 20%

**85** Colour: dark-red cherry, garnet rim. Nose: fruit preserve, roasted coffee. Palate: long, flavourful.

ADOREMUS VENDIMIA SELECCIONADA 2001 T
tinta de toro

**84**

FLOR DEL SAUCO

## BODEGAS Y PAGOS MATARREDONDA

Ctra. Toro-Valdefinjas, s/n, km. 2,5
49800 Toro (Zamora)
☎: 980 059 981 - Fax: 980 059 981
libranza@vinolibranza.com
www.vinolibranza.com

JUAN ROJO 2005 T
tinta de toro 100%

**91** Colour: cherry, garnet rim. Nose: ripe fruit, creamy oak, toasty, complex, aromatic coffee, balsamic herbs. Palate: powerful, flavourful, toasty, round tannins.

LIBRANZA 2005 T
tinta de toro 100%

**88** Colour: cherry, garnet rim. Nose: ripe fruit, spicy, creamy oak, toasty, complex, undergrowth. Palate: powerful, flavourful, toasty, round tannins.

## BODEGAS Y VIÑEDOS ANZIL

Camino El Pego, s/n
Ctra. Toro - Villabuena del Puente, km. 9,4

49800 Toro (Zamora)
☎: 915 006 000 - Fax: 915 006 006
barcelo@habarcelo.es
www.habarcelo.es

VIÑA MAYOR TORO 2006 T
tinta de toro 100%

**88** Colour: bright cherry. Nose: ripe fruit, sweet spices, creamy oak, expressive. Palate: flavourful, fruity, toasty, round tannins, smoky aftertaste.

FINCA ANZIL 2005 T
tinta de toro 100%

**90** Colour: bright cherry. Nose: creamy oak, expressive, aromatic coffee, fruit preserve, ripe fruit. Palate: flavourful, fruity, toasty, round tannins.

## BODEGAS Y VIÑEDOS BURLÓN

Perú, 10 4º Dcha.
47004(Valladolid
☎: 983 302 245 - Fax: 983 308 553
info@bodegasburlon.com
www.bodegasburlon.com

VIÑA EL TORILÓN 2005 TC
tinta de toro 100%

**91** Colour: cherry, garnet rim. Nose: fruit preserve, cocoa bean, sweet spices. Palate: flavourful, great length, round tannins.

VIÑA EL TORILÓN 2004 TR

**89** Colour: deep cherry, garnet rim. Nose: fruit preserve, fruit liqueur notes, sweet spices. Palate: light-bodied, good acidity, warm, flavourful, round tannins.

## BODEGAS Y VIÑEDOS MAURODOS S.A.

Ctra. N-122, km. 412 Villaester
47195 Pedrosa del Rey (Valladolid)
☎: 983 784 118 - Fax: 983 784 018
sanroman@bodegasmauro.com
www.bodegasanroman.com

PRIMA 2007 T
tinta de toro 90%, garnacha 10%

**90** Colour: very deep cherry. Nose: sweet spices, creamy oak, cocoa bean, fruit preserve. Palate: flavourful, full, elegant.

SAN ROMÁN 2006 T
tinta de toro 100%

**93** Colour: cherry, garnet rim. Nose: creamy oak, toasty, complex, mineral, fruit preserve, aromatic coffee. Palate: powerful, flavourful, toasty, round tannins, good acidity.

# DO TORO

## BODEGAS Y VIÑEDOS PINTIA

Ctra. de Morales s/n
47530 San Román de Hornija (Valladolid)
☎: 983 784 178 - Fax: 983 680 263
vegasicilia@vega-sicilia.com
www.vega-sicilia.com

PINTIA 2007 T
tinta de toro 100%

**96** Colour: bright cherry, purple rim. Nose: powerfull, ripe fruit, red berry notes, balanced, sweet spices, cocoa bean. Palate: flavourful, fleshy, fruity, round tannins.

PINTIA 2006 T
tinta de toro

**93** Colour: bright cherry. Nose: elegant, balanced, sweet spices, ripe fruit. Palate: flavourful, fleshy, spicy, long, round tannins.

## BODEGAS Y VIÑEDOS VALDUERO

Ctra. de Aranda, s/n
09443 Gumiel de Mercado (Burgos)
☎: 947 545 459 - Fax: 947 545 609
valduero@bodegasvalduero.com
www.bodegasvalduero.com

ARBUCALA 2006 T

**90** Colour: cherry, garnet rim. Nose: ripe fruit, spicy, creamy oak, toasty, complex, aromatic coffee. Palate: powerful, flavourful, toasty, round tannins.

## BUIL & GINÉ

Ctra. de Gratallops - Vilella Baixa, km. 11,5
43737 Gratallops (Tarragona)
☎: 977 839 810 - Fax: 977 839 811
info@builgine.com
www.builgine.com

BUIL 2005 T
tinta de toro 100%

**89** Colour: cherry, garnet rim. Nose: ripe fruit, spicy, creamy oak, toasty, complex, cocoa bean. Palate: powerful, flavourful, toasty, round tannins.

## CAMPIÑA SOCIEDAD COOP. C. Y L.

Ctra. Toro - Veniablo, km. 6,9
49882 Valdefinjas (Zamora)
☎: 980 568 125
info@bodegascampina.com
www.bodegascampina.com

CAMPIÑA WINE&ARTS 2007 T
tinta de toro 100%

**85** Colour: bright cherry. Nose: ripe fruit, sweet spices, creamy oak, expressive. Palate: flavourful, fruity, toasty, round tannins.

CAMPIÑA WINE&ARTS 2006 TC
tinta de toro

**87** Colour: cherry, garnet rim. Nose: toasty, sweet spices. Palate: flavourful, fruity aftestaste, great length.

CAMPIÑA WINE&ARTS 2006 T ROBLE
tinta de toro

**85** Colour: cherry, garnet rim. Nose: overripe fruit, roasted coffee, warm. Palate: flavourful, spirituous, fine tannins.

## CAÑADA DEL PINO, S.L.

Polígono 6 Parcela 83
49810 Morales de Toro (Zamora)
☎: 676 701 918 - Fax: 980 698 318
fincayerro@terra.es

FINCA YERRO 2007 T

**88** Colour: cherry, purple rim. Nose: expressive, red berry notes, floral, candied fruit. Palate: flavourful, fruity, good acidity, round tannins.

**FINCA Yerro**

**TORO**
DENOMINACIÓN DE ORIGEN

AMERIKAN OAK          ROBLE AMERICANO

FINCA YERRO 2006 T

**87** Colour: cherry, garnet rim. Nose: spicy, toasty, complex, balsamic herbs, red berry notes, new oak. Palate: powerful, flavourful, toasty, round tannins.

## CARMEN RODRÍGUEZ MÉNDEZ

Ctra. Salamanca, ZA 605, km. 1,650
49800 Toro (Zamora)
☎: 980 568 005
crcarodorum@yahoo.es

CARODORUM SELECCIÓN ESPECIAL 2006 TC
tinta de toro 100%

**87** Colour: bright cherry. Nose: sweet spices, expressive, dark chocolate, fruit liqueur notes. Palate: flavourful, fruity, toasty, round tannins.

CARODORUM 2006 TC
tinta de toro 100%

**84**

CARODORUM ISSOS 2006 T
tinta de toro 100%

**84**

## CEPAS Y BODEGAS

Pº de Zorrilla 77-3º
47007 Valladolid
☎: 983 355 543 - Fax: 983 340 824
info@cepasybodegas.com
www.cepasybodegas.com

ARCO DE GUÍA ROBLE ESPAÑOL 2006 T ROBLE
tinta de toro 85%, garnacha 15%

**90** Colour: bright cherry. Nose: ripe fruit, sweet spices, creamy oak, expressive. Palate: flavourful, fruity, toasty, round tannins.

VIÑALCASTA 2006 TC
tinta de toro 100%

**88** Colour: cherry, garnet rim. Nose: ripe fruit, spicy, creamy oak, toasty, complex. Palate: powerful, flavourful, toasty, fine tannins.

## COMPAÑIA DE VINOS DE TELMO RODRÍGUEZ

El Monte s/n
01308 Lanciego (Alava)
☎: 945 628 315 - Fax: 945 628 314

contact@telmorodriguez.com
www.telmorodriguez.com

GAGO 2007 T
tinta de toro

**90** Colour: cherry, garnet rim. Nose: powerfull, ripe fruit, toasty, sweet spices. Palate: flavourful, powerful, fleshy, ripe fruit.

PAGO LA JARA 2006 T
tinta de toro

**95** Colour: cherry, garnet rim. Nose: powerfull, ripe fruit, mineral, toasty, new oak. Palate: flavourful, fleshy, fruity, fresh, round tannins.

DEHESA GAGO

## CORAL DUERO

Ascensión, s/n
49154 El Pego (Zamora)
☎: 980 606 333 - Fax: 980 606 391
paula@rompesedas.com
www.rompesedas.com

ROMPESEDAS 2005 T
tinta de toro 100%

**90** Colour: very deep cherry. Nose: neat, varietal, fruit preserve, sweet spices, cedar wood. Palate: flavourful, fruity, pruney, round tannins, long.

ROMPESEDAS
TORO DENOMINACIÓN DE ORIGEN

ROMPESEDAS 2006 T
tinta de toro 100%

**91** Colour: bright cherry. Nose: ripe fruit, sweet spices, creamy oak, expressive, balsamic herbs, undergrowth. Palate: flavourful, fruity, toasty, round tannins.

## DOMAINES MAGREZ ESPAGNE

Plaça Catalunya, 5
43739 Porrera (Tarragona)
☎: 977 828 016 - Fax: 977 828 016
trosdelpadri-bernardmagrez@hotmail.com

PACIENCIA 2006 T

**94** Colour: bright cherry. Nose: ripe fruit, creamy oak, characterful, powerfull, aged wood nuances. Palate: flavourful, fruity, toasty, fine tannins, classic aged character.

TEMPERANCIA 2006 T

**93** Colour: cherry, garnet rim. Nose: ripe fruit, spicy, creamy oak, complex, fine reductive notes. Palate: powerful, flavourful, toasty, round tannins.

SPIRITUS SANCTI 2006 T

**92** Colour: cherry, garnet rim. Nose: ripe fruit, spicy, toasty, complex, earthy notes, tobacco. Palate: powerful, flavourful, toasty, round tannins.

## DOMINIO DEL BENDITO

Plaza Santo Domingo, 8
49800 Toro (Zamora)
☎: 980 693 306 - Fax: 980 694 991
tintadetoro@yahoo.com

DOMINIO DEL BENDITO 2007 T ROBLE
tinta de toro 100%

**93** Colour: very deep cherry. Nose: ripe fruit, sweet spices, creamy oak. Palate: good structure, balanced, elegant.

EL TITAN DEL BENDITO 2006 T

**93** Colour: cherry, garnet rim. Nose: macerated fruit, toasty. Palate: flavourful, long, fine tannins.

EL TITAN DEL BENDITO 2005 T
tinta de toro 100%

**92** Colour: bright cherry. Nose: sweet spices, creamy oak, expressive, floral, macerated fruit, balsamic herbs, mineral. Palate: flavourful, fruity, toasty, round tannins.

## ESTANCIA PIEDRA S.L.

Ctra. Toro Salamanca, km 5

49800 Toro (Zamora)
☎: 980 693 900 - Fax: 980 693 901
info@estanciapiedra.com
www.estanciapiedra.com

PIEDRA 2008 RD
tinta de toro 100%

**87** Colour: rose, purple rim. Nose: fresh fruit, floral, expressive, violet drops. Palate: rich, fruity, powerful, good finish.

PIEDRA AZUL 2008 T
tinta de toro 100%

**86** Colour: very deep cherry. Nose: varietal, expressive, ripe fruit, fresh fruit. Palate: round tannins, good acidity, fruity.

PIEDRA ROJA 2005 TC
tinta de toro 100%

**91** Colour: deep cherry, garnet rim. Nose: mineral, sweet spices, new oak, elegant, fruit preserve. Palate: full, fruity, powerful, slightly dry, soft tannins.

PIEDRA PAREDINAS 2004 T
tinta de toro 100%

**90** Colour: cherry, garnet rim. Nose: ripe fruit, spicy, creamy oak, toasty, wet leather. Palate: powerful, flavourful, toasty, round tannins.

PIEDRA PLATINO SELECCIÓN 2003 TC
tinta de toro 100%

**90** Colour: deep cherry. Nose: ripe fruit, scrubland, sweet spices, cocoa bean. Palate: flavourful, fleshy, spicy, round tannins.

## FRUTOS VILLAR

Eras de Santa Catalina s/n
49800 Toro (Zamora)
☎: 983 586 868 - Fax: 983 580 180
bodegasfrutosvillar@bodegasfrutosvillar.com
www.bodegasfrutosvillar.com

MURUVE 2008 T
tinta de toro 100%

**86** Colour: bright cherry. Nose: sweet spices, expressive, fruit liqueur notes, fruit preserve. Palate: flavourful, fruity, toasty, fresh fruit tannins.

MURUVE 2006 TC
tinta de toro 100%

**89** Colour: bright cherry. Nose: ripe fruit, sweet spices, creamy oak, expressive, earthy notes. Palate: flavourful, fruity, toasty, round tannins.

MURUVE ÉLITE 2006 T
tinta de toro 100%

**89** Colour: bright cherry. Nose: ripe fruit, sweet spices, expressive, raspberry, balsamic herbs. Palate: flavourful, fruity, toasty, round tannins.

MIRALMONTE 2006 TC
tinta de toro 100%

**88** Colour: bright cherry. Nose: ripe fruit, sweet spices, creamy oak, expressive, balsamic herbs. Palate: flavourful, fruity, toasty, round tannins, varietal.

MURUVE 2004 TR
tinta de toro 100%

**90** Colour: cherry, garnet rim. Nose: ripe fruit, spicy, creamy oak, toasty, complex, elegant. Palate: powerful, flavourful, toasty, round tannins.

## GRUPO YLLERA

Ctra. Madrid - Coruña, km. 173, 5
47490 Rueda (Valladolid)

☎: 983 868 097 - Fax: 983 868 177
grupoyllera@grupoyllera.com
www.grupoyllera.com

GARCILASO 2003 T

**88** Colour: bright cherry. Nose: ripe fruit, sweet spices, creamy oak, smoky. Palate: flavourful, fruity, toasty, round tannins.

## HACIENDA TERRA D'URO

Campanas, 4
47001 (Valladolid)
☎: 983 362 591
haciendaterraduro@yahoo.es

TERRA D'URO 2007 T

**89** Colour: dark-red cherry, garnet rim. Nose: powerfull, toasty, spicy, ripe fruit. Palate: flavourful, powerful, fleshy, round tannins.

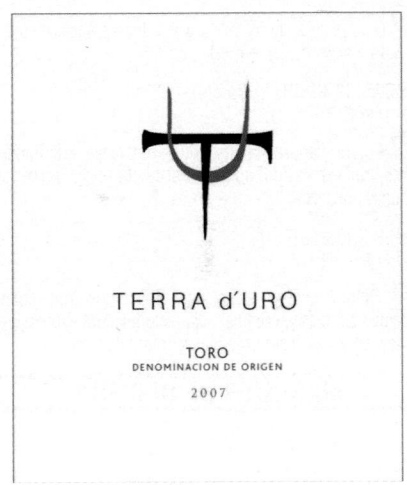

TERRA D'URO 2006 T

**87** Colour: cherry, garnet rim. Nose: powerfull, fruit liqueur notes, overripe fruit, toasty, spicy, dark chocolate. Palate: flavourful, fleshy, spicy, ripe fruit.

## LIBERALIA ENOLÓGICA

Camino del Palo, s/n
49800 Toro (Zamora)
☎: 980 692 571 - Fax: 980 692 571

byvliberalia@hotmail.com
www.liberalia.es

**LIBERALIA CERO 2008 T FERMENTADO EN BARRICA**
tinta de toro 100%

## 84

**LIBERALIA TRES 2007 T ROBLE**
tinta de toro 100%

**92** Colour: deep cherry. Nose: creamy oak, cocoa bean, spicy, ripe fruit. Palate: flavourful, good structure, concentrated, round tannins.

**LIBERALIA CUATRO 2006 TC**
tinta de toro 100%

**88** Colour: bright cherry. Nose: sweet spices, creamy oak, expressive, balsamic herbs, fruit expression. Palate: flavourful, fruity, toasty, round tannins.

**LIBERALIA CABEZA DE CUBA 2005 TC**
tinta de toro 100%

**92** Colour: deep cherry. Nose: warm, toasty, ripe fruit, dried flowers. Palate: fleshy, powerful, full.

**LIBERALIA CINCO 2004 TR**
tinta de toro 100%

**92** Colour: dark-red cherry, garnet rim. Nose: fruit liqueur notes, fruit expression, mineral. Palate: flavourful, powerful, reductive nuances.

**LIBER 2003 TGR**
tinta de toro 100%

**91** Colour: cherry, garnet rim. Nose: ripe fruit, spicy, creamy oak, toasty, complex, characterful, fruit expression. Palate: powerful, flavourful, toasty, round tannins.

## MARQUÉS DE OLIVARA

Eras de Santa Catalina, s/n
49800 Toro (Zamora)
☎: 980 693 425 - Fax: 980 693 409
marquesdeolivara@marquesdeolivara.com
www.marquesdeolivara.com

**VIÑAS DE OLIVARA 2008 T**
tinta de toro

**86** Colour: cherry, purple rim. Nose: floral, cocoa bean, fruit preserve, fruit liqueur notes. Palate: flavourful, fruity, good acidity, powerful tannins.

**VIÑAS DE OLIVARA 2007 T**
tinta de toro 100%

## 84

**MARQUÉS DE OLIVARA 2006 TC**
tinta de toro 100%

**90** Colour: cherry, garnet rim. Nose: fruit liqueur notes, toasty, wild herbs. Palate: flavourful, long, mineral.

**M.O. DE OLIVARA VENDIMIA SELECCIONADA 2006 T BARRICA**
tinta de toro 100%

**90** Colour: cherry, garnet rim. Nose: fruit preserve, fruit liqueur notes, toasty, balsamic herbs. Palate: concentrated, spirituous, complex, round tannins.

**MARQUÉS DE OLIVARA 2004 TR**
tinta de toro 100%

**88** Colour: cherry, garnet rim. Nose: toasty, fine reductive notes. Palate: round, elegant, fine tannins.

## PAGOS DEL REY

Avenida de los Comuneros, 90
49810 Morales de Toro (Zamora)
☎: 980 698 023 - Fax: 980 698 020
toro@pagosdelrey.com
www.pagosdelrey.com

**BAJOZ 2008 B**
malvasia

## 79

**FINCA LA MEDA 2008 B**
malvasia

## 78

**CAÑO 2008 B**
malvasia

## 77

**FINCA LA MEDA 2008 RD**
tinta de toro

**85** Colour: cherry, purple rim. Nose: red berry notes, ripe fruit. Palate: warm, flavourful.

**BAJOZ 2008 RD**
tinta de toro

## 83

**CAÑO 2008 RD**
tinta de toro

## 82

CAÑO TEMPRANILLO 2008 T
tinta de toro

**85** Colour: cherry, garnet rim. Nose: ripe fruit, spicy, creamy oak, toasty, complex, fruit preserve. Palate: powerful, toasty, round tannins.

FINCA LA MEDA 2008 T
tinta de toro

**83**

BAJOZ 2008 T JOVEN
tinta de toro

**80**

CAÑO TEMPRANILLO GARNACHA 2007 T

**84**

GRAN BAJOZ 2005 TC
tinta de toro

**91** Colour: cherry, garnet rim. Nose: ripe fruit, wild herbs, toasty. Palate: flavourful, good structure, slightly dry, soft tannins.

FINCA LA MEDA 2005 TC
tinta de toro

**90** Colour: cherry, garnet rim. Nose: fruit liqueur notes, fine reductive notes, spicy. Palate: flavourful, good structure, fine tannins.

FINCA LA MEDA ALTA EXPRESIÓN 2005 T
tinta de toro

**88** Colour: cherry, garnet rim. Nose: sweet spices, dark chocolate, toasty. Palate: flavourful, roasted-coffee aftertaste.

CAÑO 2005 TC
tinta de toro

**88** Colour: cherry, garnet rim. Nose: spicy, floral, fine reductive notes. Palate: powerful, flavourful, slightly dry, soft tannins.

BAJOZ 2005 TC
tinta de toro

**87** Colour: cherry, garnet rim. Nose: macerated fruit, wild herbs. Palate: good structure, flavourful, fine bitter notes, slightly dry, soft tannins.

FINCA LA MEDA 2004 TR
tinta de toro

**92** Colour: very deep cherry. Nose: toasty, dark chocolate, wild herbs, complex. Palate: flavourful, full, good structure, fine tannins.

## PALACIO DE VILLACHICA

Ctra. Nacional 122, km. 433
49800 Toro (Zamora)
☎: 983 372 289 - Fax: 983 381 356
admin@palaciovillachica.com
www.palaciodevillachica.com

PALACIO DE VILLACHICA 3T 2007 T
tinta de toro 100%

**86** Colour: cherry, garnet rim. Nose: ripe fruit, spicy. Palate: flavourful, full, slightly dry, soft tannins.

PALACIO DE VILLACHICA 2007 T ROBLE
tinta de toro 100%

**86** Colour: dark-red cherry. Nose: creamy oak, sweet spices. Palate: powerful, warm, harsh oak tannins.

PALACIO DE VILLACHICA 5T 2003 T
tinta de toro 100%

**91** Colour: cherry, garnet rim. Nose: ripe fruit, spicy, creamy oak, toasty, complex, undergrowth. Palate: powerful, flavourful, toasty, round tannins.

PALACIO DE VILLACHICA SELECCIÓN 2002 T
tinta de toro 100%

**89** Colour: cherry, garnet rim. Nose: ripe fruit, spicy, creamy oak, toasty, complex, mineral. Palate: powerful, flavourful, toasty, round tannins, sweetness.

## QUINOLA

Ctra. Nacional 122, km. 412
47540 Pedrosa del Rey, Villaesther de Arriba
(Valladolid)
☎: 625 227 321
garagewine@quinola.es
www.quinola.es

QUINOLA GARAGE WINE 2006 T ROBLE
tinta de toro 100%

**90** Colour: cherry, garnet rim. Nose: powerfull, ripe fruit, mineral, earthy notes, sweet spices, creamy oak. Palate: flavourful, powerful, fleshy, round tannins.

## QUINTA DE LA QUIETUD

Camino de Bardales, s/n. Apdo. de Correos 34
49800 Toro (Zamora)
☎: 980 568 019 - Fax: 980 568 081
info@quintaquietud.com

www.quintaquietud.com

**CORRAL DE CAMPANAS 2008 T**
tinta de toro 100%

**89** Colour: cherry, purple rim. Nose: expressive, fresh fruit, red berry notes. Palate: flavourful, fruity, good acidity, round tannins.

**QUINTA QUIETUD 2005 T**
tinta de toro 100%

**94** Colour: cherry, garnet rim. Nose: spicy, creamy oak, toasty, complex, elegant, fruit liqueur notes, mineral. Palate: powerful, flavourful, toasty, round tannins.

**LA MULA DE LA QUIETUD 2005 T**
tinta de toro 100%

**91** Colour: very deep cherry. Nose: fruit preserve, sweet spices, creamy oak. Palate: flavourful, fruity, full, round tannins.

## SITIOS DE BODEGA

Cuatro Calles s/n
47491 La Seca (Valladolid)
☎: 983 103 223 - Fax: 983 816 561
oficina@sitiosdebodega.com
www.sitiosdebodega.com

**PALACIOS DE CASTILLA 2006 T**
tinta de toro 100%

**85** Colour: cherry, garnet rim. Nose: macerated fruit, toasty. Palate: flavourful, slightly dry, soft tannins.

## TARDENCUBA BODEGAS Y VIÑEDOS

Camino de la Centinela
49153 Venialbo (Zamora)
☎: 667 751 990 - Fax: 980 573 241
bodegastardencuba@yahoo.es
www.tardencuba.es

**TARDENCUBA AUTOR INSPIRACIÓN 2007 T**
tinta de toro 100%

**86** Colour: bright cherry. Nose: ripe fruit, sweet spices, creamy oak. Palate: flavourful, toasty, round tannins, spirituous.

**TARDENCUBA 2007 T ROBLE**
tinta de toro 100%

**83**

**TARDENCUBA 2006 TC**
tinta de toro 100%

**87** Colour: cherry, garnet rim. Nose: ripe fruit, spicy, creamy oak, toasty, complex. Palate: powerful, flavourful, toasty, round tannins, sweetness.

**VALNUEVO SELECCIÓN 2005 T**
tinta de toro 100%

**87** Colour: very deep cherry. Nose: floral, rose petals, toasty. Palate: good structure, long, flavourful.

## TERA Y CASTRO

Serrano, 222 - Local
28016 Madrid (Madrid)
☎: 915 902 529 - Fax: 915 644 431
info@teraycastro.com
www.teraycastro.com

**PENTIO TORO 2006 T ROBLE**
tinta de toro

**88** Colour: bright cherry, garnet rim. Nose: medium intensity, ripe fruit, fruit liqueur notes, cocoa bean, sweet spices. Palate: flavourful, fresh, spicy, roasted-coffee aftertaste.

## TERNA BODEGAS

Cuatro Calles s/n
47491 La Seca (Valladolid)
☎: 983 103 223 - Fax: 983 816 561
oficina@sitiosdebodega.com
www.sitiosdebodega.com

**MORFEO 2006 T**
tinta de toro 100%

**92** Colour: cherry, garnet rim. Nose: macerated fruit, toasty, cocoa bean, wild herbs. Palate: fleshy, powerful, slightly dry, soft tannins.

**MORFEO 2005 T**
tinta de toro 100%

**88** Colour: cherry, garnet rim. Nose: ripe fruit, wild herbs. Palate: flavourful, long, round tannins.

## TESO LA MONJA

Paraje Valdebuey, Ctra. ZA-611, km. 6,3
49882 Valdefinjas (Zamora)
☎: 980 568 143 - Fax: 980 508 144
info@eguren.com
www.eguren.com

**VICTORINO 2007 T**
tinta de toro

**94** Colour: dark-red cherry, garnet rim. Nose: warm, earthy notes, sweet spices, elegant, ripe fruit. Palate: powerful, fruity, good acidity, round tannins, spicy.

**ALABASTER 2007 T**

**92** Colour: dark-red cherry. Nose: fresh fruit, creamy oak, cocoa bean. Palate: fleshy, powerful, flavourful, fruity, good structure.

ALMIREZ 2007 T
tinta de toro

**91** Colour: very deep cherry, garnet rim. Nose: ripe fruit, red berry notes, creamy oak, dark chocolate. Palate: powerful, fruity, good acidity, round tannins, pruney.

## VALBUSENDA

Peleagonzalo
49880 Toro (Zamora)
☎: 980 557 403 - Fax: 980 670 824
bodega@hotelbodegasvalbusenda.com
www.hotelbodegasvalbusenda.com

EKLIOS 2008 RD

**85** Colour: rose, purple rim. Nose: powerfull, ripe fruit, red berry notes, expressive. Palate: fleshy, powerful, fruity, fresh.

EKLIOS 2006 T ROBLE

**84**

VALBUSENDA 2004 TR

**89** Colour: cherry, garnet rim. Nose: ripe fruit, spicy, creamy oak, toasty, complex. Palate: powerful, flavourful, toasty, round tannins.

EKLIOS 2003 TC

**83**

## VALSANZO

Manuel Azaña, 9
Edificio Ambassador, Local 15
47014 Valladolid
☎: 983 150 150 - Fax: 983 150 151
valsanzo@valsanzo.com
www.valsanzo.com

DAMALISCO 2006 TC
tinta de toro 100%

**85** Colour: deep cherry. Nose: overripe fruit, warm, toasty. Palate: flavourful, concentrated, round tannins.

## VETUS, S.L.

Ctra. ZA-605 Toro-Fuentesauco, km. 9,5
49820 Villabuena del Puente (Zamora)
☎: 945 609 086 - Fax: 945 609 261
izadi@izadi.com

VETUS 2006 T
tinta de toro 100%

**87** Colour: deep cherry, garnet rim. Nose: fresh fruit, sweet spices, new oak, balanced, red berry notes. Palate: unctuous, flavourful, fruity, good acidity, grainy tannins.

## VIÑAGUAREÑA

Ctra. Toro-Salamanca, km. 12,5
49800 Toro (Zamora)
☎: 980 568 013 - Fax: 980 568 134
info@vinotoro.com
www.vinotoro.com

MUNIA 2008 T
tinta de toro 100%

**84**

ETERNUM VITI 2007 T
tinta de toro 100%

**85** Colour: cherry, garnet rim. Nose: ripe fruit, spicy, creamy oak, toasty, complex, fruit liqueur notes. Palate: powerful, flavourful, toasty, round tannins.

MUNIA 2006 TC
tinta de toro 100%

**82**

## VIÑEDOS DE VILLAESTER

Villaester de Arriba
47540 Pedrosa del Rey (Valladolid)
☎: 948 645 008 - Fax: 948 645 166
info@familiabelasco.com
www.familiabelasco.com

TAURUS 2005 TC

**89** Colour: bright cherry, garnet rim. Nose: warm, ripe fruit, sweet spices, cocoa bean. Palate: creamy, ripe fruit, round tannins.

TAURUS 2005 T ROBLE

**88** Colour: dark-red cherry, garnet rim. Nose: fruit preserve, powerfull, sweet spices, cocoa bean. Palate: powerful, flavourful, round tannins, good finish.

VILLAESTER 2003 T

**91** Colour: dark-red cherry, garnet rim. Nose: fruit preserve, powerfull, spicy, aromatic coffee, dark chocolate. Palate: powerful, full, fruity, spicy, round tannins.

SOME OTHER WINERIES WITHIN THE DO:

**BIENVENIDA DE VINOS S.L.**
**BODEGA FLORENCIO SALGADO NARROS**
**BODEGA INDUSTRIA ALIMENTARIA VICENTE S.L.**
**BODEGAS MÄHLER-BESSE**
**BODEGA TAURINO S.L.**
**BODEGA VALPICULATA**
**DELISPAIN BODEGAS**
**NUNTIA VINI**

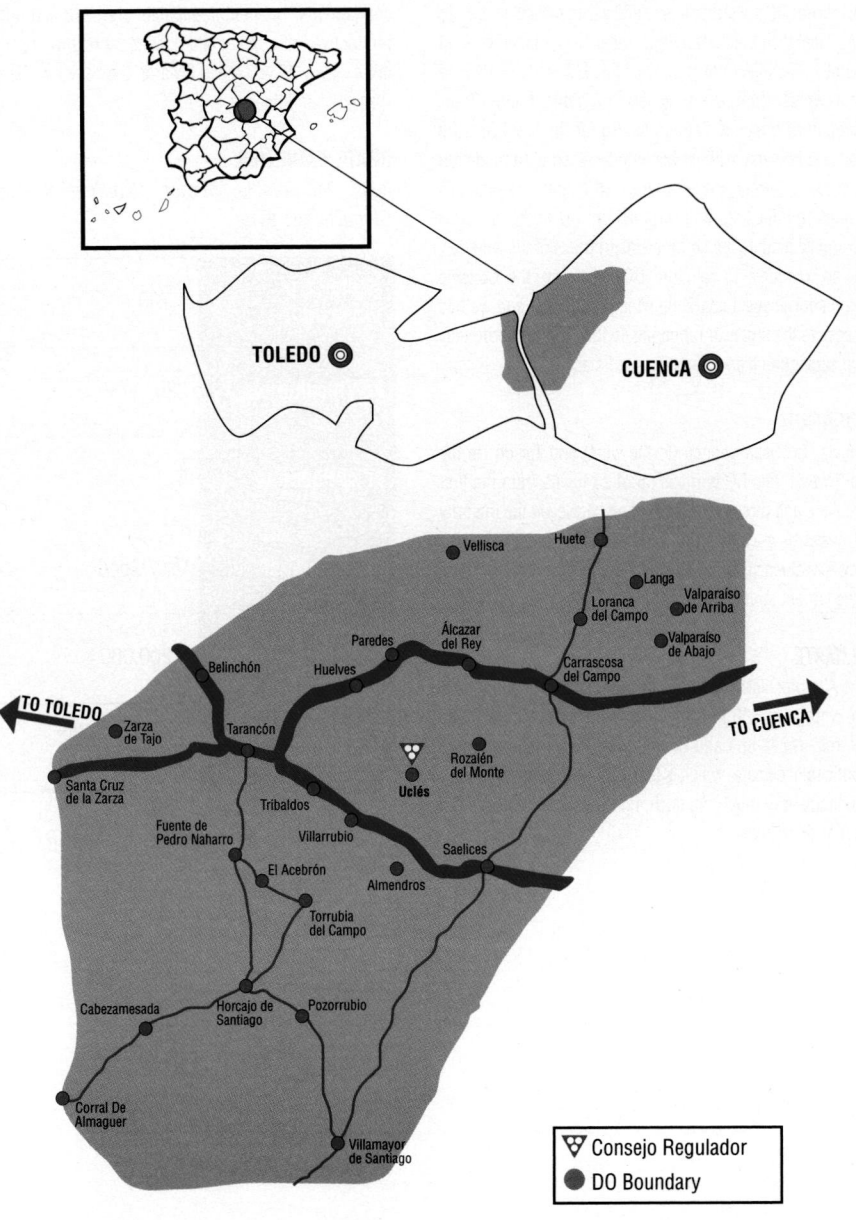

TOLEDO ◉

CUENCA ◉

Vellisca
Huete
Langa
Loranca
del Campo
Valparaíso
de Arriba
Álcazar
del Rey
Paredes
Carrascosa
del Campo
Valparaíso
de Abajo
Belinchón
Huelves
◀ TO TOLEDO
Zarza
de Tajo
Tarancón
Rozalén
del Monte
Uclés
TO CUENCA ▶
Santa Cruz
de la Zarza
Tribaldos
Fuente de
Pedro Naharro
Villarrubio
Saelices
El Acebrón
Almendros
Torrubia
del Campo
Cabezamesada
Horcajo de
Santiago
Pozorrubio
Corral De
Almaguer
Villamayor
de Santiago

▽ Consejo Regulador
● DO Boundary

# DO UCLÉS

## NEWS

The wineries from the province of Cuenca that have joined this recent DO are struggling to add wines to its cause, while they label their best renderings under DO La Mancha or VT Castilla. The initial philosophy of this DO was to catch the best wines from every winery to bottle them in the mandatory troncoconical bottle. So far the most forward house is Fontana, with its Misterio label, surely a model for the rest. Burocracy interferes with new regulations regarding labelling and production methods and this obviously hinders the commercial progress of the wineries. As an incentive to join the DO, this year the Consejo Regulador allowed sparkling wine production, and we had access to the first ever rendering on this kind, a chardonnay and sauvignon blanc from Finca la Estacada.

## LOCATION

Midway between Cuenca (to the west) and Toledo (to the northwest), this DO is made up of 25 towns from the first province and three from the second. However, the majority of vineyards are situated in Tarancón and the neighbouring towns of Cuenca, as far as Huete - where La Alcarria starts - the largest stretch of border in the DO.

## CLIMATE

The Altamira sierra forms gentle undulations that rise from an average of 600 metres in La Mancha, reaching 1,200 metres. These ups and downs produce variations in the continental climate, which is less extreme, milder and has a Mediterranean touch. As such, rain is scarce, more akin to a semi-dry climate.

## SOILS

Despite spreading over two provinces with different soil components, the communal soils are deep and not very productive, of a sandy and consistent texture, becoming more clayey as you move towards the banks of the rivers Riansares and Bendija.

## GRAPE VARIETIES:

**Reds**: *Tempranillo, Merlot, Cabernet Sauvignon, Garnacha* and *Syrah*.

| Hectares of Vineyard | 1,700 |
|---|---|
| Nº Viticulturists | 220 |
| Nº of Bodegas | 5 |
| 2008 Harvest | Very Good |
| 2007 Production | 1,200,000 l. |
| Marketing | 70% domestic 30% export |

**CONSEJO REGULADOR**
Plaza Pelayo Quintero, 1
16450 Uclés (Cuenca)
☎: 969 135 056 - Fax: 969 135 056
@ info@vinosdeucles.com
www.vinosdeucles.com

## GENERAL CHARACTERISTICS OF THE WINES:

| | |
|---|---|
| **REDS** | The majority are *Cencibel*, producing young and also slightly aged wines, defined by aromas of very fresh grape skins, a very flavoursome and rounded body, and fruit with an alcohol content/acidity balance better controlled than in other nearby areas of La Mancha. Far removed from those more rustic wines, a hint of terroir and extra minerals is detected in these, due to the presence of minerals dissolved in the soils. |

## 2008 VINTAGE RATING:

# AVERAGE

## BODEGA LA DEFENSA

Avda. de Castilla La Mancha, 38
45370 Santa Cruz de la Zarza (Toledo)
☎: 925 143 234 - Fax: 925 125 154
bodegasladefensa@bodegasladefensa.es
www.bodegasladefensa.es

VICUS 2007 T ROBLE
tempranillo 100%

**81**

VICUS 2006 TC
tempranillo 100%

**84**

VICUS 2006 T
tempranillo 100%

**78**

## COOPERATIVA NUESTRA SEÑORA DE LA SOLEDAD

Ctra. Tarancón, s/n
16411 Fuente de Pedro Naharro (Cuenca)
☎: 969 125 039 - Fax: 969 125 907
info@bodegasoledad.com
www.bodegasoledad.com

BISIESTO 2005 TC
tempranillo 100%

**78**

## FINCA LA ESTACADA

Ctra. N-400, km. 103
16400 Tarancón (Cuenca)
☎: 969 327 099 - Fax: 969 327 199
fincalaestacada@fincalaestacada.com
www.fincalaestacada.com

FINCA LA ESTACADA 2008 B
chardonnay, sauvignon blanc

**75**

FINCA LA ESTACADA 6 MESES BARRICA 2008 T
ROBLE
tempranillo

**85** Colour: dark-red cherry. Nose: ripe fruit, creamy oak, fruit expression. Palate: spicy, fruity, flavourful, fleshy.

LA ESTACADA 2008
syrah, merlot

**87** Colour: deep cherry. Nose: ripe fruit, balsamic herbs, sweet spices. Palate: ripe fruit, creamy, round tannins.

## FONTANA

Extramuros, s/n
16411 Fuente de Pedro Naharro (Cuenca)
☎: 969 125 433 - Fax: 969 125 387
bf@bodegasfontana.com
www.bodegasfontana.com

MISTERIO DE FONTANA 2006 T ROBLE

**89** Colour: cherry, purple rim. Nose: medium intensity, ripe fruit, sweet spices, cocoa bean, balanced. Palate: flavourful, powerful, fleshy, spicy.

SOME OTHER WINERIES WITHIN THE DO:

**LA VID Y LA ESPIGA S.C., C-LM**

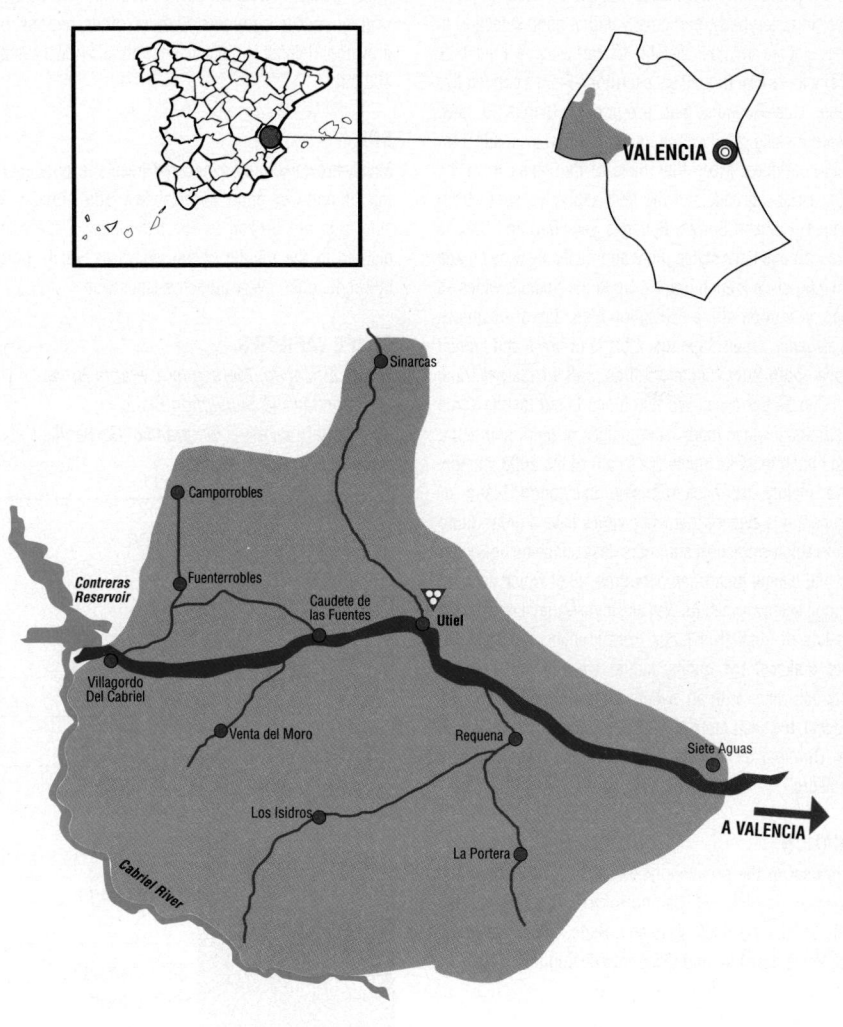

Consejo Regulador

DO Boundary

## NEWS

Utiel-Requena is progressing adequately and is even surprising everybody, particularly with a good selection of whites that are an unusual sight –to start with– in a red, bulk and single-varietal (bobal) wine territory. From a cooperative region, Utiel-Requena has progressed thanks to new, forward-looking wineries and fresh, young wines made from foreign varieties. More than 60% of the wines from the region travel abroad, and the best examples come from wineries (Hispano Suizas, Bodegas Vegalfaro and Chozas Carrascal) that have styled more approachable wines made from long-cycle French grapes. Up in our podium wines as varied as Impromptu, a sauvignon blanc full of freshness and elegance, Quod Superius, a blend of bobal and French grapes –both from Hispano Suizas, and a cabernet franc from Chozas Carrascal. We also found in our tasting some experimental wines made from malbec or pinot noir and a good bunch of white wines (44 in all) of the 2008 vintage, made mainly from chardonnay, sauvignon blanc or macabeo. It is evident that white wines have a great future in this region with short summers, less sunshine hours per year and overall higher temperatures, all of which account for good acidity levels. As well as single-varietal renderings with lots of fresh fruit made from French grapes, in the lower ranks of the quality ladder we still find creamy, spirituous wines with an evident excess of oak ageing. As for bobal, the best, more elegant renderings are Arte Mayor, from Dominio de la Vega, and Corolilla, from Bodegas Murviedro.

## LOCATION

In thewest of the province of Valencia. It comprises the municipal districts of Camporrobles, Caudete de las Fuentes, Fuenterrobles, Requena, Siete Aguas, Sinarcas, Utiel, Venta del Moro and Villagordo de Cabriel.

## CLIMATE

Continental,with Mediterranean influences, coldwinters and slightly milder summers than in other regions of the province. Rainfall is quite scarcewith an annual average of 400 mm.

## SOIL

Mainly brownish-grey, almost red limestone, poor in organic matter andwith good permeability. The horizon of the vineyards are broken by the silhouette of the odd tree planted in the middle of the vineyards,which, bordered bywoods, offer a very attractive landscape.

## GRAPE VARIETIES:

**White:** *Macabeo, Merseguera, Planta Nova, Chardonnay* and *Sauvignon Blanc.*
**Red:** *Bobal* (majority), *Tempranillo, Garnacha, Cabernet Sauvignon, Merlot, Syrah.*

| | |
|---|---|
| Hectares of Vineyard | 40,606 |
| Nº Viticulturists | 7,500 |
| Nº of Bodegas | 115 |
| 2008 Harvest | Good |
| 2007 Production | 35,328,849 l. |
| Marketing | 38% domestic 62% export |

**CONSEJO REGULADOR**
Sevilla, 12. Apdo. Correos 61
46300 Utiel (Valencia).
☎: 962 171 062 - Fax: 962 172 185
@ info@utielrequena.org
www.utielrequena.org

## GENERAL CHARACTERISTICS OF THE WINES:

| | |
|---|---|
| **WHITES** | Firstly, there are the most traditional from *Merseguera*, fresh with wild notes; secondly, the more modern variety from *Macabeo*, with greater aromatic potency, fresh and light; and finally, single variety wines from *Chardonnay*, some fermented in barrels. |
| **ROSÉS** | Produced from *Bobal*, they have a pink to salmon colour; their aromas are fresh and fruity,with some what wild and vegetative aromas; on the palate they are fresh and pleasant. |
| **REDS** | As opposed to the traditional wines from *Bobal*, with a lot of colour but with some what rustic notes, the *Garnacha* variety gives rise to young, fresh, fruity and very correct red wines. For the Crianza wines some *Bobal* is included. Those of this type are flavourful, rounded and, on occasion, some what warm. |
| **ESPUMOSOS** | Cavas and Espumosos are produced according to the traditional methods not included in the DO Cava. |

## 2008 VINTAGE RATING:

## GOOD

## ALVAREZ NÖLTING

Finca El Pinarejo, Camino del Pinarejo, s/n
46390 San Antonio de Requena (Valencia)
☎: 963 290 696 - Fax: 963 445 463
info@alvareznolting.com
www.alvareznolting.com

ALVAREZ NÖLTING CHARDONNAY 2007 BFB
chardonnay 80%, sauvignon blanc 20%

**89** Colour: bright yellow. Nose: ripe fruit, fresh, creamy oak, smoky, wild herbs. Palate: powerful, flavourful, rich, creamy.

ALVAREZ NÖLTING MAGNUM 2006 T
tempranillo 70%, cabernet sauvignon 30%

**89** Colour: dark-red cherry. Nose: complex, varietal, mineral, smoky. Palate: fresh, fruity, flavourful, ripe fruit, fruity aftestaste.

SOLEDAD DE ALVAREZ NÖLTING 2006 T
cabernet sauvignon 25%, tempranillo 75%

**88** Colour: dark-red cherry. Nose: expressive, varietal, fresh, macerated fruit, mineral. Palate: powerful, flavourful, fruity, complex, creamy, fruity aftestaste.

## BODEGA SEBIRAN

Pérez Galdos, 1
46352 Campo Arcis-Requena (Valencia)
☎: 962 301 326 - Fax: 962 303 966
info@bodegasebiran.com
www.bodegasebiran.com

TERRANEO 2008 B
macabeo 100%

**83**

TERRANEO BOBAL 2008 RD
bobal 100%

**85** Colour: rose, purple rim. Nose: ripe fruit, red berry notes, floral. Palate: fleshy, powerful, fruity, fresh.

COTO D´ARCIS BOBAL 2007 T
bobal 100%

**84**

COTO D'ARCIS TEMPRANILLO 2007 T
tempranillo 100%

**84**

TERRÁNEO 2007 T

**84**

COTO D'ARCIS 2005 TC
cabernet sauvignon 55%, tempranillo 30%, bobal 10%, garnacha 5%

**85** Colour: very deep cherry. Nose: medium intensity, fruit liqueur notes, spicy. Palate: powerful, spicy, round tannins.

COTO D'ARCIS 2003 TR
tempranillo 70%, cabernet sauvignon 20%, merlot 10%

**85** Colour: cherry, garnet rim. Nose: ripe fruit, spicy, creamy oak, toasty. Palate: powerful, flavourful, toasty, round tannins.

COTO D'ARCIS VENDIMIA SELECCIONADA 2001 T
tempranillo 80%, cabernet sauvignon 15%, garnacha 5%

**85** Colour: pale ruby, brick rim edge. Nose: elegant, spicy, fine reductive notes, wet leather, aged wood nuances, fruit liqueur notes. Palate: spicy, fine tannins, elegant, long.

COTO D'ARCIS 1999 TGR
tempranillo 75%, cabernet sauvignon 15%, garnacha 5%, bobal 5%

**83**

COTO D´ARCIS ESPECIAL BR

**87** Colour: bright yellow, pale. Nose: neat, fruit expression, dried flowers, fine lees. Palate: flavourful, fruity, good acidity.

COTO D´ARCIS BR

**83**

COTO D´ARCIS BN

**85** Colour: yellow, bright straw. Nose: candied fruit, floral. Palate: fresh, fruity, long.

## BODEGAS ARANLEÓN

Ctra. Caudete, 3
46310 Los Marcos -Caudete de las Fuentes (Valencia)
☎: 963 631 640 - Fax: 963 636 534
bgarcia@aranleon.com
www.aranleon.com

ARANLEÓN SÓLO 2007 T

**85** Colour: cherry, garnet rim. Nose: fruit preserve, overripe fruit, warm, spicy, toasty. Palate: sweetness, powerful, concentrated.

ARANLEÓN SELECCIÓN ESPECIAL 2007 T
tempranillo, cabernet sauvignon, bobal

**85** Colour: black cherry. Nose: expressive, overripe fruit, dark chocolate, sweet spices, toasty. Palate: flavourful, full, harsh oak tannins.

EL ARBOL BLANCO 2005 TC

**90** Colour: cherry, garnet rim. Nose: ripe fruit, spicy, creamy oak, toasty, complex. Palate: powerful, flavourful, toasty, round tannins.

## BODEGAS ATRIO

Apostol Santiago, 42
46330 Camporrobles (Valencia)
☎: 629 661 183 - Fax: 962 181 518
administracion@bodegasatrio.es
www.bodegasatrio.es

MATTICES DE LA BODEGA 2007 B
sauvignon blanc, chardonnay

**83**

SEDUCCIÓN DE LA BODEGA 2005 TC
bobal, syrah, tempranillo

**86** Colour: cherry, garnet rim. Nose: characterful, ripe fruit, spicy. Palate: flavourful, powerful, spicy.

PASSION DE LA BODEGA 2005 TR
bobal, merlot, cabernet sauvignon

**85** Colour: cherry, garnet rim. Nose: toasty, caramel, ripe fruit. Palate: powerful, spirituous, spicy.

## BODEGAS CASA DEL PINAR

Los Isidros - Venta del Moro, s/n
46310 Venta del Moro (Valencia)
☎: 962 139 121 - Fax: 962 139 120
diment@telefonica.net
www.casadelpinar.com

CASA DEL PINAR 2002 TR
bobal, merlot, cabernet sauvignon, tempranillo, syrah

**86** Colour: dark-red cherry, orangey edge. Nose: dark chocolate, fruit preserve, sweet spices, old leather. Palate: powerful, flavourful, ripe fruit, harsh oak tannins.

VERDERÓN
SANFIR

## BODEGAS CERROGALLINA

Artana, 22
12540 Villareal de los Infantes (Castellón)

☎: 676 897 251
beatrizrequena@cerrogallina.com
www.cerrogallina.com

HORMA DEL HOYO 2007 T
cabernet sauvignon 45%, merlot 45%, syrah 10%

**86** Colour: cherry, garnet rim. Nose: powerfull, ripe fruit, pattiserie. Palate: flavourful, powerful, round tannins.

## BODEGAS COVILOR

Antonio Bartual, 21
46313 Cuevas de Utiel (Valencia)
☎: 962 182 053 - Fax: 962 182 055
laboratorio@bodegascovilor.com
www.bodegascovilor.com

ALTO CUEVAS MACABEO 2008 B
macabeo 100%

**86** Colour: bright straw. Nose: fresh, fresh fruit, white flowers, expressive. Palate: flavourful, fruity, good acidity, balanced.

ALTO CUEVAS 2008 RD
bobal 100%

**85** Colour: rose, purple rim. Nose: ripe fruit, red berry notes, floral. Palate: fleshy, powerful, fruity, fresh.

ALTO CUEVAS TEMPRANILLO 2007 T
tempranillo 100%

**84**

SUCESIÓN BOBAL 2005 T FERMENTADO EN BARRICA
bobal 100%

**83**

SUCESIÓN BOBAL 2004 TR
bobal 100%

**85** Colour: cherry, garnet rim. Nose: dark chocolate, spicy, fruit liqueur notes. Palate: flavourful, concentrated, spicy.

SUCESIÓN BOBAL 2004 TC
bobal 100%

**83**

## BODEGAS CUEVA

Mayor, 2
46357 La Portera (Valencia)
☎: 963 557 328 - Fax: 963 555 672
info@bodegascueva.com
www.bodegascueva.com

**CUEVA 2008 T**
tempranillo, bobal, garnacha, cabernet sauvignon

**82**

**CUEVA SELECCIÓN FINCA 2007 T**

**86** Colour: cherry, garnet rim. Nose: powerful, ripe fruit, warm, scrubland. Palate: powerful, good structure, concentrated.

**CUEVA BARRICA SELECCIÓN 2006 T**

**90** Colour: cherry, garnet rim. Nose: powerful, sweet spices, pattiserie. Palate: powerful, flavourful, spicy, ripe fruit. Personality.

## BODEGAS HISPANO SUIZAS

Travesía de la Industria, 5
46370 Campos Arcis (Requena) (Valencia)

☎: 661 894 200 - Fax: 963 523 975
ceo@bodegashispanosuizas.com
www.bodegashispanosuizas.com

**IMPROMPTU 2008 B**
sauvignon blanc 100%

**93** Colour: bright yellow. Nose: ripe fruit, sweet spices, creamy oak, fragrant herbs, elegant. Palate: rich, flavourful, fresh, good acidity.

**BASSUS PREMIUM 2007 T**
bobal, cabernet sauvignon, merlot, petit verdot

**90** Colour: dark-red cherry. Nose: characterful, fruit liqueur notes, sweet spices, dark chocolate. Palate: fleshy, fruity, great length, harsh oak tannins.

**BASSUS PINOT NOIR 2007 T**
pinot noir 100%

**88** Colour: very deep cherry. Nose: medium intensity, characterful, aromatic coffee, toasty, ripe fruit. Palate: flavourful, powerful, spicy, ripe fruit.

**QUOD SUPERIUS 2006 T**
bobal, merlot, syrah, cabernet sauvignon

**93** Colour: cherry, garnet rim. Nose: powerful, spicy, mineral, ripe fruit, fruit expression, creamy oak. Palate: flavourful, long, ripe fruit, creamy.

**BASSUS PREMIUM 2006 T**
bobal, cabernet sauvignon, merlot, syrah

**90** Colour: very deep cherry. Nose: ripe fruit, expressive, fragrant herbs, mineral. Palate: flavourful, good structure, fruity, fresh, round tannins.

**BASSUS PINOT NOIR 2006 T**
pinot noir

**85** Colour: very deep cherry. Nose: fruit preserve, sweet spices, new oak, toasty. Palate: good structure, fruity, fresh, powerful, round tannins.

## BODEGAS IRANZO

Ctra. de Madrid, 60
46315 Caudete de las Fuentes (Valencia)
☎: 962 319 282 - Fax: 962 319 282
comercial@bodegasiranzo.com
www.bodegasiranzo.com

**BODEGAS IRANZO TEMPRANILLO SELECCIÓN 2008 T**
tempranillo 100%

**80**

## CAÑADA HONDA 2008 T
tempranillo 70%, cabernet sauvignon 30%

**75**

## FINCA CAÑADA HONDA 2007 T BARRICA
cabernet sauvignon 30%, tempranillo 70%

**82**

## FINCA CAÑADA HONDA 2005 TC
tempranillo 70%, cabernet sauvignon 30%

**85** Colour: cherry, garnet rim. Nose: fruit preserve, powerfull, aromatic coffee. Palate: powerful, sweetness, round tannins.

## FINCA CAÑADA HONDA 2004 TR
tempranillo 70%, cabernet sauvignon 30%

**84**

## BODEGAS MURVIEDRO

Ampliación Pol. El Romeral, s/n
46340 Requena (Valencia)
☎: 962 329 003 - Fax: 962 329 002
murviedro@murviedro.es
www.murviedro.es

### CUEVA DE LA ESPERANZA 2008 B
chardonnay 80%, pinot noir 20%

**85** Colour: yellow, pale. Nose: floral, fragrant herbs, tropical fruit, complex. Palate: fresh, fruity, easy to drink.

### ROSA DE MURVIEDRO 2008 RD
cabernet sauvignon 75%, sauvignon blanc 25%

**86** Colour: rose, purple rim. Nose: powerful, ripe fruit, red berry notes, floral, expressive. Palate: fleshy, powerful, fruity, fresh.

### CUEVA DE LA CULPA 2007 T
bobal 60%, merlot 40%

**90** Colour: dark-red cherry. Nose: powerful, ripe fruit, raspberry, spicy. Palate: flavourful, fleshy, good structure, ripe fruit, round tannins.

### COROLILLA 2006 TC
bobal 100%

**88** Colour: cherry, garnet rim. Nose: ripe fruit, spicy, creamy oak, toasty, complex. Palate: powerful, flavourful, toasty, round tannins.

### COROLILLA 2005 TR
bobal 100%

**87** Colour: cherry, garnet rim. Nose: ripe fruit, spicy, creamy oak, toasty, complex. Palate: powerful, flavourful, toasty, round tannins.

## BODEGAS PALMERA

Paraje Corral Charco de Agut
46300 Utiel (Valencia)
☎: 962 320 720 - Fax: 962 320 720
klauslauerbach@hotmail.com
www.bodegas-palmera.com

### VIÑA CABRIEL 2007 T
tempranillo 65%, merlot 20%, cabernet sauvignon 15%

**86** Colour: cherry, garnet rim. Nose: medium intensity, fruit liqueur notes, ripe fruit, spicy. Palate: flavourful, powerful, spicy.

### PALMERA BOBAL Y TEMPRANILLO 2007 T
tempranillo 50%, bobal 50%

**80**

### VIÑA CABRIEL SUPERIOR 2006 T
tempranillo 70%, merlot 20%, cabernet sauvignon 10%

**87** Colour: cherry, garnet rim. Nose: medium intensity, ripe fruit, scrubland. Palate: flavourful, good structure, spicy.

### L'ANGELET 2006 TC
tempranillo 55%, cabernet sauvignon 40%, bobal 5%

**85** Colour: cherry, purple rim. Nose: warm, fruit liqueur notes, spicy. Palate: fleshy, powerful, grainy tannins.

## BODEGAS SIERRA NORTE

P.I. El Romeral. Transporte, Parc. C2
46340 Requena (Valencia)
☎: 962 323 099 - Fax: 962 323 048
info@bodegasierranorte.com
www.bodegasierranorte.com

### CERRO BERCIAL SELECCIÓN 2008 B
chardonnay, sauvignon blanc

**88** Colour: bright yellow. Nose: powerful, sweet spices, creamy oak, fragrant herbs, fruit preserve. Palate: rich, smoky aftertaste, flavourful, fresh, good acidity.

### FUENTESECA 2008 B
macabeo 80%, sauvignon blanc 20%

**87** Colour: bright straw. Nose: fresh, fresh fruit, white flowers, expressive. Palate: flavourful, fruity, good acidity, balanced.

## HERACLIO 2007 B
macabeo 60%, sauvignon blanc 20%, chardonnay 20%

**88** Colour: bright yellow. Nose: powerful, ripe fruit, sweet spices, creamy oak, fragrant herbs. Palate: rich, smoky aftertaste, flavourful, fresh, good acidity.

## CERRO BERCIAL EL ROSADO 2008 RD
bobal 40%, merlot 40%, garnacha 20%

**87** Colour: rose, purple rim. Nose: powerful, ripe fruit, red berry notes, floral, expressive. Palate: fleshy, powerful, fruity, fresh.

## CERRO BERCIAL 2008 RD
bobal 100%

**82**

## FUENTESECA 2008 T
bobal 60%, syrah 40%

**84**

## CERRO BERCIAL 2006 T FERMENTADO EN BARRICA
tempranillo 65%, bobal 35%

**88** Colour: cherry, purple rim. Nose: expressive, fruit liqueur notes, dark chocolate, sweet spices. Palate: good structure, flavourful, long, great length.

## FUENTESECA 2006 TC
tempranillo 100%

**86** Colour: bright cherry. Nose: ripe fruit, sweet spices, creamy oak. Palate: flavourful, fruity, toasty, round tannins.

## CERRO BERCIAL PARCELA "LADERA LOS CANTOS" 2005 T
bobal 63%, cabernet sauvignon 37%

**90** Colour: cherry, garnet rim. Nose: powerful, ripe fruit, creamy oak, sweet spices. Palate: flavourful, powerful, spicy.

## CERRO BERCIAL 2005 TC
tempranillo 57%, bobal 43%

**87** Colour: cherry, garnet rim. Nose: ripe fruit, spicy, creamy oak, toasty, complex. Palate: powerful, flavourful, toasty, round tannins.

## HERACLIO 2005 T
bobal 60%, cabernet sauvignon 40%

**82**

## CERRO BERCIAL 2004 TR
tempranillo 65%, bobal 20%, cabernet sauvignon 15%

**88** Colour: cherry, garnet rim. Nose: ripe fruit, spicy, creamy oak, toasty. Palate: powerful, flavourful, toasty, round tannins.

# BODEGAS TORROJA

Nogueral, 3
46357 Azagador (Valencia)
☎: 962 304 232 - Fax: 962 303 833
herve@bodegastorroja.com
www.bodegastorroja.com

## CAÑADA MAZÁN TARDANA 2008 B
tardana 100%

**84**

## SYBARUS TARDANA 2008 B
tardana 100%

**83**

## CAÑADA MAZÁN 2008 RD
bobal

**88** Colour: rose, purple rim. Nose: powerful, ripe fruit, red berry notes, floral, expressive. Palate: fleshy, powerful, fruity, fresh.

## DULCE DE BOBAL 2008 T
bobal 100%

**88** Colour: bright cherry. Nose: expressive, raspberry, violet drops, candied fruit. Palate: good structure, sweet, flavourful, spirituous.

## CAÑADA MAZÁN 2007 T FERMENTADO EN BARRICA

**83**

## SYBARUS SYRAH 2006 T
syrah 100%

**84**

## SYBARUS BOBAL 2005 TC
bobal 100%

**85** Colour: pale ruby, brick rim edge. Nose: fruit liqueur notes, ripe fruit, spicy, old leather. Palate: concentrated, flavourful, long, harsh oak tannins.

## CAÑADA MAZÁN 2004 TC
tempranillo, cabernet sauvignon

**74**

## SYBARUS CABERNET SAUVIGNON 2003 TC
cabernet sauvignon 100%

**83**

## SYBARUS 2002 TR
tempranillo, merlot, cabernet sauvignon

**84**

## BODEGAS UTIELANAS

San Fernando, 18
46300 Utiel (Valencia)
☎: 962 171 157 - Fax: 962 170 801
modesto@bodegasutielanas.com
www.bodegasutielanas.com

VEGA INFANTE 2007 BFB
macabeo

**88** Colour: bright yellow. Nose: powerful, ripe fruit, sweet spices, creamy oak, fragrant herbs. Palate: rich, smoky aftertaste, flavourful, fresh, good acidity.

SUEÑOS DEL MEDITERRANEO 2008 T
bobal, tempranillo

**84**

VEGA INFANTE MADURADO EN BARRICA 2008 T
bobal, tempranillo

**90** Colour: cherry, purple rim. Nose: fresh fruit, floral, fruit expression, undergrowth, characterful. Palate: flavourful, fruity, good acidity, round tannins.

VEGA INFANTE 2004 TC
bobal, tempranillo

**83**

VEGA INFANTE 2003 TR
bobal

**85** Colour: cherry, garnet rim. Nose: powerful, fruit preserve, spicy, toasty. Palate: powerful, fleshy, round tannins.

## BODEGAS Y VIÑEDOS DE UTIEL

Finca El Renegado, s/n
46315 Caudete de las Fuentes (Valencia)
☎: 962 174 029 - Fax: 962 171 432
ventas@bodegasdeutiel.com
www.bodegasdeutiel.com

NODUS CHARDONNAY 2008 B
chardonnay 100%

**85** Colour: bright yellow. Nose: powerful, ripe fruit, fragrant herbs. Palate: rich, flavourful, fresh, good acidity.

ACTUM 2008 B
sauvignon blanc 100%

**83**

ACTUM VARIETAL 2007 T
merlot 50%, cabernet sauvignon 50%

**87** Colour: cherry, purple rim. Nose: red berry notes, ripe fruit, floral. Palate: spicy, great length, flavourful, slightly dry, soft tannins.

NODUS MERLOT DELIRIUM 2007 T
merlot 100%

**84**

NODUS TINTO DE AUTOR 2006 TC
merlot 45%, syrah 15%, cabernet sauvignon 25%, bobal 15%

**87** Colour: cherry, garnet rim. Nose: caramel, fruit preserve, powerfull. Palate: fleshy, slightly overripe, round tannins.

CAPELLANA 2006 TC
tempranillo 100%

**75**

ACTUM 2005 TC
merlot 50%, cabernet sauvignon 50%

**86** Colour: cherry, garnet rim. Nose: powerful, fruit preserve, sweet spices. Palate: flavourful, fruity, round tannins.

NODUS RESERVA DE FAMILIA 2004 TR
tempranillo 65%, cabernet sauvignon 20%, syrah 15%

**87** Colour: cherry, garnet rim. Nose: powerful, fruit preserve, spicy. Palate: pruney, round tannins.

CAPELLANA 2004 TR
tempranillo 50%, cabernet sauvignon 50%

**86** Colour: cherry, garnet rim. Nose: medium intensity, ripe fruit, roasted coffee. Palate: powerful, concentrated, round tannins.

NODUS SUMMUN 2003 TR
tempranillo 60%, cabernet sauvignon 20%, merlot 20%

**83**

## CHERUBINO VALSANGIACOMO S.A.

Ctra. Cheste-Godelleta, km. 1
46370 Chiva (Valencia)
☎: 962 510 451 - Fax: 962 511 361
cvalsangiacomo@cherubino.es
www.cherubino.es

MARQUÉS DE CARO 2008 RD
bobal 100%

**83**

SELECCION DE OTOÑO 2004 TC
tempranillo 50%, cabernet sauvignon 50%

**85** Colour: cherry, garnet rim. Nose: spicy, pattiserie, ripe fruit. Palate: flavourful, spicy, round tannins.

## CHOZAS CARRASCAL

Vereda San Antonio
46390 San Antonio de Requena (Valencia)
☎: 963 410 395 - Fax: 963 168 067
chozas@chozascarrascal.es
www.chozascarrascal.es

LAS TRES 2008 BFB
chardonnay, sauvignon blanc, macabeo

**89** Colour: bright straw. Nose: sweet spices, powerfull, candied fruit, scrubland. Palate: flavourful, fleshy, complex.

LAS CUATRO 2008 RD
tempranillo, garnacha, syrah, merlot

**88** Colour: brilliant rose. Nose: elegant, candied fruit, dried flowers, fragrant herbs, red berry notes. Palate: flavourful, good acidity, long, spicy.

EL CABERNET DE CHOZAS CARRASCAL 2007 T
cabernet franc

**91** Colour: black cherry. Nose: ripe fruit, sweet spices, dark chocolate, aromatic coffee. Palate: flavourful, powerful, good structure, harsh oak tannins.

LAS OCHO 2006 T
bobal Syrah, garnacha, merlot, tempranillo, monastrell, cabernet franc, cabernet sauvignon

**89** Colour: deep cherry. Nose: spicy, ripe fruit, varietal. Palate: flavourful, good structure, round tannins, spicy, balanced, toasty.

JUANPEDROS 2006 T
garnacha, syrah

**88** Colour: bright cherry. Nose: ripe fruit, sweet spices, creamy oak. Palate: flavourful, fruity, toasty, round tannins.

## COVIÑAS COOP. V.

Avda. Rafael Duyos s/n
46340 Requena (Valencia)
☎: 962 300 680 - Fax: 962 302 651
covinas@covinas.com
www.covinas.com

VIÑA ENTERIZO 2008 B
macabeo

**84**

AULA MACABEO BLANCO DE LÁGRIMA 2008 B
macabeo

**83**

VIÑA ENTERIZO BOBAL 2008 RD
bobal

**87** Colour: rose, purple rim. Nose: powerful, ripe fruit, red berry notes, floral, expressive. Palate: fleshy, powerful, fruity, fresh.

AULA BOBAL ROSADO DE LÁGRIMA 2008 RD
bobal

**85** Colour: rose, purple rim. Nose: ripe fruit, powerfull. Palate: warm, ripe fruit.

VIÑA ENTERIZO TEMPRANILLO 2007 T
tempranillo

**84**

VIÑA ENTERIZO 2006 TC
garnacha, bobal, tempranillo

**88** Colour: cherry, garnet rim. Nose: ripe fruit, spicy, creamy oak. Palate: powerful, flavourful, fleshy.

AULA MERLOT 2005 TC
merlot

**89** Colour: cherry, garnet rim. Nose: medium intensity, fruit preserve, spicy. Palate: spicy, ripe fruit, round tannins.

AULA SYRAH 2004 TC
syrah

**88** Colour: cherry, garnet rim. Nose: aromatic coffee, dark chocolate, ripe fruit. Palate: powerful, spicy.

AULA CABERNET SAUVIGNON 2004 TC
cabernet sauvignon

**87** Colour: cherry, garnet rim. Nose: medium intensity, sweet spices, toasty. Palate: flavourful, powerful, ripe fruit.

ENTERIZO 2002 TR
garnacha

**79**

## CRIADORES ARTESANOS S.L.

Avda. Virgen de Tejeda, 28
46320 Sinarcas (Valencia)
☎: 962 170 028 - Fax: 962 306 175
bodega@vinospasiego.com
www.vinospasiego.com

PASIEGO 2008 B

**87** Colour: bright straw. Nose: white flowers, fruit preserve. Palate: flavourful, fruity, good acidity, balanced.

PASIEGO DE AUTOR 2005 TC

**89** Colour: cherry, garnet rim. Nose: ripe fruit, spicy, creamy oak, toasty, complex. Palate: powerful, flavourful, toasty, round tannins.

PASIEGO 2005 TC

**86** Colour: cherry, garnet rim. Nose: fruit preserve, ripe fruit, spicy, toasty. Palate: powerful, spirituous, round tannins.

PASIEGO 2004 TR

**85** Colour: cherry, garnet rim. Nose: ripe fruit, powerfull, sweet spices. Palate: flavourful, powerful, ripe fruit, round tannins.

## DOMINIO DE LA VEGA

Ctra. Madrid - Valencia, km. 270,6
46390 San Antonio. Requena (Valencia)
☎: 962 320 570 - Fax: 962 320 330
info@dominiodelavega.com
www.dominiodelavega.com

SAUVIGNON BLANC DOMINIO DE LA VEGA 2008 BFB
sauvignon blanc, chardonnay, macabeo

**81**

DOMINIO DE LA VEGA 2006 T ROBLE
bobal, cabernet

**85** Colour: dark-red cherry, orangey edge. Nose: medium intensity, ripe fruit, creamy oak, sweet spices. Palate: flavourful, fruity, round tannins, spicy.

DOMINIO DE LA VEGA 2005 TC

**86** Colour: light cherry, bright ochre rim. Nose: fruit liqueur notes, toasty, caramel. Palate: light-bodied, toasty, spirituous, round tannins, roasted-coffee aftertaste.

DOMINIO DE LA VEGA 2004 TR

**85** Colour: cherry, garnet rim. Nose: fruit liqueur notes, spicy, aged wood nuances, powerfull. Palate: flavourful, good structure, powerful, round tannins.

ARTE MAYOR III T
bobal

**89** Colour: dark-red cherry, orangey edge. Nose: powerful, elegant, ripe fruit, cocoa bean, spicy, warm. Palate: flavourful, powerful, fruity, round tannins.

AÑACAL DOMINIO DE LA VEGA

## DOMINIO DEL ARENAL

Pedanía de San Juan s/n
46390 Requena (Valencia)
☎: 962 320 001 - Fax: 962 320 624
info@dominiodelarenal.com
www.dominiodelarenal.com

VIÑA CALDERÓN 2007 B
macabeo 100%

**75**

DOMINIO DEL ARENAL DULCE BOBAL 2007 T
bobal

**86** Colour: cherry, garnet rim. Nose: medium intensity, candied fruit, overripe fruit. Palate: sweet, good acidity, balanced.

DOMINIO DEL ARENAL SHIRAZ 2006 T
syrah 100%

**83**

DOMINIO DEL ARENAL MERLOT 2005 T
merlot 100%

**81**

VIÑA CALDERON 2004 TC
tempranillo

**83**

DOMINIO DEL ARENAL 2002 TR
tempranillo 50%, syrah 50%

**83**

DOMINIO DEL ARENAL 2002 TC
tempranillo 50%, syrah 50%

**82**

## ELVIWINES S.L.

Granollers, 27 G
08173 Sant Cugat (Barcelona)
☎: 935 343 026 - Fax: 935 441 374
info@elviwines.com
www.elviwines.com

MAKOR DE ELVIWINES 2007 T
bobal 85%, cabernet sauvignon 15%

**86** Colour: cherry, garnet rim. Nose: powerful, ripe fruit, fragrant herbs, balsamic herbs. Palate: flavourful, powerful, spicy.

## EMILIO CLEMENTE

Camino de San Blas, s/n
46340 Requena (Valencia)
☎: 963 173 584 - Fax: 963 173 726
info@eclemente.es
www.eclemente.es

FLORANTE 2007 BFB
chardonnay 50%, sauvignon blanc 30%, tardana 20%

**88** Colour: bright yellow. Nose: powerful, ripe fruit, sweet spices, creamy oak, fragrant herbs. Palate: rich, smoky aftertaste, flavourful, fresh, good acidity.

EMILIO CLEMENTE 2006 TC
tempranillo 45%, cabernet sauvignon 25%, merlot 25%, bobal 5%

**85** Colour: pale ruby, brick rim edge. Nose: fruit preserve, fruit liqueur notes, wet leather. Palate: fleshy, grainy tannins.

PEÑAS NEGRAS 2005 T
tempranillo 55%, cabernet sauvignon 25%, merlot 20%

**85** Colour: cherry, garnet rim. Nose: fruit preserve, ripe fruit, dark chocolate, roasted coffee. Palate: flavourful, powerful, spicy, round tannins.

EMILIO CLEMENTE EXCELENCIA 2006 CRIANZA
tempranillo 20%, cabernet sauvignon 20%, merlot 50%

**88** Colour: cherry, garnet rim. Nose: fruit liqueur notes, toasty, spicy, wet leather. Palate: flavourful, spicy, great length.

EXCELENCIA

## FINCA CASA LO ALTO

Ctra. Caudete - Los Isidros
46310 Venta del Moro (Valencia)
☎: 962 139 381
info@casa-lo-alto.es
www.casa-lo-alto.es

FINCA CASA LO ALTO 2006 TC

**82**

FINCA CASA LO ALTO 2004 TR

**87** Colour: cherry, garnet rim. Nose: fruit liqueur notes, fruit liqueur notes, aged wood nuances. Palate: fleshy, harsh oak tannins.

FINCA CASA LO ALTO ESP

**80**

## FINCA SAN BLAS

Partida de San Blas s/n
46340 Requena (Valencia)
☎: 963 375 617 - Fax: 963 370 707
info@fincasanblas.com
www.fincasanblas.com

FINCA SAN BLAS 2008 B
merseguera, chenin blanc, chardonnay

**81**

FINCA
SAN BLAS

BLANC08

ELEGANCIA, EQUILIBRIO Y PERSONALIDAD

LOMALTA 2005 TC
bobal, merlot, tempranillo, cabernet sauvignon, syrah

**82**

LABOR DEL ALMADEQUE MERLOT 2004 TC
merlot

**84**

LABOR DEL ALMADEQUE 2003 TR
cabernet sauvignon, tempranillo

**87** Colour: black cherry, orangey edge. Nose: characterful, cocoa bean, fruit expression, sweet spices, aged wood nuances, old leather. Palate: concentrated, fleshy, powerful tannins.

## LATORRE AGROVINICOLA

Ctra. Requena, 2
46310 Venta del Moro (Valencia)
☎: 962 185 028 - Fax: 962 185 422
vinos@latorreagrovinicola.com
www.latorreagrovinicola.com

PARREÑO 2008 B
macabeo 100%

**81**

CATAMARAN 2006 BFB
macabeo 100%

**82**

PARREÑO 2008 RD
bobal 100%

**82**

PARREÑO 2008 T
tempranillo 100%

**83**

DUQUE DE ARCAS COSECHA SELECCIONADA 2007
T FERMENTADO EN BARRICA
tempranillo 90%, bobal 10%

**83**

DUQUE DE ARCAS 2005 TC
bobal 33%, tempranillo 33%, cabernet sauvignon 33%

**75**

DUQUE DE ARCAS GRAN DUQUE SELECCIÓN
2001 TGR
bobal 100%

**86** Colour: cherry, garnet rim. Nose: aromatic coffee, toasty, fruit liqueur notes. Palate: flavourful, spicy, classic aged character.

DUQUE DE ARCAS BOBAL 2001 TR
bobal 100%

**83**

DUQUE DE ARCAS SELECCIÓN DE FAMILIA
1999 TGR
bobal 50%, tempranillo 50%

**83**

DUQUE DE ARCAS TEMPRANILLO 2001 TR
tempranillo 100%

**84**

## MAS DE BAZÁN

Ctra. Villar de Olmos, km. 2
46340 (Valencia)
☎: 962 303 586 - Fax: 986 555 799
export@agrodebazansa.es
www.agrodebazansa.es

MAS DE BAZÁN 2008 RD
bobal 65%, merlot 25%, syrah 10%

**84**

MAS DE BAZÁN TEMPRANILLO 2006 TC
tempranillo 100%

**86** Colour: cherry, garnet rim. Nose: powerful, ripe fruit, roasted coffee. Palate: powerful, fleshy, spicy.

MAS DE BAZÁN MERLOT 2006 TC
merlot 100%

**85** Colour: cherry, garnet rim. Nose: powerful, ripe fruit, warm, roasted coffee. Palate: powerful, concentrated, spicy, round tannins.

MAS DE BAZÁN BOBAL 2006 TC
bobal 100%

**84**

MAS DE BAZÁN CABERNET SAUVIGNON 2006 TC
cabernet sauvignon 100%

**82**

MAS DE BAZÁN SYRAH 2006 TC
syrah 100%

**82**

## PAGO DE THARSYS

Ctra. Nacional III, Km 274
46340 Requena (Valencia)
☎: 962 303 354 - Fax: 962 329 000
pagodetharsys@pagodetharsys.com
www.pagodetharsys.com

CARLOTA SURIA 2004 TR
tempranillo 60%, cabernet franc 40%

**87** Colour: cherry, garnet rim. Nose: mineral, ripe fruit, spicy. Palate: flavourful, good structure, spicy.

## TORRE ORIA

Ctra. Pontón - Utiel, km. 3
46390 El Derramador (Valencia)
☎: 962 320 289 - Fax: 962 320 311
santiago.sancho@natra.es
www.torreoria.com

MARQUÉS DE REQUENA 2008 B

**82**

MARQUES DE REQUENA 2008 RD JOVEN

**86** Colour: rose, bright. Nose: expressive, raspberry, floral, lactic notes. Palate: fruity, flavourful, easy to drink.

MARQUÉS DE REQUENA 2005 TC

**82**

LOS CLAUSTROS DE TORRE ORIA 2004 TC

**82**

MARQUÉS DE REQUENA 2004 TC

**82**

LOS CLAUSTROS DE TORRE ORIA 2002 TR

**84**

## VERA DE ESTENAS

Junto N-III, km. 266
46300 Utiel (Valencia)
☎: 962 171 141 - Fax: 962 174 352
estenas@veradeestenas.es
www.veradeestenas.es

VIÑA LIDÓN CHARDONNAY 2008 BFB
chardonnay 100%

**87** Colour: bright yellow. Nose: ripe fruit, sweet spices, creamy oak, fragrant herbs. Palate: rich, smoky aftertaste, flavourful, fresh, good acidity.

VERA DE ESTENAS 2008 B JOVEN
macabeo, chardonnay

**85** Colour: bright straw. Nose: fresh, fresh fruit, white flowers, expressive. Palate: flavourful, fruity, good acidity, balanced.

VERA DE ESTENAS 2008 RD
bobal

**87** Colour: rose, purple rim. Nose: powerful, ripe fruit, red berry notes, floral, expressive. Palate: fleshy, powerful, fruity, fresh.

MARTÍNEZ BERMELL MERLOT 2008 T
FERMENTADO EN BARRICA
merlot 100%

**86** Colour: cherry, purple rim. Nose: ripe fruit, floral. Palate: flavourful, powerful, spicy, harsh oak tannins.

VERA DE ESTENAS 2007 T BARRICA
bobal, cabernet sauvignon, merlot, tempranillo, syrah

**83**

VERA DE ESTENAS 2006 TC
tempranillo 50%, cabernet sauvignon 45%, merlot 5%

**82**

CASA DON ÁNGEL BOBAL 2005 T
bobal 93%, merlot 7%

**88** Colour: cherry, garnet rim. Nose: powerful, characterful, fruit liqueur notes, roasted coffee. Palate: powerful, warm, spicy.

VERA DE ESTENAS 2002 TR
tempranillo 50%, cabernet sauvignon 45%, merlot 5%

**85** Colour: cherry, garnet rim. Nose: warm, fruit expression, fruit liqueur notes, old leather. Palate: flavourful, long, powerful tannins.

VERA DE ESTENAS 2000 TGR
tempranillo 50%, cabernet sauvignon 45%, merlot 5%

**88** Colour: cherry, garnet rim. Nose: medium intensity, candied fruit, spicy. Palate: flavourful, spicy, round tannins.

CASA DON ÁNGEL MALBEC 05-06 T
malbec 100%

**88** Colour: bright cherry. Nose: ripe fruit, sweet spices, creamy oak, expressive. Palate: flavourful, fruity, toasty, round tannins.

ARGES CUA 2008 BN
macabeo, chardonnay

**85** Colour: bright straw. Nose: medium intensity, fresh fruit, dried herbs, fine lees, floral. Palate: fresh, fruity, flavourful, good acidity.

## VICENTE GANDIA PLA

Ctra. Cheste a Godelleta s/n
46370 Chiva (Valencia)
☎: 962 524 242 - Fax: 962 524 243
info@vicentegandia.com
www.vicentegandia.com

FINCA DEL MAR CHARDONNAY 2008 B
chardonnay 100%

**83**

HOYA DE CADENAS 2008 B
chardonnay 50%, sauvignon blanc 30%, viura 20%

**82**

HOYA DE CADENAS GARNACHA-BOBAL 2008 RD
garnacha 50%, bobal 50%

**83**

HOYA DE CADENAS 2008 RD
bobal 100%

**83**

FINCA DEL MAR MERLOT 2008 T
merlot 100%

**83**

FINCA DEL MAR CABERNET SAUVIGNON 2007 T
cabernet sauvignon 100%

**83**

FINCA DEL MAR TEMPRANILLO 2007 T
tempranillo 100%

**76**

HOYA DE CADENAS SHIRAZ 2006 T
syrah

**87** Colour: deep cherry. Nose: ripe fruit, spicy, medium intensity, warm. Palate: flavourful, ripe fruit, round tannins.

GENERACIÓN 1 2004 T
bobal 70%, syrah 15%, cabernet sauvignon 15%

**88** Colour: cherry, garnet rim. Nose: ripe fruit, dried flowers, spicy. Palate: good structure, flavourful, roasted-coffee aftertaste, round tannins.

HOYA DE CADENAS RESERVA PRIVADA 2004 TR
tempranillo 85%, cabernet sauvignon 15%

**86** Colour: dark-red cherry. Nose: overripe fruit, sweet spices, fine reductive notes. Palate: flavourful, full, harsh oak tannins, great length.

CEREMONIA 2004 TR
tempranillo 60%, cabernet sauvignon 30%, bobal 10%

**85** Colour: bright cherry. Nose: warm, ripe fruit, toasty. Palate: fruity, flavourful, spicy, fine tannins.

HOYA DE CADENAS 2004 TR
tempranillo 100%

**84**

## VINÍCOLA DEL OESTE S.A.

Ctra. N-III, km. 271
46390 San Antonio Requena (Valencia)
☎: 962 320 002 - Fax: 962 320 533
info@castaro.com
www.castaro.com

VIÑA CASTARO 2005 TC
cabernet sauvignon 52%, tempranillo 48%

**85** Colour: cherry, garnet rim. Nose: warm, fruit preserve, fruit liqueur notes, sweet spices, toasty. Palate: concentrated, flavourful, full, powerful tannins.

## VIÑEDOS Y BODEGAS VEGALFARO

Ctra. Pontón - Utiel, km. 3
46340 Requena (Valencia)
☎: 962 320 680 - Fax: 962 321 126
rodolfo@vegalfaro.com
www.vegalfaro.com

VEGALFARO 2008 B
chardonnay, sauvignon blanc

**88** Colour: bright yellow. Nose: powerful, ripe fruit, sweet spices, creamy oak. Palate: rich, smoky aftertaste, flavourful, fresh, good acidity.

VEGALFARO 2008 RD
merlot, bobal

**83**

VEGALFARO 2008 T
tempranillo, merlot, bobal

**86** Colour: cherry, purple rim. Nose: powerful, ripe fruit, warm. Palate: powerful, fruity, warm.

VEGALFARO 2006 TC
tempranillo, merlot, syrah

**90** Colour: cherry, garnet rim. Nose: expressive, raspberry, fruit expression, sweet spices. Palate: flavourful, ripe fruit, balanced.

PAGO DE LOS BALAGUESES SYRAH 2006 TC
syrah 100%

**90** Colour: bright cherry. Nose: ripe fruit, sweet spices, creamy oak, expressive. Palate: flavourful, fruity, toasty, round tannins.

SOME OTHER WINERIES WITHIN THE DO:

**ASTURIANA DE VINOS**
**BODEGAS DAGÓN**
**BODEGAS DEL INTERIOR**
**BODEGAS FUSO**
**BODEGAS VEREDA REAL**
**BODEGAS Y VIÑEDOS TORRES LUNA**
**COMERCIAL GRUPO FREIXENET S.A.**
**COOP. NUESTRA SEÑORA DE LAS VIÑAS**

**COOP. VINÍCOLA LA PROTECTORA**
**COOP. VINÍCOLA VITIVINICULTORES STA RITA**
**CRIANZO S.L.**
**DISCOSTA NORTE BODEGAS**
   **CASTILLO SAN DAMIÁN**
**ECOVITIS**
**EJARQUE S.L.**
**HIJOS DE ERNESTO CÁRCEL S.L.**
**IBERVINO S.L.U.**
**ORTIZ LATORRE**
**PEDRO MORENO 1940 S.L.**
**PROEXA S.L.**
**RESERVAS Y CRIANZAS REQUENENSES**
**ROMERAL VINÍCOLA**
**VINOS VIURE S.L.**
**VIÑEDOS LA MADROÑERA**

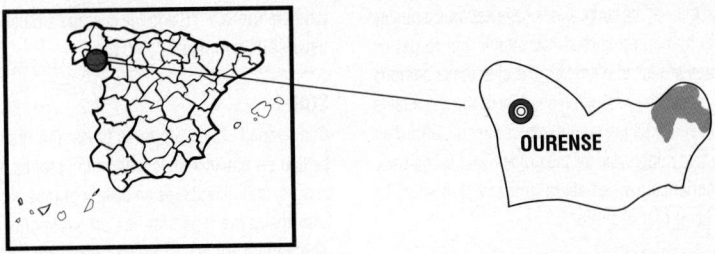

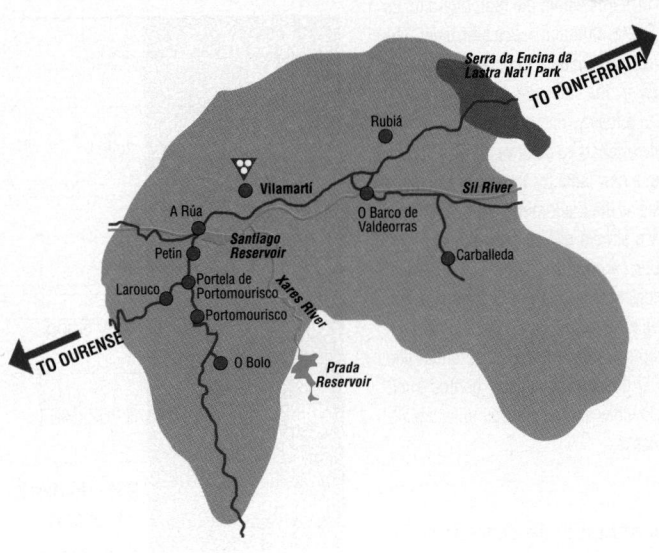

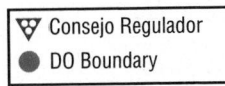

Consejo Regulador

DO Boundary

# DO VALDEORRAS

## NEWS

Although Valdeorras has been the traditional territory for godello, given the way its white wines have become a quality standard both home and abroad, we should not forget its reds have a similar sort of potential. The climatic conditions of the region, under the protecting shadow of the mountains and with an overall fresher, continental influence, afford an almost perfect ripening cycle for the grapes, and particularly the most experienced winemakers in the region seem to have got the hang of it beautifully.

Both garnacha tintorera and sousón have been added to blends with mencía, a grape variety that on 2008 shows a higher acidity level and some meatiness that reveal also some grape skin nuances. The mineral note from the slate soils typical of some vineyards within the region remind us of those from Ribeira Sacra, although a wee bit fruitier. The wines from Val de Lurres and Joaquín Rebolledo are pretty interesting, particularly in the red side of things with a succulent mencía full of a toasty, rich quality. The Consejo Regulador has a couple of goals to achieve, to classify the soils and come up with a new label for the wines that have one of the main varieties as the predominant one. As for the white godello wines, we should differentiate those with a richer, fatter character from the more commercial renderings, full of atypical aromas. To the pioneering houses Godeval and Guitián, we have to add Rafael Palacios as well as some other producers with the greatest potential like Avanthia, from Jorge Ordóñez. The reason behind such success seems to be old vines and very Burgundian ageing methods in 500 litres casks.

## LOCATION

The DO Valdeorras is situated in the northeast of the province of Orense. It comprises the municipal areas of Larouco, Petín, O Bolo, A Rua, Vilamartín, O Barco, Rubiá and Carballeda de Valdeorras.

## CLIMATE

Continental, with Atlantic influences. The average annual temperature is 11°C and the average annual rainfall ranges between 850 mm and 1,000 mm.

## SOIL

Quite varied. There are three types: the first type which is settled on shallow slate with many stones and a medium texture; the second type on deeper granite with a lot of sand and finally the type that lies on sediments and terraces, where there are usually a lot of pebbles.

## GRAPE VARIETIES:

**White:** *Godello, Dona Blanca, Palomino (Jerez)*.
**Red:** *Mencía, Merenzao, Grao Negro* and *Garnacha*.

| | |
|---|---|
| Hectares of Vineyard | 1,342 |
| Nº Viticulturists | 1,961 |
| Nº of Bodegas | 45 |
| 2008 Harvest | Very Good |
| 2007 Production | 3,262,640 l. |
| Marketing | 96% domestic 4% export |

**CONSEJO REGULADOR**
Ctra. Nacional 120, Km 463
32340 Vilamartín de Valdeorras (Orense)
☎: 988 300 295 - Fax: 988 336 887
@ consello@dovaldeorras.com
www.dovaldeorras.com

## GENERAL CHARACTERISTICS OF THE WINES:

| | |
|---|---|
| **WHITES** | Produced from the *Godello* variety, they offer high quality. They are straw yellow or pale yellow in colour. Aromatically, they are not excessively intense, although fine and delicate, with pleasant floral notes. On the palate, they are characterised by their tastiness, excellent acidity and, often, by their oily essence. |
| **REDS** | The *Mencía* variety is used, with which mainly young red wines are produced with a markedly Atlantic character, defined aromas of blackberries; they are dry and fruity on the palate. |

## 2008 VINTAGE RATING:

## VERY GOOD

## A TAPADA S.A.T.

Finca A Tapada
32310 Rubiá (Ourense)
☎: 988 324 197 - Fax: 988 324 197

**GUITIÁN GODELLO SOBRE LÍAS 2008 B**
godello 100%

**92** Colour: bright yellow. Nose: sweet spices, fragrant herbs, complex, citrus fruit, scrubland. Palate: rich, smoky aftertaste, flavourful, fresh, good acidity.

**GUITIÁN GODELLO 2008 B**
godello 100%

**90** Colour: bright straw. Nose: fresh, fresh fruit, white flowers, expressive, spicy. Palate: flavourful, fruity, good acidity, balanced.

**GUITIÁN GODELLO 2007 BFB**
godello 100%

**91** Colour: straw. Nose: scrubland, expressive, ripe fruit, pattiserie. Palate: great length, fruity, elegant, good acidity.

## ADEGA ALAN

San Roque, 36
32350 A Rúa (Orense)
☎: 988 311 457 - Fax: 988 311 457
alandeval@alandeval.com
www.adegaalan.com

**ALAN DE VAL GODELLO 2008 B**
godello 100%

**78**

**ALAN DE VAL MENCÍA 2007 T**
mencía 100%

**85** Colour: bright cherry. Nose: sweet spices, expressive, red berry notes. Palate: flavourful, fruity, round tannins, rich.

**ALAN DE VAL PEDRAZAIS MENCÍA 2006 T BARRICA**
mencía 100%

**82**

**ALAN DE VAL ESCADA GARNACHA 2006 T**
garnacha 100%

**78**

## ADEGA DA PINGUELA

Camino del Disco, 18 1B
32350 Rua (Ourense)

☎: 654 704 753

**VENTURA 2008 B**

**78**

## ADEGA MELILLAS

A Coroa s/n
32350 A Rua (Ourense)
☎: 988 310 510
lagardocigur@adegamelillas.com
www.adegamelillas.com

**LAGAR DO CIGUR 2008 B**
godello

**83**

**LAGAR DO CIGUR 2008 T JOVEN**
mencía

**89** Colour: cherry, purple rim. Nose: expressive, floral, red berry notes, ripe fruit. Palate: flavourful, fruity, good acidity, round tannins.

**LAGAR DO CIGUR 2007 T BARRICA**

**87** Colour: dark-red cherry. Nose: ripe fruit, fruit liqueur notes, mineral, floral, dark chocolate. Palate: powerful, fleshy, roasted-coffee aftertaste.

## ADEGA O CASAL

Pumarega, 22
32310 Rubiá de Valdeorras (Ourense)
☎: 689 675 800 - Fax: 988 324 286
casalnovo@casalnovo.es
casalnovo.es

**CASAL NOVO GODELLO 2008 B**
godello

**89** Colour: bright yellow, pale. Nose: fresh fruit, wild herbs. Palate: powerful, flavourful, fruity.

**CASAL NOVO MENCÍA 2008 T**

**84**

## ADEGAS A COROA S.A.T.

A Coroa, s/n
32350 A Rúa (Ourense)
☎: 988 310 648 - Fax: 988 311 439
acoroa@acoroa.com
www.acoroa.com

A COROA 2008 B
godello 100%

**87** Colour: bright yellow, greenish rim. Nose: fresh fruit, grassy, citrus fruit. Palate: flavourful, good structure, full.

GODELLO

A

COROA

VALDEORRAS

## ADEGAS DÍA-NOITE

Ctra. Carballal, s/n
32356 Petin de Valdeorras (Ourense)
☎: 988 311 462 - Fax: 988 311 462
galiciano@galiciano.com
www.galiciano.com

GALICIANO GODELLO DÍA 2008 B
godello 100%

**84**

VIÑA LADEIRA 2008 B JOVEN
palomino 60%, godello 40%

**82**

GALICIANO MENCÍA NOITE 2008 T
mencía 100%

**86** Colour: cherry, purple rim. Nose: expressive, fresh fruit, red berry notes, floral. Palate: flavourful, fruity, good acidity, soft tannins.

DANZA COVA 2007 BR
godello 100%

**80**

## BODEGA COOPERATIVA JESÚS NAZARENO

Florencio Delgado Gurriarán, 62
32300 O Barco de Valdeorras (Ourense)
☎: 988 320 262 - Fax: 988 320 242
coopbarco@infonegocio.com
www.vinosbarco.com

VIÑA ABAD GODELLO 2008 B
godello 100%

**85** Colour: bright yellow. Nose: fresh fruit, grassy. Palate: rich, round, unctuous.

MENCIÑO 2008 T
mencía 100%

**83**

ALBAR
AURENSIS
MOZAFRESCA
VALDOURO

## BODEGA SEÑORÍO DE ROBLIDO

Curros Enríquez, 10
32350 A Rua (Ourense)
☎: 679 958 874 - Fax: 988 312 343
bdga.sr.roblido@terra.es
www.bodegasgruporoblido.com

SEÑORÍO DE ROBLIDO GODELLO 2008 B

**78**

SEÑORÍO DE ROBLIDO 2008 T JOVEN
mencía , garnacha

**83**

MIL ROBLES
VIÑA AS PEDREIRAS

## BODEGAS AVANTHIA

Avda. de Galicia s/n
32413 O Barco de Valdeorras (Ourense)
☎: 968 435 022 - Fax: 968 716 051
info@orowines.com

AVANTHIA GODELLO 2008 B
godello 100%

**95** Colour: bright straw. Nose: fragrant herbs, ripe fruit, tropical fruit, sweet spices, mineral. Palate: flavourful, fleshy, complex, balanced, long.

## BODEGAS GODEVAL

Avda. Galicia, 20
32300 El Barco de Valdeorras (Ourense)
☎: 988 108 282 - Fax: 988 325 309
godeval@godeval.com
www.godeval.com

GODEVAL CEPAS VELLAS 2008 B
godello 100%

**92** Colour: bright straw. Nose: fresh, white flowers, expressive, fresh fruit. Palate: flavourful, fruity, good acidity, balanced.

GODEVAL 2008 B

**89** Colour: bright straw. Nose: fresh fruit, citrus fruit, dry nuts, fine lees. Palate: flavourful, fine bitter notes, good structure.

## BODEGAS RUCHEL, S.L.

Ctra. de Cernego, s/n
32340 Vilamartin de Valdeorras (Ourense)
☎: 986 253 345 - Fax: 986 253 345
info@vinosruchel.com
www.vinosruchel.com

RUCHEL GODELLO 2008 B
godello 100%

**83**

GRAN RUCHEL GODELLO 2006 B BARRICA
godello 100%

**87** Colour: straw, yellow. Nose: citrus fruit, fine lees, spicy, balsamic herbs. Palate: flavourful, fruity, fresh, balsamic.

RUCHEL GODELLO 2006 B BARRICA
godello 100%

**83**

RUCHEL MENCÍA 2007 T
mencía 100%

**85** Colour: deep cherry. Nose: macerated fruit, floral, balsamic herbs. Palate: flavourful, fruity, fresh.

RUCHEL MENCÍA 2006 T BARRICA
mencía 100%

**85** Colour: bright cherry. Nose: ripe fruit, sweet spices, expressive. Palate: flavourful, fruity, toasty, round tannins.

## BODEGAS SAMPAYOLO

Ctra. de Barxela s/n
32356 Petín de Valdeorras (Ourense)
☎: 679 157 977
info@sampayolo.com
www.sampayolo.com

SAMPAYOLO GODELLO 2008 B
godello

**83**

SAMPAYOLO GODELLO B BARRICA
godello 100%

**87** Colour: bright yellow. Nose: powerful, ripe fruit, sweet spices, creamy oak, fragrant herbs. Palate: rich, smoky aftertaste, flavourful, fresh, good acidity.

SAMPAYOLO MENCÍA 2008 T

**85** Colour: deep cherry. Nose: ripe fruit, balsamic herbs, spicy. Palate: flavourful, fruity, fresh.

SAMPAYOLO LAGAR DE BRIMEDA T
garnacha , mencía , tempranillo

**84**

## COMPAÑIA DE VINOS DE TELMO RODRÍGUEZ

El Monte, s/n
01308 Lanciego (Alava)
☎: 945 628 315 - Fax: 945 628 314
contact@telmorodriguez.com
www.telmorodriguez.com

GABA DO XIL 2008 B
godello

**92** Colour: bright straw. Nose: powerful, ripe fruit, fragrant herbs, white flowers. Palate: flavourful, fleshy, ripe fruit.

## COOPERATIVA SANTA MARIA DE LOS REMEDIOS

Langullo, 11
32358 Larouco (Orense)
☎: 988 348 043 - Fax: 988 348 043
bodegaslarouco@terra.es
www.bodegas-larouco.com

ARUME 2008 B
godello 100%

**79**

MEDULIO 2008 T
mencía 100%

**80**

## GERMÁN RODRÍGUEZ PRADA

Progreso, 24
32350 A Rua (Ourense)

☎: 619 350 638
galgueira@hotmail.com

**GALGUEIRA SELECCIÓN 2008 B**

**90** Colour: bright straw. Nose: fresh, fresh fruit, white flowers, expressive. Palate: flavourful, fruity, good acidity, balanced.

## JOAQUÍN REBOLLEDO

San Roque, 11
32350 A Rúa (Ourense)
☎: 988 372 307 - Fax: 988 371 427
info@joaquinrebolledo.com
www.joaquinrebolledo.com

**JOAQUÍN REBOLLEDO GODELLO 2008 B**
godello 100%

**85** Colour: bright straw. Nose: fruit expression, citrus fruit, scrubland, spicy. Palate: rich, flavourful, full, balsamic.

**JOAQUÍN REBOLLEDO GODELLO SELECCIÓN DE AÑADA 2007 B BARRICA**
godello 100%

**78**

**JOAQUÍN REBOLLEDO MENCÍA 2008 T**
mencía

**82**

**JOAQUÍN REBOLLEDO MENCÍA 2007 T BARRICA**
mencía 90%, tempranillo 10%

**85** Colour: deep cherry. Nose: red berry notes, fruit expression, balsamic herbs. Palate: flavourful, fruity, fresh, easy to drink.

**JOAQUÍN REBOLLEDO 2006 T BARRICA**

**86** Colour: very deep cherry. Nose: powerful, dark chocolate, ripe fruit. Palate: flavourful, powerful, spicy.

## MANUEL CORZO MACÍAS

Chandoiro
32370 O Bolo (Ourense)
☎: 680 850 103
manuelcorzorodriguez@yahoo.es

**VIÑA CORZO GODELLO 2008 B**
godello 100%

**87** Colour: bright yellow, pale. Nose: fresh fruit, citrus fruit, wild herbs. Palate: fresh, fruity, unctuous.

**VIÑA CORZO MENCÍA 2008 T**
mencía 100%

**83**

## RAFAEL PALACIOS

Av. de Somoza, 81
32350 A Rua (Ourense)
☎: 988 310 162 - Fax: 988 310 162
export@rafaelpalacios.com
www.rafaelpalacios.com

**LOURO DO BOLO 2008 B**
godello 92%, treixadura 8%

**94** Colour: bright yellow. Nose: fresh fruit, grapey, scrubland, dried flowers, fine lees. Palate: full, flavourful, complex, balsamic, creamy.

**AS SORTES 2007 B**
godello 100%

**93** Colour: bright straw. Nose: powerful, ripe fruit, white flowers, cocoa bean, spicy. Palate: fleshy, flavourful, fruity, fresh, good acidity.

## VAL DE IURRES S.L.

A Coroa s/n
32350 A Rua (Ourense)
☎: 988 540 578

**TERRA LOMBARDA 2008 B**
godello 100%

**84**

**SANTORUM 2007 B**
godello 100%

**86** Colour: bright yellow. Nose: ripe fruit, dried flowers, spicy. Palate: flavourful, full, good acidity.

**TERRA LOMBARDA 2008 T**
mencía 100%

**87** Colour: cherry, purple rim. Nose: expressive, red berry notes, earthy notes, balsamic herbs. Palate: flavourful, fruity, good acidity.

**SANTORUM TINTO DE AUTOR 2007 T BARRICA**
garnacha , mencía

**87** Colour: cherry, purple rim. Nose: expressive, fresh fruit, red berry notes, spicy. Palate: flavourful, fruity, good acidity, round tannins.

# DO VALDEORRAS

## VIÑA SOMOZA BODEGAS Y VIÑEDOS

Avda. Somoza, s/n
32350 A Rua (Ourense)
☎: 656 407 857 - Fax: 988 310 918
bodega@vinosomoza.com
www.vinosomoza.com

VIÑA SOMOZA GODELLO SOBRE LIAS 2008 B
godello 100%

**85** Colour: yellow, bright straw. Nose: neat, fresh fruit, grassy. Palate: good structure, fruity, fresh.

VIÑA SOMOZA GODELLO SELECCIÓN 2007 B
ROBLE
godello 100%

**88** Colour: yellow, bright golden. Nose: smoky, fruit expression, mineral. Palate: good structure, unctuous.

SOME OTHER WINERIES WITHIN THE DO:

**ADEGA AVELINA S.A.T.**
**ADEGAS DON MARIO**
**ADEGAS O RIBOUZO S.A.T.**
**BOAS MARCAS DE ESPAÑA, S.L.**
**BODEGA COOPERATIVA VIRGEN DE LAS VIÑAS**
**BODEGAS BENEITEZ S.L.**
**BODEGAS TESTEIRO S.A.T.**
**BODEGAS VALDESIL**
**CARBALLAL**
**GERMÁN RODRÍGUEZ SALGADO**
**JESÚS RAFAEL NÚÑEZ RODRÍGUEZ**
**JUAN ARES**
**LADERA SAGRADA**
**SANTA MARTA**
**VIRXEN DE GALIR S.A.T.**

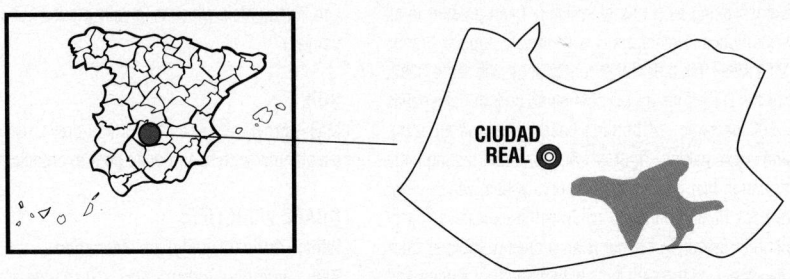

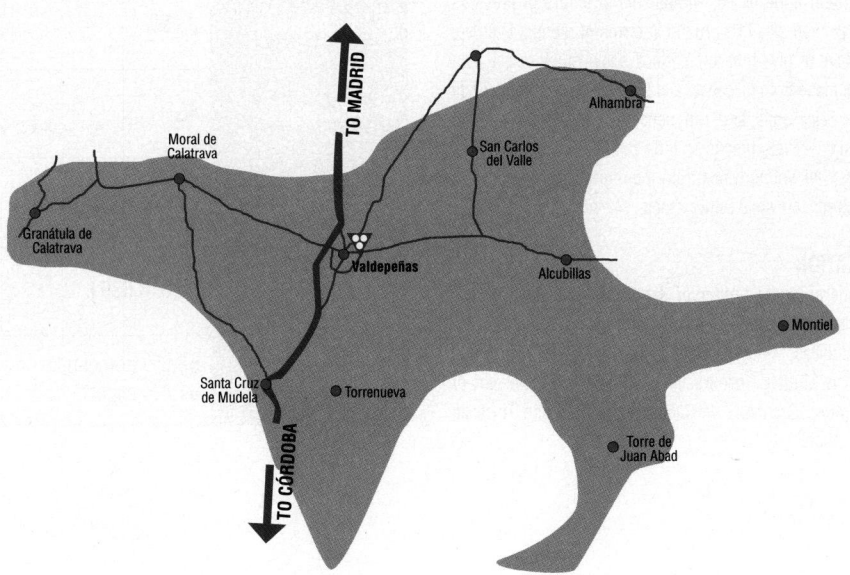

## NEWS

Still one of the most recognizable labels for the Spanish consumer, being as it has historically been present in all supermarkets and restaurants with hugely popular brands like Viña Albali (ten different products under the same label), part of the Félix Solís group, that owns only in Valdepeñas over 500 hectares, 14 bottling lines and some amazing, leading winemaking figures. As for our tasting, the confirmation that classic aged reserva wines, which a few years back finally managed to drop the excessive toasty wood notes favouring fresher crianza ones with better fruit-oak balance, lead the pack now with some fruit liqueur and finely oxidized nuances, pretty much in the best Riojan style. As in the neighbouring region of La Mancha, Valdepeñas had an overall cooler vintage with some unexpected rains that affected mainly airén vines with some rot. All in all, white wines from the region show poorly, with just some fresh and floral notes, without the structure of previous vintages, so they lost ground in terms of ratings. Even so, we have to give that airén wines show much better than those made from macabeo; and again, long aged renderings from Félix Solís and red cencibel wines with optimal ripening –levels thanks to little rainfall– steal this year's show. Still, young wines from the region, an alternative to aged reds, are solid future assets.

## LOCATION

On the southern border of the southern plateau, in the province of Ciudad Real. It comprises the municipal districts of Alcubillas, Moral de Calatrava, San Carlos del Valle, Santa Cruz de Mudela, Torrenueva and Valdepeñas and part of Alhambra, Granátula de Calatrava, Montiel and Torre de Juan Abad.

## CLIMATE

Continental in nature, with cold winters, very hot summers and little rainfall, which is usually around 250 and 400 mm per year.

## SOIL

Mainly brownish-red and brownish-grey limestone soil with a high lime content and quite poor in organic matter.

## GRAPE VARIETIES:

**White:** *Airén* (majority) and *Macabeo.*
**Red:** *Cencibel* (*Tempranillo*), *Garnacha* and *Cabernet Sauvignon.*

| | |
|---|---|
| Hectares of Vineyard | 28,195 |
| Nº Viticulturists | 3,755 |
| Nº of Bodegas | 43 |
| 2008 Harvest | Excellent |
| 2007 Production | 50,618,639 l. |
| Marketing | 58.6% domestic 41.4% export |

**CONSEJO REGULADOR**
Constitución, 23
13300 Valdepeñas (Ciudad Real)
☎: 926 322 788 - Fax: 926 321 054.
@ c.r.dovaldepenas@telefonica.net
www.dovaldepenas.es

## GENERAL CHARACTERISTICS OF THE WINES:

| | |
|---|---|
| **WHITES** | These are produced from *Airén*. They have a pale or straw yellow colour; on the nose they are fresh and fruity and may develop aromas reminiscent of banana or pineapple; on the palate, they are fresh and pleasant, although they have slightly low acidity. |
| **ROSÉS** | Raspberry pink or salmon pink in colour, they are fresh, fruity, pleasant and easy drinking. |
| **REDS** | The young wines from *Cencibel* have a deep cherry-red colour with violet nuances; the aroma is fresh and fruity, almost always with good intensity; on the palate, the freshness and the fruity nuances that make them so pleasant to drink are very noticeable. Those aged in wood start to benefit from the cleaner aromas of oak due to the use of newer barrels. They are supple and quite flavourful on the palate. |

## 2008 VINTAGE RATING:

# EXCELLENT

## BODEGAS ARÚSPIDE

Ciriaco Cruz, 2
13300 Valdepeñas (Ciudad Real)
☎: 926 347 075 - Fax: 926 347 875
info@aruspide.com
www.aruspide.com

ÁGORA 2008 B MACERACIÓN CARBÓNICA
verdejo 100%

**82**

ÁGORA 2007 TC
tempranillo 100%

**88** Colour: cherry, purple rim. Nose: fresh fruit, red berry notes, sweet spices, fine lees. Palate: flavourful, fruity, fresh.

## BODEGAS FERNANDO CASTRO

Pº Castelar, 70
13730 Santa Cruz de Mudela (Ciudad Real)
☎: 926 342 168 - Fax: 926 349 029
fernando@bodegasfernandocastro.com
www.bodegasfernandocastro.com

RAÍCES 2008 B
airén

**83**

VALDEMONTE 2008 T
tempranillo

**75**

RAÍCES SYRAH SELECCIÓN 2005 T
syrah

**83**

CASTILLO DE BAÑOS 2003 TR
tempranillo

**83**

CASTILLO SANTA BÁRBARA 2001 TGR
tempranillo

**83**

## BODEGAS J.A. MEGÍA E HIJOS

Magdalena, 33
13300 Valdepeñas (Ciudad Real)
☎: 926 347 828 - Fax: 926 347 829
jamegia@corcovo.com
www.corcovo.com

CORCOVO 2008 B
airén

**84**

CORCOVO VERDEJO 2008 B
verdejo 100%

**83**

CORCOVO 2008 RD
tempranillo 75%, syrah 25%

**87** Colour: rose, purple rim. Nose: powerful, ripe fruit, red berry notes, floral, expressive. Palate: fleshy, powerful, fruity, fresh.

## CORCOVO TEMPRANILLO 2007 T ROBLE
tempranillo 100%

**88** Colour: bright cherry. Nose: ripe fruit, sweet spices, creamy oak, expressive, lactic notes. Palate: flavourful, fruity, toasty, round tannins.

## CORCOVO SYRAH 2007 T
syrah 100%

**87** Colour: cherry, purple rim. Nose: medium intensity, ripe fruit, fresh fruit. Palate: flavourful, fruity, fresh, varietal.

## CORCOVO 2005 TC
tempranillo 100%

**86** Colour: cherry, garnet rim. Nose: sweet spices, dark chocolate, creamy oak, ripe fruit. Palate: good acidity, flavourful, round tannins.

## CORCOVO 2003 TR
tempranillo 100%

**83**

## BODEGAS JUAN RAMÍREZ

Torrecilla, 138
13300 Valdepeñas (Ciudad Real)
☎: 926 322 021 - Fax: 926 320 495
info@bodegasjuanramirez.com
www.bodegasjuanramirez.com

## ALBA DE LOS INFANTES 2008 BFB
airén 100%

**83**

## ALBA DE LOS INFANTES 2002 TC
tempranillo 70%, cabernet sauvignon 30%

**84**

## ALBA DE LOS INFANTES 2001 TR
tempranillo 100%

**85** Colour: bright cherry, orangey edge. Nose: medium intensity, ripe fruit, spicy. Palate: flavourful, spicy, classic aged character.

## BODEGAS LOS LLANOS

Ctra. N-IV, km. 200, 5
13300 Valdepeñas (Ciudad Real)
☎: 926 347 860 - Fax: 926 322 742
gbvinartis@gbvinartis.com
www.gbvinartis.com

## SEÑORIO DE LOS LLANOS 2006 TC

**82**

ARMONIOSO
DON OPAS
TORNEO
PATA NEGRA

## BODEGAS NAVARRO LÓPEZ

Autovía Madrid-Cádiz, km. 193
13300 Valdepeñas (Ciudad Real)
☎: 902 193 431 - Fax: 902 193 432
laboratorio@navarrolopez.com
www.navarrolopez.com

## DON AURELIO MACABEO VERDEJO 2008 B
macabeo, verdejo

**83**

## DON AURELIO 2008 RD
tempranillo 100%

**84**

## DON AURELIO TEMPRANILLO 2008 T
tempranillo 100%

**84**

## DON AURELIO 2007 T BARRICA
tempranillo 100%

**84**

## DON AURELIO 2006 TC
tempranillo 100%

**84**

## DON AURELIO 2004 TR
tempranillo 100%

**80**

DON AURELIO 2002 TGR
tempranillo 100%

**82**

## BODEGAS REAL

Finca Marisánchez
Ctra. de Valdepeñas a Cózar, km. 12,8
13300 Valdepeñas (Ciudad Real)
☎: 914 577 588 - Fax: 914 577 210
comunicacion@bodegas-real.com
www.bodegas-real.com

BONAL MACABEO 2008 B
macabeo 100%

**85** Colour: bright yellow, pale. Nose: neat, medium intensity, fresh fruit, grassy. Palate: balanced, fruity, flavourful.

BONAL TEMPRANILLO 2008 T
tempranillo 100%

**87** Colour: cherry, purple rim. Nose: expressive, fresh fruit, red berry notes, floral. Palate: flavourful, fruity, good acidity, round tannins.

PALACIO DE IBOR 2004 TR
tempranillo 80%, cabernet sauvignon 20%

**86** Colour: dark-red cherry, orangey edge. Nose: expressive, fruit liqueur notes, toasty. Palate: flavourful, spicy, great length.

## CANUTO BODEGAS DE VALDEPEÑAS

Caldereros, 33
13300 Valdepeñas (Ciudad Real)
☎: 926 322 009 - Fax: 926 322 009
cabovasa@cabovasa.com
www.cabovasa.com

MONTECLARO 2008 T
tempranillo 100%

**84**

MONTECLARO 2004 TC
tempranillo 100%

**83**

MONTECLARO 1999 TR
tempranillo 100%

**84**

MONTECLARO 1998 TGR
tempranillo 100%

**85** Colour: pale ruby, brick rim edge. Nose: elegant, spicy, fine reductive notes, wet leather, aged wood nuances, fruit liqueur notes. Palate: spicy, fine tannins, elegant, long.

## DIONISOS

Unión, 82
13300 Valdepeñas (Ciudad Real)
☎: 926 313 248 - Fax: 926 322 813
info@labodegadelasestrellas.com
www.labodegadelasestrellas.com

DIONISOS TEMPRANILLO 2008 T
tempranillo 100%

**84**

## FÉLIX SOLÍS

Autovía de Andalucía, km. 199
13300 Valdepeñas (Ciudad Real)
☎: 926 322 400 - Fax: 926 322 417
bfs@felixsolis.com
www.felixsolis.com

VIÑA ALBALI VERDEJO 2008 B
verdejo

**84**

LOS MOLINOS TRADICIÓN 2008 B
viura, airén

**83**

VIÑA ALBALI SEMIDULCE 2008 B
airén

**83**

ALBALI ARIUM VERDEJO 2008 B
verdejo

**83**

ALBALI ARIUM TEMPRANILLO 2008 RD

**85** Colour: brilliant rose. Nose: floral, candied fruit, red berry notes, raspberry. Palate: light-bodied, fruity, flavourful.

VIÑA ALBALI TEMPRANILLO 2008 RD
tempranillo

**84**

LOS MOLINOS TRADICIÓN 2008 RD

**82**

## ALBALI ARIUM TEMPRANILLO 2008 T

**87** Colour: cherry, purple rim. Nose: fresh fruit, red berry notes, floral. Palate: flavourful, fruity, good acidity, round tannins.

## VIÑA ALBALI TEMPRANILLO 2008 T

**85** Colour: cherry, purple rim. Nose: expressive, fresh fruit, red berry notes, floral. Palate: flavourful, fruity, good acidity, round tannins.

## LOS MOLINOS TRADICIÓN 2008 T
tempranillo

**84**

## LOS MOLINOS 2005 TC

**83**

## VIÑA ALBALI 2004 TC

**84**

## VIÑA ALBALI 2003 TR

**85** Colour: deep cherry, brick rim edge. Nose: medium intensity, ripe fruit, spicy. Palate: flavourful, reductive nuances, long, great length.

## ALBALI ARIUM 2003 TR

**85** Colour: cherry, garnet rim. Nose: medium intensity, candied fruit, fruit preserve, spicy, aged wood nuances. Palate: flavourful, spicy, classic aged character.

## LOS MOLINOS 2003 TR
tempranillo

**83**

## VIÑA ALBALI CABERNET SAUVIGNON 2003 TR
cabernet sauvignon

**82**

## VIÑA ALBALI SELECCIÓN PRIVADA 2001 TGR

**90** Colour: pale ruby, brick rim edge. Nose: elegant, spicy, fine reductive notes, wet leather, aged wood nuances, fruit liqueur notes. Palate: spicy, fine tannins, elegant, long.

## ALBALI ARIUM 2001 TGR

**89** Colour: cherry, garnet rim. Nose: medium intensity, ripe fruit, spicy, aged wood nuances, fruit liqueur notes. Palate: flavourful, spicy, classic aged character.

## LOS MOLINOS 2001 TGR

**87** Colour: pale ruby, brick rim edge. Nose: fruit liqueur notes, candied fruit, wet leather, caramel. Palate: flavourful, spicy, round tannins.

## VIÑA ALBALI 2001 TGR

**86** Colour: pale ruby, brick rim edge. Nose: spicy, fine reductive notes, wet leather, aged wood nuances, fruit liqueur notes, medium intensity. Palate: spicy, fine tannins, elegant, long.

## VIÑA ALBALI GRAN RESERVA DE LA FAMILIA 1998 TGR

**87** Colour: pale ruby, brick rim edge. Nose: spicy, wet leather, aged wood nuances, fruit liqueur notes, fruit preserve. Palate: spicy, fine tannins, elegant, long.

## DIEGO DE ALMAGRO

# MERCANTIL MARÍN PERONA

Castellanos, 99
13300 Valdepeñas (Ciudad Real)
☎: 926 313 192 - Fax: 926 313 347
bodegas@merxi.com
www.tejeruelas.com

## TEJERUELAS 2008 B

**81**

## TEJERUELAS TEMPRANILLO S.C. T

**82**

## CALAR VIEJO 2007 TC
tempranillo

**83**

## MARÍN PERONA 2004 TR
tempranillo

**85** Colour: pale ruby, brick rim edge. Nose: expressive, fruit liqueur notes, ripe fruit, sweet spices. Palate: powerful, fleshy, great length.

## MARÍN PERONA 2000 TGR

**85** Colour: pale ruby, brick rim edge. Nose: spicy, aged wood nuances, elegant. Palate: light-bodied, spirituous, spicy, fine tannins.

## VIÑA ALDANTE

## MIGUEL CALATAYUD S.A.

Postas, 20
13300 Valdepeñas (Ciudad Real)
☎: 926 348 070 - Fax: 926 322 150
vegaval@vegaval.com
www.vegaval.com

**VEGAVAL PLATA VERDEJO 2008 B JOVEN**
verdejo 100%

**84**

**VEGAVAL PLATA TEMPRANILLO 2006 T ROBLE**
tempranillo 100%

**81**

**VEGAVAL PLATA 2003 TR**
tempranillo 100%

**86** Colour: cherry, garnet rim. Nose: expressive, ripe fruit, red berry notes, sweet spices, cocoa bean, dark chocolate. Palate: flavourful, fruity, spicy, round tannins.

**VEGAVAL PLATA 2001 TGR**
tempranillo 100%

**80**

## SANCTI PAULI

Pº Estación, 47
13300 Valdepeñas (Ciudad Real)
☎: 926 316 938 - Fax: 926 316 007
sanctipauli@wanadoo.es

**SANCTI PAULI 2005 TC**
tempranillo 100%

**88** Colour: bright cherry. Nose: ripe fruit, sweet spices, creamy oak. Palate: flavourful, fruity, toasty, round tannins.

SOME OTHER WINERIES WITHIN THE DO:

**BODEGAS ESPINOSA
GALÁN S.L.
LOS MARCOS
MÁRQUEZ C.B.
PEDRO SÁNCHEZ MOLERO LARA
VICENTE NAVARRO Y HERMANOS
VIÑEDOS Y BODEGAS VISÁN**

# DO VALENCIA

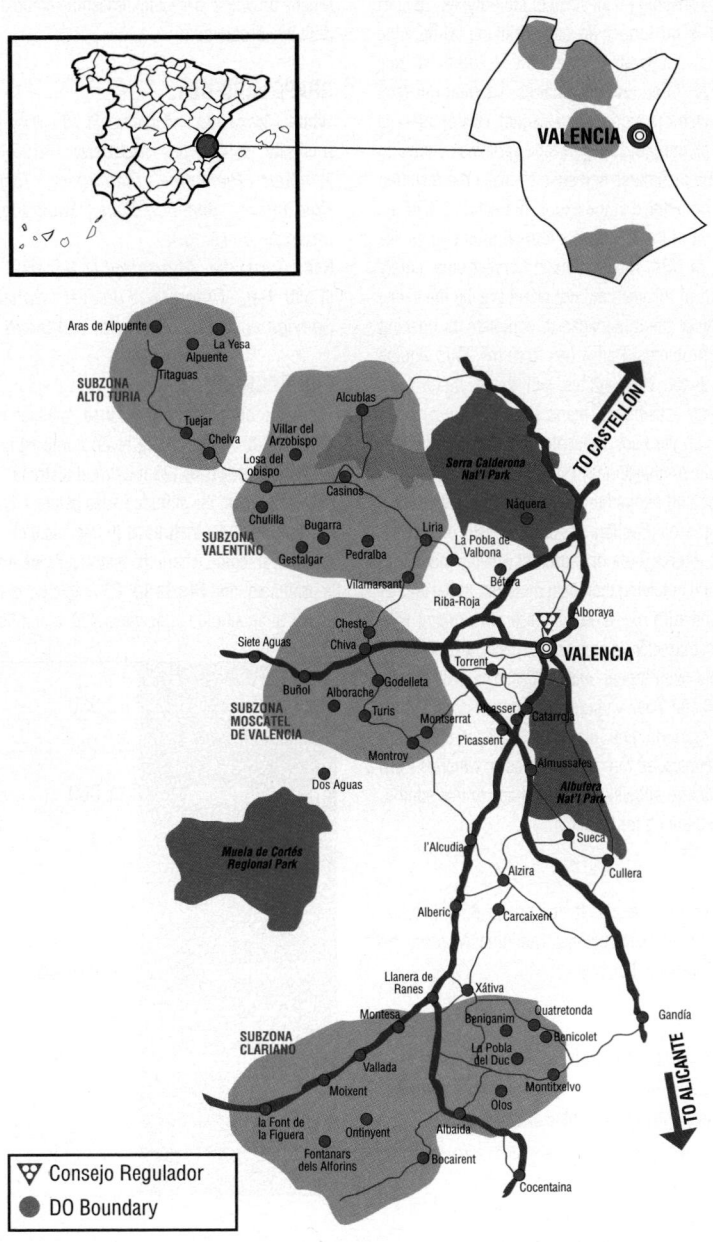

VALENCIA

SUBZONA ALTO TURIA

Aras de Alpuente
La Yesa
Alpuente
Titaguas
Tuejar
Chelva
Villar del Arzobispo
Losa del obispo
Alcublas
Casinos
Serra Calderona Nat'l Park
Náquera

SUBZONA VALENTINO

Chulilla
Bugarra
Gestalgar
Pedralba
Vilamarsant
Liria
La Pobla de Valbona
Riba-Roja
Bétera
Alboraya

TO CASTELLON

VALENCIA

Cheste
Siete Aguas
Chiva
Godelleta
Buñol
Alborache
Turis
Montserrat
Montroy
Dos Aguas

SUBZONA MOSCATEL DE VALENCIA

Torrent
Alcasser
Picassent
Almussafes

Catarroja

Albufera Nat'l Park

Muela de Cortés Regional Park

l'Alcudia
Alzira
Alberic
Carcaixent

Sueca
Cullera

Llanera de Ranes
Montesa
Xátiva
Beniganim
Quatretonda
Benicolet
Gandía

SUBZONA CLARIANO

Vallada
Moixent
La Pobla del Duc
Montitxelvo
Olos
Albaida
la Font de la Figuera
Ontinyent
Fontanars dels Alforins
Bocairent
Cocentaina

TO ALICANTE

▽ Consejo Regulador
● DO Boundary

*Peñín Guide to Spanish Wine* **841**

# DO VALENCIA

## NEWS
Valencia keeps shaking off all sorts of stereotypes. To start with, the DO is no longer an easy-drinking white wine territory or a cooperative one. The leaders of this oenological revolution are the wineries, handing out reds that show much more modern and elegant. One of the keys has been the planting of foreign grape varieties suitable to the region's microclimates and soils to make the resulting wines more competitive in the export markets. 72% of the total production of the DO travels abroad to countries like Germany, UK or USA. Heavy rains at harvest time, surely the crucial part of the year, did not affect greatly the vines, so the majority of them managed to complete its ripening cycle without problems. Red wines from the 2008 vintage show a little better than whites, but these, made from garnacha blanca, sauvignon blanc (Pasamonte) or even rarer blends of verdejo, moscatel de grano menudo, sauvignon blanc or chardonnay (El Angosto) are altogether pretty aromatic and altogether very qualitative. White local varietieties like verdil (Enguera has come up with an icewine made from it), merseguera or moscatel (mainly made into sweet wines) are not living their best moment. In the area of experimentation with red varieties there are working with cabernet franc, marselán (a cross of garnacha and cabernet sauvignon) and even tannat and malbec. The best ratings go to the 2006 and 2007 vintages, and to wines with short wood-ageing periods and plenty of varietal character. Bodegas Los Frailes, as well as some classic wineries from the area of Clariano showing in great shape in this edition, are a promising bunch for Valencia.

## LOCATION
In the province of Valencia. It comprises 66 municipal districts in 4 different sub-regions: Alto Turia, Moscatel de Valencia, Valentino and Clariano.

## CLIMATE
Mediterranean, marked by strong storms and downpours in summer and autumn. The average annual temperature is 15°C and the average annual rainfall is 500 mm.

## SOIL
Mostly brownish-grey with limestone content; there are no drainage problems.

## GRAPE VARIETIES:
**White:** *Macabeo, Malvasía* (1,700 Ha), *Merseguera* (majority 4,440 Ha), *Moscatel* (3,100 Ha), *Pedro Ximénez, Plantafina, Plantanova, Tortosí, Verdil, Chardonnay, Semillon Blanc, Sauvignon Blanc* and *Moscatel de Hungría.*
**Red:** *Garnacha, Monastrell* (1,180 Ha), *Tempranillo* (1,680 Ha), *Tintorera, Forcayat, Bobal, Cabernet Sauvignon, Merlot, Pinot Noir* and *Syrah.*

## SUB-REGIONS:
There are four in total: **Alto Turia,** the highest sub-region (700 to 800 m above sea level) comprising 6 municipal districts; **Valentino** (23 municipal districts), in the centre of the province; the altitude varies between 250 m and 650 m; **Moscatel de Valencia** (9 municipal districts), also in the central region where the historical wine from the region is produced; and **Clariano** (33 municipal districts), to the south, at an altitude of between 400 m and 650 m.

| | |
|---|---|
| Hectares of Vineyard | 13,030 |
| Nº Viticulturists | 11,800 |
| Nº of Bodegas | 85 |
| 2008 Harvest | Very Good |
| 2007 Production | 71,961,612 l. |
| Marketing | 28% domestic 72% export |

**CONSEJO REGULADOR**
Quart, 22. 46001 Valencia
☎: 963 910 096. Fax: 963 910 029.
@ info@vinovalencia.org
www.vinovalencia.org

## GENERAL CHARACTERISTICS OF THE WINES:

| | |
|---|---|
| **WHITES** | The most classic, young and fresh with pleasant wild nuances, are produced from *Merseguera*. Also typical are those made from *Moscatel* (the historic variety of the region), and are used both for dry white wines, very aromatic and light, and for the characteristic Mistelas of the region, which have a pale colour when they are from the latest harvest and golden yellow if they are older. They are all characterised by their musky and grapy aromas. |
| **ROSÉS** | The current trend is towards raspberry pink coloured rosés, which are fresh and light, with a good fruity and aromatic potency. |
| **REDS** | The most characteristic wines are produced from *Monastrell* and *Garnacha*; the wines are slightly warm with notes of ripe fruit, although with less vigour than those from Utiel-Requena and lighter than those from Alicante. Wines from other varieties have begun to be produced recently, mainly *Tempranillo* and *Cabernet Sauvignon*, which give supple, flavourful red wines with a Mediterranean character. |

## 2008 VINTAGE RATING:

## VERY GOOD

## ANDRÉS VALIENTE E HIJOS

Ctra. Pontón - Utiel, km. 3
46430 El Derramador-Requena (Valencia)
☎: 962 320 680 - Fax: 962 321 126
info@vegalfaro.com
www.vegalfaro.com

**PASAMONTE 2008 B**
sauvignon blanc, garnacha blanca

**91** Colour: bright straw. Nose: fresh, fresh fruit, white flowers, expressive, varietal. Palate: flavourful, fruity, good acidity, balanced.

**PASAMONTE 2006 T**

**91** Colour: bright cherry. Nose: ripe fruit, sweet spices, roasted coffee, balsamic herbs. Palate: flavourful, fruity, toasty, round tannins.

**PASAMONTE 2005 T**
garnacha

**90** Colour: cherry, purple rim. Nose: red berry notes, floral, toasty. Palate: flavourful, full, harsh oak tannins.

## ANTONIO ARRAEZ

Arcediano Ros, 35
46630 Fuente La Higuera (Valencia)
☎: 962 290 031 - Fax: 962 290 339
info@bodegasarraez.com
www.antonioarraez.com

**A2 VERDIL 2007 B**
verdil, malvasia, moscatel

**85** Colour: bright straw. Nose: fresh, fresh fruit, white flowers, expressive, grassy. Palate: flavourful, fruity, good acidity, balanced.

**CASAS DE HERENCIA B JOVEN**

**84**

**A2 MONASTRELL 2007 T ROBLE**
monastrell, tintorera

**85** Colour: cherry, garnet rim. Nose: powerful, spicy, toasty, ripe fruit. Palate: flavourful, spicy, round tannins, ripe fruit.

**A2 SYRAH 2007 T ROBLE**
syrah

**84**

**CASAS DE HERENCIA T ROBLE**
monastrell, tempranillo, tintorera

**85** Colour: cherry, garnet rim. Nose: red berry notes, spicy. Palate: fruity, flavourful, great length.

**LAGARES TC**
cabernet sauvignon

**83**

**CABEZUELAS**

## BATALLER S.A.

Camí Real, 94-96
46841 Castelló de Rugat (Valencia)
☎: 962 813 017 - Fax: 962 813 017
vinosbenicadell@telepolis.com

**D'ALBA VARIETAL MOSCATEL S.C. B**

**82**

**BENICADELL B**

**72**

**BENICADELL RD**

**70**

**BENICADELL 2006 TC**

**78**

**BENICADELL VARIETAL TEMPRANILLO T**

**81**

**BENICADELL T**
monastrell, garnacha

**78**

## BODEGA J. BELDA

Av. Conde Salvaterra, 54
46635 Fontanars dels Alforins (Valencia)
☎: 962 222 245 - Fax: 962 222 245
info@danielbelda.com
www.danielbelda.com

**DANIEL BELDA VERDIL 2008 B**
verdil

**83**

CHARDONNAY DANIEL BELDA 2007 BFB
chardonnay

**84**

CA'BELDA 2006 T
garnacha tinta 50%, monastrell 50%

**91** Colour: bright cherry. Nose: ripe fruit, sweet spices, creamy oak, expressive. Palate: flavourful, fruity, toasty, round tannins.

DANIEL BELDA MERLOT 2004 TR
merlot

**86** Colour: cherry, garnet rim. Nose: ripe fruit, spicy, complex, roasted coffee. Palate: powerful, flavourful, toasty, round tannins.

DANIEL BELDA 2004 TR
cabernet sauvignon

**83**

DANIEL BELDA 75 ANYS 2003 T
monastrell, garnacha, syrah

**85** Colour: cherry, garnet rim. Nose: spicy, aged wood nuances, fruit liqueur notes. Palate: spirituous, spicy, round tannins.

## BODEGA LA VIÑA

Portal de Valencia, 52
46630 La Font de la Figuera (Valencia)
☎: 962 290 078 - Fax: 962 232 039
info@vinosdelavina.com
www.vinosdelavina.com

ICONO CHARDONNAY 2008 B
chardonnay 100%

**85** Colour: bright straw. Nose: ripe fruit, fragrant herbs. Palate: fruity, fresh.

SEQUIOT MACABEO CHARDONNAY 2008 B
macabeo 90%, chardonnay 10%

**83**

SEQUIOT CABERNET SAUVIGNON 2008 RD
cabernet sauvignon 60%, tempranillo 40%

**80**

SEQUIOT TEMPRANILLO CABERNET SAUVIGNON 2008 T
tempranillo 50%, cabernet sauvignon 50%

**84**

ICONO TEMPRANILLO 2007 T
tempranillo 100%

**87** Colour: cherry, garnet rim. Nose: characterful, red berry notes, scrubland. Palate: flavourful, sweetness, powerful tannins.

CASA L'ANGEL 2007 T
cabernet sauvignon 50%, tempranillo 50%

**87** Colour: cherry, purple rim. Nose: powerful, ripe fruit, floral. Palate: powerful, fruity, good structure.

CASA L'ANGEL VENDIMIA SELECCIONADA 2007 T

**87** Colour: cherry, garnet rim. Nose: ripe fruit, sweet spices, aromatic coffee. Palate: spicy, round tannins.

ICONO SYRAH 2007 T
syrah 100%

**85** Colour: cherry, garnet rim. Nose: spicy, aged wood nuances, fruit expression. Palate: flavourful, long, good finish.

ICONO CABERNET SAUVIGNON 2007 T
cabernet sauvignon 100%

**84**

ICONO MONASTRELL 2007 T
monastrell 100%

**84**

ICONO MERLOT 2007 T
merlot 100%

**82**

VENTA DEL PUERTO 12 2006 T
tempranillo 40%, cabernet sauvignon 40%, merlot 10%, syrah 10%

**91** Colour: bright cherry. Nose: ripe fruit, sweet spices, creamy oak, expressive, powerfull. Palate: flavourful, fruity, toasty, round tannins.

VENTA DEL PUERTO 18 VENDIMIA SELECCIONADA 2006 T BARRICA
tempranillo 40%, cabernet sauvignon 40%, merlot 10%, syrah 10%

**88** Colour: cherry, garnet rim. Nose: fruit liqueur notes, creamy oak. Palate: flavourful, round tannins.

## BODEGAS EL ANGOSTO

Ctra. Fontanares CV 660, Km. 24
46870 Ontinyent (Valencia)
☎: 962 380 638 - Fax: 962 911 349
info@bodegaelangosto.com
www.bodegaselangosto.com

## ANGOSTO 2008 B

**89** Colour: bright straw. Nose: white flowers, fresh fruit, fruit expression, grassy, complex. Palate: fresh, fruity, ripe fruit.

## LA TRIBU 2008 T
monastrell, syrah

**88** Colour: cherry, purple rim. Nose: fresh fruit, red berry notes, floral. Palate: flavourful, fruity, good acidity, round tannins.

## ANGOSTO 2007 T

**92** Colour: bright cherry. Nose: ripe fruit, sweet spices, creamy oak, expressive. Palate: flavourful, fruity, toasty, round tannins.

## ANGOSTO VIÑA LOS ALMENDROS 2007 T
syrah 40%, garnacha tinta 30%, marselan 30%

**92** Colour: bright cherry. Nose: ripe fruit, sweet spices, creamy oak, expressive, lactic notes, mineral. Palate: flavourful, fruity, toasty, round tannins.

## BODEGAS ENGUERA

Ctra. CV - 590, km. 51, 1
46810 Enguera (Valencia)
☎: 962 224 318 - Fax: 961 364 167
bodega@cessa.es
www.bodegasenguera.com

## VERDIL DE GEL 2008 B
verdil 100%

**88** Colour: bright straw. Nose: ripe fruit, candied fruit, fragrant herbs. Palate: sweetness, fresh, flavourful.

## MEGALA 2007 T
monastrell 50%, syrah 50%

**90** Colour: cherry, garnet rim. Nose: powerful, ripe fruit, toasty, dark chocolate, aromatic coffee. Palate: powerful, spicy, fine bitter notes, round tannins.

## DISTINTO 2007 T BARRICA
tempranillo 50%, syrah 50%

**87** Colour: cherry, garnet rim. Nose: candied fruit, fruit liqueur notes, spicy. Palate: flavourful, spicy, round tannins.

## PARADIGMA 2007 T
monastrell 100%

**85** Colour: cherry, garnet rim. Nose: spicy, toasty, aromatic coffee, ripe fruit. Palate: flavourful, spicy, balsamic.

## ANGELICAL 2006 T
syrah 40%, tempranillo 30%, monastrell 30%

**87** Colour: cherry, purple rim. Nose: red berry notes, floral, ripe fruit, spicy. Palate: flavourful, fruity, good acidity, round tannins.

## SUEÑO DE MEGALA 2005 T
monastrell 60%, tempranillo 20%, merlot 20%

**91** Colour: very deep cherry. Nose: powerful, ripe fruit, sweet spices, mineral. Palate: flavourful, powerful, spicy, toasty.

## BODEGAS LOS FRAILES

Casa Los Frailes s/n
46635 Fontanares (Valencia)
☎: 963 339 845 - Fax: 963 363 153
info@bodegaslosfrailes.com
www.bodegaslosfrailes.com

## EFE MONASTRELL 2008 RD BARRICA
monastrell 100%

**85** Colour: rose. Nose: candied fruit, dried flowers, fragrant herbs, red berry notes, spicy. Palate: light-bodied, flavourful, good acidity, long, spicy.

## EFE MONASTRELL 2008 T
monastrell 100%

**82**

## MOMA DELS FRADES 2006 T
monastrell 50%, marselan 50%

**91** Colour: deep cherry, garnet rim. Nose: powerful, ripe fruit, cedar wood, toasty, new oak. Palate: flavourful, powerful, rich, fruity, round tannins.

## TRILOGÍA 2006 T
monastrell 70%, cabernet sauvignon 20%, tempranillo 10%

**90** Colour: cherry, garnet rim. Nose: ripe fruit, fruit expression, sweet spices, creamy oak. Palate: flavourful, powerful, spicy, round tannins.

## BILOGÍA 2005 T
monastrell 50%, tempranillo 50%

**89** Colour: bright cherry. Nose: ripe fruit, sweet spices, creamy oak, expressive. Palate: flavourful, fruity, toasty, round tannins.

## EFE 2005 T BARRICA
monastrell 80%, cabernet sauvignon 20%

**83**

# DO VALENCIA

AFTER 3 VENDIMIA TARDÍA 2005 TINTO DULCE
monastrell 100%

**87** Colour: cherry, garnet rim. Nose: candied fruit, overripe fruit, spicy. Palate: fruity, sweet, flavourful.

## BODEGAS LOS PINOS

Casa Los Pinos s/n
46635 Fontanars dels Alforins (Valencia)
☎: 962 222 090 - Fax: 962 222 086
bodegaslospinos@bodegaslospinos.com
www.bodegaslospinos.com

DOMINIO LOS PINOS SALVATGE 2008 BFB
moscatel, sauvignon blanc, viognier

**82**

DOMINIO LOS PINOS SELECTION WHITE SALVATGE 2008 B
moscatel, sauvignon blanc

**81**

DOMINIO LOS PINOS 2006 BFB
moscatel, sauvignon blanc

**83**

DOMINIO LOS PINOS SELECTION ROSÉ SALVATGE 2008 RD
garnacha

**80**

LOS PINOS 0 % 2008 T
garnacha, monastrell, syrah

**88** Colour: dark-red cherry, purple rim. Nose: fresh fruit, wild herbs, lactic notes. Palate: concentrated, powerful, flavourful, powerful tannins.

DOMINIO LOS PINOS SELECTION RED SALVATGE 2008 T
monastrell, cabernet sauvignon

**85** Colour: cherry, garnet rim. Nose: medium intensity, candied fruit, scrubland. Palate: fruity, fresh, round tannins.

DOMINIO LOS PINOS 2006 T BARRICA
cabernet sauvignon, syrah, merlot

**83**

L. OLAECHEA 2005 TC
monastrell, merlot, cabernet sauvignon

**84**

DOMINIO LOS PINOS 2004 TC
monastrell, merlot, cabernet sauvignon

**83**

DOMINIO LOS PINOS CUM LAUDE 2001 TR
merlot, cabernet franc, cabernet sauvignon, monastrell

**85** Colour: cherry, garnet rim. Nose: spicy, aged wood nuances, wet leather. Palate: spicy, classic aged character, round tannins.

DOMINIO LOS PINOS 2006 CRIANZA

**87** Colour: very deep cherry, garnet rim. Nose: macerated fruit, sweet spices, creamy oak, balanced. Palate: full, flavourful, round tannins, toasty.

## BODEGAS MAMERTO DE LA VARA

Pol. Ind. Castilla, parcela 9-10b
46380 Cheste (Valencia)
☎: 962 511 545 - Fax: 962 511 514
export@mamertodelavara.es
www.mamertodelavara.es

MAMERTO DE LA VARA MOSCATEL SELECCIÓN 2008 B
moscatel 100%

**87** Colour: bright golden. Nose: candied fruit, overripe fruit, honeyed notes, floral. Palate: sweet, fresh, fruity.

DOLCE VITA MOSCATEL 2008 VINO DE LICOR
moscatel 100%

**86** Colour: bright golden. Nose: fruit liqueur notes, honeyed notes, varietal. Palate: spirituous, sweet, flavourful.

## BODEGAS MURVIEDRO

Ampliación Polígono El Romeral, s/n
46340 Requena (Valencia)
☎: 962 329 003 - Fax: 962 329 002
murviedro@murviedro.es
www.murviedro.es

ALBA DE MURVIEDRO 2008 B
sauvignon blanc 75%, moscatel 25%

**83**

MURVIEDRO EXPRESIÓN 2006 TC
monastrell 55%, garnacha 45%

**91** Colour: cherry, garnet rim. Nose: ripe fruit, spicy, creamy oak, complex, roasted coffee. Palate: powerful, flavourful, toasty, round tannins.

# DO VALENCIA

## LOS MONTEROS 2006 TC
monastrell 60%, merlot 40%

**88** Colour: cherry, garnet rim. Nose: powerful, ripe fruit, sweet spices, cocoa bean. Palate: flavourful, spicy, ripe fruit, round tannins.

## MURVIEDRO 2005 TR
tempranillo 40%, monastrell 40%, cabernet sauvignon 20%

**88** Colour: cherry, garnet rim. Nose: ripe fruit, spicy, creamy oak, toasty, complex. Palate: powerful, flavourful, toasty, round tannins.

## ESTRELLA 10 2008 BLANCO DULCE
moscatel 100%

**85** Colour: bright straw. Nose: candied fruit, honeyed notes, citrus fruit. Palate: fruity, sweetness.

## BODEGAS ONTINIUM

Avenida Almansa, 17
46870 Ontinyent (Valencia)
☎: 962 380 849 - Fax: 962 384 419
info@coopontinyent.com
www.coopontinyent.com

ONTINIUM 2008 B
**73**

ONTINIUM SYRAH 2008 T
syrah

**88** Colour: cherry, purple rim. Nose: powerful, ripe fruit, floral. Palate: flavourful, powerful, round tannins.

ONTINIUM TEMPRANILLO 2008 T
tempranillo

**84**

ONTINIUM 2006 T BARRICA
**83**

CODOLLA
VIÑA DON CARLOS
VIÑA UMBRIA

## BODEGAS TORREVELLISCA

Ctra. L'Ombria, km. 1
46635 Fontanars dels Alforins (Valencia)
☎: 962 222 261 - Fax: 961 190 858
info@bodegas-torrevellisca.com
www.bodegas-torrevellisca.com

TORREVELLISCA MERLOT 2004 TC

**85** Colour: dark-red cherry. Nose: fruit preserve, powerfull, creamy oak. Palate: creamy, ripe fruit, round tannins, spicy.

## BODEGAS TORROJA

Nogueral, 3
46357 Azagador (Valencia)
☎: 962 304 232 - Fax: 962 303 833
herve@bodegastorroja.com
www.bodegastorroja.com

SYBARUS CHARDONNAY 2006 BFB
chardonnay 100%

**84**

## BODEGAS VEGAMAR S.L.

Camino de la Garcesa, s/n
46175 Calles (Valencia)
☎: 962 109 813 - Fax: 962 100 320
maripaz@bodegasvegamar.com
www.bodegasvegamar.com

VIÑA COSTOSA 2008 B
**78**

VIÑA AMÉRICA 2006 TC
tempranillo, syrah
**83**

VIÑA CARRASSES 2005 TC
**83**

VEGAMAR COLECCIÓN PRIVADA 2005 TC
merlot, cabernet sauvignon

## 84

**VEGAMAR 2005 TC**
tempranillo, cabernet sauvignon

## 82

### CELLER DEL ROURE S.L.

Ctra. de Les Alcusses, km. 11,5
46640 Moixent (Valencia)
☎: 962 295 020 - Fax: 962 295 142
info@cellerdelroure.es

**LES ALCUSSES 2006 T**
monastrell, otras

**91** Colour: cherry, garnet rim. Nose: spicy, ripe fruit, scrubland, aged wood nuances. Palate: flavourful, spicy, round tannins, good acidity, mineral.

**MADURESA 2006 T**
mandó, syrah, cabernet sauvignon, otras

**91** Colour: bright cherry. Nose: ripe fruit, sweet spices, creamy oak, expressive, mineral. Palate: flavourful, fruity, toasty, round tannins.

### CHERUBINO VALSANGIACOMO S.A.

Ctra. Cheste-Godelleta, km. 1
46370 Chiva (Valencia)
☎: 962 510 451 - Fax: 962 511 361
cvalsangiacomo@cherubino.es
www.cherubino.es

**MARQUÉS DE CARO ALTO TURIA 2008 B**
merseguera 80%, moscatel 20%

## 84

**MARQUÉS DE CARO MOSCATEL 2007 B**
moscatel 100%

## 82

**MARQUÉS DE CARO TEMPRANILLO 2008 T**
tempranillo 100%

**87** Colour: cherry, purple rim. Nose: neat, rose petals, red berry notes. Palate: flavourful, good structure, sweetness, long.

**MARQUÉS DE CARO CABERNET SAUVIGNON 2007 T**
cabernet sauvignon 100%

**88** Colour: cherry, garnet rim. Nose: ripe fruit, spicy, tropical fruit. Palate: balanced, flavourful, great length.

**MARQUÉS DE CARO SHIRAZ 2007 T**
syrah 100%

## 80

**MARQUÉS DE CARO 2006 TC**
syrah, cabernet sauvignon, bobal

## 83

**MARQUÉS DE CARO 2005 TR**
tempranillo 50%, cabernet sauvignon 50%

## 83

**VITTORE 2007 MISTELA**
moscatel 100%

**87** Colour: bright golden. Nose: dried fruit, overripe fruit, honeyed notes. Palate: sweet, flavourful, good acidity.

### CHESTE AGRARIA COOP. V. ANECOOP BODEGAS

María Carbonell, 2
46380 Cheste (Valencia)
☎: 962 511 671 - Fax: 962 511 732
bodega@chesteagraria.com

**MARQUES DE VALENCIA 2008 B**
moscatel, malvasia, merseguera

## 83

**MARQUES DE VALENCIA 2008 T**
tempranillo, syrah, merlot, cabernet sauvignon

## 84

**REYMOS ESP**
moscatel

## 80

**LA CARTUJA VIACOELI 2008 VINO DE LICOR**
moscatel

**85** Colour: bright golden. Nose: candied fruit, overripe fruit, honeyed notes. Palate: flavourful, sweet, balanced.

### COVIBEX COOPERATIVA VINICOLA

Ctra. Nacional III, km. 314
46370 Chiva (Valencia)
☎: 962 522 200 - Fax: 962 521 678
covibex@covibex.com
www.covibex.com

**VIÑA BÁRBARA SEMILLÓN BLANC 2008 B**

## 82

# DO VALENCIA

VIÑA BÁRBARA ALTO TURIA 2008 B
merseguera

## 80

## CV BODEGAS POLO MONLEÓN

Ctra. Valencia - Ademuz, km. 86
46178 Titaguas (Valencia)
☎: 961 634 148 - Fax: 961 634 148

HOYA DEL CASTILLO ALTO TURIA 2008 B
merseguera 70%, macabeo 30%

## 83

## HERETAT DE TAVERNERS

Ctra. Fontanars - Moixent, km. 1,8
46635 Fontanars dels Alforins (Valencia)
☎: 962 132 437 - Fax: 962 222 298
info@heretatdetaverners.com
www.heretatdetaverners.com

HERETAT DE TAVERNERS REIXIU 2008 BC
chardonnay, sauvignon blanc

**89** Colour: bright straw. Nose: fresh, white flowers, expressive. Palate: flavourful, fruity, good acidity, balanced.

HERETAT DE TAVERNERS GRACIANO 2005 TR
graciano 100%

**90** Colour: cherry, garnet rim. Nose: ripe fruit, spicy, creamy oak, toasty, complex, balsamic herbs. Palate: powerful, flavourful, toasty, round tannins.

HERETAT DE TAVERNERS EL VERN 2005 T
tempranillo 40%, cabernet sauvignon 40%, monastrell 20%

**88** Colour: cherry, garnet rim. Nose: ripe fruit, spicy, toasty. Palate: flavourful, fruity, spicy, round tannins.

HERETAT DE TAVERNERS MALLAURA 2005 TR
cabernet sauvignon 40%, tempranillo 35%, monastrell 15%, garnacha 10%

**87** Colour: cherry, garnet rim. Nose: warm, fruit liqueur notes. Palate: flavourful, balanced.

## LA BARONIA DE TURIS

Ctra. de Godelleta, 22
46389 Turis (Valencia)
☎: 962 526 011 - Fax: 962 527 282
baronia@baroniadeturis.es
www.baroniadeturis.es

LA LUNA DE MAR 2008 B JOVEN
moscatel 100%

## 83

CASTILLO DE TURIS 2007 T
tempranillo 100%

**86** Colour: cherry, garnet rim. Nose: sweet spices, pattiserie, slightly evolved. Palate: spicy, balsamic, easy to drink.

LA LUNA DE MAR 2007 T JOVEN
merlot, syrah, cabernet sauvignon, tempranillo

**86** Colour: ruby red, purple rim. Nose: expressive, ripe fruit, sweet spices, toasty. Palate: flavourful, sweetness, long, slightly dry, soft tannins.

GRAN BARÓN DE TURIS 2007 TC
tempranillo 60%, merlot 40%

**85** Colour: cherry, garnet rim. Nose: ripe fruit, spicy, toasty. Palate: powerful, flavourful, toasty, round tannins.

BARÓN DE TURIS 2006 TC
tempranillo 50%, monastrell 25%, garnacha 25%

**87** Colour: cherry, garnet rim. Nose: powerful, ripe fruit, sweet spices. Palate: flavourful, spicy, ripe fruit.

MISTELA MOSCATEL TURÍS 2008 VINO DE LICOR
moscatel

**87** Colour: yellow, bright straw. Nose: candied fruit, grapey, honeyed notes. Palate: sweet, spirituous, unctuous, elegant.

## LA CASA DE LAS VIDES
## BODEGUES I VINYES

Corral el Galtero s/n
46890 Agullent (Valencia)
☎: 962 135 003 - Fax: 962 135 494
bodega@lacasadelasvides.com
www.lacasadelasvides.com

VALLBLANCA 2008 B
verdil, macabeo

## 83

ROSA ROSAE 2008 RD
garnacha, cabernet sauvignon

## 82

ACVLIVS 2007 T
tempranillo, syrah, merlot, monastrell, garnacha

**90** Colour: bright cherry. Nose: ripe fruit, sweet spices, creamy oak, expressive. Palate: flavourful, fruity, toasty, round tannins.

CVP 2007 T
tempranillo, syrah

**86** Colour: cherry, purple rim. Nose: fruit preserve, toasty, sweet spices.

## LEOPOLDO

San Jaime, 3
03760 Ondara (Alicante)
☎: 965 766 314 - Fax: 965 766 241
correo@bodegasleopoldo.com
www.bodegasleopoldo.com

VIÑA SANTA ANA 2006 T
**76**

## PAGO CASA GRAN

Crta. Cv 652, km. 9,5
46640 Mogente (Valencia)
☎: 962 261 004 - Fax: 962 261 004
comercial@pagocasagran.com

REPOSO 2008 B
gewürztraminer, moscatel

**88** Colour: bright straw. Nose: fresh, fresh fruit, white flowers, expressive, grassy. Palate: flavourful, fruity, good acidity, balanced.

REPOSO 2007 T
merlot, syrah, monastrell
**82**

FALCATA ARENAL 2006 T
garnacha tintorera, monastrell

**89** Colour: cherry, purple rim. Nose: sweet spices, toasty, ripe fruit. Palate: flavourful, powerful, spicy, round tannins.

FALCATA CASA GRAN 2006 T
garnacha tintorera, syrah, monastrell
**84**

## RAFAEL CAMBRA S.L.

Plaza Concepción, 13 - 19
46870 Ontinyent (Valencia)
☎: 616 463 245 - Fax: 962 383 855
rafael@rafaelcambra.es
www.rafaelcambra.es

RAFAEL CAMBRA DOS 2007 T
cabernet sauvignon, cabernet franc, monastrell

**91** Colour: very deep cherry, purple rim. Nose: fruit preserve, cocoa bean, sweet spices, wild herbs. Palate: fleshy, good structure, long, slightly dry, soft tannins.

RAFAEL CAMBRA UNO 2006 T
monastrell

**88** Colour: cherry, garnet rim. Nose: powerful, fruit preserve, toasty, dark chocolate.

## SAN PEDRO APOSTOL. MOIXENT

Plaza de la Hispanidad, 4
46640 Moixent (Valencia)
☎: 962 260 020 - Fax: 962 260 560
icalabuig.moixent@coop.credit.es

CLOS DE LA VALL 2008 BFB
pedro ximénez

**85** Colour: bright straw. Nose: powerful, sweet spices, cocoa bean, ripe fruit. Palate: fruity, flavourful, ripe fruit.

CLOS DE LA VALL 2008 B
macabeo, moscatel
**80**

CLOS DE LA VALL 2008 T
tempranillo, monastrell

**87** Colour: cherry, purple rim. Nose: expressive, fresh fruit, red berry notes, floral. Palate: flavourful, fruity, good acidity, round tannins.

CLOS DE LA VALL 2006 TC
monastrell, tempranillo, cabernet sauvignon

**89** Colour: bright cherry. Nose: ripe fruit, sweet spices, creamy oak, expressive. Palate: flavourful, fruity, toasty, round tannins.

CLOS DE LA VALL 2005 TR
monastrell, cabernet sauvignon, tempranillo

**88** Colour: cherry, garnet rim. Nose: expressive, sweet spices, creamy oak, fruit preserve. Palate: flavourful, full, slightly dry, soft tannins.

## VICENTE GANDIA PLA

Ctra. Cheste a Godelleta s/n
46370 Chiva (Valencia)
☎: 962 524 242 - Fax: 962 524 243
info@vicentegandia.com

www.vicentegandia.com

## EL MIRACLE CHARDONNAY-SAUVIGNON BLANC 2008 B
chardonnay 60%, sauvignon blanc 40%

**85** Colour: yellow, bright straw. Nose: neat, grassy, tropical fruit. Palate: flavourful, rich, fruity, great length.

## FUSTA NOVA BLANC 2008 B
chardonnay 45%, sauvignon blanc 35%, moscatel 20%

**83**

## CASTILLO DE LIRIA SEMI DULCE 2008 B
viura 80%, sauvignon blanc 20%

**81**

## CASTILLO DE LIRIA 2008 B
viura 80%, sauvignon blanc 20%

**81**

## CASTILLO DE LIRIA 2008 RD
bobal 100%

**80**

## EL MIRACLE TEMPRANILLO SHIRAZ 2007 T
tempranillo 65%, syrah 35%

**84**

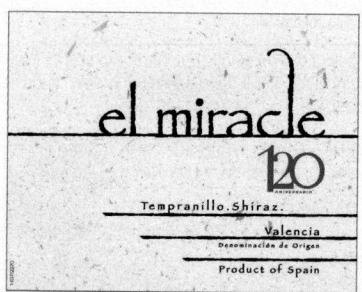

## CASTILLO DE LIRIA 2007 T
bobal 80%, syrah 20%

**82**

## CASTILLO DE LIRIA 2005 TC
tempranillo 100%

**81**

## CASTILLO DE LÍRIA 2004 TR
tempranillo 100%

**81**

## FUSTA NOVA MOSCATEL 2008 BLANCO DULCE
moscatel 100%

**85** Colour: yellow, bright golden. Nose: powerful, warm, grapey, honeyed notes. Palate: sweet, unctuous, fine bitter notes, spirituous.

## CASTILLO DE LIRIA 2008 MOSCATEL
moscatel 100%

**85** Colour: bright yellow. Nose: neat, grapey, honeyed notes. Palate: sweet, rich, fine bitter notes, great length.

## SOME OTHER WINERIES WITHIN THE DO:

**BODEGAS COMECHE**
**BODEGAS DE VENACLOIG S.L.**
**BODEGAS EL VILLAR S.C.V.**
**BODEGAS VIDAL**
**BODEGAS Y DESTILERÍAS CARMELITANO**
**COMPAÑIA VALENCIANA DE VINS**
   **I ESPIRITUOSOS**
**COOP. VINÍCOLA DE QUATRETONDA**
**COOP. AGRÍCOLA STA BÁRBARA DE CASINOS**
**COOP. SANTA BÁRBARA DE TITAGUAS**
**COOP. VINÍCOLA SAN ANTONIO ABAD**
**COOP. VINÍCOLA SAN PEDRO APÓSTOL**
**COOP. VINÍCOLA VINICA CHIVANA**
**ENRIQUE BENAVENT BENAVENT**
**HERMANOS NOGUEROLES S.L.**
**SDAD COOP. AGROVINÍCOLA DE MONTSERRAT**
**VIÑAS DEL PORTILLO S.L.**
**VITIVINÍCOLA DE LA POBLA DEL DUC**

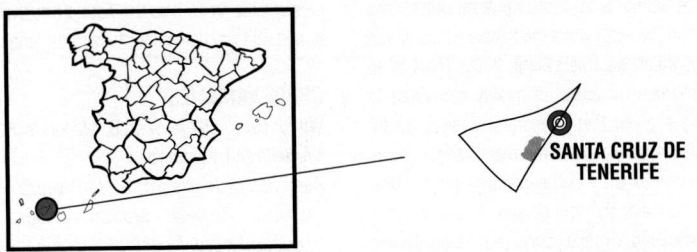

SANTA CRUZ DE
TENERIFE

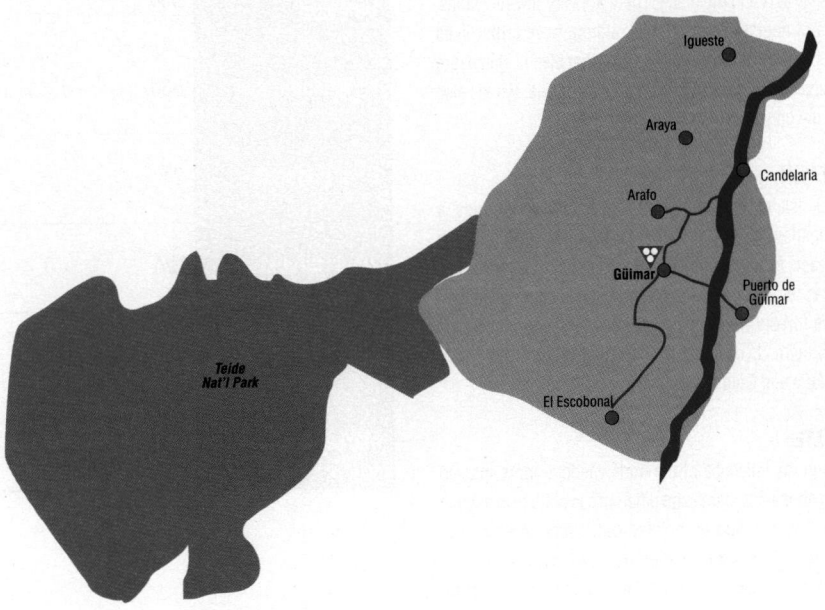

Igueste

Araya

Candelaria

Arafo

Güímar

Puerto de
Güímar

Teide
Nat'l Park

El Escobonal

▼ Consejo Regulador
● DO Boundary

# DO VALLE DE GÜÍMAR

## NEWS

Abona's neighbouring region located to the southeast of Tenerife, Valle de Güímar is a DO full of brilliant white wines (much better than the reds) when the Sahara winds do not spoil the party, which was the case in 2008. There is an obvious improvement in terms of quality compared to previous vintages given that temperatures were milder during harvest. Listán blanca is the main variety and is present in these wines wit a high percentage (up to 60%) and is showing increasingly more elegant, with some fresh herbs notes and a supple, round palate, even when blended with other local grape varieties like gual. The best-rated dry wines are El Borujo and Viña Herzas, beside the sweet Gran Virtud, made from raisins. Also on the increase are blends from malvasía and moscatel. There are very few red wines, blends of negramoll and tintilla, although we rather liked wines like Contiempo or Viña Chagua that blend listán negra with smaller amounts of foreign grape varieties. Here is also made the only sparkling wine in Tenerife.

## LOCATION

On the island of Tenerife. It practically constitutes a prolongation of the Valle de la Orotava region to the southeast, forming a valley open to the sea, with the Las Dehesas region situated in the mountains and surrounded by pine forests where the vines grow in an almost Alpine environment. It covers the municipal districts of Arafo, Candelaria and Güímar.

## CLIMATE

Although the influence of the trade winds is more marked than in Abona, the significant difference in altitude in a much reduced space must be pointed out, which gives rise to different microclimates, and pronounced contrasts in day-night temperatures, which delays the harvest until 1st November.

## SOIL

Volcanic at high altitudes, there is a black tongue of lava crossing the area where the vines are cultivated on a hostile terrain with wooden frames to raise the long vine shoots.

## GRAPE VARIETIES:

**White:** *Gual, Listán Blanco, Malvasía, Moscatel, Verdello* and *Vijariego.*

**Red:** *Bastardo Negro, Listán Negro* (15% of total), *Malvasía Rosada, Moscatel Negro, Negramoll, Vijariego Negro, Cabernet Sauvignon, Merlot, Pinot Noir, Ruby Cabernet, Syrah* and *Tempranillo.*

| | |
|---|---|
| Hectares of Vineyard | 634 |
| Nº Viticulturists | 560 |
| Nº of Bodegas | 21 |
| 2008 Harvest | N/A |
| 2007 Production | 380,000 l. |
| Marketing | 100% domestic |

**CONSEJO REGULADOR**
Tafetana, 14. 38500 Güímar (Tenerife)
☎: 922 514 709 - Fax: 922 514 485
@ consejo@vinosvalleguimar.com
www.vinosvalleguimar.com

## GENERAL CHARACTERISTICS OF THE WINES:

| | |
|---|---|
| **WHITES** | These are the most characteristic product of the area, with more than 80% of the production. They are produced from *Listán Blanco*, and the best stand out for their expressivity, refinement and complexity. They have a pale yellow colour; delicate aromas of flowers and fruit; on the palate they are complex, flavourful and persistent. |
| **REDS** | These play a minor role in the overall production. Deep cherry-red coloured, they tend to be fruity with wild nuances; on the palate they are dry, fruity and light. |

## 2008 VINTAGE RATING:

## VERY GOOD

## AGUSTÍN PÉREZ GARCÍA

Urb. Las Cruces, 28
38500 Güimar (Tenerife)
☎: 922 524 114

LOS CUATRO REALES 2008 B
**78**

## ANTONIO RAUL FUENTES BRITO

La Hoya. Finca La Sabina
38500 Güimar (Tenerife)
☎: 922 512 585 - Fax: 922 512 585

TIZÓN DEL SUR 2008 T BARRICA
listán negro 60%, syrah 20%, merlot 20%
**82**

## ARCA DE VITIS

Chinguaro, 26-B San Francisco Javier
38500 Güimar (Tenerife)
☎: 922 512 552 - Fax: 922 512 552
arcadevitis@arcadevitis.com
www.arcadevitis.com

CONTIEMPO VIDUEÑOS SECO 2008 B
marmajuelo 13,5%, verdejo %, malvasia %, gual %, moscatel %
**88** Colour: pale. Nose: grassy, wild herbs, fresh fruit, ripe fruit. Palate: flavourful, fruity, fresh.

CONTIEMPO MOSCATEL AFRUTADO 2008 B
moscatel
**87** Colour: bright straw. Nose: powerful, varietal, ripe fruit, citrus fruit, floral. Palate: flavourful, fruity, fresh, light-bodied, sweetness.

CONTIEMPO MALVASÍA SECO 2008 B
malvasia
**83**

CONTIEMPO MALVASÍA 2007 B
malvasia
**85** Colour: bright straw. Nose: fruit liqueur notes, honeyed notes. Palate: fruity, fleshy, ripe fruit, warm.

CONTIEMPO 2008 T
listán negro, tempranillo, syrah
**86** Colour: cherry, garnet rim. Nose: powerful, ripe fruit, scrubland. Palate: flavourful, powerful, fleshy.

CONTIEMPO TINTO DE POSTRE 2008 T
baboso negro
**86** Colour: cherry, garnet rim. Nose: smoky, earthy notes, ripe fruit, fruit preserve. Palate: powerful, sweet, spicy, fleshy.

CONTIEMPO 2006 TC
listán negro
**83**

CONTIEMPO MALVASÍA DULCE 2008 B DULCE
malvasia
**85** Colour: bright straw. Nose: powerful, slightly evolved, candied fruit, honeyed notes, balsamic herbs. Palate: flavourful, powerful, fleshy, sweet.

## BODEGA PICO ARGUAMA

Lomo la Arena, 9
38530 Igueste Candelaria (Tenerife)
☎: 922 501 110

PICO ARGUAMA 2008 T
**81**

## BODEGAS VIÑA DEL MACHADO

Avda. Santa Cruz, 27
38500 Güimar (Santa Cruz de Tenerife)
☎: 922 512 544 - Fax: 922 514 651
ferreol@melosar.com
www.melosar.com

VIÑA MELOSAR AFRUTADO 2008 B
**86** Colour: pale. Nose: fresh fruit, citrus fruit, floral. Palate: flavourful, fruity, fresh, sweetness.

VIÑA MELOSAR 2008 B
listán blanco 75%, gual 25%
**82**

VIÑA MELOSAR 2008 T BARRICA
tintilla, listán negro, merlot, syrah
**85** Colour: cherry, garnet rim. Nose: creamy oak, new oak, cocoa bean, ripe fruit. Palate: flavourful, fleshy, toasty, harsh oak tannins.

MELOSAR NATURALMENTE DULCE 2007 T
listán negro 60%, syrah 40%
**85** Colour: black cherry, orangey edge. Nose: medium intensity, tar, varnish, fruit preserve, candied fruit, warm. Palate: flavourful, powerful, fleshy, sweet, astringent.

HEREDAMIENTO
DOÑA ARGENTA

## EL BORUJO

Subida Los Loros, km. 4,2
38550 Arafo (Santa Cruz de Tenerife)
☎: 922 511 676 - Fax: 922 513 643
el_borujo@hotmail.com

EL BORUJO 2008 B ROBLE
gual 50%, listán blanco 50%

**91** Colour: bright straw. Nose: sweet spices, cocoa bean, creamy oak, ripe fruit, citrus fruit, tropical fruit. Palate: flavourful, ripe fruit, spicy.

EL BORUJO 2008 B
listán blanco 90%, moscatel 10%

**87** Colour: bright straw. Nose: powerful, jasmine, ripe fruit, citrus fruit. Palate: flavourful, fruity, fresh, ripe fruit.

EL BORUJO 2008 T
tempranillo 50%, listán negro 50%

**83**

## FERRERA

Calvo Sotelo, 44
38550 Arafo (Tenerife)
☎: 649 487 835 - Fax: 922 237 359
carmengloria@bodegaferrera.com

FERRERA 2008 B
listán blanco 70%, albillo 20%, moscatel 10%

**78**

## LOS PELADOS

Hoya Cartaya, 32 - Chacona
38500 Güimar (Tenerife)
☎: 922 512 786 - Fax: 922 514 485
bodegaslospelados@hotmail.com

LOS PELADOS 2008 B
listán blanco 100%

**84**

LOS PELADOS 2008 T
listán negro 80%, negramoll 20%

**84**

## MIGUEL ANGEL HERNÁNDEZ

Morras del Tanque
38550 Arafo (Santa Cruz de Tenerife)
☎: 922 511 405 - Fax: 922 290 064
mangel3@comtf.es

VIÑAS HERZAS 2008 B

**89** Colour: bright straw. Nose: fresh, fresh fruit, white flowers, expressive, tropical fruit. Palate: flavourful, fruity, good acidity, balanced.

VIÑAS HERZAS 2008 T

**83**

## SAT VIÑA LAS CAÑAS

Barranco Badajoz
38500 Güimar (Santa Cruz de Tenerife)
☎: 922 512 716 - Fax: 922 512 716
vegalascanas@hotmail.com

GRAN VIRTUD MALVASIA 2008 B
malvasia 100%

**88** Colour: pale. Nose: white flowers, jasmine, ripe fruit, fresh fruit, fragrant herbs. Palate: flavourful, fruity, fleshy.

VEGA LAS CAÑAS 2008 B
listán blanco 100%

**87** Colour: pale. Nose: mineral, earthy notes, ripe fruit, fresh fruit, floral. Palate: flavourful, fruity, fresh, fleshy.

GRAN VIRTUD 2008 B
listán blanco 100%

**86** Colour: pale. Nose: grassy, powerfull, varietal, white flowers. Palate: flavourful, fruity, fresh, fleshy.

GRAN VIRTUD 2007 B
uvas pasas 100%

**91** Colour: bright golden. Nose: powerful, candied fruit, honeyed notes, dry nuts, citrus fruit. Palate: flavourful, powerful, fleshy, sweet.

VEGA LAS CAÑAS 2008 T
listán negro 60%, syrah 30%, cabernet sauvignon 10%, merlot %

**83**

VEGA LAS CAÑAS AFRUTADO 2008 SS
listán blanco 60%, moscatel 40%

**82**

## TOMÁS GUZMÁN MESA RODRÍGUEZ (VIÑAS MESAS)

Sosa, 2
38550 Arafo (Tenerife)
☎: 922 510 450 - Fax: 922 510 450
tomasgmg@hotmail.com

VIÑAS MESAS SEMI 2008 B
listán blanco 100%

**77**

VIÑAS MESAS 2008 B
listán blanco 80%, moscatel 20%

**75**

VIÑAS MESAS 2008 RD
listán negro 100%

**87** Colour: rose, purple rim. Nose: fresh fruit, red berry notes, fruit expression. Palate: fruity, fleshy, flavourful.

VIÑAS MESAS 2008 T
listán negro, tempranillo

**83**

## VIÑA CHAGUA

Lomo Grande Abajo, 29
38500 Güimar (Santa Cruz de Tenerife)
☎: 922 511 168 - Fax: 922 511 168
bodegachagua@hotmail.com

VIÑA CHAGUA 2008 B
listán blanco 80%, Vigiriego 20%, gual %, moscatel %

**84**

VIÑA CHAGUA 2008 T
listán negro 80%, merlot 10%, syrah 10%

**85** Colour: cherry, purple rim. Nose: red berry notes, ripe fruit, raspberry, floral. Palate: flavourful, fruity, fresh.

## VITICULTORES COMARCA DE GÜIMAR

Apdo. Correos 179
38500 Güimar (Tenerife)
☎: 922 510 437 - Fax: 922 510 437
info@bodegacomarcalguimar.com
www.bodegacomarcalguimar.com

BRUMAS DE AYOSA 2008 B
listán blanco

**86** Colour: pale. Nose: floral, ripe fruit, fresh fruit, sweet spices. Palate: flavourful, fruity, fleshy.

BRUMAS DE AYOSA AFRUTADO 2008 B
listán blanco, moscatel

**84**

BRUMAS DE AYOSA 2008 BFB
listán blanco

**84**

BRUMAS DE AYOSA SELECCIÓN 2008 B
malvasia, moscatel, marmajuelo, listán blanco

**82**

BRUMAS DE AYOSA 2008 RD
listán negro

**78**

BRUMAS DE AYOSA 2007 RD
malvasia rosado

**82**

BRUMAS DE AYOSA VARIETAL 2008 T
merlot, tempranillo, cabernet sauvignon, listán negro

**81**

BRUMAS DE AYOSA 2008 T
listán negro

**73**

BRUMAS DE AYOSA MALVASÍA 2005 B DULCE
malvasia

**87** Colour: bright straw. Nose: fresh, expressive, balsamic herbs, grassy, fresh fruit, citrus fruit. Palate: flavourful, sweet, fruity.

BRUMAS DE AYOSA 2007 BN
listán blanco

**82**

SOME OTHER WINERIES WITHIN THE DO:

**AGUSTÍN JULIÁN HERNÁNDEZ
JOSÉ M. GARCÍA DELGADO
JUAN TACORONTE CEJAS
LA ROCIERA ( EL TRINQUE)
LUIS OLIVA RODRÍGUEZ
M. DEL CARMEN HERNÁNDEZ GARCÍA
MANUEL JESÚS RAMOS PÉREZ
MODESTO DÍAZ GONZÁLEZ
TIZÓN**

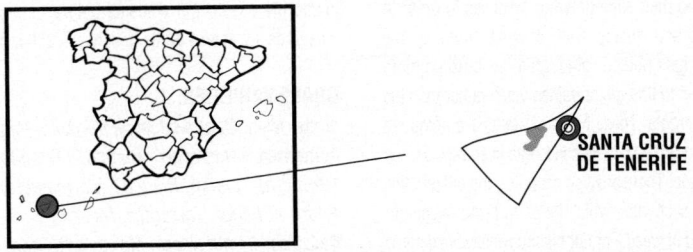

SANTA CRUZ
DE TENERIFE

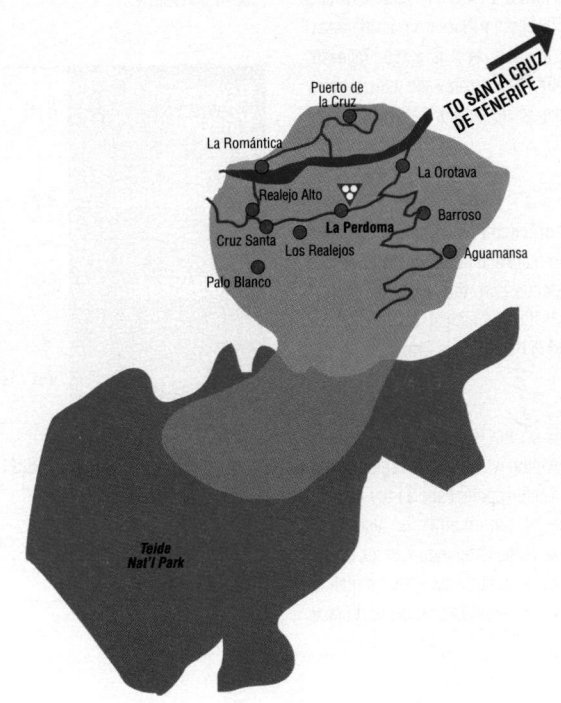

Puerto de
la Cruz

TO SANTA CRUZ
DE TENERIFE

La Romántica

La Orotava

Realejo Alto

Barroso

Cruz Santa

La Perdoma

Los Realejos

Aguamansa

Palo Blanco

Teide
Nat'l Park

▽ Consejo Regulador
● DO Boundary

## NEWS

In the valley at the foothills of the northern face of mount Teide there are changing their wine-growing practices in order to get better yields and quality. Still, a great chunk of the production never gets bottled, although it has become more and more common to find guyot trained vines rather than the traditional high pergola. These types of plants are unique in the world, reaching up to 15 meters in length in some old vines over 50 years of age. There are also dropping the old practice of digging round each vine, which helps to bring oxygen to the root and get rid of weed. For our tasting we have had some mid-table white and red wines, mostly young 2008 renderings which show some sort of varietal expression, with floral and balsamic herbs nuances. The best are those from listán blanca, juicy and aromatic, and the very best is a red, Tajinaste Vendimia Seleccionada 2007, full of creamy and mineral notes of the wood and the volcanic soil nuances of the region, simply singular.

## LOCATION

In the north of the island of Tenerife. It borders to the west with the DO Ycoden-Daute-Isora and to the east with the DO Tacoronte-Acentejo. It extends from the sea to the foot of the Teide, and comprises the municipal districts of La Orotava, Los Realejos and El Puerto de la Cruz.

## CLIMATE

As with the other regions on the islands, the weather is conditioned by the trade winds, which in this region result in wines with a moderate alcohol content and a truly Atlantic character. The influence of the Atlantic is also very important, in that it moderates the temperature of the costal areas and provides a lot of humidity. Lastly, the rainfall is rather low, but is generally more abundant on the north face and at higher altitudes.

## SOIL

Light, permeable, rich in mineral nutrients and with a slightly acidic pH due to the volcanic nature of the island. The vineyards are at an altitude of between 250 mm and 700 m.

## GRAPE VARIETIES:

**White:** Main: *Güal, Malvasía, Verdello, Vijariego.*
Authorized: *Bastardo Blanco, Forastera Blanca (Gomera), Listán Blanco, Marmajuelo, Moscatel, Pedro Ximénez, Torrontés, Moscatel.*
**Red:** Main: *Listán Negro, Malvasía Rosada, Negramoll.*
Authorized: *Bastardo Negro, Moscatel Negra, Tintilla, Vijariego Negra.*

| | |
|---|---|
| Hectares of Vineyard | 616 |
| Nº Viticulturists | 935 |
| Nº of Bodegas | 32 |
| 2008 Harvest | Very Good |
| 2007 Production | 688,916 l. |
| Marketing | 99% domestic 1% export |

**CONSEJO REGULADOR**
Parque Recreativo El Bosquito, nº1
Urb. La Marzagana II-La Perdona 38315 La Orotava.
☎: 922 309 922 / 23 - Fax: 922 309 924
@ orotava@vinos-de-canarias.org
www.dovalleorotava.com

## GENERAL CHARACTERISTICS OF THE WINES:

| | |
|---|---|
| **WHITES** | These are similar to those from Tacoronte in that they share the same Atlantic character. They have a straw yellow colour and are fresh and fruity with somewhat herbaceous notes, and in the best of the examples can reproduce the refinement of fennel or mint. |
| **ROSÉS** | Although the production is much lower, there are some fine examples of modern rosés with a raspberry colour, very fruity aromas, which are fresh and pleasant on the palate. |
| **REDS** | These are young wines, with a deep cherry-red colour, good aromatic intensity and notes of red berries in line with their Atlantic character; on the palate they are light, flavourful and pleasant. |

## 2008 VINTAGE RATING:

## GOOD

## BALCÓN DEL VALLE

Lordelos, 11
38315 La Perdoma (La Orotava)
☎: 922 331 427 - Fax: 922 324 454
balcondelvalle@yahoo.es

BALCÓN DEL VALLE 2008 B

**75**

BALCÓN DEL VALLE 2008 T

**86** Colour: cherry, garnet rim. Nose: powerfull, creamy oak, sweet spices, ripe fruit. Palate: flavourful, fleshy, spicy.

BALCÓN DEL VALLE VENDIMIA SELECCIONADA 2008 T BARRICA

**83**

BALCÓN DEL VALLE VENDIMIA SELECCIONADA 2008 T

**78**

## BODEGA LA SUERTITA

La Cruz Santa - Los Realejos
38410 (Santa Cruz de tenerife)
☎: 669 408 761
informacion@lasuertita.com
www.lasuertita.com

LA SUERTITA 2008 B BARRICA

**87** Colour: bright straw. Nose: roasted almonds, toasty, new oak, candied fruit, fruit preserve, citrus fruit. Palate: flavourful, powerful, fleshy, spicy.

LA SUERTITA 2008 B

**83**

## BODEGA TAFURIASTE

Las Candias
38312 La Orotava (Santa Cruz Tenerife)
☎: 922 336 027 - Fax: 922 336 027
vinos@bodegatafuriaste.com
www.bodegatafuriaste.com

TAFURIASTE 2008 B
listán blanco, moscatel, pedro ximénez, gual

**83**

VINOS TAFURIASTE VENDIMIA SELECCIONADA 15 MESES 2007 T
listán negro, castellana, negramoll

**86** Colour: cherry, garnet rim. Nose: powerfull, ripe fruit, dark chocolate, sweet spices, balsamic herbs. Palate: flavourful, fleshy, spicy, ripe fruit.

VINOS TAFURIASTE VENDIMIA SELECCIONADA 8 MESES 2007 T
listán negro

**83**

PRUNUS

## BODEGA TAJINASTE

El Ratiño, 5
38315 La Orotava (Tenerife)
☎: 922 308 720 - Fax: 922 308 720
bodega@tajinaste.net
www.tajinaste.net

TAJINASTE 2008 B
listán blanco

**85** Colour: bright straw. Nose: white flowers, fresh fruit. Palate: fruity, fresh, easy to drink.

TAJINASTE AFRUTADO 2008 B
listán blanco

**79**

TAJINASTE 2008 RD
listán negro

**83**

TAJINASTE TRADICIONAL 2008 T
listán negro

**87** Colour: cherry, purple rim. Nose: fresh fruit, red berry notes, floral, balsamic herbs. Palate: flavourful, fruity, good acidity, round tannins.

TAJINASTE 2008 T BARRICA
listán negro

**86** Colour: cherry, garnet rim. Nose: medium intensity, ripe fruit, balsamic herbs, scrubland. Palate: flavourful, fruity, spicy, round tannins.

TAJINASTE 2008 T MACERACIÓN CARBÓNICA
listán negro

**82**

**TAJINASTE VENDIMIA SELECCIONADA 2007 T**
listán negro

**89** Colour: bright cherry. Nose: ripe fruit, sweet spices, creamy oak, mineral. Palate: flavourful, fruity, toasty, round tannins.

## EL VALLE S.L.

Ctra. de Medianía, 156
38315 La Perdoma - La Orotava (Tenerife)
☎: 922 213 813 - Fax: 922 213 477
info@bodegaelvalle.com
www.bodegaelvalle.com

SEÑORÍO DEL VALLE AFRUTADO 2008 B

**82**

VIÑA EL VALLE 2008 B

**72**

VIÑA EL VALLE 2008 T

**78**

## FRANCISCO GONZÁLEZ PERDIGÓN

San Juan, 26
38300 La Orotava (Tenerife)
☎: 922 331 662

DEHESA ALTA 2008 T

**71**

## LOS GUINES

Pista Los Guines, s/n El Horno
38410 Los Realejos (Tenerife)
☎: 922 343 320 - Fax: 922 353 855
www.bodegalosguines.com

LOS GÜINES 2008 B

**81**

LOS GÜINES 2008 T BARRICA

**82**

## SOAGRANORTE

Ctral. Gral. La Perdoma, Las Suertes
(Finca El Esquilón) s/n
38300 La Orotava (Santa Cruz de Tenerife)

☎: 922 501 300 - Fax: 922 503 462
ventas@suertesdelmarques.com
www.suertesdelmarques.com

SUERTES DEL MARQUÉS SECO 2008 B
listán blanco

**87** Colour: bright straw. Nose: fresh, fresh fruit, white flowers, expressive. Palate: flavourful, fruity, good acidity, balanced.

7 FUENTES AFRUTADO 2008 B
listán blanco

**83**

SUERTES DEL MARQUÉS AFRUTADO 2008 B
listán blanco

**80**

SUERTES DEL MARQUÉS 2008 T

**86** Colour: cherry, purple rim. Nose: earthy notes, ripe fruit, raspberry, sweet spices. Palate: powerful, flavourful, ripe fruit.

7 FUENTES 2008 T
listán negro

**78**

## VALLEORO

Ctra. General La Oratova - Los Realejos, km. 4,5
38315 La Pedoma (Santa Cruz de Tenerife)
☎: 922 308 600 - Fax: 922 308 233
info@bodegavalleoro.com
www.bodegavalleoro.com

GRAN TEHYDA AFRUTADO 2008 B
listán blanco 100%

**85** Colour: pale. Nose: medium intensity, fresh fruit, white flowers. Palate: flavourful, fruity, sweetness.

VALLEORO TRADICIÓN 2008 B BARRICA
listán blanco 100%

**84**

VALLEORO AFRUTADO 2008 B
listán blanco 100%

**80**

GRAN TEHYDA 2008 RD
listán negro 100%

**84**

# DO VALLE DE LA OROTAVA

VALLEORO 2008 RD
listán negro 100%
## 82

GRAN TEHYDA 2008 T MACERACIÓN CARBÓNICA
listán negro 100%
## 83

VALLEORO 2008 T MACERACIÓN CARBÓNICA
listán negro 100%
## 82

SOME OTHER WINERIES WITHIN THE DO:

**BODEGA EL CALVARIO S.L.**
**EL PENITENTE S.L.**
**ERAS DEL MARQUÉS**
**FINCA LA SIERRA**
**HERMÓGENES DELGADO GUERRA**
**HORACIO LLANOS DÉVORA**
**JUAN E. LUIS BRAVO**
**MIGUEL LUIS GONZÁLEZ GONZÁLEZ**
**MONTESCLAROS**
**MONTIJO S.L.**
**RAIMUNDO HERNÁNDEZ JORGE**
**VIÑA MOCAN S.L.**
**VIÑA PIÑERA**

## NEWS

The wines from Madrid have started to get the recognition they deserve. A great achievement is the fact that in Madrid, the sales of wines from the region are now higher that those from Somontano or the albariños from Rías Baixas. The 2008 vintage in shorter in terms of production –a whole 25%, probably due to real estate interests– but not in quality, thanks to cooler night temperatures that delayed the ripening cycle. There are also a good bunch of new wines from young winemakers that have discovered the benefits of the old vines from the town of de San Martín de Valdeiglesias. Also novelties are Bernabeleva and Navaherreros, made in a Burgundian fashion from old garnacha under the consulancy of Raúl Pérez, and full of terroir expression. Great news are also the potential of the white grape albillo with two great renderings, Villamil and Cantocuerdas. Bodegas Marañones have also come up with powerful, creamy whites full of varietal expression in the same area of rocky slate soil to the west of Madrid, bordering with the province of Ávila. The cool vintage of 2008 has yielded a whole catalogue of young white wines of real stature, fresh, floral, with some fine herbal and balsamic notes and very expressive palates. The rosé renderings, almost all of them made from garnacha and tempranillo, abound in aromatic notes of red fruit. The reds, though, show some 'green' notes. Of the aged renderings we see two kinds: some that bring the ripening to the limit and get too much concentration, and a new trend, that of Raúl Pérez, that are defending the terroir expression and elegance. In the near future we will have an even broader catalogue of wines coming from two new areas in the process of being included within the DO, El Molar and Venturada, with fine slate soils.

## LOCATION

In the south of the province of Madrid, it covers three distinct sub-regions: Arganda, Navalcarnero and San Martín de Valdeiglesias.

## CLIMATE

Extreme continental, with cold winters and hot summers. The average annual rainfall ranges from 461 mm in Arganda to 658 mm in San Martín.

## SOIL

Rather unfertile soil and granite subsoil in the sub-region of San Martín de Valdeiglesias; in Navalcarnero the soil is brownish-grey, poor, with a subsoil of coarse sand and clay; in the sub-region of Arganda the soil is brownish-grey, with an acidic pH and granite subsoil.

## GRAPE VARIETIES:

**White:** *Malvar* (2,056 Ha), *Airén* (1,179 Ha), *Albillo, Parellada, Macabeo, Torrontés* and *Moscatel de Grano Menudo.*

**Red:** *Tinto Fino* (Tempranillo 1,036 Ha), *Garnacha* (2,772 Ha), *Merlot, Cabernet Sauvignon* and *Syrah.*

## SUB-REGIONS:

**San Martín.** It comprises 9 municipal districts and has more than 3,821 Ha of vineyards, with mainly the Garnacha (red) and Albillo (white) varieties.

**Navalcarnero.** It comprises 19 municipal districts with a total of about 2,107 Ha. The most typical wines are reds and rosés based on the Garnacha variety.

**Arganda.** With 5,830 Ha and 26 municipal districts, it is the largest sub-region of the DO. The main varieties are the white Malvar and the red Tempranillo or Tinto Fino.

| | |
|---|---|
| **Hectares of Vineyard** | 7,461 |
| **Nº Viticulturists** | 2,550 |
| **Nº of Bodegas** | 45 |
| **2008 Harvest** | Good |
| **2007 Production** | 17,816,604 l. |
| **Marketing** | 72% domestic 28% export |

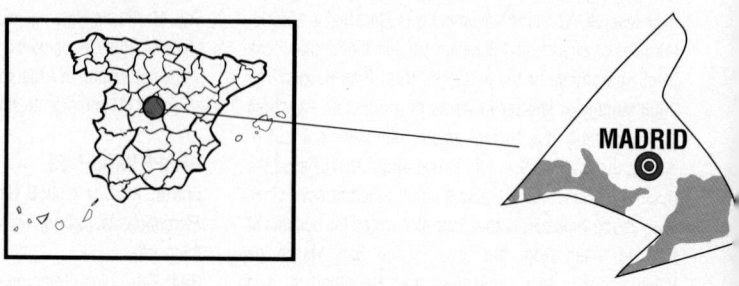

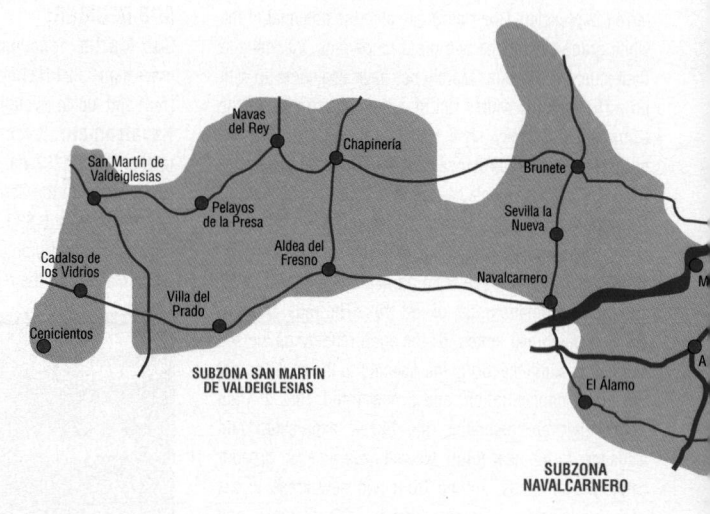

# DO VINOS DE MADRID

MADRID
Navas del Rey
Chapinería
San Martín de Valdeiglesias
Pelayos de la Presa
Brunete
Sevilla la Nueva
Aldea del Fresno
Cadalso de los Vidrios
Villa del Prado
Navalcarnero
Cenicientos
SUBZONA SAN MARTÍN DE VALDEIGLESIAS
El Álamo
SUBZONA NAVALCARNERO
Consejo Regulador
DO Boundary

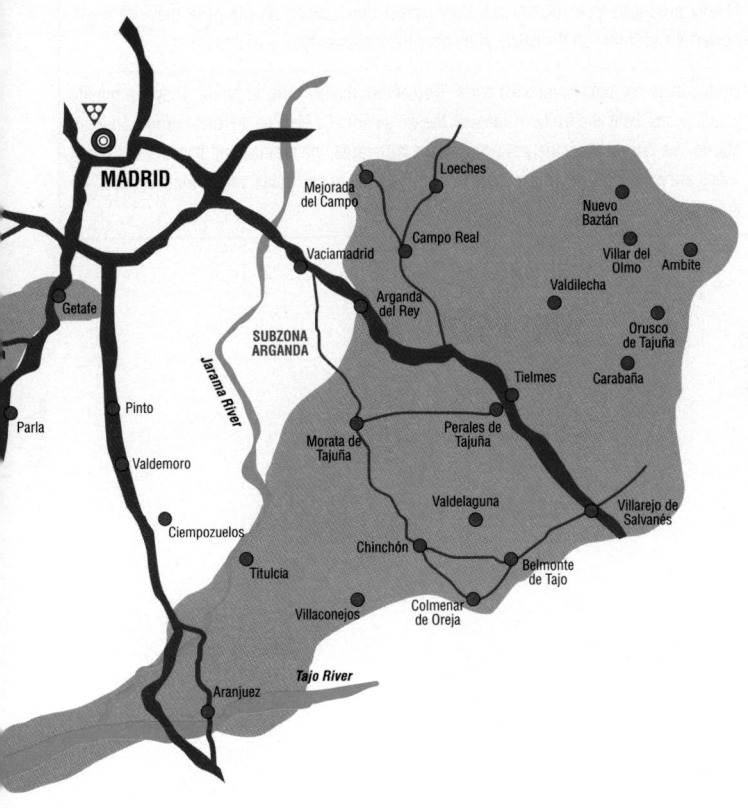

**CONSEJO REGULADOR**
Bravo Murillo, 101, 3º. 28020 Madrid
☎: 915 348 511 / 915 347 240 - Fax: 915 538 574
@ consejo@vinosdemadrid.es
www.vinosdemadrid.es

## GENERAL CHARACTERISTICS OF THE WINES:

| | |
|---|---|
| **WHITES** | The most characteristic are those produced from *Malvar* in the sub-region of Arganda. Fruity and pleasant, on occasion they have wild notes; on the palate they are fresh, flavourful and supple. They are also produced from traditional 'sobremadre' wines (they follow a barrelling process with the skins lasting about three months) and, in line with more modern trends, white wines fermented in barrels. |
| **ROSÉS** | Mainly produced from *Garnacha*, they have a pink colour; on the nose they are fresh, powerful and fruity; on the palate, they have the tastiness typical of this variety. |
| **REDS** | Firstly, there are those produced from *Tinto Fino*, mainly from Arganda. They are mostly young wines, light and fruity, in line with the wines from La Mancha. In Navalcarnero and San Martín, the *Garnacha* variety is used. In the latter area, the aromas and flavours of the red wines are concentrated, with a character of ripe fruit, earthy notes, meaty and flavourful on the palate. |

### 2008 VINTAGE RATING:

## VERY GOOD

## BERNABELEVA

Alfonso XI, nº 7
28014 Madrid (Madrid)
☎: 915 091 909
www.bernabeleva.com

### VILLAMIL 2007 B
albillo

**92** Colour: bright golden. Nose: powerful, characterful, ripe fruit, creamy oak, cocoa bean. Palate: flavourful, fruity, rich, fine bitter notes, long.

### CANTOCUERDAS 2007 B
albillo 100%

**91** Colour: bright yellow. Nose: powerful, ripe fruit, sweet spices, creamy oak, fragrant herbs. Palate: rich, smoky aftertaste, flavourful, fresh, good acidity.

### BERNABELEVA VIÑA BONITA 2007 T
garnacha 100%

**95** Colour: dark-red cherry. Nose: complex, expressive, varietal, dried herbs, spicy, aromatic coffee. Palate: spicy, balsamic, spirituous, mineral, smoky aftertaste.

### BERNABELEVA "CARRIL DEL REY" 2007 T
garnacha 100%

**93** Colour: dark-red cherry. Nose: mineral, ripe fruit, fruit liqueur notes, powerfull, expressive, varietal, warm, spicy, smoky, dried herbs, scrubland. Palate: powerful, fruity, full, flavourful, balsamic, mineral.

### BERNABELEVA "ARROYO DE TÓRTOLAS" 2007 T
garnacha 100%

**93** Colour: dark-red cherry. Nose: closed, complex, sweet spices, creamy oak. Palate: powerful, flavourful, complex, fleshy, toasty, mineral.

### NAVAHERREROS 2007 T
garnacha 100%

**91** Colour: light cherry. Nose: powerful, complex, varietal, warm, wild herbs, undergrowth, earthy notes. Palate: balsamic, creamy, mineral, smoky aftertaste.

## BODEGA DEL REAL CORTIJO DE CARLOS III

León Ruiz, s/n Real Cortijo de San Isidro
28300 Aranjuez (Madrid)
☎: 915 357 735 - Fax: 915 547 037
bodega@realcortijo.com
www.realcortijo.com

### HOMET 2004 TR
70% tempranillo, 10% merlot, 10% cabernet suvignon, 10% syrah

**85** Colour: dark-red cherry, garnet rim. Nose: ripe fruit, sweet spices, creamy oak, cocoa bean. Palate: fruity, flavourful, good acidity, round tannins.

## BODEGA ECOLÓGICA LUIS SAAVEDRA

Ctra. de Escalona, 5
28650 Cenicientos (Madrid)
☎: 914 606 053 - Fax: 914 606 053
info@bodegasaavedra.com
www.bodegasaavedra.com

### CORUCHO ALBILLO MOSCATEL 2008 B
albillo 95%, moscatel 5%

**87** Colour: golden. Nose: fruit expression, fresh fruit, white flowers, grassy. Palate: fruity, flavourful, good acidity.

### CORUCHO 2008 RD
garnacha tinta 100%

**82**

### LUIS SAAVEDRA GARNACHA CEPAS VIEJAS 2006 TC
garnacha 90%, tinto fino 10%

**89** Colour: ruby red. Nose: varietal, spicy, fine reductive notes. Palate: light-bodied, full, flavourful.

CORUCHO GARNACHA CEPAS VIEJAS 2006 T
garnacha 100%

**87** Colour: light cherry. Nose: fruit liqueur notes, fruit liqueur notes, dry nuts, spicy, tobacco. Palate: light-bodied, fresh, flavourful.

## BODEGA MARAÑONES

Hilero, 7 Nave 9
28696 Pelayos de la Presa (Madrid)
☎: 615 640 888
fernandogarcia@bodegamaranones.com

PICARANA 2008 B
albillo

**92** Colour: bright straw. Nose: powerful, ripe fruit, citrus fruit, tropical fruit, mineral, dry stone. Palate: flavourful, powerful, fleshy, spicy.

## BODEGA Y VIÑEDOS GOSÁLBEZ ORTI

Real, 14
28813 Pozuelo del Rey (Madrid)
☎: 918 725 399 - Fax: 918 725 399
bodega@qubel.com
www.qubel.com

MAYRIT 2008 B
albillo 100%

**81**

QUBÉL EXCEPCIÓN 2006 T
garnacha 100%

**90** Colour: cherry, garnet rim. Nose: powerful, ripe fruit, grassy, balsamic herbs. Palate: flavourful, powerful, spicy, ripe fruit.

MAYRIT 2006 T
tempranillo 80%, cabernet sauvignon 20%

**86** Colour: cherry, garnet rim. Nose: powerful, ripe fruit, raspberry, sweet spices. Palate: flavourful, powerful, fleshy.

MAYRIT ECO 2006 T
tempranillo 50%, cabernet sauvignon 20%, merlot 15%, syrah 15%

**85** Colour: cherry, garnet rim. Nose: powerful, grassy, balsamic herbs. Palate: flavourful, spicy, balsamic.

QUBÉL NATURE 2005 TC
tempranillo 80%, cabernet sauvignon 10%, garnacha 10%

**91** Colour: cherry, purple rim. Nose: ripe fruit, sweet spices, creamy oak, cocoa bean. Palate: powerful, good structure, warm, good acidity, sweet tannins.

QUBÉL NATURE 2004 T
tempranillo 80%, cabernet sauvignon 10%, syrah 10%

**89** Colour: very deep cherry, garnet rim. Nose: ripe fruit, balsamic herbs, sweet spices, creamy oak, dark chocolate. Palate: sweetness, fleshy, concentrated, good acidity, round tannins.

QUBÉL PACIENCIA 2004 TR
tempranillo 80%, syrah 10%, cabernet sauvignon 10%

**88** Colour: very deep cherry, garnet rim. Nose: fruit preserve, warm, sweet spices, dark chocolate. Palate: flavourful, fruity, grainy tannins, pruney.

## BODEGAS CASTEJÓN

Ronda de Watres, 29
28500 Arganda del Rey (Madrid)
☎: 918 710 264 - Fax: 918 713 343
castejon@bodegascastejon.com
www.bodegascastejon.com

VIÑA REY TEMPRANILLO 2008 T
tempranillo 100%

**85** Colour: cherry, purple rim. Nose: powerful, balsamic herbs, scrubland, smoky. Palate: flavourful, powerful, fleshy, fine bitter notes.

VIÑA REY "70 BARRICAS" 2007 T
tempranillo 100%

**85** Colour: cherry, garnet rim. Nose: ripe fruit, scrubland, balsamic herbs, toasty, new oak. Palate: powerful, fleshy, fine bitter notes.

VIÑARDUL SELECCIÓN VARIETALES 2005 T
tempranillo 85%, garnacha 10%, cabernet sauvignon 5%

**88** Colour: cherry, garnet rim. Nose: powerful, mineral, dry stone, ripe fruit, balsamic herbs. Palate: flavourful, powerful, fleshy, round tannins.

VIÑARDUL 2004 TC
tempranillo 100%

**83**

VIÑARDUL 2003 TR
tempranillo 100%

**84**

TISOL

## BODEGAS LICINIA

Carrera de Poniente, 10
28530 Morata de Tajuña (Madrid)
☎: 918 731 579 - Fax: 918 731 579
o.fernandez@licinia.es
www.bodegaslicinia.es

**LICINIA 2007 T**
tempranillo 60%, cabernet sauvignon 40%

**92** Colour: deep cherry. Nose: powerful, fruit expression, ripe fruit, mineral, sweet spices, cocoa bean, dark chocolate, lactic notes. Palate: powerful, fleshy, fruity, round tannins.

**LICINIA 2006 T**
syrah 40%, tempranillo 30%, cabernet sauvignon 30%          21€

**89** Colour: cherry, garnet rim. Nose: powerful, ripe fruit, creamy oak. Palate: flavourful, fleshy, powerful, round tannins.

## BODEGAS NUEVA VALVERDE S.A.

Santo Domingo de Silos, 6 bajo dcha.
28036 (Madrid)
☎: 915 640 191 - Fax: 914 114 718
info@bodegasnuevavalverde.com
www.bodegasnuevavalverde.com

**TEJONERAS ALTA SELECCIÓN 2006 T**
tempranillo, syrah, cabernet sauvignon, merlot, garnacha

**86** Colour: bright cherry. Nose: ripe fruit, sweet spices, creamy oak, expressive. Palate: flavourful, fruity, toasty, round tannins.

**750 2005 T**
merlot, cabernet sauvignon, syrah

**90** Colour: cherry, garnet rim. Nose: powerful, ripe fruit, sweet spices, creamy oak. Palate: flavourful, fleshy, powerful, ripe fruit, round tannins.

## BODEGAS ORUSCO

Alcalá, 54
28511 Valdilecha (Madrid)
☎: 918 738 006 - Fax: 918 738 336
bo@bodegasorusco.com
www.bodegasorusco.com

**VIÑA MAÍN 2008 B**
malvar

**84**

**VIÑA MAÍN 2008 RD**
tempranillo

**82**

**VIÑA MAÍN 2008 T**
tempranillo

**84**

**MAÍN 2005 TC**
tempranillo

**80**

## BODEGAS PABLO MORATE

Avda.Generalísimo, 33 - 34
28391 Valdelaguna (Madrid)
☎: 918 937 172 - Fax: 918 937 172
bodegasmorate@bodegasmorate.com
www.bodegasmorate.com

**VIÑA CHOZO S/C B**

**78**

**VIÑA CHOZO S/C T**

**81**

**SEÑORÍO DE MORATE GRAN SELECCIÓN 2005 TC**
tempranillo

**83**

**SEÑORÍO DE MORATE GRAN SELECCIÓN 2004 TC**

**85** Colour: cherry, garnet rim. Nose: scrubland, powerfull, ripe fruit. Palate: flavourful, fleshy, powerful, fine bitter notes.

**SEÑORÍO DE MORATE GRAN SELECCIÓN 2003 TR**

**84**

**SEÑORÍO DE MORATE SELECCIÓN 2000 TGR**

**83**

## BODEGAS TAGONIUS

Ctra. Ambite, km. 4,4
28550 Tielmes (Madrid)
☎: 918 737 505 - Fax: 918 746 161
tagonius@tagonius.com
www.tagonius.com

# DO VINOS DE MADRID

## TAGONIUS VARIETAL SYRAH 2007 T
syrah 100%

**90** Colour: very deep cherry, garnet rim. Nose: fruit preserve, floral, sweet spices, creamy oak, varietal. Palate: concentrated, fruity, flavourful, good acidity, sweet tannins.

## TAGONIUS VARIETAL MERLOT 2007 T
merlot 100%

**88** Colour: very deep cherry, garnet rim. Nose: fruit preserve, spicy, aromatic coffee, expressive. Palate: ripe fruit, concentrated, good acidity, round tannins.

## TAGONIUS 2006 T ROBLE
tempranillo 15,5%, cabernet sauvignon 54%, sumoll 22%, merlot 8,5%

**89** Nose: fruit preserve, dark chocolate, sweet spices, creamy oak. Palate: powerful, round, good acidity, sweet tannins.

## TAGONIUS CENTENARIO GRAN VIA 2005 TR
merlot 50%, tempranillo 50%

**91** Colour: cherry, garnet rim. Nose: ripe fruit, spicy, creamy oak, toasty, scrubland, balsamic herbs. Palate: powerful, flavourful, toasty, round tannins.

## TAGONIUS 2005 TC
tempranillo 20%, cabernet sauvignon 25%, syrah 45%, merlot 10%

**89** Colour: cherry, purple rim. Nose: powerful, ripe fruit, creamy oak, toasty, grassy. Palate: flavourful, powerful, fleshy, round tannins.

## TAGONIUS MARIAGE 2005 TR
tempranillo 50%, merlot 50%

**89** Colour: cherry, garnet rim. Nose: powerful, ripe fruit, candied fruit, dark chocolate, aromatic coffee. Palate: flavourful, fleshy.

## TAGONIUS GRAN VINO SELECCIÓN 2004 TR
cabernet sauvignon 50%, syrah 15%, merlot 25%, tempranillo 10%

**90** Colour: cherry, garnet rim. Nose: ripe fruit, spicy, creamy oak, roasted coffee. Palate: powerful, flavourful, toasty, round tannins.

## TAGONIUS 2004 TR
tempranillo 30%, cabernet sauvignon 50%, syrah 20%

**89** Colour: cherry, garnet rim. Nose: powerful, ripe fruit, grassy, varietal. Palate: flavourful, fleshy, fruity, sweetness, round tannins.

## TIKVAH KOSHER 2004 TC
tempranillo 80%, cabernet sauvignon 20%

**88** Colour: cherry, garnet rim. Nose: spicy, toasty, ripe fruit, scrubland, balsamic herbs. Palate: flavourful, powerful, fleshy.

PUNTO DIEZ

## FIGUEROA

Convento, 19
28380 Colmenar de Oreja (Madrid)
☎: 918 944 859 - Fax: 918 944 859
bodegasjesusfigueroa@hotmail.com

## FIGUEROA 2008 B
malvar 100%

**85** Colour: straw. Nose: fresh fruit, dried herbs, expressive, fresh. Palate: fruity, fine bitter notes, fresh.

## FIGUEROA 2008 T
tempranillo 100%

**85** Colour: cherry, purple rim. Nose: expressive, red berry notes, floral, ripe fruit. Palate: flavourful, fruity, good acidity, round tannins.

## FIGUEROA 2006 TC
tempranillo 100%

**84**

## JESÚS DÍAZ

Convento, 38
28380 Colmenar de Oreja (Madrid)
☎: 918 943 378 - Fax: 918 944 890
bodegasjdiaz@interbook.net
www.bodegasjesusdiaz.com

## EL BLANCO DE JESÚS DÍAZ 2008 B
malvar 100%

**77**

## JESÚS DÍAZ 2008 RD
tempranillo 100%

**83**

## JESÚS DÍAZ 2008 T
tempranillo 80%, merlot 20%

**87** Colour: cherry, purple rim. Nose: expressive, fresh fruit, red berry notes, floral. Palate: flavourful, fruity, good acidity, round tannins.

## HEREDAD TORRESANO 2006 T ROBLE
tempranillo 100%

**87** Colour: cherry, garnet rim. Nose: powerful, ripe fruit, fruit preserve, creamy oak. Palate: flavourful, powerful, fleshy, round tannins.

**HEREDAD TORRESANO LA CUEVA DEL CONVENTO 2005 TC**
tempranillo

**87** Colour: cherry, garnet rim. Nose: ripe fruit, spicy, creamy oak, toasty. Palate: powerful, flavourful, toasty, round tannins.

**HEREDAD TORRESANO 2005 TC**
tempranillo 100%

**85** Colour: bright cherry. Nose: ripe fruit, creamy oak. Palate: flavourful, fruity, toasty, round tannins.

## PAGOS DE FAMILIA MARQUÉS DE GRIÑÓN (EL RINCÓN)

Dominio de Valdepusa Ctra. CM 4015, km. 23
45692 Malpica de Tajo (Toledo)
☎: 917 450 999 - Fax: 914 114 202
info@pagosdefamilia.com
www.pagosdefamilia.com

**EL RINCÓN 2005 T**

**85** Colour: deep cherry. Nose: fruit preserve, sweet spices, dark chocolate. Palate: sweetness, spirituous, good structure, fleshy.

**EL RINCÓN 2004 T**

**88** Colour: deep cherry. Nose: ripe fruit, fruit liqueur notes, creamy oak. Palate: powerful, flavourful, sweetness, spirituous.

## RICARDO BENITO S.L.

Las Eras, 5
28600 Navalcarnero (Madrid)
☎: 918 110 097 - Fax: 918 112 663
bodega@ricardobenito.com
www.ricardobenito.com

**TAPÓN DE ORO 2008 B JOVEN**
malvar

**85** Colour: bright straw. Nose: floral, ripe fruit, citrus fruit. Palate: fruity, fresh, fleshy.

**CASTIZO 2008 T**

**87** Colour: cherry, garnet rim. Nose: powerful, ripe fruit, red berry notes, fragrant herbs. Palate: flavourful, fruity, fresh.

**DUÁN 2007 T**

**86** Colour: cherry, purple rim. Nose: scrubland, balsamic herbs, ripe fruit. Palate: flavourful, fruity, fresh.

**MADRILEÑO DE RICARDO BENITO 2007 T**

**84**

**DIVO GRAN VINO DE GUARDA 2006 T**

**92** Colour: cherry, garnet rim. Nose: ripe fruit, spicy, creamy oak, toasty. Palate: powerful, flavourful, toasty, round tannins.

**ASIDO 2006 T**

**88** Colour: cherry, purple rim. Nose: powerful, red berry notes, fruit expression, violet drops. Palate: flavourful, fruity, fresh, fleshy.

**SEÑORÍO DE MEDINA**

## VINÍCOLA DE ARGANDA SOCIEDAD COOPERATIVA MADRILEÑA

Camino de San Martín de la Vega, 16
28500 Arganda del Rey (Madrid)
☎: 918 710 201 - Fax: 918 710 201
vinicola@cvarganda.e.telefonica.net

**PAGO VILCHES 2008 B**
malvar 100%

**83**

**BALADÍ 2007 B**
malvar 100%

**86** Colour: bright golden. Nose: powerful, toasty, cocoa bean, candied fruit. Palate: powerful, flavourful, fleshy.

**PAGO VILCHES 2008 RD**
tempranillo 100%

**85** Colour: rose, purple rim. Nose: fresh fruit, raspberry, fruit expression. Palate: fresh, fruity, good acidity, flavourful.

**PAGO VILCHES 2008 T**
tempranillo 100%

**85** Colour: cherry, purple rim. Nose: fresh fruit, red berry notes, herbaceous. Palate: rich, fruity, full, good acidity, fruity aftestaste.

**VIÑA RENDERO SELECCIÓN ESPECIAL 2007 T ROBLE**
tempranillo 100%

**84**

VIÑA RENDERO 2007 T
tempranillo 100%

**80**

VIÑA RENDERO 2006 TC
tempranillo 100%

**85** Colour: very deep cherry, garnet rim. Nose: ripe fruit, sweet spices, new oak. Palate: fruity, good acidity, spicy, round tannins.

PERUCO 2005 TR
tempranillo 100%

**85** Colour: dark-red cherry, garnet rim. Nose: fruit preserve, spicy, caramel. Palate: fruity, powerful, grainy tannins, sweetness.

## VINOS JEROMÍN

San José, 8
28590 Villarejo de Salvanés (Madrid)

☎: 918 742 030 - Fax: 918 744 139
comercial@vinosjeromin.com
www.vinosjeromin.com

PUERTA CERRADA 2008 B
malvar 60%, airén 40%

**84**

PUERTA DEL SOL MALVAR 2008 BFB
malvar 100%

**84**

PUERTA DE ALCALÁ 2008 B
malvar 100%

**84**

PUERTA CERRADA 2008 RD
tempranillo 50%, garnacha 40%, malvar 10%

**83**

PUERTA DE ALCALÁ 2008 RD JOVEN
tempranillo 60%, garnacha 40%

**83**

PUERTA DE ALCALÁ 2008 T
tempranillo 100%

**85** Colour: deep cherry, purple rim. Nose: fresh fruit, red berry notes, varietal, herbaceous. Palate: flavourful, fruity, round tannins.

PUERTA CERRADA 2008 T
tempranillo 60%, garnacha 40%

**83**

GREGO 2007 T ROBLE
tempranillo 65%, syrah 35%

**88** Colour: cherry, garnet rim. Nose: powerful, ripe fruit, balsamic herbs, scrubland. Palate: flavourful, powerful, fleshy, ripe fruit.

GREGO GARNACHA CENTENARIAS 2007 T ROBLE
garnacha 100%

**85** Colour: cherry, garnet rim. Nose: floral, ripe fruit, grassy. Palate: flavourful, powerful, fleshy.

PUERTA DEL SOL VARIETALES 2006 TC
cabernet sauvignon 60%, merlot 30%, tempranillo 10%

**81**

GREGO 2005 TC
tempranillo 60%, syrah 30%, garnacha 10%

**88** Colour: cherry, garnet rim. Nose: sweet spices, creamy oak, ripe fruit, fruit preserve. Palate: flavourful, fleshy, sweetness, round tannins.

PUERTA DEL SOL TEMPRANILLO 2005 TC
tempranillo 100%

**82**

MANU VINO DE AUTOR 2004 TC
tempranillo, syrah, garnacha, merlot, cabernet sauvignon

**91** Colour: bright cherry. Nose: ripe fruit, sweet spices, creamy oak, raspberry, mineral. Palate: flavourful, fruity, toasty, round tannins.

PUERTA DE ALCALÁ 2004 TC
tempranillo 100%

**88** Colour: cherry, garnet rim. Nose: powerful, ripe fruit, toasty, dark chocolate. Palate: powerful, fleshy, sweetness.

DOS DE MAYO 2004 TC
tempranillo 100%

**86** Colour: cherry, garnet rim. Nose: powerful, ripe fruit, fruit preserve, warm. Palate: powerful, fleshy, sweetness, spicy.

PUERTA DE ALCALÁ 2004 TR
tempranillo 100%

**84**

FÉLIX MARTÍNEZ CEPAS VIEJAS 2001 TR
tempranillo 90%, syrah 10%

**90** Colour: dark-red cherry, garnet rim. Nose: ripe fruit, new oak, tobacco, sweet spices. Palate: full, powerful, complex, round tannins, mineral.

FÉLIX MARTÍNEZ

MANU VINO DE AUTOR 2005 CRIANZA
tempranillo, syrah, garnacha, merlot, cabernet sauvignon

**90** Colour: cherry, garnet rim. Nose: powerful, lactic notes, ripe fruit, sweet spices. Palate: flavourful, powerful, fleshy, round tannins.

## VINOS Y ACEITES LAGUNA

Illescas, 5
28360 Villaconejos (Madrid)
☎: 918 938 196 - Fax: 918 938 344
vyalaguna@eresmas.com
www.lagunamadrid.com

ALMA DE VALDEGUERRA 2008 T
tempranillo 100%

**87** Colour: cherry, purple rim. Nose: powerful, ripe fruit, raspberry, scrubland. Palate: flavourful, powerful, fleshy, ripe fruit.

EXUN PASIÓN 2006 T
tempranillo 70%, cabernet sauvignon 30%

**90** Colour: cherry, garnet rim. Nose: ripe fruit, spicy, creamy oak, toasty, complex, new oak. Palate: powerful, flavourful, toasty, round tannins.

LACUNA 2005 TC
tempranillo 100%

**87** Colour: cherry, garnet rim. Nose: toasty, cocoa bean, powerfull, fruit preserve, ripe fruit. Palate: flavourful, powerful, fleshy, round tannins.

## VIÑAS DE EL REGAJAL

Antigua Ctra. N-IV, km. 50,5
28300 Aranjuez (Madrid)
☎: 913 078 903 - Fax: 913 576 312
dgpita@garip.es

EL REGAJAL SELECCIÓN ESPECIAL 2007 T

**93** Colour: dark-red cherry. Nose: powerful, ripe fruit, fruit expression, creamy oak. Palate: flavourful, powerful, fleshy, ripe fruit.

SOME OTHER WINERIES WITHIN THE DO:

**ALEX
BODEGA ECOLÓGICA ANDRÉS MORATE
BODEGAS DEL FRESNO
BODEGAS FRANCISCO CASAS S.A.
BODEGAS PERAL (LUIS ANTONIO
PERAL HEREZA)**

# DO VINOS DE MADRID

**BODEGAS Y VIÑEDOS PEDRO GARCÍA**
**COOPERATIVA NUESTRA SEÑORA**
**DE LA SOLEDAD**
**COOPERATIVA VINÍCOLA SAN ROQUE**
**DON ÁLVARO DE LUNA**
**EL ARCO**
**S.A.T. 1.431 SAN ESTEBAN PROTOMÁRTIR**
**SAN ANDRÉS DE VILLAREJO DE SALVANÉS**
**SAN ISIDRO DE BELMONTE S.C.**
**SOLERA BODEGAS**
**VALLE DEL SOL S.A.T. 4478**
**VIÑA BAYONA**
**VIRGEN DE LA POVEDA S.A.T.**

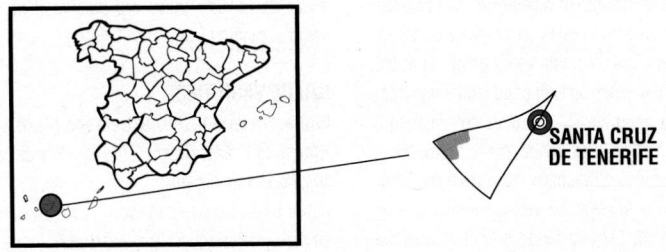

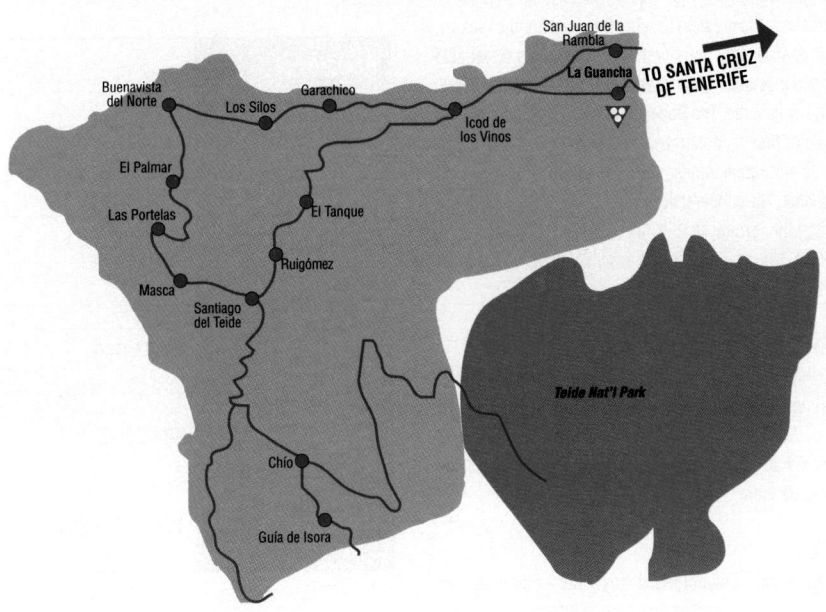

▽ Consejo Regulador
● DO Boundary

## NEWS

If there is a relevant feature that singles out Ycoden, that is probably its great, ancestral sweet wines from malvasía, the so-called Canary shoved off to every part of the world from the port of Garachico, but we should also point out at the fact that they try hard to come up with good renderings from local varieties like negramoll, marmajuelo, vijariego, verdello, güal, or tintilla. The wines made from these varieties are few, but very different to those from the other islands. The usual way to asset the vintage, a poor one by every standard, given that strong winds in April affected the buds, is through young wines, and this year we particularly liked those from tintilla like Tágara and Viñátigo, with their singular nose of mountain herbs and earth. As for the whites, the wines from marmajuelo show some singularity. Nevertheless, the greatest assets of Ycoden are the creamy, sweet malvasía renderings, with good alternating sweet-acid notes and a singular ashy character that age magnificently in barrel or in bottle. The Bodega Comarcal de Icod is a good example of how a cooperative with selected vineyards can come up with great wines, in its case bottled under the El Ancón label. The cooperative is part of Bodegas Insulares de Tenerife, the group that is also behind Viña Norte in Tacoronte, being both coops an essential drive for the most qualitative Canary wines.

## LOCATION

Occupying the northeast of the island of Tenerife and comprising the municipal districts of San Juan de La Rambla, La Guancha, Icod de los Vinos, Los Silos, El Tanque, Garachico, Buenavista del Norte, Santiago del Teide and Guía de Isora.

## CLIMATE

Mediterranean, characterised by the multitude of microclimates depending on the altitude and other geographical conditions. The trade winds provide the humidity necessary for the development of the vines. The average annual temperature is 19°C and the average annual rainfall is around 540 mm.

## SOIL

Volcanic ash and rock on the higher grounds, and clayey lower down. The vines are cultivated at very different heights, ranging from 50 to 1,400 m.

## GRAPE VARIETIES:

**White:** Preferred: *Bermejuela* (or *Marmajuelo*), *Güal, Malvasía, Moscatel, Pedro Ximénez, Verdello, Vijariego* and *Albillo*.
Authorized: *Bastardo Blanco, Forastera Blanca, Listán Blanco* (majority), *Sabro, Torrontés*.
**Red:** Preferred: *Tintilla, Listán Negro* (majority), *Malvasía Rosada, Negramoll* and *Castellana*.
Authorized: *Bastardo Negra, Moscatel Negra, Vijariego Negra*.

| Hectares of Vineyard | 310 |
|---|---|
| Nº Viticulturists | 765 |
| Nº of Bodegas | 20 |
| 2008 Harvest | Very Good |
| 2007 Production | 384,210 l. |
| Marketing | 100% domestic |

**CONSEJO REGULADOR**
La Palmita, 10
38440 La Guancha -Tenerife.
☎: 922 130 246 - Fax: 922 828 159
@ ycoden@ycoden.com
www.ycoden.com

## GENERAL CHARACTERISTICS OF THE WINES:

| | |
|---|---|
| **WHITES** | The most characteristic wines of the DO are the white wines produced from *Listán*, which are fresh, flavourful and quite expressive. They are produced as dry, semi sec and sweet wines and there are also examples of wines fermented in barrels. |
| **ROSÉS** | These have a strawberry colour, good fruit expression and are pleasantly herbaceous. |
| **REDS** | These have a deep cherry-red colour; they are fruity and fresh; on occasion they develop soothing aromas: eucalyptus and autumn leaves. |

## 2008 VINTAGE RATING:

# GOOD

## BODEGA COMARCAL DE ICOD

Camino Cuevas del Rey, 1
38430 Icod de los Vinos (Tenerife)
☎: 922 122 395 - Fax: 922 814 688
icod@bodegasinsularestenerife.es
www.bodegasinsularestenerife.es

EL ANCÓN MALVASIA 2006 B BARRICA

**92** Colour: bright straw. Nose: earthy notes, creamy oak, sweet spices, cocoa bean, ripe fruit. Palate: flavourful, fleshy, sweet, long, creamy.

EL ANCÓN 2008 T

**87** Colour: cherry, purple rim. Nose: powerful, ripe fruit, red berry notes. Palate: flavourful, fleshy, long.

EL ANCÓN 2006 T BARRICA

**83**

MIRADERO 2008 BLANCO AFRUTADO

**87** Colour: bright straw. Nose: ripe fruit, citrus fruit, grassy. Palate: flavourful, fruity, fresh.

MIRADERO 2008 ROSADO AFRUTADO

**85** Colour: brilliant rose. Nose: elegant, red berry notes, fresh fruit, floral. Palate: flavourful, fruity, fresh, light-bodied.

EL ANCÓN NEGRAMOLL 2006 TINTO DULCE

**90** Colour: cherry, garnet rim. Nose: powerful, candied fruit, overripe fruit, balsamic herbs. Palate: flavourful, sweet, fleshy.

## BODEGAS BILMA

Carretera Gral. Chío-Bocatauce, km. 1
38689 Guía de Isora (Tenerife)
☎: 922 850 641 - Fax: 922 852 318
bodegasbilma@bodegasbilma.com
www.bodegasbilma.com

TÁGARA 2008 B

**85** Colour: pale. Nose: medium intensity, fresh fruit, grassy. Palate: flavourful, fruity, fresh.

TÁGARA AFRUTADO 2008 B

**82**

TÁGARA 2007 BFB

**85** Colour: bright golden. Nose: powerful, candied fruit, honeyed notes, floral. Palate: flavourful, powerful, sweet, fleshy.

TÁGARA 2008 RD

**84**

TÁGARA 2007 T BARRICA

**80**

TÁGARA TINTILLA 2006 T
tintilla

**87** Colour: cherry, garnet rim. Nose: scrubland, fragrant herbs, ripe fruit, sweet spices. Palate: flavourful, fruity, fresh, easy to drink.

## BODEGAS VIÑÁTIGO

Cabo Verde, s/n
38440 La Guancha (Tenerife)
☎: 922 828 768 - Fax: 922 829 936
vinatigo@vinatigo.com
www.vinatigo.com

VIÑÁTIGO MARMAJUELO 2008 B
marmajuelo 100%

**88** Colour: bright straw. Nose: ripe fruit, candied fruit, honeyed notes, tropical fruit. Palate: flavourful, fleshy, sweetness, good acidity.

VIÑÁTIGO 2008 B
listán blanco 100%

**85** Colour: bright straw. Nose: powerful, candied fruit, citrus fruit. Palate: flavourful, sweetness, fruity.

VIÑÁTIGO VERDELLO 2008 B
verdello 100%

**85** Colour: bright straw. Nose: scrubland, ripe fruit, fresh fruit. Palate: flavourful, powerful, fleshy.

VIÑÁTIGO VIJARIEGO 2007 B
vijariego 100%

**85** Colour: bright straw. Nose: powerful, fruit liqueur notes, candied fruit, citrus fruit. Palate: flavourful, powerful, fleshy.

VIÑÁTIGO GUAL 2007 B
gual 100%

**78**

**VIÑÁTIGO MALVASÍA 2006 B**
malvasia 100%

**90** Colour: bright golden. Nose: ripe fruit, citrus fruit, honeyed notes, tropical fruit. Palate: flavourful, powerful, fleshy, sweetness.

**VIÑÁTIGO 2008 RD**
listán negro 100%

**85** Colour: brilliant rose. Nose: ripe fruit, red berry notes, floral. Palate: flavourful, fruity, fleshy, spicy.

**VIÑÁTIGO NEGRAMOLL 2008 T**
negramoll 100%

**82**

**VIÑÁTIGO BABOSO 2007 T**
baboso negro 100%

**83**

**VIÑÁTIGO TINTILLA 2006 T ROBLE**
tintilla 100%

**87** Colour: cherry, garnet rim. Nose: powerful, spicy, burnt matches, earthy notes. Palate: flavourful, spicy, ripe fruit, round tannins.

## CUEVA DEL REY

Camino Cuevas del Rey, 8
38430 Icod de los Vinos (Tenerife)
☎: 922 121 414 - Fax: 922 121 414

CUEVA DEL REY 2008 B

**83**

CUEVA DEL REY 2008 T

**82**

## FRANCISCO JAVIER GÓMEZ PIMENTEL

La Patita, 63
38430 Icod de los Vinos (Tenerife)
☎: 922 810 237 - Fax: 922 810 237
bodegasacevino@yahoo.es

ACEVIÑO SEMISECO 2008 B
listán blanco 100%

**84**

**ACEVIÑO 2008 B**
listán blanco 100%

**80**

**ACEVIÑO 2008 B BARRICA**
listán blanco 100%

**80**

**ACEVIÑO 2008 RD**
listán blanco, listán negro

**87** Colour: brilliant rose. Nose: floral, fresh fruit, red berry notes, elegant. Palate: flavourful, fruity, fresh.

**ACEVIÑO 2008 T MACERACIÓN CARBÓNICA**
listán negro 100%

**85** Colour: cherry, purple rim. Nose: powerful, red berry notes, fresh fruit, balsamic herbs. Palate: flavourful, fruity, fresh, fleshy.

**ACEVIÑO 2008 T BARRICA**
listán negro 100%

**82**

**ACEVIÑO 2008 T**
listán negro 100%

**73**

## VIÑA SPINOLA

Camino Esparragal, s/n
38470 Los Silos (Tenerife)
☎: 922 840 977 - Fax: 922 840 977

VIÑA SPINOLA MALVASÍA SECO 2004 B

**88** Colour: bright straw. Nose: petrol notes, honeyed notes, candied fruit. Palate: flavourful, powerful, fine bitter notes.

VIÑA SPINOLA B

**75**

VIÑA SPINOLA 2008 RD

**76**

VIÑA SPINOLA 2008 T

**70**

VIÑA SPINOLA MALVASÍA SECO 2008 B DULCE

**70**

## VIÑA ZANATA

El Sol, 3
38440 La Guancha (Santa Cruz de Tenerife)
☎: 922 828 166 - Fax: 922 828 166
zanata@zanata.net
www.zanata.net

VIÑA ZANATA 2008 B

**83**

VIÑA ZANATA MARMAJUELO 2008 B BARRICA

**83**

VIÑA ZANATA 2008 RD

**70**

TARA TINTILLA 2007 T

**78**

## YEBENES MONTESDEOCA

Camino La Suerte, 18
38430 Icod de los Vinos (Tenerife)
☎: 922 121 554

TINOCA 2008 B
marmajuelo

**86** Colour: pale. Nose: powerful, grassy, balsamic herbs, ripe fruit. Palate: flavourful, fruity, fresh.

TINOCA 2008 T

**83**

SOME OTHER WINERIES WITHIN THE DO:

**C.B. BALJA
C.B. LUIS I., ANTONIO Y JAVIER LÓPEZ DE AYALA Y AZNAR
COOPERATIVA AGRARIA CHINYERO
CUEVAS DEL VIENTO S.L.
CUMBRES DE BOLICO
GREGORIO GONZÁLEZ MARTEL
HERMABRI
JUANDANA S.L.
M. ELISA VICTORIA LÓPEZ DE AYALA LEÓN-HUERTA
PATIO REAL
PEDRO M. DORTA GRILLO
ROBERTO PÉREZ LUIS
VIÑA EL PALMAR S.L.
VIÑAMONTE**

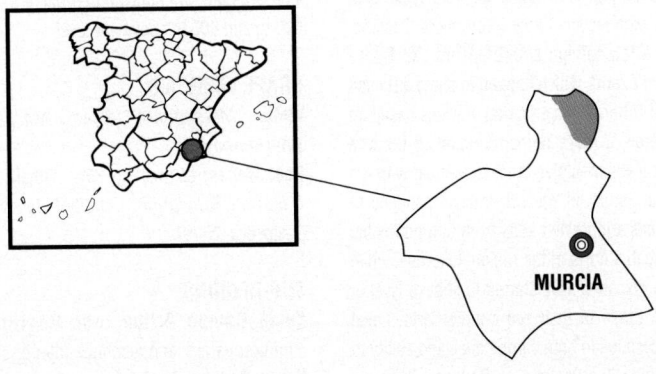

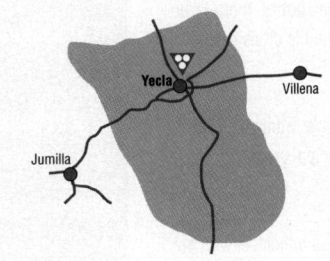

## NEWS

There are very few Spanish wine regions that show wines more modern and homogenous than those from Yecla. With just about eleven wineries and to the forerunners, Castaño, we have to add a few foreign entrepreneurs like Trenza Wines and Vinnico Export, which happen to share a Danish winemaker, David Tofterup and a myriad of wines based on the local monastrell, a more refined version of the one offered by the local wineries given that is blended with the Bordelaise varietal bunch. In Yecla they have managed to profit from old vines and fresher soils from Campo Arriba, the higher area located north of the region. Likewise, white wines made from macabeo have started to show a level of quality similar to those of their red counterparts. Local wineries have succeeded in both competence and ability to renovate, companies like Castaño or Bodegas Purísima Concepción, the latter a great pioneer which controls 60% of the DO's grape production and sells its wines in thirty countries. But quality is very homogenous, as well as diverse, throughout the DO, for there can be found intense and deeply mineral examples beside lighter every day wines. And with an average price of 6 € per bottle, there is no wonder Yecla will manage to overcome the crisis easily.

## LOCATION

In the northeast of the province of Murcia, within the plateau region, and comprising a single municipal district, Yecla.

## CLIMATE

Continental, with a slight Mediterranean influence, with hot summers and cold winters, and little rainfall, which is usually around 300 mm per annum.

## SOIL

Fundamentally deep limestone, with good permeability. The vineyards are on undulating terrain at a height of between 400 m and 800 m above sea level.

## GRAPE VARIETIES:

**White:** *Merseguera, Airén, Macabeo, Malvasía, Chardonnay.*

**Red:** *Monastrell* (majority 85% of total), *Garnacha Tinta, Cabernet Sauvignon, Cencibel (Tempranillo), Merlot, Tintorera, Syrah.*

## SUB-REGIONS:

**Yecla Campo Arriba,** with Monastrell as the most common variety and alcohol contents of up to 14°, and **Yecla Campo Abajo,** whose grapes produce a lower alcohol content (around 12° for reds and 11.5° for whites).

| Hectares of Vineyard | 7,320 |
|---|---|
| Nº Viticulturists | 836 |
| Nº of Bodegas | 11 |
| 2008 Harvest | Good |
| 2007 Production | 4,898,900 l. |
| Marketing | 20% domestic 80% export |

**CONSEJO REGULADOR**
Centro de Desarrollo Local.
Poeta Francisco A. Jiménez, s/n.
Polígono Industrial Urbayecla II.
☎: 968 792 352 - Fax: 968 792 352.
@ info@yeclavino.com
www.yeclavino.com

### GENERAL CHARACTERISTICS OF THE WINES:

| | |
|---|---|
| **WHITES** | These have a straw yellow colour; they are fruity and have quite a good aromatic intensity, although on the palate their acidity is somewhat low. |
| **ROSÉS** | Although they are not the most representative wines of the region, the best wines are produced according to modern techniques for this type of wine and they are therefore quite fruity, fresh and pleasant. |
| **REDS** | Thes are the most characteristic wines of the region and also the most abundant. Produced mainly from *Monastrell*, they have either a violet cherry or deep cherry-red colour. Their aroma is of ripe fruit and there may sometimes be hints of raisining, due to the strong sunshine of the region. They are meaty, warm and supple on the palate. |

### 2008 VINTAGE RATING:

## GOOD

# DO YECLA

## BODEGAS CASTAÑO

Carretera Fuentealamo, 3 Apdo. 120
30510 Yecla (Murcia)
☎: 968 791 115 - Fax: 968 791 900
info@bodegascastano.com
www.bodegascastano.com

CASTAÑO MACABEO CHARDONNAY BFB

**86** Colour: bright straw. Nose: fresh, fresh fruit, white flowers, expressive. Palate: flavourful, fruity, good acidity.

CASTAÑO MONASTRELL 2008 RD JOVEN
monastrell

**84**

CASTAÑO MONASTRELL 2007 T
monastrell

**87** Colour: cherry, purple rim. Nose: expressive, red berry notes, floral, fruit preserve. Palate: flavourful, fruity, good acidity, round tannins, balsamic.

VIÑA AL LADO DE LA CASA 2006 T

**91** Colour: bright cherry. Nose: sweet spices, expressive, varietal, fruit preserve. Palate: flavourful, fruity, toasty, round tannins, balsamic.

DETRÁS DE LA CASA SYRAH 2006 T
syrah

**91** Colour: bright cherry. Nose: ripe fruit, sweet spices, creamy oak, expressive, mineral, dry stone. Palate: flavourful, fruity, toasty, slightly dry, soft tannins.

DETRÁS DE LA CASA CABERNET SAUVIGNON-TINTORERA 2006 TC
garnacha tinta, cabernet sauvignon

**92** Colour: dark-red cherry. Nose: characterful, expressive, dry stone, mineral, aromatic coffee. Palate: powerful, flavourful, complex, fruity, balsamic, ripe fruit.

HÉCULA 2006 T
monastrell

**88** Colour: bright cherry. Nose: sweet spices, expressive, fruit preserve, varietal, toasty. Palate: flavourful, fruity, toasty, round tannins.

CASTAÑO COLECCIÓN 2005 T
monastrell 80%, cabernet sauvignon 20%

**91** Colour: cherry, garnet rim. Nose: spicy, creamy oak, toasty, complex, fruit preserve, varietal, mineral. Palate: powerful, flavourful, toasty, round tannins.

CASTAÑO MONASTRELL DULCE T

**88** Colour: cherry, garnet rim. Nose: overripe fruit, fruit preserve, sun-drenched nuances. Palate: flavourful, powerful, fruity, sweet, balanced.

POZUELO
MO

## BODEGAS LA PURÍSIMA

Carretera de Pinoso, 3 Apdo. Correos 27
30510 Yecla (Murcia)
☎: 968 751 257 - Fax: 968 795 116
ventas@bodegaslapurisima.com
www.bodegaslapurisima.com

VALCORSO MACABEO 2008 BFB
macabeo 100%

**88** Colour: bright straw. Nose: fresh, fresh fruit, white flowers. Palate: flavourful, fruity, good acidity, balanced.

ESTÍO 2008 B
macabeo 100%

**81**

ESTÍO 2008 RD
monastrell 70%, syrah 20%, tempranillo 10%

**82**

VALCORSO MERLOT 2008 T
merlot 100%

**88** Colour: cherry, purple rim. Nose: expressive, fresh fruit, red berry notes, floral, varietal. Palate: flavourful, fruity, good acidity, round tannins.

ESTÍO 2008 T
monastrell 70%, syrah 30%

**87** Colour: cherry, purple rim. Nose: expressive, red berry notes, floral, ripe fruit. Palate: flavourful, fruity, good acidity, round tannins, balanced.

VALCORSO SYRAH 2008 T
syrah 100%

**86** Colour: cherry, purple rim. Nose: red berry notes, floral, ripe fruit, earthy notes. Palate: flavourful, good acidity, round tannins.

VALCORSO MONASTRELL ECOLÓGICO 2008 T
monastrell 100%

**82**

VALCORSO MONASTRELL 2007 T BARRICA
monastrell 100%

**89** Colour: bright cherry. Nose: sweet spices, expressive, fruit preserve. Palate: flavourful, fruity, toasty, round tannins.

ESTÍO MONASTRELL ECOLÓGICO 2007 TC
monastrell 100%

**86** Colour: bright cherry. Nose: ripe fruit, sweet spices, expressive, scrubland. Palate: flavourful, fruity, toasty, round tannins, balsamic.

TRAPÍO 2006 T
monastrell 100%

**90** Colour: cherry, garnet rim. Nose: spicy, creamy oak, toasty, complex. Palate: powerful, flavourful, toasty, round tannins.

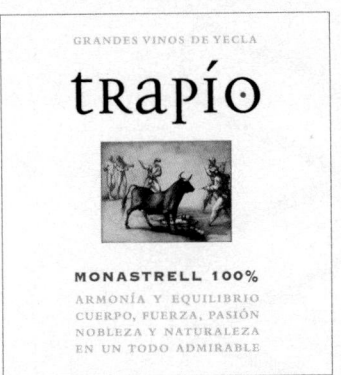

IV EXPRESIÓN 2006 T
monastrell, syrah, garnacha

**88** Colour: cherry, garnet rim. Nose: spicy, toasty, complex, fruit preserve, tar, mineral. Palate: powerful, flavourful, toasty, round tannins.

IGLESIA VIEJA 2005 TC
monastrell 70%, cabernet sauvignon 15%, tempranillo 15%

**86** Colour: cherry, garnet rim. Nose: ripe fruit, spicy, toasty, dark chocolate, aged wood nuances. Palate: powerful, flavourful, toasty, round tannins.

IGLESIA VIEJA 2003 TR
monastrell 70%, cabernet sauvignon 15%, tempranillo 15%

**86** Colour: cherry, garnet rim. Nose: spicy, toasty, complex, fruit liqueur notes, fruit preserve, dark chocolate. Palate: powerful, toasty, round tannins, classic aged character.

## BODEGAS SEÑORÍO DE BARAHONDA

Ctra. de Pinoso. Km.3,5
30510 Yecla (Murcia)

☎: 968 718 696 - Fax: 968 790 928
acandela@barahonda.com
www.barahonda.com

BARAHONDA 2008 B
macabeo 100%

**83**

BARAHONDA 2008 RD
monastrell 100%

**81**

CARRO 2008 T
monastrell, merlot, syrah, tempranillo

**86** Colour: cherry, purple rim. Nose: expressive, red berry notes, floral, fruit preserve. Palate: flavourful, fruity, good acidity, round tannins, balsamic.

BARAHONDA SUMMUM 2007 T
monastrell

**91** Colour: bright cherry. Nose: sweet spices, creamy oak, expressive, fruit preserve, mineral. Palate: flavourful, fruity, toasty, round tannins, balsamic.

BARAHONDA 2007 TC
monastrell 100%

**88** Colour: cherry, garnet rim. Nose: spicy, toasty, fruit preserve, varietal. Palate: powerful, flavourful, toasty, round tannins, balsamic.

HEREDAD CANDELA MONASTRELL 2007 T
monastrell 100%

**88** Colour: cherry, garnet rim. Nose: toasty, complex, fruit preserve, fruit liqueur notes. Palate: powerful, flavourful, toasty, balsamic.

BARAHONDA MONASTRELL 2007 T
monastrell 100%

**85** Colour: cherry, garnet rim. Nose: expressive, ripe fruit, dried flowers. Palate: flavourful, fruity, good acidity, round tannins.

BARAHONDA BARRICA 2006 T
monastrell 70%, cabernet sauvignon 30%

**86** Colour: bright cherry. Nose: ripe fruit, sweet spices, creamy oak, expressive. Palate: flavourful, fruity, toasty, round tannins.

BELLUM EL REMATE 2005 T
monastrell 100%

**89** Colour: bright cherry. Nose: ripe fruit, sweet spices, expressive, dark chocolate. Palate: flavourful, fruity, toasty, round tannins, sweet.

BELLUM PROVIDENCIA
NABUKO

## BODEGAS Y VIÑEDOS EVINE

Camino Sax, km. 7
30510 Yecla (Murcia)
☎: 968 718 250 - Fax: 968 718 250
info@bodegasevine.com
www.bodegasevine.com

KYATHOS 2005 T
monastrell 100%

**88** Colour: cherry, garnet rim. Nose: spicy, toasty, complex, overripe fruit, aged wood nuances. Palate: powerful, flavourful, toasty, round tannins.

LLANO QUINTANILLA 2005 TC
monastrell 100%

**86** Colour: cherry, garnet rim. Nose: spicy, toasty, complex, fruit liqueur notes, caramel. Palate: powerful, flavourful, toasty, round tannins.

EVINE

## LONG WINES

Avda. del Monte, 46
28120 Algete (Madrid)
☎: 916 221 305 - Fax: 916 220 029
william@william-long.com
www.longwines.com

CASA DEL CANTO 2006 T BARRICA
monastrell, syrah

**87** Colour: cherry, garnet rim. Nose: spicy, creamy oak, toasty, complex, fruit liqueur notes. Palate: powerful, flavourful, toasty, round tannins.

CASA DEL CANTO 2004 TR
monastrell, tempranillo, cabernet sauvignon, petit verdot

**89** Colour: cherry, garnet rim. Nose: ripe fruit, spicy, creamy oak, toasty, complex, mineral. Palate: powerful, flavourful, round tannins, roasted-coffee aftertaste.

## TRENZA WINES S.L.

Avda. Matías Saenz Tejada s/n Edif. Fuengirola Center Local 1
29640 Fuengirola (Málaga)
☎: 615 343 320 - Fax: 952 588 467
www.trenzawines.com

TRENZA FAMILY COLECTION 2006 T
monastrell 53%, cabernet sauvignon 10%, merlot 14%, garnacha tinta 6%, syrah 17%

**92** Colour: bright cherry. Nose: ripe fruit, sweet spices, creamy oak, expressive. Palate: flavourful, fruity, toasty, round tannins.

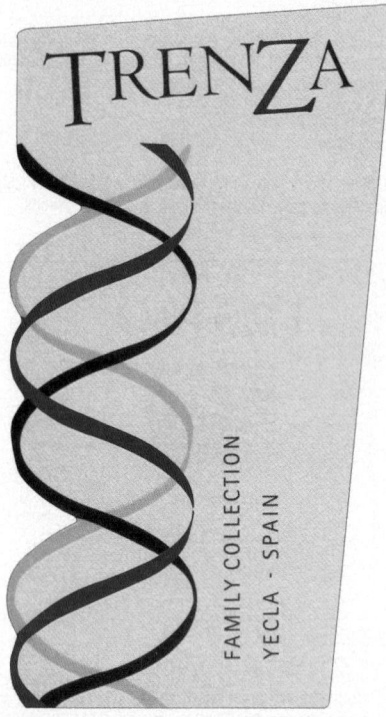

TRENZA FAMILY COLECTION 2004 T
monastrell 48%, cabernet sauvignon 32%, syrah 14%, garnacha tinta 6%

**90** Colour: cherry, garnet rim. Nose: creamy oak, toasty, complex, fruit liqueur notes, powerfull. Palate: powerful, flavourful, toasty, round tannins.

## VINNICO EXPORT

Calle de la Muela, 16
03730 Jávea (Alicante)
☎: 965 791 967 - Fax: 966 461 471
info@vinnico.com
www.vinnico.com

PAU 2008 B
macabeo 50%, airén 50%

**85** Colour: bright straw. Nose: powerful, ripe fruit, tropical fruit. Palate: flavourful, fleshy, ripe fruit.

**PAU 2008 T**
monastrell 100%

**88** Colour: cherry, purple rim. Nose: floral, red berry notes, wild herbs. Palate: flavourful, full, balsamic, great length.

**FLOR DEL MONTGÓ OLD VINES MONASTRELL 2007 T**

**86** Colour: cherry, garnet rim. Nose: spicy, toasty, complex, fruit liqueur notes. Palate: powerful, flavourful, toasty, round tannins.

SOME OTHER WINERIES WITHIN THE DO:

**BODEGAS Y VIÑEDOS DE MURCIA S.L,**
**BODEGAS Y VIÑEDOS DEL MEDITERRÁNEO**
**CASA DE LAS ESPECIAS**

**PICOS DEL MONTGÓ BARREL SELECT 2006 T**
monastrell 50%, merlot 10%, syrah 20%, cabernet sauvignon 5%, garnacha tinta 15%

**89** Colour: cherry, garnet rim. Nose: ripe fruit, spicy, toasty, complex, earthy notes. Palate: powerful, flavourful, toasty, round tannins.

**CREENCIA 2006 T**
monastrell 100%

**88** Colour: bright cherry. Nose: ripe fruit, creamy oak, powerfull, roasted coffee. Palate: flavourful, fruity, toasty, harsh oak tannins.

**MONTGÓ MONASTRELL SHIRAZ 2006 T**
monastrell, syrah, cabernet sauvignon

**84**

# VINOS DE PAGO

Vinos de Pago –somehow the Spanish equivalent to grand crus– is a new category, slightly superior to a DO, that designates singular wines that come from an specific area with distinct climatic and soil condition and is awarded by every Autonomous Government to properties that fulfil those and other requirements, such as a five-year probation period under a Vino de Calidad (VCPRD) label.

Castilla-La Mancha pioneered this sort of recognition with **Finca Élez,** the property that Manuel Manzaneque owns in the municipality of El Bonillo (Albacete) at an altitude of a thousand meters and which broke into the market with a *Chardonnay* and is working nowadays with syrah and other great red blends.

**Dehesa del Carrizal**, in Retuerta de Bullaque (to the north of Ciudad Real) has also a high altitude and a continental climate and works mainly with foreign –French– varieties.

**Dominio de Valdepusa**, in Malpica de Tajo (Toledo) and owned by Carlos Falcó was the first property to incorporate *Cabernet Sauvignon* and *Chardonnay* to its varietal range as well as the training systems of Richard Smart for hot-country viticulture. His wines, made mainly with varieties with a long vegetative cycle, have a fleshy palate and elegant tannins.

*Pago del Guijoso*, the last property to be awarded the Vino de Pago category by Castilla-La Mancha, is placed on a 3.000 hectares woodland area between the provinces of Albacete and Ciudad Real. Divinus, made from *Chardonnay*, is their best wine.

Navarra has awarded as well to **Señorío de Arínzano** the first Vino de Pago label within the autonomous region. Placed in Aberín (Estella) in a territory with evident Atlantic influences, the Chivite family are making there their Colección 125 white wines and their brand-new red wines, Señorío de Arínzano, made from the classic French grapes.

## DEHESA DEL CARRIZAL

### DEHESA DEL CARRIZAL

Ctra. Navas de Estena, km. 5,000
13194 Retuerta del Bullaque (Ciudad Real)
☎: 925 421 773 - Fax: 925 421 761
bodega@dehesadelcarrizal.com
www.dehesadelcarrizal.com

DEHESA DEL CARRIZAL CHARDONNAY 2007 B

**89** Colour: bright yellow. Nose: ripe fruit, fruit expression, tropical fruit. Palate: fleshy, powerful, fruity, fresh, good finish.

DEHESA DEL CARRIZAL MV ROJO 2007 T

**89** Colour: cherry, garnet rim. Nose: ripe fruit, spicy, toasty, complex, floral. Palate: powerful, flavourful, toasty, round tannins.

DEHESA DEL CARRIZAL MV AZUL 2007 T

**88** Colour: deep cherry, purple rim. Nose: ripe fruit, varietal, expressive, sweet spices. Palate: full, powerful, good acidity, toasty.

DEHESA DEL CARRIZAL SYRAH 2006 T

**90** Colour: bright cherry. Nose: ripe fruit, sweet spices, creamy oak, expressive, mineral. Palate: flavourful, fruity, toasty, round tannins.

DEHESA DEL CARRIZAL MV ROJO 2005 T

**88** Colour: bright cherry. Nose: ripe fruit, sweet spices, creamy oak, dark chocolate. Palate: flavourful, fruity, toasty, round tannins.

DEHESA DEL CARRIZAL COLECCIÓN PRIVADA 2004 T

**92** Colour: very deep cherry, garnet rim. Nose: ripe fruit, elegant, mineral, sweet spices. Palate: powerful, full, good acidity, round tannins, great length.

DEHESA DEL CARRIZAL CABERNET SAUVIGNON 2004 T

**89** Colour: deep cherry, garnet rim. Nose: ripe fruit, sweet spices, balanced, mineral. Palate: creamy, powerful, fruity, round tannins.

## DOMINIO DE VALDEPUSA

### PAGOS DE FAMILIA MARQUÉS DE GRIÑÓN

Dominio de Valdepusa Ctra. CM-4015, km. 23
45692 Malpica de Tajo (Toledo)
☎: 925 877 423 - Fax: 925 789 416
service@pagosdefamilia.com
www.pagosdefamilia.com

CALIZA 2006 T

**88** Colour: dark-red cherry. Nose: creamy oak, cedar wood, macerated fruit. Palate: sweetness, good structure, powerful, flavourful, creamy.

DOMINIO DE VALDEPUSA SYRAH 2005 T

**92** Colour: deep cherry. Nose: powerfull, fruit liqueur notes, fruit preserve, fruit expression, creamy oak, spicy, dark chocolate.

MARQUÉS DE GRIÑÓN DOMINIO DE VALDEPUSA CABERNET SAUVIGNON 2005 T
cabernet sauvignon 100%

**90** Colour: dark-red cherry. Nose: cedar wood, creamy oak, ripe fruit, damp undergrowth. Palate: complex, fleshy, flavourful, varietal.

CALIZA 2005 T

**86** Colour: dark-red cherry. Nose: candied fruit, fruit liqueur notes, ripe fruit, mineral, spicy, caramel. Palate: fleshy, fruity, powerful, flavourful, sweetness.

MARQUÉS DE GRIÑÓN DOMINIO DE VALDEPUSA PETIT VERDOT 2004 T

**92** Colour: dark-red cherry. Nose: ripe fruit, varietal, expressive, dark chocolate, spicy. Palate: good structure, fleshy, toasty, mineral, ripe fruit.

MARQUÉS DE GRIÑÓN DOMINIO DE VALDEPUSA EMERITVS 2004 TR

**92** Colour: deep cherry. Nose: fruit preserve, fruit liqueur notes, candied fruit, sweet spices, dark chocolate. Palate: sweetness, rich, powerful, smoky aftertaste, toasty, spirituous.

SVMMA VARIETALIS DOMINIO DE VALDEPUSA 2004 T

**91** Colour: deep cherry. Nose: spicy, smoky, cedar wood, ripe fruit, fruit liqueur notes, candied fruit. Palate: spirituous, powerful, flavourful, fleshy.

**TRIPLE A 2004 T**
graciano 100%

**91** Colour: deep cherry. Nose: ripe fruit, fruit expression, fruit liqueur notes, dark chocolate, spicy. Palate: spirituous, good structure, fruity, roasted-coffee aftertaste, ripe fruit.

**MARQUÉS DE GRIÑÓN DOMINIO DE VALDEPUSA SYRAH 2004 T**
syrah 100%

**90** Colour: very deep cherry. Nose: cedar wood, roasted coffee, sweet spices. Palate: sweet tannins, powerful, flavourful, spirituous.

## PAGO FINCA ÉLEZ
### MANUEL MANZANEQUE

Ctra. Ossa de Montiel a El Bonillo
02610 El Bonillo (Albacete)
☎: 967 585 003 - Fax: 967 585 056
info@manuelmanzaneque.com
www.manuelmanzaneque.com

**MANUEL MANZANEQUE CHARDONNAY 2007 BFB**
chardonnay 100%

**87** Colour: bright yellow. Nose: toasty, creamy oak, caramel, powerfull, candied fruit. Palate: toasty, rich, lacks fruit, fine bitter notes.

**MANUEL MANZANEQUE NUESTRA SELECCIÓN 2006 T**
cabernet sauvignon 45%, tempranillo 45%, merlot 10%

**90** Colour: bright cherry, garnet rim. Nose: varietal, ripe fruit, sweet spices. Palate: flavourful, unctuous, spicy, creamy, round tannins.

**MANUEL MANZANEQUE ESCENA 2006 T**
tempranillo 90%, cabernet sauvignon 10%

**89** Colour: bright cherry. Nose: expressive, spicy, floral. Palate: flavourful, fruity, toasty, round tannins.

**MANUEL MANZANEQUE SYRAH 2006 T**
syrah 100%

**88** Colour: dark-red cherry, garnet rim. Nose: ripe fruit, sweet spices, warm. Palate: light-bodied, powerful, fruity, good finish, round tannins.

**MANUEL MANZANEQUE FINCA ÉLEZ 2004 TC**

**88** Colour: dark-red cherry, garnet rim. Nose: ripe fruit, balanced, sweet spices, new oak, warm. Palate: powerful, flavourful, fruity, good acidity, round tannins.

## PAGO GUIJOSO
### BODEGAS Y VIÑEDOS SÁNCHEZ MULITERNO S.L.

Ctra. de Ossa de Montiel a El Bonillo, km. 11
02610 El Bonillo (Albacete)
☎: 967 193 222 - Fax: 967 193 292
bodegas@sanchez-muliterno.com
www.sanchez-muliterno.com

**DIVINUS 2007 BFB**
chardonnay

**87** Colour: bright straw. Nose: ripe fruit, creamy oak, expressive, tropical fruit. Palate: creamy, powerful, fruity, spicy.

**VEGA GUIJOSO 2007 T**

**89** Colour: cherry, garnet rim. Nose: powerfull, ripe fruit, red berry notes, creamy oak, toasty. Palate: flavourful, fruity, fresh.

**VIÑA CONSOLACIÓN 2004 TR**

**88** Colour: cherry, garnet rim. Nose: powerfull, ripe fruit, sweet spices, cocoa bean. Palate: flavourful, spicy, ripe fruit, good acidity.

**MAGNIFICUS**

## PAGO PRADO DE IRACHE
### IRACHE

Monasterio de Irache, 1
31240 Ayegui (Navarra)
☎: 948 551 932 - Fax: 948 554 954
irache@irache.com
www.irache.com

**PRADO IRACHE VINO DE PAGO 2006 T**
tempranillo 70%, cabernet sauvignon 20%, merlot 10%

**91** Colour: bright cherry. Nose: sweet spices, creamy oak, expressive, balsamic herbs, lactic notes, ripe fruit. Palate: flavourful, fruity, toasty, round tannins.

## PAGO SEÑORÍO DE ARÍNZANO
### VIÑEDOS Y BODEGAS SEÑORÍO DE ARÍNZANO

All the wines reviewed in this section are produced according to the traditional method known as second fermentation in bottle (the same method used for the production of Cava), and come from regions which do not fall under the DO Cava or any other DOs.

In fact, they represent a very small portion of the sparkling wines produced in Spain and their production figures do not come close to those of Cava. As far as the quality of these wines is concerned, they are generally somewhat inferior to the Catalonian Cavas.

# SPARKLING WINES-TRADITIONAL METHOD

## AGROALIMENTARIA VIRGEN DEL ROCÍO

Avda. de Cabezudos, s/n
21730 Almonte (Huelva)
☎: 959 406 146 - Fax: 959 407 052
administracion@raigal.com
www.raigal.com

RAIGAL BR

**82**

## BARRANCO OSCURO

Cortijo Barranco Oscuro
18440 Cádiar (Granada)
☎: 958 343 066 - Fax: 958 343 496
info@barrancooscuro.com
www.barrancooscuro.com

BARRANCO OSCURO BRUT NATURE 2007 BN
Vigiriego

**82**

## DOMINIO BUENAVISTA

Ctra. de Almería, s/n
18480 Ugíjar (Granada)
☎: 958 767 254 - Fax: 958 767 254
info@veleta.com
www.dominiobuenavista.com

VELETA ROSADO BLANC DE NOIR 2006 ESP
tempranillo 60%, garnacha 40%

**75**

VELETA BLANCO 2006 ESP
Vigiriego 80%, chardonnay 20%

**75**

## JESÚS DÍAZ

Convento, 38
28380 Colmenar de Oreja (Madrid)
☎: 918 943 378 - Fax: 918 944 890
bodegasjdiaz@interbook.net
www.bodegasjesusdiaz.com

EL BRUT NATURAL JESUS DIAZ 2006 ESP
macabeo , parellada

**82**

## JORDAN DE ASSO

Cariñena, 55
50408 Aguarón (Zaragoza)
☎: 976 620 291 - Fax: 976 230 270
info@jordandeasso.com
www.jordandeasso.com

JORDAN DE ASSO 2006 BN
macabeo 80%, chardonnay 20%

**82**

## LIBERALIA ENOLÓGICA

Camino del Palo, s/n
49800 Toro (Zamora)
☎: 980 692 571 - Fax: 980 692 571
byvliberalia@hotmail.com
www.liberalia.es

ARIANE 2007 ESP

**79**

## LOBBAN WINE

Creueta, 24
08784 St. Jaume Sesoliveres (Barcelona)
☎: 667 551 695
pamelageddes@terra.es
www.lapamelita.com

LA ROSITA 2003 ROSADO ESPUMOSO
monastrell 100%

**79**

LA PAMELITA 2003 TINTO ESPUMOSO
monastrell 95%, tempranillo 5%

**84**

## PAGO DE THARSYS

Ctra. Nacional III, Km 274
46340 Requena (Valencia)
☎: 962 303 354 - Fax: 962 329 000
pagodetharsys@pagodetharsys.com
www.pagodetharsys.com

THARSYS ÚNICO BLANC DE NEGRE 2006 ESP RESERVA
bobal 100%

**81**

# SPARKLING WINES-TRADITIONAL METHOD

## SERRANO

Finca La Cabaña, 30
30594 Pozo Estrecho (Cartagena) (Murcia)
☎: 968 556 298 - Fax: 968 556 298
vinos@bodegaserrano.com
www.bodegaserrano.com

GALTEA 2007 ESP
chardonnay 40%, malvasia 40%, moscatel 20%

**82**

SOME OTHER WINERIES:

**IBAÑEZ ARDO APARTSUAK
MENCÍAS DE DOS S.L.
SERRAT DE MONTSORIU
VIÑEDOS Y BODEGAS GARVA**

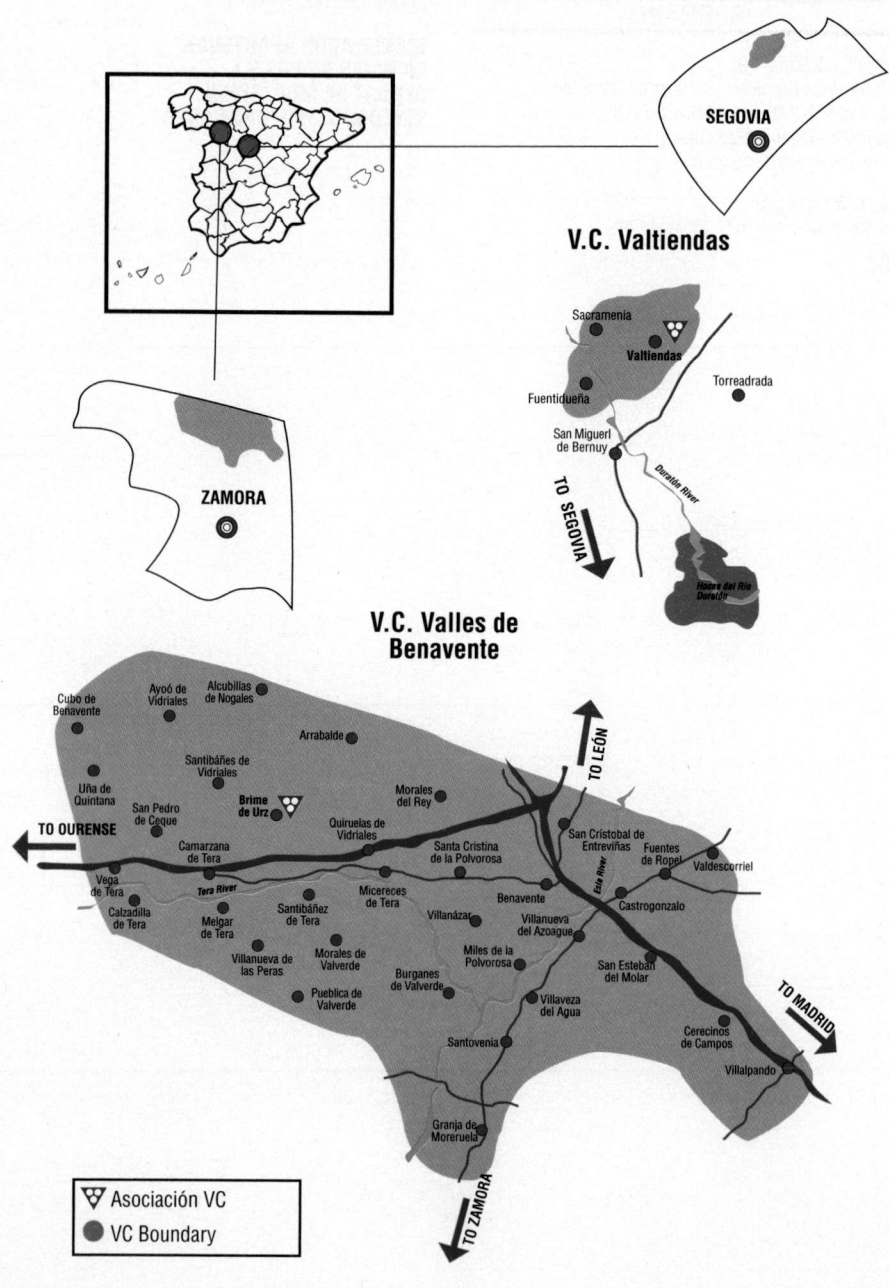

SEGOVIA

## V.C. Valtiendas

Sacramenia
Valtiendas
Torreadrada
Fuentidueña
San Miguerl
de Bernuy

ZAMORA

Duratón River

TO SEGOVIA

Hoces del Río
Duratón

## V.C. Valles de Benavente

Cubo de Benavente
Ayoó de Vidriales
Alcubillas de Nogales
Arrabalde
TO LEÓN
Santibáñes de Vidriales
Morales del Rey
Uña de Quintana
San Pedro de Ceque
Brime de Urz
Quiruelas de Vidriales
San Cristobal de Entreviñas
Fuentes de Ropel
Valdescorriel
TO OURENSE
Camarzana de Tera
Santa Cristina de la Polvorosa
Vega de Tera
Tera River
Micereces de Tera
Benavente
Castrogonzalo
Esla River
Calzadilla de Tera
Melgar de Tera
Santibáñez de Tera
Villanázar
Villanueva del Azoague
Villanueva de las Peras
Morales de Valverde
Miles de la Polvorosa
San Esteban del Molar
TO MADRID
Pueblica de Valverde
Burganes de Valverde
Villaveza del Agua
Cerecinos de Campos
Santovenia
Villalpando
Granja de Moreruela
TO ZAMORA

▽ Asociación VC
● VC Boundary

## VINO DE CALIDAD DE LOS VALLES DE BENAVENTE

Recognized by the Autonomous Government of Castilla y León since September 2000, the VC currently covers over 50 towns and 3 bodegas located in the towns of Benavente, Santibáñez de Vidriales and San Pedro de Ceque. The region has 5 wine-growing regions: Valle Vidriales, Valle del Tera, Valle Valverde, La Vega and Tierra de Campos, which surround Benavente as a natural centre, and 4 rivers (Tera, Esla, Órbigo and Valderadey, all tributaries of the Duero) which mark the outline of the geographical area of the region.

## VINO DE CALIDAD VALTIENDAS

This region to the north of Segovia is known for the brand Duratón, also the name of the river near which many wineries have emerged. The wines are mainly made from the local *Tempranillo* grape, known here as *Tinta del País*. and are much more fruity and have higher acidity levels than those from Ribera del Duero, thanks to an average altitude of 900 metres and soils composed of clay and smooth stones.

## VALLES DE BENAVENTE

### BODEGA EL TESORO SOC. COOP.

Pol. La Mata Camino Viñas, s/n
4962 Brime de Urz (Zamora)
☎: 980 643 138
bodega_el_tesoro@terra.com

URZ 2007 T
prieto picudo 70%, tempranillo 30%

**87** Colour: garnet rim. Nose: ripe fruit, varietal, expressive, floral. Palate: flavourful, full, concentrated, good finish.

PETAVONIUM 2006 T ROBLE
tempranillo 70%, prieto picudo 30%

**88** Colour: cherry, garnet rim. Nose: cocoa bean, ripe fruit, sweet spices, creamy oak. Palate: flavourful, good structure, creamy, balanced, round tannins.

### BODEGAS OTERO

Avda. El Ferial, 22
49600 Benavente (Zamora)
☎: 980 631 600 - Fax: 980 631 722
info@bodegasotero.es
www.bodegasotero.es

VALLEOSCURO 2008 B
verdejo 100%

**84**

VALLEOSCURO 2008 RD
prieto picudo 100%

**86** Colour: rose, purple rim. Nose: ripe fruit, red berry notes, floral, expressive, candied fruit. Palate: fleshy, powerful, fruity, fresh, carbonic notes.

VALLEOSCURO 2008 RD
prieto picudo , tempranillo

**86** Colour: brilliant rose. Nose: candied fruit, fresh, expressive. Palate: flavourful, fruity, fresh, full.

VALLEOSCURO 2007 T
prieto picudo , tempranillo

**90** Colour: cherry, garnet rim. Nose: ripe fruit, spicy, creamy oak, toasty, complex. Palate: powerful, flavourful, toasty, round tannins.

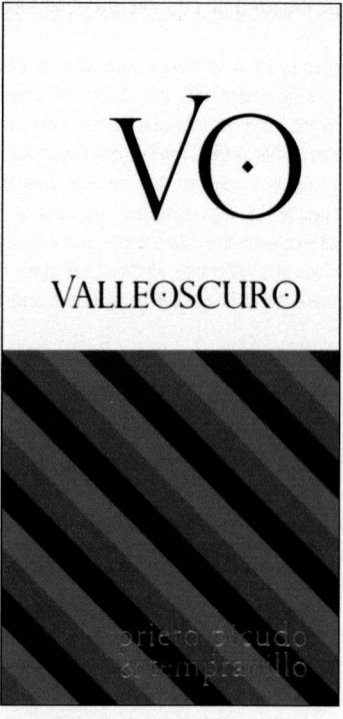

OTERO 2006 TC
prieto picudo 100%

**87** Colour: cherry, garnet rim. Nose: powerful, ripe fruit, earthy notes, aromatic coffee, toasty. Palate: powerful, fleshy, concentrated, toasty.

SOME OTHER WINERIES WITHIN THE DO:

**BODEGAS GARCÍA BUENO
BODEGAS VERDES
BODEGAS Y VIÑEDOS RAMÓN PAZ
COOPERATIVA SAN ISIDRO
(SAN PEDRO DE CEQUE)**

## VALTIENDAS

### BODEGAS OTERO

Avda. El Ferial, 22
49600 Benavente (Zamora)
☎: 980 631 600 - Fax: 980 631 722

info@bodegasotero.es
www.bodegasotero.es

**OTERO 2005 TC**
prieto picudo 100%

**88** Colour: bright cherry. Nose: ripe fruit, sweet spices, expressive, dark chocolate. Palate: flavourful, fruity, toasty, round tannins.

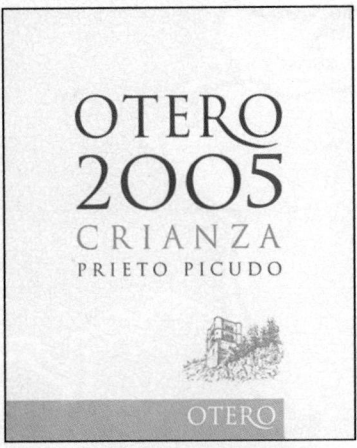

## VAGAL S.L.

La Fuente, 19
40314 Valtiendas (Segovia)
☎: 921 527 331 - Fax: 921 527 332
vagal@bodegasvagal.com
www.vagal.com

**VAGAL CUVÉE JOANA 2007 T**
tinta del país

**90** Colour: cherry, garnet rim. Nose: powerful, ripe fruit, scrubland. Palate: flavourful, fleshy, spicy, round tannins.

**VAGAL PAGO ARDALEJOS 2005 T**

**90** Colour: cherry, garnet rim. Nose: powerful, mineral, earthy notes, sweet spices. Palate: flavourful, fruity, fresh, ripe fruit, round tannins.

## ZARRAGUILLA S.L.

Iglesia, 14
40237 Sacramenia (Segovia)
☎: 921 527 126 - Fax: 921 527 270

informacion@bodegaszarraguilla.es
www.bodegaszarraguilla.es

**ALTAMENIA 2007 T ROBLE**

**85** Colour: cherry, purple rim. Nose: ripe fruit, red berry notes, scrubland. Palate: flavourful, fruity, fresh.

**VENNUR 2006 T ROBLE**

**89** Colour: cherry, garnet rim. Nose: ripe fruit, spicy, creamy oak, toasty, mineral. Palate: powerful, flavourful, toasty, round tannins.

**ZARRAGUILLA 2006 T ROBLE**

**87** Colour: bright cherry. Nose: ripe fruit, sweet spices, creamy oak, expressive. Palate: flavourful, fruity, toasty, round tannins.

**ZETA 37 2005 T**

**86** Colour: cherry, garnet rim. Nose: powerful, ripe fruit, sweet spices, dark chocolate. Palate: flavourful, fleshy, ripe fruit, round tannins.

### SOME OTHER WINERIES WITHIN THE DO:

**BODEGA TINTO REDREJA**
**BODEGA VALVIÑA**
**BODEGA VIÑA SANCHA**
**BODEGAS Y VIÑEDOS ANDREA**
**GUTIÉRREZ FERREAS**
**GALGO WINES**

# VINOS DE LA TIERRA

1 - Betanzos
2 - Barbanza e Iria          *Galicia*
3 - Val Do Miño-Ourense

4 - Cangas                   *Asturias*

5 - Liébana                  *Cantabria*
6 - Costa de Cantabria

7 - Valles de Sadacia        *La Rioja*

8 - Ribera del Queiles       *Navarra-Aragón*

9 - Ribera del Gállego-Cinco Villas
10 - Ribera del Jiloca
11 - Valdejalón              *Aragón*
12 - Bajo Aragón
13 - Valle del Cinca

14 - Castelló                *Valencia*
15 - El Terrerazo

16 - Abanilla                *Murcia*
17 - Campo de Cartagena

18 - Laujar-Alpujarra
19 - Desierto de Almería
20 - Ribera del Andarax
21 - Contraviesa-Alpujarra
22 - Granada Suroeste
23 - Norte de Granada
24 - Sierra Sur de Jaén      *Andalucía*
25 - Bailén
26 - Córdoba
27 - Sierra Norte de Sevilla
28 - Los Palacios
29 - Cádiz
41 - Torreperogil
42 - Sierra de las Estancias
       y los Filabres

⬤ VT Boundary

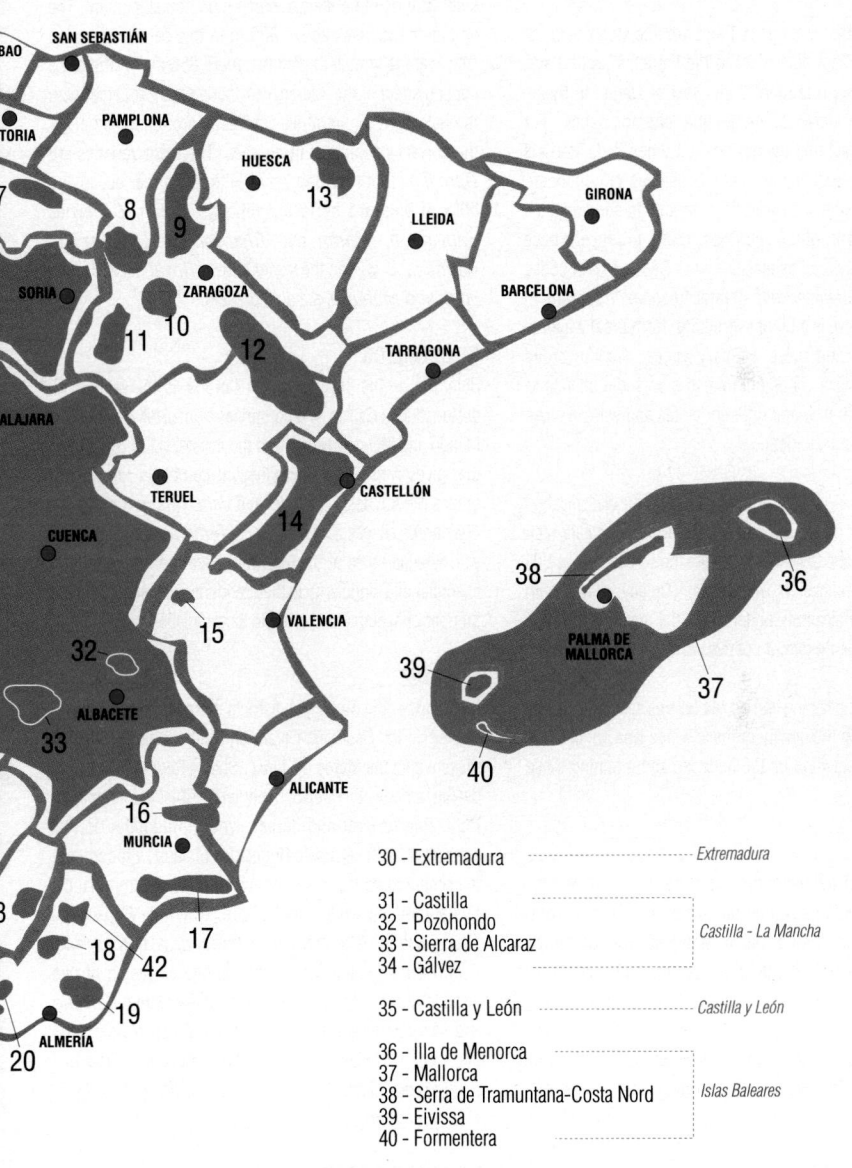

30 - Extremadura ·············· *Extremadura*

31 - Castilla
32 - Pozohondo
33 - Sierra de Alcaraz       *Castilla - La Mancha*
34 - Gálvez

35 - Castilla y León ·············· *Castilla y León*

36 - Illa de Menorca
37 - Mallorca
38 - Serra de Tramuntana-Costa Nord       *Islas Baleares*
39 - Eivissa
40 - Formentera

The different Vinos de la Tierra designations have been listed in alphabetical order.

Theoretically, the Vinos de la Tierra are one step below the DO wines, and are equivalent to the French Vins de Pays, pioneers in the promotion of this sort of status. In Spain, however, they have some unique characteristics. For example, the fact that the designation Vinos de la Tierra is not always the goal in itself, but it is used as a springboard to achieve the highly desired DO category. In addition, as it has happened in other countries, many producers have opted for this type of association with less stringent codes to produce their wines with greater freedom. Therefore, in this section there is a bit of everything: from great wines to other simpler and more ordinary wines. But the broad spectrum of these wines offers also a splendid chance to experiment with new and different tastes and with all types of local or regional varieties.

The new Ley del Vino (Wine Law) maintains the classification of Vinos de la Tierra, but establishes an intermediate step between these and DO wines. They are the so-called 'Vinos de Calidad con Indicación Geográfica' (Quality Wines with Geographical Indication), under which the region in question must remain for a minimum of five years.

In the light of the tasting carried out for this section, a steady improvement in the quality of these wines was noticed and also fewer misgivings by the bodegas about joining these associations.

## VT BAILÉN

The area comprised under the "Vinos de la Tierra de Bailén" covers 350 hectares in the municipal districts of Bailén, Baños de la Encina, Guarromán, Mengíbar, Torredelcampo and Villanueva de la Reina, in the province of Jaén. From the grapes produced in these vineyards white, rosé and red wines are made, as long as the varieties used are *Pedro Ximénez* for whites or *Tempranillo, Cabernet Sauvignon, Garnacha* or the original and indigenous *Molinera* for reds.

## VT BAJO ARAGÓN

The most Mediterranean region of Aragón, bordering the provinces of Tarragona, Castellón and Teruel, comprises four different areas: Campo de Belchite, Bajo Martín, Bajo Aragón and Matarraña, all of which share clay and limestone soils very rich in minerals with a high potash content. The altitude never rises above 600 m in this semi-arid region (the average annual rainfall is a mere 350 mm), where the cooling effect of the 'Cierzo' (northerly wind), together with the day-night temperature contrasts, are fundamental for the correct ripening of the grapes. The main varieties are *Garnacha* (both red and white, with the former occupying 80% of vineyard surface), although *Syrah, Cabernet Sauvignon, Merlot* and *Chardonnay Tempranillo, Cariñena*, as well as the lesser known *Royal, Romero de Híjar and Muniesa*, are also present.

## VT BETANZOS

Betanzos, in the province of La Coruña, is the second VT designation in Galicia, and comprises a small hill between the Mendo and Mandeo Rivers and the coastal valley (Betanzos) that gives it its name. The vineyard combines *local* white grapes like Agudelo (*Godello*) and *Jerez* with red grapes like *Garnacha*, as well as *Mencía* and *Tempranillo*. Producers, with Adegas Vinsa at the forefront, have been trying to add character and singularity to their renderings by increasing the number of hectares dedicated to local varieties.

## VT CÁDIZ

It comprises the municipal districts of Arcos, Prado del Rey, Setenil de las Bodegas, Olvera and Villamartín, as well as those within the Marco de Jerez –Sherry Region– (Sanlúcar de Barrameda, El Puerto, Trebujena, Chiclana, Chipiona, Rota, Puerto Real and Jerez), where production is still controlled by the Consejo Regulador of Jerez, although not the resulting wines, a somehow peculiar crummstance. The authorised white varieties are: *Garrido, Palomino, Chardonnay, Moscatel de Chipiona, Macabeo and Colombard* (which means the definite exclusion of two historic varieties from the vineyards of the region: *Perruno* and *Mantúa*, practically extinct and of very low yield); and the red varieties: *Tempranillo, Syrah, Cabernet Sauvignon, Garnacha, Monastrell, Merlot, Tintilla de Rota and Pinot Noir.*

## VT CAMPO DE CARTAGENA

The only two VTs in the Region of Murcia, Abanilla and Campo de Cartagena, share common regulations that stipulates the authorised varieties (Red: *Bonicaire, Cabernet Sauvignon, Forcallat Tinta, Garnacha Tintorera, Merlot, Moravia Dulce (Crujidera), Syrah and Petit Verdot*; White: *Chardonnay, Malvasía, Moscatel de Grano Menudo and Sauvignon Blanc*) and the recommended ones (Red: *Garnacha, Monastrell, Tempranillo*; White: *Airén, Merseguera, Moscatel de Alejandría, Pedro Ximénez, Verdil and Viura (Macabeo)*). The only production comes from Bodegas Serrano, which has a vineyard surface of 25 hectares.

## VT CANGAS

The vineyards around the municipality of Cangas del Narcea, in the province of Asturias, on the provincial border with León, are located on siliceous, very sandy slate soils somewhat similar –even in their terraced structure– to those from Priorat, in Catalunya. The high annual rainfall (1000 mm) is the most distinctive climatic feature of the area. Indigenous varieties predominate: *Verdejo Negro, Carrasquín (María Ordoña), Mencía* and *Albarín Negro* for red wines, and *Albarín Blanco* for white wines.

## VT CASTELLÓ

It comprises the wines of the sub-regions of Alto Palanca, Alto Mijares, Sant Mateu and Las Useras-Vilafamés.

## VT CASTILLA

Castilla-La Mancha, which has the largest vineyard surface on the planet (600,000 Ha, equivalent to 6% of the world's total vineyard surface, and to half of Spain's) used this geographic indication of Vinos de la Tierra in 1999 to label all the wines produced outside the different DOs within the region: Valdepeñas, La Mancha, Manchuela, Méntrida, Mondéjar, Ribera del Júcar, Almansa and part of Jumilla. There has been some conflict of interest with the VT Castilla y León regarding the use of the word 'Castilla' on its labels, which, given the size of the vineyard and the volume bottled in Castilla-La Mancha, has increased its exports to the detriment of those of Castilla y León.

## VT CASTILLA Y LEÓN

Another of the regional 'macro-designations' for wines produced in a total of 317 municipal districts of the provinces of Ávila, Burgos, León, Palencia, Salamanca, Segovia, Soria, Valladolid and Zamora. A continental climate with little rainfall, together with diverse soil patterns, are the most distinctive characteristics of a region, which, on the whole, can be divided into the Duero basin and part of the central plateau, alongside the mountainous perimeter that surrounds them both.

## VT CONTRAVIESA-ALPUJARRA

The altitude of the vineyards (up to 1300 meters, the highest in Europe) of this region in the province of Granada makes vine-growing quite difficult, in spite of the abundant sunlight hours, its cooler climate and the absence of irrigation put a serious obstacle to complete the grape's growing cycle. In the production of white wines, red wines and rosés from Contraviesa-Alpujarra, the red *Tempranillo, Garnacha, Vijiriego Negra, Cabernet Sauvignon* and *Merlot* are used, along with the white *Chardonnay* and *Sauvignon Blanc* are used.

## VT CÓRDOBA

Born in 2002 as a geographical indication to label the red and rosé wines made in the province of Córdoba, as well as quality table wines excluded by the DO Montilla-Moriles. It comprises some 300 hectares and the following varieties: *Merlot, Syrah, Tempranillo, Pinot Noir* and *Tintilla de Rota.*

## VT COSTA DE CANTABRIA

These are the wines made between the coast of Cantabria and the inland valleys up to a height of 600 metres.

## VT DESIERTO DE ALMERÍA

Approved in the summer of 2003, the production area comprises the municipal districts of Alcudia de Monteagud, Benitagla, Benizalón, Castro de Filabres, Lubrín, Lucainena de las Torres, Olula de Castro, Senés, Sorbas, Tabernas, Tahal, Turrillas, Uleila del Campo and Velefique. It produces white wines from *Chardonnay, Moscatel, Macabeo* and *Sauvignon Blanc*, and red and rosé wines from *Tempranillo, Cabernet Sauvignon, Monastrell, Merlot, Syrah* and *Garnacha.*

## VT EIVISSA

The production area includes the entire island of Ibiza (Eivissa), with the vineyards located in small valleys amongst the mountains –which are never higher than 500 meters– on brownish-reddish soil covered by a thin limestone crust. The low rainfall levels and the hot, humid summers are the most interesting climatic features. The authorized red varieties are *Monastrell, Tempranillo, Cabernet Sauvignon, Merlot* and *Syrah*, and the white are *Macabeo, Parellada, Malvasía, Chardonnay* and *Moscatel.*

## VT EL TERRERAZO

The production area is limited exclusively to the area known as El Terrerazo, within the municipal district of Utiel, in Valencia, a property that belongs to the Sarrión family, the owners of Mustiguillo, the only bodega included in the DO, with the ubiquitous Sara Pérez in charge of winemaking.

## VT EXTREMADURA

In December 1990, the regional government passed the regulation submitted by the Comisión Interprofesional de Vinos de la Tierra de Extremadura, and approved the creation of the "Vino de la Tierra de Extremadura" geographical designation, which comprises the six wine regions within the provinces of Cáceres and Badajoz (Tierra de Barros, Ribera Alta del Guadiana, Ribera Baja del Guadiana, Montánchez, Cañamero and Matanegra). Very little known in Spain and abroad, it is, nonetheless, the second biggest "Vino de la Tierra" designation in terms of production.

## VT FORMENTERA

A new geographical indication designed to include the wines produced in the island of Formentera with the red varieties *Monastrell, Fogoneu, Tempranillo, Cabernet Sauvignon* and *Merlot*, and the whites *Malvasía, Premsal Blanc* (or *Moll*, which is yielding such great wines in the Majorcan DO of Pla I Llevant) and *Chardonnay*. Thus, in August 2004, the designation of "Vino de la Tierra de Formentera" was created. The relatively small production area (60 hectares) represents, however, 12.5% of the total agricultural surface area of the island. With nearly half of the vineyards planted with Monastrell, it is clear that the best wines from Formentera have to be red and rosé renderings. The subtropical, dry, Mediterranean climate, characterised by abundant

sunshine and summers with high temperatures and humidity levels but little rain, evidently require grape varieties well adapted to this type of weather. The soils are varied, although sandy soils are predominant, with significantly high clay content.

## VT GÁLVEZ

In the province of Toledo, it comprises the municipalities of Cuerva, Gálvez, Guadamur, Menasalvas, Mazarambraz, Polán, Pulgar, San Martín de Montalbán and Totanes.

## VT GRANADA SUROESTE

This VT comprises wines produced in some 50 municipal districts of the province of Granada, from *Vijariego, Macabeo, Pedro Ximénez, Palomino, Moscatel de Alejandría, Chardonnay* and *Sauvignon Blanc* white grape varieties and the red varieties *Garnacha, Perruna, Tempranillo, Cabernet Sauvignon, Merlot, Syrah* and *Pinot Noir.*

## VT ILLA DE MENORCA

In the island of Menorca, declared a Biosphere Reserve in 1993, wine production has been very important for many centuries and especially during the English occupation, which began in 1708 and ended in the 19th century. The gentle slopes, the brownish limestone soil with a complex petrological substratum of limestone, sandstone and slate, the Mediterranean climate and the winter winds from the north are the most significant features from a viticultural point of view. Of all the different varieties, the red ones are *Cabernet Sauvignon, Merlot, Monastrell, Tempranillo* and *Syrah*; and the whites *Chardonnay, Macabeo, Moscatel, Parellada, Moll* and *Malvasía*, the latter yielding surely the best examples of this variety in the whole of the Mediterranean.

## VT LAUJAR-ALPUJARRA

It comprises some 700 hectares of vineyard in and around the town of Laujar, in the province of Almería, as well as the municipal districts of Alcolea, Bayárcal, Paterna del Río, Laujar del Andarax, Fondón, Fuente Victoria, Benecid, Baires, Almócita, Padules, Ohanes and Canjáyar.

## VT LIÉBANA

It comprises the production area of the municipalities of Potes, Pesagüero, Cabezón de Liébana, Camaleón, Castro Cillarigo and Vega de Liébana.

## VT LOS PALACIOS

It includes the production area of the municipal districts of Los Palacios y Villafranca, Utrera, Dos Hermanas and Alcalá de Guadaira in the province of Seville.

## VT MALLORCA

The production area is that of the island of Mallorca, which enjoys a Mediterrranean climate of mild temperatures– particularly the lower ones– and limestone soils with abundant clay and sandstone. Red varieties are *Cabernet Sauvignon, Merlot, Syrah, Monastrell, Tempranillo, Fogoneu, Callet* and *Manto Negro*, and the white ones *Chardonnay, Moscatel, Moll, Parellada, Macabeo* and *Malvasía*.

## VT NORTE DE GRANADA

It includes the vineyard surface of a total of 43 municipal districts in and around the town of Guadix, with the white *Chardonnay, Baladí, Verdejo, Airén* and *Torrontés*, and the red *Tempranillo, Monastrell* and *Garnacha* as main varieties, as well as *Palomino, Pedro Ximénez* and *Macabeo* (white), and *Cabernet Sauvignon* and *Merlot* (red) as complementary ones, suitable for the production of white, red and rosé wines.

## VT POZOHONDO

It comprises the municipal districts of Alcadozo, Peñas de San Pedro and Pozohondo, in the province of Albacete.

## VT RIBERA DEL ANDARAX

It comprises the municipal districts of Alboloduy, Alhabia, Alhama de Almería, Alicún, Almócita, Alsodux, Beires, Bentarique, Canjáyar, Enix, Félix, Jergal, Huécija, Illar, Instinción, Nacimiento, Ohanes, Padules, Rágol, Santa Cruz de Marchena and Terque in the province of Almería.

## VT RIBERA DEL GÁLLEGO-CINCO VILLAS

Ribera del Gállego-Cinco Villas comprises a vast territory along the Gállego river virtually down to the city of Zaragoza.

The northernmost bodega within the VT, Bodegas y Viñedos Reino de los Mallos, is located in Murillo de Gállego, a town on the provincial border between Zaragoza and Huesca, and at the opposite end of the area of the five historical towns (Cinco Villas) that give the region its name: Sos del Rey Católico, Ejea de los Caballeros, Uncastillo, Sádaba and Tauste. The average altitude in the region is 600 metres, which, along with the presence of the wind known as 'alariez' –similar to the north wind that blows through the Ebro valley, known as 'cierzo'– account for a slow ripening pattern. The soils are in general stony (the typical gravel) in nature, allowing good drainage. *Garnacha* and *Tempranillo*, along with *Cabernet Sauvignon, Merlot* and the white *Macabeo* are all planted in the region.

## VT RIBERA DEL JILOCA

The Jiloca is, together with the Jalón, one of the main tributaries of the Ebro river. Located in the valley and close to mount Moncayo, Ribera del Jiloca is divided in three different areas: Sierra de Santa Cruz (to the northwest, with the town of Abanto), and Jiloca Valley and Sierras de Peco-Herrera to the northeast. The cooperatives represent 95% of the total production in the region. Other towns with bodegas of interest are Daroca, San Martín del Río and Báguena. As with the neighbouring DO Calatayud, the vines are planted on old river terraces on limestone rocky soils, with *Garnacha* as the main variety, followed by *Macabeo* (white). A dry climate, abundant sunlight and cold winters are the features that account for the excellent quality of the local grapes.

## VT RIBERA DEL QUEILES

A new geographic indication for wines produced exclusively from the varieties *Cabernet Sauvignon, Graciano, Garnacha, Tempranillo, Merlot* and *Syrah*, it comprises nine municipal districts in Aragón (Grisel, Lituénigo, Los Fayos, Malón, Novallas, Santa Cruz de Moncayo, Tarazona, Torrellas and Vierlas) and seven in Navarra (Ablitas, Barillas, Cascante, Monteagudo, Murchante, Tulebras and the part of the town of Tudela to the south of the Ebro river) near the Queiles river. The project was initiated by Bodegas Guelbenzu, in Cascante, that was initially hoping to gain exclusive rights over the VT.

## VT SERRA DE TRAMUNTANA-COSTA NORD

This VT comprises 18 municipal districts in the island of Mallorca, between the cape of Formentor and the southwest coast of Andratx, with mainly brownish-grey and limestone soils. Single-varietal wines from white grapes (mainly *Malvasía* and *Chardonnay*) and red ones from *Cabernet Sauvignon* and *Merlot* stand out.

## VT SIERRA DE LAS ESTANCIAS Y LOS FILABRES

Located in the namesake mountain region in the province of Almería, it was approved along with its regulations in 2008. It comprises the municipalities of Alcóntar, Serón, Bacares, Bayarque, Tíjola, Armuña, Sierro, Suflí, Lúcar, Somontín, Urrácal, Purchena, Olula del Río, Macael, Laroya, Fines, Partaloa, Oria, Líjar, Chercos, Albánchez, Cóbdar, Cantoria, Albox, Taberno, Arboleas and Zurgena. The special geo-climatic conditions include intense sunlight for most of the day, cooler nights and little rainfall. The French varieties predominate in the vineyard.

## VT SIERRA NORTE DE SEVILLA

Vinos de la Tierra de la Sierra Norte de Sevilla got its status at the beginning of February 2005. This region, located in the north of the province of Sevilla at the foothills of Sierra Morena, has a landscape of gentle hills and altitudes that go from 250 to almost 1000 metres. The climate in the region is Mediterranean, with hot, dry summers, mild winters and a fairly high average rainfall, reaching occasionally over 800 mm. Since 1998, grape varieties such as *Tempranillo, Cabernet Franc, Syrah, Merlot, Pinot Noir, Cabernet Sauvignon* and the whites *Chardonnay* and *Viognier* have been planted in the region. The soils are varied, with presence of both limestone and slate. As well as Cazalla, the towns included in the designation are Alanís, Almadén de la Plata, Constantina, Guadalcanal, Las Navas de la Concepción, El Pedroso, La Puebla de los Infantes, El Real de la Jara and San Nicolás del Puerto.

## VT SIERRA SUR DE JAÉN

It comprises the towns of Alcalá La Real, Castillo de Locubín, Frailes, Fuensanta de Martos, Los Villares, Valdepeñas de Jaén and the mountain areas that are part of the municipal districts of Alcaudete and Martos.

## VT TORREPEROGIL

Approved in 2006, this geographic indication in the province of Jaén comprises 300 hectares in the area of La Loma and the municipal districts of Úbeda, Sabiote, Rus, Cabra de Santo Cristo, Canena and Torreperogil, the latter being the main town. The wines are a blend of *Garnacha, Syrah, Cabernet Sauvignon* and *Tempranillo* (reds), as well as *Jaén* blanco and *Pedro Ximénez* for the white renderings.

## VT VAL DO MIÑO

Annex I of the Order of the Ministerio de Agricultura, Pesca y Alimentación (Spanish Agriculture Ministry) of 7th January 1998 establishes the geographical limits of this VT, i.e., the municipal districts of Pereiro de Aguiar, Coles, Barbadás, San Cibrao das Viñas, Toén in the province of Ourense, as well as those of the capital city, Ourense, all of them in the Miño river valley.

## VT VALDEJALÓN

Established in 1998, it comprises 36 municipal districts in the mid- and lower-Jalón valley and its tributaries, Aranda, Isuela and Grío. The vines are planted on brownish-grey limestone and alluvial soils, with low rainfall levels of 350 mm. They are some 1000 hectares planted with white (*Macabeo, Garnacha Blanca, Moscatel* and *Airén*) and red varieties (*Garnacha, Tempranillo, Cabernet Sauvignon, Syrah, Monastrell* and *Merlot*).

## VT VALLE DEL CINCA

Located in the southeast of the province of Huesca, Valle del Cinca enjoys favourable climatic and soil conditions for vine growing, similar to a certain extent to those of Somontano and Costers del Segre. The soil is mainly limestone and clay, and the average annual rainfall barely reaches 300 mm, so irrigation is usually required.

## VT VALLES DE SADACIA

A designation created to include wines made in La Rioja from *Moscatel*, a variety which was practically lost with the phylloxera that has been recuperated to produce two types of wine: 'vino de licor' (a blend of wine, must and, in some cases, some 'aguardiente' or wine spirits), and the white *Moscatel* wine which, depending on wine-making, may either be dry, semi-dry or sweet. The wines come mainly from the Cidacos (known as Sádicos in the past) river valley, from which the region gets its name.

## VT VIÑEDOS DE ESPAÑA

A new geographical designation approved in 2006 by the Spanish Ministry of Agriculture and so far used for very few wines. The European Comission rejected the label as well as that of its French counterpart once the autonomous governments from Castilla y León and La Rioja challenged its legality. The label is being used by some wineries from different VT from Andalucía, Aragón, Baleares, Canarias, Castilla-La Mancha, Cataluña, Extremadura, Comunidad de Madrid, Región de Murcia, Navarra and the Comunidad Valenciana that prefer that umbrella and more commercial label, which somehow helps them to jump the boundaries of a given autonomous region with the goal of international recognition.

## BAILÉN
### SOCIEDAD ANDALUZA DE LA VID SANTA GERTRUDIS

Prolongacion Baeza, s/n ó Ctra. N IV Km. 296
23710 Bailen (Jaen)
☎: 953 671 256 - Fax: 953 671 256
sta_gertrudis@bailen.org

DUQUE DE BAILEN 2005 B

**85** Colour: golden. Nose: creamy oak, sweet spices, balsamic herbs, earthy notes. Palate: flavourful, rich, good acidity, correct.

ATARDECER ANDALUZ
MARIA BELLIDO
BATALLA 1808
BORJA
RIBERA DEL GUADIEL
MARQUÉS DE PORTUGALETE
SHAMPÁNY

## BAJO ARAGÓN
### BODEGAS LECERANAS

Ignacio de Ara, 3
50002 Zaragoza
☎: 976 461 056 - Fax: 976 461 558
bodegasevohe@terra.es

EVOHE 2008 T
garnacha 100%

**90** Colour: cherry, garnet rim. Nose: fresh, varietal, damp undergrowth, balsamic herbs, scrubland. Palate: good acidity, fresh, powerful, flavourful, fruity, light-bodied.

## BODEGAS TEMPORE

Ctra. Zaragoza-Montalbán, s/n
50131 Lécera (Zaragoza)
☎: 976 835 040 - Fax: 976 835 040
info@bodegastempore.com
www.bodegastempore.com

TEMPORE JOVEN 2008 T
garnacha 50%, tempranillo 50%

**84**

TEMPORE TERRAE GARNACHA 2007 T
garnacha 100%

**83**

TEMPORE 2005 T ROBLE
tempranillo 100%

**88** Colour: cherry, garnet rim. Nose: sweet spices, dark chocolate, fruit preserve. Palate: spicy, soft tannins, fleshy.

## DOMINIO MAESTRAZGO

Royal, 13
44550 Alcorisa (Teruel)
☎: 978 840 642 - Fax: 978 841 054
bodega@dominiomaestrazgo.com
www.dominiomaestrazgo.com

SANTOLEA 2007 T
garnacha 60%, tempranillo 20%, cariñena 20%

**83**

DOMINIO MAESTRAZGO MAGNUM 2005 T BARRICA
garnacha 65%, tempranillo 20%, syrah 15%

**86** Colour: cherry, garnet rim. Nose: powerful, fruit liqueur notes, toasty, spicy, wet leather. Palate: flavourful, spicy, ripe fruit, fine tannins.

REX DEUS 2004 T
garnacha 85%, cabernet sauvignon 10%, syrah 5%

**89** Colour: cherry, garnet rim. Nose: ripe fruit, spicy, creamy oak, toasty. Palate: powerful, flavourful, toasty, round tannins.

REX DEUS MAGNUM 2004 T
garnacha 85%, cabernet sauvignon 10%, syrah 5%

**88** Colour: cherry, garnet rim. Nose: ripe fruit, creamy oak, toasty, complex, dark chocolate. Palate: powerful, flavourful, toasty, round tannins.

## VENTA D'AUBERT S.L.

Ctra. Valderrobres a Arnes, km. 28
44623 Cretas (Teruel)
☎: 978 769 021 - Fax: 978 769 031
ventadaubert@gmx.net
www.ventadaubert.com

VENTA D'AUBERT VIOGNIER 2008 B
viognier 100%

**91** Colour: bright straw. Nose: fresh, fresh fruit, white flowers, expressive. Palate: flavourful, fruity, good acidity, balanced.

VENTA D'AUBERT 2007 B
chardonnay 60%, garnacha blanca 20%, viognier 20%

**92** Colour: bright yellow. Nose: ripe fruit, sweet spices, creamy oak, fragrant herbs. Palate: rich, smoky aftertaste, flavourful, fresh, good acidity.

VENTUS 2005 TR
cabernet sauvignon 48%, merlot 24%, garnacha 22%, syrah 6%

**90** Colour: cherry, garnet rim. Nose: ripe fruit, spicy, creamy oak, toasty, complex. Palate: powerful, flavourful, toasty, round tannins.

VENTA D'AUBERT SYRAH 2005 T
syrah 100%

**90** Colour: dark-red cherry, orangey edge. Nose: ripe fruit, expressive, characterful. Palate: fruity, flavourful, rich, full, round tannins.

DIONUS 2004 TR
cabernet sauvignon 50%, merlot 40%, cabernet franc 10%

**86** Colour: dark-red cherry, orangey edge. Nose: fruit preserve, spicy, dark chocolate, cocoa bean. Palate: flavourful, fruity, rich, round tannins.

## VINOS MONTANER

Avda. Aragón 85
50710 Maella (Zaragoza)
☎: 976 638 748 - Fax: 976 638 384
vinosmontaner@telefonica.net

FINCA MAS NOU BARONO 2008 T
cabernet sauvignon 50%, syrah 25%, garnacha 25%

**85** Colour: cherry, purple rim. Nose: fresh fruit, red berry notes, floral. Palate: flavourful, fruity, good acidity, round tannins.

BARONO

---

SOME OTHER WINERIES WITHIN THE VT:

**COOP. SANTA MARÍA LA MAYOR
FANBAR S.L.
GRUPO MAGALIA
LAMARCA WINES**

# BETANZOS

**ADEGAS VINSA S.L.**

# CÁDIZ

## BODEGA SANATORIO

Olivo, 1
11130 Chiclana de la Frontera (Cádiz)
☎: 956 400 756 - Fax: 956 532 907
administracion@bodegamanuelaragon.com
www.bodegasanatorio.com

MANUEL ARAGÓN SAUVIGNON BLANC 2007 B
sauvignon blanc

**78**

MANUEL ARAGÓN 2006 T JOVEN
tempranillo, syrah

**78**

## BODEGAS BARBADILLO

Luis de Eguilaz, 11
11540 Sanlúcar de Barrameda (Cádiz)
☎: 956 385 500 - Fax: 956 385 501
barbadillo@barbadillo.com
www.barbadillo.com

ANTONIO BARBADILLO CASTILLO DE SAN DIEGO 2008 B
palomino

**87** Colour: bright straw. Nose: fresh, fresh fruit, white flowers, expressive. Palate: flavourful, fruity, good acidity, balanced.

MAESTRANTE SEMI DULCE 2008 B
palomino

**81**

GIBALBÍN 2006 T
tempranillo, syrah, merlot, cabernet sauvignon

**85** Colour: cherry, purple rim. Nose: expressive, fresh fruit, red berry notes, floral. Palate: flavourful, fruity, good acidity, round tannins.

## BODEGAS OSBORNE

Fernán Caballero, 7
11500 El Puerto de Sta. María (Cádiz)
☎: 956 869 000 - Fax: 956 869 026
comunicaciones@osborne.es
www.osborne.es

GADIR 2008 B

**83**

## CORTIJO DE JARA

Medina, 79
11402 Jerez de la Frontera (Cádiz)
☎: 956 338 163 - Fax: 956 338 163
puerta.nueva@terra.es
www.cortijodejara.com

CORTIJO DE JARA TEMPRANILLO-MERLOT-SYRAH 2006 T

**84**

CORTIJO DE JARA TEMPRANILLO-MERLOT-SYRAH 2006 T ROBLE

**84**

## FINCA MONCLOA

Manuel María González, 12
11403 Jerez de la Frontera (Cádiz)
☎: 956 357 000 - Fax: 956 357 043
nacional@gonzalezbyass.es
www.gonzalezbyass.com

FINCA MONCLOA 2006 T
cabernet sauvignon 51%, syrah 36%, merlot 12%, tempranillo 1%

**87** Colour: cherry, garnet rim. Nose: ripe fruit, medium intensity, creamy oak, spicy, aromatic coffee. Palate: flavourful, spicy, ripe fruit.

## HEREDEROS DE ARGÜESO S.A.

Mar, 8
11540 Sanlúcar de Barrameda (Cádiz)
☎: 956 385 116 - Fax: 956 368 169
argueso@argueso.es
www.argueso.es

BLANCO ARGÜESO 2008 B
palomino 100%

**77**

## HUERTA DE ALBALÁ

Ctra. Ca-6105, km. 4
11630 Arcos de la Frontera (Cádiz)
☎: 647 746 048 - Fax: 856 023 053
bodega@huertadealbala.com
www.huertadealbala.com

BARBAROSA 2008 RD
syrah 100%

**87** Colour: rose, purple rim. Nose: fresh fruit, violet drops, floral. Palate: light-bodied, fruity, flavourful, good acidity, fruity aftestaste.

TABERNER 2008 RD

**82**

BARBAZUL 2007 T
tintilla 50%, syrah 30%, merlot 20%

**88** Colour: bright cherry. Nose: ripe fruit, sweet spices, creamy oak, expressive. Palate: flavourful, fruity, toasty, round tannins.

TABERNER Nº 1 2006 T
syrah 80%, merlot 17%, cabernet sauvignon 3%

**90** Colour: cherry, garnet rim. Nose: ripe fruit, spicy, creamy oak, toasty, dark chocolate. Palate: powerful, flavourful, toasty, round tannins.

TABERNER 2006 T
syrah 70%, merlot 25%, cabernet sauvignon 5%

**88** Colour: cherry, garnet rim. Nose: spicy, roasted almonds, dark chocolate, ripe fruit. Palate: flavourful, fleshy, spicy, round tannins.

## SÁNCHEZ ROMATE HERMANOS

Lealas 26-30
11403 Jerez de la Frontera (Cádiz)
☎: 956 182 212 - Fax: 956 185 276
comercial@romate.com
www.romate.com

MOMO 2008 B

**80**

SOME OTHER WINERIES WITHIN THE VT:

**BODEGAS BARÓN**
**BODEGAS GARVEY**
**BODEGAS VALDIVIA**
**LUIS CABALLERO**
**WILLIAMS & HUMBERT S.A.**

## CAMPO DE CARTAGENA
### SERRANO

Finca La Cabaña, 30
30594 Pozo Estrecho (Cartagena) (Murcia)
☎: 968 556 298 - Fax: 968 556 298
vinos@bodegaserrano.com
www.bodegaserrano.com

VIÑA GALTEA SEMISECO 2008 B
moscatel 35%, chardonnay 35%, malvasia 30%

**82**

VIÑA GALTEA SEMIDULCE B
malvasia 60%, moscatel 40%

**78**

DARIMUS CABERNET SYRAH 2006 T BARRICA
cabernet sauvignon 80%, syrah 20%

**82**

DARIMUS SYRAH DULCE 2008 TINTO DULCE
syrah 100%

**88** Colour: bright cherry. Nose: fruit liqueur notes, candied fruit, dark chocolate, sweet spices, dry stone. Palate: powerful, full, creamy, good finish.

## CANGAS
### BODEGAS ANTÓN CHICOTE

La Galiana,88 Limés
33800 Cangas de Narcea (Asturias)
☎: 985 810 934

PENDERUYOS 2008 T
verdejo tinto, carrasquin, albarin tinto, mencia

**87** Colour: cherry, garnet rim. Nose: expressive, ripe fruit, fruit expression. Palate: good acidity, balanced, fruity, flavourful.

PENDERUYOS SELECCIÓN 2008 T

**85** Colour: bright cherry. Nose: ripe fruit, red berry notes, balsamic herbs, earthy notes. Palate: fleshy, fresh, fruity.

### BODEGAS DEL NARCEA S.L.

Las Barzaniellas - Limés
33817 Cangas del Narcea (Asturias)
☎: 985 813 103 - Fax: 985 813 103
bodegadelnarcea@hotmail.com
www.bodeganarcea.com

PESGOS 2008 B
albarín 80%, albillo 20%

**86** Colour: bright straw. Nose: fragrant herbs, fruit preserve, caramel. Palate: fruity, fresh, varietal.

PESGOS 2006 T
mencía, carrasquín, albarín

**89** Colour: bright cherry. Nose: fresh, red berry notes, raspberry, mineral. Palate: fresh, fruity, light-bodied, balsamic.

PESGOS 2006 T ROBLE
mencía, carrasquín, albarín tinto, verdejo tinto

**87** Colour: deep cherry. Nose: mineral, raspberry, fruit expression, cedar wood. Palate: flavourful, powerful, balsamic.

PESGOS SELECCIÓN 2005 T
albarín tinto, carrasquín, verdejo tinto, mencía

**86** Colour: bright cherry. Nose: ripe fruit, sweet spices, expressive, balsamic herbs, scrubland. Palate: flavourful, fruity, toasty, round tannins.

### VIÑEDOS OBANCA

Obanca 12
33800 Cangas del Narcea (Asturias)
☎: 985 811 539

CASTRO DE LIMES S.C. T
carrasquín

**83**

OBANCA
VIÑEDOS OBANCA

SOME OTHER WINERIES WITHIN THE VT:

**BODEGA MONASTERIO DE CORIAS**
**BODEGAS LA MURIELLA S.L.**
**CHACÓN-BUELTA S.L.**

## CASTELLÓN
### MASIA DE LA HOYA

Avda. Navarro Reverter, 1
12400 Segorbe (Castellón)
☎: 964 710 050 - Fax: 964 713 484
masiadelahoya@masiadelahoya.com
www.masiadelahoya.com

MASÍA DE LA HOYA 2008 T
syrah 100%

**87** Colour: deep cherry, garnet rim. Nose: ripe fruit, floral, spicy. Palate: rich, good acidity, fruity, spicy, round tannins.

MASÍA DE LA HOYA 2008 T
merlot 100%

**81**

SOME OTHER WINERIES WITHIN THE VT:

**VIÑEDOS Y BODEGAS MAYO CASANOVA
BODEGA LES USERES**

## CASTILLA
### ALTOLANDON

Ctra. N-330, km. 242
16330 Landete (Cuenca)
☎: 677 228 974 - Fax: 962 300 662
altolandon@altolandon.com
www.altolandon.com

L´AME MALBEC 2007 T
malbec 100%

**90** Colour: very deep cherry, garnet rim. Nose: ripe fruit, spicy, balsamic herbs, varietal, scrubland. Palate: fleshy, complex, round tannins, fine bitter notes.

### AMADIS DE GAULA

Geronimo Ceballos, 2
13270 Almagro (Ciudad Real)
☎: 926 562 424
www.amadisdegaula.com

REQUIEBRO VERDEJO 2008 B
verdejo

**89** Colour: bright yellow. Nose: fruit expression, complex, varietal, balanced, fragrant herbs. Palate: flavourful, fruity, fine bitter notes, good acidity.

REQUIEBRO 2006 T
syrah

**88** Colour: dark-red cherry, orangey edge. Nose: spicy, creamy oak, ripe fruit. Palate: fruity, rich, flavourful, full, round tannins.

REQUIEBRO 2005 T
syrah, cabernet

**87** Colour: dark-red cherry. Nose: smoky, cocoa bean, creamy oak, fruit preserve. Palate: powerful, good structure, grainy tannins.

REQUIEBRO 2004 T
syrah, cabernet

**87** Colour: bright cherry. Nose: ripe fruit, sweet spices, creamy oak, expressive, dark chocolate. Palate: flavourful, fruity, toasty, round tannins.

REQUIEBRO SELECCION 2004 T
tempranillo

**86** Colour: dark-red cherry, bright ochre rim. Nose: varietal, sweet spices, new oak, aromatic coffee, overripe fruit. Palate: powerful, good structure, fruity, round tannins.

### ANA BOMBAL

Ctra. de Chozas
45510 Fuensalida (Toledo)
☎: 605 222 658

DESTIEMPO 2007 T
syrah, garnacha

**88** Colour: deep cherry. Nose: fresh, expressive, red berry notes, fruit expression, spicy. Palate: flavourful, fleshy, complex, fruity.

### BANÚS

Caldereros, 2
13300 Valdepeñas (Ciudad Real)
☎: 693 299 449
banus@banus.eu
www.banus.eu

BANÚS 2008 B
sauvignon blanc 100%

**86** Colour: bright straw. Nose: fresh, fresh fruit, white flowers, fine lees. Palate: flavourful, fruity, good acidity, balanced.

**BANÚS 2008 RD**
tempranillo 60%, garnacha 40%

**87** Colour: rose. Nose: fresh fruit, red berry notes, expressive, dried flowers. Palate: flavourful, fruity, good acidity, fine bitter notes.

**BANÚS SELECCIÓN ESPECIAL 2007 T**
tempranillo 100%

**83**

## BODEGA FINCA EL RETAMAR

Camino Los Palacios, s/n
45100 Sonseca (Toledo)
☎: 687 765 400 - Fax: 925 380 950
bodega@peces-barba.com
www.peces-barba.com

**CONDE DE ORGAZ SYRAH 2006 T**
syrah 100%

**88** Colour: cherry, purple rim. Nose: ripe fruit, creamy oak, spicy, mineral. Palate: balanced, slightly dry, soft tannins, flavourful, fruity.

**CONDE DE ORGAZ CABERNET-MERLOT 2003 T**
cabernet sauvignon 50%, merlot 50%

**83**

**BARBAROS 2008 ESPUMOSO ROSADO**
garnacha 75%, tempranillo 25%

**79**

## BODEGA LA DEFENSA

Avda. de Castilla La Mancha, 38
45370 Santa Cruz de la Zarza (Toledo)
☎: 925 143 234 - Fax: 925 125 154
bodegasladefensa@bodegasladefensa.es
www.bodegasladefensa.es

**CLARIUS 2008 RD**
tempranillo 100%

**79**

## BODEGA LOS ALJIBES

Finca Los Aljibes
02520 Chinchilla de Montearagón (Albacete)
☎: 918 843 472 - Fax: 918 844 324
info@fincalosaljibes.com
www.fincalosaljibes.com

**VIÑA ALJIBES 2008 B**
sauvignon blanc 80%, chardonnay 20%

**87** Colour: bright straw. Nose: fresh, fresh fruit, white flowers, expressive, fine lees. Palate: flavourful, fruity, good acidity, balanced, fine bitter notes.

**VIÑA ALJIBES 2008 RD**
syrah 100%

**87** Colour: rose, purple rim. Nose: powerful, ripe fruit, red berry notes, floral, expressive. Palate: fleshy, powerful, fruity, fresh.

**VIÑA ALJIBES 2007 T**
merlot 55%, cabernet sauvignon 45%

**82**

**ALJIBES CABERNET FRANC 2006 T**
cabernet franc 100%

**88** Colour: deep cherry, garnet rim. Nose: fresh fruit, red berry notes, dry stone, characterful, sweet spices. Palate: creamy, fruity, powerful, round tannins.

**ALJIBES SYRAH 2005 T**
syrah 100%

**90** Colour: bright cherry. Nose: sweet spices, creamy oak, expressive, ripe fruit, red berry notes. Palate: flavourful, fruity, toasty, round tannins.

**ALJIBES 2005 T**
merlot 35%, cabernet sauvignon 35%, cabernet franc 30%

**89** Colour: cherry, garnet rim. Nose: ripe fruit, spicy, toasty, complex, damp earth, macerated fruit. Palate: powerful, toasty, fine tannins, fresh.

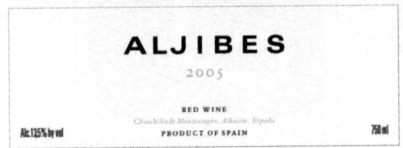

SELECTUS

## BODEGA TIKALO

Finca Guadianeja - Ctra. Catellar de Santiago-Torre de Juan Abad, km. 29,200
13343 Villamanrique (Ciudad Real)
☎: 916 613 543 - Fax: 916 623 734
info@bodegatikalo.com
www.bodegatikalo.com

## ALBALIZA 2008 RD
tempranillo 50%, garnacha 25%, cabernet sauvignon 25%

**78**

## RUBENS 2007 T
tempranillo 100%

**87** Colour: cherry, purple rim. Nose: expressive, fresh fruit, red berry notes, floral. Palate: flavourful, fruity, good acidity, soft tannins.

## ALBALIZA 2007 T
tempranillo 65%, garnacha 35%

**86** Colour: deep cherry, purple rim. Nose: fresh fruit, red berry notes, expressive, balsamic herbs. Palate: fruity, flavourful, powerful, fresh.

## KIOS 2004 T
tempranillo 100%

**88** Colour: very deep cherry, garnet rim. Nose: ripe fruit, sweet spices, creamy oak, powerfull. Palate: powerful, fruity, unctuous, good acidity, toasty, round tannins.

## KIOS ELITE 2003 T
tempranillo 100%

**87** Colour: bright cherry. Nose: ripe fruit, sweet spices, creamy oak, expressive. Palate: flavourful, fruity, toasty, round tannins.

## KIOS CABERNET SAUVIGNON 2003 T
cabernet sauvignon 100%

**87** Colour: bright cherry. Nose: ripe fruit, sweet spices, creamy oak, expressive. Palate: flavourful, fruity, toasty, round tannins, rich.

## BODEGA VENTA DE LA OSSA

Finca Sierra de la Solana. CR-P 1343. Km. 1,6
13640 Herencia (Ciudad Real)
☎: 926 691 107 - Fax: 926 691 162
info@ventalaossa.com
www.ventalaossa.com

## VENTA LA OSSA SYRAH 2007 T
syrah 100%

**93** Colour: cherry, garnet rim. Nose: powerful, lactic notes, ripe fruit, creamy oak, new oak. Palate: flavourful, fleshy, rich, fruity, creamy, round tannins.

## VENTA LA OSSA 2007 T
tempranillo 80%, petit verdot 10%, merlot 10%

**92** Colour: bright cherry. Nose: sweet spices, creamy oak, expressive, red berry notes, ripe fruit. Palate: flavourful, fruity, toasty, round tannins.

## BODEGAS ARÚSPIDE

Ciriaco Cruz, 2

13300 Valdepeñas (Ciudad Real)
☎: 926 347 075 - Fax: 926 347 875
info@aruspide.com
www.aruspide.com

**ALARIS 2008 B**
airén 100%

**86** Colour: bright straw. Nose: candied fruit, fruit expression, varietal. Palate: easy to drink, fruity, fresh, flavourful.

**ARDALES AIRÉN 2008 B**
airén 100%

**84**

**AUTOR DE ARÚSPIDE CHARDONNAY 2007 B BARRICA**
chardonnay 100%

**90** Colour: bright yellow. Nose: powerful, sweet spices, creamy oak, fragrant herbs. Palate: rich, smoky aftertaste, flavourful, fresh, good acidity.

**ALARIS 2008 T**
tempranillo 100%

**88** Colour: deep cherry, purple rim. Nose: ripe fruit, red berry notes, expressive. Palate: flavourful, fruity, good acidity, sweet tannins, good finish.

**ARDALES 2007 T BARRICA**
tempranillo 100%

**87** Colour: bright cherry. Nose: ripe fruit, sweet spices, creamy oak. Palate: flavourful, fruity, toasty, round tannins.

**AUTOR DE ARÚSPIDE TEMPRANILLO 2006 T**
tempranillo 100%

**92** Colour: cherry, garnet rim. Nose: ripe fruit, spicy, creamy oak, complex, macerated fruit, undergrowth. Palate: flavourful, toasty, round tannins, complex.

## BODEGAS ARVA VITIS

Morago, 7 Bajo
13200 Manzanares (Ciudad Real)
☎: 926 611 065 - Fax: 926 611 065
arvavitis@arvavitis.com
www.arvavitis.es

**GRIAL DE AMADIS 2002 T**
syrah

**90** Colour: dark-red cherry, garnet rim. Nose: fruit preserve, aromatic coffee, sweet spices, cedar wood, earthy notes. Palate: full, flavourful, fresh, fine tannins.

ARVA VITIS

AVALON DE ARVA VITIS
SIERRA DE SILES

## BODEGAS BONJORNE

Ctra. La Roda Muntra, km. 2.3
02630 La Roda (Albacete)
☎: 967 601 754 - Fax: 967 601 754
export@bonjorne.es
www.bonjorne.es

**BONJORNE SELECCIÓN 2007 BFB**
chardonnay

**79**

**BONJORNE 6 MESES BARRICA 2006 T**

**84**

ALTOS DEL MAJANAR

## BODEGAS CASA DE LA VIÑA

Ctra. de la Solana a Infantes, km. 15
13248 Alambra (Ciudad Real)
☎: 926 696 044 - Fax: 926 696 068
casadelavina@domecqbodegas.com
www.bodegascasadelavina.com

**CASA DE LA VIÑA TEMPRANILLO 2008 T**
tempranillo

**90** Colour: cherry, purple rim. Nose: expressive, fresh fruit, red berry notes, floral. Palate: flavourful, fruity, good acidity, round tannins.

CASA DE LA VIÑA TEMPRANILLO 2006 T BARRICA

**87** Colour: dark-red cherry. Nose: fresh, fruit expression, creamy oak. Palate: flavourful, powerful, fruity, toasty.

CASA DE LA VIÑA EDICIÓN LIMITADA 2005 T

**88** Colour: bright cherry. Nose: sweet spices, creamy oak, overripe fruit, warm. Palate: flavourful, fruity, toasty, round tannins.

ALBOR

## BODEGAS CORONADO

Ctra. San Isidro, s/n
16620 La Alberca de Záncara (Cuenca)
☎: 676 463 483 - Fax: 967 150 107
informacion@bodegascoronado.com
www.bodegascoronado.com

CHARCÓN SAUVIGNON BLANC 2008 B
sauvignon blanc 100%

**79**

VIÑA CHARCÓN 2006 T ROBLE
cabernet sauvignon 50%, cencibel 50%

**83**

VIÑA CHARCÓN SYRAH 2005 T
syrah 100%

**84**

## BODEGAS EL LINZE

Duque de Liria, 9
28015 Madrid
☎: 636 161 479
info@ellinze.com
www.ellinze.com

EL LINZE 2007 T
syrah

**90** Colour: cherry, purple rim. Nose: varietal, red berry notes, lactic notes, scrubland, sweet spices, creamy oak. Palate: fresh, fruity, correct, soft tannins.

## BODEGAS ERCAVIO

Plazuela de la Iglesia, 1
45311 Dosbarrios (Toledo)
☎: 925 122 281 - Fax: 925 137 033
masquevinos@fer.es
www.bodegasercavio.com

ERCAVIO 2008 B

**89** Colour: bright straw. Nose: fresh, fresh fruit, white flowers, expressive. Palate: flavourful, fruity, good acidity.

ERCAVIO 2008 RD
tempranillo

**85** Colour: raspberry rose. Nose: red berry notes, lactic notes, floral. Palate: flavourful, fruity, good acidity, balanced, easy to drink.

ERCAVIO 2007 T ROBLE

**87** Colour: dark-red cherry. Nose: ripe fruit, spicy, creamy oak. Palate: round tannins, powerful, flavourful, spirituous.

LA MESETA 2006 T
tempranillo 50%, syrah 50%

**87** Colour: dark-red cherry. Nose: fruit expression, ripe fruit, spicy, creamy oak. Palate: flavourful, fruity, powerful, varietal.

LA PLAZUELA 2005 T

**91** Colour: dark-red cherry. Nose: ripe fruit, fruit liqueur notes, dry stone, dark chocolate, creamy oak. Palate: fleshy, powerful, flavourful, spicy, ripe fruit.

ERCAVIO LIMITED RESERVE 2004 T

**89** Colour: dark-red cherry. Nose: ripe fruit, fruit expression, undergrowth, creamy oak, toasty. Palate: good structure, fruity, flavourful, ripe fruit.

## BODEGAS GAZULES

Ríos Rosas, 44-A 7G
28003 Madrid
☎: 620 796 713
jcamacho.martinez@yahoo.es
wwww.bodegasgazules.com

PRIVILEGIO DE GAZULES 2006 T
syrah 80%, cabernet sauvignon 20%

**88** Colour: cherry, garnet rim. Nose: powerful, ripe fruit, red berry notes, sweet spices. Palate: flavourful, fleshy, fruity.

## BODEGAS JUAN RAMIREZ

Torrecilla, 138
13300 Valdepeñas (Ciudad Real)
☎: 926 322 021 - Fax: 926 320 495
info@bodegasjuanramirez.com
www.bodegasjuanramirez.com

AMPELO 2008 B JOVEN
chardonnay 100%

**81**

AMPELO 2008 B JOVEN
verdejo 100%

**80**

AMPELO 2008 T
syrah 100%

**84**

CÉSAR LUCENDO

## BODEGAS LAHOZ

Ctra.N-310 (Tomelloso-Villarrobledo) km. 108,500
13630 Socuéllamos (Ciudad Real)
☎: 926 699 083 - Fax: 926 514 929
info@bodegaslahoz.com
www.bodegaslahoz.com

RECATO SAUVIGNON BLANC 2008 BFB

**88** Colour: bright straw. Nose: ripe fruit, tropical fruit, powerfull, creamy oak, scrubland. Palate: unctuous, flavourful, fruity, spicy.

RECATO 9 MESES 2007 T BARRICA
tempranillo

**87** Colour: deep cherry, purple rim. Nose: ripe fruit, varietal, medium intensity. Palate: flavourful, fruity, easy to drink, good finish.

ABAD DE SOTO 2007 T

**84**

## BODEGAS LÓPEZ PANACH

Finca El Calaverón
02600 Villarrobledo (Albacete)
☎: 967 573 140 - Fax: 967 573 297
bodegas@lopezpanach.com
www.lopezpanach.com

LÓPEZ PANACH VERDEJO 2008 B
verdejo 100%

**85** Colour: straw. Nose: ripe fruit, scrubland. Palate: fruity, varietal, good acidity.

LÓPEZ PANACH TEMPRANILLO 2008 T
tempranillo 100%

**78**

LÓPEZ PANACH SELECCIÓN 2006 T
tempranillo 100%

**86** Colour: cherry, garnet rim. Nose: powerful, toasty, dark chocolate, ripe fruit. Palate: flavourful, powerful, fleshy, spicy.

LÓPEZ PANACH COUPAGE 2006 T
tempranillo 50%, cabernet sauvignon 25%, merlot 12,5%, syrah 12,5%

**85** Colour: cherry, garnet rim. Nose: powerful, ripe fruit, balsamic herbs. Palate: flavourful, spicy, ripe fruit.

LÓPEZ PANACH TEMPRANILLO CABERNET 2006 T ROBLE
tempranillo 50%, cabernet sauvignon 50%

**85** Colour: cherry, garnet rim. Nose: powerful, balsamic herbs, grassy, toasty. Palate: flavourful, fleshy, spicy.

LÓPEZ PANACH SYRAH 2005 T
syrah 100%

**82**

LÓPEZ PANACH MERLOT 2005 T
merlot 100%

**82**

LÓPEZ PANACH TEMPRANILLO 2004 T
tempranillo 100%

**87** Colour: cherry, garnet rim. Nose: powerful, fruit preserve, dark chocolate. Palate: powerful, fleshy.

LÓPEZ PANACH CABERNET SAUVIGNON 2004 T
cabernet sauvignon 100%

**81**

## BODEGAS MANO A MANO

Ctra. CM 412, km. 100
13248 Alhambra (Ciudad Real)
☎: 915 942 076 - Fax: 916 160 246
malvarez@avpositivo.com

MANO A MANO 2008 T ROBLE

**91** Colour: dark-red cherry. Nose: spicy, dark chocolate, fruit liqueur notes, fresh fruit, mineral. Palate: powerful, flavourful, concentrated, round tannins.

## BODEGAS MARTÚE LA GUARDIA

Campo de la Guardia s/n
45760 La Guardia (Toledo)
☎: 925 123 333 - Fax: 925 123 332
bodegasenlaguardia@martue.com
www.martue.com

MARTÚE CHARDONNAY 2008 B
chardonnay 100%

**85** Colour: bright yellow. Nose: ripe fruit, dried flowers, sun-drenched nuances. Palate: full, fruity, creamy.

MARTÚE 2007 T
tempranillo 47%, merlot 15%, syrah 1%, cabernet sauvignon 37%

**87** Colour: dark-red cherry, orangey edge. Nose: ripe fruit, creamy oak, spicy. Palate: flavourful, rich, fruity, round tannins.

MARTÚE 2006 T
tempranillo, merlot, syrah, cabernet sauvignon

**87** Colour: deep cherry. Nose: powerful, ripe fruit, varietal, fruit liqueur notes. Palate: powerful, fleshy, sweetness, spicy.

MARTÚE SYRAH 2006 T
syrah 100%

**87** Colour: very deep cherry, purple rim. Nose: ripe fruit, floral, sweet spices, creamy oak. Palate: powerful, fruity, sweetness, round tannins, spicy.

MARTÚE ESPECIAL 2006 T
cabernet sauvignon 68%, merlot 20%, syrah 12%

**85** Colour: dark-red cherry, orangey edge. Nose: powerful, fruit preserve, caramel, dark chocolate. Palate: flavourful, powerful, spirituous, pruney, balanced, round tannins.

## BODEGAS MÁXIMO S.L.

Camino Viejo de Logroño, 26
01320 Oyón (Álava)
☎: 945 622 216 - Fax: 945 622 315
maximo@bodegasmaximo.com
www.bodegasmaximo.com

MÁXIMO VERDEJO 2008 B
verdejo, sauvignon blanc

**86** Colour: bright yellow. Nose: ripe fruit, grassy, varietal. Palate: flavourful, good acidity, fine bitter notes.

MÁXIMO TEMPRANILLO 2008 RD
tempranillo

**87** Colour: raspberry rose. Nose: raspberry, fresh. Palate: flavourful, fruity, balanced, fine bitter notes.

MÁXIMO MERLOT 2007 T
merlot

**87** Colour: bright cherry. Nose: ripe fruit, sweet spices, creamy oak, expressive. Palate: flavourful, fruity, toasty, round tannins.

MÁXIMO TEMPRANILLO 2007 T

**86** Colour: cherry, garnet rim. Nose: powerful, ripe fruit, sweet spices, cocoa bean. Palate: flavourful, powerful, fleshy.

MÁXIMO SYRAH 2007 T

**85** Colour: cherry, garnet rim. Nose: powerful, ripe fruit, dark chocolate, sweet spices. Palate: flavourful, fleshy, spicy, round tannins.

MÁXIMO CABERNET SAUVIGNON 2007 T
cabernet sauvignon

**85** Colour: cherry, garnet rim. Nose: powerful, ripe fruit, sweet spices, dark chocolate. Palate: powerful, flavourful, spicy, round tannins.

## BODEGAS MONTALVO WILMOT

Ctra. Ruidera km. 10,2
13710 Argamasilla de Alba (Ciudad Real)
☎: 926 699 069 - Fax: 926 699 069
maria@montalvowilmot.com
www.montalvowilmot.com

MONTALVO WILMOT SYRAH 2008 T ROBLE
syrah 100%

**86** Colour: very deep cherry, purple rim. Nose: floral, sweet spices, ripe fruit, balanced. Palate: fruity, easy to drink, correct.

MONTALVO WILMOT TEMPRANILLO 2008 T
tempranillo 85%, cabernet sauvignon 15%

**84**

MONTALVO WILMOT CABERNET SAUVIGNON 2008 T
cabernet sauvignon 100%

**83**

MONTALVO WILMOT SYRAH 2006 T ROBLE
syrah 100%

**86** Colour: cherry, garnet rim. Nose: varietal, ripe fruit, spicy, cocoa bean. Palate: fruity, spicy, round tannins, good acidity.

MONTALVO WILMOT COLECCIÓN PRIVADA 2004 T
tempranillo 75%, cabernet sauvignon 25%

**86** Colour: cherry, garnet rim. Nose: fruit preserve, toasty. Palate: fleshy, good acidity, round tannins.

MONTALVO WILMOT CABERNET DE FAMILIA 2003 T
cabernet sauvignon 100%

**88** Colour: cherry, garnet rim. Nose: ripe fruit, sweet spices, balanced. Palate: fruity, powerful, pruney, round tannins, spicy.

## BODEGAS NAVARRO LÓPEZ

Autovía Madrid-Cádiz, km. 193
13300 Valdepeñas (Ciudad Real)
☎: 902 193 431 - Fax: 902 193 432
laboratorio@navarrolopez.com
www.navarrolopez.com

PREMIUM 1904 2007 T
tempranillo 70%, petit verdot 30%

**85** Colour: cherry, purple rim. Nose: expressive, medium intensity, ripe fruit, creamy oak. Palate: flavourful, long, good finish, soft tannins.

## BODEGAS PALOMAR SÁNCHEZ

Ctra. de Ocaña Km. 1,5
16400 Tarancón (Cuenca)
☎: 646 539 032 - Fax: 969 324 493
bodegas@palomarsanchez.com
www.bodegaspalomarsanchez.com

CAMPOS DE TARANZ 2007 T ROBLE

**85** Colour: cherry, garnet rim. Nose: ripe fruit, fruit liqueur notes, spicy. Palate: fresh, flavourful, balanced, easy to drink.

CAMPOS DE TARANZ 18 MESES 2006 T

**84**

VIÑA SABUCO 2005 T

**87** Colour: cherry, garnet rim. Nose: powerful, ripe fruit, toasty, sweet spices. Palate: flavourful, powerful, fleshy, round tannins.

## BODEGAS REAL

Finca Marisánchez
Ctra. de Valdepeñas a Cózar, km. 12,8
13300 Valdepeñas (Ciudad Real)
☎: 914 577 588 - Fax: 914 577 210
comunicacion@bodegas-real.com
www.bodegas-real.com

FINCA MARISÁNCHEZ CHARDONNAY 2008 B
chardonnay 100%

**83**

MOSCATEL FINCA MARISÁNCHEZ 2008 B
moscatel 100%

**80**

VIÑA IBOR 2007 T ROBLE
tempranillo 100%

**87** Colour: cherry, purple rim. Nose: lactic notes, red berry notes, ripe fruit, scrubland. Palate: flavourful, fruity, fleshy.

FINCA MARISÁNCHEZ 2006 T ROBLE
tempranillo 80%, merlot 10%, syrah 10%

**88** Colour: bright cherry. Nose: ripe fruit, sweet spices, creamy oak, dark chocolate. Palate: flavourful, fruity, toasty, round tannins.

VEGA IBOR TEMPRANILLO 2005 T BARRICA
tempranillo 100%

**87** Colour: cherry, garnet rim. Nose: ripe fruit, red berry notes, sweet spices. Palate: flavourful, fruity, fresh, fleshy.

## BODEGAS SAN ISIDRO DE P. MUÑOZ

Ctra El Toboso, 1
13620 Pedro Muñoz (Ciudad Real)
☎: 926 586 057 - Fax: 926 568 380
jesusr@viacotos.com
www.viacotos.com

## CARRIL DE COTOS AIRÉN 2008 B
airén 100%

**81**

## CARRIL DE COTOS SEMIDULCE B
airén 100%

**78**

## CARRIL DE COTOS TEMPRANILLO 2008 T
tempranillo 100%

**88** Colour: deep cherry. Nose: varietal, red berry notes, ripe fruit. Palate: round tannins, fruity, varietal.

## CARRIL DE COTOS TEMPRANILLO 2006 T
tempranillo 100%

**78**

## CARRIL DE COTOS 2005 T BARRICA
cabernet sauvignon 100%

**85** Colour: deep cherry. Nose: varietal, ripe fruit, creamy oak, spicy. Palate: ripe fruit, balsamic, round tannins.

## BODEGAS VERUM

Ctra. de Argmasilla de Alba, km. 0,8
13700 Tomelloso (Ciudad Real)
☎: 926 511 404 - Fax: 926 515 047
info@bodegasverum.com
www.bodegasverum.com

VERUM 2008 B
sauvignon blanc, gewürztraminer

**87** Colour: bright straw. Nose: fresh, fresh fruit, white flowers, expressive. Palate: flavourful, fruity, good acidity, balanced.

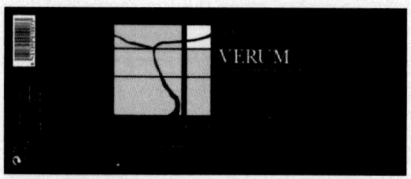

## BODEGAS Y VIÑEDOS BARREDA

Ramalazo, 2
45880 Corral de Almaguer (Toledo)
☎: 925 207 223 - Fax: 925 207 223
bodegas-barreda@bodegas-barreda.com
www.bodegas-barreda.com

## TORRE DE BARREDA AMIGOS 2006 T
tempranillo, cabernet sauvignon, syrah

**88** Colour: cherry, garnet rim. Nose: fruit preserve, fruit liqueur notes, sweet spices, aromatic coffee. Palate: rich, flavourful, good acidity, full, round tannins.

## TORRE DE BARREDA PAÑOFINO 2006 T
tempranillo

**87** Colour: very deep cherry, garnet rim. Nose: fruit preserve, powerfull, earthy notes, sweet spices, aromatic coffee. Palate: full, good acidity, fruity, round tannins.

## TORRE DE BARREDA PAÑOFINO 2005 T
tempranillo

**89** Colour: dark-red cherry, garnet rim. Nose: fruit preserve, warm, sweet spices, balanced. Palate: rich, fruity, good finish, round tannins, powerful.

## BODEGAS Y VIÑEDOS CASA DEL VALLE

Ctra. de Yepes-Añover de Tajo, km. 47,700
Finca Valdelagua
45313 Yepes (Toledo)
☎: 925 155 533 - Fax: 925 147 019
casadelvalle@bodegasolarra.es
www.bodegacasadelvalle.es

## HACIENDA CASA DEL VALLE CABERNET SAUVIGNON 2006 T
cabernet sauvignon 100%

**85** Colour: deep cherry, garnet rim. Nose: ripe fruit, earthy notes, sweet spices, herbaceous. Palate: fruity, grainy tannins, good acidity, spicy.

## HACIENDA CASA DEL VALLE SHIRAZ 2006 T
syrah 100%

**85** Colour: very deep cherry, purple rim. Nose: ripe fruit, spicy, balanced, warm. Palate: fruity, good acidity, spicy, round tannins.

## FINCA VALDELAGUA 2005 T
cabernet sauvignon 40%, syrah 40%, merlot 20%

**87** Colour: deep cherry, garnet rim. Nose: fruit liqueur notes, warm, sweet spices, cocoa bean. Palate: flavourful, fruity, good acidity, spicy, slightly dry, soft tannins.

## BODEGAS Y VIÑEDOS CASTIBLANQUE

Isaac Peral, 19
13610 Campo de Criptana (Ciudad Real)
☎: 926 589 147 - Fax: 926 589 148

info@bodegascastiblanque.com
www.bodegascastiblanque.com

BALDOR CHARDONNAY 2008 BFB
chardonnay 100%

**83**

ILEX AIRÉN 2008 B
airén 100%

**80**

ILEX 2008 RD
syrah 100%

**82**

ILEX 2008 T
tempranillo 60%, garnacha 25%, syrah 15%

**86** Colour: cherry, purple rim. Nose: fresh fruit, red berry notes, floral. Palate: flavourful, fruity, good acidity, round tannins.

ILEX COUPAGE 2006 T
tempranillo 50%, garnacha 25%, syrah 15%, cabernet sauvignon 10%

**87** Colour: cherry, garnet rim. Nose: ripe fruit, spicy, creamy oak, toasty. Palate: powerful, flavourful, toasty, round tannins.

BALDOR TRADICIÓN SYRAH 2006 T
syrah 100%

**86** Colour: deep cherry. Nose: ripe fruit, fruit expression, floral, sweet spices. Palate: powerful, pruney, round tannins, flavourful.

BALDOR CABERNET SAUVIGNON OLD VINES 2006 T
cabernet sauvignon 100%

**86** Colour: cherry, garnet rim. Nose: aged wood nuances, dark chocolate, toasty, ripe fruit. Palate: powerful, spicy.

BALDOR TRADICIÓN TEMPRANILLO 2004 T
tempranillo 100%

**86** Colour: cherry, garnet rim. Nose: powerful, grassy, smoky, warm. Palate: sweetness, fine bitter notes, round tannins.

BALDOR TRADICIÓN CABERNET SAUVIGNON 2004 T
cabernet sauvignon 100%

**82**

## BODEGAS Y VIÑEDOS PINUAGA

Ctra. N-301, km. 95,5
45880 Corral de Almaguer (Toledo)
☎: 914 577 117 - Fax: 914 577 117
info@bodegaspinuaga.com

www.bodegaspinuaga.com

PINUAGA LA SENDA 2008 T
merlot 80%, tempranillo 20%

**87** Colour: deep cherry, purple rim. Nose: fresh fruit, fruit expression, red berry notes. Palate: flavourful, fruity, good acidity, fresh.

PINUAGA NATURE TEMPRANILLO 2007 T
tempranillo

**87** Colour: cherry, purple rim. Nose: red berry notes, lactic notes, violets, ripe fruit. Palate: balanced, fruity, good acidity.

PINUAGA TEMPRANILLO (12 MESES EN BARRICA) 2005 T
tempranillo 100%

**89** Colour: cherry, garnet rim. Nose: sweet spices, fresh fruit, powerfull, balsamic herbs. Palate: flavourful, fresh, fine bitter notes, complex.

## BODEGAS Y VIÑEDOS TAVERA

Ctra. Valmojado - Toledo, km. 22
45182 Arcicóllar (Toledo)
☎: 637 847 777 - Fax: 925 590 218
info@bodegastavera.com
www.bodegastavera.com

TAVERA ANTIGUOS VIÑEDOS 2008 RD
garnacha 100%

**81**

TAVERA 2008 T MACERACIÓN CARBÓNICA
syrah 60%, tempranillo 20%, garnacha 20%

**87** Colour: cherry, purple rim. Nose: fresh fruit, red berry notes, floral. Palate: flavourful, fruity, good acidity, round tannins.

TAVERA ANTIGUOS VIÑEDOS 2007 T
garnacha 100%

**85** Colour: cherry, garnet rim. Nose: powerful, ripe fruit, red berry notes, spicy. Palate: flavourful, ripe fruit, round tannins.

TAVERA VENDIMIA SELECCIONADA 2006 T
tempranillo 70%, syrah 20%, garnacha 10%

**87** Colour: cherry, garnet rim. Nose: powerful, mineral, ripe fruit, sweet spices. Palate: flavourful, fleshy, spicy.

## BODEGAS Y VIÑEDOS URIBES MADERO (BOD. CALZADILLA)

Ctra. Huete-Cuenca, km. 3,2
16500 Huete (Cuenca)
☎: 969 143 020 - Fax: 969 147 047

um@pagodecalzadilla.net
www.pagodecalzadilla.net

OPTA CALZADILLA 2006 T
tempranillo, syrah, garnacha

**89** Colour: deep cherry, garnet rim. Nose: ripe fruit, varietal, toasty, overripe fruit. Palate: powerful, warm, round tannins, pruney.

CALZADILLA 2005 T
tempranillo, cabernet sauvignon, garnacha, syrah

**89** Colour: very deep cherry, garnet rim. Nose: ripe fruit, lactic notes, red clay notes, dark chocolate. Palate: good structure, warm, grainy tannins, flavourful.

CALZADILLA SYRAH 2004 TC

**89** Colour: very deep cherry, garnet rim. Nose: ripe fruit, sweet spices, aromatic coffee, fruit liqueur notes. Palate: fleshy, powerful, round tannins, pruney, spicy.

## CASALOBOS

CM-412, km. 6,5
13196 Picón (Ciudad Real)
☎: 915 745 734 - Fax: 914 092 869
bodega@casalobos.es

CASALOBOS 2006 T

**89** Colour: deep cherry. Nose: undergrowth, fruit liqueur notes, ripe fruit, sweet spices, toasty, cedar wood. Palate: fleshy, spirituous, sweetness, flavourful.

## COOP. NTRA. SRA. DE LA SOLEDAD

Ctra. Tarancón, s/n
16411 Fuente de Pedro Naharro (Cuenca)
☎: 969 125 039 - Fax: 969 125 907
info@bodegasoledad.com
www.bodegasoledad.com

OBÍAS 2008 B
airén 50%, chardonnay 50%

**81**

OBÍAS 2008 T
tempranillo 100%

**82**

## COOP. PURÍSIMA CONCEPCIÓN

Ctra. Minaya-San Clemente, km. 10
16610 Casas de Fernando Alonso (Cuenca)

☎: 969 383 043 - Fax: 969 383 153
info@vinoteatinos.com
www.vinoteatino.com

AIRAZ COLECCIÓN 2008 B

**82**

AIRAZ COLECCION 2008 T

**89** Colour: cherry, purple rim. Nose: expressive, fresh fruit, red berry notes, floral. Palate: flavourful, fruity, good acidity, round tannins.

TEATINOS DULCE MOSCATEL B DULCE

**87** Colour: yellow. Nose: candied fruit, floral, pattiserie, balsamic herbs. Palate: flavourful, elegant, good acidity, creamy.

## COOP. UNIÓN CAMPESINA INIESTENSE

San Idefonso, 1
16235 Iniesta (Cuenca)
☎: 967 490 120 - Fax: 967 490 777
comercial@cooperativauci.com
www.cooperativauci.com

SEÑORIO DE INIESTA SAUVIGNON BLANC 2008 B
sauvignon blanc 100%

**76**

SEÑORÍO DE INIESTA BOBAL 2008 RD
bobal 100%

**85** Colour: rose. Nose: neat, fresh fruit, red berry notes, lactic notes, dried flowers. Palate: rich, fruity, flavourful.

SEÑORÍO DE INIESTA 2008 T
tempranillo 100%

**83**

SEÑORÍO DE INIESTA CABERNET SAUVIGNON 2008 T
cabernet sauvignon 100%

**80**

SEÑORÍO DE INIESTA SYRAH 2008 T
syrah 100%

**78**

SEÑORÍO DE INIESTA 2006 T ROBLE
tempranillo 50%, cabernet sauvignon 50%

**87** Colour: light cherry, bright ochre rim. Nose: fruit liqueur notes, spicy, aged wood nuances, cocoa bean. Palate: rich, fruity, flavourful, toasty, round tannins.

## COSECHEROS Y CRIADORES

Diputación, s/n
01320 Oyón (Álava)
☎: 945 601 944 - Fax: 945 622 488
nacional@cosecherosycriadores.com
www.familiamartinezbujanda.com

INFINITUS GEWÜRZTRAMINER 2008 B

**88** Colour: bright straw. Nose: floral, varietal, ripe fruit. Palate: rich, flavourful, powerful, fruity, good finish.

INFINITUS CHARDONNAY VIURA 2008 B

**81**

INFINITUS TEMPRANILLO CABERNET FRANC 2008 RD

**86** Colour: rose, purple rim. Nose: fresh fruit, red berry notes, lactic notes. Palate: rich, fruity, fresh, flavourful.

INFINITUS CABERNET SAUVIGNON 2008 T

**87** Colour: very deep cherry, garnet rim. Nose: ripe fruit, elegant, varietal, herbaceous. Palate: fleshy, powerful, fruity, varietal.

INFINITUS MERLOT 2008 T

**87** Colour: deep cherry, purple rim. Nose: ripe fruit, spicy, characterful. Palate: rich, fruity, good acidity, round, soft tannins.

INFINITUS SYRAH 2008 T

**86** Colour: deep cherry, purple rim. Nose: ripe fruit, elegant, balsamic herbs. Palate: rich, fruity, balanced, round tannins.

INFINITUS TEMPRANILLO 2008 T

**86** Colour: deep cherry, purple rim. Nose: ripe fruit, red berry notes, balsamic herbs. Palate: rich, fruity, flavourful, soft tannins.

INFINITUS MALBEC 2008 T

**86** Colour: deep cherry, purple rim. Nose: ripe fruit, spicy, earthy notes. Palate: unctuous, fruity, good acidity, spicy.

INFINITUS CABERNET SAUVIGNON-TEMPRANILLO 2007 T

**86** Colour: deep cherry, purple rim. Nose: ripe fruit, balsamic herbs, sweet spices, new oak. Palate: fruity, good acidity, unctuous, round tannins, toasty.

## DEHESA DE HILARES

Ctra. Almagro - Bolaños, s/n Aptdo. Correos 70
13260 Bolaños de Calatrava (Ciudad Real)
☎: 696 538 087
dehesadehilares@gmail.com

DEHESA DE HILARES 2006 T
merlot 80%, cabernet franc 20%

**89** Colour: deep cherry. Nose: ripe fruit, fresh, powerfull, varietal. Palate: fleshy, fruity, fresh, flavourful.

## DIONISOS

Unión, 82
13300 Valdepeñas (Ciudad Real)
☎: 926 313 248 - Fax: 926 322 813
info@labodegadelasestrellas.com
www.labodegadelasestrellas.com

PAGOS DEL CONUCO 2006 T
tempranillo 100%

**88** Colour: bright cherry. Nose: ripe fruit, sweet spices, creamy oak, expressive. Palate: flavourful, fruity, toasty, round tannins.

VINUM VITAE 2005 TC
tempranillo 100%

**87** Colour: cherry, garnet rim. Nose: expressive, fruit preserve, fruit liqueur notes, new oak. Palate: flavourful, long, spicy, fine tannins.

EGO PRIMUS 2005 TC
tempranillo 70%, cabernet sauvignon 15%, syrah 15%

**87** Colour: cherry, garnet rim. Nose: ripe fruit, sweet spices, balanced. Palate: flavourful, round tannins, good acidity, great length.

## DOMECQ BODEGAS + CINCO CASAS

Virgen de las Nieves, 2
13720 Cinco Casas (Ciudad Real)
☎: 926 529 010 - Fax: 926 526 070
jcutilla@domecqbodegas.com
www.domecqbodegas.com

ELEGIDO SELECCIÓN 2005 T

**76**

## DOMINIO DE EGUREN

San Pedro, s/n

01309 Páganos (Álava)
☎: 945 600 117 - Fax: 945 600 554
info@eguren.com
www.eguren.com

CÓDICE 2007 T

**88** Colour: deep cherry. Nose: aromatic coffee, fresh fruit, powerfull, expressive. Palate: powerful, flavourful, fruity.

## EL PROGRESO SOCIEDAD COOP. CLM

Avda. de la Virgen, 89
13670 Villarubia de los Ojos (Ciudad Real)
☎: 926 896 088 - Fax: 926 896 135
elprogreso@cooprogres.com
www.bodegaselprogreso.com

MI CHUPITO 2008 B
airén 100%

**78**

## ENVÍNATE

Ramón y Cajal, 27 - bajo
02630 La Roda (Albacete)
☎: 627 564 495 - Fax: 967 444 194
asesoria.envinate@gmail.com

PUZZLE 2008 T
garnacha 25%, monastrell 25%, tempranillo 25%, others 25%

**89** Colour: deep cherry, purple rim. Nose: powerful, ripe fruit, red berry notes, sweet spices. Palate: flavourful, fleshy, fruity.

## FÉLIX SOLÍS

Autovía de Andalucía, km. 199
13300 Valdepeñas (Ciudad Real)
☎: 926 322 400 - Fax: 926 322 417
bfs@felixsolis.com
www.felixsolis.com

ORQUESTRA 2008 B

**87** Colour: bright straw. Nose: ripe fruit, warm, tropical fruit. Palate: fresh, unctuous, fine bitter notes, good finish.

CONSIGNA CHARDONNAY 2008 B

**85** Colour: bright straw. Nose: ripe fruit, varietal, warm, floral. Palate: rich, fruity, fine bitter notes.

CONSIGNA TEMPRANILLO 2008 RD

**84**

ORQUESTRA 2008 T

**87** Nose: powerful, ripe fruit, scrubland. Palate: flavourful, spicy, ripe fruit.

CONSIGNA TEMPRANILLO 2008 T

**87** Colour: cherry, purple rim. Nose: fresh fruit, red berry notes, floral. Palate: flavourful, fruity, good acidity, round tannins.

CONSIGNA MERLOT 2008 T
merlot

**85** Colour: cherry, garnet rim. Nose: powerful, ripe fruit, balsamic herbs, creamy oak. Palate: flavourful, powerful, fleshy, toasty.

ORQUESTRA MERLOT 2008 T

**84**

CONSIGNA CABERNET SAUVIGNON 2008 T

**83**

CONSIGNA SHIRAZ 2008 T

**80**

ORQUESTRA CABERNET SAUVIGNON 2008 T JOVEN

**80**

## FEMAL, BODEGAS Y VIÑEDOS LA SOLANA

Ctra.Porzuna-Cno. Cristo del Humilladero Km. 3
13420 Malagón (Ciudad Real)
☎: 983 681 146 - Fax: 983 681 147
bodega@pagoflorentino.com
www.pagoflorentino.com

PAGO FLORENTINO 2007 T

**89** Colour: bright cherry, garnet rim. Nose: dark chocolate, ripe fruit, aged wood nuances, sweet spices. Palate: fleshy, rich, creamy, round tannins.

## FINCA CASA ALARCÓN

Ctra. Montealegre km 4,5
02660 Caudete (Albacete)
☎: 965 828 266 - Fax: 965 229 405
comercial@casalarcon.com

www.casalarcon.com

**NEA 2007 T**
petit verdot

**85** Colour: dark-red cherry, garnet rim. Nose: ripe fruit, sweet spices. Palate: rich, fruity, sweetness, soft tannins.

**CASA ALARCÓN CHARDONNAY 2008 B**
chardonnay

**85** Colour: bright yellow. Nose: ripe fruit, tropical fruit, medium intensity, sweet spices. Palate: fleshy, fruity, spicy.

**CASA ALARCÓN ROSADO DE SYRAH 2008 RD**
syrah

**84**

**BLAU 2008 T**
monastrell, merlot

**89** Colour: cherry, purple rim. Nose: expressive, fresh fruit, red berry notes, floral, dark chocolate. Palate: flavourful, fruity, good acidity, round tannins.

**DON JAIME DE CASA ALARCÓN 2007 T**
temrpanillo, cabernet, syrah

**88** Colour: cherry, purple rim. Nose: ripe fruit, new oak, creamy oak, spicy. Palate: balanced, good acidity, round tannins, flavourful, fruity.

**TRIA ROBLE FRANCÉS 2007 T**
syrah, petit verdot, merlot

**87** Colour: very deep cherry, garnet rim. Nose: ripe fruit, fruit expression, red berry notes, sweet spices. Palate: full, good acidity, fruity, concentrated.

**TRIA ROBLE AMERICANO 2007 T**
syrah, petit verdot, merlot

**85** Colour: cherry, garnet rim. Nose: powerful, ripe fruit, smoky, toasty. Palate: powerful, toasty, spicy, round tannins.

## FINCA CASA CARRIL CRUZADO

Ctra. Iniesta-Villagarcía del Llano, km. 13
16236 Villagarcía del Llano (Cuenca)
☎: 967 571 154 - Fax: 967 571 155
bodega@casacarrilcruzado.com
www.casacarrilcruzado.com

**CASA CARRIL CRUZADO SYRAH 2006 TC**
syrah 100%

**86** Colour: bright cherry. Nose: ripe fruit, sweet spices, creamy oak, raspberry, floral. Palate: flavourful, fruity, toasty, round tannins, fruity aftestaste.

**CASA CARRIL CRUZADO PETIT VERDOT 2006 T**
petit verdot 100%

**85** Colour: bright cherry. Nose: sweet spices, creamy oak, expressive, jasmine, macerated fruit. Palate: flavourful, fruity, toasty, round tannins.

**CASA CARRIL CRUZADO 2006 T BARRICA**
cabernet sauvignon, syrah, tempranillo, petit verdot

**81**

## FINCA CONSTANCIA

Camino del Bravo s/n
45543 Otero (Toledo)

☎: 925 861 535 - Fax: 925 861 533
lslara@gonzalezbyass.es
www.gonzalezbyass.es

**FINCA CONSTANCIA 2007 T**
syrah, cabernet sauvignon, petit verdot, tempranillo, graciano,
cabernet franc

**90** Colour: deep cherry. Nose: ripe fruit, fruit expression, fruit liqueur notes. Palate: balanced, round tannins, spicy, fruity, flavourful, powerful.

**FINCA CONSTANCIA 2006 T**

**88** Colour: cherry, garnet rim. Nose: powerful, warm, spicy, ripe fruit. Palate: spicy, fine bitter notes, fine bitter notes.

**FINCA CONSTANCIA 2005 T**

**87** Colour: cherry, garnet rim. Nose: powerful, fruit preserve, warm, spicy. Palate: flavourful, fleshy, spicy, round tannins.

ALTOZANO

## FINCA CORONADO

Sevilla, s/n
13440 Argamasilla de Calatrava (Ciudad Real)
☎: 618 614 888
info@fincacoronado.com
www.fincacoronado.com

**FINCA CORONADO 2006 T**
tempranillo 30%, cabernet sauvignon 30%, syrah 20%, petit verdot 10%, graciano 5%, merlot 5%

**90** Colour: deep cherry. Nose: ripe fruit, warm, spicy, toasty, caramel. Palate: flavourful, powerful, fleshy, spicy, round tannins.

## FINCA EL REGAJO

Lope de Vega, 24
02651 Fuentealamo (Albacete)
☎: 967 112 323

**PUERTO PINAR VIOGNIER 2008 B**
viognier

**85** Colour: bright straw. Nose: floral, fresh fruit. Palate: fruity, good acidity, rich, flavourful.

**PETIT VERDOT 2008 T**

**88** Colour: bright cherry. Nose: sweet spices, creamy oak, expressive, fruit preserve, mineral. Palate: flavourful, fruity, toasty, round tannins.

**MACEDONIO 2007 T**
monastrell, petit verdot

**82**

## FINCA LA ESTACADA

Ctra. N-400, km. 103
16400 Tarancón (Cuenca)
☎: 969 327 099 - Fax: 969 327 199
fincalaestacada@fincalaestacada.com
www.fincalaestacada.com

**SECUA DULCE 2007 B**
chardonnay

**82**

**FINCA LA ESTACADA 2008 RD**
garnacha

**86** Colour: onion pink. Nose: elegant, candied fruit, fragrant herbs, red berry notes, spicy. Palate: flavourful, long, spicy, sweetness.

**FINCA LA ESTACADA 12 MESES BARRICA 2007 T**
tempranillo

**89** Colour: dark-red cherry, orangey edge. Nose: expressive, fruit expression, ripe fruit, new oak, cocoa bean. Palate: round tannins, fruity, rich, good structure.

**SECUA CABERNET-SYRAH 2005 T**
cabernet sauvignon, syrah

**89** Colour: dark-red cherry, orangey edge. Nose: ripe fruit, undergrowth, cocoa bean, dark chocolate, creamy oak, expressive. Palate: fruity, flavourful, spicy, round tannins, fruity aftestaste.

**FINCA LA ESTACADA SELECCIÓN VARIETALES 2005 T**
tempranillo, cabernet sauvignon, merlot, syrah

**87** Colour: deep cherry, orangey edge. Nose: ripe fruit, creamy oak, dark chocolate, sweet spices. Palate: round tannins, spicy, creamy, fruity.

## FINCA LA VALONA
## VIÑEDOS Y BODEGAS

Paraje los Pinares de Rubielos
16230 Villanueva de la Jara (Cuenca)
☎: 967 496 600 - Fax: 967 495 495
info@fincálavalona.com

**FINCA LA VALONA 2007 T**
tempranillo 100%

**89** Colour: very deep cherry. Nose: ripe fruit, creamy oak, sweet spices. Palate: balanced, elegant, round tannins, flavourful, fruity.

## FINCA LORANQUE

Finca Loranque s/n
45593 Bargas (Toledo)
☎: 669 476 849 - Fax: 925 590 316
fincaloranque@fincaloranque.com
www.fincaloranque.com

LACRUZ DE FINCA LORANQUE 2007 T
tempranillo, syrah

**85** Colour: cherry, purple rim. Nose: ripe fruit, red berry notes, medium intensity. Palate: fruity, good acidity, ripe fruit.

LACRUZ DE FINCA LORANQUE CABERNET
SAUVIGNON 2005 T
cabernet sauvignon 100%

**88** Colour: cherry, garnet rim. Nose: varietal, ripe fruit, damp undergrowth, grassy. Palate: flavourful, powerful, fleshy, spicy, ripe fruit.

LACRUZ DE FINCA LORANQUE SYRAH 2005 T
sumoll 100%

**86** Colour: cherry, garnet rim. Nose: medium intensity, ripe fruit, spicy, toasty. Palate: flavourful, ripe fruit, round tannins.

FINCA LORANQUE SYRAH-TEMPRANILLO 2005 T
syrah 50%, tempranillo 50%

**83**

## FINCA LOS ALIJARES
## BODEGA Y VIÑEDOS

Avda. de la Paz, 5
45180 Camarena (Toledo)
☎: 918 174 364 - Fax: 918 174 364
gerencia@fincalosalijares.com
www.fincalosalijares.com

FINCA LOS ALIJARES VIOGNIER 2008 B
viognier 100%

**78**

9 COTAS 2008 RD
garnacha 50%, syrah 50%

**86** Colour: rose, purple rim, bright. Nose: fresh fruit, red berry notes, violet drops. Palate: flavourful, fruity, good acidity.

FINCA LOS ALIJARES PETIT VERDOT 2008 T
petit verdot 100%

**88** Colour: cherry, purple rim. Nose: powerful, ripe fruit, red berry notes, cocoa bean, new oak. Palate: flavourful, fruity, fresh, round tannins.

FINCA LOS ALIJARES 2008 T
petit verdot 50%, syrah 50%

**82**

FINCA LOS ALIJARES GRACIANO 2007 TC
graciano 100%

**87** Colour: bright cherry. Nose: expressive, fruit preserve, dark chocolate, faded flowers. Palate: flavourful, fruity, toasty, round tannins.

FINCA LOS ALIJARES 2008 MOSCATEL
moscatel 100%

**85** Colour: bright straw. Nose: varietal, medium intensity, candied fruit. Palate: flavourful, fruity, sweetness, easy to drink.

## FINCA LOS NEVADOS
## BODEGA Y VIÑEDOS

Camino del Rosillo, s/n
13630 Socuéllamos (Ciudad Real)
☎: 926 118 908 - Fax: 667 430 396
info@fincalosnevados.es
www.fincalosnevados.es

FINCA LOS NEVADOS 2008 B
chardonnay 60%, sauvignon blanc 40%

**88** Colour: bright straw. Nose: ripe fruit, powerfull, warm, scrubland, sweet spices. Palate: rich, flavourful, fine bitter notes, unctuous.

MINSTRAL 2008 BFB
viognier 100%

**88** Colour: yellow. Nose: ripe fruit, sweet spices, creamy oak, warm. Palate: rich, fruity, good acidity, spicy.

MINSTRAL 2007 B
viognier

**88** Colour: straw. Nose: medium intensity, elegant, ripe fruit, citrus fruit, floral. Palate: fruity, fresh, flavourful, fleshy.

FINCA LOS NEVADOS 2007 T
tempranillo, garnacha, merlot

**88** Colour: very deep cherry, garnet rim. Nose: ripe fruit, lactic notes, varietal, fruit expression. Palate: creamy, fruity, powerful, fruity aftertaste.

**LEBECHE 2006 T**
tempranillo 60%, petit verdot 40%

**87** Colour: dark-red cherry, garnet rim. Nose: ripe fruit, elegant, spicy, new oak. Palate: flavourful, fruity, grainy tannins, spicy.

**SYRIACUS 2005 T**
syrah 100%

**89** Colour: very deep cherry, garnet rim. Nose: ripe fruit, fruit expression, floral, sweet spices, creamy oak. Palate: unctuous, round, fruity, good acidity, round tannins.

**GREGAL 2005 T**
garnacha 50%, cabernet sauvignon 50%

**84**

BOREAS

## FONTANA

Extramuros, s/n
16411 Fuente de Pedro Naharro (Cuenca)
☎: 969 125 433 - Fax: 969 125 387
bf@bodegasfontana.com
www.bodegasfontana.com

**QUERCUS 2005 T**
tempranillo 100%

**91** Colour: bright cherry. Nose: ripe fruit, sweet spices, creamy oak, undergrowth, earthy notes. Palate: flavourful, fruity, toasty, round tannins, creamy.

**GRAN FONTAL VENDIMIA SELECCIONADA 2005 TR**
tempranillo 100%

**90** Colour: cherry, garnet rim. Nose: powerful, toasty, sweet spices, ripe fruit. Palate: flavourful, fleshy, powerful, ripe fruit.

**DUETO DE FONTANA 2004 T**
cabernet sauvignon 50%, merlot 50%

**88** Colour: deep cherry, garnet rim. Nose: powerful, expressive, varietal, spicy. Palate: balanced, ripe fruit, round tannins.

**PAGO EL PÚLPITO 2005 VINO DE LICOR**
tempranillo 100%

**91** Colour: cherry, garnet rim. Nose: fruit expression, ripe fruit, dry stone, undergrowth, cedar wood, cigar. Palate: pruney, creamy, good structure, good acidity.

MESTA

## JESUS DEL PERDÓN - BODEGAS YUNTERO S.C.C.M.

Pol. Ind., Ctra. s/n
13200 Manzanares (Ciudad Real)
☎: 926 610 309 - Fax: 926 610 516
yuntero@yuntero.com
www.yuntero.com

**LAZARILLO SEMIDULCE 2008 B**
airén 100%

**82**

**LAZARILLO 2008 B**
airén 100%

**82**

**LAZARILLO TEMPRANILLO 2008 T**
tempranillo 100%

**85** Colour: cherry, purple rim. Nose: fresh fruit, red berry notes, fruit expression. Palate: fruity, good acidity, flavourful, correct.

## LOBECASOPE S.L.

Menasalbas, 18
45120 San Pablo de los Montes (Toledo)
☎: 679 443 792
flequi@ziries.es
www.lobecasope.com

**ZIRIES 2008 T**

**91** Colour: deep cherry. Nose: ripe fruit, wild herbs, red berry notes, scrubland, dark chocolate, spicy. Palate: round, fruity, good acidity, complex, flavourful, varietal.

**NAVALEGUA 2008 T BARRICA**
garnacha tinta 70%, tempranillo 15%, cariñena 15%

**89** Colour: dark-red cherry. Nose: varietal, powerfull, expressive, fresh fruit, wild herbs, scrubland, smoky. Palate: complex, fresh, flavourful.

**ZIRIES 2007 T**
garnacha 90%, cencibel 10%

**90** Colour: bright cherry. Nose: sweet spices, creamy oak, expressive, mineral, ripe fruit. Palate: flavourful, fruity, toasty, round tannins.

## MONT REAGA S.L.

Ctra. N-420, km. 333,2 Apdo. de correos nº 6
16649 Monreal del Llano (Cuenca)
☎: 645 769 801 - Fax: 637 370 892
mont-reaga@mont-reaga.com
www.mont-reaga.com

BLANCO DE MONTREAGA 2007 BFB
sauvignon blanc 100%

**85** Colour: bright yellow. Nose: tropical fruit, spicy, creamy oak, sun-drenched nuances, fruit preserve. Palate: rich, flavourful, creamy, smoky aftertaste.

ISOLA DE MONTREAGA 2008 RD
tempranillo 50%, syrah 50%

**84**

ISOLA DE MONTREAGA 2008 T
merlot 100%

**84**

TEMPO DE MONTREAGA 2006 T
cabernet sauvignon, merlot

**86** Colour: dark-red cherry, orangey edge. Nose: ripe fruit, creamy oak, spicy. Palate: fruity, rich, flavourful.

LA ESENCIA DE MONTREAGA 2005 T
syrah 100%

**89** Colour: bright cherry, garnet rim. Nose: neat, varietal, fresh fruit. Palate: fruity, flavourful, good acidity, soft tannins.

MONTREAGA CLÁSICO 2004 T
syrah 100%

**89** Colour: cherry, garnet rim. Nose: spicy, ripe fruit, medium intensity, red berry notes, balsamic herbs. Palate: fruity, balanced, great length.

TEMPO DE MONTREAGA LA ESPERA 2004 T
cabernet sauvignon 70%, merlot 30%

**87** Colour: cherry, garnet rim. Nose: ripe fruit, powerfull, expressive, spicy, aromatic coffee. Palate: correct, balanced, fleshy.

FATA MORGANA TINTO DULCE
merlot 100%

**89** Colour: dark-red cherry. Nose: overripe fruit, fruit liqueur notes, toasty. Palate: powerful, flavourful, sweetness.

## NTRA. SRA. DEL PILAR
## SOC. COOP. DE CLM

Extramuros, s/n

45810 Villanueva de Alcardete (Toledo)
☎: 925 166 375 - Fax: 925 166 611
alcardet@terra.es

FINCA ALMEDO 2007 T
tempranillo 80%, cabernet sauvignon 20%

**85** Colour: deep cherry, purple rim. Nose: red berry notes, fruit expression, varietal. Palate: light-bodied, fruity, flavourful.

## ORGANIC SIGNATURE WINES

Extramuros, s/n
02260 Fuentealbilla (Albacete)
☎: 967 472 503 - Fax: 967 472 516
info@franchete.com
www.franchete.com

FRANCHETE ECOLÓGICO ASSEMBLAGE 2007 T

**82**

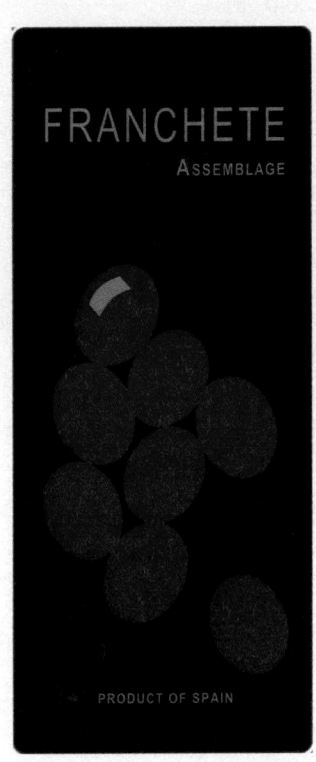

FRANCHETE ECOLÓGICO ASSEMBLAGE 2008 T

**85** Colour: cherry, garnet rim. Nose: powerful, fruit preserve, smoky, balsamic herbs. Palate: spicy, ripe fruit, round tannins.

FRANCHETE CABERNET SAUVIGNON ECOLÓGICO 2007 T JOVEN

**82**

FRANCHETE TINTO BARRICA 2005 T

**83**

## OSBORNE MALPICA DE TAJO

Ctra. Malpica-Pueblanueva, Km 6
45692 Malpica de Tajo (Toledo)
☎: 956 869 000 - Fax: 956 869 026
comunicacion@osborne.es
www.osborne.es

SOLAZ VIURA 2008 B
viura

**85** Colour: bright straw. Nose: fruit expression, candied fruit, citrus fruit, warm. Palate: fruity, fresh, flavourful.

FINCA DE MALPICA 2008 RD

**89** Colour: rose, purple rim, bright. Nose: fresh fruit, red berry notes, floral, powerfull. Palate: flavourful, fruity, good structure.

SOLAZ MULTIVARIETAL 2008 RD

**85** Colour: rose, purple rim. Nose: fresh fruit, lactic notes, expressive. Palate: light-bodied, flavourful, fruity, good acidity.

SOLAZ SELECCION FAMILIAR 2006 T

**89** Colour: bright cherry. Nose: ripe fruit, sweet spices, creamy oak, expressive, scrubland. Palate: flavourful, fruity, toasty, round tannins.

DOMINIO DE MALPICA
VENDIMIA SELECCIONADA 2006 T

**87** Colour: light cherry, bright ochre rim. Nose: macerated fruit, sweet spices, aromatic coffee, warm. Palate: spirituous, roasted-coffee aftertaste, round tannins.

SOLAZ TEMPRANILLO-CABERNET SAUVIGNON 2006 T

**85** Colour: light cherry, bright ochre rim. Nose: fruit liqueur notes, sweet spices, new oak. Palate: light-bodied, fruity, good acidity, harsh oak tannins, easy to drink.

SOLAZ CABERNET SAUVIGNON-SHIRAZ 2006 T

**85** Colour: light cherry, orangey edge. Nose: fruit liqueur notes, fruit liqueur notes, sweet spices. Palate: flavourful, fruity, good acidity, round tannins.

FINCA DE MALPICA 2005 T

**87** Colour: light cherry, bright ochre rim. Nose: macerated fruit, sweet spices, dark chocolate, balanced. Palate: rich, spirituous, smoky aftertaste, round tannins.

PLURAL 2004 T

**86** Colour: light cherry, bright ochre rim. Nose: fruit preserve, sweet spices, new oak. Palate: good acidity, round tannins, roasted-coffee aftertaste, spirituous.

## PAGO CASA DEL BLANCO

Ctra. Manzanares-Moral de Calatrava, km. 23,200
13200 Manzanares (Ciudad Real)
☎: 917 480 606 - Fax: 913 290 266
quixote@pagocasadelblanco.com
www.pagocasadelblanco.com

PILAS BONAS 2007 B
sauvignon blanc

**83**

QUIXOTE PETIT VERDOT 2005 T
petit verdot 100%

**87** Colour: bright cherry. Nose: ripe fruit, sweet spices, creamy oak, new oak. Palate: flavourful, fruity, toasty, round tannins.

QUIXOTE CABERNET SAUVIGNON SYRAH 2005 T
cabernet sauvignon 50%, syrah 50%

**86** Colour: cherry, garnet rim. Nose: smoky, tar, powerfull, overripe fruit. Palate: fleshy, powerful, spicy.

QUIXOTE 2005 T
merlot 53%, tempranillo 27%, petit verdot 20%

**86** Colour: cherry, garnet rim. Nose: powerful, ripe fruit, toasty, sweet spices. Palate: powerful, fleshy, flavourful, round tannins.

QUIXOTE TEMPRANILLO MERLOT 2005 T
tempranillo, merlot

**84**

QUIXOTE TEMPRANILLO 2005 T
tempranillo 100%

**83**

PILAS BORRAS

## PAGO DE LUNA

Tomás Navarro Tomás, 4 Bajo
02630 La Roda (Albacete)
☎: 967 548 508 - Fax: 967 548 022
contacto@pagodeluna.com
www.pagodeluna.com

PAGO DE LUNA 2007 T
merlot 40%, cabernet sauvignon 25%, syrah 25%, tempranillo 10%

**87** Colour: deep cherry. Nose: ripe fruit, sweet spices, dark chocolate, creamy oak. Palate: balanced, spicy, slightly dry, soft tannins, flavourful.

## PAGO DE VALLEGARCÍA

Claudio Coello, 35 Bajo C
28001 (Madrid)
☎: 925 421 407 - Fax: 925 421 822
info@vallegarcia.com
www.vallegarcia.com

VALLEGARCÍA VIOGNIER 2007 BFB
viognier 100%

**94** Colour: bright yellow. Nose: powerful, ripe fruit, sweet spices, creamy oak, dried herbs. Palate: rich, smoky aftertaste, flavourful, fresh, good acidity.

VALLEGARCIA SYRAH 2006 T
syrah 100%

**91** Colour: bright cherry, garnet rim. Nose: medium intensity, red berry notes, ripe fruit, spicy. Palate: complex, full, rich, toasty, round tannins.

HIPPERIA 2005 T
merlot 47%, cabernet franc 2%,
cabernet sauvignon 46%, petit verdot 5%

**87** Colour: dark-red cherry, bright ochre rim. Nose: spicy, overripe fruit, boiled fruit notes, toasty. Palate: rich, fruity, spicy, round tannins.

## PAGO DEL VICARIO

Ctra. Ciudad Real-Porzuna, km. 16
Apdo. 1303
13080 Ciudad Real (Ciudad Real)
☎: 902 092 926 - Fax: 926 666 029
info@pagodelvicario.com
www.pagodelvicario.com

BLANCO DE TEMPRANILLO 2008 B
tempranillo 100%

**82**

TALVA 2006 BFB
chardonnay 50%, sauvignon blanc 50%

**82**

PAGO DEL VICARIO CORTE DULCE 2006 B
chardonnay 50%, sauvignon blanc 50%

**78**

PAGO DEL VICARIO PETIT VERDOT 2008 RD
petit verdot 100%

**84**

PAGO DEL VICARIO AGIOS 2006 T
tempranillo 70%, garnacha 30%

**87** Colour: cherry, garnet rim. Nose: powerful, toasty, dark chocolate, ripe fruit. Palate: good structure, roasted-coffee aftertaste, round tannins.

PAGO DEL VICARIO 50-50 2006 T
cabernet sauvignon 50%, tempranillo 50%

**87** Colour: bright cherry, garnet rim. Nose: ripe fruit, sweet spices. Palate: flavourful, balanced, fine bitter notes, ripe fruit.

**PAGO DEL VICARIO MONAGÓS 2006 T**
syrah 90%, garnacha 10%

**87** Colour: bright cherry, garnet rim. Nose: macerated fruit, ripe fruit, medium intensity, aromatic coffee. Palate: complex, elegant, round tannins.

**PENTA 2006 T**
tempranillo 55%, cabernet sauvignon 25%, merlot 18%, petit verdot 2%

**87** Colour: bright cherry. Nose: ripe fruit, sweet spices, creamy oak. Palate: flavourful, fruity, toasty, soft tannins.

**PAGO DEL VICARIO MERLOT DULCE 2004 T**
merlot 100%

**84**

## VINNICO EXPORT

De la Muela, 16
03730 Jávea (Alicante)
☎: 965 791 967 - Fax: 966 461 471
info@vinnico.com
www.vinnico.com

**CAPA AIRÉN VERDEJO 2008 B**
verdejo 70%, airén 30%

**81**

**CEPUNTO ORO S/C T**
cabernet sauvignon, tempranillo

**84**

**DOS PUNTOS 2008 T**
tempranillo 85%, syrah 15%

**87** Colour: dark-red cherry. Nose: ripe fruit, creamy oak, spicy. Palate: fruity, flavourful, spicy, ripe fruit, round tannins.

**CAPA TEMPRANILLO 2008 T**
tempranillo 90%, syrah 10%

**83**

## VINOS COLOMAN

Goya, 17
13620 Pedro Muñoz (Ciudad Real)
☎: 926 586 410 - Fax: 926 586 656
coloman@satcoloman.com
www.satcoloman.com

**PEDROTEÑO AIRÉN 2008 B**
airén 100%

**83**

**PEDROTEÑO CENCIBEL 2008 T**
tempranillo 100%

**80**

## VINOS Y BODEGAS

Ctra. de las Mesas, km. 1
13630 Socuéllanos (Ciudad Real)
☎: 926 531 067 - Fax: 926 532 249
roman@vinosybodegas.com
www.vinosybodegas.com

**TEMPLUM B**
sauvignon blanc

**81**

**TEMPLUM CABERNET SAUVIGNON 2008 T**
cabernet sauvignon

**81**

**TEMPLUM SYRAH 2008 T**
syrah

**80**

**TEMPLUM TEMPRANILLO 2006 T**

**81**

**TEMPLUM MERLOT 2006 T**

**78**

**MIRADOR DE CASTILLA SELECCION 2003 T**
tempranillo, cabernet sauvignon, syrah

**85** Colour: cherry, garnet rim. Nose: powerful, overripe fruit, fruit liqueur notes, spicy. Palate: flavourful, long, powerful tannins.

**MIRADOR DE CASTILLA SELECCION 2003 T**
tempranillo, cabernet sauvignon, syrah

**84**

## VIÑEDOS CIGARRAL SANTA MARÍA

Cerro del Emperador, s/n
45001 Toledo (Toledo)
☎: 925 252 991 - Fax: 925 253 198
vinedos@adolfo-toledo.com
www.adolfo-toledo.com

**PAGO DEL AMA SYRAH 2006 T BARRICA**
syrah

**91** Colour: bright cherry. Nose: sweet spices, creamy oak, ripe fruit, red berry notes, varietal. Palate: flavourful, fruity, toasty, round tannins.

PAGO DEL AMA CABERNET SAUVIGNON 2005 T BARRICA

**91** Colour: bright cherry. Nose: sweet spices, expressive, fruit preserve, dark chocolate, caramel. Palate: flavourful, fruity, toasty, round tannins.

## VIÑEDOS MEJORANTES

Ctra. de Villafranca, km. 2
45860 Villacañas (Toledo)
☎: 925 201 036 - Fax: 925 200 023
portillejo@portillejo.com
www.portillejo.com

VAL DE PORT 2008 B
airén 90%, verdejo 10%

**79**

VAL DE PORT 2007 T
cabernet sauvignon 70%, tempranillo 20%, merlot 10%

**84**

## VIÑEDOS Y BODEGAS MUÑOZ

Ctra. Villarrubia, 11
45350 Noblejas (Toledo)
☎: 925 140 070 - Fax: 925 141 334
info@bodegasmunoz.com
www.bodegasmunoz.com

LEGADO MUÑOZ CHARDONNAY 2008 B
chardonnay

**86** Colour: bright straw. Nose: powerful, ripe fruit, sweet spices. Palate: flavourful, fleshy, spicy.

LEGADO MUÑOZ TEMPRANILLO 2008 T

**86** Colour: deep cherry, purple rim. Nose: fresh fruit, varietal, expressive. Palate: flavourful, powerful, fruity.

LEGADO MUÑOZ MERLOT 2007 T
merlot

**85** Colour: cherry, purple rim. Nose: varietal, fresh, ripe fruit. Palate: fruity aftestaste, round tannins, good acidity, easy to drink.

LEGADO MUÑOZ GARNACHA 2007 T

**84**

FINCA MUÑOZ

## VITIS TERRARUM S.L.

Ronda de Segovia, 35
28005 Madrid
☎: 913 656 001 - Fax: 913 656 001
info@vitisterrarum.es
www.vitisterrarum.es

VITIS TERRARUM SYRAH 2006 T
syrah 100%

**87** Colour: cherry, garnet rim. Nose: powerful, ripe fruit, sweet spices. Palate: powerful, fleshy, flavourful.

SOME OTHER WINERIES WITHIN THE VT:

**AGROVILLARTA
ALBAVINSA S.A.
BACO, BODEGAS ASOCIADAS COOP.
BERBERANA
BODEGA ECOLÓGICA BRUNO RUIZ
BODEGA HNOS. MATEOS HIGUERA
BODEGA PALAREA
BODEGA PINTO POLO
BODEGA SAN GINÉS
BODEGA SAN JOSÉ
BODEGA SEÑORÍO DEL JÚCAR
BODEGA Y VIÑEDOS LA CANDELARIA
BODEGAS ARESAN S.L.
BODEGAS BAÑUSTES
BODEGAS CALAR
BODEGAS CANTÓ
BODEGAS CASA ANTONETE
BODEGAS CASAQUEMADA
BODEGAS CASTILLO DE CONSUEGRA
BODEGAS CELAYA
BODEGAS DEL MUNI
BODEGAS EGUREN
BODEGAS EL TANINO
BODEGAS ENOMAR
BODEGAS GARDEL
BODEGAS HACIENDA ALBAE
BODEGAS HNOS. CATALÁN CAMBRONERO
BODEGAS HNOS. RUBIO
BODEGAS ISLA
BODEGAS LA REMEDIADORA
BODEGAS LOMA CASANOVA S.L.
BODEGAS MARTÍNEZ SÁEZ
BODEGAS MONTEAGUDO RODRÍGUEZ
BODEGAS MORALIA
BODEGAS OLCAVIANA
BODEGAS ROMERO DE ÁVILA SALCEDO**

**BODEGAS SANTA MARGARITA**
**BODEGAS SANVIVER**
**BODEGAS VIÑA OBDULIA**
**BODEGAS Y VIÑEDOS JESÚS RECUERO**
**BODEGAS Y VIÑEDOS SÁNCHEZ MULITERNO**
**CAPILLA DEL FRAILE**
**CASA DE PUEBLAS**
**CASA GUALDA**
**CASAGRANDE**
**CERVANTINO**
**COOP. NTRA. SRA. DE LA SOLEDAD S.C.L.**
**COOP. NTRA. SRA. DE LOS REMEDIOS**
**DUELA MAESTRA**
**FINCA DE VERAGUA**
**FINCA LABAJOS**
**FINCA SANDOVAL**
**FORO DE FORMACIÓN Y CULTURA DEL VINO**
**GALGO WINES**
**LA VID Y LA ESPIGA S.C., C-LM**
**LOS AGUILEROS**
**MIGUEL CALATAYUD S.A.**
**SDAD. COOP. AGRARIA NTRA. SRA. DE RUS**
**SDAD. COOP. AGRÍCOLA SAN ANTONIO ABAD**
**SDAD. COOP. NTRA. SRA. DEL ESPINO**
**UNIÓN CELLERS DEL NOYA S.A.**
**VINÍCOLA DE CASTILLA**
**VINÍCOLA MORALES, S.L.**
**VIÑEDOS DE CAMARENA, SDAD. COOP. DE CLM**
**VIÑEDOS Y BODEGAS EL CASTILLO**
**VIÑEDOS Y BODEGAS GARVA**
**VIÑEDOS Y BODEGAS VISÁN**
**VIÑEDOS Y RESERVAS**
**VITIS NATURA**

## CASTILLA Y LEÓN

### ABADIA RETUERTA

Ctra. N-122 Km. 332,5
47340 Sardón de Duero (Valladolid)
☎: 983 680 314 - Fax: 983 680 286
info@abadia-retuerta.es
www.abadia-retuerta.es

PAGO NEGRALADA 2006 T
tempranillo 100%

**90** Colour: bright cherry. Nose: ripe fruit, sweet spices, creamy oak, expressive, powerfull, earthy notes. Palate: flavourful, fruity, toasty, round tannins.

PAGO LA GARDUÑA SYRAH 2006 T
syrah 100%

**90** Colour: deep cherry, garnet rim. Nose: cocoa bean, creamy oak, ripe fruit, lactic notes. Palate: complex, flavourful, spicy, ripe fruit, round tannins.

ABADÍA RETUERTA SELECCIÓN ESPECIAL 2006 T
tempranillo 75%, cabernet sauvignon 20%, merlot 5%

**88** Colour: bright cherry, garnet rim. Nose: cocoa bean, sweet spices, medium intensity. Palate: creamy, flavourful, round tannins.

### AGRÍCOLA CASTELLANA S.C.L.

Ctra. Rodilana, s/n
47491 La Seca (Valladolid)
☎: 983 816 320 - Fax: 983 816 562
info@agricolacastellana.com
www.agricolacastellana.com

CABALLERO DE CASTILLA TEMPRANILLO 2008 T
tempranillo 100%

**84**

CASA MARÍA TEMPRANILLO 2008 T
tempranillo 100%

**83**

### ANTA BANDERAS

Ctra. Palencia-Aranda, km. 68
09443 Villalba de Duero (Burgos)
☎: 947 613 050 - Fax: 947 613 051
natura@antaempresas.com
www.antabodegas.com

LANAVA CHARDONNAY 2008 B
chardonnay 100%

**87** Colour: bright straw. Nose: fresh, fresh fruit, expressive, tropical fruit. Palate: flavourful, fruity, good acidity, balanced.

### ARRIAGA Y MIMÉNDEZ COMPAÑÍA DE VINOS

c/Capitán Cortés, 6 Piso 4 Puerta 3
26003 Logroño (La Rioja)
☎: 941 287 072 - Fax: 941 287 072
info@arriagaymimendez.com
www.arriagaymimendez.com

MITERNA CORTE DOS 2006 T BARRICA
prieto picudo 100%

**86** Colour: deep cherry, garnet rim. Nose: fruit preserve, sweet spices, varietal, creamy oak, premature reduction notes. Palate: unctuous, powerful, grainy tannins, sweetness.

## BELONDRADE

Camino del Puerto
47491 La Seca (Valladolid)
☎: 983 481 001 - Fax: 600 590 024
info@belondradeylurton.com
www.belondradeylurton.com

QUINTA APOLONIA 2008 B
verdejo 100%

**89** Colour: yellow, pale. Nose: fresh fruit, citrus fruit, wild herbs. Palate: fruity, flavourful, fresh, good finish, fruity aftestaste.

QUINTA CLARISA 2008 RD
tempranillo 100%

**89** Colour: rose, purple rim. Nose: fresh fruit, red berry notes, fragrant herbs. Palate: rich, fruity, elegant, fruity aftestaste.

## BODEGA CÁMBRICO

Paraje El Guijarral, s/n
37658 Villanueva del Conde (Salamanca)
☎: 923 281 006 - Fax: 923 213 605
info@cambrico.com
www.cambrico.com

575 UVAS DE CÁMBRICO 2006 T
tempranillo 75%, rufete 14%, calabrés 11%

**93** Colour: cherry, garnet rim. Nose: powerful, lactic notes, warm, fruit liqueur notes, red berry notes, toasty, dark chocolate. Palate: flavourful, powerful, fleshy, spicy.

CÁMBRICO TEMPRANILLO 2005 T
tempranillo 100%

**91** Colour: cherry, purple rim. Nose: powerful, ripe fruit, fruit expression, fragrant herbs, sweet spices. Palate: flavourful, powerful, fleshy, spicy, round tannins.

CÁMBRICO RUFETE 2005 T
rufete 100%

**90** Colour: cherry, garnet rim. Nose: powerful, warm, ripe fruit, spicy, scrubland. Palate: spicy, ripe fruit, soft tannins.

## BODEGA CASTO PEQUEÑO

Calvario, s/n
24220 Valderas (León)
☎: 987 762 426 - Fax: 987 763 147
bodega@castopequeno.com
www.castopequeno.com

QUINTA HINOJAL 2008 B
verdejo, viura

**83**

COTOVAL 2008 RD
prieto picudo

**86** Colour: brilliant rose. Nose: fresh fruit, floral, varietal, fresh. Palate: fruity, flavourful, fresh.

QUINTA HINOJAL 2008 RD
tempranillo 100%

**84**

QUINTA HINOJAL 2004 T
tempranillo 100%

**83**

## BODEGA EMINA MEDINA

Ctra. Medina del Campo-Olmedo, km. 1,2
47400 Medina del Campo (Valladolid)
☎: 902 430 170 - Fax: 902 430 189
eminarueda@emina.es
www.eminarueda.es

EMINA GEWURZTRAMINER 2008 B
gewürztraminer 100%

**86** Colour: bright straw. Nose: fruit expression, rose petals, powerfull, fruit preserve. Palate: fruity, fresh, sweetness.

EMINA CHARDONNAY 2007 B
chardonnay 100%

**86** Colour: bright yellow. Nose: powerful, ripe fruit, sweet spices, creamy oak, fragrant herbs. Palate: rich, smoky aftertaste, flavourful, fresh, good acidity.

## BODEGA FRANÇOIS LURTON

Camino Magarin, s/n
47529 Villafranca del Duero (Valladolid)
☎: 983 034 030 - Fax: 983 034 040
bodega@jflurton.es
www.jflurton.es

HEREDEROS LURTON 2007 T
tempranillo 100%

**86** Colour: cherry, garnet rim. Nose: spicy, toasty, ripe fruit, scrubland. Palate: flavourful, ripe fruit, spicy.

CUESTA GRANDE 2006 T
tinta de toro 100%

**89** Colour: bright cherry. Nose: sweet spices, creamy oak, expressive, red berry notes. Palate: flavourful, fruity, toasty, round tannins.

## BODEGA PALACIO DE BORNOS

Ctra. Madrid-Coruña km. 170,7
47490 Rueda (Valladolid)
☎: 983 868 336 - Fax: 983 868 432
bodegasbccv@interbook.net
www.bodegasdecastilla.com

EXXENCIA DE BORNOS 1999 B

**91** Colour: old gold, amber rim. Nose: powerful, candied fruit, dry nuts, honeyed notes. Palate: flavourful, sweet, slightly overripe.

## BODEGA Y VIÑEDOS LUNA BEBERIDE

Ctra. Madrid-Coruña, km. 402
24540 Cacabelos (León)
☎: 987 549 002 - Fax: 987 549 214
info@lunabeberide.es
www.lunabeberide.es

LUNA BEBERIDE 2007 T ROBLE

**86** Colour: very deep cherry. Nose: powerful, ripe fruit, new oak, toasty. Palate: concentrated, sweetness, spirituous, powerful, flavourful.

TIERRAS DE LUNA

## BODEGAS ALDEASOÑA S.L.

Casa del Mayorazgo
Ctra. Peñafiel San Ildefonso, s/n
40235 Aldeasoña (Segovia)
☎: 983 878 052 - Fax: 983 873 052
cpitarch@bodegaconvento.com

ALDEASOÑA 2005 T
tinta del país 100%

**91** Colour: very deep cherry. Nose: powerful, ripe fruit, toasty, scrubland. Palate: powerful, fleshy, round tannins.

## BODEGAS ANTAÑO

Arribas, 7-9
47490 Rueda (Valladolid)
☎: 983 868 533 - Fax: 983 868 514
comercial@bodegasantano.com

www.bodegasantano.com

ANTAÑO CHARDONNAY 2006 B
chardonnay 100%

**89** Colour: yellow. Nose: ripe fruit, lactic notes, tropical fruit, creamy oak. Palate: rich, fruity, good acidity, roasted-coffee aftertaste.

BRAVÍA 2007 T ROBLE
tempranillo 100%

**82**

COBRANZA 2006 T
tempranillo 100%

**85** Colour: deep cherry. Nose: floral, expressive, fruit preserve. Palate: full, fruity, grainy tannins, flavourful.

COBRANZA VENDIMIA SELECCIONADA 2005 T ROBLE

**89** Colour: deep cherry, garnet rim. Nose: fruit preserve, sweet spices, cocoa bean, balanced. Palate: full, powerful, fruity, good acidity, round tannins.

COBRANZA VENDIMIA SELECCIONADA 2004 T
tempranillo 100%

**88** Colour: cherry, garnet rim. Nose: ripe fruit, spicy, roasted coffee. Palate: powerful, flavourful, toasty, round tannins.

## BODEGAS DE LOS HEREDEROS DEL MARQUÉS DE RISCAL

Torrea, 1
01340 Elciego (Álava)
☎: 945 606 000 - Fax: 945 606 023
marquesderiscal@marquesderiscal.com
www.marquesderiscal.com

RISCAL 1860 2007 T
tempranillo

**87** Colour: cherry, purple rim. Nose: ripe fruit, fruit expression, powerfull, varietal. Palate: spicy, round tannins, good acidity, balanced.

## BODEGAS ESCUDERO

Ctra. de Arnedo, s/n
26587 Gravalos (La Rioja)
☎: 941 398 008 - Fax: 941 398 070
escudero@bodegasescudero.com
www.bodegasescudero.com

CREPÚSCULO 2006 T
tinta del país 100%

## 84

## BODEGAS GARCÍA NIÑO

Avda. Julio,s/n
09410 Arandilla (Burgos)
☎: 916 192 294 - Fax: 916 126 072
fernando@bodegasgarcianino.es
www.bodegasgarcianino.es

ALTORREDONDO 2007 T ROBLE
tempranillo 100%

**88** Colour: cherry, garnet rim. Nose: powerful, ripe fruit, scrubland, balsamic herbs, toasty. Palate: powerful, fleshy, ripe fruit.

ALTORREDONDO 14 MESES 2005 T
tempranillo 100%

**87** Colour: very deep cherry, garnet rim. Nose: fruit preserve, fruit liqueur notes, sweet spices, cocoa bean. Palate: full, fruity, grainy tannins, good structure.

ALTORREDONDO 24 MESES 2004 TC
tempranillo 100%

**89** Colour: dark-red cherry, purple rim. Nose: elegant, expressive, macerated fruit, creamy oak, cocoa bean, sweet spices. Palate: creamy, spicy, round tannins, flavourful, powerful.

## BODEGAS JIMÉNEZ LANDI

Avda. Solana, 45
45930 Méntrida (Toledo)
☎: 918 178 213 - Fax: 918 178 213
jose@jimenezlandi.com
www.jimenezlandi.com

EL REVENTON 2007 T
garnacha 100%

**93** Colour: deep cherry. Nose: wild herbs, mineral, burnt matches, fruit liqueur notes, fruit expression, roasted almonds, cedar wood. Palate: spirituous, complex, powerful, flavourful.

## BODEGAS LEDA VIÑAS VIEJAS

Mayor, 48
47320 Tudela de Duero (Valladolid)
☎: 983 403 094 - Fax: 983 403 146
b.leda@bodegasleda.com
www.bodegasleda.com

MÁS DE LEDA 2007 TC
tempranillo

**91** Colour: deep cherry, garnet rim. Nose: ripe fruit, sweet spices, balanced, undergrowth. Palate: round, fruity, powerful, good acidity, grainy tannins.

LEDA VIÑAS VIEJAS 2005 T
tempranillo

**90** Colour: very deep cherry, garnet rim. Nose: ripe fruit, mineral, powerfull, sweet spices. Palate: powerful, full, grainy tannins, good structure.

## BODEGAS MAURO

Cervantes, 12
47320 Tudela de Duero (Valladolid)
☎: 983 521 972 - Fax: 983 521 973
info@bodegasmauro.com
www.bodegasmauro.com

MAURO 2007 T ROBLE

**90** Colour: bright cherry, garnet rim. Nose: ripe fruit, sweet spices, cocoa bean. Palate: flavourful, good structure, round tannins.

MAURO VENDIMIA SELECCIONADA 2005 T

**91** Colour: very deep cherry, garnet rim. Nose: fruit preserve, new oak, dark chocolate, cocoa bean. Palate: powerful, fleshy, toasty.

TERREUS PAGO DE LA CUEVA BAJA 2005 TC

**91** Colour: cherry, garnet rim. Nose: powerful, fruit preserve, toasty, dark chocolate, aromatic coffee. Palate: fleshy, powerful, ripe fruit, slightly dry, soft tannins.

## BODEGAS MONTE LA REINA S.C.L.

Ctra. Toro-Zamora, km. 436,7
49881 Toro (Zamora)
☎: 980 082 011 - Fax: 980 082 012
bodega@montelareina.es
www.montelareina.es

VIZORRO 2008 B

## 80

VIZORRO 2008 RD
tempranillo

## 83

VIZORRO 2008 T

**85** Colour: bright cherry. Nose: ripe fruit, red berry notes, spicy. Palate: flavourful, fruity, fresh.

## BODEGAS SANTA RUFINA

Pago Fuente La Teja Polígono 3, Parcela 102
47290 Cubillas de Santa Marta (Valladolid)
☎: 983 585 202 - Fax: 983 585 202
info@bodegassantarufina.com
www.bodegassantarufina.com

ULTIMATUM 2004 T
tempranillo 100%

**83**

## BODEGAS VALDEÁGUILA S.L.

Avda. de la Paz, 26
37658 Garcibuey (Salamanca)
☎: 923 437 168 - Fax: 923 437 168
info@valdeaguila.com
www.valdeaguila.com

VIÑA SALAMANCA 2008 B
malvasia 60%, verdejo, pedro ximénez 40%,

**82**

VIÑA SALAMANCA RUFETE-TEMPRANILLO 2008 RD
rufete 65%, tempranillo 35%

**83**

VIÑA SALAMANCA RUFETE-TEMPRANILLO 2007 T
rufete 50%, tempranillo 50%

**85** Colour: light cherry. Nose: ripe fruit, red berry notes, neat. Palate: fruity, good acidity, flavourful, round tannins.

## BODEGAS VINOS DE LEÓN

La Vega, s/n
24190 Armunia (León)
☎: 987 209 712 - Fax: 987 209 800
info@bodegasvinosdeleon.es
www.bodegasvinosdeleon.es

PALACIO DE LEÓN S.C. B
verdejo 100%

**85** Colour: bright straw. Nose: varietal, fresh, mineral, red clay notes, fresh fruit. Palate: fresh, fruity, light-bodied, flavourful.

PALACIO DE LEÓN RD
tempranillo 100%

**71**

PALACIO DE LEÓN CUVÉE 2005 T
tempranillo 100%

**79**

PALACIO DE LEÓN CUVÉE 2004 T

**81**

## BODEGAS VIÑAS ZAMORANAS

Ctra. La Estación, s/n
49530 Coreses (Zamora)
☎: 980 500 995 - Fax: 980 500 611
bvz@bodegaszamoranas.es
www.bodegaszamoranas.es

TRESANTOS 2006 T ROBLE

**85** Colour: cherry, garnet rim. Nose: powerful, ripe fruit, toasty, dark chocolate. Palate: flavourful, powerful, fleshy, round tannins.

TRESANTOS VENDIMIA SELECCIONADA 2005 T
tempranillo 100%

**89** Colour: cherry, purple rim. Nose: powerful, varietal, fragrant herbs, balsamic herbs, creamy oak. Palate: flavourful, fleshy, ripe fruit, round tannins.

## BODEGAS VIZAR

Ctra. N-122, km. 341
Villabañez (Valladolid)
☎: 983 682 690
alberto@bodegasvizar.es
www.bodegasvizar.es

VIZAR SYRAH 2007 T
syrah 100%

**90** Colour: cherry, purple rim. Nose: powerful, red berry notes, ripe fruit, lactic notes, new oak. Palate: flavourful, fleshy, fruity, spicy.

VIZAR SELECCIÓN 2006 T
tempranillo 50%, syrah 50%

**91** Colour: cherry, garnet rim. Nose: ripe fruit, spicy, creamy oak, toasty, complex, fruit preserve. Palate: powerful, flavourful, toasty, round tannins.

VIZAR 12 MESES 2006 T
tempranillo 85%, cabernet sauvignon 15%

**88** Color bright cherry. Aroma ripe fruit, sweet spices, creamy oak, expressive. Palate: flavourful, fruity, toasty, round tannins.

## BODEGAS Y VIÑEDOS BURLÓN

Calle Perú, 10 4º Dcha.
47004 (Valladolid)
☎: 983 302 245 - Fax: 983 308 553
info@bodegasburlon.com
www.bodegasburlon.com

PRADO BURLÓN 2006 T
tempranillo 100%

**85** Colour: cherry, garnet rim. Nose: medium intensity, fresh fruit, spicy. Palate: flavourful, balanced, fruity, round tannins, good acidity.

## BODEGAS Y VIÑEDOS GARMENDIA

Finca Santa Rosalia, s/n Revilla Vallegera
34260 Vizmalo (Burgos)
☎: 947 166 171 - Fax: 947 166 147
maria@bodegasgarmendia.com
www.bodegasgarmendia.com

GARMENDIA 2008 B
verdejo 60%, viura 40%

**83**

GARMENDIA SELECCIÓN 2004 T
tempranillo 95%, merlot 5%

**87** Colour: deep cherry, brick rim edge. Nose: fruit liqueur notes, sweet spices, warm, balanced. Palate: light-bodied, fruity, good acidity, roasted-coffee aftertaste, round tannins.

GARMENDIA 2004 T BARRICA
tempranillo 90%, graciano 5%, garnacha 5%

**84**

## BODEGAS Y VIÑEDOS LA MEJORADA

Monasterio de La Mejorada
47410 Olmedo (Valladolid)
☎: 606 707 041 - Fax: 983 483 061
contacto@lamejorada.es
www.lamejorada.es

LA MEJORADA LAS CERCAS 2006 T ROBLE
tempranillo 60%, syrah 40%

**92** Colour: cherry, garnet rim. Nose: powerful, expressive, mineral, ripe fruit, fresh fruit, sweet spices. Palate: flavourful, fleshy, complex, spicy, round tannins.

LA MEJORADA LAS NORIAS 2006 T
tempranillo

**88** Colour: cherry, garnet rim. Nose: powerful, fruit preserve, ripe fruit, sweet spices, creamy oak. Palate: flavourful, fleshy, sweetness, spicy.

VILLALAR 2006 T ROBLE
cabernet sauvignon

**87** Colour: deep cherry. Nose: creamy oak, ripe fruit, varietal. Palate: fruity, powerful, flavourful, sweetness, spirituous.

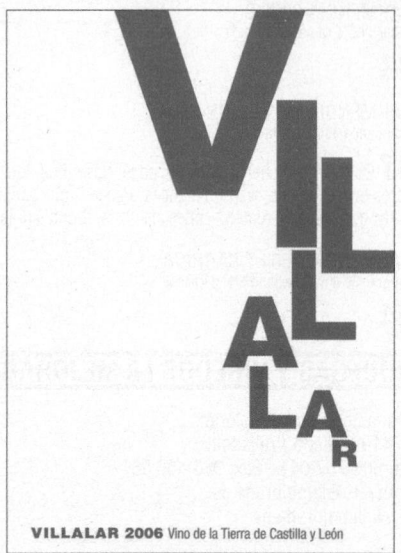

**VILLALAR 2006** Vino de la Tierra de Castilla y León

## COMPAÑIA DE VINOS DE TELMO RODRÍGUEZ

El Monte s/n
01308 Lanciego (Álava)
☎: 945 628 315 - Fax: 945 628 314
contact@telmorodriguez.com
www.telmorodriguez.com

PEGASO 2006 T
garnacha

**91** Colour: dark-red cherry. Nose: medium intensity, fresh, varietal, complex, wild herbs, mineral. Palate: flavourful, balsamic, ripe fruit, fleshy.

## COMPAÑIA DE VINOS MIGUEL MARTÍN

Ctra. Burgos - Portugal, km. 101
47290 Cubillas de Santa María (Valladolid)
☎: 983 250 319 - Fax: 983 250 329
exportacion@ciadevinos.com
www.ciadevinos.com

MARTÍN VERÁSTEGUI VENDIMIA SELECCIONADA
2008 B
verdejo

**84**

RETOLA 2008 B

**82**

RETOLA S/C RD

**79**

RETOLA 2005 T BARRICA

**84**

MARTÍN VERÁSTEGUI VENDIMIA SELECCIONADA
2004 T
tempranillo 75%, garnacha 25%

**86** Colour: pale ruby, brick rim edge. Nose: fruit preserve, creamy oak, spicy. Palate: round tannins, flavourful, fruity, fleshy.

RETOLA 2004 TC

**84**

RETOLA TEMPRANILLO T

**83**

MARTÍN VERÁSTEGUI VINO DE LICOR

**88** Colour: amber. Nose: dry nuts, candied fruit, mineral, citrus fruit. Palate: flavourful, full, spirituous, creamy, toasty.

## CUEVAS DE CASTILLA

Ctra. Madrid-Coruña, km. 171
47490 Rueda (Valladolid)
☎: 983 868 336 - Fax: 983 868 432
bodegasbccv@interbook.net
www.bodegasdecastilla.com

PALACIO DEL ALMIRANTE CHARDONNAY 2007 BFB
chardonnay

**87** Colour: bright yellow. Nose: powerful, ripe fruit, sweet spices, fragrant herbs. Palate: rich, smoky aftertaste, flavourful, fresh, good acidity.

HUERTA DEL REY 2008 RD
tempranillo

**87** Colour: rose, purple rim. Nose: powerful, ripe fruit, red berry notes, floral, expressive. Palate: fleshy, powerful, fruity, fresh.

ALMIRANTAZGO 2002 T
tempranillo

**85** Colour: cherry, garnet rim. Nose: sweet spices, ripe fruit, toasty. Palate: spicy, ripe fruit, round tannins.

## DE ALBERTO

Ctra. de Valdestillas, 2
47239 Serrada (Valladolid)
☎: 983 559 107 - Fax: 983 559 084
info@dealberto.com
www.dealberto.com

FINCA VALDEMOYA 2008 RD
tempranillo 100%

**88** Colour: onion pink. Nose: fresh fruit, expressive, rose petals, elegant. Palate: carbonic notes, fruity, good acidity, flavourful.

MENELAO 2005 T BARRICA
tempranillo 80%, cabernet 20%

**85** Colour: very deep cherry. Nose: ripe fruit, spicy, creamy oak. Palate: warm, slightly dry, soft tannins, spicy, powerful.

CCCL 2004 T ROBLE
tempranillo 80%, cabernet sauvignon 20%

**87** Colour: dark-red cherry. Nose: fruit preserve, creamy oak, dark chocolate. Palate: round tannins, fruity, flavourful, powerful.

## DEHESA DE CADOZOS

Pº Pintor Rosales, 72 Bajo
28008 Madrid
☎: 914 550 253 - Fax: 915 448 142
nmaranon@cadozos.com
www.cadozos.com

SAYAGO 2006 T
tinta fina, pinot noir

**90** Colour: very deep cherry. Nose: ripe fruit, earthy notes, dried herbs, cocoa bean, spicy, expressive. Palate: slightly dry, soft tannins, balanced, flavourful, powerful, ripe fruit.

CADOZOS 2005 T
tinta fina, pinot noir

**90** Colour: cherry, purple rim. Nose: damp earth, ripe fruit, spicy, cocoa bean, pattiserie, elegant. Palate: flavourful, fleshy, round tannins, elegant, balanced, good acidity.

CADOZOS 2004 T
tinta fina, pinot noir

**91** Colour: very deep cherry. Nose: elegant, ripe fruit, spicy, cocoa bean, aromatic coffee, earthy notes. Palate: elegant, balanced, flavourful, powerful, round tannins.

## DOMINIO DEL BENDITO

Pza. Santo Domingo, 8
49800 Toro (Zamora)
☎: 980 693 306 - Fax: 980 694 991
tintadetoro@yahoo.com

PERLARENA RD

**78**

ANTOJO RUBIO 2005 B DULCE

**88** Colour: old gold. Nose: fruit liqueur notes, candied fruit, dry nuts, sun-drenched nuances, pattiserie. Palate: flavourful, full, elegant, unctuous, good acidity.

## DOMINIO DOSTARES, S.L.

Los Barredos, 4 (P.I.B.A.)
24318 San Román de Bembibre (León)
☎: 987 514 550 - Fax: 987 514 570
info@dominiodetares.com
www.dominiodetares.com

TOMBÚ 2008 RD

**90** Colour: rose, purple rim. Nose: complex, varietal, red berry notes, fruit expression. Palate: complex, good structure, fresh, flavourful, varietal.

ESTAY 2006 T
prieto picudo 100%

**87** Colour: dark-red cherry. Nose: varietal, powerfull, fresh, creamy oak, red clay notes, mineral. Palate: powerful, flavourful, fruity, roasted-coffee aftertaste.

CUMAL 2005 T ROBLE
prieto picudo 100%

**94** Colour: deep cherry. Nose: varietal, powerfull, complex, fruit expression, spicy, creamy oak, toasty. Palate: powerful, flavourful, complex, varietal, balsamic, roasted-coffee aftertaste.

LEIONE 2005 T
prieto picudo 100%

**89** Colour: deep cherry. Nose: damp earth, undergrowth, fresh fruit, spicy, cocoa bean, toasty. Palate: spicy, creamy, good acidity, fruity.

BRYSAL

## ERMITA DEL CONDE

Camino de la Torre, 1

09410 Coruña del Conde (Burgos)
☎: 917 702 554
aris3@telefonica.net

ERMITA DEL CONDE 2006 T
tempranillo 95%, merlot 5%

**92** Colour: bright cherry. Nose: ripe fruit, sweet spices, creamy oak, expressive, red berry notes, mineral. Palate: flavourful, fruity, toasty, round tannins.

ERMITA DEL CONDE TRES HECTÁREAS 2006 T
tempranillo 95%, merlot 5%

**89** Colour: cherry, purple rim. Nose: mineral, ripe fruit, expressive, creamy oak, spicy. Palate: fruity, spicy, balsamic, fruity aftestaste.

## ESTANCIA PIEDRA S.L.

Ctra. Toro Salamanca, km 5
49800 Toro (Zamora)
☎: 980 693 900 - Fax: 980 693 901
info@estanciapiedra.com
www.estanciapiedra.com

CANTADAL TIERRA DE CANTOS B

**80**

CANTADAL 2005 T
tinta de toro 25%, garnacha 25%, cabernet sauvignon 25%, merlot 25%

**88** Colour: deep cherry, orangey edge. Nose: sweet spices, ripe fruit, elegant, creamy oak, cocoa bean. Palate: fruity, flavourful, rich, soft tannins.

## ESTEFANÍA

Ctra. Dehesas - Posada, s/n
24390 Ponferrada (León)
☎: 987 420 015 - Fax: 987 420 015
info@tilenus.com
www.tilenus.com

CLAN CHARCO LAS ÁNIMAS 2008 RD
prieto picudo 100%

**86** Colour: rose, purple rim. Nose: fresh fruit, red berry notes, fruit expression, lactic notes. Palate: carbonic notes, fruity, good acidity, easy to drink.

CASTILLO DE ULVER 2006 T
tempranillo, mencía

**88** Colour: dark-red cherry, orangey edge. Nose: fruit preserve, creamy oak, sweet spices, aromatic coffee, scrubland. Palate: round tannins, flavourful, powerful, rich, good structure.

CLAN CHARCO LAS ÁNIMAS 2006 T ROBLE
prieto picudo 100%

**84**

## FINCA CÁRDABA

Coto de Cárdaba s/n
40314 Valtiendas (Segovia)
☎: 921 527 470 - Fax: 921 527 470
info@fincacardaba.com
www.fincacardaba.com

VIÑA SANCHA 2007 RD
tempranillo 100%

**85** Colour: light cherry. Nose: fresh fruit, red berry notes, medium intensity. Palate: unctuous, flavourful, fruity, correct.

FINCA CÁRDABA 2005 T
tempranillo 100%

**85** Colour: bright cherry. Nose: ripe fruit, sweet spices, creamy oak. Palate: fruity, toasty, round tannins, fleshy, full.

FINCA CÁRDABA SELECCIÓN 2004 T
tempranillo 100%

**87** Colour: cherry, garnet rim. Nose: powerful, smoky, roasted coffee. Palate: powerful, toasty, powerful tannins.

## FINCA LA RINCONADA S.L.

Finca La Rinconada
47520 Castronuño (Valladolid)
☎: 983 034 892 - Fax: 983 866 016
fincalarinconada@fincalarinconada.es
www.fincalarinconada.es

BARCOLOBO 2007 T
tempranillo 80%, cabernet sauvignon 15%, syrah 5%

**88** Colour: cherry, purple rim. Nose: powerful, ripe fruit, lactic notes, toasty, new oak. Palate: flavourful, powerful, fleshy, ripe fruit.

**BARCOLOBO**

2007
VENDIMIA

12 MESES EN BARRICA

VINO DE LA TIERRA DE CASTILLA Y LEÓN
Product of Spain

Elaborado por
FINCA LA RINCONADA, S.L.
CASTRONUÑO · VALLADOLID · ESPAÑA

## FINCA VILLAMARÍA

Ctra. Sanabria, km. 3,800
24750 La Bañeza (León)
☎: 987 605 918 - Fax: 987 632 020
gaspar@legumbresluengo.es

VILLA MARIA 2006 T ROBLE
cabernet sauvignon, merlot
**83**

## FRUTOS VILLAR

Ctra. Burgos, km. 113,7
47270 Cigales (Valladolid)
☎: 983 586 868 - Fax: 983 580 180
bodegasfrutosvillar@bodegasfrutosvillar.com
www.bodegasfrutosvillar.com

DON FRUTOS 2008 B JOVEN
verdejo 90%, sauvignon blanc 10%

**80**
TASCO 2008 T
tempranillo 90%, cabernet sauvignon 10%

**83**

SEÑORÍO DE BALBOA

## GARNACHA ALTO ALBERCHE

Camino del Pimpollar, s/n
05100 Navaluenga (Avila)
☎: 616 416 542
info@altoalberche.es
www.altoalberche.es

7 NAVAS SELECCIÓN 2006 T
garnacha 100%

**89** Colour: cherry, garnet rim. Nose: ripe fruit, spicy, creamy oak. Palate: sweetness, powerful, flavourful, spirituous.

## GORDONZELLO

Alto de Santa Marina, s/n
24294 Gordoncillo (León)
☎: 987 758 030 - Fax: 987 757 201
comercial@gordonzello.com
www.gordonzello.com

CANDIDUS 2008 B
verdejo 100%

**88** Colour: pale. Nose: ripe fruit, tropical fruit, scrubland, characterful. Palate: rich, flavourful, fruity, full.

## GRUPO YLLERA

Ctra. Madrid - Coruña, km. 173, 5
47490 Rueda (Valladolid)
☎: 983 868 097 - Fax: 983 868 177
grupoyllera@grupoyllera.com
www.grupoyllera.com

OLIVANTE DE LAURA SEMIDULCE B
**80**

CUVI 2008 RD
**84**

CUVI 2007 T ROBLE
**84**

YLLERA 25 ANIVERSARIO 2005 T

**91** Colour: bright cherry. Nose: ripe fruit, sweet spices, creamy oak, expressive. Palate: flavourful, fruity, toasty, round tannins.

### YLLERA DOMINUS GRAN SELECCIÓN VIÑEDOS VIEJOS 2004 T

**90** Colour: dark-red cherry, orangey edge. Nose: ripe fruit, creamy oak, cocoa bean, sweet spices. Palate: round tannins, fruity, flavourful, good acidity, smoky aftertaste

### YLLERA ROBLE FRANCÉS Y AMERICANO 2004 T ROBLE

**88** Colour: cherry, garnet rim. Nose: ripe fruit, spicy, toasty. Palate: powerful, flavourful, toasty, round tannins.

### YLLERA VENDIMIA SELECCIONADA 2002 T BARRICA

**89** Colour: cherry, garnet rim. Nose: powerfull, ripe fruit, red berry notes, toasty. Palate: flavourful, fleshy, spicy, round tannins.

## HACIENDA MARQUÉS DE LA CONCORDIA

Ctra. El Ciego, s/n
26350 Cenicero (La Rioja)
☎: 914 365 900 - Fax: 914 365 932
info@haciendas-espana.com
www.haciendas-espana.com

DURIUS NATURAL RESERVE SYRAH 2005 T
syrah

**89** Colour: black cherry. Nose: powerful, ripe fruit, toasty, spicy, smoky. Palate: powerful, fleshy, spicy, ripe fruit.

DURIUS NATURAL RESERVE 2004 T
tempranillo, merlot

**85** Colour: very deep cherry, garnet rim. Nose: fruit preserve, tobacco, sweet spices, fruit liqueur notes. Palate: powerful, fruity, good acidity, ripe fruit, round tannins.

## JOSÉ CARLOS MARTÍN SÁNCHEZ

Salas Pombo, s/n
Santibáñez de la Sierra (Salamanca)
☎: 923 435 260
info@bodegasrochal.com
www.bodegasrochal.com

ZAMAYÓN 2008 T
rufete

**85** Colour: cherry, purple rim. Nose: ripe fruit, red berry notes. Palate: flavourful, fruity, fresh.

CALIXTO 2006 T

**89** Colour: cherry, garnet rim. Nose: powerful, mineral, earthy notes, ripe fruit, sweet spices. Palate: flavourful, fruity, spicy.

ZAMAYÓN OSIRIS 2006 T
rufete, tempranillo

**88** Colour: bright cherry. Nose: ripe fruit, sweet spices, creamy oak, expressive, mineral. Palate: flavourful, fruity, toasty, round tannins.

## LIBERALIA ENOLÓGICA

Camino del Palo, s/n
49800 Toro (Zamora)
☎: 980 692 571 - Fax: 980 692 571
byvliberalia@hotmail.com
www.liberalia.es

LIBERALIA UNO 2008 B DULCE
moscatel 90%, albillo 10%

**79**

## OSSIAN VIDES Y VINOS, S.L.

San Marcos, 5
40447 Nieva (Segovia)
☎: 696 159 121 - Fax: 921 594 207
ossian@ossian.es
www.ossian.es

OSSIAN 2007 BFB
verdejo

**94** Colour: bright straw. Nose: elegant, expressive, white flowers, ripe fruit, toasty, sweet spices. Palate: creamy, ripe fruit, fleshy, flavourful, good acidity.

## PAGOS GALAYOS

Camino Pimpollar
05100 Navaluenga (Ávila)
☎: 918 611 696 - Fax: 918 612 553
dvrcru@gmail.com
www.pagosgalayos.com

ZERBEROS "ARENA DE GRANITO" 2006 T ROBLE
garnacha 100%

**93** Colour: dark-red cherry. Nose: varietal, powerfull, expressive, scrubland, mineral, cocoa bean, creamy oak. Palate: complex, sweetness, powerful, spirituous.

ZERBEROS "ARENA DE PIZARRA" 2006 T ROBLE
garnacha 100%

**90** Colour: cherry, garnet rim. Nose: faded flowers, wild herbs, complex, earthy notes, creamy oak. Palate: spirituous, powerful, flavourful, sweetness, sweet tannins.

ZERBEROS FINCA PIZARRA 2006 T ROBLE
garnacha 100%

**89** Colour: cherry, garnet rim. Nose: mineral, earthy notes, macerated fruit, spicy, aromatic coffee, creamy oak, wild herbs. Palate: fresh, fruity, flavourful, balsamic, mineral, smoky aftertaste.

## RAMIRO WINE CELLAR

Camino Viejo de Simancas km. 3,5
47008 Valladolid
☎: 983 274 202 - Fax: 983 274 202
bodega@ramirowinecellar.com
www.ramirowinecellar.com

RAMIRO'S 2006 T
tempranillo 100%

**89** Colour: deep cherry. Nose: ripe fruit, spicy, cocoa bean, elegant. Palate: powerful, flavourful, fruity, round tannins, balanced.

CÓNDITA 2006 T
tempranillo 100%

**88** Colour: cherry, garnet rim. Nose: powerful, ripe fruit, sweet spices, toasty. Palate: flavourful, fleshy, toasty, round tannins.

## SITIOS DE BODEGA

Cuatro Calles s/n
47491 La Seca (Valladolid)
☎: 983 103 223 - Fax: 983 816 561
oficina@sitiosdebodega.com
www.sitiosdebodega.com

ABRILEÑO 2008 RD

**84**

## TERNA BODEGAS

Cuatro Calles s/n
47491 La Seca (Valladolid)
☎: 983 103 223 - Fax: 983 816 561
oficina@sitiosdebodega.com
www.sitiosdebodega.com

E TERNA SELECCIÓN PRIETO PICUDO 2006 T

**89** Colour: deep cherry, garnet rim. Nose: ripe fruit, sweet spices, balanced, dry stone. Palate: unctuous, full, good acidity, good structure, round tannins.

E TERNA SELECCIÓN GARNACHA CEBREROS 2006 T

**88** Colour: cherry, garnet rim. Nose: ripe fruit, sweet spices, balanced. Palate: flavourful, good structure, good acidity, fruity, round tannins.

## VINOS DE ALISTE

Pza.de España, 4
49520 Figueruela de Abajo (Zamora)
☎: 676 986 570 - Fax: 944 231 816
javier@hacedordevino.com
www.vinosdealiste.com

GEIJO 2008 BFB
viura 90%, verdejo 5%, chardonnay 5%

**82**

MARINA DE ALISTE 2007 TC
tempranillo 90%, syrah 10%

**88** Colour: bright cherry. Nose: sweet spices, creamy oak, expressive, ripe fruit. Palate: flavourful, fruity, toasty, round tannins.

ALISTE 2007 T ROBLE
tempranillo 90%, syrah 10%

**86** Colour: cherry, garnet rim. Nose: powerful, ripe fruit, balsamic herbs, scrubland. Palate: flavourful, ripe fruit, spicy, round tannins.

VIÑA CARRERON 2006 T
garnacha 33%, mencía 33%, tempranillo 33%

**86** Colour: bright cherry. Nose: medium intensity, ripe fruit, red berry notes, spicy. Palate: flavourful, fruity, fresh, spicy, easy to drink.

## VIÑAS DE LA VEGA DEL DUERO

Casa s/n Granja Sardón
47340 Sardon de Duero (Valladolid)
☎: 650 498 353 - Fax: 983 339 622
jbgnd@telefonica.net

QUINTA SARDONIA Q2 2007 T

**90** Colour: bright cherry. Nose: ripe fruit, sweet spices, creamy oak, expressive, mineral. Palate: flavourful, fruity, toasty, round tannins.

QUINTA SARDONIA 2006 T

**94** Colour: very deep cherry. Nose: ripe fruit, expressive, caramel, creamy oak. Palate: flavourful, fruity, toasty, round tannins.

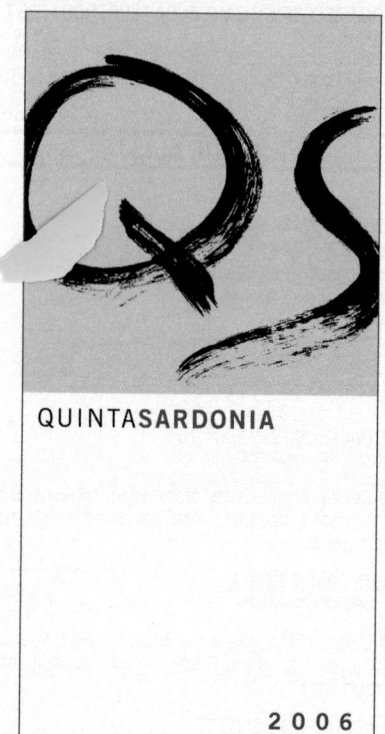

QUINTASARDONIA

2 0 0 6

BODEGA GÓTICA
BODEGA M. CRUZ MARINELLI GARCÍA
BODEGA SOLAR DE MUÑOSANCHO
BODEGAS AGEJAS S.L.
BODEGAS CASTELO DE MEDINA
BODEGAS FÉLIX LORENZO CACHAZO S.L.
BODEGAS TORINOS
BODEGAS TORRESMANUR, S.L.
BODEGAS Y VIÑEDOS ALONSO TORIBIO
BODEGAS Y VIÑEDOS FERNÁNDEZ RIVERA
BODEGAS Y VIÑEDOS RIBERA DEL DURATÓN
BODEGAS Y VIÑEDOS VALDUERO
COOP. SAN ESTEBAN
DEHESA DE RUBIALES S.L.
EL TERRERO
FARIÑA
FINCA TORREMILANOS BOD. PEÑALBA LÓPEZ
HIJA DE FRANCISCO PÉREZ ADRIÁ
MARQUÉS DE IRÚN
PALACIO DE ARGANZA S.A.
PEÑASCAL
RIBAS DEL CÚA
TODA EUROPA INTERCOMERCIAL
VALSARDO DE PEÑAFIEL S.L.
VERMILIÓN DE VALBUENA DE DUERO
VILLACEZÁN
VINOS SANZ
VIÑA ALBARES

## CONTRAVIESA-ALPUJARRA

### BODEGA GARCÍA DE VERDEVIQUE

Los García de Verdevique
18439 Castaras (Granada)
☎: 958 342 439
info@bodegasgarciadeverdevique.com
www.bodegasgarciadeverdevique.com

LOS GARCÍA DE VERDEVIQUE 2005 T BARRICA
tempranillo, cabernet sauvignon

**86** Colour: cherry, garnet rim. Nose: medium intensity, ripe fruit, sweet spices. Palate: flavourful, fruity, fresh.

LOS GARCÍA DE VERDEVIQUE 2004 T BARRICA
tempranillo 80%, cabernet sauvignon 20%

**88** Colour: cherry, garnet rim. Nose: powerful, ripe fruit, toasty, creamy oak, dark chocolate. Palate: flavourful, powerful, fleshy, spicy.

LOS GARCIAS DE VERDEVIQUE ESP
Vigiriego

**75**

## VIÑEDOS DE VILLAESTER

Villaester de Arriba
47540 Pedrosa del Rey (Valladolid)
☎: 948 645 008 - Fax: 948 645 166
info@familiabelasco.com
www.familiabelasco.com

AVUTARDA 2008 T
tempranillo, cabernet sauvignon

**90** Colour: cherry, purple rim. Nose: powerful, expressive, red berry notes, raspberry, lactic notes. Palate: flavourful, fruity, good acidity, balanced, fruity aftestaste.

SOME OTHER WINERIES WITHIN THE VT:

**ALTA PAVINA**
**AVELINO VEGAS**
**BEGOÑA CARRILLO ROMERO S.A.**
**BODEGA COOP. DE CIGALES**

## DOMINIO BUENAVISTA

Ctra. de Almería, s/n
18480 Ugíjar (Granada)
☎: 958 767 254 - Fax: 958 767 254
info@veleta.com
www.dominiobuenavista.com

VELETA CHARDONNAY 2008 B
chardonnay 100%

**88** Colour: bright golden. Nose: ripe fruit, dry nuts, powerfull, toasty, creamy oak. Palate: flavourful, fruity, spicy, toasty, long.

VELETA VIJIRIEGA 2007 B
Vigiriego 90%, chardonnay 10%

**87** Colour: bright straw. Nose: toasty, ripe fruit, medium intensity, citrus fruit. Palate: flavourful, fresh, balanced.

VELETA TEMPRANILLO ROSÉ 2008 RD
tempranillo 70%, garnacha 30%

**78**

VELETA CABERNET SAUVIGNON 2007 T
cabernet sauvignon 90%, merlot 10%

**85** Colour: dark-red cherry, garnet rim. Nose: ripe fruit, creamy oak, aged wood nuances. Palate: flavourful, fruity, round tannins.

VELETA TEMPRANILLO 2007 T
tempranillo 90%, cabernet sauvignon 10%

**82**

VELETA NOLADOS 2006 T
cabernet sauvignon 40%, cabernet franc 40%, tempranillo 20%

**89** Colour: bright cherry. Nose: sweet spices, expressive, fruit liqueur notes, toasty. Palate: flavourful, fruity, toasty, round tannins.

## LOS BARRANCOS

Ctra. Cádiar-Albuñol, km. 9, 4
18449 Lobras (Granada)
☎: 958 343 218 - Fax: 958 343 412
peter.hilgard@t-online.de
www.losbarrancos.es

CORRAL DE CASTRO 2007 T ROBLE
tempranillo 85%, cabernet sauvignon 10%, merlot 5%

**88** Colour: cherry, garnet rim. Nose: ripe fruit, spicy, balsamic herbs, scrubland. Palate: powerful, flavourful, toasty, round tannins.

CERRO DE LA RETAMA EDICIÓN ESPECIAL 2006 T
tempranillo 70%, cabernet sauvignon 15%, merlot 15%

**87** Colour: deep cherry, garnet rim. Nose: ripe fruit, toasty, spicy. Palate: fleshy, good structure, round tannins.

SOME OTHER WINERIES WITHIN THE VT:

**BODEGAS LORENTE
CUATRO VIENTOS
EL SOTILLO
JOSÉ CARA E HIJOS
PIEDRAS BLANCAS**

## CÓRDOBA
## COOPERATIVA AGRICOLA LA UNIÓN

Avda. de Italia, 1
14550 Montilla (Córdoba)
☎: 957 651 855 - Fax: 957 657 135
info@cooperativalaunion.com

LOS OMEYA 2008 RD
syrah 100%

**78**

LOS OMEYA 2007 T
syrah 100%

**82**

LOS OMEYA 2004 T ROBLE
syrah

**86** Colour: cherry, garnet rim. Nose: dark chocolate, sweet spices. Palate: ripe fruit, warm, round tannins.

RIO DE LA HOZ

SOME OTHER WINERIES WITHIN THE VT:

**ALVEAR
BODEGAS LA AURORA
BODEGAS JESÚS NAZARENO, S.C.A.
BODEGAS LAMA
COOP. VITIVINÍCOLA LA PURÍSIMA
NAVISA**

## COSTA DE CANTABRIA
### BODEGAS VIDULAR

Barrio Río Lastra, 264
39761 Junta de Voto (Cantabria)
☎: 942 631 324 - Fax: 942 631 324
info@riberadelason.com
www.riberadelason.com

RIBERA DEL ASÓN 2008 B
albariño 80%, chardonnay 20%

**87** Colour: straw. Nose: fresh, fresh fruit, white flowers, expressive. Palate: flavourful, fruity, good acidity, balanced.

### LANCINA VIÑEDOS Y BODEGA

B. Tuebre, 31
39790 Bárcena de Cicero (Cantabria)
☎: 942 64 2 2
lancina@lancina.es

LANCINA 2008 B
riesling 50%, godello 50%

**90** Colour: bright straw. Nose: fresh, fresh fruit, white flowers, expressive. Palate: flavourful, fruity, good acidity, balanced.
LANCINA SOBRE LÍAS 2008 B
riesling 50%, godello 50%

**90** Colour: old gold. Nose: white flowers, creamy oak, expressive, ripe fruit. Palate: fruity, rich, flavourful, full, great length.

## DESIERTO DE ALMERÍA
BODEGAS AGROSOL

## EIVISSA
### CAN RICH DE BUSCATELL

Cami de Sa Vorera, s/n
07820 San Antonio (Baleares)
☎: 971 803 377 - Fax: 971 803 377
info@bodegascanrich.com
www.bodegascanrich.com

CAN RICH 2008 B
chardonnay 60%, malvasia 40%

**82**

CAN RICH 2008 RD
tempranillo 80%, merlot 20%

**81**

LAUSOS CABERNET SAUVIGNON° 2006 T
cabernet sauvignon 100%

**87** Colour: pale ruby, brick rim edge. Nose: ripe fruit, wild herbs, toasty. Palate: flavourful, fine tannins.

CAN RICH VI NEGRE 2006 T
tempranillo 60%, merlot 30%, cabernet sauvignon 10%

**82**

CAN RICH SELECCIÓN 2005 T
cabernet sauvignon 60%, tempranillo 30%, merlot 10%

**82**

CAN RICH DULCE 2007 VINO DE LICOR
malvasia 100%

**83**

### SA COVA

Sa Cova
07816 Sant Mateu D'Albarca (Baleares)
☎: 971 187 046 - Fax: 971 187 811
sacova-ibiza@telefonica.net

SA COVA BLANC DE BLANC 2008 B
malvasia 90%, moscatel 10%

**82**

SA COVA 9 2007 T

**79**

SA COVA PRIVAT 2004 T

**80**

SA COVA CLOT D'ALBARCA 2004 T

**78**

### VINOS CAN MAYMÓ

Casa Can Maymó
07816 Sant Mateu d'Albarca (Balears)
☎: 971 805 100 - Fax: 971 805 100
info@bodegascanmaymo.com

CAN MAYMÓ 2008 B
malvasia 60%, moscatel 40%

**85** Colour: bright straw. Nose: white flowers, candied fruit, wild herbs. Palate: flavourful, unctuous, great length.

**CAN MAYMÓ 2008 RD**
monastrell 80%, syrah 20%

**80**

**CAN MAYMÓ TRADICIÓN 2008 T**
monastrell 80%, syrah 20%

**80**

**CAN MAYMÓ 2007 T**
merlot

**87** Colour: cherry, garnet rim. Nose: sweet spices, creamy oak, floral. Palate: flavourful, toasty, slightly dry, soft tannins. Personality.

**CAN MAYMÓ 2007 T BARRICA**
tempranillo 60%, merlot 40%

**86** Colour: light cherry. Nose: sweet spices, creamy oak, wild herbs, fruit expression. Palate: flavourful, slightly dry, soft tannins.

SOME OTHER WINERIES WITHIN THE VT:

**VINS DE TANYS MEDITERRANIS**

## EL TERRERAZO
### MUSTIGUILLO VIÑEDOS Y BODEGA

Ctra. N-330, km 196,5 El Terrerazo
46300 Utiel (Valencia)
☎: 962 168 260 - Fax: 962 168 259
info@bodegamustiguillo.com
www.bodegamustiguillo.com

**FINCA TERRERAZO 2007 T**
bobal, tempranillo, cabernet sauvignon

**94** Colour: bright cherry. Nose: ripe fruit, sweet spices, creamy oak, earthy notes. Palate: flavourful, fruity, toasty, round tannins.

**QUINCHA CORRAL 2007 T**
bobal 100%

**93** Colour: cherry, garnet rim. Nose: ripe fruit, spicy, creamy oak, toasty, powerfull, mineral. Palate: powerful, flavourful, toasty, round tannins.

**MESTIZAJE 2008 T**
bobal, tempranillo, syrah, cabernet sauvignon, merlot

**90** Colour: cherry, garnet rim. Nose: ripe fruit, sweet spices, creamy oak, cocoa bean. Palate: flavourful, powerful, fleshy, spicy, ripe fruit.

**MESTIZAJE 2007 T**
bobal 50%, tempranillo, syrah, cabernet sauvignon and merlot 50%

**89** Colour: cherry, garnet rim. Nose: medium intensity, ripe fruit, spicy, toasty. Palate: flavourful, powerful, fine bitter notes.

## EXTREMADURA
### BODEGA DE MIRABEL

Avda. de Monfragüe, 41
Trujillo (Cáceres)
☎: 927 323 154

**MIRABEL 2007 T ROBLE**
tempranillo 70%, syrah 30%

**92** Colour: dark-red cherry. Nose: mineral, fruit expression, ripe fruit, red berry notes. Palate: full, powerful, flavourful, sweetness.

### BODEGA PERALES

Autovía A 5 km - 360 Extremadura
06800 Mérida (Badajoz)
☎: 913 191 508 - Fax: 913 088 450
contact@marquesdevaldueza.com
www.marquesdevaldueza.com

**MARQUÉS DE VALDUEZA 2007 T**
cabernet sauvignon 37%, syrah 48%, merlot 15%

**92** Colour: cherry, garnet rim. Nose: powerful, ripe fruit, sweet spices, scrubland, toasty, dark chocolate. Palate: flavourful, fleshy, spicy, round tannins.

**VALDUEZA 2007 T**
cabernet sauvignon 46%, syrah 33%, merlot 21%

**90** Colour: deep cherry. Nose: spicy, fruit expression, warm. Palate: flavourful, toasty, powerful, fruity.

**MARQUÉS DE VALDUEZA 2006 T**
cabernet sauvignon 50%, syrah 50%

**92** Colour: bright cherry. Nose: sweet spices, creamy oak, expressive, dark chocolate, ripe fruit. Palate: flavourful, fruity, toasty, round tannins.

## BODEGAS ALAUDE

Semillero de Empresas, N-2
06120 Oliva de la Frontera (Badajoz)
☎: 924 740 174 - Fax: 924 740 178
info@bodegasalaude.com
www.bodegasalaude.com

**QVINTA ALAVDE 2007 T ROBLE**
tempranillo 80%, merlot 20%

**85** Colour: cherry, garnet rim. Nose: powerful, ripe fruit, spicy, creamy oak. Palate: flavourful, fleshy, spicy.
**ALIVS 2006 T**
tempranillo 60%, cabernet sauvignon 20%

**83**

## BODEGAS CAÑALVA

Coto, nº 54
10136 Cañamero (Cáceres)
☎: 927 369 405 - Fax: 927 369 405
info@bodegascañalva.com
www.bodegascañalva.com

**CAÑALVA COUPAGE ESPECIAL 2008 TC**
cabernet sauvignon 25%, syrah 25%, merlot 25%, tempranillo 25%

**87** Colour: cherry, garnet rim. Nose: ripe fruit, sweet spices, cocoa bean. Palate: flavourful, powerful, spicy, round tannins.

**CAÑALVA CABERNET SAUVIGNON 2008 T ROBLE**
cabernet sauvignon 100%

**86** Colour: cherry, garnet rim. Nose: powerful, ripe fruit, red berry notes, sweet spices, cocoa bean. Palate: flavourful, fresh, spicy, ripe fruit.

**CAÑALVA SYRAH 2006 T**
syrah 100%

**83**

**CAÑALVA TINTO FINO 2004 TC**
tempranillo 100%

**81**

**LUZ 2008 SEMIDULCE**
macabeo 100%

**85** Colour: bright straw. Nose: fruit preserve, citrus fruit, grassy. Palate: flavourful, sweetness, fruity, fresh.

## BODEGAS DE AGUILAR

La Radio, 10
06760 Navalvillar de Pela (Badajoz)
☎: 924 861 252 - Fax: 924 824 238
comunicacion@bodegasdeaguilar.es
www.bodegasdeaguilar.es

**AGUILAR 2008 B**
alarije 100%

**74**

**AGUILAR 2008 RD**
cabernet sauvignon 100%

**75**

**AGUILAR ROBLE 2006 T**
tempranillo 85%, graciano 15%

**77**

**AGUILAR GRAN ROBLE 2006 T**
cabernet sauvignon 90%, graciano 10%

**77**

## BODEGAS HABLA

Ctra. N-V, P.K. 259
10200 Trujillo (Cáceres)
☎: 927 659 180 - Fax: 927 659 181
habla@bodegashabla.com
www.bodegashabla.com

**HABLA Nº 5 2006 T**
tempranillo 70%, cabernet sauvignon 25%, petit verdot 5%

**92** Colour: bright cherry. Nose: ripe fruit, sweet spices, creamy oak, expressive, mineral, dark chocolate. Palate: flavourful, fruity, toasty, round tannins.

**HABLA Nº 4 2006 T**
syrah 100%

**92** Colour: deep cherry, garnet rim. Nose: sweet spices, cocoa bean, red berry notes, ripe fruit. Palate: flavourful, fleshy, fruity, spicy, round tannins.

## BODEGAS ORTIZ

Ctra de Sevilla 34
06200 Almendralejo (Badajoz)
☎: 924 662 811 - Fax: 924 665 406
info@bodegasortiz.com
www.bodegasortiz.com

**SEÑORÍO DE ORÁN 2005 TC**
tempranillo

**85** Colour: bright cherry, orangey edge. Nose: pattiserie, sweet spices, ripe fruit. Palate: flavourful, sweetness, spirituous.

CHARNECAL

## BODEGAS RUIZ TORRES

Ctra. EX 116, KM-33,8
10136 Cañamero (Cáceres)
☎: 927 369 024 - Fax: 927 369 302
info@ruiztorres.com
www.ruiztorres.com

**ANTEROS 2008 T**
petit verdot 100%

**87** Colour: cherry, garnet rim. Nose: powerful, ripe fruit, sweet spices, toasty. Palate: fruity, fleshy, spicy.

**TRAMPAL 2005 TC**
tempranillo 80%, garnacha 20%

**78**

**FELIPE RUIZ 2001 TR**
cabernet sauvignon 60%, graciano 40%

**74**

## BODEGAS VENTURA DE VEGA

Badajoz, 70
06200 Almendralejo (Badajoz)
☎: 924 671 105 - Fax: 924 677 205
bodegas@vegaesteban.com
www.vegaesteban.com

CADENCIAS DE VEGA ESTEBAN PARDINA 2008 B SEMIDULCE

pardina

**81**

TALLANT DE VEGA ESTEBAN

## BODEGAS Y VIÑEDOS ÁNGEL SÁNCHEZ REDONDO

Avda. Martín Palomino, 49
10600 Plasencia (Cáceres)
☎: 927 116 250 - Fax: 927 418 102
ana@vinaplacentina.com
www.fincaelpalomar.com

**VIÑA PLACENTINA COUPAGE CABERNET SAUVIGNON Y MERLOT 2004 T**
cabernet sauvignon 75%, merlot 25%

**81**

**VIÑA PLACENTINA PAGO DE LOS ÁNGELES CABERNET SAUVIGNON 2003 T**
cabernet sauvignon 100%

**79**

**VIÑA PLACENTINA ECOLÓGICO CABERNET SAUVIGNON 2003 T**
cabernet sauvignon 100%

**78**

**VIÑA PLACENTINA CABERNET SAUVIGNON ETIQUETA NEGRA 2002 T**
cabernet sauvignon 100%

**81**

## LAR DE BARROS - INVIOSA

Aptdo. de Correos 291
Ctra. Ex-300, p.k. 55,9
P.I. Dehesa del Pedregal, Naves 4-5-6
06200 Almendralejo (Badajoz)
☎: 924 671 235 - Fax: 924 687 231
info@lardebarros.com
www.lardebarros.com

**LAR DE ORO 2008 B**
chardonnay 100%

**84**

**LAR DE ORO 2008 T**
cabernet sauvignon 100%

**83**

## LUIS GURPEGUI MUGA

Avda. Celso Muerza, 8
31570 San Adrián (Navarra)
☎: 948 670 050 - Fax: 948 670 259
eroman@gurpegui.com
www.gurpegui.es

GURPEGUI TEMPRANILLO CABERNET SAUVIGNON
2008 T

**85** Colour: bright cherry, purple rim. Nose: medium intensity, red berry notes, ripe fruit. Palate: fruity, easy to drink, balanced.

5 VIÑAS 2008 T

**85** Colour: bright cherry, purple rim. Nose: medium intensity, red berry notes. Palate: fruity, correct, fresh.

PINTORESCO 2008 T

**83**

RANCHO VIEJO

## PAGO DE LAS ENCOMIENDAS, VIÑEDOS Y BODEGA

Camino San Isidro, s/n
06220 Villafranca de los Barros (Badajoz)
☎: 924 118 280
pagodelasencomiendas@pagodelasencomiendas.es
www.pagodelasencomiendas.es

NADIR 2008 RD
tempranillo, syrah, petit verdot

**87** Colour: rose, purple rim. Nose: powerful, ripe fruit, red berry notes, floral, expressive. Palate: fleshy, powerful, fruity, fresh.

NADIR 2007 T

**86** Colour: cherry, garnet rim. Nose: powerful, ripe fruit, red berry notes, creamy oak. Palate: flavourful, fleshy, powerful.

XENTIA 2007 T
tempranillo 85%, petit verdot 15%

**84**

## SDAD.COOP. VIRGEN DE LA ESTRELLA

Mérida, 1
06230 Los Santos de Maimona (Badajoz)

☎: 924 544 094 - Fax: 924 572 490
export@maimona.com
www.maimona.com

DULCE EVA 2008 B
eva 100%

**81**

## VIÑA EXTREMEÑA

Ctra. de Alange, s/n
06200 Almendralejo (Badajoz)
☎: 924 670 158 - Fax: 924 670 159
info@vinexsa.com
www.vinexsa.com

PALACIO DE MONSALUD 2007 T
tempranillo 100%

**83**

MONASTERIO DE TENTUDIA 2006 T
tempranillo 100%

**82**

PALACIO DE VALDEINFANTE 2004 T
tempranillo 100%

**83**

CORTE REAL PLATINUM 2002 T
cabernet sauvignon 50%, merlot 50%

**87** Colour: pale ruby, brick rim edge. Nose: elegant, spicy, fine reductive notes, wet leather, aged wood nuances, fruit liqueur notes. Palate: spicy, fine tannins, elegant, long.

MONASTERIO DE TENTUDIA TRADICIÓN 2002 T
tempranillo 50%, cabernet sauvignon 50%

**86** Colour: pale ruby, brick rim edge. Nose: wet leather, fruit liqueur notes, spicy, aromatic coffee. Palate: spicy, classic aged character, fine bitter notes.

CASTILLO DE VALDESTRADA
ADVENTUS
VEGA ADRIANA

## VIÑA SANTA MARINA

Ctra. N-630, km. 634 - Apdo. 714
06800 Mérida (Badajoz)
☎: 902 506 364 - Fax: 924 027 675
bodega@vsantamarina.com
www.vsantamarina.com

**ALTARA 2008 B**
montua 80%, viognier 20%

**84**

**VIOGNIER SECO 2008 B**
viognier 100%

**83**

**VIOGNIER VENDIMIA TARDIA 2006 B**
viognier 100%

**86** Colour: bright straw. Nose: powerful, ripe fruit, candied fruit, fragrant herbs. Palate: flavourful, sweet, ripe fruit.

**VIÑA SANTA MARINA 2008 RD**
merlot 100%

**83**

**CELTUS TEMPRANILLO 2007 T**
tempranillo 100%

**86** Colour: cherry, garnet rim. Nose: ripe fruit, mineral, spicy, floral. Palate: flavourful, fruity, spicy, round tannins.

**EQUUS 2006 T ROBLE**
tempranillo 85%, cabernet sauvignon 10%, syrah 5%

**85** Colour: cherry, garnet rim. Nose: ripe fruit, toasty, sweet spices, scrubland. Palate: flavourful, fruity, spicy, balsamic.

**VIÑA SANTA MARINA CABERNET SAUVIGNON-SYRAH 2006 T BARRICA**
cabernet sauvignon 70%, syrah 30%

**85** Colour: cherry, garnet rim. Nose: powerful, ripe fruit, scrubland, fragrant herbs. Palate: flavourful, fine bitter notes, spicy, round tannins.

**MIRACULUS 2006 TR**
merlot, cabernet sauvignon, cabernet franc, syrah, petit verdot

**81**

## SOME OTHER WINERIES WITHIN THE VT:

**BODEGAS AGAPITA RUBIO BRAVO**
**BODEGA LAS GRANADAS**
**BODEGAS MIGUEL GRUESO**
**BODEGAS ROMALE**
**BODEGA SAN MARCOS**
**BODEGAS SANI S.L.**
**BODEGAS TORIBIO**
**CATALINA ARROYO**
**COLOMA VIÑEDOS Y BODEGAS**
**DOLORES MORENAS**
**FRANCO-SÁNCHEZ S.L.**
**GASPAR SANTOS E HIJOS S.A.**

**JUAN LEANDRO ROMERO LÓPEZ (BODEGAS ROMERO)**
**MARCELINO DÍAZ**
**SANTA MARTA VIRGEN**
**VADE MECUM BODEGAS**
**VÍA DE LA PLATA**
**VINIFICACIONES EXTREMEÑAS**

## FORMENTERA

### CAP DE BARBARIA

Ctra.Cap de Barbaria, km. 5,8
07860 Formentera (Baleares)
☎: 617 460 629
info@capdebarbaria.com
www.capdebarbaria.com

**CAP DE BARBARIA 2007 T**

**95** Colour: dark-red cherry, garnet rim. Nose: fruit expression, fresh fruit, powerfull, varietal, characterful, mineral, undergrowth, cocoa bean. Palate: elegant, powerful, flavourful, fruity, fruity aftestaste, toasty.

### TERRAMOLL

Ctra. de La Mola, km. 15,5
07872 Formentera (Baleares)
☎: 971 327 257 - Fax: 971 327 257
info@terramoll.es
www.terramoll.es

**TERRAMOLL BLANC DE NOIRS 2008 B**
merlot

**84**

**TERRAMOLL 2008 B**

**84**

**PRIMUS 2008 B**
viognier, malvasia

## 84

**TERRAMOLL 2008 RD**

**87** Colour: rose, purple rim. Nose: macerated fruit, characterful, dry stone, red berry notes. Palate: fruity, flavourful, easy to drink, good finish.

**TERRAMOLL ES MONESTIR 2007 T**
monastrell

**89** Colour: cherry, garnet rim. Nose: powerful, ripe fruit, toasty, smoky. Palate: flavourful, powerful, fleshy, roasted-coffee aftertaste.

**TERRAMOLL 2005 TC**

**88** Colour: cherry, garnet rim. Nose: ripe fruit, spicy, creamy oak, toasty, balsamic herbs. Palate: powerful, flavourful, toasty, round tannins.

**PÉTILLANT NOIR ESP**
merlot 50%, cabernet sauvignon 50%

**85** Colour: bright cherry. Nose: smoky, red berry notes, burnt matches. Palate: sweetness, fruity, carbonic notes, balsamic.

# GRANADA-SUROESTE
## BODEGAS FONTEDEI

Doctor Horcajadas, 10
18570 Deifontes (Granada)
☎: 958 427 306 - Fax: 958 427 306
bodegasbodegran@gmail.com

**PICO DEL LLANO FONTEDEI 2008 B**

## 80

**FONTE DEI SYRAH MERLOT 2007 T ROBLE**
syrah 70%, merlot 30%

**90** Colour: bright cherry. Nose: ripe fruit, sweet spices, creamy oak, expressive. Palate: flavourful, fruity, toasty, round tannins.

**FONTE DEI PRADO NEGRO 2007 T ROBLE**
tempranillo 70%, cabernet sauvignon 30%

**86** Colour: cherry, garnet rim. Nose: powerful, ripe fruit, spicy, toasty. Palate: flavourful, powerful, fleshy, round tannins.

## BODEGAS SEÑORIO DE NEVADA

Ctra. de Cónchar, s/n
18659 Villamena (Granada)
☎: 958 777 092 - Fax: 958 777 062
info@senoriodenevada.es

www.bodegassenoriodenevada.es

**SEÑORÍO DE NEVADA SYRAH SELECCIÓN 2006 T**
syrah 100%

**87** Colour: cherry, garnet rim. Nose: toasty, fruit preserve, caramel. Palate: powerful, good structure, spicy, pruney.

**SEÑORÍO DE NEVADA CABERNET / MERLOT 2005 T**
cabernet sauvignon 60%, merlot 40%

**86** Colour: cherry, garnet rim. Nose: toasty, warm, boiled fruit notes. Palate: toasty, powerful, spicy, fleshy.

**SEÑORÍO DE NEVADA SELECCIÓN 2005 T**
cabernet sauvignon 80%, merlot 20%

**86** Colour: bright cherry, orangey edge. Nose: caramel, fruit preserve, boiled fruit notes. Palate: powerful, fleshy.

**SEÑORÍO DE NEVADA SYRAH-MERLOT 2005 T**
syrah 60%, merlot 40%

## 81

## GREGORIO GARCÍA DOMÍNGUEZ

Nueva de la Virgen, 31
18005 Granada
☎: 958 295 357
gregoriogarcia@ibagar.com

**ARS 2008 T**
tempranillo, merlot

**86** Colour: cherry, purple rim. Nose: ripe fruit, red berry notes, fruit expression. Palate: flavourful, fleshy, powerful, pruney.

SOME OTHER WINERIES WITHIN THE VT:

**BODEGA LOS MORENOS S.L.**
**BODEGA LOS NEVEROS**
**BODEGAS H. CALVENTE**
**VINÍCOLA ALHAMEÑA SIERRA TEJEDA**

# ILLA DE MENORCA
## CELLER SOLANO DE MENORCA

Cugullonet Nou. Camí de Sa Forana s/n,
Sant Climent
07712 Mahón (Menorca)
☎: 607 242 510
saforana@saforana.com
www.saforana.com

**SA FORANA 2008 T**
cabernet sauvignon, ull de llebre, syrah

**88** Colour: bright cherry, purple rim. Nose: violets, red berry notes, expressive. Palate: fruity, flavourful, good acidity, fine bitter notes, round tannins.

## VINYA SA CUDIA

Cos de Gracia, 7
07702 Mahón (Menorca)
☎: 629 330 162 - Fax: 971 353 607
info@vinyasacudia.com
www.vinyasacudia.com

VINYA SA CUDÍA 2008 B
malvasia 100%

**88** Colour: straw, pale. Nose: ripe fruit, balsamic herbs, elegant, floral. Palate: unctuous, fruity, good acidity, sweetness, good finish.

SOME OTHER WINERIES WITHIN THE VT:

**BODEGAS BINIFADET S.A.T.**
**CRISPÍN MARIANO VADELL**

## LAUJAR-ALPUJARRA

### BODEGA EL CORTIJO DE LA VIEJA

Ctra. A-348 (Lanjarón-Almería)km. 85
Paraje de la Vieja
04480 Alcolea (Almería)
☎: 950 343 919 - Fax: 950 343 919
comercial@iniza.net
www.iniza.net

INIZA MACABEO 2008 B
macabeo 90%, others 10%

**77**

INIZA 2008 RD
petit verdot 100%

**82**

INIZA 2008 T MACERACIÓN CARBÓNICA
garnacha 75%, tempranillo 25%

**88** Color cherry, purple rim. Aroma expressive, fresh fruit, red berry notes, floral. Taste flavourful, fruity, good acidity, round tannins.

INIZA 4 CEPAS 2007 T
tempranillo 30%, merlot 30%, syrah 20%, petit verdot 20%

**83**

SOME OTHER WINERIES WITHIN THE VT:

**BODEGA FUENTE VICTORIA**
**CORTIJO EL CURA**
**SELECCIÓN DE VINOS DE FONDÓN S.L.**
**VALLE DE LAUJAR**

## LIÉBANA

### BODEGA PICOS DE CABARIEZO

Barrio Cabariezo, s/n
39571 Cabezón de Liébana (Cantabria)
☎: 942 735 177 - Fax: 942 735 176
info@vinosylicores.es
www.vinosylicorespicos.com

PICOS DE CABARIEZO 2007 T
mencía 40%, tempranillo 30%, garnacha 30%

**78**

PICOS DE CABARIEZO 2006 T ROBLE
mencía 100%

**87** Colour: deep cherry, garnet rim. Nose: fresh fruit, balsamic herbs, spicy, balanced. Palate: flavourful, fruity, good acidity, round tannins.

## RÍO SANTO

Cillorigo de Liébana
39584 Esanos (Cantabria)
☎: 652 286 474
info@riosanto.es
www.riosanto.es

LUSIA 2007 T ROBLE
mencía 85%, tempranillo 15%

**86** Colour: bright cherry. Nose: red berry notes, fresh fruit, balsamic herbs, mineral. Palate: flavourful, light-bodied, fresh, slightly dry, soft tannins.

## MALLORCA
### 4 KILOS VINÍCOLA

Finca Son Vell Nou, 266
07509 Manacor (Baleares)
☎: 660 226 641 - Fax: 971 465 255
fgrimalt@4kilos.com
www.4kilos.com

4 KILOS 2007 T

**94** Colour: bright cherry. Nose: sweet spices, creamy oak, expressive, fresh fruit. Palate: flavourful, fruity, toasty, round tannins, powerful, sweetness.

12 VOLTS 2007 T
syrah 30%, merlot 30%, cabernet sauvignon 20%, callet and fogoneu 20%

**93** Colour: bright cherry. Nose: ripe fruit, creamy oak, expressive, cedar wood, cocoa bean, dry stone. Palate: flavourful, fruity, toasty, round tannins, powerful, mineral, fruity aftestaste.

4 KILOS 2006 T

**93** Colour: dark-red cherry. Nose: creamy oak, spicy, fruit liqueur notes, ripe fruit. Palate: varietal, powerful, flavourful, fruity, good structure.

## AN NEGRA VITICULTORS S.L.

3ª Volta 18
07200 Falanitx (Balears)
☎: 971 584 481 - Fax: 971 584 482
animanegra@annegra.com

QUÍBIA 2008 B

**91** Colour: bright straw. Nose: powerful, ripe fruit, citrus fruit, white flowers. Palate: flavourful, powerful, fleshy, rich.

QUÍBIA 2005 B

**87** Colour: bright yellow. Nose: ripe fruit, sweet spices, rancio notes. Palate: rich, smoky aftertaste, flavourful, fresh, fine bitter notes.

AN/2 2007 T

**89** Colour: cherry, garnet rim. Nose: powerful, sweet spices, roasted coffee, ripe fruit. Palate: flavourful, fleshy, spicy, ripe fruit.

ÀN 2006 TC

**92** Colour: very deep cherry, orangey edge. Nose: powerful, balsamic herbs, scrubland, ripe fruit, toasty. Palate: flavourful, spicy, ripe fruit, round tannins.

## BINIGRAU

Fiol, 33
07143 Biniali (Illes Balears)
☎: 971 512 023 - Fax: 971 886 495
info@binigrau.es
www.binigrau.es

NOU NAT 2008 B
prensal 60%, chardonnay 40%

**92** Colour: bright yellow. Nose: fruit preserve, tropical fruit, wild herbs. Palate: flavourful, good structure.

OBAC DE BINIGRAU 2006 TC
manto negro, callet, merlot, cabernet sauvignon, syrah

**84**

BINIGRAU SELECCIÓ 2004 T

**86** Colour: pale ruby, brick rim edge. Nose: ripe fruit, spicy, warm. Palate: flavourful, powerful, toasty, great length.

## BODEGA SON ARTIGUES

Camino de Son Artigues s/n
07260 Porreres (Illes Baleares)
☎: 971 181 314 - Fax: 647 880 184
info@sonartigues.com
www.sonartigues.com

SON ARTIGUES 2006 T
merlot, syrah

**87** Colour: cherry, garnet rim. Nose: spicy, balsamic herbs, ripe fruit. Palate: fleshy, full, great length, powerful tannins.

## SON ARTIGUES CALLET 2006 T
callet 86%, syrah 7%, merlot 7%

**85** Colour: pale ruby, brick rim edge. Nose: overripe fruit, floral, toasty. Palate: flavourful, balanced, fine bitter notes, soft tannins. Personality.

## SON ARTIGUES CALLET 2005 T
callet

**87** Colour: pale ruby, brick rim edge. Nose: overripe fruit, sweet spices, cocoa bean, balsamic herbs. Palate: flavourful, full, fine tannins.

## SON ARTIGUES GRAN 2005 T
callet, syrah, merlot

**86** Colour: cherry, garnet rim. Nose: overripe fruit, toasty, spicy. Palate: flavourful, long, great length.

## BODEGAS CA'N VIDALET

Ctra. Alcudia-Pollença PMV 220-1 km. 4,85
07460 Pollença (Baleares)
☎: 971 531 719 - Fax: 971 535 395
info@canvidalet.com
www.canvidalet.com

### CA'N VIDALET CHARDONNAY 2008 B
chardonnay 100%

**84**

### CA'N VIDALET BLANC DE BLANCS 2008 B
chardonnay, sauvignon blanc

**83**

### CA'N VIDALET BLANC DE NEGRES 2008 B
merlot, cabernet sauvignon, syrah

**83**

### CA'N VIDALET MOSCATELL 2008 B
moscatel 100%

**80**

### CA'N VIDALET SYRAH 2006 T
syrah 100%

**85** Colour: cherry, purple rim. Nose: wild herbs, floral, fruit expression. Palate: fruity, flavourful, great length.

### CA'N VIDALET CABERNET SAUVIGNON 2005 T
cabernet sauvignon 100%

**88** Colour: cherry, garnet rim. Nose: varietal, grassy, spicy, ripe fruit. Palate: toasty, great length, slightly dry, soft tannins.

### CA'N VIDALET MERLOT 2005 T
merlot 100%

**86** Colour: pale ruby, brick rim edge. Nose: toasty, spicy, balsamic herbs. Palate: toasty, flavourful, great length.

## BODEGAS RIBAS

Montanya, 2
07330 Consell (Balears)
☎: 971 622 673 - Fax: 971 622 746
info@bodegaribas.com
www.bodegaribas.com

### SIO BLANC 2007 B
prensal 40%, viognier 30%, chardonnay 20%, chenin blanc 10%

**87** Colour: bright yellow. Nose: fruit preserve, smoky. Palate: flavourful, full, long.

### SIÓ 2007 T
manto negro, syrah, cabernet sauvignon, merlot

**90** Colour: cherry, garnet rim. Nose: wild herbs, ripe fruit, sweet spices. Palate: flavourful, powerful, slightly dry, soft tannins.

### RIBAS 2007 T
manto negro 60%, syrah %, cabernet sauvignon 40%, merlot %

**85** Colour: bright cherry. Nose: ripe fruit, sweet spices, balsamic herbs. Palate: flavourful, fruity, round tannins.

### RIBAS DE CABRERA 2006 T
manto negro, syrah, cabernet sauvignon, merlot

**92** Colour: cherry, garnet rim. Nose: ripe fruit, spicy, toasty, complex, mineral. Palate: powerful, flavourful, toasty, round tannins.

## BODEGAS SON PUIG

Finca Son Puig, s/n
07194 Puigpunyent Mallorca (Illes Balears)
☎: 971 614 184 - Fax: 971 614 184
info@sonpuig.com
www.sonpuig.com

### SONPUIG 2007 B BARRICA
chardonnay 52%, prensal 48%

**91** Colour: bright yellow. Nose: powerful, ripe fruit, sweet spices, creamy oak, fragrant herbs. Palate: rich, smoky aftertaste, flavourful, fresh, good acidity.

### SONPUIG ESTIU 2007 T
tempranillo 60%, cabernet sauvignon 20%, merlot 20%

**85** Colour: cherry, garnet rim. Nose: white flowers, ripe fruit. Palate: flavourful, great length, slightly dry, soft tannins.

### SONPUIG 2006 T
tempranillo 60%, cabernet sauvignon 20%, merlot 20%

**88** Colour: bright cherry. Nose: ripe fruit, sweet spices, dried flowers. Palate: fruity, round tannins, flavourful.

GRAN SONPUIG 2005 T
tempranillo 41%, cabernet sauvignon 18%, merlot 33%, callet 8%

**89** Colour: pale ruby, brick rim edge. Nose: dried flowers, sweet spices, ripe fruit. Palate: flavourful, spicy, round tannins.

## FINCA SON BORDILS

Ctra. Inca-Sineu, km. 4
07300 Inca (Illes Balears)
☎: 971 182 200 - Fax: 971 612 583
info@sonbordils.es
www.sonbordils.es

SON BORDILS MUSCAT 2008 B
moscatel 100%

**87** Colour: bright yellow, greenish rim. Nose: varietal, grapey, fruit preserve, wild herbs. Palate: fruity, light-bodied, fresh, varietal.

SON BORDILS BLANC DE RAÏM BLANC 2008 B
prensal 94%, chardonnay 6%

**85** Colour: bright straw. Nose: fresh, fresh fruit, white flowers, expressive. Palate: flavourful, fruity, good acidity, balanced.

FINCA SON BORDILS CHARDONNAY 2008 B
chardonnay 97%, riesling 3%

**83**

SON BORDILS ROSAT DE MONASTRELL 2008 RD
monastrell 86%, merlot 14%

**83**

SON BORDILS MERLOT 2005 T
merlot 86%, manto negro 14%

**87** Colour: pale ruby, brick rim edge. Nose: spicy, cedar wood, ripe fruit, cocoa bean. Palate: flavourful, toasty, slightly dry, soft tannins.

SON BORDILS CABERNET SAUVIGNON 2005 T
cabernet sauvignon 100%

**86** Colour: pale ruby, brick rim edge. Nose: balsamic herbs, varietal, spicy. Palate: balanced, fleshy, round tannins.

SON BORDILS SYRAH 2005 T
syrah 100%

**83**

SON BORDILS NEGRE 2004 T
merlot 58,3%, cabernet sauvignon 28,7%, manto negro 9,6%, callet 3,1%, syrah %

**88** Colour: pale ruby, brick rim edge. Nose: reduction off-odours, fruit preserve, balsamic herbs. Palate: flavourful, great length, roasted-coffee aftertaste, fine tannins.

## JAUME DE PUNTIRÓ

Pza. Nova, 23
07320 Santa María del Cami (Mallorca (Baleares))
☎: 971 620 023 - Fax: 971 620 023
pere@vinsjaumedepuntiro.com
www.vinsjaumedepuntiro.com

PORPRAT 2007 T
merlot 100%

**85** Colour: cherry, garnet rim. Nose: overripe fruit, toasty, floral. Palate: flavourful, powerful, round tannins.

## JOSÉ L. FERRER (FRANJA ROJA)

Conquistador, 103
07350 Binissalem (Balears)
☎: 971 511 050 - Fax: 971 870 084
info@vinosferrer.com
www.vinosferrer.com

D2UES MOLL CHADONNAY 2008 B
chardonnay, prensal

**81**

D2UES MANTONEGRO CABERNET 2006 T
manto negro, cabernet sauvignon

**89** Colour: bright cherry. Nose: ripe fruit, sweet spices, creamy oak, expressive. Palate: flavourful, fruity, toasty, round tannins.

D2UES CALLET SYRAH 2006 T
callet, syrah

**87** Colour: bright cherry. Nose: ripe fruit, sweet spices, floral. Palate: flavourful, fruity, slightly dry, soft tannins.

## SON VIVES

Font de la Vila
07191 Banyalbufar (Illes Balears)
☎: 609 601 904 - Fax: 971 718 065
toni@darder.com
www.sonvives.com

JUXTA MARE 2008 B
malvasia

**85** Colour: bright straw. Nose: fresh, fresh fruit, white flowers, expressive. Palate: flavourful, fruity, good acidity, balanced.

FUSIÓ DE BLANCS 2006 B
malvasia, chardonnay, prensal

**88** Colour: bright yellow. Nose: ripe fruit, sweet spices, creamy oak, fragrant herbs. Palate: rich, smoky aftertaste, flavourful, good acidity.

ROELLA 2008 RD

**82**

NEGRE 2007 T

**86** Colour: bright cherry. Nose: ripe fruit, sweet spices, creamy oak, expressive. Palate: flavourful, fruity, toasty, round tannins.

## VINS NADAL

Ramón Llull, 2
07350 Binissalem (Balears)
☎: 971 511 058 - Fax: 971 870 150
albaflor@vinsnadal.com
www.vinsnadal.com

COUPAGE 110 VINS NADAL 2007 T
manto negro, cabernet sauvignon, merlot, syrah

**84**

SYRAH 110 VINS NADAL 2006 T
syrah 100%

**84**

MERLOT 110 VINS NADAL 2005 T
merlot 100%

**83**

## VINYES I VINS CA SA PADRINA

Camí dels Horts. s/n
07140 Sencelles (Balears)
☎: 686 933 991 - Fax: 971 612 400
cellercasapadrina@gmail.com

MOLLET GONZÁLEZ SUÑER 2008 B JOVEN
prensal, chardonnay

**86** Colour: bright straw. Nose: fresh, fresh fruit, white flowers, expressive. Palate: flavourful, fruity, good acidity, balanced.

## VINYES MORTITX

Ctra. Pollensa Lluc, km. 10,9
07315 Escorca (Illes Balears)
☎: 971 182 339 - Fax: 971 531 914
bodega@vinyesmortitx.com
www.vinyesmortitx.com

DOLÇ DE GEL MORTITX 2008 B
riesling 50%, malvasia 50%

**88** Colour: bright yellow. Nose: candied fruit, warm, floral, elegant. Palate: unctuous, good acidity, flavourful, great length.

BLANC MORTITX 2008 B
malvasia

**79**

FLAIRES DE MORTITX 2008 RD
monastrell 80%, tempranillo 20%

**81**

NEGRE MORTITX 2007 T
merlot 35%, syrah 30%, cabernet sauvignon 20%, monastrell 15%

**87** Colour: bright cherry. Nose: red berry notes, lactic notes, spicy. Palate: flavourful, fruity, round tannins.

L'U DE MORTITX 2006 T
merlot 60%, cabernet sauvignon 20%, syrah 20%

**90** Colour: dark-red cherry, cherry, purple rim. Nose: ripe fruit, cedar wood, cocoa bean, expressive. Palate: fleshy, full, round tannins.

RODAL PLA DE MORTITX 2006 T
syrah 60%, merlot 20%, cabernet sauvignon 20%

**85** Colour: cherry, garnet rim. Nose: overripe fruit, wild herbs, spicy. Palate: flavourful, fruity, easy to drink.

SOME OTHER WINERIES WITHIN THE VT:

**BODEGA BINIAGUAL**
**ES VERGER SAT**
**FLORIANÓPOLIS**
**SON PRIM PETIT CELLER**
**VINORICA (CASTELL MIQUEL)**

## NORTE DE GRANADA
### ANTONIO VILCHEZ VALENZUELA

Fuente Vieja, 26
18516 Marchal (Granada)
☎: 958 690 146 - Fax: 958 690 146
naranjuez@vinossingulares.com
www.vinossingulares.com

NARANJUEZ PINOT NOIR 2006 T

**85** Colour: dark-red cherry, orangey edge. Nose: ripe fruit, creamy oak, dark chocolate, warm. Palate: round tannins, fruity, flavourful.

### BODEGAS SEÑORÍ NAZARI (BODEGAS MUÑANA)

Ctra. de Cortes y Graena a La Peza,
Finca Peñas Prietas s/n
18517 Cortes y Graena (Granada)
☎: 958 670 715
jbustamante@bodegasmunana.com
www.bodegasmunana.com

MUÑANA 3 CEPAS 2007 T
syrah 60%, cabernet sauvignon 35%, merlot 5%

**90** Colour: bright cherry. Nose: sweet spices, creamy oak, expressive, ripe fruit. Palate: flavourful, fruity, toasty, round tannins.

MUÑANA CABERNET SAUVIGNON 2007 T
cabernet sauvignon 100%

**89** Colour: cherry, garnet rim. Nose: powerful, ripe fruit, toasty, sweet spices. Palate: flavourful, fleshy, fruity, fresh.

MUÑANA 2007 T
tempranillo 60%, cabernet sauvignon 30%, monastrell 10%

**87** Colour: cherry, garnet rim. Nose: medium intensity, candied fruit, fruit expression, spicy. Palate: flavourful, ripe fruit, spicy, round tannins.

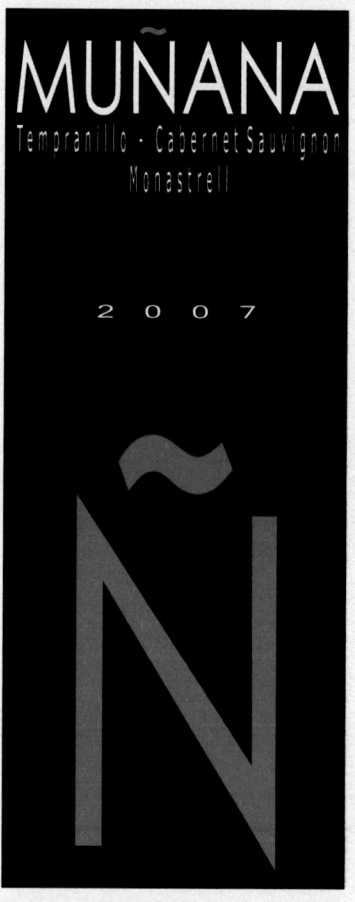

## MARQUÉS DE CASA PARDIÑAS C.B.

Finca San Torcuato
18540 Huélago (Granada)
☎: 630 901 094
flopezjusticia@wanadoo.es

SPIRA VENDIMIA SELECCIONADA 2008 T

**89** Colour: dark-red cherry. Nose: macerated fruit, red berry notes, creamy oak, spicy, smoky, earthy notes. Palate: flavourful, rich, fine tannins, balsamic.

SPIRA VENDIMIA SELECCIONADA 2007 T

**90** Colour: cherry, garnet rim. Nose: ripe fruit, spicy, creamy oak, toasty, mineral. Palate: powerful, flavourful, toasty, round tannins.

## RAMÓN SAAVEDRA SAAVEDRA

Avda. Andalucía, 18
18517 Cortes y Graena (Granada)
☎: 958 670 634
ramon.saavedra@ggrunert.de

IRADEI CAUZÓN 2006 T

**88** Colour: deep cherry. Nose: fruit liqueur notes, fruit preserve, earthy notes, smoky. Palate: good structure, fresh, fruity.

CAUZÓN 2006 T

**88** Colour: very deep cherry, garnet rim. Nose: fruit preserve, expressive, earthy notes, sweet spices. Palate: round, fruity, good acidity, sweetness, sweet tannins.

SOME OTHER WINERIES WITHIN THE VT:

**BODEGA JABALCÓN**
**BODEGA ROMERO GARCÍA C.B.**
**BODEGAS FERNÁNDEZ HERRERO**
**BODEGAS VILLAGRAN**
**DOMINGO Y QUILES**
**GARCÍA MARTOS S.L.**
**MÉNDEZ MOYA**
**PAGO DE ALMARAES**
**VIÑAS DE PURULIO**

## RIBERA DEL ANDARAX
### FINCA ANFORA

Barranco del Obispo, s/n.
04729 Enix (Almeria)
☎: 629 131 370 - Fax: 950 341 614
info@vegaenix.com
www.vegaenix.com

VEGA ENIX EXENSYS 2005 T

**90** Colour: cherry, garnet rim. Nose: candied fruit, overripe fruit, powerfull. Palate: flavourful, sweetness, fleshy, balanced.

VEGA ENIX SANTYS 2005 T

**87** Colour: cherry, garnet rim. Nose: spicy, creamy oak, toasty, overripe fruit. Palate: powerful, flavourful, toasty, round tannins.

VEGA ENIX LAURENTI 2004 T

**91** Colour: cherry, garnet rim. Nose: medium intensity, ripe fruit, sweet spices, dark chocolate, toasty. Palate: flavourful, fleshy, spicy, ripe fruit, round tannins.

VEGA ENIX CALIDON 2004 T

**89** Colour: cherry, garnet rim. Nose: ripe fruit, spicy, creamy oak, toasty. Palate: powerful, flavourful, toasty, round tannins.

VEGA ENIX SANTYS 2003 T

**88** Colour: cherry, garnet rim. Nose: powerful, overripe fruit, honeyed notes, dark chocolate. Palate: powerful, fleshy, spirituous.

VEGA ENIX MONTENEO 2002 T

**87** Colour: cherry, garnet rim. Nose: ripe fruit, dark chocolate, toasty. Palate: flavourful, spicy, ripe fruit.

SOME OTHER WINERIES WITHIN THE VT:

**FINCA LA MORALEA (PACO FERRE)**
**LA BODEGA DE ALBOLODUY**

## RIBERA DEL GÁLLEGO
## CINCO VILLAS

### BODEGAS EJEANAS

Prolongación Paseo del Muro, 18
50600 Ejea de los Caballeros (Zaragoza)
☎: 976 663 770 - Fax: 976 663 770
info@bodegasejenas.com
www.bodegasejenas.com

VEGA DE LUCHÁN 2008 RD
garnacha, cabernet sauvignon

**80**

VEGA DE LUCHÁN 2006 T
cabernet sauvignon 100%

**83**

UVA NOCTURNA GARNACHAS VIEJAS 2005 T
garnacha 100%

**89** Colour: deep cherry. Nose: ripe fruit, varietal, cocoa bean, creamy oak, spicy. Palate: fine tannins, flavourful, powerful, fruity, fresh.

VEGA DE LUCHÁN 2004 T BARRICA
tempranillo, cabernet sauvignon

**78**

### BODEGAS UNCASTELLUM S.L.

Ctra. Uncastillo-Sos del Rey Católico, s/n
50678 Uncastillo (Zaragoza)
☎: 976 679 110 - Fax: 976 679 110
uncastellum@umcastellum.com
www.uncastellum.com

UNCASTELLUM 2008 RD
tempranillo 60%, garnacha 40%

**87** Colour: brilliant rose. Nose: fresh, candied fruit, raspberry. Palate: easy to drink, fruity, good acidity.

UNCASTELLUM 2006 T BARRICA
tempranillo 50%, garnacha 30%, merlot 10%, cabernet sauvignon 10%

**84**

UNCASTELLUM AUREUM 2005 T
tempranillo 25%, garnacha 25%, merlot 25%, cabernet sauvignon 25%

**87** Colour: cherry, garnet rim. Nose: spicy, toasty, complex, aromatic coffee, fruit liqueur notes. Palate: powerful, flavourful, toasty, round tannins.

## BODEGAS Y VIÑEDOS
## REINO DE LOS MALLOS

Ctra. A-132, km. 37,2
22808 Murillo de Gállego (Hoya de Huesca) (Zaragoza)
☎: 974 383 015 - Fax: 974 380 156
bodega@reinodelosmallos.es
www.reinodelosmallos.es

REINO DE LOS MALLOS MACABEO 2007 BFB
macabeo 90%, garnacha blanca 10%

**85** Colour: bright yellow. Nose: powerful, ripe fruit, sweet spices, creamy oak. Palate: rich, smoky aftertaste, flavourful, fresh, good acidity.

REINO DE LOS MALLOS MONOVARIETALES
GARNACHA 2008 RD
garnacha 100%

**83**

REINO DE LOS MALLOS MONOVARIETALES SYRAH 2007 T
syrah 100%

**87** Colour: deep cherry, bright ochre rim. Nose: fruit preserve, red berry notes, sweet spices, dark chocolate. Palate: unctuous, powerful, flavourful, round tannins, good finish.

REINO DE LOS MALLOS MONOVARIETALES
MERLOT 2006 T
merlot 100%

**88** Colour: deep cherry, orangey edge. Nose: powerful, ripe fruit, dark chocolate, aged wood nuances. Palate: powerful, ripe fruit, round tannins.

REINO DE LOS MALLOS MONOVARIETALES
CABERNET 2006 T
cabernet sauvignon 100%

**85** Colour: very deep cherry, bright ochre rim. Nose: fruit preserve, expressive, sweet spices, new oak. Palate: confected, pruney, toasty, round tannins.

REINO DE LOS MALLOS CABERNET MERLOT 2004 T
cabernet sauvignon 40%, merlot 40%, garnacha 20%

**88** Colour: cherry, garnet rim. Nose: powerful, ripe fruit, dry nuts, aromatic coffee, dark chocolate. Palate: flavourful, spicy, easy to drink, round tannins.

## EDRA BODEGA Y VIÑEDOS

Ctra A 132, km 26
22800 Ayerbe (Huesca)
☎: 679 420 455 - Fax: 974 380 829
edra@bodega-edra.com
www.bodega-edra.com

EDRA GRULLAS DE PASO 2007 T
merlot 50%, cabernet sauvignon 40%, tempranillo 10%, garnacha %

**85** Colour: bright cherry. Nose: ripe fruit, sweet spices, woody. Palate: flavourful, fruity, toasty, harsh oak tannins.

EDRA XTRA SYRAH 2005 TR
syrah 100%

**90** Colour: cherry, purple rim. Nose: expressive, neat, varietal, sweet spices, cedar wood, red berry notes, ripe fruit. Palate: flavourful, powerful, fleshy, fruity, good structure.

EDRA MERLOT SYRAH 2005 TC
syrah, merlot

**88** Colour: very deep cherry. Nose: ripe fruit, fruit preserve, sweet spices. Palate: flavourful, powerful, fruity, concentrated.

SOME OTHER WINERIES WITHIN THE VT:

**LAMARCA WINES**

# RIBERA DEL JILOCA
## BODEGA SANTO TOMÁS DE AQUINO

Avda. Madrid, 39
50360 Daroca (Zaragoza)
☎: 976 800 277 - Fax: 976 800 777
cooperativa@daroca.info

PUERTA BAJA S/C RD

**72**

MARQUÉS DE DAROCA VIÑAS VIEJAS 2007 T

**82**

MARQUÉS DE DAROCA GARNACHA TEMPRANILLO 2005 T
garnacha 30%, tempranillo 70%

**85** Colour: dark-red cherry, orangey edge. Nose: fruit preserve, sweet spices, creamy oak. Palate: warm, sweetness, fruity, grainy tannins.

PUERTA BAJA T

**81**

## BODEGAS VINAE MURERI S.L.

Ctra. Murero-Atea
Finca La Moratilla
50366 Murero (Zaragoza)
☎: 976 808 033 - Fax: 976 808 034
info@vinaemureri.com
www.vinaemureri.com

MURERO ELITE 2005 T
garnacha 100%

**91** Colour: bright cherry. Nose: ripe fruit, sweet spices, creamy oak, expressive, powerfull, mineral. Palate: flavourful, fruity, toasty, fleshy, powerful tannins.

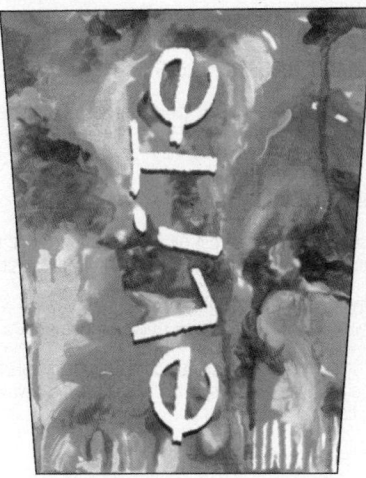

MURET ORO 2007 T
garnacha 100%

**88** Colour: cherry, purple rim. Nose: powerful, ripe fruit, creamy oak, toasty, dark chocolate. Palate: flavourful, fleshy, spicy.

# VINOS DE LA TIERRA

## MURET VIDADILLO 2007 T
vidadillo 80%, bobal 20%

**88** Colour: cherry, garnet rim. Nose: powerful, fruit preserve, dark chocolate, aromatic coffee. Palate: powerful, spicy, balsamic.

SOME OTHER WINERIES WITHIN THE VT:

**COMERCIAL GRUPO FREIXENET S.A.**

# RIBERA DEL QUEILES
## GUELBENZU

San Juan, 14
31520 Cascante (Navarra)
☎: 976 191 000 - Fax: 948 850 097
info@guelbenzu.es
www.guelbenzu.com

GRACIANO GUELBENZU 2006 T

**87** Colour: dark-red cherry, garnet rim. Nose: fruit preserve, sweet spices, aromatic coffee. Palate: powerful, fruity, round tannins, long.

LOMBANA 2006 T

**86** Colour: cherry, garnet rim. Nose: ripe fruit, varietal, balsamic herbs. Palate: flavourful, fruity, fruity aftestaste.

LAUTUS GUELBENZU 2004 T
tempranillo 40%, merlot 25%, cabernet sauvignon 25%, garnacha 10%

**89** Colour: deep cherry. Nose: cocoa bean, spicy, ripe fruit, fruit liqueur notes. Palate: slightly dry, soft tannins, flavourful, fruity, fleshy, great length.

VIERLAS GUELBENZU T

**88** Colour: cherry, garnet rim. Nose: medium intensity, cocoa bean, ripe fruit. Palate: ripe fruit, flavourful, powerful, fruity.

EVO GUELBENZU
AZUL GUELBENZU
RED GUELBENZU
LOMBANA GUELBENZU

SOME OTHER WINERIES WITHIN THE VT:

**WINERY ARTS**

# SERRA DE TRAMUNTANA COSTA NORD
## COOP. MALVASÍA DE BANYALBUFAR

Esperit Sant, 13
07191 Banyalbufar (Balears)
☎: 616 537 146
cooperativa@malvasiadebanyalbufar.com
www.malvasiadebanyalbufar.com

CORNET 2008 B
malvasia 100%

**91** Colour: bright yellow. Nose: fresh fruit, citrus fruit, grassy. Palate: flavourful, long, fresh.

## SA VINYA DE CAN SERVERA

Sa Creu s/n
07313 Selva (Mallorca)
☎: 629 282 758
info@divins.es
www.divins.es

DIVINS SELECCIÓ 2007 T
syrah 84%, manto negro 8%, callet 8%

**83**

DIVINS 2007 T
cabernet sauvignon 92%, manto negro 4%, callet 4%

**81**

SOME OTHER WINERIES WITHIN THE VT:

**FLORIANÓPOLIS
VINORICA (CASTELL MIQUEL)**

# SIERRA NORTE DE SEVILLA
## COLONIAS DE GALEÓN

Plazuela, 39
41370 Cazalla de la Sierra (Sevilla)
☎: 955 710 092 - Fax: 955 710 093
info@coloniasdegaleon.com
www.coloniasdegaleon.com

OCNOS 2007 BFB
chardonnay 100%

**85** Colour: bright golden. Nose: ripe fruit, creamy oak, smoky. Palate: creamy, rich, fleshy.

COLONIAS DE GALEÓN 2008 T MACERACIÓN CARBÓNICA
cabernet franc 50%, tempranillo 30%, syrah 20%

**82**

COLONIAS DE GALEÓN 2006 T ROBLE
cabernet franc 40%, tempranillo 30%, merlot 15%, syrah 15%

**83**

SILENTE SELECCIÓN 2005 T ROBLE
cabernet franc, tempranillo, merlot, syrah

**85** Colour: dark-red cherry, orangey edge. Nose: fruit preserve, roasted coffee, sweet spices, tobacco. Palate: fruity, flavourful, fine tannins.

## SIERRA DE LAS ESTANCIAS Y LOS FILABRES

### FINCA ONEGAR

Paraje Onegar
04870 Purchena (Almería)
☎: 950 126 135 - Fax: 950 445 545
central@fincaonegar.com
www.fincaonegar.com

ONEGAR 2007 TC
tempranillo 85%, cabernet sauvignon 10%, petit verdot 5%

**86** Colour: cherry, garnet rim. Nose: powerful, fruit preserve, smoky, dark chocolate, toasty. Palate: powerful, fine bitter notes, round tannins.

ONEGAR 2006 TC
tempranillo 90%, cabernet sauvignon 10%

**89** Colour: cherry, garnet rim. Nose: powerful, varietal, sweet spices, creamy oak. Palate: flavourful, fleshy, spicy, ripe fruit.

## VAL DO MIÑO-OURENSE

### ADEGAS LAGARIÑOS S.L.
### BODEGA SEÑORÍO DE ROBLIDO

## VALDEJALÓN

### EPILENSE DE VINOS Y VIÑEDOS S.C.

San Agustín, 7

50290 Épila (Zaragoza)
☎: 976 603 835 - Fax: 976 603 553
valdecella@terra.es

VALDECELLA 2008 B
macabeo 70%, garnacha blanca 30%

**86** Colour: bright straw. Nose: fresh, medium intensity, ripe fruit. Palate: flavourful, good structure, good acidity.

VALDECELLA 2008 RD
garnacha 90%, tempranillo 10%

**81**

VALDECELLA GARNACHA 2008 T
garnacha 100%

**85** Colour: dark-red cherry, purple rim. Nose: fresh, expressive, varietal, fresh fruit. Palate: good acidity, flavourful, fruity.

VALDECELLA TEMPRANILLO MERLOT 2008 T
tempranillo 60%, merlot 40%

**85** Colour: dark-red cherry, purple rim. Nose: fruit expression, fresh fruit, fresh. Palate: fruity, flavourful, fresh.

VALDECELLA 2008 T
garnacha 50%, tempranillo 30%, merlot 20%

**83**

VALDECELLA COSECHA SELECCIÓN EXTRA 2007 T
garnacha 40%, tempranillo 40%, merlot 20%

**86** Colour: very deep cherry, garnet rim. Nose: ripe fruit, red berry notes, toasty, aromatic coffee. Palate: fruity, powerful, good acidity, grainy tannins.

VALDECELLA 2007 T FERMENTADO EN BARRICA
garnacha 100%

**84**

VALDECELLA 2006 TC
tempranillo 40%, garnacha 40%, merlot 20%

**84**

VALDECELLA MOSCATEL 2008 VINO DE LICOR
moscatel 100%

**87** Colour: old gold. Nose: candied fruit, grapey, dry nuts, balsamic herbs, smoky. Palate: unctuous, elegant, confected.

SOME OTHER WINERIES WITHIN THE VT:

**COOP.DEL CAMPO SAN PEDRO ARBUÉS**
**VIÑEDOS DE MANCUSO S.L.**

## VALLE DEL CINCA
### NUVIANA

Ctra. A-1241 Zaidín-Tamarit, km 11
22549 San Miguel-Belver de Cinca (Huesca)
☎: 974 478 800 - Fax: 974 478 802
v.sanchez@codorniu.es
www.grupocodorniu.es

NUVIANA 2008 B
chardonnay, sauvignon blanc

**78**

NUVIANA 2008 RD
cabernet sauvignon, syrah

**84**

NUVIANA 2008 T

**83**

### VALONGA BODEGAS Y VIÑEDOS

Apartado Correos, 29
22500 Binéfar (Huesca)
☎: 974 435 127 - Fax: 974 339 101
bodegas@valonga.com
www.valonga.com

VALONGA CHARDONNAY 2008 B
chardonnay

**81**

VALONGA 2008 RD
tempranillo, merlot

**83**

MONTE VALONGA TEMPRANILLO 2008 T
tempranillo

**87** Colour: deep cherry. Nose: varietal, expressive, mineral, ripe fruit, fresh fruit. Palate: flavourful, full, fruity.

MONTE VALONGA SYRAH 2008 T
syrah

**85** Colour: very deep cherry. Nose: varietal, ripe fruit, warm. Palate: flavourful, fruity, spicy, balsamic.

MONTE VALONGA SYRAH 2007 T

**85** Colour: dark-red cherry. Nose: varietal, ripe fruit, creamy oak, new oak. Palate: grainy tannins.

CAMPO GABÁS 2005 TC

**82**

SOME OTHER WINERIES WITHIN THE VT:

**MONTE JULIA**

## VALLES DE SADACIA
### BODEGAS ONTAÑON

Avda. de Aragón, 3
26006 Logroño (La Rioja)
☎: 941 234 200 - Fax: 941 270 482
comunicacion@ontanon.es
www.ontanon.es

RIBERAS DE MARCO FABIO DE MOSCATEL SS

**90** Colour: pale. Nose: powerful, varietal, fresh fruit. Palate: flavourful, fruity, fresh.

SOME OTHER WINERIES WITHIN THE VT:

**CASTILLO DE MAETIERRA**

## VIÑEDOS DE ESPAÑA
### BODEGA VIÑALMANZORA

Polígono La Zalea, Parcela 2B2
04890 Serón (Almería)
☎: 609 436 248 - Fax: 950 421 202
diegogea@hotmail.com
www.vinalmanzora.es

SAETÍAS 2007 B ROBLE
airén 100%

**80**

DIDACUS SYRAH 2008 T
syrah 100%

**85** Colour: cherry, garnet rim. Nose: varietal, fresh, ripe fruit, spicy. Palate: fruity, flavourful, balanced.

DIDACUS 2007 T BARRICA
tempranillo 100%

**85** Colour: black cherry, garnet rim. Nose: ripe fruit, creamy oak, spicy. Palate: fruity, flavourful, round tannins, good acidity.

## CHERUBINO VALSANGIACOMO S.A.

Ctra. Cheste-Godelleta, km. 1
46370 Chiva (Valencia)
☎: 962 510 451 - Fax: 962 511 361
cvalsangiacomo@cherubino.es
www.cherubino.es

DRASSANES 2006 T
syrah 60%, cabernet sauvignon 40%

**88** Colour: dark-red cherry. Nose: ripe fruit, green pepper, creamy oak, dark chocolate, spicy. Palate: spicy, great length, fruity, varietal, round tannins.

## VEGA GRANDE DE GUADALUPE

Pza.de Guadalupe, 1 Ctra. GC-500 (Juan Grande)
35107 San Bartolomé de Tirajana (Las Palmas de Gran Canaria)
☎: 928 336 279 - Fax: 928 310 876
bfidalgo@invercasti.com

CONDE DE LA VEGA GRANDE DE GUADALUPE
2008 T
cabernet sauvignon

**84**

# TABLE WINES

The different wines reviewed in the following pages are produced in geographical regions which are not included in any DO or integrated in any Vinos de la Tierra association, although many of them are produced in areas with a certain wine-making tradition.

What follows does not pretend to be an exhaustive summary of the usually mundane Vinos de Mesa, but rather an attempt to rescue the most outstanding wines, in terms of quality, from the remaining "unlabelled" wines within the Spanish wine-producing arena.

All the wineries are sorted by Autonomous Communities. Amongst the brands tasted, the reader will discover wines with singular characteristics and, in many cases, of excellent quality, which may be of great interest to all those who are looking for new offerings and interesting alternatives to serve at the table

---

## ANDALUCÍA

### ANTONIO VILCHEZ VALENZUELA

Fuente Vieja, 26
18516 Marchal (Granada)
☎: 958 690 146 - Fax: 958 690 146
naranjuez@vinossingulares.com
www.vinossingulares.com

NARANJUEZ PRISA MATA 2007 T

**83**

NARANJUEZ PRISA MATA 2006 T

**86** Colour: deep cherry, orangey edge. Nose: powerful, fruit liqueur notes, toasty, spicy. Palate: flavourful, spirituous, spicy.

### BARRANCO OSCURO

Cortijo Barranco Oscuro
18440 Cádiar (Granada)
☎: 958 343 066 - Fax: 958 343 496
info@barrancooscuro.com
www.barrancooscuro.com

BLANCAS NOBLES 2006 BC
Vigiriego, sauvignon blanc, riesling, moscatel, morisco, albariño

**83**

BLANCAS NOBLES CLÁSICO 2006 BC
Vigiriego, vermentino, viognier, sauvignon blanc, riesling, moscatel, albariño, chardonnay

**77**

TRES UVES 2006 B
Vigiriego, vermentino, viognier

**68**

RUBAIYAT BARRANCO OSCURO 2005 T
syrah

**91** Colour: cherry, garnet rim. Nose: ripe fruit, spicy, creamy oak, toasty, smoky. Palate: powerful, flavourful, toasty, round tannins.

BO2 BARRANCO OSCURO 2005 T
tempranillo, otras

**88** Colour: black cherry. Nose: balsamic herbs, scrubland, damp undergrowth. Palate: powerful, concentrated.

BORGOÑON GRANATE BARRANCO OSCURO 2005 TC
pinot noir

**85** Colour: cherry, garnet rim. Nose: ripe fruit, spicy, toasty, complex, balsamic herbs. Palate: powerful, flavourful, toasty, round tannins.

TEMPRANILLO Y MÁS 2005 T
tempranillo, garnacha, cabernet sauvignon, cabernet franc, merlot

**83**

1368 BARRANCO OSCURO PAGO CERRO LAS MONJAS 2003 TC
garnacha, syrah, cabernet sauvignon, merlot, cabernet franc

**88** Colour: deep cherry, garnet rim. Nose: ripe fruit, toasty, balsamic herbs, aged wood nuances. Palate: fruity, flavourful, powerful, round tannins.

### BODEGAS PRIVILEGIO DEL CONDADO S.L.

San José, 2
21710 Bollullos del Condado (Huelva)
☎: 959 410 261 - Fax: 959 410 171
comercial@vinicoladelcondado.com
www.vinicoladelcondado.com

LANTERO SYRAH 2007 T

**81**

LANTERO ROBLE SYRAH 2006 T ROBLE
syrah

**84**

### EQUIPO NAVAZOS

Cartuja nº1 - módulo 6
11401 Jerez de la Frontera (Cádiz)
☎: 649 435 979
equipo@navazos.com
www.equiponavazos.com

NAVAZOS NIEPOORT 2008 B
palomino

**93** Colour: straw. Nose: fresh fruit, grassy, flor yeasts. Palate: good acidity, fresh, light-bodied, balsamic, complex, fine bitter notes.

### JORGE ORDÓÑEZ & CO

Pº de la Axarquia, 19
29718 Almáchar (Málaga)
☎: 952 504 706 - Fax: 976 852 764
office@jorge-ordonez.es

# TABLE WINES

JORGE ORDÓÑEZ & CO. ESENCIA 2004 B

**95** Colour: old gold, amber rim. Nose: citrus fruit, ripe fruit, candied fruit, expressive. Palate: flavourful, fleshy, complex, sweet.

## JOSÉ GALLEGO GÓNGORA S.A.

Cristo de la Vera Cruz, 59
41808 Villanueva del Ariscal (Sevilla)
☎: 954 113 700 - Fax: 954 113 239
direccion2@bodegasgongora.com
www.bodegasgongora.com

GÓNGORA AMONTILLADO MUY VIEJO AM
garrido fino 100%

**84**

GÓNGORA PATA DE HIERRO FI
garrido fino 100%

**84**

DUQUE DE CARMONA ORANGE WINE OL
garrido fino 60%, moscatel 20%, pedro ximénez 20%

**86** Colour: mahogany, iodine. Nose: spicy, aromatic coffee, roasted almonds, citrus fruit, candied fruit. Palate: flavourful, full, fresh, fruity aftestaste.

OLOROSO GÓNGORA OL
garrido fino 100%

**86** Colour: iodine, amber rim. Nose: powerful, elegant, dry nuts, toasty, dark chocolate, aged wood nuances. Palate: rich, fine bitter notes, fine solera notes, long, spicy.

GÓNGORA SOLERA 1840 OL
garrido fino 75%

**83**

GÓNGORA PX DULCE AÑEJO SELECCIÓN IMPERIAL
pedro ximénez 100%

**84**

## MARENAS VIÑEDOS & BODEGA

Ctra. N-331 (Córdoba - Málaga), km 47
14550 Montilla (Córdoba)
☎: 957 655 724
info@bodegamarenas.com
www.bodegamarenas.com

MARENAS LUCÍA 2005 TC
syrah 100%

**89** Colour: dark-red cherry, garnet rim. Nose: macerated fruit, earthy notes, expressive, floral. Palate: rich, powerful, grainy tannins, fruity.

MARENAS ALVARO 2004 TC
syrah 50%, monastrell 50%

**84**

## RAMÓN SAAVEDRA SAAVEDRA

Avda. Andalucía, 18
18517 Cortes y Graena (Granada)
☎: 958 670 634
ramon.saavedra@ggrunert.de

CAUZÓN 2007 B

**78**

CAUZÓN 2007 T
pinot noir

**87** Colour: cherry, garnet rim. Nose: ripe fruit, creamy oak, spicy. Palate: fruity, full, flavourful, round tannins.

IRADEI CAUZÓN 2007 T

**86** Colour: very deep cherry, garnet rim. Nose: expressive, new oak, fruit preserve. Palate: unctuous, powerful, ripe fruit, round tannins, pruney.

# ARAGÓN
## EDRA BODEGA Y VIÑEDOS

Ctra A 132, km 26
22800 Ayerbe (Huesca)
☎: 679 420 455 - Fax: 974 380 829
edra@bodega-edra.com
www.bodega-edra.com

EDRA BLANCOLUZ 2008 B
viognier 100%

**84**

# BALEARES
## BINIGRAU

Fiol, 33
07143 Biniali (Illes Balears)
☎: 971 512 023 - Fax: 971 886 495
info@binigrau.es
www.binigrau.es

BINIGRAU 2008 B
chardonnay

**87** Colour: bright straw. Nose: fresh, fresh fruit, expressive, tropical fruit. Palate: flavourful, fruity, good acidity, balanced.

## BINIGRAU DOLÇ 2006 T
manto negro 60%, merlot 40%

**87** Colour: dark-red cherry. Nose: characterful, fruit liqueur notes, fruit liqueur notes, candied fruit. Palate: flavourful, sweetness, long, balanced.

## VINS TONI GELABERT

Camí dels Horts de Llodrá km. 1,3
07500 Manacor (Balears)
☎: 610 789 531 - Fax: 971 552 409
info@vinstonigelabert.com
www.vinstonigelabert.com

TORRE DES CANONGE 2008 B
giro blanco

**88** Colour: bright yellow. Nose: powerful, ripe fruit, sweet spices, fragrant herbs. Palate: rich, good acidity, fruity, unctuous.

# CANARIAS
## BODEGAS VIÑATIGO

Cabo Verde, s/n
38440 La Guancha (Tenerife)
☎: 922 828 768 - Fax: 922 829 936
vinatigo@vinatigo.com
www.vinatigo.com

VIÑAS DE TACANDE 2006 T
baboso negro, Vigiriego, tintilla, negramoll

**90** Colour: cherry, garnet rim. Nose: powerful, ripe fruit, scrubland, earthy notes. Palate: flavourful, fleshy, powerful.

# CANTABRIA
## BODEGA PICOS DE CABARIEZO

Barrio Cabariezo, s/n
39571 Cabezón de Liébana (Cantabria)
☎: 942 735 177 - Fax: 942 735 176
info@vinosylicores.es
www.vinosylicorespicos.com

HIELU DE PICOS 2008 VINO DULCE NATURAL
gewürztraminer 60%, riesling 40%

**82**

# CASTILLA-LA MANCHA
## BODEGAS CORONADO

Ctra. San Isidro, s/n
16620 La Alberca de Záncara (Cuenca)
☎: 676 463 483 - Fax: 967 150 107
informacion@bodegascoronado.com
www.bodegascoronado.com

CHARCÓN 2008 T
cabernet sauvignon 50%, syrah 50%

**81**

## BOD. Y VIÑEDOS CASTIBLANQUE

Isaac Peral 19
13610 Campo de Criptana (Ciudad Real)
☎: 926 589 147 - Fax: 926 589 148
info@bodegascastiblanque.com
www.bodegascastiblanque.com

SOLAMENTE 2008 B
airén 100%

**83**

SOLAMENTE 2008 RD
syrah 100%

**86** Colour: light cherry. Nose: red berry notes, fresh fruit, expressive. Palate: fruity, creamy, powerful, fresh.

SOLAMENTE 2008 T
tempranillo 60%, garnacha 25%, syrah 15%

**84**

## DOMECQ BODEGAS + CINCO CASAS

Virgen de las Nieves, 2
13720 Cinco Casas (Ciudad Real)
☎: 926 529 010 - Fax: 926 526 070
jcutilla@domecqbodegas.com
www.domecqbodegas.com

ELEGIDO B

**75**

ELEGIDO RD

**65**

ELEGIDO S/C T

**80**

BLANCO EMPARRADO SEMI-DULCE

**80**

## CASTILLA Y LEÓN
### ALVARO ARRANZ

Ctra. de Valoria, s/n
47315 Pesquera (Valladolid)
☎: 983 339 581 - Fax: 983 339 581
info@alvaroarranz.com
www.alvaroarranz.com

ELIAZAR 2006 RD
tempranillo 100%

**87** Colour: onion pink, coppery red. Nose: medium intensity, elegant, candied fruit, fruit liqueur notes. Palate: flavourful, fleshy, spicy, round tannins.

### ARZUAGA NAVARRO

Ctra. N-122, km. 325
47350 Quintanilla de Onésimo (Valladolid)
☎: 983 681 146 - Fax: 983 681 147
bodeg@arzuaganavarro.com
www.arzuaganavarro.com

FAN D. ORO 2008 BFB
chardonnay 100%

**87** Colour: old gold, amber rim. Nose: dried herbs, creamy oak, ripe fruit, balsamic herbs. Palate: creamy, easy to drink, flavourful, fruity, fleshy.

### BODEGA RAMÓN RAMOS

Pozo, 35
49153 Venialbo (Zamora)
☎: 980 573 080 - Fax: 980 573 241
info@bodegaramonramos.com
www.bodegaramonramos.com

RICARDO SANCHEZ 2005 T
tempranillo

**86** Colour: dark-red cherry. Nose: macerated fruit, creamy oak. Palate: flavourful, round tannins.

RAMÓN RAMOS

## BODEGAS MARCOS MIÑAMBRES

Camino de Pobladura, s/n
24234 Villamañan (León)
☎: 987 767 038 - Fax: 987 767 371
satvined@picos.com

M. MIÑAMBRES 2008 B
albarín 100%

**88** Colour: straw, pale. Nose: ripe fruit, dry stone, varietal, expressive. Palate: powerful, fresh, fruity, good acidity.

M. MIÑAMBRES 2008 RD
prieto picudo, tempranillo

**81**

M. MIÑAMBRES 2006 T
prieto picudo, tempranillo

**79**

## BODEGAS Y VIÑEDOS CASTRO VENTOSA

Finca El Barredo, s/n
24530 Valtuille de Abajo (León)
☎: 987 562 148 - Fax: 987 562 191
castroventosa@telefonica.net
www.castroventosa.com

AIROLA 2008 B
chardonnay

**88** Colour: bright straw. Nose: varietal, expressive, ripe fruit, fruit expression. Palate: fruity, rich, flavourful, fleshy.

## ESTANCIA PIEDRA S.L.

Ctra. Toro - Salamanca, km 5
49800 Toro (Zamora)
☎: 980 693 900 - Fax: 980 693 901
info@estanciapiedra.com
www.estanciapiedra.com

LA GARONA 2004 TC
tinta de toro 75%, garnacha 25%

**90** Colour: cherry, garnet rim. Nose: powerful, earthy notes, sweet spices, aromatic coffee, dark chocolate. Palate: flavourful, fruity, fleshy, spicy.

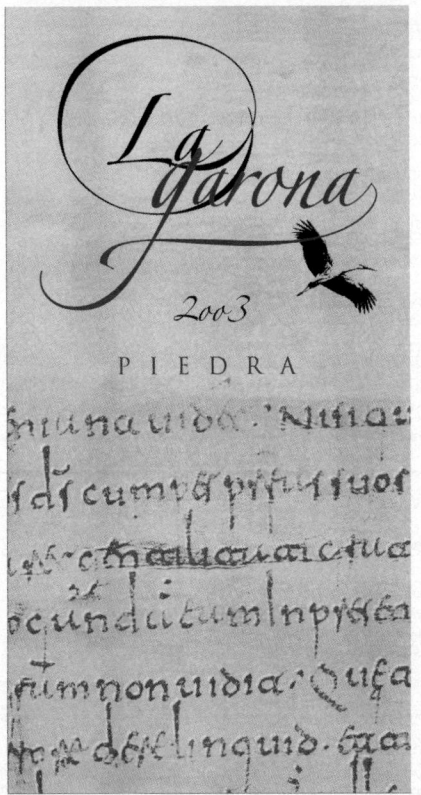

## LIBERALIA ENOLÓGICA

Camino del Palo, s/n
49800 Toro (Zamora)
☎: 980 692 571 - Fax: 980 692 571
byvliberalia@hotmail.com
www.liberalia.es

DURADERO 2007 T
tinta de toro 50%, tinta roriz 40%, touriga 10%

**91** Colour: bright cherry. Nose: ripe fruit, sweet spices, creamy oak, expressive, scrubland. Palate: flavourful, fruity, toasty, round tannins.

## PÉREZ CARAMÉS S.A.

Peña Picón, s/n
24500 Villafranca del Bierzo (León)
☎: 987 540 197 - Fax: 987 540 314
info@perezcarames.com
www.perezcarames.com

CASAR DE SANTA INÉS V 2005 T
merlot

**88** Colour: dark-red cherry. Nose: dark chocolate, sweet spices, fruit liqueur notes, fruit liqueur notes, undergrowth. Palate: fleshy, rich, fruity, mineral.

## QUINTA DE LA QUIETUD

Camino de Bardales, s/n
Apartado de Correos 34
49800 Toro (Zamora)
☎: 980 568 019 - Fax: 980 568 081
info@quintaquietud.com
www.quintaquietud.com

LA DULCE QUIETUD 2006 BLANCO DULCE
albillo, palomino, verdejo, malvasia, moscatel

**93** Colour: bright golden. Nose: candied fruit, fruit liqueur notes, acetaldehyde. Palate: flavourful, concentrated, sweet, spirituous, fleshy, great length, long.

## VIÑA MARINA

Jardines, 15
49123 Benejiles (Zamora)
☎: 690 036 102
soteropintado@gmail.com

VIÑA MARINA 2006 T ROBLE

**82**

VIÑA MARINA 2005 TC

**84**

VIÑA MARINA 2004 TR
tempranillo

**88** Colour: cherry, garnet rim. Nose: ripe fruit, spicy, creamy oak, toasty, dark chocolate. Palate: powerful, flavourful, toasty, round tannins.

# CATALUÑA
## CAVAS DEL AMPURDÁN

Pza. del Carme, 1
17491 Perelada (Girona)
☎: 972 538 011 - Fax: 972 538 277
perelada@castilloperelada.com
www.blancpescador.com

BLANC PESCADOR VINO DE AGUJA 2008 B
macabeo 60%, parellada 20%, xarel.lo 20%

**84**

CRESTA AZUL 2008 B
moscatel, macabeo, xarel.lo, parellada

**80**

CRESTA ROSA 2008 RD
tempranillo 40%, cariñena 40%, garnacha 20%

**80**

BLANC PESCADOR PREMIUM 2008 BLANCO DE AGUJA
xarel.lo 67%, chardonnay 33%

**84**

CRESTA ROSA PREMIUM 2008 ROSADO DE AGUJA
pinot noir 85%, syrah 15%

**83**

## CELLER MARIOL

Joan Miro, s/n
43786 Batea (Tarragona)
☎: 934 367 628 - Fax: 934 500 281
celler@cellermariol.es
www.cellermariol.es

JO! 2008 B
verdejo

**88** Colour: bright straw. Nose: powerful, ripe fruit, scrubland. Palate: flavourful, fruity, fresh, rich.

## CELLER RAMÓN SADURNI

Can Sadurni
08799 Olerdola (Barcelona)
☎: 666 771 308
auladelvi@hotmail.com

RR SADURNI 2008 B
xarel.lo

**85** Colour: bright straw. Nose: mineral, dry stone, fresh fruit. Palate: fine bitter notes, good acidity, easy to drink, fruity.

SADURNI 2008 RD
merlot

**87** Colour: onion pink. Nose: floral, fresh fruit, raspberry, expressive, fresh. Palate: balanced, fine bitter notes, fruity.

RR SADURNI 2004 T
cabernet sauvignon 50%, merlot 50%

**86** Colour: deep cherry, bright ochre rim. Nose: macerated fruit, creamy oak, sweet spices. Palate: fruity, good acidity, sweetness, round tannins.

## CLOS DE N'ARGÓ

Migdia, 6
43125 Gratallops (Tarragona)
☎: 699 503 099

CLOS DE N'ARGÓ 2007 T
garnacha, cabernet franc, cariñena, merlot, syrah

**78**

## DG VITICULTORS

Raval, 87
08737 Torrelles de Foix (Barcelona)
☎: 938 971 938 - Fax: 938 971 941
dgviticultors@dgviticultors.com
www.dgviticultors.com

CALIGO VI DE BOIRA 2005 B
chardonnay 100%

**91** Colour: bright golden. Nose: citrus fruit, candied fruit, honeyed notes, scrubland. Palate: fruity, rich, flavourful, good acidity, creamy.

# Caligo

VI DE BOIRA

DOLCE · DOCE

DOLCE · SÜSS · SWEET · DOUX · DULCE · DOLÇ

37,5 cl. · 12,5% vol.

Embotellat per R.E. 1600200CAT
per a DG Viticultors, S.L.
08796 Barcelona · SPAIN
VI DE TAULA

## HERETAT MONT-RUBÍ

L'Avellà, 1
08736 Font Rubí (Barcelona)
☎: 938 979 066 - Fax: 938 979 066
hmr@mont-rubi.com
www.mont-rubi.com

ADVENT 2007 B
xarel.lo 100%

**89** Colour: old gold. Nose: dry nuts, candied fruit, fruit liqueur notes, pattiserie, spicy. Palate: elegant, round, unctuous, good acidity.

DURONA 2005 T
sumoll, garnacha, cariñena, syrah, merlot

**91** Colour: dark-red cherry, orangey edge. Nose: ripe fruit, sweet spices, expressive, powerfull, elegant. Palate: ripe fruit, spicy, round tannins, flavourful, fruity, elegant.

GAINTUS 2005 T
sumoll 100%

**89** Colour: cherry, garnet rim. Nose: smoky, cedar wood, fruit expression, fruit preserve, earthy notes. Palate: flavourful, complex, fine tannins, balsamic.

GAINTUS 2004 T
sumoll

**89** Colour: bright cherry, garnet rim. Nose: expressive, balanced, fruit liqueur notes, sweet spices. Palate: flavourful, good structure, easy to drink, ripe fruit, long.

## JOAN SARDÀ

Ctra. Vilafranca- St. Jaume dels Domenys, km. 8,1
08732 Castellví de la Marca (Barcelona)
☎: 937 720 900 - Fax: 937 721 495
joansarda@joansarda.com
www.joansarda.com

BLANC DE SALOBRE BLANCO DULCE
pedro ximénez, moscatel, garnacha, macabeo

**87** Colour: old gold, amber rim. Nose: pattiserie, aged wood nuances, toasty, fruit liqueur notes. Palate: full, rich, flavourful, fine solera notes.

## PAGO DIANA

Manso Sant Mateu
17464 Sant Jordi Desvalls (Gerona)
☎: 636 572 693 - Fax: 934 172 279
manager@pagodiana.com

DIANEL.LO 2008 RD
temrpanillo

**85** Colour: onion pink. Nose: fresh fruit, floral, fresh. Palate: flavourful, fruity, fresh, full.

TERIA 2006 T

**87** Colour: bright cherry, orangey edge. Nose: fruit liqueur notes, red berry notes, caramel, aromatic coffee. Palate: spicy, ripe fruit, warm.

CLOS DIANA 2006 T

**87** Colour: cherry, garnet rim. Nose: medium intensity, ripe fruit, spicy, balsamic herbs. Palate: flavourful, spicy, easy to drink.

## PARDAS

Finca Can Comas, s/n
08775 Torrelavit (Barcelona)
☎: 938 995 005
pardas@cancomas.com
www.pardas.net

PARDAS SUMOLL ROSAT 2008 RD
sumoll 100%

**89** Colour: rose, purple rim. Nose: complex, fresh, expressive, red berry notes. Palate: flavourful, powerful, fruity, varietal.

## VINS DE TALLER

Nou, 5
17469 Siurana d'Empordà (Girona)
☎: 934 816 434 - Fax: 934 816 434
info@vinsdetaller.com
www.vinsdetaller.com

VINS DE TALLER CO 2008 BFB
cortese 100%

**84**

VINS DE TALLER VRM 2007 BFB
viognier 55%, rousanne 33%, marsanne 12%

**90** Colour: bright straw. Nose: fragrant herbs, ripe fruit, tropical fruit. Palate: flavourful, fleshy, ripe fruit.

VINS DE TALLER MM 2006 TC
merlot 69%, marselan 31%

**89** Colour: bright cherry. Nose: ripe fruit, sweet spices, creamy oak, expressive, scrubland, earthy notes. Palate: flavourful, fruity, toasty, round tannins.

## GALICIA
### BODEGAS FORJAS DEL SALNÉS

As Lovas, 5
36968 Xil (Santa Eulalia) (Pontevedra)
☎: 699 446 113 - Fax: 986 742 131
rodri@movistar.net

SKETCH 2007 B BARRICA
albariño 100%

**90** Colour: bright golden. Nose: scrubland, powerfull, characterful, creamy oak. Palate: powerful, flavourful, mineral, smoky aftertaste.

## LA RIOJA
### BODEGA LOS TINOS

Tinos 52
Alberite (La Rioja)
☎: 941 436 304

PRENSA REAL S/C T

**83**

VALVIEJO S/C T

**78**

VEGA ROBLE T

**76**

## HACIENDA MARQUÉS
## DE LA CONCORDIA

Ctra. El Ciego, s/n
26350 Cenicero (La Rioja)
☎: 914 365 900 - Fax: 914 365 932
info@haciendas-espana.com
www.haciendas-espana.com

PRÍNCIPE ALFONSO DE HOHENHOLE RESERVA
PRIVADA 2006 TR
cabernet sauvignon, tempranillo, syrah

**87** Colour: cherry, garnet rim. Nose: fruit preserve, balsamic herbs, sweet spices, cocoa bean. Palate: flavourful, fruity, grainy tannins, warm.

### ÁNDALUS PETIT VERDOT 2005 T
petit verdot 100%

**92** Colour: dark-red cherry, garnet rim. Nose: ripe fruit, sweet spices, dark chocolate, powerfull. Palate: unctuous, round, fruity, sweetness, spicy, round tannins.

## MURCIA
### BODEGA BALCONA

Democracia, 7
30180 Bullas (Murcia)
☎: 968 652 891
bodegabalcona@larural.es
www.partal-vinos.com

### CASA DE LA CRUZ 2005 T
syrah, merlot, cabernet sauvignon

**88** Colour: cherry, garnet rim. Nose: creamy oak, toasty, complex, fruit preserve. Palate: powerful, flavourful, toasty, round tannins.

### BODEGAS CASTAÑO

Ctra. Fuentealamo, 3 Apdo. 120
30510 Yecla (Murcia)
☎: 968 791 115 - Fax: 968 791 900
info@bodegascastano.com
www.bodegascastano.com

### CASA CISCA T

**93** Colour: cherry, garnet rim. Nose: ripe fruit, cocoa bean, aromatic coffee, expressive, elegant, complex. Palate: spicy, balsamic, fine tannins, balanced, spirituous, round tannins.

## PAÍS VASCO
### DOMINIO DE EGUREN

San Pedro, s/n
01309 Páganos (Álava)
☎: 945 600 117 - Fax: 945 600 554
info@eguren.com
www.eguren.com

### PROTOCOLO 2008 B

**83**

### PROTOCOLO 2008 RD

**87** Colour: rose, purple rim. Nose: violet drops, raspberry. Palate: powerful, flavourful, fruity, fresh.

### PROTOCOLO 2008 T

**86** Colour: dark-red cherry. Nose: fresh fruit, neat, varietal. Palate: flavourful, fresh, fruity, slightly dry, soft tannins.

## VALENCIA
### CELLER LA MUNTANYA

Rotonda Quatrecamins-Camí Alquerieta
03830 Muro de l'Alcoi (Alicante)
☎: 965 531 248 - Fax: 965 531 248
info@cellerlamuntanya.com
www.cellerlamuntanya.com

### ALBIR 2008 B
macabeo 40%, malvasia 40%, merseguera 15%, moscatel 5%

**87** Colour: bright straw. Nose: medium intensity, citrus fruit. Palate: flavourful, full, fruity, balanced, good acidity, fine bitter notes.

### CELLER LA MUNTANYA 2008 T
monastrell 43%, giró 20%, bobal 17%, garnacha 10%, bomicaire 10%

**90** Colour: dark-red cherry. Nose: fresh fruit, fruit expression, expressive, balsamic herbs. Palate: spicy, mineral, round tannins, good acidity.

### ALMOROIG 2006 T
monastrell 69%, giró 23%, garnacha 8%

**89** Colour: bright cherry. Nose: sweet spices, creamy oak, undergrowth, macerated fruit, complex. Palate: flavourful, fruity, toasty, round tannins.

### ALMOROIG 2005 T
monastrell 50%, giró 30%, garnacha tintorera 20%

**90** Colour: very deep cherry, garnet rim. Nose: warm, sweet spices, ripe fruit, mineral. Palate: flavourful, sweetness, round tannins, fruity.

### PAGO DE THARSYS

Ctra. Nacional III, Km 274
46340 Requena (Valencia)
☎: 962 303 354 - Fax: 962 329 000

# TABLE WINES

pagodetharsys@pagodetharsys.com
www.pagodetharsys.com

PAGO DE THARSYS VENDIMIA NOCTURNA 2008 B
albariño 80%, godello 20%

**89** Colour: bright straw. Nose: fresh, ripe fruit, citrus fruit, sweet spices. Palate: flavourful, fruity, fleshy, ripe fruit.

PAGO DE THARSYS NUESTRO BOBAL 2005 T
bobal 85%, cabernet franc 15%

**88** Colour: cherry, garnet rim. Nose: red berry notes, wild herbs, spicy. Palate: concentrated, fleshy, full, slightly dry, soft tannins.

PAGO DE THARSYS 2004 T
merlot 70%, cabernet franc 30%

**88** Colour: dark-red cherry, garnet rim. Nose: fresh fruit, varietal, cedar wood, aromatic coffee. Palate: flavourful, fruity, smoky aftertaste, spicy, soft tannins.

PAGO DE THARSYS SELECCIÓN BODEGA 2003 T
merlot 90%, cabernet franc 10%

**89** Colour: dark-red cherry. Nose: earthy notes, fruit preserve, creamy oak, toasty, spicy, characterful. Palate: fleshy, sweetness, spirituous, flavourful, powerful.

## PAGOS DEL MOLINO

Víctor Elías Martínez, 1 pta. 14
46340 Requena (Valencia)
☎: 615 267 249 - Fax: 962 305 102
dani@pagosdelmolino.com
www.pagosdelmolino.com

FUSSION DE BOBAL 2005 T
bobal, merlot, syrah, cabernet sauvignon, cabernet franc, petit verdot

**90** Colour: bright cherry. Nose: ripe fruit, sweet spices, creamy oak, expressive. Palate: flavourful, fruity, toasty, round tannins, fresh.

ARRAS DE BOBAL 2004 T
bobal 100%

**87** Colour: very deep cherry, bright ochre rim. Nose: fruit preserve, sweet spices, cocoa bean, warm. Palate: round, powerful, good acidity, round tannins.

## SALVADOR POVEDA

CV 830 - Ctra. Salinas, km. 3
03640 Monovar (Alicante)
☎: 966 960 180 - Fax: 965 473 389
salvadorpoveda@salvadorpoveda.com

www.salvadorpoveda.com

CANTALUZ 2007 B

**80**

ROSELLA RD

**82**

## VINS DEL COMTAT

Turballos, 1-3
03820 Alicante
☎: 965 593 194 - Fax: 965 593 590
info@vinsdelcomtat.com
www.vinsdelcomtat.com

ROSADO MONASTRELL 2008 RD

**88** Colour: rose, purple rim. Nose: powerful, ripe fruit, red berry notes, floral, expressive. Palate: fleshy, powerful, fruity, fresh, spirituous.

MONTCABRER 2005 T

**90** Colour: cherry, garnet rim. Nose: ripe fruit, spicy, creamy oak, toasty, complex, elegant. Palate: powerful, flavourful, toasty, round tannins, good structure.

PENYA CADIELLA SELECCIÓ 2005 T

**88** Colour: cherry, garnet rim. Nose: ripe fruit, spicy, creamy oak, toasty, complex, dry stone, balsamic herbs. Palate: powerful, flavourful, toasty, round tannins, warm, elegant.

PEÑA CADIELLA 2005 T ROBLE

**87** Colour: cherry, garnet rim. Nose: ripe fruit, spicy, creamy oak, toasty, complex, scrubland. Palate: powerful, flavourful, toasty, round tannins, spirituous.

VERDEVAL

## VIÑEDO Y BODEGA HERETAT DE CESILIA

Paraje Alcaydias, 4
03660 Novelda (Alicante)
☎: 965 603 763 - Fax: 965 603 763
comercial@casa-sicilia.com
www.heretatdecesilia.com

AZAL B

**89** Colour: bright straw. Nose: fresh, fresh fruit, white flowers, expressive. Palate: flavourful, fruity, good acidity, balanced.

CESILIA 2008 RD

**88** Colour: onion pink. Nose: elegant, candied fruit, dried flowers, fragrant herbs, red berry notes. Palate: light-bodied, flavourful, good acidity, long, spicy.

AD GAUDE 2005 T
monastrell 70%, syrah 15%, petit verdot 15%

**90** Colour: very deep cherry. Nose: toasty, dark chocolate, ripe fruit, fruit expression, fruit liqueur notes. Palate: powerful, flavourful, sweetness, spirituous, complex, toasty, mineral, ripe fruit.

HERETAT DE CESILIA SELECCIÓN DE BARRICAS T

**89** Colour: cherry, garnet rim. Nose: spicy, creamy oak, toasty, complex, fruit preserve. Palate: powerful, flavourful, toasty, round tannins.

LIZANA T
**83**

CARDENAL ALVAREZ 2005 TINTO

**89** Colour: pale ruby, brick rim edge. Nose: fruit preserve, dry nuts, dark chocolate, aged wood nuances, roasted almonds, cedar wood. Palate: fresh, flavourful.

SEÑOR DE SIRERA

## VIÑEDOS Y BODEGAS MAYO CASANOVA

San Antonio, 90
12192 Vilafamés (Castellón)
☎: 964 329 312 - Fax: 964 329 312
mail@mayocasanova.com
www.mayocasanova.com

MAGNANIMVS VINO DE AUTOR SERIE ORO 2006 T
merlot 30%, syrah 30%, cabernet sauvignon 30%, otras 10%

**89** Colour: cherry, garnet rim. Nose: powerful, aged wood nuances, cocoa bean, cedar wood. Palate: flavourful, powerful, spicy, slightly dry, soft tannins.

# GLOSARY

## AND

## INDEXES

## VOCABULARY

### TERMINOLOGY RELATED TO COLOUR.

**AMBER.** The first step in the oxidative ageing of sherry generoso wines, brandies, whiskies and rum, somewhere between yellow and coppery red.

**BEADS.** The slow rising string of bubbles in a sparkling wine.

**BRICK RED.** An orangey hue, similar to that of a brick, used to describe reds aged in bottle for more than 10 years or in barrel for longer than six.

**BRILLIANT.** Related to a young and neat wine.

**CANDY CHERRY.** This is used to define a colour lighter than a red but darker than a rosé.

**CLEAN.** Utterly clean, immaculate.

**CLOUDY.** Lacking clarity.

**COPPERY.** A reddish nuance that can be appreciated in whites aged in wood for a long period, generally amontillados and some palo cortados.

**CHERRY.** Commonly used to express red colour. It can take all sort of degrees from 'light' all the way to 'very dark' or almost 'black cherry'.

**DARK.** This often refers to a tone slightly lighter than 'deep' and synonymous to "medium-intensity".

**DEEP.** A red with a very dark colour, which hardly lets us see the bottom of the glass.

**DULL.** A wine lacking in liveliness, usually with an ochre hue.

**GARNET RED.** A common nuance in medium to light reds. If the wine is an intense cherry red it could have a garnet rim only if it comes from cooler regions; if it is more luminous and open than the violet rim of a dark wine, it generally would be a young wine.

**GOLDEN.** Gold in colour with yellow –predominantly– to reddish tones.

**GLIMMER.** A vague brilliance.

**IODINE.** A tone similar to iodine tincture stains (old gold and brownish) displayed by rancio and generoso wines have after their long oxidative ageing.

**LIVELY.** A reflection of the youth of a wine through bright, brilliant colours.

**MAHOGANY.** Describes the second stage of ageing in brandies, rum and generoso sherry (fortified) wines. A hue between brown and yellow displayed by wines when long aged.

**OCHRE.** Yellow-orangey hue, the last colour phase of a table wine, generally found in wines with a long oxidative ageing; it is a sign of their decline.

**OILY.** A wine that appears dense to the eye, usually sweet and with high alcohol content.

**OLD GOLD.** Gold colour with the brownish tones found in amontillados and a bit lighter than the mahogany nuance predominant in oloroso sherry.

**ONION SKIN.** A touch lighter than salmon colour.

**OPAQUE.** A wine with such depth of colour we cannot see the bottom of the glass. Generally found in very old pedro ximénez and therefore akin to caramelised notes.

**OPEN.** Very pale, not at all intense.

**ORANGEY EDGE.** Intermediate phase between a deep red and brick red found towards the rim in red wines of a medium age. It generally appears sooner in wines with higher alcohol content and it is also typical of wines made from pinot noir.

**RASPBERRY.** Sort of pinkish colour with a bluish rim, it is the optimal colour for rosé wines since it denotes freshness, youth and a good acidity.

**RIM.** Also known as 'edge', it refers to the lighter colour the wine displays at the edge of the oval when we hold the glass at 45°, as opposed to the 'core' or main body of colour right in the centre. If it is a young red, it will show normally violet or raspberry nuances; when slightly older, it will be a deeper red or garnet, and if has been in the bottle for more than five years it might be anything from ruby to tawny through brick red and orangey.

**RUBY.** Slightly orangey hue with a yellow nuance found in old wines that have lost part of their original cherry colour.

**SALMON.** A tone slightly redder than pink found in rosé wines with less acidity and more alcohol.

**STEELY.** Pale colour with metallic reflections (reminiscent of those from steel) found in some whites.

**STRAW-COLOURED.** This term should be understood as straw yellow, the colour found in the majority of young white wines, halfway between yellow and green. It can also be described as "lemony".

## TERMINOLOGY RELATED TO AROMA.

**ACETONE.** Very close notes to those of nail varnish, typical of very old eau de vie.

**ALCOHOL.** It is not a pejorative term for an excess of alcohol –in which case we would refer to it as burning–, but just a predominant, non-aggressive note.

**ALDEHYDE.** A sensory note of oxidized, slightly rancid alcohol, typical of old wines with high alcohol content that have undergone oxidative ageing.

**ANIMAL.** Not a positive note, generally the result of long storage in bottle, also referred to as 'wet dog' or 'wet hide' and normally associated with a lack of hygiene. If it is found in younger vintages, then it could be a symptom of "brett" (see brett).

**ATTIC.** An aroma associated with that of old dry wood and dust typical of attics, mainly found in fortified wines aged in wood and in very old wines aged for a long period in old barrels which happen to have also been bottled for more than ten years.

**BALSAMIC.** A trait usually associated to wood-aged wines in hot regions, where high temperatures accelerate their evolution. It also refers to the aroma of dry herbs such as eucalyptus and bay leaf, as well as incense and tar.

**BLACK FRUIT.** It refers to the sort of toasted aromas of very ripe grapes, those almost 'burnt skin' notes found in reds that have undergone a long vatting period in contact with the skins.

**"BRETT".** This is the abbreviation for a new term (brettanomyces) to describe an old problem: the aroma of stables, henhouse, and wet new leather generally found along with reductive off-odours in wines that have been in the bottle for more than ten years. These aromas were considered part of the sensory complexity of old wines and therefore tolerated. Nowadays, due to better olfactory research and more hygienic working conditions in the wineries, they are easily detected and considered more a defect. In addition, today brett is often found in younger wines as this particular bacteria or yeast usually develops better in wines with higher ph levels. The increase in the ph of wines is quite common these days due to global warming, riper grapes and the use of fertilizers over the past thirty-five years.

**BROOM.** An aroma reminiscent of Mediterranean shrubs, only a bit dryer.

**CANDIED FRUIT.** This is a sweet nuance, somewhere between toasted and jammy, which is found in whites with a long oxidative ageing and in some sweet white wines.

**CAROB.** Anybody who has chewed or smelt one of those beans cannot would easily recall its typical blend of sweetness and toasted notes, as well as the slightly rustic nuance. It is usually found in old brandy aged in soleras of pedro ximénez and in deep, concentrated wines made from very ripe grapes.

**CEDAR.** The somewhat perfumed aroma of cedar, a soft wood commonly found in Morocco.

**CITRUS.** An aroma reminiscent of lemon, orange and grapefruit.

**CLASSIC RIOJA.** A note named after the more traditional and popular style of Rioja, with predominantly woody notes (normally from very old wood) along with a typical character of sweet spices and occasionally candle wax nuances instead of fruit, given the oxidative character provided by long ageing periods.

**CLEAR.** A wine with no defects, neither in the nose nor in the palate.

**CLOSED.** A term to describe a faint or not properly developed nose. Almost always found in concentrated wines from a good vintage, which evolve very slowly in the bottle, but it can also be found in wines recently bottled.

**COCOA.** Delicate, slightly toasted aroma found in wines aged in wood for a moderately long time that have evolved very well in the bottle.

**COMPLEX.** A wine abundant in aromas and flavours related either to grape variety, soil or ageing, although none of those features is particularly prominent.

**CREAMY.** Aroma of finely toasted oak (usually French) with notes of caramelised vanilla.

**DATES.** A sweet aroma with hints of dates and a raisiny nuance.

**EARTHY.** An aroma somewhere between clay and dust typical of red wines made from ripe grapes and with high alcohol content. It can also refer in some wines to a mineral nuance.

**ELEGANT.** A harmonious combination of fine, somewhat restrained aromatic notes related to perfumed wood, and a light, pleasantly balanced richness or complexity (see complex).

**ETHEREAL.** This is used to describe spirits, fortified wines and wines with a certain intensity of alcohol in their oxidative evolution; the strength of the alcohol reveals the rancid-type aromas. It has a lot to do with age.

**WITHERED FLOWERS.** This is a sort of 'toasty' nuance typical of good champagnes made with a high percentage of pi-

not noir and some cavas which have aged perfectly in the bottle and on their lees for a long time.

**FINE.** A synonym for elegant.

**FINE LEES.** This is an aroma between herbaceous and slightly toasty that is produced by the contact of the wine with the lees (dead yeasts cells) after the fermentation has taken place, a process called autolysis that helps to make the wine more complex and to give it a richer aroma.

**FLOR.** This is a pungent, saline aroma typically found in sherry wines, particularly fino, manzanilla and, to a lesser degree, amontillado. It is caused by a film-forming yeast known as 'flor' in Spanish (literally flower), which transfers to the wine its singular smell and flavour.

**FLORAL.** Reminiscent of the petals of certain flowers –such as roses and jasmine–noticeable in certain northern withes or in quality reds after a bottle-ageing spell that also delivers some spicy notes.

**FRAGRANT HERBS.** An aroma similar to soaps and perfumes made from lavender, rosemary, lemon, orange blossom or jasmine. It is found in white wines that undergo pre-fermentative cold skin maceration.

**FRESH.** A wine with lively aroma and hardly any alcohol expression.

**FRESH FRUIT.** These are fruity notes produced by a slow grape-ripening cycle typical of mild climates.

**FRUIT EXPRESSION.** Related to different flavours and aromas reminiscent of various fruits and fine herbs.

**FRUITY.** Fruit notes with a fine herbal character and even hints of green grass.

**HERBACEOUS.** A vague note of vine shoots, scrub and geranium leaf caused by an incomplete maturation of the grape skin.

**INTENSE.** A powerful aroma that can be immediately referred to as such when first nosing the wine.

**IODINE.** This refers to iodine tincture, a combination of the sweetish smell of alcohol, toasted notes, liniment and varnish or lacquer.

**JAM.** Typical notes of very ripe black fruit slightly caramelised by a slow oxidative ageing in oak barrels. Very similar to forest fruit jam (prunes, blackberries, blueberries, redcurrants, cherries…). Found in red wines –generally from southern regions– with a high concentration of fruit notes giving that they are made resorting to long vatting periods, which provide longer contact with the skins.

**MACERATION.** These are aromas similar to those produced during fermentation and that –logically– found in young wines.

**MEDITERRANEAN.** An aroma where various prominent notes (sweetness, alcohol, burning and raisiny notes, caramel…) produced by grapes grown in hot regions blend in to characterize the wines.

**MINERAL NOTES.** Used to describe wines that have a subtle nose with plenty of notes reminiscent of flint, slate, hot stones or dry sand.

**MUSK.** A term to describe the sweet and grapey notes typical of highly aromatic varieties such as moscatel, riesling and gewürztraminer.

**ROASTED COFFEE.** (See terms of taste).

**SUBDUED FRUIT.** It generally refers to aromas produced by a fast ripening of the grapes typical of warm climates.

**EVOLUTION NOTES.** Generally used to describe wines aged prematurely by either oxygen or heat, e.g., a wine that has been left in a glass for several hours.

**NUTS.** Notes generally found in white wines with oxidative ageing; the oxygen in the air gives rise to aromas and flavours reminiscent of nuts (bitter almond, hazelnut, walnut…). When ageing spells are longer and –most importantly– take place in older casks, there will appear notes that are closer to fruits like figs, dates and raisins.

**ORANGE PEEL.** Typical fruity aroma found in certain white wines with, above all, a vibrant spicy character.

**ORGANIC NOTES.** A way to define the fermentative aromas – essentially related to yeast– and typical of young white wines and also fortified generoso wines from the sherry region.

**OVERRIPE FRUIT.** An aroma typical of young wines that are already slightly oxidized and reminiscent of grape bunches with some signs of rot –noble or not–, or simply bruised or recently pressed grapes.

**OXIDATIVE EVOLUTION.** Notes related to the tendency of a wine to age by the action of oxygen that passes through the pores of the cask or barrel (micro-oxidation), or during racking.

**PATISSERIE.** An aroma between sweet and toasted with hints of caramelised sugar and vanilla typical of freshly baked cakes. It is found in wines –generally sweet– that have been aged in oak for a long time and it is caused by both oxidative evolution and the aromatic elements (mainly vanillin) found in oak.

**PEAT.** A slightly burnt aroma that occurs when the notes of ripe grapes blend in with the toasted aromas of new oak in wines with a high alcohol content.

**PHENOLIC.** A short and derivative way to describe polyphenols (a combination of the tannins and anthocyanins, vegetal elements of the grape), it describes aromas of grape skins macerated for a long time that yield notes somewhere between ink and a pressed bunch of grapes.

**TAR.** The pitchy, petrolly aromas of very toasted wood, associated with concentrated red wines with lots of colour, structure and alcohol.

**PORT.** This is the sweet aroma of wine made from somewhat raisiny or overripe grapes and reminiscent of the vintage Ports made with a short oxidative ageing.

**PUNGENT.** A prominent aromatic note produced by the combination of alcohol, wood and flor notes and typical of –particularly– fino sherry wines.

**RANCIO.** This is not a defect but a note better known as "sherryfied" and brought about by oxidative ageing.

**RED FRUIT.** An aromatic note that refers to forest red fruits (blackberries, redcurrants, mulberries) as well as slightly unripe cherries and plums.

**REDUCTION.** A wine aroma caused by the lack of oxygen during long bottle ageing, which gives rise to notes like tobacco, old leather, vanilla, cinnamon, cocoa, attic, dust, etc.

**REDUCTION OFF-ODOURS.** This is a negative set of aromas, halfway between boiled cabbage and boiled eggs, produced by the lees in wines that have not been properly aerated or racked.

**REDUCTIVE TANK OFF-ODOURS.** A smell between metal and boiled fruit typical of wines stored in large vats at high temperatures. The sulphur added –probably in excess– combines with the wine and reduces its freshness and the expression of fruit notes. This phenomenon is largely found in the production of bulk wines.

**RIPE GRAPE SKIN.** The aroma that a very ripe grape gives off when squeezed, similar to that of ink or of ripe grape bunches just pressed.

**SALINE.** This is the note acquired by a fino that has aged in soleras under flor yeast.

**SEASONED WOOD.** It refers to notes that may appear in wines aged in barrel for a long period –more than four or five years– which have lost the fine toasted aromas and flavours of new oak.

**SHRUB.** An aroma typically herbal found in Mediterranean regions, a mixture of rosemary, thyme and other typically semi-arid herbs. It refers to the dry, herbaceous note found generally in white and red wines from warmer regions.

**SOLERA.** An aroma close to the damp, seasoned, aged aroma of an old bodega for oloroso wines.

**SPICY.** It refers to the most common household spices (pepper, cloves, cinnamon) that appear in wines that undergo long and slow oxidative ageing in oak casks or barrels.

**SPIRITUOUS.** Both a flavour and an olfactory feature related to high alcohol content but without burning sensations. It is an almost 'intellectual' term to define alcohol, since that product is nothing else but the "spirit of wine".

**STEWED FRUIT.** Notes of stewed or 'cooked' fruit appear in wines made from well-ripened –not overripe– grapes and are similar to those of jam.

**TERROIR.** An aromatic note determined by the soil and climate and therefore with various nuances: mountain herbs, minerals, stones, etc.

**TOASTED SUGAR.** Sweet caramelised aromas.

**TOFFEE.** A note typical of the milk coffee creams (lactic and toasted nuances mixed together) and present in some crianza red wines.

**TROPICAL NOTES.** The sweet white fruit aromas present in white wines made from grapes that have ripened very quickly and lack acidity.

**TRUFFLE.** Similar note to that of a mixture of damp earth and mushrooms.

**UNDERGROWTH.** This is the aromatic nuance between damp earth, grass and fallen leaves found in well-assembled, wood-aged reds that have a certain fruity expression and good phenolic concentration.

**VANILLA.** A typical trait of wines –also fortified– aged in oak, thanks to the vanillin, an element contained in that type of wood.

**VARIETAL EXPRESSION.** This is the taste and aroma of the variety or varieties used to make the wine.

**VARNISH.** A typical smell found in very old or fortified wines due to the oxidation of the alcohol after a long wood-ageing period. The varnished-wood note is similar to the aroma of eau de vie or spirits aged in wood.

**VISCOUS.** The sweet taste and aromatic expression of wines with high alcohol content.

**VOLATILE.** A note characteristic of wines with high volatile acidity, i.e., just the first sign of them turning into vinegar. It is typical of poorly stabilized young wines or aged wines either with a high alcohol content or that have taken on this note during the slow oxidative wood-ageing phase, although we should remember it is a positive trait in the case of generoso wines.

**WINE PRESS.** The aroma of the vegetal parts of the grape after fermentation, vaguely reminiscent of pomace brandy, grapeskins and ink.

**CHARACTERFUL.** Used to express the singularity of a wine above the rest. It may refer to winemaking, terroir or the peculiarities of its ageing.

**WOODY.** It describes an excess of notes of wood in a wine. The reason could be either a too long ageing period or the wine's lack of structure.

**VARNISHED WOOD.** A sharp note typical of wines aged in wood for a long period, during which the alcohol oxidises and gives off an aroma of acetone, wood or nail varnish.

**YEASTY.** The dry aroma of bread yeast that can be perceived in young cavas or champagnes, or wines that have just been bottled.

## TERMINOLOGY RELATED TO THE PALATE

**ALCOHOL.** A gentle, even sweet note of fine spirits; it is not a defect.

**ALCOHOLIC EDGES.** A slight excess of alcohol perceived on the tongue, but which does not affect the overall appreciation of the wine.

**BITTER.** A slight, non-aggressive note of bitterness, often found in some sherry wines (finos, amontillados) and the white wines from Rueda; it should not be regarded as a negative feature, quite on the contrary, it helps to counterbalance soft or slightly sweet notes.

**CARAMELISED.** A very sweet and toasted note typical of some unctuous wines aged in oloroso or pedro ximénez casks.

**DENSE.** This is related to the body of the wine, a thick sensation on the palate.

**FATNESS.** "Gordo" (fat) is the adjective used in Jerez to describe a wine with good body; it is the antonym of "fino" (light).

**FLABBY.** Used to describe a wine low in acidity that lacks freshness.

**FLAVOURFUL.** A pronounced and pleasant sensation on the palate produced by the combination of various sweet nuances.

**FULL.** A term used to describe volume, richness, some sweetness and round tannins; that is, a wine with a fleshy character and an almost fat palate.

**AMPLE.** A term used to describe richness. It is a sensation generally experienced on the attack.

**LIGHT.** The opposite of meaty, dense or concentrated; i.e., a wine with little body.

**LONG.** This refers to the persistence of the flavour after the wine has been swallowed.

**MEATY.** A wine that has body, structure and which can almost literally be "chewed".

**NOTES OF WOOD.** Well-defined notes somewhere between woody and resin generally found in wines matured in younger casks.

**OILY.** This is the supple, pleasantly fat sensation produced by glycerine. It is more prominent in older wines –thanks to the decrease in acidity– or in certain varieties such as riesling, gewürztraminer, chardonnay, albariño and godello.

**OXIDATIVE AGEING.** It refers to the influence of the air in the evolution of wine. Depending on the level of oxygen in the air, oxidation will take place in wine to a greater or lesser extent. Oxidative ageing happens when the air comes in contact with the wine either during racking –which ages the wine faster– or through the pores of the wood.

**PASTY.** This is not a pejorative term, simply a very sweet and dense taste.

**ROASTED COFFEE.** The sweet and toasted note of caramelised sugar typically found in wines aged in oak barrels –generally burnt inside–, or else the taste of very ripe (sometimes even overripe) grapes.

**ROUGH TANNINS.** Just unripe tannins either from the wood or the grape skins.

**ROUND.** This is an expression commonly used to describe a wine without edges, supple, with volume and body.

**SWEETENED.** Related to sweetness, only with an artificial nuance.

**SWEETNESS.** A slightly sweet note that stands out in a wine with an overall dry or tannic character.

**SOFT TANNINS.** Both alcohol and adequately ripened grapes help to balance out the natural bitter character of the tannins. They are also referred to as fat or oily tannins.

**TANNIC.** This is term derived from tannin, a substance generally found in the skin of the grape and in the wood that yields a somewhat harsh, vegetal note. In wines, it displays a slightly harsh, sometimes even grainy texture.

**UNCTUOUS.** This refers to the fat, pleasant note found in sweet wines along with their somewhat sticky sweetness.

**VELVETY.** A smooth, pleasant note on the palate typical of great wines where the tannins and the alcohol have softened down during ageing.

**VIGOROUS.** A wine with high alcohol content.

**WARM.** The term speaks of alcohol in a more positive way.

**WELL-BALANCED.** A term that helps to define a good wine: none of the elements that are part of it (alcohol, acidity, dry extract, oak) is more prominent than the other, just pure balance.

# THE BEST WINES FROM EACH REGION

## ABONA

90 ..TIERRA DE FRONTOS TINTO CLÁSICO 2008 T ......................39
89 ..FLOR DE CHASNA 2007 T .............................................40
89 ..FLOR DE CHASNA 2008 T BARRICA...............................40
89 ..TIERRAS DE APONTE MALVASÍA DULCE 2006 B ...............41
88 ..LOS TABLEROS 2008 B BARRICA ...................................39
88 ..MAGMATICO 2008 T ....................................................40
88 ..MARQUES DE FUENTE B ..............................................40
88 ..TESTAMENTO MALVASÍA ESENCIA 2006 B DULCE ...........40
87 ..LOS TABLEROS 2007 T BARRICA....................................39
87 ..TESTAMENTO MALVASÍA 2008 B BARRICA .......................39
87 ..TESTAMENTO MALVASÍA DRY 2008 B .............................39
87 ..VIÑA TAMAIDE 2008 B ..................................................40
86 ..FLOR DE CHASNA 2008 T ..............................................40
86 ..TIERRA DE FRONTOS BLANCO CLÁSICO 2008 B ...............39
86 ..TIERRA DE FRONTOS ECOLÓGICO 2008 B .......................39
86 ..VIÑA ARESE AFRUTADO 2008 B......................................40
85 ..FLOR DE CHASNA SEMISECO 2008 B .............................39
85 ..MENCEY DE CHASNA 2008 B .........................................39
85 ..PAGOS REVERÓN 2007 T BARRICA..................................40
85 ..TIERRA DE FRONTOS BLANCO SELECCIÓN 2007 B ..........39

## ALELLA

92 ..MARFIL MUY DULCE 2003 B ............................................45
90 ..ALTA ALELLA ORBUS 2007 TC ........................................45
90 ..DADES ALTA ALELLA BLANC DOLÇ 2008 B.......................45
90 ..IN VITA 2008 B .............................................................46
90 ..MARFIL GENEROSO SEMI 1976 B ...................................45
90 ..MARFIL VIOLETA 2003 T ................................................45
89 ..ALTA ALELLA LANIUS 2008 B ........................................45
89 ..MARQUÉS DE ALELLA ALLIER 2007 BFB .........................46
88 ..ALTA ALELLA PARVUS SYRAH 2007 T..............................45
88 ..IVORI 2008 B ...............................................................45
88 ..MARFIL GENEROSO SEC 1976 B DULCE ..........................45
88 ..MARQUÉS DE ALELLA PANSA BLANCA 2008 B ..................46
87 ..ALTA ALELLA DOLÇ MATARÓ 2008 TINTO DULCE ..............45
87 ..ALTA ALELLA PARVUS 2008 RD.......................................45
87 ..MARQUÉS DE ALELLA PANSA BLANCA XAREL.LO 2008 B ..46
87 ..MARQUÉS DE ALELLA VIOGNIER 2008 B ..........................46
86 ..ROURA CRIANZA TRES CEPS 2006 TC ............................46
85 ..EXEO 2008 B ...............................................................45
85 ..MARFIL 2006 TC ..........................................................45
85 ..ROURA MERLOT ROSAT 2008 RD ...................................46

## ALICANTE

94 ..BERYNA SELECCIÓN 2005 T ..........................................56
94 ..CASA BALAGUER 2006 T ...............................................56
94 ..EL SEQUÉ 2007 T ROBLE ..............................................60
94 ..SALINAS 1237 2006 T....................................................59
93 ..CASTA DIVA ESENCIAL 2008 B........................................57
93 ..CASTA DIVA FONDILLÓN 1987 1987 FONDILLÓN ..............58
93 ..ENRIQUE MENDOZA SANTA ROSA 2004 TR ......................61
93 ..MIRA SALINAS 2006 T ...................................................59
92 ..BERYNA 2007 T ...........................................................55
92 ..CASTA DIVA FONDILLÓN 1999 FONDILLÓN .......................58
92 ..CASTA DIVA FONDILLÓN SOLERA 1978 FONDILLÓN...........58
92 ..CASTA DIVA FURTIVA LÁGRIMA 2008 B ............................57
92 ..CASTA DIVA RESERVA REAL 2002 B RESERVA ..................57
91 ..CASTA DIVA COSECHA MIEL 2008 B ................................57
91 ..EL SEQUÉ 2006 T ROBLE ..............................................60

91 ..ENRIQUE MENDOZA MOSCATEL DE LA
MARINA 2008 B ..........................................................60
91 ..ENRIQUE MENDOZA SHIRAZ 2005 TC..............................60
91 ..ESTRECHO MONASTRELL 2005 T ...................................60
91 ..MIRA SALINAS 2007 T ...................................................59
90 ..BAHIA DE DÉNIA MOSCATEL DE LA MARINA
ALTA 2008 B JOVEN ....................................................55
90 ..BOCA NEGRA MONASTRELL 2006 TC ..............................52
90 ..CAMPS DE GLORIA 2006 B............................................59
90 ..CASTA DIVA RECONDITA ARMONIA 2007 T ......................57
90 ..CRISTAL.LI B ..............................................................63
90 ..FONDILLÓN 1987 1987 GE GRAN RESERVA......................63
90 ..LEVA DANIEL'S 2006 T ..................................................54
90 ..MIGUEL NAVARRO SELECCIÓN 2008 B.............................60
90 ..MIGUEL NAVARRO SELECCIÓN MONASTRELL
TEMPRANILLO 2007 T .................................................60
90 ..MIGUEL NAVARRO SELECCIÓN SYRAH MERLOT 2007 T ....60
90 ..PUERTO SALINAS 2006 T ..............................................59

## ALMANSA

91 ..ADARAS 2006 T ...........................................................68
91 ..LA HUELLA DE ADARAS 2007 T JOVEN.............................68
90 ..ADARAS 2005 T ...........................................................68
90 ..ADARAS SELECCIÓN 2008 B..........................................68
90 ..ATALAYA 2008 T ..........................................................69
89 ..HIGUERUELA 2008 T.....................................................69
88 ..1752 2006 T BARRICA...................................................69
88 ..ATALAYA 2007 T ..........................................................69
88 ..LA VEGA DE ADARAS 2005 T .........................................68
87 ..TUDON'S 2006 T ..........................................................68
86 ..CASTILLO DE ALMANSA SELECCIÓN 2004 TR ..................69
85 ..EL CALIZO DE ADARAS 2008 T.......................................68

## ARABAKO TXAKOLINA

86 ..SEÑORÍO DE ASTOBIZA 2008 B .....................................73

## ARLANZA

90 ..BUEZO NATTAN 2004 TC ...............................................79
89 ..BUEZO PETIT VERDOT 2004 TC ......................................79
89 ..BUEZO TEMPRANILLO 2004 TC ......................................79
88 ..BUEZO VARIETALES 2004 TC .........................................79
88 ..VIÑA VALDABLE 2008 T .................................................78
87 ..DOMINIO DE MANCILES 2007 B ......................................78
87 ..PAGOS DE NEGREDO MAGNUM 2005 TC ..........................79
87 ..TINTO LERMA 2006 TC ..................................................79
86 ..DOMINIO DE MANCILES 2007 T ROBLE ............................78
86 ..GARMENDIA 2008 T ......................................................78
86 ..VALDEMANSILLA 2002 TC .............................................78

## ARRIBES

92 ..LA SETERA SELECCIÓN ESPECIAL 2007 T .......................84
92 ..TERRAZGO 2006 T.........................................................85
91 ..CONDADO DE FERMOSEL"TRANSITIUM DURII" 2005 T .......85
91 ..CONDADO DE FERMOSEL"TRANSITIUM DURII" 2006 T .......85
90 ..DURIUS MAGISTER 2005 T .............................................84
90 ..GRAN ABADENGO 2005 TR .............................................84
89 ..BRUÑAL 2004 TC..........................................................84
89 ..LA SETERA 2006 TC ......................................................84
88 ..ABADENGO JUAN GARCÍA 2007 T ROBLE...........................84

# THE BEST WINES FROM EACH REGION

# THE BEST WINES FROM EACH REGION

## EMPORDÀ

# THE BEST WINES FROM EACH REGION

## MONTSANT

## NAVARRA

# THE BEST WINES FROM EACH REGION

## RIAS BAIXAS

# THE BEST WINES FROM EACH REGION

# THE BEST WINES FROM EACH REGION

# THE BEST WINES FROM EACH REGION

**90** ..VIÑA SASTRE 2007 T ROBLE .................................555
**90** ..VIÑEDOS Y BODEGAS LA PLANTA 2008 T ROBLE ...........543
**90** ..VIYUELA 10 2006 T .........................................567

## RIBERA DEL GUADIANA

**93** ..HUNO MATANEGRA 2007 TC .............................604
**92** ..ALUNADO 2008 BFB ......................................604
**91** ..HUNO 2007 TC ............................................604
**90** ..MACARENO 2006 TC ......................................606
**90** ..VIÑA PUEBLA CHARDONNAY 2008 B ..................602
**89** ..VEGA HERRERA 2008 B ..................................604
**89** ..VIÑA PUEBLA SELECCIÓN 2008 T ......................602
**88** ..VIÑA PUEBLA 2008 BFB ..................................602
**88** ..ZALEO SELECCIÓN 2007 T ..............................605
**87** ..FUENTE CORTIJO 2005 TC ...............................601
**87** ..RASGO 2006 T ROBLE .....................................606
**87** ..SEÑORÍO DE ALANGE SYRAH 2008 T ...................606
**87** ..SEÑORÍO DE ALANGE TEMPRANILLO 2008 T ...........606
**87** ..TORREMAYOR 2003 TR ....................................606
**87** ..VEGA HERRERA 2007 T ROBLE ..........................604
**87** ..VIÑA PUEBLA ESENZIA 2006 TC ........................602
**87** ..VIÑA ROJA COUPAGE 2005 TC ..........................601

## RIBERA DEL JÚCAR

**88** ..ADAR 2007 T ...............................................611
**88** ..CINCO ALMUDES TEMPRANILLO 2008 T ...............610
**88** ..CINCO ALMUDES TRADICIÓN JÚCAR 2007 T ...........610
**88** ..TEATINOS CLAROS DE CUBA 2005 TR ..................611
**87** ..ALBAK 2005 T ..............................................611
**87** ..FURIA DE ELVIWINES 2005 TC ...........................611
**87** ..NESS 2008 T ................................................611
**87** ..TEATINOS TEMPRANILLO 2008 T ........................611
**87** ..VEGA MORAGONA TEMPRANILLO 2007 T JOVEN ........612
**86** ..CASA GUALDA SYRAH 2007 T ...........................611
**86** ..NESS 2008 B ...............................................611
**86** ..VEGA MORAGONA 2006 TC ..............................612

## RIOJA

**98** ..VIÑA EL PISÓN 2007 T ....................................664
**97** ..CASTILLO YGAY 2001 TGR ...............................685
**97** ..CONTADOR 2007 T ........................................622
**96** ..AVRVS 2005 T .............................................674
**96** ..CIRSION 2007 T ............................................656
**96** ..DALMAU 2005 TR ..........................................684
**96** ..FINCA EL BOSQUE 2007 T................................692
**96** ..LA VIÑA DE ANDRÉS ROMEO 2007 T ...................622
**95** ..ARTADI PAGOS VIEJOS 2007 T ..........................664
**95** ..CASTILLO YGAY 2000 TGR ...............................685
**95** ..DALMAU 2004 TR ..........................................684
**95** ..DIGMA 2005 T .............................................631
**95** ..MALPUESTO 2007 T ......................................651
**95** ..MARTIRES 2008 B .........................................673
**95** ..SIERRA CANTABRIA COLECCIÓN PRIVADA 2007 T ......692
**94** ..ALTOS DE LANZAGA 2006 T .............................669
**94** ..AMANCIO 2006 T ..........................................692
**94** ..ARO 2005 T .................................................648
**94** ..CALVARIO 2006 T ..........................................673
**94** ..CALVARIO 2007 T ..........................................673
**94** ..CAPELLANIA 2004 B .......................................684
**94** ..CAPELLANIA 2005 B .......................................684

**94** ..CIRSION 2006 T ............................................656
**94** ..CONTINO VIÑA DEL OLIVO 2007 T .......................699
**94** ..CULMEN 2005 TR ..........................................681
**94** ..DIGMA 2006 T .............................................631
**94** ..GAUDIUM GRAN VINO 2004 TR ..........................683
**94** ..GLORIA DE OSTATU 2005 T ..............................652
**94** ..GRAN RESERVA 904 RIOJA ALTA 1997 TGR..............681
**94** ..LA CUEVA DEL CONTADOR 2007 T ......................622
**94** ..LA NIETA 2007 T ...........................................699
**94** ..PLÁCET VALTOMELLOSO 2008 B .........................689
**94** ..REMELLURI 2005 TR .......................................676
**94** ..REMÍREZ DE GANUZA 2004 TR ..........................638
**94** ..SIERRA CANTABRIA 2004 TGR ...........................692
**93** ..ALLENDE 2007 B ...........................................673
**93** ..AVRVS 2006 T .............................................673
**93** ..CAMPILLO FINCA CUESTA CLARA 2004 T................668
**93** ..CONTINO VIÑA DEL OLIVO 2005 T .......................700
**93** ..EGOMEI ALMA 2005 T.....................................674
**93** ..FINCA TORREA 2006 TR ...................................633
**93** ..IMPERIAL 2004 TR .........................................671
**93** ..INSPIRACIÓN VALDEMAR COLECCIÓN
          VARIETALES 2005 T ...................................661
**93** ..INSPIRACIÓN VALDEMAR EDICIÓN LIMITADA 2004 T ...661
**93** ..LA VICALANDA 2004 TR ...................................629
**93** ..LETRAS 2006 T ............................................617
**93** ..LUIS MEDRANO GRACIANO 2007 T.......................647
**93** ..MARQUÉS DE ARIENZO VENDIMIA SELECCIONADA
          2006 T RESERVA ESPECIAL ............................635
**93** ..MARQUÉS DE CÁCERES 2004 TR ........................684
**93** ..MARQUÉS DE RISCAL 2003 TGR...........................633
**93** ..MARQUES DE RISCAL SELECCIÓN GEHRY 2001 T .........633
**93** ..MC MARQUÉS DE CÁCERES 2006 T ......................683
**93** ..MENTOR ROBERTO TORRETTA 2005 T....................647
**93** ..PAISAJES VIII LA PASADA 2006 T ........................689
**93** ..QUÉ BONITO CACAREABA 2008 B ........................621
**93** ..REAL DE ASÚA 2004 T ....................................671
**93** ..REMELLURI 2007 B..........................................676
**93** ..RODA I 2005 TR.............................................656
**93** ..SIERRA CANTABRIA ORGANZA 2007 B ...................692
**93** ..VIÑA ARDANZA 2001 TR....................................681
**92** ..ABEL MENDOZA GRACIANO GRANO A GRANO 2006 T ......621
**92** ..ABEL MENDOZA TEMPRANILLO GRANO A
          GRANO 2006 T ........................................621
**92** ..ALBA DE BRETÓN 2004 TR................................630
**92** ..ALLENDE 2004 T ...........................................673
**92** ..AMAREN GRACIANO 2006 TC .............................626
**92** ..ANTIÓN PREMIUM 2005 T .................................628
**92** ..BARÓN LADRÓN DE GUEVARA DE AUTOR 2006 TC ......660
**92** ..CERRADO DEL CASTILLO 2005 T ........................669
**92** ..CONTINO GRACIANO 2006 T ..............................699
**92** ..GLORIA DE OSTATU 2006 T ..............................652
**92** ..HIRU 3 RACIMOS 2006 T ..................................645
**92** ..LAN EDICIÓN LIMITADA 2006 T ..........................681
**92** ..LANZAGA 2006 T ..........................................670
**92** ..LOS DOMINIOS DE BERCEO PREFILOXÉRICO 2006 TC ......629
**92** ..MARIA REMIREZ DE GANUZA 2004 T ....................638
**92** ..MARQUÉS DE CÁCERES 2001 TGR .......................684
**92** ..MARQUÉS DE MURRIETA 2004 TR ........................684
**92** ..MARQUÉS DE VARGAS HACIENDA PRADOLAGAR
          2004 TR ...............................................645
**92** ..MARQUÉS DE VARGAS RESERVA PRIVADA 2005 TR ......645
**92** ..OSTATU 2005 TR ..........................................652
**92** ..PREDICADOR 2007 T ......................................622

# THE BEST WINES FROM EACH REGION

# THE BEST WINES FROM EACH REGION

## TIERRA DEL VINO DE ZAMORA

93 ..CENIT 2006 T ................................................782
93 ..CENIT 2007 T ................................................782
91 ..DEMORA 2006 T ...........................................782
91 ..DEMORA 2007 T ...........................................782
91 ..VENTA MAZARRÓN 2007 T ............................782
87 ..NOVO 2005 T ROBLE......................................782
86 ..ALTER ENOS 2006 B ......................................782

## TORO

96 ..PINTIA 2007 T ...............................................796
95 ..PAGO LA JARA 2006 T ...................................797
95 ..TERMANTHIA 2006 T .....................................788
94 ..ELÍAS MORA 2004 TR .....................................787
94 ..GRAN ELÍAS MORA 2005 T..............................787
94 ..NVMANTHIA 2006 T .......................................788
94 ..PACIENCIA 2006 T .........................................798
94 ..QUINTA QUIETUD 2005 T ................................802
94 ..VICTORINO 2007 T .........................................802
93 ..CYAN PAGO DE LA CALERA 2001 TR ................786
93 ..DOMINIO DEL BENDITO 2007 T ROBLE..............798
93 ..EL ALBAR BARRICAS 2006 T ...........................787
93 ..EL ALBAR EXCELENCIA 2006 T ........................787
93 ..EL TITAN DEL BENDITO 2006 T .......................798
93 ..ELÍAS MORA 2006 TC ....................................787
93 ..PINTIA 2006 T ...............................................796
93 ..SAN ROMÁN 2006 T .......................................795
93 ..TEMPERANCIA 2006 T ....................................798
92 ..ALABASTER 2007 T.........................................802
92 ..DOMINIO DE VALDELACASA 2006 T .................787
92 ..EL TITAN DEL BENDITO 2005 T .......................798
92 ..FINCA LA MEDA 2004 TR ................................801
92 ..LIBERALIA CABEZA DE CUBA 2005 TC .............800
92 ..LIBERALIA CINCO 2004 TR..............................800
92 ..LIBERALIA TRES 2007 T ROBLE ......................800
92 ..MORFEO 2007 T .............................................802
92 ..SPIRITUS SANCTI 2006 T ...............................798
92 ..VEGA SAÚCO "TO" 2005 TC ............................795
91 ..ADOREMUS 2004 TR .......................................795
91 ..ALMIREZ 2007 T ............................................803
91 ..CAMPO ELISEO 2004 T ..................................787
91 ..FINCA SOBREÑO 2005 TC...............................793
91 ..GRAN BAJOZ 2005 TC.....................................801
91 ..INARAJA 2005 T .............................................792
91 ..JUAN ROJO 2005 T .........................................795
91 ..LA MULA DE LA QUIETUD 2005 T ....................802
91 ..LIBER 2003 TGR .............................................800
91 ..NOVELLUM REJADORADA 2006 TC ...................793
91 ..PALACIO DE VILLACHICA 5T 2003 T ................801
91 ..PEÑA REJAS 2004 TR .....................................789
91 ..PIEDRA ROJA 2005 TC ...................................798
91 ..ROMPESEDAS 2006 T .....................................798
91 ..VALMORO 2006 T ...........................................786
91 ..VILLAESTER 2003 T ........................................803
91 ..VIÑA EL TORILÓN 2005 TC..............................795
90 ..ARBUCALA 2006 T..........................................796
90 ..ARCO DE GUÍA ROBLE ESPAÑOL 2006 T ROBLE ...797
90 ..CASTILLO MONTE LA REINA 2007 T ROBLE.......791
90 ..CASTILLO MONTE LA REINA VENDIMIA
      SELECCIONADA 2005 T ................................792
90 ..CYAN PRESTIGIO 2003 T ROBLE .....................786

90 ..FINCA ANZIL 2005 T .......................................795
90 ..FINCA LA MEDA 2005 TC ................................801
90 ..FRONTAURA 2005 TR ......................................787
90 ..GAGO 2007 T .................................................797
90 ..GRAN COLEGIATA CAMPUS 2004 TC................790
90 ..M.O. DE OLIVARA VENDIMIA SELECCIONADA
      2006 T BARRICA ..........................................800
90 ..MARQUÉS DE OLIVARA 2006 TC ......................800
90 ..MURUVE 2004 TR ...........................................799
90 ..PEÑAMONTE 2006 T BARRICA.........................794
90 ..PIEDRA PAREDINAS 2004 T ............................799
90 ..PIEDRA PLATINO SELECCIÓN 2003 TC .............799
90 ..PRIMA 2007 T ................................................795
90 ..PRIMERO 2008 T MACERACIÓN CARBÓNICA ....790
90 ..QUINOLA GARAGE WINE 2006 T ROBLE............801
90 ..ROMPESEDAS 2005 T .....................................797
90 ..SANGO DE REJADORADA 2005 TR ...................793

## UCLÉS

89 ..MISTERIO DE FONTANA 2006 T ROBLE..............808
87 ..LA ESTACADA 2008 T ....................................808
85 ..FINCA LA ESTACADA 6 MESES BARRICA 2008 T ROBLE....808

## UTIEL-REQUENA

93 ..IMPROMPTU 2008 B ......................................814
93 ..QUOD SUPERIUS 2006 T ................................814
91 ..EL CF DE CHOZAS CARRASCAL 2007 T............818
90 ..BASSUS PREMIUM 2006 T ..............................814
90 ..BASSUS PREMIUM 2007 T ..............................814
90 ..CERRO BERCIAL PARCELA "LADERA LOS
      CANTOS" 2005 T ..........................................816
90 ..CUEVA BARRICA SELECCIÓN 2006 T................814
90 ..CUEVA DE LA CULPA 2007 T ...........................815
90 ..EL ARBOL BLANCO 2005 TC............................813
90 ..PAGO DE LOS BALAGUESES SYRAH 2006 TC ...824
90 ..VEGA INFANTE MADURADO EN BARRICA 2008 T ....817
90 ..VEGALFARO 2006 TC......................................824
89 ..ALVAREZ NÖLTING CHARDONNAY 2007 BFB .....812
89 ..ALVAREZ NÖLTING MAGNUM 2006 T ...............812
89 ..ARTE MAYOR III T ..........................................819
89 ..AULA MERLOT 2005 TC ...................................818
89 ..LAS OCHO 2006 T ..........................................818
89 ..LAS TRES 2008 BFB .......................................818
89 ..PASIEGO DE AUTOR 2005 TC ..........................819

## VALDEORRAS

95 ..AVANTHIA GODELLO 2008 B ...........................829
94 ..LOURO DO BOLO 2008 B ................................831
93 ..AS SORTES 2007 B .........................................831
92 ..GABA DO XIL 2008 B ......................................830
92 ..GODEVAL CEPAS VELLAS 2008 B ....................830
92 ..GUITIÁN GODELLO SOBRE LÍAS 2008 B ...........828
91 ..GUITIÁN GODELLO 2007 BFB..........................828
90 ..GALGUEIRA SELECCIÓN 2008 B ......................831
90 ..GUITIÁN GODELLO 2008 B ..............................828
89 ..CASAL NOVO GODELLO 2008 B .......................828
89 ..GODEVAL 2008 B ............................................830
89 ..LAGAR DO CIGUR 2008 T JOVEN .....................828
88 ..VIÑA SOMOZA GODELLO SELECCIÓN 2007 B ROBLE ....832
87 ..A COROA 2008 B ............................................829

87 ..GRAN RUCHEL GODELLO 2006 B BARRICA ......................830
87 ..LAGAR DO CIGUR 2007 T BARRICA ...............................828
87 ..SAMPAYOLO GODELLO B BARRICA ..............................830
87 ..SANTORUM TINTO DE AUTOR 2007 T BARRICA ..............831
87 ..TERRA LOMBARDA 2008 T..........................................831
87 ..VIÑA CORZO GODELLO 2008 B .....................................831

## VALDEPEÑAS

90 ..VIÑA ALBALI SELECCIÓN PRIVADA 2001 TGR ...................839
89 ..ALBALI ARIUM 2001 TGR ............................................839
88 ..ÁGORA 2007 TC......................................................836
88 ..CORCOVO TEMPRANILLO 2007 T ROBLE.........................837
88 ..SANCTI PAULI 2005 TC.............................................840
87 ..ALBALI ARIUM TEMPRANILLO 2008 T ............................839
87 ..BONAL TEMPRANILLO 2008 T ......................................838
87 ..CORCOVO 2008 RD ..................................................836
87 ..CORCOVO SYRAH 2007 T ...........................................837
87 ..LOS MOLINOS 2001 TGR ............................................839
87 ..VIÑA ALBALI GRAN RESERVA DE LA FAMILIA 1998 TGR ..839

## VALENCIA

92 ..ANGOSTO 2007 T ....................................................846
92 ..ANGOSTO VIÑA LOS ALMENDROS 2007 T ........................846
91 ..CA'BELDA 2006 T.....................................................845
91 ..LES ALCUSSES 2006 T ..............................................849
91 ..MADURESA 2006 T ...................................................849
91 ..MOMA DELS FRADES 2006 T ......................................846
91 ..MURVIEDRO EXPRESIÓN 2006 TC ................................847
91 ..PASAMONTE 2006 T .................................................844
91 ..PASAMONTE 2008 B .................................................844
91 ..RAFAEL CAMBRA DOS 2007 T .....................................851
91 ..SUEÑO DE MEGALA 2005 T ........................................846
91 ..VENTA DEL PUERTO 12 2006 T ....................................845
90 ..ACVLIVS 2007 T......................................................850
90 ..HERETAT DE TAVERNERS GRACIANO 2005 TR ................850
90 ..MEGALA 2007 T.......................................................846
90 ..PASAMONTE 2005 T .................................................844
90 ..TRILOGÍA 2006 T .....................................................846
89 ..ANGOSTO 2008 B ....................................................846
89 ..BILOGÍA 2005 T ......................................................846
89 ..CLOS DE LA VALL 2006 TC .........................................851
89 ..FALCATA ARENAL 2006 T ...........................................851
89 ..HERETAT DE TAVERNERS REIXIU 2008 BC .....................850

## VALLE DE GÜIMAR

91 ..EL BORUJO 2008 B ROBLE..........................................857
91 ..GRAN VIRTUD 2007 B ...............................................857
89 ..VIÑAS HERZAS 2008 B ..............................................857
88 ..CONTIEMPO VIDUEÑOS SECO 2008 B ...........................856
88 ..GRAN VIRTUD MALVASIA 2008 B ..................................857
87 ..BRUMAS DE AYOSA MALVASÍA 2005 B DULCE ................858
87 ..CONTIEMPO MOSCATEL AFRUTADO 2008 B ...................856
87 ..EL BORUJO 2008 B ...................................................857
87 ..VEGA LAS CAÑAS 2008 B ...........................................857
87 ..VIÑAS MESAS 2008 RD ..............................................858
86 ..BRUMAS DE AYOSA 2008 B ........................................858
86 ..CONTIEMPO 2008 T ..................................................856
86 ..CONTIEMPO TINTO DE POSTRE 2008 T ..........................856
86 ..GRAN VIRTUD 2008 B................................................857
86 ..VIÑA MELOSAR AFRUTADO 2008 B................................856

## VALLE DE LA OROTAVA

89 ..TAJINASTE VENDIMIA SELECCIONADA 2007 T ................863
87 ..LA SUERTITA 2008 B BARRICA .....................................862
87 ..SUERTES DEL MARQUÉS SECO 2008 B ..........................863
87 ..TAJINASTE TRADICIONAL 2008 T ..................................862
86 ..BALCÓN DEL VALLE 2008 T .........................................862
86 ..SUERTES DEL MARQUÉS 2008 T...................................863
86 ..TAJINASTE 2008 T BARRICA .......................................862
86 ..VINOS TAFURIASTE VENDIMIA SELECCIONADA
       15 MESES 2007 T...............................................862

## VINOS DE MADRID

95 ..BERNABELEVA VIÑA BONITA 2007 T..............................869
93 ..BERNABELEVA "ARROYO DE TÓRTOLAS" 2007 T ............869
93 ..DIVO GRAN VINO DE GUARDA 2006 T ...........................873
93 ..EL REGAJAL SELECCIÓN ESPECIAL 2007 T ....................875
93 ..LICINIA 2007 T........................................................871
92 ..BERNABELEVA "CARRIL DEL REY" 2007 T .......................869
92 ..PICARANA 2008 B ...................................................870
92 ..VILLAMIL 2007 B .....................................................869
91 ..CANTOCUERDAS 2007 B ............................................869
91 ..MANU VINO DE AUTOR 2004 TC ..................................875
91 ..NAVAHERREROS 2007 T.............................................869
91 ..QUBÉL NATURE 2005 TC ...........................................870
91 ..TAGONIUS CENTENARIO GRAN VIA 2005 TR ...................872
90 ..750 2005 T ............................................................871
90 ..EXUN PASIÓN 2006 T ...............................................875
90 ..FÉLIX MARTÍNEZ CEPAS VIEJAS 2001 TR.......................875
90 ..MANU VINO DE AUTOR 2005 TC ..................................875
90 ..QUBÉL EXCEPCIÓN 2006 T.........................................870
90 ..TAGONIUS GRAN VINO SELECCIÓN 2004 TR ..................872
90 ..TAGONIUS VARIETAL SYRAH 2007 T..............................872

## YCODEN-DAUTE-ISORA

92 ..EL ANCÓN MALVASIA 2006 B BARRICA ..........................880
90 ..EL ANCÓN NEGRAMOLL 2006 TINTO DULCE ...................880
90 ..VIÑÁTIGO MALVASÍA 2006 B .......................................881
88 ..VIÑA SPINOLA MALVASÍA SECO 2004 B .........................881
88 ..VIÑÁTIGO MARMAJUELO 2008 B ..................................880
87 ..ACEVIÑO 2008 RD ...................................................881
87 ..EL ANCÓN 2008 T ...................................................880
87 ..MIRADERO 2008 BLANCO AFRUTADO ...........................880
87 ..TÁGARA TINTILLA 2006 T............................................880
87 ..VIÑÁTIGO TINTILLA 2006 T ROBLE ...............................881

## YECLA

92 ..DETRÁS DE LA CASA CABERNET SAUVIGNON
       TINTORERA 2006 TC .........................................886
92 ..TRENZA FAMILY COLECTION 2006 T ..............................888
91 ..BARAHONDA SUMMUM 2007 T....................................887
91 ..CASTAÑO COLECCIÓN 2005 T .....................................886
91 ..DETRÁS DE LA CASA SYRAH 2006 T..............................886
91 ..VIÑA AL LADO DE LA CASA 2006 T ...............................886
90 ..TRAPÍO 2006 T........................................................887
90 ..TRENZA FAMILY COLECTION 2004 T ..............................888
89 ..BELLUM EL REMATE 2005 T ........................................887
89 ..CASA DEL CANTO 2004 TR .........................................888
89 ..PICOS DEL MONTGÓ BARREL SELECT 2006 T.................889
89 ..VALCORSO MONASTRELL 2007 T BARRICA .....................886

# THE BEST WINES FROM EACH REGION

# THE BEST WINES FROM EACH REGION

# WINE REGIONS BY AUTONOMOUS COMMUNITY

# THE BEST WINES FROM EACH REGION

# WINERIES

# WINERIES

# WINERIES

# WINERIES

# WINES

# WINES

# WINES

# WINES

# WINES

# WINES

# WINES

# WINES

# WINES

# WINES

# WINES

# WINES

# WINES

# WINES

# WINES

# WINES

# WINES

# WINES